A COMMENTARY
ON THE ARISTOTELIAN
ATHENAION POLITEIA

PREFACE

This is a long commentary on a short text: my excuse for perpetrating it lies in the importance of the text, and in the fact that it has not received a comprehensive commentary in any language since Sandys' 2nd edition of 1912. There is, however, no shortage of books and articles dealing with parts of the *Athenaion Politeia*: if I had tried to read everything that might be relevant my own book would never have been finished, but I hope that I have not missed much of importance.

Though I must accept the blame for all that appears here, many friends have helped me in my work. I am not a practised decipherer of papyri, and my own opinions on difficult readings would be worthless: I am therefore particularly grateful to my colleague Dr J. D. Thomas, who has examined difficult passages for me and has allowed me to quote his readings, and to Dr T. S. Pattie of the British Library, for making the London papyrus available to him and supplying photographs of parts of it. The whole book has been read in draft by Professor A. Andrewes and Dr D. M. Lewis, and parts by Professors M. H. Chambers, S. Dow, W. G. Forrest, J. J. Keaney and D. M. MacDowell: it has benefited greatly from their comments, but I owe it to them to make it clear that I have not always accepted their advice. The burden of reading the proofs has been shared by Dr D. Bargrave-Weaver (to whom some of the Addenda are due), Miss T. A. S. Barron and Dr E. D. Hunt. I must thank collectively those who have supplied translations from obscure languages, the publishers who have responded patiently to my enquiries about their editions of *A.P.*, and the many friends who have allowed me to pick their brains and in some cases to make use of their unpublished work, but I acknowledge here permission from Professor A. L. Boegehold, Mr I. A. Robinson and Dr D. H. Thomas to cite their dissertations.

The University of Durham has generously supported me in my work, providing a congenial setting for the study of Greek history, allowing me sabbatical leave in 1972 and sabbatical leave and leave of absence in 1978/9, and making grants from its Research Fund and Sabbatical Leave Fund. In 1972 the Fellows of Wadham College, Oxford, made me a member of the Senior Common Room; Professor and Mrs M. F. Wiles provided ideally central hospitality then and on subsequent occasions also; in 1978/9 I was elected a Fellow of the Center for Hellenic Studies, Washington, D.C. (under

PREFACE

the aegis of Harvard University), and enjoyed the Center's admirable facilities.

The Oxford University Press has proceeded with this monstrous book in lean times, and (as connoisseurs will realise) has indulged its opinionated author beyond his wildest expectations; and the printers have risen to the challenge with great skill.

I offer my sincere thanks to all these, and to my wife and to everyone else who has encouraged me and suffered me in an obsession which is not yet at an end.

P. J. R.

Durham
Easter Term 1981

Work on the *Athenaion Politeia* has continued apace since this *Commentary* was first published. In particular, 1991 saw the centenary of the publication of the first modern edition of *A.P.*, and that was marked by celebratory conferences in Italy and Switzerland; M. H. Chambers has produced a revised Teubner text (1986) and a German translation and commentary (1990); J. J. Keaney has produced a book on the language of *A.P.* (1992); I followed this *Commentary* with an annotated Penguin Classics translation (1984). I have taken advantage of this paperback reissue to add a little material which ought to have been included in the original edition, and to review more recent work.

P. J. R.

Durham
Michaelmas Term 1992

CONTENTS

	page
LIST OF ILLUSTRATIONS	ix
REFERENCES	xi

INTRODUCTION

1.	The Rediscovery of the *Athenaion Politeia*	1
2.	The First Part of the *Athenaion Politeia*	5
3.	The Second Part of the *Athenaion Politeia*	30
4.	Language and Style	37
5.	Date of the *Athenaion Politeia*; Insertions and Revisions	51
6.	Aristotle and the *Athenaion Politeia*	58

COMMENTARY

A.	The Lost Beginning	65
B.	Cylon (1)	79
C.	Between Cylon and Solon (2–4)	84
D.	Solon (5–12)	118
E.	Between Solon and Pisistratus (13)	179
F.	The Tyranny (14–19)	189
G.	From Cleisthenes' Reforms to Xerxes' Invasion (20–2)	240
H.	The Mid Fifth Century (23–8)	283
I.	The Four Hundred and the Five Thousand (29–34. i *init.*)	362
J.	The Thirty and the Ten (34–41. i)	415
K.	Conclusion to First Part (41. ii–iii)	482
L.	Registration and Training of Citizens (42)	493
M.	Officials, Sortitive and Elective: The Boule (43–9)	510
N.	Sortitive Annual Officials (50–4)	571
O.	The Archons (55–9)	612
P.	The Athlothetae (60)	668
Q.	Elective Military Officials (61)	676
R.	Concluding Note on Officials (62)	689
S.	Jury-Courts (63–9)	697

CONTENTS

	page
APPENDIX	737
BIBLIOGRAPHY	
i. Editions, Translations and Commentaries	739
ii. Other Books	747
SELECT ADDENDA	767
INDEXES	
i. Passages from Aristotle	785
ii. Inscriptions, Papyri and Other Manuscripts	788
iii. General Index	797

LIST OF ILLUSTRATIONS

page

Fig. 1 A πινάκιον, validated for both dicastic and magisterial allotments 704
(From a photograph of Brooklyn Museum, New York, 34.678 = J. H. Kroll, *Athenian Bronze Allotment Plates*, no. 86; reproduced by permission of the Brooklyn Museum. Actual size)

Fig. 2 A pair of κληρωτήρια, for dicastic allotments 707
(Adapted from plate accompanying article by S. Dow, *HSCP* l 1939, 1–34; reprinted by permission of Prof. Dow and Harvard University Press)

Fig. 3 Map of Attica 763

Fig. 4 Plan of Athens 764

REFERENCES

1. *Ancient Texts*

I refer both to the Aristotelian *Athenaion Politeia* and to its author as
A.P. The following other abbreviations should be noticed:

A.	Aeschines
Ar.	Aristophanes
Arist.	Aristotle
D.	Demosthenes
H.	Herodotus
Isae.	Isaeus
Is.	Isocrates
L.S.	*Lexica Segueriana*, in I. Bekker, *Anecdota Graeca*, i (Berlin: Nauck, 1814)
Plat.	Plato
Pl.	Plutarch
Thph.	Theophrastus
Thp.	Theopompus
T.	Thucydides
X.	Xenophon

References in the form, Phil. 328 F 64, are to texts in F. Jacoby, *Die Fragmente der griechischen Historiker* (Berlin: Weidmann/Leiden: Brill, 1926–58). Books of Aristotle's *Politics* are numbered in manuscript order (as in the Oxford Text); speeches of Hyperides are numbered in the order of the Oxford and Loeb texts; chapters of Pausanias are divided into sections as in the Teubner text of F. Spiro (1903; the new Teubner text of M. H. Rocha-Pereira, not yet complete when this Commentary was finished, normally but not always uses the same divisions); chapters of Plutarch's *Lives* are divided into sections as in the Teubner text. In cases where the question of authorship does not matter for my purposes I have been content to echo the judgments of editors.

I use again here two conventions which I used in *The Athenian Boule*. (*a*) While for most purposes, including page and line numbers and chapter numbers of ancient texts, I use 'old style' arabic numerals (1234567890), for many serial numbers, especially of literary fragments and inscriptions and papyri, I use 'modern' numerals (1234567890). (*b*) I cite the periodical *Hesperia* by volume and year (as in other references to periodicals) when referring to pages, but by volume only when referring to an inscription by its serial number

REFERENCES

(in the annual series of Agora inscriptions except when otherwise indicated).

2. Modern Works

Articles in periodicals are cited in sufficient detail for identification in the course of the Commentary. In general I use the abbreviations of *L'Année philologique*, with the usual English divergences (e.g. *AJP* for *AJPh*); but the publications of the German academies are abbreviated as *Abh. Berlin, Sb. Leipzig*, etc., the *Mitteilungen des Deutschen Archäologischen Instituts, Athenische Abteilung*, as *AM*, and the *Zeitschrift der Savigny-Stiftung für Rechtsgeschichte, Romanistische Abteilung*, as *ZSS*. Superior figures indicate the second and subsequent series of a periodical (e.g. CQ^2 xiii 1963).

Editions of, translations of and commentaries on *A.P.* (listed in part i of the Bibliography, pp. 739–47) are cited by editor's name and number of edition alone, except that Kenyon's later editions are identified as follows:

edition of 1903	Berlin ed.
edition of 1920	O.C.T.
translation of 1920	Oxford Translation

The names of Herwerden and Leeuwen are used without further reference for suggestions thus attributed in Herwerden & Leeuwen; the name of Wilcken is used without further reference for his readings reported in Kaibel & Wilamowitz[3].

Details of books cited in the course of the Commentary will be found in part ii of the Bibliography, pp. 747–62 (with the exception of editions of and commentaries on ancient texts other than *A.P.*, and such standard compilations as *C.A.H.* and *RE*). For some frequently cited works I use a shortened form of the title; and the following abbreviations should be noted:

A.T.L.	Meritt *et al.*, *The Athenian Tribute Lists*
Beazley, *A.B.V.*	*Attic Black-Figure Vase-Painters*
Beazley, *A.R.V.*[2]	*Attic Red-Figure Vase-Painters*[2]
Busolt [& Swoboda], *G.S.*	*Griechische Staatskunde*
Davies, *A.P.F.*	*Athenian Propertied Families, 600–300 B.C.*
Gilbert, *C.A.S.A.*	*The Constitutional Antiquities of Sparta and Athens*
Harrison, *L.A.*	*The Law of Athens*
Hignett, *H.A.C.*	*A History of the Athenian Constitution to the End of the Fifth Century B.C.*
Jacoby, *F.G.H.*	*Die Fragmente der griechischen Historiker*

REFERENCES

Jacoby, *Supp.* i/ii	*op. cit.*, Dritter Teil, b (Supplement), i/ii
Jones, *A.D.*	*Athenian Democracy*
Kahrstedt, *U.M.A.*	*Untersuchungen zur Magistratur in Athen*
Kirchner, *P.A.*	*Prosopographia Attica*
Lipsius, *A.R.*	*Das attische Recht und Rechtsverfahren*
Meisterhans & Schwyzer, *G.a.I.*	*Grammatik der attischen Inschriften*
Meyer, *G.d.A.*	*Geschichte des Altertums*
Rhodes, *A.B.*	*The Athenian Boule*
Wilamowitz, *A.u.A.*	*Aristoteles und Athen*
G.G.	*Griechische Geschichte*
H.G.	*Histoire grecque* or *History of Greece*

INTRODUCTION

1. The Rediscovery of the ATHENAION POLITEIA

Aristotle's *Nicomachaean Ethics* ends with a transitional passage leading to the *Politics*, in which he says that he will first draw on the works of his predecessors and then base his investigation on 'the collection' of constitutions' (ἐκ τῶν συνηγμένων πολιτειῶν).[1] The best ancient lists of the works of Aristotle include a collection of 158 πολιτεῖαι. Item 143 in the list of Diogenes Laertius reads:

πολιτεῖαι πόλεων δυοῖν δεούσαιν ρξ´ · κατ᾽ εἴδη · δημοκρατικαί, ὀλιγαρχικαί, τυραννικαί, ἀριστοκρατικαί.[2]

Item 135 in the list of Hesychius reads:

πολιτείας πόλεων ἰδιωτικῶν καὶ δημοκρατικῶν καὶ ὀλιγαρχικῶν ⟨καὶ⟩ ἀριστοκρατικῶν καὶ τυραννικῶν ρνη´.[3]

Various Syriac and Arabic texts are derived from a Greek life of Aristotle and catalogue of his works by one Ptolemy. The version of Usaibia includes:

86. His book on the government of the cities, entitled πολιτεῖαι. In this he deals with the government of many peoples and cities, Greek and others, and their different constitutions; the number of peoples and cities he mentions is 171.

[πολιτεῖαι πόλεων ροα´.

---

[1] Arist. *E.N.* x. 1180 b 20–1181 b 24, esp. 1181 b 15–24.
[2] D.L. v. 27 (V. Rose, Teubner ed. of Arist.'s fragments, pp. 8–9; P. Moraux, *Les Listes anciennes des ouvrages d'Aristote*, 27; I. Düring, *Aristotle in the Ancient Biographical Tradition*, 50). κατ᾽ εἴδη Moraux: καὶ ἴδια (ἴδιαι) codd.; ⟨κοιναὶ⟩ καὶ ἴδιαι Bernays; κατ᾽ ἰδίαν Düring. Cf. J. J. Keaney, *AJP* lxxxiv 1963, 52–63, esp. 62–3, who suggests that the πολιτεῖαι were arranged in four categories in the library of the Peripatus, and that this list of Aristotle's works is derived from the Peripatetic Ariston. The view that there was an alphabetic sequence of πολιτεῖαι, with the Athenian in first place, rests on three texts: ἐν τῇ α´ Ἀθηναίων Πολιτείᾳ in one MS of Harp. θεσμοθέται (simply a dittography), ἐν τῇ Ἰθακησίων Πολιτείᾳ μβ´ in Phot., Suid. (Σ 718), σκυτάλη (a corruption of μέμνηται vel sim.: cf. Sandys², xxviii), ἃς ἐκδέδωκε κατὰ στοιχεῖον in Elias, *Comm. Arist. Gr.* xviii. i. 113. 32–3 (Rose, *op. cit.*, p. 258) (not stated in his sources but his own inference); cf. Keaney, *CP* lxiv 1969, 213–18. The epitomes of Heraclides (cf. below) begin with Athens but do not continue in alphabetical order.
[3] Rose, *op. cit.*, p. 16; Düring, *op. cit.*, 87.

I

INTRODUCTION

95. His book on the life (ways of life) of the cities, entitled πολιτεία, in two books. [πολιτείας β'.⁴
It has been argued from the arrangement of the list that the later entry has been corrupted from ... β' δεούσαιν ρξ', and the earlier entry is an interpolation.⁵ Other biographers credited Aristotle with 250 πολιτεῖαι,⁶ which is perhaps corrupted from 150 as an approximation to 158.⁷ 158 may be accepted as the authentic number of the πολιτεῖαι. The *Epitome of Heraclides*, entitled ἐκ τῶν Ἡρακλείδου περὶ πολιτειῶν, gives a brief summary of the Ἀθηναίων Πολιτεία followed by still briefer excerpts from 43 other πολιτεῖαι.⁸ None of the πολιτεῖαι is included in the *corpus Aristotelicum* transmitted to us, but we have many quotations from and references to them by later writers.⁹

The **Berlin Papyrus** of *A.P.* was originally P. Berol. 163 of the Aegyptische Museum, Berlin, and is now no. 5009 in the Papyrussammlung of the Staatliche Museen, East Berlin. It was acquired in 1879; published by F. Blass, *Hermes* xv 1880, 366–82; first identified as a text of *A.P.* by T. Bergk, *RM*² xxxvi 1881, 87–115 (but he could not believe that *A.P.* contained the extensive quotation from Solon in fr. Ia, and not all accepted his identification¹⁰); the publication of the London papyrus confirmed the identification. What survive are two leaves from a codex:

on fr. Ia, 12. iii–iv;   on fr. Ib, 13. i–v;
on fr. IIa, 21. iv–22. iv;   on fr. IIb, 22. iv–viii.

---

⁴ Trans. Düring, *op. cit.*, 229–30: the versions of Qifti and Usaibia are combined in a Latin translation by M. Steinschneider in the Berlin ed. of Aristotle, v (these items, 1472–3), set side by side in a German translation by A. Baumstark, *Syrisch-arabische Biographieen des Aristoteles* (69–70); Rose, *op. cit.* (pp. 21–2), gives simply the Greek titles, and his figure against the first is ρξα' = 161, which is repeated by Moraux, *op. cit.*, 303.

⁵ Baumstark, *Philologisch-historische Beiträge C. Wachsmuth* ... *überreicht*, 145–6, *Syrisch-arabische Biographieen*, 80, 88–9; Moraux, *op. cit.*, 303–4.

⁶ Ammonius, *Comm. Arist. Gr.* IV. iv. 3. 27–8 (ἀμφὶ τὰς ν' καὶ διακοσίας); Olympiodorus, *ibid.* XII. i. 6. 15, 8. 2; Elias, *ibid.* XVIII. i. 33. 7–8, 113. 31–3; *Vit. Lat.* 23 (pp. 446 Rose, 154 Düring); *Vit. Vulg.* 23 (pp. 440 Rose, 135 Düring) (σνε'); in *Vit. Marc.* 23 (pp. 431 Rose, 100–1 Düring) the numeral is omitted. Cf. Rose, *op. cit.*, p. 258.

⁷ R. Weil, *Aristote et l'histoire*, 98.

⁸ The whole edited by C. Müller, *F.H.G.*, ii. 197–224; by Rose, *op. cit.*, as fr. 611; by M. R. Dilts, *Heraclidis Lembi Excerpta Politiarum* (*G. R. & B. Mon.* v 1971); the Athenian portion edited by most editors of *A.P.*

⁹ Last collected by Rose, *op. cit.*: frs. 381–603 are assigned to 68 (or perhaps 69: *op. cit.*, p. 324) of the πολιτεῖαι, of which 51 are actually cited by title; three further fragments, from πολιτεῖαι already represented in Rose's collection, are added by Weil, *op. cit.*, 101 with n. 38; frs. 381–471 relate to Athens. Sandys², xxviii–xxxix, reviews the ancient writers who mention the πολιτεῖαι; the fate of the πολιτεῖαι in the late Roman Empire is discussed by J.-P. Callu, *REL* liii 1975, 268–315.

¹⁰ E.g. Rose, *op. cit.*, p. 260.

INTRODUCTION

This papyrus also contains *marginalia*, not now decipherable; it was probably written in the second century A.D. For further details see the only edition undertaken since the publication of the London papyrus, that of M. H. Chambers, *TAPA* xcviii 1967, 49–66.

The **London Papyrus** is P. Lond. 131, of the British Library (formerly of the British Museum). It was among the purchases made for the Museum in 1888–9 by E. A. T. W. Budge; the text on the verso[11] was identified as *A.P.* by F. G. Kenyon on 26 February 1890;[12] the first public announcement was made in two articles in *The Times*, 19 January 1891, 9, cols i–ii and iv–v; [13] Kenyon's *editio princeps* was published on 30 January 1891; a facsimile was published on 1 March 1891. Small additional fragments of the same papyrus, acquired later, were first used in Kenyon's Berlin ed. of 1903.

This papyrus consists of four rolls, the first three headed α, β (these two headings not by the original scribe), and γ τόμος:

on roll α,	cols i–xi	= chs 1–29. i;
on roll β,	cols xii–xxiv	= chs 29. ii–46. i;
on roll γ,	cols xxv–xxx	= chs 46. i–63. iv;
on roll ⟨δ⟩,	cols xxxi–xxxvi	= chs 64. i–69. ii.[14]

Kenyon saw in this text the work of four scribes: Kaibel & Wilamowitz at first proposed to reduce the number to two, but they were persuaded that Kenyon was right.[15] The work is divided between the scribes as follows:

1. α–β, cols i–xii   = chs 1–30. vi;
2. β, cols xiii–xx *med*.   = chs 31. i–41. ii (... πλεῖστα συνέβη);
3. β, cols xx *med*.–xxiv   = chs 41. ii (τὴν πόλιν ...)–46. i (... βουλῆς λαμβάνουσιν);

---

[11] Ambiguities in the use of the terms recto and verso are discussed by E. G. Turner, *Actes du XVe congrès international de papyrologie, 1977*, i: the accounts are on the side of the papyrus which was used first, and that is the side with horizontal fibres.

[12] See Budge, *By Nile and Tigris*, ii. 147–50; Turner, *Greek Papyri: An Introduction*, 22–4 with 176 n. 12. The announcement in *The Times* referred to 'a source in Egypt which, for obvious reasons, it is not expedient to specify too particularly'; according to Budge, *loc. cit.*, the papyrus came from a tomb to the east of Khemenu (Hermopolis), but other writers have given different accounts.

[13] Extracts in *CR* v 1891, 70–2.

[14] Wilcken claimed to read δ at the head of col. xxxi, but Kenyon in his Berlin ed. reported that he could see no trace of it; in early editions this roll was estimated to contain not six but seven columns.

[15] Four scribes, Kenyon[1], xi–xii; 1 = 4 and 2 = 3, Kaibel & Wilamowitz[1], v–vii; four scribes confirmed, Kenyon[3], xii n. 1, Blass[1], iv–vii, Kaibel & Wilamowitz[3], v–vi (reporting concurrence of Wilcken).

INTRODUCTION

4. γ, cols xxv–xxx   = chs 46. i (ποιεῖται δὲ ...)–63. iv;

3 again. ⟨δ⟩, cols xxxi–xxxvi = chs 64. i–69. ii.

There are corrections by the fourth scribe throughout. Rolls β (scribe 3) and γ (scribe 4) end in mid-column; ⟨δ⟩ (scribe 3) ends in mid-column with a flourish. The beginning of the work is missing, and appears to have been missing from the text from which this papyrus was copied; the end of col. xxxvi is certainly the end of the text which these scribes copied, and almost certainly the end of the complete work.[16] The text of *A.P.* is written on the reverse of accounts dated to the 10th and 11th years of Vespasian, A.D. 77/8 and 78/9:[17] *A.P.*'s first three rolls are on the reverse of the 11th year (col. xi, whose recto is blank, was added to roll α when *A.P.* was written; lacunae in the accounts show that the ends of rolls β and γ were abandoned when *A.P.* was written); the fourth is on the reverse of the 10th year. Part of the reverse of roll α had already been used for a *hypothesis* to and the beginning of a commentary on D. xxi. *Mid.*:[18] this occupies 1½ columns after the half-column x (after Σοφωνίδου in 25. i). The text of *A.P.* was written late in the first or very early in the second century A.D. For further information on this papyrus, and on the hands and abbreviations of the four scribes, see *CR* v 1891, 183, Herwerden & Leeuwen, 163–79, and the plates of Herwerden & Leeuwen and Oppermann; Kenyon[3], x–xvi, xix–xx, lxviii; Kenyon, Berlin ed., vi–x; Sandys[2], xliii–xlix; H. J. M. Milne, *Catalogue of the Literary Papyri in the British Museum* (*P. Lit. Lond.*), 84, no. 108; E. G. Turner, *Greek Manuscripts of the Ancient World*, 102–3, pl. 60.

A small fragment from Oxyrhynchus[19] is restored by M. H. Chambers, *TAPA* cii 1971, 43, to give a version of 7. iii; but the extent to which it diverges from the London papyrus indicates that, if correctly identified, it is not a text of *A.P.* but a paraphrase. Cf. *ad loc.*

i–xxx = 1–63 was divided into chapters by Kenyon[1], and Kenyon's chapters were subdivided into sections by Kaibel & Wilamowitz[1]; xxxi–xxxvi = 64–9 was divided into chapters and sections by Kenyon in his Berlin ed. Some early commentators cite not by chapters but by pages of Kenyon[1].

[16] For attempts to calculate how much has been lost before ch. 1 see p. 65.
[17] Published by Kenyon in *Greek Papyri in the British Museum: Catalogue with Texts*, i (1893), 166–91; the first three rolls re-edited by A. Świderek, *Ac. Sci. Pol., Bibl. Ant.* i (1960).
[18] Published by Herwerden & Leeuwen, 180–5 (from the facsimile), Kenyon[3], 215–19.
[19] Not yet published in *P. Oxy.*

INTRODUCTION

Kenyon's *editio princeps* was produced with admirable speed; it contained errors which might have been avoided with less speed, but these were soon detected. Herwerden & Leeuwen give a line-by-line transcription (from the facsimile) and a reconstructed text on facing pages. Kaibel & Wilamowitz[3] (with the readings of Wilcken) and Kenyon's Berlin ed. are the most authoritative editions for the readings of the London papyrus. Oppermann gives an up-to-date line-by-line text of xxxi–xxxvi = 64–9. The best indexes and collections of *testimonia* are in Kenyon's Berlin ed. and Sandys[2]; Sandys[2] consolidates the first generation of work on *A.P.*, and gives a full bibliography to 1912 (but omits one or two of the items listed in Sandys[1]), and Oppermann gives a more selective bibliography which has been brought up to date in successive reprints; I have attempted to give a complete list of texts, translations and commentaries in the first part of my Bibliography, pp. 739–47.

2. The First Part of the ATHENAION POLITEIA

The contents of *A.P.* fall into two parts: from the lost beginning to ch. 41, a history of the πολιτεία to its last 'change', the restoration of the democracy in 403; and from ch. 42 to ch. 69, an account of the working of the πολιτεία in the author's own day.[20]

The first part may be analysed as follows; the letters in the left-hand column refer to the sections of this commentary, and the bracketed roman numerals and short headings on the right refer to the 'changes' of 41. ii.

A	——	The lost beginning, from the foundation of the monarchy to the annual archonship.	[I Ion; II Theseus]
B	1	Cylon.	
C	2–4	Between Cylon and Solon.	
	2	Causes of στάσις: poor enslaved to rich.	
	3	Causes of στάσις: ἀρχαία πολιτεία.	
	4	Draco.[21]	[— Draco]
D	5–12	Solon.	[III Solon]
	5	Solon's background.	
	6	σεισάχθεια.	
	7–8	Laws and πολιτεία.	

[20] R. Weil, *Aristote et l'histoire*, 102, remarks that it is not clear from the fragments that all the πολιτεῖαι were thus arranged.

[21] I believe that the 'Draconian constitution' is a late insertion in the text of *A.P.*, but that the first sentence of ch. 4 is part of the original text and may originally have been followed by further material on Draco's θεσμοί. Cf. pp. 45–6, 53, 60.

INTRODUCTION

		9	Solon and democracy.
		10	Measures, weights, coinage.
		11. i	Solon's ἀποδημία.
		11. ii–12	Solon in middle ground between two parties.
E	13		Between Solon and Pisistratus.
		13. i–ii	στάσις over archonship.
		13. iii–v	The three parties.
F	14–19		The tyranny. [IV Pisistratus]
		14–15	The rise of Pisistratus.
		16	The rule of Pisistratus.
		17–18	The end of the tyranny: Hipparchus.
		19	The end of the tyranny: Hippias.
G	20–2		From Cleisthenes' reforms to Xerxes' invasion. [V Cleisthenes]
		20. i–iii	Cleisthenes and Isagoras.
		20. iv–v	The Alcmaeonids and the end of the tyranny.
		21	Reforms of Cleisthenes.
		22	From Cleisthenes to Xerxes' invasion.
H	23–8		The mid fifth century.
		23. i–ii	Ascendancy of the Areopagus. [VI Areopagus]
		23. ii–24	Naval power. [VII Aristides ...
		25	Reform of Ephialtes. ... and Ephialtes]
		26. i	Cimon.
		26. ii–iv	Changes of the 450's.
		27	Pericles.
		28	Deterioration after Pericles: aristocratic and democratic leaders.
I	29–34. i		The Four Hundred and the Five Thousand. [VIII The Four Hundred]
		29	The institution of the Four Hundred.
		30	'Future' constitution.
		31	'Immediate' constitution.
		32	The rule of the Four Hundred.
		33–34. i	The intermediate régime.
J	34–41. i		The Thirty and the Ten.
		34. i–ii	The restored democracy. [IX Democracy]
		34. iii	The institution of the Thirty. [X The Thirty ...
		35	The rule of the Thirty.
		36	The opposition of Theramenes.
		37	Theramenes eliminated.
		38	The democrats at Munichia. ... and the Ten]

INTRODUCTION

	39	Terms of reconciliation.
	40	Moderation of restored democracy.
	41. i	The democracy restored. [XI Democracy]
K	41. ii–iii	Conclusion to first part.
	41. ii	Changes in the constitution.
	41. iii	Payment for attending the assembly.

41. ii provides the clearest guide to the author's intentions: to list the changes which the Athenian constitution had undergone between the earliest times and the achievement of its present form. Aristotle believed that the πόλις exists by nature and man is a πολιτικὸν ζῷον;[22] nature does nothing without a purpose;[23] accordingly, the works of nature can be analysed and explained, and human and political phenomena are susceptible of the same kinds of explanation as 'natural' phenomena.[24] He distinguished four causes of the existence of any given thing: the material cause (τὸ ἐξ οὗ), the formal (τὸ εἶδος), the efficient (τὸ ποιοῦν) and the final (τὸ τέλος);[25] the last three often coalesce into one.[26] The constitution which had developed in Athens was a democracy, and democracy is not a 'straight' form of constitution but a perversion (παρέκβασις);[27] democracy is not therefore conducive to the natural τέλος of the state, which is the good life,[28] but it can be said that any form of constitution has its own τέλος, that of democracy being freedom.[29] On this basis it could be argued that the form ultimately taken by the Athenian constitution was the 'final' form towards which it had been moving from the beginning, and that the history of the constitution would show how this movement had reached its goal.[30] On the other hand, in his more pragmatic moments Aristotle was well aware that history is not as tidy as this, that a state can equally easily change from a first form of constitution to a second or from

---

[22] Arist. *Pol.* I. 1252 B 27–1253 A 18, III. 1278 B 15–30.

[23] E.g. Arist. *Pol.* I. 1253 A 9, 1256 B 20–1; other references collected by Bonitz, *Index Aristotelicus*, s.v. φύσις, 836 B 28–37.

[24] An analogy between the parts of an animal and the parts of a state is drawn in *Mot. An.* 703 A 29–36, *Pol.* IV. 1290 B 23–38.

[25] *Phys.* II. 194 B (16–)23–195 A 26 = *Met.* Δ. 1013 A 24–B 28.

[26] *Phys.* II. 198 A 22–7.

[27] *Pol.* III. 1279 A 22–B 10.

[28] *Pol.* III. 1278 B 15–30, 1280 A 31–1281 A 8.

[29] *Rhet.* I. 1366 A 2–7.

[30] Cf. *Pol.* III. 1286 B 8–22 (not specifically referring to Athens) on the development from kingship to democracy, concluding that since states have become larger it is perhaps not easy for any constitution other than democracy to come about; II. 1264 A 1–5 suggests that man's development is more or less complete and finality has been achieved. Similarly we read in *Poet.* 1449 A 9–15 that tragedy, πολλὰς μεταβολὰς μεταβαλοῦσα, has reached its final form: ἐπαύσατο, ἐπεὶ ἔσχε τὴν αὑτῆς φύσιν.

7

INTRODUCTION

the second to the first;[31] and both in the *Politics* and in *A.P.* it is sensibly maintained that Solon did not intend everything that followed in due course from his reforms.[32] The history of Athens at the end of the fifth century exemplified the truth that it was possible both for democracy to change to oligarchy and for oligarchy to change to democracy; in 321, on the orders of Antipater, the stable democracy of the fourth century was to give way to oligarchy once more, and further changes were to follow. Those changes were still in the future when *A.P.* was written; but, if the form of the constitution in the fourth century was thought to be its final and intended form, it had been attained not by a steady advance towards this goal but by a series of advances and setbacks.

The words τέλος and φύσις are not used at all with teleological implications in *A.P.*, and we are nowhere directly told that the present form of the constitution is its 'final' form; but in the series of changes which the author lists each move in the direction of democracy takes Athens further than the previous such move. (I) Ion gave Athens her first institutions. (II) Under Theseus the state had 'some semblance of a constitution', μικρὸν παρεγκλίνουσα τῆς βασιλικῆς (41. ii), but still the constitution before Solon was ὀλιγαρχικὴ πᾶσι (2. iii). [(—) Draco could be accommodated, in that he gave Athens her first written laws.] (III) Solon's constitution was the one ἀφ' ἧς ἀρχὴ δημοκρατίας ἐγένετο, but he did not intend all that later followed from his reforms (9, 41. ii). (IV) Pisistratus ruled well (14. iii, 16), but his rule was still a tyranny and under it Solon's laws fell into disuse (22. i). (V) Cleisthenes' πολιτεία was δημοτικωτέρα πολὺ τῆς Σόλωνος (22. i, 41. ii), and in the years that followed his reforms the city and the democracy increased (23. i). (VI) The Persian Wars were followed by the ascendancy of the Areopagus, under which there was a decline (25. i).[33] (VII) Then Ephialtes took away the politically important powers of the Areopagus: we are not told here that his πολιτεία was more democratic than Cleisthenes', but since he transferred to organs of the δῆμος powers which they had not previously possessed the author presumably believed that it was;[34] the strengthening of the demo-

---

[31] Cf. *Pol.* v. 1316 a 1–b 27, arguing against the degenerative scheme of Plat. *Rep.* IV. 445 c 1–e 4, VIII. 543 a 1–IX. 576 b 10.

[32] *Pol.* II. 1273 b 35–1274 a 21, *A.P.* 9. ii. Throughout this Introduction, when I refer to passages in *A.P.*, the recommendation 'see *ad loc.*' should be understood.

[33] In 25. i καίπερ ὑποφερομένη κατὰ μικρόν is followed immediately by αὐξανομένου δὲ τοῦ πλήθους. *A.P.* has tried to combine the view that the Persian Wars were followed by a period of Areopagite ascendancy with the view that they were followed by the growth of the Delian League and the strengthening of the democracy: cf. pp. 48–9.

[34] Cf. 29. iii with its implication that the constitution had become more democratic since the time of Cleisthenes.

INTRODUCTION

cracy was anticipated in 23. ii–24 and is continued in 26–8 (in 26. i the πολιτεία becomes 'slacker', in 27. i it becomes δημοτικωτέραν ἔτι, and in 28. i things become 'much worse' after Pericles' death; cf. 41. ii). (VIII) This development is interrupted by the oligarchy of the Four Hundred and the Five Thousand;[35] (IX) then democracy is restored; (X) the end of the Peloponnesian War leads to the oligarchy of the Thirty and the Ten; (XI) then the democracy is restored again.

Ch. 41 begins, not entirely in accord with what has gone before, by stating that in 403 τότε δὲ κύριος ὁ δῆμος γενόμενος τῶν πραγμάτων ἐνεστήσατο τὴν νῦν οὖσαν πολιτείαν; the remark that this was the eleventh change leads to the summary of changes in the constitution, ending with the restoration of 403, ἀφ' ἧς διαγεγένηται μέχρι τῆς νῦν ἀεὶ προσεπιλαμβάνουσα τῷ πλήθει τὴν ἐξουσίαν.[36] As an instance of this 41. iii mentions payments for attendance at the assembly, which Aristotle regarded as characteristic of the most extreme kind of democracy[37] but which Athens did not adopt until after 403. The doctrine is nowhere explicitly stated, but *A.P.* may be said to illustrate the doctrine that extreme democracy was the final and intended form of the Athenian πολιτεία, towards which (gradually, and with setbacks) it had all the time been developing;[38] and a man writing in the 330's and 320's could be forgiven for thinking that the constitution had reached its final form, as there had been no major upheaval since the restoration of 403, and in contrast with the preceding two hundred years or more this was stability indeed.[39]

Aristotle regarded virtue as a mean between extremes,[40] and believed that the state should be based on the middle sort of citizens;[41] the forms of constitution which came closest to this ideal were aristocracy and πολιτεία (the forms of which oligarchy and democracy are perversions).[42] The 'moderate' political opinions expressed in *A.P.* are consonant with the doctrines of the *Politics*, but they are not of course opinions peculiar to Aristotle and his school. Under the ascendancy of the Areopagus after the Persian Wars

---

[35] For the view of the Five Thousand implied in *A.P.*'s summary see on 41. ii.

[36] Whether this claim is justified is open to doubt.

[37] *Pol.* VI. 1292 B 41–1293 A 10, 1299 B 38–1300 A 4, VI. 1317 B 30–5.

[38] Cf. Wilamowitz, *A.u.A.*, i. 187, J. J. Keaney, *HSCP* lxvii 1963, 115–46, esp. 115–20.

[39] This is sufficient to explain why *A.P.*'s historical account ends where it does, and there is no need to invoke an *ur-A.P.* written early in the fourth century: cf. pp. 18, 33. The date of *A.P.* will be discussed below, pp. 51–8: it is apparent from the second part that the original version was written towards the end of the 330's and revised in the first half of the 320's; there is no reason to suppose that the first part is earlier.

[40] *E.N.* II. 1104 A 11–27, 1106 A 26–1109 B 26.

[41] *Pol.* IV. 1295 A 25–1297 A 13.

[42] *Pol.* IV. 1293 A 35–1294 B 41.

INTRODUCTION

ἐπολιτεύθησαν Ἀθηναῖοι καλῶς κατὰ τούτους τοὺς καιρούς (23. ii); after Ephialtes' reform the πολιτεία became 'slacker' because of the demagogues, and the Athenians did not adhere to the νόμοι as they had done in the past (26. i–ii); under Pericles' leadership things were not too bad, but after his death they became much worse as less respectable men came to be leaders of the δῆμος (28. i); Nicias, Thucydides and Theramenes, described in 28. ii–iii as leaders of the γνώριμοι, were the best of the more recent politicians (28. v); under the intermediate régime of 411/0 δοκοῦσι ... καλῶς πολιτευθῆναι κατὰ τούτους τοὺς καιρούς (33. ii); and there is praise for Rhinon and the moderation of the restored democracy of 403 (38. iv, 40. i–iii).[43] The complaint of 26. ii that under the democracy the Athenians did not adhere to the laws as they had done in the past is characteristically Aristotelian,[44] and it reappears in 41. ii *fin.*, which also recalls the *Politics* in its reference to the transfer of the boule's κρίσεις to the δῆμος,[45] and in the claim that οἱ πολλοί are less easily corrupted than οἱ ὀλίγοι.[46] There are other passages which show a strong affinity with the *Politics*. Both in *A.P.* 5. iii and in *Pol.* IV. 1296 A 18–20 Solon is said to be one of the μέσοι πολῖται.[47] Both in *A.P.* 9. ii and in *Pol.* II. 1273 B 35–1274 A 21 it is maintained, in connection with the δικαστήρια, that Solon did not intend all that later followed from his legislation. *Pol.* V. 1304 A 20–4 seems to say that the battle of Salamis resulted both in a more oligarchic constitution under the control of the Areopagus and in the strengthening of Athens' naval power and the democracy; and these two themes reappear in *A.P.* 23–4, where control by the Areopagus seems to be an immediate consequence of Salamis and the growth of the Delian League and economic benefits for the δῆμος a long-term consequence. *A.P.* 34–40 and *Pol.* V. 1305 B 22–7 both write of the régime of the Thirty without mentioning Plato's relative Critias, who appears in our other sources as the leader of the extreme oligarchs.[48]

To this extent we may accept that *A.P.*'s first part gives an Aristotelian view of Athens' political history; but Day & Chambers, in *Aristotle's History of Athenian Democracy*, have claimed a great deal more than this. In *Pol.* IV. 1291 B 30–1292 A 38 Aristotle distinguishes

---

[43] 41. ii *fin.* is reminiscent of [X.] *A.P.* in appraising on its own terms a régime which is not to the writer's taste; but cf. also the closing chapters of *Pol.* II.

[44] Cf. *Pol.* IV. 1292 A 4–7, 23–5, 32–7; also III. 1282 B 1–6, IV. 1293 A 30–4, 1298 A 28–33.

[45] *Pol.* IV. 1299 B 38–1300 A 1, VI. 1317 B 30–5.

[46] *Pol.* III. 1286 A 26–35 cf. 1281 A 39–B 21.

[47] Cf. the statement in 15. iv that Megacles' party pursued τὴν μέσην πολιτείαν.

[48] Notice also *A.P.* 3. ii–iii with *Pol.* III. 1285 B 13–19 (not specifically referring to Athens) on the weakening of the basileus, *A.P.* 14. iii. 16, with the good tyrant of *Pol.* V. 1314 A 29–1315 B 10, and the Aristotelian expressions in *A.P.* cited on p. 39; but see pp. 60–1 for some historical disagreements between *A.P.* and *Pol.*

INTRODUCTION

five kinds of democracy: one based on equality, one with a low property qualification for full citizenship, one in which full citizenship is open to all who are unobjectionable (in birth[49]) but the law rules, one in which citizenship is open to all (free men[50]) but the law rules, and a last kind in which it is not the law which rules but the πλῆθος with its decrees. In IV. 1292 B 25–1293 A 12 the first is omitted but the other four are repeated; what distinguishes the last from the preceding kinds of democracy is that the provision of stipends enables the poorer citizens to exercise their rights. Finally, in VI. 1318 B 6–1319 B 32 there is a further reference to the four kinds of democracy; different kinds of citizen population are discussed (agricultural, pastoral and so on); and it is said that the last form of democracy is one in which all are partners. The similarity between the ἔμμισθος πόλις of Pericles' time and after, where the πλῆθος has subsidised leisure and rules by decrees and law-court verdicts, and the 'last' democracy of the *Politics* is clear enough;[51] but Day & Chambers claim that the summary in *A.P.* 41. ii contains four, and only four, forms of democracy, those initiated by changes III, V, VI and VII,[52] and it is the main thesis of their book that these four forms are intended to represent the four forms of the *Politics*, and that the author has invented or distorted the facts to fit his theory.[53] For instance, Androtion and *A.P.* disagreed on the date of the institution of ostracism;[54] the fact that they could disagree shows that there was no evidence available in the fourth century to settle the question; Androtion chose the later date in order not to make Cleisthenes seem too democratic, *A.P.* chose the earlier in order to make the democracy of Cleisthenes seem more advanced than that of Solon.[55] But I fear it is Day & Chambers who have distorted the facts to fit their theory: the ascendancy of the Areopagus, brought about by change VI, is clearly represented not as a move towards democracy but as a move away from

---

[49] Cf. 1292 B 35–6. The use of the term ἀνυπεύθυνοι is puzzling: it may be derived from a particular non-Athenian context; certainly there is nothing in Athenian history that will enable us to make sense of it.
[50] Cf. 1292 B 38–9.
[51] On the ἔμμισθος πόλις in Pl. *Per.* 12. iv–vi see A. Andrewes, *JHS* xcviii 1978, 3–4.
[52] *A.H.A.D.*, 66–7.
[53] Cf. Chambers, *TAPA* xcii 1961, 20–36.
[54] For this problem, see on 22. iii.
[55] *A.H.A.D.*, 13–15; cf. 107: 'The *nomoi* in chapter 22 reached him through Androtion, neatly summarized and dated. Only one date, that of the ostracism law, had to be corrected in the light of Aristotle's theory.' For their view of Androtion on ostracism cf. Jacoby, *Supp.* i. 120.

INTRODUCTION

democracy,[56] and it is incredible that this régime should have been invented 'to close the gap between the second democracy of Cleisthenes and the radical fourth democracy begun by Ephialtes'.[57] Day & Chambers make much of the connection in the *Politics* between the balance of population and the form of government, by which the existence of a large number of lower-class men eligible for citizenship is conducive to democracy but the existence of a small number is conducive to oligarchy:[58] the losses among the upper class in 26. i, they claim, were fabricated to provide a change in the balance of the state and explain the continuing move towards democracy after Ephialtes' reform; Pericles with his citizenship law tried to reverse the trend (26. iv: διὰ τὸ πλῆθος τῶν πολιτῶν), but afterwards he turned to demagogy (27). 26. i is one of the most difficult passages in *A.P.*, but by the end of it *A.P.* has decided that the losses fell on the better sort of men in both the lower and the upper classes; *A.P.* does not state what Day & Chambers infer, that the citizenship law was an anti-democratic measure, in conflict with the view of Pericles given in 27, but if it was so this would surely show that *A.P.* respected the facts and did not twist them to fit his theory.[59] If Cleisthenes readmitted to citizenship men of impure descent (21. iv with 13. v) and Pericles made the requirements for citizenship more stringent, it is hard to find 'second' and 'third' democracies in *A.P.*

Day & Chambers also stress the use of the word συμβαίνειν.[60] To express 'happen' *A.P.* sometimes uses the neutral γίγνεσθαι (which they do not discuss),[61] and occasionally τυγχάνειν, which they believe 'is used only to state what is the case, without a necessary connotation that something has happened by chance',[62] but they count twenty-five uses of συμβαίνειν and four of συμπίπτειν (all in the first part), which they find more significant. These verbs can be used in their 'causally least committal sense',[63] or they can be used

---

[56] Cf. N. G. L. Hammond, *CR*² xxiv 1964, 36, D. Kagan, *CP* lix 1964, 189–90, G. L. Cawkwell, *JHS* lxxxvi 1966, 247, reviewing *A.H.A.D.* W. L. Newman in his ed. of Arist. *Pol.*, iv, pp. xl–xli, doubted whether a connection can be established between Athenian history and the successive kinds of democracy.

[57] *A.H.A.D.*, 126.

[58] *A.H.A.D.*, 25–37; e.g. *Pol.* VI. 1319 B 6–14, 1320 B 25–1321 A 4.

[59] Cf. Hammond, *op. cit.*, 35–6.

[60] *A.H.A.D.*, 42–50, cf. Day, *TAPA* xcii 1961, 52–65. Contr. F. W. Gilliard, *Hist.* xx 1971, 433–5, who remarks that *A.P.* frequently uses συμβαίνειν of the results of moral choice.

[61] E.g. 22. i, 34. i, 39. i.

[62] 2. iii, 18. iii, 24. ii, 32. iii, 37. i (*bis*), 53. v, cf. Solon *ap.* 12. iv, v: *A.H.A.D.*, 42–3.

[63] Day, *op. cit.*, 53 with n. 3, citing 13. iii, 16. vi, 28. v (with Kaibel, *Stil und Text*, 185), 40. ii *fin.*, 41. i, cf. H. II. 120. iii, T. I. 98. iv.

INTRODUCTION

for the chance convergence of two independent chains of events;[64] but for Aristotle συμβαίνειν could be a technical term with a more precise meaning—in a discussion of it in the *Metaphysics* he gives these examples:

οἷον ἐπὶ κυνὶ ἂν χειμὼν γένηται καὶ ψῦχος, τοῦτο συμβῆναί φαμεν, ἀλλ' οὐκ ἂν πνῖγος καὶ ἀλέα, ὅτι τὸ μὲν ἀεὶ ἢ ὡς ἐπὶ τὸ πολὺ τὸ δ' οὔ. καὶ τὸν ἄνθρωπον λευκὸν εἶναι συμβέβηκεν (οὔτε γὰρ ἀεὶ οὔθ' ὡς ἐπὶ τὸ πολύ), ζῷον δ' οὐ κατὰ συμβεβηκός[65]—

and Day & Chambers believe that συμβαίνειν and συμπίπτειν are often used in *A.P.* of what happens, in this sense, accidentally, not according to and sometimes in frustration of nature and its τέλος. 'In effect, for Aristotle the state has a history mostly by accident.'[66] Day claims to find this technical sense of συμβαίνειν and συμπίπτειν particularly in their three occurrences in 26. i.[67] Those who seek are apt to find; but I can detect no significant difference between μετὰ δὲ ταῦτα συνέβαινεν πολλῷ τραχυτέραν εἶναι τὴν τυραννίδα (19. i) and τούτων δὲ γενομένων δημοτικωτέρα πολὺ τῆς Σόλωνος ἐγένετο ἡ πολιτεία (22. i), between κατὰ γὰρ τοὺς καιροὺς τούτους συνέπεσε μηδ' ἡγεμόνα ἔχειν τοὺς ἐπιεικεστέρους (26. i) and ἐτύγχανεν γὰρ οὗτος μὲν δεχόμενος ὁ δ' Ἵππαρχος ἀποστέλλων τὴν πομπήν (18. iii).[68] Aristotle did have a technical concept of συμβεβηκότα, and he could when he chose emphasize the part played by chance in history;[69] but I am not persuaded that metaphysical 'accidents' are implied by any of the instances of συμβαίνειν and συμπίπτειν in *A.P.* Whereas Day concludes that 'theory pervades and controls the historical chapters of the *Ath. Pol.*',[70] I find remarkably few traces of Aristotelian theory in *A.P.*[71]

[64] Day, *op. cit.*, 54-7 with 55-6 n. 10, citing 6. ii, 16. iv, 21. iii, 23. ii, 37. i, cf. H. VII. 166, T. V. 14. i.
[65] *Met. E.* 1026 A 33–1027 A 28, quoting 1026 B 33–7.
[66] *A.H.A.D.*, 50.
[67] Day, *op. cit.*, 60, suggests as other instances of this usage 16. vii, 19. i, 22. i, 23. ii (but contr. n. 64, above), 24. iii, 27. i, 34. i, 34. ii, 41. ii (VII).
[68] Cf. in *Pol.* V ὅπερ ἐν Ἀπολλωνίᾳ συνέβη τῇ ἐν τῷ Πόντῳ (1306 A 8–9) and ὅπερ καὶ ἐν Ἡρακλείᾳ ἐγένετο τῇ ἐν τῷ Πόντῳ (1305 B 36). For the extent to which *A.P.* avoids verbal monotony see pp. 42-4.
[69] E.g. συμβαίνει δ' ἐνίοτε τοῦτο καὶ διὰ τύχας (*Pol.* V. 1303 A 3): contrast καὶ τοῦτο συμβαίνει κατὰ λόγον (*Pol.* VII. 1328 A 12–13). In *Poet.* 1459 A 21–7 Aristotle writes in these words of the coincidence of Himera and Salamis: . . . καὶ μὴ ὁμοίας ἱστορίαις τὰς συνθέσεις εἶναι (thus Kassel's O.C.T.), ἐν αἷς ἀνάγκη οὐχὶ μιᾶς πράξεως ποιεῖσθαι δήλωσιν ἀλλ' ἑνὸς χρόνου, ὅσα ἐν τούτῳ συνέβη περὶ ἕνα ἢ πλείους, ὧν ἕκαστον ὡς ἔτυχεν πρὸς ἄλληλα. ὥσπερ γὰρ κατὰ τοὺς αὐτοὺς χρόνους ἥ τ' ἐν Σαλαμῖνι ἐγένετο ναυμαχία καὶ ἡ ἐν Σικελίᾳ Καρχηδονίων μάχη οὐδὲν πρὸς τὸ αὐτὸ συντείνουσαι τέλος . . .
[70] Day, *op. cit.*, 64.
[71] Cf. G. L. Huxley, *GR&BS* xiii 1972, 161-2. It was noted above, p. 8, that τέλος and φύσις are not used in a teleological sense in *A.P.*; ἔργον appears only

INTRODUCTION

J. J. Keaney has suggested another way in which Aristotelian teleology may have affected *A.P.*'s presentation of his material.[72] He believes that *A.P.* saw in Solon the beginnings of Athenian democracy,[73] and for this reason chronicled constitutional changes after Solon more fully than changes before: that may well be right, but I cannot accept the further suggestion that *A.P.* is really divided not into two parts but into three, with ch. 3 marking the transition from first to second as 41 marks the transition from second to third; 3 like 2 is needed where it is to explain the grievances which Solon sought to redress, and Solon is treated in detail because, probably for the first time, *A.P.* had reached a topic on which details were available in his sources; Pisistratus is given a similarly detailed treatment, since detailed material was available, though he did not contribute similarly to the development of the democracy. Nor do I see the same centrality as Keaney in Ephialtes' reform of the Areopagus: he stresses that the δῆμος to achieve sovereignty had to take over the powers first of the archons, then of the Areopagus and finally of the boule, notes that the weakening of the archons is implied in the first of his three parts (3), that of the Areopagus in the second (23. i, 25) and that of the boule in the third (45. i, 45. iii, 49. iii, 55. ii), and thinks it significant that the ascendancy of the Areopagus was achieved by the sixth of the eleven changes;[74] but I think that if *A.P.* had wanted to make that point he would have done so more obviously.†

A.P. does recount how the Athenian democracy arrived at its final form, a view of constitutional history which would not surprise us in Aristotle; and his remarks on that final form closely resemble the remarks on 'last' democracy in the *Politics*; but subtler traces of Aristotelian philosophy are to be seen only in the eye of the beholder. When *A.P.* expresses a political opinion, that opinion again is of the kind which we should expect from Aristotle. However, I believe that, although he is sincere in the opinions which he expresses, when he expresses them he is usually not reacting spontaneously to what he found in his sources as bare fact but is repeating with his approval a comment which he found in one of his sources. This is most clearly

---

in 28. v *fin.*, where the author gives his choice between conflicting judgments on Theramenes. Gilliard, *op. cit.*, 430–5, remarks that for Aristotle groups of men like individual men are not teleologically determined but are capable of making good or bad choices.

[72] *HSCP* lxvii 1963, 115–46, esp. 120–31.

[73] Cf. 41. ii (III). Who was the founder of the democracy, and what part Solon had played, were questions much discussed in the fourth century: cf. pp. 159, 261, 376, 428.

[74] *Op. cit.*, 131–6. For Keaney's view of the descriptive part of *A.P.* cf. below, p. 37.

INTRODUCTION

the case in 33. ii, where (though it is given a different slant) *A.P.*'s praise of the intermediate régime of 411/0 coincides with that expressed by Thucydides (VIII. 97. ii), from whom his facts on the institution of that régime are derived. 28. ii–iii (–iv) gives a list of προστάται τοῦ δήμου and τῶν γνωρίμων, which since it does not entirely match the author's main narrative must have been taken over from some earlier writer. In §v Nicias, Thucydides, and Theramenes are said to be the best of the more recent politicians; the praise of Nicias and Thucydides is said to command general agreement but that of Theramenes is admitted to be controversial and is justified. I suggest that *A.P.* found these men praised in connection with the list; his own contribution is the realisation that Theramenes' part in history was controversial and that praise of him required justification,[75] as in 6. ii–iv when confronted with rival versions of the story that Solon gave advance warning of the σεισάχθεια to his friends *A.P.* had to make up his own mind and decided that the less creditable story is inconsistent with what we know of Solon's character. Similarly I believe that the praise of the Areopagite ascendancy (23. ii), the comment on the deterioration after Pericles' death (28. i), and the praise of Rhinon and Archinus (38. iv, bound up with the false account of a second board of Ten; 40. ii), though sincere, are not original to *A.P.* On the other hand, the comment in 40. iii on other democracies and γῆς ἀναδασμός is likely to have originated later than the composition of the source which *A.P.* used on the events of 404–403.

This leads to the question of the sources used in the first half of *A.P.* The use of Solon's poems in 5 and 12, and of scolia in 19. iii and 20. v and documents in 30–1 and 39 is obvious; the dependence of parts of *A.P.*'s narrative on Herodotus and Thucydides was quickly detected, and scholars began arguing whether Xenophon's *Hellenica* and Ephorus were used. But much of the narrative can be seen to be independent of these, and two kinds of writing in particular have been considered as further sources of *A.P.*, the *Atthides* (and especially that of Andotion, written not long before *A.P.*), and partisan political writings produced late in the fifth and early in the fourth century.

Wilamowitz devoted the first volume of his *Aristoteles und Athen* to an analysis of *A.P.* and a search for its sources. He argued that the material with a definite oligarchic bias was derived from an oligarchic pamphlet, written in the autumn of 404 by Theramenes as a

---

[75] I am not persuaded by P. E. Harding, *Phoen.* xxviii 1974, 101–11, that *A.P.* was the first to defend Theramenes as a 'moderate'.

15

manifesto for his party;[76] the austerely chronological material, and the material with a democratic slant, came from the *Atthides* and especially from Androtion;[77] Xenophon[78] and Ephorus[79] were not used; except for the events of 404–403,[80] *A.P.* did not undertake historical research but closely followed his sources.[81] Busolt in his *Griechische Geschichte*, ii². 32–54 (written before but published after the appearance of *Aristoteles und Athen*), began his survey of *A.P.*'s sources with Androtion, and suggested that where *A.P.* records a difference of opinion he may not have consulted the conflicting works himself but have found the difference noted for him by Androtion;[82] he too believed in an oligarchic pamphlet (though he attributed less to the pamphlet and more to Androtion than did Wilamowitz), and originally accepted the suggestion of F. Duemmler[83] that its author was Critias,[84] but in his preface and *addenda* he announced his conversion to the view that the author was Theramenes or at any rate a supporter of his;[85] Xenophon was used only in ch. 36, and it was likelier that *A.P.* and Ephorus had a common source on the Thirty than that *A.P.* used Ephorus.[86] W. Buseskul, in a book in Russian on *Aristotle's Athenaion Politeia as a Source for Athenian Constitutional History to the End of the Fifth Century*,[87] ch. iii, argued that *A.P.* used Ephorus but not Xenophon, used the *Atthides* for documentary material, and used not one but several partisan works; various other sources must be taken into account, including Solon, comedy, anecdotes and oral tradition. Schoeffer thought that *A.P.*'s knowledge of oligarchic slanders could come

---

[76] *A.u.A.*, i, esp. 161–9 (167 admits that we have no evidence that Theramenes wrote anything). E. M. Walker, *CR* viii 1894, 206, argued that if *A.P.* used an oligarchic source of this kind we should expect his account of 404–403 to come from it also, and that is impossible if the pamphlet is ascribed to Theramenes.

[77] *A.u.A.*, i. 260–90; 276–7 suggests that *A.P.* consulted several *Atthides* but all supported the democracy under which they were written. On Wilamowitz' theory of an austere early chronicle, expanded into an *Atthis* by an unknown writer *c*. 380, see Jacoby, *Atthis, passim*.

[78] *A.u.A.*, i. 122.

[79] *A.u.A.*, i. 304–7.

[80] *A.u.A.*, i. 122–3.

[81] *A.u.A.*, i. 373.

[82] *G.G.*, ii². 34–5. For extensive use of Androtion cf. B. Keil, *Die solonische Verfassung in Aristoteles Verfassungsgeschichte Athens*, 190–4.

[83] *Hermes* xxvii 1892, 260–86 = *Kliene Schriften*, ii. 417–42; T. Reinach, *REG* iv 1891, 143–58, had suggested that the interpolations which he claimed to detect in *A.P.* (cf. below, pp. 53–4) were from a work by Critias.

[84] *G.G.*, ii². 13, 42 n., 50.

[85] *G.G.*, ii². viii, 800–1, cf. III. i. 25–7, III. ii. 606–9, 703.

[86] *G.G.*, ii². 54 with n. 2, cf. *Hermes* xxxiii 1898, 71–86.

[87] *Afinskaja politija Aristotelja kak istotschik dlja isstorii gossudarsstwennowa sstroja Afinn*, known to me from *JAW* xxiii Bibl. = lxxxvi 1895, 62, V. von Schoeffer, *JAW* xxiii. i = lxxxiii 1895, 203–5 no. 22 and 215–21.

INTRODUCTION

from a democratic Atthidographer's reply and his knowledge of documents from an *Atthis* or from direct consultation; the oligarchic pamphlet could be dismissed as *ein ziemlich wesenloser Schatten*.[88] Busolt when he returned to the subject felt able to attribute an increasing amount of the material in *A.P.* to Androtion, and thought that what remained might come from a variety of sources.[89]

This view that Androtion was *A.P.*'s principal source has become orthodox doctrine. Jacoby in his *Atthis* and *F.G.H.* suggested that the Atthidographers do not represent a uniform tradition but different writers had different political attitudes: Clidemus was a supporter of the democracy, and may perhaps be detected behind *A.P.*'s allusions to οἱ δημοτικοί;[90] Androtion was a pupil of Isocrates and a sympathiser with the 'moderate' views of Theramenes, and his presentation of Athenian history will therefore have been particularly congenial to *A.P.*;[91] Phanodemus' interests were religious and educational rather than political.[92] In his more cautious moments Jacoby suggested that *A.P.* used more than one *Atthis*, and also a variety of poems, documents and partisan pamphlets;[93]

> ...but even when eliminating everything that is doubtful we may confidently maintain that A. stands as a source for Aristotle beside, or even before, Herodotos and Thukydides, who could be used as a basis for certain portions only because they did not treat Attic history in its full extent. The *Atthis* of A. is the book which gave Aristotle the general framework, and which was used in the historical introduction for the details of Attic history and Attic institutions mostly, even if not alone.[94]

Day & Chambers repeat as a view of his sources which is 'universally accepted' that *A.P.* made some use of Clidemus and depended most heavily on Androtion, and regard the suggested oligarchic pamphlet as an unnecessary complication.[95] In the most recent extended study of *A.P.*'s sources J. H. Schreiner has followed up Jacoby's remarks on the different political standpoints of the different Atthidographers: he suggests that *A.P.* worked almost exclusively from three sources, relying most heavily on the 'moderate' Androtion, but drawing pro-democratic material from Clidemus and extreme anti-democratic material from Phanodemus (he supposes that each

---

[88] *Op. cit.*, 216.
[89] *G.S.*, i. 91–7.
[90] *Atthis*, 75 with 294 n. 25, *Supp.* i. 81–2.
[91] *Atthis*, 78, *Supp.* i. 87–8, 95–9.
[92] *Atthis*, 78, *Supp.* i. 172–3.
[93] Esp. *Atthis*, 234–5 n. 36, *Supp.* ii. 100; cf. below, p. 21 n. 128.
[94] *Supp.* ii. 101. See in general *Atthis*, 156, 213, 384 n. 30; *Supp.* ii. 91–3 n. 86, 99 n. 124, i. 103–4 with ii. 99–102 n. 127, ii. 107 n. 27, i. 145 with ii. 133 n. 17.
[95] *A.H.A.D.*, 5–12.

of these wrote in order to rebut his predecessor's account); the many awkwardnesses in *A.P.*'s narrative result from his failure to resolve satisfactorily the conflicting accounts which he found in these three histories.[96]†

In contrast to this emphasis on the Atthidographers, O. Seeck[97] and A. von Mess[98] developed Wilamowitz' idea of a Theramenist pamphlet. Seeck, noting that *A.P.*'s first part mentions nothing later than the raising of assembly pay to 3 obols in the late 390's (41. iii), supposed that the whole of the first part is based on a Theramenist work of *c.* 390, to which Aristotle added in his own copy a few notes from the researches of Demetrius of Phalerum; Mess declared more forcefully that Aristotle never opened Herodotus, Thucydides or an Atthidographer, but at most used superficially in addition to this work his school's antiquarian researches on the archonship. This view, which makes *A.P.* a mere transcript of an *ur-A.P.* written some sixty years before, is not necessary to explain why the historical narrative ends where it does,[99] and has rightly been rejected; Wilamowitz' view that *A.P.* used both the *Atthides* and a Theramenist pamphlet was revived by Hignett.[100]

A more thorough investigation of *A.P.*'s sources was undertaken by G. Mathieu in *Aristote, Constitution d'Athènes: essai sur la méthode suivie par Aristote dans la discussion des textes.*[101] According to him *A.P.* made limited use of Herodotus and Thucydides; otherwise, only the most austerely chronological material is derived from the *Atthides*, and by far the larger part comes from partisan writings. *A.P.* did not confine his attention to one work: many passages in his narrative are of a pro-democratic slant, and must come from a work by an unknown democratic author; also he had two anti-democratic sources, of different kinds, a pamphlet dealing in personal invective, by Critias (or a member of his circle),[102] and a theoretical work on political institutions, by a supporter of Theramenes. As Schreiner was to argue later in connection with his theory of three *Atthides*, Mathieu claimed that inconsistencies and obscurities in *A.P.*'s narrative result from his failure to solve the problems presented by his differing sources. This view of *A.P.*'s sources has been repeated by A. Tovar.[103]

---

[96] *SO* Supp. xxi 1968, esp. 13–20.
[97] *Klio* iv 1904, 270–326, esp. 282–92.
[98] *RM*² lxiii 1908, 382–4, *VDP* I 1909, 147–9, *RM*² lxvi 1911, 356–92.
[99] Cf. pp. 9 with n. 39, 33.
[100] *H.A.C.*, 5–6, 28.
[101] Conclusions summarised pp. 114–28; cf. Mathieu & Haussoullier, iv–xiv.
[102] By Critias, *Aristote*, 119–21; by Critias or a disciple, Mathieu & Haussoullier, vi.
[103] Tovar, 31–4.

INTRODUCTION

Recently P. E. Harding has argued in a series of articles that Androtion's political career does not show any kind of ideological commitment,[104] that the aim of Clidemus and Androtion in writing their *Atthides* was not to interpret Athens' history on 'democratic' and 'moderate' lines but simply to give an accurate account of it, and that, although some of the facts in *A.P.* may be drawn from the *Atthides*, the orthodox view attaches far too much importance to them and too little to other possible sources, including Aristotle's own opinions and research.[105] Harding's attack on orthodoxy is justified, but his own case is over-stated. Evidence for Clidemus' attitudes is minimal: that he was awarded a crown for his *Atthis* by the δῆμος in the middle of the fourth century does not prove democratic bias;[106] 323 FF 7–8 do not prove that he regarded Cleisthenes rather than Solon as the founder of the democracy, nor, if he did, would that prove democratic bias;[107] it should be accepted that F 21 gives a pro-Themistocles account of the provision of money before Salamis whereas *A.P.* 23. i gives an anti-Themistocles account,[108] and that men associated with Themistocles were responsible for weakening the Areopagus in the interests of democracy in the 460's whereas Cimon opposed them,[109] but this one instance is meagre support for the view that Clidemus consistently displayed democratic bias. Androtion probably was the son of the Andron who under the intermediate régime of 411/0 proposed the trial of Antiphon and others;[110] he was a pupil of Isocrates,[111] who was himself a pupil of Theramenes,[112] and whose works consistently show a distaste for extreme democracy;[113] his own career, like that of other fourth-century politicians, shows that he acquiesced in the

---

[104] *Hist.* xxv 1976, 186–200.
[105] *Phoen.* xxviii 1974, 282–9, *Hist.* xxvi 1977, 148–60, cf. *Phoen.* xxviii 1974, 101–11.
[106] Tert. *An.* 52 = Clid. 323 T 2, with Harding, *Hist.* xxvi 1977, 151–2, against Jacoby *ad loc.*
[107] Harding, *op. cit.*, 152, against Jacoby *ad loc.*
[108] Jacoby *ad loc.*, contr. Harding, *op. cit.*, 153–4.
[109] Cf. on 25. i.
[110] Crat. 342 F 5 ap. Harp. Ἄνδρων, [Pl.] *X. Or.* 833 E; but D. XXII. *Andr.* 33–4, 56, 68, omits to mention this to the discredit of Androtion's father: e.g. Jacoby, *Supp.* i. 87 with ii. 80 n. 25.
[111] Evidence collected at Andr. 324 T 2.
[112] D. H. 535. *Is.* 1, [Pl.] *X. Or.* 836 F–837 A, *Vit. Is.* (Baiter & Sauppe, ii, p. 3 A; Mathieu & Brémond, Budé ed. of Is., i, p. xxxiii), schol. Ar. *Ran.* 541, Suid. (Δ 234) δέξιος.
[113] Harding attacks the view of Isocrates as a trainer of conservative politicians in *CSCA* vi 1973, 137–49, esp. 138–40. I agree with N. H. Baynes, *Byzantine Studies and Other Essays*, 144–67, that Isocrates is not to be taken too seriously as a political thinker, but I see no reason to doubt that he did dislike extreme democracy. Pupils are not bound to accept their masters' views, but neither are they bound to reject them. On *A.P.* and Isocrates see the following paragraph.

INTRODUCTION

democracy but does not show whether his acquiescence was enthusiastic or reluctant.[114] On the actual or supposed fragments which have been thought to betray his bias, I agree with Harding that *A.P.* 23. i, disagreeing with Clidemus, cannot reliably be derived from Androtion,[115] and that Androtion did not attempt for political reasons to detach ostracism from Cleisthenes,[116] but I continue to think that the object of Androtion's eccentric interpretation of the σεισάχθεια in 324 F 34 was to free Solon from the charge of having undertaken so dangerous a measure as the cancellation of debts.[117] This fragment is evidence that Androtion could be biased against extreme democracy; but it has not been proved that his work was permeated by such bias, or that any of the seriously biased material in *A.P.* is derived from him.

Correspondences have been noticed between *A.P.* and Isocrates.[118] Most strikingly, 26. i resembles Is. VIII. *Pace*, 86–8, on the casualties in Athens' fifth-century wars; the number of Athenians killed by the Thirty is given as 1,500 in 35. iv and in Is. VII. *Areop.* 67, xx. *Lochit.* 11 (and A. III. *Ctes.* 235);[119] notice also 23. ii with Is. VII. *Areop.* 50–5 and other passages cited *ad loc.*, 28. iv with Is. VIII. *Pace*, 75, and with XII. *Panath.* 132–3.[120] The pupils of Isocrates included Androtion, but he had many other pupils too; his writings were well known to Aristotle,[121] and Aristotle shared his dislike of extreme democracy. In 35. iv and perhaps in 26. i we should think of a common source; of the other resemblances we ought perhaps to say no more than that themes treated by Isocrates gained a wide currency.

My own view of *A.P.*'s sources resembles that of Buseskul, or Jacoby at his most cautious. *A.P.* did use Herodotus and Thucydides where they treated Athenian topics fully enough to be of use to him;[122] he did not use Xenophon, but ch. 36 and Xenophon both draw on the same defence of Theramenes; it is unlikely that he used Ephorus on the events of 404–403, but there is a little material on

---

[114] Harding, *Hist.* xxv 1976, 186–200. On ideology in fourth-century politics see Rhodes, *LCM* iii 1978, 207–11.

[115] *Hist.* xxvi 1977, 154–5: cf. above.

[116] *Op. cit.*, 157–8, cf. J. J. Keaney, *Hist.* xix 1970, 9–11, against the view of Jacoby and Day & Chambers, cited above, p. 11 with n. 55.

[117] *Pace* Harding, *Phoen.* xxviii 1974, 282–9: cf. on 6. i.

[118] See especially W. L. Newman, *CR* v 1891, 160–1.

[119] Schol. A. I. *Tim.* 39 gives 1,500 as the figure of ἔνιοι, 2,500 as the figure of Lysias.

[120] Cf. pp. 39–40 on traces of Isocratean language in *A.P.*

[121] Cf. Newman, *loc. cit.*; W. D. Ross, *Aristotle*, 3, observes that 'there is no writer (except Homer) whom he quotes so often in the *Rhetoric*.'

[122] I do not agree with Levi, i. 203, 205, that an intermediary must be postulated to explain the small differences between *A.P.* and Herodotus.

INTRODUCTION

the tyranny which may come from him.[123] The material which can most reliably be attributed to an *Atthis* is the chronological—probably the account of the kings in the lost beginning; the chronological notes on the period after Solon's reforms and on the tyranny; possibly the account of Cleisthenes' reforms in 21, linked to the archonship of Isagoras, and more certainly the series of political *fasti* in 22 (including the passage on the institution of ostracism, for which the dependence of *A.P.* on Androtion seems assured); and the laws of the 450's in 26. ii–iv. Direct points of contact between *A.P.* and fragments of the *Atthides* are in fact very few. With Hellanicus (*c.* 400[124]) there are none. With Clidemus (*c.* 350[125]) there are two points of disagreement, between 21. v and 323 F 8 on the ναυκραρίαι, and between 23. i and F 21 on the provision of money before Salamis; on Phye, the woman who posed as Athena for Pisistratus, *A.P.* is aware of different versions, but 14. iv does not mention what is distinctive in F 15, and I doubt if we can conclude much from the fact that both use the participle of παραιβατεῖν but Herodotus does not.[126] The fragments of Androtion (*c.* 340[127]) offer three serious points of contact: between 6. i and 10 and 324 F 34 on Solon's σεισάχθεια and reform of measures, weights, and coinage, revealing that they disagreed certainly on the σεισάχθεια and also, I believe, on how the relationship between the drachma and the mina was altered; 22. iii–iv and F 6 on the institution of ostracism, where I believe that Androtion is reported correctly by *A.P.* and incorrectly in F 6; 29. ii and F 43 against T. VIII. 67. i on the συγγραφεῖς of 411, where they agree and I believe are right.[128] With Phanodemus (*c.* 335[129]) we again have no points of contact. However, the *Atthides* existed, and it is hard to imagine that *A.P.* would not have used them where they offered the kind of detail that he wanted.

Partisan literature was undoubtedly written in the late fifth and early fourth centuries, and probably in some quantity. We have long known the *Athenaion Politeia* preserved with the works of Xenophon.[130] More recently a Heidelberg papyrus has been recognised as a

---

[123] The attempt of R. Werner, *Ath.*² xxxvi 1958, 48–89, to detect extensive use of Ephorus in the chapters on the tyranny and in 21–2 is unconvincing.

[124] Jacoby, *Supp.* i. 5.

[125] *Ibid.* 58; but the argument from F 8 (cf. below, p. 680) is unsatisfactory.

[126] Contr. Sandys², xlvii.

[127] Jacoby, *Supp.* i. 103; but the restoration of Did. *In Dem.* viii. 14–15 = Andr. 324 T 13 has been challenged by G. L. Cawkwell, *CQ*² xiii 1963, 131 n. 1, Harding, *Hist.* xxv 1976, 197–8.

[128] There is no good reason to think that FF 10–11 prove the use of Androtion in *A.P.* 38, or F 35 in 15. iii, or F 37 in 28. iii: cf. Jacoby *ad locc.*

[129] Jacoby, *Supp.* i. 173.

[130] In fact iii. 4 of that work and *A.P.* 24. iii, at the end of the list of τρεφόμενοι, make the same surprising combination of war orphans and keepers of the gaol, which they presumably owe to a common source.

fragment of a similar work, of similar date;[131] and the 'Theramenes papyrus' is probably part of a defence of Theramenes, written early in the fourth century by a man who knew Lys. XII. *Erat.* 68–70 and XIII. *Agor.* 8–11, and probably that or a work like it is the common source of Xenophon and *A.P.* on Theramenes' objections to the extremists among the Thirty.[132] Antiphon's speech in his own defence, under the intermediate régime of 411/0, was admired by Thucydides (who was not in Athens to hear it delivered) and by others:[133] there are papyrus fragments at Geneva which are normally thought to belong to this speech; some have doubted the attribution, but if this is not the defence of Antiphon it is a defence of one of the other extremists of 411;[134] plausible but not conclusive cases have been made both for Antiphon's defence and for Androtion's *Atthis* as the source of *A.P.*'s non-Thucydidean material on the revolutions of 411.[135] Speeches by Andocides and Lysias for political trials survive, and many other political speeches which do not now survive will have been put into circulation. If we believe that *A.P.* used writings of this kind we are not inventing unnecessary entities but assuming that he used material which we know existed.[136]†

We must also take into consideration a kind of writing which is represented for us by three non-Athenians. Stesimbrotus of Thasos wrote at the end of the fifth century περὶ Θεμιστοκλέους καὶ Θουκυδίδου καὶ Περικλέους:[137] this was long assumed to be a political pamphlet directed against Athens' oppression of her allies;[138] that view was undermined by F. Schachermeyr, who regarded Stesimbrotus' work as a character-centred biographical history, not political at all;[139] most recently K. Meister has accepted that this was a history rather than a political pamphlet but has shown that it was biased in favour

[131] P. Heid. 182 with M. Gigante, *Maia* ix 1957, 68–74.
[132] P. Mich. 5982, published by R. Merkelbach and H. C. Youtie, *ZPE* ii 1968, 161–9, cf. W. Luppe, *ibid.* xxxii 1978, 14–16, interpreted by A. Henrichs, *ibid.* iii 1969, 101–8, A. Andrewes, *ibid.* vi 1970, 35–8. An alternative interpretation by B. R. I. Sealey, *ibid.* xvi 1975, 279–88, is possible but I think less likely.
[133] T. VIII. 68. ii, Arist. *E.E.* III. 1232 B 6–9 (quoting Agathon), [Pl.] *X. Or.* 833 B.
[134] J. Nicole, *L'Apologie d'Antiphon*, cf. the standard editions of Antiphon: attribution doubted by G. Pasquali, *SSAC* i 1908, 46–57, Beloch, *G.G.*², II. i. 392 n. 1, P. Roussel, *REA* xxvi 1925, 5–10.
[135] Cf. pp. 366–7.
[136] It was of course harder for an ancient writer than for a modern to make use of a large number of texts, as is stressed by Schreiner, *SO* Supp. xxi 1968, 13–14; but if it is credible that Plutarch read a fair proportion of the many works which he cites in his writings it must also be credible that *A.P.* should have consulted several works.
[137] Ath. XIII. 589 E = Stes. 107 F 10a: see FF 1–11.
[138] E.g. Wilamowitz, *Hermes* xii 1877, 361–7 = *Kleine Schriften*, iii. 35–40, Jacoby *ad auct.*
[139] *Sb. Wien* CCXLVII. V 1965 = *Forschungen und Betrachtungen*, 151–71.

INTRODUCTION

of Sparta and aristocracy.[140] Theopompus of Chios, who wrote perhaps a little earlier than *A.P.* or perhaps about the same time as *A.P.*, included in book x of his *Philippica* a digression περὶ τῶν Ἀθήνησι δημαγωγῶν and in book xxv a further digression on fifth-century Athens.[141] The tradition was continued in the third century by Idomeneus of Lampsacus, who wrote ⟨περὶ τῶν Ἀθήνησι⟩ν δημαγωγῶν.[142] Stesimbrotus' fragments offer no point of contact with *A.P.* Theopompus, 115 F 89, and *A.P.* 27. iii both write of the generosity of Cimon, diverging to some extent but agreeing that Pericles' generosity with the state's resources was a gambit to counter Cimon's generosity with his own, so that a common source has been suggested;[143] F 92 and 28. iii use very similar language of the demagogy of Cleon, and here too a common source has been suggested.[144] *A.P.* 28 contains a list of successive aristocratic and democratic leaders, which appears to have been taken over from some earlier work:[145] Gomme and Raubitschek have suggested that Theopompus was the source of this list;[146] I am not so confident, but the compiler was surely not an Atthidographer, and may well have been a writer in this tradition rather than an Athenian pamphleteer. There are other places where Gomme has suggested that Theopompus lies behind *A.P.* and Stesimbrotus lies behind Theopompus: in the criticism of Solon cited in 6. ii and 9. ii,[147] in ch. 24 with its list of τρεφόμενοι[148] (but I am not as sure as most scholars that this list was compiled by a man of oligarchic bias who disapproved of τροφή), and in 26. i on Cimon's leadership and Athens' losses in war[149] (but an apologetic anti-democratic source in Athens seems likelier).†

On the revolutions of 411 and 404 *A.P.* gives us material derived ultimately from documents: most obviously the two constitutions in 30–1 and the terms of reconciliation in 39; also the decree of Pythodorus and the rider of Clitophon in 29. i–iii; the report in 29. iv, more specific than that of Thucydides, of the withdrawal of safeguards by the συγγραφεῖς and the report in 29. v of the resolutions

---

[140] *Hist.* xxvii 1978, 274–94.
[141] Ath. iv. 166 D = Thp. 115 F 100: see FF 85–100 (x), 153–6 (xxv). On these digressions see W. R. Connor, *Theopompus and Fifth-Century Athens*; on his date, pp. 4–5, 109–10.
[142] *L.S.* 249. 27 = Idom. 338 F 2: see FF 1–15.
[143] Wade-Gery, *AJP* lix 1938, 131–4 = *Essays*, 235–8, cf. Connor, *op. cit.*, 110.
[144] Connor, *op. cit.*, 108–10 cf. 48–9; Gomme, *Hist. Comm. Thuc.*, i. 48 n. 1, had suggested that *A.P.* used Theopompus.
[145] Cf. p. 15.
[146] Gomme, *loc. cit.*; Raubitschek, *Phoen.* ix 1955, 125, xiv 1960, 82–3.
[147] *Op. cit.*, 47 n. 2.
[148] *Op. cit.*, 47–8, cf. *CR* xl 1926, 8.
[149] *Op. cit.*, 48 n. 1.

adopted by the assembly at Colonus; the precise dates in 32; the reference to the decree of Dracontides in 34. iii; perhaps the archon of 404/3 and the early acts of the Thirty, in 35. i–ii; the laws used as an excuse for the elimination of Theramenes, in 37. i. We have 'laws of Solon which they no longer use' in 8. iii and an ancient law against tyranny in 16. x. 5 and 12 quote extracts from Solon's poems, 7. iv quotes an epigram, implying that it is still visible on the Acropolis, and 19. iii and 20. v quote scolia. The documents of the oligarchs were probably not consulted in the archives by *A.P.* but quoted for him by one of his sources: with the exception of financial records, needed for continuity, the democrats will not have been anxious to preserve oligarchic documents; and in 29. i the reference to Melobius' speaking to the motion, and possibly the demotic of Pythodorus, suggest that the documents came to *A.P.* accompanied by a certain amount of narrative. The epigram in 7. iv is said to be part of the evidence adduced by ἔνιοι; and it is not *A.P.* but Thucydides who cites the dedications of the younger Pisistratus (VI. 54. vi) and the stele commemorating the downfall of the tyrants (VI. 55. i–ii: in view of his error over Thessalus *A.P.* can hardly have examined the stele).[150] Similarly I suspect that the relevant poems of Solon were quoted for *A.P.* by one of his sources: a man living in fourth-century Athens will of course have known Solon's poems, but from the end of the fifth century men had looked back to Solon or earlier for the origins of the democracy,[151] and, given the use that Thucydides was prepared to make of Homer,[152] I should be surprised if Solon's poems on political themes were not exploited until the time of *A.P.* This is perhaps confirmed by 5. iii, where *A.P.* introduces with the words ἐν τοῖσδε τοῖς ποιήμασιν a quotation of four consecutive lines; there is no other use of the plural to denote the lines of a single poem earlier than Dionysius of Halicarnassus; and this quotation conspicuously fails to prove the point which it is said to prove, though it is followed by a comment which is appropriate. The explanation may be that *A.P.* was following a source which did at this point include a quotation which seemed to show that Solon was one of the μέσοι πολῖται, but in abbreviating from this source he omitted that quotation while retaining the passage which introduced it.[153] As it is unlikely that

---

[150] I doubt the suggestion of Wade-Gery, *CQ* xxvii 1933, 18 = *Essays*, 136–7, that a small divergence from Herodotus in 20. iii depends on an inscription.

[151] Cf. pp. 159, 261, 376, 428.

[152] T. I. 9–10.

[153] On 5. iii cf. also p. 41. The possibility that *A.P.* found Solon's poems quoted by his source is strengthened by the fact that *A.P.* and Pl. *Sol.*, which probably have a common source, agree to a considerable extent but not entirely in their selections from the poems.

INTRODUCTION

the author went directly to the archives or to the collected works of Solon, I doubt if he made direct use of old comedy: comedy may have contributed to the list of τρεφόμενοι in 24. iii, and to the idea of a succession of προστάται and more particularly to the description of Cleon in 28. ii–iii, but I should expect to find clearer traces if *A.P.* had consulted the plays himself. However, even when he relies largely on earlier written accounts, a writer may from time to time introduce what he simply happens to know: the scolia in 19. iii and 20. v may fall into this category; since the works of the Aristotelian school included five books on Solon's ἄξονες, *A.P.* may have inserted his quotations from ancient laws from his own knowledge;[154] and I suspect that the brief and inaccurate passage in 34. i which bridges the gap between 410 and 404 may be due not to a bad source but to the author's writing out what he thought he knew without bothering to check his facts.

A.P. does not tell us how he knows what he knows. In eleven places he indicates that there is a difference of opinion:[155] all concern what are for his purpose secondary issues; in six of them he states his own preference; in one of the others he says that the difference is unimportant. Three times he goes out of his way to indicate unanimity, each time in connection with Solon: 'Every one agrees, and he has mentioned it in his poetry.'[156] There are a number of issues, often more important issues, on which we know that disagreements existed but *A.P.* does not acknowledge the fact. 22. vii conflicts with H. VII. 144. i on Themistocles' shipbuilding programme; 17–18 agrees with Herodotus and Thucydides that Hipparchus was not the reigning tyrant and his murder did not put an end to the tyranny, but disagrees with all previous accounts known to us on the Pisistratid family and the member of the family who was the cause of the trouble; disagreements with Clidemus and Androtion have been noted above;[157] 8. i–ii disagrees with Arist. *Pol.* II. 1273 B 40–1274 A 2[158] on Solon and the election of magistrates; and these are all silent diagreements. When *A.P.* does refer to a disagreement, he usually mentions the champions of rival views simply as οἱ μέν and οἱ δέ, or τινες, or ἔνιοι; uniquely in 14. iv he ascribes one version to Herodotus; but in 18. iv, on the bearing of

---

[154] No. 140 in Hesychius' list of Aristotle's works: Rose's Teubner ed. of the fragments, p. 16, Düring, *Aristotle in the Ancient Biographical Tradition*, 87. 35. ii quotes a law which the Thirty annulled: it was a notorious law, and I doubt if *A.P.* verified the text.
[155] 3. iii, *6. ii–iv, *7. iv, *9. ii, 14. iv, *17. ii, 17. iv, *18. iv, 18. v, (27. iv), *28. v: preference indicated in asterisked passages, difference said to be unimportant in 3. iii.
[156] 5. iii, 6. iv, 12. i; cf. also 28. v (below).
[157] P. 21.
[158] Cf. 1274 A 16–17, III. 1281 B 25–34.

25

arms in the Panathenaic procession, he says that ὁ λεγόμενος λόγος...
οὐκ ἀληθής ἐστιν without telling us that this λόγος is to be found in
Thucydides. In three places he does not identify his sources
but does characterise them: in 6. ii the τινες who told the story
that Solon gave advance notice of the σεισάχθεια to his friends are
subdivided into οἱ δημοτικοί and οἱ βουλόμενοι βλασφημεῖν; in 18. v,
when Aristogiton under torture denounces friends of the Pisistratids,
οἱ δημοτικοί regard this as a device to weaken the tyranny while
ἔνιοι regard the denunciation as true; in 28. v, after naming Nicias,
Thucydides and Theramenes as the best of the more recent politicians,
A.P. says that nearly all agree on the first two but there is a dispute
over Theramenes—but 'to those who do not judge superficially'
Theramenes seems not a destroyer of all régimes ὥσπερ αὐτὸν
διαβάλλουσι but a supporter of all lawful régimes. Jacoby suggested
tentatively, and Schreiner firmly asserted, that when he refers to
οἱ δημοτικοί *A.P.* means Clidemus,[159] but I suspect that when he
applies this kind of label to his sources *A.P.* is alluding to more
obviously partisan writings; similarly on 28. v it has already been
suggested by Andrewes that 'those who do judge superficially' are
the authors of political pamphlets hostile to Theramenes.[160]

When *A.P.* tells us why he prefers one account to another, he says
not that he has evidence which proves that one is right (which is not
to say that there was no evidence) but that one seems more reasonable. οὐ γὰρ εἰκός that Solon would behave dishonourably in small
things when he behaved honourably in great; ταύτην μὲν οὖν χρὴ
νομίζειν ψευδῆ τὴν αἰτίαν εἶναι (6. ii–iv). Those who believe that the
ἱππεῖς were so called because they were men who could maintain a
horse adduce as a σημεῖον the name of the class and equestrian
dedications by members of it; οὐ μὴν ἀλλ' εὐλογώτερον that the same
kind of criterion should be used for ἱππεῖς as for πεντακοσιομέδιμνοι
(7. iv). οὐ μὴν εἰκός to suppose that Solon deliberately incorporated
ambiguities in his laws; οὐ γὰρ δίκαιον to judge from present-day
practice rather than from the rest of his πολιτεία (9. ii). One criterion
which *A.P.* is willing to employ is chronology: those who say that
Solon was Pisistratus' lover φανερῶς ληροῦσιν: οὐ γὰρ ἐνδέχεται ταῖς
ἡλικίαις (17. ii). It is untrue that Hippias caught his brother's
assassins by telling the members of the Panathenaic procession to
stand aside from their arms: the armed procession did not exist
then but was instituted later (18. iv). Praise of Theramenes is
justified by interpretation: he was not a wrecker of all régimes but
a supporter of all lawful régimes (28. v). Similarly (on a point
which *A.P.* does not suggest was controversial) the statement that
the archon was the most recently created of the three senior

[159] Cf. p. 17.
[160] *ZPE* vi 1970, 37–8.

magistrates is supported by the σημεῖον that he is not responsible for 'traditional' ceremonies as the other two are (3. iii). That the headquarters of the basileus used to be the Bucoleum is confirmed by the σημεῖον that the sacred marriage of the βασίλιννα and Dionysus is still held there (3. v). That Solon provided for the appointment of the archons by lot according to property-class is supported by the σημεῖον that the comparable law on the appointment of the treasurers of Athena is still in force (8. i). The struggle over the archonship after Solon's reforms makes it δῆλον that that was the most important office (13. ii). That Pisistratus' party included men not of pure Athenian descent is supported by the σημεῖον of a διαψηφισμός on the fall of the tyranny (13. v).

Wilamowitz was right to claim that *A.P.* was not an original researcher, as far as the historical part is concerned. He relied on those previous writings in which he could find detailed accounts of the matters in which he was interested (and matters of marginal relevance to his theme might be treated at disproportionate length if detailed accounts happened to be available, as they were for the beginning and the end of the tyranny). If these previous writers quoted evidence he was happy to follow them, but he did not look for further evidence himself: when his sources disagreed he followed the one that seemed to him to be more reasonable; and his divergence from all his predecessors on the Pisistratid family, and his insertion of the 'Draconian constitution' (if he made that insertion himself[161]) suggest that sometimes what he thought most reasonable was simply what was most precise or most up to date. But frequently he tried to combine what he read in different sources rather than choose between them. In 14–15 his combination of an Atthidographer's chronology with Herodotus nearly succeeds, but that chronology seems to have been based partly on the misunderstanding of one of the data provided by Herodotus, with the result that in 14. iii and 15. i *A.P.* repeats from Herodotus that Pisistratus remained in power only for a short time but adds from his *Atthis* that that time was of several years' duration. More disastrously, 18. i prepares us for a story of Hipparchus' murder in which Hipparchus was the villain whose advances to Harmodius provoked the murderers, but in 18. ii Hipparchus' place is taken by Thessalus.[162] The list of προστάται in 28. ii–iii does not correspond to *A.P.*'s main narrative: there Miltiades is the opponent of Xanthippus but in 22 he is not mentioned; Themistocles and Aristides are on opposite sides there (I believe) but on the same side in 23. iii; Cimon is the opponent of Ephialtes there but does not appear until after Ephialtes' death in 25–6; Thucydides is the opponent of Pericles there but does not

[161] Cf. pp. 45–6, 53, 60.
[162] Cf. pp. 50, 54–5.

INTRODUCTION

appear in 27. Although I dissent from their conclusions, because I think *A.P.* read more widely than they are prepared to allow, I believe that Mathieu and Schreiner were in principle right to examine these awkwardnesses as evidence for *A.P.*'s combination of material from different sources.

I have done what I can in the course of the commentary, and in particular in the introductions to the successive sections, to indicate what sources *A.P.* has used. Here I summarise my findings; an asterisk draws attention to a passage in which one or more variants are noted.

—	The lost beginning. Probably from one or more *Atthides*.
1	Cylon. Treated by H. and T., but neither was *A.P.*'s main source; same source used in Pl. *Sol.* 12.
2–3*	στάσις before Solon. Same source used in Pl. *Sol.* 13. Chs. 2–12 form an organised whole,[163] and it is likely that the same main source was used throughout.
4	'Draconian constitution.' Fabricated late c5 or c4, and late insertion in *A.P.*; but insertion probably displaced section on Draco's θεσμοί.
5–12*	Solon. Main source not Androtion; probably included quotations from Solon; same source used in Pl. *Sol.*; either an *Atthis* or a separate work on Solon. 9. ii shows affinity with Arist. *Pol.*; 10, disagreeing with Androtion, interrupts arrangement[164] and may not be from main source.
13	στάσις after Solon. At any rate §§i–ii from an *Atthis*. Parties (§§iii–v) treated by H. but he was not *A.P.*'s source; Pl. *Sol.* 13 similar to *A.P.* but dates parties before Solon.
14–15*	Rise of Pisistratus. H. main source; chronology from an *Atthis*; some other matter.
16	Rule of Pisistratus. Unclear how far *A.P.* put material together, how far a source did this.
17–18*	Murder of Hipparchus. Chronology of 17. i from an *Atthis*; T. used but *A.P.* diverges on Pisistratid family and other details; on family disagrees with all known earlier writers; 18. i–ii incoherent combination of incompatible sources.
19	Expulsion of Hippias. H. main source; chronology from an *Atthis*; some other matter.
20. i–iii	Cleisthenes and Isagoras. From H.

---

[163] Cf. pp. 14, 45–7.
[164] Cf. pp. 47, 54.

INTRODUCTION

20. iv–v	Alcmaeonid opposition to tyranny. From author's general knowledge?
21	Cleisthenes' reforms. Perhaps from Androtion.
22	*Fasti* after Cleisthenes. From Androtion.
23. i–ii^a, 27–28. i*	Oligarchic view of mid C5.
23. ii^b–24, 25. i–ii	Democratic view of mid C5. Both parts of 23 show affinity with Arist. *Pol*.
25. iii–iv	Themistocles and Ephialtes. Late insertion in *A.P.*
26. i	Cimon. Misplaced by *A.P.*; perhaps from apologetic anti-democratic source.
26. ii–iv	Laws of 450's. From an *Atthis*, perhaps that of Androtion.
28. ii–v*	Democratic and aristocratic leaders. Perhaps from writer in tradition of Stesimbrotus.
29–33	The Four Hundred and the Five Thousand. T. combined with apologetic source which quoted documents (perhaps Antiphon's defence, perhaps Androtion).[165]
34. i–ii	Between 410 and 404. From author's general knowledge?
34. iii–40	The Thirty, the Ten and the democratic restoration. Treated by X. *H.* and Ephorus but neither used by *A.P.*; defence of Theramenes used by X. *H.* and *A.P.*; *A.P.* perhaps from one main source, quoting documents and with 'moderate' bias.
41	Author's own summary. Comments on restored democracy show affinity with Arist. *Pol*.

If *A.P.* did not engage in original historical research, his value to the modern historian lies in what he preserves of material that is now lost, and in what he shows us of the way in which a fourth-century writer tried to reconcile conflicting sources and to solve historical problems. In 21–2 and 26. ii–iv we have valuable factual material which we did not have until *A.P.* was recovered. 25. i–ii

---

[165] There is one motif common to 29–33, 34. i–ii and 34. iii–40 (which does not necessarily prove that all three sections are from the same main source: probably *A.P.* is inserting an apologia which was commonly resorted to in the fourth century). In 411 the Athenians were compelled to set aside the democracy and substitute an oligarchy (ἠναγκάσθησαν, 29. i; *A.P.* does not say, as Arist. *Pol.* v. 1304 B 7–15 does, that the oligarchs used deceit); the δῆμος was deceived in the trial of the generals, and when the Spartans offered peace (ἐξαπατηθέντος, ἐξαπατηθέντες, 34. i); the δῆμος was terrified and compelled to appoint the Thirty (καταπλαγεὶς ... ἠναγκάσθη, 34. iii); cf. the reference to deceit in 28. iii. D.S. agrees with *A.P.* on Sparta's peace offer (XIII. 53. iii) and the institution of the Thirty (XIV. 3. vii), but not on the institution of the Four Hundred or the trial of the generals.

preserves a favourable account of Ephialtes' reform whereas previously we had only an unfavourable account. 29–33 incorporates a view of the setting-up of the oligarchy in 411 as the oligarchs wished it to appear; and although we may well think Thucydides' account, which stresses the terror and lawlessness of the revolution, a better one, *A.P.* has added to our understanding of the revolution a dimension which previously we did not possess. Similarly *A.P.*'s account of the Thirty appears to be wrong on the chronology, and in distinguishing two boards of Ten, for reasons of political bias, but the different defences of Theramenes in *A.P.* and Diodorus add to our understanding, and, particularly in chs. 39–40, *A.P.* here too preserves factual material not available to us in any other texts.

Where he could, *A.P.* tried to combine material from different sources, but he did not always appreciate the extent of their disagreements, and at times this has led to incoherence in his own account. When he was aware of a disagreement he looked not for proof but for reasonableness. He could be sensible in his judgments: it does not much affect the picture of Athens' constitutional development whether the first life archon was Medon or his son Acastus (3. iii); we are not likely to think that Solon left ambiguities in his laws deliberately, to place more power in the hands of juries, if we consider all that we know about his reforms (9. ii). On the other hand, the account of Pisistratus' sons which *A.P.* accepted was recent but wrong, and he failed to produce a coherent account of the murder of Hipparchus; the documents in chs. 30–1, though authentic documents of the oligarchs of 411, led him to a mistaken view of how the Four Hundred were appointed. We are greatly enriched by the recovery of *A.P.*'s narrative, but we must use his material more critically than he did.

3. *The Second Part of the* ATHENAION POLITEIA

The second part of *A.P.*, chs 42–69, is devoted to an analysis of the constitution in the author's own day. It may be summarised as follows: I quote the introductory (I) and resumptive (R) phrases which mark the beginnings and ends of *A.P.*'s principal sections;[166] the letters in the left-hand column refer to the sections of this commentary.

I^1 ἔχει δ' ἡ νῦν κατάστασις τῆς πολιτείας τόνδε τὸν τρόπον. (42. i)
I^2 μετέχουσιν μὲν τῆς πολιτείας ... (42. i)

---

[166] On his use of these phrases cf. pp. 44–5.

INTRODUCTION

L 42   REGISTRATION AND TRAINING OF CITIZENS.

R² τὰ μὲν οὖν περὶ τὴν τῶν πολιτῶν ἐγγραφὴν καὶ τοὺς ἐφήβους τοῦτον ἔχει τὸν τρόπον. (43. i)

I³ τὰς δ' ἀρχὰς τὰς περὶ τὴν ἐγκύκλιον διοίκησιν . . . (43. i)

M 43–62   OFFICIALS, SORTITIVE AND ELECTIVE.

I⁴ βουλὴ δὲ . . . (43. ii)

43. ii–49   The boule.

	43. ii–44	Prytanes, epistates; meetings of boule and assembly.
	45. i–iii	Powers of boule: judicial (not κυρία).
	45. iv	προβούλευσις.
	46. i	Navy.
	46. ii	Public works.

I⁵ συνδιοικεῖ δὲ καὶ ταῖς ἄλλαις ἀρχαῖς τὰ πλεῖστα. (47. i)

	47–8	Financial officials.
	49	δοκιμασίαι.

R⁵ συνδιοικεῖ δὲ καὶ ταῖς ἄλλαις ἀρχαῖς τὰ πλεῖσθ', ὡς ἔπος εἰπεῖν. (49. v)

R⁴ τὰ μὲν οὖν ὑπὸ τῆς βουλῆς διοικούμενα ταῦτ' ἐστίν. (50. i)

I⁶ κληροῦνται δὲ καὶ . . . (50. i)

N 50–4   Sortitive annual officials.

	50–1	Concerned with city facilities.
	52–3	Concerned with justice.

I⁶ ᵇⁱˢ κληροῦσι δὲ καὶ τάσδε τὰς ἀρχάς. (54. i)

	54	Various.

R⁶ αὗται μὲν οὖν αἱ ἀρχαὶ κληρωταί τε καὶ κύριαι τῶν εἰρημένων [πάντ]ων εἰσίν. (55. i)

I⁷ οἱ δὲ καλούμενοι ἐννέα ἄρχοντες . . . (55. i)

O 55–9   The archons.

	55–56. i	Appointment.
	56. ii–vii	Archon.
	57	Basileus.
	58	Polemarch.
	59. i–vi	Thesmothetae.
	59. vii	The whole college.

R⁷ τὰ μὲν οὖν περὶ τοὺς θ' ἄρχοντας τοῦτον ἔχει τὸν τρόπον. (60. i)

I⁸ κληροῦσι δὲ καὶ ἀθλοθέτας . . . (60. i)

INTRODUCTION

P 60 The athlothetae (sortitive, quadrennial).
I⁹ χειροτονοῦσι δὲ καὶ τὰς πρὸς τὸν πόλεμον ἀρχὰς ἀπάσας. (61. i)
Q 61 Elective military officials.
R 62 Concluding note on officials.

I¹⁰ τὰ δὲ δικαστήρια ... (63. i)
S 63–9 JURY-COURTS.
63–5 Allotment of jurors to courts.
66. i Allotment of magistrates to courts.
66. ii–iii Allotment of courtroom officials.
67 Timing of trials.
68. i Size of juries.
68. ii–69. i Voting.
69. ii τίμησις; payment of jurors.

After ch. 42, on the registration and training of young citizens, *A.P.* subdivides his analysis of the πολιτεία by authorities: the boule, with which are treated financial officials working directly under the supervision of the boule; miscellaneous sortitive officials; the archons; the athlothetae (treated separately as quadrennial officials); elective military officials; and finally the δικαστήρια. [D.] xxv. *Aristog. i.* 20 mentions as the four main manifestations of the state's working the meeting of the boule, the assembly of the δῆμος, the manning of the courts, and the succession of one year's ἀρχαί by those of the following year. A similar basic arrangement to *A.P.*'s can be found in the discussion of the best form of constitution in the closing chapters of Arist. *Pol.* IV, which treats first the citizen body (1296 B 13–1297 B 34), and then the τρία μόρια τῶν πολιτειῶν πασῶν (which resemble but are not identical with the conventional modern division into legislature, executive, and judicature) (1297 B 35–1298 A 9): τὸ βουλευόμενον περὶ τῶν κοινῶν (1298 A 9–1299 A 2), τὸ περὶ τὰς ἀρχάς (1299 A 3–1300 B 12) and τὸ δικάζον (1300 B 13–1301 A 15). However, *A.P.* has no separate treatment of τὸ βουλευόμενον περὶ τῶν κοινῶν, attaching what he does say on this theme to the boule and including that in his treatment of the ἀρχαί (with the result that the νομοθέται are omitted altogether); similarly, though he ends with an account of the δικαστήρια, much that concerns the administration of justice is treated in connection with the appropriate ἀρχαί. *A.P.*'s fairly systematic cataloguing of the various officials (but there is a striking distinction between officials working under the supervision of the boule, in 47–8, and other officials, in 50–4) corresponds to nothing in the discussion of the ἀρχαί in *Pol.* IV, which is devoted largely to the suitability of different offices to different kinds of constitution, and to methods of appointment

32

INTRODUCTION

(*A.P.* does not neglect the latter theme); but there is a survey of the kinds of official needed by a city-state at the end of *Pol.* VI (1321 B 4–1323 A 10), which at some points reflects Athenian practice but is not directly based on Athens.[167] In that survey six offices are said to be ἀναγκαιόταται (1321 B 6–1322 A 30):

1. ἀγορανόμοι   Cf. *A.P.* 51. i–iii.
2. ἀστυνόμοι   Cf. *A.P.* 50. ii, also 54. i (ὁδοποιοί).
3. ἀγρονόμοι   No Athenian equivalent.
4. ἀποδέκται   Cf. *A.P.* 48. i–ii.
5. ἱερομνήμονες   No direct Athenian equivalent.
6. Executors of sentences   Cf. *A.P.* 52. i.

Four kinds of offices are ἀναγκαίας μὲν οὐθὲν ἧττον, ἐν σχήματι δὲ μείζονι τεταγμένας (1322 A 30–B 29):

1. Military   Cf. *A.P.* 61.
2. Accounting   Cf. *A.P.* 48. iii–v, 54. ii.
3. Probouleutic   Cf. *A.P.* 43. ii–44, 45. iv.
4. Religious   Cf. *A.P.* 47. i, 50. i, 54. vii–viii, and on the archons.

Then follows a fresh summary of the kinds of office that are needed (1322 B 30–1323 A 6):

1. Religious; military; financial.
2. Concerned with facilities.
3. Judicial.
4. Deliberative.
5. (In some cities) disciplinary.

A.P.'s analysis thus uses the same kind of categories as Aristotle in the *Politics*, but neither work is in this respect directly dependent on the other.

In theory *A.P.* could have obtained his information from a study of the laws of Athens, or from observation of current practice, or from earlier analyses of the constitution. However, there is no evidence that any earlier analyses existed (though one such, his *Atthis* of *c.* 380, was postulated by Wilamowitz[168]), whereas the existence of a code of νόμοι revised at the end of the fifth century[169] will have made direct study of the laws in the fourth century a fairly easy task. Moreover, there are indications that it may have

[167] Discussed by Wilamowitz, *A.u.A.*, i. 234–8. For an earlier essay on the same theme see Plat. *Legg.* VI. 751 A 1–768 E 3.

[168] *A.u.A.*, i. 256–9 cf. 214–15, 225–6; cf. on 53. iv. But in the account of the ἐφηβεία, reorganised *c.* 335/4, he detected a freshness due to the author's writing from his own knowledge (194), and similarly he believed the account of the δικαστήρια in 63–9 to be written from direct knowledge (204–5). On the alleged *Atthis* of *c.* 380 cf. above, pp. 9 with n. 39, 18.

[169] Cf. pp. 441–2.

INTRODUCTION

been the organisation of that code of νόμοι which provided the pattern for the organisation of *A.P.*'s chapters on the ἀρχαί: *IG* i² 114 seems to have contained a collection, made in the early stages of the process of revision, of the laws relating to the boule;[170] and a law providing for the annual review of the new code divides the laws of Athens into four categories: τῶν βουλευτικῶν, τῶν κοινῶν, οἳ κεῖνται τοῖς ἐννέα ἄρχουσιν, τῶν ἄλλων ἀρχῶν.[171] Each section could be further subdivided: for instance, Ath. vi. 235 c quotes a provision ἐν τῷ τοῦ βασιλέως νόμῳ; we have references to the νόμος τῶν διαιτητῶν,[172] the εἰσαγγελτικὸς νόμος,[173] and the νόμοι τελωνικοί;[174] cf. *A.P.*'s usage in 8. iv, 22. i, iii. If the κοινοὶ νόμοι are those which are common to all ἀρχαί,[175] and for the most part need not be included in an analysis of the πολιτεία, the other three categories correspond to the three main subdivisions of *A.P.* 43–62 (but suggest that 50–4 would be better placed after 55–9, so as to lead directly to 60–2): in particular the use of βουλευτικοί as one of these categories may explain why *A.P.* attaches to the boule what he has to say about the assembly and about those officials whose work was directly supervised by the boule.

Wilamowitz[176] compares the law quoted in [D.] XLIII. *Mac.* 75 with *A.P.* 56. vii, where it is clear that what we have in *A.P.* is a summary of the law, transposed into the indicative mood; similarly the extracts from the homicide law in D. XXIII. *Arist.* 22 with 24, 53, 77, are summarised in *A.P.* 57. iii; and although throughout this second part *A.P.* uses language which does not prescribe what should be done but describes what is done, he often inserts such expressions as ὁ νόμος κελεύει or οἱ νόμοι κελεύουσιν.[177] There are several notes on differences between past and current practice:[178] these may be derived from an original law and an amending law, or from the author's general knowledge (and the latter must be

---

[170] Cf. Rhodes, *A.B.*, 195–9.
[171] *Ap.* D. xxiv. *Tim.* 20: the Review Law of D. M. MacDowell, *JHS* xcv 1975, 62–74.
[172] Lys. fr. 44 Sauppe, D. xxi. *Mid.* 94, *IG* ii² 179, 8.
[173] Hyp. IV. *Eux.* 3.
[174] D. xxiv. *Tim.* 101.
[175] MacDowell, *op. cit.*, 67; this is preferable to the suggestion of E. Ruschenbusch, *Hist.* Einz. ix 1966, 27–31, that they are the laws governing the behaviour of private citizens.
[176] *A.u.A.*, i. 258–9.
[177] 43. vi, 49. iv, 51. iii, 53. v, 53. vi; also 45. i, 48. i, 51. i, 57. iv, 60. ii, 67. i, 69. ii; also the use of expressions like δεῖ or οὐκ ἔξεστιν in 44. i, 44. iii, 44. iv, 45. iv, 46. i, 47. iii, 47. v, 48. i, 48. iv, 53. v, 54. i, 54. ii, 55. iv, 56. iii, 58. ii, 62. iii, 63. iii.
[178] 45. i (with the story of Eumelides and Lysimachus), 45. iii, 49. iii, 51. iii, 53. i, 53. iv, 54. iii, 54. vii, 55. i, 55. ii with iv, 56. iii, 56. iv, 60. ii, 61. i, 62. i, and apparently 67. iv–v.

invoked at any rate for the story in 45. i, and for the notes on obsolete provisions in the laws in 60. ii and 61. ii);[179] most of them read as integral parts of *A.P.*'s text, but 54. vii is clearly a late insertion (which, with its archontic date 329/8, probably derives from its author's direct knowledge of the change), and other insertions are likely in 46. i and 51. iii.[180] Occasionally we meet an expression which is unlikely to correspond to anything in the laws (e.g. οὗτος δὲ καλεῖται ἐμ[πήκτ]ης, in 64. ii, and the narrative language of 54. ii;[181] in 43. vi χρηματίζουσιν δ' ἐνίοτε καὶ ἄνευ προχειροτονίας is probably *A.P.*'s summary of a law which specified when προχειροτονία was not required[182]). For the most part, however, it is likely that *A.P.* has done what in 56. vii and 57. iii he can be seen to have done, and has presented us with a summary—*pace* Wilamowitz, presumably his own summary—of the laws concerning the πολιτεία.[183] In addition we must remember that he will have been able to see the machinery of state working, and, if he was not Aristotle or a young or non-Athenian pupil but an Athenian who had reached a sufficient age, to take part in its working.

We have already noticed that by treating the assembly in connection with the boule *A.P.* totally fails to mention the νομοθέται.[184] Other omissions may likewise be due to his reliance on the organisation of Athens' laws: taxation and liturgies are not treated comprehensively but are alluded to where they concern one of the officials (e.g. tax-collecting and the poletae, 47. ii; choregi and the archon, 56. iii; trierarchs and the στρατηγὸς ἐπὶ τὰς συμμορίας, 61. i); the registration of citizens is dealt with in 42, but one aspect is reserved for 53. iv–v, vii, and there is no similar treatment of metics, who are again alluded to where they happen to concern one of the ἀρχαί.[185] The council of the Areopagus receives only casual mention (47. ii, 57. iii–iv, 59. vi, 60. ii, iii); and nothing is said of the im-

---

[179] I doubt if Haussoullier was right in suggesting that these notes come from an *Atthis*: Mathieu & Haussoullier, xvi, xxiii–xxiv.
[180] Cf. pp. 55–6.
[181] Cf. διὸ καὶ νῦν . . . οὐδ' ἂν εἰς εἴποι θητικόν, 7. iv.
[182] For a similar condensation see 52. i *fin.*
[183] First argued by B. Bursy, *De Aristotelis Π. A. Partis Alterius Fonte et Auctoritate*, 1–51, and widely accepted (e.g. Busolt, *G.S.*, i. 97 with n. 1).
[184] P. 32; cf. 512–13. According to Harp. θεσμοθέται the annual revision of the laws was treated by Theophrastus in book III of his *Νόμοι* (fr. 4 Hager, *JP* vi 1876, 1–27), and some have seen in *Pol.* v. 1309 B 14–15 an allusion to the undertaking of that work in Aristotle's lifetime (e.g. H. Usener, *Pr.J.* liii 1884, 21–2 = *Vorträge und Aufsätze*, 97–8, Gilbert, *C.A.S.A.*, xxxvi n. 3, comparing Philod. *Rhet.* ii. 57 Sudhaus; contr. Newman *ad loc.* and most translators, also H. Bloch, *HSCP* Supp. i 1940, 363–6); but I am not persuaded that νομοθεσία was omitted from *A.P.* because it was to be dealt with in another work (developed from Usener by Haussoullier *ap.* Mathieu & Haussoullier, xxiv–xxvi).
[185] Noticed by D. Whitehead, *PCPS* Supp. iv 1977, 104 n. 106.

INTRODUCTION

portant financial office held by Lycurgus and his friends at the time when *A.P.* was written.[186] From among *A.P.*'s other omissions we may note that 43. v and 59. ii include two of the three kinds of προβολή known to us but omit the third; 53. i simplifies in implying that all private lawsuits except those mentioned in 52. ii–iii were handled by the Forty and the διαιτηταί; the treatment of secretaries and of ἱεροποιοί in 54. iii–vii is selective; the list of lawsuits handled by the thesmothetae, in 59, is incomplete.[187] Some of *A.P.*'s alleged omissions have led to controversy: 42. i does not state that citizens had to be born in wedlock; 42. ii and 53. iv–v do not state that thetes were excluded from service as ephebi and διαιτηταί; 43. ii sets out a pattern for the division of the year into prytanies which ignores intercalary years and even in ordinary years may not have been followed invariably; 63. iii does not state that there was a fixed number of jurors registered each year.

As in his first part *A.P.* has treated some matters at what seems disproportionate length,[188] similarly his second part contains unexpectedly lengthy treatment of some topics. Most striking is the devotion of chs 63–9 to the organisation of the δικαστήρια: Keil suggested that the organisation set out by *A.P.* was new when he wrote and that this novelty explains *A.P.*'s extensive account;[189] but the latest evidence for a clearly different system is Aristophanes' *Plutus*, of 388, most scholars have preferred a date about the 370's for the institution of the system described by *A.P.*,[190] and the πινάκια used for the daily allotments by κληρωτήριον support this earlier date.[191] My own view is that fourth-century Athenians took some pride in this elaborately random procedure for assigning jurors to courts, and that *A.P.* was fascinated by the details and recorded them at length for that reason.[192] The same may be said of his treatment of the διαιτηταί and the forty-two year-classes in 53. iv–vii: this system of year-classes is older than the reorganisation of the ἐφηβεία in the mid 330's (but the change from whitewashed boards to a bronze stele, mentioned in 53. iv, is perhaps to be associated with that reform), and again I suspect the explanation of *A.P.*'s lengthy account to be that he was fascinated by elaborate arrange-

[186] Cf. pp. 53, 515–16.
[187] Cf. p. 661.
[188] Cf. p. 27.
[189] *Anonymus Argentinensis*, 267–9, cf. Haussoullier *ap.* Mathieu & Haussoullier, xix–xx.
[190] E.g. G. Colin, *REG* xxx 1917, 82–4, H. Hommel, *Philol.* Supp. xix. ii 1927, 128–34, cf. Harrison, *L.A.*, ii. 241. The daily allotment of magistrates to courts (66. i) was not introduced until *c.* 340.
[191] Cf. on 63. iv: *A.P.*'s boxwood πινάκια seem to have replaced bronze for this purpose *c.* 350.
[192] Cf. p. 697.

ments of this kind. On the other hand, his attention to the details of the ἐφηβεία in 42. ii–v may well be due to the recent reorganisation which had produced a compulsory two years' national service for all young Athenians of hoplite class or above:[193] if the author was an Athenian citizen he may have been one of the first young men to undergo this service.

In this second part *A.P.* keeps strictly to his task of describing the constitution currently in force. Sometimes current practice is contrasted with earlier practice; but there is only one anecdote, that of Eumelides and Lysimachus in 45. i; outside that anecdote no men are mentioned by name except Solon, in 47. i as author of a law still in force, Harmodius and Aristogiton, in 58. i as objects of cult, and Cephisophon, as the archon of 329/8 in an insertion at the end of 54. vii. Argument is rarer in the second part than in the first, but notice the comment on the ninth prytany at the end of 47. iv, and the appeal to inscriptions to support the greater importance of the old-style secretary in 54. iii. There are two cross-references to the first part, in 47. i on the Solonian property classes and the appointment of the treasurers of Athena, and in 55. i on the history of the appointment of the archons; on the distribution of 'traditional' and 'added' festivals among the three senior archons 3. iii (a σημεῖον) and 57. i disagree, and 57. i appears to be correct; on the circumstances in which an archon may be required to dedicate a statue 55. v is more specific than 7. i and is probably correct. There is no comment on the merits and defects of the constitution described, and no comparison between practice in Athens and in other cities. J. J. Keaney has suggested that in beginning his account of the boule's functions with judicial matters in which it used to be κυρία but is no longer (45. i–iii), and in ending his second part with an extended treatment of the δικαστήρια, *A.P.* is focusing attention on the point made in 41. ii *fin.*, καὶ γὰρ αἱ τῆς βουλῆς κρίσεις εἰς τὸν δῆμον ἐληλύθασιν;[194] but I am not persuaded that this purpose governed the arrangement of his material, and think that if he had wanted to point this moral he would have done so more obviously.

4. Language and Style

A.P. immediately strikes the reader as being utterly different from the other works of the Aristotelian corpus. It is not a speculative work, in which the author attacks a series of ἀπορίαι (and the

---

[193] Haussoullier *ap.* Mathieu & Haussoullier, xvii–xix, cf. Wilamowitz, *A.u.A.*, i. 194.
[194] *HSCP* lxvii 1963, 121–2, 136, *AJP* xc 1969, 412.

vocabulary of such a work—ἀπορεῖν, ζητεῖν, θεωρεῖν, λύειν and the like—is conspicuously absent[195]), nor is it like the biological works, which generalise from a multitude of observed instances. The first part is a history of the πολιτεία, using earlier writings as source material, not in order to set out earlier views and then criticise them or give the author's own views, as is done elsewhere in the corpus,[196] but to attempt to extract from them a coherent narrative. The second part is not a generalisation from many instances but an account of one instance, the working of the Athenian πολιτεία in the author's own day, based on the actual laws which regulated the working of the πολιτεία. In view of the author's objectives, we should not be surprised that the general manner of A.P. is far more straightforward than that of the other works of the corpus, and in view of his dependence on written sources we should not be surprised that his language shows the influence of those sources.

Where we can compare A.P. with one of his sources (14–15, 19–20. iii, with Herodotus, 56. vii, 57. iii, with the laws), we see that he followed them closely, and this fact explains some features of his vocabulary. In 14. iii ἐρριζωμένης is repeated from ἐρριζωμένην in H. I. 60. i, and Herodotus' τὠυτὸ φρονήσαντες becomes in A.P. the equally Herodotean ὁμοφρονήσαντες; περιελαυνόμενος and ἐπικηρυκεύειν in 14. iv are repeated from H. I. 60. ii; after noting different accounts of Phye A.P. uses παραιβατούσης, a verb which is not in Herodotus' account but is in Clid. 323 F 15 and may have been used by some one else before him; 19. iv uses χρηστηριάζεσθαι, which is a Herodotean word, though not used in v. 63. i; the ἑσσούμενος ... τὸν δῆμον προσεταιρίζεται of H. v. 66. ii becomes ἡττώμενος δὲ ταῖς ἑταιρείαις ... προσηγάγετο τὸν δῆμον in 20. i; ἀγηλατεῖν is used both in H. v. 72. i and in A.P. 20. iii. 56. vii follows the law (ap. [D.] XLIII. Mac. 75) in the use of such terms as ἐπιμελεῖσθαι, ὀρφανοί, ἐπίκληροι, ἐπιβάλλειν, but substitutes the commoner fourth-century terms σκήπτεσθαι for φάσκειν[197] and δικαστήριον for ἡλιαία; 57. iii follows the law (ap. D. XXIII. Arist. 22 cf. 24, 53) in using the technical terms φόνου, τραύματος, ἐκ προνοίας, πυρκαιᾶς, ἐν πολέμῳ ἀγνοήσας (but the law's ἐν ἄθλοις ἄκων has become ἐν ἄθλῳ ἀγωνιζόμενος). In 61. i A.P. does not use what came to be the standard terminology for the regular postings of the generals, but it is possible that his language does correspond to that of the laws which instituted these postings, and that the standard terminology

---

[195] The closest we come to that is the use of θεωρεῖν in 9. ii, one of the passages most closely related to the *Politics*; ἀμφισβήτησις and its cognates are used in 3. iv, 5. ii, 9. ii, 28. v, 35. ii (cf. below).

[196] E.g. Arist. *H.A.* III. 511 B 10–513 A 15 with 513 A 16–515 A 26, *Pol.* II. 1260 B 27–1269 B 28.

[197] But φάσκειν is used in the anecdote in 45. i.

INTRODUCTION

did not correspond to that; in 61. vii he uses "Ἄμμωνος of the sacred trireme which came to be known as Ἀμμωνιάς. Thus the fact that many words are used in *A.P.* which are not found elsewhere in the Aristotelian corpus or in other fourth-century prose need cause no surprise. It is more striking that, apart from constitutional technicalities such as προεδρικός (59. ii) and quantitative terms such as ἑπτάχους (67. ii), there are many words and usages in *A.P.* which are found elsewhere not at all or not until much later: ὅρκια ποιεῖν active (3. iii), αὐτοτέλης = κύριος (3. v, 53. ii), πολιτεία = the body of those possessing citizenship (4. ii ['Draconian constitution'], 37. i, 38. ii), ποιήματα = lines of one poem (5. iii),[198] παραστρατηγεῖν, already metaphorical (6. ii), καταφατίζειν (7. i), προδιασπείρειν (14. iv), ἐκκλησιάζειν = hold assembly (of chairman) or address assembly (15. iv), ἐγκαταγηράσκειν (17. i), προσοργίζεσθαι (19. v), ἐπιλείπεσθαι with personal subject and dative (20. ii, 27. iv, cf. 34. iii), ἐξαπορεῖν (23. i), δεσποτικωτέρως (24. ii), μονοχίτων (25. iii), ἀντιδημαγωγεῖν (27. iii), προσαναζητεῖν (Clitophon's rider, 29. iii), ἄλλοσε not of place (Colonus resolutions, 29. v), ἐπεισκαλεῖν and ἐπείσκλητος = invite(d) in addition ('future' constitution, 30. iv), διαβουλεύειν = complete boule's year, and ἐκδιαιτᾶν = complete arbitration (32. i, 53. v), συναρέσκεσθαι middle (33. ii), γίγνεσθαι ὑπό (33. ii), παροργίζειν active (34. i), διαπίπτειν of interval of time (35. iv), οὐχ οἷον . . . ἀλλὰ καί (40. iii), προεξαλείφειν (47. v), προδρομεύειν (49. i), ἔκθυμα = expiatory sacrifice (in title of office, 54. vi), διαρρινᾶν (68. iv). There are, on the other hand, some expressions which are distinctively Aristotelian: τάξις τῆς πολιτείας (3. i, 5. i, cf. 41. ii), ἀριστίνδην καὶ πλουτίνδην (3. i, vi), μήτε . . . ἀλλά (16. iii), ἀμφισβήτησις (9. ii, 28. v, cf. 3. iv, 5. ii, 35. ii), δυσκολία (35. ii), and perhaps γεγωνεῖν (15. iv)—but apart from the vocabulary of teleology[199] and speculation, and other philosophical terms, many favourite terms of Aristotle are absent, such as εὐλαβεῖσθαι, ἐφίεσθαι, ὀρέγεσθαι, ὑπολαμβάνειν; πολίτευμα, προαίρεσις (but προαιρεῖσθαι in 27. ii); 'nothing is ἄτοπον and no person or thing is either σπουδαῖος or φαῦλος'.[200] There are also expressions in *A.P.* which are characteristic of Isocrates, and may be derived from him either directly or through an intermediary: κολάζουσα . . . τοὺς ἀκοσμοῦντας (3. vi), βλασφημεῖν (6. ii), ἐνσημαίνεσθαι sc. τὴν ὀργήν (18. ii), κακοπράγμων of συκοφάνται (35. iii), θαρρεῖν of the δῆμος (22. iii, 24. i, 27. i), and perhaps διοικεῖν τὰ κοινά/τὰ περὶ τὴν πόλιν πολιτικῶς

---

[198] But I suspect that the intended reference is to two poems and one quotation has been omitted: cf. p. 24.
[199] Cf. p. 8.
[200] H. Richards, *CR* v 1891, 273; Richards claimed to find 'no word that has a distinct Aristotelian stamp'. On the extent to which Aristotelian ideas can be found in *A.P.* see pp. 7–15.

INTRODUCTION

(14. iii, 16. ii).²⁰¹ προδανείζειν = (simply) lend (16. ii) is very much a word of *A.P.*'s generation.

Early commentators, without the aid of a computer, paid some attention to *A.P.*'s use of particles and conjunctions. In general, particles are used far more sparingly in *A.P.* than in the rest of the Aristotelian corpus: ἄρα, γε and γοῦν, κἂν εἰ, τε γάρ, τοίνυν and τοίγαρ are not found at all, μέντοι only once (emendation in 28. v), περ only in a limited range of compounds, οὖν only twice alone (19. iv, 60. iii), μήν only in οὐ μὴν ἀλλά, ἀλλά in every instance except one (40. iii) after a negative; on the other hand, there is one instance of δή after a superlative (40. iii), a use not found in the corpus.²⁰² (Usage within the corpus is not uniform: καίτοι and μέντοι are common in *Physics*, *Metaphysics* and *Politics* but not in *Rhetoric*; οὐ μὴν ἀλλά is common in *Politics* but, except in quotations, appears only once in *Rhetoric*.) These phenomena have not disconcerted those who believe that *A.P.* was written by Aristotle. Sandys², lix, writes:

> In the above statement such divergences as have been noticed may be fairly attributed to the different character of the works compared. There is clearly less scope for a multiplicity of particles, or of conjunctions (such as κἂν εἰ and τοίνυν and ἄρα), in a consecutive exposition of constitutional history and antiquities, than in the course of a philosophical discussion.

I concur with that judgment, and do not believe that further stylometric studies would enable us to determine whether Aristotle himself was the author of *A.P.*²⁰³

A.P. aimed not merely at setting down the facts in the simplest possible way but at writing readable Greek. Where he could easily do so, he avoided hiatus, if not with as great determination as Isocrates; but hiatus is to be found in those passages in the first part which are derived from a documentary original,²⁰⁴ and is found increasingly as we proceed through the second part. (Headlam compared Aristotle's tendency to avoid hiatus in the introductions to works, and sometimes to separate books, but increasingly to allow it thereafter, especially when using technical language; Kaibel remarked on the absence of hiatus from the fragments of the dialogues.)²⁰⁵

There are signs of a taste for balanced elements within the

---

[201] On *A.P.* and Isocrates cf. p. 20.

[202] Cf. J. B. Mayor, *CR* v 1891, 123, H. Richards, *ibid.* 273, Herwerden & Leeuwen, 216 *s.v. particulae*, Kaibel, *Stil und Text*, 73–80, Sandys², lviii–lix.

[203] Cf. pp. 61–3.

[204] Notice the motion of Pythodorus and the resolutions setting up the oligarchy of the Four Hundred, in 29, and the documents in 30–1, 39.

[205] J. W. Headlam, *CR* v 1891, 270–2, Kaibel, *Stil und Text*, 9–16, cf. Sandys², lxi–lxii.

sentence. The most striking instance is in 38. iv (and may be derived from a source early enough to have been written under the influence of Gorgias):[206]

a^1 οἱ δὲ περὶ τὸν ῾Ρίνωνα
b^1 διά τε τὴν εὔνοιαν τὴν εἰς τὸν δῆμον ἐπῃνέθησαν,
c^1 καὶ λαβόντες τὴν ἐπιμέλειαν ἐν ὀλιγαρχίᾳ
c^2 τὰς εὐθύνας ἔδοσαν ἐν δημοκρατίᾳ,
b^2 καὶ οὐδεὶς οὐδὲν ἐνεκάλεσεν αὐτοῖς
d^1 οὔτε τῶν ἐν ἄστει μεινάντων
d^2 οὔτε τῶν ἐκ Πειραιέως κατελθόντων,
a^2 ἀλλὰ διὰ ταῦτα καὶ στρατηγὸς εὐθὺς ᾑρέθη ῾Ρίνων.

Another sentence which comes close to perfect balance is in 6.i:

κύριος δὲ γενόμενος τῶν πραγμάτων ὁ Σόλων
a^1 τόν τε δῆμον ἠλευθέρωσε
b^1 καὶ ἐν τῷ πάροντι καὶ εἰς τὸ μέλλον,
c^1 κωλύσας δανείζειν ἐπὶ τοῖς σώμασιν,
a^2 καὶ νόμους ἔθηκε | καὶ χρεῶν ἀποκοπὰς ἐποίησε
b^2 καὶ τῶν ἰδίων καὶ τῶν δημοσίων
c^2 ἃς σεισάχθειαν καλοῦσιν, ὡς ἀποσεισάμενοι τὸ βάρος.

Since the words καὶ νόμους ἔθηκε disturb the sense as well as the balance of the sentence, Kaibel & Wilamowitz deleted them:[207] I sympathise, but prefer to think that these words were written by A.P., in a rather clumsy attempt to foreshadow the non-economic reforms which are to follow in 7–8. Typical of A.P. is a sentence in 5. iii which starts with a precise balance but fails to maintain it:

ἦν δ᾽ ὁ Σόλων
a^1 τῇ μὲν φύσει καὶ τῇ δόξῃ τῶν πρώτων,
a^2 τῇ δ᾽ οὐσίᾳ καὶ τοῖς πράγμασιν τῶν μέσων,
b^1 ὡς ἔκ τε τῶν ἄλλων ὁμολογεῖται
b^2 καὶ αὐτὸς ἐν τοῖσδε τοῖς ποιήμασιν μαρτυρεῖ,
c παραινῶν τοῖς πλουσίοις μὴ πλεονεκτεῖν.[208]

Also there are passages in A.P. where metrical patterns have been detected, which the author may have intended. An example may be given from 55. iv:

a^1 ἐπειδὰν | δὲ παράσχηται τοὺς μάρτυρας,   ∪ ∪ − − − − − ∪ ≍
a^2 ἐπερωτᾷ "τούτου βούλεταί   ∪ ∪ − − − − − ∪ ≍
b^1 τις κατηγορεῖν;" κἂν μὲν ᾖ   − ∪ − ∪ − − ∪ −
b^2 τις κατήγορος, δοὺς κατη | γορίαν.   − ∪ − ∪ − − ∪ −

[206] Cf. G. Rudberg, *Eranos* xxii 1924, 217–19.
[207] Cf. Kaibel, *Stil und Text*, 81–2, 134: he discusses A.P.'s sentence construction in pp. 64–86 (balance within sentence, 81–6). See also below, pp. 46–7.
[208] On 5. iii cf. p. 24.

INTRODUCTION

A more problematic instance is to be found in 48. iv:

a^1	τῶν εὐθύνων, οἷς ἀναγκαῖόν ἐστι	_ _ _ _ _ ∪ _ _ ∪ _ ⏑
b^1	ταῖς ἀγοραῖς[209] κα-	⏑ ∪ ∪ _ ∪
b^2	τὰ τὸν ἐπώνυ-	⏑ ∪ ∪ _ ∪
a^2	μον τὸν τῆς φυλῆς ἑκάστης καθῆσθαι·	_ _ _ _ _ ∪ _ _ ∪ _ ⏑
(c^1)	κἂν[210] τις βούληταί τι-	(⏑) _ _ _ _ _ ∪
c^2	νι τῶν τὰς εὐθύνας ἐν	⏑ _ _ _ _ _ ∪
d^1	τῷ δικαστηρίῳ δεδωκότων ἐν-	_ ∪ _ _ ∪ _ ∪ _ ∪ _ ⏑
d^2	τὸς τριῶν[211] ἡμερῶν ἀφ' ἧς ἔδωκε	_ ∪ _ _ ∪ _ ∪ _ ∪ _ ⏑
c^3	τὰς εὐθύνας εὔθυναν.	⏑ _ _ _ _ _ ∪

How far such phenomena are intended, and how far they occur without the author's conscious intention, in the course of his trying to write readable Greek, has been disputed; but most have agreed that Blass (particularly in his 4th ed.) went a great deal too far in searching for such patterns and in emending the papyrus' text to obtain them. Occasional verse rhythms may be found in *A.P.* which the author presumably did not intend, such as the iambic trimeters in 14. i and 26. ii,

λαβὼν δὲ τοὺς κορυνηφόρους καλουμένους,   ∪ _ ∪ _ | ∪ ∪ _ ∪ _ | ∪ _ ∪ _
εἰ μή τι παρεωρᾶτο τῶν ἐν τοῖς νόμοις,   _ _ ∪ ∪ ∪ | _ _ ∪ _ | _ _ ∪ _

and the dactylic hexameter in 56. iv,

οὓς πρότερον μὲν ὁ δῆμος ἐχειροτόνει δέκα ὄντας.[212]

_ ∪ ∪ | _ ∪ ∪ | _ ∪ ∪ | _ ∪ ∪ | _ ∪ ∪ | _ ⏑

In the choice and arrangement of words it would be easy to produce a very high degree of monotony, particularly in the annalistic passages, the summaries in 28. ii–iii and 41. ii, and the lists of officials in 47–8 and 50–4. *A.P.* has done a little to mitigate this. πρῶτον μὲν γὰρ οἱ ταμίαι τῆς Ἀθηνᾶς εἰσὶ μὲν δέκα, κληροῦται δ' εἷς ἐκ τῆς φυλῆς (47. i) is matched almost exactly by ἔπειθ' οἱ πωληταὶ ι' μέν εἰσι, κληροῦται δ' εἷς ἐκ τῆς φυλῆς (47. ii), but *A.P.* then varies his presentation with εἰσὶ δ' ἀποδέκται δέκα, κεκληρωμένοι κατὰ φυλάς (48. i), κληροῦσι δὲ καὶ λογιστὰς ἐξ αὐτῶν οἱ βουλευταὶ δέκα (48. iii),

---

[209] But the restoration ἀγοραῖς, which fits this scheme, is very far from certain.
[210] Blass⁴ printed καὶ ἂν *metri gratia*.
[211] Most editors read γ'; Wilcken read τ' (τριακοσίων), which gives an impossible sense; Kenyon in his Berlin ed. thought λ' (τριάκοντα) possible, and I believe that gives a preferable sense.
[212] On metrical patterns in *A.P.* see Blass' prefaces, esp. ⁴xvi–xxv, B. Keil, *Die solonische Verfassung in Aristoteles Verfassungsgeschichte Athens*, 18–39, and the sober remarks of Kaibel, *Stil und Text*, 87–95. For Aristotle's views on rhythm in prose see *Rhet.* III. 1408 B 21–1409 A 21.

INTRODUCTION

κληροῦσι δὲ καὶ εὐθύνους ἕνα τῆς φυλῆς ἑκάστης (48. iv).[213] Similar variety is to be found in the introductions of the different officials in 50-4; to carry the variety beyond the introduction, 51. i and ii are very nearly parallel, but §i mentions the Piraeus before the city whereas §ii mentions the city first, §i continues τούτοις δὲ ὑπὸ τῶν νόμων προστέτακται whereas §ii uses the more direct καὶ οὗτοι, §i uses the passive πωλήσεται[214] but §ii uses οἱ πωλοῦντες.

Attempts to avoid monotony in the first part have sometimes led to ambiguity. In 28. ii part of the list of προστάται reads

μετὰ δὲ ταῦτα τοῦ μὲν δήμου προειστήκει Ξάνθιππος, τῶν δὲ γνωρίμων Μιλτιάδης·
ἔπειτα Θεμιστοκλῆς καὶ Ἀριστείδης·
μετὰ δὲ τούτους Ἐφιάλτης μὲν τοῦ δήμου, Κίμων δ' ὁ Μιλτιάδου τῶν εὐπόρων:

if ch. 28 stood in isolation readers would automatically assume that Themistocles was a democratic leader and Aristides an aristocratic, and I believe that that is what is intended here; but in 23. iii both men are said to be προστάται τοῦ δήμου, and most scholars, believing that *A.P.* could not thus have contradicted himself within so short a space, have assumed that the same must be intended in 28. ii. The search for variety in the summary of changes in the constitution, in 41. ii, has led *A.P.* to use the strange expressions ἑβδόμη καὶ μετὰ ταύτην ... and ὀγδόη δ' ἡ τῶν τετρακοσίων κατάστασις, καὶ μετὰ ταύτην, ἐνάτη δέ, δημοκρατία πάλιν: corruption has been suspected, particularly in the latter instance, where attempts have been made to insert a reference to the Five Thousand, but there is no need for emendation. The first sentence of 22. ii begins πρῶτον μὲν οὖν ἔτει πέμπτῳ ... ἐφ' Ἑρμοκρέοντος ἄρχοντος; the second sentence begins simply ἔπειτα; 22. iii begins ἔτει δὲ μετὰ ταῦτα δωδεκάτῳ ... ἐπὶ Φαινίππου ἄρχοντος: the papyrus' text does not yield enough years between 508/7 (21. i) and 490/89 (22. iii), and some have supposed that, to avoid monotony, *A.P.* used the bare ἔπειτα when he might have given another archontic date, but here I believe that ἔπειτα is logical rather than temporal, both sentences of §ii refer to the same year, and πέμπτῳ is corrupt. However, as Kaibel pointed out, *A.P.* could have done much more than he has done to avoid monotony if he had set a high priority on doing so: for instance, in 7. i-ii there are three occurrences of νόμους and one of νόμων in four consecutive sentences, though the meaning could easily have been conveyed

---

[213] The texts of surviving decrees suggest that the corresponding clauses in the laws will not have displayed the greatest possible uniformity. For variations on the theme in 50-4 see on 51. iv, 54. v; proposals to emend in the interests of uniformity (as in 47. i) are misguided.

[214] Corrected from the papyrus' πωλῆται.

43

INTRODUCTION

without such repetition;[215] in 52. i there is a long string of future participles, which could easily have been interrupted.[216]

The most obvious style for the presentation of a historical outline is a sequential style, such as we find in ch. 22: in one year A happened; in a second year B happened, and also C; in a third year D happened. The summary in 41. ii shows that *A.P.* thought of his first part as a review of the series of changes, some of them advances and others setbacks, by which the constitution had arrived at its final form; and the underlying pattern of the first part is sequential. On the other hand, an account of how the constitution now works calls for an analytic style, which does not simply list one law after another but divides and subdivides to produce a coherent arrangement. This is what *A.P.* has done in his second part, and to a limited extent he has marked the principal divisions and subdivisions by the device of ring composition, using to round off a section a phrase recalling the phrase which introduced it.[217] In Herodotus, I, we find:

a^1 ἱστορέων δὲ εὕρισκε Λακεδαιμονίους τε καὶ Ἀθηναίους προέχοντας (56. ii)
a^2 τούτων δὴ ὦν τῶν ἐθνέων τὸ μὲν Ἀττικὸν κατεχόμενόν τε καὶ διεσπασμένον ἐπυνθάνετο ὁ Κροῖσος
b^1 ὑπὸ Πεισιστράτου τοῦ Ἱπποκράτεος ... τυραννεύοντος Ἀθηναίων (59. i)
b^2 καὶ Πεισίστρατος μὲν ἐτυράννευε Ἀθηνέων (64. iii)
a^3 τοὺς μὲν νῦν Ἀθηναίους τοιαῦτα τὸν χρόνον τοῦτον ἐπυνθάνετο ὁ Κροῖσος κατέχοντα,
c^1 τοὺς δὲ Λακεδαιμονίους ... ἐόντας ἤδη τῷ πολέμῳ κατυπερτέρους Τεγεητέων (65. i)
c^2 πολλῷ κατυπέρτεροι τῷ πολέμῳ ἐγίγνοντο οἱ Λακεδαιμόνιοι (68. vi)
a^4 ταῦτα δὴ ὦν πάντα πυνθανόμενος ὁ Κροῖσος (69. i)

On pp. 30–2 I have given an analysis of *A.P.*'s second part, quoting the principal introductory and resumptive phrases. Subdivisions are sometimes marked in the same way, as in:

a^1 οἱ δὲ καλούμενοι ἐννέα ἄρχοντες (55. i)
b^1 καὶ ὁ μὲν ἄρχων (56. ii)
b^2 καὶ ὁ [μὲν ἄρχων ἐπιμελεῖτ]αι τούτων·
c^1 ὁ δὲ βασιλεὺς (57. i)

---

[215] *Stil und Text*, 50–1.
[216] *Stil und Text*, 26.
[217] Ring composition in *A.P.* is discussed by J. J. Keaney, *AJP* xc 1969, 406–23. I have throughout consulted Keaney's analyses, but the analyses printed here are my own.

d^1 ὁ δὲ πολέμαρχος (58. i)
d^2 ταῦτα τοῖς μετοίκοις ὁ πολέμαρχος (58. iii)
e^1 οἱ δὲ θεσμοθέται (59. i)
a^2 τοὺς δὲ δικαστὰς κληροῦσι πάντες οἱ ἐννέα ἄρχοντες (59. vii)
a^3 τὰ μὲν οὖν περὶ τοὺς θ' ἄρχοντας τοῦτον ἔχει τὸν τρόπον (60. i)

His rings are often incomplete, as his rhythmic patterns often show an imperfect responsion and his sentences are often not exactly balanced; but we have a single ring in:

a^1 μετέχουσιν μὲν τῆς πολιτείας (42. i)
a^2 τὰ μὲν οὖν περὶ τὴν τῶν πολιτῶν ἐγγραφὴν καὶ τοὺς ἐφήβους τοῦτον ἔχει τὸν τρόπον (43. i)

and instances of a small ring within a larger in the example given above, on the archons, and in:

a^1 κληροῦσι δὲ καὶ (50. i)
b^1 κληροῦσι δὲ καὶ ⟨τοὺς⟩ τετταράκοντα (53. i)
    from whom A.P. passes to the arbitrators
    from whom he digresses to the forty-two year-classes
b^2 κληροῦσι δὲ καὶ τάσδε τὰς ἀρχάς (54. i)
a^2 αὗται μὲν οὖν αἱ ἀρχαὶ κληρωταί τε καὶ κύριαι τῶν εἰρημένων [πάντ]ων εἰσίν (55. i)

In the first part the essentially sequential arrangement is not affected by the occasional use of a resumptive remark at the end of one section before the next is introduced, as in:

ἡ μὲν οὖν τῶν Ἀρεοπαγιτῶν βουλὴ τοῦτον τὸν τρόπον ἀπεστερήθη τῆς ἐπιμελείας. | μετὰ δὲ ταῦτα ... (26. i);

but there are passages which have a genuinely analytic structure. One of the most striking is:

a^1 συνέβη στασιάσαι τούς τε γνωρίμους καὶ τὸ πλῆθος πολὺν χρόνον (2. i)
b^1 ἦν γὰρ αὐτῶν ἡ πολιτεία τοῖς τε ἄλλοις ὀλιγαρχικὴ πᾶσι,
c^1 καὶ δὴ καὶ ἐδούλευον οἱ πένητες τοῖς πλουσίοις (2. ii)
c^2 χαλεπώτατον μὲν οὖν καὶ πικρότατον ἦν τοῖς πολλοῖς τῶν κατὰ τὴν πολιτείαν τὸ δουλεύειν (2. iii)
b^2 ἦν δ' ἡ τάξις τῆς ἀρχαίας πολιτείας [[τῆς πρὸ Δράκοντος]][218] τοιάδε.
d^1 τὰς μὲν ἀρχὰς καθίστασαν ἀριστίνδην καὶ πλουτίνδην (3. i)
d^2 ἡ γὰρ αἵρεσις τῶν ἀρχόντων ἀριστίνδην καὶ πλουτίνδην ἦν (3. vi)
b^3 ἡ μὲν οὖν πρώτη πολιτεία ταύτην εἶχε τὴν ὑπογραφήν.

[218] The bracketed words were inserted when the 'Draconian constitution' was inserted.

INTRODUCTION

e^1 μετὰ δὲ ταῦτα ... Δράκων τοὺς θεσμοὺς ἔθηκεν (4. i)[219]
b^4 τοιαύτης δὲ τῆς τάξεως οὔσης ἐν τῇ πολιτείᾳ,
c^3 καὶ τῶν πολλῶν δουλευόντων τοῖς ὀλίγοις,
a^2 ἀντέστη τοῖς γνωρίμοις ὁ δῆμος. ἰσχυρᾶς δὲ τῆς στάσεως οὔσης καὶ πολὺν χρόνον ἀντικαθημένων ἀλλήλοις (5. i–ii)

Keaney in his analysis of ch. 2 regards this pattern as showing that the economic background to Solon's reforms is enclosed within, and thus shown to be less important than, the political background;[220] but it could as well be argued from his analysis of 2. i–5. i[221] that the political background is enclosed within, and thus shown to be less important than, the economic background. I suspect that neither conclusion should be drawn: rather, like Herodotus in the extract quoted above, *A.P.* announces that there were two causes of dissatisfaction, one political and the other economic, and (ὕστερον πρότερον, Ὁμηρικῶς) proceeds to deal first with the second and secondly with the first. Keaney uses this pattern to confirm that the 'Draconian constitution' in ch. 4 is an interpolation;[222] but as he says the technique is flexible, and as we have seen *A.P.* tends not to carry through stylistic schemes to a perfect completion: it seems to me, and I have tried to show in my analysis, that the pattern of these chapters could accommodate a section on Draco's θεσμοί.

Similarly a pattern, partly sequential and partly analytic, can be seen in the chapters on Solon:[223]

a εἵλοντο κοινῇ διαλλακτὴν καὶ ἄρχοντα Σόλωνα καὶ τὴν πολιτείαν ἐπέτρεψαν αὐτῷ (5. ii)
b κύριος δὲ γενόμενος τῶν πραγμάτων Σόλων
c^1 τόν τε δῆμον ἠλευθέρωσε ...
d^1 καὶ νόμους ἔθηκε
c^2 καὶ χρεῶν ἀποκοπὰς ἐποίησε ... (6. i)
e^1 πολιτείαν δὲ κατέστησε
d^2 καὶ νόμους ἔθηκεν ἄλλους (7. i)
d^3 κατέκλεισεν δὲ τοὺς νόμους εἰς ἑκατὸν ἔτη
e^2 καὶ διέταξε τὴν πολιτείαν τόνδε ⟨τὸν⟩ τρόπον (7. ii)
f^1 τὰς δ' ἀρχὰς ἐποίησε ... (8. i)

---

[219] If when the 'Draconian constitution' was inserted it displaced a section on Draco's θεσμοί, that section may have ended with a phrase answering to e^1. There is a summary of ch. 2 in 4. v, which was probably written when the 'constitution' was inserted.
[220] *Op. cit.*, 415, cf. *HSCP* lxvii 1963, 124 with 143 n. 25.
[221] *Op. cit.*, 416.
[222] *Op. cit.*, 415 n. 20.
[223] Discussed briefly by Keaney, *op. cit.*, 417. 2. i–5. ii and 5. ii–13. i *init.* may be regarded as the two halves of an organised section on Solon's reforms (cf. p. 14).

INTRODUCTION

f^2 τὰ μὲν οὖν περὶ τὰς ἀρχὰς τοῦτον εἶχε τὸν τρόπον.
g^1 δοκεῖ δὲ τῆς Σόλωνος πολιτείας τρία ταῦτ' εἶναι τὰ δημοτικώτατα (9. i)
g^2 ἐν μὲν οὖν τοῖς νόμοις ταῦτα δοκεῖ θεῖναι δημοτικά,
c^3 πρὸ δὲ τῆς νομοθεσίας ποιῆσαι τὴν τῶν χρεῶν ἀποκοπὴν
h καὶ μετὰ ταῦτα τήν τε τῶν μέτρων καὶ σταθμῶν καὶ τὴν τοῦ νομίσματος αὔξησιν (10. i)
e^3 διατάξας δὲ τὴν πολιτείαν ὅνπερ εἴρηται τρόπον (11. i)
i^1 ἀποδημίαν ἐποιήσατο (11. i)
i^2 τὴν μὲν οὖν ἀποδημίαν ἐποιήσατο διὰ ταύτας τὰς αἰτίας. Σόλωνος δ' ἀποδημήσαντος ... (13. i)

In 6. i the words καὶ νόμους ἔθηκε have been seen as an awkward intrusion into the account of Solon's economic reform, and into what would without them be a perfectly balanced sentence, and accordingly some have deleted them;[224] but I prefer to let the words stand, and suppose that *A.P.* has attempted more clumsily here what he did at the beginning of ch. 2, announcing a (political and) legal and an economic reform and proceeding to deal first with the economic. Ch. 10 is a more serious interruption: *A.P.* has introduced Solon in ch. 5, has dealt with the economic reform in 6 and the legal and political reform in 7–8, and has singled out 'democratic' features in 9; then further measures of Solon are added in 10 before we proceed to the sequel of the reforms in 11 as if 10 did not exist. I do not suggest that 10 is not the work of *A.P.*, or even that it is an insertion in a text originally written without it;[225] but it does interrupt the structure of the text,[226] and I imagine that, having written from a source other than Androtion a discussion of Solon which gives the orthodox view of the σεισάχθεια, *A.P.* decided to add his own version of the measures which Androtion had applied to his reinterpretation of the σεισαχθεία.[227]

Chs. 20–1 contain an account of Cleisthenes and Isagoras, based on Herodotus; next a note on the Alcmaeonids' responsibility for the ending of the tyranny; and then an account of Cleisthenes' laws. The note on the Alcmaeonids seems oddly placed, and Keaney suggests that this may be explained through a further use of ring composition:[228]

a^1 καταλυθείσης δὲ τῆς τυραννίδος ἐστασίαζον πρὸς ἀλλήλους Ἰσαγόρας ὁ Τεισάνδρου φίλος ὢν τῶν τυράννων καὶ Κλεισθένης τοῦ γένους ὢν τῶν Ἀλκμεωνιδῶν.
b^1 ἡττώμενος δὲ ταῖς ἑταιρείαις ὁ Κλεισθένης προσηγάγετο τὸν δῆμον, ἀποδιδοὺς τῷ πλήθει τὴν πολιτείαν.

---
[224] Cf. p. 41.
[225] Ch. 10 was regarded as an interpolation by Seeck: cf. p. 54.
[226] As remarked by Wilamowitz, *A.u.A.*, i. 41.
[227] Cf. p. 28.   [228] *Op. cit.*, 417–20.

c^1 ὁ δὲ Ἰσαγόρας ἐπιλειπόμενος τῇ δυνάμει πάλιν ἐπικαλεσάμενος τὸν Κλεομένην (20. i–ii)

c^2 οἱ μὲν περὶ τὸν Κλεομένην καὶ Ἰσαγόραν κατέφυγον εἰς τὴν ἀκρόπολιν (20. iii)

b^2 κατασχόντος δὲ τοῦ δήμου τὰ πράγματα Κλεισθένης ἡγεμὼν ἦν καὶ τοῦ δήμου προστάτης.

a^2 αἰτιώτατοι γὰρ σχεδὸν ἐγένοντο τῆς ἐκβολῆς τῶν τυράννων οἱ Ἀλκμεωνίδαι καὶ στασιάζοντες τὰ πολλὰ διετέλεσαν (20. iv)

b^3 διὰ μὲν οὖν ταύτας τὰς αἰτίας ἐπίστευεν ὁ δῆμος τῷ Κλεισθένει. τότε δὲ τοῦ πλήθους προεστηκὼς ... (21. i)

When one sets out the material like this one is probably being far more deliberate about it than the author was. But if he did not deliberately construct these schemes he was a man to whom it came naturally to present his more complex material in this way, and this helps us to understand the placing of the Alcmaeonids, which to us is illogical.

One further section with an analytic structure is 23. i–25. i:[229]

a^1 τότε μὲν οὖν μέχρι τούτου προῆλθεν ἡ πόλις ἅμα τῇ δημοκρατίᾳ κατὰ μικρὸν αὐξανομένη·

b^1 μετὰ δὲ τὰ Μηδικὰ πάλιν ἴσχυσεν ἡ ἐν Ἀρείῳ πάγῳ βουλὴ καὶ διῴκει τὴν πόλιν (23. i)

(b^2) διὰ ταύτην δὴ τὴν αἰτίαν παρεχώρουν αὐτῆς τῷ ἀξιώματι, καὶ ἐπολιτεύθησαν Ἀθηναῖοι καλῶς κατὰ τούτους τοὺς καιρούς.

c^1 συνέβη γὰρ αὐτοῖς περὶ τὸν χρόνον τοῦτον ... τὴν τῆς θαλάττης ἡγεμονίαν λαβεῖν (23. ii)

a^2 μετὰ δὲ ταῦτα θαρρούσης ἤδη τῆς πόλεως καὶ χρημάτων ἠθροισμένων πολλῶν,

c^2 συνεβούλευεν ἀντιλαμβάνεσθαι τῆς ἡγεμονίας

d^1 καὶ καταβάντας ἐκ τῶν ἀγρῶν οἰκεῖν ἐν τῷ ἄστει·

e^1 τροφὴν γὰρ ἔσεσθαι πᾶσι,

(e^2) τοῖς μὲν στρατευομένοις, τοῖς δὲ φρουροῦσι,

d^2 τοῖς δὲ τὰ κοινὰ πράττουσι,

c^3 εἶθ᾽ οὕτω κατασχήσειν τὴν ἡγεμονίαν.

f^1 πεισθέντες δὲ ταῦτα καὶ λαβόντες τὴν ἀρχὴν (24. i–ii)

(f^2) ... ἄρχειν ὧν ἔτυχον ἄρχοντες.[230]

e^3 κατέστησαν δὲ καὶ τοῖς πολλοῖς εὐπορίαν τροφῆς (24. ii–iii)

e^4 ἡ μὲν οὖν τροφὴ τῷ δήμῳ διὰ τούτων ἐγίγνετο.

b^3 ἔτη δὲ ἑπτακαίδεκα μάλιστα μετὰ τὰ Μηδικὰ διέμεινεν ἡ πολιτεία προεστώτων τῶν Ἀρεοπαγιτῶν, καίπερ ὑποφερομένη κατὰ μικρόν.

a^3 αὐξανομένου δὲ τοῦ πλήθους ... (25. i)

---

[229] Discussed by Keaney, *op. cit.*, 412–13.

[230] Cited by Keaney in his analysis of the passage. This corresponds verbally but not in meaning to f^1.

INTRODUCTION

Here A.P. had to fit in two apparently incompatible themes, the ascendancy of the Areopagus and the growth of naval democracy, and within the latter he had to deal both with Athenian power and with the resulting benefits for the δῆμος: the analytic style was clearly suitable for this.

In contrast to these signs that A.P. took some care over the composition of his work, many passages have been found which are awkward in language, logic, or both. Some have been noticed above: in 5. iii ἐν τοῖσδε τοῖς ποιήμασιν introduces a quotation from a single poem, which does not prove the point which it is said to prove;[231] in 6. i καὶ νόμους ἔθηκε interrupts both the sense and the balance of the sentence;[232] ch. 10 interrupts an otherwise well-planned account of Solon.[233] 22. i arouses the expectation that the law of ostracism will be discussed, but in §ii πρῶτον μὲν οὖν takes us to the bouleutic oath and the election of generals, and we return to ostracism only in §iii; 22. iv–vi reports the ostracism of Hipparchus and Megacles, and adds that for three years the friends of the tyrants were ostracised but does not give the name of the third victim; 57. iii–iv distinguishes between the different kinds of homicide trial, and specifies the court for each kind except the last (which we know from other evidence to have been held at the prytaneum): in each case some have suspected a lacuna in the text, but more probably there is a lacuna in A.P.'s composition and he has omitted material which he could have given and we should have expected him to give. The problem is particularly great when A.P. reports the contents of a document: the 'future' constitution in 30 contains many obscurities, which may be due either to careless drafting or to careless condensation of a fuller original; similarly, when the terms of reconciliation in 39 fail to give enough information on registration for settlement at Eleusis (§iv) or on the juries to hear εὔθυναι (§vi), it is hard to decide whether the blame should rest with the authors of the document or with A.P., or with the intermediary in whose narrative A.P. found the document.[234] Again, A.P.'s complicated material on the organisation of the δικαστήρια is not set out in the best order for the reader's understanding: we do not know how the relevant laws were arranged, but I suspect that much of the fault here is A.P.'s. A compressed passage in 43. vi mentions προχειροτονία only to say that sometimes it is not used; and the reference to προβουλεύματα in 44. iv does not make sense until one has read 45. iv.

24. ii–iii contains many oddities of grammar and sense, which

[231] Pp. 24, 41.
[232] Pp. 41, 46–7.
[233] Pp. 28, 46–7.
[234] Cf. p. 23.

INTRODUCTION

some editors have attempted to correct: in §ii ἀρχή suddenly replaces the ἡγεμονία of §i; the τε before συμμάχοις has no correlative; ἑῶντες governs first an accusative without a verb and after that an infinitive without an accusative, and it would be more normal to insert τὰς before παρ' αὐτοῖς; in §iii ἀπὸ τῶν φόρων καὶ τῶν τελῶν καὶ τῶν συμμάχων forms a strange trio; ἔνδημοι μὲν εἰς ἑπτακοσίους ἄνδρας, ὑπερόριοι δ' εἰς ἑπτακοσίους can hardly be right; νῆες αἱ τοὺς φόρους . . . δισχιλίους ἄνδρας is unsatisfactory both in syntax and in sense; and that is followed by the very bald ἔτι δὲ πρυτανεῖον καὶ ὀρφανοὶ καὶ δεσμωτῶν φύλακες. It is normal to give *A.P.* the benefit of the doubt and blame a copyist at any rate for the repeated ἑπτακοσίους; but I believe that much that is unsatisfactory here is due to *A.P.*'s trying to confine within a reasonable compass material which was set out more fully by his source. Similarly there have been attempts to improve on οἷον περὶ . . . ποιήσαντες καθάπαξ in 35. ii, and some have tried to restore a main verb in the long sentence μετὰ δὲ ταῦτα . . . τὴν πολιτείαν in 15. i–ii, but probably what we read in the papyrus is what *A.P.* wrote. Some difficulties seem to have resulted from *A.P.*'s trying to combine statements from different sources which are not in fact compatible, as when 18. i prepares us to see Hipparchus as the frustrated lover of Harmodius but in 18. ii his place is taken by Thessalus,[235] or when 30. i and 32. i tell us that a hundred ἀναγραφεῖς were appointed by the Five Thousand but 32. iii says that the Five Thousand λόγῳ μόνον ᾑρέθησαν. Copyists do sometimes make nonsense of sensible texts, but far too much in *A.P.* is vulnerable to this kind of criticism for us to blame all imperfections on copyists and reconstruct an original, pure *A.P.*

A.P. is thus a very uneven work. There are passages where the sequence of thought has been carefully worked out, where there are guiding phrases to help the reader to follow this sequence, and where attention has been given to such matters as the balance of the sentences and perhaps even the rhythm; but there are also passages that are inconsistent with one another, passages where the meaning is obscure, and a few passages which are grammatically incoherent. Many have concluded from its imperfections that it is an unfinished work. Kaibel supposed that Aristotle had intended the work for publication but left it unrevised at his death, and it was then published by a pupil or friend;[237] and of more recent writers E. Drerup suggested that Aristotle did not complete the revision of his material but made additional notes which were interpolated by

---

[235] Cf. pp. 27, 54–5.

[236] *No* n. 236.]

[237] *Stil und Text*, 27, cf. 21–2, also 229, 247–8, and B. Keil, *BPW* xi 1891, 618, *Die solonische Verfassung in Aristoteles Verfassungsgeschichte Athens*, 50–3.

INTRODUCTION

an editor who did not always understand them,[238] while Tovar argued that *A.P.* is too inelegant to be one of the ἐξωτερικοὶ λόγοι praised by ancient critics,[239] but that Aristotle kept it up to date as he did all his writings, by touching up a working manuscript from time to time.[240] With Tovar's view we may compare that of R. Shute, written before the discovery of *A.P.*:

> But of the Politeae, as of the History of Animals and of the ἱστορίαι generally, we must always bear in mind that they represent not any fixed work of Aristotle or of anyone else, but merely a continuously open note-book.[241]

We shall see in the next section of this Introduction that insertions have been made in the text of *A.P.*, but insertions like corruptions will not explain all that we find unsatisfactory. The carelessness in *A.P.*, as well as the care, is the author's own work.

5. *Date of the* ATHENAION POLITEIA; *Insertions and Revisions*

In the first part of *A.P.* there is no allusion to anything later than the increase in assembly pay to 3 obols (41. iii), which is earlier than Aristophanes' *Ecclesiazusae*, of the late 390's.[242] Though I do not accept the contention of Keaney that material in the second part is selected and displayed in order to support the conclusion drawn at the end of the first part,[243] I see no reason to suppose that an appreciable interval separates the composition of the second part from that of the first.[244]

For the second part a *terminus post quem* is provided by the description of the ἐφηβεία as a compulsory programme of two years'

---

[238] *Mnem.*³ x 1942, 1–7.
[239] Cic. *Acad. Pr.* II. 119, *Inv.* II. 6, *Orat.* I. 49, *Top.* I. 3; D.H. 430. *Imit.* 6. iv; Quint. x. i. 83; cf. Kaibel, *Stil und Text*, 114–16. I doubt if much should be concluded about the style of the πολιτεῖαι from the inclusion of κτίσεις καὶ πολιτεῖας Ἀριστοτέλους among the histories whose reading gives innocent pleasure by Pl. *Non Posse Suav.* 1093 B–C.
[240] *REC* iii 1948, 153–9, cf. Tovar, 27–31. On the views of Drerup and Tovar cf. below, pp. 54–6.
[241] *On the History of the Process by which the Aristotelian Writings arrived at their Present Form*, 72.
[242] Hence the assumption of Wilamowitz and others that *A.P.* transcribed a source written not long after that: cf. pp. 15–18 and 9 with n. 39.
[243] Cf. p. 37.
[244] J. Zürcher, *Aristoteles' Werk und Geist*, who believes the *corpus Aristotelicum* to be the result of a generation's revision by Theophrastus, in pp. 257–8 accepts the obvious date for the second part of *A.P.* but regards the first as a youthful work of Aristotle. This seems no more plausible than the rest of his thesis (on which see G. B. Kerferd, *CR*² v 1955, 60–1).

national service (42. ii–v): this programme was instituted c. 335/4, and *A.P.*'s account of it, which must have been written later than that, shows no sign of not being part of the original text.[245] 54. iv mentions, again with no sign of insertion, the secretary ἐπὶ τοὺς νόμους, who seems still not to exist in 335/4 (but the presumably parallel ἐπὶ τὰ ψηφίσματα, not mentioned by *A.P.*, is already attested in 343/2); 56. iv mentions a change in the appointment of epimeletae of the Dionysia, which occurred certainly after the middle of the century and perhaps in the mid 330's, and here too there is no sign that *A.P.*'s text has been changed. 61. i mentions the στρατηγὸς ἐπὶ τὰς συμμορίας, an appointment which seems still not to have existed in 334/3,[246] and two generals assigned to the Piraeus, which is confirmed for 325/4 whereas as late as 333/2 there was only one;[247] this section also mentions that generals are no longer appointed on a tribal basis, a change which seems from our incomplete knowledge of fourth-century generals to have taken place after 357/6 but before 323/2.[248] 66. i, without mentioning that earlier practice was different, writes of a daily allotment of presiding magistrates (with their cases) to particular lawcourts, whereas a speech of the late 340's cites as still current a law stipulating that δίκαι σίτου are to be tried at the Odeum.[249] A general *terminus ante quem* is provided by the suppression at the beginning of 321/0, on the orders of Antipater, of the democratic constitution whose working *A.P.* describes in the present tense,[250] and a *terminus* of 322 may be deduced from the reference at the end of 62. ii to Samos, which Athens lost at the end of that year.[251]

It has been thought that some passages enable the limits to be narrowed further. 54. vii contains a reference to the archontic year 329/8;[252] but that, I shall argue, is a late insertion in a text originally written without it.[253] 46. i begins and ends with triremes but at one point refers to triremes and quadriremes: the earliest surviving navy list to mention quadriremes is that of 330/29,

[245] Cf. p. 56, on 53. iv; on the date of the institution see pp. 494–5.

[246] *IG* ii² 1623, 147–59: noticed by C. Torr, *CR* v 1891, 119, B. Keil, *BPW* xi 1891, 613, cf. Busolt, *G.G.*, ii². 17 n. 1.

[247] O. W. Reinmuth, *Mnem.* Supp. xiv 1971, no. 15, l.h.s.–r.h.s., contr. 5, 7, 9, ii. 9–11. Here again there is no sign of revision in the text of *A.P.*

[248] Tod 153, 20–4; J. Sundwall, *Klio* Bhft. iv 1906, 23–4, 25.

[249] [D.] LIX. *Neaer.* 52, cf. 54. However, in 52. ii ἔτι need not be a sign that additions have been made to the list of δίκαι ἔμμηνοι, either in the law or in *A.P.*

[250] Cf. W. S. Ferguson, *Hellenistic Athens*, 22 with n. 1.

[251] D.S. XVIII. 18. ix.

[252] Kenyon¹ *ad loc.* (but cf. below, p. 55 n. 272). C. Torr, *CR* v 1891, 277, thought that the reference to a sexennial Delian festival pointed to a change decided after 330; it is far from certain that he is right, but if he is this reference too could be a later addition.

[253] Cf. pp. 55–6.

quinqueremes are still not mentioned in 326/5 and make their first appearance in 325/4: some early commentators concluded from this that *A.P.* was written before 325,[254] but again it seems likely that the passage has been revised and an original version of *A.P.* mentioned triremes only.[255] In 61. vii the sacred triremes are given the names Πάραλος and Ἄμμωνος: some dated the change from Σαλαμινία to Ἀμμωνιάς (which seems to be the correct form of the name) in 324, making this the latest reference in *A.P.*,[256] more have thought the change followed shortly after Alexander's visit to the oracle of Ammon in 332/1,[257] but in fact there is no reliable *terminus post quem* for Athens' adoption of the name Ἀμμωνιάς, and our latest reference to the Σαλαμινία is in 373.[258] No mention is made in 43. i or elsewhere of the financial office held in the late 330's and early 320's by Lycurgus, and so Schoeffer dated an original version *c*. 350;[259] but this is inconsistent with our other evidence, and we must admit that *A.P.* has omitted an office which we should have expected him to include.[260]

There are passages in *A.P.* which appear to be late insertions into the text (I use that term as being neutral between 'additions' made by the author and 'interpolations' made by some one other than the author). It is most widely agreed that the 'Draconian constitution' in ch. 4 is an insertion: Arist. *Pol.* II. 1274 B 15–16 states that Draco enacted laws for the existing constitution, and there is no other sign of a constitution of Draco in surviving literature; awkward passages in 3. i, 41. ii and perhaps 7. iii are best explained as pieces of patchwork undertaken to fit this 'constitution' into a text originally written without it. T. Reinach, one of the first to recognise that insertion,[261] claimed to identify two other insertions in the first part of *A.P.*: 8. i on the appointment of archons, which he thought incompatible with 13. ii as well as with Arist. *Pol.*;[262] and the story of Themistocles and Ephialtes in 25. iii–iv, which seems chronologically impossible, is mentioned nowhere else except in the *hypothesis* to Is. VII. *Areop.* (which refers to *A.P.* but gives a different

[254] *IG* ii² 1627, 275–8, 1628, 495–7, 1629, 808–12: noticed by C. Torr, *CR* v 1891, 119 n. 1 (who admitted the possibility of revision).
[255] Cf. pp. 55–6.
[256] E.g. H. Weil, *JS* 1891, 199–200, Tovar, cited p. 55.
[257] E.g. Busolt, *G.G.*, ii². 18 n.
[258] X. *H.* VI. ii. 14.
[259] V. Sheffer, *Afinskoe Grazhdanstvo i Narodnoe Sobranie* (*Athenian Citizenship and People's Assembly*), i. 12–16, cf. *JAW* XXI. i = lxxv 1893, 32–3, XXIII. i = lxxxiii 1895, 212.
[260] Cf. pp. 35–6, 515–16.
[261] *REG* iv 1891, 82–5, 143–58.
[262] For *A.P.* and Arist. *Pol.* on the archonship cf. p. 60; αἱρεῖν in 13. ii need not mean anything more specific than 'appoint', and if that is so *A.P.* tells a consistent story.

INTRODUCTION

version of the story), and fits very awkwardly with the last sentence of ch. 25.[263] The theory of an insertion is not necessary to explain 8. i, but I believe Reinach was right to regard 25. iii–iv as an insertion. O. Seeck agreed that the 'Draconian constitution' is an insertion (and with it rejected the whole of ch. 3 and the cross-reference in 8. iv); did not discuss 25. iii–iv; defended 8. i and instead rejected 13. i–ii and 22. v; and regarded ch. 10 on measures, weights and coinage as a further insertion.[264] His treatment of the passages on the archonship is no more acceptable than that of Reinach, but his suspicion of ch. 10 is more tempting. Androtion's account is preserved by Plutarch, but we have no other account of these measures of Solon; 10 interrupts the flow of *A.P.*'s narrative,[265] and its introduction is awkwardly phrased; on the other hand, the silence of antiquity on the 'Draconian constitution' and on Themistocles' involvement with Ephialtes suggest that these were not to be found in the *Atthides* which were consulted for the original version of *A.P.* but were inserted later when they were discovered in some other text, but it was already official doctrine at the end of the fifth century that there were measures and weights of Solon,[266] and we know that the subject was treated by Androtion, so here I think it likelier that, in spite of its awkwardness, ch. 10 did form part of the original version of *A.P.*

Further suspicions were expressed by E. Drerup, who claimed to detect signs that Aristotle had not finished his revision of *A.P.* and his notes had been incorporated by an editor at several points in 41, in the various unspecific chronological notes in the opening chapters, in 2 (where he saw unnecessary duplication), in 3. i (where he regarded τὰς μὲν ἀρχὰς καθίστασαν ἀριστίνδην καὶ πλουτίνδην as an anticipation of §vi), and in the correspondence between 3. vi and 8. iv on the powers of the Areopagus.[267] Others have detected insertions in *A.P.*'s account of the tyranny. Mathieu sought to solve the chronological problem by supposing that *A.P.* unemended gives a coherent set of data except in 15. ii, where he repeats Herodotus' figure for the duration of the second exile, and R. Weil saw in the awkward ἐνδεκάτῳ πάλιν ἔτει τό τε πρῶτον ἀνασώσασθαι a sign that the text has been revised at this point.[268] The awkwardness of 18.

---

[263] The last point was not made by Reinach; he believed that the story is also legally impossible, but I am among those who accept that Themistocles was condemned by the Areopagus.

[264] *Klio* iv 1904, 270–82, cf. (on ch. 10) 164–81.

[265] Cf. pp. 28, 46–7.

[266] Decree of Tisamenus *ap*. And. 1. *Myst*. 83.

[267] *Mnem.*³ x 1942, 1–7, cf. above, pp. 50–1. Some of the expressions in 2–3 which he thought redundant are to be explained as elements in *A.P.*'s ring composition: cf. pp. 45–6.

[268] Mathieu, *Aristote, Constitution d'Athènes*, 31–3; Weil, *Aristote et l'histoire*, 112–14.

INTRODUCTION

i–ii, in the course of which Thessalus supplants Hipparchus as the villain among Pisistratus' sons, has tempted many to delete Thessalus.[269] However, not every piece of awkwardness is proof that the author changed his mind: we cannot rule out the possibility that on occasions *A.P.* wrote out a passage from one of his sources and then tried to adapt it on discovering that another text disagreed; but the 'Draconian constitution' (with associated adjustments elsewhere) and the story of Themistocles and Ephialtes are the only passages in the first part of which I am confident that there was an original version which did not contain them and which in that form passed out of the author's hands.

More recently, attention has been focused on the second part. Tovar saw at three points signs that additions have been made to the original text:[270] 46. i, which begins with the boule's responsibility for already existing triremes, continues καὶ ποιεῖται [[δὲ]] τριήρεις ἢ τετρήρεις, ὁποτέρας ἂν ὁ δῆμος χειροτονήσῃ, but ends with triremes alone once more;[271] 54. vii, which ends by mentioning an addition to the list of quadrennial festivals, dated 329/8;[272] and 61. vii, where Tovar is among those who believe that the name Ἀμμωνιάς was not used for one of the sacred triremes until 324.[273] J. J. Keaney has surveyed all the notes in the second part of *A.P.* on a difference between earlier and current practice, and has concluded that two in particular are likely to be late insertions:[274] the change in the number of σιτοφύλακες, in 51. iii, which can plausibly be dated to the early 320's (and whose mention calls for explanation since there were other, similar changes which are not mentioned[275]); and the addition to the list of quadrennial festivals, in 54. vii; the other two instances discussed by Tovar he regards as possible insertions. It had already been remarked by Reinach that Plutarch and the lexicographers appear to have used a version of *A.P.* which did not contain the insertions in the first part.[276] Keaney observes that Harp. σιτοφύλακες seems to have used a text of *A.P.* which did not

---

[269] Done first by Herwerden & Leeuwen; most recently and most carefully by C. W. Fornara, *Hist.* xvii 1968, 411–18. Cf. above, pp. 27, 50.

[270] *REG* iii 1948, 153–9, cf. Tovar, 27–31.

[271] R. Weil, *op. cit.*, 111–12, rejected Tovar's reconstruction of an original text containing the δέ, but agreed that an insertion has been made in this passage.

[272] It was already remarked by Kenyon¹ that this 'might have been added after the main bulk of the work was written'.

[273] Cf. p. 53.

[274] *Hist.* xix 1970, 326–36.

[275] In fact neither of the instances given by Keaney, *op. cit.*, 331 n. 2 (56. i, 57. i) is certain; but there are many certain changes to which *A.P.* does not draw attention, such as those cited above, pp. 51–2, as providing a *terminus post quem* for the composition of the work.

[276] *REG* iv 1891, 152, cf. Wilcken, *Apophoreton*, 97, Seeck, *Klio* iv 1904, 280–2, and on ch. 4 Keaney, *op. cit.*, 332 n. 29.

contain the insertion in 51. iii (but Phot. *s.v.* derives from a version which did contain it), and Poll. VIII. 107 to have used a text which did not contain the insertion in 54. vii (justifiably, he is less confident in this case than in the first); on the other hand, the change in the way in which members of the forty-two year-classes were listed, in 53. iv, is repeated in Harp. στρατεία ἐν τοῖς ἐπωνύμοις, and if that change is to be associated with the reorganisation of the ἐφηβεία *c.* 335/4 its mention by Harpocration may support the view that the original version of *A.P.* was written after that reorganisation.[277]

The end of 54. vii, with the only archontic date in the second half of *A.P.*, should certainly be regarded as an insertion; insertion in 46. i is probable, and in 51. iii is made probable by the silence of Harpocration and the likelihood that the change was made in the 320's (though I should not have suspected an insertion on the basis of *A.P.*'s text alone); I do not suspect an insertion in 61. vii. A good case has been made for the view that the version of *A.P.* which was most widely current in antiquity did not contain these insertions:[278] this version was written towards the end of the 330's, and was 'published' in the sense that a text passed out of the author's hands and was copied thereafter; but the London papyrus gives us a version in which insertions were made during the first half of the 320's. The insertions in the second part might have been a user's *marginalia* which a copyist incorporated in the text; but the addition of the story of Themistocles and Ephialtes in 25, and, even more, the insertion of the 'Draconian constitution' in 4 and the modification of other passages to fit it into *A.P.*, are surely deliberate modifications made in the Aristotelian school, and the fact that in Is. VII. *Areop.*, *hyp.*, and Phot. σιτοφύλακες we have two texts derived from this later version of *A.P.* confirms that the insertions are not simply notes made by a reader in his own copy some centuries later. We cannot tell whether the edition of the London papyrus was intended to be the final edition; but it is possible that, if Aristotle had not left Athens in 323 and died in 322, or if the democracy had not been suppressed in 321, the attempt to keep *A.P.* up to date would have continued.

Of the fragments attributed to *A.P.* by Rose in his Teubner ed., 381, 384 and 385 refer to the lost beginning; 382, 386, 392, 394 (on λυκόποδες), 399, 401, 415 and 456 are not in our text of *A.P.*, but they simply cite 'Aristotle' and may refer to other works; in 389

---

[277] Cf. pp. 51–2.

[278] However, the London papyrus of 27. iv, representing the revised text, and Pl. *Per.* 9. ii, presumably derived from an unrevised text, agree on the erroneous Δαμωνίδου τοῦ Οἴηθεν, so there we must assume that the error was already present in the original text of *A.P.*

INTRODUCTION

(Photius, ii) Ἀριστοτέλης is a corruption of Ἀριστοφάνης;[279] at fr. 406 Rose printed an emended text which does not match *A.P.*, but the manuscripts' text does match *A.P.* and the emendation is thus shown to be wrong. More seriously, 439 (Harp. ἀντιγραφεύς) cites *A.P.* for that official, whom our text does not mention;[280] 447 cites *A.P.* for an account of the λογισταί and συνήγοροι different from that of 54. ii, so either the citation is wrong[281] or the passage is badly corrupt;[282] 461 cites Ἀριστοτέλης ἐν πολιτείαις for material on jury pay which is not in *A.P.*;[283] fr. 15 in Kaibel & Wilamowitz³ (not in Rose) cites Ἀριστοτέλης ἐν τῇ πολιτείᾳ for material which is not in *A.P.* None of these four fragments provides very strong grounds for supposing that there was an edition of *A.P.* in circulation in antiquity which contained material omitted by the London papyrus: the author was himself responsible for the omissions of which readers complain.[284]

I add a note on alleged changes in practice which are not mentioned in *A.P.* It has already been remarked that 46. i mentions quadriremes but not quiqueremes, whereas quinqueremes are included for the first time in the navy list of 325/4:[285] if this passage was revised, it was revised before that year and not further revised later. E. E. Cohen has resolved a clash between 59. v with 52. ii and Poll. VIII. 101 by suggesting that earlier δίκαι ἐμπορικαί were handled by the εἰσαγωγεῖς but *c*. 330 they were transferred to the thesmothetae;[286] but neither passage in *A.P.* mentions a change or shows signs of disruption, and this tends to support the normal view that Pollux is simply wrong. 56. vi states that εἰσαγγελίαι κακώσεως are ἀζήμιοι τῷ βουλομένῳ διώκειν: originally, it seems, that was true of all kinds of prosecution of which the word εἰσαγγελία was used, but not long before 330 it ceased to be true of εἰσαγγελίαι for major public offences; either when the law was changed for εἰσαγγελίαι of that kind it was not changed for εἰσαγγελίαι κακώσεως or in this respect *A.P.* was not brought up to date. Dittenberger claimed that *A.P.* was already out of date in writing in 57. i that there were not two but four epimeletae of the Mysteries;[287] but *A.P.*'s four epimeletae are now found in a law to be dated shortly before the middle of the fourth century, and it seems improbable that two of the four

---

[279] See fr. 8 in Kaibel & Wilamowitz³.
[280] Cf. Rhodes, *A.B.*, 238.
[281] Kenyon *ad loc.*
[282] Kaibel, *Stil und Text*, 226–7, cf. fr. 6 in Kaibel & Wilamowitz³.
[283] Cf. p. 356.
[284] Cf. pp. 35–6. I do, however, suspect that when the 'Draconian constitution' was inserted it displaced material on Draco's θεσμοί: cf. pp. 5 n. 21, 45–6, 60.
[285] Pp. 52–3 cf. 55.
[286] *Ancient Athenian Maritime Courts*, 158–98.
[287] Note on *IG* ii² 661 = *SIG*³ 384.

INTRODUCTION

were abolished before the time of *A.P.* and by no means certain that two were abolished even later.

6. *Aristotle and the* ATHENAION POLITEIA

At the beginning of this Introduction I cited the passage in the *Nicomachaean Ethics* in which Aristotle says that the *Politics* will be based on his collection of constitutions. Aristotle and his school collected information on particular states for the study of politics in the same way as they collected information on particular plants and animals for the study of biology;[288] and in the *Politics* we do in fact find allusions to a variety of points in the history and constitutions of different states. In addition to the πολιτεῖαι, we know of several other historical works undertaken by the school: νόμιμα (βαρβαρικά), νόμοι, περὶ τῶν Σόλωνος ἀξόνων, δικαιώματα, ὑπομνήματα ἱστορικά, ὀλυμπιονῖκαι and πυθιονῖκαι, διδασκαλίαι, περὶ τραγῳδιῶν, ἀπορήματα Ὁμηρικά, παροιμίαι, and πέπλος.[289]

If the *Politics* were based directly on the collections of evidence, we should expect the collections to be comparatively early works and the *Politics* to be comparatively late; but in fact we have seen that *A.P.* was originally written towards the end of the 330's and revised in the early 320's,[290] while the latest unambiguous reference in the *Politics* is to the murder of Philip of Macedon in 336.[291] The *Politics* as we have it does not form a single coherent treatise: in the nineteenth century many scholars tried to make it more coherent by changing the order of the books, while in the twentieth many have followed W. W. Jaeger in supposing that different parts of the *Politics* represent different stages in the development of Aristotle's thought,[292] a view which remains attractive in principle though it has proved hard to secure agreement on the separation of early material from late.[293] The most extensive attempt to test the

[288] For the analogy cf. p. 7 with n. 24. The importance of this accumulation of facts is stressed by G. L. Huxley, *GR&BS* xiii 1972, 157–69, who cites Arist. *H.A.* I. 491 A 7–14 on the need to collect facts before investigating causes, and *P.A.* I. 644 B 22–645 A 4 on the different attractions of studying the heavenly bodies and the various perishable objects of this world.

[289] Discussed by R. Weil, *Aristote et l'histoire*, 116–44.

[290] Pp. 51–8. Arist. fr. 529 Teubner *ap.* Poll. IX. 62 (from the Κυρηναίων Πολιτεία) refers to the gold coinage of Cyrene, which began to be issued *c.* 340 (C. M. Kraay, *Archaic and Classical Greek Coins*, 299).

[291] v. 1311 B 1–3: attempts to detect later references are rightly dismissed by Weil, *op. cit.*, 181–95.

[292] *Aristoteles: Grundlegung einer Geschichte seiner Entwicklung*, translated as *Aristotle: Fundamentals of the History of his Development*, esp. ch. x; this approach was anticipated by Wilamowitz, *A.u.A.*, i. 355–9.

[293] See the review of the question by Weil, *op. cit.*, 57–84.

INTRODUCTION

Politics against the historical works is that of R. Weil,[294] who agrees with Jaeger that books IV–VI, most fully supplied with references to particular instances, are the latest part of the *Politics*, but unlike him does not limit Aristotle's interest in factual, historical enquiry to the latest period in his life.[295] He makes the very dubious assumption that, where the *Politics* makes a detailed reference to a historical point, this was written when there did not yet exist a detailed treatment in the relevant πολιτεία, but where there is only a casual allusion, either there did already exist a detailed treatment in a πολιτεία or the point was too well known to need a detailed exposition; but I see no reason to doubt that at any rate some parts of the *Politics* are earlier than some of the πολιτεῖαι, and some of the allusions to Athens are likely to be earlier than *A.P.*[296] Aristotle did not first assemble or cause his pupils to assemble the 158 πολιτεῖαι and then write the *Politics* on the basis of this accumulated material; but I assume that he did from the beginning regard politics as a study which required knowledge of actual constitutions, and as he and his pupils collected more information he fitted more information into his treatment of the subject.

The first part of *A.P.* quotes documents (e.g. 30–1, 39), the poems of Solon (5, 12) and Athenian scolia (19. iii, 20. v), and refers to a dedication on the Acropolis (7. iv); it argues for conclusions which are reasonable (e.g. 7. iv), and cites familiar facts as a σημεῖον or τεκμήριον to support the reasonableness of a conclusion (e.g. 8. i). This is in keeping with what we know of the other historical works of the school,[297] and indeed with other Greek histories: Thucydides, for instance, quotes treaties (e.g. v. 18–19, 23–4), makes use of Homer (I. 9–10) and, albeit in a sceptical spirit, oracles (II. 54), refers to the stele commemorating the expulsion of the tyrants (VI. 55. i–ii), uses the argument from reasonableness (e.g. II. 29. iii), and cites σημεῖα and τεκμήρια (e.g. II. 50. ii). However, we have seen reason to believe that *A.P.* did not look for further historical evidence himself: he read widely in the histories and the partisan literature available to him, and he may have added a little from his own knowledge, but most of the evidence which he cites had already been pressed into service by one of his sources.[298] What is distinctive about the first half of *A.P.* is its purpose: to supply not a universal history or a history of a great war or even a general history of Athens, but a history of the πολιτεία, showing the stages

---

[294] *Op. cit.*, esp. 179–323.
[295] Cf. Huxley, *op. cit.*, 158–9, 163.
[296] On the theories of J. Zürcher see p. 51 n. 244.
[297] Cf. Huxley, *op. cit.*, *GR&BS* xiv 1973, 271–86, xv 1974, 203–13, also xii 1971, 505–15.
[298] Cf. pp. 15–30.

by which it had developed to its present (and apparently final) form. On the whole the author has kept to his brief, though he has not entirely resisted the temptation to deal in detail with episodes on which detailed information happened to be available. But it is the second part of the work which is more original. This provides what no earlier writer is known to have provided, a straightforward factual account of how the Athenian πολιτεία worked in the author's own day; and, though observation and general knowledge have doubtless contributed something, this account is based on the laws which regulated the working of the πολιτεία.[299] As a historian *A.P.* is mediocre (though by no means useless to us), but as a describer of constitutional practice he is first in the field.

We have seen that *A.P.* displays the political attitude which we should expect to find in a work of the Aristotelian school; that its first part is Aristotelian in seeking to trace the development of the Athenian constitution to the present and final form of democracy, and that its second part uses the same kinds of category as are used in the *Politics*; but beyond that it does not appear that *A.P.*'s presentation of Athens' history and current practice has been conditioned by Aristotelian political theory.[300] The style is very different from that of the rest of the Aristotelian corpus; and, although some characteristically Aristotelian expressions may be found in *A.P.*, many expressions which we regard as distinctively Aristotelian are conspicuous by their absence.[301]

Similarly, when we turn from presentation to content, there are some significant agreements between *A.P.* and the *Politics*,[302] but against them we must set some striking disagreements. *Pol.* II. 1274 B 15–16 says that Draco enacted laws for an already existing constitution, whereas *A.P.* 4 quotes what purports to be the constitution of Draco—but we have seen that the 'Draconian constitution' is a late insertion in the text of *A.P.*, and may have displaced a section on Draco's θεσμοί which did not conflict with the *Politics*.[303] *Pol.* II. 1273 B 40–1274 A 2 (cf. 1274 A 16–17) and III. 1281 B 25–34 say that Solon left unaltered the appointment of magistrates by election, but according to *A.P.* 8. i–ii and 22. v Solon instituted κλήρωσις ἐκ προκρίτων in place of election by the Areopagus, and this was abandoned under the tyranny but revived in 487/6: here too a late insertion in *A.P.* was suspected by Reinach, but I do not think it can be doubted that from the beginning *A.P.* gave an account of Solon's law on the archons which was in conflict with the *Politics*.[304] *Pol.* V contains two references to the oligarchy of the Four Hundred: 1304 B 12–15 says outright that those who held out the prospect of Persian help against Sparta were deceitful, which is compatible

[299] Cf. pp. 32–7.   [300] Cf. pp. 5–15, 32–3.   [301] Cf. pp. 37–40.
[302] Cf. pp. 9–10.   [303] Cf. pp. 5 n. 21, 53.   [304] Cf. pp. 53–4.

INTRODUCTION

with *A.P.* 29. i but is not actually stated there; 1305 B 22–7 mentions the demagogy of Phrynichus within the Four Hundred, which corresponds to nothing in *A.P.*[305] (Of other apparent disagreements, *Pol.* V. 1315 B 31–4 seems to have applied a different method of reckoning to the same data on the chronology of the tyranny as were used by *A.P.*;[306] VI. 1319 B 19–27 does not necessarily imply that Cleisthenes created new phratries, in conflict with *A.P.* 21. vi; III. 1284 A 17–22, B 15–22, V. 1302 B 15–21, 1308 B 16–19, writes in general of ostracism as a democratic device to check those who are too powerful, which does not exclude the reference to the tyranny in *A.P.* 22. iii–iv; the brief mention of Ephialtes and Pericles as attackers of the Areopagus in II. 1274 A 7–8 is compatible either with the two successive attacks of *A.P.* 25. i–ii, 27. i, or with the joint attack of Pl. *Cim.* 15. ii, *Per.* 9. v, 10. vii.) There is no difficulty in believing that information was available when *A.P.* was written which was not readily accessible to Aristotle when a corresponding passage in the *Politics* was written. The man who revised *A.P.* by inserting the 'Draconian constitution' and the story of Themistocles and Ephialtes was fooled by material which we can see was not authentic, and changed *A.P.* for the worse by these insertions; but I am prepared to accept that study of the ἄξονες had shown that what was said in the *Politics* about Solon and the appointment of archons was wrong, but the *Politics* was not carefully indexed and the necessary corrections were not made there.[307] There may have been some revisions in parts of the *Politics* that are essentially early, but we need not be alarmed if passages survived which Aristotle came not to believe.

I have left to the end the much-discussed question whether Aristotle himself was the author of *A.P.* No one would now deny that *A.P.* is the Ἀθηναίων Πολιτεία from the collection of πολιτεῖαι attributed in the ancient world to Aristotle, that it was written in the 330's and 320's when Aristotle was in Athens, and that it is a product of the Aristotelian school; but it continues to be disputed whether Aristotle wrote the work himself or entrusted it to a pupil. The question is more important to the student of Aristotle than to the student of Athenian history.[308] The case in favour of Aristotelian authorship depends on the attribution of antiquity; but this is a weak foundation unless one is prepared to believe that Aristotle

---

[305] Our text of *A.P.* does not mention Phrynichus at all, but I am inclined to blame a copyist rather than the author for his omission from the list of oligarchic leaders in 32. iii (based on T. VIII. 68, which includes Phrynichus).

[306] Cf. p. 194.

[307] I thus cannot agree with Hignett, *H.A.C.*, 29, that if 'Aristotle had changed his mind since he wrote the *Politics* . . . it is remarkable that in every instance the change seems to have been for the worse'.

[308] Cf. Hignett, *H.A.C.*, 28.

INTRODUCTION

himself wrote all the 158 πολιτεῖαι and all the other works attributed to him. Some have argued that the Athenian constitution was particularly important, so Aristotle must have reserved that for himself;[309] but although Aristotle was in Athens when *A.P.* was written he was not an Athenian and did not admire the Athenian democracy, so the Athenian constitution may not have seemed particularly important to him.[310] On the other hand, it is certain that Aristotle could not have produced single-handed all the works attributed to him, but must have set his pupils to work collecting material in various fields.[311] The stylistic differences between *A.P.* and the rest of the corpus[312] could be due to the different nature of the work and in particular to the influence of the sources used. The factual disagreements with the *Politics* mentioned above[313] could be due to Aristotle's changing his mind as a result of further reading. A further argument used against Aristotelian authorship is that the first part of *A.P.* is of indifferent quality as a work of history[314]— Hignett remarked on 'the immeasurable superiority of the *Politics* to the *Athenaion Politeia* in breadth of treatment and soundness of judgement'[315]—but *A.P.* is not a work which requires breadth of treatment as the *Politics* does, it is not obvious that the *Politics* displays superior historical judgment to *A.P.*, and it is possible to conclude with Wilamowitz that Aristotle was not a great historian.[316] Nevertheless, I am struck by the absence of Aristotelian expressions which we might have expected to find in *A.P.*, and by the small number of passages which have a strongly Aristotelian flavour. Some suggested that a pupil did much of the work but Aristotle himself

[309] E.g. Busolt, *G.G.*, ii². 29, E. M. Walker in J. U. Powell & E. A. Barber, *New Chapters in the History of Greek Literature*, i. 136.

[310] Cf. Hignett, *H.A.C.*, 30. On the argument that *A.P.* was the first of an alphabetic series of πολιτεῖαι and so may have been written first by Aristotle to serve as a model for his pupils (supposed by J. J. Keaney, *Hist.* xix 1970, 327 n. 6, to be the basis of Jaeger, *Aristoteles*, 350 = Engl. trans.², 327, Tovar, *REC* iii 1948, 154–5) see p. 1 n. 2; we cannot date the other πολιτεῖαι (apart from one indication that the Κυρηναίων Πολιτεία was written after *c*. 340: p. 58 n. 200), but the lateness of *A.P.* makes it not very likely that that was finished before the rest of the collection was begun.

[311] The classic study of the organisation of Aristotle's school is H. Usener, *Pr. J.* liii 1884, 1–25 = *Vorträge und Aufsätze*, 67–102, esp. 21–2 = 97–8. For a study of the school's historical work see F. Duemmler, *RM*² xlii 1887, 179–97 = *Kleine Schriften*, ii. 463–81; and, more recently, H. Bloch, *HSCP* Supp. i 1940, 367–76, cf. J. P. Lynch, *Aristotle's School*, 85–90.

[312] Stressed by some of the first English commentators, esp. H. Richards, *CR* v 1891, 184–5, 272–3, 333–4.

[313] Used as a basis for argument by F. Cauer, *Hat Aristoteles die Schrift vom Staate der Athener geschrieben?* 4, 45–7.

[314] Cauer, *op. cit.*, esp. 30–7; F. Rühl, *RM*² xlvi 1891, 426–64.

[315] *H.A.C.*, 29.

[316] *A.u.A.*, i. 373.

revised it.[317] This also must be regarded as a possibility, but the 'Aristotelian' ch. 9 fits into the pattern of *A.P.*'s treatment of Solon and I am not disposed to regard it as a comment inserted by Aristotle into a collection of facts by his pupil; more probably the pupil showed stronger Aristotelian influence when he attempted to assess the significance of his facts. It is true, as Hignett complained, that many who accept *A.P.* as the work of Aristotle have been anxious to believe statements and silences which they would not have been anxious to believe on the authority of a mere pupil[318] (though more recently Day & Chambers[319] and Schreiner[320] have attributed *A.P.* to Aristotle but have not been anxious to believe what they read in it). On the evidence which we have, Aristotle could have written this work himself, but I do not believe he did. That does not diminish the interest and importance of *A.P.*†

---

[317] E.g. L. Whibley, *CR* v 1891, 223, J. H. Wright, *HSCP* iii 1892, 22 with n. 2. The joint production of pictures by leading painters and their pupils provides a parallel from more recent times.
[318] *H.A.C.*, 28–9.
[319] *A.H.A.D.*
[320] *SO* Supp. xxi 1968.

COMMENTARY

A. *The Lost Beginning*

Two texts purport to summarise the historical part of *A.P.* One is *A.P.* 41. ii, at the end of the historical part, listing the μεταβολαί or μεταστάσεις by which the Athenian constitution developed to its 'final' form, fourth-century democracy (cf. *ad loc.*); the other is the *Epitome of Heraclides* (on which see Introduction, p. 2). What is included in *Epit. Heracl.* is clearly derived from *A.P.* (fully argued by H. von Holzinger, *Philol.* l 1891, 436–46), though we cannot rely on it to have retained *A.P.*'s order of narration (cf. §§5–7, restored to *A.P.*'s order by Kenyon), and the excerptor showed no sense of proportion in his selection of material (cf. §4, which omits Pisistratus' rise to power but mentions his death after 33 years' tyranny, next mentions the assassination of Hipparchus and the continuation of Hippias' tyranny, but then omits the expulsion of Hippias, the struggle between Isagoras and Cleisthenes, and Cleisthenes' tribal reform, and passes directly to the introduction of ostracism and its use in the 480's.

By combining these two summaries we obtain the following list of items to be supplied before the affair of Cylon: (*a*) Athens was originally under the rule of kings (*Epit.*); (*b*) Ion settled in Attica and was responsible for the creation of the four tribes (41. ii, *Epit.*, cf. frs. 1, 3); (*c*) there was στάσις after Pandion divided the rule among his sons (*Epit.*); (*d*) Theseus derogated from the monarchy, making a proclamation of equity (41. ii, *Epit.*, cf. fr. 2); (*e*) the story of Theseus' death was told, with an anticipatory digression on Cimon's recovery of his bones from Scyros (*Epit.*, cf. fr. 4); (*f*) the kingship was abolished ἀπὸ τῶν Κοδριδῶν (*Epit.*); (*g*) the story of Hippomenes, the last ruler from the house of the Codridae, was told (*Epit.*). Although other writers supply a variety of material on these topics, only the four fragments noted above claim to be derived from 'Aristotle'.

Sandys[2] (lxv) and M. H. Chambers (*TAPA* xcviii 1967, 63–5) have both calculated that the lost beginning, including the missing part of the chapter on Cylon, should have occupied four to six pages of the Berlin papyrus, which I calculate as equivalent to four to six pages of Kenyon's O.C.T.

(a) The kings of Athens: For the legend of the kings, built up gradually on the basis of an extremely meagre tradition, see the following sections, and commentary on 3. i, iii. The outline accepted by *A.P.* is essentially that found in the later chronographers: after Cecrops I there were fourteen kings of the original, Erechtheid, dynasty, from Cranaus to Thymoetes (for the sake of orientation I shall give Eratosthenes' dates as established by Jacoby [Castor, 250 F 4], though they are of course as artificial as the history to which they are attached: he placed the beginning of Cecrops' reign in 1556/5); a new dynasty began with Melanthus (1127/6); after the death of Melanthus' son Codrus his son Medon was the first of a series of ἄρχοντες elected for life from the royal house (1069/8; for a variant, see §f and 3. iii with commentary); after thirteen of these life archons there was a series of archons each elected for a term of ten years (beginning 753/2); after Hippomenes' archonship (723/2–714/3) the office was opened to all Eupatrids (§g); and the annual archonship began with Creon in 683/2. Few of these kings are known to Herodotus; the original construction of the list seems to have been the work of Hellanicus (see Jacoby, *Atthis*, 125–7, commentary on 323a F 23), and *A.P.* clearly had access to a full reconstruction with some variants.

(b) Ion: When Erechtheus was king (1487/6–1438/7 according to Eratosthenes) Eleusis and the Thracians under Eumolpus made war on Athens, and Ion, son of king Xuthus of the Peloponnese and Erechtheus' daughter Creusa, was made commander or polemarch of the Athenians and led them to victory (for references see on 3. ii). Those who compiled the list of kings did so without making room in it for Ion, the son of a foreign father; but at an early date he had become regarded as the ancestor of the Ionians, and of their senior branch, the Athenians, in reflection of the tradition that after the fall of the Mycenaean kingdoms men had migrated from various parts of Greece to Athens and had set out from Athens to found new homes in Asia Minor (e.g. Solon, fr. 4a West *ap. A.P.* 5. ii; also H. I. 146. ii, 147. ii, VIII. 44. ii, IX. 106. iii, T. I. 2. v–vi, 6. iii, 12. iv, II. 15. iv), and the four 'Ionian' tribes found in Athens and elsewhere were said to be named after his sons (e.g. H. v. 66. ii, 69. i: cf. p. 67).†

A direct allusion to Ion's activity is found in **fr. 1** (*Epit. Heracl.* 1, Harp. Ἀπόλλων πατρῷος ὁ Πύθιος, schol. Ar. *Av.* 1527, etc.). *Epit. Heracl.* reports that Ion settled with the Athenians (συνοικήσαντος δὲ Ἴωνος αὐτοῖς, codd.), and Harpocration that he settled in Attica (τούτου γὰρ οἰκήσαντος τὴν Ἀττικήν, codd.), while we read in *A.P.*'s own summary in 41. ii that Ion and his followers settled (Ἴωνος καὶ τῶν μετ' αὐτοῦ συνοικησάντων). In 41. ii Kenyon originally retained the papyrus's συνοικισάντων; συνοικησάντων has come to be accepted as the correct text (cf. *ad loc.*), but, however unjustifiably, the idea of a synoecism by Ion has persisted: it survives in Kenyon's Oxford Translation of 41. ii, and it was imported into *Epit. Heracl.* by Kaibel & Wilamowitz, who emended to αὐτούς (cf. Kenyon, Berlin ed. and O.C.T., Moore, 311); Kenyon emended to ⟨συν⟩-οικήσαντος in Harpocration (Berlin ed., O.C.T.), which may be correct if we suppose that *A.P.* used συνοικήσαντος and τὴν Ἀττικήν has been supplied as object in the process of excerpting. Fr. 1 tells us that Ion settled in Attica, and gave it a cult of Apollo πατρῷος, a suitable diety to preside over his kinship organisation (and a deity chosen to be his father in an alternative version of the legend [Eur. *Ion*, 8–36, followed by Plat. *Euthyd.* 302 D 1, Arr. *Anab.* VII. 29. iii, schol. Ar. *Av.* 1527]—but this never became standard doctrine, and it would be rash to claim on the basis of the lexicographers that it must have been the doctrine of *A.P.*).

Wade-Gery has argued (*CQ* xxv 1931, 2–6 = *Essays*, 88–92) that we should also associate with Ion **fr. 3** (schol. [Plat.] *Axioch.* 371 D, *Lex. Patm.* γεννῆται [*BCH* i 1877, 152 = K. Latte & H. Erbse, *Lexica Graeca Minora*, 162], etc.): these texts mention, together with the division of the people into four tribes and their subdivisions, a twofold division into γεωργοί and δημιουργοί; whereas other texts, including *A.P.* 13. ii and Pl. *Thes.* 25. ii, add the εὐπατρίδαι to these to yield a threefold division. Some have regarded the twofold division as a defective version of the threefold, and have inserted the εὐπατρίδαι in fr. 3 (e.g. Kaibel & Wilamowitz; Gomme, *CR* xlii 1928, 226), but Wade-Gery makes a good case for the view that *A.P.* believed in a twofold division associated with the four tribes and therefore with Ion. The εὐπατρίδαι must (according to *A.P.*) have come into existence later: though it may be doubted whether Kenyon and Wade-Gery were right to regard Pl. *Thes.* 25. i–ii as well as the beginning of iii as derived from *A.P.* (Kenyon's fr. 2), it is likely enough that where Plutarch ascribes to Theseus the whole threefold division *A.P.* believed Theseus to have separated the εὐπατρίδαι from the original two classes (cf. §d). A variant form of *A.P.*'s account is found in Str. 383. VIII. vii. 1: ἐπέτρεψαν αὐτῷ (*sc.* τῷ Ἴωνι) τὴν πολιτείαν Ἀθηναῖοι; he divided the people first into four tribes and then into four βίοι—γεωργοί, δημιουργοί, ἱεροποιοί, φύλακες (but εὐπατρίδαι are not mentioned)—and left his name to the country.

The four 'Ionian' tribes in Athens were called Αἰγικορεῖς, Ἀργαδεῖς, Γελέοντες, Ὅπλητες (e.g. H. v. 66. ii, Eur. *Ion*, 1575–81; cf. Poll. VIII. 109, claiming to know two earlier sets of tribal names, whose regional connotations are discussed by D. Kienast, *HZ* cc 1965, 274–7): the names, with two more (Βορεῖς, Οἰνῶπες), are found in other Ionian states, though with less regularity than the names of the three Dorian tribes in Dorian states (cf. Gilbert, *C.A.S.A.*, 103–4 n. 3,

Busolt & Swoboda, *G.S.*, ii. 769, Hignett, *H.A.C.*, 51, A. J. Toynbee, *Some Problems of Greek History*, 43–4 n. 2). Some sought a more rational explanation of the names than the derivation from Ion's sons and suggested that they denoted distinct occupational classes (Pl. *Sol.* 23. v; and perhaps Strabo's four βίοι are intended to explain the four tribes): some modern scholars have accepted this suggestion (e.g. Gilbert, *C.A.S.A.*, 103); but the occupational classes are more likely to be a product of fifth- and fourth-century philosophy than a genuine element in early Athenian society (cf. pp. 71–2), and we should more probably look for the origin of the tribal names in the cult titles of the gods worshipped by the tribes (e.g. E. Maass, *GGA* 1889, 805–8, 1890, 353–4 n. 3, Busolt & Swoboda, *G.S.*, ii. 770).

Fr. 3 suggests with implausible neatness that each tribe was divided into three parts known as τριττύες or φρατρίαι, each of those was divided into thirty γένη, and each γένος comprised thirty men: to lessen our confidence still further, it offers a comparison with the seasons, months and days of the year (which does not favour the theory of J. H. Oliver, *GR&BS* xiii 1972, 99–103 cf. 107, that at the time of the hoplite revolution thirty γένη in all were created). The division of each tribe into three trittyes is repeated in *A.P.* 8. iii and 21. iii, and need not be doubted; Cleisthenes similarly divided each of his ten new tribes into three trittyes (21. iv), and although by analogy with similar words τριττύς ought to mean something which is itself divided into three parts there is no evidence that in Athens either the old or the new trittyes were so divided; in Athenian usage τριττύς seems to have meant a third part of a tribe (cf. C. W. J. Eliot, *Phoen.* xxi 1967, 80–3, Rhodes, *Hist.* xx 1971, 400–1; S. C. Humphreys, *ASNP*[3] iv 1974, 351 = *Anthropology and the Greeks*, 195, suggests that there were three phratries to a trittys). Cleisthenes' trittyes (like his tribes and demes) were local units, and it has often been supposed that the trittyes into which the old tribes were divided were local too (e.g. Gilbert, *C.A.S.A.*, 105, Busolt & Swoboda, *G.S.*, ii. 770; H. Hommel, *RE*, viiA [1939/48], 334–42, suggested a link with the twelve πολεῖς of Phil. 328 F 94, but see Jacoby *ad loc.*), but the supposition rests on no secure foundation; we now know that one of the trittyes of the tribe Geleontes was called Λευκοταίνιοι, 'white-ribboned' (*Hesp.* iv 2, 35–7, cf. W. S. Ferguson, *Classical Studies . . . E. Capps*, 151–8). On the relationship between trittyes and phratries we have no direct evidence apart from the texts contributing to fr. 3, which make them identical. We shall see that this must be wrong; meanwhile it may be noted that no reader of *A.P.* 21. iii, vi, who did not possess fr. 3 would suspect that *A.P.* made trittyes and phratries identical.†

When we turn to the composition of phratries ('brotherhoods'), we find a fragment of Philochorus which records a law obliging phratries to accept as members καὶ τοὺς ὀργεῶνας καὶ τοὺς ὁμογάλακτας οὓς γεννήτας καλοῦμεν (328 F 35), and decrees of the Δεκελειεῖς and Δημοτιωνίδαι which show one phratry in the 390's containing a privileged group, while the whole is divided into θίασοι (*IG* ii² 1237 with Wade-Gery, *CQ* xxv 1931, 129–43 = *Essays*, 116–34, W. E. Thompson, *SO* xlii 1968, 51–68). It used to be thought that the two categories of Philochorus' law together included all the members of the phratries, and that the law was enacted at a time when the citizenship was being extended, to oblige the phratries to receive into membership the newly enfranchised ὀργεῶνες as well as the long-established γεννῆται (e.g. Jacoby *ad loc.*; this view is still held by N. G. L. Hammond, *JHS* lxxxi 1961, 76–82, 95–8 = *Studies*, 105–15, 136–41, with further comment 142–4); but Andrewes has argued (*JHS* lxxxi 1961, 1–15) that ὀργεῶνες and γεννῆται are both privileged groups, whose members are to be admitted to the phratry without scrutiny because they have already passed a more rigorous scrutiny to secure membership of their smaller groups, that the Δημοτιωνίδαι are a γένος, and that it was common if not universal for a single γένος to form the aristocratic core of a phratry (ὀργεῶνες were another, relatively obscure, upper-class minority). It should at any rate be accepted that the phratries, in the time of Draco and probably at all times before Cleisthenes' creation of a new basis for citizenship, were organisations through which all the citizens of Athens were distributed (cf. M&L 86, 18–19), whereas the γένη, 'clans', contained only the more aristocratic citizens (on the relationship between γεννῆται and εὐπατρίδαι see pp. 75–6). If Andrewes is right, as I think likely, the scheme of fr. 3 will be wrong in various respects: the phratries will have been far more than twelve in number (as many had suspected before Andrewes wrote: e.g. Hignett, *H.A.C.*, 59–60); they therefore cannot have been identical with the trittyes (though this is still maintained by F. J. Frost, *AJAH* i 1976, 67), but it is likely that all members of the same phratry belonged to the same tribe (cf. Hom. *Il.* II. 362–3, not of course referring to Athens) and possible but not necessary that all belonged to the same trittys; the γένος will not be a subdivision of a phratry but will have stood in a one-to-one (perhaps sometimes two- or three-to-one) relationship to it; and there will have been members of the phratry who did not belong to any γένος. The obscurest point is the relationship between the trittys and the phratry: tribe and trittys, and tribe, phratry and γένος, seem to be two sets of institutions which have been artificially combined to produce a single series.†

These units all depend on supposed common ancestors in the mythical past. As a smaller and more genuine kinship group we should notice the οἰκία, the family in a fairly broad sense: a γένος might comprise several οἰκίαι. Herodotus uses οἰκίη of Isagoras' family (v. 66. i) and the elder Miltiades' family (vi. 35. i); he uses γένος of the Γεφυραῖοι, who undoubtedly were a γένος (v. 55); of the Alcmaeonids he uses οἰκίη when thinking of a particular moment in time (vi. 125. i) and γένος when thinking more of the whole line (v. 62. ii). But γένος could be used non-technically (for Herodotus' application of the word to families elsewhere in Greece and beyond cf. especially I. 7. i, IV. 147. ii, 150. ii, VII. 117. i, 208. i, IX. 33. i), and the Alcmaeonids were probably not a γένος in the technical sense. Paus. II. 18. ix derives τὸ Παιονιδῶν γένος καὶ Ἀλκμαιωνιδῶν from the Neleids of Pylos (cf. pp. 186–7), and H. v. 70–1 writes of 'the Alcmaeonids' in connection with Cylon (cf. on ch. 1); but H. VI. 125. i says that the family became distinguished from the time of Solon's contemporary Alcmaeon and his son Megacles, and elsewhere the term Alcmaeonid is applied only to the descendants of that Alcmaeon (Wade-Gery, *CQ* xxv 1931, 82–3 = *Essays*, 106–8, Davies, *A.P.F.*, 369–70, and cf. below, p. 84; contr. P. J. Bicknell, *Hist.* Einz. xix 1972, 59–60).†

Cleisthenes deprived them of their political significance, and it probably ceased to be true that all citizens belonged to them, but thanks to religious and social pressure these kinship organisations survived into the fifth and fourth centuries, and to belong was normal rather than abnormal (cf. Ar. *Av.* 1669–70, *Ran.* 418, Plat. *Euthyd.* 302 C 4–D 3). Philochorus' law, quoted from book IV of his *Atthis*, should belong to the Periclean period (Andrewes, *op. cit.*, 2, 13–14); a sacrifice of the Λευκοταίνιοι was included in the revised sacrificial calendar of 403/2 (*Hesp.* iv 2, 35–7); the phratry of the Δεκελειεῖς ordered a scrutiny of its members in 396/5 (*IG* ii² 1237, 9–12); when a foreigner was awarded Athenian citizenship he was offered membership not only of the (Cleisthenic) tribe and deme of his choice but also of the phratry of his choice (e.g. M&L 85, 15–17, Tod 133, 30–3, 178, 15–22). If the kinship organisations were not changed except in so far as membership of them ceased to be an essential concomitant of citizenship (8. iii, 21. vi, with commentary), fourth-century writers should have known the relationship between the different units, even though they did not know when or how they originated. If phratries and trittyes were different entities it is not credible that in the fourth century *A.P.* made the mistake of identifying them: no doubt he did ascribe to Ion all the kinship units named in fr. 3, almost certainly he did believe that in the original scheme every member of a phratry was a γεννήτης and the non-γεννῆται were relative newcomers, and beyond that he probably did not fully explain units whose nature was familiar in Athens and throughout the Greek world. R. Weil (*Entret. Hardt* xi 1964, 164–5), compares the use of the number 5,040 in Plat. *Legg.* v. 737 E 1–738 B

COMMENTARY ON THE *ATH. POL.*

I, VI. 771 A 5–C 7, and wonders whether *A.P.* believed in this scheme or merely reported it as someone else's theory; more probably, despite the references to 'Aristotle', this scheme is the work of a later writer who was not in touch with the surviving institutions and sought to explain what *A.P.* had taken for granted.[1]

As to when and how the kinship organisations actually did come into existence, Andrewes has again issued a disturbing challenge to what had been the accepted view (*Hermes* lxxxix 1961, 129–40): whereas most have believed that these organisations were survivals of very ancient institutions (e.g. Busolt & Swoboda, *G.S.*, i. 129–32, ii. 768–9, Hignett, *H.A.C.*, 47–55), he has stressed that they are foreign not only to the bureaucracy of the Mycenaean kingdoms but also to the Homeric poems (*Il.* II. 362–3, in which Nestor proposes that the army should be marshalled κατὰ φῦλα, κατὰ φρήτρας, is an intrusion with no effect on the subsequent action and no parallel), and suggests that, though comparable organisations may have existed earlier, the whole network of kinship organisations as found in classical Greece was a creation of the dark ages, a system in which competing nobles and groups of nobles could organise their retainers and dependants (cf. the earlier hints of E. Meyer, *Forschungen*, ii. 529–30, *Geschichte des Altertums*, iii². 285–7). A. J. Toynbee argued that the tribes originated in dark age Asia Minor, to be copied in mainland Greece (*Some Problems of Greek History*, 43–4), and that is probably right; but F. Cassola (*La Ionia nel mondo miceneo*, 246–56) has claimed that they were survivals from a Greek settlement of Ionia in the Mycenaean period.

Fr. 3 mentions also a twofold division into occupational classes, γεωργοί and δημιουργοί. The first (whichever Greek word is used of them: cf. below) are farmers of some kind. The second appear in Hom. *Od.* XVII. 383–5, XIX. 135, and later as the men who ply specialised crafts; and the word is found in many places as the title of a magistrate. Usually it is explained as denoting those who work for the δῆμος, but L. R. Palmer has argued vigorously from the Pylos tablets (where δῆμος has been found but not δημιουργοί) that it should originally have denoted those who work δῆμος-land as opposed to land held from another source (*TPS* 1954, 18–53b, esp. 37–45; for the subsequent debate see especially K. Murakawa, *Hist.*

---

[1] ἔθνη in Harp. τριττύς, Poll. VIII. 111, is certainly wrong. It suggested to Busolt (*G.G.*, ii². 107–8 n. 3) the doubtful idea that the lexicographers have misconstrued a text of *A.P.* which divided the tribes not into three trittyes = phratries but in three separate ways. More recently F. R. Wüst has suggested on the basis of Pollux that within each tribe one trittys corresponded to each of the three classes, εὐπατρίδαι, γεωμόροι and δημιουργοί (*Hist*, vi 1957, 178–86), and on the basis of D.S. I. 28. iv–v, and Lydus, *Mag. Rom.* I. 47, that the classes and trittyes were in fact a creation of Solon, later attributed to Theseus (*Hist.* viii 1959, 1–11)—which finds no support in our best evidence for Solon.

vi 1957, 385–415, M. I. Finley, *Hist.* vi 1957, 133–59, *EcHR*[2] x 1957/8, 128–41, esp. 137–9, 140 with n. 3, Palmer, *EcHR*[2] xi 1958/9, 87–96, esp. 91–3). This simple division is at first sight more credible than the fourfold division postulated to explain the four tribes (cf. pp. 67–8); but apart from the attribution to Theseus of the separation of the εὐπατρίδαι from these two classes (cf. §d) and the puzzling appearance of the resulting three classes in connection with the archonship in 13. ii (cf. *ad loc.*) this distinction plays no part whatever in Athenian history, though the distinction between εὐπατρίδαι and other citizens is a real one and is important especially in the archaic state. Some have suggested that the γεωργοί and δημιουργοί were originally local officials (B. R. I. Sealey, *Hist.* ix 1960, 178–80, x 1961, 512–14 = *Essays*, 30–4, 39–41; C. Roebuck, *Hesp.* xliii 1974, 485–93, esp. 491–3), but I suspect that the application of this division to early Athens rests not on reliable tradition but on philosophers' teaching—perhaps inspired by vague memories of bronze age society—as to what elements ought to be found in the πόλις (cf. L. Gernet, *RPh*[3] xii 1938, 216–27, Day & Chambers, *A.H.A.D.*, 173).

The farmers are called γεωργοί in fr. 3 (cf. *L.S.* 257. 7–11, *E.M.* [395. 50] εὐπατρίδαι, Hes. [*A* 820] ἀγροιῶται), ἄγροικοι in 13. iii (cf. D.H. *A.R.* II. 8. ii), γεωμόροι in fr. 2 (Pl. *Thes.* 25. ii, cf. Poll. VIII. 111) and in D.S. I. 28. iv–v (deriving the three classes from Egypt); the δημιουργοί are called ἐπιγεώμοροι in *L.S.* and *E.M.*, and are omitted by D.H. There has been much discussion of the three words used of the 'farming' class: in some cities the γεωμόροι were the landed aristocracy (e.g. Syracuse, H. VII. 155. ii, Samos, T. VIII. 21), ἄγροικος is commonly used with the implication 'boorish' or 'stupid' and its application to this class is surprising (e.g. Ar. *Nub.* 47, 628, 646, cf. K. J. Dover, *Greek Popular Morality*, 113), γεωργός is a neutral term; for instance, γεωμόροι was rejected by Busolt & Swoboda as 'unrichtig' (*G.S.*, ii. 859 n. 3) and by Jacoby as 'not Aristotelian' but defended by Wüst as the *difficilior lectio* (*Hist.* vi 1957, 189–91). It is impossible to say which word *A.P.* used in attributing a twofold division to Ion (γεωργοί is at any rate not necessarily his word; but the use of ἄγροικοι in 13. ii does not guarantee that that word was used earlier); but to search for 'the original' names of the three classes is in any case misdirected effort, and it is more important to see the whole theory of a division against the background of the philosophy which produced it (see in particular Plat. *Tim.* 24 A 3–B 3, *Critias*, 110 C 3–7, 112 B 1–5; *Rep.* II. 369–76, etc., criticised by Arist. *Pol.* II. 1262 A 25–1265 A 1; Arist. *Pol.* II. 1267 B 30–3 and 1268 A 17–20 (ascribing a doctrine of three classes in the state to Hippodamus of Miletus), IV. 1291 B 2–4, VII. 1328 B 20–4, etc.).

COMMENTARY ON THE *ATH. POL.*

Discussion may be postponed until later of one division of the citizen body not attested for the lost beginning of *A.P.* but found in the surviving chapters: the ναυκραρίαι, said to have numbered twelve to each tribe (8. iii with commentary) and to have been replaced in Cleisthenes' reform by the demes (21. v with commentary).

(c) Pandion: King Erechtheus was succeeded by Cecrops II (1347/6–1308/7 according to Eratosthenes), and Cecrops by Pandion II (1307/6–1283/2); in *Epit. Heracl.* Pandion is described as βασιλεύσας μετὰ 'Ερεχθέα, but the omission of Cecrops is no doubt due to the epitomator rather than to *A.P.* In the version which became canonical Pandion was driven out of Athens by the sons of Metion, went to Megara, married the daughter of king Pylas and became king there himself; his four sons returned to Athens after his death, expelled the Metionidae and partitioned the kingdom of Athens-and-Megara (Apoll. *Bibl.* III. 205–6, Paus. I. 5. iii–iv cf. 41. vi [Pandion's tomb in Megara]); but there are traces of an alternative version, followed according to *Epit. Heracl.* by *A.P.*, in which Pandion acquired Megara without losing Athens, and was himself responsible for dividing the enlarged kingdom between his sons (Soph. fr. 872 Nauck[2] *ap.* Str. 392. IX. i. 6, schol. Ar. *Lys.* 58 cf. schol. *Vesp.* 1223); it is not clear which version was followed by Phil. 328 F 107 *ap.* Str. *loc. cit.* For a discussion of the story and its connection with the rivalry between Megara and Athens in the seventh and sixth centuries (cf. on 1, 2. ii, 14. i) see Jacoby's commentary on 328 F 107: he thinks it 'very probable' that in Pandion Athens has adopted a figure from Megarian legend, while Megara in turn tried to lay claim to Aegeus by suggesting that his father was not Pandion but Scyrius (Apoll. *Bibl.* III. 206, cf. Pl. *Thes.* 13. i).

Aegeus, as the eldest son, obtained the city of Athens and the surrounding plain (Eratosthenes dated his reign 1282/1–1235/4), Pallas the παραλία, Lycus the διακρία (thus foreshadowing the regional divisions of the sixth century: cf. on 13. iv) and Nisus Megara. It was believed that Aegeus came into conflict with his brothers—he expelled Lycus, who fled to Asia Minor and became the ancestor of the Lycians (H. I. 173. iii cf. VII. 92, Str. 573. XII. viii. 5, 667. XVI. iii. 10, Paus. I. 19. iii); and after recognising Theseus as his son and heir he was attacked by Pallas, whom Theseus defeated (Pl. *Thes.* 13, schol. Eur. *Hipp.* 35 [including Phil. 328 F 108], cf. Apoll. *Epit.* I. 11)—while Nisus was killed and Megara captured by Minos in the course of his campaign against the joint kingdom to avenge the death of his son Androgeos (Apoll. *Bibl.* III. 209–11). 'Atthidography, following earlier speculations, had dated the trichotomy of (Attica) back to Pandion, and to Atthidography fell the

COMMENTARY ON THE *ATH. POL.*

task of eliminating it' (Jacoby, *Supp.* i. 431): with Aegeus' brothers all removed, Attica could be reunited by Theseus.

(d) **Theseus' proclamation**: Theseus, who succeeded Aegeus (1234/3–1206/5 according to Eratosthenes), was believed to have accomplished the definitive synoecism by which the whole of Attica was incorporated in the πόλις of Athens (T. II. 15. ii, Is. x. *Hel.* 35, [D.] LIX. *Neaer.* 74–5, *Marm. Par.* 239 A 20, D.S. IV. 61. viii, Pl. *Thes.* 24. i–iv), having previously consisted of twelve πόλεις (Phil. 328 F 94 *ap.* Str. 397. IX. i. 20), and been divided among the sons of Pandion (§c). He is said to have been a king with democratic leanings, who in a manner which is not very clear gave up the kingship or some of the power pertaining to it and established a form of democracy (Eur. *Suppl.* 399–408, cf. 350–3, 429–41, Is. x. *Hel.* 34–7, XII. *Panath.* 126–9, [D.] LIX. *Neaer.* 74–5, LX. *Epit.* 28, *Marm. Par.* 239 A 20, D.S. IV. 61. viii, Pl. *Thes.* 24. ii, 24. v–25. iii; cf. the attack on this view by Paus. I. 3. iii; E. Ruschenbusch, *Hist.* vii 1958, 408–18, exaggerates the difference between versions written before the late 340's and those written after). *A.P.* 41. ii describes Theseus' régime as ἔχουσα πολιτείας τάξιν and μικρὸν παρεγκλίνουσα τῆς βασιλικῆς (cf. *ad loc.*), and *Epit. Heracl.* records a proclamation and the bringing together of τούτους ἐπ᾽ ἴσῃ καὶ ὁμοίᾳ: the first seems to be echoed in Pl. *Thes.* 25. iii, ὅτι δὲ πρῶτος ἀπέκλινε πρὸς τὸν ὄχλον, ὡς Ἀριστοτέλης φησί, while §i records τὸ 'δεῦρ᾽ ἴτε πάντες λεῴ' κήρυγμα and §ii states that Theseus created the three classes of εὐπατρίδαι, γεωμόροι and δημιουργοί, gave the εὐπατρίδαι special privileges and τοῖς ἄλλοις ὥσπερ εἰς ἴσον κατέστησε. Kenyon printed the whole of this part of ch. 25 as **fr. 2**, and his derivation of it from *A.P.* was supported by Wade-Gery (*CQ* xxv 1931, 4–6 = *Essays* 91–2: cf. above, p. 67) but rejected by Jacoby, *Atthis*, 247–8 n. 49, and Hammond, *JHS* lxxxi 1961, 78 n. 9 = *Studies*, 107–8 n. 4. Theseus' proclamation was doubtless a standard element in the story, so more than the basic fact is needed to link *Thes.* 25. i securely to *A.P.* (as Jacoby suggests, the proclamation may both originally and in *A.P.* have belonged to the synoecism, but *Epit. Heracl.* is too unreliable to prove it); 25. ii ascribes to Theseus the creation of the three classes, whereas *A.P.* more probably ascribed to him the separation of the εὐπατρίδαι from Ion's two (p. 67); the sentence ὅτι δὲ πρῶτος ... reads like the insertion of a reference to 'Aristotle' into an account derived from elsewhere. *A.P.* could be the ultimate source of §§i–ii, but is unlikely to be the direct source; whether there is any material from *A.P.* in *Thes.* 24 it is hard to say, but §iii is clearly derived from T. II. 15. ii. In *A.P.*'s account Theseus will have reunited Attica after its division among Pandion's sons (probably this was the purpose of the proclamation), have separated a privileged caste of εὐπατρίδαι from the γεωργοί and δημιουργοί who made up the citizen body, and have lessened the power of the monarchy. Perhaps, as suggested by M. Sironić, Z. Ant. v 1955, 281, the εὐπατρίδαι were represented in A.P. as the local chieftains of the old, divided Attica; what was involved in Theseus' inclination to the ὄχλος is not clear, unless even the giving of privileges to the εὐπατρίδαι was thought to be the first step in the direction of democracy.[2] We cannot be sure that in A.P. as in Pl. Thes. 25. ii the εὐπατρίδαι were to supply ἄρχοντες; but they may at any rate have supplied the Areopagus: cf. p. 79.

The composition of an aristocracy is capable of changing, but (in peaceful conditions) of changing only gradually; the capacity for change can in some circumstances be cut off. The Eupatrid aristocracy of Athens probably became fixed in its membership in the late seventh and early sixth centuries, when Draco provided written laws for a state in which appointment to office was made ἀριστίνδην καὶ πλουτίνδην (cf. 3. i, vi, 4. i, with commentary) and Solon substituted a new basis for appointment which was to cut the tie between political privilege and noble birth (cf. 7. iii–8. i with commentary). The Eupatrid families of archaic and classical Athens were the families which before Solon's reforms held the monopoly of political and religious offices: essentially they will have been the leading families with which Athens emerged from the dark age following the fall of the Mycenaean kingdoms, almost certainly families of *nobiles* rather than *patricii*, who acquired their leading position as the fittest who survived during the dark age rather than by any act of creation (cf. C. Roebuck, *Hesp.* xliii 1974, 487–90).[3] But Athens' legendary history required a fountain of honour, and the tradition of a democratic king required a rational explanation, so Theseus became the creator of the Eupatrids, who by giving privileges to them (and perhaps also in other ways which we cannot recover) reduced the power of the monarchy.

The Eupatrids were the aristocrats of the seventh and sixth centuries, no doubt mostly men whose land lay near the city of Athens and who had ready access to the seat of power (cf. A. W. Gomme, *The Population of Athens*, 37–9; also Sealey, *Hist.* ix 1960, 178–80, x 1961, 512–14 = *Essays*, 30–4, 39–41—but Sealey makes too much of regional and too little of other considerations, and unnecessarily doubts that the Eupatrids of the fifth and fourth centuries

---

[2] [D.] LIX. *Neaer*. 74–5 alleges that after Theseus' reforms the king was appointed by χειροτονία ἐκ προκρίτων.

[3] Wade-Gery, *CQ* xxv 1931, 4 with n. 3 = *Essays*, 90 with n. 3, hinted at another technical term, ἰθαγενεῖς: the word means 'authentic' or 'autochthonous', but I know no parallel to its application by Hesychius to certain Athenian γένη (e.g. [H 921] ‘Ησυχίδαι, [Λ 1391] Λυκομίδαι).

were the descendants of the archaic aristocracy); the γεννῆται were the members of the γένη which formed the nuclei of the phratries (cf. §b). Earlier writers assumed that εὐπατρίδαι and γεννῆται were coextensive classes (e.g. H. Francotte, *La Polis grecque*, 10–11, etc., Busolt, *G.S.*, i. 776 n. 2), but this view was challenged by Wade-Gery (*CQ* xxv 1931, 1–11, 77–89 = *Essays*, 86–115). It must be true, both of what actually happened and of what was believed by later Greeks to have happened, that the Eupatrids were always a narrower circle within the wider circle of the γεννῆται. Until the reforms of Cleisthenes every citizen belonged to a phratry, and later it was probably believed that until immigrants were admitted to citizenship every citizen had been a member of a γένος, in which case Theseus' Eupatrids must have been regarded as a privileged minority among the γεννῆται. If Andrewes' explanation of the actual origin of the phratries is correct, there will never in fact have been a time when all citizens were γεννῆται; but whereas in every part of Attica there will have been γένη which built up phratries around themselves not every γένος will have had members who gained an established position in the politics of the city, so again the Eupatrids will have been a smaller group than the γεννῆται. (When a man did make his mark he will perhaps have gained Eupatrid status only for his οἰκία rather than for his whole γένος.)†

It seems established that in the Hellenistic and Roman periods there was a γένος called Εὐπατρίδαι (but on the Delphic evidence see G. Daux, *Delphes au II*ᵉ *et au I*ᵉʳ *siècle*, 551–4), and Is. xvi. *Big.* 25 has suggested to some that this was true also of the archaic and classical periods (e.g. Wilamowitz, *Aus Kydathen*, 119 n. 34, *Hermes* xxii 1887, 121 n. 1, J. Toepffer, *Hermes* xxii 1887, 479–83), but there are strong arguments against this (Wade-Gery, *CQ* xxv 1931, 82–5 = *Essays*, 106–10, Davies, *A.P.F.*, 11–12): almost certainly in the archaic and classical periods εὐπατρίδαι was never anything but the name of a caste; the name fell into disuse, and in the Hellenistic period was revived as the name of a γένος.

As for the synoecism with which Theseus is credited, most scholars agree that even if there was a single Attic state in the bronze age there must have been a fresh synoecism early in the archaic period, with the incorporation of Eleusis in the united state coming comparatively late (e.g. A. M. Snodgrass, *Archaeology and the Rise of the Greek State*, 16–21). I accept that, but there are some who believe in a definitive bronze age synoecism (e.g. R. A. Padgug, *GR&BS* xiii 1972, 135–50, J. N. Coldstream, *Geometric Greece*, 70–1).‡

(e) The death of Theseus: It is clear from *Epit. Heracl.* and **fr. 4** that *A.P.* told the story of Theseus' death on Scyros and of Cimon's recovery of Theseus' bones after the Persian Wars. These two episodes are in themselves of no importance for the πολιτεία, and though he sometimes strays A.P. does normally keep within sight of the πολιτεία, so it is likely here that A.P. also gave an account of the events leading to Theseus' death, which are of more relevance to his theme. Theseus and the Lapith Pirithous captured Helen from Sparta, and were then themselves captured in an attempt to carry off Persephone from the underworld (D.S. IV. 63, Apoll. Epit. I. 23–4, Hyg. Fab. 79) or, in the rationalised version of the legend, from Epirus (Pl. Thes. 31, Ael. V.H. IV. 5 [both retaining the names of the dramatis personae], Paus. I. 17. iv–v). In his absence Menestheus, son of Peteos and great-grandson of Erechtheus, roused the nobles and people against Theseus and with the aid of Helen's brothers was made king in his place; Theseus was released by Heracles, but on returning to Athens he was unable to gain control; so he sent his children to Euboea (if that had not already been done for him when Menestheus seized power) and sailed to Scyros (in some versions he set out for Crete but was carried to Scyros by the wind), where he was lured to his death by Lycomedes (Pl. Thes. 32–5, Paus. I. 17. v–vi, cf. D.S. IV. 62. iv, Apoll. Epit. I. 24, Ael. V.H. IV. 5). One of Athens' first achievements after the Persian War of 480–479 was the capture of Scyros: Delphi had ordered Athens to bring back the bones of Theseus, and Cimon brought to Athens a suitably impressive skeleton (Pl. Thes. 36. i–iii, Cim. 8. iii–vii, Paus. I. 17. vi; cf. T. I. 98. ii, D.S. XI. 60. ii). For Scyros in the fourth century see 62. ii with commentary.

Theseus had to be ousted by Menestheus, to explain how Menestheus came to be commander of the Athenians in the Trojan War (Hom. Il. II. 546–56), and with Spartan help, to explain why the cult of Heracles was important in Athens and that of Theseus comparatively late and unimportant (cf. p. 211). The story could conveniently abolish the premature 'democracy' attributed to Theseus, for those who wished to give the credit for founding the democracy to a later figure (on the different candidates see Ruschenbusch, Hist. vii 1958, 398–424; Pl. Thes. 25. iii adduces the characterisation of the Athenians as δῆμος in Hom. Il. II. 547 as confirmation of Theseus' democracy, but A.P. 2. ii describes the state before Draco and Solon as ὀλιγαρχικὴ πᾶσι). For discussion of how the Atthidographers may have treated the story see Jacoby's commentary on Hell. 323a FF 18–19, Phil. 328 FF 18–19.

(f) Abolition of the kingship: For the treatment of this episode in the lost beginning of the work we have only the evidence of Epit. Heracl., but A.P. returns to the topic in 3. i, iii. In the version which became canonical Codrus was the last king (1090/89–1070/69 according to Eratosthenes) and his son Medon (1069/8–1050/49) was persuaded to hold the office of archon for life instead of the kingship; 3. iii quotes a variant, that (Medon was king and) his son Acastus was the first of the life archons, and concludes that it does not much matter which version is right. For the alleged softness of the kings cf. 3. ii with commentary, where *A.P.* alleges a similar reason for the creation of the polemarchy. Jacoby, *Supp.* i. 45 with ii. 54 n. 29, suggests that the text used by *Epit. Heracl.* here conflicted with 3. iii and followed the version in which all the rulers down to Hippomenes were kings (cf. §g); but behind *Epit. Heracl.* more probably lies a version consistent with 3. iii, in which Hippomenes was not king but tried to regain what his forebears had lost (cf. J. J. Keaney, *HSCP* lxvii 1963, 139–41).

(g) The story of Hippomenes: Although the canonical account made Codrus the last king of Athens, there are traces of an older tradition in which all the rulers of Athens down to Hippomenes (the fourth of the seven ten-year archons: 723/2–714/3) bore the title βασιλεύς (*Marm. Par.* 239 A 27–31, cf. Plat. *Symp.* 208 D 4–5, Arist. *Pol.* v. 1310 B 34–7 with Jacoby, *Supp.* ii. 53–4 n. 28, Paus. I. 3. iii, IV. 13. vii), and the monarchy was abolished after Hippomenes' cruel punishment of a daughter caught in adultery (Hippomenes is βασιλεύς in the account given in Suid. [Π 655] Πάριππον καὶ κόρην). This tradition was reconciled with the alternative by the supposition that all the archons down to Hippomenes were chosen from the royal house, and that after Hippomenes had disgraced himself the archonship was thrown open to all the Eupatrids (Hippomenes is ἄρχων in the accounts of D.S. VIII. 22, Nic. Dam. 90 F 49, Suid. [I 573] Ἱππομένης; in the last two he ἐξέπεσε τῆς ἀρχῆς—no doubt conveniently at the end of his ten years). *Epit. Heracl.* shows that the story was told by *A.P.*, representing Hippomenes as εἷς τῶν Κοδριδῶν and as wanting to give the lie to the reputation for softness under which the family had lived since it was deprived of the kingship; doubtless *A.P.* gave as the result of Hippomenes' behaviour the opening of the archonship to all Eupatrids. For a full discussion of the rival versions see Jacoby's commentary on Hell. 323a F 23.†

We can now build up an outline of how Athens' early history is likely to have been treated in the opening chapters of *A.P.* First an account must have been given of the foundation of the monarchy: of Cecrops, the first king, and of Cranaus and the dynasty which he founded. Then those episodes in the legendary history of Athens will have been narrated which involved a change either in the royal house or in the political standing of the people: Ion's settlement, with the creation of the two classes (γεωργοί and δημιουργοί) and the four tribes, and the institution of the office of polemarch for him to hold; Pandion's division of the kingdom between his sons, foreshadowing the regional divisions of the early sixth century; Theseus' unification of Attica, his creation of the Eupatrid order and his 'democratic' reduction of the powers of the monarchy; Menestheus' ousting of Theseus and his abolition of the 'democracy' (but not of the Eupatrid order). Next (presumably, though there is no evidence that can be adduced in support) will have come the recovery of the throne by Theseus' son Demophon, either as a result of Menestheus' dying at Troy (Pl. *Thes.* 35. viii) or by expelling him after the Trojan War (schol. T. I. 12. ii); and the change of dynasty which occurred when Melanthus, a fugitive from Pylos, accepted on behalf of the aged Thymoetes a challenge from Xanthus of Boeotia on condition that he should become king if he won (H. v. 65. iii, Hell. 323a F 23, Str. 393. IX. i. 7, Paus. II. 18. viii–ix, schol. Ar. *Ach.* 146, schol. *Pax*, 890, Suid. [*A* 2940] Ἀπατούρια; for the tradition that the Alcmaeonid and Pisistratid families shared Melanthus' Pylian origin see on 13. iv). This will have been followed by the death of Melanthus' son Codrus and (it seems) the story that his sons were soft and given to luxury and that for this reason Medon was induced to accept the newly created life archonship instead of the kingship; the reduction of the term of office from life to ten years; the opening of the archonship to all Eupatrids after Hippomenes' cruelty to his daughter; and the further reduction of the term of office to one year with the appointment of Creon for 683/2. *A.P.* may then have passed directly to Cylon's attempt to make himself tyrant (ch. 1). Other material may have been included in the lost chapters, such as the foundation of the council of the Areopagus, which can hardly have made its first appearances at 3. vi, [4. iv] and 8. iv (perhaps it was thought to have been founded by Theseus when he created the Eupatrid order: cf. p. 75 and commentary on 3. vi); but we have only a few pages to fill (cf. p. 65). This paragraph sets out as a minimum, a rather more generous minimum than that of M. Sironić, *Ž. Ant.* v 1955, 278–82, what must have been included.

B. *Cylon* (1)

The principal accounts of the Cylonian episode and its aftermath are in H. v. 71, T. I. 126. iii–xii, Pl. *Sol.* 12. i–ix, and schol. Ar. *Eq.* 445 (= 443 Dindorf: the scholia give three accounts, which I designate §§a, b and c in the order in which they are printed in the editions of Dindorf, Dübner and Jones & Wilson).

Cylon, an Olympic victor (H. §i, T. §iii, cf. Suid. [Π 1179] Περικλῆς) married to the daughter of Theagenes tyrant of Megara (T.

§iii, schol. §b, cf. Suid.), assembled a band of supporters (τῶν ἡλικεωτέων, H. §i) including a force from Megara (T. §v, schol. §b) and attempted to seize the Acropolis (H. §i, T. §v, schol. §§b, c, cf. a). On consulting Delphi he had been advised to make his attempt during the greatest festival of Zeus, and had picked the Olympic festival rather than Athens' greatest festival of Zeus, the Diasia (T. §§iv–vi, schol. §b): it is attractively suggested that Thucydides is here contradicting a rival version, perhaps underlying Herodotus' account, in which Cylon did choose the Diasia (M. H. Jameson, *BCH* lxxxix 1965, 167–72; on the Diasia see L. Deubner, *Attische Feste*, 155–7, J. D. Mikalson, *The Sacred and Civil Calendar of the Athenian Year*, 117, 120–1, H. W. Parke, *Festivals of the Athenians*, 120–2, Jameson, *op. cit.*, 159–67; M. L. Lang, *CP* lxii 1967, 243–9, notes that Megara, Delphi and a festival are all absent from Herodotus' account and rejects them as embellishments.

According to Herodotus the attempt failed and Cylon and his supporters became suppliants at τὸ ἄγαλμα: they were persuaded to move by οἱ πρυτάνιες τῶν ναυκράρων, οἵ περ ἔνεμον τότε τὰς Ἀθήνας, on the understanding that their lives would be spared; but they were killed and the Alcmaeonid family was blamed for this. In Thucydides' story (§§v–xi, cf. schol. §b and more briefly §c) Cylon and his supporters occupied the Acropolis but the people came πανδημεὶ ἐκ τῶν ἀγρῶν (§v; in the rival version, ἐκ τῶν Ἀγρῶν, on the left bank of the Ilissus, where they were celebrating the Diasia?) and besieged them; after a while the citizens wearied of the siege and entrusted the whole matter to the nine archons (τότε δὲ τὰ πολλὰ τῶν πολιτικῶν οἱ ἐννέα ἄρχοντες ἔπρασσον: §viii); Cylon and his brother escaped, and the others went as suppliants to the altar on the Acropolis; the guard persuaded them to move, promising them their lives, but killed them; what became of Cylon and his brother is not stated. Plutarch (§i, cf. schol. §a) begins at the point where τοὺς συνωμότας τοῦ Κύλωνος had become suppliants of Athena: Megacles the archon (who in Suid. [Κ 2673] Κυλώνειον ἄγος, [Π 1179] Περικλῆς, becomes Pericles) persuaded them to stand trial; to maintain their hold on divine protection they attached a thread to the statue before leaving, but when the thread broke Megacles and his colleagues turned on the suppliants and the people killed them.

Herodotus and the scholia (all three §§) merely say that those responsible for the killing fell under a curse. Thucydides (§xii) says that the accursed were expelled, and were expelled again by Cleomenes of Sparta (in 508/7: cf. 20. iii with commentary), and (apparently on the second occasion) the bones of those of the accursed who had died and had been buried were removed; but later the accursed returned. According to Plutarch (§§ii–ix) the surviving Cylonians became strong again and there was στάσις between them and τοὺς ἀπὸ Μεγακλέους, until Solon, ἤδη δόξαν ἔχων, persuaded the accursed to stand trial: Myron of Phlya prosecuted, the accursed were convicted, the living were expelled and the bones of the dead were removed; but Megara captured Nisaea and Salamis from Athens and the city was filled with fear, until the Athenians called in Epimenides of Crete, who befriended and advised Solon and purified the city. (In 11. i Plutarch names [Megacles' son] Alcmaeon as στρατηγός of the Athenians in the First Sacred War, the first part of which ended in 591/0 [T. J. Cadoux, *JHS* lxviii 1948, 99–101; for doubts on the historicity of the war see N. Robertson, *CQ*² xxviii 1978, 38–73]—but it is not unthinkable that in spite of the curse Alcmaeon's command may have preceded the return of the Alcmaeonids to Athens [Davies, *A.P.F.*, 371].)†

Cylon's Olympic victory was assigned to Ol. xxxv = 640 (Euseb. Arm. 92 Karst), and a reign in the second half of the seventh century would be acceptable for Theagenes of Megara (F. Schachermeyr, *RE* va [1934], 1342–4); Plutarch associates Epimenides' purification with Solon and his reforms (cf. D.L. 1. 110, with the date Ol. xlvi = 596/5–593/2, but see p. 83; it is dated between Ol. xlv. 4 = 597/6 and Ol. xlvi. 4 = 593/2 by Euseb. Arm. 187 Karst, Hieron. 99b Helm; Suid. [E 2471] Ἐπιμενίδης dated it Ol. xliv = 604/3–601/0), and his story implies that Cylon's *coup* was at least one generation earlier. But there are texts from which a much later dating has been inferred: Herodotus, whose account of the affair is a digression from the struggle between Isagoras and Cleisthenes, notes ταῦτα πρὸ τῆς Πεισιστράτου ἡλικίης ἐγένετο; Thucydides implies that the bones of the dead Alcmaeonids were removed at the time of that struggle; Is. xvi. *Big.* 26 amalgamates this persecution of the Alcmaeonids with their exile under the tyranny, and so represents it as an undeserved punishment (cf. on 19. iii); Plato dates Epimenides' visit to Athens not in the time of Solon but πρὸ τῶν Περσικῶν δέκα ἔτεσιν πρότερον (*Legg.* 1. 642 D 4–E 4). Accordingly De Sanctis (*Ἀτθίς*, ¹274–82 = ²280–9) and Beloch (*G.G.*², 1. ii. 302–9) associated Cylon's *coup* with the episodes involving Megacles in Pisistratus' rise to power (13. iii–15. i), and accepted a date of *c.* 510–500 for Epimenides' purification, claiming as further supporting evidence that the prosecutor Myron ought not to be described as Φλυεύς (Pl. *Sol.* 12. iv) before Cleisthenes' reforms: on Epimenides, though not on Cylon, they found many supporters (cf. Schachermeyr, *Klio* xxv 1932, 339 = *Forschungen und Betrachtungen*, 65). Recently E. Lévy (*Hist.* xxvii 1978, 513–21) has advocated a less drastic down-dating and, adopting the suggestion of T. Lenschau (*Philol.* xci 1936, 396–411) that the first forty-nine

Olympiads were annual, has placed Cylon's Olympic victory in 598/7 and his *coup* in 597/6 or 596/5. However, for Herodotus, who says nothing of Draco and little of Solon, πρὸ τῆς Πεισιστράτου ἡλικίης ἐγένετο need not exclude a date in the seventh century; Thucydides' text need not mean that the bones of dead Alcmaeonids were removed on the second occasion but not on the first; Isocrates does not reliably date the removal of the bones; and rural 'demotics' are entirely possible before Cleisthenes' institution of the demes as political units (Jacoby, *Atthis*, 367–8 n. 81; cf. 14. iv, 21. iv, with commentary). The evidence of Plato is not enough to upset the main tradition, which is now commonly and rightly accepted (first championed by H. Diels, *Sb. Berlin* 1891, 387–403; for a full defence see L. Moulinier, *REA* xlviii 1946, 182–202).†

Tyranny and the killing of suppliants were both offences in the eyes of the Athenians, and it is natural that different stories should have developed, differently assigning the blame for the whole unfortunate series of events. Herodotus accepts that the Cylonians were wrongly killed, but his mention of the πρυτάνιες τῶν ναυκράρων (whoever they were: cf. on 8. iii) has usually been seen as an attempt to divert the blame from the Alcmaeonids. Thucydides, who conspicuously fails to mention the Alcmaeonids or Megacles, is clearly engaging in polemic against a version which he rejects: as Jameson has shown (*BCH* lxxxix 1965, 167–72) his mention of the Diasia makes little sense except as a reply to a version in which Cylon made his *coup* at the Diasia (W. G. Forrest, *BCH* lxxx 1956, 39–40, writing before the discovery of the inscription used by Jameson, explained the note as Delphi's defence against the charge of giving Cylon bad advice—but we may wonder whether in the fifth century, when tyranny was generally execrated, Delphi would admit to having encouraged a man who made an unsuccessful bid for tyranny), and since the Diasia was a festival of purification there may have been a version which emphasised that Cylon committed the first sin (cf. schol. §§b, c, which in general agree with Thucydides but claim that Cylon looted the temple of Athena); and his note on the function of the nine archons must surely be a reply to the version blaming the πρυτάνιες τῶν ναυκράρων (later Paus. VII. 25. iii was diplomatically neutral on the question). It is too simplistic to claim that Herodotus' account is a defence of the Alcmaeonids and Thucydides' is a rebuttal of that defence (e.g. R. W. Macan, ed. of H. IV–VI, i. 214: Jacoby, *Atthis*, 186, could as plausibly argue that both favour the Alcmaeonids; cf. F. R. Wüst, *Hist.* vi 1957, 176–8, C. Mossé, *La Tyrannie dans la Grèce antique*, 51, also the sceptical account of M. L. Lang, *CP* lxii 1967, 243–9), but it should be accepted as certain that they disagree on the supreme magistrates of Athens (*pace* Wüst, *loc. cit.*, B. Jordan, *CSCA* iii 1970, 153–75).

There may also have been disagreement on the part played by Epimenides. There are signs that he was connected with Delphi before the Sacred War, in which case his purification would most naturally be a cleansing of the city for the Cylonians after the Alcmaeonids had been expelled (Pl. *Sol.* 13. i, cf. Jacoby, *Atthis*, 40–1, 272 n. 227, Forrest, *op. cit.*, 41–2, R. J. Hopper, *BSA* lvi 1961, 212); on the other hand, in Pl. *Sol.* 12 and D.L. I. 110 he is associated with Solon, and since Solon and Alcmaeon are both connected with Athens' participation in the Sacred War (A. III. *Ctes.* 107–12, Pl. *Sol.* 11. i–ii, Paus. x. 37. vi) Epimenides' purification ought logically to be linked with the Alcmaeonids' return (though no text survives which spells out this conclusion, and in Pl. *Sol.* 12. iii Solon persuades the Alcmaeonids to submit to the trial which leads to their exile). Most probably the link with Solon is a later fiction of the kind which readily became attached to Solon's name, and dates in the 590's for Epimenides' purification are derived from that fiction; Epimenides' original position is on the Cylonian side.†

The *coup* and its aftermath did not only affect Athens' relations with Delphi: they were important in the history of relations between Athens and Megara (see especially the reconstruction of Hopper, *op. cit.*, 208–17), and for the way in which the curse could be invoked against the Alcmaeonid family by its enemies on many subsequent occasions (see especially G. W. Williams, *Hermath.* lxxviii 1951, 32–49, lxxix 1952, 3–21, lxxx 1952, 58–71). We do not know what combination of motives led Cylon to make his attempt, but if the causes of discontent revealed in *A.P.* 2–3 were already present they were clearly not present in such force as to make the citizens think that any change of régime must be a change for the better.

Epit. Heracl. 2 shows that *A.P.* like Pl. *Sol.* 12. i–ii gave an account in which οἱ περὶ Μεγακλέα were mentioned and were blamed for the death of the suppliants. M. Sironić, *Z. Ant.* v 1955, 274–8, argues from the appearance in Thucydides of some of the words used by *Epit.* that *A.P.* used his account, but they are words which might occur in any account of the affair: on the basis of what survives we cannot deny that *A.P.* made any use of Herodotus and Thucydides, but neither can have been his main source for the story. At the beginning of our text of *A.P.* we have the end of the affair: as in Pl. *Sol.* 12. iii–iv Myron prosecutes in a special court of aristocrats (for swearing καθ' ἱερῶν cf. 29. v with commentary; for ἀριστίνδην cf. 3. i with commentary), and as in Plutarch the expulsion extends to the bones of the dead, and so must be presumed to occur at least a generation after Cylon's *coup*; the involvement of Epimenides is reduced to one short sentence. In that sentence ἐπὶ τούτοις has been variously interpreted: Poste rendered it as 'subsequently', and E.

Lévy as 'immediately afterwards' (*Hist.* xxvii 1978, 514 with n. 8), Sandys 'besides' and Moore 'in connection with this matter', but most probably it means 'on these terms' (cf. Kenyon's Oxford Translation, Fritz & Kapp): Epimenides' purification is not merely subsequent to the expulsion of the Alcmaeonids but (as in Pl. *Sol.* 13. i) is associated with it; here too, though briefer than Plutarch, *A.P.* is in agreement with him. In the penultimate sentence γένος denotes the 'issue' of the actual offenders, whose bones were removed from Attica: it should not be cited as evidence for the view that the Alcmaeonids constituted a γένος in the technical sense of that word (cf. p. 70).

A.P. narrates the whole story of Cylon before proceeding to the στάσις which Solon tried to resolve; he mentions Draco's legislation immediately before the reforms of Solon (cf. pp. 86–7 for a defence of the positioning of 4. i). Myron's prosecution and Epimenides' purification may well have been appended to the story of Cylon so as not to interrupt a narration which would have to be interrupted if the author kept to chronological order, so it would be wrong to claim that *A.P.* has any date for these two episodes. However, Cylon's *coup* must be placed in one of the Olympic years between his victory in 640/39 and Draco's legislation in 621/0 (cf. on 4. i), but we have seen that *A.P.* and Plutarch follow a version in which the expulsion and purification were at least a generation later than the *coup*, probably *c.* 600. Whether the bones of the dead were in fact removed on this occasion, and whether the expulsion and purification are rightly dated as late as *c.* 600, must remain uncertain.

The text of the London papyrus starts at the beginning of a roll, and the roll has been headed α (not by the original scribe): cf. Introduction, p. 3. The lost beginning of the work was already missing from the text from which this copy was made.

C. *Between Cylon and Solon* (2–4)

Ch. 2 describes a state of στάσις between γνώριμοι and πλῆθος, which Solon attempted to resolve; ch. 3 purports to describe ἡ τάξις τῆς ἀρχαίας πολιτείας τῆς πρὸ Δράκοντος, and in fact concentrates on the archons; ch. 4 calls the content of 3 ἡ . . . πρώτη πολιτεία and moves on to describe the τάξις which resulted from the θεσμοί of Draco; ch. 5 introduces the account of Solon with references both to τῆς τάξεως οὔσης ἐν τῇ πολιτείᾳ and to the enslavement of the many and the στάσις of ch. 2.

Commentators on *A.P.* were quick to suspect ch. 4: its contents were found to be anachronistic and reminiscent of the intermediate régime of 411/0 (cf. commentary on ch. 4), and they in no way justify the allegation of oligarchic oppression made in 2. ii–iii; elsewhere in ancient literature there is no trace of a Draconian πολιτεία (apart from a vague reference in [Plat.] *Axioch.* 365 D 7–8; Arist. *Pol.* II. 1274 B 15–18 explicitly states that Draco enacted laws for the existing constitution) or of the material contained in this chapter; and indications were found that this chapter was not part of 'the original' version of *A.P.* (Draco is nowhere properly 'introduced'; and τῆς πρὸ Δράκοντος in 3. i, when Draco has not been previously mentioned, καθάπερ διῄρητο καὶ πρότερον in 7. iii, and the clumsy treatment of Theseus and Draco in 41. ii have all been regarded as unskilful pieces of patchwork undertaken to fit ch. 4 into a text originally written without it). Already in 1891 the 'Draconian constitution' was dismissed as an interpolation derived from the oligarchs of 411 by J. W. Headlam, *CR* v 1891, 166–8, and T. Reinach, *REG* iv 1891, 82–5, 143–58, cf. F. Cauer, *Hat Aristoteles die Schrift vom Staate der Athener geschrieben?* 70–1. Defenders commonly admitted that the 'Draconian constitution' was rediscovered by the fifth-century oligarchs and awkwardly inserted by the author into the narrative which he derived from the *Atthides* (e.g. Busolt, *Philol.* l 1891, 393–400, Wilamowitz, *A.u.A.*, i. 49–50, 57–9, 76–98, cf. ii. 55–6): E. Meyer regarded the 'constitution' as a later invention, but accepted it as a fully constituent part of *A.P.*, though not derived from the author's main source (*Forschungen*, i. 236–9, cf. Mathieu, *Aristote, Constitution d'Athènes*, 112–13: later writers ignored it because they knew it to be inauthentic). The sceptical view that the 'constitution' is neither historically authentic nor an authentic component of *A.P.* was reinforced by De Sanctis (*Ἀτθίς*, [1]162–7 = [2]161–6) and Wilcken (*Apophoreton* [1903], 85–98), and has become widely accepted (for a convenient summary see Busolt, *G.S.*, i. 52–8, with bibliography 53 n. 2).

More recently there have been signs of uneasiness at this solution. Wade-Gery found 3. vi as dubious historically as 4, but 'no ingenuity has yet managed to extract the poison from the body of the treatise and leave no wound' (*CQ* xxv 1931, 77–8 = *Essays*, 101); Jacoby briefly suggested that the whole of 3–4 forms a later addition (*Atthis*, 387–8 n. 62: cf. the earlier hints of O. Seeck, *Klio* iv 1904, 274–6, Adcock, *Klio* xii 1912, 1); Fritz & Kapp have argued that 3 and 4 are both historically unacceptable but should nevertheless be accepted as authentic components of *A.P.*, two sketches of the same constitution, not integrated with each other and thereby betraying that *A.P.* as we have it was not finished for publication (8–12, cf. Fritz, *CP* xlix 1954, 73–93 = *Schriften zur ... Verfassungsgeschichte*, 71–98, and earlier P. Meyer, *Des Aristoteles Politik und die Ἀθηναίων Πολιτεία*, 31–44); Hammond has described *A.P.* 3 as 'one of its finest chapters' (*JHS* lxxxi 1961, 82 = *Studies*, 114); F. P.

Rizzo has attempted a defence of 3 and 4 on fundamentalist lines (*Mem. Ist. Lomb.* xxvii 1960–3, 271–308). In response to those who would reject 3 as well as 4, or would retain both, J. J. Keaney has argued from the use of 'ring composition' that the early chapters of *A.P.* have been very carefully put together, and that there is an elaborate scheme which runs through 2 and 3 and into 5 but is interrupted by 4 (*AJP* xc 1969, 406–23, esp. 415–17). Among sceptics a later date for the invention of the 'Draconian constitution' has been canvassed, to assign it not to the end of the fifth century but to the last quarter of the fourth, perhaps as the work of Demetrius of Phalerum (Jacoby, *Atthis*, 385 n. 51, developed by A. Fuks, *The Ancestral Constitution*, 84–101, Ruschenbusch, *Hist.* vii 1958, 398–424, esp. 421–2).†

It should not be denied that 3 and 4 both represent theoretical reconstruction rather than well-documented history (cf. commentary, below; Rizzo's fundamentalist defence is unconvincing), and that there is a good deal of awkwardness in the presence of 3 and 4 side by side (in particular there is no cross-reference between 3. vi and 4. ii on the appointment of magistrates, or between the very similar 3. vi and 4. iv on the Areopagus; but Fritz' view that the two chapters give different accounts of the same constitution cannot be right). However, a reconstruction which does not deceive us might have deceived Aristotle or his pupil, and there are other places where the author has failed to integrate material drawn from different sources (cf. Introduction, pp. 43, 50). But the evidence of patchwork at any rate in 3. i and 41. ii (I am less sure that καθάπερ διῄρητο καὶ πρότερον in 7. iii was added for the sake of the 'Draconian constitution': cf. *ad loc.*) makes it clear that the 'constitution' is in some sense an insertion in the text of *A.P.* The insertion runs from ἡ δὲ τάξις αὕτη (4. i) to παρ' ὃν ἀδικεῖται νόμον (4. iv); the résumé of 2 in 4. v, defended by Wilcken (*Apophoreton*, 93–5), should probably be regarded as another piece of patchwork, written to help fit the insertion into the original text.

Ch. 3 and 4. i need not be condemned as further insertions: the appointment of the archons, no less than the condition of the peasantry, was a matter on which Solon was moved to take action, and for that reason 3 is needed, and is needed where it is found rather than at some point before ch. 1. At the beginning of 4. i ἡ μὲν οὖν . . . τὴν ὑπογραφήν is a typical concluding sentence, inseparable from 3, and the next sentence (μετὰ δὲ ταῦτα . . . τοὺς θεσμοὺς ἔθηκεν) referring to θεσμοί rather than a πολιτεία, is in line with the tradition about Draco and distinct from what follows. μετὰ δὲ ταῦτα in 4. i could refer either to the unsuccessful *coup* of Cylon (or to the purification by Epimenides which rounded off the affair— but probably *A.P.*'s source placed that after Draco's legislation: cf.

p. 84) or to the state reached at the end of the political development outlined in ch. 3: Wilcken (*loc. cit.*) took it in the first sense, and moved 4. i + v to between 1 and 2; H. Hommel moved 4. i to between 2 and 3 (*Festschrift F. Zucker*, 195–209). But 2 and 3 belong together as two aspects of the situation which Solon tried to remedy, and the pattern in *A.P.*'s phraseology noted by Keaney underlines the connection, so if a transposition is to be made at all Wilcken's is the better; but if *A.P.* has treated Draco's legislation as part of the background to Solon's reforms rather than as an appendix to Cylon's *coup* it will perhaps be better to reconcile ourselves to a careless use of μετὰ δὲ ταῦτα and leave the sentence in its place. Wherever the sentence stands, further information or explanation is needed to make sense of it—there is no need to suspect the reference to Draco's θεσμοί in 7. i, and his laws surely demand fuller treatment than is contained in this one sentence (cf. B. L. Gildersleeve, *AJP* xii 1891, 98–9)—and I suggest that the sentence is correctly placed, and that it was originally followed by further material on Draco which was omitted when the 'constitution' was inserted.

On the use of 'ring composition' in these early chapters of *A.P.* see Introduction, pp. 45–7. Keaney is right to observe that these chapters show a carefully worked out pattern: from 2 to the beginning of 5 *A.P.* sets out the economic and political background of Solon's reforms, and from 5 to the beginning of 13 he gives an equally carefully articulated account of the reforms and Athens' reception of them; introductory and resumptive phrases mark the stages in his thought. Keaney sees in this pattern confirmation that ch. 4 was not included in the original version of *A.P.*, but the pattern can be developed in more than one way, and it does not seem impossible to me that *A.P.* should originally have contained a passage on Draco's θεσμοί in place of the present ch. 4.

Whether the insertion of the 'Draconian constitution' was made by the author of *A.P.* or by someone else is a question more important for those who believe in Aristotelian authorship but wish to exonerate Aristotle from charges of credulity and clumsiness than for the sceptics. The lack of other references to this 'constitution' is a fact to be taken seriously, and suggests that it was absent from the version of *A.P.* which circulated most widely in antiquity (first suggested by Reinach, *REG* iv 1891, 143–58: cf. Introduction, pp. 53–6); but the modifications made elsewhere in *A.P.* to accommodate the insertion indicate that we are dealing not with the accidental interpolation of material noted by a private reader in his own copy but with a deliberate revision made presumably in the Aristotelian school. The source of the 'constitution' must remain uncertain: invention in the late fifth and in the fourth century both seem possible.

Although variants are noted, as in 3. iii, the careful organisation of these chapters suggests that in them *A.P.* is relying on a single main source, possibly an *Atthis* or possibly a separate work on Solon. Little was remembered about Athens before Solon's reforms, and chs. 2–3 represent theorists' reconstruction rather than unbroken tradition. For ch. 2 the reconstruction was based on good material, the poems and laws of Solon: according to Poll. VII. 151 the term ἐπίμορτυς γῆ was found παρὰ Σόλωνι, and *A.P.* and Plutarch both mention the technical term ἑκτήμορος as a word needing explanation to their readers (on the survival of Solon's laws see on 7. i). On the machinery of state, however, there is likely to have been little evidence: one or two isolated incidents may have been remembered, and Solon's laws may in places have specified that a particular institution was to be retained, modified or abolished (Pl. *Sol.* 19. iii–v quotes his amnesty law to prove that the council of the Areopagus existed before his reforms; for the laws of Draco and Solon as evidence for what preceded them see R. S. Stroud, *Athens Comes of Age*, 22); but ch. 3 records 'what ought to have been' rather than what was known to have been.

2. i. μετὰ δὲ ταῦτα: Ch. 1 by implication places the expulsion of the accursed and after it Epimenides' purification at least a generation later than Cylon's *coup*, i.e. *c.* 600 (cf. p. 84); this sentence claims that there was a long period of στάσις before the legislation of Draco and the reforms of Solon. We should therefore assume that the expulsion and purification were narrated out of chronological sequence as an appendix to the story of Cylon, and that the reference here is to the *coup* and its immediate consequences: Cylon's bid for tyranny is seen as the first incident in a period of στάσις lasting (probably: cf. on 13. i) until Pisistratus succeeded in establishing himself as tyrant.

τούς τε γνωρίμους καὶ τὸ πλῆθος: *A.P.* frequently writes of Athens as divided between the great (γνώριμοι, or sometimes ἐπιφανεῖς, εὐγενεῖς, εὔποροι [all in 28. ii]) and the mass of the people (πλῆθος or δῆμος), and names individual politicians as champions of one group or the other (προστάται τῶν γνωρίμων κτλ., προστάται τοῦ δήμου: a schematic list in 28. ii–iii, individual προστάται in 2. ii, 20. iv, 23. iii, 25. i, 26. i, 28. i, cf. 36. i; see *ad locc.*). This rigid polarisation is not found in Herodotus, but it is a commonplace in [X.] *A.P.* (i. 2, 4, etc.), Thucydides (e.g. III. 27. ii [Mytilene], 72. ii etc. [Corcyra], IV. 66. iii [προστάται τοῦ δήμου in Megara], V. 82. ii [Argos], VIII. 21, 73. ii [Samos]) and fourth-century writers, and facts came to match theory as men and cities labelled themselves oligarchic or democratic (while using the same words to cover a variety of shades of political attitude). δῆμος in particular was a conveniently ambiguous word, which could be used to denote the whole citizen community, the whole subject community as opposed to its ruler or rulers, or the mass of the lower orders as opposed to the γνώριμοι; and in the last use the line between γνώριμοι and δῆμος could be drawn at various levels according to circumstances. Thucydides represents Alcibiades as saying that πᾶν . . . τὸ ἐναντιούμενον τῷ δυναστεύοντι δῆμος ὠνόμασται, his family's προστασία τοῦ πλήθους is derived from its opposition to tyranny, and τοῦ ξύμπαντος προέστημεν (VI. 89. iv–vi); in X. *M*. IV. ii. 37–9 the assumption that δῆμος may be defined as τοὺς πένητας τῶν πολιτῶν is used as the basis of a Socratic enquiry. (On the variety of terms used by *A.P.* see Kaibel, *Stil und Text*, 51–3; on the uses of δῆμος in the archaic period see W. Donlan, *PP* xxv 1970, 381–95, and more briefly J. A. O. Larsen, *CP* lxviii 1973, 45–6; on δῆμος and δημοκρατία in the fifth century see B. R. I. Sealey, *CSCA* vi 1973, 253–95, and on the polarisation of 'democrats' and 'oligarchs' see on 24. ii and J. Bleicken, *Hist.* xxviii 1979, 148–72, esp. 166–71.)

There seem at this time to have been two causes of discontent, in relation to which the line should be drawn at two different levels: there is oppression of the poor by the rich, and there is an aristocratic monopoly of public office which impinges (as *A.P.* fails to make clear) not on the poor, who in archaic Athens would never aspire to office, but on the non-aristocratic rich.[4] Each is an instance of στάσις between γνώριμοι and πλῆθος, but the categories are differently defined.

πολὺν χρόνον [[τὸν δῆμον]]: τὸν δῆμον is confidently deleted by Kenyon as *glossam manifestam* (in his O.C.T. the words are printed in the *apparatus* only), and most editors have rightly followed him. J. E. B. Mayor argued unconvincingly that τούς τε γνωρίμους καὶ τὸ πλῆθος is the subject of στασιάσαι and τὸν δῆμον the object (*CR* v 1891, 106); Thalheim preferred to delete καὶ τὸ πλῆθος and read . . . πολὺν χρόνον ⟨καὶ⟩ τὸν δῆμον, but though δῆμος is *A.P.*'s usual word for the mass of the people it is likelier that here he used πλῆθος and his usual word has been added.

2. ii. ἡ πολιτεία: *A.P.* raises first a political theme, to which he will return in ch. 3, that the state was oligarchic in all respects, and then an economic theme, with which he proceeds to deal immediately, that the poor were enslaved to the rich. On this arrangement of the material cf. Introduction, pp. 45–6. πολιτεία in *A.P.* most commonly means 'régime', 'constitution', 'government of the state'

---

[4] A. J. Holladay, *G&R*[2] xxiv 1977, 47, doubts whether there were many rich non-Eupatrids at this time; but Solon's reform, and the discontent which followed (13. i–ii with commentary), make little sense unless there was a significant body of such men.

(cf. Kaibel, *Stil und Text*, 56–7): the use of the word here is typical; κατὰ τὴν πολιτείαν in §iii is less so, but is intelligible enough as a reference to this sentence; for extensions of this sense see 9. ii, 28. v, with commentary. Sometimes the word means 'control of the government', and so 'citizenship' (e.g. 4. ii with commentary), and in three passages in *A.P.* it refers to the body of those possessing citizenship (4. iii, 37. i *fin.*, 38. ii, with commentary).

ἐδούλευον οἱ πένητες τοῖς πλουσίοις: Cf. Pl. *Sol.* 13. iv–v:

ἅπας μὲν γὰρ ὁ δῆμος ἦν ὑπόχρεως τῶν πλουσίων. ἢ γὰρ ἐγεώργουν, ἐκείνοις ἕκτα τῶν γινομένων τελοῦντες, ἐκτημόριοι προσαγορευόμενοι καὶ θῆτες, ἢ χρέα λαμβάνοντες ἐπὶ τοῖς σώμασιν, ἀγώγιμοι τοῖς δανείζουσιν ἦσαν, οἱ μὲν αὐτοῦ δουλεύοντες, οἱ δ' ἐπὶ τὴν ξένην πιπρασκόμενοι. πολλοὶ δὲ καὶ παῖδας ἰδίους ἠναγκάζοντο πωλεῖν—οὐδεὶς γὰρ νόμος ἐκώλυε—καὶ τὴν πόλιν φεύγειν διὰ τὴν χαλεπότητα τῶν δανειστῶν.

All the land of Attica was in a few hands; the poor were indebted or enslaved to the rich, some working the land as their dependants, others being seized as slaves because they defaulted on their dues to their masters or on repayment of what they had borrowed on the security of their persons. These apparently simple statements have proved anything but simple, and there has been a great variety of attempts to explain the state of the land and the peasantry in seventh-century Attica: for a convenient survey of modern views see F. Cassola, *PP* xix 1964, 26–34.

The peasants were freed from their grievous state by Solon's σεισάχθεια: *A.P.* and Plutarch believe that this comprised a cancellation of all debts, a ban for the future on δανείζειν ἐπὶ τοῖς σώμασιν, and the liberation of those who had already been enslaved for debt (cf. 6. i with commentary); Solon himself claims to have liberated the enslaved earth by uprooting the ὅροι planted in it, and to have restored to home and freedom many Athenians sold abroad as slaves (fr. 36. 1–17 West *ap. A.P.* 12. iv, Pl. *Sol.* 15. vi; cf. also fr. 4. 23–5). Thus *A.P.* and Plutarch have Solon's authority for distinguishing (as Plutarch does more clearly than *A.P.*) between two states of servitude: one which can metaphorically be described as the enslavement of the earth, marked by ὅροι planted in it; and actual chattel slavery, a state in which the slave might be sold abroad by an owner who did not wish to keep him.

Various names are given to the men in the first state of servitude, who worked on the land. A πελάτης (*A.P.*) is one who approaches another, in verse simply a neighbour, in prose one who is dependent on or works for another: the noun is found rarely but clearly did not need to be explained; the verb πελατεύειν occurs in a papyrus fragment of Aeschylus (*P. Oxy.* xviii 2161, ii. 22 = fr. 275. 20 Lloyd-Jones [Loeb. ed. of Aeschylus, rev. 1957, vol. ii] = fr. 474. ii. 22

Mette); late writers use πελάτης as the equivalent of the Latin *cliens* (e.g. D.H. *A.R.* I. 83. iii); lexicographers give it the same meaning as the next word to be discussed, θής (schol. Plat. *Euthyph.* 4 c and texts quoted by Greene *ad loc.*). A θής (Pl.) is one who labours for another, commonly for a fixed wage, as a free man (or at any rate less unfree than a δμώς or δοῦλος (Hom. *Od.* IV. 644, Hes. *Op.* 602; the verb θητεύειν Hom. *Il.* XXI. 444, *Od.* XI. 489, XVIII. 357, cf. H. VIII. 137. ii); the noun was to be used as the name of the lowest of Solon's four property classes (7. iii with commentary). The lexicographers offered a third equivalent: λατρίς (e.g. Ar. Byz. fr. 39 Nauck, *ap.* Eust. 1246. 9–16 *ad Il.* XXI. 450, Hes. πελάται), a servant of a man or god, with the cognate abstract λατρεία and verb λατρεύειν (e.g. Soph. *Trach.* 35, 70; the verb is used by Solon, fr. 1. 48 West, of a man working on the land). Two of these words are used together in Plat. *Euthyph.* 4 c 3–5: ὅ γε ἀποθανὼν πελάτης τις ἦν ἐμός, καὶ ὡς ἐγεωργοῦμεν ἐν τῇ Νάξῳ, ἐθήτευεν ἐκεῖ παρ' ἡμῖν. D.H. *A.R.* II. 9. ii says ἐκάλουν δὲ Ἀθηναῖοι μὲν θῆτας τοὺς πελάτας ἐπὶ τῆς λατρείας; and Poll. III. 82, at the end of a section on δοῦλοι, says πελάται δὲ καὶ θῆτες ἐλευθέρων ἐστὶν ὀνόματα διὰ πενίαν ἐπ' ἀργυρίαν δουλευόντων. θής was a general term for a paid labourer, and Prof. Andrewes suggests that πελάται may have been dependent labourers working on their master's demesne; but the word proper to the dependent peasant in Attica was evidently ἑκτήμορος (the lexicographers mostly confirm *A.P.*'s form of the word). *A.P.* states that these were so called because they worked the land κατὰ ταύτην ... τὴν μίσθωσιν, and Plutarch makes clear what *A.P.* perhaps leaves ambiguous, that they retained five-sixths of the produce and had to surrender one-sixth. Scholiasts and lexicographers were divided on this (Plutarch is supported by Hes. [*E* 4985] ἐπίμορτος, opposed by Eust. 1854. 31 *ad Od.* XIX. 28; other texts are ambiguous), and so are modern scholars; but although some have thought retention of five-sixths unduly generous it is hard to believe that a peasant could keep himself and his family on one-sixth of the produce of 'his' land (the Messenians apparently surrendered half of their produce: Tyrt. fr. 6 West), and Plutarch is probably right (see K. von Fritz, *AJP* lxi 1940, 54–61, lxiv 1943, 24–43 = *Schriften zur ... Verfassungsgeschichte*, 110–16, 117–34). Land worked on these terms by ἑκτήμοροι, and perhaps other land worked by share-croppers on other terms, was called ἐπίμορτος γῆ (the adjective was probably applicable to the men as well as to the land), and the part of the produce which they surrendered was their μορτή (Poll. VII. 151, Hes. *loc. cit.*, Eust. *loc. cit.*).[5]

---

[5] G. Kirk, *Hist.* xxvi 1977, 369–70, draws attention to an Iranian system of share-cropping by which five elements were taken into account (land, water,

COMMENTARY ON THE *ATH. POL.*

Cassola in his review of modern interpretations distinguishes three schools of thought as to how the ἑκτήμοροι came into existence and what their status was: some believe that all farming land was the hereditary property of one or other of the aristocratic γένη, and the ἑκτήμοροι were a hereditary class of serfs dependent on the aristocrats and working the land for them; others think that the peasants were originally smallholders who owned and could dispose of their land, and that when they had contracted debts and defaulted on them their creditors retained them on the land as ἑκτήμοροι; the third view is that the peasants owned their land but could not dispose of it, and because their land was inalienable could only be retained on it as ἑκτήμοροι when they defaulted on their debts. Cassola advances a fourth view, for which he relies heavily on Solon, fr. 4. 12–13 West—

οὔθ' ἱερῶν κτεάνων οὔτε τι δημοσίων
φειδόμενοι κλέπτουσιν ἀφαρπαγῇ (ἐφ' ἁρπαγῇ?) ἄλλοθεν ἄλλος—

that early Attica was a patchwork of private land and temple and communal land, and the rich had unlawfully added temple and communal land to their private estates, driving off the poor who depended on the use of that for their livelihood, and the poor were therefore obliged to work for the rich, sometimes on land thus acquired and sometimes to bring marginal land under cultivation (*PP* xix 1964, 26–68, esp. 35–41, 49–51, cf. xxviii 1973, 75–87: he compares Hom. *Od.* XVIII. 357–61).

The Athenians believed that they were autochthonous, and that in the dark age men had migrated from other parts of Greece to Athens and from Athens to the Aegean and Asia Minor (cf. p. 66): it would be inconsistent with this to believe that in Athens, as in many colonies of the archaic and classical periods, parcels of land had once been allocated to the citizens, and that these κλῆροι were the inalienable possessions of the original holders and their descendants (cf. Arist. *Pol.* VI. 1319 A 10–11: ἦν δὲ τό γε ἀρχαῖον ἐν πολλαῖς πόλεσι νενομοθετημένον μηδὲ πωλεῖν ἐξεῖναι τοὺς πρώτους κλήρους). The Athenians may of course have held incompatible views about their past, but I know of no evidence for inalienable κλῆροι in Attica. On the other hand, what we know of primitive societies suggests that, even when theoretically possible, it will in fact have been rare for land to change hands outside the family: a man's livelihood depended on his large estate or his small plot, and if he parted with that he would have little opportunity of sustaining life in any other way. At the outbreak of the Peloponnesian War most Athenians lived where their families had lived as long as they could

---

animals, seed, labour) and one share of the produce went to the provider of each element; but there is no evidence for such a system in archaic Greece.

remember (T. II. 14. ii, 16), and it was believed that before Solon there had not been even limited rights to bequeath property outside the family (Pl. *Sol.* 21. iii); but rarity of opportunity and a ban on bequests do not prove that there was a formal ban on disposal *inter vivos*: Hesiod, in Boeotia *c.* 700, lived in a world in which the fortunate man might buy the κλῆρος of the unfortunate (*Op.* 340–1; cf. Hom. *Il.* XIV. 119–24, *Od.* XIV. 61–4). On inalienability in general see M. I. Finley, *Eirene* vii 1968, 25–32 = *The Use and Abuse of History*, 153–60.

Most modern scholars have thought that it was through pressure of debt that Athenian peasants became ἑκτήμοροι. The theories of W. J. Woodhouse, *Solon the Liberator*, esp. 42–97, based on the assumption that land was inalienable, have with modifications found many supporters (e.g. N. Lewis, *AJP* lxxii 1941, 144–56, J. V. A. Fine, *Hesp.* Supp. ix 1951, 167–208, esp. 179–84; also N. G. L. Hammond, *JHS* lxxxi 1961, 76–98 = *Studies*, 104–41); but the best explanation on economic lines, allowing the theoretical possibility of sale, is that worked out by A. French, CQ^2 vi 1956, 11–25, and E. Will, *IIe Conférence internationale d'histoire économique, 1962*, i. 59–73. On this view, the population of Attica expanded as life became more secure, and to feed the growing population more land was brought under cultivation (the archaeological record points to a substantial increase in population and in settlement throughout Attica, from very modest beginnings, and a decline in trade beyond the borders of Attica, towards the end of the eighth century: J. N. Coldstream, *Greek Geometric Pottery*, 360–2, *Geometric Greece*, 109, 133, cf. 78, A. M. Snodgrass, *Archaeology and the Rise of the Greek State*, 10–18); in due course this led to deforestation on the hills and declining fertility in the plains (cf. Theogn. 959–62, Plat. *Critias*, 111 A 2–D 8), so that a farm which had once been just adequate to feed a farmer and his family became inadequate; a man whose supplies ran out before the harvest would have to borrow from a richer neighbour, and might proceed around the vicious circle until he was hopelessly indebted and at his creditor's mercy; rather than enslave a man whom (with his family) he would then have to feed, the creditor chose to keep the debtor on his land as a dependent peasant, and at some stage (perhaps when the laws were written down by Draco: cf. on 4. i) the condition of these dependent peasants was standardised, to make them ἑκτήμοροι, bound to surrender a sixth of their produce. Since a man who found it hard to make ends meet on the whole of his produce would find it harder on five sixths, some ἑκτήμοροι fell into debt on their μορτή, and their masters did then seize them as chattel slaves and dispose of them, keeping their land and perhaps turning it over to the production of olives or vines, which require less labour than cereals.

The ὅροι of which Solon writes will have been markers planted in the land of the ἑκτήμοροι as a sign of their obligation. Compare the laws of Gortyn, where a debtor may either voluntarily undertake (κατακείμενος) or have imposed upon him (νενικαμένος) a form of servitude: *I. Cret.* iv 41, cols. v–vi, 72 (= Gortyn Code), i. 56–ii. 2, cf. R. F. Willetts, *Aristocratic Society in Ancient Crete*, 36, 54–6, *The Law Code of Gortyn*, 14, 57.†

However, some have denied that there was such a crisis of population and productivity (G. Ferrara, *PP* xv 1960, 29–30, C. G. Starr, *The Economic and Social Growth of Early Greece, 800–500 B.C.*, 251 n. 38). In addition, theories of this kind encounter a serious obstacle in the supposition that the peasant farmers twice fell hopelessly into debt, on the first occasion being repreived and set up again as ἑκτήμοροι. It would have been naïve of the creditors to suppose that men who had failed when they controlled all the produce of their land would succeed when they were given a fresh start but with a sixth of their produce bespoken. That a man mortgaged his farm before his person conflicts with *A.P.*'s plain statement, οἱ δανεισμοὶ πᾶσιν ἐπὶ τοῖς σώμασιν ἦσαν μέχρι Σόλωνος; the theory that the form of mortgage used was a fictitious sale, πρᾶσις ἐπὶ λύσει, advocated by Woodhouse, is unlikely to be correct for a society in which genuine sales were rare, and neither solves the problem of double default nor gives the creditor the security he needs. Ruschenbusch, *Hist.* xxi 1972, 753–5, avoids double default by supposing that enslavement for debt occurred in an earlier period and repreive of debtors to become ἑκτήμοροι in a later, but this again conflicts with *A.P.* Neither *A.P.* nor Plutarch states that the ἑκτήμοροι had arrived at that status through falling into debt. It seems better, therefore, to revert to the first kind of theory reviewed by Cassola, that the ἑκτήμοροι were not defaulting debtors given another chance but (if the terminology of mediaeval Europe may be borrowed) men in a feudal state of hereditary serfdom. At some date, perhaps long before Solon, small men unable to cope alone with the various pressures of life (among which economic pressures may certainly be included) had voluntarily or semi-voluntarily accepted this status, binding themselves to work the land for a master in exchange for his protection and support (cf. W. G. Forrest, *The Emergence of Greek Democracy*, 144–50, citing Genesis, xlvii. 13–26, where in a time of famine farmers become πεντάμοροι [but the word is not used] of the pharaoh without previously being his debtors). The institution may have been extended, or perhaps introduced, in the period of expansion in the eighth century, when we may guess that younger sons set out with some of their family's dependants to bring new land under cultivation. On this kind of servitude see M. I. Finley, *RD*[4] xliii 1965,

159–84, and compare Andrewes' theory of the origin of tribes and phratries, discussed above, p. 71.

The question, who owned the land worked by the ἑκτήμοροι, is apt to be discussed in anachronistic terms. In a community which has no written laws, and little or no writing of any kind, ownership as a legal concept can hardly exist. X farms the land bounded by the stream, the wood and the land farmed by Y, and his ancestors farmed it before him: this, together with his neighbours' knowledge of it, is his title to the land. It will have been a similar fact of common knowledge that a sixth of the produce of X's land was due to the local lord, and that if X defaulted the lord would dispose of X and his land as he saw fit. The land 'belonged' to X in the sense that as long as he paid his μορτή no one could challenge his claim to it; it 'belonged' to X's whole family in the sense that if X died while in occupation of it the land would pass to his sons; but it also 'belonged' to the lord in the sense that the μορτή was due to him and if it was not paid he could enslave X and take over the land. There must also have been some land more completely in the possession of the lord, worked by his own family and perhaps by πελάται (cf. pp. 90–1). Finally, though neither *A.P.* nor Plutarch mentions them, it is likely that there will have remained some independent farmers, neither ἑκτήμοροι themselves nor overlords of ἑκτήμοροι; their land was not δι' ὀλίγων and (unless they were driven to borrow from them) they were not ὑπόχρεοι τῶν πλουσίων: perhaps it was partly to distinguish them from the independent farmers that the lords planted their ὅροι in the lands of the ἑκτήμοροι. Some citizens will have had sources of income other than agriculture (cf. Solon, fr. 13. 43–62 West), but few if any will not have possessed some land and depended at least in part on the produce of it. It is likely enough that Cassola is right to insist that there were also temple lands and communal lands, but he leans too much on a few words of Solon: there may have been some landowners who in the late seventh century were encroaching on such lands and thereby making life harder for others, but without further evidence we should not suppose that this happened on so large a scale as to be the chief cause of distress.

By the late seventh century a situation which presumably had been tolerable was becoming intolerable. One cause may well have been overcropping, which reduced the fertility of the land and made what had once been an adequate farm inadequate; increasing population, division of family land between too many sons, and encroachment by the rich on land previously available to the poor, may be other causes. In addition it is likely that one important factor was the beginning of a move away from a purely self-subsistent economy in Attica: before the end of the seventh century

Athens was involved in war with Aegina (H. v. 82–8 with T. J. Dunbabin, *BSA* xxxvii 1936/7, 83–91; eighth century preferred by Coldstream, *Greek Geometric Pottery*, 361 with n. 10, *Geometric Greece*, 135), with Megara over the possession of Salamis (Pl. *Sol.* 8–10, 12. v: cf. *A.P.* 14. i with commentary) and, further afield, with Mytilene over the possession of Sigeum, at the entrance to the Hellespont (H. v. 94. ii–95, Str. 599–600. XIII. i. 38–9, with D. L. Page, *Sappho and Alcaeus*, 152–61), and we may assume that she had begun to export olive oil and import corn; it seems increasingly likely that coins were not struck in Athens until some time after Solon's reforms and that few if any coins had yet reached Attica from elsewhere (cf. on 8. iii and 10), but wealth was beginning to include silver and gold as well as beasts on a man's land and corn in his barn (Solon, fr. 24. 1–3 West). There were growing opportunities and growing incentives for those who were rich to become richer, and for a few men of moderate means to acquire sudden wealth (cf. Solon, frs. 4. 11, 12 sqq., 6. 3–4, 15), and the gap between rich and poor was probably widening. Almost certainly it would be wrong to assume that all ἐκτήμοροι were poor, all their overlords rich and all independent farmers moderately prosperous: more probably some ἐκτήμοροι were prospering and some independent farmers had fallen into debt in circumstances of the kind suggested by French and Will.†

Like the origin of the ἐκτήμοροι, however, the distress in Attica at the end of the seventh century should not be attributed to economic causes alone. *A.P.* began this chapter with the distinction between γνώριμοι and πλῆθος; in §ii he writes ἐδούλευον οἱ πένητες τοῖς πλουσίοις, and those words are appropriate to the economic subjection with which he is concerned in this section; but in §iii he insists χαλεπώτατον μὲν οὖν καὶ πικρότατον ἦν τοῖς πολλοῖς τῶν κατὰ τὴν πολιτείαν τὸ δουλεύειν, and although this serves to round off his treatment of Athens' economic ills (cf. Introduction, pp. 45–6) the reference to the πολιτεία and the political section which follow suggest that he is thinking generally of the subjection of the many and not only of the status of the ἐκτήμοροι and of those enslaved for debt. The nature of Solon's political reform (chs 7–8) makes it clear that there were some Athenians whose complaint was that they were as prosperous as the aristocrats but were denied political equality with them, that appointments were made ἀριστίνδην as well as πλουτίνδην (3. i, vi); even among the poor some may have been irked as much by their subservience as by their poverty (and not all the acts of the rich were lawful: cf. Solon, frs. 4. 11, 36, 36. 8–10 West). Cylon's bid for tyranny, made with Megarian support, and unsuccessful, may have been in part an attempt to exploit this situation, when the discontent was not yet sufficient to guarantee him the support he needed. Then came Draco's publication of a code of laws, which if it defined the status of the ἑκτήμοροι and the right of a creditor to enslave a defaulting debtor may have made life harder for some whose masters had previously been more lenient than Draco prescribed (cf. Forrest, *The Emergence of Greek Democracy*, 150). A generation later Solon had to be appointed as mediator.

οὗτος δὲ πρῶτος ἐγένετο τοῦ δήμου προστάτης: For the use of δῆμος to denote the mass of the unprivileged, in whatever sense is appropriate to the occasion, cf. on §i. προστάτης (on which see W. R. Connor, *The New Politicians of Fifth-Century Athens*, 110–5) is the standard word for a political leader in Herodotus, Thucydides, Xenophon's *Hellenica* and Plato, which tended to be supplanted in other fourth-century writing by δημαγωγός (cf. on 26. i): Herodotus in his Persian debate says that under a democracy cliques arise until προστάς τις τοῦ δήμου makes himself tyrant (III. 82. iv); Thucydides often writes of προστάται τοῦ δήμου (III. 75. ii, 82. i, IV. 46. iv, 66. iii, VI. 35. ii, VIII. 89. iv, cf. VI. 89. iv). In *A.P.* 28. ii–iii Solon and Pisistratus are listed as προστάται τοῦ δήμου and then follow pairs of opposing προστάται τοῦ δήμου and τῶν γνωρίμων from Cleisthenes and Isagoras to the end of the fifth century; an earlier list, in Is. XV. *Antid.* 230–6, also makes Solon the first of the προστάται τοῦ δήμου.

2. iii. οὐδενὸς γάρ, ὡς εἰπεῖν, ἐτύγχανον μετέχοντες: In rounding off his section on the economic plight of the ordinary Athenians *A.P.* at the same time looks ahead to the political section which follows (cf. p. 96): the citizens 'had a share in nothing'—neither in the wealth of their land nor in justice or political power.

3. i. ἦν δ' ἡ τάξις τῆς ἀρχαίας πολιτείας: Ch. 3, anticipated by the opening words of 2. ii, explains the aristocratic basis of the archaic state, which Solon sought to undermine. τάξις, primarily the draw-up of an army, came to be used also of other orderly dispositions: in Arist. *Pol.* we read ἔστι δὲ πολιτεία πόλεως τάξις τῶν τε ἄλλων ἀρχῶν καὶ μάλιστα τῆς κυρίας πάντων (III. 1278 B 8–10, cf. IV. 1289 A 15–18), and it is possible to refer to ἡ Κρητικὴ τάξις (II. 1271 B 40–1). Is. IV. *Paneg.* 39 claims that Athens πρώτη γὰρ καὶ νόμους ἔθετο καὶ πολιτείαν κατεστήσατο.

τῆς πρὸ Δράκοντος: Inserted when the 'Draconian constitution' was inserted in ch. 4, as at the same time a reference to Draco was inserted in 41. ii and, it has been claimed, a reference to their already existing was added to what is said of Solon's property classes in 7. iii: cf. pp. 85, 86.

ἀριστίνδην καὶ πλουτίνδην: Repeated in §vi. For this characterisation of aristocratic appointments cf. Arist. *Pol.* II. 1273 A 23–4, IV. 1293 B 10–11, also (ἀριστίνδην only) II. 1272 B 35–7, Plat. *Legg.* IX. 855 C 6–D 1; and for the kind of 'excellence' underlying ἀριστίνδην cf.

on 12. iii. That offices had been open only to men who satisfied this double requirement could safely be inferred from Solon's making wealth the sole qualification for office (8. i): no doubt the restriction was a convention not at first explicitly formulated, and unchallenged until the late seventh century; if Draco felt it necessary to include the restriction in his law code (cf. on 4. i) he may perhaps have stated it more specifically; but his law on homicide, republished in 409/8, shows us that the characterisation of appointments as ἀριστίνδην was not impossible in early Athens (M&L 86, 18–19, cf. [D.] XLIII. *Mac.* 57: this clause is surely not a later addition or modification). For *A.P.*'s claim that τὸ ... ἀρχαῖον appointments were made by the Areopagus see 8. ii with commentary.

τὸ μὲν πρῶτον διὰ [βίου], μετὰ δὲ ταῦτα [δε]καέτειαν: On the list of Athenian kings, life archons and ten-year archons see Wilamowitz, *A.u.A.*, ii. 126–44, *Hermes* xxxiii 1898, 119–29, Busolt, *G.G.*, ii². 124–35, De Sanctis, Ἀτθίς, ¹73–116, = ²77–116, A. Ledl, *Studien zur älteren athenischen Verfassungsgeschichte*, 107–272, Hignett, *H.A.C.*, 38–46, Jacoby, commentary on Hell. 323a F 23; the chronographers' lists are reconstructed by Jacoby, *Klio* ii 1902, 406–39, revised in *F.G.H.* (Castor, 250 F 4 with commentary); for the treatment of the kings in the lost beginning of *A.P.* see pp. 65–79. As noted on p. 66, the account accepted in *A.P.*, derived from Hellanicus and his successors, corresponds to that on which the chronographers were to base their lists: after the death of king Codrus his son Medon was the first of a series of ἄρχοντες elected for life from the royal house (in 1069/8 according to Eratosthenes and his successors) (for a variant see §iii with commentary, below); after thirteen of these life archons there was a series of seven archons each elected for a term of ten years (beginning with Charops in 753/2); after the fourth of these ten-year archons, Hippomenes (723/2–714/3), had disgraced himself, the archonship was thrown open to all Eupatrids; then the term of office was further reduced to one year, beginning with Creon (683/2) (see especially Vell. Pat. I. 2. ii, 8. iii, Paus. IV. 5. x; Just. II. 7. i–ii passes straight from Codrus to the annual archonship). The history of the kings and archons was rationalised and expanded from a very scanty core of traditional material (the list known in the fifth century had to be lengthened to yield a monarchy of suitable antiquity: see conveniently Busolt & Swoboda, *G.S.*, ii. 784 with n. 1), and in contrast with the list that became canonical there are traces of an alternative account, in which all the rulers down to Hippomenes were kings and he was deposed for his outrageous behaviour (cf. pp. 77–8). Nothing can be relied on beyond the basic fact that Athens passed from monarchy to an aristocratic régime with three principal magistrates (archon, basileus and polemarch), perhaps in several stages but not necessarily in the stages indicated by *A.P.* In the second half of the fifth century a list of Athenian archons was published on stone (M&L 6): probably that list contained all the annual archons from Creon; Plat. *Hipp. Mai.* 285 E 3-6 refers to the possibility of reciting a list of archons ἀπὸ Σόλωνος, but this does not suffice to prove that in the late fifth or early fourth century Athens had a complete list of archons as far back as Solon but no farther.

3. ii. μέγισται δὲ καὶ πρῶται τῶν ἀρχῶν: When *A.P.* was written there was a 'college' of nine ἄρχοντες—the archon, basileus, polemarch and six thesmothetae—made up to ten by the addition of a secretary to the thesmothetae so that one could be appointed from each of Cleisthenes' ten tribes (55. i with commentary): the archon was the eponymous magistrate, giving his name to the year, and in the seventh and sixth centuries had apparently been the senior magistrate of Athens (cf. 13. ii with commentary); it is likely enough that the separately-named archon, basileus and polemarch were of greater antiquity than the thesmothetae. In this chapter we have a good sample of fourth-century rationalism, set out in the standard language of such work (ὅθεν καὶ ... τεκμήριον ... σημεῖον ... διὸ καὶ ... σημεῖον ... : cf. Introduction, pp. 26-7). Apart from the faith placed in the story of Ion (compare the 'rational' use of Homer in T. I. 9-10) the reasoning is sensible enough; though we may doubt whether the archon was created later than the more specifically named polemarch (De Sanctis, *Ἀτθίς*, ¹124 = ²124, Hignett, *H.A.C.*, 42) we can easily understand how the basileus who was once king of Athens had his civil power transferred to an archon and his military power transferred to a polemarch (not necessarily for the reason given by *A.P.*: cf. next note) but that the Athenians did not dare to undermine his religious supremacy (cf. H. IV. 161, on Cyrene; Arist. *Pol.* III. 1285 B 13-19, Pl. *Q.R.* 279 C-D, on cities in general). *A.P.* suggests that the new offices were at first held for life and subsequently all three were reduced in tenure: we may guess that more probably the new offices were limited in tenure from the start and, perhaps not immediately, the position of basileus was made a magistracy comparable to them, but we have no evidence apart from what the Athenians later believed.†

The discussion of who was the first life archon suggests that *A.P.* has not simply transcribed what he found in a single source. The first τεκμήριον which he mentions below is derived from ἔνιοι, but much of the reasoning and adducing of σημεῖα in this chapter may be his own.

διὰ τὸ γενέσθαι ... τὰ πολέμια μαλακούς: Cf. *Epit. Heracl.* 1 with pp. 77-8, where a similar reason is alleged for the institution of the archonship. Failure in war may have provided the pretext, but resentment of royal power which was felt to be excessive is as likely a motive as scorn for a royal house which was felt to be incapable of using its power. For πολέμια cf. on 23. iii: Blass, *LZB* 1891, 303, proposed πολεμικά, but unnecessarily.

ὅθε]ν κ]αὶ τὸν Ἴωνα μετε[πέ]μψαντο: It was said that in the reign of Erechtheus (1487/6–1438/7 according to Eratosthenes) Eleusis and the Thracians under Eumolpus made war on Athens, and Ion, son of king Xuthus of the Peloponnese and Erechtheus' daughter Creusa, was made commander of the Athenians and led them to victory (H. VIII. 44. ii [where he is στρατάρχης], T. II. 15. i, Phil. 328 F 13, Str. 383. VIII. vii. 1, Paus. I. 31. iii [where he ἐπολεμάρχησε], VII. 1. ii, v, schol. Ar. *Av.* 1527 [again as πολέμαρχος]). On the legend of Ion see pp. 66–73; since he is cited here to account for the institution of the polemarchy *A.P.* presumably believed that he was the first polemarch and that the office was a regular one from that time onwards (cf. J. J. Keaney, *HSCP* lxvii 1963, 128).

Schol. Plat. *Phaedr.* 235 D describes the polemarch as ὥσπερ λοχαγὸς τοῦ βασιλέως, ὃς καὶ ἀπόντος αὐτοῦ ἐπιμελεῖται τῶν κατὰ τὴν πόλιν: that is without parallel and its source is unknown.

3. iii. [ο]ἱ μὲν γὰρ πλείους ἐπὶ Μέδοντος, ἔνιοι δ' ἐπὶ Ἀκάστου: In the chronographers' scheme Codrus' son Medon (1069/8–1050/49) was the first of the life archons and Medon's son Acastus (1049/8–1014/13) the second: here *A.P.* mentions non-committally an alternative theory which on account of the appearance of Acastus' name in the archontic oath (cf. below) made him the first life archon. The rival versions may well have been sponsored by different Atthidographers. *A.P.*'s comment on the disagreement is striking: presumably he thought he had no way of deciding which was the correct version; and of course he is right to say that whichever version is preferred our picture of Athens' constitutional development is not much affected.

οἱ ἐννέα ἄρχοντες ὀμνύουσι[ν ὥ]σπερ [ἐ]πὶ Ἀκάστου τὰ ὅρκια ποιήσειν: Dr J. D. Thomas tells me that the traces before ἐπὶ do not really suit either Kenyon's ὥσπερ or Wilcken's ΗΤΑ; Kenyon's τὰ before ὅρκια, not read by Wilcken, he finds acceptable. In §ii *A.P.* argued from Ion; here he says that those who make Acastus the first life archon argue from a clause (not otherwise attested) in the archons' oath. On the oath cf. 7. i, 55. v, with commentary: the latter passage reveals that the newly appointed archons took two oaths, at the Stoa of the Basileus and on the Acropolis, and this enabled Sandys to make some sense, though not very good sense, of the rendering 'swear that they will swear'. 'Swear' is certainly what ὅρκια/ὅρκον ποιεῖσθαι means in the passages cited by LSJ (H. I. 141. iv, 143. i, X. *Lac. Pol.* xv. 7, *SIG*[3] 591, 32); but here the verb is active, and the meaning required is 'swear that they will perform their oaths' (e.g. Kenyon's Oxford Translation, Fritz & Kapp, Moore): there seems no room for doubt about the reading of the papyrus at that point, though Kenyon[3] records some drastic suggestions for emendation.

ὡς ἐπὶ τούτου ... τῷ ἄρχοντι δωρεῶν: 'Since in his time the Codridae gave up the kingship in exchange for the privileges given to the archon' (and thereafter held the archonship instead) should be the meaning of the Greek (cf. Kenyon's Oxford Translation, Fritz & Kapp, Hignett, *H.A.C.*, 40, Moore): that is, according to ἔνιοι it was in the reign of Acastus that the life archonship was instituted and the Codridae agreed to hold that instead of the kingship. Kaibel, *Stil und Text*, 123, construed ἐπὶ with τῆς βασιλείας, surely wrongly; Kenyon[1-3], followed by Poste, Mathieu & Haussoullier and others, explained the meaning as 'withdrew from the kingship' (in respect of the powers transferred from that position, which they retained, to the archonship), but this is a very strained interpretation of the Greek. Suggested emendations, mostly put forward in support of that interpretation—τῶν ἀποδοθεισῶν, Kaibel; ἀνταποδοθεισῶν, Sandys[1]; the deletion of ἀντὶ, Thalheim, Sandys[2], Mathieu & Haussoullier—do not make the text any easier. The remark at the end of this section, that the archonship has only νεωστὶ become ἡ ἀρχὴ μεγάλη, need not be fatal to the natural interpretation of the Greek here: cf. below.

As for the basis of the argument, we may accept that ὥσπερ ἐπὶ Ἀκάστου certainly appeared in the archons' oath in the second half of the fourth century and probably had appeared since the time to which it referred; but although even Hignett accepted the phrase as guaranteeing the historicity of king Acastus (*H.A.C.*, 39, 45-6, but with doubts on p. 46) the Acastus mentioned here might be an unknown man who held the archonship in the seventh or sixth century rather than Medon's son. The name is not to my knowledge attested for a historical Athenian.

[τὸ] μηδὲν τῶν πατρίων τὸν ἄρχ[ο]ντα διοικεῖν: Cf. 57. i (ὡς δ' ἔπος εἰπεῖν καὶ τὰς πατρίους θυσίας διοικεῖ οὗτος πάσας [*sc.* ὁ βασιλεύς], disagreeing with this sentence on the polemarch), and Plat. *Polit.* 290 E 6-8; [D.] LIX. *Neaer.* 74 remarks that originally (before Theseus' 'democracy') the king performed all the sacrifices. No doubt here too the author is thinking of religious observances (contrast the use of διοικεῖν in §vi, below); and if he could not prove that all that were the concern of the basileus were ancient (57. i with commentary), he was perhaps more certain of the comparative modernity of those which were the concern of the archon. In fact most of the festivals assigned by *A.P.* to the archon were fairly recent institutions (56. iii-v with commentary), but the same must be said of those which he assigns to the polemarch (58. i with commentary): what is said in 57. i is more accurate than what is said here.

τὰ ἐπίθετα: 'Additional', more recent (cf. Is. VII. *Areop.* 29: τὰς πατρίους θυσίας ... τὰς μὲν ἐπιθέτους ἑορτάς); contrast 25. ii with commentary, where the word has a pejorative sense.

νεωστί: In 13. ii the archonship is said to have been the most powerful office in the early sixth century; presumably here the word is not to be pressed and *A.P.* means little more than that the archonship was more recent than the offices of basileus and polemarch and came to supplant the kingship as the principal office of state.

3. iv. θ[εσ]μοθέται: θεσμός was the oldest Greek word for law (cf. 4. i, 12. iv, with commentary, and M. Ostwald, *Nomos and the Beginnings of the Athenian Democracy*, 12–20), and a θεσμοθέτης ought to be a lawgiver. But whereas νομοθέτης and the verb νομοθετεῖν regularly do have that meaning, θεσμοθέτης (except in Longin. 9. ix, used of Moses) and θεσμοθετεῖν (except in Paus. IX. 36. viii, used of Draco: cf. on 4. i) seem to be used only of the office in Athens and of similar offices elsewhere. In the fourth century the thesmothetae had a general responsibility for the law courts (59. i, v, cf. 63. v, 64. i, 66. i, with commentary); their only concern with making law as opposed to applying it was a duty, probably not acquired until after 403/2 or even *c.* 350, to search annually for contradictions in the laws and to initiate the procedure of νομοθεσία to remove any contradictions which they found (A. III. *Ctes.* 38–9 with Rhodes, *A.B.*, 48–52, D. M. MacDowell, *JHS* xcv 1975, 62–74, esp. 71–2). We may assume that the thesmothetae were instituted before the reforms of Solon (as *A.P.* believed: §v), and very probably before the legislation of Draco, since otherwise we should surely have more information on their institution (*pace* Ruschenbusch, *Untersuchungen zur Geschichte des athenischen Strafrechts*, 78–9 n. 237); but if they did exist before the legislation of Draco, and if Draco did give Athens her first written laws, the thesmothetae cannot have been created to perform the etymologically acceptable duty given to them here, ὅπως ἀναγράψαντες τὰ θέσμια φυλάττωσι πρὸς τὴν τῶν ἀμφισβητούντων κρίσιν. It is in any case not very likely that such a duty would be given to six annual magistrates (cf. M. Cary, *C.A.H.*, iii[1]. 593: it is often claimed, e.g. by Gomme, *CR* xl 1926, 161, Ostwald, *op. cit.*, 174–5, that θέσμια here means 'judgments' in individual cases, and R. S. Stroud, *Athens Comes of Age*, 22, suggests that the information is derived from a law of Draco or Solon requiring the thesmothetae to perform this duty 'as before', but I am not certain that the word can bear that meaning). Probably this is a guess on the part of *A.P.* or his source, which has not been reconciled with the tradition about Draco (cf. Mathieu, *Aristote, Constitution d'Athènes*, 7); we have no material on which to base a better guess.†

ἤδη κατ' ἐνιαυτὸν αἱρουμέ[νων] τὰς ἀρχάς: The list inscribed on stone in the second half of the fifth century was a list of eponymous archons only (cf. pp. 98-9), and we have no evidence for similar lists of early βασιλεῖς, polemarchs and thesmothetae; but if the published list of archons was based on written records similar records of the other magistrates ought to have survived too. We do not know whether *A.P.* is repeating what was regarded as certain knowledge or is adopting a hypothesis which some would have rejected.

τῶν ἀμφι[σ]βητ[ού]ντων: As a technical term in Athenian law ἀμφισβητεῖν means 'lay claim to', of property (LSJ *s.v.*, I. 3. b). This word and its cognates are favourites of Aristotle and of *A.P.* to refer more generally to 'disputes' (cf. 5. ii, 9. ii, 28. v, 35. ii).

3. v. ἦσαν δ' οὐχ ἅμα πάντες: Misreported as οὐκ ἐξῆν αὐτοῖς ἅμα δικάζειν by *L.S.* 449. 17 and Suid. (*A* 4119) ἄρχων, which derive from this passage.

τὸ νῦν καλούμενον Βουκολεῖον: Comparison with the 'Ἐπιλύκειον, below, suggests that *A.P.* believed that it was originally called the βασιλεῖον (Poll. VIII. 111 gives the name βασιλεῖον to the headquarters of the φυλοβασιλεῖς, situated παρὰ τὸ Βουκολεῖον); the βουκολία of Ath. VI. 235 C is presumably to be identified with the Βουκολεῖον, and the Βουζύγιον, the field of sacred ox-ploughing (Pl. *Coni. Praec.* 144 A-B) was possibly nearby. The name Βουκολεῖον probably derives from the worship of Dionysus (e.g. Ar. *Vesp.* 9-10, Eur. *Bacch.* 100, 618, 920-2, 1017, 1159; cf. below). In the classical period the basileus used the Stoa of the Basileus at any rate for some of his business (Plat. *Euthyph.* 1 A 1-4), a building at the northwest corner of the Agora, now dated to the second quarter of the fifth century; partitioning of the stoa before the end of the century may have provided an office for the basileus in the left-hand third of it (for the stoa and its date see on 7. i). The location of the buildings mentioned in this section (except the 'Ἐπιλύκειον) depends on that of the prytaneum, discussed in the next note.

πλησίον τοῦ πρυτανείου: The prytaneum known to Pausanias (I. 18. iii) was situated to the north of the Acropolis, near the securely-identified cave of Aglaurus, and it is most likely that the prytaneum was always located there. However, there have been various attempts to place the original prytaneum elsewhere. Harp. Πάνδημος Ἀφροδίτη = Apoll. 244 F 113 refers to an ἀρχαία ἀγορά: E. Curtius, *Attische Studien*, ii. 54-7 cf. 44-9, placed that and the 'prytaneum of Theseus' south of the Acropolis; Judeich, *Topographie von Athen*[2], placed the Old Agora to the west of the Acropolis (62, 285-305), with the original prytaneum in the gap between the Acropolis and the Areopagus (296-9 cf. 304-5); H. A. Thompson, *JHS* lxxxvi 1966, 273, tries to locate the Old Agora from Pausanias' location of the prytaneum; the problem of the Old Agora is cautiously discussed by R. E. Wycherley, *Phoen.* xx 1966, 285-93. L. B. Holland believed that until 480 the prytaneum occupied the site of the Mycenaean palace on the Acropolis, on which was built in the second half of the sixth century what is usually regarded as the Old Temple of Athena (*AJA*² xliii 1939, 289-98, cf. Curtius, *op. cit.*, 55 ['pre-Thesean prytaneum']: he claimed the support of Poll. IX. 40, but contrast VIII. 128). For recent attempts to place the prytaneum and its neighbours see R. J. Hopper, *The Acropolis*, 81 fig. 6; J. Travlos, *Pictorial Dictionary of Ancient Athens*, 8 fig. 5 (placing the buildings north of the Acropolis but the Βουζύγιον between the Acropolis and the Areopagus); S. G. Miller, *Hesp.* xxxix 1970, 227-31 (placing the Βουκολεῖον north and the Βουζύγιον south-west of the Acropolis), and *The Prytaneion*, 38-54 (placing the prytaneum north of the Acropolis and to the east, perhaps some way to the east, of the Eleusinium).[6] See also on the prytaneum and other buildings M. de G. Verrall & J. E. Harrison, *Mythology and Monuments of Ancient Athens*, 166-8, J. G. Frazer, *Pausanias's Description of Greece*, ii. 170-3, I. C. T. Hill, *The Ancient City of Athens*, 103, H. A. Thompson & R. E. Wycherley, *The Athenian Agora*, xiv. 46-7.†

ἡ σύμμειξις ἐνταῦθα γίγνεται τῷ Διονύσῳ καὶ ὁ γάμος: It is now agreed that the ἱερὸς γάμος of the βασίλιννα and Dionysus took place not at the Dionysia, as some thought (still claimed by Moore, 212), but on 12 Anthesterion (viii), at the Χόες, the central day of the Anthesteria. The principal text is [D.] LIX. *Neaer.* 73-8. Representations of the 'marriage' have been identified in vase paintings: British Museum, 1906. 1-13. 1 = L. Deubner, *Attische Feste*, Taf. 10; Museo Nazionale, Tarquinia, RC 4197 = Beazley, *A.R.V.*², ii. 1057 no. 96 = *C.V.A.*, *Mus. Naz. Tarquiniense*, ii (*Italia*, xxvi), tav. 16 (1195); Staatliche Museen, Berlin, 2589 = Beazley *op. cit.*, ii. 1301 no. 7 = Deubner, *op. cit.*, Taf. 18. 2 = H. W. Parke, *Festivals of the Athenians*, pl. 46; also Metropolitan Museum, New York, 24. 97. 34 = Deubner, *op. cit.*, Taf. 11. 3-4 = Parke, *op. cit.*, pl. 44 (children imitating the ceremony). See Deubner, *op. cit.*, 99-111, 120, E. Simon, *AK* vi 1963, 6-22, esp. 11-12, A. W. Pickard-Cambridge rev. J. P. A. Gould & D. M. Lewis, *The Dramatic Festivals of Athens*, 11-13, Parke, *op. cit.*, 112-3, 118-9.‡

Some have been embarrassed by the fact that if σύμμειξις denotes intercourse it should logically follow γάμος rather than precede it;

---

[6] I mention because it has been used by S. Rossiter, *Blue Guide: Greece*, the proposal by K. S. Pittakys, *L'Ancienne Athènes*, 132-9, to identify as the prytaneum the site which is now usually regarded as the Diogeneum (e.g. Travlos, *Pictorial Dictionary*, 281 with 282 fig. 362): in Rossiter's 3rd ed. this site is marked as the

but Wilhelm argued convincingly that the word for intercourse should be μεῖξις, and here σύμμειξις is the ceremonial meeting of the partners before their marriage (*Anz. Wien* lxxiv 1937, 39–57 = *Akademieschriften*, ii. 582–600: not noticed in LSJ or 1968 Supplement).

τὸ πρυτανεῖον: The importance of the prytaneum as the religious heart of the city was stressed by N. D. Fustel de Coulanges, *La Cité antique*, liv. III, ch. vi (166 with n. 1, ed. of 1916); cf. Miller, *The Prytaneion*, 13–16. In the classical period the prytaneum remained the ceremonial headquarters of the state: it contained the ἑστία, *par excellence*, of Athens, from which fire was taken to colonies at their foundation (Poll. I. 7, IX. 40, schol. Aristid. XIII. *Panath.* 103 [iii. 48. 8–10 Dindorf], *E.M.* [694. 28] πρυτανεῖα, cf. H. I. 146. ii, [Pl.] *X. Or.* 847 D, Paus. I. 18. iii); it was the place where the city entertained the citizens and foreigners whom it wished to honour (cf. p. 308); and was adorned with various statues ([Pl.] *X. Or.* 847 D–E, Paus. I. 18. iii, IX. 32. viii, Ael. *V.H.* IX. 39). Thucydides was presumably thinking of a supposed ancestor of this building when he wrote that Theseus ἓν βουλευτήριον ἀποδείξας καὶ πρυτανεῖον ξυνῴκισε πάντας (II. 15. ii). The prytaneum should not be confused, as it frequently was by lexicographers and scholiasts, with the Tholos, which as the meeting- and dining-place of the prytanes (43. ii with commentary) was the working headquarters of the state: cf. D. Levi, *ASAA* vi–vii 1923–4, 1–25, E. Vanderpool, *Hesp.* iv 1935, 470–5, S. Dow, *Hesp.* Supp. i 1937, 22–4, Rhodes, *A.B.*, 16 n. 5. Texts relating to the prytaneum are conveniently assembled by R. E. Wycherley, *The Athenian Agora*, iii, pp. 166–74.

For the location of the prytaneum see pp. 103–4. The statues of the ἐπώνυμοι of Cleisthenes' ten tribes stood in the Agora, from the mid fourth century near the Tholos (cf. on 21. iv), and it is surely a resultant error that leads *L.S.* 449. 17 and Suid. (*A* 4119) ἄρχων to place the archon's headquarters παρὰ τοὺς ἐπωνύμους (though Travlos, *Pictorial Dictionary*, 210, uses the texts as evidence for an earlier set of ἐπώνυμοι near the prytaneum).

τὸ Ἐπιλύκειον: Cf. Hes. (*E* 4947) Ἐπιλύκειον; it is corrupted to ἐν Λυκείῳ in *L.S.* 449. 17 and Suid. (*A* 4119) ἄρχων. A connection with the Lyceum, a gymnasium used as a military training-ground (north-east of the Acropolis, extending from Σύνταγμα to the National Garden: Travlos, *op. cit.*, 345), would be appropriate to the polemarch and has commonly been preferred to *A.P.*'s story of the polemarch Epilycus (e.g. Kenyon, Sandys, Busolt, *G.G.*, ii². 166–7 n. 8).

---

prytaneum in the plan on p. 106 but the text of p. 136 gives the current orthodoxy. There is no good evidence to support Pittakys' identification, and his site seems too far north.†

3. v] COMMENTARY ON THE *ATH. POL.*

τὸ θεσμοθετεῖον: θεσμοθέσιον, schol. Plat. *Prot.* 337 D, *L.S.* 449. 17, Suid. (*A* 4119) ἄρχων; θεμίστιον, schol. Plat. *Phaedr.* 235 D; θεσμοφορεῖον, Hes. πρυτανεῖον: *A.P.* doubtless gives the correct form. It has been suggested that the South Stoa in the Agora, built in the late fifth century, may have served as the thesmotheteum (H. A. Thompson & R. E. Wycherley, *The Athenian Agora*, xiv. 77–8; *Agora Guide*[3], 158–60, is less specific). The thesmotheteum is mentioned once, and the nine archons several times, in *IG* ii[2] 46 (cf. p. 667).

ἐπὶ δὲ Σόλωνος: Cf. D.L. I. 78. It is not known on what evidence this statement is based; but although Solon altered the method of appointment of the archons he did not alter their duties, so we have no particular reason to suspect this as a false inference. The Stoa of the Basileus is later than Solon (cf. pp. 103, 134).

τὰς δίκας αὐτοτελεῖς [κρίν]ειν: With the meaning 'complete in itself', 'self-sufficient', αὐτοτελής is a favourite word of Aristotle; later writers use it as a synonym of αὐτοκράτωρ or κύριος (D.C. LII. 22. i, cf. Polyb. III. 9. v, Pl. *Amat.* 754 D). Here it is used in conjunction with κύριος to emphasise the difference between the archons' full judicial powers in the past and their restricted powers in the time of *A.P.*; in 53. ii it is used (with infinitive) instead of κύριος: cf. Kaibel, *Stil und Text*, 39–40. The normal view of the history of Athenian jurisdiction is that originally all decisions lay with one of the archons or with the ex-archons assembled in the council of the Areopagus; Solon gave litigants dissatisfied with the archon's verdict the right of ἔφεσις to the ἡλιαία (9. i with commentary); in the first half of the fifth century, by abrupt reform or (more probably) by a gradual development, the archons' jurisdiction in most of the cases which came their way was changed to a preliminary enquiry (προανακρίνειν), followed by automatic reference of all cases which were technically in order to a δικαστήριον in which the archon who had conducted the enquiry presided (cf. on 25. ii); for procedure in the fourth century see 63–9 with commentary. Uncertainties about the later stages in this history are discussed below in their place; there need be no doubt that before Solon the archons were αὐτοτελεῖς in whatever jurisdiction they possessed, but we have no information on how jurisdiction was divided between individual archons and the Areopagus.†

3. vi. ἡ δὲ τῶν Ἀρεοπαγιτῶν βουλή: It is likely that in the days of the monarchy the king had a more or less informal council of senior aristocratic advisers (for Homeric society see, e.g. G. Glotz, *La Cité grecque*, 54–8, trans. *The Greek City*, 46–50, G. M. Calhoun and T. B. L. Webster in A. J. B. Wace & F. H. Stubbings, *A Companion to Homer*, 436–7 and 457–8, M. I. Finley, *The World of Odysseus*[2],

79–83), and that, by whatever stages the monarchy gave way to an aristocracy, the council which had advised the kings remained in existence to advise the magistrates, and its power was increased as that of the kings was reduced. At some date it was laid down that the nine archons should automatically (except in cases of misconduct) join the ranks of the Areopagus at the end of their year of office (Pl. *Sol.* 19. i, Poll. VIII. 118, cf. *A.P.* 60. iii, law *ap.* D. XXIV. *Tim.* 22: see D. M. MacDowell, *Athenian Homicide Law*, 40–1): even after the institution of nine annual archons there may have been a period when this was normal practice rather than a legal requirement; but in early Athens archons and Areopagites will inevitably have come from the same restricted class even if there was no formal connection between the two positions. Pl. *Sol.* 19. iii–iv reports the view of οἱ πλεῖστοι that the Areopagus was created by Solon, and to prove that it was older than that cites Solon's amnesty law: cf. on 8. iv.†

It is scarcely credible that this sentence should be *A.P.*'s first mention of the Areopagus, a body much discussed by the many fourth-century writers who represented the past as better than the present. Very probably the lost beginning of *A.P.* stated when and with what functions the Areopagus was created, and gave a fuller introduction to it in connection with its creation; the occasion chosen was perhaps Theseus' separation of the Eupatrids from the other citizens (cf. pp. 75, 79), and the functions assigned to the Areopagus must have included jurisdiction, especially in cases of homicide (cf. 25. ii with commentary).

τὴν μὲν τάξιν εἶχε τοῦ διατηρεῖν τοὺς νόμους: Other uses of τάξις are based on its military use (cf. on §i): τάξιν ἔχειν is thus to have a position or assignment. On guarding the laws cf. 4. iv, 8. iv and especially 25. ii with commentary, where I suggest that at or before the time of Draco's legislation the Areopagus was given the title φύλαξ τῶν νόμων *vel simile quid* as a description of the powers which it then possessed, and subsequently used this title as a pretext for assuming new powers in changed circumstances. As long as the archonship remained the principal office of state the Areopagus contained the accumulated political wisdom of Athens: in the seventh century it will have 'watched over the laws and administered most and the greatest of the city's affairs' very much as the Senate of the Roman Republic was to do, by giving the magistrates advice on which they were likely to act unquestioningly, and by acting as a court of law. For other references to the Areopagus as guardian of the state or the laws see Aesch. *Eum.* 704–6 (quoted p. 315), Is. VII. *Areop.* 37, 46; there is something of the same idea in the recommendation of Arist. *Pol.* V. 1308 B 20–2.

διῴκει δὲ τὰ πλεῖστα καὶ τὰ μέγιστα τῶν ἐν τῇ πόλει: Cf. 8. iv (καὶ τά τε ἄλλα τὰ πλεῖστα καὶ τὰ μέγιστα τῶν πολιτ⟨ικ⟩ῶν διετήρει), and the reference to τῶν διῳκημένων in 25. ii. διοικεῖν came to be used of administration in general and financial administration in particular (cf. διοίκησις in 24. iii *fin.*, 43. i, with commentary), but in §iii and 57. i the word is used of religious administration, and here the participles suggest that the author is thinking primarily of judicial activity.

καὶ κολάζουσα καὶ ζημιοῦσα πάντας τοὺς ἀκοσμοῦντας κυρίως: Cf. again 8. iv (καὶ τοὺς ἁμαρτάνοντας ηὔθυνεν κυρία οὖσα καὶ ζημιοῦν καὶ κολάζειν). The verb κολάζειν is used of legal punishments by dramatists, orators and Plato rather than by historians. For τοὺς ἀκοσμοῦντας cf. Is. vii. *Areop.* 37, 39, 42, 46 (and *IG* i² 84, 27, *Hesp.* xlix 1980, 258–88, 32, 36, both concerned with festivals); and since κολάζειν also occurs frequently in that speech, twice with ἀκοσμοῦντας as object (§§42, 46, cf. 22, 26) it is likely that this description of the Areopagus is derived ultimately from Isocrates (but Isocrates was too widely influential for us to conclude that it reached *A.P.* through Androtion: cf. Introduction, pp. 20, 39–40); διοικεῖν again is a favourite word of Isocrates, though by no means peculiar to him (e.g. vii. *Areop.* 20, 31, 56, 67); but the language in which this view of the Areopagus is restated in 8. iv is less markedly Isocratean. Though Isocrates' romantic accounts of the past are a poor basis for historical reconstruction, it need not be doubted that what is said here of the Areopagus is essentially correct.

For powers of punishment cf. on the archons, §v with commentary: the Areopagus was deprived of most of its judicial powers in 462/1 on the grounds that they were ἐπίθετα (25. ii with commentary), but what remained to it remained inappellable. For the Atthidographers' view of the Areopagus as a court in early Athens see Phil. 328 F 3, Andr. 324 FF 3, 4 = Phil. 328 FF 4, 20, Phanod. 325 F 10 = Phil. 328 F 196.

ἡ γὰρ αἵρεσις τῶν ἀρχόντων ἀριστίνδην καὶ πλουτίνδην ἦν: Repeated from §i to round off what *A.P.* says about the ἀρχαί: cf. Introduction, p. 45. διὸ καὶ μόνη τῶν ἀρχῶν αὕτη μεμένηκε διὰ βίου καὶ νῦν: Despite διό, *A.P.* has not explained why membership of the Areopagus should be for life: presumably we must supply the normal Greek assumption that councils of ex-magistrates do serve for life. Here ἀρχή includes the Areopagus, as in 43–62 and specifically in 62. iii it includes the boule of five hundred: ch. 8 is ambiguous; but the last sentence of §v implied a distinction between Areopagus and ἀρχαί, cf. 4. ii with iii. Arist. *Pol.* iii. 1275 A 23–32 wonders whether the term ἀρχή can be extended to members of assemblies and juries, and for want of a better term regards these as holding a (temporally) ἀόριστος ἀρχή.

4. i. ἡ μὲν οὖν πρώτη πολιτεία: This sentence rounds off what has gone before, but with a new element: what in 3. i was described as

COMMENTARY ON THE *ATH. POL.* [4. i

the ἀρχαία πολιτεία is here labelled πρώτη. In 41. ii as it now stands the original government of Athens was altered first by Ion; secondly, and so as to involve a πολιτείας τάξις, by Theseus; next by Draco. πρώτη is surprising applied to the constitution in force after the abolition of the monarchy and the creation of the nine archons; but the original version of 41. ii had nothing between Theseus and Solon (cf. *ad loc.*), and the word is perhaps to be explained as indicating that this is the first point at which *A.P.* has given an outline of the πολιτεία as opposed to a history of events which impinged on the πολιτεία.

μετὰ δὲ ταῦτα: The reference could be either to Cylon's *coup* and its immediate consequences (cf. μετὰ δὲ ταῦτα in 2. i) or to the state supposed to have been reached at the conclusion of the political development sketched in ch. 3; χρόνου τινὸς οὐ πολλοῦ διελθόντος suggests that *A.P.* is thinking of a definite event and so favours the first interpretation, though with 2-3 intervening the reference is far from obvious. Some have proposed to move this sentence to the end of 1 or the end of 2, but more probably *A.P.* has used these words carelessly to introduce 'what happened next', and the sentence is in its correct place: cf. pp. 86-7.

ἐπ' Ἀρισταίχμου ἄρχοντος: *A.P.* links Draco's legislation with an archon not otherwise attested. The chronographers dated it somewhere in Ol. xxxix = 624/3-621/0 (evidence conveniently summarised by A. E. Samuel, *Greek and Roman Chronology*, 200, cf. T. J. Cadoux, *JHS* lxviii 1948, 92); a possible reading in D.S. ix. 17 places it 27 years before Solon, and this if we count from his archonship in 594/3 (cf. on 5. ii) yields by the exclusive reckoning appropriate to cardinal numerals Ol. xxxix. 4 = 621/0; 27 years may also underlie what we find in schol. A. 1. *Tim.* 6 and Tzetzes, *Chil.* v. 350-1; and so 621/0 should be accepted as the canonical date established by later Greeks. See H. F. Clinton, *Fasti Hellenici*, i. 211-3, R. S. Stroud, *U. Calif. Pub. Cl. Stud.* iii 1968, 66-70 (this evidence is not mentioned by Samuel).

Δρά[κ]ων τοὺς θεσμοὺς ἔθηκεν: Our earliest surviving reference to Draco is Cratinus, fr. 274 Kock *ap.* Pl. *Sol.* 25. ii:

πρὸς τοὺς Σόλωνος καὶ Δράκοντος οἶσι νῦν
φρύγουσιν ἤδη τὰς κάχρυς τοῖς κύρβεσιν.

A decree of 409/8 ordered τὸ[ν] Δράκοντος νόμον τὸμ περὶ τô φό[ν]ο ἀναγρα[φ]σά[ν]τον οἱ ἀναγραφές τὸν νόμον (M&L 86, 4-6); in 403 a decree inaugurating the restored democracy stipulated νόμοις δὲ χρῆσθαι τοῖς Σόλωνος καὶ μέτροις καὶ σταθμοῖς, χρῆσθαι δὲ καὶ τοῖς Δράκοντος θεσμοῖς οἷσπερ ἐχρώμεθα ἐν τῷ πρόσθεν χρόνῳ, and then went on to make arrangements for supplementing those laws (decree *ap.* And. 1. *Myst.* 83, cf. 81-2: see pp. 441-2). The orators of the fourth

109

century tended to attribute the current law on homicide to Draco, as they tended to attribute the current code of law as a whole to Solon (J. C. S. Schreiner, *De Corpore Iuris Atheniensium*, 29–53 [Solon], 74–91 [Draco]), and it is arguable that this is what is meant by the references to Draco of the decree quoted by Andocides (especially in view of the qualification which is added) and of Andocides himself, and probably also of X. *Oec.* xiv. 4. But it was not believed that Draco's law on homicide had been his only law: *A.P.* 7. i states that under Solon τοῖς δὲ Δράκοντος θεσμοῖς ἐπαύσαντο χρώμενοι πλὴν τῶν φονικῶν (see *ad loc.*, and cf. Pl. *Sol.* 17), and there was a tradition that the penalties in Draco's laws had been uniformly severe (Herodicus [or Prodicus] *ap.* Arist. *Rhet.* II. 1400 B 19–23, Arist. *Pol.* II. 1274 B 15–18, Demades *ap.* Pl. *Sol.* 17. iii); Lysias ascribed to Draco the νόμος ἀργίας otherwise attributed to Solon or Pisistratus (frs. 35, 94, Sauppe, cf. Pl. *Sol.* 17. ii; contrast H. II. 177. ii, Thph. fr. 99 Wimmer *ap.* Pl. *Sol.* 31. v). The passage cited from Arist. *Pol.* begins Δράκοντος δὲ νόμοι μὲν εἰσί, πολιτείᾳ δ' ὑπαρχούσῃ τοὺς νόμους ἔθηκεν, and this has been combined with *A.P.* 41. ii, ἡ (*sc.* μετάστασις) ἐπὶ Δράκοντος, ἐν ᾗ καὶ νόμους ἀνέγραψαν πρῶτον, to yield the orthodox modern view that Draco gave Athens her first written laws by codifying existing practice, perhaps with slight improvements (e.g. Adcock, *C.A.H.*, iv[1]. 28: for the clash between this and what is said of the thesmothetae in 3. iv see *ad loc.*).

Various doubts have been expressed. Most extreme, as often, was Beloch, who doubted whether Draco as a human being had ever existed (*G.G.*[2], I. ii. 358–62); but Adcock defended the tradition (*CHJ* ii 1926–8, 95–109), and Sealey, himself inclined to scepticism, pointed out that the elimination of Draco would solve nothing, since it seems reliably enough attested that someone gave Athens written laws, at least on homicide, before the reforms of Solon (*Hist.* ix 1960, 156–8 = *Essays*, 10–12). Many who accept Draco's existence and his responsibility for the law of homicide believe that that was his only law and there were no others for Solon to repeal (e.g. I. M. Linforth, *Solon the Athenian*, 68–9, 275–6, Hignett, *H.A.C.*, 307–8, Sealey, *loc. cit.*, *History of the Greek City States*, 99–105). But it is not surprising that little should be remembered of a code of law superseded after a generation, and there is no good reason why the Athenians should have invented such a code if it had never existed: in conditions of στάσις after an unsuccessful bid for tyranny it is entirely credible that there should have been demands for the publication of the law, and not only in the field of homicide.

Beyond this it is hard to tell how far one can safely go. Stroud, *op. cit.*, 75–82, assembles the evidence for measures with which Draco has been credited and energetically seeks to throw the burden of proof on the doubters, but he tends to place too much trust in the accuracy of the Athenians' 'memory' of laws annulled at the beginning of the sixth century. Ruschenbusch, *Hist.* ix 1960, 147–52, suggests that Draco did not cover the whole field of law but did provide a criminal law for offences against individuals, by which the injured party had to obtain judicial sanction for the exercise of his previously unrestricted right of self-help against the offender (compare his view, argued in *Untersuchungen zur Geschichte des athenischen Strafrechts*, 11–15, that ἀτιμία was the one penalty specified in Solon's code and death or fines were forms of satisfaction which an injured party might demand rather than penalties prescribed by law—in which case Solon will not have lightened penalties but will have carried written law into fields not touched by Draco). For ἀτιμία see 8. v with commentary. With one exception (Poll. ix. 61—from what source, we do not know) no penalty is said to have been laid down by a law of Draco except death (which might be ἀτιμία misremembered) or ἀτιμία, and Solon enacted an amnesty law to restore rights to ἄτιμοι, so it is plausible that Draco's laws should have regulated the conditions in which self-help was allowed; if we accept that Draco is likely to have enacted laws in fields other than homicide, which Solon repealed, we must conclude that Solon set some limits to the satisfaction which could be demanded from various categories of offender. We may guess that there were laws of Draco concerned with ἑκτήμοροι (perhaps standardising their status for the first time) and with debt: pre-Solonian debtors were ἄτιμοι *vis-à-vis* their creditors, and in fr. 36. 8–12 West *ap.* 12. iv Solon admits that some men had been lawfully enslaved. There is no good evidence, however, for constitutional laws of Draco, and he may well have left the constitution to the force of custom.

For the law of homicide we have the inscription of 409/8, cleaned and republished by Stroud (*op. cit.*, cf. M&L 86). The text begins with the law on unintentional homicide; Stroud establishes that the text inscribed on this stele was more extensive than had been imagined, and that there is a heading, [δεύτ]ερος [ἄχσον], in line 56 corresponding to the πρῶτος ἄχσον in line 10; he argues forcefully that the ἀναγραφεῖς, ordered to publish Draco's law, ought to have published Draco's law and not whatever law on homicide was currently valid (60-4), and that the embarrassment of the καὶ ἐὰμ with which the law begins (line 11) should be avoided by translating it not as 'and if' but as 'even if' (34–40). On the first point a large part of his conclusion may be accepted though his argument is insufficient: I am not convinced that by 'Draco's law' the Athenians must have meant 'the original law of Draco, without any additions or modifications'; but all that we know of their legislative practice suggests that any alterations, particularly in so sensitive a field as homicide, would have been made not by tampering with the original text but by means of supplementary decrees: particular clauses might thus have been rendered obsolete, and *pace* Stroud might have been omitted in republication; but such clauses would be few—to a considerable extent the law on homicide will still have been Draco's law—and the ἀναγραφεῖς will have begun by copying either the whole of Draco's law or all except the clauses which were no longer in force. καὶ ἐάμ is an extremely harsh beginning to the law, however it is translated, and here at least it is best to postulate some loss or omission (cf. M&L, p. 266). Ruschenbusch, *Hist.* ix 1960, 129–54, attempts to reconstruct 'the original' Draconian law of homicide, but in contrast to Stroud's fundamentalism he is rather too willing to envisage major changes between the end of the seventh century and the end of the fifth (see also his review of Stroud in *Gnomon* xlvi 1974, 815–7).†

We do not know who Draco was, nor how he came to be appointed as lawgiver nor what his position was *vis-à-vis* the other ἀρχαί. It is clear from *A.P.* that he was not archon. Paus. ix. 36. viii, Δράκοντος Ἀθηναίοις θεσμοθετήσαντος, should be regarded as an unusual but perfectly intelligible use of the verb rather than as implying that Draco was one of the thesmothetae or a substitute for all of them, or that Pausanias thought that he was (cf. on 3. iv): the verb is used here by analogy with νομοθετεῖν of a man whose enactments were known as θεσμοί (cf. 7. i [but νόμους in the corresponding passage in Pl. *Sol.* 17. i, and in *A.P.* 41. ii], M&L 86, 20 [restored; but νόμον in the decree of 409/8, line 5], And. 1. *Myst.* 81, decree *ap.* 83). For the significance of θεσμός and νόμος see on 12. iv; the active of τιθέναι is regularly used of individual lawgivers (cf. e.g. 6. i), but the middle is used of the δῆμος or bodies representative of the δῆμος (31. ii, 45. i).

It is as surprising that *A.P.* says no more about Draco's θεσμοί as that it follows this sentence with the notoriously implausible 'Draconian constitution', and I suspect that before or when the 'constitution' was inserted in our text of *A.P.* further information on the θεσμοί was omitted: cf. pp. 86–7.

4. ii. ἀπεδέδοτο μὲν ἡ πολιτεία: The pluperfect is correct in relation to the other verbs, which describe in the imperfect how the state functioned when this 'constitution' was in force (H. Richards, *CR* v 1891, 467, cf. Sandys²). In the middle of the chapter the description switches to the accusative-and-infinitive construction, returning to imperfect indicatives before the end: probably the source from which the 'Draconian constitution' is derived used accusatives and infinitives throughout, and the man responsible for the insertion made a half-hearted job of recasting the 'constitution' in narrative form.

πολιτεία in *A.P.* most commonly refers to the government of the state, but here and in a few other passages that shades into 'franchise' or 'citizenship': cf. the indexes in Sandys² and, less helpfully, Kenyon's Berlin ed.; for a more unusual use of the word see §iii with commentary.

τοῖς ὅπλα παρεχομένοις: This is stated explicitly as the qualification for citizenship in the intermediate régime of 411/0 (33. i, T. VIII. 97. i), and must be what was meant by the propaganda phrase of early 411, τοῖς δυνατωτάτοις καὶ τοῖς σώμασιν καὶ τοῖς χρήμασιν λητουργεῖν (29. v, T. VIII. 65. iii). For the pre-Solonian state this is at once too inclusive and too exclusive: office-holding was a monopoly of the rich and aristocratic (3. i), while the assembly, on the few occasions when it met, was probably open to all free Athenians, though only the rich and aristocratic would speak in it (cf. on 7. iii).

τοὺς ταμίας: The treasurers of Athena: cf. 7. iii, 8. i, 47. i, with commentary.

οὐσίαν κεκτημένους οὐκ ἐλάττω δέκα μνῶν ἐλευθέραν: This invites suspicion first on account of the means of assessing a man's wealth —Solon a generation after Draco used the produce of a man's land as his criterion (7. iii–iv with commentary), and even then Athens had no coinage (cf. on 8. iii and 10)—and secondly because it sets a higher qualification for generals and hipparchs than for archons and treasurers, and this, at any rate in the relative standing of archons and generals, reflects the political realities of the late fifth century rather than the late seventh century (cf. 3. iii, 13. ii, 22. ii, v, 26. ii, with commentary). It is pointless to estimate what a man's land might produce and how much its produce might be worth, and to compare the categories implied by this section with Solon's property classes. In terms of the time when the 'Draconian constitution' is likely to have been invented the figures are surprisingly low: the qualifications specified are 10 minas (= ⅙ talent) and 100 minas (= 1⅔ talents), whereas the general qualification for liturgic service in the fourth century was about 4 talents (Davies, *A.P.F.*, xxiii–xxiv) and under the law in force from 357 to 340 those liable to the trierarchy (a fixed number, 1,200, not those with a fixed property qualification, but the actual coverage was probably similar) were about 4% of the citizen body (Rhodes, *A.B.*, 5–6 with 3 n. 6). From the time of Solon the qualification for hoplite service was probably that for membership of the class of zeugitae (cf. on 7. iii); at any rate, the figures available make it clear that the hoplite class was considerably wider than the liturgic, amounting in the fifth and fourth centuries to about half of the citizen body (Gomme, *Population of Athens*, 1–35 with 26 table 1).

τὰς δ' ἄλλας ἀρχὰς ⟨τὰς⟩ ἐλάττους: τὰς (H. Richards, *CR* v 1891, 176) is necessary; τὰς μὲν (Gomme, *CR* xxxix 1924, 152) is not.

COMMENTARY ON THE *ATH. POL.*

στρατηγούς: For στρατηγοί before Cleisthenes see on 22. ii: it is not likely that there was a regular office of στρατηγός in the time of Draco.

ἱππάρχους: For hipparchs see 61. iv with commentary, and for the cavalry in early Athens see p. 143.

παῖδας ἐκ γαμετῆς γυναικὸς γνησίους ὑπὲρ δέκα ἔτη γεγονότας: The only other texts mentioning a requirement of this kind are the inscribed Decree of Themistocles, M&L 23, 18–22 (τριη[ρ]ά[ρχους . . .] . . . ἐκ τῶν κ[εκ]τημέν[ω]ν γ[ῆν] τ[ε κ]αὶ [οἰκί]αν Ἀθ[ή]νησι καὶ οἷς ἂμ παῖδ[ες] ὦσι γνή[σιοι]), and Din. i. *Dem.* 71, of 323 (τοὺς νόμους προλέγειν τῷ ῥήτορι καὶ τῷ στρατηγῷ . . . παιδοποιεῖσθαι κατὰ τοὺς νόμους, γῆν ἐντὸς ὅρων κεκτῆσθαι); but compare Pericles' funeral oration, T. II. 44. iii. ῥήτωρ in the sense required in Dinarchus' law ('speaker' in the assembly, i.e. politician) first appears in Athens in the 440's (M&L 49, 21) and is common in the late fifth and fourth centuries (W. R. Connor, *The New Politicians of Fifth-Century Athens*, 116–19, S. Perlman, *Ath.*² xli 1963, 328–30): we may allow some delay, and suspect that a clause laying down qualifications for ῥήτορες would not ante-date the codification of the law at the end of the fifth century; but requirements of this kind may well be survivals from the archaic state (e.g. Busolt & Swoboda, *G.S.*, ii. 836 with n. 4: Mathieu, *REG* xl 1927, 113–14, offers no solid arguments against), and their appearance in the Decree of Themistocles need not be regarded as an anachronism.

τούτους δ' ἔδει διε[γγ]υᾶν . . . τοὺς ἔνους μεχρὶ εὐθυνῶν: διεγγυᾶν can apparently mean either 'give security' (*SIG*³ 976, 49, D.H. *A.R.* VII. 12. ii) or 'take security' (*SIG*³ 629, 20): here the most natural rendering of the Greek is, 'And these were required to take security from the prytanes, generals and hipparchs of the previous year until their euthynae, accepting as guarantors four men from the same (property) class as the generals and hipparchs' (cf. Kenyon's Oxford Translation; for stipulations about the class of guarantors cf. bouleutic oath *ap.* D. XXIV. *Tim.* 144). Various alternatives have been advanced—Wilamowitz, *A.u.A.*, i. 86–7 (after A. Schulthess) translated 'to give security for the prytanes' and then deleted καὶ τοὺς στρατηγοὺς καὶ τοὺς ἱππάρχους; Fritz & Kapp, cf. Moore, offer 'These officers [that is, the newly elected Generals and Hipparchs] were to be held to bail by the Prytanes, as were the Generals and Hipparchs of the previous year until the completion of their audit' —but obtain a no more credible procedure by a more awkward rendering of the Greek. τούτους is perhaps intended to refer to all the ἀρχαί, not only to the generals and hipparchs; πρυτανεῖς are probably envisaged as a standing committee of the council to be mentioned below (e.g. Wilamowitz, *A.u.A.*, i. 87—but not necessarily four in number), not as the archons reappearing under a different title (considered by Sandys). It is strange that we have prytanes, generals and hipparchs in the first half of the sentence, generals and hipparchs in the second half, and archons and treasurers in neither; but any attempt at emendation would more probably improve on the original text than restore it.

The institution of εὔθυναι, a check on a man's performance at the end of a term of office, is attested in a deme inscription of *c.* 460 (*IG* i² 188; cf. εὔθυνος in Aesch. *Pers.* 828, of 472) and seems to have been an ancient one (Hignett, *H.A.C.*, 203–5, Sealey, *CP* lix 1964, 18–20 = *Essays*, 52–4); but the rule apparently given here, that the new magistrates are to demand guarantors and see that their predecessors submit to examination, is not attested in Athens (neither is any alternative rule which can be extracted from any alternative text). For the pre-Ephialtic procedure see on 9. i, 25. ii; and for fourth-century procedure see 48. iii–v, 54. ii, with commentary.

4. iii. βουλεύειν δὲ τετρακοσίους καὶ ἕνα: Solon instituted a council of four hundred (8. iv with commentary), and Cleisthenes a council of five hundred (21. iii, 43. ii, with commentary) which with changes in membership to match changes in the number of tribes lasted throughout the history of Athens; the extreme oligarchic régime of 411 was based on a council of four hundred (29. v, 31. i, with commentary). Draco's council could well have been invented in the circles which speculated more or less seriously about the πάτριος πολιτεία; it is not credible that in Draco's time Athens had a council other than the Areopagus (J. H. Oliver, *The Athenian Expounders of the Sacred and Ancestral Law*, 68–9, did find it credible, and emended to 501; but he was sufficiently answered by M. N. Tod, *JHS* lxxi 1951, 270–1). The choice of 401 rather than 400 is reminiscent of the δικαστήρια (cf. 53. ii, 68. i, with commentary); Cyrene at the end of the fourth century had a gerousia of 101 (*SEG* ix 1, §3).

τοὺς λαχόντας ἐκ τῆς πολιτείας: Appointment by lot, resulting in the 'fair' distribution of offices among those considered equally eligible rather than the appointment of the best or the most popular candidates, was particularly favoured by democrats (cf. the Persian debate, H. III. 80. vi). However, oligarchs had no cause to object to sortition if those among whom the lots were to be drawn were suitably restricted: in 411 the Four Hundred πρυτάνεις ... σφῶν αὐτῶν ἀπεκλήρωσαν (T. VIII. 70. i); sortition has a part to play in the constitutional documents of chs. 30–1 (cf. *ad loc.*); and in Arist. *Pol.*, though sortition is labelled democratic in VI. 1317 B 17–21 (–1318 A 11), the choice between election and sortition is conspicuously not used as an indication of the complexion of a form of government in the complicated discussion in IV. 1300 A 8–B 12. In V. 1309 A 33–B 14 Aristotle considers as qualities sought in candidates for office φιλίαν πρὸς τὴν καθεστῶσαν πολιτείαν, δύναμιν . . . τῶν ἔργων τῆς ἀρχῆς and ἀρετὴν καὶ δικαιοσύνην . . . τὴν πρὸς τὴν πολιτείαν, and we may reflect that, whereas to secure the second election seems desirable, it would probably be thought sufficient to exclude by δοκιμασία any candidates not possessed of the first or the third; a fragment of Theophrastus considers the criteria of ἀρετή, κτῆσις ἀρκοῦσα and φρόνησις and adds that εὔνοια is κοινόν (MS Vat. Gr. 2306, B 36–105, published by J. J. Keaney & A. Szegedy-Maszak, *TAPA* cvi 1976, 227–40, J. H. Oliver, *GR&BS* xviii 1977, 326–9).

As noted on §ii, πολιτεία sometimes means 'franchise' or 'citizenship': here it has to mean 'those possessed of the citizenship', which is not a normal use of the word. (*Pace* LSJ, the word does not have this meaning in Arist. *Pol.* IV. 1292 A 34; πολίτευμα is used with this meaning in *Pol.* V. 1302 B 16–17, 1305 B 34, VI. 1321 A 30–1, VII. 1332 B 31, and in Hellenistic inscriptions.) The closest parallels to this use of πολιτεία are elsewhere in *A.P.*: ἔξω . . . τῆς πολιτείας in 37. i, τῶν ἐν τῇ πολιτείᾳ in 38. ii.

κληροῦσθαι δὲ καὶ ταύτην: Sc. τὴν βουλήν or τὴν ἀρχήν.

καὶ τὰς ἄλλας ἀρχάς: Sandys is probably right to exclude at any rate the generals and hipparchs: the Athenians always recognised that military commanders required skill, and did not appoint them by lot (cf. ch. 61 and [X.] *A.P.* i. 3; and for the views of the oligarchs in 411 see 30. ii, 31. ii).

τοὺς ὑπὲρ τριάκοντ' ἔτη γεγονότας: In the classical period this was the age requirement for jurors (63. iii with commentary), bouleutae (X. *M.* I. ii. 35 [oligarchy of 404/3]; cf. D. XXII. *Andr.*, *hyp.* i. 1), and probably most regular officials (cf. p. 510); the same requirement is found in the constitutions of 411 (30. ii, 31. i).

καὶ δὶς τὸν αὐτὸν μὴ ἄρχειν: Cf. 62. iii, with commentary on the exceptions. The principle springs from the same desire to ensure fair shares for all who are entitled to a share as the use of sortition, and like that is not confined to democratic régimes (cf. the 'immediate' constitution of 411, 31. iii; in seventh-century Dreros the same man could not be κόσμος again for ten years [M&L 2]). In Arist. *Pol.* the ban on repetition is, like sortition, politically neutral in a discussion in IV (1299 A 8–12) but listed as a democratic feature in VI (1317 B 17–24 [–1318 A 11]); in IV. 1298 A 15–17 and 1300 A 25–6 it is not democratic *per se* but is mentioned as a possible way of applying the democratic principle that all should rule; cf. also II. 1261 A 32–B 6, 1264 B 6–13, III. 1275 A 23–6, V. 1308 A 14–18.

ἐξελθεῖν: 'ξ *paene totum periit*,' Kenyon, Berlin ed.; 'εξ *non certum*,' Kenyon, O.C.T.; δ[ι]ελθεῖν, Wilcken; δ[ι]ελθεῖν, M. H. Chambers, *TAPA* cii 1971, 42, and Dr J. D. Thomas reports that the traces suit δ quite well. Arist. *Pol.* IV uses a different construction, from which it would be dangerous to argue: ἕως ἄν διεξέλθη (vv.ll. διέλθη, ἐξέλθη) διὰ πάντων, 1298 A 16–17; ἕως ἄν διέλθη διὰ πάντων τῶν πολιτῶν, 1300 A 25–6—in each case with the office as subject. With a personal subject ἐξελθεῖν, 'retire from office', should be correct: cf. Arist. *Pol.* II. 1273 A 16, decree *ap.* And. I. *Myst.* 77.

εἰ δέ τις τῶν βουλευτῶν . . . ἐκλείποι τὴν σύνοδον: Cf. the 'future' constitution of 411, 30. vi: there is no evidence that such fines were ever in fact imposed in Athens. The fine for non-attendance was a standard oligarchic device to ensure that members of official bodies did their duty; democracies instead offered a stipend for attendance (e.g. Arist. *Pol.* IV. 1294 A 37–B 1, 1297 A 17–19, 21–4, 35–B 1, 1298 B 17–19; and cf. 24. iii, 27. iii–iv, 41. iii, 62. ii, with commentary). ἕδρα, common in documents in the sense 'meeting', recurs in the 'future' constitution of 411, 30. iv.

ἀπέτινον ὁ μὲν πεντακοσιομέδιμνος . . . ζευγίτης δὲ μίαν: Having been ignored in §ii, the property classes on which Solon based political rights (7. iii–iv) make a surprising appearance; as above, reckoning in terms of coinage is attributed to a time when Athens had no coinage (though it is possible that standard weights of silver were used in this way as early as the beginning of the sixth century: cf. on 8. iii). In the 'future' constitution of 411 fines for absence from the boule are threatened at a flat rate of 1 drachma a day; under the democracy bouleutae were paid 5 obols a day in the 320's and probably less earlier (62. ii with commentary).

4. iv. ἡ δὲ βουλὴ ἡ ἐξ Ἀρείου πάγου: The role of guardian of the laws which the Areopagus lost in 462/1 (3. vi, 8. iv, 25. ii, with commentary) must have been discussed at the end of the fifth century, since in 403/2 the Areopagus was ordered to ἐπιμελεῖσθαι . . . τῶν νόμων, ὅπως ἄν αἱ ἀρχαὶ τοῖς κειμένοις νόμοις χρῶνται (decree *ap.* And. I. *Myst.* 84: I do not know what, in practical terms, its author meant by this, and I doubt whether he knew); for further evidence that the Areopagus was discussed at that time cf. Lys. fr. 178 Sauppe. ἐξῆν δὲ τῷ ἀδικουμένῳ πρὸ[ς τὴν τῶν] Ἀρεοπαγιτῶν βουλὴν εἰσαγγέλλειν: For Solon's institution of εἰσαγγελία to the Areopagus in cases of attempted tyranny cf. 8. iv with commentary; for the fourth-century procedure see 43. iv with commentary. It is not clear whether the inventor of the 'Draconian constitution' is thinking of that procedure for major offences against the state, or of prosecutions of magistrates (taking this sentence with the previous one: cf. 45. ii with commentary), or even of denunciations of offenders in general (not restricting εἰσαγγέλλειν to its later technical senses).

4. v. ἐπὶ δὲ τοῖς σώ[μ]ασιν ἦσαν οἱ δανεισμοί: καθάπερ εἴρηται proves that this sentence has at any rate been adapted to its context in

A.P. Most probably the inserted 'constitution' ends with the previous sentence, and this sentence, summarising ch. 2, was written at the time of the insertion to help to fit it into its context in *A.P.*: cf. p. 86 and Introduction, p. 46 n. 219.

D. *Solon* (5–12)

Herodotus has little to say about Solon, and treats him as a sage, a lawgiver and a poet, but not as an economic and constitutional reformer (I. 29–33 cf. 86. iii, II. 177. ii, V. 113. ii); Thucydides does not mention him at all. Of the references to him in Arist. *Pol.* the most important is II. 1273 B 35–1274 A 21, which reviews current judgments on him. There is an anecdotal account in *D.L.* I. 45–67; but apart from *A.P.* our other major source is Plutarch's *Solon*. *A.P.* and Plutarch both make considerable use of Solon's poems (their selections coincide to a great extent, but not entirely); both refer to specific laws of Solon; and similarities of general outline and narrative detail suggest that Plutarch used *A.P.* or his source or both. Plutarch makes explicit references to 'Aristotle' in *Sol.* 25. i (*A.P.* 7. i), *Them.* 10. vi (23. i), *Cim.* 10. ii (27. iii), *Per.* 9. ii (27. iv), 10. viii (25. iv) and *Nic.* 2. i (28. v); but occasional use of *A.P.* would not be incompatible with his also drawing independently on *A.P.*'s source: agreement between *A.P.* and Pl. *Sol.* extends back to ch. 1 on Cylon and ch. 2 on the ἐκτήμοροι, and on Cylon Plutarch is fuller than *A.P.*; we have reason to think that *A.P.* found the quotations from the poems in his source (cf. p. 124 and Introduction, p. 24), and the fact that Plutarch's selection is similar but not identical again suggests that he consulted the same source. Adcock, *Klio* xii 1912, 1–16, argued that the material common to the two is from a narrative source of democratic tendency, whom he believed to be Androtion, and that 'Aristotle' imposed on this narrative a commentary based on his own view of Solon as a μέσος πολίτης, which has no parallel in Plutarch (cf. *Pol.* IV. 1296 A 18–20); but his separation of the two strands is not wholly successful, and the common source ought not to be Androtion, who held a view of the σεισάχθεια, fundamental to the interpretation of Solon's work, which *A.P.* 6. i, 10, and Pl. *Sol.* 15. iii–vi agree in rejecting (on the political views of Androtion see Introduction, pp. 19–20). Ch. 10, on Solon's reform of measures, weights, and coinage, interrupts what is otherwise a well-planned account (cf. pp. 47, 54), and I believe that on Solon and on the crisis with which he tried to deal *A.P.* used a single main source, either an *Atthis* other than Androtion's or a separate work on Solon, but has added some material from elsewhere (cf. pp. 28, 88).

In addition to Solon's poems, his laws were available (cf. on 7. i), so in dealing with him we pass from the reconstruction of what Athens' history was imagined to have been to an episode on which there was reliable information. Hignett concluded from the failure of Herodotus to treat Solon as a major reformer that it was only in the propaganda battles of the late fifth century that he became canonised as the founding hero of the democracy (*H.A.C.*, 2–8; cf. the over-schematic attempt by Ruschenbusch, *Hist.* vii 1958, 398–424, to date the first appearance of various men as democratic heroes, with Solon's début dated *c.* 356): there is some truth in Hignett's view—certainly Solon cannot have become a democratic hero until there was a self-conscious democracy which needed a hero, and until the end of the fifth century Cleisthenes seems to have occupied that position—but he is too sceptical in supposing that most of our 'tradition' about Solon is in fact later invention.†

The outline on which *A.P.* and Plutarch agree is that the Athenians, in a state of tension between rich and poor, chose Solon, a μέσος πολίτης, to be archon and mediator (*A.P.* 5, Pl. *Sol.* 14–15. i); Solon liberated the people by cancelling debts and banning loans on the security of the person (*A.P.* 6, *Sol.* 15. ii–16. iv); he divided the citizens into four classes according to the produce of their land, and based the distribution of political power on this classification (*A.P.* 7–8, *Sol.* 16. v–19); by three measures in particular he strengthened the position of the common people and laid the foundations of the later democracy, by banning loans on personal security, and in the judicial sphere by allowing any citizen to institute proceedings on behalf of an injured party and by allowing appeals from the decision of a magistrate to the heliaea, but he did not deliberately make his laws ambiguous to increase the power of the courts (*A.P.* 9, *Sol.* 18. iii–vii); also he altered Athens' system of measures, weights and coinage (*A.P.* 10, *Sol.* 15. iii–iv). Finding that he had pleased neither side, being too drastic for one but not drastic enough for the other, he left Athens for ten years, during which his laws were not to be altered (*A.P.* 11–12, *Sol.* 25. vi–28. i); but even in his absence there was trouble, and in due course Pisistratus made himself tyrant (*A.P.* 13 sqq., *Sol.* 29–31. iv). Arist. *Pol.* II, like *A.P.* 9. ii, insists that Solon did not intend all that was later built on his foundations: some praise Solon for making a good mixture and establishing δημοκρατίαν . . . τὴν πάτριον, others reproach him for making the lawcourt master of all and so paving the way for the radical democracy, but that was not Solon's intention and it seems that he gave the δῆμος only τὴν ἀναγκαιοτάτην . . . δύναμιν, and did not intend the γνώριμοι and εὔποροι to lose their power (cf. the quotations from Solon's poems in 12. i–ii).

It appears both from chs 2–4 and from what Solon actually did that he was concerned essentially with two problems: agrarian discontent, arising from the servitude of the ἑκτήμοροι and the risk that they and others would fall hopelessly into debt and be enslaved; and political discontent, at all levels because, though Draco had published the laws for all to know, their administration by the aristocratic magistrates was not trusted by all, and among the rich because a limited number of aristocratic families, though not richer or more 'useful' to the state than certain other families, nevertheless retained a monopoly of political power. The quotations from Solon's poems suggest that before his appointment as mediator he had been a champion of the poor and unprivileged (5. iii); but, substantial as his reforms were, he was no revolutionary, and the measures which he judged appropriate fell far short of what some of the poor and unprivileged had wanted (12): in the fourth century Solon could be praised both by those who emphasised his reforms and by those who emphasised his moderation. His measures failed to satisfy the Athenians, and discontent persisted to be exploited by Pisistratus in the next generation.

Of the many modern books on Solon the most useful is I. M. Linforth, *Solon the Athenian*; W. J. Woodhouse, *Solon the Liberator*, offers an influential but I believe mistaken account of the σεισάχθεια (cf. pp. 93–5).

5. i–ii. τοιαύτης δὲ τῆς τάξεως . . . ἀντικαθημένων ἀλλήλοις: The chapter begins with expressions rounding off in reverse order the description of Athens' political and economic situation which *A.P.* has given above: the πολιτεία had the τάξις set out in ch. 3, the many were enslaved to the few as explained in 2. ii–iii, and so the δῆμος rose against the γνώριμοι and there was a long period of στάσις as stated in 2. i. Cf. Introduction, pp. 45–6.

5. ii. εἵλοντο κοινῇ διαλλακτὴν καὶ ἄρχοντα Σόλωνα: Cf. Pl. *Sol.* 14. iii (ἄρχων . . . καὶ διαλλακτὴς καὶ νομοθέτης), 16. v (τῆς πολιτείας διορθωτὴν καὶ νομοθέτην), *Amat.* 763 D (εἵλοντο κοινῇ διαλλακτὴν καὶ ἄρχοντα καὶ νομοθέτην).

Cypselus, archon three years before Solon, was dead by *c.* 585 (M&L 6, fr. *a*, with Pl. *Sol.* 14. iii, discussed by M. F. McGregor, *Polis and Imperium: Studies . . . E. T. Salmon*, 31–4), and in the chronographic tradition Solon's archonship is dated 594/3 (e.g. Sosicrates *ap.* D.L. I. 62: see Jacoby, *Apollodors Chronik*, 165–78, T. J. Cadoux, *JHS* lxviii 1948, 93–9, A. E. Samuel, *Greek and Roman Chronology*, 201; cf. above, p. 109); but *A.P.* 14. i dates Solon's legislation in the 32nd year before the archonship of Comeas, and if that year is 561/0 (cf. pp. 191–9) *A.P.*'s date for Solon must be 592/1. Hammond, *JHS* lx 1940, 71–83 = *Studies*, 145–62, with further discussion

162–9, tries to accept both dates, placing the σεισάχθεια in 594/3 and the political reform in 592/1; but the two must surely be variant dates for Solon's archonship (cf. Cadoux, *loc. cit.*, and commentary on 10. i). G. V. Sumner, *CQ*² xi 1961, 49–54, suggested that the archon list used by *A.P.* placed Solon's archonship in 592/1, but comparison with other records obliged later chronographers to add two archons between Solon and 587/6 and to place Solon in 594/3 in their revised list. M. Miller, *Klio* xxxvii 1959, 42–52, suggested that 594/3 is merely a theoretical date for Solon derived from a supposed beginning of the 42-year cycles of ἐπώνυμοι (on which see 53. iv with commentary), in *Klio* xli 1963, 85–7, she suggested as the actual date of his archonship 573/2, half a cycle later, and her views are further elaborated in *Arethusa* i 1968, 62–81, ii 1969, 62–86, iv 1971, 25–47—but this reconstruction is itself purely theoretical, and there is no good reason for her assumption that the Athenian archon list was authentic as far back as the 550's but no farther. Sumner's explanation of the discrepancy between *A.P.* and the chronographers is ingenious and may be right; but it remains possible and perhaps likelier that the troubles following Solon's reforms (13. i–ii with commentary) led *A.P.* or his source to miscalculate and to lose two years.†

A.P. and Plutarch agree in placing at least some of Solon's reforms in his archonship, though the legislation of Draco before him (4. i) and of Cleisthenes after him (21. i) are placed in the archonships of others, and Cleisthenes did (in 525/4, before his reforms: M&L 6, *c* 3) hold the archonship. Jacoby suggested, rather improbably, that the archon list described Solon as ἄρχων καὶ διαλλακτής (*Atthis*, 175–6); but Hignett doubted whether any evidence survived to link Solon's reforms with his archonship, and supposed that the link was merely an inference made by the Atthidographers: he rejected the link, placing Solon's reforms about the late 570's, after the troubles mentioned in 13. i–ii (*H.A.C.*, 316–21). Similar scepticism had been expressed by T. Case, *CR* ii 1888, 241–2, and many have found Hignett's arguments persuasive (e.g. Sealey, *Hist.* ix 1960, 159 with n. 31 = *Essays*, 12 with 35 n. 31, *History of the Greek City States*, 121–3, *Hist.* xxviii 1979, 238–41, Davies, *A.P.F.*, 323, cf. W. H. Plommer, *CR*² xix 1969, 126–9, expressing general scepticism on early archontic dates, and Miller, cited above); but I believe he was wrong. Of the synchronisms which he cited, that with Philocyprus is authentic and that with Amasis may be authentic, but they need not affect the date of the reforms (cf. on 11. i), while the others could easily have been invented by men ignorant or careless of chronology; the failure of H. 1. 29. i to mention Solon's archonship proves nothing; that Solon should have been accepted as mediator at the age of about 30–35 (Davies, *loc.*

cit.) may not have seemed so startling at the time as it does now (Pisistratus was about 40–45 when he made his first bid for tyranny [Davies, *A.P.F.*, 445], in 407 Cyrus, son of Darius II, was given a superior command in Asia Minor at the age of 16 [Pl. *Art.* 2. iv with D. M. Lewis, *Sparta and Persia*, 134 n. 151], and likewise Alexander the Great was made regent in Philip's absence and commanded a minor expedition at 16 [Pl. *Alex.* 9. i]); while evidence in favour of the link may be extracted from those laws of Solon which refer to his archonship (*ap.* Pl. *Sol.* 19. iv; [D.] XLIV. *Leoch.* 68, XLVI. *Steph. ii.* 14). If Solon's poems were kept in circulation, facts about their author could have been preserved also: the tradition associating Solon's laws with his archonship should be accepted.

How long Solon's work of reform lasted it is impossible to say (Plutarch's division of it into two distinct phases is without foundation: cf. on 10. i); but we have more than enough candidates for the archonship in the years following 594/3 (Cadoux, *op. cit.*, 99–101, Samuel, *op. cit.*, 201), and we may assume that his tenure of that office was not prolonged. How he came to be appointed simultaneously to the archonship and to a special commission is again uncertain (R. J. Hopper, *BSA* lvi 1961, 213, suggests that success in the war against Megara helped to win him a following: cf. on 14. i); but the poem quoted in this chapter seems to show (as *A.P.* recognises) that Solon had pronounced on Athens' troubles before he was called upon to heal them, and other lines quoted (esp. fr. 34. 7–8 West *ap.* 12. iii) bear out the statement of 11. ii that he could if he had wished have become tyrant.

γιγνώσκω . . . : Fr. 4a West, quoted only here. In commenting on the state of affairs in Attica before his archonship the fragments of Solon in this chapter resemble fr. 4 (*ap.* D. XIX. *F.L.* 255), and perhaps belong to the same poem (cf. Linforth, *Solon the Athenian*, 178).

There is an edition of the fragments with commentary and translation by Linforth, *op. cit.*, 129–245; A. Masaracchia, *Solone*, 201–362, gives a commentary and Italian translation; the most recent edition of the text is by M. L. West, *Iambi et Elegi Graeci ante Alexandrum Cantati*, ii. 119–45; some of the fragments, including 5, 6 and 36, are included (as frs. 5, 24) in D. A. Campbell, *Greek Lyric Poetry: A Selection*. There are discussions of the attitudes underlying Solon's poems by G. Vlastos, *CP* xli 1946, 65–83, A. W. H. Adkins, *Moral Values and Political Behaviour in Ancient Greece*, 47–57, E. A. Havelock, *The Greek Concept of Justice*, 249–62.

πρεσβυτάτην . . . γαῖαν 'Ιαονίας: For the belief that Athens was the mother city of the Ionians cf. p. 66.

καινομένην: Read by Blass[4] and approved by Kenyon in his Berlin ed. and O.C.T.; Wilcken's κλινομένην, regarded by Kenyon as possible but less likely (Dr J. D. Thomas concurs), is preferred by Oppermann and West; suggestions by others seeking an easier metaphor include καρφομένην (Diels *ap*. Blass⁴, claiming to read that in the papyrus) and καιομένην (T. Hudson-Williams: cf. Lys. XXXIII. *Olymp.* 7). We have no independent way of determining whether Solon thought of Attica as 'being slain', 'tottering', 'being withered' or 'being burned': it would be dangerous to insist that the same verb must be read here as in Lysias, and no alternative is so clearly preferable as to justify the rejection of the word given by the papyrus, which is most probably καινομένην.

ἐν ᾗ πρὸς ἑκατέρους ὑπὲρ ἑκατέρων μάχεται καὶ διαμφισβητεῖ: In the lines quoted in §iii, thought by editors but not stated by *A.P.* to come from the same poem, Solon ranges himself unambiguously on the side of the poor; it is arguable that the criticisms of fr. 4 West also are aimed at the rich, but it can also be said that in that fragment he κοινῇ παραινεῖ καταπαύειν τὴν ἐνεστῶσαν φιλονικίαν; cf. fr. 5. 5–6 *ap.* 12. i and fr. 37. 9–10 *ap.* 12. v. διαμφισβητεῖν and its cognates are favourite words of Aristotle and of *A.P.* (cf. 3. iv with commentary; διαμφισβήτησις is used in 35. ii): Solon 'fights and disputes' on behalf of each side against the other.

5. iii. ἦν δ' ὁ Σόλων ... τῶν μέσων: Cf. Pl. *Sol.* 1–3, esp. 1. ii; Arist. *Pol.* IV. 1296 A 18–20 says that the best lawgivers come from the μέσοι πολῖται and that Solon's poems show that he was one of these; for a modern discussion of Solon's family see Davies, *A.P.F.*, 322–4 cf. 334–5. Solon is said to have been doubly related to Pisistratus (H. V. 65. iii, Pl. *Sol.* 1. ii, D.L. III. 1; Her. Pont. fr. 147 Wehrli *ap.* Pl. *Sol.* 1. iii), and more tenuously related to the family of Dropides (archon 645/4: *Marm. Par.* 239 A 34) and his sons Critias and Dropides, that is, the family of Critias the late-fifth-century oligarch, with which Plato was connected (Plat. *Charm.* 155 A 2–3, 157 E 4–158 A 1, *Tim.* 20 E 1–3, on which later writers embroidered: cf. p. 429): that and the fact of his appointment as archon make it certain that he was τῶν πρώτων. Davies is sceptical about the tradition of his μεσότης, and notes that what survives from his poems attests no more than a hostility to ill-gotten but a desire for legitimate wealth (esp. fr. 13. 7–8 West): *A.P.* proceeds to a quotation which is said to prove this point but does not (cf. next note), and Arist. *Pol.* also claims that this is proved by his poems; perhaps other verses by Solon did prove what the surviving verses do not, or perhaps passages like the one which follows, in which Solon speaks on behalf of the poor, were pressed too far. Plutarch reports from Hermippus that Solon's father Execestides had reduced his property through charitable expenditure and that Solon in consequence became a merchant (*Sol.* 2. i); but though it is clear from his poems that Solon travelled (cf. on 11. i) the tradition that he was a trader, and that he travelled and traded in his youth, cannot be confirmed. If it is true it may not be a sign of his family's impoverishment: S. C. Humphreys, *Anthropology and the Greeks*, 165–8, suggests that a period of youthful travels in search of wealth formed part of the normal life cycle of the sons of archaic Greek nobles and peasant farmers.

ἐν τοῖσδε τοῖς ποιήμασιν: ποιήματα should be 'poems' (LSJ cites no use of the plural to denote consecutive lines of a single poem earlier than D.H. 13. *Comp.* 3, *A.R.* 1. 41. iii); but what follows is a single extract from one poem, which fails to prove the point asserted by *A.P.* in this sentence (cf. next note), though it is followed by a comment which is appropriate to it. It may be a further sign that something is wrong that what began as a carefully balanced sentence loses its balance in the concluding words, παραινῶν τοῖς πλουσίοις μὴ πλεονεκτεῖν (cf. Introduction, p. 41). This prompts the suspicion that the quotations from Solon in *A.P.* have not been inserted from his own knowledge by the author (though a man working in Athens in the fourth century should have known the poems) but were already present in his source, and that at this point his source gave more than one quotation, the first being intended to confirm Solon's μεσότης, and that *A.P.* in abbreviating has retained the introduction but not the quotation which it introduced (cf. p. 118).

ὑμεῖς δ' . . . : Fr. 4c West, quoted only here: editors assign it to the same poem as the lines quoted in §ii. These lines and the comment which follows do not display the impartiality alleged in *A.P.*'s comment on the previous quotation (though other lines, not now surviving, may have reproached the poor on behalf of the rich); nor do they show that Solon was τῶν μέσων, either τῇ οὐσίᾳ or τοῖς πράγμασι (though it is conceivable that words such as these, coming from a known aristocrat, were imagined to show this); but they do show that at some time before his reforms Solon expressed the grievances of the poor against the rich. 11. ii–12, with quotations from other poems, shows that afterwards he was subjected to complaints from both sides, was prepared to attribute to some of the poor (fr. 34. 1 *ap.* 12. iii) the lust for ἁρπαγή which he had earlier attributed to the rich (fr. 4. 13 *ap.* D. xix. *F.L.* 255), and held a 'moderate' view of what was due to the δῆμος (cf. Linforth, *Solon the Athenian*, 9: Masaracchia, *Solone, passim*, makes too much of Solon's avoidance of revolution and too little of his willingness to blame and offend the rich).

ἡσυχάσαντες . . . ἦτορ: For this transitive use cf. Plat. *Rep.* ix. 572 A 5.

ἐς κόρον [ἡ]λάσατε: Cf. Tyrt. fr. 11. 10 West.

ἄρτια πά[ντ']: Solon also uses ἄρτιος, 'wholesome', in fr. 4. 32, 39, West *ap.* D. xix. *F.L.* 255, fr. 6. 4 *ap.* *A.P.* 12. ii. πά[ντ'], used with ἄρτια in fr. 4, was first read by Kaibel & Wilamowitz, and has been accepted by most editors, including Kenyon in his O.C.T.; M. H. Chambers, *TAPA* cii 1971, 42, reads πά[ν]τ'. τα[ῦτ'] was first read by Herwerden & Leeuwen, was read by Wilcken (but rejected by Kaibel & Wilamowitz[3]) and accepted by Kenyon in his Berlin ed. and Oppermann; West reads τα[ῦ]τ', and Dr J. D. Thomas finds that virtually certain. Because he did so once, Solon should not be required always to use πάντα with ἄρτια, and ταῦτ' gives a better sense here.

τήν τε φι[λαργυρ]ίαν: Fr. 4b West. Cf. Pl. *Sol.* 14. iii (δεδοικὼς τῶν μὲν τὴν φιλοχρηματίαν, τῶν δὲ τὴν ὑπερηφανίαν), which forms the basis of the various synonyms which have been suggested to fill the lacuna; also the oracle said to have been given to the Spartan Lycurgus at Delphi, *ap.* D.S. VII. 12. v. Most editors have accepted the pentameter yielded by Kenyon's φι[λαργυρ]ίαν and the emendation of the second τε to θ' by J. B. Mayor and H. Jackson (*CR* v 1891, 107), the unmetrical τε being retained by Kaibel & Wilamowitz and by Kenyon in his Berlin ed.; Wilcken read φσ ... ειαν and denied that the letter before ε could be ρ, but Kaibel & Wilamowitz[3] were not dissuaded and Diels *ap.* Kenyon's Berlin ed. read φι[λαργ]υρείαν; but Blass[3] read φ[ιλοπλου]τίαν, Chambers, *TAPA* xcvi 1965, 34, reads φιλ[οπλο]υτίαν (an ending which Dr J. D. Thomas regards as possible) and supposes that *A.P.* here quotes Solon unmetrically and inaccurately, and West prints φ [..] .. [..] .. τιαν, suspects that *A.P.* like Plutarch may have written φιλοχρηματίαν, and suggests that Solon may have written something like

ἦ γὰρ ἔγωγε δέδοικ' ... ἐσορῶν
χρήματα τιμῶντας πάντῃ θ' ὑπερηφανέοντας.

In a chapter which has already given two *verbatim* quotations and which here says καὶ ἐν ἀρχῇ τῆς ἐλεγείας δεδοικέναι φησὶ ... we should expect a third to follow: most probably *A.P.* intended to quote again but carelessly used the wrong word, φιλοπλουτίαν.

6. i. τόν τε δῆμον ἠλευθέρωσε καὶ ἐν τῷ π[α]ρόντι καὶ εἰς τὸ μέλλον: In *A.P.* the economic reform of Solon comprises two main elements, a ban for the future on δανείζειν ἐπὶ τοῖς σώμασιν and the liberation of those who have already been enslaved for debt (cf. 2. ii; also Solon, fr. 36. 8–15 West *ap.* 12. iv), and the σεισάχθεια proper, χρεῶν ἀποκοπὰς ... καὶ τῶν ἰδίων καὶ τῶν δημοσίων (cf. Pl. *Sol.* 15. ii–v, noting but rejecting Androtion's different account [cf. below]; also Phil. 328 F 114, and lexica cited by Jacoby *ad loc.*).

To abolish enslavement for debt presents no problems of interpretation (though it must have been difficult to find and to liberate those already enslaved, especially those outside Attica, which Solon in fr. 36 claims to have done). In fact, although it is generally true that after Solon's reforms debts were not incurred on the security of the person, there are signs that slavery for debt was not entirely impossible in later Athens: see [D.] LIII. *Nic.* 11 with L. Beauchet, *L'Histoire du droit privé*, ii. 414–15, Harrison, *L.A.*, i. 39; Lys. XII. *Erat.* 98, Ar. *Plut.* 147–8, Is. XIV. *Plat.* 48, with C. Mossé, *La Fin de la démocratie athènienne*, 189 n. 3; Men. *Her.* 20, 36, *hyp.* 3, Ter. *Heaut.* 500 sqq., 793, with the commentary of Gomme & Sandbach on *Her.* 36.†

The cancellation of all debts is more problematic. It requires some exercise of the imagination to envisage what the range of debts can have been in a community which did not yet use coinage: it is possible that a man who had borrowed corn when his own supplies had run out, to keep himself and his family alive until the next harvest, would have been freed from the obligation to repay that; but it is harder to believe that a man who at the crucial time had borrowed a hoe from his neighbour would have been freed from the obligation to return it. In the opening lines of fr. 36 West Solon claims to have uprooted the ὅροι and to have liberated the earth, which suggests that the principal debts cancelled were the obligations of the ἑκτήμοροι to pay their overlord a sixth of their produce (cf. on 2. ii; the terms μορτή and ἐπίμορτος γῆ seem to have been used in Solon's laws [Poll. VII. 151]). From Solon's description of what he did, and from the fact that Attica when we know more about it is a land of small farmers, it follows that the freed ἑκτήμοροι became the owners of the land which they continued to occupy (cf. Masaracchia, *Solone*, 146–8, arguing that Solon restored 'the old rights' of the peasants); though some, believing that this land had previously been 'owned', in an anachronistic sense of that word, by the overlords, and noting that Solon abstained from γῆς ἀναδασμός (11. ii, Pl. *Sol.* 16. i, cf. Solon, fr. 34. 8–9, *ap. A.P.* 12. iii), have been forced to the improbable conclusion that the overlords continued to own the land (e.g. A. French, *CQ*[2] vi 1956, 20–5, Day & Chambers, *A.H.A.D.*, 168–9). In addition to this standardised obligation of the ἑκτήμοροι Solon may have cancelled other debts to individuals, such as debts of produce; and it may be, as *A.P.* suggests, that some men were also burdened by public debts, i.e. debts to the state or to a temple or local religious organisation, and that these debts too were cancelled (here all must be speculative: see on the ναυκραρίαι, 8. iii with commentary); but the simple χρεῶν ἀποκοπάς ... καὶ τῶν ἰδίων καὶ τῶν δημοσίων is almost certainly an anachronistic reformulation of what Solon actually did (cf. M. Mühl, *RM*[2] xcvi 1953, 214–23—but *pace* Mühl Plutarch surely equated τῶν συμβολαίων ἀναίρεσιν with the cancellation of debts, and in *Sol.* 15. ii and v alludes twice to the same interpretation of the σεισάχθεια).†

Andr. 324 F 34 used the reform of measures, weights and coinage which *A.P.* describes in ch. 10 to argue that the σεισάχθεια was not an ἀποκοπὴ χρεῶν but simply a reduction of interest rates. In Athens after the Peloponnesian War it was accepted that ἀποκοπαὶ χρεῶν would be an undesirable overturning of the established order (e.g. And. I. *Myst.* 88, Is. XII. *Panath.* 259); ἀποκοπαὶ χρεῶν are commonly associated with γῆς ἀναδασμός (e.g. Is., *loc. cit.*), a measure from which Solon had abstained (cf. above). It is commonly thought that Androtion's reinterpretation of the σεισάχθεια arose from a desire to dissociate Solon from so revolutionary a measure as ἀποκοπαὶ χρεῶν (e.g. Busolt, *G.S.*, i. 94–5, Jacoby, *Supp.* i. 145): this view has been challenged by P. E. Harding, *Phoen.* xxviii 1974, 282–9, who objects that in fourth-century Athens there is no sign of men who approve of such revolutionary measures; but this consensus did not obtain elsewhere in the fourth century, so it is entirely possible that fourth-century Athenians should have been conscious of cancellation of debts and redistribution of land as revolutionary acts to be avoided, and the view that Androtion has for that reason deliberately reinterpreted the σεισάχθεια may stand (cf. Introduction, p. 20). Philochorus (328 F 114) seems to have held to the orthodox view of the σεισάχθεια.‡

Mathieu, *Aristote, Constitution d'Athènes*, 13, claims that *A.P.* places the ban for the future on personal security before the σεισάχθεια but Pl. *Sol.* 15. ii implies that the σεισάχθεια came first, and that *A.P.*'s order is intended to make the σεισάχθεια seem less revolutionary by representing it as the retrospective extension of an existing law (cf. B. Keil, *Die solonische Verfassung in Aristoteles Verfassungsgeschichte Athens*, 44–5). This seems too subtle: both writers clearly regard the σεισάχθεια and the ban for the future on personal security as parts of the same reform, and I do not think that either intends a chronological distinction between the two parts (cf. on 10. i).

As has often been stressed, Solon did nothing to make economically viable a plot of land which had not been viable, and he may even have made life harder for some of the poor in that they would probably find it more difficult to borrow after his reform than before. Although he made the ἑκτήμοροι the unencumbered owners of their plots, his reform must in the long term if not immediately have driven some men off the land in search of an alternative livelihood: his ban on the export of natural products other than olive oil (Pl. *Sol.* 24. i) would appeal to large-scale rather than small-scale farmers, and he encouraged both native and immigrant craftsmen (*ibid.* 22. i–iii, 24. iv).

καὶ νόμους ἔθηκε: These words interrupt what is otherwise a care-

6. i] COMMENTARY ON THE *ATH. POL.*

fully balanced sentence (Kaibel, *Stil und Text*, 81–2 cf. 134) and, placed between the ban on δανείζειν ἐπὶ τοῖς σώμασιν and χρεῶν ἀποκοπάς, they also interrupt the sense. Kaibel & Wilamowitz supposed them to be an anticipation of νόμους ἔθηκεν ἄλλους in 7. i and deleted them, and some other early editors followed their lead. The criticisms are justified, but I suspect that these words are nevertheless an authentic part of *A.P.*'s text, and that he has done more clumsily here what he did at the beginning of ch. 2: there he announced a political and an economic cause of distress, proceeded to deal immediately with the economic and returned to the political in ch. 3; here he deals immediately with Solon's economic reform and in 7–8 with his legal and political reform, and the purpose of these words is to give forewarning of the second topic before he deals with the first. Cf. Introduction, pp. 41, 46–7.

ἃς σεισάχθειαν καλοῦσιν: Cf. Pl. *Sol.* 15. ii, *Alex. Fort.* II. 343 c, claiming that the name was Solon's; *Sol.* 16. v, where the name is given to a festival in which the liberation of the ἑκτήμοροι was celebrated. In *Sol.* 15. ii, *Praec. Ger. Reip.* 807 E, the name is a σόφισμα or ὑποκόρισμα χρεῶν ἀποκοπῆς. The plural καλοῦσιν suggests that, despite the implication of Plutarch, *A.P.* did not find the name in Solon's poems.

6. ii. ἐν οἷς πειρῶνταί τιν[ες] διαβάλλ[ει]ν αὐτόν: Cf. Pl. *Sol.* 15. vii–ix, *Praec. Ger. Reip.* 807 D–E, and the brief allusion in Suid. (Σ 779) Σόλων. The story that Solon 'leaked' his intention of cancelling debts to some of his friends, who took advantage of it, evidently became an accepted part of the tradition: οἱ δημοτικοί believed that Solon's behaviour was naïve but innocent; οἱ βουλόμενοι βλασφημεῖν believed that he himself was one of those who profited from this foreknowledge; there is no sign that any one tried to deny the whole story. *A.P.* believes that Solon, behaving honourably in great things, could not have behaved dishonourably in small, and so prefers the former version. This argument from character is presented in language typical of fourth-century rationalism (πιθανώτερος ὁ ... λόγος· οὐ γὰρ εἰκὸς ... μαρτυρεῖ ... χρὴ νομίζειν); 9. ii will similarly argue that we should judge from all that we know about Solon; and we need not doubt that the comment on his conflicting sources is *A.P.*'s own (cf. Introduction, pp. 25–7).

Those who profited from the leakage *A.P.* describes simply as τισι τῶν γνωρίμων; Pl. *Sol.* names Conon, Clinias and Hipponicus as the leading profiteers, and in defence of Solon claims that he in fact lost by the cancellation of debts: descendants of the three men named (Conon, Alcibiades, Callias) were simultaneously prominent towards the end of the Peloponnesian War, and it has been plausibly suggested (by E. Fabricius, *ap.* F. Duemmler, *Hermes* xxvii 1892,

262 = *Kleine Schriften*, ii. 419, cf. Wilamowitz, *A.u.A.*, i. 62–3: Duemmler, *opp. citt.*, 260–86 = 417–42, esp. 261–5 = 418–22, guessed at a pamphlet by Critias) that the story was invented at that time, primarily to discredit those men; and Davies, *A.P.F.*, 12, 255, 506, dismisses the need even to recognise the historicity of the three ancestors. *A.P.*'s failure to name the culprits serves no obvious purpose of his own: since he knew conflicting versions of the story and no one seems to have denied it altogether, we may suspect that among those who narrated it were some who did not wish to discredit Conon, Alcibiades and Callias and who suppressed the names of their ancestors (and possibly even substituted other names); *A.P.* pronounced on the disagreement over Solon, and ignored this second disagreement, which does not affect our judgment on Solon.[7]

There are further grounds for suspecting that the whole story is a later invention: even if the account of the σεισάχθεια given above (on 6. i) is mistaken, it can hardly have been possible, in a society in which land changed hands with difficulty and coinage was not yet used, at short notice to borrow capital and acquire land in exchange for it (cf. J. V. A. Fine, *Hesp.* Supp. ix 1951, 180–1 n. 45). ὅθεν φασὶ ... παλαιοπλούτους (§ii) confirms that the story was used in propaganda against Athenians of a later generation; Lys. XIX. *Bon. Arist.* 49 (of the 380's) distinguishes between τῶν ἀρχαιοπλούτων and τῶν νεωστὶ ἐν δόξῃ γεγενημένων, and in §§34–41, 48, mentions Conon and Callias as men whose property turned out to be worth far less than had been imagined. For a fanciful reconstruction, crediting the story with a genuine core, see Woodhouse, *Solon the Liberator*, 182–90; and for a more recent attempt at rationalisation see M. Miller, *Arethusa* i 1968, 70–3.

οἱ δημοτικοί: On *A.P.*'s sources and his labelling of them see Introduction, pp. 15–30: it has been suggested that when he refers to οἱ δημοτικοί he means the Atthidographer Clidemus, but I suspect that when he uses a label such as this he is thinking of the more obviously partisan writings.

παραστρατηγη[θ]ῆναι: 'Was outgeneralled': this is the only use of the passive recorded in LSJ, and the active is not recorded until the Roman period; but some one must presumably have used the word literally before it occurred to *A.P.* to use it metaphorically.

οἱ β[ουλ]όμενοι βλασ[φ]ημεῖν: βλασφημεῖν, of the defamation of human beings, is a favourite word of the orators; in particular Kaibel, *Stil und Text*, 135, compares Is. XV. *Antid.* 32, τῶν βλασφημεῖν καὶ διαβάλλειν βουλομένων; *A.P.* uses the word again in 28. v, of the de-

---

[7] Mathieu, *Aristote, Constitution d'Athènes*, 19, is hypercritical in asserting that the opponents of the δημοτικοί could not have agreed that the beneficiaries were γνώριμοι.

tractors of Theramenes (cf. also 23. iv). Again we do not know whom *A.P.* has in mind: Gomme, *Hist. Comm. Thuc.*, i. 47 n. 2, suggested that here and in 9. ii the detractors of Solon included Theopompus; we cannot be sure that Theopompus wrote early enough to be used by *A.P.*, but Athenians of different political complexions agreed that Solon was a man to be praised, so criticism of this kind is more likely to have been found in the writings of a man like Theopompus (cf. Introduction, p. 23).

6. iii. κοινόν: 'Neutral', 'impartial', as in T. III. 53. ii, 68. i; Fritz & Kapp and Moore translate it as 'public-spirited', devoted to objectives which were κοινά rather than ἴδια, but it is hard to find a parallel to this.

ἐξὸν αὐτῷ ... τυραννεῖν τῆς πόλεως: Cf. 11. ii, 12. iii with quotation from Solon, fr. 34 West; also Pl. *Sol.* 14. iii–15. i with quotation of frs. 32 and 33, *Comp. Sol. Publ.* 2. v.

ἀμφοτέροις ἀπεχ[θέ]σθαι: Again repeated in 11. ii and confirmed by the quotations from Solon's poems in 12.

φανεροῖς: The basic meaning of the word is 'visible', and in one of its metaphorical uses a man who has committed an offence becomes φανερός if found out (e.g. Lys. VII. *Ol.* 12): here *A.P.*'s meaning is that this act of πλεονεξία is one which would all too easily be detected.

καταρρυπαίνειν: 'Defile', used of a ἑστία, Plat. *Legg.* XI. 919 E 8–9, used metaphorically of virtues or virtuous acts, *ibid.*, 937 D 8, Is. XII. *Panath.* 63.

7. i. πολιτείαν δὲ κατέστησε: *A.P.* announces Solon's reform of the πολιτεία and his legislation, deals briefly with his legislation in §§i–ii, and then deals with the πολιτεία in 7. iii–8. v. The political reform amounts to less than the establishment of a new constitution, but some scholars have made unduly heavy weather over this: it certainly marks a new stage in the development of the πολιτεία; and if any constitutional laws had been included in Draco's code they will have been superseded by new laws of Solon, so that when he completed his work his will have been the only currently valid constitutional laws.

καὶ νόμους ἔθηκεν ἄλλους: Possibly, with reference to what follows, laws other than those of Draco; but more probably laws other than those which are regarded as constituting the πολιτεία. Solon's laws are already referred to as νόμοι by H. I. 29. i, ii, II. 177. ii, but Solon himself called his laws θεσμοί: cf. on 12. iv.

τοῖς δὲ Δράκοντος θεσμοῖς ... πλὴν τῶν φονικῶν: Cf. Pl. *Sol.* 17. i. For the ordinances of Draco, and for the tendency of fourth-century Athenians to regard their current code of laws as comprising the homicide law of Draco and on other matters the laws of Solon, see on 4. i. Sceptics like Hignett have concluded that by the end of the fifth century it was impossible to distinguish between the original enactments of Draco and Solon and later additions to the code (*H.A.C.*, 17–27), but this scepticism is unjustified: see next note. However, it was later the Athenians' practice to destroy the official texts when they annulled laws (e.g. decree *ap*. And. 1. *Myst*. 79, Tod 123, 31–5): the laws of Solon are a special case, since he produced a complete code which was superseded only piecemeal, so there is no problem in *A.P.*'s being able to quote obsolete laws of Solon (8. iii); but the whole of Draco's code was superseded at once apart from his law on homicide, and I doubt the suggestion of R. S. Stroud that these laws may have survived physically for two hundred years or more (*Athens Comes of Age*, 24, cf. *U. Calif. Pub. Cl. Stud.* xix 1979, 43).

ἀναγράψαντες δὲ τοὺς νόμους εἰς τοὺς κύρβεις: Cf. Pl. *Sol*. 25. i–ii: κατεγράφησαν εἰς ξυλίνους ἄξονας ἐν πλαισίοις †περιέχουσι† στρεφομένους, fragments of which were preserved in Plutarch's day; he refers to 'Aristotle' for the alternative name, κύρβεις, quotes a couplet of the fifth-century comedian Cratinus (cf. p. 109: the κύρβεις of Solon and Draco are now used for roasting barley), and says that ἔνιοι believe that the sacred laws and sacrificial calendar were contained in the κύρβεις and the rest in the ἄξονες. That some sacrifices were recorded in the κύρβεις is confirmed by Lys. xxx. *Nic*. 17, 18, 20, and an inscription of 363/2 (*Hesp*. vii 1, 87); the homicide law of Draco which was inscribed on stone in 409/8 was derived from at least two numbered ἄξονες (M&L 86, 10, 56); laws of Solon are cited from ἄξονες numbered i (Pl. *Sol*. 24. ii), v (schol. Hom. *Il*. xxi. 282), xiii (said to be law no. 8) (Pl. *Sol*. 19. iv), xvi (*ibid*. 23. iv) and xxi (Harp. ὅτι οἱ ποιηταί); cf. also D. xxiii. *Arist*. 28, 31 (with Cobet's emendation), Harp. σῖτος, Themist. *Orat*. xxvi. *Dic*. 315 A (with Kesters' emendation); Hesychius' list of Aristotle's works includes a treatise in five books περὶ τῶν Σόλωνος ἀξόνων (discussed by Ruschenbusch, *Hist. Einz*. ix 1966, 40–2; cf. Introduction, p. 58 with n. 289). It is certain that both names were in use in the century before *A.P.* was written; numbers are used only with the term ἄξονες. In later antiquity there was much discussion of the ἄξονες and κύρβεις and of how, if at all, the two differed: some texts repeat or modify the distinction made by Plutarch's ἔνιοι on the grounds of content (e.g. Harp. ἄξονι, κύρβεις); and two other distinctions are attempted—on the grounds of material used (e.g. Harp. *locc. citt*.; but the texts disagree, and wood is the material most commonly attributed to each), and of shape (contrasting τετράγωνοι ἄξονες with τρίγωνοι κύρβεις, e.g. Poll. viii. 128; or representing the κύρβεις as upright, capped stelae, e.g. Harp. κύρβεις).†

Modern scholars have taken full advantage of the variety of ancient theories. Of more recent studies J. H. Oliver, *Hesp.* iv 1935, 9–13, suggested that strictly ἄξονες denotes the physical objects and κύρβεις the body of law contained in the ἄξονες; L. B. Holland, *AJA*² xlv 1941, 346–62, argued from the chronology of references to them that ἄξονες and κύρβεις were different sets of similar objects, of different dates; S. Dow, *Proc. Mass. Hist. Soc.* lxxi 1953–7, 24–35, made the distinction of content primary and argued that the different contents required different kinds of monument for their display (cf. H. Hansen, *Philol.* cxix 1975, 39–45). Ruschenbusch, *op. cit.*, 14–25, and A. Andrewes, Φόρος: *Tribute to B. D. Meritt*, 21–8, argue that attempts to distinguish ἄξονες and κύρβεις as different objects or objects with different contents are merely guesses by the uninformed, puzzled by the use of the two words, that the words must in fact denote the same objects, perhaps thought of in different ways, and that these objects, of which fragments survived in Plutarch's time, were seen in Athens by Eratosthenes in the third century B.C. and by Polemon in the second. Stroud (*U. Calif. Pub. Cl. Stud.* xix 1979, esp. 12–13, 41–4, cf. *Athens Comes of Age*, 23–4) like Holland attacks the evidence chronologically: relying on Anax. 72 F 13 (quoted below, p. 134) he argues that the ἄξονες and κύρβεις were different sets of objects, and suggests that the laws of Draco and Solon were originally inscribed on revolving wooden beams called ἄξονες but at some time before 462/1 were copied on to capped bronze stelae called κύρβεις.

I doubt if the fragment of Anaximenes will bear the weight that Stroud places on it. It seems clear that in the Hellenistic period the ἄξονες survived and could be seen by those who wished to see them; and that it was known that the term κύρβεις also had been applied to the inscribed collection of the ancient laws, but that there was then no certain knowledge of how if at all the κύρβεις had differed from the ἄξονες: I conclude with Ruschenbusch and Andrewes that most probably both terms had been applied to the same set of objects. The most important Hellenistic texts are those which cite the views of Eratosthenes and Polemon, which Jacoby conveniently assembles as Erat. 241 F 37: Eratosthenes regarded ἄξονες and κύρβεις as identical (F 37a); and whereas he believed them to be τρίγωνοι Polemon noted that the ἄξονες were really τετράγωνοι but ὅταν ἐπὶ τὸ στενὸν κλιθῶσι τῆς γωνίας they might appear τρίγωνοι; they were man-sized, with rectangular wooden faces, and with pivots at the ends which enabled readers to rotate them (F 37b, c). An ἄξων should be an axle, or an object which revolves on an axle (e.g. Hom. *Il.* xvi. 378), and the requirement will best be met by wooden beams of square section, inscribed (doubtless βουστροφηδόν: Euphorion *ap.* Harp., Phot., Suid. [*O* 104], ὁ κάτωθεν νόμος) on all four faces; a viewer who saw the beams with the angle projecting towards him, and did not examine them closely, might imagine that they were of triangular section. Most scholars, including Ruschenbusch, have envisaged the ἄξονες as set vertically in a frame (cf. *L.S.* 204. 3; 413. 15 = *E.M.* [115. 45] ἄξονες); Andrewes and Stroud follow L. H. Jeffery (*Local Scripts of Archaic Greece*, 51–2) in preferring a horizontal setting, but this is perhaps more than should be extracted from ἑκατέρωθεν (F 37b) and the fact that the axles of vehicles are horizontal.[8] The meaning of κύρβεις must remain uncertain: Miss Jeffery (*op. cit.*, 53–5) and Andrewes are among those who follow Oliver in giving it an abstract meaning, as in Apoll. 244 F 107b; Ruschenbusch (*op. cit.*, 20–2) refers κύρβεις to the complete monuments and ἄξονες specifically to the rotating beams.

The ἄξονες survived substantially intact to the time of Polemon, who apparently saw them in the prytaneum. Citations of laws from numbered ἄξονες confirm that they survived long enough for their contents to be copied by later Greeks; Androtion quotes a law naming the colacretae, whose office was abolished *c*. 411 (324 F 36: cf. on §iii), and *A.P.* quotes from τοῖς νόμοις τοῖς Σόλωνος οἷς οὐκέτι χρῶνται; in the republication of (post-Solonian) laws concerning the boule a curious lacuna seems to indicate that the ἀναγραφεῖς appointed in 410 were scrupulously careful not to tamper with ancient texts (*IG* i² 114, 44 [line 43, Wade-Gery, *BSA* xxxiii 1932/3, 113–22, and *IG* i³ 105], with D. M. Lewis, *JHS* lxxxvii 1967, 132); and Ruschenbusch and Andrewes produce further arguments for the survival of an authentic text of Solon's laws. Though an orator might ascribe to Solon any law which he wished to cite with approval, it was possible to discover which were in fact the laws of Solon and to quote their texts: the objections of Hignett (*H.A.C.*, 22–7 cf. 313) are not fatal.[9] Ruschenbusch produced a calculation of the number of ἄξονες needed to contain Solon's code (*op. cit.*,

---

[8] Dow's revival in *AJA*² lxv 1961, 349–51, of a suggestion by Σ. Α. Κουμανούδης, 'Εφ. Ἀρχ. iii 1885, 215–18, that the curiously-shaped stone on which *IG* i² 2 is inscribed is evidence for an ἄξων resembling a paddle-wheel in section, is certainly to be rejected: cf. Ruschenbusch, *op. cit.*, 24 n. 48.

[9] D. H. Thomas ('Aristotle's Treatment of Historical Material in the *Politics*', i. 134–8 with ii. 460–7) has argued that ἄξονες did survive to the fifth and fourth centuries, but what they contained was not the original Solonian code but a revision of it by Cleisthenes: (*a*) if Solon's legislation is dated to his archonship the reference to the Isthmian Games in the law *ap*. Pl. *Sol*. 23. iii, D.L. 1. 55, is impossible, if it is dated later πρὶν ἢ Σόλωνα ἄρξαι in the law *ap*. Pl. *Sol*. 19. iv is unacceptably ambiguous, and in either case if the first coins are post-Solonian the drachmae of the laws *ap*. Pl. *Sol*. 23, esp. iv, are impossible; (*b*) 8. iv looks anachronistic as a formulation of Solon's νόμος εἰσαγγελίας; (*c*) the formulation of the law *ap*. 16. x is not anachronistic, but the preface θέσμια τάδε Ἀθηναίων ἐστὶ καὶ πάτρια can hardly be Solonian; (*d*) the use of a σημεῖον in 8. i suggests that the

25), but this is extremely precarious (see Stroud, *U. Calif. Pub. Cl. Stud.* iii 1968, 59–60).

ἔστησαν ἐν τῇ στοᾷ τῇ βασιλείῳ: After earlier attempts to bestow this title on other buildings (e.g. H. A. Thompson, *Hesp.* vi 1937, 64–76, 225–6; *Agora Guide*[2], 61–4), the Stoa of the Basileus was found in the excavations of 1970. It is the northernmost building on the west side of the Agora; the earliest date considered for it is the middle of the sixth century, and on account of the reused material in it Thompson now assigns it to the second quarter of the fifth (T. L. Shear, jr., *Hesp.* xl 1971, 243–60 with plates 45–50, xliv 1975, 365–70 with plate 82, H. A. Thompson & R. E. Wycherley, *The Athenian Agora*, xiv. 83–90, *Agora Guide*[3], 82–7; Thompson's later date announced in a lecture given to the Archaeological Institute of America in Washington, D.C., 20 October 1978, cf. *Agora Guide*[3], 84; cf. Paus. I. 3. i, 14. vi). This cannot therefore have been the original location of the ἄξονες, but by the end of the fifth century it had become their home: Draco's homicide law was obtained from the basileus and republished in front of the stoa (M&L 86, 7–8); on its completion the revised code of laws was displayed ἐν τῇ στοᾷ, ... εἰς τὸν τοῖχον, ἵνα περ πρότερον ἀνεγράφησαν (And. I. *Myst.* 82, decree *ap.* 84). According to Anax. 72 F 13, τοὺς ἄξονας καὶ τοὺς κύρβεις ἄνωθεν ἐκ τῆς ἀκροπόλεως εἰς τὸ βουλευτήριον καὶ τὴν ἀγορὰν μετέστησεν Ἐφιάλτης; Poll. VIII. 128 substitutes the prytaneum for the bouleuterium: many have been persuaded by Wilamowitz, *A.u.A.*, i. 45 n. 7, that this was a metaphorical way of saying that Ephialtes made the government of the state more democratic, but Jacoby *ad loc.* was prepared to accept it as a literal statement. Prof. Thompson suggests that the stoa was built to provide a new home for the ἄξονες (which were placed on the platform at the foot of the walls); that the revised code was written in ink on the back wall (cf. *IG* i[2] 94, 22–5; contr. below, pp. 441–2), perhaps as a

---

content of the ἄξονες was known not to be identical with the Solonian code. The most serious point is the first (*a*), in reply to which I should say that I date Solon's legislation to his archonship (5. ii with commentary); the law *ap.* Pl. *Sol.* 23. iii is not said to come from the ἄξονες, and many have doubted its authenticity (e.g. Adcock, *C.A.H.*, iv[1]. 44; Ruschenbusch, *op. cit.*, includes it as F 143 in his category *Unbrauchbares, Zweifelhaftes, Falsches*), but in any case it is possible that there were games called Isthmian before the refoundation which Eusebius dated 581/0 (cf. Busolt, *G.G.*, i[2]. 653); I accept that coinage is post-Solonian (10 with commentary) but believe that it was already possible in Solon's time to refer to standard weights of uncoined silver (8. iii with commentary). (*b*) I agree with Thomas that 8. iv is anachronistic, but do not feel obliged to believe that this formulation of the law was to be found on the ἄξονες; (*c*) I imagine that the addition of the preface to the law *ap.* 16. x belongs to a separate stele rather than to the ἄξονες; (*d*) I believe that the purpose of the σημεῖον in 8. i is not to establish a fact but to confirm the reasonableness of a known fact.

temporary measure; and that the stones on which the code was inscribed were set up not in the stoa but in front of it (he now doubts the excavators' claim that the building was adapted to receive them), and were later moved to the area of the Tholos and bouleuterium. Stroud, who distinguishes between ἄξονες and κύρβεις, suggests that Ephialtes placed the ἄξονες as museum pieces in the prytaneum and the κύρβεις in the stoa (*Athens Comes of Age*, 24, *U. Calif. Pub. Cl. Stud.* xix 1979, 12–13, 44). If there was only one set of objects, not two, that set will have been placed in the stoa by Ephialtes and will perhaps have been moved to the prytaneum when the revised code was published at the beginning of the fourth century; at the beginning of the second century Polemon saw the ἄξονες in the prytaneum (Erat. 241 F 37c); by about 50 B.C. they had been seriously damaged (Ruschenbusch, *op. cit.*, 37–8); and by the time of Plutarch only small fragments survived, still in the prytaneum (Pl. *Sol.* 25. i).†

καὶ ὤμοσαν χρήσεσθαι πάντες: The text implies that the oath was taken at the end of the process, when Solon produced his new code, as does the reference to an oath taken by the boule in Pl. *Sol.* 25. iii (likewise mentioned after the publication of the laws); but in H. I. 29. ii the Athenians ὁρκίοισι ... μεγάλοισι κατείχοντο δέκα ἔτεα χρήσεσθαι νόμοισι τοὺς ἄν σφι Σόλων θῆται (cf. on §ii), and that indefinite clause should imply that the oath was taken in advance, when Solon was given his commission. In view of the dissatisfaction which Solon's reforms provoked, an oath when he was appointed is more likely.

One is tempted to think, particularly in the light of Plutarch's limitation of the oath to the boule, that πάντες must be wrong and that in a city state embracing the whole of Attica the taking of an oath by all the citizens was not feasible; but it was thought feasible in 410 (decree *ap.* And. I. *Myst.* 97: κατὰ φυλὰς καὶ κατὰ δήμους) and 403 (And. I. *Myst.* 90), and instances can be found in other, admittedly less populous, cities (Megara in 424, T. IV. 74. ii; Cyrene *c.* 400, D.S. XIV. 34. vi; Mytilene and Tegea in 324, Tod 201, 31–2, 202, 57 sqq.; Tauric Chersonese *c.* 300, *SIG*[3] 360; Cos and Calymnus end C3, *Svt.* 545), so the temptation should be resisted. Cleisthenes' deme organisation did not yet, of course, exist: probably the oath was administered through the phratries.

οἱ δ' ἐννέα ἄρχοντες ὀμνύοντες πρὸς τῷ λίθῳ: Cf. 55. v, where this piece of information about the archontic oath is repeated and further details are added (there it is said, more specifically and more plausibly, that the dedication is required from archons who accept δῶρα); in Pl. *Sol.* 25. iii this oath is taken by ἕκαστος τῶν θεσμοθετῶν, and there and in Plat. *Phaedr.* 235 D 8–E 1 the statue is to be life-sized and is to be dedicated at Delphi. The λίθος has now been found by the excavators in front of the Stoa of the Basileus, near the north wing (T. L. Shear, jr, *Hesp.* xl 1971, 259–60, H. A. Thompson & R. E. Wycherley, *The Athenian Agora*, xiv. 88, *Agora Guide*[3], 85; cf. Poll. viii. 86): Mrs E. T. Vermeule *ap. Agora Guide*[3], 315, suggests that it is a stone salvaged from the lintel of a Mycenaean tholos tomb and regarded as something both royal and sacred.

κατεφάτιζον: Cf. Pl. *Sol.* 25. iii (καταφατίζων). No other instance of the verb is cited in LSJ, and it is not repeated in 55. v; but Aristotle uses κατάφασις and καταφατικός in his logical works, e.g. *Cat.* 12 B 5–16. Wilamowitz, *A.u.A.*, i. 47–8, suggests that the verb is an archaic word of Ionic origin, used here as appropriate to the solemn declaration.

7. ii. κατέκλεισεν: Blass[2] was the first to read κατέκληισεν, which was accepted by Kaibel & Wilamowitz[3] and by Kenyon in his Berlin ed.; but that form would be surprising as late as the second half of the fourth century (Meisterhans & Schwyzer, *G.a.I.*, 36–8), and in the *corrigenda* of his Berlin ed. and his O.C.T. Kenyon preferred the later form. The verb means 'shut up': Sandys[2] cited And. III. *Pace*, 7, D. IV. *Phil. i.* 33, both of which refer to the 'shutting up' of Athens' resources νόμῳ to prevent their being squandered; here the νόμοι themselves are 'shut up' to prevent their being altered or repealed.

εἰς ἑκατὸν ἔτη: Cf. Pl. *Sol.* 25. i; but only ten years, H. i. 29. ii. Herodotus links this with the Athenians' oath to observe Solon's laws (cf. §i, above), and with the ten years of Solon's absence from Attica (i. 29. i, cf. *A.P.* 11. i with commentary, Pl. *Sol.* 25. vi): this makes sense, though it is odd that they have become separated in the later accounts. Those who appointed Solon and agreed to abide by his laws would be dead before a hundred years had passed, and until the fourth century most peace treaties and alliances were entered into for a fairly short period (but in M&L 17 Elis and Heraea make a hundred-year alliance, and a few perpetual alliances from the sixth and fifth centuries are known: see F. E. Adcock & D. J. Mosley, *Diplomacy in Ancient Greece*, 221), so it is more likely that he bound the Athenians to keep his laws only for ten years.

διέταξε τὴν πολιτείαν: Cf. τάξις in 3. i and 5. i. The verb means 'he ordered' or 'disposed': properly it is used of issuing commands, and in view of Solon's commission it must carry its full meaning here; contrast 29. v with commentary, where I argue that the subject of διέταξαν is probably οἱ αἱρεθέντες, who merely made recommendations which were accepted as binding by an assembly of the citizens.

7. iii. τιμήματι: τίμημα is a valuation in general, and a valuation of property for political purposes in particular. In the fourth century the tax called εἰσφορά was levied on the τίμημα of all citizens and metics whose declared property was worth more than a certain amount (e.g. D. xiv. *Symm*. 19); a state in which political rights depended on a property qualification could be described as a πολιτεία ἀπὸ τιμημάτων (Is. xii. *Panath*. 131, Pl. *Phoc*. 27. v, cf. D.S. xviii. 18. iv), and in an unparalleled phrase the terms of reconciliation of 403 describe those who possess such a qualification as τοῖς τὰ τιμήματα παρεχομένοις (39. vi with commentary); the use of the word in M&L 78, *c* 2, is obscure. Here τιμήματι was first read by C. Wessely, and has been accepted by Kenyon and other editors: insertion or emendation have been proposed by some who find the text harsh, but it is better to accept the harshness. In 8. i *A.P.* writes of sortition ἐκ τῶν τιμημάτων (cf. Theophrastus, quoted p. 551); Poll. viii. 129 calls the four classes τιμήματα, but *A.P.* here calls them τέλη.

διεῖλεν εἰς τέτταρα τέλη ... καὶ πρότερον: Cf. Pl. *Sol*. 18. i–ii; Arist. *Pol*. ii. 1274 A 19–21 lists the classes in the wrong order, with τῆς καλουμένης ἱππάδος between ζευγιτῶν and τὸ θητικόν (καλουμένης may be due to the use of the feminine for this class only [cf. pp. 142–3], or may perhaps hint at the disagreement on the significance of the term which *A.P.* discusses below).

In Plutarch there is no suggestion that the classes already existed (cf. Harp. ἱππάς, πεντακοσιομέδιμνον), but in our text of *A.P.* pre-existing classes are given a new significance. Many have sought to obtain an easier sentence and agreement between *A.P.* and Plutarch by condemning καθάπερ διῄρητο καὶ πρότερον as one of the insertions made with the 'Draconian constitution' to fit that into *A.P.* (cf. pp. 85, 86); but it would be very surprising if the man responsible for the insertion should have thought of altering this sentence while leaving many other affected sentences untouched (3. i and 41. ii are far more obvious targets for alteration), later writers who used *A.P.* were not bound to repeat these words, and although the awkward expression may perhaps betray *A.P.*'s fitting a piece of information from another source into his main narrative we should not necessarily lay the blame on 'Draco' here. The nomenclature suggests that the πεντακοσιομέδιμνοι are a later addition to a structure in which ἱππεῖς, ζευγῖται and θῆτες already existed (but had not existed for very long: see below): probably what Solon did was to distinguish the very richest citizens from the other ἱππεῖς, and for the first time give the classes a precise definition and a political function.[10]

---

[10] Moore, 218, supposes that all four classes already existed and πεντακοσιομέδιμνοι is a new name for the class previously styled εὐπατρίδαι. E. L. Smithson, *Hesp*. xxxvii 1968, 92–7, suggests that a chest with five model 'granaries' on its lid,

It has usually been thought that the old division into three classes, like Solon's division into four, was primarily economic and occupational—that the ἱππεῖς were men who could keep a horse, the ζευγῖται were men who could keep a pair of oxen, and the θῆτες were men who, not rising to the latter level, were not economically independent (in §iv *A.P.* rejects this economic interpretation, but it is accepted in Poll. VIII. 129–31 cf. 132). Some, however, have claimed that military considerations were primary, the ἱππεῖς being the aristocratic class of cavalry and the ζευγῖται (as in Pl. *Pel.* 23. iv) the hoplites (C. Cichorius, *Griechische Studien H. Lipsius dargebracht*, 135–40, cf. Beloch, *G.G.*², I. i. 303 with n. 1); more recently this explanation has been preferred by Andrewes, *The Greek Tyrants*, 87, and L. H. Jeffery, *Archaic Greece*, 93 with 107 n. 6; G. E. M. de Ste. Croix in an unpublished essay believes that the three classes were always based on military status and suspects that (unlike the πεντακοσιομέδιμνοι) even after Solon they may not have been defined in economic terms. On the qualifications see §iv with commentary. The military explanation of the ἱππεῖς and ζευγῖται seems the better (in particular ζευγῖται ought to denote those who are yoked, not those who own a yoke-pair), but the men below hoplite level had no serious part to play in the warfare of archaic Greece, and the word used of them, θῆτες, is undoubtedly economic and occupational (cf. p. 91): this need not be disconcerting, particularly if the threefold division was in common use before Solon gave it official significance. ζευγίτης, in referring to a hoplite, refers to his being a member of a phalanx: since the introduction of the hoplite phalanx in Greece is to be dated not earlier than the beginning of the seventh century (cf. A. M. Snodgrass, *JHS* lxxxv 1965, 110–22, esp. 110–16, J. B. Salmon, *JHS* xcvii 1977, 84–101, esp. 85–93), the classification which Solon adopted was not more than a century old.†

For theories supposing the existence of other economic classes in earlier Athens see pp. 68, 71–2.

τὰς μὲ[ν ἄλλ]ας ἀρχὰς: First suggested by Wilcken, and by Diels *ap.* Kenyon's Berlin ed., and accepted by most editors; but με[γάλ]ας was suggested by Fritz & Kapp, 155 n. 18 (cf. Arist. *Pol.* III. 1282 A 41), and M. H. Chambers, *TAPA* xcvi 1965, 34–5, read μεγάλας; [[με[γίστ]ας]] was restored and deleted by Blass[1], and Chambers in *TAPA* cii 1971, 43, identifies in a separate papyrus fragment from Oxyrhynchus a version of this passage with the reading μεγίστας, and so accepts that as the word to be restored in the London

---

† found in a grave of the mid ninth century, was intended to advertise its owner's status as a πεντακοσιομέδιμνος (cf. the use of horses on funerary vases by men of 'knightly' status: J. N. Coldstream, *Geometric Greece*, 76–7), but I doubt if so specific a message was intended.

papyrus; Dr J. D. Thomas finds μεγάλας a likelier reading than μὲν ἄλλας, and does not think μεγίστας possible. Strictly any adjective is superfluous here, since the thetes' membership of the ecclesia and heliaea ought not to rank as an ἀρχή at all (cf. §iv; but see also p. 108). Despite the attractions of μὲν, μεγάλας or μεγίστας gives a better sense than ἄλλας; μεγίστας has its attractions (cf. Plat. Theag. 127 E 2, πολλὰς ἤδη ἀρχὰς καὶ τὰς μεγίστας Ἀθηναίοις ἦρξας; but in A.P. 3. ii μέγισται... καὶ πρῶται τῶν ἀρχῶν characterises the three senior archonships); but Chambers' fragment if correctly identified diverges too much from the London papyrus to be a *verbatim* quotation of A.P., and μεγάλας is therefore to be preferred.

τοὺς ἐννέα ἄρχοντας: Cf. 8. i with commentary. The archons are treated at length in the second part of A.P., chs 55–9, and a reconstruction of the early history of the office has been given in 3. i–v.

τοὺς ταμίας: The treasurers of Athena. These were appointed from the highest class only (8. i), and that fact is repeated in 47. i, where they are treated further.

τοὺς πωλητάς: The 'sellers', makers of state contracts and sellers of confiscated property. They are treated in 47. ii–iii.

τοὺς ἕνδεκα: Gaolers and executioners, treated in 52. i. If the theory of Ruschenbusch were correct, that the one penalty of the Solonian code was ἀτιμία and that sentences which had to be acted on were introduced later, there would be no need for the Eleven as early as this; but I doubt if he is right (cf. p. 111). K. Freeman, *The Work and Life of Solon*, 76, suggests that the number was tied to the ten tribes and that these officers did not number eleven before Cleisthenes' reform; but there is no obvious reason why ten tribes should have produced eleven gaolers, and I suspect that the number survived from an earlier date.

τοὺς κωλακρέτας: 'Collectors of hams' (compare the original meaning of ταμίας, one who carves or dispenses, e.g. Hom. *Il.* XIX. 44; in *Il.* IV. 84 Zeus is ἀνθρώπων ταμίης πολέμοιο, and that usage persists, especially in verse; but in prose from H. II. 121. a. ii onwards a ταμίας is most commonly a treasurer). This title (found also at Cyzicus: *CIG* 3660) stands in contrast to the immediately intelligible titles of most Athenian offices, and must be old; in the latter part of the fifth century the colacretae were the paying officers of the state treasury (and whereas most officials served for a year these served only for one prytany: A. Wilhelm, *Sb. Wien* CCXVII. v 1939, 52–72); *c.* 411, when Athens' financial position in the Peloponnesian War was critical, the office was abolished and an enlarged board of Hellenotamiae administered both the city's funds and the funds of the Delian League (cf. 30. ii with commentary); in the fourth century the Athenians ceased to maintain one central treasury and instead allocated funds to a variety of spending authorities (cf. 48. ii with commentary). See Rhodes, *A.B.*, 102–3, cf. 99 n. 4.

ἀνάλογον τῷ μεγέθει τοῦ τιμήματος: See on 8. i for the archons and the treasurers of Athena; it is not known what qualifications were required for other offices.

τοῖς δὲ τὸ θητικὸν τελοῦσιν: (*sc. τέλος*). This is the standard formula for 'those belonging to the thetic class' (cf. Ste. Croix, *C&M* xiv 1953, 42–4). The original meaning of the word is 'perform' or 'pay'; the latter is its normal meaning in classical prose, especially with reference to the payment of taxes; and since Greeks were often divided into categories for purposes of taxation τελεῖν εἴς τινας came to mean 'belong to a certain class' (e.g. H. II. 51. ii, VI. 53. i, 108. v: in VI. 108 the sense of paying what is due may also be present). This inevitably prompts the question, whether θητικὸν τελεῖν and the parallel expressions used in §iv are fossilised expressions meaning 'belong to the thetic class' and no more, or originally they also carried the more literal meaning 'pay taxes as a member of the thetic class'. Poll. VIII. 129–30 (from what source is not known) specifies the sums which the different classes ἀνήλισκον εἰς τὸ δημόσιον (and VIII. 86 misinterprets as a reference to membership of the Solonian classes a question at the archons' δοκιμασία about payment of taxes: cf. on 55. iii); Böckh, *Staatshaushaltung der Athener*[3], i. 583–91, based on this a theory of the Solonian classes as taxation classes, which won some support, but it was denounced by Beloch, *Hermes* xx 1885, 237–61, and Hignett was able to write that it 'has long been exploded' (*H.A.C.*, 100). Pollux' figures, expressed in terms of the talent and mina, can hardly be authentic for the Solonian period, and there is no sign that in the fifth and fourth centuries there was any connection between taxation and the Solonian classes; but we know so little about the financing of early Athens (cf. 8. iii with commentary, on the ναυκραρίαι) that it would be unwise to rule out the possibility that Solon did base some form of taxation on these classes.

ἐκκλησίας: Cf. Arist. *Pol.* II. 1274 A 15–21, III. 1281 B 31–4. It is implied rather than clearly stated (2. ii–iii, cf. 'Draconian constitution', 4. ii *init.*) that previously the thetes were excluded from the assembly: many have accepted the implication, believing that the thetes were first admitted to the assembly by Solon (e.g. Busolt, *G.G.*, ii[2]. 273 n. 1, Kahrstedt, *Staatsgebiet und Staatsangehörige in Athen*, 59); Hignett believed on *a priori* grounds that they were excluded until the tyranny and finally admitted by Cleisthenes (*H.A.C.*, 79, 84, 98, 117–23, 143); on the other hand Masaracchia argued that in this respect as in others Solon did not give the poor a new right but reaffirmed an old one (*Solone*, 164–7). Suspicion is indeed better directed against the assumption that the thetes were

COMMENTARY ON THE *ATH. POL.* [7. iii

excluded from the assembly before Solon: ζευγῖται and θῆτες were probably then convenient labels of no practical importance except when hoplites were needed for fighting, and it is unlikely that there was a formal distinction between full citizens, who could attend the assembly, and inferior citizens, who could not. More probably every citizen could attend, though as in the case of Thersites (Hom. *Il.* II. 84 sqq.) the lower-class men were expected, both before Solon's reforms and for some time after (cf. Solon, fr. 6. 1 West *ap. A.P.* 12. ii), to attend as 'brute votes' rather than active members; and assemblies were rarely held and little business was laid before them. Solon will have strengthened the assembly not by adding the thetes to it but by giving it a probouleutic council independent of the Areopagus, and perhaps by prescribing regular meetings (8. iv with commentary). For a non-committal discussion of the Solonian assembly see G. T. Griffith, *Ancient Society and Institutions . . . V. Ehrenberg*, 115–38, esp. 117–22.

δικαστηρίων: Cf. ch. 9 with commentary.

7. iv. πεντακόσια μέτρα τὰ συνάμφω ξηρὰ καὶ ὑγρά: We are not told how wet and dry measures, μέδιμνοι of grain (the principal crop being barley) and μετρηταί (equivalent to ¾ μέδιμνος) of olive oil or wine, were combined in a single scale: the yield of olives and vines is more variable than that of grain; a μετρητής of oil or wine would be more valuable than a μέδιμνος of wheat, and wheat would be more valuable than barley. A recent estimate suggests as likely average yields per acre[11] 8 bushels (rather more than 5½ μέδιμνοι) of barley (but this figure should be halved to allow for alternate years of fallow), 10 imperial gallons (rather less than 1¼ μετρηταί) of oil, or 100–150 imperial gallons (11½–17½ μετρηταί) of wine (A. French, *The Growth of the Athenian Economy*, 20–1 cf. 176; cf. also A. Jardé, *Les Céréales dans l'antiquité grecque*, i. 59–60, 186, C. G. Starr, *The Economic and Social Growth of Early Greece, 800–500 B.C.*, 153–4); in fact a farmer would not normally cultivate one crop to the total exclusion of the others. Explanations too sophisticated to be credible for early Attica must be avoided; and it is possible that we should keep to the crude if obvious interpretation of the texts, that the μέδιμνοι of grain and μετρηταί of oil and wine which a man's land produced were simply added together as 'measures' of produce. Alternatively, if a slightly greater degree of fairness and sophistication is thought possible, we should follow a line of thought first indicated by K. M. T. Chrimes, *CR* xlvi 1932, 2–4: she suggested that all land was assessed in terms of its potential grain yield (which

[11] The equivalent yields per hectare are: 7·2 hectolitres (rather more than 13¼ μέδιμνοι) of barley, 112 litres (rather less than 3 μετρηταί) of oil and 1,120–1,685 litres of wine (30–45 μετρηταί).

itself does not seem likely and is certainly not what *A.P.* and Plutarch are saying); G. Thomson, *Studies* . . . *D. M. Robinson*, ii. 848, suggests more attractively that all produce was assessed on a 'wheat standard', and Ste. Croix in an unpublished essay corrects this to a 'barley standard'—that is, a μέδιμνος of barley was reckoned as the equivalent of (say) ½ μέδιμνος of wheat or ¼ μετρητής of oil, so that a man whose land produced 300 μέδιμνοι of barley and 100 μετρηταί of oil might be assessed at 700 measures of produce. Presumably farmers were asked to declare how much they grew in a 'normal' year, or perhaps in a stated year, and their declaration was accepted unless someone challenged it.

The classification as reported takes no account of other forms of wealth, such as ownership of animals or the proceeds of trade, though in fr. 13. 43–62 West Solon mentions agriculture merely as one means of livelihood among many: as long as agriculture was of primary importance for most citizens a classification on this rough and ready basis will not have been conspicuously unfair (and Ste. Croix points out that as a qualification for offices which might tempt the holders to embezzlement agricultural land gives better security than income from trade or even possession of a herd of cattle). Some scholars reluctant to believe that agricultural produce was the sole basis of classification have adduced Pl. *Sol.* 23. iii, εἰς μέν γε τὰ τιμήματα τῶν θυσιῶν λογίζεται πρόβατον καὶ δραχμὴν ἀντὶ μεδίμνου: Wilcken, *Hermes* lxiii 1928, 236–8, proposed to read οὐσιῶν for θυσιῶν and to use the sentence as evidence that other kinds of wealth were after all taken into account; but C. M. A. van den Oudenrijn, *Mnem.*[4] v 1952, 19–27, demonstrated convincingly that it refers not to the Solonian classes but to sacrificial offerings (for a recent discussion of that vexing passage see K. H. Waters, *JHS* lxxx 1960, 185–8). It has been widely assumed that later generations applied a new means of classification, with a monetary basis (e.g. Hignett, *H.A.C.*, 142–3, 225–6; denied by Kahrstedt, *Staatsgebiet und Staatsangehörige in Athen*, 251, 255–60): such a change would have been sensible, though there is no evidence that it was ever made, but *pace* Hignett the assessment can never have been in terms of annual income. As for the purposes of εἰσφορά, men's wealth in monetary terms was regularly reckoned on a basis of capital (cf. Busolt, *G.G.*, ii[2]. 269); *SEG* ix 1, 6–15, an inscription of the late fourth century from Cyrene, defines the qualification for citizenship in terms of capital securely possessed by or owed to the citizen. For the extent to which this subdivision of the citizen body persisted in the fifth and fourth centuries see pp. 145–6.

ἱππάδα: *Sc.* τάξιν, though the other three classes have a neuter adjective with τέλος understood. The same phraseology is used in Pl. *Sol.* 18. i, Isae. VII. *Her. Apoll.* 39; cf. Arist. *Pol.* II. 1274 A 21, which switches to the feminine immediately after τρίτου τέλους: the adjective appears to be an old one.

ὡς δ' ἔνιοί φασι τοὺς ἱπποτροφεῖν δυναμένους: See on §iii for the significance of the terms ἱππεῖς, ζευγῖται, θῆτες. Clearly the question was debated in the fourth century: ἔνιοι cite the name of the class and (presumably, equestrian) dedications by members of it (cf. p. 137 n. 10); A.P. considers the economic and occupational criterion, is silent on the military criterion, and finds it εὐλογώτερον that the lower classes like the highest should have been defined in terms of produce. How the classes acquired their names, and how Solon defined membership of the classes, are questions which he does not distinguish. It has regularly been accepted that his is the right answer to the second question, and that Solon defined each of the classes in terms of produce: Ste. Croix in an unpublished essay suggests that only the πεντακοσιομέδιμνοι were so defined, while the ἱππεῖς and ζευγῖται were simply the cavalry and the hoplites and it was left to a citizen's patriotism (and his neighbour's jealousy) to ensure that he was correctly registered; D. M. MacDowell, *The Law in Classical Athens*, 160, dealing simply with military service, believes that men could choose whether to serve as hoplites or as light-armed troops or oarsmen. There is no evidence for reassessments apart from Athemion's epigram (on which see next note), and we might expect to find some if they had occurred at all often; but not all Athenians were always eager to do their patriotic duty, and it is hard to believe that the liability to cavalry and to hoplite service were never defined (for the requirement of health and wealth in the cavalry see 49. ii with commentary). I therefore think it likelier that all four classes were defined, as *A.P.* states, but suspect that a man would retain his class membership, and a son would inherit his father's class membership, unless he took positive steps to have it changed.

On the kinds of argument to which *A.P.* resorts on disputed points see Introduction, pp. 26–7. εὔλογος is used regularly in Arist. *Pol.* of the reasonableness of what is known to be the case (e.g. I. 1258 B 2, II. 1269 B 40, III. 1279 A 39), and εὐλογώτερον here should not be taken as a sign that the criterion used by Solon was not known (cf. below, on the σημεῖον in 8. i).

Διφίλου Ἀνθεμίων ... : The statue must be that of Anthemion: the error (which is avoided in Poll. VIII. 131) should perhaps be blamed on a copyist rather than the author, and can most simply be corrected by deleting Διφίλου after εἰκών (E. S. Thompson, *CR* v 1891, 225, C. Radinger, *Philol.* l 1891, 400; A. S. Murray, *CR* v 1891, 108, said by Kenyon [Berlin ed., O.C.T.] to delete Διφίλου and by Sandys[2] to defend it, in fact accepted that the statue was Anthemion's and proposed the less likely correction Διφίλου ⟨Ἀνθεμίωνος⟩). In inscriptions pentameters used otherwise than in elegiac couplets are rare but do occur (see F. D. Allen, *P. Am. Sch. Ath.* iv 1885/6, 42–3, K. F. Smith, *AJP* xxii 1901, 173–82, A. E. Raubitschek, *Dedications from the Athenian Akropolis*, pp. 205–7); here editors' suspicion has been aroused by the pair of pentameters, and to produce an elegiac couplet attempts have been made to restore a hexameter with the aid of some MSS of Pollux. J. B. Mayor's Διφίλου Ἀνθεμίων τήνδ' ⟨εἰκόν'⟩ ἔθηκε θεοῖσι is the most attractive reconstruction (*CR* v 1891, 177); but it is possible that *A.P.*'s quotation is correct.

Anthemion's statue and epigram are part of the evidence adduced by ἔνιοι, and the present ἀνάκειται does not guarantee that *A.P.* has checked the evidence, but we may presume that a statue which was standing when his source wrote was still standing when he wrote. The statue will almost certainly postdate the return of the Athenians after the Persian sack in 480–479, and it is an attractive guess (but by no means certain: other rich Anthemions are known) that the Anthemion who rose to be a ἱππεύς is the father of the politician Anytus, active at the end of the fifth and the beginning of the fourth century (cf. 27. v, 34. iii, with commentary: this was suggested by W. Aly, *NJA* xvi 1913, 170, Raubitschek, *op. cit.*, p. 206, cf. Davies, *A.P.F.*, 40–1). The name Diphilus is fairly common in Athens: the earliest known bearer of it is the Δίπιλος καλός of Beazley, *A.R.V.*[2], i. 371 no. 24, by the Brygos painter (*c.* 500–480).

The above note follows the normal assumption that θητικοῦ ἀντὶ τέλους ἱππάδ' ἀμειψάμενος means 'acquiring hippad in place of thetic rank', but this has not gone unchallenged. Miss L. H. Jeffery in an unpublished note points out that the pair of pentameters is not the only obstacle to straightforward acceptance of what *A.P.* says: Diphilus is an aristocratic kind of name rather than a name that a θής might bear; a ἱππεύς whose father had been a θής might well not wish to advertise that fact; and θεοῖς has no parallel among surviving epigrams on the Acropolis (we should expect θεῷ, sc. Ἀθηναίᾳ). She therefore suggests that Anthemion's change of status should be interpreted with the aid of Pl. *Cim.* 5. ii–iii: Anthemion is to be thought of as an ἑταῖρος of Cimon in 480, who though a ἱππεύς volunteered to serve as a ναύμαχος ἀνήρ (i.e. an ἐπιβάτης, a kind of fighter normally recruited from the thetic class: see T. vi. 43 with Dover's commentary; the hoplite ἐπιβάται of viii. 24. ii are exceptional), and vowed a dedication to a plurality of gods if all turned out well; the first line alone belongs to Anthemion's dedication, while the second was perhaps added by a contemporary wit but fooled later readers. A θής might bear an ambitious name, and a man who had risen in the world might be proud of the fact; the plurality of gods is unusual but does not necessarily prove that the second line does not belong to Anthemion's dedication. What is crucial is the use of the verb: LSJ reports that the active ἀμείβειν is normally used with the accusative of what is obtained, but there is at least one instance where what is obtained is in the genitive and what is given up is in the accusative (Hom. *Il.* VI. 235-6); similarly the middle ἀμείβεσθαι is normally used with the accusative of what is obtained, and the nearest approach to the contrary that I have found is ἀμείψασθαι sc. *accus.* πρὸς νόμισμα = 'give up in exchange for money' in Pl. *Aem.* 23. ix: while it is not impossible that the words should have the meaning which Miss Jeffery suggests it is unlikely, and we should continue to understand them as they were understood by *A.P.*†

ζευγίσιον δὲ τελεῖν τοὺς διακόσια ... ποιοῦντας: *E.M.* (410. 1) ζευγίσιον, with material in Gaisford's commentary, confirms that this is the correct form; but the MSS of Poll. VIII. 131 and other lexica listing Solon's classes give ζευγήσιον. The papyrus' figure of 200 measures is confirmed by Poll. VIII. 130 and other texts derived from *A.P.*; but in a law *ap.* [D.] XLIII. *Mac.* 54 a next of kin who does not wish to marry an heiress must give her a dowry of 500 drachmae if he is a πεντακοσιομέδιμνος, 300 if he is a ἱππεύς, or 150 if he is a ζευγίτης, from which Böckh (*Staatshaushaltung der Athener*³, i. 581) argued that the qualification for the ζευγῖται ought to be 150 measures rather than 200. Ste. Croix (who believes that only the πεντακοσιομέδιμνοι had a qualification defined in terms of produce: cf. p. 143) agrees with Böckh in finding it incredible that the qualifications of the ἱππεῖς and the ζευγῖται were in the proportion 3:2, and supposes that *A.P.* was guessing on the basis of a law which resembled that in [D.] XLIII. *Mac.* 54 but yielded the proportion 5:3:2—but we have no information which would justify us in rejecting *A.P.*'s figures as correct for Solon's definition of the classes.

οὐδεμιᾶς μετέχοντας ἀρχῆς: Cf. §iii with commentary.

ἔρηται τὸν μέλλοντα κληροῦσθαί τιν' ἀρχήν: The subject is probably ὁ θεσμοθέτης, as suggested by Sandys (cf. A. III. *Ctes.* 13); the question was presumably asked when men submitted their names as candidates. Attempts to restore a question on membership of a Solonian class in *A.P.*'s account of the archons' δοκιμασία, after the allotment had taken place (55. iii), are misguided: cf. *ad loc.*

οὐδ' ἂν εἰς εἴποι θητικόν: In 457/6 the zeugitae were admitted to the archonship but the thetes were not (26. ii), and the distinction between the two classes must still have been taken seriously; some have argued from [X.] *A.P.* i. 2 that by the time of that work the thetes were no longer legally excluded from office (e.g. Busolt, *G.G.*, III. i. 292 n. 6), but that is not a necessary conclusion; in the 350's the bouleutic oath still contained an undertaking not to imprison an accused man (except on certain charges) if he could produce three guarantors τὸ αὐτὸ τέλος τελοῦντας (D. XXIV. *Tim.* 144), and Isaeus could still complain of a man's making a low assessment of his property for εἰσφορά but claiming ἱππάδα τελεῖν (VII. *Her. Apoll.* 39). Apparently by the time of *A.P.* the law which excluded the thetes from all offices had not been repealed but had become a dead letter. Probably the allocation of men to the Solonian classes continued but no one took it seriously and any man wishing to stand for any office would claim to belong to the requisite class. It is likely that the basis of classification, even if redefined in terms of capital, was not revised to keep pace with changes in values and in individual men's fortunes (cf. pp. 142–3), and as the classification became increasingly unrealistic there would be an increasing temptation to ignore it: possibly by the time of *A.P.* one could be a πεντακοσιομέδιμνος and so legally qualified to be treasurer of Athena, but yet πάνυ πένης (47. i with commentary).

8. i. τὰς δ' ἀρχὰς ἐποίησε κληρωτὰς ἐκ προκρίτων: Contrast Arist. *Pol.* II. 1273 B 35–1274 A 3, 1274 A 16–17, III. 1281 B 25–34, claiming that Solon retained the 'aristocratic' principle of election to office (in IV. 1298 B 8–11, 1300 A 34–B 1, the mixture of election and sortition is associated with the kind of constitution called πολιτεία); Plutarch does not pronounce on the question. Texts which have been cited in support of *A.P.*'s view that κλήρωσις ἐκ προκρίτων was an ancient institution include Is. VII. *Areop.* 22–3, XII. *Panath.* 145, [D.] LIX. *Neaer.* 75 (but little importance can be attached to D. XX. *Lept.* 90, a conventional ascription to Solon of the current law); also Pl. *Per.* 9. iv, Paus. IV. 5. x. The language of 13. ii has been thought, wrongly, to conflict with this passage (cf. *ad loc.*). To most of those who accept Aristotelian authorship *A.P.* gives Aristotle's later and therefore better judgment, or else what is said in *Pol.* can be regarded as covering κλήρωσις ἐκ προκρίτων (e.g. Wilamowitz, *A.u.A.*, i. 72–3, Gilbert, *C.A.S.A.*, 136 with n. 1, Fritz & Kapp, 155–6 n. 22), though some have dissented (e.g. Busolt, *G.G.*, ii². 274–7, Moore, 220–1); to the sceptical Hignett this is one of the main points on which *Pol.* expresses a better opinion than *A.P.*, and is therefore evidence against Aristotelian authorship (*H.A.C.*, 29, 321–6).†

Since *Pol.* insists that Solon made no change in the method of appointment, we must accept that the two texts disagree. *A.P.* quotes in support of his account the law governing the appointment of the treasurers of Athena, ᾧ χρώμενοι διατελοῦσιν ἔτι καὶ νῦν (which mentions κλήρωσις but not ἐκ προκρίτων; cf. 47. i); he believes that for a while this process was replaced by election, and that in 487/6 κλήρωσις ἐκ προκρίτων was restored τότε μετὰ τὴν τυραννίδα πρῶτον (22. v, whose credibility is weakened, but not fatally, by the accompanying claim that there were 500 πρόκριτοι each year: cf. *ad loc.*); later he remarks that (apparently at the time of Ephialtes' reform)

τὴν ... τῶν ἐννέα ἀρχόντων αἴρεσιν οὐκ ἐκίνουν, ἀλλ' ἕκτῳ ἔτει μετὰ τὸν Ἐφιάλτου θάνατον ἔγνωσαν καὶ ἐκ ζευγιτῶν προκρίνεσθαι τοὺς κληρωσομένους τῶν ἐννέα ἀρχόντων, καὶ πρῶτος ἦρξεν ἐξ αὐτῶν Μνησιθείδης

(457/6: 26. ii); when *A.P.* was written the 'college' of archons had been made up to ten by the addition of a secretary, ten προλαχόντες were allotted from each tribe, and one archon or the secretary was allotted from each group of ten (8. i with 55. i). *A.P.* tells a consistent story; Solon's laws survived, and were available for him to consult (cf. on 7. i); it can easily be argued that Aristotle did not make a thorough investigation when commenting on Solon in *Pol.*, and did not revise what he had said in *Pol.* when later he or a pupil did investigate (cf. Introduction, pp. 60–1). But *A.P.* requires more energetic defence than this: he quotes a law of Solon, but unfortunately not the law on the appointment of the archons, which would have established his case irrefutably; and this, together with the conflict between *A.P.* and *Pol.*, has inevitably given rise to the suspicion that the law on the appointment of the archons was not available, and that he was merely arguing from the procedures of his own day (e.g. Hignett, *H.A.C.*, 323–4, Day & Chambers, *A.H.A.D.*, 80–2). However, we should not demand too much of *A.P.*'s σημεῖον: even if Solon's laws were available for consultation, they were doubtless not consulted very often, and in referring to the still valid law on the treasurers of Athena *A.P.* may be not giving the evidence on which his belief is based so much as citing a familiar fact to confirm the reasonableness of an unfamiliar one (cf. the conclusion in 7. iv that the definition of the ἱππεῖς in terms of produce is εὐλογώτερον, with commentary *ad loc.*).

Sceptics find it improbable that sortition should have been used so early in Athens, and can see no reason why Solon should have introduced it for appointment to the archonship. Hignett claims that Is. XII. *Panath.* 145 and VII. *Areop.* 22–3 contradicts himself by attributing κλήρωσις ἐκ προκρίτων to different periods in the golden age of the past (*H.A.C.*, 323); but almost certainly Ste. Croix is right to argue, in an unpublished essay, that in both places Isocrates is using προκρίνειν not as a technical term meaning 'choose as members of the short list' but with its more usual meaning of 'choose', *tout court.* [D.] LIX. *Neaer.* 75 does allege χειροτονία ἐκ προκρίτων for the appointment of the king after the 'democratic reform' of Theseus, which may reflect a genuine tradition that appointment in two stages was a practice with a long history. We ought not to doubt the clear statement of 8. i and 47. i that the treasurers of Athena were still in *A.P.*'s own day appointed in accordance with a law of Solon which prescribed sortition within the class of πεντακοσιομέδιμνοι. The use of sortition to decide between men considered equally eligible was not peculiar to democratic constitutions (cf. on 4. iii), and in fact Solon's purpose in using κλήρωσις ἐκ προκρίτων for the archons may easily be imagined: the πρόκρισις of a large number of candidates would give a reasonable chance both to the Eupatrids and to the non-aristocratic rich now for the first time made eligible (cf. on §ii), while the use of the lot to make the final decision, if honestly performed, would make it hard for either class to gain an unfair predominance. Our conclusion should therefore be that *Pol.* is wrong and *A.P.* is right, and that Solon did introduce κλήρωσις ἐκ προκρίτων for the appointment of the archons. For the troubles which ensued see 13. i–ii with commentary.

The property qualification for the archonship is not stated. The office was opened to the zeugitae in 457/6 (26. ii): some have thought that it had been open to the first two classes from the time of Solon (e.g. Hignett, *H.A.C.*, 101–2, cf. 142, 156); others note that the archonship is limited to the same class as the treasurers of Athena in the 'Draconian constitution' (4. ii) and to the highest class by Demetrius of Phalerum (228 F 43 *ap.* Pl. *Arist.* 1. ii, writing of 489/8), and suppose that Solon restricted the archonship to the first class and the second was admitted later, though perhaps not as late as 489 (e.g. E. S. Staveley, *Greek and Roman Voting and Elections*, 33 with 239 n. 49). A final decision is impossible, but if from the beginning the archonship could be held only once in a man's life (stated for the fourth century in 62. iii, and no evidence suggests that the rule did not apply earlier) we may wonder whether the πεντακοσιομέδιμνοι were numerous enough for limitation to that class to be feasible.

ἑκάστη δέκα: If *A.P.* is right on the basic mechanism of appointment there is no reason why he should not be right on this detail: the fact that in his time there were ten προλαχόντες from each of the (Cleisthenic) tribes may as easily be evidence for Athenian conservatism as for false inference by a writer with no reliable information.
καὶ ‹ἐκ› τού[των ἐκ]λήρουν: Adopted hesitantly by Kenyon (Berlin ed., noting *correctura in papyro facta locum pravatum indicat*, and O.C.T.) from Kaibel & Wilamowitz[1]; he added in his Berlin ed. that if the word existed ἐξεκλήρουν would fit the traces on the papyrus. Thalheim and Oppermann restore καὶ τού[των ἐκ]λήρουν without adding ἐκ. Wilcken read τοὺς θ' ἐκλήρουν, but Kenyon in his Berlin ed. judged that insufficient to fill the space. Kenyon[1] had restored καὶ τού[τους ἐκ]λήρουν, and that is supported by Chambers, *TAPA*

xcvi 1965, 35, who reads καὶ τούτους ἐκλήρουν. The demonstrative must refer not to the men finally appointed but to the πρόκριτοι, and to express that meaning Kenyon's text should be right (cf. 30. iv, 47. i, as well as ἐκ τούτων κυαμεύειν immediately below).

ὅθεν ἔτι διαμένει ... τὸ δέκα κληροῦν ἑκάστην: The survival was not continuous: see 22. v with commentary. When the use of κληρωτήρια and πινάκια was taken over from the allotment of juries to the appointment of magistrates, c. 370, it is likely that each tribe was expected to find one of its προλαχόντες from each of the ten sections A–K (cf. p. 704).

κυαμεύειν: κληροῦν denotes drawing lots in general, while κυαμεύειν strictly denotes drawing lots with beans as counters. The latter word is commonly used with reference to Athenian allotments in the fifth century (H. VI. 109. ii, IG i² 41, 19, Pl. Per. 27. ii–iii, Ar. Av. 1022, T. VIII. 66. i, A.P. 24. iii, 32. i, decree ap. And. I. Myst. 96; cf. the constitution imposed by Athens on Erythrae, M&L 40, 9–13). In the fourth century more sophisticated allotment procedures were introduced, with counters called κύβοι released one by one from a tube in a κληρωτήριον (cf. pp. 708–9): throughout the second part of the treatise we find κληροῦν and its cognates used to describe the fourth-century procedures; κυαμεύειν may have been retained in the fourth-century law on the appointment of the archons, or A.P. may have used this word here simply for variety.

ἐκ τῶν τιμημάτων: Equivalent to ἐκ τῶν τελῶν: cf. p. 137.

ὁ περὶ τῶν ταμιῶν νόμος: Cf. 47. i. This law confirms the use of sortition and of the Solonian classes, but not the use of an elected short list. MS Vat. Gr. 2306, B 36–46 (a fragment of Theophrastus, accessible in J. J. Keaney & A. Szegedy-Maszak, TAPA cvi 1976, 227–40, and J. H. Oliver, GR&BS xviii 1977, 326–39), distinguishes offices for which wealth is required, those for which ἀρετή is required and those for which both are required; ἐν μὲν γὰρ τῇ ταμιείᾳ, καθάπερ εἴρηται, τὰς οὐσίας τηροῦσιν. ταμίαι, probably of Athena, are attested in the mid sixth century: IG i² 393, cf. L. H. Jeffery, Local Scripts of Archaic Greece, 72, 77, no. 21.

8. ii. [Σόλ]ων μὲν οὖν ... περὶ τῶν ἐννέα ἀρχόντων: The last four words were deleted by Kaibel & Wilamowitz² (cf. Wilamowitz, A.u.A., i. 49 n. 15); but Kaibel objected (Stil und Text, 140–1), and in Kaibel & Wilamowitz³ the deletion is merely suggested in the apparatus. We should not delete: the treasurers were mentioned to support what is said about the archons, and with these words A.P. closes the digression.

τὸ γὰρ ἀρχαῖον: Thus Kenyon, followed by most editors; but Herwerden & Leeuwen and Wilcken thought τὸ δ' a likelier reading, and I understand that Chambers concurs; according to Dr J. D.

Thomas the letter looks like γ with no mark of abbreviation. Neither gives an impossible sense, but in a sentence which does not add further information on Solon's πολιτεία (as do the sentences with δέ which follow in §iii) but explains the practice which his practice superseded, γάρ is preferable.

The statement of Arist. *Pol.* 11. 1273 B 35–1274 A 2 that Solon retained the 'aristocratic' principle of αἵρεσις (in contrast with κλήρωσις) need not conflict with *A.P.*'s statement that previously appointments had been made by the Areopagus. As noted above (p. 147) all that we can safely read in Isocrates' glowing accounts of the past is that deliberate choice of some kind was preferred to random sortition. It is most unlikely that there was documentary evidence available to later generations except on the new principle of appointment introduced by Solon; but *A.P.* 3. i and vi tell us what we should have expected, that in post-monarchic Athens office-holding became the monopoly of a limited number of families (cf. on 3. i, and on the Eupatrids pp. 74–6), and it is rightly assumed that a major purpose of Solon's classification by produce was to break this monopoly by making wealth the sole qualification for office. It is not intrinsically unlikely that the ex-archons in the Areopagus should have made the appointments, either directly or by inviting the assembly to confirm their choice; but we can only guess, and in all probability fourth-century Athenians could do no more.

ἀνακαλεσαμένη καὶ κρίνασα καθ' αὑτήν: *A.P.* seems to envisage a surprisingly modern procedure, by which candidates were summoned to an interview to determine which should be appointed: he or his source is perhaps thinking of the δοκιμασία, the check on a man's suitability for office which in later Athens followed his selection and which for the major offices may until the reforms of Ephialtes have been conducted by the Areopagus (cf. on 25. ii).

[διατάξα]σα: Read by Kenyon, who noted it in his Berlin ed. as *lectio non certa*; Wilcken read \ . . . . TA, which Kenyon thought possible but less likely, and from which Kaibel *ap.* Kaibel & Wilamowitz[3] restored [ἄρξον]τα; Dr J. D. Thomas reads]ασα. Either word gives an acceptable sense.

8. iii. φυλαὶ δ' ἦσαν δ' καθάπερ πρότερον: Cf. pp. 67–9.

καὶ φυλοβασιλεῖς τέτταρες: The heads of the tribes: cf. 41. ii, where their creation, like that of the tribes, is ascribed to Ion. Poll. VIII. 111 writes:

οἱ δὲ φυλοβασιλεῖς, ἐξ εὐπατριδῶν ὄντες, μάλιστα τῶν ἱερῶν ἐπεμελοῦντο, συνεδρεύοντες ἐν τῷ βασιλείῳ παρὰ τὸ Βουκολεῖον.

(For the βασιλεῖον and Βουκολεῖον see 3. v with commentary.) What tribal activities the φυλοβασιλεῖς presided over in early Athens it is impossible to say. In the revised sacrificial calendar of the end of the fifth century the φυλοβασιλεῖς and the formula ἐκ τῶν φυλοβασιλικῶν are found (*IG* ii² 1357, *a* 3–8, *Hesp.* iv 2, 30–43, 44–58, *Hesp.* x 2, 44–6): the formula used to be interpreted as a reference to the fund to which the sacrifices were charged, but S. Dow has shown that it is a source citation, giving as the authority for these sacrifices the law (?) of the φυλοβασιλεῖς (*Proc. Mass. Hist. Soc.* lxxi 1953–7, 15–21, 25–7). For the judicial function which they retained in certain categories of homicide trial see 57. iv with commentary.

τριττύες μὲν τρεῖς: Fr. 3 implausibly identifies the trittyes with the phratries, but it is hard to believe that this identification was made by *A.P.*: cf. pp. 68–9.

ναυκραρίαι δὲ δώδεκα: Not mentioned in the account of the tribes and their subdivisions in fr. 3; *A.P.* does not say, what Poll. VIII. 108 deduced, that each trittys was divided into four ναυκραρίαι (cf. Hignett, *H.A.C.*, 71, rejecting Pollux' deduction). Information on the ναυκραρίαι is scanty. The obsolete laws quoted here, if they may be trusted, prove that ναυκραρίαι existed in the time of Solon and that their officers, the ναύκραροι, had charge of ἀργύριον (cf. below); 21. v suggests that they were abolished by Cleisthenes, but Clid. 323 F 8 claims that Cleisthenes divided his new tribes into fifty ναυκραρίαι (cf. *ad loc.*); they are mentioned in other quotations from laws (Andr. 324 F 36, Phot. ναυκραρία); and attempts to describe their function are made in *L.S.* 283. 20, Poll. VIII. 108 (supply of ships), and Hes. (*N* 118) ναύκλαροι (*sic*; local taxation). The view that they had a local basis may be supported by the note in *L.S.* 275. 20, Phot. Κωλιάς, that one of the ναυκραρίαι bore that name (the name of a promontory south-east of Phalerum, probably the modern Hagios Kosmas: H. VIII. 96. ii, Paus. I. 1. v, cf. Hammond, *Studies*, 291 n. 1, Raubitschek, Φόρος: *Tribute to B. D. Meritt*, 137–8). By etymology ναύκραρος should mean 'ship-chief': the word and its cognates are found only in connection with the Athenian institution.†

The organisation of ναυκραρίαι must have begun as one through which the citizens contributed to the cost of supplying and maintaining Athens' warships. How early Athens built up a fleet is not clear: before the end of the seventh century she had been involved in war with Aegina, with Megara over the possession of Salamis, and with Mytilene over the possession of Sigeum (cf. p. 96); in 498 she sent twenty ships to assist in the Ionian Revolt (H. v. 97. iii, 99. i), and *c.* 491 she possessed fifty ships and acquired a further twenty from Corinth (H. VI. 89 cf. 132, with L. H. Jeffery, *AJP* lxxxiii 1962, 53–4). Beyond this almost all is speculative. The ναυκραρίαι may have acquired other administrative functions; they may well have had a local basis (but Hes., *loc. cit.*, may simply have over-exploited the statement of *A.P.* 21. v that Cleisthenes replaced the ναυκραρίαι by the demes); whether *A.P.* or Clidemus is right on Cleisthenes cannot be determined, though some see support for Clidemus in Athens' fleet of fifty ships. Herodotus, in an account of the affair of Cylon which apparently seeks to exculpate the archon Megacles and the Alcmaeonid family, makes the puzzling statement that the πρυτάνιες τῶν ναυκράρων . . . ἔνεμον τότε τὰς Ἀθήνας (v. 71. ii: cf. on ch. 1, above): an attempt has been made by B. Jordan, *CSCA* iii 1970, 153–75, to deny that Herodotus and T. 1. 126. viii are in conflict, and to show that in the seventh century the ναύκραροι were the chief revenue collectors of Athens (reading ἐνέμον⟨το⟩ in Herodotus); but in the texts which he cites νέμεσθαι is used of men who draw revenues for their own enjoyment, and the conflict between Herodotus and Thucydides seems certain and fatal to his arguments. The speculations of F. R. Wüst, *Hist.* vi 1957, 176–8, identifying the ναύκραροι with the Areopagus and their πρυτάνιες with the archons, are equally unsatisfactory. ναυκραρίαι had undoubtedly ceased to exist when Herodotus was writing, and what information underlies his statement is unknown. A. French, *JHS* lxxvii 1957, 238, suggests that the ναυκραρίαι originated in cooperation between owners of merchant ships; for a sceptical discussion of the institution see Hignett, *H.A.C.*, 67–74.

It is maintained in this commentary that Solon's reforms are rightly associated with his archonship in 594/3 (see on 5. ii), that the text of his laws survived to be studied by later Greeks (see on 7. i), and that Athens had no coinage at the time of Solon's archonship or for some time after (see on 10). Here *A.P.* quotes from τοῖς νόμοις τοῖς Σόλωνος οἷς οὐκέτι χρῶνται "ἀναλίσκειν ἐκ τοῦ ναυκραρικοῦ ἀργυρίου"; ἀργύριον appears in another of τοὺς νόμους τοὺς Σόλωνος τοὺς παλαιούς, quoted in Lys. x. *Theomn. i*. 18 (cf. 15); cf. the fines and values of sacrificial victims expressed in drachmae in the laws *ap.* Pl. *Sol.* 23, one of them (§iv) said to be from ἄξων xvi. At first sight it might appear that we must abandon any one of the three tenets stated at the beginning of this paragraph if we wish to maintain the other two (cf. Rhodes, *NC*[7] xv 1975, 6–7); but it seems increasingly likely that coinage was not introduced into Attica even by the later date which some prefer for Solon's reforms, and I now believe that the explanation should be sought in the use of uncoined silver. By the time of Solon a rich man would have silver and gold among his possessions (Solon, fr. 24. 1–3 West, where this is the first form of wealth to be mentioned), and it is credible that the use of coins, standard pieces of silver of guaranteed weight and purity, was adopted as an improvement on an earlier system which reckoned in standard weights of silver but had no standard and officially recognised pieces corresponding to those weights (cf. C. M. Kraay, *Archaic and Classical Greek Coins*, 313-14, on Pheidon of Argos). If this was so, we can accept that Solon in 594/3 enacted laws which expressed values in drachmae, and which referred to the ναυκραρικὸν ἀργύριον; LSJ cites no use of ἀναλίσκειν earlier than the fifth century, but it is not impossible that that should have been used of the spending of uncoined silver before the introduction of coinage.

ἦν δ' ἐπί: Conjectured by Herwerden & Leeuwen and read by Wilcken, accepted hesitantly by Kenyon (Berlin ed. and O.C.T.) and other editors. M. H. Chambers, *TAPA* cii 1971, 43, reads [ἦ]ν [δ' ἐπὶ].

τὰς εἰσφορὰς: In fifth- and fourth-century Athens εἰσφορά was an occasional tax levied on the property of all who admitted to possessing more than a certain amount; but here the contrast with τὰς δαπάνας suggests that *A.P.* is using the word in the more general sense of 'revenue': he envisages the ναύκραροι as financial officers in charge of revenue and expenditure.

ἐν τοῖς νόμοις τοῖς Σόλωνος οἷς οὐκέτι χρῶνται: On the survival of Solon's laws, including those which were superseded, see pp. 131-5.

8. iv. β[ου]λὴν δ' ἐποίησε τετρακοσίους: Cf. 21. iii, Pl. *Sol.* 19. i–ii: it is an attractive suggestion that Plutarch's comparison of the two βουλαί with a ship's two anchors (§ii) derives from one of Solon's poems (G. F. Schömann, *Die Verfassungsgeschichte Athens nach G. Grote's History of Greece kritisch geprüft*, 78, K. Freeman, *The Work and Life of Solon*, 79 with n. 1, F. Stähelin, *Hermes* lxviii 1933, 345). Despite the clear statements of *A.P.* and Plutarch, the existence of Solon's boule of four hundred has been strongly contested: see, for a full statement of the sceptics' case, Hignett, *H.A.C.*, 92-6; for a full defence, P. Cloché, *REG* xxxvii 1924, 1-26. There is no need for scepticism: the fact that the new boule failed to prevent Pisistratus from becoming tyrant does not prove that there was no new boule (D.L. 1. 49 alleges that it supported him, which could be true); the boule which resisted Cleomenes in 508/7 is best identified with the Solonian four hundred (cf. on 21. iii); there seems no compelling reason why the oligarchs of the late fifth century should have invented a boule of four hundred if none had existed (cf. on 31. i); of inscriptions, M&L 8 makes it very likely that two βουλαί co-existed in Chios before *c.* 550, and M&L 14, 12, ends with a mention of the boule but may well not be pre-Cleisthenic. Hignett, *H.A.C.*, 96, found no purpose for the new boule to fulfil; but the Eupatrids, whose monopoly of power Solon was trying to break, would for at least a generation continue to dominate the Areopagus, and this is sufficient to explain the creation of a new council to guide the assembly.

According to Plutarch Solon created the new boule because he saw τὸν δῆμον οἰδοῦντα καὶ θρασυνόμενον τῇ τῶν χρεῶν ἀφέσει, and specified as its function προβουλεύειν ... τοῦ δήμου καὶ μηδὲν ἐᾶν ἀπροβούλευτον εἰς ἐκκλησίαν εἰσφέρεσθαι (cf. 45. iv with commentary); and this preparation of business for the assembly was probably its only major duty, though it may also have had docimastic and disciplinary powers over its own members (cf. Rhodes, *A.B.*, 178, 204–7, 209–11). If this probouleutic council was to justify its existence, it is likely that Solon prescribed regular meetings both for it and for the assembly (cf. pp. 140–1; and for a comparable stage in the development of Sparta cf. the Great Rhetra *ap.* Pl. *Lyc.* 6. ii). Previously the occasional meetings of the assembly had probably been convened with little notice, to the advantage of the convening magistrates: the institution of the new council, and the requirement that it must give prior consideration to all business brought before the assembly, should have protected the assembly against the excessive influence both of the archons and Areopagus and of pressure groups of any kind, which thrive on the opportunity to present business without warning at meetings thinly attended by their opponents. προβούλευσις became standard Greek practice. Homeric assemblies might shout, remain ominously silent, or even mutiny; in the classical period, in Athens and elsewhere, votes were counted and, subject to certain safeguards, the will of the majority prevailed.[12] When and in what kind of body votes were first counted is not known, but it is hard to believe that in Athens the counting of votes in the council and assembly was introduced later than Solon's reforms (cf. J. A. O. Larsen, *CP* xliv 1949, 164–81, A. L. Boegehold, *Hesp.* xxxii 1963, 366–74, G. E. M. de Ste. Croix, *The Origins of the Peloponnesian War*, 348–9); in Draco's homicide law as republished in 408/9 an unintending killer may be pardoned only by the unanimous agreement of the closest available kinship group, but it may be suspected that the 51 ἐφέται decide by majority vote (M&L 86, 13–20).

The boule comprised 100 members from each tribe, thetes evidently being excluded. Plutarch seems to say (though this is perhaps to read too much into his words) that the original four hundred were picked by Solon; Adcock, accepting this, supposed that appointment was for life and vacancies were filled by election (*C.A.H.*, iv[1]. 53–4); but it is better to confess our ignorance.

τὴν δὲ τῶν Ἀρεοπαγιτῶν ἔταξεν ἐπὶ [τὸ] νομοφυλακεῖν: Cf. 3. vi, 4. ii ('Draconian constitution') and 25. ii with commentary; also Pl. *Sol.* 19. ii. In §§iii–v Plutarch reports a majority view that the Areopagus was created by Solon, which he rightly rejects, quoting a

---

[12] In an assembly attended by some thousands a second vote is more likely than a precise count on occasions when there was not a clear majority: cf. on 30. v.

Solonian amnesty law from which men condemned for homicide or 'tyranny' by the Areopagus or other authorities are excluded; but the Council of the Areopagus will not have needed a distinctive name until a second council was created (though the name may have been used sometimes before), and the Areopagus remained The Council, *par excellence*, for some time afterwards (cf. on 25. i, 45. i). There may never have been a law giving the Areopagus probouleutic powers, but no doubt in pre-Solonian Athens on the occasions when an assembly was held the archons who (very probably: Hignett, *H.A.C.*, 74, 92, 98–9, 150–1, Rhodes, *A.B.*, 21 n. 4) presided had been armed with the Areopagus' advice. For the powers of the Areopagus in early Athens see on 3. vi; for the powers which it lost in 462/1 see on 25. ii; for the powers which it retained thereafter see 57. iii (cf. 47. ii, 59. vi) and 60. ii with commentary.

ὥσπερ ὑπῆρχεν καὶ πρότερον ἐπίσκοπος οὖσα τῆς πολιτείας: Those who believe ch. 3 as well as ch. 4 to have been inserted into the original text of *A.P.* must condemn this clause as one of the modifications made to accommodate the insertion: this was done by O. Seeck, *Klio* iv 1904, 270–82. See pp. 84–8 (where ch. 3 is defended as part of the original version of *A.P.*) and Introduction, pp. 53–4.

καὶ τά τε ἄλλα τὰ πλεῖστα καὶ τὰ μέγιστα τῶν πολιτ<ικ>ῶν διετήρει: Cf. 3. vi (διῴκει δὲ τὰ πλεῖστα καὶ τὰ μέγιστα τῶν ἐν τῇ πόλει).

καὶ τοὺς ἁμαρτάνοντας ηὔθυνεν κυρία οὖσα καὶ [ζη]μιοῦν καὶ κολάζειν: Cf. again 3. vi (καὶ κολάζουσα καὶ ζημιοῦσα πάντας τοὺς ἀκοσμοῦντας κυρίως). 3. vi appears to be derived ultimately from Isocrates (cf. *ad loc.*); but here the same picture of the Areopagus is repeated in less markedly Isocratean language, as if what had been copied from a source there is repeated from memory here. The earliest meaning of εὐθύνειν is 'guide straight' or 'direct' (like the Homeric ἰθύνειν); from that it came to denote making the crooked straight (e.g. Solon, fr. 4. 36 West), and then calling to account or punishing (e.g. Aesch. *Pers.* 828, T. I. 95. v); a special instance of that is the Athenian institution of εὔθυναι, the examination of an official's conduct on his retirement (48. iv–v, cf. 54. ii, with commentary). In Arist. *Pol.* II. 1274 A 15–18, III. 1281 B 32–4, τὰς ἀρχὰς εὐθύνειν is said to have been given by Solon to the δῆμος: whatever Aristotle may have meant by that, it is unlikely that εὔθυναι took place before the assembly in archaic Athens (cf. Hignett, *H.A.C.*, 204), and it does not conflict with this passage (*pace* Mathieu, *Aristote, Constitution d'Athènes*, 24–5) since the reference here is not to the εὔθυναι of magistrates but to the punishment of offenders in general.†

καὶ τὰς ἐκτίσεις ἀνέφερεν εἰς πόλιν: ἔκτ(ε)ισις is regularly used of the payment of financial dues, including fines; before the use of coinage had become normal the 'payments' required for a wrong done to the state rather than to an individual probably took the form of a compulsory dedication to be placed in the temple of Athena or one of the gods (compare the requirement of a gold statue from an offending archon: 7. i, 55. v, with commentary). Probably there were records which listed penalties without the reason for their imposition, which survived to be read by *A.P.* or one of his sources and prompted the doubtful inference that no reason had been stated or known when the penalty was imposed; misconduct in office by an official is the most obvious form which a wrong to the state as such might have taken.

To call the Acropolis πόλις was old-fashioned by the fourth century, but the usage persisted in this and other prepositional phrases: see T. II. 15. vi, and Wyse's commentary on Isae. v. *Her. Dic.* 44 (pp. 476–7).

π[ρ]όφασιν δι' ὃ [τὸ ἐ]κτ[ίν]εσθαι: Thus Kenyon, hesitantly, in his Berlin ed. and O.C.T., followed by most subsequent editors; R. Y. Tyrrell, *CR* v 1891, 177, had suggested πρόφασι[ν τοῦ ἐκτίν]εσθαι. Blass, *LZB* 1891, 303, proposed πρόφασι[ν τοῦ εὐθύν]εσθαι, which was accepted by Herwerden & Leeuwen and Kenyon[3]; Wilcken read and Kaibel & Wilamowitz[3] deleted πρόφασιν [[διὰ τὸ [εὐ]θύ[ν]εσθαι]]; and I understand that M. H. Chambers finds Wilcken's θυ 'fairly clear' on the papyrus, as does Dr J. D. Thomas.

καὶ τοὺς ἐπὶ καταλύσει τοῦ δήμου συνισταμένους . . . εἰσα[γγ]ελ[ία]ς περὶ αὐτῶν: The formulation is more at home in the late fifth and fourth centuries (e.g. decree of 410 *ap*. And. I. *Myst*. 96–7; law of 336, *SEG* xii 87, 7–10; νόμος εἰσαγγελτικός *ap*. Hyp. IV. *Eux*. 7–8) than in the early sixth; but bids for tyranny by Cylon before Solon and Pisistratus after, and the fact that Solon could himself have become tyrant (cf. 6. iii–iv, 11. ii, 12. iii), make it credible that Solon should have enacted a law against would-be tyrants. The amnesty law quoted in Pl. *Sol*. 19. iv suggests that before Solon's reforms the Areopagus had claimed the right to condemn ἐπὶ τυραννίδι. Contrast, however, the scepticism of M. H. Hansen, *Eisangelia*, 17–19 cf. 56–7.

On the various Athenian laws of this kind, which from their nature could be enforced only against an unsuccessful transgressor, see 16. x with commentary. On the procedure of εἰσαγγελία for major public offences see 25. ii, 43. iv, 59. ii, with commentary. The same term was used also for charges against magistrates (45. ii cf. 4. iv), against διαιτηταί (53. vi), and against those who maltreated their parents or wards (commentary on 56. vi). Ruschenbusch, *Untersuchungen zur Geschichte des athenischen Strafrechts*, 73–4, suggests that it was the original term for any verbal denunciation to the authorities; it may at any rate be true that the prosecutions which when written denunciation had become normal were called γραφαί were earlier called εἰσαγγελίαι.

8. v. ὁρῶν δὲ ... : §v has no obvious relevance to what precedes, and 9. i sums up 7. iii–8. iv with the words τὰ μὲν οὖν περὶ τὰς ἀρχὰς τοῦτον εἶχε τὸν τρόπον as if this section did not exist. But we need not suspect revision or interpolation: probably the Areopagus' jurisdiction over τοὺς ἐπὶ καταλύσει τοῦ δήμου συνισταμένους has led *A.P.* to the subject of στάσις and so to Solon's famous law against neutrality in times of στάσις. Contrast Fritz, cited below.

[ἀγα]πῶντας τὸ αὐτόματον: ἀγαπῶντας was first suggested by Kaibel & Wilamowitz[1] and is generally accepted: Kaibel, *Stil und Text*, 143, compares Plat. *Rep.* III. 399 C 1 (τὰ ἀποβαίνοντα ἀγαπῶντα). For the use of τὸ αὐτόματον as equivalent to τὸ ἀπὸ τύχης Kaibel compares Arist. *M.M.* II. 1199 A 9, A. III. *Ctes.* 167, D.S. XII. 38. iv.

νόμον ἔθηκεν ... ἴδιον: Cf. Pl. *Sol.* 20. i (ἴδιος μὲν μάλιστα καὶ παράδοξος), *Praec. Ger. Reip.* 823 F, *Ser. Num. Vind.* 550 B–C, Cic. *Ep. Att.* x. 1. ii, Gell. II. 12 (the last citing *A.P.*); for later Athenian dislike of ἀπράγμονες cf. Pericles' funeral oration, T. II. 40. ii. Lysias, in a speech against a man who withdrew from Attica in 404/3 rather than live under the régime of the Thirty, claims that no one has ever thought it necessary to legislate against such behaviour (XXXI. *Phil.* 27–8): but a law which had rarely if ever been enforced, and may not have been included in the revised law code adopted on the restoration of the democracy, could have been ignored by an orator, or it may be that leaving Attica was treated as a separate offence from staying there but remaining neutral (R. Develin, *Hist.* xxvi 1977, 508); so *pace* Hignett (*H.A.C.*, 26–7) this is less than conclusive proof that Solon cannot have enacted the law against neutrality for which he later became famous. See also, in favour of authenticity, B. Lavagnini, *RFIC*[3] xxv 1947, 81–93 (reprinted with postscript, *Att. Palermo*[4] vi 1945/6 [*sic*], 19–34), J. A. Goldstein, *Hist.* xxi 1972, 538–45, V. Bers, *Hist.* xxiv 1975, 493–8; against, E. Graf, *HG* xlvii 1936, 34–5, B. Λαούρδας, 'Αθ. liii 1949, 119–29, K. von Fritz, *Hist.* xxvi 1977, 245–7. Goldstein suggests, ingeniously if not convincingly (his argument presupposes more widespread knowledge of an unused law than is likely; and see next note), that Philon's behaviour was not covered by Solon's law but Lysias, while denying the law's relevance, made use of its wording. Fritz, suggesting that *A.P.* presents this as a supplementary law which will not have been inscribed on the ἄξονες and of which an authentic text is not likely to have survived (which I doubt: cf. above), notes that Solon claims in the poems quoted in ch. 12 that he has been neutral between γνώριμοι and δῆμος.†

μ[ὴ] θῆται τὰ ὅπλα μηδὲ μεθ' ἑτέρων: The basic meaning of the expression is 'rest arms' (e.g. H. IX. 52 *fin.*, T. IV. 44. i): see LSJ s.v. τίθημι, A. II. 10. Goldstein, *loc. cit.*, notes that the normal expression for 'take up arms' is (ἀνα)λαμβάνειν τὰ ὅπλα, and suggests

157

that 'θέσθαι τὰ ὅπλα appears to have been a technical legal term, found in contexts dealing with fitness for civic rights as it is in the speech against Philon and in the law ascribed to Solon.' But there is no reason why a different but no less common verb should be used in such contexts, and in almost every case where Goldstein regards θέσθαι as equivalent to (ἀνα)λαμβάνειν (but not in Plat. *Legg.* VI. 753 B 5–6, which constitutes an exception to his rule also) the reference is not to taking up one's arms but to placing one's arms, whether literally or metaphorically, at the disposal of one side against another. See T. II. 2. iv with Gomme's commentary, ii. 4; IV. 68. iii; Plat. *Rep.* IV. 440 E 5–6 with Adam's commentary, i. 257; D. XXI. *Mid.* 145 with Goodwin's commentary, 85; A. I. *Tim.* 29; Lyc. *Leocr.* 43; *IG* ii² 505, 38–9; 666, 10–12.

ἄτιμον εἶναι: On ἀτιμία as loss of rights see Ruschenbusch, *Untersuchungen zur Geschichte des athenischen Strafrechts*, 11–47, Harrison, *L.A.*, ii. 169–76, M. H. Hansen, *Apagoge, Endeixis and Ephegesis*, 75–82, Rhodes, *CQ*² xxviii 1978, 89–90. In archaic Athens the ἄτιμος lost not merely his rights as a citizen but his rights as a person, vis-à-vis the individual(s) whom he had injured or (as in this case) the community as a whole, who might inflict on him death or any lesser penalty (for Ruschenbusch's suggestion that ἀτιμία was the only penalty provided for in the laws of Draco and Solon see above, p. 111). Later, as the area in which a man might rely on self-help was reduced and that in which he must have recourse to law was increased, the concept of ἀτιμία was correspondingly tamed, and in most circumstances it came to denote loss of civic rights only (but the rights lost included that of recourse to law to protect one's personal rights), but I agree with Harrison that the stronger sense of ἀτιμία did not wholly disappear in the fifth and fourth centuries (for the contrast between the two senses of ἀτιμία see D. IX. *Phil. iii.* 44). The ἀτιμία in question here will be the primitive, untamed kind: apathy in a domestic crisis is being treated as equivalent to treachery.†

καὶ τῆς πόλεως μὴ μετέχειν: Cf. 26. iv (possibly from Pericles' text), 36. i, Lys. VI. *And.* 48 (Ἀνδοκίδης . . . ἀξιοῖ νυνὶ μετέχειν τῆς πόλεως); also Lys. XXX. *Nic.* 15, Is. III. *Nic.* 15, 16, XVIII. *Call.* 16, 42, 48, 49, XXI. *Euth.* 2, where μετέχειν τῆς πολιτείας is used of those who have political rights under a particular (especially a non-democratic) régime. μετέχειν τῆς πόλεως is probably the older expression (cf. B. Lavagnini, *RFIC* lxxv = ²xxv 1947, 85 n. 1). If primitive ἀτιμία is intended the offender will be deprived not only of his share in the city's government and corporate activities but also of the protection of its laws, especially its laws against homicide. However strong the ἀτιμία is taken to be, this clause will have added nothing to a fourth-century reader's understanding of ἄτιμον εἶναι: it should be not the author's comment on that clause but an elaboration which was included in Solon's law.

9. i. τὰ μὲν οὖν [περὶ τὰ]ς ἀρχὰς ... τὸν τρόπον: *A.P.* ignores his digression to deal with the law against neutrality, and sums up the discussion of the ἀρχαί in 7. iii–8. iv: cf. on 8. v.

δοκεῖ ... τρία ταῦτ᾽ εἶναι τὰ δημοτικώτατα: Cf. the list of constitutional changes in 41. ii (τρίτη ... ἡ ἐπὶ Σόλωνος, ἀφ᾽ ἧς ἀρχὴ δημοκρατίας ἐγένετο) and the judgment in 22. i, 41. ii, that Cleisthenes' πολιτεία was δημοτικωτέρα πολὺ τῆς Σόλωνος, with commentary *ad locc*. Ruschenbusch in his attempt to date the appearances of different Athenians as founders of the democracy (*Hist.* vii 1958, 398–424: on Solon, 399–408, cf. J. A. O. Larsen, *Studies ... G. H. Sabine*, 1–16, Masaracchia, *Solone*, 1–78) has found Solon first thus characterised in Is. vii. *Areop.* 16–17, ἐκείνην τὴν δημοκρατίαν ... ἣν Σόλων μὲν ὁ δημοτικώτατος ἐνομοθέτησε ... ἧς οὐκ ἂν εὕροιμεν οὔτε δημοτικωτέραν οὔτε τῇ πόλει μᾶλλον συμφέρουσαν (which he dates to 356), D. xxii. *Andr.* 30–1, associating Solon with δημοκρατία (which he dates to 355), and later speeches, esp. Is. xv. *Antid.* 231–2, D. lvii. *Eub.* 31–2, A. iii. *Ctes.* 257, D. xviii. *Cor.* 6, Hyp. iii. *Ath.* 21. This is too neat and schematic: some date Is. vii. *Areop.* later than 356 (e.g. G. L. Cawkwell, *O.C.D.*², 554), and some date D. xxii. *Andr.* earlier than 355 (E. Schweigert, *Hesp.* viii 1939, 12–17, D. M. Lewis, *BSA* xlix 1954, 43–4; contr. B. R. I. Sealey, *REG* lxviii 1955, 89–92, G. L. Cawkwell, *C&M* xxiii 1962, 50–5); and in any case there is not so wide a chasm as Ruschenbusch would have us believe between the texts cited above and the decision of the restored democracy in 403 to use 'the laws of Solon and the ordinances of Draco' after some of the laws of Solon had been repealed by the Thirty (And. i. *Myst.* 81–3 with *A.P.* 35. ii, schol. A. i. *Tim.* 39). Nevertheless it is true that in surviving texts Solon is often described as δημοτικός and linked with δημοκρατία in and after the 350's but rarely before (he is φιλόδημος in Ar. *Nub.* 1187), and it was not until the end of the fifth century that the democrats looked further back than Cleisthenes for their founding hero. For the impact of such discussions on the Aristotelian school cf. Arist. *Pol.* ii. 1273 b 35–1274 a 21.

Of the three features singled out here, the ban on loans against personal security has been mentioned above (6. i); but the provision for ὁ βουλόμενος to prosecute has not been mentioned at all, and apart from the allusion to δικαστήρια in 7. iii nothing has been said about ἡ εἰς τὸ δικαστήριον ἔφεσις.

τὸ ἐξεῖναι τῷ βουλομένῳ τιμωρ[εῖ]ν ὑπὲρ τῶν ἀδικουμένων: Cf. Pl. *Sol.* 18. vi–vii. Previously the right to initiate proceedings had in all cases been limited to the injured party (and where necessary his next of kin); Solon distinguished a category of cases in which any citizen in full possession of his rights might initiate proceedings. The best explanation is that of G. Glotz, *La Solidarité de la famille*, 369–82 (cf. Ruschenbusch, *Untersuchungen zur Geschichte des athenischen Strafrechts*, 47–53), based on an analysis of the charges to which this provision applied, that it was needed in those cases of private injury where the injured party was unable, either in law or for obvious personal reasons, to prosecute on his own account; for different views see Lipsius, *A.R.*, 237–8 with n. 1, K. Latte, *Hermes* lxvi 1931, 30–48 = *Kleine Schriften*, 252–67. In classical Athenian law most cases in which ὁ βουλόμενος might prosecute, 'public' lawsuits, were γραφαί; 'private' lawsuits, in which only the injured party might prosecute, were δίκαι (cf. Lipsius, *A.R.*, 237–44, Harrison, *L.A.*, ii. 76–8).

φασιν: A reflection of the fourth-century debate on the origin of the democracy and the nature of Solon's constitution which underlies this chapter: cf. above.

ἡ εἰς τὸ δικαστή[ριον] ἔφε[σι]ς: Cf. Pl. *Sol.* 18. ii–iii, *Comp. Sol. Publ.* 2. ii, also Arist. *Pol.* II. 1273 B 35–1274 A 5, 1274 A 15–18. Though *A.P.* and Plutarch both write of τὸ δικαστήριον (and *A.P.* 7. iii and Arist. *Pol.* have the plural) the word is almost certainly anachronistic. There cannot have been a plurality of δικαστήρια as early as this (Grote, *H.G.* [1869–84], v. 211–3, S. B. Smith, *TAPA* lvi 1925, 106–19); and Solon's word will have been ἡλιαία (for the smooth breathing see Wade-Gery, *BSA* xxxvii 1936/7, 265 n. 3 = *Essays*, 173 n. 4, Dover on Ar. *Nub.* 863, MacDowell on Ar. *Vesp.* 195; I retain the aspirate when transliterating), found in a law quoted by Lysias to illustrate the retention of archaic language in the laws (Lys. x. *Theomn. i.* 16, cf. D. xxiv. *Tim.* 105) and sometimes used of the later δικαστήρια (for an analysis of Athenian uses of the word see Busolt & Swoboda, *G.S.*, ii. 1151 n. 3, and for the heliaea as a courtroom see 68. i with commentary). Cognate words in other dialects denote the assembly (e.g. H. I. 125. ii, v. 29. ii, 79. ii, VII. 134. ii, *SIG*³ 56 [=M&L 42, *B*], 44, 594, 2, 715, 1), so Solon's heliaea should be a judicial session of the whole assembly: M. H. Hansen, *Eisangelia*, 51–2, argues from Arist. *Pol.* that the heliaea was a court of sworn jurors, but I do not believe that that text proves his point (cf. Rhodes, *JHS* xcix 1979, 103–6).[13]†

ἔφεσις strictly denotes not an appeal but the removal of a case from one plane to another for a fresh hearing (see Ruschenbusch,

---

[13] In the sixth-century inscription from Chios, M&L 8, the δημοσίη βολή probably judges appeals without reference to the assembly (*pace* Wade-Gery, *Essays*, 198–9), and it has been suggested, though I am not persuaded, that it was the boule of four hundred which was to hear appeals in Athens (L. H. Jeffery, *Archaic Greece*, 93–4, 231–2).

ZSS lxxviii 1961, 386–90, Harrison, *L.A.*, ii. 72–4: there were, for instance, some circumstances in which ἔφεσις was obligatory, e.g. 45. i–iii, 55. ii, with commentary); but 'appeal' by a dissatisfied litigant is intended in 53. ii, and here does not misrepresent the ἔφεσις instituted by Solon (cf. H. J. Wolff, *Traditio* iv 1946, 78–9 with n. 214, D. M. MacDowell, *The Law in Classical Athens*, 30–2). ἔφεσις was probably allowed from the decisions of an individual magistrate only, not from the decisions of the Areopagus: this is perhaps supported by Plutarch's ὅσα ταῖς ἀρχαῖς ἔταξε κρίνειν, and the Areopagus' jurisdiction was inappellable in cases which it still heard after 462/1 (cf. Ant. v. *Caed. Her.* 87, VI. *Chor.* 3); as in classical Athens, magistrates' penalties up to a certain limit will not have been subject to appeal (52. iii, 53. ii, 56. vii, 61. ii, with commentary, cf. MacDowell, *loc. cit.*).

However, the law quoted by Lysias and Demosthenes is an embarrassment to this view, since it seems to expect the heliaea to play a larger part in judicial procedure than the hearing of appeals would give it:

δεδέσθαι δ' ἐν τῇ ποδοκάκκῃ τὸν πόδα πένθ' ἡμέρας καὶ νύκτας ἴσας, ἐὰν προστιμήσῃ ἡ ἡλιαία. προστιμᾶσθαι δὲ τὸν βουλόμενον, ὅταν περὶ τοῦ τιμήματος ᾖ.
ἐὰν δέ τις ἀπαχθῇ, τῶν γονέων κακώσεως ἑαλωκὼς ἢ ἀστρατείας ἢ προειρημένον αὐτῷ τῶν νομ⟨ίμ⟩ων εἴργεσθαι, εἰσιὼν ὅποι μὴ χρή, δησάντων αὐτὸν οἱ ἕνδεκα καὶ εἰσαγόντων εἰς τὴν ἡλιαίαν, κατηγορείτω δὲ ὁ βουλόμενος οἷς ἔξεστιν. ἐὰν δ' ἁλῷ, τιμάτω ἡ ἡλιαία ὅ τι χρὴ παθεῖν αὐτὸν ἢ ἀποτεῖσαι.

(Laws *ap.* D. XXIV. *Tim.* 105.)

Some have therefore supposed that Solon required the magistrates to sit not alone but with a court in all cases (e.g. Adcock, *C.A.H.*, iv[1]. 56) or in all contested cases (Ruschenbusch, *Untersuchungen zur Geschichte des athenischen Strafrechts*, 78–82, cf. *Hist.* xiv 1965, 381–4); others think that the law is sufficiently explained if, to discourage frivolous appeals, Solon allowed the heliaea to impose an additional penalty when it confirmed a magistrate's condemnation (Lipsius, *A.R.*, 440, Bonner & Smith, *Administration of Justice*, i. 179); Wilamowitz thought that ἔφεσις was obligatory if a magistrate wished to impose a penalty above a certain limit, as later the boule was required to refer a case within its jurisdiction to a δικαστήριον if it wanted a penalty in excess of a 500-dr. fine (*A.u.A.*, i. 60: cf. on 45. i). Lipsius' is the best explanation of the first law quoted; the second law concerns men already convicted and pronounced ἄτιμοι who are arrested after infringing their ἀτιμία (clearer in Demosthenes' paraphrase, §103), and these should perhaps be regarded as having by their actions challenged the magistrate's sentence of ἀτιμία.

κύριος γὰρ ὢν ὁ δῆμος ... τῆς πολιτείας: Cf. 41. i, 41. ii *fin.*, Arist. *Pol.* II. 1274 A 2–7 (in all of which the word κύριος recurs), Pl. *Sol.* 18. iii; also *A.P.* 35. ii (τὸ κῦρος ὃ ἦν ἐν τοῖς δικασταῖς), Ar. *Vesp.* 518 (ὅστις ἄρχω τῶν ἁπάντων), Lyc. *Leocr.* 3–4: the epigrammatic sentence may well not be original to *A.P.* The δικαστήρια did in the developed democracy enjoy considerable political power, through their rights to hold the δοκιμασίαι of magistrates before they entered office (45. iii, 55. ii–iv, 59. iv) and to pronounce on their εὔθυναι at the end of their year of office (48. iv–v, 54. ii, with commentary; on Arist. *Pol.* II. 1274 A 15–18, III. 1281 B 32–4, see p. 155), and to hear political charges such as the γραφαὶ παρανόμων and νόμον μὴ ἐπιτήδειον θεῖναι; but meetings of the undivided heliaea cannot have been frequent, and it is unlikely that the first generations to which the right of ἔφεσις was available made great use of it.

9. ii. διὰ τὸ μὴ γέγραφθ[αι το]ὺς νόμους ἁπλῶς μηδὲ σαφῶς: Cf. Pl. *Sol.* 18. iv, also *Sol.* 25. vi with *A.P.* 11. i and commentary. There is no need to suppose that Solon was intentionally ambiguous (on this point *A.P.* is eminently sensible): the accusation probably arose in the late fifth century, when the Athenians' addiction to litigation was notorious, experience had shown that there were difficult cases not adequately covered by Solon's laws, and his archaic language was beginning to seem obscure (cf. Ar. fr. 222 Kock, and p. 161). One of the first acts of the Thirty in 404 was

καθεῖλον ... τῶν Σόλωνος θεσμῶν ὅσοι διαμφισβητήσεις εἶχον, καὶ τὸ κῦρος ὃ ἦν ἐν τοῖς δικασταῖς κατέλυσαν, ὡς ἐπανορθοῦντες καὶ ποιοῦντες ἀναμφισβήτητον τὴν πολιτείαν (35. ii).

Fourth-century theorists shared the view of the Thirty and insisted that the laws should be framed so as not to allow too much latitude to the jurors: Arist. *Rhet.* I. 1354 A 27–30, B 11–16, cf. Plat. *Polit.* 294 A 10–295 A 7. The power of the courts in relation to gaps and ambiguities in the laws is explored by Ruschenbusch, *Hist.* vi 1957, 257–74.

ὁ περὶ τῶν κλήρων καὶ ἐπικλήρων: 35. ii cites as an example of the ambiguities removed by the Thirty Solon's list of circumstances in which a testator's wishes could be disregarded (where the 'disputes' lay in the fact that a jury would have to decide, for example, whether the testator's eccentricity amounted to madness or senility: cf. *ad loc.*). Quotations from Solon's law are given in Ar. *Av.* 1660–6, [D.] XLVI. *Steph. ii.* 14, and further parts of the law of inheritance as it stood in the fourth century are found in Isae. VI. *Her. Phil.* 47, [D.] XLIII. *Mac.* 51 (with reference to the state's fresh start in 403/2), also

[D.] XLIII. *Mac.* 16, 54, XLVI. *Steph. ii.* 22; see also FF 49-53 in Ruschenbusch, *Hist.* Einz. ix 1966, 86-9, Isae. III. *Her. Pyrrh.* 64, VII. *Her. Apoll.* 20, XI. *Her. Hagn.* 1-2, with Wyse's commentary (pp. 347-9, 351-2, 564-5, 680-1), and for a recent discussion of the law with references to earlier literature Harrison, *L.A.*, i. 122-62. An ἐπίκληρος is the heiress of a man who leaves no legitimate male issue: to prevent the extinction of the family she would be married to a man who would be adopted as son and would hold the property in trust for the sons of that marriage; failing that the male next of kin would have the right to marry her and inherit the property. Pl. *Sol.* 20. ii-iv (cf. other texts assembled in Ruschenbusch's FF 51-2) comments on further provisions for the marriage of ἐπίκληροι: the husband must have intercourse with the ἐπίκληρος at least three times a month, and if he proves impotent she may take another partner.

ἀμφισβητήσεις: A philosophers' word, and a favourite of Aristotle and of *A.P.* (cf. p. 103): 35. ii on the same subject uses διαμφισβήτησις and ἀναμφισβήτητος.

οἴονται μὲν οὖν τινες: *A.P.* is still quoting arguments used by others in the debate on Solon and the origin of the democracy. Gomme, *Hist. Comm. Thuc.*, i. 47 n. 2, suggests that the τινες include Theopompus: cf. p. 130 and Introduction, p. 23.

διὰ τὸ μὴ δύνασθαι καθόλου περιλαβεῖν τὸ βέλτιστον: This clause is *A.P.*'s explanation of ἀσαφεῖς αὐτὸν ποιῆσαι τοὺς νόμους.

οὐ γὰρ [δ]ίκ[αιον] ἐκ τῶν νῦν γιγνομένων: Cf. Arist. *Pol.* II. 1274 A 5-21, where it is again argued that Solon is not to be blamed for τὴν νῦν δημοκρατίαν, which came about οὐ κατὰ τὴν Σόλωνος ... προαίρεσιν, ἀλλὰ μᾶλλον ἀπὸ συμπτώματος. Although it is combined with the attribution to Solon of a method of appointing magistrates which conflicts with 8. i, the similarity between that passage and the assessment of Solon's work in this chapter is one of the more striking correspondences between *Pol.* and *A.P.*: cf. Introduction, pp. 10, 63.

ἐκ τῆς ἄλλης πολιτείας: On the use of πολιτεία in *A.P.* see pp. 89-90: here the reference is to the rest of Solon's political dispensation, his 'constitution' in the broadest sense. Solon's βούλησις is revealed also by the verses quoted in ch. 12.

10. i. πρὸ δὲ τῆς νομοθεσίας: After a chapter which the reader would expect to conclude *A.P.*'s treatment of Solon a further item is added. Androtion had exploited the reform of measures, weights and coinage to give an account of the σεισάχθεια which freed Solon from the charge of adopting so drastic a remedy as the cancellation of debts (cf. p. 127): *A.P.*, who rejected that account, here interrupts the plan of his chapters on Solon to give his own version of that reform (cf. p. 118 and Introduction, pp. 47, 54).

It is unlikely that there can have survived any evidence as to the order in which Solon's reforms were enacted (cf. Jacoby, *Supp*. i. 147, but contrast Hammond, *JHS* lx 1940, 71–83 = *Studies*, 145–62, with further note 162–9, M. Miller, *Arethusa* i 1968, 62–81: as Hammond suggests some one may have drawn chronological conclusions from the order of the numbered ἄξονες). *A.P.* has not suggested above any distinction of time between the economic reform of ch. 6 and the legal and political reform of 7–8. Plutarch does make a distinction: he describes the economic reform in *Sol*. 15; in 16 he says that at first that caused discontent, but the discontent evaporated and Solon was given a fresh appointment to reform the state; in 17–25. v he writes of the political and legal reform. Almost certainly what was originally a logical distinction has had a chronological significance read into it, and once the misunderstanding had occurred it was embroidered upon.[14]

ποιῆσαι: Kaibel & Wilamowitz[1] restored ποιῆσα[ς], regarding the use of θεῖναι and ποιῆσαι, as grammatically parallel infinitives dependent on δοκεῖ, as impossibly awkward (cf. Kaibel, *Stil und Text*, 145, noting the shift to participles after δοκεῖ + infinitive in 40. ii); Wilcken read and Kaibel & Wilamowitz[3] deleted ποιήσας [[καὶ]]; Kenyon in his Berlin ed. reaffirmed his reading of ποιῆσαι and could not see Wilcken's superscript καὶ; M. H. Chambers, *TAPA* cii 1971, 43, reads ποιήσας. The participle is to be preferred.

μετὰ ταῦτα: The reference is uncertain, and the awkwardness is presumably due to *A.P.*'s attempting to fit this additional material into his main narrative. Logically the reform of measures should precede the classification of the citizen body according to measures of produce; Plutarch includes the reform of measures in the economic reform (*Sol*. 15. iii) because he reaches it through Androtion's use of it to explain the σεισάχθεια.

10. i–ii. τὴν τε τῶν μέτρων καὶ σταθμῶν καὶ τὴν τοῦ νομίσματος αὔξησιν. . . . καὶ τοῖς ἄλλοις σταθμοῖς: Cf. Andr. 324 F 34 *ap*. Pl. *Sol*. 15. iii–iv:

> . . . καὶ τὴν ἅμα τούτῳ (*sc*. the reduction of interest rates) γενομένην τῶν τε μέτρων ἐπαύξησιν καὶ τοῦ νομίσματος τιμῆς.[15] ἑκατὸν γὰρ ἐποίησε δραχμῶν τὴν μνᾶν, πρότερον ἑβδομήκοντ' ἄγουσαν,[16] ὥστ' ἀριθμῷ μὲν ἴσον, δυνάμει δ' ἔλαττον ἀποδιδόντων, ὠφελεῖσθαι μὲν τοὺς ἐκτίνοντας μεγάλα, μηδὲν δὲ βλάπτεσθαι τοὺς κομιζομένους.

[14] I do not believe that either author intended to draw a chronological distinction between the ban for the future on δανείζειν ἐπὶ τοῖς σώμασιν and the σεισάχθεια: cf. on 6. i.   [15] τιμῆς Sintenis: τιμήν codd.
[16] ἑβδομήκοντ' ἄγουσαν T. Reinach, *Hermes* lxiii 1928, 238–40: ἑβδομήκοντα καὶ τριῶν οὖσαν codd. Not all have accepted it, but this emendation seems to me to be certain.

These passages have been much discussed, and agreement on them seems as far away as ever; I have argued for my view of them in *NC*⁷ xv 1975, 1–11, xvii 1977, 152.

In *A.P.* the end of §i refers first to measures, then to weights and finally to coinage, and we should expect §ii to deal with these topics in the same order (K. Kraft, *JNG* x 1959/60, 21–46, xix 1969, 7–14, C. M. Kraay, *Essays ... Stanley Robinson*, 1–9). §ii begins with the statement that Athens' measures were made larger than the 'Pheidonean'; the next sentence, stating that the mina, which previously weighed 70 drachmae, was 'filled up with the 100', should refer to weights; and the 'increase in the value of the coinage' should be sought in one or both of the last two sentences, that (whereas the later standard coin was the tetradrachm) the old standard coin was the didrachm (Kraay), and that for purposes of coinage Solon established a proportion of (not 60 but) 63 minas to the talent (Kraft). Androtion as reported by Plutarch writes first of measures and secondly of coinage, and to explain the second he introduces the change from a mina of 70 drachmae to a mina of 100 drachmae —from which he argues that this enabled debtors to pay less while creditors still received all that was due to them. Earlier commentators assumed that *A.P.*'s account like Plutarch's is derived from Androtion and that it too must refer to the coinage in writing of the change in the drachma or mina, and it has often been thought that *A.P.* and Plutarch envisaged the same change (for a recent version of this doctrine see M. H. Crawford, *Eirene* x 1972, 5–8); but since *A.P.* rejected Androtion's explanation of the σεισάχθεια we should not automatically assume that his account of what Solon did in this area is derived from Androtion or agrees with him.

Measures are straightforward enough. Pheidon of Argos (probably to be dated to the first half of the seventh century, e.g. Busolt, *G.G.*, i². 611–25, Wade-Gery, *C.A.H.*, iii¹. 761–2; an eighth-century date is preferred by G. L. Huxley, *BCH* lxxxii 1958, 588–601, cf. *Early Sparta*, 28–31; T. Kelly, *A History of Argos to 500 B.C.*, 94–129, argues for the sixth-century date implied by Herodotus, but that is unlikely to be right) is variously credited with measures, weights and coinage, of which measures are the best attested (H. vi. 127. iii; Eph. 70 FF 115, 176, *ap.* Str. 358. viii. iii. 33, 376. viii. vi. 16; *Marm. Par.* 239 A 30; *E.M.* [612. 57] ὀβελίσκος). Surviving (post-Solonian) measures of capacity in Athens indicate no change in standard (M. L. Lang [& M. Crosby], *The Athenian Agora*, x. 48); in the fourth century 5 'Delphic' μέδιμνοι were equivalent to 8 'Pheidonean' μέδιμνοι (Tod 140, 80–7); Delphi was very probably using either the Athenian standard or the 'Aeginetan'; Sparta's μέδιμνος, which presumably was the 'Aeginetan', was equivalent to

1½ Athenian μέδιμνοι (Dicaearchus *ap*. Ath. IV. 141 C, Pl. *Lyc*. 12. iii); either possibility for Delphi will yield an Athenian μέδιμνος larger than the 'Pheidonean'.

Weights are more difficult. A change from a mina of 70 drachmae to a mina of 100 drachmae can be achieved either by enlarging the mina or by reducing the drachma: Androtion evidently believed that the drachma was reduced, but the more natural interpretation of what *A.P.* says is that the mina was enlarged. Classical Athens undoubtedly had a system in which there were 100 drachmae to the mina: Kraft thought it incredible that she should earlier have had a system in which there were 70 drachmae to the mina, and supposed that Solon in fact increased both drachma and mina in the proportion 70:100 (*JNG* x 1959/60, 27–32, xix 1969, 17–20); but there is evidence for such a system not only in Delphi, where it could have come about by a combination of different standards to suit the needs of a sanctuary visited by men from many cities, but in various other places, and so a mina of 70 drachmae is not to be ruled out as impossible (cf. Crawford, *op. cit.*, 7 with n. 7). Here *A.P.* does not refer to any outside standard; but it has often been pointed out that 70 drachmae in Aeginetan coinage weigh the same as 100 drachmae in Athenian coinage (there is no change of standard in either city between the earliest coins and the time of *A.P.*), and that proportion was in fact observed as a rate of exchange (Tod 140, 21–3); it may well be that there were 70 drachmae to the mina in the 'Aeginetan' system. In that case, if Solon reduced the drachma, as Androtion believed, Athens will have used the 'Aeginetan' drachma and mina before his reform and will have combined the 'Euboeic' drachma with the 'Aeginetan' mina after; if he enlarged the mina, as *A.P.* seems to say, she will have used the 'Euboeic' drachma and an idiosyncratic mina before his reform and the 'Euboeic' drachma and the 'Aeginetan' mina after.

Although it is not reflected in the coinage, there was at least one increase in Athens' weight standards, applying to all units in the system, between the time of Solon and the time of *A.P.* Three bronze standard weights of *c*. 500 or a little earlier point to a stater (=2 minas) of 756–95 g.; next there may have been a period when the stater weighed *c*. 860 g.; in the late fifth and fourth centuries the stater weighed *c*. 900–20 g. (Lang, *op. cit.*, 18–21, M. H. Chambers, *CSCA* vi 1973, 11–12: the stater of 860 g. is postulated by Chambers but regarded by Lang as within the limits of tolerance of the stater of 900–20 g.; on Lang's alleged heavier stater of the Peloponnesian War see Rhodes, *NC*[7] xv 1975, 8). We have no evidence for weight standards in Aegina, but it is likely that the Athenian and Aeginetan drachmae were in the proportion 70:100 at the time when coinage was introduced, and that this proportion was maintained for the coinage in spite of subsequent changes in weight standards.

The change in the coinage implied by *A.P.*'s next sentence is authentic: in the oldest Athenian coin series, the *Wappenmünzen* (on which cf. p. 169), the standard coin was the didrachm; but there are a few tetradrachms at the end of the series, and the tetradrachm was the standard coin in the 'Owl' series which followed (cf. Kraay, *Archaic and Classical Greek Coins*, 57, 60).

The final sentence has usually been thought to mean that (presumably, to cover the mint's expenses) Solon had his coins made slightly under weight, 63 minas' worth of coins being struck from each 60 minas' weight of silver: Kraay, accepting this, supposes that the previous sentence is intended to explain the 'increase' in the coinage and this last sentence is a supplementary note. Kraft, however, believed this sentence to mean that Solon had his coins made slightly over weight, 60 minas' worth of coins being struck from each 63 minas' weight of silver: for him the previous sentence was a parenthesis and this making the coins over weight was Solon's 'increase'. When we set the unchanging weights of the coins against the different weight standards mentioned above, we find that on the earliest standard 53–5 minas' worth of coins will have been struck from 60 minas' weight of silver; if there was a stater of 860 g., on that standard 60 minas' worth of coins will have been struck from 60 minas' weight of silver; on the later standard 63–4 minas' worth of coins will have been struck from 60 minas' weight of silver. *Pace* Kraft, I find it hard to believe that Athens' earliest coins were deliberately made over weight: more probably, though the principle had been adopted that there should be 100 drachmae to the mina, the relationship of the small unit to the large was not at first worked out with sufficient care (a didrachm will have been $\frac{2}{3}$–1 g. heavier than it should have been on the earliest weight standard known to us). What *A.P.* is normally thought to be saying, that 63 minas' worth of coins were struck from 60 minas' weight of silver, was true of his own day: I suspect that he did not know that the earlier standard weights were lighter, and with that proviso I accept Kraay's interpretation of what he says about the coinage. Chambers (*op. cit.*, 7–15) suggests instead that *A.P.* is referring to the change from his 860 g. to the 900–20 g. weight standard, describing it in terms of the 'coin mina'.

Since the publication of articles by P. Jacobsthal and E. S. G. Robinson on the Artemisium at Ephesus (*JHS* lxxi 1951, 85–95, 156–67) the dates of the earliest coins have been steadily lowered. M. J. Price and N. M. Waggoner argue that the first electrum coins were issued shortly before 560, Croesus' silver coins in the 550's and then the first Aeginetan coins *c.* 550; in Athens the

Wappenmünzen began *c.* 545 or later and the Owls *c.* 510–506 (*Ancient Greek Coinage; The Asyut Hoard*, 64–8, 73–6, 78–9, 122–3); Kraay in reply dates the electrum coins before 600, the first Aeginetan coins *c.* 565–560 and Croesus' silver coins after that; the *Wappenmünzen c.* 560–550 and the Owls *c.* 527–520 (*NC*[7] xvii 1977, 195–6, 197–8). Some have tried to maintain the higher dates which used to be accepted (e.g. H. A. Cahn, *Kleine Schriften*, 81–97, L. Weidauer, *Probleme der frühen Elektronprägung*), but on the evidence we now have it appears that we must choose between the extreme downdating of Price & Waggoner and the moderate downdating of Kraay; any further lowering of the initial dates, however, would make it very hard to accommodate the Athenian issues which must be dated before the Persian sack of 480. We must accept that the earliest Athenian coins, and even the earliest Aeginetan coins, were issued long after Solon's archonship, and even after the later date which some prefer for his reforms (cf. on 5. ii): he cannot have reformed Athens' coinage, or even have introduced coinage to Athens, though passages from his laws indicate that at the time of his reforms standard weights of uncoined silver served as a form of currency (cf. on 8. iii).†

Crawford suggests that not merely the reform of coinage but all the reforms attributed to Solon in this chapter are spurious: Athens' μέδιμνος was larger than the 'Pheidonean'; Athens divided the mina into 100 drachmae whereas Aegina divided into it 70; classical Athens' standard coin was the tetradrachm whereas Aegina's was the didrachm (he does not believe even that it was remembered that Athens' earliest coin had been the didrachm); fourth-century theory regarded these three differences as 'increases', and attributed the 'increases' to Solon. If, as I believe, Solon's laws survived and could be consulted in the fourth century (cf. on 7. i), this degree of scepticism is excessive. I suggest that Solon's laws did enjoin the use of standard measures and weights; that his measures of capacity were larger than the 'Pheidonean' and happen still to have been in use at the time of *A.P.*; that his weight system used the same mina as the 'Aeginetan' but divided it into 100 drachmae whereas the 'Aeginetan' divided it into 70, and on one or more subsequent occasions the Athenians changed to a heavier set of standards but they continued to think of their weights, as they thought of their measures, as 'Solonian'; and that later they wrongly assumed that Solon's standards represented a departure from the standards previously used in Athens (and disagreed as to what their earlier weight system had been). Since coins were named after the weights of silver which they represented, if there was no record of when coinage had been introduced it was easy to assume that Solon must have reformed Athens' coinage as well as her weights.

10. ii. ἔχ[ο]υσα: Read by Wilcken, and by Kenyon in his Berlin ed. and O.C.T. Originally Kenyon read only [ἔχο]υσα, and W. Wyse suggested the more specific ἄγουσα or ἕλκουσα (*CR* v 1891, 108); ἄγειν is the verb normally used in fourth-century texts, and is used at the corresponding point in Plutarch's account (cf. p. 164 with n. 16); Chambers, *TAPA* xcvi 1965, 35, reads ἄγ[ο]υσα.

ἦν δ' ὁ ἀρχαῖος χαρακτὴρ δίδραχμον: The well-known 'Owls' were tetradrachms (cf. p. 167). Phil. 328 F 200, commenting on the Owls, states that the old didrachms had a bull stamped on them, and is followed in this by Poll. ix. 60–1; incredibly, Pl. *Thes.* 25. iii attributes the 'Bull' coinage to Theseus. From the evidence of the actual coins we learn that the Owl tetradrachms were indeed preceded by didrachms; but the coins in question were the *Wappenmünzen*, bearing a variety of devices which C. T. Seltman interpreted as the badges of the aristocratic clans (*Athens: Its History and Coinage*, 19–38). N. Yalouris (*MH* vii 1950, 52–4) suggested that all the badges have some connection with the Panathenaea and can be regarded as symbols of Athena ἱππία, and Seltman's aristocratic badges have been disposed of by R. J. Hopper (*CQ*² x 1960, 242–7), but at any rate the attribution of these coins to Athens seems securely established. The Bull is indeed found (cf. Kraay, *Archaic and Classical Greek Coins*, 57 with pl. 9 no. 170), but only as one design among many.

11. i. διατάξας δὲ τὴν πολιτείαν ὅνπερ εἴρηται τρόπον: 7. i begins πολιτείαν δὲ κατέστησε, and 7. ii introduces the account of Solon's constitutional reform with διέταξε τὴν πολιτείαν τόνδε ⟨τὸν⟩ τρόπον; the assessment of Solon in 9 ends with a reference to his πολιτεία. Ch. 10, as we have noted, interrupts the plan of *A.P.*'s treatment of Solon (cf. p. 163); this resuming phrase ignores 10 and refers to 7–9.

ἐπειδὴ προσιόντες αὐτῷ περὶ τῶν νόμων ἐνώχλουν: Cf. Pl. *Sol.* 25. vi. Though neither *A.P.* nor Plutarch quotes Solon it is not unlikely that this statement is derived, whether securely or not, from material in Solon's poems.

ἀποδημίαν ἐποιήσατο: Cf. Pl. *Sol.* 25. vi–28. i, H. i. 29. i. Herodotus, almost certainly rightly, links this with the 10 years (100 in *A.P.* and Pl.) during which Solon's laws were to remain unaltered: cf. 7. ii with commentary. The most thorough modern discussion of Solon's travels is that of Linforth, *Solon the Athenian*, 297–302. Plutarch gives an account based at least in part on Solon's poems (*Sol.* 26. i, iv), confirming from them *A.P.*'s statement that he visited Egypt (*Sol.* 26. i), and accepting despite chronological difficulties the story of his meeting Croesus of Lydia (*Sol.* 27. i). This last story, not included in *A.P.*, was current as early as the time of Herodotus

(1. 29–33); but *pace* Plutarch the chronological difficulties are too great for it to be acceptable: the date of 560/59 for Solon's death cannot be relied upon but is plausible (Phaen. fr. 21 Wehrli *ap.* Pl. *Sol.* 32. iii, with Davies, *A.P.F.*, 323–4; Jacoby, *JHS* lxiv 1944, 50 n. 64 = *Abhandlungen*, 285–6 n. 64, *Atthis*, 365 n. 70, suspected that Solon did not return to Athens or live as late as 560); Croesus' accession is to be dated *c.* 560 (for attempts at greater precision see H. Kaletsch, *Hist.* vii 1958, 1–47, esp. 1–25, 39–47, M. Miller, *Klio* xli 1963, 59–67); and as Grote remarked the fact that in this connection Plutarch does not give a quotation from Solon's poems 'amounts to negative evidence of some value' (*H.G.* [1869–84], iii. 150 n.). D.L. 1. 49–54, 62, dates Solon's travels later, as a reaction to the rise of Pisistratus, but this is because he believes that Solon could not have lived under Pisistratus' rule (cf. on 14. ii). No more is heard of Solon between his leaving Athens and the rise of Pisistratus, and we may doubt whether he returned permanently to Athens when the ten years had expired (cf. K. Freeman, *The Work and Life of Solon*, 181: for this reason if for no other we should draw no conclusion from the statement in Plat. *Tim.* 21 C 5–D 1 that he returned from Egypt to find στάσις). If he did continue to travel, the synchronisms with Amasis of Egypt, whose reign began in 570 or 569 (H. I. 30. i, II. 177. ii), and with Philocyprus of Cyprus, whose son was alive in 497 (H. v. 113. ii, Pl. *Sol.* 26. ii–iv, confirmed by a quotation from the poems; in *Vit. Arat. i* [p. 7 Martin] Philocyprus becomes Cypranor), need not be an obstacle to belief in the orthodox date for his archonship and reforms (cf. A. J. Holladay, *G&R*² xxiv 1977, 53–4, and commentary on 5. ii; for the use of these synchronisms as evidence against the orthodox date see Hignett, *H.A.C.*, 320, S. S. Markianos, *Hist.* xxiii 1974, 1–20, Ἑλληνικά xxviii 1975, 5–28 with English summary 239).

κατ' ἐμπορίαν: That in the course of his travels Solon engaged in trade is possible, and even likely, but cannot be confirmed and may be based on no more than the assumption that as one of the μέσοι Solon must have been a trader: cf. on 5. iii.

καὶ θεωρίαν: Cf. H. 1. 29. i (κατὰ θεωρίης πρόφασιν).

οὐ γὰρ οἴεσθαι ... τοὺς νόμους ἐξηγεῖσθαι παρών: This, together with the statement that he would not return for ten years, is grammatically dependent on εἰπών, and that supports the suggestion made above, that Solon may have given the reasons for his departure from Athens in his poems. The explanation is more graphically expressed in Pl. *Sol.* 25. vi: Solon was under continual pressure from men urging him to expound or alter his laws. For the allegation that his laws were obscure cf. 9. ii with commentary.

11. ii. τὰς στάσεις ἀμφοτέρας μεταθέσθαι: That is, they regretted their agreement to appoint him and to accept the measures which he judged appropriate. For dissatisfaction with what Solon had done cf. Pl. *Sol.* 14. ii, 16. i–iv (between his economic and his political and legal reform: cf. on 10. i), 25. iv. That Solon's reforms displeased both sides, being more drastic than the rich and aristocratic would have liked but less drastic than at any rate some of the poor and ignoble had wanted, is clear from his poems, quoted in *A.P.* 12 and elsewhere; and that they failed to provide a wholly satisfactory solution to Athens' problems is shown by the ensuing troubles over the archonship, reported in 13. i–ii, and by the tyranny of Pisistratus.

πάντ' ἀνάδαστα ποιήσειν: Cf. Solon, fr. 34. 8–9 West *ap.* 12. iii; also Pl. *Sol.* 16. i, citing the 'Lycurgan' distribution of equal κλῆροι to the Spartan ὅμοιοι. On γῆς ἀναδασμός in the classical period see 40. iii with commentary. It is not clear what Solonian legislation on land tenure Aristotle had in mind in *Pol.* II. 1266 B 14–17.

εἰς τὴν αὐτὴν τάξιν: εἰς was deleted by Kaibel & Wilamowitz[1],[3] (cf. Arist. *Pol.* IV. 1296 A 39–40), emended to ἢ by Kaibel & Wilamowitz[2] (cf. Kaibel, *Stil und Text*, 146–7, citing such passages as Arist. *Pol.* IV. 1296 A 37–8). Both changes won some support, but Aristotle uses εἰς ... τὴν τάξιν with other verbs (e.g. *Phys.* II. 196 A 27–8), and it is not incredible that *A.P.* should have written what we read in the London papyrus.†

καὶ ἐξὸν αὐτῷ ... τυραννεῖν εἵλετο πρὸς ἀμφοτέρους ἀπεχθέσθαι: Cf. 6. iii–iv, Solon, fr. 34. 7–8 West *ap.* 12. iii; also Pl. *Sol.* 15. i with quotation of frs 32, 33, *Comp. Sol. Publ.* 2. v. In view of his earlier support of the poor and unprivileged against the rich and powerful (5. ii–iii with commentary), it is easy to suppose that Solon might have become tyrant as champion of the poor, less easy to suppose that he might have done so as champion of the rich whom he had been attacking; but fr. 36. 22–5 *ap.* 12. iv suggests that he could have supported either side against the other, and 5. ii claims that in his earlier poetry he 'fought and disputed on behalf of each side against the other'. We must remember that Solon was Eupatrid if not rich (5. iii with commentary), and εἵλοντο κοινῇ διαλλακτὴν καὶ ἄρχοντα (5. ii).

ἀπεχθέσθαι is the correction of W. Wyse, *CR* v 1891, 108, for the papyrus' ἀπεχθεσθῆναι: Aristid. XLVI. *Quatt.* (ii. 360, Dindorf), in a paraphrase of 11. ii–12. i, uses the present infinitive, ἀπεχθάνεσθαι. σώσας τὴν πατρίδα καὶ τὰ βέ[λτι]στα νομοθετήσας: Probably to be read as a formulation of what Solon thought he was doing, rather than as an expression of *A.P.*'s enthusiastic approval.

12. i. οἱ τ' ἄλλοι συμφωνοῦσι πάντες καὶ αὐτὸς ἐν τῇ ποιήσει μέμνηται: *A.P.* has twice before remarked that all agree and Solon provides

COMMENTARY ON THE *ATH. POL.*

confirmation in his poems, in 5. iii on his μεσότης, and in 6. iv on the opportunity he had to become tyrant: cf. Introduction, p. 25. The discussion of Solon ends with a selection of quotations from his poems, made to illustrate the moderation of his reforms. The contrast with 5. ii–iii and the poems quoted there makes it clear that at some time before his reforms he had expressed the grievances of the poor against the rich; but afterwards he was subjected to complaints from both sides, and in his later poems he claims to have resisted the excessive demands of both, he attributes to some of the poor a lust for ἁρπαγή (fr. 34. 1 West *ap.* 12. iii), and he professes a 'moderate' view of what is due to the δῆμος (frs 5. 1–2 *ap.* 12. i, 6 *ap.* 12. ii, 36. 20–2 *ap.* 12. iv, 37. [6–]7–8 *ap.* 12. v). Nevertheless he claims that he has not betrayed the trust of the poor and unprivileged, and that what he has done for them, though less than some had hoped for, is all that he had promised and more than they could have dreamed of (frs 34. 6 *ap.* 12. iii, 36. 1–2, 15–17, *ap.* 12. iv, 37. 1–3 *ap.* 12. v).

δήμῳ μὲν γὰρ ἔδωκα . . . : Fr. 5 West, quoted also in Pl. *Sol.* 18. v; Arist. *Pol.* II. 1274 A 15–16 (cf. Wilamowitz, *A.u.A.*, i. 71 n. 43) and Aristid. XLIV. *Rhod. Conc.*, XLVI. *Quatt.* (i. 829, ii. 360, Dindorf) are derived from this fragment. δῆμος can refer either to the whole community or to the mass of the lower orders as opposed to the γνώριμοι (cf. on 2. i): here the contrast with οἳ . . . εἶχον δύναμιν καὶ χρήμασιν ἦσαν ἀγητοί makes it clear that the latter meaning is intended.

γέρας ὅσσον ἀπαρκεῖ: Plutarch has κράτος ὅσσον ἐπαρκεῖ, and uses ἐπαρκεῖν immediately afterwards, in §vi; ἀπαρκεῖ had already been conjectured, by Coraes, before the discovery of *A.P.*; but Brunck read ἐπαρκεῖν and is followed by West. It is doubtful whether Solon would regard what he had given to the δῆμος as κράτος; the only other instance noted in LSJ of ἐπαρκεῖν without an object is Soph. *Ant.* 612, so *A.P.*'s verb is to be preferred, but K. Ziegler argues strongly for a generic infinitive rather than a specific indicative (*Miscellanea . . . Augusto Rostagni*, 656). I should print γέρας ὅσσον ἀπαρκεῖν.

οὔτ' ἐπορεξάμενος: Usually taken to mean 'nor holding out the hope of greater' (Linforth); but the normal meaning of the word is 'reach out for', and Prof. P. H. J. Lloyd-Jones suggests to me that here it should mean 'nor reaching out for it', not contrasting with ἀφελών but reinforcing it. This yields a better parallelism between the two couplets. (Cf. on βιαζόμενος in §ii.)

μηδὲν ἀεικὲς ἔχειν: 'Suffer no indignity' (Linforth): cf. H. III. 15. i, ἔχων οὐδὲν βίαιον.

ἀμφιβαλὼν κρατερὸν σάκος ἀμφοτέροισι: Usually rendered 'holding out my strong shield over both of them' (Fritz & Kapp), but what follows makes it likelier that Solon claimed to have held out his shield not in protection of both sides but in defence against both (C. Rogge, *PhW* xliv 1924, 797–8: cf. frs 36. 26–7 West *ap.* 12. iv, 37. 9–10 *ap.* 12. v).†

12. ii. δῆμος δ' ὧδ' ἂν ἄριστα . . . : Fr. 6 West. Lines 1–2 are quoted also in Pl. *Comp. Sol. Publ.* 2. vi. Lines 3–4 are variously quoted and attributed: they are ascribed to Theognis (153–4) in the form

τίκτει τοι κόρος ὕβριν, ὅταν κακῷ ὄλβος ἕπηται
ἀνθρώπῳ καὶ ὅτῳ μὴ νόος ἄρτιος ᾖ,

and the two versions are contrasted by Clem. Alex. *Strom.* VI. 8. vii; line 3, with the wording of 'Theognis', is quoted and ascribed to Homer by schol. Pind. *Ol.* xiii. 12e; cf. also D.L. I. 59, Diogenianus, VIII. 22, and other texts cited by West. Solon doubtless wrote what is quoted in *A.P.* or something similar, but we cannot hope to discover the original author of the proverb or the original form of words.

μήτε βιαζόμενος: Plutarch has πιεζόμενος, but that seems too strong a word for the context. Like πιεζόμενος, βιαζόμενος is normally read as passive and contrasted with λίαν ἀνεθείς, 'neither left too free nor subjected to too much restraint' (Linforth). In combining the second couplet with the first Solon must have been thinking more of the danger of giving the δῆμος too much freedom than of that of giving it too little (cf. Linforth, *Solon the Athenian*, 181), and the possibility should be considered that βιαζόμενος is middle and a reinforcement of λίαν ἀνεθείς, 'not unleashed too much nor allowed to work violence' (cf. on ἐπορεξάμενος in §i: this suggestion is not to be blamed on Lloyd-Jones); but the usual interpretation is more obvious and is probably right.

12. iii. οἳ δ' ἐφ' ἁρπαγαῖσιν ἦλθον: Fr. 34 West. Lines 4–5 are quoted in Pl. *Sol.* 16. iii; lines 6–7 (ἃ μὲν . . . ἔερδον) in Aristid. XLIX. Παραφθ. (ii. 536, Dindorf), with ἄελπτα for εἶπα in line 6. Disappointed members of the δῆμος claimed that Solon had let them down, and he replies that he has done what he promised, and that they were wrong to expect a more ruthless purpose to be concealed behind his mild words (με κωτίλλοντα λείως). We have insufficient information to judge between him and his accusers here; but frs 4a and 4c, quoted in 5. ii–iii, show that not all his words were mild and suggest that if men did read into his words a more ruthless purpose than he really had they may not have been wholly to blame.

At the beginning οἵ is standard in editions of *A.P.*, but West's οἳ is no less likely; for ἐφ' ἁρπαγαῖσιν ἦλθον H. Richards suggested ἐφ' ἁρπαγῇ συνῆλθον (*CR* vii 1893, 212: cf. ἐφ' ἁρπαγῇ, the probable reading in fr. 4. 13), but there is no reason why Solon should not have used plural noun and simple verb here.

12. iii] COMMENTARY ON THE *ATH. POL.*

τι [ῥέζ]ειν: The restoration of Kenyon[1] has become standard in editions of *A.P.*, but J. B. Bury suggested [κιν]εῖν (*CR* v 1891, 178), and West prints τι[..] . ε[ι]ν.

οὐδὲ πιεί[ρ]ας χθονὸς ... ἰσομοιρίαν ἔχειν: This confirms that, as *A.P.* remarks in introducing the quotation and also in 11. ii, there were extremists among the poor who wanted not merely the unencumbered possession of the land which they occupied but a redistribution of land. In the contrast κακοῖσιν ἐσθλοὺς Solon adheres to the convention in which these words refer to a man's standing in society rather than his character (see especially A. W. H. Adkins, *Merit and Responsibility*, 30–40, 75–9, 159–63, *Moral Values and Political Behaviour in Ancient Greece*, 12–21).

ἐσθ[λοὺς] is the first word decipherable in fr. Ia of the Berlin papyrus of *A.P.*, which runs from here to ἀνδρῷ[ν] at the end of §iv (line 25 of the quotation). On the Berlin papyrus see briefly Introduction, pp. 2–3, and for this fragment see M. H. Chambers, *TAPA* xcviii 1967, 55–7.

12. iv. [πάλιν]: Restored by Kenyon, who commented in his Berlin ed. *lectio incerta, sed haec vestigiis non incongruens est; potest etiam littera ultima s esse* (and Dr J. D. Thomas doubts the ν). This is almost certainly right (cf. πάλιν δ' in §ii, καὶ πάλιν δ' in §iii, καὶ πάλιν in §v); but Κ. Σ. Κόντος suggested λέγει (*Ἀθ.* iii 1891, 332), and Wilcken read ... *EI*, offering *N, M* or *C* as the previous letter. ἐγὼ δὲ τῶν μὲν ... : Fr. 36 West. All but the first two lines are quoted in Aristid. xlix. Παραφθ. (ii. 536–8, Dindorf); lines 6–7, 11–14 (γλῶσσαν ... ἔχοντας) and 16 are quoted in Pl. *Sol.* 15. vi, vi and i respectively. Here again Solon is replying to extremists among the δῆμος, and begins with the insistence that he has done what he set out to do—by liberating the earth, ransoming slaves, and providing justice for all. Another man in Solon's position might (have gratified the extremists and) not have given Athens a moderate solution; but if the δῆμος had not been restrained the result would not have been acceptable to the rich, and civil war would have followed.

In the first two lines 'many emendations have been proposed, in almost every syllable' (Linforth, *Solon the Athenian*, 184), but the version of Kenyon's Berlin ed. and O.C.T. has become generally accepted. The reading ξ[υ]νήγαγον is due to A. Platt, *CR* v 1891, 178; the punctuation is due to R. C. Jebb, *ap.* Sandys, cf. *JP* xxv 1897, 98–105; and the couplet is best translated, 'Of the purposes for which I assembled the people, is there any which I stopped before achieving?' Sandys considered two possible interpretations of ξυνήγαγον δῆμον: 'I formed the popular party, or (less probably) gathered the people into one (by healing the divisions which separated the various orders in the state).' In lines 3–17 Solon goes on to say what he has done for those in debt or exiled, but in 18–27 he proceeds to claim that what he did was fair to all and that another man in his position might not have restrained the δῆμος (where that word evidently denotes not the whole people but the mass of the unprivileged), and 22–5 suggests that he could have supported either side against the other. Seen in the context of the whole poem, δῆμον in line 2 should denote the whole people rather than the oppressed lower classes, and the best interpretation is one which Sandys did not consider, 'called the people to an assembly' (Campbell, *Greek Lyric Poetry*, 251, citing T. I. 120, i, II. 60. i; cf. Moore).

ἐν δίκῃ χρόνου (l. 3): Sandys again considers two possibilities: 'before the tribunal of time ... or, less probably, in the justice of time, i.e. justice which time eventually brings', and συμμαρτυροίη points to legal proceedings; but it would be surprising to find δίκη used to mean 'trial' or 'court' as early as this, and although the effect is very much the same Solon's thought must be closer to 'when time delivers judgment'. For the idea of time as the vindicator of the just Linforth quotes Pind. *Ol.* x. 53, fr. 145 Bowra, Soph. *O.T.* 614, X. *H.* III. iii. 2; see also Solon, frs 4. 16, 28–9, 13. 8, 28–32, West, with W. W. Jaeger, *Sb. Berlin* 1926, 79 = *Scripta Minora*, i. 329, trans. *Five Essays*, 90–1; Aesch. *P.V.* 981. For the use of δίκη by Solon and other early writers see M. Gagarin, *CP* lxviii 1973, 81–94, lxix 1974, 186–97 (on Solon, 190–2).†

μήτηρ μεγίστη ... Γῆ (ll. 4–5): The soil of Attica is here personified as Γῆ: Sandys compares Plat. *Legg.* v. 740 A 2–7, 741 C 1–2; and for Earth as the mother of the gods and of all things Linforth compares Hes. *Theog.* 116–18 (cf. 126–8), *Hymn. Hom.* xxx. *Terr.*, Eur. fr. 839 Nauck[2].

ὅρους ἀνεῖλον (l. 6): The ὅροι will have been marker posts set up in the land as evidence of an overlord's claim on the land and on the ἑκτήμοροι who worked it (cf. pp. 94, 95). By uprooting the ὅροι Solon abolished this claim, and so liberated the land and the ἑκτήμοροι: cf. on 2. ii and 6. i.‡

πρόσθεν δὲ (l. 7): All sources agree on this, but γε would give a better sense: it was proposed by H. Stadtmüller, *Festschrift zur 36. Versammlung deutscher Philologen und Schulmänner, 1882*, 71, and in *A.P.* by J. B. Mayor, *CR* v 1891, 109.

πολλοὺς δ' Ἀθήνας ... ἀνήγαγον πραθέντας (ll. 8–9): Solon's claim is clear enough, but it is not clear how he tracked down these men or, in the case of those sold into slavery outside Attica, induced their owners to part with them; and there must surely in fact have been a number of slaves whom he failed to redeem.

ὑπὸ χρειοῦς (ll. 10–11): This is the reading of the London papyrus

(West dots all but the first letter and the last), the Berlin papyrus reads χρεῶν, and Aristides the obviously wrong χρησμὸν λέγοντας. The singular is regularly accepted. Hammond, *JHS* lxxxi 1961, 89 = *Studies*, 125, supposes that the word whose genitive Solon uses here is χρέος, and translates, 'through stress of debt' (cf. M. H. Chambers, *TAPA* xcviii 1967, 56; Moore, translation with p. 225); but usually, and surely rightly, it has been thought that the noun is χρεώ and the meaning is 'through dire necessity' (cf. Hom. *Il.* VIII. 57)—and Hammond and Chambers both retain the perispomenon accentuation appropriate to that. But Solon seems to have been misunderstood in antiquity too: the scribe who wrote the plural χρεῶν in the Berlin papyrus was probably thinking of debts.

ὡς ἄν (l. 12): This would be unusual in early poetry: A. Platt, *JP* xxiv 1896, 251–2, suggested ὥστε; West prints ὡς δή.

δουλίην (l. 13): Possibly the reference is to men who had been enslaved but not sold abroad, but more probably here as in line 7 Solon is considering as slavery the state of the ἑκτήμοροι.

ἤθη δεσποτῶν τρομευμέν[ους] (l. 14): 'Trembled at their masters' whims' (Linforth).

κράτει νόμου (ll. 15–16): The London papyrus reads κρατεεινομου, the Berlin κράτη ὁμοῦ, Aristides κράτη or κράτει ὁμοῦ, and Plutarch (not quoting line 15) ὁμοῦ; editors have been divided between νόμου and ὁμοῦ, but κράτει νόμου as 'by force of law' is very hard to accept, and κράτει, ὁμοῦ should be the correct text (cf. V. L. Ehrenberg, *Charisteria A. Rzach . . . dargebracht*, 22–3 = *Polis und Imperium*, 149–50, trans. *Aspects of the Ancient World*, 82–3; Chambers, *TAPA* xcviii 1967, 56–7; M. Ostwald, *Nomos and the Beginnings of the Athenian Democracy*, 3 n. 5).

βίαν τε καὶ δίκην συναρμόσας (l. 16): 'βίην repeats the idea of κράτει, and the line is an apology of the lawgiver for resorting to force at all' (Linforth, *Solon the Athenian*, 187)—but when and how did Solon resort to force? We should not be surprised at the use of force by the Solon of frs 4c and 4b West (*ap.* 5. iii), the Solon who could if he wished have become tyrant (11. ii, fr. 34 *ap.* 12. iii); but force is not usually associated with the man whom both sides agreed to accept as mediator. He did not seize power by violence, and he claims that by his moderation he prevented violence and bloodshed (lines 20–5; cf. fr. 34. 7–8 *ap.* 12. iii, expressing distaste for the βία associated with tyranny). βία and δίκη are normally contrasted as means of resolving a dispute (cf. M. Gagarin, *CP* lxviii 1973, 81–94), though Masaracchia, *Solone*, 348, cites a number of passages in which a combination of βία and δίκη or their equivalents is mentioned (e.g. Hom. *Il.* XVI. 542). Most probably the reference here is not to physical force, but we should think of such passages as fr. 5. 5–6 *ap.* 12. i, lines 20–2 of this fr., and fr. 37. 7–10 *ap.* 12. v: Solon resisted the demands of both rich and poor, and constrained both to acquiesce in a just settlement.

θεσμούς θ' ὁμοίως (l. 18): This is the reading of the London papyrus, with θ' corrected from an original τε; the Berlin papyrus has θε[σ]μὸν δ' ὁμοίως; Aristides has θεσμοὺς θ' ὁμοίως or ὁμοίους. Solon is turning to a new theme, after concluding the previous theme with ταῦτα μέν ..., so δ' is preferable to θ'; ὁμοίους is attractive, but is unlikely to be right against both papyri and most MSS of Aristides.

It was later customary to refer to the θεσμοί of Draco and the νόμοι of Solon (cf. on 7. i), but here Solon uses θεσμός of his own enactments: cf. 35. ii and Pl. *Sol.* 19. iv. Ostwald, *Nomos and the Beginnings of the Athenian Democracy*, 9–56, characterises θεσμός as a regulation imposed by an external authority and νόμος as a norm accepted by the whole community, while F. Quass, *Nomos und Psephisma*, 11–23, suggests that θεσμός like nearly all the other words meaning 'law' denotes a decision of the legislative authority, whether that authority be a single man or a council or assembly, while νόμος alone denotes a norm to be observed. In the later part of his book Ostwald revives the suggestion of R. Hirzel, *Abh. Leipzig* xx. i 1900–3, 49, that Athens owes the adoption of the term νόμος to Cleisthenes, who distinguished the decrees which he carried through the assembly (cf. on 21. i) from the statutes of Draco and Solon. The remarks of Quass and the criticisms of J. K. Davies (*CR*[2] xxiii 1973, 225–7) are not fatal to what Ostwald says of the significance of this change: θεσμός at any rate can be used of a regulation imposed from outside, while the later Athenian alternative to νόμος, ψήφισμα, clearly denotes a decision reached by democratic vote (for νόμοι and ψηφίσματα cf. on 26. ii).

τῷ κακῷ τε κἀγαθῷ (l. 18): This, the reading of the London papyrus, gives a much better sense than the καλῷ of the Berlin papyrus: Solon enacted laws which were fair to the lower and upper classes alike. For the use of these words with social rather than moral significance cf. §iii with commentary.

[κ]ακοφραδής τε καὶ φιλοκτήμων; (l. 21): κακοφραδής means 'bad in counsel', whether through malice or through folly: the combination with φιλοκτήμων, suggesting that the champions of the oppressed tend to be self-seeking, indicates that here, as in Hom. *Il.* XXIII. 483, the former meaning is intended.

εἰ γὰρ ἤθελον ... ἠδ' ἐχηρώθη πόλις (ll. 22–5): 'For if I had been willing to do what pleased the enemies of the people at that time, or again what *their* opponents planned for *them*, (there would have been civil war and) this city would have been deprived of many of her sons' (Fritz & Kapp). The ἃ το[ῖς and ἃ τ[οῖσιν of the Berlin papyrus, supported by Aristides (all MSS in the first instance, most

COMMENTARY ON THE *ATH. POL.*

in the second), is clearly right against the αὐτοῖς and αὐτοῖσιν of the London papyrus.

ὡς ἐν κύσιν ... λύκος: (l. 27): Linforth compares Hom. *Il.* xii. 41–2 (not 43), where the same image is used but featuring a boar or lion.

12. v. μεμψιμοιρίας: The word is rare, but is found in Hipp. *Ep.* xx (ix. 386 Littré), Thph. *Char.* 17. i, [Arist.] *V.V.* 1251 B 25.

δήμῳ μὲν εἰ χρὴ ... : Fr. 37. 1–5 West, quoted only here. In lines 1–3 the ungrateful δῆμος is reminded that Solon has given it (not as much as it would like but) more than it would previously have dreamed of; lines 4–5 are addressed to the rich aristocrats, and Solon's message to them is presumably that they should thank him for saving them from tyranny and revolution. Fr. 37 may belong to the same poem as fr. 36 (Linforth, *Solon the Athenian*, 182).

αἰνοῖεν: 'Would praise me.' West suggests σαίνοιεν, 'would fawn on me': this would be very appropriate, and the σ could easily have been lost after ἀμείνονες, but his index records several instances of αἰνεῖν in poetry of this kind and none of σαίνειν, so I hesitate to emend.

οὐκ ἂν κατέσχε δῆμον ... : Fr. 37. 7–10 (West counts the introductory clause as line 6). Lines 7–8 are quoted by Pl. *Sol.* 16. iv, and the whole is paraphrased by Aristid. XLVI. *Quatt.* (ii. 360 Dindorf). These lines take up the theme of fr. 36. 20–7, that another man in Solon's position would have acted as a whole-hearted champion of the δῆμος, with disastrous results.

πρὶν ἀνταράξας πῖαρ ἐξεῖλεν γάλα: πῖαρ, 'fat', is the reading of Plutarch; the London papyrus has πῦαρ, 'beestings' (the milk given by a cow immediately after calving). A. Platt, *JP* xxiv 1896, 255–7, championed πῦαρ, but failed to give a convincing explanation of ἐξεῖλεν γάλα. πῖαρ seems more likely, and has generally been preferred. Several constructions are theoretically possible, but most probably πῖαρ and γάλα are both accusatives governed by ἐξεῖλεν (Linforth, *Solon the Athenian*, 192–3). Linforth saw in the line an allusion to the process of skimming butter off milk and to the thin liquid which remains when this is done (cf. H. iv. 2, Hippocr. *De Morbis*, ii. 358 Kuhn; the same interpretation was adopted by W. W. Jaeger, *Hermes* lxix 1929, 31 = *Scripta Minora*, ii. 16); but butter-making was a barbarian activity, while ἐκ πῖαρ ἑλέσθαι is found in Hom. *Il.* xi. 550. T. C. W. Stinton more plausibly suggests: ' "... before, having stirred it [*sc.* the milk] up, he had deprived the milk of its cream", that is, by mixing up the cream with the milk and so dissipating it': this hypothetical other man 'would have so stirred up the existing order as to deprive the state of its best element, viz. the aristocracy' (*JHS* xcvi 1976, 159–60).

ἐγὼ δὲ τούτων ὥσπερ ἐν μεταιχμίῳ ὅρος κατέστην: The image of a ὅρος (whether a boundary post, or a marker like those which Solon uprooted) in the space between the contestants is difficult. Jaeger proposed to read ⟨δ⟩όρος (*opp. citt.*, 31–2 = 16–18, citing Eur. *Heracl.* 803, *Phoen.* 1361–3, where δόρος is used with μεταίχμιον; contr. E. Römisch, *Studien zur älteren griechischen Elegie*, 77–9). Stinton suggests that ὅρος is an error for οὖρος, 'guardian' (if they are not the same word), as in οὖρος Ἀχαιῶν (e.g. Hom. *Il.* VIII. 80), and τούτων does not depend on μεταιχμίῳ and denote the two sides but depends on οὖρος and denotes the aristocrats (*op. cit.*, 161–2). Stinton may be right, but I am not sure that the explanation of this sentence has yet been found.

E. *Between Solon and Pisistratus* (13)

§§i–ii, recounting the struggle over the archonship in the years after Solon's reforms, have no parallel in extant literature: their ultimate source is presumably the archon list, expounded by one or other of the Atthidographers (cf. Jacoby, *Atthis*, 174–5). The details of this struggle and its final resolution seemed to Hignett inappropriate to the aftermath of Solon's reforms, and this is one of his reasons for lowering the date of the reforms (*H.A.C.*, 319–20: cf. on 5. ii); but the fact that Pisistratus was able to make himself tyrant is sufficient evidence that Solon did not solve all Athens' problems, and it is not incredible that Solon's attempt to break the Eupatrids' monopoly of power should have been followed by a period of strife leading to a compromise between the Eupatrids and the others.

§§iii–v describe and seek to explain the division of Attica into three locally based factions, which enabled Pisistratus to become powerful. H. I. 59. iii has a brief note on the factions, leading like *A.P.*'s note to an account of Pisistratus' seizures of power, but significantly different from *A.P.* Pl. *Sol.* 13. i–iii gives an account of the factions, including a political interpretation on the same lines as *A.P.*, before the appointment of Solon as archon and mediator (cf. *Amat.* 763 D, *Praec. Ger. Reip.* 805 D–E), and 29. i names the leaders of the factions after Solon's reforms. Cf. also Ar. *Vesp.* 1223, *Lys.* 35, with scholia (schol. *Vesp.* 1223 introduces a note on the factions with the incredible κατὰ γὰρ τοὺς Σόλωνος νόμους τρεῖς ἦσαν αἱ τάξεις), Arist. *Pol.* V. 1305 A 23–4, D.H. *A.R.* I. 13. iii, D.L. I. 58, and notes on the factions' names in the lexica. For the retrojection of this tripartite division of Attica to Pandion see p. 73. It is only in the period of Pisistratus' rise to power that the three factions are reliably attested, and we may assume that this particular grouping was in fact a short-lived phenomenon (but Sealey, *Hist.*

ix 1960, 155–80 = *Essays*, 9–38, makes regional issues fundamental throughout early Athenian history).

§ii ends with the comment that the disputes over the archonship show that that was the most important office in Athens, which is likely to be the author's own comment. §v introduces the διαψηφισμός after the fall of the tyranny as a σημεῖον to support the statement that Pisistratus' faction included men who were not of pure Athenian descent: this might be the author's contribution again, or might be an argument used before him by an earlier writer who added a political dimension to Herodotus' regional account of the factions.

13. i. τὴν μὲν οὖν ἀποδημίαν ἐποιήσατο: Resuming 11. i, after explaining why Solon had pleased neither side and had left Athens for ten years.

ἔτι τῆς πόλεως τεταραγμένης: *A.P.* probably regarded Cylon's *coup* as the first incident in a period of στάσις; μετὰ δὲ ταῦτα συνέβη στασιάσαι τούς τε γνωρίμους καὶ τὸ πλῆθος πολὺν χρόνον (2. i); ἰσχυρᾶς δὲ τῆς στάσεως οὔσης καὶ πολὺν χρόνον ἀντικαθημένων ἀλλήλοις Solon was given his special commission (5. ii); since he pleased no one, Athens remained in a disturbed state. *A.P.* presumably envisages the στάσις as ending at last when Pisistratus seized power for the third time, established himself securely, and ruled the city well (16).

τῷ δὲ πέμπτῳ μετὰ τὴν Σόλωνος ἀρχὴν οὐ κατέστησαν ἄρχοντα: τῷ δὲ [πέμπ]τῳ is the beginning of fr. Ib of the Berlin papyrus, which runs to [καθαροὶ] διὰ in §v: see M. H. Chambers, *TAPA* xcviii 1967, 58–9.

If Solon was archon in 594/3 (cf. on 5. ii), the simplest interpretation of the data is that the years of ἀναρχία were 590/89 and 586/5, and that Damasias, legitimate archon for 582/1, clung to the office for the whole of 581/0 and the first two months of 580/79. This assumes that the counting includes both terminal years (as usual with Greek ordinals), that the reference is to Solon's archonship rather than his departure and thereafter to the archon's year of office rather than to the year in which the appointment was made, and that the curious phrase διὰ τῶν αὐτῶν χρόνων in §ii means 'after the same lapse of time' (it is preceded by μετὰ δὲ ταῦτα, and cf. διὰ τινῶν ὡρισμένων χρόνων in Arist. *Pol.* III. 1275 A 25–6). N. Robertson (*CQ*[2] xxviii 1978, 61 with n. 3) describes the expression as 'perfectly commonplace', but what is at issue is not the use of διά + genitive (implied by his citation of H. W. Smyth, *Greek Grammar*, §1685. 1. c) but the meaning of τῶν αὐτῶν χρόνων; others who have adopted this interpretation include Kenyon, Hammond (*JHS* lx 1940, 72–5 = *Studies*, 146–50), T. J. Cadoux (*JHS* lxviii 1948, 93–103) and Hignett (*H.A.C.*, 319), and I believe it to be correct. One year in the 580's is occupied by another archon: 588/7, the year of Philippus (Clem. Alex. *Strom.* I. 127. i, Syncellus, i. 429 Dindorf). The other evidence that can be brought to bear on the question concerns the Delphic festivals: *Marm. Par.* 239 A 37-8 very probably placed Simon, in whose archonship the ἀγὼν χρηματίτης was held, in 591/0, and Damasias, in whose archonship the ἀγὼν στεφανίτης was instituted, in 582/1 (Cadoux, *op. cit.*, 83-6, 104-6; the other possibilities would be 590/89 and 581/0); Paus. x. 7. iv-v dates the 'first Pythiad', the last occasion when ἆθλα were awarded, to Ol. xlviii. 3 = 586/5, and associates with the 'second Pythiad' the first ἀγὼν στεφανίτης; of the *hypotheses* to Pind. *Pyth.*, b dates the ἀγὼν χρηματίτης to the archonship of 'Simonides', the final defeat of the Cirrhaeans μετὰ ... χρόνον ἑξαετῆ, and the ἀγὼν στεφανίτης, (apparently) after that, to the archonship of Damasias, while d dates the ἀγὼν χρηματίτης to the archonship of Simon and the ἀγὼν στεφανίτης to the archonship of 'Damasis', ἔτει ἕκτῳ. Probably we should place Simon and the ἀγὼν χρηματίτης in 591/0 (a special victory celebration need not be in a 'Pythian' year; Robertson, who doubts the historicity of the First Sacred War, suggests that 591/0 was later calculated as the date of the last festival in the old eight-yearly cycle [*op. cit.*, 62-3]), the final defeat of the Cirrhaeans in 586/5, and Damasias and the first ἀγὼν στεφανίτης in 582/1: this is compatible with Kenyon's interpretation of *A.P.*

Two other interpretations, which have recently been canvassed, deserve mention; both take διὰ τῶν αὐτῶν χρόνων to mean 'during the same period of time', i.e. between the first and the second ἀναρχία, and identify the second ἀναρχία with the second year of Damasias. M. Miller, *Klio* xxxvii 1959, 46-8, starts from Solon's archonship in 594/3, places the ἀναρχίαι in 589/8 and 585/4, and (relying on the *hypotheses* to Pindar) makes Damasias' first year 586/5—all of which she regards not as authentic but as unreliable later reconstruction. G. V. Sumner, *CQ*² xi 1961, 49-54, starts from *A.P.*'s implied date of 592/1 for Solon's archonship, places the ἀναρχίαι in 587/6 and 582/1, and makes Damasias' first year 583/2 (supposing that *Marm. Par.*'s entry for 582/1 should read Δαμασίου τοῦ δευτέρου ⟨τὸ δεύτερον⟩). Neither of these persuades me that Kenyon's interpretation is wrong.†

It may be literally true that on two occasions οὐ κατέστησαν ἄρχοντα, and the office of archon remained vacant, or perhaps some one did hold office as archon but his archonship was subsequently expunged from the list as invalid: in view of what we are told about Damasias, the latter is less likely. In later Athenian history, Isagoras kept his place in the list as the archon of 508/7 (21. i with commentary), but on the fall of the Four Hundred early in 411/0 their archon for that year was deposed and replaced by a suffect (33. i with commentary), and 404/3, although the Thirty appointed an archon for that year, was subsequently regarded as a year of ἀναρχία (35. i with commentary).

διὰ τὴν αὐτὴν αἰτίαν: This is the reading of the London papyrus (τ' αὐτ' αἰτίαν); the Berlin papyrus has the less appropriate ταύτην τὴν [αἰτίαν] (M. H. Chambers, *TAPA* xcviii 1967, 58).

13. ii. διὰ τῶν αὐτῶν χρόνων: Cf. on §i. The phrase is best interpreted as meaning 'after the same lapse of time'; but some have preferred 'during the same period of time', and others have regarded it as impossible Greek and deleted it as an interpolation (e.g. Kaibel & Wilamowitz, cf. Kaibel, *Stil und Text*, 153).

Δαμασίας: *P.A.* 3110. *Marm. Par.* 239 A 38 identifies him as Δαμασίου τοῦ δευτέρου, which can only mean 'Damasias the younger' (Cadoux, *JHS* lxviii 1948, 102 n. 162), the elder Damasias being the archon of 639/8 (D.H. *A.R.* III. 36. i): the name is a rare one, and it is likely that the two men were related and the younger Damasias was therefore a Eupatrid. Two later occasions are known when, in exceptional circumstances, one man was archon for more than a single year: Olympiodorus, in 294/3 and 293/2 (W. K. Pritchett & B. D. Meritt, *Chronology of Hellenistic Athens*, pp. xvi-xvii); and Medeus, in 91/0, 90/89 and 89/8 after an earlier term in 101/0 (*IG* ii² 1713, 9–11; 2336, 89, 91 [100/99, *IG*]).

αἱρεθεὶς ἄρχων: Probably correctly, *A.P.* has ascribed to Solon a change after which archons were appointed by κλήρωσις ἐκ προκρίτων (8. i with commentary). Some have been tempted to see in αἱρεθείς and ἐλέσθαι here signs that this passage is derived from a different source, according to which the post-Solonian archons were directly elected (e.g. T. Reinach, *REG* iv 1891, 146–9, O. Seeck, *Klio* iv 1904, 276–9, each believing one passage or the other to be interpolated; Mathieu, *Aristote, Constitution d'Athènes*, 22); but the word can mean no more than 'appoint' in contexts where the method of appointment is immaterial (cf. αἵρεσις in 26. ii), and the use of it here need have no implications for the method by which the archons were appointed. Cf. Introduction, pp. 53–4.†

ἐξηλάθη: The London and Berlin papyri agree on ἐξηλάσθη, but that is a late form: the earlier was substituted by Herwerden & Leeuwen, cf. H. Richards, *CR* v 1891, 226.

ἄρχοντας ἐλέσθαι δέκα: The most plausible interpretation of what *A.P.* actually says is that a board of ten replaced the (eponymous) archon, perhaps for the remainder of the year in which Damasias was ousted rather than τὸν μετὰ Δαμασίαν ... ἐνιαυτόν. This may be what happened; but *A.P.*'s silence suggests that afterwards the regular appointment of archons was resumed, and the substitution of a board for an individual simply for what was left of that one year would hardly have resolved the difficulties (though it is accepted by some, e.g. H. Berve, *Die Tyrannis bei den Griechen*, i. 45). It is an attractive guess of E. Cavaignac, *RPh*² xlviii 1924, 144–8, cf. Wade-Gery, *CQ* xxv 1931, 79 = *Essays*, 102–3, that the ten men were not a board doing duty for the archon but the ten πρόκριτοι put up by each tribe for the final sortition, and that this remedy was adopted not on one occasion but indefinitely (in fact, until sortition was abandoned under the tyranny: cf. on 16. ix, 22. v). Solon's adoption of wealth as the sole qualification for office had led to strife between the Eupatrids and other rich citizens, and to give both sides a fair chance the Athenians now laid down how each tribe's list of πρόκριτοι was to be composed. As Wade-Gery admitted, this is not what *A.P.* says; but it may be what he ought to have said.†

This is the only time during the historical period when the three classes εὐπατρίδαι, ἄγροικοι (or γεωργοί or γεωμόροι) and δημιουργοί, make an appearance: very probably in the lost beginning of *A.P.* the two occupational classes, 'farmers' and 'craftsmen', were ascribed to Ion and the separation of the Eupatrids from these was said to be the work of Theseus, while in fact the Eupatrids were the *nobiles* of pre-Solonian Athens and the occupational classes were the product of later theory (cf. pp. 71–2, 74–6). To find a role for ἄγροικοι (or one of the other, more plausible names) and δημιουργοί in the sixth century is well-nigh impossible, even for those who place Solon's reforms after this crisis (those who place them before it, as I do, must suppose that all the men concerned will have satisfied Solon's property qualification for the archonship: cf. p. 148), and L. Gernet accordingly supposed that the whole story of the compromise was invented by later theorists (*RPh*³ xii 1938, 216–27, cf. Day & Chambers, *A.H.A.D.*, 173). I suspect that the theorists may rather have added to an authentic nucleus: after Damasias had been ousted it was decided that each tribe's πρόκριτοι for the archonship should comprise five Eupatrids and five non-Eupatrids, and later the theorists proceeded to divide the non-Eupatrids into ἄγροικοι and δημιουργοί. If, as is likely, Damasias was a Eupatrid (cf. above), his illegal retention of office will presumably have been a blow against the non-Eupatrids, and so the compromise should be seen as a defeat for the Eupatrids (Wade-Gery, *CQ* xxv 1931, 79 = *Essays*, 103). Hammond (*JHS* lxxxi 1961, 78 with n. 9 = *Studies*, 107–8 with n. 4, supposes that in this chapter εὐπατρίδαι is used not of the pre-Solonian nobility but in contrast to οἱ τῷ γένει μὴ καθαροί (§v), but this is an unnecessary and unlikely complication.

Chambers' study of the Berlin papyrus confirms that it has corrupted ἀγροίκων into ἀποίκων, but shows that another difficulty was illusory: the Berlin papyrus agrees with the London that there were to be five Eupatrids (not four, as originally thought), three ἄγροικοι and two δημιουργοί (*TAPA* xcviii 1967, 58, cf. Kenyon, *CR* xiv 1900, 413).

ᾧ καὶ δῆλον ... περὶ ταύτης τῆς ἀρχῆς: This comment is of more relevance to *A.P.*'s particular interest, the history of the πολιτεία, than to the general history of Athens, and if *A.P.*'s source for the troubles concerning the archonship is an *Atthis* (cf. p. 179, and Introduction, p. 21) we may suspect that he has added it himself. By the mid fifth century the archonship had ceased to be the climax, or even an essential step, of a political career (cf. on 22. v), but *A.P.* rightly concludes that earlier the archonship must have been the most important office of state (cf. 3. ii–v with commentary).

13. iii. ὅλως δὲ διετέλουν νοσοῦντες τὰ πρὸς ἑαυτούς: Cf. §i with commentary: Solon failed to put an end to Athens' troubles, and she remained in a state of disturbance until Pisistratus finally established himself as tyrant. *A.P.*'s grounds for discontent make a strange collection: one applicable to the rich (that the σεισάχθεια had made them poor: this complaint reappears in §v), one applicable to the Eupatrids (that the changes in the constitution had deprived them of power), and a third applicable to any one but perhaps especially to rich non-Eupatrids (personal ambition). Discontent among the poor, who had hoped for more drastic measures from Solon (11. ii–12) and whose champion Pisistratus was about to become (13. iv–v) is conspicuously absent; the poor were not involved in competition for the archonship or in other political activity, but they might provide material and support for those who were.

τὴν τῶν χρεῶν ἀποκοπήν: For this description of the σεισάχθεια see 6. i with commentary. The principal debts which Solon cancelled will have been the obligations of the ἑκτήμοροι to surrender a sixth of their produce to an overlord: the overlords will have lost their dependants' sixths, and this blow will no doubt have fallen more heavily on some than on others, but most will probably have retained enough land in their own possession to remain among the richer members of the community.

οἱ δὲ τῇ πολιτείᾳ δυσχεραίνοντες: These must be Eupatrids who were previously in a powerful position and were angered by the alterations made in the constitution by Solon and after the archonship of Damasias.

13. iv. ἦσαν δ' αἱ στάσεις τρεῖς: Other texts mentioning the three factions are listed on p. 179. Of modern discussions the most thorough is R. J. Hopper, *BSA* lvi 1961, 189–219; see also A. French, *JHS* lxxvii 1957, 241–2, *G&R*² vi 1959, 46–57, B. R. I. Sealey, *Hist.* ix 1960, 155–80 = *Essays*, 9–38, D. M. Lewis, *Hist.*

xii 1963, 22–6, C. Mossé, *AC* xxxiii 1964, 401–13, A. J. Holladay, *G&R*² xxiv 1977, 40–56.†

On the identification of the first two στάσεις, as men of the plain and men of the coast, there is no disagreement in the sources; the third faction is labelled ὑπεράκριοι by H. I. 59. iii but διάκριοι by *A.P.* and almost all other writers (ὑπεράκριοι recurs in D.H. *A.R.* I. 13. iii; Pl. *Amat.* 763 D has ἔπακροι, perhaps through a copyist's error; D.L. I. 58 has ἐξ ἄστεως, certainly wrongly), and Herodotus alone regards this faction as a later creation, intervening in the rivalry between the other two. Herodotus is earlier than our other sources; Διακρία was widely used as a name for the hilly region of north-east Attica (e.g. Ar. *Vesp.* 1223: see Hopper, *op. cit.*, 189–94, J. S. Traill, *Hesp.* xlvii 1978, 94–6; the fact can be used on either side of the argument). H. W. Pleket has suggested that each name was used of Pisistratus' supporters by a different group of Athenians (*Τάλαντα* i 1969, 41), but more probably these men were originally called ὑπεράκριοι, those 'beyond the hills', out of sight from the plain of Athens (Wade-Gery, *JHS* lxxi 1951, 219 n. 40 = *Essays*, 167 n. 2). In any case there is little doubt about the three regions involved: the πέδιον is the plain of Athens, the παραλία is essentially the coastal strip running from Phalerum to Sunium, and the third region is the north-east of Attica, including at least part of the east coast (cf. below, on Pisistratus). Though seafarers would not live inland, and the third region has rather worse farming land than the other two, Hopper rightly stresses that the three regions were not peopled with distinct occupational and economic classes: most of the inhabitants of all three would still be farmers, some more prosperous than others (*op. cit.*, 201–5), though a generation after Solon's reforms we should expect the number of men earning their living in other ways to have begun to grow (cf. on 6. i).

Herodotus gives the three factions regional characteristics only; Arist. *Pol.* v. 1305 A 23–4, cf. 1310 B 30–1, regards Pisistratus στασιάσας πρὸς τοὺς πεδιακούς as an instance of a leader trusted by the δῆμος because of its hatred of the rich; for *A.P.* (followed by Plutarch) they εἶχον . . . τὰς ἐπωνυμίας ἀπὸ τῶν τόπων ἐν οἷς ἐγεώργουν, but also had distinct political ideologies—the men of the plain oligarchic, the men beyond the hills led by the δημοτικώτατος Pisistratus, and the men of the coast favouring τὴν μέσην πολιτείαν. We should certainly expect to find the greatest proportion of Eupatrids, families important in the running of pre-Solonian Athens, in the plain, and the greatest proportion of the poor and unprivileged in the faction of Pisistratus, while Megacles' faction at least occupied the middle ground in the sense that the ensuing narrative shows it capable of joining with either of the others; but the ideological interpretation as formulated by *A.P.* and Plutarch must arouse suspicion. The μέση (*A.P.*) or μεμειγμέν(η) (Pl. *Sol.* 13. iii) πολιτεία was a philosophers' ideal, and particularly an Aristotelian ideal (e.g. Arist. *Pol.* IV. 1295 B 34–1296 A 21; cf. also Is. XII. *Panath.* 153, Plat. *Legg.* IV. 712 D 2–E 5), wholly out of place in the early sixth century; and the labels 'oligarchic' and 'democratic', though less obviously inapplicable, are likewise the product of later thought about how cities ought to be governed (for an early specimen, in which the word δημοκρατία still does not appear, see the notorious Persian debate in H. III. 80–2).

Some account should also be taken of personal rivalry within the aristocracy. The three leaders were all prominent Eupatrids (cf. below), competing for personal ascendancy, who rallied in their support their neighbours and dependants from the localities where their influence was strongest. This is probably more important than considerations of ideology in explaining the difference between the following of Lycurgus and that of Megacles; but it is likely that Pisistratus, drawing support from the part of Attica that was poorest and farthest from Athens, claimed to represent the interests of various kinds of unprivileged Athenian and is not unfairly described as δημοτικώτατος. Personal and local rivalries, and attitudes to the Solonian dispensation, both had a part to play, and *A.P.*'s account, although it goes beyond Herodotus' and is not expressed in language appropriate to the period, is not fundamentally wrong.

Μεγακλῆς ὁ 'Ἀλκμέωνος: *P.A.* 9692. Grandson of the Megacles who was archon when Cylon tried to make himself tyrant (cf. on 1), and presumably the senior member in his generation of the Alcmaeonid family: he is the Megacles who married Agariste, daughter of Cleisthenes of Sicyon (H. VI. 126–31; but F. W. Mitchel, *TAPA* lxxxviii 1957, 127–30, perversely tries to make two men out of one), and whose children included the Athenian Cleisthenes (cf. on 20. i). In and after the fifth century, Alcmaeonids are found in three demes lying between the city of Athens and the coast (Agryle, Alopece and Xypete [D. M. Lewis, *Hist.* xii 1963, 23 cf. 39]; Sealey would add Leuconoe, perhaps north of the city [*Hist.* ix 1960, 163 = *Essays*, 16, with n. 41]), but there are grounds for thinking that they had earlier lived and perhaps later retained land and dependants on the coastal strip running from Phalerum to Sunium, the παραλία *par excellence* (L. H. Jeffery, *BSA* lvii 1962, 143–4, 57, C. W. J. Eliot, *Hist.* xvi 1967, 279–86, Davies, *A.P.F.*, 372, 374, 599, P. J. Bicknell, *Hist.* Einz. xix 1972, 74).

Like the Pisistratids (below) and the later kings of Athens (p. 79), the Alcmaeonids were said to be of Pylian origin (Paus. II. 18. viii–ix: this may underlie Is. XVI. *Big.* 25, which makes the Pisistratids and Alcmaeonids kinsmen and is rejected by most scholars but believed by A. E. Raubitschek, *RM*[2] xcviii 1955, 262 with n. 9), and the list of life archons includes a Megacles and an Alcmaeon (cf. Castor, 250 F 4). This tradition, however, is not found in Herodotus (e.g. v. 62. ii, vi. 125. i); and although they were certainly Eupatrids the weight of the evidence suggests that the Alcmaeonids were not of long-established nobility (Davies, *A.P.F.*, 369–70).

Λυκοῦργος: *P.A.* 9248. H. I. 59. iii adds his father's name, Aristolaides. The name Lycurgus is rare in Attica, and this bearer of it is very probably an ancestor of the fourth-century financier Lycurgus, of the γένος which, when its name (Βουτάδαι) was given to a city deme west of the Agora, took to calling itself 'Ετεοβουτάδαι (Sealey, *Hist.* ix 1960, 163 = *Essays*, 16 with nn. 42–4. D. M. Lewis, *Hist.* xii 1963, 22–3, 26, Davies, *A.P.F.*, 348; cf. below, p. 257). That deme would provide a very suitable home for the leader of the πεδίον.

Πεισίστρατος: H. I. 59. iii again adds his father's name, Hippocrates. The family claimed to be of Pylian and royal descent (H. v. 65. iii; the name is given to a son of Nestor in Hom. *Od.* III. 400–1); a Pisistratus was archon in 669/8 (Paus. II. 24. vii). For Solon's connection with the family see on 5. iii; for Pisistratus' earlier career see on 14. i. The family home was in the region on the east coast known as Βραυρών, later given the deme-name Φιλαΐδαι ([Plat.] *Hipparch.* 228 B 4–5, Pl. *Sol.* 10. iii; other evidence for their local possessions and influence discussed by D. M. Lewis, *Hist.* xii 1963, 23–4 cf. 26–7, Davies, *A.P.F.*, 452–5; and see below, p. 257).†

Hopper, *BSA* lvi 1961, 205, remarks on the absence from this set of political rivals of Miltiades son of Cypselus, whose home was to the west of Βουτάδαι at Λακιάδαι, and who ἐδυνάστευε in the time of Pisistratus and Croesus (H. vi. 34–38. i: cf. pp. 217, 257–8, and on the chronology 198).

13. v. προσεκεκόσμηντο: The use of προσκοσμεῖν for προστάσσειν is unique (and has not been noticed by LSJ or the 1968 Supplement), but there is no need for the emendations suggested by early commentators (assembled by Sandys[2]). The usage is probably Ionic (W. Wyse *ap.* Sandys): H. IX. 31. ii uses κοσμεῖν for τάσσειν. The προσ- indicates that the impoverished rich and the men of impure descent are additional to Pisistratus' main source of support, which *A.P.* presumably believes to be the poor men of his own region.

οἵ τε ἀφ[η]ρημένοι τὰ χρέα: 'Those who had been deprived of the debts due to them' (Kenyon's Oxford Translation): cf. §iii with commentary. Those who had been creditors and overlords will of course have lost by Solon's reforms, and there may have been some whose losses were severe, but *A.P.*'s view of their poverty is due at least in part to his view of the σεισάχθεια as a cancellation of all debts. We should expect to find more poverty and distress among the former ἐκτήμοροι and debtors whom Solon had freed from their obligations but whose farming he had not otherwise assisted (but I am not persuaded by Hopper, *BSA* lvi 1961, 195 with n. 73, that this phrase means 'those who had been freed from debt').

οἱ τῷ γένει μὴ καθαροί: Though it is not stated by *A.P.*, Solon was believed to have encouraged immigrant craftsmen to settle in Athens (cf. on 6. i), and *A.P.* is probably thinking of these men and of their descendants, some of the latter no doubt being the products of mixed marriages. He mentions as a σημεῖον the deletion of men from the citizen registers on the fall of the tyranny (cf. next note), and it is unlikely that he had any more direct evidence that there were men of this kind supporting Pisistratus. It is likely enough that some such men were included in Pisistratus' following, but it is hard to believe that they were numerically important; by the time of Hippias' expulsion Athens had another category of doubtful citizens in the tyrants' mercenaries and their sons. See further p. 256.

μετὰ τὴν [τῶν] τυράννων κατάλυσιν ἐποίησαν διαψηφισμόν: διαψηφισμόν is the correction of Sandys (*CR* v 1891, 110) for the papyrus' δ(ια)φημισμό(ν): this word is used by Ath. v. 218 A, of the condemnation of the generals after Arginusae; the word used of the check made in 346/5 was διαψήφισις (A. 1. *Tim.* 77, D. LVII. *Eub.* 26).

This check is not mentioned in its chronological place, but there is no need to doubt it (*pace* Jacoby, *Supp.* i. 158–60, Day & Chambers, *A.H.A.D.*, 118). *A.P.* probably believes that it is those who were deprived of citizenship on this occasion who were shortly afterwards readmitted by Cleisthenes (see 21. iv with commentary, and the sensible discussion of K.-W. Welwei, *Gymnasium* lxxiv 1967, 423–37); but I doubt the inference of K. H. Kinzl from ἐφυλέτευσε in Arist. *Pol.* III. 1275 B 37 (quoted below, p. 255) that at this stage Cleisthenes had men enfranchised through the four Ionian tribes (*Greece and the Eastern Mediterranean* ... F. Schachermeyr, 200 with n. 8): μετὰ τὴν τῶν τυράννων ἐκβολήν need not mean immediately after Hippias' expulsion. R. S. Stroud (*Athens Comes of Age*, 29–30) believes it to be as likely as not that this decree was published in a permanent form, and suggests that the decree included a definition of the qualification for citizenship; but as early as this the *onus probandi* should rest with those who believe in permanent publication. Subsequent general checks on the registers of citizens are attested in 445/4 and 346/5 (cf. pp. 332–3, 500–1).

εἶχον δὲ ἕκαστοι ... ἐν οἷς ἐγεώργουν: ἕκαστοι surely refers to the three factions as a whole, not simply to their leaders (*pace* Hopper, *BSA* lvi 1961, 194).

F. *The Tyranny* (14–19)

Our information on the tyranny falls into three divisions—the rise of Pisistratus, the rule of Pisistratus, the ending of the tyranny—of which the second is more thinly treated than the first and last, both in *A.P.* and elsewhere. *A.P.*'s treatment of the first and last divisions might well be judged excessive in a history of the πολιτεία; but detailed material was available in Herodotus and Thucydides, and controversy had been aroused and had continued into the fourth century, and so *A.P.* did not omit the details.

Chs 14–15 cover the rise of Pisistratus. There is another account in H. I. 59. iv–64, and similarities of wording and substance make it clear that *A.P.* has made use of that account, almost certainly directly (uniquely, he names Herodotus as a source in 14. iv). From another source, presumably an *Atthis*, he has added a series of chronological details which conflict with Herodotus, and which have left signs of strain in 14. iii and 15. i; he has also added to Herodotus' account the story of Solon's reaction to Pisistratus (14. ii–iii *init.*, cf. 17. ii) and some narrative details.

Ch. 16, on the rule of Pisistratus, meagre as it is, is the fullest connected account of the subject that we have, though other accounts of individual items can be found elsewhere. There are parallels with Aristotle's *Politics*; we cannot tell how far *A.P.* had to put together the material in this chapter himself, how far it had already been assembled by an earlier writer.

Chs 17–19 are devoted to the downfall of the tyranny, in two stages. Of the assassination of Hipparchus (17–18) we have earlier accounts in H. v. 55–61 (mostly concerned with the family of Harmodius and Aristogiton), vi. 123. ii, and T. i. 20. ii, vi. 54–9, both protesting against the standard view that this was the act by which Athens had been liberated. That view had been adopted by Hellanicus (Jacoby, *Atthis*, 158–9, C. W. Fornara, *Hist.* xvii 1968, 381–3, K. J. Dover, in Gomme *et al.*, *Hist. Comm. Thuc.*, iv. 320–3), and was maintained in the fourth century by Plato (*Symp.* 182 c 5–7) and probably by Ephorus (D.S. x. 17); [Plat.] *Hipparch.* 228 B 4–229 D 7 followed the standard view in making Hipparchus the eldest son and sole or joint ruler until his death, but took over from Herodotus and Thucydides the fact that Hippias continued the tyranny thereafter, and exaggerated their statement that the tyranny was harsher in this final period. In the major controversy *A.P.* is firmly on the side of Herodotus and Thucydides; but he disagrees with all previous writers known to us on the Pisistratid family and on the identity of the Pisistratid whose interest in Harmodius was the cause of the trouble (17. iii–iv, 18. ii: the divergent material has been ineptly fitted into the narrative, but I am not persuaded that this is not the work of *A.P.*); on other points of detail he disagrees with Thucydides, sometimes making use of the rival version, and once directly (though without naming him) contradicting Thucydides (18. iv). In the major controversy it is clear that Herodotus and Thucydides were right and fifth-century orthodoxy and Hellanicus were wrong; but the truth was unpalatable to those fifth-century Athenians who were not well disposed towards the Alcmaeonid family or Sparta, and Harmodius and Aristogiton were therefore pressed into service as more acceptable heroes (see pp. 230, 289, 308). There may be some points on which Thucydides' account can be faulted (in particular, in insisting that Hippias must have been sole ruler he perhaps mistakes the nature of a family tyranny: cf. on 17. iii), but *A.P.*'s departures from it seem due to further elaboration of the legend as the controversy continued rather than to reliable information which Thucydides had missed. See T. R. Fitzgerald, *Hist.* vi 1957, 275–86, C. W. Fornara, *Hist.* xvii 1968, 400–24, Davies, *A.P.F.*, 446–9; M. Hirsch, *Klio* xx 1926, 129–67, was too sceptical in arguing that Thucydides was trying to reconstruct a coherent story out of what was already in his time legendary material; the defence of *A.P.* by M. L. Lang, *Hist.* iii 1954–5, 395–407, must be judged a failure.†

Ch. 19 relates the ousting of Hippias. The story is told in H. v. 62. ii–65, from which *A.P.*'s account is mainly derived; some chronological and other matter has been added from elsewhere (the Lipsydrium scolium in 19. iii perhaps from the author's direct knowledge), and on one point the development of the legend can be traced. Herodotus represents the Alcmaeonids as able to enlist Delphi's support, in the form of oracular pressure on Sparta, because of the generosity they had shown in the rebuilding of the temple there; fourth-century writers seem to have deduced from Herodotus, wrongly, that the contract for rebuilding the temple was made after Hipparchus' murder; in the middle of the fourth century Is. xv. *Antid.* 232 and D. xxi. *Mid.* 144 (with schol. 623. 14 Dindorf) claim that the Alcmaeonids borrowed money from Delphi to liberate Athens, presumably by hiring mercenaries; another scholium on Demosthenes (622. 27 Dindorf) follows a version less favourable to the Alcmaeonids, in which they misappropriated the building funds; *A.P.* 19. iv repeats Herodotus' story of oracular pressure on Sparta but combines with it a version, probably the latter, of the fourth-century story; later in Phil. 328 F 115 we find another part of Herodotus' story reconciled with the fourth-century chronology, in the claim that the Alcmaeonids did a more expensive job than they had contracted to do out of gratitude, in fulfilment of a vow, presumably after the Spartans had been persuaded to expel Hippias (cf. W. G. Forrest, *GR&BS* x 1969, 277–86: I am not sure that he is right to attribute the pro-Alcmaeonid account to Clidemus and the anti-Alcmaeonid to Androtion, but the rest of his reconstruction can stand without this). In all probability Herodotus' version of the story was right, and by the time of Hippias' expulsion the Alcmaeonids had already displayed enough generosity to earn the gratitude of Delphi. *A.P.* had read Herodotus and had also read a more recent account, and tried to combine the two.

A.P.'s chapters on the tyranny are a mixture of material from different sources, and at least some of the mixing has been done by *A.P.* himself. For chs 14–15 he used Herodotus as his main source, added the chronology of an *Atthis*, and other material perhaps from other sources; ch. 16 he may have had to put together from items found in various places; chs 17–18 show acquaintance with Thucydides but use also material which is not in agreement with him, while the awkwardness of the passage on Thessalus suggests that *A.P.* has tried to fit that into a more orthodox account; ch. 19 like 14–15 is based on Herodotus, with the addition of chronology from an *Atthis* and some other matter. Ephorus may have been used in 16. vi, but 18. i–ii differs from the Ephoran account of Pisistratus' sons which we find in Diodorus, and in 18. iv–vi, where different accounts of the torture of Aristogiton are contrasted, the version which appears in Diodorus is ascribed to δημοτικοί; the attempt of R. Werner, *Ath.*² xxxvi 1958, 48–89, to detect extensive use of Ephorus in these chapters and in 21–2 is unconvincing. Many of *A.P.*'s departures from fifth-century sources are not improvements: he has given the latest information, and the latest information was not always the best.

For modern studies of the Pisistratid tyranny see especially A. Andrewes, *The Greek Tyrants*, 100–15, H. Berve, *Die Tyrannis bei den Griechen*, i. 47–77 with ii. 543–63, C. Mossé, *La Tyrannie dans la Grèce antique*, 49–78.

The chronology of the tyranny has to be pieced together from several passages, and is best discussed in a single note. Apart from *A.P.*, the principal relevant texts are Herodotus, Thucydides and Aristotle's *Politics*; most other texts are compatible with the conclusions that can be drawn from these four, though there are a few rogue passages. I have argued for the views which I express here in *Phoen.* xxx 1976, 219–33; most of my citations are of the more recent discussions; a conspectus of older views is given by F. Schachermeyr, *RE*, xix (1937/8), 171–2.

Herodotus gives no indication of when Pisistratus first seized power; he was first expelled μετὰ ... οὐ πολλὸν χρόνον, with his tyranny οὔ κω κάρτα ἐρριζωμένην (1. 60. i); for his second *coup* there is again no indication; his second exile was due to his refusal to beget children by Megacles' daughter (1. 61. i–ii), so ought again to be after a fairly short time; his third and final *coup* occurred διὰ ἑνδεκάτου ἔτεος (1. 62. i), and the implication of the whole digression in 1. 53 sqq. is that this preceded the outbreak of the war in which Croesus of Lydia fell to Cyrus. Herodotus does not mention Pisistratus' death; Hipparchus was killed when sending off the Panathenaic procession (v. 56): after that the tyranny continued ἐπ' ἔτεα τέσσερα (v. 55); Hippias and his family were then expelled ἄρξαντες ... Ἀθηναίων ἐπ' ἔτεα ἕξ τε καὶ τριήκοντα (v. 65. iii).

Thucydides gives chronological details in connection with the fall of the tyranny: Hipparchus was killed at the Great Panathenaea (VI. 56. ii); Hippias continued to rule ἔτη τρία ... ἔτι and was deposed ἐν τῷ τετάρτῳ (VI. 59. iv); he came to Marathon with the Persians ὕστερον ἔτει εἰκοστῷ (*ibid.*). The Four Hundred were established ἐπ' ἔτει ἑκατοστῷ μάλιστα ἐπειδὴ οἱ τύραννοι κατελύθησαν (VIII. 68. iv).

Aristotle's *Politics*, discussing the durations of tyrannies, says that Pisistratus ἐν ἔτεσι τριάκοντα καὶ τρισὶν ἑπτακαίδεκα ἔτη τούτων ἐτυράννησεν, ὀκτωκαίδεκα δὲ οἱ παῖδες, ὥστε τὰ πάντα ἐγένετο ἔτη τριάκοντα καὶ πέντε (V. 1315 B 31–4).

A.P. gives more details than any other surviving text: Pisistratus first seized power ἔτει δευτέρῳ καὶ τριακοστῷ μετὰ τὴν τῶν νόμων θέσιν, ἐπὶ Κωμέου ἄρχοντος (14. i); he was first expelled οὔπω ... τῆς ἀρχῆς ἐρριζωμένης, ... ἕκτῳ ἔτει μετὰ τὴν πρώτην κατάστασιν, ἐφ' Ἡγησίου ἄρχοντος (14. iii); he seized power for the second time ἔτει ... δωδεκάτῳ μετὰ ταῦτα (14. iv); he was expelled for the second time ἔτει μάλιστα ἑβδόμῳ μετὰ τὴν κάθοδον, after ruling οὐ ... πολὺν χρόνον and failing to have intercourse with Megacles' daughter (15. i); he seized power for the third time ἑνδεκάτῳ πάλιν ἔτει (15. ii); he died ἐπὶ Φιλόνεω ἄρχοντος ἀφ' οὗ μὲν κατέστη τὸ πρῶτον τύραννος ἔτη τριάκοντα καὶ τρία βιώσας, ἃ δ' ἐν τῇ ἀρχῇ διέμεινεν ἑνὸς δέοντα εἴκοσι (17. i); Hipparchus was killed τοῖς Παναθηναίοις (18. iii); Hippias was expelled ἔτει ... τετάρτῳ μάλιστα μετὰ τὸν Ἱππάρχου θάνατον (19. ii), ἐπὶ Ἁρπακτίδου ἄρχοντος, ... μετὰ τὴν τοῦ πατρὸς τελευτὴν ἔτη μάλιστα ἑπτακαίδεκα, τὰ δὲ σύμπαντα σὺν οἷς ὁ πατὴρ ἦρξεν ἑνὸς δεῖ πεντήκοντα (19. vi); Cleisthenes enacted his laws ἔτει τετάρτῳ μετὰ τὴν τῶν τυράννων κατάλυσιν, ἐπὶ Ἰσαγόρου ἄρχοντος (21. i); [for the archonship of Hermocreon see 22. i with commentary]; Marathon was fought ἐπὶ Φαινίππου ἄρχοντος (22. iii). The Four Hundred were established ἐπὶ Καλλίου μὲν ἄρχοντος, ἔτεσιν δ' ὕστερον τῆς τῶν τυράννων ἐκβολῆς μάλιστα ἑκατόν (32. ii).

For completeness' sake I list the data found in other texts. Is. XVI. *Big.* 26 states that the στάσις associated with the tyranny lasted 40 years (perhaps reckoned from Pisistratus' third *coup* to the reforms of Cleisthenes: A. E. Raubitschek, *RM*² xcviii 1955, 260); [Plat.] *Hipparch.* 229 B 3–4 says that after Hipparchus' death τρία ἔτη ἐτυραννεύθησαν ᾿Αθηναῖοι ὑπὸ ῾Ιππίου. *Marm. Par.* dates Pisistratus' first *coup* in the archonship of Comeas, 561/0 or 560/59, and the murder of Hipparchus and the expulsion of the Pisistratids (presumably derived from an account in which the killing of Hipparchus put an end to the tyranny: cf. Jacoby, *Atthis*, 371 n. 97) in the archonship of Harpactides, 512/1 or 511/0 (239 A 40, 45: in favour of 561/0 and 511/0 see T. J. Cadoux, *JHS* lxviii 1948, 83–6, 106–9); *Chron. Rom.* dates Pisistratus' (first) *coup* 563/2 and the murder of Hipparchus (probably again identified with the ending of the tyranny) 512/1 (*IG* xiv 1297 = *F.G.H.* 252, B 5, 8). Justin, II. 8. x, says that Pisistratus after obtaining a bodyguard *per annos xxxiii/xxxiv regnavit* (MSS divided). Eusebius has four relevant entries (I give the text of Jerome, with the dates of the Armenian version according to Karst, pp. 188–90; for variant dates in the MSS of Jerome see most conveniently M. Miller, *Klio* xxxvii 1959, 44–5): *Pisistratus Atheniensium tyrannus in Italiam transgreditur*, 562/1; *Pisistratus secunda vice Athenis regnat*, 543/2; *Hipparchus et Hippias Athenis tyrannidem exercent*, 528/7; *Armodius et Aristogiton Hipparchum tyrannum interfecerunt*, 518/7. Schol. Ar. *Vesp.* 502 = Erat. 241 F 40 says that the duration of the tyranny is given as 50 years by Eratosthenes, 41 by Aristotle (*sic*), 36 by Herodotus; schol. Ar. *Lys.* 619 says that Hippias' tyranny lasted 3 years, but some say 4, Herodotus says 6 (*sic*).

When periods of time are reckoned in ordinal numerals, it is standard Greek practice to include both terminal years; with cardinal numerals it is usual to include the year in which a state of affairs began but not that in which it ended, but it is possible to include both terminal years: of the passages quoted above, T. VI. 59. iv illustrates the normal use of both ordinals and cardinals, H. V. 55 on the same period illustrates the alternative use of cardinals (cf. Rhodes, *Phoen.* xxx 1976, 220–1). *A.P.* gives a series of intervals reckoned in ordinals, where we should expect the interval before each fixed point to have been calculated from the immediately preceding fixed point, even in the cases where this is not explicitly stated, and the reckoning to be inclusive; and he gives summary figures in cardinals, which we should expect to have been obtained by deducting one from each of the ordinals in the series. He is capable of contradicting himself when he tries to combine material from incompatible sources, and I shall argue that the awkwardness in 14. iii and 15. i. is due to his trying to combine Herodotus' narrative with a chronology different from that implied by Herodotus; but the extent of the chronological data that he gives suggests that he had access to a complete chronology of the tyranny, which we should expect to be internally consistent: if we can do so without great violence to the text, we ought to interpret *A.P.* on the assumption that his chronological notes are consistent with one another.†

The chronological notes in the text of the London papyrus are not consistent with one another, but only two corrections are needed to obtain consistency. (*a*) The figures for the separate periods in Pisistratus' career conflict with the summary figures in 17. i (and leave an implausibly short time for his third period of tyranny). The figures in 17. i appear to be sound (since the figures of Arist. *Pol.* seem to have been calculated, in a different way, from the same series of dates: cf. Rhodes, *Phoen.* xxx 1976, 222 n. 8); they yield 14 years for the two periods of exile, while 14. iv and 15. ii yield 21 years; the figure in 15. ii is confirmed by H. 1. 62. i, so it is the figure in 14. iv which is wrong, and there we must correct δωδεκάτῳ to πέμπτῳ (first proposed by Wilamowitz, *A.u.A.*, i. 22–3). (*b*) In 19. vi τὰ ... σύμπαντα σὺν οἷς ὁ πατήρ ἦρξεν are said to amount to 49 years, but the 33 years from Pisistratus' first *coup* to his death (17. i) and the 17 of Hippias' rule (19. vi) amount to 50 in all (the total given by Eratosthenes). Some have emended to 51 (which is an easier correction palaeographically, and is the total of the figures in Arist. *Pol.*, but does not suit the arithmetic of *A.P.*); but the words used by *A.P.* should denote not the whole period from Pisistratus' first *coup* to Hippias' expulsion but the total duration of the tyranny within this period, and on *A.P.*'s arithmetic that amounts to 19 + 17 = 36 years (in Arist. *Pol.* 17 + 18 = 35): 36 is the total needed here (G. V. Sumner, *CQ*² xi 1961, 41). (For *A.P.*'s placing of Pisistratus' first *coup* in the 32nd year after Solon's legislation see on 5. i: I believe the likeliest explanation is not that *A.P.* implies a date of 592/1 for Solon or that the papyrus' text of 14. i is corrupt, but that the troubles over the archonship during this period have led *A.P.* or his source to miscalculate the interval.)

These two corrections yield an internally consistent chronology in *A.P.*, but they do not yield agreement between *A.P.* and Herodotus. The total of 36 years is found in H. v. 65. iii, but there scholars agree that it refers not to the total duration of the tyranny from the first *coup* to Hippias' expulsion but the duration of the continuous tyranny from the final *coup* to Hippias' expulsion. Many have thought that a single chronological scheme underlies Herodotus and *A.P.*, and have been prepared to make drastic emendations in the text of *A.P.* to obtain agreement between the two, but I prefer to accept the disagreement as authentic (cf. F. Heidbüchel, *Philol.* ci 1957, 70–89, Sumner, *op. cit.*, 37–48). Herodotus does not give durations for either of the first two periods of tyranny, but his narrative implies that both were very short; *A.P.* reproduces Herodotus' narrative, but he makes the first period of tyranny end in the 6th year and the second in the 7th, and (with 14. iv corrected as above) implies that Pisistratus died in the 9th year of the third period: the awkward combinations of chronology and narrative in 14. iii and 15. i confirm that the chronology of *A.P.* differs from that implied by Herodotus.

The latest items in the series present no difficulty, and allow us to convert relative to absolute dates. The battle of Marathon and the archonship of Phaenippus can be dated with certainty to 490/89 (Cadoux, *op. cit.*, 117, A. E. Samuel, *Greek and Roman Chronology*, 205); Isagoras was archon in 508/7 (D. H. *A.R.* 1. 74. vi cf. v. 1. i: Cadoux, *op. cit.*, 113–14, Samuel, *op. cit.*, 204); the year of Harpactides' archonship and Hippias' expulsion, the fourth year before that, must be 511/0 (Cadoux, *op. cit.*, 113–14, Samuel, *op. cit.*, 204). Thucydides' 20th year from the battle of Marathon is therefore a round number; but his 100th year from the establishment of the Four Hundred, though qualified with μάλιστα, is precise.

Table 1 shows the results obtained so far: archons' names are in capital letters; information deduced from other material in the same column is enclosed in square brackets.

Table 1

	Herodotus	Thucydides	Arist. *Pol.*	*A.P.*
Solon's reforms				SOLON, 594/3
Pisistratus' first coup				'in 32nd year' (error for 34th), COMEAS, 561/0 (14. i)
First expulsion	after short time (1. 60. i)			after short time, in 6th year, HEGESIAS, 556/5 (14. iii)
Second coup				'in 12th year' [corrupted from 5th, 552/1] (14. iv)
Second expulsion	(after short time) (1. 61. i–ii)			after short time, in 7th year, [546/5] (15. i)
Third coup	in 11th year (1. 62. i), before war ending in fall of Sardis (1. 53 sqq.), trad. date 546/5 (cf. below)			in 11th year, [536/5] (15. ii)

Table 1—contd.

	Herodotus	Thucydides	Arist. Pol.	A.P.
Pisistratus' death				[in 9th year], PHILONEOS, 528/7 (17. i)
Years in power Years in exile Years from first *coup* to death			17 [16] 33 (V. 1315 B 31–4)	19 [14] 33 (17. i)
Murder of Hipparchus Expulsion of Hippias	Panathenaea (V. 56) after 4 years (V. 55)	Great Panathenaea (VI. 56. ii) in 4th year (VI. 59. iv)		Panathenaea [514/3] (18. iii) in 4th year, HARPACTIDES, 511/0 (19. ii, vi)
Years of Hippias' rule			18 (*ibid.*)	17 (19. vi)
Years of tyranny in all (see above on period intended)	36 (V. 65. iii)		35 (*ibid.*)	'49' [corrupted from 36] (19. vi)
Cleisthenes' reforms				in 4th year, ISAGORAS, 508/7 (21. i) (ISAGORAS— HERMOCREON— PHAENIPPUS corrupt, 22. i–iii)
Battle of Marathon		in 20th year from expulsion of Hippias (VI. 59. iv)		PHAENIPPUS, 490/89 (22. iii)
Establishment of Four Hundred		about 100th year after end of tyranny (VIII. 68. iv)		CALLIAS, 412/1, about 100 years after end of tyranny (32. ii)

A.P.'s chronological scheme presumably comes from the Atthidographers, and we must ask what authority they had for it. Sceptics believe that they had no authoritative material except that provided by Herodotus; they misunderstood the significance of his 36 years, and with the expulsion of Hippias in 511/0 as their one fixed date they allocated half a generation to Hippias and a whole generation to Pisistratus; intervals of time which could not be derived from Herodotus were arbitrarily supplied (Heidbüchel, *op. cit.*). I accept that Herodotus' account provided the starting-point from which the Atthidographers' chronology was developed, but I do not accept the sceptics' doctrine that no authentic tradition can have survived which was not recorded by Herodotus. Each point in the Atthidographers' scheme which does not depend on Herodotus must be judged on its own merits.

All our fifth- and fourth-century evidence is compatible with the view that Hipparchus was killed in the 4th year before Hippias was expelled; that will be 514/3, and unless there was an unattested irregularity the Great Panathenaea will have been held in that year; if the year of Hippias' expulsion was remembered the year of Hipparchus' murder should also have been remembered, and this date need not be doubted. The date of 528/7 for Pisistratus' death is independent of Herodotus, but again need not be doubted: Hippias was archon in 526/5 (M&L 6, *c* 2), and it is striking that the scheme places Pisistratus' death not in 527/6, where rational reconstruction might be expected to place it, but in the previous year; probably Pisistratus died late in 528/7, when the next year's archon had already been appointed, and Hippias took the first vacant year for himself (Andrewes, *The Greek Tyrants*, 109). The earlier dates are more difficult. Herodotus implies that Pisistratus' third *coup* was in 547/6 or 546/5 (cardinal numeral), and his second expulsion in 557/6 or 556/5; *A.P.* places his third *coup* in 536/5 and his second expulsion in 546/5: it is hard to believe that the third and final *coup* was in fact as late as 536/5, and I accept the suggestion that *A.P.*'s chronology depends on the misunderstanding of Herodotus' 36 years, and perhaps on the assumption that 546/5 and 556/5 were Herodotean dates which had to be fitted into the scheme somehow, even if they could not be kept at the points where Herodotus put them. If Herodotus is right on these points, *A.P.* must be wrong not only on the second expulsion and the third *coup* but also on the first expulsion and the second *coup*. 561/0 as the date of the first *coup* remains possible: nothing can be done to confirm or to refute it, but the year when Pisistratus first tried to make himself tyrant could well have been remembered, and this date may be given the benefit of the doubt. If the first *coup* was in 561/0 and the second expulsion in 557/6 or 556/5 it is theoretically possible that one other detail in *A.P.* is authentic: the first and second periods of tyranny will both be very short, and the figures given for them must be wrong, but it may be that the length of the first period of exile was remembered like that of the second, and that that did end in the 5th year. Table 2 sets out the chronology which I propose; I prefer the later of the dates which might be implied by Herodotus on account of the fall of Sardis, for which see below.

Table 2

	implied by H	A.P.	Rhodes
First *coup*		561/0	561/0?
First expulsion		556/5	(561/0 or 560/59??)
Second *coup*		552/1	(557/6 or 556/5??)
Second expulsion	557/6 or 556/5	546/5	556/5?
Third *coup*	547/6 or 546/5	536/5	546/5?
Pisistratus' death		528/7	528/7
Murder of Hipparchus	514/3	514/3	514/3
Expulsion of Hippias	511/0	511/0	511/0

Various external arguments have been invoked in connection with this problem; there is a recent review of them by J. G. F. Hind, CQ^2 xxiv 1974, 14–17. Miltiades the son of Cypselus went out to the Chersonese when Pisistratus was tyrant, and in due course he was captured by the Lampsacenes and rescued by Croesus (H. VI. 34–38. i: cf. p. 217): Wade-Gery thought that this should belong to the securely established tyranny, and devised a scheme in which it could fall after Pallene but before the fall of Sardis (*JHS* lxxi 1951, 218–9 with n. 38 = *Essays*, 166 with n. 3), but Miltiades was born before *c.* 585 (Davies, *A.P.F.*, 299), so to place his departure in one of the earlier spells of tyranny is possible and perhaps preferable (cf. L. H. Jeffery, *Archaic Greece*, 96). Cimon the son of Stesagoras won three Olympic chariot races with the same team; on the first two occasions he was in exile from Pisistratus' tyranny, on the second he secured his recall to Athens by having the victory announced in Pisistratus' name, and after the third he was put to death by Pisistratus' sons, Pisistratus having died (H. VI. 103. i–iii): some place his first victory in 532 (e.g. N. G. L. Hammond, CQ^2 vi 1956, 117 with n. 4, M. E. White, *Polis and Imperium: Studies . . . E. T. Salmon*, 81–95), but it is far more likely that it was in 536 (e.g. Wade-Gery, *opp. citt.*, 212–4 = 156–8, Davies, *A.P.F.*, 300), and if he was exiled by Pisistratus before the summer of 536 it is unlikely that the third *coup* was as late as 536. Pisistratus helped to install Lygdamis as tyrant of Naxos, and Lygdamis subsequently helped Polycrates to power in Samos, but these events are themselves too insecurely dated to be of help here (cf. on 15. iii). At the time of Pisistratus' second *coup* his sons Hippias and Hipparchus were νεανίαι (ἐνηλίκιοι in Pl. *Cat. Mai.* 24. viii), able to object to the Alcmaeonid liaison, and at the beginning of the second exile Pisistratus is said to have consulted Hippias (H. I. 61. i–iii); but Hippias as an elderly man accompanied the Persians to Marathon in 490 (e.g. H. VI. 107): if he was born *c.* 570 (Davies, *A.P.F.*, 446), he will have been about fifteen in 556/5 and about eighty in 490. *A.P.* 17. iv states that at Pallene reinforcements were brought to Pisistratus from Argos by Hegesistratus, his son by a marriage made during his first period of rule or first exile (H. 1. 61. iv mentions the reinforcements but not Hegesistratus), and if Pallene is dated 546/5 Hegesistratus cannot have been older than fifteen at the time. We might dismiss the references to the sons in H. 1. 61 as embroidery, and condemn the story of Hegesistratus as an invention based on his name and his mother's Argive origin (e.g. Beloch, *G.G.*², 1. ii. 298, on Hegesistratus); but men of about fifteen could be treated as young adults (cf. pp. 121–2), and these stories may be true without being fatal to the date of 546/5 for Pallene. Herodotus' account of Pisistratus' rise to power implies that Pallene preceded the fall of Sardis. The date of the Greek chronographers for that appears to have been 546/5, and there is no reliable evidence for any alternative (Sumner, *op. cit.*, 42–3 n. 4). It has become orthodox doctrine that this cannot be the war recorded in the *Nabonidus Chronicle* under 547/6, since Cyrus spared Croesus' life (H. 1. 86–90) but killed the king of Lu—: in fact the reading Lu— is uncertain (A. K. Grayson, *Texts from Cuneiform Sources*, v. 282); on the other hand, the verb may mean either 'kill' or 'defeat', and Grayson in his translation prefers the latter (*op. cit.*, 107). It must remain uncertain whether it is the war against Croesus which is recorded in the *Chronicle*. Sumner stresses that Herodotus does not make Pallene and the fall of Sardis contemporaneous but places Pallene before the beginning of the war (*op. cit.*, 45–6): I agree that this is what his narrative implies, but suspect that his method of narrating one in a digression from the other has led him to distort a tradition that the two were contemporaneous: the two events could have occurred in the same year whether the fall of Sardis is to be dated 546/5 (as seems more likely) or 547/6.†

14. i. δημοτικώτατος δ' εἶναι δοκῶν: Resuming 13. iv.
καὶ σφόδρ' εὐδοκιμηκὼς ἐν τῷ πρὸς Μεγαρέας πολέμῳ: Cf. H. 1. 59. iv (πρότερον εὐδοκιμήσας ἐν τῇ πρὸς Μεγαρέας γενομένῃ στρατηγίῃ, Νίσαιάν τε ἑλὼν καὶ ἄλλα ἀποδεξάμενος μεγάλα ἔργα), Just. 11. 8. i–v. On Athens' war with Megara over the possession of Salamis see Pl. *Sol.* 8–10, 12. v, with A. French, *JHS* lxxvii 1957, 241, R. J. Hopper, *BSA* lvi 1961, 208–17, L. Piccirilli, *ASNP*³ viii 1978, 1–13; Plutarch's confusing account gives the impression that Pisistratus and Solon were colleagues in the war (*Sol.* 8. iii–iv), but *A.P.* 17. ii dismisses as chronologically impossible the story (found in Pl. *Sol.* 1. iv–v, Ael. *V.H.* viii. 16) that Pisistratus was loved by Solon and was general ἐν τῷ πρὸς Μεγαρέας πολέμῳ περὶ Σαλαμῖνος. Hopper suggests that Athens gained and lost Salamis several times: one conquest was

instigated by Solon, and that success helped to carry him to the archonship; subsequently Salamis was lost again, and Pisistratus played a prominent part in its reconquest shortly before he made his first bid for the tyranny. Piccirilli agrees except that he does not believe Athens lost Salamis again before the war in which, to strengthen her hold on the island, Pisistratus captured Nisaea.†

κατατραυματίσας ἑαυτὸν: Cf. H. I. 59. iv (*τραυματίσας ἑωυτόν τε καὶ ἡμιόνους ἤλασε ἐς τὴν ἀγορὴν τὸ ζεῦγος ὡς ἐκπεφευγὼς τοὺς ἐχθρούς, . . . ἐδέετό τε τοῦ δήμου φυλακῆς τινος πρὸς αὐτοῦ κυρῆσαι*), D.S. XIII. 95. v–vi, Pl. *Sol.* 30. i–ii, Polyaen. I. 21. iii, Just. II. 8. vi–x; also Arist. *Rhet.* I. 1357 B 31–3, D.L. I. 60. This became a favourite means of acquiring a bodyguard and setting oneself up as tyrant: Plat. *Rep.* VIII. 566 B 5–8, Arist. *Rhet.* I. 1357 B 30–6 (in general; Arist. cites Dionysius I of Syracuse and Theagenes of Megara as well as Pisistratus); *Pol.* III. 1286 B 39–40, D.S. XIII. 95. iii–vi (Dionysius).

Ἀριστίωνος γράψαντος τὴν γνώμην: Cf. Pl. *Sol.* 30. iii (*Ἀρίστωνος δὲ γράψαντος*); this detail is not given by Herodotus. That documentary evidence of Aristion's motion survived is very unlikely; that it is correctly remembered and that it is a later invention are both serious possibilities, though the use of *γράψαντος* is surely anachronistic (C. Mossé, *La Tyrannie dans la Grèce antique*, 63). Many have tried to identify Aristion with the man whose gravestone, dating from *c.* 510, has been found at Belanideza, a headland on the east coast slightly south of 38° N., in Pisistratid country (*IG* i² 1024, cf. Kirchner, *P.A.* 1728, L. H. Jeffery, *Local Scripts of Archaic Greece*, 75, 78, no. 42, G. M. A. Richter with M. Guarducci, *Archaic Gravestones of Attica*, 47, 170, no. 67: champions of the identification include Wilamowitz, *A.u.A.*, i. 261, Day & Chambers, *A.H.A.D.*, 175); the inscribed ostraca earlier than the institution of ostracism include one bearing the name Πισίσ⟨τ⟩ρατος and one bearing Ἀριστίον, and E. Vanderpool has suggested that these men may be the tyrant and his supporter (*Hesp.* Supp. VIII 1949, 405–8; cf. below, p. 268). Both identifications are attractive, but Aristion is a common name and neither can be regarded as certain.

τοὺς κορυνηφόρους καλουμένους: Cf. H. I. 59. v (*τῶν ἀστῶν . . ἄνδρας τούτους οἳ δορυφόροι μὲν οὐκ ἐγένοντο Πεισιστράτου, κορυνηφόροι δέ· ξύλων γὰρ κορύνας ἔχοντες εἵποντο οἱ ὄπισθε*), Pl. *Sol.* 30. iii, v (where they number fifty), Polyaen. I. 21. iii (three hundred), schol. Plat. *Rep.* VIII. 566 B (three hundred). In schol. Plat. these men are called δορυφόροι: the mercenaries of the finally established tyranny are referred to by that word in T. VI. 57. i, iv, Ar. *Eq.* 447–9, *A.P.* 18. iv, Polyaen. I. 22, and are called ἐπίκουροι in H. I. 64. i, T. VI. 55. iii, Polyaen. I. 21. ii; but the unusual κορυνηφόροι is clearly the correct term for the citizen bodyguard which Pisistratus was allowed on this occasion. C. Mossé, *La Tyrannie dans la Grèce antique*, 62-4, compares the κορυνηφόροι or κατωνακοφόροι of Sicyon (*ibid.*, 41 n. 2, E. Will, *Doriens et Ioniens*, 48-50), and suspects that Pisistratus' bodyguard was recruited from his lower-class supporters; J. Boardman, *RA* 1972, 62, describes them as 'more like riot police than military', and suggests that there may be a deliberate echoing of Heracles, the κορυνηφόρος *par excellence* (cf. on 14. iv and 15. iv).

ἐπαναστὰς μετὰ τούτων τῷ δήμῳ κατέσχε τὴν ἀκρόπολιν: Cf. H. 1. 59. vi (συνεπαναστάντες δὲ οὗτοι ἅμα Πεισιστράτῳ ἔσχον τὴν ἀκρόπολιν), Pl. *Sol.* 30. v. Likewise in the seventh century Cylon had tried to seize the Acropolis (cf. p. 80), in 511/0 Hippias was expelled from the Acropolis (19. v-vi), and in 508/7 Isagoras and Cleomenes when they encountered resistance occupied the Acropolis (20. iii).

ἔτει δευτέρῳ καὶ τριακοστῷ ... ἐπὶ Κωμέου ἄρχοντος: See pp. 191-9 and commentary on 5. ii. Solon was archon and at any rate began the enactment of his reforms in 594/3; *A.P.*'s date for Comeas' archonship and Pisistratus' first seizure of power is 561/0, the 34th year after 594/3. Some have emended the text here, others have argued that *A.P.* dates at any rate part of Solon's legislation 592/1, but most probably the troubles over the archonship mentioned in 13. i-ii have led *A.P.* or his source to miscalculate the interval.

14. ii. λέγεται δὲ Σόλωνα ... ἀντιλέξαι: The story alluded to in this section is told in two versions. The fullest presentation of the first is in Pl. *Sol.* 30. i-31. ii: Solon had previously tried to dissuade Pisistratus and the other leaders (*ibid.*, 29. ii-v); when Pisistratus wounded himself Solon reproached him for acting the part of Odysseus; at the assembly which voted Pisistratus a bodyguard he spoke against the proposal, and when he had failed to persuade the citizens he departed saying that he was τῶν μὲν ... σοφώτερος, τῶν δ' ἀνδρειότερος; when Pisistratus had seized the Acropolis and Megacles and the Alcmaeonids had gone into exile, he again harangued the people and again failed to persuade them, and then went home and displayed his arms at the door of his house; many wanted him to flee, but he replied that he trusted in his old age, and in fact Pisistratus respected and even consulted him; Solon died in the year after Pisistratus' first *coup* (*ibid.*, 32. iii: cf. on 17. ii). Elements of this version appear also in D.S. ix. 4, 20, Pl. *An Seni*, 794 F, Ael. *V.H.* viii. 16, Aristid. xli. *Ep. Smyrn.* (i. 765 Dindorf). The story has a different conclusion in D.L. 1. 49-54 cf. 65-7: Solon went armed into the assembly (so also D.S.) to urge opposition to Pisistratus; when he failed to persuade the citizens he said that he was τῶν μὲν σοφώτερος, τῶν δὲ ἀνδρειότερος, but the boule, Πεισιστρατίδαι ὄντες, said he was mad; Solon then displayed his arms πρὸ τοῦ στρατηγείου and went on his travels (cf. on 11. i), dying in Cyprus at the age of eighty (ch. 62); letters said to have been written by or to Solon are quoted, with details which accord with this version of the story. This second version is found also in Gell. xvii. 21. iv, V.M. v. iii. ext. 3, VIII. ix. ext. 1, schol. D. XLV. *Steph. i.* 64, schol. Plat. *Rep.* x. 599 E, cf. also Her. Pont. fr. 148 Wehrli *ap.* Pl. *Sol.* 32. iii; consistent with it is a story found only in a fragment of an unknown writer's philosophical dialogue, perhaps of the fourth or third century B.C.: Solon went abroad before the tyranny when his warning was ignored; the speaker stayed in Athens until after the *coup*, when he joined Solon in Ionia, but he returned to Athens in due course, on the insistence of Pisistratus and his other friends and on the advice of Solon (*P. Oxy.* iv 664. 1-15). Three fragments from the poems are said to date from this period in Solon's life: 9 West, a piece of generalisation on tyranny, is quoted by D.S., Plutarch and D.L., and is said to be a warning written before Pisistratus seized power; 10, quoted by D.L. alone says that time will reveal the basis of Solon's 'madness'; 11, again quoted by D.S., Plutarch and D.L., is said to have followed the *coup* and is addressed to men who πεπόνθατε λυγρὰ δι' ὑμετέρην κακότητα, who τούτους ηὐξήσατε ... καὶ διὰ ταῦτα κακὴν ἔσχετε δουλοσύνην. The story of Solon's reaction to Pisistratus (to whom he was related: cf. on 5. iii) is discussed by Wilamowitz, *A.u.A.*, i. 261-6, Linforth, *Solon the Athenian*, 303-7; on its later elaboration see M. Mühl, *RM*² xcix 1956, 315-23, blaming much of it on Phaenias. Already in the time of *A.P.* a detailed story existed, garnished with sayings attributed to Solon; hardly any confirmation can be derived from the surviving fragments of Solon's poems. Plutarch's version of the story is probably the older (DL's version depends on the assumption that Solon could not have lived under the rule of the tyrant: cf. K. Freeman, *The Work and Life of Solon*, 155-7), and appears to be the version behind *A.P.*'s allusion. It is possible that Solon lived to 560/59 and witnessed Pisistratus' first *coup* (cf. on 11. i), and fr. 11 may confirm this; otherwise nearly all is probably invention.

ὅσοι μὲν γὰρ ἀγνοοῦσι ... ὅσοι δ' εἰδότες κατασιωπῶσιν: Pl. *Sol.* 30. iv interprets this in terms of economic classes: the poor supported Pisistratus, not realising what support for him would lead to, while the rich realised but were afraid to oppose him. The saying presupposes that the tyranny was bad for all, which *A.P.* did not believe (§iii, 16 *passim*).

ἐξαράμενος: Here Solon merely displays his arms at his door, as also in Pl. *Sol.* 30. vii (*pace* B. Lavagnini, *Att. Palermo*⁴ vi 1945/6, 32-4 cf. 31-2 n. 2), and versions in which Solon appears in his armour (D.S. IX. 4, 20. i; cf. D.L. I. 49, but in 50 cf. 65 he afterwards lays up his arms) are the result of further embroidery on the original story.

βεβοηθηκέναι τῇ πατρίδι: Pl. *Sol.* 30. vii adds καὶ τοῖς νόμοις—and if Solon's law against neutrality is authentic (8. v with commentary) Solon may have considered himself legally as well as morally obliged to make at least token resistance to Pisistratus.

14. iii. Πεισίστρατος ... διῴκει τὰ κοινὰ πολιτικῶς μᾶλλον ἢ τυραννικῶς: Cf. ch. 16 (where §ii repeats these words with ὥσπερ εἴρηται; also H. I. 59. vi (οὔτε τιμὰς τὰς ἐούσας συνταράξας οὔτε θέσμια μεταλλάξας, ἐπί τε τοῖσι κατεστεῶσι ἔνεμε τὴν πόλιν καλῶς τε καὶ εὖ, likewise on Pisistratus' first period of tyranny). T. VI. 54. v–vi (on the tyranny as a whole). Arist. *Pol.* v. 1314 A 29–1315 B 10 gives advice on how to preserve a tyranny by ruling well: the tyranny should be not τυραννικωτέραν but βασιλικωτέραν (1314 A 34–5); δεῖ μὴ τυραννικὸν ἀλλ' οἰκονόμον καὶ βασιλικὸν εἶναι φαίνεσθαι τοῖς ἀρχομένοις καὶ μὴ σφετεριστὴν ἀλλ' ἐπίτροπον (1315 A 41–B 2). Pisistratus is not mentioned here, as he is in the survey of how tyranny can be preserved by successful bad rule (1313 A 34–1314 A 29: Pisistratus, 1313 B 23), but his reputation may nevertheless have contributed to the description of the 'good' tyrant. πολιτικός and πολιτικῶς, in the sense 'devoted to the interests of the πόλις', are favourite words of Isocrates (e.g. IV. Paneg. 79, 151, IX. *Evag.* 46), and he too uses τὰ κοινά as object of διοικεῖν (XI. *Bus.* 16, XV. *Antid.* 285: both words are common in Arist. *Pol.*, but he does not use them together); but his only references to Pisistratus are strongly hostile (XII. *Panath.* 148, XVI. *Big.* 25–6).

οὔπω δὲ τῆς ἀρχῆς ἐρριζωμένης ὁμοφρονήσαντες: Cf. H. I. 60. i (μετὰ δὲ οὐ πολλὸν χρόνον τὠυτὸ φρονήσαντες οἵ τε τοῦ Μεγακλέος στασιῶται καὶ οἱ τοῦ Λυκούργου ἐξελαύνουσί μιν. οὕτω μὲν Πεισίστρατος ἔσχε τὸ πρῶτον Ἀθήνας καὶ τὴν τυραννίδα οὔ κω κάρτα ἐρριζωμένην ἔχων ἀπέβαλε). ὁμοφρονεῖν, though not used here by Herodotus, is a Herodotean word (VII. 229. i, VIII. 3. i, 75. iii, IX. 2. ii), and ὁμολογήσαντος occurs a few lines below, in I. 60. iii.

ἕκτῳ ἔτει ... ἐφ' Ἡγησίου ἄρχοντος: 556/5. Into the narrative which he derives from Herodotus *A.P.* inserts chronological notes derived from an *Atthis*; so long a period for the first period of tyranny is hard to reconcile with the Herodotean narrative, and more probably Pisistratus remained in power only for a few months (cf. pp. 191–9).

14. iv. ἔτει δὲ δωδεκάτῳ μετὰ ταῦτα: Herodotus gives no indication of how long the first period of exile lasted; *A.P.*'s figures for the separate periods can most easily be reconciled with his summary figures if here we substitute πέμπτῳ for δωδεκάτῳ (Wilamowitz,

A.u.A., i. 22-3), so that in *A.P.*'s scheme this will be 552/1; if the first and second periods of tyranny were both very short it could be true that Pisistratus began the second in the 5th year (cf. again pp. 191-9).

περιελαυνόμενος ὁ Μεγακλῆς τῇ στάσει: Cf. H. i. 60. ii (περιελαυνόμενος δὲ τῇ στάσι ὁ Μεγακλέης ἐπεκηρυκεύετο Πεισιστράτῳ, εἰ βούλοιτο οἱ τὴν θυγατέρα ἔχειν γυναῖκα ἐπὶ τῇ τυραννίδι): Megacles was 'harassed' (*sc.* by Lycurgus' party) in the rivalry between the factions. According to schol. Ar. *Nub.* 48 cf. 800, Suid. (*E* 87) ἐγκεκοισυρωμένην, Megacles' daughter was called Coesyra; other statements about a woman of that name seem to make her the wife of the Megacles who was ostracised in 487/6 (Ar. *Ach.* 614 with schol., cf. schol. *Nub.* 46). Some have denied the authenticity of any Coesyra in the Alcmaeonid family (e.g. Wilamowitz, *A.u.A.*, i. 111 n. 20, Dover on Ar. *Nub.* 48); Davies accepts Coesyra as the wife of the fifth-century Megacles but thinks the application of the name to Pisistratus' third wife 'an imaginative expansion of Herodotos' account' (*A.P.F.*, 380-1); but T. L. Shear, jr, has argued for the existence of three women of this name, the mother of the Megacles contemporary with Pisistratus, his daughter, and the wife of the fifth-century Megacles (*Phoen.* xvii 1963, 99-112; the Coesyra who married Pisistratus is accepted also by Berve, *Die Tyrannis bei den Griechen*, i. 49 with ii. 545, P. J. Bicknell, *Hist.* Einz. xix 1972, 81). The ostraca found in the Ceramicus (cf. p. 275) have added a further complication: one names Μεγακλῆς ἱπποκρατός καὶ Κοισύρας (cf. H. B. Mattingly, *U. Leeds R.* xiv 1971, 283); Hippocrates will have been a brother of the Alcmaeonid woman who married Pisistratus (e.g. Davies, *A.P.F.*, 375 with 379), so this ostracon may confirm that Shear's second Coesyra did exist and allege, not necessarily truthfully, that she had an incestuous union with her brother.

ἀρχαίως καὶ λίαν ἁπλῶς: 'In a primitive and excessively simple manner'; Pl. *Sol.* 3. vi (ἐν δὲ τοῖς φυσικοῖς ἁπλοῦς ἐστι λίαν καὶ ἀρχαῖος [*sc.* ὁ Σόλων], with an example from fr. 9 West, one of the fragments said to embody Solon's reaction to Pisistratus) is probably an echo of this; H. i. 60. iii says μηχανῶται ... πρῆγμα εὐηθέστατον, ὡς ἐγὼ εὑρίσκω, μακρῷ.

προδιασπείρας: Herodotus has nothing directly corresponding to this. No other use of this double compound is noted in LSJ; διασπείρειν is found most commonly in the historians, and has the object λόγον in X. *H.* v. i. 25.

γυναῖκα μεγάλην καὶ καλήν: H. i. 60. iv gives her height as 3 fingers short of 4 cubits, i.e. 5 ft 7 in.–6 ft 4 in. (1715–1936 mm.) according to the standard used, and this modest figure tells in favour of the account's authenticity.

COMMENTARY ON THE *ATH. POL.* [14. iv

ὡς μὲν 'Ηρόδοτός φησιν: This is the only place where *A.P.* names a source other than Solon's poems.

ἐκ τοῦ δήμου τῶν Παιανέων: Cf. H. i. 60. iv (ἐν τῷ δήμῳ τῷ Παιανέϊ). Paeania lay due east of Athens, on the eastern slopes of Hymettus (cf. J. S. Traill, *Hesp.* Supp. xiv 1975, 43); the main route from the east coast to Athens passed not far to the north of it. There is no need for alarm at such references to a δῆμος, or local community, before the reforms of Cleisthenes (cf. pp. 81–2 and commentary on 21. iv).

ὡς δ' ἔνιοι ... Θρᾷτταν: In Clid. 323 F 15 (superseding Anticl. 140 F 6) she is called Phye the daughter of Socrates (who was presumably a citizen: Wilamowitz, *A.u.A.*, i. 29 n. 1) and is said to have been given in marriage to Hipparchus (but see Davies, *A.P.F.*, 452); before making his quotation from Clidemus, Ath. XIII. 609 c says that she was a στεφανόπωλις, which he perhaps derived from Phylarchus (81 F 21); by a simple error schol. Ar. *Eq.* 449 calls her Myrrhine, the name of Hippias' wife, and supposes that she was married to Pisistratus. The ascription of a foreign woman to an Attic δῆμος would be unusual: Jacoby (*Supp.* i. 72) confidently proclaims that the original dispute was simply over Phye's deme, and that στεφανόπωλιν Θρᾷτταν in *A.P.* is an insertion of what may originally have been a marginal note; alternatively it may be that *A.P.* knew both the major and the minor divergence from Herodotus and carelessly amalgamated them. Collytus was in the city of Athens, south of the Acropolis (cf. Traill, *op. cit.*, 40): it is not so obviously appropriate for a supporter of Pisistratus, though there is no reason why she should not have come from there; but this alternative version may have been used to cast a slur on Phye, 'the reputation of this popular residential quarter not being above reproach' (Jacoby, *loc. cit.*, citing Pl. *Dem.* 11. v). We cannot tell who ἔνιοι were; on *A.P.*'s references to disagreements among his sources see Introduction, pp. 25–7.

For this story see also Polyaen. i. 21. i, Pl. *Her. Mal.* 858 c, V.M. i. iii. 3, Hermogenes, *Inv.* i. 3 with Max. Plan. *ad loc.* (v. 378 Walz). The story was rejected by Beloch, *RM*[2] xlv 1890, 469–71, cf. *G.G.*[2], i. ii. 288 (believing that Pisistratus seized power only twice and was exiled only once), E. Meyer, *Forschungen*, ii. 248–50, but defended by B. Niese, *Hermes* xlii 1907, 464–8, [How &] Wells on H. i. 60; P. N. Ure, *The Origin of Tyranny*, 54–6, suggested that it is a variation on the story of the Paeonian woman in H. v. 12–13 (cf. Nic. Dam. 90 F 71). More recently there have been more sophisticated attempts at rationalisation by M. Delcourt, *Oedipe ou la légende du conquérant*, 177–80, and L. Gernet, *Éventail de l'histoire vivante: hommage à L. Febvre*, ii. 52–3 = *Anthropologie de la Grèce antique*, 358. J. Boardman describes the episode as 'a charade recalling nothing more than

Athena's introduction of Herakles to Olympus by chariot' (*Athenian Black Figure Vases*, 221, cf. 224 and *RA* 1972, 57–72; and see also on §i and 15. iv); whether or not that is how Pisistratus intended it to be understood, there is no need to doubt that the charade was performed.†

παραιβατούσης: The παρα(ι)βάτης was the warrior who stood beside the driver of the chariot (e.g. Hom. *Il.* XXIII. 132). The verb—'dies gewiss ionische Wort' (Kaibel, *Stil und Text*, 45, cf. Sandys)—is not used in Herodotus' account; Clid. 323 F 15 has τὴν παραιβατήσασαν αὐτῶι γυναῖκα, but *A.P.* does not mention what is distinctive in that passage, so unlike Sandys[2], lxvii, I am not confident that he provided *A.P.* with the word (Clidemus and *A.P.* may have found it in the account of the same predecessor); Παραιβάτες is a proper name in *IG* i[2] 5, 1.

προσκυνοῦντες: προσκυνεῖν was an act of homage paid by Persians to their human superiors (e.g. H. I. 134. i) but by Greeks only to the gods; the original meaning of the Greek word is 'blow a kiss', and this is the essential part of the act, but it might on occasions be accompanied by physical abasement (see J. P. V. D. Balsdon, *Hist.* i 1950, 374–5 = G. T. Griffith [ed.], *Alexander the Great: The Main Problems*, 190–1, J. Hofstetter, *Hist.* Einz. xviii 1972, 106–7, R. J. Lane Fox, *Alexander the Great*, 300–1, 535–6). H. I. 60. v says προσεύχοντό . . . τὴν ἄνθρωπον καὶ ἐδέκοντο Πεισίστρατον.

15. i. ὡς ἐξέπεσε . . . : The sentence is grammatical nonsense, with no main verb, and some have corrected it: Kaibel & Wilamowitz deleted ὡς; A. Gennadios, *CR* v 1891, 274, and Herwerden & Leeuwen substituted αὖθις; but more probably we should accept that the author has failed to work out his long sentence.

ἔτει μάλιστα ἑβδόμῳ μετὰ τὴν κάθοδον: In *A.P.*'s scheme this is 546/5; but as in 14. iii he has inserted into the narrative derived from Herodotus (cf. next note) chronological material derived from an *Atthis* which is hard to reconcile with that narrative, and as there we should prefer the implication of the narrative, that this period of tyranny was very short (cf. pp. 191–9).

οὐ γὰρ πολὺν χρόνον κατέσχεν: The story of Pisistratus' marrying Megacles' daughter as he had promised, but avoiding intercourse (or at any rate conception), is told at greater length in H. I. 61. i–ii (where it is not explicitly stated that this second period of tyranny was short: by stating what Herodotus implies *A.P.* has added to his embarrassment). W. Wyse, *CR* v 1891, 110, proposed to substitute κατεῖχεν for κατέσχεν, which some editors accepted (cf. Kaibel, *Stil und Text*, 156), but the aorist may be retained.

φοβηθεὶς ἀμφοτέρας τὰς στάσεις ὑπεξῆλθεν: Cf. H. I. 61. ii, explaining as *A.P.*'s shorter narrative fails to do why he should be afraid of both the other factions (ὀργῇ δὲ ὡς εἶχε [sc. ὁ Μεγακλέης] καταλλάσσετο τὴν ἔχθρην τοῖσι στασιώτῃσι. μαθὼν δὲ ὁ Πεισίστρατος τὰ ποιεύμενα ἐπ' ἑωυτῷ ἀπαλλάσσετο ἐκ τῆς χώρης τὸ παράπαν); this time Pisistratus did not wait to be driven out. It is alleged that on one occasion of his expulsion his property was confiscated, and only Callias, of the Κήρυκες (a family later found in Alopece with the Alcmaeonids), dared to bid for his property: H. VI. 121. ii.

15. ii. καὶ πρῶτον μὲν συνῴκισε περὶ τὸν Θερμαῖον κόλπον: H. I. 61. ii omits Pisistratus' visit to the northern Aegean and takes him straight to Eretria, but I. 64. i reveals that in his third period of tyranny he received revenues from the Strymon. Nothing more is heard of the Athenian settlement: the settlers, if authentic, must be adherents of Pisistratus who chose to leave Attica with him; J. W. Cole believes that Pisistratus went first to Eretria on leaving Athens (but see below on *A.P.*'s πάλιν) and suggests that the settlement may have been a joint foundation of Pisistratus and the Eretrians (*G&R*[2] xxii 1975, 43).†

'Ραίκηλος: See C. F. Edson, *CP* xlii 1947, 188–91, N. G. L. Hammond, *History of Macedonia*, i. 186–8, Cole, *op. cit.*, 42–3. Lycophr. 1236–7 mentions Rhaecelus and Mt. Cissus together, and schol. *ad loc.* associates with Cissus the πόλις called Αἶνος, presumably the Αἴνεια of H. VII. 123. ii–iii, the last city reached by Xerxes' fleet in 480 as it sailed along Pallene into the Thermaic Gulf. Only schol. Lycophr. and Steph. Byz. 'Ράκηλος call it a πόλις. Aenea is to be placed on Megálo Karaburnú (cf. Admiralty: Naval Intelligence Division, *Greece*, i, fig. 48); Edson argues that Rhaecelus was the ancient name of the cape, and of Pisistratus' short-lived settlement on it, and Hammond thinks Rhaecelus the last part of the table-land running north-west towards Aenea; Cole argues that Rhaecelus ought to be a specific place, and agrees that it should be near to but distinct from Aenea, which should be correct (but S. Casson, *Macedonia, Thrace and Illyria*, 82–5, placed Rhaecelus at Kalamaria, on Mikró Karaburnú).

τοὺς περὶ Πάγγαιον τόπους: Mt. Pangaeum, in an area famous for its gold and silver mines, stands a few miles inland from the Thracian coast, east of the R. Strymon: see Casson, *op. cit.*, 63–6, stressing that the gold and silver deposits were around the mountain rather than on it. Pisistratus' activity marks the beginning of a long history of Athenian attempts to gain a foothold in the region and to exploit its gold, silver and timber: various fifth-century attempts at colonisation culminated in the foundation of Amphipolis in 437/6, but Amphipolis went over to Sparta in the Archidamian War and Athens never succeeded in recovering it.

καὶ στρατιώτας μισθωσάμενος: Herodotus, who omits Pisistratus' visit to this region (cf. above), omits also his obtaining mercenaries from it, but he knows that Pisistratus acquired a large number of mercenaries (1. 61. iii–iv, 64. i). Thrace was a source from which the Greeks frequently obtained mercenaries (e.g. T. IV. 129. ii, V. 6. iv, VII. 27–30), and Thracian warriors appear on Athenian vases from c. 540 (cf. J. G. P. Best, *Thracian Peltasts and their Influence on Greek Warfare*, 5–7).

ἐλθὼν εἰς Ἐρέτριαν: Cf. H. 1. 61. ii, 62. i.

ἐνδεκάτῳ πάλιν ἔτει τό‹τε› πρῶτον: Cf. H. 1. 62. i (ἐξ Ἐρετρίης δὲ ὁρμηθέντες διὰ ἑνδεκάτου ἔτεος ἀπίκοντο ὀπίσω). Ten years must be the duration of the second period of exile (*pace* G. Sanders, *Nouv. Clio* vii–ix 1955–7, 161–79), and πάλιν marks this as the latest in *A.P.*'s series of intervals of time (*pace* Sandys and others, most recently J. W. Cole [cited above], who suppose it to mean that Pisistratus returned to Eretria, having been there before he went to Rhaecelus). The correction of τὸ to τό‹τε› was first made by Blass, *LZB* 1891, 303, and despite the defence of τὸ by Tovar, *REC* iii 1948, 162–3, is surely necessary. With this correction the expression is still clumsy but its meaning is clear, that it was only after ten years of exile that Pisistratus made his final attempt; there is no need to follow R. Weil, *Aristote et l'histoire*, 112–14, in detecting a sign of revision here (cf. Introduction, p. 54). In *A.P.*'s chronology this final *coup* was made in 536/5, but the date implied by Herodotus, which is to be preferred, is 547/6 or 546/5 (cf. pp. 191–9).

ἀνασώσασθαι βίᾳ τὴν ἀρχήν: Cf. H. 1. 106. ii, III. 65. vii, 73. i; but in 1. 61. iii on Pisistratus (cf. III. 73. ii) Herodotus writes ἀνακτᾶσθαι ὀπίσω τὴν τυραννίδα.

συμπροθυμουμένων: Cf. H. 1. 61. iv, quoted below.

Θηβαίων: Cf. H. 1. 61. iii (πολλῶν δὲ μεγάλα παρασχόντων χρήματα Θηβαῖοι ὑπερεβάλοντο τῇ δόσι τῶν χρημάτων). We have no information on Pisistratus' previous contacts with Thebes.

Λυγδάμιος τοῦ Ναξίου: Cf. H. 1. 61. iv (καὶ Νάξιός σφι ἀνὴρ ἀπιγμένος ἐθελοντής, τῷ οὔνομα ἦν Λύγδαμις, προθυμίην πλείστην παρείχετο, κομίσας καὶ χρήματα καὶ ἄνδρας). Between the Thebans and Lygdamis Herodotus adds the Argives, for whom see 17. iv with commentary.

τῶν ἱππέων τῶν ἐχόντων ἐν Ἐρετρίᾳ τὴν πολιτείαν: Herodotus says nothing of these. At some date the Eretrian aristocracy of ἱππεῖς (cf. the ἱπποβόται of neighbouring Chalcis [H. V. 77. ii], and also Arist. *Pol.* IV. 1289 B 38–40) was overthrown by one Diagoras (Arist. *Pol.* V. 1306 A 5–6); H. VI. 100–1 shows Eretria in a state of στάσις in 490. ἐχόντων... τὴν πολιτείαν means 'having control of the state'.

15. iii. νικήσας δὲ τὴν ἐπὶ Παλληνίδι μάχην: There is a detailed account in H. 1. 62–3: Pisistratus landed at Marathon (near Eretria, and in the eastern coastal region on which his support was based: cf. on

13. iii, iv), and when he set out for the city οἱ ἐκ τοῦ ἄστεος came to resist him; the two forces met ἐπὶ Παλληνίδος Ἀθηναίης ἱρὸν (62. iii); Pisistratus attacked his opponents at lunch time and defeated them; suitable messages to the citizens prevented further resistance (cf. Polyaen. I. 21. i). ἐπὶ Παλληνίδι recurs at 17. iv; Polyaenus uses ἐπὶ Παλληνίδος; schol. Ar. *Ach.* 234 cites Androtion (324 F 35) and *A.P.* as authorities for a battle in the δῆμος Παλληνεῖς or ἐν Παλλήνη; ἐν Παλληνίδι is used of the temple in Ath. VI. 234 F, 235 A. And. I. *Myst.* 106 claims that Andocides' great-grandfather Leogoras was general in a victory 'against the tyrants' ἐπὶ Παλληνίῳ, while And. II. *Red.* 26 (unemended) claims that his great-great-grandfather Leogoras στασιάσας πρὸς τοὺς τυράννους ὑπὲρ τοῦ δήμου could have come to terms with them but εἵλετο μᾶλλον ἐκπεσεῖν μετὰ τοῦ δήμου: possible interpretations are listed and discussed by D. M. MacDowell, ed. of And. I. *Myst.*, pp. 212–13, Davies, *A.P.F.*, 27–8. And. I. *Myst.* 106 surely intends to refer to the expulsion of Hippias in 511/0, but may well be guilty 'of a faulty reproduction of the name (Παλληνίῳ) and a faulty transference of it to a wrong context' (Davies, against MacDowell); II. *Red.* 26 may be either a garbled reference to the same occasion (as both MacDowell and Davies believe) or an attempt to say something about an earlier occasion.

Pallene and the temple of Athena Παλληνίς lay in the col between Hymettus and Pentelicon, on the longer but easier route from Marathon to Athens (cf. J. S. Traill, *Hesp.* Supp. xiv 1975, 54). For the cult of Athena Παλληνίς and the local association which observed the cult see R. Schlaifer, *HSCP* liv 1943, 35–67, D. M. Lewis, *Hist.* xii 1963, 33–4, 39.

τὴν [π]όλιν: First read by Wilcken, and generally accepted; Kenyon had originally restored [τὴν ἀρχὴ]ν. πόλις here means not the Acropolis, which is so called in §iv (contrast 8. iv, where πόλις is used of the Acropolis), but the city: we may assume, however, that Pisistratus did again occupy the Acropolis.

παρελόμενος τοῦ δήμου τὰ ὅπλα: Cf. §iv with commentary.

κατεῖχεν ἤδη τὴν τυραννίδα βεβαίως: Cf. H. I. 64. i (πειθομένων δὲ τῶν Ἀθηναίων, οὕτω δὴ Πεισίστρατος τὸ τρίτον σχὼν Ἀθήνας ἐρρίζωσε τὴν τυραννίδα).

καὶ Νάξον ἑλὼν ἄρχοντα κατέστησε Λύγδαμιν: Cf. H. I. 64. i–ii (ὁμήρους ... καταστήσας ἐς Νάξον—καὶ γὰρ ταύτην ὁ Πεισίστρατος κατεστρέψατο πολέμῳ καὶ ἐπέτρεψε Λυγδάμι), schol. Ar. *Vesp.* 355; also Arist. *Pol.* V. 1305 A 37–B 1, fr. 558 Teubner *ap.* Ath. VIII. 348 A–C (from the Ναξίων Πολιτεία), on Lygdamis as a man who became tyrant from within the ruling class. Some have thought that he had two spells as tyrant, and was in exile after the first when he helped Pisistratus at Pallene (e.g. J. Toepffer, *RM*² xlix 1894, 244–6, Glotz & Cohen, *H.G.*, i. 291; contr. Busolt, *G.G.*, ii². 324 with n. 3, stressing that there is no hint of this in Herodotus or *A.P.*). In the course of the 530's Lygdamis helped Polycrates to power in Samos (Polyaen. I. 23. ii: on the date see J. P. Barron, *CQ*² xiv 1964, 210 n. 1, H. Berve, *Die Tyrannis bei den Griechen*, i. 79, 107, ii. 583); *c.* 525 or *c.* 517 his tyranny was ended by the Spartans (Pl. *Her. Mal.* 859 D cf. *Apophth. Lac.* 236 C–D, schol. A. II. *F.L.* 77).

15. iv. παρείλε⟨το⟩ δὲ τοῦ δήμου τὰ ὅπλα: Cf. Polyaen. I. 21. ii; but contrast T. VI. 56. ii, 58, claiming that under the tyranny the citizens wore arms to take part in the Panathenaic procession and that the disarming was the work of Hippias—which *A.P.* 18. iv directly denies. Many have pronounced in favour of Thucydides (e.g. Busolt, *G.G.*, ii². 326 n. 1 cf. 383 n. 1, Hignett, *H.A.C.*, 125 n. 3, Day & Chambers, *A.H.A.D.*, 20–1), but Dover points out that we have no reliable way of deciding who is right (Gomme *et al.*, *Hist. Comm. Thuc.*, on VI. 58. ii); A. J. Holladay suggests that Pisistratus may have disarmed the citizens but not permanently (*G&R*² xxiv 1977, 52). *A.P.* or his source may have known a decree of the democracy ordering the wearing of arms in the procession, and such a decree may either have made it clear that this was an innovation or have misled the reader into thinking so; like many other elements in the story of Hipparchus' murder, this could have been put to purposes of propaganda, since it would have been less shameful that the citizens failed to rally in the tyrannicides' support if they were unarmed. Arist. *Pol.* V. 1311 A 12–13 notices disarming the people as a device of tyrannies and oligarchies, and 1315 A 38 remarks that 'good' tyrants do not need to do this; another tyrant who did it was Aristodemus of Cumae (D.H. *A.R.* VII. 8. ii–iii); oligarchies which disarmed the unprivileged included the Thirty at Athens in 404/3 (37. ii with commentary); but those in Mytilene who had been unarmed and were given arms in 428/7 (T. III. 27. ii) were probably men below the hoplite class, who had been unable to afford to arm themselves (cf. Hermocrates in T. VI. 72. iv).

The middle παρείλε⟨το⟩ was first urged by W. G. Rutherford, *CR* v 1891, 110, and was accepted by Kenyon and many others; but the active of the papyrus has been retained by Thalheim, Mathieu & Haussoullier, Oppermann and Tovar (who argues for it in *REC* iii 1948, 159–61). Although the middle is used in 25. iv and 37. ii, the active is defensible here and in 25. ii, and emendation is unnecessary. ἐξοπλασίαν: 'Armed parade'. The more usual form is ἐξοπλισία (e.g. X. *Anab.* I. vii. 10), but ἐξοπλασία is found also in *IG* xii (v) 647, 39 (Ceos, C3) and *SIG*³ 410, 10 (Erythrae, C3), and in some MSS of D.S. XV. 79. iv, XVI. 3. i, XIX. 3. ii: *pace* Kenyon[1] and some other editions it need not be expunged here.

ἐν τῷ Θησείῳ: Polyaen. I. 21. ii locates the parade in the Anaceum (whence Kenyon[1] read Ἀνακείῳ) and has the confiscated arms taken to the shrine of Aglaurus. Paus. I. 17. ii–vi gives an account of the Theseum, situated near the Gymnasium of Ptolemy (cf. Pl. *Thes.* 36. iv), and ends with the statement that the Theseum was founded when Cimon brought the bones of Theseus to Athens, after the Persian Wars (cf. p. 77); immediately afterwards he discusses the shrine of the Dioscuri (I. 18. i: they were sometimes called the Ἄνακες [e.g. Pl. *Thes.* 33. ii, *IG* ii² 4796], whence the name Ἀνακεῖον), 'above' that the shrine of Aglaurus (§ii), and then the prytaneum (§iii). The cave and shrine of Aglaurus are securely identified, on the north side of the Acropolis (e.g. W. Judeich, *Topographie von Athen*², 303–4, Travlos, *Pictorial Dictionary*, 8 fig. 5, R. J. Hopper, *The Acropolis*, 29–30, 50–3, with 25 fig. 3, 81 fig. 6), and the other buildings must be nearby (e.g. Travlos, *op. cit.*, 578–9, Hopper, *op. cit.*, 81 fig. 6). Cf. pp. 103–4; and see also M. de G. Verrall & J. E. Harrison, *Mythology and Monuments of Ancient Athens*, 143–68, J. G. Frazer, *Pausanias's Description of Greece*, ii. 145–9, 164–8, I. C. T. Hill, *The Ancient City of Athens*, 92–101, H. A. Thompson & R. E. Wycherley, *The Athenian Agora*, xiv. 124–6, J. P. Barron, *JHS* xcii 1972, 20–2, E. Vanderpool, *Hesp.* xliii 1974, 308–10.†

Pausanias says in the last sentence of I. 17. vi that the Theseum was created in the time of Cimon, and in the first sentence of I. 18. i that the Anaceum was ἀρχαῖον. The Anaceum was an enclosure in which a cavalry parade (And. I. *Myst.* 45) or a sizeable meeting (T. VIII. 93. i) could be held, while there is no evidence apart from *A.P.* for any Theseum, let alone an enclosure capable of containing an armed parade, on this site before the fifth century (allotments of magistracies in the Theseum are mentioned in 62. i); so it is likely that, whether or not the story is true, *A.P.* or his source is guilty of an anachronism and on this point Polyaenus gives a more acceptable version (but see Phil. 328 F 18 with Jacoby *ad loc.*). J. Boardman has pointed out that Theseus became popular in Athens only after 510, whereas the tyrants preferred the cult of Heracles (*RA* 1972, 57–72, cf. commentary on 14. i and iv, and his further exploration of Pisistratus' interest in Heracles in *JHS* xcv 1975, 1–12): the evidence for interest in Heracles and in Theseus is assembled by F. Brommer, *Vasenlisten zur griechischen Heldensage*³, 1–209 and 210–58, *Denkmälerlisten zur griechischen Heldensage*, i and ii. 1–28; see also T. B. L. Webster, *Potter and Patron in Classical Athens*, 82–90, 252–3 (associating Theseus particularly with the Alcmaeonids and Cimon), C. G. Starr, *The Economic and Social Growth of Early Greece, 800–500 B.C.*, 172 (contrasting the archaic Heracles with the civilised Theseus).‡

ἐκκλησιάζειν: Usually 'to hold an assembly', with the members as subject (e.g. T. VII. 2. i, VIII. 93. i, Lys. XII. *Erat.* 73); in Aen. Tact.

COMMENTARY ON THE *ATH. POL.*

9. i, D.S. xxi. 16. iv and the Septuagint it means 'to summon to an assembly' (with a direct object); here it must mean 'to hold an assembly' (as chairman) or 'to address in assembly', a usage not noticed in LSJ or the 1968 Supplement. In Thucydides' account of the disarming (vi. 58) Hippias tells the men to leave their arms and they expect him to address them.

κ(αὶ) [χρ(όνον)] προσηγό]ρευεν μικρόν: Thus Kenyon, in his Berlin ed. and O.C.T., as *lectio valde incerta*; he had originally restored [φωνῇ δ' ἐξεκλησί]ασεν μικρόν, and in the Berlin ed. he still thought]ασεν possible;]δεστεγεν (with Γ^ω before), read by Wilcken, approved by Kaibel & Wilamowitz[3], and dotted thus by Oppermann, he thought impossible. Kenyon's later restoration is adopted by Oppermann and Tovar, and 'has the advantage of tense' (Gomme, *CR* xlii 1928, 225); Dr J. D. Thomas reports that προσηγ]όρεψεν is quite a good reading; but many other guesses have been made,[17] of which the one that has found most favour is Thalheim's κ(αὶ) [χρ(όνον) μὲν ἠκκλησί]ασεν μικρόν, adopted by Sandys[2], Mathieu & Haussoullier and others. The latter would involve a more violent departure from the normal meaning of ἐκκλησιάζειν than we have noticed above, and Kenyon's text is to be preferred. Polyaenus adds a detail which is appropriate to the story, that Pisistratus deliberately spoke quietly.

τὸ πρόπυλον: 'Apparently used on purpose to avoid the grander term προπύλαια, which ... would have suggested the Propylaea of the time of Pericles' (Sandys). The word is rare in the singular, but instances of it include *IG* i[2] 891, *SEG* x 379, xiv 27 (not necessarily from the Piraeus), *IG* ii[2] 1046, 13. For the pre-Periclean gateways to the Acropolis see C. H. Weller, *AJA*[2] viii 1904, 35–70, W. Judeich, *Topographie von Athen*[2], 66–7, 225–7, G. P. Stevens, *Hesp.* xv 1946, 73–83, I. C. T. Hill, *The Ancient City of Athens*, 143 with 239 n. 13, W. H. Plommer, *JHS* lxxx 1960, 127–8, 146–50, Travlos, *Pictorial Dictionary*, 482, Hopper, *The Acropolis*, 28, 129–31, with 25 fig. 3, 81 fig. 6.†

γεγωνῇ: γεγωνεῖν, 'to make oneself heard by shouting', is rare except in Homer and tragedy, but its appearances in prose include a number of instances in Aristotle (esp. *Aud.* 804 B 24, *Probl.* xix. 2. 917 B 21), also Plat. *Hipp. Mai.* 292 D 4.

οἱ ἐπὶ τούτῳ τεταγμένοι: When men are appointed to a task the noun or pronoun following ἐπί may be accusative or dative or (less frequently) genitive: the papyrus has τούτ(ων), most editors have followed W. G. Rutherford and J. E. B. Mayor, *CR* v 1891, 110, in

---

[17] To those listed by Sandys[2] add one of Σ. Ν. Δραγούμης, Ἀθ. xxvii 1915, 34, [φωνεῖν δ' ἐσπούδ]ασεν, and two of Π. Σ. Φωτιάδης, *EE* ii 1925, 25–31 (cf. 33–4, quoting an unfavourable letter from Kenyon), καὶ [πλῆθος εἴσω ἐχώρη]σεν and καὶ [τοῦτο (sc. τὸ Θησεῖον) πλῆθ]ος ἔστεγεν.

emending to τούτῳ, Kaibel & Wilamowitz preferred τοῦτο; Kaibel, *Stil und Text*, 157, cited H. iv. 84. ii and wondered whether to keep τούτων, but I doubt if that is right.

[κατα]κλείσαντες: Kenyon originally restored [συγ], and Wilcken claimed to read παρα; [κατα]κλῆσαντες was first restored by Blass[2], and that should be the right compound (cf. Kaibel, *op. cit.*, 157). As in 7. ii Kenyon rightly corrected the ηι of the papyrus to the form normal in the second half of the fourth century, ει.

εἰς τὰ πλησίον οἰκήματα τοῦ Θησείου: In Polyaenus' version of the story this becomes εἰς τὸ ἱερὸν τοῦ Ἀγραύλου. There are references to οἰκέματα on the Acropolis in *IG* i[2] 4, 2, 17 (485/4).

ἀπελθόντας ἐπὶ τῶν ἰδίων εἶναι: Cf. 16. iii, and Pisistratus' message to the Athenians after Pallene, H. I. 63. ii (θαρσέειν τε κελεύοντες καὶ ἀπιέναι ἕκαστον ἐπὶ τὰ ἑωυτοῦ); similar expressions are used, not in connection with Pisistratus, in A. III. *Ctes.* 8, Arist. *Pol.* V. 1309 A 4–7.

16. i. μεταβολὰς ἔσχεν τοσαύτας: Cf. 41. ii, summarising the μεταβολαί or μεταστάσεις in the history of the Athenian constitution, and the frequent references in Arist. *Pol.* to μεταβολαί of the πολιτεία. Here the 'changes' are Pisistratus' seizures of power and withdrawals into exile.

16. ii. διῴκει δ' ὁ Πεισίστρατος . . . μᾶλλον πολιτικῶς ἢ τυραννικῶς: Cf. 14. iii with commentary, where *A.P.* says the same of Pisistratus' first period of tyranny. There *A.P.* like Isocrates uses τὰ κοινὰ as object of διοικεῖν; here he uses another Isocratean expression: διοικεῖν has τὰ περὶ τὴν πόλιν as object in Is. XII. *Panath.* 124, XV. *Antid.* 158, cf. Plat. *Laches*, 179 C 4–5, [Arist.] *Oec.* II. 1348 B 4.†

φιλάνθρωπος ἦν καὶ πρᾶος καὶ τοῖς ἁμαρτάνουσι συγγνωμονικός: φιλάνθρωπος is used particularly by orators and philosophers, and is a favourite word of Isocrates; X. *M.* I. ii. 60 describes Socrates as δημοτικὸς καὶ φιλάνθρωπος. πρᾶος is used by writers of all kinds, is a favourite word of Isocrates and Plato, but is comparatively rare in Herodotus and Thucydides (cf. J. de Romilly, *The Rise and Fall of States according to Greek Authors*, 66). συγγνωμονικός is not used by Isocrates or Plato but is a favourite word of Aristotle (*E.N.* IV. 1126 A 3, VI. 1143 A 21–2, *Rhet.* II. 1384 B 3, [Arist.] *V.V.* 1251 B 33).

The papyrus has πρᾶος without iota here (confirmed by M. H. Chambers, *TAPA* xcvi 1965, 32) and πραότητι in 22. iv, but πράιοι with iota in 16. x. Almost all editors supply the iota where it is absent, but πρᾶος appears to be the correct form (cf. Meisterhans & Schwyzer, *G.a.I.*, 64 with n. 547, citing the proper name Πρᾶος in *IG* ii[2] 1928, 20 [beg. c4]; LSJ *s.v.*).

τοῖς ἀ[πό]ροις προεδάνειζε χρήματα: Not attested elsewhere except, in a more dramatic form, in Ael. *V.H.* ix. 25; but Thph. fr. 99 Wimmer *ap.* Pl. *Sol.* 31. v ascribes to Pisistratus the νόμος ἀργίας which others ascribed to Draco or Solon (cf. p. 110). We need not doubt that Pisistratus did make loans to poor farmers: the loans are presumably to be associated with the tax on produce mentioned in §iv. προδανείζειν can mean simply 'lend in advance' and so 'lend', without implying 'before' or 'first'; it is very much a word of *A.P.*'s own time, being found in *IG* ii² 333, *c* 9 (335/4), vii 4254 = *SIG*³ 298, 38 (Oropus, 329/8), decree *ap.* [Pl.] *X. Or.* 852 B (307/6), and also *OGIS* 46, 5 (Halicarnassus, c3). See W. Wyse, *CR* vi 1892, 254–7, vii 1893, 21, who suggests that it came to have the special meaning 'lend without interest'.

διατρέφεσθαι: Not found often before the Roman period, but instances include T. iv. 39. ii, X. *M.* ii. vii. 6, *Vect.* i. 1.

16. iii. ἵνα μήτε ἐν τῷ ἄστει ... ἐπιμελεῖσθαι τῶν κοινῶν: The two objectives ascribed to Pisistratus are two aspects of one: the citizens should be freed from the temptation to engage in politics or to unite against the tyrant by employment in farming, which will ensure both distance from the city and lack of leisure. The first point about farmers is made by Arist. *Pol.* vi. 1319 A 26–32, and the second in iv. 1292 B 25–9, vi. 1318 B 9–16; in v. 1311 A 13–15 it is said that both tyrannies and oligarchies remove the ὄχλος from the city; in v. 1313 B 21–5 the Pisistratids are said to have had the temple of Olympian Zeus started (and other tyrants to have had other works done) in order to ensure ἀσχολία. However, neither an occupied peasantry nor public works are necessarily signs of oppression: in the Good Old Days of Is. vii. *Areop.* 33, 48–55, men did not frequent the city and its distractions but were busy with their work in the country, and the rich gave assistance to the poor; in Arist. *Pol.* v. 1314 B 37–8 the 'good' tyrant is advised to κατασκευάζειν ... καὶ κοσμεῖν τὴν πόλιν, but ὡς ἐπίτροπον ὄντα καὶ μὴ τύραννον. Dio Chr. vii. *Eub.* 107–8, xxv. *Daem.* 3, remarks on Pisistratus' keeping the Athenians scattered in the countryside; the latter passage says that Attica was planted with olives on his orders; cf. §ii with commentary, on Pisistratus' loans to farmers.

Pisistratus may have had the political objective here ascribed to him, but it is likely that he also had an economic objective: Solon had freed the ἑκτήμοροι and perhaps other debtors from their obligations, but otherwise had done nothing to make life easier for peasant farmers struggling at subsistence level (cf. on 6. i), and a tyrant who taxed produce and made loans to farmers (and perhaps redistributed land confiscated from his opponents) was probably trying to improve the lot of the poorer farmers at the expense of the more prosperous. In particular, the loans may have been intended to tide poorer farmers over the years of waiting in a change from the cultivation of cereals to that of olives and vines (cf. A. J. Holladay, *G&R*² xxiv 1977, 40–56).†

μήτε ... ἀλλά: The combination is not listed in the index to J. D. Denniston, *The Greek Particles*². Kaibel, *Stil und Text*, 158, compares Arist. *Pol.* v. 1308 B 11–12 (μήτ' ... ἀλλά), *Rhet.* I. 1355 B 8–9 (οὔτε ... ἀλλά, but Ross's O.C.T. emends), II. 1394 A 22–4 (οὔτε ... ἀλλά), Galen, *Protr.* 1 (οὔτε ... ἀλλά).

τῶν μετρίων: 'Reasonable means of subsistence': cf. 27. iii.

16. iv. συνέβαινεν αὐτῷ καὶ τὰς προσόδους γίγνεσθαι μείζους: *A.P.* writes as if the proceeds of the tax went to Pisistratus himself rather than to the state; and as far as we know the tax was abolished on the fall of the tyranny: probably no clear distinction was made between the revenue of the tyrant and the revenue of the state.

ἐπράττετο γὰρ ἀπὸ τῶν γιγνομένων δεκάτην: Cf. D.L. I. 53, Zenob. IV. 76 and other late writers; but T. VI. 54. v writes of Pisistratus' sons Ἀθηναίους εἰκοστὴν μόνον πρασσόμενοι τῶν γιγνομένων. Day & Chambers, *A.H.A.D.*, 95, believe that *A.P.* is wrong; many suppose that both are right and Pisistratus' sons reduced the rate of tax (e.g. Sandys; Berve, *Die Tyrannis bei den Griechen*, i. 53, 65–6, with ii. 548; H. W. Pleket, *Τάλαντα* i 1969, 46 n. 95). However, Thucydides' context provides a sufficient explanation of the μόνον without our having to suppose that a higher rate of tax had been levied earlier: the best explanation of the discrepancy is not that *A.P.* is wrong but rather that 'the specific term εἰκοστή may be subsumed under the generic δεκάτη, ... and in principle the more precise evidence is preferable to the more general' (Dover on T., *loc. cit.*; cf. earlier F. Cornelius, *Die Tyrannis in Athen*, 53 n. 5). I doubt if P. Cloché was right in suggesting that Pisistratus was continuing a tax already in existence (*La Démocratie athénienne*, 3 with n. 2).

16. v. τοὺς κατὰ δήμους κατεσκεύασε δικαστάς: Not attested elsewhere (but a confused note in Dem. Phal. 228 F 31 attributes to οἱ περὶ Σόλωνα the institution of δήμαρχοι, on whom see 21. v with commentary, as local justices), and rejected, unnecessarily, by De Sanctis, *Ἀτθίς*, ¹305 = ²313, Day & Chambers, *A.H.A.D.*, 95–6. Later, probably on the fall of the tyranny, the appointment of travelling magistrates was discontinued; and the institution was revived in 453/2 (26. iii with commentary) and modified at the beginning of the fourth century (53. i with commentary). The fact that the fifth-century magistrates numbered thirty (a convenient number for post-Cleisthenic Athens) proves nothing for those of the sixth century.

ὅπως μὴ ... παραμελῶσι τῶν ἔργων: The motive is consistent with that ascribed to Pisistratus for encouraging small farmers; but it is unlikely that the minor disputes which these magistrates will have been competent to settle will previously have been brought to Athens, and more probable that Pisistratus was substituting representatives of the central authority for whatever arbitration the disputants had been able to obtain locally—usually, no doubt, from the local nobility (e.g. Hignett, *H.A.C.*, 115).

16. vi. συμβῆναί φασι τὰ περὶ τὸν ἐν τῷ [Ὑμ]ηττῷ γεωργοῦντα: The story, introduced here by φασι, is found also in D.S. IX. 37. ii–iii, Suid. (*K* 1206) καὶ σφάκελοι ποιοῦσιν ἀτέλειαν, (*Σ* 1711) σφακελισμός, Zenob. IV. 76, and other late compilations. The account in *A.P.* seems to have been remembered as an explanation of the χωρίον ἀτελές; the compilers' version is given as an explanation of the proverb καὶ σφάκελοι ποιοῦσιν ἀτέλειαν (attributed to Demon by O. Crusius, *Analecta Critica ad Paroemiographos Graecos*, 77, cf. 132–3, with the approval of Wilamowitz, *A.u.A.*, i. 272–3; but see the doubts of Jacoby, *Supp.* i. 204 with ii. 168 nn. 18–21). D.S. as preserved by *Exc. Vat.* is defective: the extract ends with the quotation of the proverb, but the farmer's reply to Pisistratus does not include the word σφάκελος and does resemble his reply in *A.P.* (ἔφησε λαμβάνειν ἐκ τοῦ χωρίου κακὰς ὀδύνας, ἀλλ' οὐθὲν αὐτῷ μέλειν· τούτων γὰρ τὸ μέρος Πεισιστράτῳ διδόναι); there are further reminiscences of *A.P.* in θαυμάσας... τὴν φιλεργίαν and καὶ γελάσας ἐποίησε τὸ χωρίον ἀτελές. In the latter part of book IX D.S. seems to have been following Ephorus (cf. IX. 26 with Eph. 70 F 181, IX. 32 with F 58), and we may guess that both *A.P.* and D.S. obtained this story from him (18. iv–vi tells another story which was also told by Ephorus, but ascribes that version to δημοτικοί). As presented by *A.P.* the story is less than satisfactory, since if the peasant did not realise that he was talking to Pisistratus his remark did not display laudable παρρησία.

παντελῶ[ς π]έτρας σκάπτοντα: Kaibel & Wilamowitz[1] suggested π... λω[ς ἐν], and C. Wessely and Blass[1] read παντελῶ[ς ἐν]; there is no room on the papyrus for the preposition, and editors were reluctant to accept this striking use of adverb with noun (cf. Kaibel, *Stil und Text*, 159–60, Sandys[2], *apparatus*), but the reading was confirmed by Wilcken and by Kenyon in his Berlin ed. For the image of digging rocks Sandys compares Philemon I, fr. 98. 5 Kock, Men. fr. 719, Com. Adesp. fr. 380, Lucian, *Phalaris*, ii. 8; notice also Is. VIII. *Pace*, 117.

16. vii. παρ‹ην›ώχλε[ι]: παροχλεῖν is the rarer verb, but it is found in Thph. *C.P.* III. 10. v and has been retained by Kenyon[1-3] and Oppermann; J. B. Mayor and W. Wyse, *CR* v 1891, 110, and others argued for παρηνώχλει (ἐνώχλουν is found in 11. i), which was accepted by Kenyon in his Berlin ed. and O.C.T. and by most other editors; but it is better to leave the *difficilior lectio* undisturbed.

αἰεὶ παρεσκε[ύ]αζεν εἰρήνην καὶ ἐτήρει τὴν ἡσυχίαν: We hear of few episodes in which soldiers were or may have been involved, though our information on the sixth century is so scanty that the silence may to some extent be misleading. No doubt the soldiers used in overseas adventures were mercenaries and not citizens, even if Pisistratus had not disarmed the citizens (cf. H. 1. 64. i, perhaps T. vi. 54. v, and 14. i, 15. iv–v, with commentary). Pisistratus' friend Lygdamis was installed as tyrant of Naxos (15. iii). Delos was 'purified' by the removal of all graves within sight of the sanctuary of Apollo (H. 1. 64. ii, T. iii. 104. i–ii). Sigeum, acquired by Athens at the end of the seventh century (cf. p. 96), was apparently lost subsequently and had to be reconquered from Mytilene by Pisistratus, who installed there his son Hegesistratus (cf. on 17. iii), ὃς οὐκ ἀμαχητὶ εἶχε τὰ παρέλαβε παρὰ Πεισιστράτου (H. v. 94. i). On the European side of the Hellespont Miltiades (cf. p. 187) accepted an invitation to rule over a settlement of the Dolonci in the Chersonese, and although Herodotus represents this as the personal venture of a man ἀχθόμενόν τε τῇ Πεισιστράτου ἀρχῇ καὶ βουλόμενον ἐκποδὼν εἶναι (vi. 34–38. i; quotation from 35. iii) it is very likely that he went with Pisistratus' support to a settlement so significantly placed (e.g. Wade-Gery, *JHS* lxxi 1951, 218–19 = *Essays*, 165–7; for a sensible discussion of the colony's status see E. Will, *Nouv. Clio* vi 1954, 424–38): he probably went out in one of the earlier periods of tyranny (cf. p. 198), but the settlement remained in the control of his family until after Darius' Scythian expedition. For the allies of the tyranny see 15. ii with commentary (Pallene), 19. v–vi with commentary (511/0).

πολλὰ κλέ[α ἐ]θρ[ύλλο]υν: Thus Kenyon in his Berlin ed. and O.C.T., as *lectio non certa, sed vestigiis satis apta*. Previously Kenyon had read πολλάκις [παρωμιάζ]ετο; C. Wessely suggested πολλάκις ἐθρύλησαν, modified by Blass[1] to πολλάκις ἐθ[ρυ]λλ[εῖ]το and by Thalheim to πολλάκ[ις ἐ]θρ[ύλλο]υν, which was accepted by Sandys[2] and Oppermann. Wilcken read ΠΟΛΛΑ . ΕΛΕΙΕΤΟΥ .. ΙΝ, on the basis of which Kaibel & Wilamowitz[3] printed πολλ .. ἐλέγετο . . . . . Π. Σ. Φωτιάδης, *EE* ii 1925, 31–3, suggested πολλὰ πάλ[α]ι θρ[υλοῦσ]ιν (cf. [Plat.] *Hipparch.* 229 B 5–7). I know no instance in prose of the plural κλέα, and should prefer Thalheim's text, but Dr J. D. Thomas supports Kenyon's πολλακλε.

ὁ ἐπὶ Κρόν[ου] βίος: The age of Cronus is represented as a golden age in Hes. *Op.* 109–26, cf. Cratinus, fr. 165 Kock; the label is applied to the rule of Pisistratus' sons before the murder of Hipparchus by [Plat.] *Hipparch.* 229 B 3–7, to the treatment of

Athens' allies in the Delian League when Aristides assessed their tribute by Pl. *Arist.* 24. iii, to the generosity of Cimon by Pl. *Cim.* 10. vii (cf. 27. iii with commentary). M. Hirsch, *Klio* xx 1926, 161-2, supposed that the tyranny was first so described by the oligarchs of the late fifth century, but the oligarchs professed that their ideal was an earlier form of the democracy (cf. 29. iii with commentary) and are not likely to have admired the tyranny: presumably the description was first applied at some time after Pisistratus' death by someone who thought the current state of affairs miserable by comparison, perhaps in the last stages of the tyranny or perhaps slightly later (but hardly very much later).

πολλῷ γενέσθαι τραχυτέραν τὴν ἀρχήν: Cf. 19. i, where συνέβαινεν πολλῷ τραχυτέραν εἶναι τὴν τυραννίδα after the killing of Hipparchus, and for the memory of Hippias' tyranny as a time of severity cf. Ar. *Vesp.* 500-2, *Lys.* 614-18. It became orthodox doctrine that tyrants ruled harshly; but Pisistratus died a natural death and bequeathed the tyranny to his sons, whereas the sons succumbed to a series of attempts to oust them, so ancient writers inevitably supposed that the father's rule was mild but the sons' rule was harsh: similarly in Corinth Cypselus ruled mildly but Periander was harsh and very soon after his death Psammetichus/Cypselus II was expelled (Nic. Dam. 70 FF 57-60, contr. H. v. 92); in Acragas Theron was mild but his son Thrasydaeus harsh (D.S. xi. 53. ii); in Syracuse Gelon was mild, Hieron was harsh and Thrasybulus harsher still (D.S. xi. 67. ii-vi). In the case of the Pisistratids, those who insisted that Hipparchus was killed solely for personal reasons and that at that time the tyranny was not yet hated had to postpone the degeneration until after Hipparchus' death (T. vi. 54. v-vi, 59. ii, cf. H. v. 55, 62. ii, vi. 123. ii; also [Plat.] *Hipparch.* 229 B 3-7; and see on 18. i), but those who regarded the killing of Hipparchus as the act of liberation could regard Hippias and Hipparchus as cruel and unjust (Ephorus *ap.* D.S. x. 17. i, Idom. 338 F 3). *A.P.* accepts the main contention of Herodotus and Thucydides, that Hipparchus was not the reigning tyrant and his death did not end the tyranny, but his account shows some traces of the alternative story: thus he makes the tyranny deteriorate after Pisistratus' death and deteriorate further after the murder of Hipparchus.

16. viii. τὸ δημοτικὸν εἶναι τῷ ἤθει καὶ φιλάνθρωπον: Pisistratus is δημοτικώτατος ... εἶναι δοκῶν in 14. i and φιλάνθρωπος in 16. ii.

ἐβ[ούλ]ετο πάντα διοικεῖν κατὰ τοὺς νόμους: Cf. H. I. 59. vi (quoted p. 203), T. vi. 54. vi (τὰ δὲ ἄλλα αὐτὴ ἡ πόλις τοῖς πρὶν κειμένοις νόμοις ἐχρῆτο), Pl. *Sol.* 31. iii (καὶ γὰρ ἐφύλαττε τοὺς πλείστους νόμους τοὺς Σόλωνος, ἐμμένων πρῶτος αὐτὸς καὶ τοὺς φίλους ἀναγκάζων— after which the story which follows in *A.P.* is repeated); but contrast

COMMENTARY ON THE *ATH. POL.* [16. viii

A.P. 22. i (συνέβη τοὺς μὲν Σόλωνος νόμους ἀφανίσαι τὴν τυραννίδα διὰ τὸ μὴ χρῆσθαι). Tyranny in an established Greek πόλις was an extra-constitutional phenomenon, and it was no doubt legally correct to describe Pisistratus as οὐδεμίαν ἑαυτῷ πλεονεξίαν διδούς. Solon's institutions will for the most part have survived, but Pisistratus will have seen that they worked in such a way as to yield the results which he wanted: despite the recommendation that the people should be occupied with their own affairs (15. v, 16. iii) the boule of four hundred and the assembly should have continued to meet; R. J. Bonner thought that the right of ἔφεσις to the heliaea was suspended (*CP* xix 1924, 359–61), but more probably it remained theoretically available but was not much used; for the archonship cf. on §ix.

[κ]αί [ποτ]ε προσκληθεὶς φόνου δίκην εἰς ῎Αρειον πάγον: Cf. Arist. *Pol.* v. 1315 B 21–2, Pl. *Sol.* 31. iii (*pace* Sandys and Wehrli [fr. 149] it is not clear that Her. Pont. was Plutarch's source for the story); in Arist. *Pol.* v. 1315 A 6–8 the 'good' tyrant awards honours himself but allows magistrates and lawcourts to impose punishments. The story may well be true. προσκαλεῖσθαι is regularly used of a prosecutor's summons to a defendant to appear before the relevant authority (cf. 29. iv with commentary).

16. ix. διὸ καὶ πολὺν χρόνον ἔμεινεν ... πάλιν ἀνελάμβανε ῥᾳδίως: Probably the author's own comment, written in conformity with the belief that a tyrant who was able to maintain and bequeath his position must have been a mild ruler. On the lengths of tyrannies see Arist. *Pol.* v. 1315 B 11–39.

ἔμεινεν ⟨ἐν⟩ [τῇ ἀρ]χ[ῇ]: [ἐν τῇ ἀρχῇ] was proposed by Blass, *LZB* 1891, 304, and Herwerden, *BPW* xi 1891, 322 (cf. 17. i, ἐν τῇ ἀρχῇ διέμεινεν); Kenyon in his Berlin ed. read the χ and Wilcken claimed to read both the α and the χ. Blass[4] for metrical reasons preferred ἔμεινεν [ἡ] ἀ[ρ]χ[ή] (cf. his pp. 129–30, citing 25. i, 33. i, διέμεινεν ἡ πολιτεία): on metre in *A.P.* see Introduction, pp. 41–2; I would not emend for the sake of metre; here the usual text, though requiring emendation, is the likelier, but Blass's alternative could be right.

ἀνελάμβανε: The papyrus' ἐπελάμβανε is clearly inappropriate: ἀνελάμβανε (H. Richards, *CR* v 1891, 226) has rightly been preferred by editors to ἀπελάμβανε (W. Wyse, *ibid.*, 110), the latter being used only of taking back what someone gives back (cf. Kaibel, *Stil und Text*, 162).

καὶ τῶν γνωρίμων καὶ τῶν δημοτικῶν: Here uniquely in *A.P.* those contrasted with the γνώριμοι are the δημοτικοί; but although the word is often used of politicians who lead or appeal to the δῆμος (e.g. 14. i, 16. viii, of Pisistratus) it can also refer to the members of the δῆμος, and is clearly intended to do so here.

16. ix] COMMENTARY ON THE *ATH. POL.*

τοὺς μὲν γὰρ ταῖς ὁμιλίαις: 'Through his friendly intercourse with them' (Fritz & Kapp); Arist. *Pol.* v. 1315 B 3–4 includes among the recommendations to the 'good' tyrant τοὺς μὲν γνωρίμους καθομιλεῖν, τοὺς δὲ πολλοὺς δημαγωγεῖν. According to H. 1. 64. i Pisistratus secured the loyalty of (presumably) the γνώριμοι by depositing their children on Naxos as hostages. Otherwise the best evidence available to us for the tyrants' dealings with the γνώριμοι is a fragment of the archon list (M&L 6, *c*, with D.H. *A.R.* VII. 3. i and T. VI. 54. vi–vii; there is an interesting discussion by M. E. White, *Polis and Imperium: Studies . . . E. T. Salmon*, 81–95): Onetorides, probably from a rich family subsequently registered in the city deme of Melite (Davies, *A.P.F.*, 421), was archon in 527/6; Hippias in 526/5 (cf. p. 197); Cleisthenes, of the Alcmaeonid family, in 525/4 (cf. on 19. iii); Miltiades son of Cimon in 524/3; an unidentified Calliades in 523/2; and probably Hippias' son Pisistratus in 522/1. T. VI. 54. vi comments αἰεί τινα ἐπεμέλοντο σφῶν αὐτῶν ἐν ταῖς ἀρχαῖς εἶναι: clearly the tyrants did not rely solely on their own family but secured the cooperation of the leading families of Athens; Andocides (II. *Red.* 26, on which cf. p. 209) claims that his great-great-grandfather Leogoras could have been reconciled with the tyrants καὶ γενομένῳ κηδεστῇ ἄρξαι μετ' ἐκείνων τῶν ἀνδρῶν τῆς πόλεως. 22. v indicates that, if Solon had provided for the appointment of archons by κλήρωσις ἐκ προκρίτων (8. i with commentary), the tyrants found it easier to secure the results they wanted by direct election.

A.P. and some of his sources will have had the archon list available to them, and *A.P.* was capable of drawing conclusions from the appearance of names in documents (54. iii with commentary): whether this observation was based on such evidence cannot be determined.

16. x. ἦσαν ... οἱ περὶ τῶν τυράννων νόμοι πρᾶοι: (Though the papyrus here has ι, πρᾶοι should be spelled without: cf. §ii with commentary.) *A.P.*'s point seems to be that the mildness of the laws made it easier for Pisistratus to acquire and to retain power.

Evidence for measures against attempts to overthrow the constitution or set up a tyranny is collected and discussed by M. Ostwald, *TAPA* lxxxvi 1955, 103–28. The following are listed in chronological order:

(*a*) One of the categories excluded from Solon's amnesty law was ὅσοι (from various courts, for crimes of homicide or) ἐπὶ τυραννίδι ἔφευγον ὅτε ὁ θεσμὸς ἐφάνη ὅδε (Pl. *Sol.* 19. iv).

(*b*) Solon established the procedure of εἰσαγγελία to the Areopagus against τοὺς ἐπὶ καταλύσει τοῦ δήμου συνισταμένους (*A.P.* 8. iv).

(c) Fear of tyranny is said to have been Cleisthenes' reason for the institution of ostracism (*A.P.* 22. iii–iv and other texts).

(d) On the restoration of the democracy in 410/09 Demophantus carried a decree ἐάν τις δημοκρατίαν καταλύῃ τὴν Ἀθήνησιν, ἢ ἀρχήν τινα ἄρχῃ καταλελυμένης τῆς δημοκρατίας; an oath incorporated in the decree repeats these charges and adds ἐάν τις τυραννεῖν ἐπαναστῇ ἢ τὸν τύραννον συγκαταστήσῃ (quoted as a 'law of Solon' [§95] in And. I. *Myst.* 96–8, cf. D. xx. *Lept.* 159, Lyc. *Leocr.* 124–7 [misdating it to 403/2]).

(e) The νόμος εἰσαγγελτικός in the consolidated code with which Athens began the fourth century included a clause ἐάν τις τὸν δῆμον τὸν Ἀθηναίων καταλύῃ ... ἢ συνίῃ ποι ἐπὶ καταλύσει τοῦ δήμου ἢ ἑταιρικὸν συναγάγῃ (Hyp. IV. *Eux.* 7–8, cf. Poll. VIII. 52, L.R.C. εἰσαγγελία).

(f) In 337/6 Eucrates carried a νόμος, ἐάν τις ἐπαναστῆι τῶι δήμωι ἐπὶ τυραννίδι ἢ τὴν τυραννίδα συγκαταστήσηι ἢ τὸν δῆμον τὸν Ἀθηναίων ἢ τὴν δημοκρατίαν τὴν Ἀθήνησιν καταλύηι (*SEG* xii 87; quotation from lines 7–10).

(g) Warnings against tyranny or the overthrow of the democracy are found also in the bouleutic oath (D. XXIV. *Tim.* 144), the heliastic oath (*ibid.*, 149) and the prayer-cum-curse with which proceedings in the boule and assembly began (Ar. *Thesm.* 335–9 with Rhodes, *A.B.*, 37); and the Athenian democracy is explicitly safeguarded in two treaties, Tod 144, 25–6 (362/1), 147, 28–9 (361/0).

The law quoted here is supposed by *A.P.* to have been current in the time of Pisistratus; Ostwald, from the absence of provision for εἰσαγγελία, supposes it to be a law of Draco, remembered and cited in support of measures taken on the fall of the tyranny (*op. cit.*, 106–9, cf. below). He suggests that the Athenians alternated between 'strong' laws which outlawed revolutionaries and authorised direct action against them, and 'weak' laws which required revolutionaries to be brought to trial. I suspect that from the time of Solon the two may rather have coexisted—even when the law permits direct action some men in some circumstances will prefer the greater safety of legal proceedings—and suggest: (i) that Ostwald is right to see the text quoted here as a reaffirmation of an ancient law (cf. below); (ii) that in 410 Demophantus' decree reaffirmed an existing law (which had not been invoked to prevent the overthrow of the democracy in 411) and required the Athenians to take an oath to observe it; (iii) that in 403 Demophantus' decree lapsed (on this I agree with Ostwald, *op. cit.*, 115, against MacDowell, commentary on And. I. *Myst.* 99; but I believe that the once-for-all oath was Demophantus' only innovation), but the new code contained a provision for the outlawing of revolutionaries, and the stele containing Demophantus' decree was allowed to stand; (iv) that in 336 Eucrates briefly reasserted the provision for outlawry before introducing his new matter, the threat against the Areopagus.

In Demophantus' decree and in Eucrates' law it is made clear that a revolutionary is to be outlawed: he loses all right to the protection of the law and may be killed with impunity. Originally ἀτιμία denoted this state of outlawry, and in the law quoted here ἄτιμος is used to prescribe outlawry for revolutionaries and their issue; but in the classical period the concept of ἀτιμία was 'tamed' and it was held to denote loss of civic rights only (cf. on 8. v). Demophantus, and Eucrates in lines 10–11, spell out the implications of 'primitive' ἀτιμία but do not use the word (Demophantus uses πολέμιος); both ἄτιμος and πολέμιος are used in the decree outlawing Arthmius of Zelea for bringing Persian gold to the Peloponnese, and Demosthenes explains that there ἄτιμος has its 'primitive' sense (D. IX. *Phil. iii*. 41–6 and other texts, collected and discussed by R. Meiggs, *The Athenian Empire*, 508–12; C. Habicht, *Hermes* lxxxix 1961, 23–5, believes the decree to be a fourth-century fabrication). There are other cases where we should expect the penalty to be outlawry but ἄτιμος continues to be used without qualification (notably the condemnation of Archeptolemus and Antiphon, *ap*. [Pl.] *X. Or.* 834 A–B; lines 20–2 of Eucrates' law): I believe that in such cases ἄτιμος does still retain its original sense (Rhodes, *CQ*[2] xxviii 1978, 89–90, cf. Harrison, *L.A.*, ii. 169–76), but others think it intolerable that the stronger and the weaker sense should exist simultaneously and maintain that in the classical period ἄτιμος without qualification must have the weaker sense (e.g. M. H. Hansen, *Apagoge, Endeixis and Ephegesis*, 75–82). It is in any case clear that *A.P.* has confused the two senses of the word, and describes the law which he quotes as mild because he supposes that ἄτιμος in it is used in the weaker sense, whereas it is in fact used in the stronger: there is no need to suppose with P. Karavites, *Ath.*[2] lii 1974, 327–8, that πρᾶος here means not 'mild' but 'inconsistent'.†

πρὸς τὴν τῆς τυραννίδος <κατάστασιν>: The papyrus' text is defective: Kenyon's original solution was to delete τήν; the insertion of κατάστασιν was suggested by Kaibel & Wilamowitz[1] in their *apparatus*, and although they never promoted it to their text it has been generally accepted.

θέσμια τάδε 'Αθηναίων ἐστὶ καὶ πάτρια: This preamble very probably marks the reaffirmation of what was already regarded at the time when it was reaffirmed as a 'traditional' law (P. L. Usteri, *Ächtung und Verbannung im griechischen Recht*, 12 n. 1, Ostwald, *TAPA* lxxxvi 1955, 108), and Ostwald suggests that the law was reaffirmed *c*. 510 to justify the expulsion of Hippias and his family. J. K. Davies thinks that πάτρια in the new preamble points to the time of

Ephialtes' reform or, more probably, to the end of the fifth century (*CR*² xxiii 1973, 225–6); but although we know that πάτρια was used as a political slogan at these two times there is no reason why it should not have been used as in this preamble at another time, and the question of when the law was reaffirmed must be left open. The original law can hardly be later than Solon: the description of the offence is more appropriate to early Athens than that used by *A.P.* with reference to Solon's law in 8. iv.†

Kenyon in his Berlin ed. and O.C.T. read after Ἀθηναίων an oblique stroke as a compendium for ἐστί, and then κ'; Blass²⁻⁴ and Wilcken did not see the oblique stroke; Kaibel & Wilamowitz¹ restored Ἀθηναίων [κατὰ τά], and retained that text in their 3rd ed. (cf. Kaibel, *Stil und Text*, 163–4, Wilamowitz, *A.u.A.*, ii. 43 n. 15), but it is unlikely to be right.

[[ἐπὶ τυραννίδι]]: Deleted as an intrusion by Kenyon and nearly all editors; but ἐπαναστῆι ... ἐπὶ τυραννίδι is now found in Eucrates' law (*SEG* xii 87, 7), so it is better to delete τυραννεῖν (N. C. Conomis, 'Ἑλληνικά xvi 1958–9, 10 n. 3, M. H. Hansen, *Apagoge, Endeixis and Ephegesis*, 77 n. 17); Ostwald, *op. cit.*, 121 n. 97, suggests that no deletion is needed, but it is hard to accept this double reference to tyranny.

ἢ συγκαθιστῆ: The change from plural to singular is violent. Some have accepted it as a sign of antiquity (e.g. Kaibel, *Stil und Text*, 165, Ostwald, *op. cit.*, 106); others have found it intolerable, and have inserted τις either before συγκαθιστῆ (Herwerden & Leeuwen, Blass, Kenyon³ and others, sometimes with further emendations) or after (Sandys², Mathieu & Haussoullier); J. K. Davies (*CR*² xxiii 1973, 225) suggests that ἐάν τινες τυραννεῖν ἐπανιστῶνται is a later addition to the original law. Here I do not find the case for emendation compelling: Davies may be right; or *A.P.* may by extracting the phrases which he wished to quote have removed grammatical coherence from a longer original (cf. the constitutional documents in 30–1, 39, with commentary).

17. i. ἐγκατεγήρασε τῆ ἀρχῆ: Cf. T. vi. 54. ii (γηραίου τελευτήσαντος ἐν τῇ τυραννίδι), V.M. viii. ix. ext. 2; Pisistratus will have been about seventy-five (cf. below). The verb is rare: it is used literally in Pl. *Phoc.* 30. v and metaphorically in Din. ii. *Aristog.* 3.

ἐπὶ Φιλόνεω ἄρχοντος ... ἔφευγε γὰρ τὰ λοιπά: In *A.P.*'s scheme this will be 528/7, and the date may be accepted as correct. Arist. *Pol.* v. 1315 B 31–4 gives the same total of 33 years from Pisistratus' first *coup*, but makes the total of Pisistratus' years in power as 17. Cf. pp. 191–9.

17. ii. διὸ καὶ φανερῶς ληροῦσιν: On *A.P.*'s treatment of disagree-

17. ii] COMMENTARY ON THE *ATH. POL.*

ments among his sources see Introduction, pp. 25-7: this is an unusually strongly worded rejection of a view which he rejects, which is all the more surprising as the chronological argument which he uses does not in fact justify rejection (cf. below). ληρεῖν is used several times by Isocrates and Plato; Aristotle does not use the verb, but in *H.A.* vi. 579 B 2–3 we find ὁ δὲ λεχθεὶς μῦθος . . . ληρώδης ἐστί.

‹οἱ› φάσκοντες ἐρώμενον εἶναι Πεισίστρα[τον] Σόλωνος: οἱ was first added by Kaibel & Wilamowitz; Tovar refrains from adding it (cf. *REC* iii 1948, 161–2, citing Is. xvii. *Trap.* 11, ἀφικνοῦνταί μοι ἀπαγγέλλοντες), but although there is a good case for omission in Isocrates the article is needed here. Which predecessors of *A.P.* told this story we do not know; despite *A.P.*'s rejection it survived to be noted as a possibility by Pl. *Sol.* 1. iv–v (ὡς ἔνιοί φασιν) and Ael. *V.H.* viii. 16 (λέγεται).

καὶ στρατηγεῖν . . . περὶ Σαλαμῖνος: Cf. 14. i with commentary: there *A.P.* accepts Pisistratus' participation in the war but says nothing of his generalship, for which cf. H. 1. 59. iv. Probably Athens gained and lost Salamis more than once, and the war instigated by Solon was not the war in which Pisistratus was general. For στρατηγοί before Cleisthenes see on 22. ii: probably there was not yet a regular office but *ad hoc* appointments could be made for wars fought outside Attica.

οὐ γὰρ ἐνδέχεται ταῖς ἡλικίαις: For the use of chronology to test a story's truth cf. Pl. *Sol.* 27. i (ἔνιοι, but not Plutarch, rejected the story of Solon's visit to Croesus on chronological grounds: cf. pp. 169–70), *Them.* 27. ii (on chronological grounds the Persian king encountered by Themistocles on his flight from Greece should be Artaxerxes rather than Xerxes).

ἐάν τις ἀναλογίζηται . . . · ἐφ' οὗ ἀπέθανεν ἄρχοντος: *A.P.* has not reported all the data available to him. He nowhere gives the date of Solon's death; Phaen. fr. 21 Wehrli *ap.* Pl. *Sol.* 32. iii places it in the year after Pisistratus' first *coup*, 560/59, and this is more likely both to be true and to be the date assumed by *A.P.* than the version which placed Solon's travels after the *coup* and therefore his death appreciably later (cf. on 11. i, 14. ii). More pertinent would be a comparison of the two men's birth dates: no ancient source gives us these, but on the information we have it seems that Solon was born *c.* 630–625 and Pisistratus *c.* 605–600 (Davies, *A.P.F.*, 323–4, 445) —in which case on chronological grounds the story is entirely possible.

17. iii. κατεῖχον οἱ υἱεῖς τὴν ἀρχήν: For a brief review of the different accounts of Pisistratus' sons and the end of the tyranny see pp. 189–91. H. v. 55 writes of Ἵππαρχον τὸν Πεισιστράτου, Ἱππίεω δὲ τοῦ τυράννου ἀδελφεόν (but contrast his references to the Πεισιστρατίδαι in vi. 39. i, 103. iii); T. vi. 54. ii polemically insists οὐχ Ἵππαρχος, ὥσπερ οἱ πολλοὶ οἴονται, ἀλλ' Ἱππίας πρεσβύτατος ὢν ἔσχε τὴν ἀρχήν (cf. vi. 55 passim and i. 20. ii; on vi. 54. iv–v see Dover, in Gomme et al., Hist. Comm. Thuc., iv. 318–19); Hellanicus seems to have made Hipparchus both eldest son and reigning tyrant until his death (perhaps reflected in Marm. Par. 239 A 45); A.P. writes of a shared tyranny (with Hippias as the leading partner: 18. i); Ephorus also wrote of a shared tyranny (D.S. x. 17. i)—it is not clear whether [Plat.] Hipparch. 228–9 followed Hellanicus or Ephorus here—and this is perhaps a deliberate compromise made in the fourth century to reconcile the conflicting views of the fifth (cf. Jacoby, Atthis, 337 n. 43). In fact there was no constitutional office of τύραννος to which a man was appointed, and it is possible that Ephorus and A.P. are correct in supposing that on Pisistratus' death power passed to his sons collectively, in which case it is likely enough that one of them, ceteris paribus the eldest, would become the leading partner (cf. D. Loenen, Mnem.⁴ i 1948, 88–9).

ἦσαν δὲ δύο ... ᾧ παρωνύμιον ἦν Θέτταλος: Herodotus mentions Hippias and Hipparchus without saying who their mother was, and in v. 94. i mentions the νόθος Hegesistratus, γεγονότα ἐξ Ἀργείας γυναικός; according to T. vi. 55. i–ii cf. i. 20. ii Pisistratus had three γνήσιοι sons, Hippias, Hipparchus and Thessalus; and on that point Ephorus probably agreed with Thucydides (D.S. x. 17. i). A.P. ascribes to Pisistratus only two sons by his Athenian wife, Hippias and Hipparchus; two more by his Argive wife, Iophon and Hegesistratus; and says that Thessalus was a παρωνύμιον of Hegesistratus (cf. Pl. Cat. Mai. 24. viii, where Pisistratus has Iophon and Thessalus by his Argive wife; also schol. Ar. Vesp. 502, where the Πεισιστρατίδαι are four in number). Pisistratus' marriages and sons are convincingly discussed by Davies, A.P.F., 445–50: he had five sons in all, Hippias, Hipparchus and Thessalus by his Athenian wife and Iophon and Hegesistratus by his Argive; A.P.'s identification of Thessalus with Hegesistratus has no independent authority but is derived from the controversy as to why and with what result Hipparchus was killed (cf. below).

By Pericles' law of 451/0 Athenian citizenship was limited to those whose parents were both Athenians (26. iv with commentary); previously, it is assumed, the son inherited his father's status and his mother's status was irrelevant. G. E. M. de Ste. Croix in an unpublished paper insists that a νόθος was the child of parents who were not legally married, and that whether a man was a νόθος and whether he was a μητρόξενος are different questions: that is certainly true of the sixth century; but by fourth-century law, if not by Pericles' law, marriages between Athenians and non-Athenians were banned and any children of such unions were therefore νόθοι. Davies, *A.P.F.*, 446, says that 'the νόθοι (*sc.* among Pisistratus' sons) were such not as sons of a non-Athenian mother but because they never became Athenian citizens by being presented and accepted for membership of their father's phratry.' However, it is doubtful whether good evidence survived of the status of Pisistratus' union with Timonassa or of the status of the sons of that union, unless the stele recording the banishment of the Pisistratids labelled some γνήσιοι and others νόθοι; more probably νόθος and the related concepts have been applied loosely and anachronistically to a union which by the laws of later Athens could not have produced citizen sons.

ἐκ τῆς γαμετῆς: 'By his wedded wife' (in contrast to Timonassa): the contrast is spoiled by *A.P.*'s use of γαμεῖν twice in §iv of Pisistratus' union with Timonassa. The identity of the Athenian wife is not known: schol. Ar. *Eq.* 449 calls her Myrrhine, and identifies her with the woman who posed as Athena to assist the second *coup*; but Myrrhine was the name of Hippias' wife, and in Clid. 323 F 15 Phye is said to have been married to Hipparchus (cf. on 14. iv).†

'Ιοφῶν: Nothing is known of him except his name and parentage.
Ἡγησίστρατος: Pisistratus reconquered Sigeum from Mytilene and installed Hegesistratus as its ruler (cf. on 16. vii); Sigeum was available as a refuge for Hippias when he was expelled from Athens (H. v. 65. iii, 91. i, 94. i, T. VI. 59. iv), and may still have been under the rule of Hegesistratus.

παρωνύμιον: In 13. v, 45. i, *A.P.* uses the normal ἐπωνυμία. Dover on T. VI. 55. i argues that in the sense 'alternative name', 'nickname', παρωνύμιον is a late word (Pherecydes, 3 F 25a need not be a *verbatim* quotation), but it could be used in the fourth century to mean 'derivative name' (cf. Plat. *Soph.* 268 C 1–2), and in this case the derivative name would also be an alternative name: this is perhaps an over-nice distinction. The only attested link between the tyranny and Thessaly is that Thessalians came to support Hippias in 511/0 (19. v).

17. iv. Γοργίλος, Τιμώνασσαν, ... Ἀρχῖνος ὁ Ἀμπρακιώτης τῶν Κυψελιδῶν: These details are found only here (except that Pl. *Cat. Mai.* 24. viii, following *A.P.* or his source on the identity of Hegesistratus and Thessalus, repeats the name of Timonassa): the stele recording the banishment of the Pisistratids (T. VI. 55. i–ii) may have identified Pisistratus' second wife, but is unlikely to have given as much information about her as this, and in view of his error over Thessalus *A.P.* can hardly have examined the stele himself. Wilcken, *Hermes* xxxii 1897, 478–92, in disgust at the muddle over Thessalus deleted the whole of §iv as a gloss, but this is not called for. On the foundation of Ambracia as a colony of Cypselid Corinth see Str. 325. VII. vii. 6, 452. x. ii. 8, and on the fall of the Cypselids from power there see Arist. *Pol.* v. 1304 A 31–3, 1311 A 39–B 1.

συνεμαχέσαντο: H. I. 61. iv mentions the support of Ἀργεῖοι μισθωτοί but not their number or Hegesistratus; *A.P.* 15. ii omits Argos from the list of Pisistratus' allies at Pallene. Some have doubted the story of Hegesistratus' bringing the Argive reinforcements, and Hude suggested that this Hegesistratus was not a son but a brother-in-law of Pisistratus, but the chronological objection need not be fatal (cf. p. 199).

οἱ μὲν ἐκπεσόντα τὸ πρῶτον, οἱ δὲ κατέχοντα τὴν ἀρχήν: During his first period of exile or his (*sc.* first) period of tyranny, i.e. on the chronology which I advocate 561/0—*c.* 556. Since there were two sons of the marriage, but Pisistratus was free to marry Megacles' daughter *c.* 556 and did not lose the support of Argos, it is likely that the marriage fell early in this period and that Timonassa was not divorced but died. As an alternative explanation L. Gernet suggested that Pisistratus did not limit himself to one wife at a time but that Timonassa's sons were brought up in Argos, which is possible but not necessary (*Éventail de l'histoire vivante: hommage à L. Febvre*, ii. 43–4 = *Anthropologie de la Grèce antique*, 346–8, cf. Berve, *Die Tyrannis bei den Griechen*, ii. 546). No other surviving text includes this detail, so we do not know who οἱ μέν and οἱ δέ are, or what is the basis of their disagreement.

18. i. ἦσαν δὲ κύριοι ... Ἵππαρχος καὶ Ἱππίας: Cf. 17. iii with commentary.

πρεσβύτερος δὲ ὢν ὁ Ἱππίας: Asserted polemically by T. I. 20. ii, VI. 54. ii, 55: Hipparchus must have been represented as the eldest son as well as the successor of Pisistratus by Hellanicus, and is represented as the eldest son by [Plat.] *Hipparch.* 228 B 5–6, Ael. *V.H.* VIII. 2 (the latter avowedly derived from the former). Hellanicus was championed by Beloch, $G.G.^2$, I. ii. 293–7, *Hermes* lv 1920, 311–17, but most scholars have rightly preferred Thucydides and *A.P.* (for a statement of the arguments see A. Scholte, $Mnem.^3$ v 1937, 69–75).

καὶ τῇ φύσει πολιτικὸς καὶ ἔμφρων: Herodotus and Thucydides say nothing of the characters of Pisistratus' sons, except that in T. VI. 55. iii Hippias διὰ τὸ πρότερον ξύνηθες τοῖς μὲν πολίταις φοβερόν, ἐς δὲ τοὺς ἐπικούρους ἀκριβές was easily able to retain power after the death of Hipparchus; but it was a natural corollary of the view that the tyranny was mild until Hipparchus' death and that Hipparchus was killed because of a private grudge (cf. p. 218) that Hippias should be regarded as a good man and Hipparchus as a bad man who brought trouble upon himself. For Ephorus, who probably followed Hellanicus in believing that the murder of Hipparchus ended the tyranny, but like *A.P.* believed that Hippias and Hipparchus were joint rulers, both were βίαιοι καὶ χαλεποί, ... πολλὰ δὲ παρανομοῦντες εἰς τοὺς Ἀθηναίους, while Thessalus was σοφὸς and ἀπείπατο τὴν τυραννίδα, ... τὴν ἰσότητα ζηλώσας (D.S. X. 17. i). [Plat.] *Hipparch.* 228 B 4–229 B 7 makes Hipparchus the eldest son and sole or part ruler: he is represented as σοφώτατος and a paragon of virtue, and only under the subsequent rule of Hippias did Athens suffer true tyranny. *A.P.* in much of his account follows Thucydides (though without close verbal reminiscences), and begins by contrasting the public-spirited (πολιτικὸς: cf. on 14. iii) and wise Hippias with the childish and amorous Hipparchus; but these bad qualities of Hipparchus are then left in the air, and the account is contaminated with the ascription to Thessalus of vicious qualities and love for Harmodius. Presumably in reaction to Ephorus' denunciation of Hipparchus and praise of Thessalus, and to [Plato]'s representation of Hipparchus as an innocent victim, an adherent of the anti-Hellanican school accepted the relevance of Thessalus and transferred Hipparchus' seduction of Harmodius to Thessalus (cf. Davies, *A.P.F.*, 448–9); *A.P.* has added to his Thucydidean nucleus the results of further controversy, and has made a very untidy job of it. However, although it is a particularly glaring instance, this is by no means the only place in *A.P.* where conflicting material has not been satisfactorily reconciled, and the untidiness does not oblige us to delete the reference to Thessalus as another man's interpolation into *A.P.*: Herwerden & Leeuwen deleted Θέτταλος ... ὑβριστής; J. M. Stahl, *RM*² 1 1895, 387–9, and Wilcken, *Hermes* xxxii 1897, 478–92, deleted καὶ τοὺς περὶ ... νεώτερος πολύ; C. W. Fornara, *Hist.* xvii 1968, 411–18, deletes καὶ φιλόμουσος ... καὶ ὑβριστής, which is correct as a separation of the alternative version from the Thucydidean.

φιλόμουσος: Hipparchus' patronage of the arts is stressed by [Plat.], *loc. cit.* One of the Hermae with verse inscriptions (*ibid.*, 228 c 6–229 B 1) has been found: see *SEG* x 345 with J. F. Crome, *AM* lx–lxi 1935–6, 300–13, esp. 305–6, B. M. W. Knox, *Athens Comes of Age*, 48–9. Herodotus reports that Hipparchus expelled Onomacritus for making fraudulent additions to the oracles of Musaeus (VII. 6. iii: cf. below). Hipparchus is credited with a wall enclosing the Academy, which became proverbial for its lavish work (Suid. [T 733] τὸ Ἱππάρχου τειχίον), but no trace of this has yet been found (Travlos, *Pictorial Dictionary*, 42). φιλόμουσος is used of culture-loving men in X. *Cyr.* V. i. 1, Plat. *Phaedr.* 259 B 5, *Rep.* VIII. 548 E 5.†

τοὺς περὶ Ἀνακρέοντα καὶ Σιμωνίδην: Cf. [Plat.] *Hipparch.* 228 C 1–3, Ael. *V.H.* VIII. 2. The lyric poet Anacreon of Teos was active in the second half of the sixth century: before coming to Athens he was at the court of Polycrates of Samos (H. III. 121. i, Str. 638. XIV. i. 16); subsequently he may like Simonides have gone to Thessaly; Paus. I. 25. i records a statue of him in Athens; he is said to have been the lover of Critias, son of Solon's relative and contemporary Dropides (schol. Aesch. *P.V.* 128 [but his alleged admiration of Aeschylus is anachronistic], cf. Plat. *Charm.* 157 E 4–158 A 1; for Dropides see p. 123). Simonides of Ceos was born *c.* 556 (fr. 77 Diehl), and was active in the last third of the sixth century and the first third of the fifth: his epigrams include one on the death of Hippias' daughter Archedice (fr. 85 Diehl *ap.* T. VI. 59. iii, attributed to Simonides by Arist. *Rhet.* I. 1367 B 20–1); for an apology for his writing for tyrants see Plat. *Protag.* 346 B 5–8; after the fall of the tyranny he went to the Pisistratids' friends the Aleuadae and the Scopadae in Thessaly (cf. fr. 37/542 Page with Plat. *Protag.* 339 A 7, Theocr. XVI. 34–47 with schol. [=fr. 23/528 Page] and with Gow *ad loc.*; also Cic. *Orat.* II. 352–3, Quint. XI. ii. 14, V.M. I. viii. ext. 7); he returned to Athens, associated with Themistocles (cf. the anecdote in Pl. *Them.* 5. vi, repeated three times in the *Moralia*; Cic. *Fin.* II. 104), and was perhaps the author of the epigram inscribed on the base of the new statues of Harmodius and Aristogiton in 477/6 (fr. 76 Diehl); he ended his life in Sicily (schol. Pind. *Ol.* ii. 29b, c, d, Callim. fr. 64 Pfeiffer).

It is characteristic of Aristotle (H. Bonitz, *Index Aristotelicus, s.v.* περί, 579 A) and of late Greek (LSJ *s.v.*, C. I. 2) to use οἱ περὶ τὸν δεῖνα to mean scarcely more than ὁ δεῖνα. In the other instances of this expression in *A.P.* (14. iii, 20. iii, 28. ii, 38. iv) the plural is genuine; but here, with τοὺς ἄλλους ποιητάς following, we seem to have the Aristotelian use.†

καὶ τοὺς ἄλλους ποιητάς: One of the other poets in the Pisistratids' court was the dithyrambist Lasus of Hermione, rival of Simonides (cf. Ar. *Vesp.* 1410–11) and teacher of Pindar; another was the oracle-collector Onomacritus, who was banished by Hipparchus when Lasus exposed his forgeries (cf. above).

18. ii. Θέτταλος δὲ νεώτερος πολὺ καὶ τῷ βίῳ θρασὺς καὶ ὑβριστής: On the sons of Pisistratus and the characters ascribed to them cf. above. The true Thessalus, a son by his first wife, must unless with Gernet we make Pisistratus a bigamist (cf. p. 227) have been born by *c.* 561/0; Hippias, the eldest son, was born *c.* 570 (cf. pp. 198–9). For *A.P.* Thessalus is a παρωνύμιον of Hegesistratus, one of two sons by Pisistratus' Argive wife, born between *c.* 560 and *c.* 556 (cf. p. 227): by representing him as νεώτερος πολὺ *A.P.* 'made his new active role as Harmodios' seducer more plausible' (Davies, *A.P.F.*, 449). It is a symptom of *A.P.*'s unsatisfactory combination of his conflicting source material that the same man (as he believes) is called Hegesistratus in 17. iv but Thessalus here.

ἀφ' οὗ: More probably masculine than neuter (Sandys).

ἐρασθεὶς γὰρ ... τῆς πρὸς αὐτὸν φιλίας: According to T. VI. 54. ii–iv cf. 56. i Hipparchus loved Harmodius and tried but failed to win him away from Aristogiton (cf. Plat. *Symp.* 182 c 5–7; Arist. *Pol.* v. 1311 A 36–9, also 1312 B 29–31, *Rhet.* II. 1401 B 11–12; D.S. x. 17. i; Pl. *Amat.* 760 c; Ath. XIII. 602 A: no doubt this is the correct version); in the apologia for Hipparchus in [Plat.] *Hipparch.* 229 c 2–D 7 Aristogiton merely imagines that Hipparchus is his rival, and Hipparchus succeeds in winning over an unnamed man loved by Harmodius. C. W. Fornara, *Hist.* xvii 1968, 411, points out that Thucydides is the first to call Harmodius and Aristogiton lovers: they are not lovers in the scolia *ap.* Ath. xv. 695 A–B or in the allusions of Aristophanes.

H. V. 57–61 dwells on Harmodius and Aristogiton as members of the family of the Γεφυραῖοι, immigrants who claimed to have originated in Eretria and who are at any rate securely linked with Tanagra. On the family and its origins see Hecat. 1 F 118, Str. 404. IX. ii. 10, with Wilamowitz, *Hermes* xxi 1886, 106–7 = *Kleine Schriften*, v. i. 16–17, Davies, *A.P.F.*, 472–9. Whatever their mixture of personal and public motives, Harmodius and Aristogiton were after the expulsion of Hippias celebrated as the men who struck the first blow against the tyranny, and in due course their cult was fostered by those who did not wish to be beholden to the Alcmaeonids and Sparta for the liberation of Athens, until Thucydides found it necessary to protest that the orthodox account of the liberation was wrong. Cf. pp. 289, 308, and 58. i with commentary; and see V. L. Ehrenberg, *WS* lxix 1956, 57–69 = *Polis und Imperium*, 253–64, A. J. Podlecki, *Hist.* xv 1966, 129–41, M. Ostwald, *Nomos and the Beginnings of the Athenian Democracy*, 121–36, Fornara, *Philol.* cxiv 1970, 155–80, H. W. Pleket, *Τάλαντα* iv 1972, 63–81, I. Calabi Limentani, *Acme* xxix 1976, 9–27.

ἐνεσημαίνετο: *Sc.* τὴν ὀργήν, 'gave signs of his anger': cf. Is. xx. *Lochit.* 22 (ἐνσημανεῖσθε Λοχίτῃ τὴν ὀργὴν τὴν ὑμετέραν αὐτῶν). On the substance contrast T. VI. 54. iv: βίαιον μὲν οὐδὲν ἐβούλετο δρᾶν, ἐν τρόπῳ δέ τινι ἀφανεῖ ὡς οὐ διὰ τοῦτο δὴ παρεσκευάζετο προπηλακιῶν αὐτόν.

μέλλουσαν αὐτοῦ τὴν ἀδελφὴν κανηφορεῖν Παναθηναίοις: Cf. T. VI. 56. i–ii (where the festival at which Hipparchus is killed is the Great Panathenaea but the festival at which Harmodius' sister is rejected as κανηφόρος is simply πομπῇ τινί: probably *A.P.* or a predecessor has been careless), Plat. *Symp.* 182 c 5–7, Arist. *Pol.* v. 1311 A 36–9, Ael. *V.H.* XI. 8, Max. Tyr. XVIII. 2. b–e Hobein (the last two both, like *A.P.*, setting the incident at the Panathenaea). On κανηφόροι (bearers of baskets containing gifts to the gods; commonly daughters of the aristocracy) in religious processions see Ar. *Ach.* 241-62 with schol. 242, *Av.* 1550-2 with schol. 1551, *Lys.* 641-7 with schol. 646, 647, *Eccl.* 730-44, and K. Mittelhaus, *RE*, x (1917/9), 1862-6; also (at the Panathenaea) Phil. 328 F 8 with Jacoby *ad loc.*

ἐκώλυσεν: ἀπήλασαν λέγοντες οὐδὲ ἐπαγγεῖλαι τὴν ἀρχὴν διὰ τὸ μὴ ἀξίαν εἶναι (T. VI. 56. i).

λοιδορήσας τι τὸν Ἁρμόδιον: Found only in *A.P.*: for other writers the rejection of his sister was a sufficient insult to Harmodius.

μετεχόντων πολλῶν: Thucydides believed that Hipparchus was killed for personal reasons only (VI. 54. i, 59. i), and that ἦσαν δὲ οὐ πολλοὶ οἱ ξυνομωμοκότες ἀσφαλείας ἕνεκα (56. iii); inconsistently with that, he believed that the original plan was to kill Hippias (57. i–iii) and overthrow the tyranny (54. iii), and that the conspirators hoped for widespread support when the deed was done (56. iii). Several early commentators inserted οὐ to bring *A.P.* into line with Thucydides (cf. Sandys², *apparatus*): that cannot be proved wrong, but *A.P.* is not following Thucydides so closely as to make the case for insertion compelling, and it is better to accept the disagreement: though he accepts the story of a personal affront to be avenged, he believes that the plot was against Hippias and the tyranny (§iii), and his many conspirators may be derived from the Hellanican vulgate (Fornara, *Hist.* xvii 1968, 407).

18. iii. παρατηροῦντες ἐν ἀκροπόλει τοῖς Παναθηναίοις Ἱππίαν: T. VI. 57. ii states explicitly that the festival was the Great Panathenaea (in fact, the festival of 514/3: cf. pp. 191-9); Παναθήναια alone may but need not refer to the greater festival (Rhodes, *A.B.*, 236). *A.P.* agrees with T. VI. 57. i–iii that the intended victim was Hippias (cf. previous note); but whereas Thucydides has Hippias ἔξω ἐν τῷ Κεραμεικῷ καλουμένῳ marshalling the procession (cf. Travlos, *Pictorial Dictionary*, 477: there was a Pompeum immediately inside the city wall, between the Sacred Gate and the Dipylon Gate, but the oldest building on that site is of *c.* 400), and Hipparchus in the Leocoreum (cf. below: in T. I. 20. ii he is τὴν Παναθηναϊκὴν πομπὴν διακοσμοῦντι there), *A.P.* more logically places Hipparchus in the Leocoreum to dispatch the procession and Hippias on the Acropolis to receive it. T. VI. 58 is consistent with Thucydides' location of Hippias, but we do not know the grounds for his belief or for *A.P.*'s different belief; it may well be that until Thucydides reinstated Hippias as 'the' tyrant no one cared where he was, and *A.P.*'s placing of him reflects not authentic tradition but fourth-century inference (Fornara, *op. cit.*, 408-9).

ἰδόντες τινὰ τῶν κοινωνούντων τῆς πρά[ξ]εως: Cf. T. I. 20. ii, VI. 57. ii.

βουλόμενοί τι δρᾶσαι πρὸ τῆς συλλήψεως: Cf. T. I. 20. ii (βουλόμενοι δὲ πρὶν ξυλληφθῆναι δράσαντές τι καὶ κινδυνεῦσαι), VI. 57. iii.

παρὰ τὸ Λεωκόρειον: In agreement with Thucydides (cf. above). The Leocoreum was within the city walls (T. VI. 57. iii), ἐν μέσῳ τῷ Κεραμεικῷ (Phanod. 325 F 8 and texts quoted by Jacoby *ad loc.*); an explanation of its name is given by Ael. *V.H.* XII. 28 (it commemorated the daughters of Leos, who to save the city were sacrificed with their father's consent); it is mentioned by Hegesias (C3) *ap.* Str. 396. IX. i. 16, but it is not mentioned by Pausanias, and probably by his time little or no trace of it survived (H. A. Thompson & R. E. Wycherley, *The Athenian Agora*, xiv. 207 n. 2). For attempts to locate it see W. Judeich, *Topographie von Athen*[2], 338–9, Travlos, *Pictorial Dictionary*, 3, 5, 8 fig. 5, modified at 578, Thompson & Wycherley, *op. cit.*, 121–3; the 'more promising site', found 'at the eleventh hour', a square enclosure east of the south wing of the Stoa of the Basileus, is described but not yet identified by T. L. Shear, jr, *Hesp.* xlii 1973, 126–34, 360–9, and 'safely ... identified' in *Agora Guide*[3], 87–90; Wycherley, *Stones of Athens*, 63–4, 98, is cautious, but Thompson, *Athens Comes of Age*, 101–2, accepts the identification.

18. iv. αὐτῶν δ' ὁ μὲν ... πολὺν χρόνον αἰκισθείς: Cf. T. VI. 57. iv. In both accounts Hipparchus has δορυφόροι: contrast the κορυνηφόροι acquired by Pisistratus at his first seizure of power (14. i with commentary).

κατηγόρησεν: The story of Aristogiton's being tortured to reveal his accomplices is not given by Thucydides: it was given by Ephorus (D.S. X. 17. ii–iii), and reappears in Sen. *De Ira*, II. 23. i, Polyaen. I. 22, Just. II. 9. ii–vi; it is told of other tyrannicides by Cic. *Tusc.* II. 52, V.M. III. iii. ext. 2, Ath. XIII. 602 B, Pl. *Garr.* 505 D, D.L. IX. 26–7.

ἐν ταῖς ἀνάγκαις: Sandys compares H. I. 116. iv–v, T. I. 99. i, Ant. VI. *Chor.* 25.

φύσει: 'By birth', as in 5. iii; contrast 18. i, where it means 'by nature'.

ἴχνος: Used metaphorically by Ant. II. *Tetr. i.* γ. 10, δ. 10; by Plato frequently (e.g. *Polit.* 290 D 5, *Crat.* 393 B 3); by Arist. *H.A.* VIII. 588 A 19, 33, IX. 608 B 4.

ὁ λεγόμενος λόγος: Found in T. VI. 58, ending ... καὶ εἴ τις ηὑρέθη ἐγχειρίδιον ἔχων· μετὰ γὰρ ἀσπίδος καὶ δόρατος εἰώθεσαν τὰς πομπὰς ποιεῖν (§ii), cf. 56. ii. Consistently with his denial of it, *A.P.* believes that the citizens were disarmed by Pisistratus after Pallene (15. iv–v with commentary).

18. v. κατηγόρει δὲ τῶν τοῦ τυράννου φίλων: The version of οἱ δημοτικοί was no doubt the original, to which that of ἔνιοι was a rejoinder (Fornara, *Hist.* xvii 1968, 407). If Hellanicus told the story, he will have given the original version, in which Aristogiton was bitterly opposed to the tyranny and in his 'revelations' did his utmost to weaken it by casting suspicion on its supporters; and this version was given by Ephorus (cf. D.S. x. 17. ii–iii); but when *A.P.* refers to sources as δημοτικοί he is more probably thinking of the more obviously partisan writers (cf. Introduction, p. 26).

ἀσεβήσαιεν: Sc. οἱ τύραννοι (the plural is continued after Hipparchus' death here and in 19. iii, vi; cf. the account of Hippias' expulsion in H. v. 62–5): they would be impious in that they killed τοὺς ἀναιτίους and weakened in that they killed φίλους ἑαυτῶν.

18. vi. καὶ τέλος ... : The melodramatic end to the story accords with the version of the δημοτικοί, in which even under torture Aristogiton maintained his opposition to the tyranny.

19. i. μετὰ δὲ ταῦτα ... τραχυτέραν εἶναι τὴν τυραννίδα: Cf. 16. vii with commentary (διαδεξαμένων τῶν υἱέων πολλῷ γενέσθαι τραχυτέραν τὴν ἀρχήν). All who knew that the tyranny continued after Hipparchus' death agreed that it then became harsher.

διὰ τὸ τιμωρεῖν τἀδελφῷ καὶ διὰ τὸ πολλοὺς ἀνῃρηκέναι καὶ ἐκβεβληκέναι: T. vi. 59. ii–iv mentions killings but not exiles; in fact it seems that the Alcmaeonids went into exile after the murder of Hipparchus (cf. on §iii).

19. ii. ἔτει δὲ τετάρτῳ μάλιστα: Cf. T. vi. 59. iv (Hippias continued to rule ἔτη τρία ... ἔτι and was deposed ἐν τῷ τετάρτῳ); in H. v. 55 the tyranny continues ἐπ' ἔτεα τέσσερα and in [Plat.] *Hipparch.* 229 B 3–4 it continues τρία ἔτη. If we grant that Herodotus has used a cardinal numeral in the less common way, all our texts are compatible with 514/3 as the year of Hipparchus' murder and 511/0 as that of Hippias' expulsion (cf. pp. 191–9).

ἐπεὶ κακῶς εἶχεν τὰ ἐν τῷ ἄστει: Presumably an inference from the fortification of Munichia, and from the increasing harshness of Hippias' rule.

τὴν Μουνιχίαν ἐπεχείρησε τειχίζειν: (Spelled Μουνυχ— here and elsewhere in the papyrus, but that form is extremely rare in inscriptions: cf. Meisterhans & Schwyzer, *G.a.I.*, 29 with n. 150). This detail is preserved only in *A.P.* Munichia is the hill on the east side of the Piraeus, facing towards Phalerum Bay: it was garrisoned by the Four Hundred in 411 (T. viii. 92. v) and occupied by Thrasybulus and the returning democrats in 403 (38. i with commentary); in the time of *A.P.* it was garrisoned by ephebi (42. iii) and one of the generals was responsible for it (61. i). Epimenides (cf. on ch. 1) is said to have warned the Athenians that Munichia would be a source of trouble to them: Pl. *Sol.* 12. x, D.L. 1. 114.

In T. VI. 59. ii–iv Hippias arranges to be able to withdraw to Lampsacus if forced to leave Athens: the dating to this period of the marriage of his daughter Archedice to Aeantides of Lampsacus is not questioned by Dover *ad loc.* or by Davies, *A.P.F.*, 452.

ὑπὸ Κλεομένους: Cf. §§v–vi.

χρησμῶν γιγνομένων: Cf. §iv.

19. iii. οἱ φυγάδες, ὧν οἱ ᾿Αλκμεωνίδαι προειστήκεσαν: Cf. H. v. 62. ii (᾿Αλκμεωνίδαι, γένος ἐόντες Ἀθηναῖοι καὶ φεύγοντες Πεισιστρατίδας, ἐπείτε σφι ἅμα τοῖσι ἄλλοισι Ἀθηναίων φυγάσι...), T. VI. 59. iv; also 20. iv, below. H. I. 64. iii, VI. 123. i, leads us to suppose that the Alcmaeonids had been in exile since Pisistratus' third *coup* (K. H. Kinzl, *RM*² cxix 1976, 311–14, argues that this implication was not intended, but I doubt if he is right); in Is. XVI. *Big.* 25–6 this is further elaborated, giving them forty years of virtuous exile, with the destruction of houses and the uprooting of the dead worked in too (from the Cylonian curse: cf. pp. 81–2), but XV. *Antid.* 232, saying that Cleisthenes was exiled by the tyrants, is not specific enough to be of use; *A.P.*, though he says nothing of men exiled after Pallene, says nothing to counter this supposition. However, we now have a fragment of the inscribed archon list in which the archon of 525/4 may be restored with certainty as [Κ]λεισθέν[ες] (M&L 6, c 3, cf. on 16. ix),[18] the son by Agariste of Sicyon (H. VI. 126–31 cf. v. 67. i, 69. i) of the Megacles whose daughter Pisistratus married (14. iv–15. i), and the reformer of 508/7 (20–1). We must assume that the Alcmaeonids were reconciled with the Pisistratids at or before Pisistratus' death, and an obvious occasion for their going into exile again is the aftermath of Hipparchus' murder (positively asserted by schol. Aristid. XIII. *Panath.* [iii. 118 Dindorf], but P. J. Bicknell, *Hist.* xix 1970, 130 n. 6, is probably right to say that this rests on no independent authority). Bicknell supposes that according to *A.P.* the Alcmaeonids were exiled after Hipparchus' death and not after Pallene, and that this is correct and Herodotus was misled by Alcmaeonid propaganda (*op. cit.*, 129–31): *A.P.* may indeed be thinking of the exiles whom he mentioned in §i, but here he is probably restating what he found in Herodotus and does not intend to disagree with him.†

οὐκ ἐδύναντο ποιήσασθαι τὴν κάθοδον, ἀλλ᾿ ἀεὶ προσέπταιον: Cf. H. v. 62. ii (οὐ προεχώρεε [κάτοδος], ἀλλὰ προσέπταιον μεγάλως πειρώμενοι κατιέναι τε καὶ ἐλευθεροῦν τὰς Ἀθήνας); προσπταίειν in this metaphorical sense is a favourite word of Herodotus (cf. LSJ *s.v.*, II).

[18] The doubts of J. W. Alexander, *CJ* liv 1958/9, 307–14, were answered by C. W. J. Eliot & M. F. McGregor, *Phoen.* xiv 1960, 27–35.

COMMENTARY ON THE *ATH. POL.* [19. iii

τειχίσαντες ἐν τῇ χώρᾳ Λειψύδριον τὸ ὑπὲρ Πάρνηθος: Cf. H. v. 62.
ii (*Λειψύδριον τὸ ὑπὲρ Παιονίης τειχίσαντες*, without further details),
schol. Ar. *Lys.* 665, 666, Hes. (Λ 564) *Λειψύδριον*, Suid. (Λ 812)
Λυκοπόδες, Suid. (Ε 2440), *E.M.* (361. 31), *ἐπὶ Λειψυδρίῳ μάχη*.
Lipsydrium has been identified with a fort on a spur of Mt Parnes
now called Karagoupholesa (but the surviving remains are of the
fourth or third century): this is on the Attic side of Parnes, north of
the deme Παιονίδαι (J. R. McCredie, *Hesp.* Supp. xi 1966, 58–61,
J. S. Traill, *Hesp.* Supp. xiv 1975, 47); there is no deme called
Παιονία, and Παιανία lies due east of Athens (cf. on 14. iv). Therefore Herodotus has given the deme name in an incorrect form
(which a non-Athenian might have done) but his ὑπέρ is acceptable.
A.P.'s ὑπὲρ Πάρνηθος cannot be correct in a work written from the
Athenian point of view—Lipsydrium is neither 'above' nor 'beyond'
the main summit of Parnes—and it is hardly credible that *A.P.*
should have made this mistake himself: schol. Ar. *Lys.* 666, claiming
to quote *A.P.*, corrects this (*Λειψύδριον· χωρίον τῆς Ἀττικῆς περὶ τὴν
Πάρνηθον εἰς ὃ συνῆλθόν τινες ἐκ τοῦ ἄστεος*); ὑπὸ Πάρνηθος is found in
the MSS of *E.M.*, but otherwise the lexica like the papyrus of *A.P.*
have ὑπὲρ Πάρνηθος. J. H. Wright suggested that we should read
ὑπὸ in *A.P.* (*HSCP* iii 1892, 54 n. 2); otherwise we should emend to
περὶ Πάρνηθα from schol. *Lys.* and suppose that ὑπὲρ Πάρνηθος is a
corruption introduced under the influence of Herodotus.

μ(ετὰ) ταύτην τὴν συμφορὰν: Suid. Ε 2440, *E.M.* 361. 31 (cf. above)
say *σκολιὸν εἰς αὐτοὺς ᾔδετο*, and *A.P.* 20. v says *ᾖδον καὶ εἰς τοῦτον
ἐν τοῖς σκολιοῖς*: probably εἰς is what *A.P.* wrote here and the more
obvious μετὰ has been substituted under the influence of ὕστερον
(Kaibel & Wilamowitz, Blass[1–3], cf. Kaibel, *Stil und Text*, 168).

αἰεί: Deleted, probably rightly, by Hude and many others as a
dittography before αἰαῖ. Apart from this place the London papyrus
contains six instances of ἀεί and six of αἰεί (see indexes in Kenyon's
Berlin ed. and Sandys); in 13. ii the London papyrus has αἰεὶ but
the Berlin ἀεὶ (confirmed by M. H. Chambers, *TAPA* xcviii 1967,
58): according to Meisterhans & Schwyzer, *G.a.I.*, 31 n. 149, 33,
the form ἀεί is standard after 361 B.C. except in decrees of θίασοι.

αἰαῖ . . . : The text is given also by Suid. Ε 2440, *E.M.* 361. 31
(reading ὁπότ᾿ ἔδειξαν in line 4), Ath. xv. 695 E (reading κύρησαν
as the last word); *μάχεσθαι | ἀγαθούς τε καὶ εὐπατρίδας* should be
retained despite attempts to improve on it. The word προδωσέταιρος
is found only in this scolium and in D.C. LVIII. 14 (cf. προδωσίκομπος,
Eust. 710. 12 *ad Il.* VIII. 229, Phot. *s.v.*, Suid. [Π 2371] *s.v.*). The
scolium has been added by *A.P.* to his Herodotus-based narrative:
it was well known, and he may well have contributed it from his
own direct knowledge and not have copied it from an earlier written
source (cf. Introduction, p. 25).

19. iv] COMMENTARY ON THE *ATH. POL.*

19. iv. ἐμισθώσαντο τὸν ἐν Δελφοῖς νεὼν οἰκοδομεῖν: Cf. H. v. 62.ii–63. i (with 66. i, 90. i, VI. 123), Is. XV. *Antid.* 232, D. XXI. *Mid.* 144 with schol. (622. 27 and 623. 14 Dindorf), Phil. 328 F 115; the narrative of *A.P.* is summarised by schol. Ar. *Lys.* 1150. The principal texts (apart from the second scholium) are collected in Jacoby's commentary on Phil., and the different versions of the story are analysed by W. G. Forrest, *GR&BS* x 1969, 277–86. According to Herodotus the Alcmaeonids obtained the contract for rebuilding the temple of Apollo at Delphi and οἷα δὲ χρημάτων εὖ ἥκοντες did a more expensive job than they had contracted to do; either in gratitude for this or, ὡς ἂν δὴ οἱ Λακεδαιμόνιοι[19] λέγουσι, as a result of bribery Delphi prefaced every response to a Spartan with instructions to liberate Athens (Pl. *Her. Mal.* 860 C–D could not believe that the Pythia was corrupted). The previous temple was burned in 548/7 (Paus. x. 5. xiii; Eusebius gives 555/4 or 549/8); Amasis of Egypt, who died in 526, made a contribution to the funds (H. II. 180): Forrest argues persuasively that Herodotus was right in the chronological implication which matters for his story, that the new temple was well advanced or finished before 511/0, and wrong in or rather careless of the implication which does not matter for his story, that the Alcmaeonids took the contract after Lipsydrium (*pace* Wilamowitz, *A.u.A.*, i. 34 with n. 10, we need not doubt that Lipsydrium followed Hipparchus' death). Fourth-century writers assumed that the contract was made after Lipsydrium, and reinterpreted Delphi's help in the terms which seemed most natural to them: Isocrates and Demosthenes (with second scholium) follow a version favourable to the Alcmaeonids, which Forrest attributes to Clidemus, in which the Alcmaeonids borrowed money from Delphi to (hire mercenaries and) liberate Athens; the first scholium follows a hostile version, which Forrest attributes to Androtion, in which the Alcmaeonids misappropriated the building funds. *A.P.*'s ὅθεν εὐπόρησαν ... βοηθείαν probably reflects the latter version; but Herodotus is his main narrative source in this chapter, and he combines with misappropriation of the building funds Herodotus' story that Delphi helped by putting oracular pressure on Sparta. Later Philochorus reconciled more of Herodotus' story with the fourth-century's chronology and account of Delphi's help: the Alcmaeonids took the contract, received money and hired mercenaries; after their success they did a more expensive job than they had contracted to do, in gratitude and to fulfil a vow.

Forrest's invocation of Clidemus and Androtion is purely speculative, but otherwise his account of the story's development is

---

[19] Schweighäuser's substitution of Λακεδαιμόνιοι for Ἀθηναῖοι in H. v. 63. i is defended by Forrest, *op. cit.*, 279–81; but contr. K. H. Kinzl, *RM*[2] xcviii 1975, 193–204, esp. 194–5 n. 8.

persuasive. K. H. Kinzl, *Hermes* cii 1974, 179–90, pertinently cites the second scholium on Demosthenes, omitted by Jacoby, and argues that the two scholia and the earlier part of Phil. 328 F 115 represent a single version; but his use of D.S. x. 17. ii to attribute this to Ephorus is unconvincing.

ὅθεν εὐπόρησαν χρημάτων: H. v. 62. iii says οἷα δὲ χρημάτων εὖ ἥκοντες, but this is to make a different point, as part of a different version of the story: probably the verbal resemblance is accidental, but it may be that *A.P.* has allowed Herodotus' wording to affect his presentation of the alternative story.†

ἡ δὲ Πυθία ... ἕως προύτρεψε τοὺς Σπαρτιάτας: Cf. H. v. 63. i (ἀνέπειθον τὴν Πυθίην χρήμασι, ὅκως ἔλθοιεν Σπαρτιητέων ἄνδρες εἴτε ἰδίῳ στόλῳ εἴτε δημοσίῳ χρησόμενοι, προφέρειν σφι τὰς Ἀθήνας ἐλευθεροῦν), Pl. *Her. Mal.* 860 C–D. χρηστηριάζεσθαι is a Herodotean word (e.g. I. 55. i, 66. i), though not used in v. 63. i.

καίπερ ὄντων ξένων αὐτοῖς τῶν Πεισιστρατιδῶν: Cf. H. v. 63. ii (... ἐξελῶντα Πεισιστρατίδας ἐξ Ἀθηνέων, ὅμως καὶ ξείνους σφι ἐόντας τὰ μάλιστα), 90. i. If we read Λακεδαιμόνιοι in v. 63. i (cf. above) this becomes less authoritative, as a story told by Spartans who soon came to regret their expulsion of Hippias, and what we know of Sparta's foreign policy at this time tells against its truth, but Forrest goes too far in saying that 'all evidence for friendship between Sparta and the Athenian tyrants disappears' (*GR&BS* x 1969, 281 n. 7). Sealey accepts the claim, and supposes that by this time the Pisistratids' friendship had been transferred from Argos to Sparta (*History of the Greek City States*, 144): cf. next note.

ἡ πρὸς τοὺς Ἀργείους τοῖς Πεισιστρατίδαις ὑπάρχουσα φιλία: Cf. 17. iii–iv with commentary, on Pisistratus' marriage to Timonassa and on the help he received from Argos at Pallene. There is no evidence of later dealings between the Pisistratids and Argos, and Herodotus does not mention Argive friendship at this point; it is unlikely that the Pisistratids maintained simultaneous friendships with Argos and with Sparta.

19. v. Ἀγχίμολον ἀπέστειλαν κατὰ θάλατταν ἔχοντα στρατιάν: Cf. H. v. 63. ii (πέμπουσι Ἀγχιμόλιον τὸν Ἀστέρος, ἐόντα τῶν ἀστῶν ἄνδρα δόκιμον, σὺν στρατῷ ἐξελῶντα Πεισιστρατίδας. ... πέμπουσι δὲ τούτους κατὰ θάλασσαν πλοίοισι). All MSS of Herodotus have Ἀγχιμόλιον; *A.P.*'s Ἀγχίμολον is repeated in schol. Ar. *Lys.* 1150. *A.P.* is simply restating what he found in Herodotus, but what little comparative material we have suggests that his is the right form of the name (cf. perhaps *SEG* xi 667, no. 21), and his form is preferred by J. Toepffer, *RE*, i (1893/4), 2105, F. Bechtel, *Die historischen Personennamen des Griechischen*, 21 cf. 323, P. Poralla, *Prosopographie der Lakedaimonier*, 13. The version on which our MSS of Herodotus agree is presum-

ably a corruption of which the text used by *A.P.* was innocent. The only other bearer of the name is an Elean sophist called Anchimolus by Hegesander *ap.* Ath. II. 44 c, Anchipylus or Archipylus by D.L. II. 126.

Nothing else is known of Anchimolus: his going by sea may indicate that opposition from Megara was feared; but Cleomenes afterwards went by land, though with a larger force.

Κινέαν βοηθῆσαι τὸν Θετταλὸν ἔχοντα χιλίους ἱππεῖς: H. v. 63. iii–iv gives a more detailed story, of which this is a summary: Anchimolus landed at Phalerum; by virtue of an alliance the Pisistratids summoned help from Thessaly, and a thousand cavalry were brought by the βασιλεύς Cineas, ἄνδρα Κονιαῖον (that adjective corresponds to the name of no known Thessalian town; various conjectures have been made; see most recently N. Robertson, *JHS* xcvi 1976, 105); these attacked the Spartan camp in the plain of Phalerum, killing Anchimolus and many others and driving the survivors back to the ships; Anchimolus was buried at Alopece (in the south-east outskirts of the city: J. S. Traill, *Hesp.* Supp. xiv 1975, 53).

προσοργισθέντες: H. v. 64. i says merely μετὰ δέ. The only other occurrences of the verb are late (Jos. *B.J.* II. 295 [*v.l.* παρ—], Pl. *Lib. Ed.* 13 D); Kaibel, *Stil und Text*, 170, explains the compound (the Spartans were already angry with the Pisistratids and this defeat increased their anger), and compares προσεμπικρανέεσθαι in H. III. 146. ii.

Κλεομένην ἐξέπεμψαν τὸν βασιλέα στόλον ἔχοντα μείζω κατὰ γῆν: Cf. H. v. 64. i (Λακεδαιμόνιοι μέζω στόλον στείλαντες ἀπέπεμψαν ἐπὶ τὰς Ἀθήνας, στρατηγὸν τῆς στρατιῆς ἀποδέξαντες βασιλέα Κλεομένεα τὸν Ἀναξανδρίδεω, οὐκέτι κατὰ θάλασσαν ἀλλὰ κατ' ἤπειρον); στόλος is particularly though not exclusively a Herodotean word. Cleomenes was Agiad king of Sparta from before 519 to *c.* 491/0 (T. III. 68. v; H. vi. 85. i in its context; both terminal dates have been challenged, I believe wrongly): his career need not be discussed here except in so far as it impinges on Athens.

τοὺς τῶν Θετταλῶν ἱππεῖς ἐνίκησεν: Cf. H. v. 64. ii: both texts state that this occurred at the entrance to Attica (*sc.* from the Megarid), and Herodotus adds that the surviving Thessalians promptly returned home.

κατακλείσας τὸν Ἱππίαν εἰς τὸ καλούμενον Πελαργικὸν τεῖχος ἐπολιόρκει μετὰ τῶν Ἀθηναίων: Cf. H. v. 64. ii (ἅμα Ἀθηναίων τοῖσι βουλομένοισι εἶναι ἐλευθέροισι ἐπολιόρκεε τοὺς τυράννους ἀπεργμένους ἐν τῷ Πελαργικῷ τείχεϊ), *Marm. Par.* 239 A 45 (Ἀθηναῖοι [ἐξανέστ]ησαν τοὺς Πεισιστρατίδας ἐκ τ[οῦ Π]ελασγικοῦ τείχους). There is no need here for a long disquisition on the name Πελασγοί applied to various pre-Greek and non-Greek peoples: older views are summarised by

[How &] Wells, *Comm. Her.*, i. 442–6 and (1928 reprint) 455–6; see also Jacoby, *Supp.* i. 405–21, A. J. Toynbee, *Some Problems of Greek History*, 86–8, 126–34. The story was told by Hecataeus (1 F 127 *ap.* H. VI. 137. ii) and repeated by the Atthidographers (cf. Clid. 323 F 16, Phil. 328 F 99, with Jacoby *ad locc.* and other texts cited by him) that the Pelasgians came to Attica, built the wall round the Acropolis for the Athenians, and were rewarded with land below Mt Hymettus; but later, when they aroused the jealousy of the Athenians, were expelled. The wall to which this story refers was presumably that built in the Late Helladic III B period (*c.* 1250–1200 B.C.), parts of which still survive. There was also τό ... Πελαργικὸν καλούμενον τὸ ὑπὸ τὴν ἀκρόπολιν, an enclosed area which was left unoccupied for religious reasons until the Peloponnesian War (T. II. 17. i) and which engaged the attention of Lampon during the war (M&L 73, 54–9), most probably at the north-west corner of the Acropolis (but some have argued for a strip running round the western half of the Acropolis): see Lucian, *Pisc.* 42, 47, *Bis Acc.* 9, M. de G. Verrall & J. E. Harrison, *Mythology and Monuments of Ancient Athens*, 535–8, J. G. Frazer, *Pausanias's Description of Greece*, ii. 355–9, W. Judeich, *Topographie von Athen*[2], 113–20, I. C. T. Hill, *The Ancient City of Athens*, 132–3, Travlos, *Pictorial Dictionary*, 52, 55, R. J. Hopper, *The Acropolis*, 22–9. The wall and the enclosure were termed not Πελασγικόν but Πελαργικόν; πελαργός means 'stork', and Πελαργοί was supposed to be a nickname for the Pelasgians or another form of their name (cf. Myrsilus, 477 F 9 *ap.* D.H. *A.R.* I. 28. iv, Str. 221. V. ii. 4, 397. IX. i. 18). In all probability the enclosure was called Πελαργικόν and was regarded as an area of religious significance, now beyond explanation, long before the Pelasgians were invoked to explain anything, and later the Mycenaean Acropolis wall was attributed to the Pelasgians and its name assimilated to that of the Πελαργικόν. Herodotus was probably thinking of the fortified Acropolis as Hippias' refuge, and *A.P.* goes on to mention the Acropolis in §vi; but the good water supply (H. v. 65. i), if authentic, may point to his having retained control of the enclosure too (cf. Gomme, *Hist. Comm. Thuc.*, ii. 64).

19. vi. προσκαθημένου δ' αὐτοῦ: According to H. v. 65. i the Spartans had not expected to mount a siege, and but for their stroke of luck would have returned home after a few days.

συνέπεσεν: Cf. H. v. 65. i (συντυχίη ... ἐπεγένετο).

ὑπεξιόντας ἁλῶναι τοὺς τῶν Πεισιστρατιδῶν υἱεῖς: Cf. H. v. 65. i (ὑπεκτιθέμενοι γὰρ ἔξω τῆς χώρης οἱ παῖδες τῶν Πεισιστρατιδέων ἥλωσαν); Hippias is the only son of Pisistratus who is known to have had children (cf. T. VI. 55. i).

ὁμολογίαν ... ἐν πένθ' ἡμέραις ἐκκομισάμενοι: Cf. H. v. 65. ii (ὥστε

ἐν πέντε ἡμέρῃσι ἐκχωρῆσαι ἐκ τῆς Ἀττικῆς). Who went with Hippias is not clear; but his grandson Hipparchus stayed in Athens to be archon in 496/5 and ostracised in 488/7 (22. iv with commentary).
ἐπὶ Ἁρπακτίδου ἄρχοντος: The year is 511/0 (cf. pp. 191–9); *A.P.* is our only source for the archon's name.
κατασχόντες . . . ἔτη μάλιστα ἑπτακαίδεκα: Since 528/7, 17 years if we reckon in the normal manner for cardinal numerals and include the first year but not the last; Arist. *Pol.* v. 1315 B 31–4 reckons in the alternative manner for cardinals and gives the total as 18 years.
τὰ δὲ σύμπαντα . . . ἑνὸς δεῖ πεντήκοντα: If the interval from Pisistratus' first *coup* to Hippias' expulsion is intended, *A.P.*'s total should be 50 years (561/0–511/0: 33 [17. i] + 17), which is the total given by Erat. 241 F 40 *ap.* schol. Ar. *Vesp.* 502; the total of the figures in Arist., *loc. cit.*, is 51 years, and since that calls for an easier emendation than 50 some have restored it here, though it does not fit *A.P.*'s arithmetic (e.g. Jacoby, *Atthis*, 373–4 n. 107). But *A.P.*'s σὺν οἷς ὁ πατὴρ ἦρξεν should refer not to the whole of this period but to the total extent of the tyranny within it, which in *A.P.*'s scheme amounts to 36 years (G. V. Sumner, CQ^2 xi 1961, 41); for ways in which the incorrect figure of 49 could have been supplied here see Wilamowitz, *A.u.A.*, i. 23, F. Heidbüchel, *Philol.* ci 1957, 86.

This is *A.P.*'s only use of the preposition σύν except in quotations from Solon: Sandys notes that, although rare in Attic prose (except for Xenophon), it is used to express numerical addition.

G. *From Cleisthenes' Reforms to Xerxes' Invasion* (20–2)

Here as in his chapters on the rise of Pisistratus and the expulsion of Hippias *A.P.* has combined material from Herodotus with material from elsewhere; but the Herodotean and the non-Herodotean material are here not interwoven but presented separately. 20. i–iii is a summary of H. v. 66, 69–73. i, on the rivalry of Isagoras and Cleisthenes, the intervention of Cleomenes of Sparta, and the eventual victory of Cleisthenes; as before, *A.P.* shows a close verbal resemblance to Herodotus, and must have made direct use of his work. 20. iv–v reverts to the responsibility of the Alcmaeonids for the ending of the tyranny, and quotes the Cedon scolium, perhaps from the author's own direct knowledge. 21 gives a detailed account of Cleisthenes' reforms, placing them in the archonship of Isagoras: it contains material not available to us in any other text; but the manner of presentation does not suggest that it is derived directly from Cleisthenes' laws, and *A.P.*'s most likely source is an *Atthis*; the author's failure to coordinate this chapter clearly with 20 has led some scholars to suppose that he disagreed with Herodotus on the chronology of the reforms (cf. pp. 244, 249). In 22 a general verdict on Cleisthenes leads to a mention of the law on ostracism and then to a dated series of events in Athens' political history down to the recall of the ostracised at the time of Xerxes' invasion: again much of the material has survived only in *A.P.*, and the annalistic framework makes it almost certain that the source is an *Atthis*. On the origin and first use of ostracism (22. iii–iv) it will be seen that *A.P.*'s source can be identified as Androtion, and we may guess that the whole series of events in 22 (in which ostracism plays a large part) is from him, and perhaps the account of Cleisthenes' laws in 21 as well.

Cleisthenes was not a specially commissioned legislator like Draco and Solon, but a man who made proposals which were adopted by the assembly as ψηφίσματα (cf. on 21. i). The Athenians did not begin to inscribe public documents on stone stelae in large quantities until the 450's, but some survive from the previous half-century, and if Cleisthenes' laws were published in permanent form they should have been inscribed on stelae rather than on ἄξονες like those of Draco and Solon (R. S. Stroud, *Athens Comes of Age*, 30–1, suggests that the balance of probabilities favours permanent publication).[20] In the fifth century Cleisthenes was regarded as the founding hero of the democracy, but he did not join the canon of legislators, and the only later reference to 'the laws of Cleisthenes' is 29. iii (Κλειτοφῶν ... προσαναζητῆσαι δὲ τοὺς αἱρεθέντας ἔγραψεν καὶ τοὺς πατρίους νόμους οὓς Κλεισθένης ἔθηκεν ὅτε καθίστη τὴν δημοκρατίαν), which suggests that in 411 they still existed or were thought to do so, but may also suggest that they were not readily available and would have to be searched for (cf. *ad loc.*). The republication of the laws begun in 410 was officially linked with the names of Draco and Solon, but what was intended was the republication of all the laws, including those of Cleisthenes, which were currently in force, so some at least of his laws should have survived in the fourth-century code, though not necessarily with his name attached or in a form which allowed them to be distinguished from other laws. Although it is not impossible, it is less likely that an Atthidographer should have been able to consult Cleisthenes' laws than that he should have been able to consult Solon's laws; and most, though not quite all, of the details in ch. 21 could have been obtained by applying to the fact of Cleisthenes' tribal reform knowledge of how the tribal system worked in the fourth century. (Wade-Gery, *CQ* xxvii 1933, 19–20 = *Essays*, 139–40, was confident that Cleisthenes' laws did survive; Hignett, *H.A.C.*, 129–31, argues that they did not.)

Except in Herodotus and *A.P.* little material on Cleisthenes

[20] For the suggestion of D. H. Thomas that the surviving ἄξονες contained Cleisthenes' revision of the laws see above, p. 133 n. 9.

survives for us to read: Clid. 323 F 8 seems to conflict with 21. v on the ναυκραρίαι; Arist. *Pol.* has two allusions to Cleisthenes, VI. 1319 B 19–27 on the creation of the new tribes, and III. 1275 B 34–9 on the enfranchisement of slaves and foreigners (a passage productive of mystery rather than enlightenment: cf. on 21. iv). As a source of information not otherwise available to us chs 21–2 are as valuable as any part of the narrative section of *A.P.*: 'es ist alles eitel gold' (Wilamowitz, *A.u.A.*, ii. 146). Since the discovery of *A.P.* the greatest further contribution to our understanding of this period has come from archaeology: in seeing how Cleisthenes put together demes to form trittyes and trittyes to form tribes we are better placed to estimate his purpose, and our knowledge of ostracism is now augmented by many thousands of ostraca.

20. i. ἐστασίαζον πρὸς ἀλλήλους: Cf. H. v. 66. i–ii (ἐν δὲ αὐτῆσι [sc. Ἀθήνῃσι] δύο ἄνδρες ἐδυνάστευον, Κλεισθένης τε ἀνὴρ Ἀλκμεωνίδης ... καὶ Ἰσαγόρης Τεισάνδρου, οἰκίης μὲν ἐὼν δοκίμου, ἀτὰρ τὰ ἀνέκαθεν οὐκ ἔχω φράσαι. ... οὗτοι οἱ ἄνδρες ἐστασίασαν περὶ δυνάμιος). Cleisthenes was the senior member in his generation of the Alcmaeonid family: he had been archon in 525/4 and had gone into exile after the death of Hipparchus (cf. on 19. iii). Isagoras has tempted modern scholars to conjecture what Herodotus could not discover: some have tried to make him a Philaid on the strength of his father's name (N. G. L. Hammond, *CQ*[2] vi 1956, 127–8, B. R. I. Sealey, *Hist.* ix 1960, 172 = *Essays*, 25, cf. more subtly P. J. Bicknell, *Hist.* Einz. xix 1972, 84–8, *Hist.* xxiii 1974, 153–4), but the name is too common to guarantee the inference, and if Isagoras were a Philaid we may suspect that Herodotus could have discovered the fact; D. M. Lewis, *Hist.* xii 1963, 25–6, used the family cult of Zeus Κάριος (H. v. 66. i) and *IG* i[2] 186 to place him in the deme Icarium, on the north-east slope of Mt Pentelicon (J. S. Traill, *Hesp.* Supp. xiv 1975, 41), but he now believes the inscription to refer to the hero Ἰκάριος (see revised text of inscription, *IG* i[3] 253).

For a comparison of 20. i–iii with H. v. 66, 69–73. i, see Wade-Gery, *CQ* xxvii 1933, 17–19 = *Essays*, 136–9, showing that almost everything said by *A.P.* is a restatement of what he found in Herodotus, without addition or divergence; the exceptions which he noted I do not believe involve intentional disagreement with Herodotus.

φίλος ὢν τῶν τυράννων: Not stated by Herodotus, and shown by him to be untrue of the time of Hippias' expulsion (v. 70. i: Cleomenes was a ξεῖνος of Isagoras ἀπὸ τῆς Πεισιστρατιδέων πολιορκίης, so Isagoras was resident in Athens but assisted in the overthrow of the tyranny). However, it is probably an inference from Herodotus' narrative rather than a piece of independent information: *A.P.* 'interprets the rivalry between the two men ... as a rivalry between the Tyrants' enemies (who had turned them out) and the Tyrants' friends (who had acquiesced in the tyranny)'— Wade-Gery, *opp. citt.* 19 = 138–9, cf. Wilamowitz, *A.u.A.*, ii. 76 n. 6.

τοῦ γένους ὢν τῶν 'Αλκμεωνιδῶν: Whether the Alcmaeonids were a γένος in the technical sense of that word is disputed, but I believe they were not. Here and in 28. ii *A.P.* uses the word of the Alcmaeonids (but he does not use it of any other γένος or family), and the technical sense is possible but not necessary; Herodotus does not use the word in v. 66, from which this sentence is derived (but does use it of the Alcmaeonids elsewhere). Cf. p. 70.

ἡττώμενος δὲ ταῖς ἑταιρείαις ὁ Κλεισθένης προσηγάγετο τὸν δῆμον: Cf. H. v. 66. ii (ἑσσούμενος δὲ ὁ Κλεισθένης τὸν δῆμον προσεταιρίζεται), also 69. i (τὸν Ἀθηναίων δῆμον πρότερον ἀπωσμένον τότε πάντως πρὸς τὴν ἑωυτοῦ μοῖραν προσεθήκατο): what we have in *A.P.* is simply a restatement of what he found in Herodotus, and provides no evidence for the existence of ἑταιρεῖαι (associations or 'clubs' of men who were on occasion prepared to cooperate for political purposes: see on 34. iii) in the time of Cleisthenes (Wade-Gery, *opp. citt.*, 19 = 138; but the proposal of G. Maddoli, *Cronologia e storia*, 81–6, to strengthen the resemblance to Herodotus by taking ταῖς ἑταιρείαις with προσηγάγετο rather than with ἡττώμενος is difficult with *A.P.*'s word order). τὸν δῆμον denotes the ordinary citizens, as opposed to the δυναστεύοντες who were contending for supremacy; K. H. Kinzl, *Greece and the Eastern Mediterranean* ... F. Schachermeyr, 201–2, argues that the support of the masses could be delivered only by their noble leaders, but I doubt if in this respect the Athenian assembly, with its straightforward voting, functioned like the Roman assemblies. That Cleisthenes' courting of the δῆμος was something new is well brought out by Hignett, *H.A.C.*, 125–6, who stresses the aristocratic nature of the scolium quoted in 19. iii.†

Neither Herodotus nor *A.P.* explains how Cleisthenes came to be 'defeated', but it has long been recognised that *A.P.* provides the material for an explanation in 21. i: Isagoras had been elected archon for 508/7 (cf. Busolt, *G.G.*, ii². 401–2; for election see on 16. ix, 22. v).[21] It was a rule of the classical democracy that a man might not hold any non-military office more than once (62. iii with commentary; for this purpose the nine archonships were probably

---

[21] D. J. McCargar, *Phoen.* xxviii 1974, 275–81, is persuaded by Frost and Badian that archons at this time were young men beginning their political career (cf. below, p. 274), and argues that to identify the archon of 508/7 with Isagoras Τεισάνδρου is 'both uncertain and unlikely'; but since no other Isagoras is attested at any date in Athens it is more likely that the identification is correct and that the election of Isagoras as archon for 508/7 was politically significant.

regarded as a single office): Cleisthenes, having been archon in 525/4, could not legitimately be a candidate for 508/7 unless either the democratic rule did not yet exist (our incomplete evidence provides no certain breach of the democratic rule, but the archons of 664/3 and 659/8 were both named Miltiades [Paus. IV. 23. x, VIII. 39. iii]; Damasias' prolonged archonship was illegitimate [13. ii with commentary]) or it was argued that service under the tyranny should be ignored (but it is unlikely that Cleisthenes would wish to draw attention to the fact that he had been archon under the tyranny). Very probably Cleisthenes wanted the archonship of 508/7 not for himself but for a friend (cf. E. Badian, *Antichthon* v 1971, 18 n. 42, 21 n. 52, with great caution): if Alcmeon, in whose archonship the tribes δέκα ἐγένοντο (Poll. VIII. 110), is to be placed in 507/6, he is the obvious candidate (Davies, *A.P.F.*, 382); if he is to be placed in 502/1, Cleisthenes' candidate remains unknown (cf. p. 263). Wilamowitz, *A.u.A.*, i. 6 (when Cleisthenes' archonship of 525/4 was not known), supposed that Cleisthenes became archon on the withdrawal of Cleomenes and Isagoras, and this is revived by Fritz & Kapp; but see on 21. i.†

ἀποδιδοὺς τῷ πλήθει τὴν πολιτείαν: Not derived from Herodotus, who at this point gives his account of Cleisthenes' tribal reform and a digression on Cleisthenes of Sicyon (v. 66. ii–69. ii). Very probably the purpose of the phrase is to note Cleisthenes' reform at the 'correct' point in the narrative sequence (for which Herodotus was *A.P.*'s sole authority), while delaying the detailed account of that reform, to supply it in 21 from a more informative source (cf. B. Niese, *HZ* lxix = ²xxxiii 1892, 49–50; Wade-Gery, *opp. citt.*, 19, 21–2, 24 = 139, 142–3, 147; R. J. Seager, *AJP* lxxxiv 1963, 287–9); the many scholars who have supposed that *A.P.* disagrees with Herodotus and places the reforms after Cleomenes' intervention (e.g. Wilamowitz, *A.u.A.*, ii. 76–7 with n. 8; most recently D. J. McCargar, *Hist.* xxv 1976, 385–95) have been misled by the way in which he has used the material from his different sources. To have won the upper hand Cleisthenes must at least have proposed his reforms at this stage, and probably had them adopted by the assembly; but there can have been no time for them to take effect before the intervention of Cleomenes (cf. Hignett, *H.A.C.*, 331–6; and 21. i, 22. ii, with commentary).

Wade-Gery translates this phrase as *universo populo tribuens rempublicam* (*opp. citt.*, 19 n. 5, 25, 26 n. 1 = 139 n. 2, 147–8, 149 n. 1). In rendering πολιτείαν as *rempublicam* he is clearly right: although 21. iv suggests that the purpose of the tribal reforms was to conceal the enfranchisement of new citizens, what Cleisthenes is here represented as offering to the πλῆθος can only be political power in the sense of control of the state, and 21. ii is best explained in the same way. But in rendering τῷ πλήθει as *universo populo* rather than *plebi* he seems to be wrong: in context the phrase must mean that Cleisthenes gave to the common people, whose support he had won, that political power which previously had been a monopoly of the δυναστεύοντες; if πλῆθος means something other than δῆμος immediately before it, and is not simply a synonym used to avoid repetition, we should expect the contrast to be made far more clearly (on misunderstandings which have arisen from *A.P.*'s attempts to avoid monotony cf. Introduction, p. 43). It is typical of *A.P.*'s lack of coordination that in his account of the reforms in 21, apart from what he says of 'mixing', he does not explain how the reorganisation gave power to the πλῆθος.

20. ii. ὁ δὲ Ἰσαγόρας ... εἶναι τῶν ἐναγῶν: Cf. H. v. 70 (ἐν τῷ μέρεϊ ἐσσούμενος ὁ Ἰσαγόρης ἀντιτεχνᾶται τάδε· ἐπικαλέεται Κλεομένεα τὸν Λακεδαιμόνιον, γενόμενον ἑωυτῷ ξεῖνον ἀπὸ τῆς Πεισιστρατιδέων πολιορκίης. ... τὰ μὲν δὴ πρῶτα πέμπων ὁ Κλεομένης ἐς τὰς Ἀθήνας κήρυκα ἐξέβαλλε Κλεισθένεα καὶ μετ' αὐτοῦ ἄλλους πολλοὺς Ἀθηναίων, τοὺς ἐναγέας ἐπιλέγων). Herodotus at this point gives a brief account of the curse on those who killed the supporters of Cylon (v. 71): *A.P.* has already given his account of Cylon (1), and offers no explanation of the curse here.

ἐπιλειπόμενος τῇ δυνάμει: This construction recurs twice in *A.P.* (27. iv, cf. 34. iii [with ἄλλως in place of the dative]), but is found nowhere else. It is convincingly championed, as a natural development from other uses of λείπειν and ἐπιλείπειν, by Kaibel, *Stil und Text*, 171, and need not be emended out of existence.

20. iii. ὑπεξελθόντος δὲ τοῦ Κλεισθένους ... ἑπτακοσίους οἰκίας: Cf. H. v. 72. i (Κλεομένης δὲ ὡς πέμπων ἐξέβαλλε Κλεισθένεα καὶ τοὺς ἐναγέας, Κλεισθένης μὲν αὐτὸς ὑπέξεσχε· μετὰ δὲ οὐδὲν ἧσσον παρῆν ἐς τὰς Ἀθήνας ὁ Κλεομένης οὐ σὺν μεγάλῃ χειρί, ἀπικόμενος δὲ ἀγηλατέει ἑπτακόσια ἐπίστια Ἀθηναίων, τὰ οἱ ὑπέθετο ὁ Ἰσαγόρης), T. i. 126. xii. ⟨ἀφικόμενος ὁ Κλεομένης⟩ was first added by Kaibel & Wilamowitz[2] and has been generally accepted: some such insertion is needed to make Cleomenes the subject of ἠγηλάτει in *A.P.* as he is in Herodotus (cf. Kaibel, *Stil und Text*, 171). Apart from these two passages, LSJ cites that verb only from Soph. *O.T.* 402.

None of the accounts of the affair of Cylon leads us to expect that those held responsible for the killing of his supporters were so numerous that their descendants about four generations later should amount to seven hundred οἰκίαι ('families' in a fairly broad sense [cf. pp. 69–70]; Herodotus' ἐπίστια has a similar meaning); the detail is justifiably suspected by Wilamowitz, *A.u.A.*, i. 31–2, How [& Wells], commentary on H. v. 72. i, but their suggestion that νεοπολῖται were added to the accursed has little to commend it. M. Ostwald, *Nomos and the Beginnings of the Athenian Democracy*, 185, pertinently asks whether Cleisthenes really considered himself subject to the curse.

ταῦτα δὲ διαπραξάμενος ... κυρίους καθιστάναι τῆς πόλεως: Cf. H. v. 72. i (ταῦτα δὲ ποιήσας δεύτερα τὴν βουλὴν καταλύειν ἐπειρᾶτο, τριηκοσίοισι δὲ τοῖσι Ἰσαγόρεω στασιώτῃσι τὰς ἀρχὰς ἐνεχείριζε). The boule which Cleomenes tried to dissolve must have been Solon's boule of four hundred (8. iv with commentary): Cleisthenes' boule of five hundred cannot yet have been brought into existence, and to abolish the venerable council of the Areopagus was probably unthinkable (*pace* Hignett, *H.A.C.*, 94–5); Cleisthenes must have won the support not only of the assembly but also of the council which prepared its business, and with this support it is not difficult to understand that his proposals could be put to the assembly despite the opposition of the reigning archon, Isagoras. It has been suggested that the three hundred supporters of Isagoras were the members of the Areopagus, of whom all but the oldest will have been archons under the tyranny (Sealey, *Hist.* ix 1960, 160 n. 35 = *Essays*, 35–6 n. 35, *History of the Greek City States*, 149–50); but at least one member of the Areopagus, Cleisthenes, was now in opposition to Isagoras.

τῆς δὲ βουλῆς ἀντιστάσης ... ἀφεῖσαν ὑποσπόνδους: Cf. H. v. 72. ii, iv–73. i (ἀντισταθείσης δὲ τῆς βουλῆς καὶ οὐ βουλομένης πείθεσθαι ὅ τε Κλεομένης καὶ ὁ Ἰσαγόρης καὶ οἱ στασιῶται αὐτοῦ καταλαμβάνουσι τὴν ἀκρόπολιν. Ἀθηναίων δὲ οἱ λοιποὶ τὰ αὐτὰ φρονήσαντες ἐπολιόρκεον αὐτοὺς ἡμέρας δύο· τῇ δὲ τρίτῃ ὑπόσπονδοι ἐξέρχονται ἐκ τῆς χώρης ὅσοι ἦσαν αὐτῶν Λακεδαιμόνιοι. ... τοὺς δὲ ἄλλους Ἀθηναῖοι κατέδησαν τὴν ἐπὶ θανάτῳ. ... οὗτοι μὲν νῦν δεδέμενοι ἐτελεύτησαν), also Ar. *Lys.* 274–82. According to Herodotus the truce applied only to the Spartans, while the Athenians with Cleomenes were put to death (but in v. 74. i Cleomenes subsequently plans to install Isagoras as tyrant), but according to *A.P.* it extended to πάντας. Schol. Ar. *Lys.* 273 reports Athens' condemnation of those who supported Cleomenes when he invaded again, commemorated by a bronze stele on the Acropolis, and Wade-Gery supposed that *A.P.* knew the stele and corrected Herodotus in the light of it (*CQ* xxvii 1933, 18 = *Essays*, 136–7, cf. Jacoby, *Atthis*, 337 n. 40): the fact that *A.P.* says nothing to suggest that the point was disputed is not conclusive evidence against this view, but he shows no interest in the further history of Cleomenes and Isagoras, and more probably he has simply been careless in his paraphrase (cf. Ostwald, *Nomos and the Beginnings of the Athenian Democracy*, 144 n. 6, suggesting that πάντας is intended to refer to the Spartans alone).

In *A.P.* the sequel to Cleisthenes' reforms is the series of political events chronicled in ch. 22. Herodotus says nothing of these, but instead gives what *A.P.* omits, the further attempts of Sparta to upset the reforms and Athens' appeal to Persia for support against Sparta. Cleomenes' next plan was a three-pronged attack on Athens from the Peloponnese, Boeotia and Chalcis, which collapsed when the Corinthians and Cleomenes' fellow king Demaratus returned home (H. v. 74–7); the Alcmaeonids' responsibility for the oracular pressure which had encouraged Sparta to expel Hippias was discovered, and the Spartans summoned Hippias from his retreat in Sigeum and proposed to a meeting of the Peloponnesians that he should be reinstated in Athens, but the Corinthians objected and were able to carry the day; Hippias returned to Sigeum and then joined the Persian satrap Artaphernes at Sardis (v. 90–6: probably Isagoras was condemned after the previous invasion and this was still the work of Cleomenes, still pursuing a policy of hostility to Cleisthenes: e.g. W. G. Forrest, *A History of Sparta, 950–192 B.C.*, 88–9, contr. G. E. M. de Ste. Croix, *The Origins of the Peloponnesian War*, 116 n. 72). Before the abortive invasion Athens sent envoys to Sardis to make an alliance with Persia, and the envoys gave tokens of submission, which led to trouble when they returned home (v. 73); when Hippias retired to Sardis the Athenians sent a deputation to protest, but achieved nothing (v. 96. ii).

Κλεισθένη δὲ καὶ τοὺς ἄλλους φυγάδας μετεπέμψαντο: Cf. H. v. 73. i (Ἀθηναῖοι δὲ μετὰ ταῦτα Κλεισθένεα καὶ τὰ ἑπτακόσια ἐπίστια τὰ διωχθέντα ὑπὸ Κλεομένεος μεταπεμψάμενοι . . .).

20. iv. κατασχόντος δὲ . . . τοῦ δήμου προστάτης: *A.P.* adds a sentence of his own to round off the narrative sequence which he has repeated from Herodotus: without a precise verbal echo, it responds to ἡττώμενος δὲ ταῖς ἑταιρείαις ὁ Κλεισθένης προσηγάγετο τὸν δῆμον, ἀποδιδοὺς τῷ πλήθει τὴν πολιτείαν, in §i (cf. Introduction, pp. 47–8).

αἰτιώτατοι γὰρ . . . οἱ Ἀλκμεωνίδαι: Herodotus (cf. VI. 123) and Thucydides (cf. VI. 59. iv) would both have agreed with this statement, but neither helps us to understand why *A.P.* has made it at this point. The reason must be sought in *A.P.*'s structural pattern: after reproducing Herodotus' narrative and adding a resumptive sentence (cf. above), he returns to the theme of conflict between Cleisthenes the Alcmaeonid and Isagoras the 'friend of the tyrants' with which he began the chapter; and the Alcmaeonids' opposition to the tyranny, as well as Cleisthenes' programme of reform, explains why he won the support of the δῆμος (21. i). Cf. J. J. Keaney, *AJP* xc 1969, 417–20.

καὶ στασιάζοντες τὰ πολλὰ διετέλεσαν: 'And for much of the time they persisted in conflict (*sc.* with the Pisistratids)'; some have wanted an insertion after στασιάζοντες (πρὸς τούτους, A. Gennadios, *CR* v 1891,

274; πρὸς αὐτούς, Kaibel, *Stil und Text*, 172), but this is unnecessary. Cleisthenes' archonship of 525/4 is unknown or conveniently forgotten: cf. on 19. iii.

20. v. ἔτι δὲ πρότερον τῶν Ἀλκμεωνιδῶν Κήδων: Two interpretations are theoretically possible: 'before the Alcmaeonids Cedon' and 'previously Cedon of the Alcmaeonids'. Nothing more is known of this Cedon, and only two other Athenian Cedons are known, from the fourth century (D.S. xv. 34. v, *IG* ii² 2308, *A*). The former interpretation is perhaps the more natural in isolation, and has generally been preferred (cf. J. J. Keaney, *Z.Ant.* xxx 1979, 73-4), but the latter gives a better sense as a sequel to the previous sentence, and that should be decisive (its champions include Wilamowitz, *A.u.A.*, i. 38, Mathieu & Haussoullier, Tovar [hesitantly] and M. Sironić, *Z.Ant.* xxi 1971, 131-3). The author may well have added the reference to Cedon, and the scolium, from his own direct knowledge (cf. Introduction, p. 24).

καὶ εἰς τοῦτον: In addition to the heroes of Lipsydrium (cf. 19. iii).

ἔγχει καὶ Κήδωνι . . . : Quoted also by Ath. xv. 695 E, with the inferior εἰ δὴ χρή at the beginning of the second line. *Pace* Sandys the fact that Athenaeus quotes this immediately after the Lipsydrium scolium does not prove that *A.P.* was his source.

21. i. διὰ μὲν οὖν ταύτας τὰς αἰτίας: At first reading the reference seems to be to the Alcmaeonids' persistent opposition to the tyranny, noted in 20. iv-v; but more probably *A.P.* is referring to the whole of ch. 20 and is thinking both of the Alcmaeonids' opposition to the tyranny and of Cleisthenes' enlistment of the δῆμος' support through his proposed reforms (20. i).

τότε δὲ τοῦ πλήθους προεστηκώς: Resuming τοῦ δήμου προστάτης from 20. iv (and not implying that it was only after his return that he attained to this position: cf. R. J. Seager, *AJP* lxxxiv 1963, 289, contr. Hignett, *H.A.C.*, 332). This chapter ascribes the reforms to Cleisthenes personally, and 22. i and 29. iii refer to the νόμοι which he ἔθηκεν, but it is noteworthy that *A.P.* does not make him the holder of any office, as he had made Solon archon (5. ii): some have thought that Cleisthenes must have been appointed to some office (e.g. Wilamowitz, *A.u.A.*, i. 6), but more probably he persuaded the assembly to adopt his proposals as ψηφίσματα (e.g. Wade-Gery, *CQ* xxvii 1933, 19-25 = *Essays*, 139-48, though his argument from 29. iii is not cogent and he later abandoned it; Ostwald, *Nomos and the Beginnings of the Athenian Democracy*, 155-9, suggesting that whereas Draco and Solon had called their laws θεσμοί Cleisthenes called his νόμοι). On the procedures by which Cleisthenes' reform was enacted and implemented see A. Andrewes, *CQ*² xxvii 1977, 241-8 (but I am less optimistic than he is about the speed with which the reorganisation could be carried out).

ἔτει τετάρτῳ μετὰ τὴν τῶν τυράννων κατάλυσιν ἐπὶ Ἰσαγόρου ἄρχοντος: 508/7 (cf. p. 195). Some have argued from the fact that *A.P.*'s detailed account of Cleisthenes' reforms follows the narrative of ch. 20 that the reforms must have followed Cleomenes' withdrawal (e.g. Wilamowitz, *A.u.A.*, ii. 76-7 with n. 8, Sandys), but this is to mistake the relationship between 20 and 21. Others have argued that Isagoras could not have continued as archon after that episode (as Wilamowitz also believed: *A.u.A.*, i. 6), and that this dating to Isagoras' archonship confirms Herodotus' placing of the reforms before Cleomenes' intervention (Wade-Gery, *opp. citt.*, 21-2 = 142-3, cf. Ostwald, *op. cit.*, 143-5, suggesting that Alcmaeon had been elected archon for the following year before Cleomenes' intervention and took office immediately after Cleomenes' withdrawal, Andrewes, *op. cit.*, 246-7), but Isagoras certainly remained alive after Cleomenes' withdrawal and there is no positive evidence that any one replaced him as archon before the end of the year. In all probability, however, Cleisthenes' proposals were approved by the assembly before Isagoras appealed to Cleomenes, and indeed it was that approval which prompted Isagoras' appeal, so that if we think of their formal enactment Herodotus mentions them at the correct point; but Cleisthenes' reorganisation cannot have been completed before Cleomenes was called in, and I argue that it did not take effect until 501/0 (cf. on 22. ii).

21. ii. πρῶτον μ(ὲν) ο(ὖν) ⟨συν⟩ένειμε πάντας: W. L. Newman, *CR* v 1891, 163, and others suggested πρῶτον μὲν συνένειμε (cf. 41. ii, and συνέταξεν in 21. iii), which was accepted by Mathieu & Haussoullier and Oppermann; Kaibel & Wilamowitz suggested πρῶτον μὲν οὖν ⟨συν⟩ένειμε, preceded by a lacuna which should be filled with a note on the enfranchisement of new citizens (cf. Wilamowitz, *A.u.A.*, i. 31 n. 3, Kaibel, *Stil und Text*, 172-4); their text was accepted but their lacuna rejected by H. Diels, *ap.* Kenyon's Berlin ed., and this is the best solution. It is true that somewhere in this chapter a note of Cleisthenes' enfranchisements is needed; but the omission more probably belongs to §iv than here (cf. *ad loc.*, and comment on ἀναμεῖξαι βουλόμενος), and that and the awkwardly abrupt beginning of §ii are as likely to be due to *A.P.*'s excessive compression of what he found in his source as to a scribe's error (cf. p. 262, on 22. i-ii).

πρῶτον μὲν οὖν marks the first in the series of measures attributed to Cleisthenes, a series interrupted by explanatory comments: the other items are ἔπειτα the remodelling of the boule (§iii); δὲ καὶ the construction of the tribes out of demes and trittyes (§iv)—after which one point leads to another as the author thinks of them.

21. ii] COMMENTARY ON THE ATH. POL.

εἰς δέκα φυλὰς ἀντὶ τῶν τεττάρων: Cf. H. v. 66. ii, 69, Arist. *Pol.* vi. 1319 B 19–27. For the four old tribes and other subdivisions of the citizen body see pp. 66–76, and for the composition of the new tribes see §iv with commentary.

ἀναμεῖξαι βουλόμενος, ὅπως μετάσχωσι πλείους τῆς πολιτείας: According to Herodotus Cleisthenes was motivated by dislike of the Ionians, as his grandfather Cleisthenes (who renamed the four tribes of Sicyon) was motivated by dislike of the Dorians; in Arist. *Pol.* vi the creation of more tribes is a κατασκεύασμα χρήσιμον πρὸς τὴν δημοκρατίαν τοιαύτην (*sc.* τὴν τελευταίαν), ... ὅπως ἂν ὅτι μάλιστα ἀναμειχθῶσι πάντες ἀλλήλοις, αἱ δὲ συνήθειαι διαζευχθῶσιν αἱ πρότερον. What *A.P.* says could be translated either 'so that more (*sc.* of the citizens) should have a share in the running of the state' (cf. ἀποδιδοὺς τῷ πλήθει τὴν πολιτείαν in 20. i; this seems to be the meaning of Arist. *Pol.* vi) or 'so that more (*sc.* men) should be members of the citizen body' (cf. §iv, where *A.P.* argues that the new organisation was intended to conceal the admission of νεοπολῖται; in 8. v and 26. iv μὴ μετέχειν τῆς πόλεως is used of ἀτιμία and of exclusion from citizenship, and in 42. i μετέχειν τῆς πολιτείας is used of citizenship); the comment on μὴ φυλοκρινεῖν which follows could be represented as appropriate to either interpretation (cf. below). I believe that it is wrong to interpret this sentence in the light of §iv, and that here as in 20. i *A.P.* is thinking of the involvement of more (existing) citizens in the running of the state (cf. Wade-Gery, *CQ* xxvii 1933, 25 n. 2 = *Essays*, 148 n. 1, K.-W. Welwei, *Gymnasium* lxxiv 1967, 423 n. 4; contr. Fritz & Kapp, Day & Chambers, *A.H.A.D.*, 111–13).

ὅθεν ἐλέχθη καὶ τὸ μὴ φυλοκρινεῖν ... βουλομένοις: φυλοκρινεῖν should originally have been used with reference to tribal membership (cf. Poll. VIII. 110, Hes. φυλοκρινεῖν), but it came to mean more generally 'make nice (or over-nice) distinctions about sorts of people' (as in T. VI. 18. ii with 11. vii, cf. the synonyms offered by Suid. [Φ 840] φυλοκρινεῖ). Similarly ἐξετάζειν τὰ γένη, used in *A.P.*'s explanation, might be used literally, with reference to the kinship groups known as γένη, or (as suggested by W. Wyse *ap.* Sandys, comparing D. LVII. *Eub.*, *hyp.* 2) more generally of an investigation into men's birth.[22]

A.P. seems to have believed that originally every citizen belonged both to a tribe and to a γένος, but at some time (probably under the tyranny: cf. 13. v) citizenship was usurped by immigrants who belonged to neither; in fact it is more likely that before Cleisthenes'

---

[22] F. R. Wüst, *Hist.* vi 1957, 178–86, supposed that within each old tribe the three trittyes corresponded to the three classes εὐπατρίδαι, γεωμόροι and δημιουργοί (cf. above, p. 71 with n. 1), and that φυλοκρινεῖν refers to that distinction, but this can hardly be right.

reform every citizen belonged to a tribe but the γεννῆται were an aristocratic minority and there was never a time when every citizen belonged to a γένος. If *A.P.* is using φυλοκρινεῖν and γένη narrowly, he will be thinking of the distinction between νεοπολῖται and established citizens (of which he certainly is thinking in §iv); but if he is using these words in a broader sense his comment will be no less appropriate to a distinction between the γνώριμοι and the δῆμος, and that is more probable (cf. Day & Chambers, *A.H.A.D.*, 113–14, supposing that *A.P.* is using these words in the narrower sense but ought to be using them in the broader). The attachment of this comment on μὴ φυλοκρινεῖν to the new tribal organisation may already have been found in *A.P.*'s source, or it may be a contribution of his own (cf. §iv *fin.*).

21. iii. τὴν βουλὴν πεντακοσίο[υ]ς ἀντὶ τετρακοσίων κατέστησεν: For Solon's boule of four hundred see 8. iv with commentary.

πεντήκοντα ἐξ ἑκάστης φυλῆς: Within each tribal contingent seats were allocated to individual demes (cf. §iv, 62. i) in proportion to their size. It is possible that members were elected at first, but appointment by lot will have been introduced not later than the middle of the fifth century (cf. the constitution imposed on Erythrae, M&L 40, 8–9); appointment was for a year, and at any rate in the fourth century no man might serve more than twice in his life (62. iii); membership was probably restricted to the three highest Solonian classes (but there is no direct evidence, and P. J. Bicknell believes that the thetes were eligible: *Hist.* xxiii 1974, 161, cf. *Hist. Einz.* xix 1972, 5), and to men who had reached the age of thirty (X. *M.* I. ii. 35, referring to the régime of the Thirty, but there is no reason to suppose that on this point the democratic rule was different; cf. D. XXII. *Andr., hyp.* i. 1). Cf. 43. ii with commentary, and Rhodes, *A.B.*, 1–14.

διὰ τοῦτο δὲ οὐκ εἰς δώδεκα φυλὰς συνέταξεν: *A.P.*'s logic is defective, for if he had wished to do so Cleisthenes could have created twelve new tribes, not by calling each of the old trittyes a tribe but by organising the citizen body afresh as he did to create his ten tribes.

ὥστ' οὐ [σ](υν)έπιπτεν <ἂν> ἀναμίσγεσθαι: μίσγειν as an alternative to μειγνύναι is largely Homeric and Ionic, but προσμίσγειν is found in T. III. 22. iii, VI. 104. ii, and μίσγειν in Plat. *Tim.* 41 D 5, 6.

21. iv. διένειμε δὲ καὶ ... πάντων τῶν τόπων: Cf. H. v. 69. ii (δέκα τε δὴ φυλάρχους ἀντὶ τεσσέρων ἐποίησε, δέκαχα [Lolling: δέκα codd.] δὲ καὶ τοὺς δήμους κατένειμε ἐς τὰς φυλάς), Psell. 'Ὀνόματα Δικῶν, 103 Boissonade (quoted in Kenyon's Berlin ed. and Sandys). The old tribes were based on actual or supposed kinship; the new were based on locality. The smallest unit in the system was the δῆμος, a village and the land around it (or, perhaps better, a village and its inhabitants: W. E. Thompson, *SO* xlvi 1971, 72–9), or a part of the city of Athens (on this use of the word see J. A. O. Larsen, *CP* lxviii 1973, 45–6); according to Str. 396. ix. i. 16 there were 170 or 174 demes in all, but in the fourth century (the earliest period for which we have sufficient evidence) there were in fact 133, six of them divided into 'upper' and 'lower' sections (cf. J. S. Traill, *Hesp.* Supp. xiv 1975, 81–103). Demes were combined to form trittyes; and trittyes were put together to form tribes in such a way that each tribe comprised one trittys from the ἄστυ, one from the παραλία and one from the μεσόγειος (on the division of the four old tribes into trittyes see p. 68). When the system was constructed each citizen was assigned to the deme in which he lived; the perpetuation of the system was hereditary, and in future each man would belong to his father's or adoptive father's deme irrespective of where he lived (adoption and the deme, Isae. vii. *Her. Apoll.* 27–8, [D.] xliv. *Leoch.* 39; ἐγκεκτημένοι, men who live in one deme but are registered in another, [D.] l. *Poly.* 8, *IG* ii² 1214, esp. 11–17, 25–8, cf. p. 279 on Themistocles' deme and house); but until the outbreak of the Peloponnesian War most Athenians still lived where their families had lived for generations (T. ii. 14. ii, 16).

There are many inscriptions which list citizens under their tribes and demes, among them those which commemorate all the members, or one tribe's members, of the boule in a particular year (see especially S. Dow, *Hesp.* Supp. i 1937, B. D. Meritt & J. S. Traill, *The Athenian Agora*, xv). These show which demes belonged to which tribe, and make it clear that different demes consistently sent different numbers of members to the boule and were presumably of different size. Students of topography have been able to place most of the demes on the map of Attica and in one of the three trittyes within their tribe (see especially Traill, *Hesp.* Supp. xiv 1975, 35–55, with index 109–12 and maps). A trittys was usually, but not always, a group of adjacent demes round which a line can be drawn on a map; the three trittyes which were combined to make a tribe might (if viewed as continuous areas of territory) meet one another at a point or on a line, or might be totally separate from one another; and the trittyes like the demes were of varying size (for modified trittyes of approximately equal size see 44. i with commentary). The three regions were different from the regions after which the 'parties' of *c.* 560 were named (13. iv with commentary): ἄστυ included not only the city but the plain of Athens including its coast, bounded by Corydallus and Aegaleos on the north-west and Hymettus on the south-east but stopping somewhat short of Parnes and Pentelicon in the north-east; παραλία comprised all the coastal strip of Attica except the part that was in ἄστυ, and included the demes in the western hills north of the plain of Eleusis; μεσόγειος comprised the rest of the interior. The island of Salamis, and the territory of Oropus at such times as it belonged to Athens (as it probably did at this time: J. Wiesner, *RE*, xviii [1939/43], 1173) were not included in this system: men who lived there and were Athenian citizens must have been registered elsewhere (notice the demotics in *IG* ii² 1225-8, and for Athenian cleruchs on Salamis see M&L 14 with commentary).†

The new tribal system supplanted the old as the basis of Athenian citizenship—to be a citizen a man had to be a member of a deme and of the trittys and tribe in which that deme was included—and it provided a framework for the organisation of Athenian public life. In the assembly men voted as individuals, and probably on most occasions could sit where they wished (A. L. Boegehold, *Hesp.* xxxii 1963, 373-4, contr. E. S. Staveley, *Greek and Roman Voting and Elections*, 81-2, 86-7). The tribes, however, were the basis of the army (22. ii, 61: the military aspect of Cleisthenes' reforms is stressed by H. van Effenterre, *REG* lxxxix 1976, 1-17), the boule (§iii, 43. ii, 62. i), and in due course various offices (e.g. 47, i, ii, 48. i; even the nine archons had a secretary added, to form a college of ten men, one from each tribe [55. i]) and the law courts (63-9). We may therefore assume that, although the demes and the trittyes were far from equal in size, the tribes must when created have been approximately equal; it may be that numbers of hoplites were more important than total numbers of citizens (cf. Gomme, *Hist. Comm. Thuc.*, ii. 73-4, W. E. Thompson, *Hist.* xiii 1964, 400-1, P. J. Bicknell, *Hist.* Einz. xix 1972, 19-21). According to *A.P.* the trittyes were put together by lot to form the tribes, and it may be that that was Cleisthenes' original intention, foreshadowed in his legislation before the detailed work was done, but if equal tribes were to be obtained from unequal trittyes we may doubt if that is what was actually done (cf. C. W. J. Eliot, *Phoen.* Supp. v 1962, 138-46, *Phoen.* xxii 1968, 3-17; contr. Thompson, *op. cit.*, 402-8, Bicknell, *op. cit.*, 49-51; Andrewes, *CQ*² xxvii 1977, 245-6, suggests that trittyes were named and allotted to tribes before their composition was worked out in detail): true or false, this is a point which could not be deduced from knowledge of how the tribes and their subdivisions were organised in the fourth century.

There have been many attempts to make political sense of Cleisthenes' reform by explaining why his tribal system should have been constructed as it was: the most fruitful are those which are based firmly on detailed knowledge of that construction (especially, Eliot, *Phoen.* Supp. v 1962, 136-47, D. M. Lewis, *Hist.* xii 1963, 22-40, and *Gnomon* xxxv 1963, 723-5 [reviewing Eliot]). Cleisthenes will at least have 'mixed up' the people, and have encouraged the unification of the state, by combining in one tribe men from different parts of Attica (it may be significant that the ἄστυ, where most of the families active in city politics must have lived, was distributed through all ten tribes: e.g. D. W. Bradeen, *TAPA* lxxxvi 1955, 22–30). Lewis attractively suggests that the mixture was more subtle than this, and that in constructing his trittyes Cleisthenes deliberately cut across older divisions, separated cult centres from their natural hinterlands, and so on (cf. Bicknell, *Mnem.*[4] xxviii 1975, 57–60, French trans. *REG* lxxxix 1976, 599–603). The old network of influences was one in which the Alcmaeonids were not well placed, and Cleisthenes could claim that he was doing away with unfair channels of influence (see Ostwald, *Nomos and the Beginnings of the Athenian Democracy*, 153–7, on Cleisthenes and ἰσονομία; Andrewes, *op. cit.*, 242–3, 247), while doing his own family a good turn; since their homes to the south of the city were assigned to three tribes, and the coastal strip towards Sunium, where they may have had land and dependants (cf. p. 186), was assigned to the same three tribes, it seems that in addition they were well placed in the new system and could count on seeing familiar faces in the meetings of their tribes.

καὶ δημότας ... σφᾶς αὐτοὺς τῶν δήμων: As stated in the previous note, citizenship was in future to depend on membership of a deme, and so the use of the δημοτικόν with the personal name to identify a man became increasingly common. But even before Cleisthenes' reforms gave the deme its new significance the demotic could be used in this way (cf. pp. 81–2, and 14. iv with commentary), and by the fourth century the demotic had not supplanted the patronymic (to which *A.P.* must refer in πατρόθεν, pace J. H. Oliver, *Hist.* ix 1960, 504–5) but had been added to it, so that the politician Demosthenes was Δημοσθένης Δημοσθένους Παιανιεύς (see Pl. *Dem.* 20. iii for the delight which Philip of Macedon took in the jingle). City demes, more artificial than rural demes, would inevitably catch on more slowly (A. E. Raubitschek, *Actes du 2ᵉ congrès international d'épigraphie grecque et latine, 1952*, 67–9 = *CJ* xlviii 1952/3, 117–19; M&L, p. 41), and it has been suggested that at the beginning of the fifth century the use of the demotic was a sign of 'democratic' leanings (E. Vanderpool, *Lectures ... L. T. Semple*, ii 1966–70, 20–2, Bicknell, *Hist.* Einz. xix 1972, 43–4); it is also used unusually frequently on ostraca against the immigrant Meno (Vanderpool, *op. cit.*, 21).

If Cleisthenes ordered the use of the demotic with a man's name to identify him officially, his order was very little obeyed until more than a century afterwards, and more probably *A.P.* is making a false inference from the practice of his own time; like the argument from μὴ φυλοκρινεῖν in §ii, this argument could have been used already by his source, but may well be his own. If the order is conjectural, its alleged purpose—to conceal the fact that the father of, say, one Callicles was Thrax and an obvious immigrant—must be conjectural likewise: this purpose could only be achieved if all cases were like my example, where an immigrant with an obviously foreign name gave his son an acceptably Athenian name, and even in such cases it is unlikely that Athenian inquisitiveness will have allowed many sons of immigrants to hide their origin.

As he fails to mention in its chronological place the διαψηφισμός by which some men were removed from the registers on the fall of the tyranny (13. v with commentary), *A.P.* fails to mention directly the enfranchisements which he invokes to explain the use of the demotic. Kaibel & Wilamowitz supposed that a note of the enfranchisements had dropped out at the beginning of §ii (cf. *ad loc.*); more probably the enfranchisements, had they been mentioned, would have been mentioned here, and their loss is due not to omission by a scribe but to *A.P.*'s compression of his source material.

Arist. *Pol.* III. 1275 B 34–9 mentions the enfranchisements in a notoriously difficult passage:

ἀλλ' ἴσως ἐκεῖνο μᾶλλον ἔχει ἀπορίαν, ὅσοι μετέσχον μεταβολῆς γενομένης πολιτείας, οἷον ⟨ἃ⟩ Ἀθήνησιν ἐποίησε Κλεισθένης μετὰ τὴν τῶν τυράννων ἐκβολήν. πολλοὺς γὰρ ἐφυλέτευσε ξένους καὶ δούλους μετοίκους. τὸ δ' ἀμφισβήτημα πρὸς τούτους ἐστὶν οὐ τίς πολίτης ἀλλὰ πότερον ἀδίκως ἢ δικαίως.

J. H. Oliver, *Hist.* ix 1960, 503–7, supposed that the references both in Arist. *Pol.* and in *A.P.* are to the institution of metics as a separate class (cf. F. R. Wüst, *Hist.* xiii 1964, 370–3, E. Grace, *Klio* lvi 1974, 353–68): he was answered by D. Kagan, *Hist.* xii 1963, 41–6; D. Whitehead, *PCPS* Supp. iv 1977, 143–7, accepts the rebuttal of Oliver's view but believes that Cleisthenes did in fact institute the class of metics. Otherwise all have agreed that this passage ascribes to Cleisthenes the enfranchisement of πολλοὺς ξένους καὶ δούλους μετοίκους—but who are they? Many have deleted μετοίκους as a gloss on ξένους interpolated at the wrong point (cf. H. Hommel, *RE* xv [1931/2], 1432–3, Jacoby, *Supp.* ii. 143 n. 15, Day & Chambers, *A.H.A.D.*, 25 n. 8, 117 with n. 57), but there are fifth-century texts which use the term ξένος μέτοικος (Soph. *O.T.* 452, Ar. *Eq.* 347, cf. Eur. *Suppl.* 892: cf. J. K. Davies, *CJ* lxxiii 1977/8, 116 [in his reference to Harrison, *L.A.*, i, read 188]), so it is perhaps better to follow Newman in taking ξένους and δούλους as parallel adjectives qualifying μετοίκους (*ad loc.* and i. 231 n. 1, cf. K.-W. Welwei, *Gymnasium* lxxiv 1967, 435–6). The phrase in fact tells us little when we reflect that if non-citizens were to be made citizens foreign immigrants and slaves were the only available candidates: we should presumably think of the immigrant craftsmen first encouraged by Solon to come to Attica (with the offer of citizenship: Pl. *Sol.* 24. iv) and no doubt encouraged by the tyrants also (e.g. Hignett, *H.A.C.*, 112, 133), and of the tyrants' mercenaries (e.g. Bicknell, *PP* xxiv 1969, 34–7: cf. D.S. xi. 72. iii–73. i, on fifth-century Sicily); Bicknell suggested the slaves might be those brought back from abroad by Solon (but in *Hist.* Einz. xix 1972, 51 n. 9, he withdrew the suggestion, and connected the slaves with the tyrants' mercenary forces; the slaves redeemed by Solon are likely to have been men whose right to citizenship was not in doubt), Welwei thought they were freedmen or descendants of freedmen. The men now given citizenship must be largely identical with those deprived of it by the διαψηφισμός of 13. v. They will have been a minority in the δῆμος, and although they may have had some influence on the assembly of citizens which adopted Cleisthenes' proposals (cf. D. M. Lewis, *Hist.* xii 1963, 38) Cleisthenes' main appeal will have been to those whose citizenship had not been challenged (cf. Wade-Gery, *CQ* xxvii 1933, 25–6 = *Essays*, 148–50).

τοὺς νεοπολίτας: *Pace* Oliver, *op. cit.*, 505, the word must mean 'new citizens'. The only other instances listed in LSJ are late: D.S. xiv. 7. iv, Ath. iv. 138 A, App. *B.C.* i. 214 (49. iv).

τῶν δήμων ἀναγορεύωσιν: Fr. IIa of the Berlin papyrus begins at ἀναγορεύωσιν and runs to Κ]λεισθέ[νης in 22. iv: see M. H. Chambers, *TAPA* xcviii 1967, 59–60.

21. v. κατέστησε δὲ καὶ δημάρχους: The demes were not merely used as the basis of Athenian citizenship but were for the first time given a corporate existence, with their own presiding magistrate, the demarch (at first perhaps elected, later appointed by lot), and assembly (for decrees of deme assemblies see *IG* i² 183–9, ii² 1172–1221, and the decrees listed by Traill, *Hesp.* Supp. xiv 1975, 74–5 n. 10; for an assembly of the deme Halimus in 346/5 see D. LVII. *Eub.* 9–14). Similarly there were to be corporate activities of the new trittyes (about which we hear little: D. M. Lewis, *Hist.* xii 1963, 34–5) and the new tribes (for decrees of tribes see *IG* ii² 1138–71). The introduction of local political machinery will have been very important, as it provided a means by which the citizens could gain political interest and experience on a domestic level and by which the supremacy of the aristocrats in local matters could in due course be challenged (cf. R. J. Hopper, *The Basis of the Athenian Democracy*, 14–18): this was rightly stressed by J. W. Headlam, *Election by Lot at Athens*, 165–8, and this aspect of his reorganisation may have played a large part in winning Cleisthenes his popularity (cf. D. Kienast, *HZ* cc 1965, 277–9, Ostwald, *Nomos and the Beginnings of the Athenian Democracy*, 149–60).

Dem. Phal. 228 F 31 is a confused note attributing to οἱ περὶ Σόλωνα the institution of δήμαρχοι as local justices: it is most unlikely that Demetrius himself made this mistake. The δικάσται κατὰ δήμους (16. v with commentary), as a Pisistratid institution, were probably abolished on the fall of the tyranny; E. Vanderpool suggested that the earlier text on a stele from Marathon which he published in *Hesp.* xi 1942, 329–37 (=*SEG* x 2, A), belongs to a Cleisthenic law entrusting the settlement of small disputes to the deme authorities (see esp. his pp. 332–3), but confirmation is still lacking.

τὴν αὐτὴν ἔχοντες ἐπιμέλειαν ... ἀντὶ τῶν ναυκραριῶν ἐποίησεν: For what little is known of the ναυκραρίαι and their officers the ναύκραροι see 8. iii with commentary. *A.P.* probably means that the ναυκραρίαι were abolished (he was so understood by the lexicographers, e.g. Poll. VIII. 108, Hes. [Δ 824] δήμαρχοι, [N 118] ναύκλαροι, Phot. ναυκραρία, ναύκραροι; but to avoid a direct clash with Clid. 323 F 8 he is interpreted by Sandys and by Bicknell, *Hist.* Einz. xix 1972, 50 n. 8, to mean that the ναυκραρίαι merely lost some of their functions). According to Clidemus, when Cleisthenes created the ten tribes he subdivided them into fifty ναυκραρίαι: most accept the conflict between this and what we read in *A.P.*; some have noted that at the beginning of the fifth century Athens' fleet comprised fifty ships (H. VI. 89 cf. 132) and have preferred Clidemus, supposing that the ναυκραρίαι were abolished by Themistocles when he enlarged the fleet (22. vii with commentary: e.g. Wilamowitz, *A.u.A.*, ii. 165–6 n. 52, Hignett, *H.A.C.*, 21–2, 69, Jacoby *ad loc.*); but our evidence is insufficient to decide the question.

προσηγόρευσε δὲ τῶν δήμων ... ἔτι τοῖς τόποις: Many of the demes are named after local features (e.g. Κηφισία, Ποταμός) or plants (e.g. Ἐλαιοῦς, Μαραθών, Φηγοῦς); frequently if not always these names were already in use as place names before Cleisthenes' reforms (e.g. Μαραθών: Hom. *Od.* VII. 80). Similarly the name Κεραμεῖς was given to the deme which included the potters' quarter of the city, the Κεραμεικός. On the other hand, several demes are given names in patronymic form, and in some cases the families after which they are named are well known: the name Βουτάδαι was given to a deme in the city, to the west of the Agora (cf. Traill, *Hesp.* Supp. xiv 1975, 48), in which one branch of the γένος Βουτάδαι lived (Davies, *A.P.F.*, 348–53; for the other branch see *A.P.F.*, 169–73), and when every citizen registered in the deme could call himself Βουτάδης the γένος in self-defence took to calling itself Ἐτεοβουτάδαι (cf. p. 187); the name Φιλαΐδαι was given to the locality on the east coast previously known as Βραυρών (the home of the Pisistratids: cf. p. 187), and although many have believed that the original or the country home of the Philaids must have been there (e.g. Wilamowitz, *A.u.A.*, ii. 73 n. 4, Sealey, *Hist.* ix 1960, 168–9 = *Essays*, 21, Bicknell, *Hist.*

21. v] COMMENTARY ON THE *ATH. POL.*

Einz. xix 1972, 3 n. 9) their only attested home is at Λακιάδαι, to the west of Βουτάδαι (D. M. Lewis, *Hist.* xii 1963, 25, Davies, *A.P.F.*, 310; location of deme, Traill, *op. cit.*, 49); two names conspicuously not used are Πεισιστρατίδαι and Ἀλκμαιωνίδαι. Lewis concludes from these examples that Cleisthenes' purpose in naming demes after families was not to honour but rather to weaken the families whose names were thus taken in vain (*op. cit.*, 26–7).

ὑπῆρχον ἔτι τοῖς τόποις: The Berlin papyrus has not ἔτι but ἐν, and this has been preferred by Blass, Kaibel & Wilamowitz[3], Thalheim and Oppermann; Π. Ν. Παπαγεώργιος, Ἀθ. iv 1892, 554, suggested ἔτι ἐν. The subject of the verb can only be δῆμοι or κτισάντες: if δῆμοι, the meaning will be something like 'for not all were still connected with a particular locality' (Moore); if οἱ κτισάντες, 'for there were no longer founders in existence for all the places', i.e. not all the founders were now known (cf. Fritz & Kapp, 165 n. 53). The latter gives a more acceptable sense, but it requires δήμοις rather than τόποις (which might be a scribal error after the preceding τόπων), and even with that correction it can hardly be said that *A.P.* has expressed himself clearly; ἔτι is preferable to ἐν.

21. vi. τὰ δὲ γένη καὶ τὰς φρατρίας καὶ τὰς ἱερωσύνας ... κατὰ τὰ πάτρια: Arist. *Pol.* VI. 1319 B 19–27, mentioning the creation of more units by Cleisthenes and in Cyrene, says φυλαί τε γὰρ ἕτεραι ποιητέαι πλείους καὶ φατρίαι, καὶ τὰ τῶν ἰδίων ἱερῶν συνακτέον εἰς ὀλίγα καὶ κοινά, and if we suppose that all this is to be applied to the work of Cleisthenes in Athens we have a *prima facie* conflict between the *Politics* and *A.P.* But it is not necessary that each of Aristotle's general points should be applicable to each of his examples (cf. Newman *ad loc.* [iv. 522], Wade-Gery, *CQ* xxvii 1933, 26–7 = *Essays*, 150–1), and Cleisthenes' creation of new tribes may be all that Aristotle had in mind. What *A.P.* says may be accepted (though some have been led by *Pol.* to suppose that Cleisthenes did create new phratries: e.g. Sandys; Hammond, *Studies*, 142–4). Having deprived the old kinship organisations of their responsibility for the citizenship, and having constructed his new organisation so as to undermine the influence of the old, Cleisthenes did not need either to abolish or to reorganise the old, but could leave them to wither. On the whole the old tribes and trittyes did wither, and *A.P.* does not think it necessary to mention that they were left alone; but the γένη, and the phratries built up around the γένη, and the old priesthoods attached to particular γένη and phratries, maintained a vigorous existence in spite of Cleisthenes.†

The regular φρατρίας is the spelling of the Berlin papyrus; the London papyrus has φατρίας (which is the form used in the MSS of Arist. *Pol.*, but the epigraphic instance cited by Meisterhans &

Schwyzer, *G.a.I.*, 82 with n. 701, has not survived in *IG* ii² 1239, 1). The London papyrus has ἱερωσύνας here (the word is not preserved on the Berlin papyrus), —ο— in 42. v and —ω— in 57. ii: Kaibel & Wilamowitz¹⁻² emended to —εω— in each case, but —ω— may stand as that, —εω— and —ειω— are all found in fourth-century inscriptions (cf. Meisterhans & Schwyzer, *G.a.I.*, 46 with n. 333, and add the instances of —εω— in *Hesp.* vii 1, 8–9, etc.).

ταῖς δὲ φυλαῖς ... οὓς ἀνεῖλεν ἡ Πυθία, δέκα: Cf. H. v. 66. ii (... ἐξευρὼν δὲ ἑτέρων ἡρώων ἐπωνυμίας ἐπιχωρίων, πάρεξ Αἴαντος· τοῦτον δέ, ἅτε ἀστυγείτονα καὶ σύμμαχον, ξεῖνον ἐόντα προσέθετο), and the lexica *s.v.* ἐπώνυμοι; Paus. I. 5. ii(–iv) gives an account of the heroes chosen, and x. 10. i reports statues of seven at Delphi (on which see P. Vidal-Naquet, *RH* ccxxxviii 1967, 281–302); there is a study of the ten heroes by U. Kron, *AM* Bhft. v 1976. The statues of the ten tribal ἐπώνυμοι (with appropriate additions and subtractions in the Hellenistic and Roman periods) were set up in the Agora, and their base served as a state notice board, where temporary notices of various kinds were displayed (e.g. 53. iv, Ar. *Pax*, 1183–4, And. I. *Myst.* 83, D. xx. *Lept.* 94, xxi. *Mid.* 103, xxiv. *Tim.* 18, 23, A. III. *Ctes.* 38–9; *testimonia* collected by R. E. Wycherley, *The Athenian Agora*, iii, pp. 85–90). The monument opposite the Old Bouleuterium by the road running along the west side of the Agora, which used to be dated to the late fifth century (R. Stillwell, *Hesp.* ii 1933, 137–9, *Agora Guide*², 54–5), is now dated a little after 350, and supposed to be the successor of a monument of *c.* 430 sited farther south (T. L. Shear, jr, *Hesp.* xxxix 1970, 145–222, cf. Travlos, *Pictorial Dictionary*, 210–12, H. A. Thompson & R. E. Wycherley, *The Athenian Agora*, xiv. 38–41, *Agora Guide*³, 70–2; identification of earlier monument doubted by Kron, *op. cit.*, 229–31); if, as we might expect, a similar monument was erected soon after the creation of the ten tribes, it has yet to be found (for Travlos' guess at a site near the prytaneum see above, p. 105).

In view of the Alcmaeonids' association with Delphi (cf. 19. iv with commentary, and Pl. *Sol.* 11. ii) it should cause no surprise that Apollo was asked to give his blessing to the new organisation by naming the ten tribes; Kron, *op. cit.*, 29–31, argues that Apollo did not choose from a longer list but approved ten heroes chosen by Cleisthenes. The ten names chosen (in what became for certain purposes an official order:[23] e.g. *IG* i² 943) were Ἐρεχθηίς, Αἰγηίς, Πανδιονίς, Λεωντίς, Ἀκαμαντίς, Οἰνηίς, Κεκροπίς, Ἱπποθωντίς, Αἰαντίς and Ἀντιοχίς; Herodotus regarded Ajax, of Salamis, as a neighbour and a foreigner, and to the Athenians Salamis was not a part of

[23] A. E. Raubitschek, *AJA*² lx 1956, 280–1 n. 4, suggested that before the mid fifth century there was a different official order, but he was answered by W. K. Prichett, *U. Calif. Pub. Cl. Arch.* IV. ii 1960, 146–7.

Attica but a possession (54. viii, 62. ii, with commentary, cf. p. 253).

Mention must be made at the end of ch. 21 of an important omission of which *A.P.* is often accused: he says nothing of any change affecting the magistrates or the Areopagus, or of any change affecting the powers (as opposed to the membership) of the boule or assembly, though there is a vague reference in 22. i to 'other laws' of Cleisthenes. Many have assumed that, although neither *A.P.* nor any other source mentions them, such changes must have been made by Cleisthenes (e.g. Grote, *H.G.* [1869–84], iv. 62 sqq., Busolt, *G.G.*, ii². 430–9, Bonner & Smith, *Administration of Justice*, i. 195–7 [in a chapter entitled 'The Judicial Reforms of Cleisthenes']), but what we know of Athens in the period between Cleisthenes and Ephialtes can be explained without such assumptions (Hignett, *H.A.C.*, 145–8, is suitably cautious; on εἰσαγγελία see below, p. 316). There is one change not in the distribution of power but in the mechanism of the state which seems likely: a change in the appointment of the archons from the tyrants' direct election to the allotment of particular offices within an elected college (see on 22. v). P. Cloché, *REG* xxxiii 1920, 28–35, supposed that when an oath was administered to the boule in 501/0 the boule must have lost substantial powers which it had been given by Cleisthenes, but I believe that the oath marks not a departure from Cleisthenes' reform but the culmination of it (cf. 22. ii with commentary).

Nothing more is heard of Cleisthenes himself, but there is no need to believe that he fell from favour: by now he may well have been over sixty, and he probably died a natural death (cf. Davies, *A.P.F.*, 375); there is no more foundation for the suggestion that like Solon he went on his travels (R. D. Cromey, *Hist.* xxviii 1979, 129–47) than for any other solution.

22. i. δημοτικωτέρα πολὺ τῆς Σόλωνος ἐγένετο ἡ πολιτεία: 9. i listed τῆς Σόλωνος πολιτείας τρία ... τὰ δημοτικώτατα, 27. i says that in the time of Pericles δημοτικωτέραν ἔτι συνέβη γενέσθαι τὴν πολιτείαν, 29. iii reports the reference of Clitophon in 411 to τοὺς πατρίους νόμους οὓς Κλεισθένης ἔθηκεν ὅτε καθίστη τὴν δημοκρατίαν and explains that an oligarch could speak of Cleisthenes in these terms ὡς οὐ δημοτικὴν ἀλλὰ παραπλησίαν οὖσαν τὴν Κλεισθένους πολιτείαν τῇ Σόλωνος; in the summary of constitutional changes in 41. ii *A.P.* includes τρίτη ... ἡ ἐπὶ Σόλωνος, ἀφ' ἧς ἀρχὴ δημοκρατίας ἐγένετο, and πέμπτη ... ἡ Κλεισθένους, δημοτικωτέρα τῆς Σόλωνος. H. VI. 131 refers to Κλεισθένης ... ὁ τὰς φυλὰς καὶ τὴν δημοκρατίην Ἀθηναίοισι καταστήσας, cf. in the fourth century Is. VII. *Areop.* 16 (ἐκείνην τὴν δημοκρατίαν ... ἣν Σόλων μὲν ὁ δημοτικώτατος γενόμενος ἐνομοθέτησε, Κλεισθένης δ' ὁ τοὺς τυράννους ἐκβαλὼν καὶ τὸν δῆμον καταγαγὼν πάλιν ἐξ ἀρχῆς κατέστησεν), XV. *Antid.* 232, 306, XVI. *Big.* 26–7, Arist. *Pol.* VI. 1319

B 20–1 (Κλεισθένης ... βουλόμενος αὐξῆσαι τὴν δημοκρατίαν); but according to Pl. *Cim.* 15. iii in 462/1 Cimon was accused of trying to τὴν ἐπὶ Κλεισθένους ἐγείρειν ἀριστοκρατίαν. These quotations speak for themselves: in the time of Ephialtes it was possible to speak disparagingly of Cleisthenes; but thereafter according to one's political standpoint one could say that he took a step in the direction of full democracy or that he revived Solon's 'respectable' democracy, and still subscribe to the view that he was a man to be praised. *A.P.*'s sympathies are not with the extreme democracy (cf. Introduction, pp. 9–10): in ch. 9, though he singled out democratic features of Solon's dispensation, he took care to dissociate him from the democracy later built on his foundations; in accordance with his view of Athens' political history as an intermittent progress towards the full democracy (41. ii with commentary, cf. pp. 7–9) he judges that Cleisthenes' régime took Athens further towards democracy than Solon's, and this judgment is correct.

On the heroes of the Athenian democracy see E. Ruschenbusch, *Hist.* vii 1958, 398–424 (on Cleisthenes, 418–21), and discussion above, p. 159. In the latter part of the fifth century the democrats regarded Cleisthenes as their founding hero, but with the antiquarian research and propaganda battles which began at the end of the century the origins of the democracy were traced further back. At the time of Cleisthenes the word δημοκρατία had probably not yet been coined, and the slogan with which he campaigned was probably ἰσονομία (cf. J. A. O. Larsen, *Essays ... G. H. Sabine*, 1–16, G. Vlastos, *AJP* lxxiv 1953, 337–66, Ostwald, *Nomos and the Beginnings of the Athenian Democracy, passim*, H. W. Pleket, *Τάλαντα* iv 1972, 63–81).[24]

καὶ γὰρ συνέβη τοὺς μὲν Σόλωνος νόμους ἀφανίσαι τὴν τυραννίδα διὰ τὸ μὴ χρῆσθαι: Contrast H. I. 59. vi (οὔτε τιμὰς τὰς ἐούσας συνταράξας οὔτε θέσμια μεταλλάξας, ἐπί τε τοῖσι κατεστεῶσι ἔνεμε τὴν πόλιν κοσμέων καλῶς τε καὶ εὖ), T. VI. 54. vi (τὰ δὲ ἄλλα αὐτὴ ἡ πόλις τοῖς πρὶν κειμένοις νόμοις ἐχρῆτο, πλὴν καθ' ὅσον αἰεί τινα ἐπεμέλοντο σφῶν αὐτῶν ἐν ταῖς ἀρχαῖς εἶναι), *A.P.* 16. viii (ἐβούλετο πάντα διοικεῖν κατὰ τοὺς νόμους), Pl. *Sol.* 31. viii (καὶ γὰρ ἐφύλαττε τοὺς πλείστους νόμους τοὺς Σόλωνος, ἐμμένων πρῶτος αὐτὸς καὶ τοὺς φίλους ἀναγκάζων); and see commentary on 16. viii. As regards the formalities, it is likely that the other texts are right and this passage is wrong, that on the whole Solon's institutions did survive but the tyrants saw to it that they worked in such a way as to yield the desired results.

The Berlin papyrus has χρᾶσθαι, not used in Attic until the Hellenistic period, for the London papyrus' χρῆσθ(αι).

[24] K. H. Kinzl, *Gymnasium* lxxxv 1978, 117–27, 312–26, suggests that δημοκρατία was coined in the time of Cleisthenes, as a slogan not for 'democracy' but for 'deme-power': this seems improbable.

22. i] COMMENTARY ON THE *ATH. POL.*

και[ν]ούς δ' άλλους θεΐναι τὸν Κλεισθένη: Apart from the law on ostracism, and possibly the institution of the ten generals, we cannot tell what 'other' laws *A.P.* has in mind.

στοχαζόμενον τοῦ πλήθους: Sandys compares Arist. *Pol.* IV. 1296 B 36–7 (στοχάζεσθαι χρὴ τῶν μέσων), Polyb. VI. 38. ii (πρὸς τὸ πλῆθος ἀεὶ στοχαζόμενος).

ἐν οἷς ἐτέθη καὶ ὁ περὶ τοῦ ὀστρακισμοῦ νόμος: Here again *A.P.* suffers from over-compression. The subject of ostracism is raised, only to be dropped without adequate explanation and then resumed in §iii. Also the figures in §§ii–iii yield too few years between Cleisthenes' reform and Marathon, and one solution that has been proposed is a lacuna at the end of §i. Probably the chronological difficulty is to be resolved by emendation in §ii (cf. *ad loc.*), and here there is not a lacuna in the strict sense but the author himself has abbreviated his material too drastically for coherence and, knowing that there is more material on ostracism to follow, has said less about it here than he ought. Cf. p. 249, on 21. i–ii.

22. ii. πρῶτον μὲν οὖν ἔτει πέμπτῳ μετὰ ταύτην τὴν κατάστασιν ἐφ' Ἑρμοκρέοντος ἄρχοντος: The archonship of Hermocreon is not attested elsewhere: the London papyrus reads Ἑρμουκρέοντος, and the beginning of the name is not preserved in the Berlin papyrus, but the correct form must be Ἑρμο— (cf. F. Bechtel, *Die historischen Personennamen des Griechischen*, 164–5).

The last date mentioned is the archonship of Isagoras, securely assigned to 508/7, and the next is the archonship of Phaenippus, securely assigned to 490/89 (21. i, 22. iii, cf. p. 195); but if Hermocreon was archon in the 5th year after Isagoras and Phaenippus in the 12th after Hermocreon there are not enough years to fill this interval. The solution most often adopted is that of Kenyon[1-3] (cf. Sandys; T. J. Cadoux, *JHS* lxviii 1948, 115–16; Hignett, *H.A.C.*, 337): the 5th year after Isagoras, 504/3, is already occupied by Acestorides (D.H. *A.R.* v. 37. i), but the 12th year before Phaenippus, 501/0, is not otherwise occupied, so Hermocreon is to be assigned to 501/0 and πέμπτῳ (in both London and Berlin papyri) corrected to ὀγδόῳ (ε' corrected to η', if we suppose that at some stage in the transmission of the text alphabetic numerals were used: in the London papyrus letters are used for ordinal numerals in 32. i, 47. iv, 54. ii). This is better than the view of Wilamowitz, *A.u.A.*, i. 24–5, that κατάστασιν refers to the year after Cleisthenes' legislation, 507/6, that πέμπτῳ is to be retained and Hermocreon placed in 503/2, and in §iii δωδεκάτῳ is to be emended to τετάρτῳ καὶ δεκάτῳ (ιβ' to ιδ'). Others refuse to emend and suppose that a third interval of time has been lost, either at the end of §i, where there should be legislation dated to 505/4 (F. Schachermeyr, *Klio* xxv 1932, 346–7 =

Forschungen und Betrachtungen, 72–3, G. V. Sumner, *CQ*² xi 1961, 35–7; but in *BICS* xi 1964, 84–5, Sumner preferred to emend, without deciding between Kenyon and Wilamowitz) or between the two sentences of §ii (considered by Cadoux, *loc. cit.*, who would then date the first to 504/3 and the second to 501/0 and suppose that Hermocreon has been named in the wrong place; preferred with the improbable assumption of exclusive counting, so that the first sentence, with Hermocreon, falls in 503/2 and the second in 502/1, by E. Meyer, *G.d.A.*, iii². 745, A. E. Samuel, *Greek and Roman Chronology*, 205). Neither of these alternatives is convincing: κατάστασιν ought to refer to a major episode, such as the enactment of the measures described in 21; and to accept the second alternative one must assume either exclusive counting or a major dislocation, while ἔπειτα here can as easily be logical as temporal (Sumner, *BICS* xi 1964, 84, against C. W. Fornara, *CQ*² xiii 1963, 104, and notice πρῶτον... ἔπειτα... in 43. iii; more recently D. J. McCargar, *RM*² cxix 1976, 315–23, has supposed that it means specifically 'in the following year'). Kenyon's remains the best explanation, and we should emend to ὀγδόῳ here.

τῇ βουλῇ τοῖς πεντακοσίοις τόν ὅρκον ἐποίησαν ὅν ἔτι καὶ νῦν ὀμνύουσιν: Although the oath was no doubt essentially the same in *A.P.*'s day as in 501/0, an undertaking to serve uncorruptly and in the best interests of Athens, various more specific undertakings are known to have been added to the oath at various later dates: on the contents of the oath see especially Wade-Gery, *BSA* xxxiii 1932/3, 113–22, Rhodes, *A.B.*, 194–9. There have been two interpretations of the introduction of the oath: that it marks a departure from Cleisthenes' dispensation, by which the boule undertook not to do various things which it had previously been able to do (P. Cloché, *REG* xxxiii 1920, 28–35, J. A. O. Larsen, *Representative Government in Greek and Roman History*, 15–18, cf. Bicknell, *Hist.* Einz. xix 1972, 36–7, *Hist.* xxiii 1974, 161, B. McM. Caven, *JHS* xcv 1975, 244); and that it marks the culmination of Cleisthenes' reforms, and perhaps was first sworn in 501/0 because that was the first year in which there was a boule of five hundred based on Cleisthenes' new tribal organisation (W. Peremans, *LEC* x 1941, 193–201, C. W. J. Eliot, *Phoen.* Supp. v 1962, 145–7 with n. 18, Rhodes, *A.B.*, 191–3); E. Capps argued that a new era for the Great Dionysia, including competitions based on the ten tribes, began in 502/1 (*Hesp.* xii 1943, 10–11, cf. A. W. Pickard-Cambridge rev. J. P. A. Gould & D. M. Lewis, *Dramatic Festivals of Athens*, 71–2, 102–3). In the latter case Alcmeon, in whose archonship the tribes δέκα ἐγένοντο (Poll. VIII. 110), should perhaps be placed not in 507/6 (Cadoux, *op. cit.*, 114, Samuel, *op. cit.*, 204–5) but in 502/1, which is otherwise unoccupied (Eliot, *loc. cit.*; cf. above, p. 244). I stand by my preference for the second interpretation: the working out of the details of Cleisthenes' new system could have taken several years, and if what happened in 501/0 represented a major departure from his dispensation we ought to hear more about it.

ἔπειτα τοὺς στρατηγοὺς ᾑροῦντο ... ὁ πολέμαρχος: For the London papyrus' ἐξ ἑκάστης φυλῆς the Berlin papyrus has ἀ]πὸ φυλῆς ἑκάστης. *A.P.* has to say many times in the course of his work that one man is appointed from each tribe: as far as possible he varies his form of expression (cf. Introduction, pp. 42–3); the form given in the London papyrus recurs (without ἕνα) in 8. iv, 31. i, 55. i, that given in the Berlin papyrus recurs (without ἕνα) in 43. ii; for other forms used see Sandys' index *s.v.* φυλή. Blass inserted the article here and wherever it is not included with ἕκαστος (cf. Kaibel, *Stil und Text*, 189–90), but we cannot be sure that *A.P.* was incapable of omitting it. On ἔπειτα see above.

In 17. ii *A.P.* writes of Pisistratus στρατηγεῖν ἐν τῷ πρὸς Μεγαρέας πολέμῳ περὶ Σαλαμῖνος, and in 22. iii he writes that Pisistratus δημαγωγὸς καὶ στρατηγὸς ὢν τύραννος κατέστη; στρατηγοί are mentioned also in the 'Draconian constitution', 4. ii–iii. Pisistratus' στρατηγίη in the Megarian war is mentioned in H. 1. 59. iv; Pl. *Sol.* 11. ii writes of the First Sacred War that ἐν ... τοῖς τῶν Δελφῶν ὑπομνήμασιν Ἀλκμαίων, οὐ Σόλων, στρατηγὸς ἀναγέγραπται. N. G. L. Hammond is thus right to insist that Cleisthenes' στρατηγοί were not a total innovation, but his assumption that the earlier στρατηγοί were regular, annual officials has no foundation, and I prefer the contrary assumption that they were occasional, *ad hoc* appointments for wars fought outside Attica (*CQ*[2] xix 1969, 111–14 = *Studies*, 346–51; *ad hoc* appointments, Sealey, *Hist.* ix 1960, 173 = *Essays*, 26, E. Badian, *Antichthon* v 1971, 26 n. 68; see also C. W. Fornara, *Hist.* Einz. xvi 1971, 1–10). He is right again to insist that ᾑροῦντο κατὰ φυλάς, ἐξ ἑκάστης φυλῆς ἕνα means simply that the generals were elected one from each tribe, and that κατὰ φυλάς does not mean that each tribe elected its own general (cf. 44. iv, quoted below): it is possible, but by no means necessary, that each tribe elected a short list of candidates, but the final selection will have been made by the assembly (*opp. citt.*, 112 = 348, comparing 22. v, 42. ii, 48. i, 56. iii, 63. i–ii, iv); I doubt the suggestion of K. H. Kinzl, *Greece and the Eastern Mediterranean ... F. Schachermeyr*, 208, that a πρόκρισις was made by the boule (cf. his emendation of 22. v, cited *ad loc.*).

The relative powers of generals and polemarch have been much disputed; what *A.P.* says has to be interpreted in the light of the Marathon campaign. Herodotus tells a detailed and consistent story: Philippides was sent to Sparta by the generals (vi. 105. i, 106. i); the army was led out by the ten generals, one of them being Miltiades (103. i), who was elected by the δῆμος (104. ii); at

Marathon the generals were equally divided and the polemarch appointed by lot, who at that time was ἑνδέκατος ψηφιδοφόρος, ... ὁμόψηφον ... τοῖσι στρατηγοῖσι, was asked to give a casting vote (109. i–ii, 110); the πρυτανηίη among the generals rotated daily, but supporters of Miltiades let him preside on their days (110); in the battle the polemarch was stationed on the right wing, as the law at that time required (111. i). This must surely be believed: the generals were not subordinate commanders of tribal contingents (that duty fell to the taxiarchs: 61. iii with commentary) but were already the real commanders of the army; the polemarch was titular commander-in-chief, who could vote with the generals, and on this exceptional occasion, when the enemy were in Attica and a full levy under all ten generals went out to meet them, he accompanied the army and took the post of honour and danger on the right wing; even so, he was not the actual commander of the army but the generals took it in turn to hold the πρυτανηίη. See Hammond, *JHS* lxxxviii 1968, 48–50 cf. 45 = *Studies*, 229–33 cf. 223–4, *CQ*[2] xix 1969, 119–23 = *Studies*, 358–64, criticised in different ways by A. R. Burn, *JHS* lxxxix 1969, 119, P. J. Bicknell, *AC* xxxix 1970, 427–42, Fornara, *op. cit.*, 72–3, Badian, *op. cit.*, 26 with n. 68, 31–2: I agree with Hammond as modified by Badian.

How the polemarch was appointed is discussed in the commentary on §v. *A.P.*'s only other notes on the appointment of generals are in 44. iv (ποιοῦσι δὲ καὶ τὰς ἀρχαιρεσίας στρατηγῶν ... ἐν τῇ ἐκκλησίᾳ, καθ' ὅ τι ἂν τῷ δήμῳ δοκῇ) and 61. i (χειροτονοῦσι ... στρατηγοὺς δέκα, πρότερον μὲν ἀφ' ⟨ἑκάστης⟩ φυλῆς ἕνα, νῦν δ' ἐξ ἁπάντων); but a little must be said here about the appointment of generals between 501/0 and the time of *A.P.* In 469/8 there was still one general from each tribe (Pl. *Cim.* 8. viii); Andr. 324 F 38 purports to name the ten generals of 441/0 but seems in fact to name eleven, including both Pericles and Glaucon from the tribe Acamantis; except perhaps when emergency appointments were made (e.g. 414/3: T. vii. 16. i) the number of generals remained ten, but it is certain that on a number of occasions after 440 one tribe provided two of the ten, and possible both that on some occasions there were greater departures from the tribal basis of appointment and that there were some departures from the tribal basis between 480 and 440; the earliest year of which we can confidently assert that the tribal basis has been abandoned is 323/2 (cf. on 61. i). Fornara, *op. cit.*, argues that there was a single change, in the late 460's, from election according to tribes to election irrespective of tribes, but some of his identifications are doubtful and it should be accepted that in the late fifth century and much of the fourth generals were elected on a modified tribal basis.

K. J. Dover, *JHS* lxxx 1960, 61–77, has established (against

Beloch, *Die attische Politik seit Perikles*, 274–88) that when a man is designated general δέκατος αὐτός, as in T. I. 116. i, he is not thereby shown to be superior to his colleagues; except when Alcibiades was ἀναρρηθεὶς ἁπάντων ἡγεμὼν αὐτοκράτωρ in 407 (X. *H*. I. iv. 20) the ten generals remained theoretically equal. A modified tribal basis might yet be intended to confer prestige on a man elected with a colleague from his own tribe; or it might be intended to give a fairer opportunity to good men in a tribe which happened to contain one outstanding man, or to allow the use of another good man from elsewhere if one tribe was lacking in talent. Nearly everyone who has written on the subject has made his own guess as to how elections on a modified tribal basis were conducted; it must be borne in mind that despite modern usage there is no authority for describing one (or more) of the generals as elected ἐξ ἁπάντων, and that our notions of fairness may differ from those of the Athenians. The most promising approach is that of M. Piérart, *BCH* xcviii 1974, 125–46: he suggests that the presiding officers in the assembly would take each tribe in turn, inviting the assembly to vote for or against each candidate until a majority in favour of one of the tribe's candidates had been obtained; if in one tribe there was not a majority in favour of any candidate, they would proceed to the next tribe, and after this first phase of the voting had been completed that place would be offered irrespective of tribe to candidates not already elected, and would be given to the first of those for whom a majority could be obtained in this second phase (cf. Hammond, CQ^2 xix 1969, 125 n. 1 = *Studies*, 366 n. 2, on the appointment of the three commanders of the Sicilian expedition of 415; and the Romans' understanding of election by majority vote, e.g. E. S. Staveley, *Greek and Roman Voting and Elections*, 179–81). If this account of the electoral procedure is right, the effect will have been to relax the rule that one general must be chosen from each tribe on those occasions when in some tribe there was not a majority for any candidate, and to allow more than one departure from the tribal basis if there was more than one tribe in which that happened. Before this modification was introduced, a second vote may have been taken on all the candidates in a tribe if on the first there was not a majority for any of them.†

22. iii. ἔτει δὲ μετὰ ταῦτα δωδεκάτῳ ... ἐπὶ Φαινίππου ἄρχοντος: For the chronology see on §ii, and p. 195: it is beyond dispute (though J. A. R. Munro tried to dispute it: *C.A.H.*, iv¹. 232–3) that Phaenippus was archon in 490/89 and that the battle of Marathon was fought at the beginning of that year.

διαλιπόντες ἔτη δύο: That is, τρίτῳ ἔτει, 488/7, when the archon was Anchises (D.H. *A.R.* VIII. I. i: thus Cadoux, *JHS* lxviii 1948, 118, Hignett, *H.A.C.*, 336–7, Samuel, *Greek and Roman Chronology*, 205;

but A. E. Raubitschek, *Hist.* viii 1959, 127-8, places this and the following ostracisms one year later). In the series of events in this chapter *A.P.* does not directly attach an archon's name to any of the ostracisms, though he knows the date of each and dates by archon other events which fell in the same years as the ostracisms of Megacles and Aristides. Ostracism was as likely to generate an official document as any other events mentioned in this chapter, and in view of the nature of ostracism the official records must have been dated. I believe that *A.P.*'s source (identifiable as Androtion: cf. next note) recorded each of the ostracisms under its year (even if he gave them in a single list rather than year by year, as suggested by Raubitschek, *C&M* xix 1958, 105-6, he must surely have dated them), and that *A.P.* has presented the material as he has done in order to avoid the monotony of an annalistic list in which each entry begins ἐπὶ —— ἄρχοντος (cf. Introduction, pp. 42-4).

22. iii-iv. θαρροῦντος ἤδη τοῦ δήμου ... βουλόμενος αὐτόν: For the first phrase cf. 24. i (θαρρούσης ἤδη τῆς πόλεως after the foundation of the Delian League), 27. i (θαρρήσαντας τοὺς πολλοὺς after Pericles προύτρεψεν τὴν πόλιν ἐπὶ τὴν ναυτικὴν δύναμιν); W. L. Newman, *CR* v 1891, 161, compares Is. vii. *Areop.* 3, xii. *Panath.* 133. The δῆμος' confidence is presumably due to the victory at Marathon (but P. Karavites, *Hist.* xxvi 1977, 134-5, suggests a shift in the balance of power after defeat in the war against Aegina).

For the institution of ostracism cf. Andr. 324 F 6 *ap.* Harp. Ἵππαρχος:

... ἄλλος δέ ἐστιν Ἵππαρχος ὁ Χάρμου. ... περὶ δὲ τούτου Ἀνδροτίων ἐν τῇ β΄ φησὶν ὅτι συγγενὴς μὲν ἦν Πεισιστράτου τοῦ τυράννου καὶ πρῶτος ἐξωστρακίσθη, τοῦ περὶ τὸν ὀστρακισμὸν νόμου τότε πρῶτον [on these two words see below] τεθέντος διὰ τὴν ὑποψίαν τῶν περὶ Πεισιστράτου, ὅτι δημαγωγὸς ὢν καὶ στρατηγὸς ἐτυράννησεν.

(In *A.P.* the London papyrus reads ὅτε before Πεισίστρατος: Kenyon[1] emended to ὅτι in the light of Andr.'s ὅτι before δημαγωγὸς; Kaibel & Wilamowitz preferred ὁ γὰρ, but Kaibel expressed doubts in *Stil und Text,* 175; M. H. Chambers, *TAPA* xcviii 1967, 60, reports that the Berlin papyrus reads ὅτι.) Ostracism was also said to have been devised by Cleisthenes as a weapon against the Pisistratids by Ephorus (cf. D.S. xi. 55. i; but Raubitschek, *C&M* xix 1958, 73-109, derives all post-Aristotelian accounts from Theophrastus) and by Phil. 328 F 30; according to Ael. *V.H.* xiii. 24 Cleisthenes not only introduced ostracism but was also its first victim. Theophrastus, writing metaphorically, described Theseus' exclusion from Athens (cf. p. 77) as ostracism, and this was taken literally by some later writers (Suid. [A 4101] ἀρχὴ Σκυρία, schol. Ar. *Plut.* 627, Hieron.

58 Helm, with Raubitschek, *op. cit.*, 78 n. 3); Ptolemaeus Chennus (CI A.D.) attributed ostracism to one Achilles son of Lyson (*ap.* Phot. *Bibl.* 152 A 39–40).

An unparalleled account of ostracism in MS Vat. Gr. 1144, 222 ʳ⁻ᵛ, republished by J. J. Keaney & A. E. Raubitschek, *AJP* xciii 1972, 87–91, asserts that ostracism was originally conducted in the boule, where over two hundred votes against the victim were required: whence this was derived I do not know, but in the absence of confirmatory evidence I am not eager to believe it. It is believed by P. J. Bicknell, *Gnomon* xlvi 1974, 818, D. J. McCargar, *CP* lxxi 1976, 248–52; an attempt to find some factual basis for it is made by R. Develin, *Antichthon* xi 1977, 10–21, who recalls the suggestion of E. Vanderpool that the Areopagus had voted with ostraca to banish Pisistratus and Aristion (cf. above, p. 200) and suggests that this text alludes to a banishment-procedure introduced by Solon.†

No one now doubts that ostracism proper was introduced after the tyranny and that the first victim was Hipparchus; but there has been much disagreement on the apparent clash between *A.P.* and Androtion (the discussions are exhaustively reviewed by R. Thomsen, *The Origin of Ostracism*, 11–60). *A.P.* says that ostracism was introduced by Cleisthenes but not used until 488/7, Androtion according to the received text of Harpocration says that ostracism was instituted when it was first used; yet they tell their different stories in remarkably similar words. Apart from one or two rogue theories there have been two main lines of interpretation. Some accept the conflict, conclude that the Atthidographers disagreed on the question and that there was therefore no reliable tradition, think a lapse of twenty years between institution and first use incredible, and so follow Androtion (e.g. Beloch, *G.G.*², I. ii. 332–3, De Sanctis, *Ἀτθίς*, ¹347 = ²370–1, Hignett, *H.A.C.*, 159–64; cf. J. H. Schreiner, *C&M* xxxi 1976, 84–97, arguing from Lyc. *Leocr.* 117–18 that ostracism was instituted after Marathon for use against τοὺς ἀλιτηρίους καὶ τοὺς προδότας), while a few accept the conflict but are not sure which version is correct (Jacoby *ad loc.*, Day & Chambers, *A.H.A.D.*, 13–15). Others stress the verbal similarity between *A.P.* and the fragment, notice that τότε πρῶτον makes excellent sense with ἐχρήσαντο in *A.P.* but nonsense with τεθέντος in the fragment, and conclude that Harpocration cannot have quoted Androtion accurately and there is no need to reject *A.P.*'s account. Early champions of the latter view supposed that, although he names Androtion, Harpocration has in fact misquoted *A.P.* (Wilamowitz, *A.u.A.*, i. 123 n. 3 cf. 115 n. 27, Kaibel, *Stil und Text*, 174–5, cf. H. Bloch, *Gnomon* xxxi 1959, 492–3); more recently a modification of this view has found favour, that *A.P.* and Harpocration both set out to reproduce the account of Androtion and *A.P.* discharged the task more faithfully (G. V. Sumner, *CQ*² xi 1961, 37 n. 1, *BICS* xi 1964, 79–86, K. J. Dover, *CR*² xiii 1963, 256–7, K. Meister, *Chiron* i 1971, 85–8; cf. earlier F. Schachermeyr, *Klio* xxv 1932, 346 n. 2 = *Forschungen und Betrachtungen*, 72 n. 2). J. J. Keaney, *Hist.* xix 1970, 1–4, cf. xxv 1976, 480–2, claims that the immediate archetype of our MSS of Harpocration had not τότε πρῶτον but the still more nonsensical τότε πρώτου, and suggests that both Androtion and Harpocration actually wrote (e.g.) πρὸ τούτου, less close to the wording of *A.P.* but in factual agreement with him: πρὸ τούτου τεθέντος does not seem very likely, and I prefer to think (with Thomsen, *op. cit.*, 54–5), that the scribes who changed τότε πρώτου to τότε πρῶτον were in fact returning to the original text, a text in which Harpocration garbled what had been written by Androtion. If this is so, the solution of Sumner and his followers is surely right: the verbal resemblance between the two passages is so close that *A.P.* must have been following Androtion; *A.P.* does not always draw attention to disagreements with his predecessors, but it would be surprising if he silently disagreed with Androtion in language so close to his; τότε πρῶτον does make sense with ἐχρήσαντο as it does not with τεθέντος (Chambers, *JHS* xcix 1979, 151–2, defends τότε πρῶτον τεθέντος as acceptable Greek, but it remains true that *A.P.*'s text gives a much better sense than the fragment's text); and *pace* Beloch it was possible 'eine solche Waffe ... 20 Jahre lang in der Scheide rosten zu lassen' (cf. below).†

On the purpose of ostracism there is general agreement in the sources: it was devised after the fall of the tyranny to prevent future tyrannies; it was aimed at those who were too prominent, originally at τοὺς τῶν τυράννων φίλους in general and Hipparchus, its first victim, in particular; and was to be regarded as a democratic institution (*A.P.* 22. i, iii–iv, vi, echoed in other accounts of the institution and of individual ostracisms). In Arist. *Pol.* we find a more general, theoretical approach (which must be based to a considerable extent on the Athenian institution: hardly any information is preserved on comparable institutions elsewhere), describing ostracism as a democratic device to check those who were too powerful (III. 1284 A 17–22, B 15–22, V. 1302 B 15–21, 1308 B 16–19); and the doctrine that ostracism was intended for use against those who were too powerful is found earlier in Thucydides' comment that Hyperbolus was ostracised οὐ διὰ δυνάμεως καὶ ἀξιώματος φόβον, ἀλλὰ διὰ πονηρίαν καὶ αἰσχύνην τῆς πόλεως (VIII. 73. iii). Keaney (*op. cit.*, 4–11) distinguishes in *A.P.* 22 two different explanations of ostracism, that it was aimed at the Pisistratids (which he attributes to Androtion) and that it was a democratic measure against those who became too prominent (which he attributes to Aristotle); but this seems too subtle: it is more likely that for *A.P.* and for Androtion before him ostracism was a 'democratic' institution, devised with particular victims in view but used for a wider purpose afterwards.

Although ancient commentators were in agreement not all have believed that they were right. That ostracism was intended for use specifically against the younger Hipparchus, or against any of the Pisistratids, is unlikely, and as a means of preventing a future tyranny ostracism was unreliable, since a man who was so influential that there was a danger of his becoming tyrant might be able to ensure that a majority of votes was cast against a candidate other than himself. Ostracism would, on the other hand, have provided a more peaceful and civilised way of resolving the conflict between Cleisthenes and Isagoras, which had resulted in Spartan intervention. It has been suggested that Cleisthenes introduced ostracism as a way of resolving such conflicts, either before Cleomenes' intervention, as a weapon with which to threaten Isagoras (G. R. Stanton, *JHS* xc 1970, 180–3, D. W. Knight, *Hist.* Einz. xiii 1970, 21–4), or after, to provide a better way of dealing with future conflicts (G. E. M. de Ste. Croix, in an unpublished essay; Moore, 243, considers both possibilities). The ancient explanation and the modern alternative are not mutually exclusive: Cleisthenes may have thought of the threat to the state both from a single man who threatened to become too powerful and from rival aristocrats who were contending for political supremacy; and if his law did not survive (cf. p. 241) or did not refer to the Pisistratids, later Athenians will easily have concluded from the fact that Hipparchus was the first to be ostracised that Cleisthenes had them in mind.†

On the mechanism of ostracism our principal sources are D.S. XI. 55. ii, Pl. *Arist.* 7. v–vi, Poll. VIII. 20, schol. Ar. *Eq.* 855, Phil. 328 F 30 (Jacoby prints the other texts in his commentary). In the sixth prytany of each year (*A.P.* 43. v; Thomsen, *op. cit.*, 135, suggests that annual consultation of the assembly was a modification of the original scheme) the assembly decided whether to hold an ostracism; if it decided in favour the ostracism was held in the Agora in the eighth prytany; each voter wrote on a potsherd the name of the man whom he most wanted to remove from Athens, and if at least six thousand votes were cast in all (Pl.; Poll., schol. Ar. and Phil. say if six thousand votes were cast against one man, but see Jacoby, and to the studies which he cites add M. Fränkel, *Die attische Geschworengerichte*, 14–19[25]) the man against whom most votes were cast was exiled, without loss of property, for ten years (D.S. gives the period as five years, and Phil. says that it was changed to five, but this is certainly wrong). T. B. L. Webster, *Potter and Patron*

---

[25] G. V. Sumner, *Phoen.* xxix 1975, 198, suggests that after the ostracism of Hyperbolus the Athenians changed to the rule that 6,000 votes must be cast against the victim, but I doubt whether this is right.

in Classical Athens, 142 with pl. 16 (*b*), suggests that the counting of votes at an ostracism is depicted on a cup by the Pan Painter (Ashmolean Museum, Oxford, 1911. 617 = Beazley, *A.R.V.*², i. 559 no. 152 = *C.V.A.*, Oxford, i [*G.B.*, iii], pl. vii. 3).

With the exception of the victim of 486/5 *A.P.* 22 names and dates all the men ostracised in the 480's. The following were or may have been ostracised subsequently: Themistocles, *c.* 470 (see on 25. iii); Cimon, in 462/1 (see on 25. i); the elder Alcibiades, *c.* 460 (Lys. xiv. *Alc. i.* 39, [And.] iv. *Alc.* 34: E. Vanderpool, *Hesp.* xxi 1952, 1–8, xxxvii 1968, 117; ostracised twice?); Meno Μενεκλείδου Γαργήττιος, *c.* 457 (Hes. [*M* 866] Μενωνίδαι: Raubitschek, *Hesp.* xxiv 1955, 286–9); Callias Διδυμίου, 440's ([And.] iv. *Alc.* 32: Vanderpool, *Lectures* ... *L. T. Semple* ii 1966–70, 239–40); Damon Δαμωνίδου Ὄαθεν, 440's or later (see on 27. iv); Thucydides Μελησίου Ἀλωπεκῆθεν, *c.* 443 (see on 28. ii); Hyperbolus Ἀντιφάνους Περιθοίδης, 417–415 (T. viii. 73. iii, Thp. 115 F 96, Pl. *Nic.* 11. i–viii, *Alc.* 13. iv–ix). More than ten thousand of the ostraca used in voting have now been found, and they range over all the men named here and many more—over 130 in all. Clearly there was no list of candidates, and some men would receive one or a few votes on account of private enmity; some men may have been important against whom only a few votes happen to have been found, but we may be sure that those against whom we have many votes were prominent men and serious candidates for ostracism. Most voters gave their candidate's name alone or with patronymic and/or demotic, but a few added further information and/or comment: some instances are mentioned below in connection with the victims of the 480's. One interesting find contains 191 votes against Themistocles, the work of only fourteen hands, and proof that the advantages of an organised effort were soon appreciated (O. Broneer, *Hesp.* vii 1938, 228–41); the institution of ostracism presupposes widespread literacy, but this find and the story in Pl. *Arist.* 7. vii–viii provide a salutary warning. On ostracism in general see especially Raubitschek, *Actes du 2ᵉ congrès international d'épigraphie grecque et latine, 1952*, 59–74 = *CJ* xlviii 1952/3, 113–22, A. R. Hands, *JHS* lxxix 1959, 69–79, M&L 21, Vanderpool, *Lectures* ... *L. T. Semple* ii 1966–70, 215–70, Thomsen, *The Origin of Ostracism*, 61–108 (listing and discussing ostraca known to 1972).†

δημαγωγὸς καὶ στρατηγός: On δημαγωγός and *A.P.*'s use of it see pp. 323–4: in this context the word may be formally equivalent to προστάτης τοῦ δήμου, but it has hostile undertones. On στρατηγοί before Cleisthenes see p. 264.

22. iv. τῶν ἐκείνου συγγενῶν Ἵππαρχος Χάρμου Κολλυτεύς: Probably Charmus was married to a daughter of Hippias (Kirchner,

P.A. 7600, Davies, *A.P.F.*, 451). Hipparchus will have been born *c*. 530 or a little earlier, and is very probably the Hipparchus who is described as καλός on vases of the late sixth century (Beazley, *A.B.V.*, 667, *A.R.V.*[2], ii. 1584) and the Hipparchus who was archon in 496/5 (D.H. *A.R.* vi. 1. i). A grandson of Hippias would naturally be suspect after Hippias had accompanied the Persians to Marathon (H. vi. 107–108. i, 109. iii), but despite much that has been written to the contrary we do not know enough to say whether the fact of his archonship is politically significant. Only twelve ostraca bearing his name are known.

ἔθηκεν ὁ Κλεισθένης: Κ]λειοθέ[νης is the last surviving word on fr. IIa of the Berlin papyrus. On fr. IIb the first surviving word is εἰωθ]-υί[α, in §iv, and the last is κατοι]κεῖν, in §viii: see M. H. Chambers, *TAPA* xcviii 1967, 60–2.

τοὺς τῶν τυράννων φίλους ... εἴων οἰκεῖν τὴν πόλιν: Whether this is *A.P.*'s own comment or is derived from Androtion must remain uncertain. It adds nothing to what is said elsewhere in *A.P.*: that τοὺς τῶν Πεισιστρατιδῶν υἱεῖς were captured and used as a bargaining counter with Hippias in 511/0 (19. vi), that Isagoras was a φίλος ... τῶν τυράννων (20. i) who did συνεξαμαρτάνειν ἐν ταῖς ταραχαῖς (*A.P.* says nothing of him after 508/7), that the first three victims of ostracism were τῶν τυράννων φίλους (22. vi).

χρώμενοι τῇ εἰωθυίᾳ τοῦ δήμου πρᾳότητι: We should retain the papyrus' πραότητι (cf. p. 213). Sandys compares Is. xv. *Antid.* 20 (describing the Athenians as in some circumstances ἐλεημονεστάτους ... καὶ πραοτάτους ἁπάντων ... τῶν Ἑλλήνων), D. xxiv. *Tim.* 51 (ὁ γὰρ τὸν νόμον τοῦτον ... θεὶς ᾔδει τὴν φιλανθρωπίαν καὶ τὴν πρᾳότητα τὴν ὑμετέραν); *A.P.* 16. x says that in the time of Pisistratus the laws against tyranny were πρᾶοι (cf. *ad loc.*), and 16. ii describes Pisistratus himself as πρᾶος.

ὧν ἡγεμὼν καὶ προστάτης ἦν Ἵππαρχος: Doubtless an inference from the fact that of the φίλοι τῶν τυράννων known to have remained in Athens he was the closest to Pisistratus and the first to be ostracised.

22. v. εὐθὺς δὲ τῷ ὑστέρῳ ἔτει ἐπὶ Τελεσίνου ἄρχοντος: 487/6; *A.P.* is our only source for the archon's name. 34. ii has τῷ ὕστερον ἔτει, which Kaibel & Wilamowitz and others have preferred here; but it would be wrong to remove an acceptable reading for the sake of consistency.

ἐκυάμευσαν τοὺς ἐννέα ἄρχοντας ... πάντες ἦσαν αἱρετοί: According to *A.P.* the archons were originally appointed by the Areopagus (8. ii); Solon introduced the procedure of κλήρωσις ἐκ προκρίτων (8. i); now we are told that the tyranny substituted direct election and κλήρωσις ἐκ προκρίτων was revived in 487/6. *A.P.*'s story is consistent, but other texts conflict with it: Arist. *Pol.* II. 1273 B 35–1274 A 3,

III. 1281 B 25–34, claims that Solon retained the 'aristocratic' principle of election to office; H. VI. 109. ii describes Callimachus at Marathon as ὁ τῷ κυάμῳ λαχὼν Ἀθηναίων πολεμαρχέειν (but contrast Paus. I. 15. iii; and Idom. 338 F 5 *ap.* Pl. *Arist.* I. viii claims that the archon of 489/8 was elected). I have argued that before Solon *A.P.* was and we are reduced to guesswork, but that *A.P.*'s account of Solonian procedure is to be accepted (see on 8. ii, i); after the illegally prolonged archonship of Damasias it was perhaps enacted that only half of each tribe's πρόκριτοι might be Eupatrids (13. ii with commentary). The tyranny, presumably after Pisistratus' third and final *coup*, changed to direct election (cf. on 16. ix), and Isagoras was surely elected archon for 508/7 (cf. on 20. i). We have seen above that Herodotus gives a detailed, consistent and credible account of the generals and the polemarch at Marathon (pp. 264–5). On the appointment of the polemarch it became standard doctrine after the discovery of *A.P.* that *A.P.* is right and Herodotus is wrong (tolerated, surprisingly, even by Hammond, *JHS* lxxxvii 1968, 50 with n. 145 = *Studies*, 232–3 with 233 n. 1), but Badian has argued strongly that we should believe Herodotus here too (*Antichthon* v 1971, 21–6; but we know too little of Athens in the early fifth century to substantiate his view that the archons appointed before 487/6 were as undistinguished as those appointed after); on the other hand, although *A.P.* is unique in telling us of a reform in 487/6 there is no reason why he should not be right. We should therefore consider as a serious possibility the suggestion attributed by Hammond to Oncken, that Cleisthenes was responsible for a change by which men were elected to the college of archons but assigned by lot to a specific post within the college (Hammond, *loc. cit.*, cf. Badian, *loc. cit.*, P. J. Bicknell, *A. Class.* xiv 1971, 147–9).

According to the preserved text of *A.P.* (both London and Berlin papyri) the practice introduced in 487/6 was sortition κατὰ φυλὰς from five hundred πρόκριτοι elected by the demes; 62. i says that some sortitive officials including the nine archons used to be appointed from the whole tribe but others were apportioned among the demes. Some have accepted what is said here (e.g. E. S. Staveley, *Greek and Roman Voting and Elections*, 38 with 239 n. 59), but as Kenyon remarked in his first edition this cannot be right: partly because in *A.P.*'s own time, when more men were eligible for the office, there were only one hundred προλαχόντες (8. i), and partly because at this time there can hardly have been many more than five hundred men eligible for the archonship in any one year (cf. Badian, *op. cit.*, 17–19; if Solon had restricted the archonship to πεντακοσιομέδιμνοι it must by this time have been opened to ἱππεῖς [cf. above, p. 148]). The number five hundred and the reference to the demes suggest confusion with the appointment of the boule, and this is perhaps likelier than the mere corruption of ἑκατὸν (ρ΄) to πεντακοσίων (φ΄) (Kenyon considered both); the correction of πεντακοσίων to πεντακοσιομεδίμνων (J. W. Headlam, *CR* v 1891, 112; more recently Bicknell, *RFIC* c = ³l 1972, 168–9) is not likely to be right; nor is the deletion of δημοτῶν, to yield πρόκρισις by the boule (K. H. Kinzl, *Greece and the Eastern Mediterranean . . . F. Schachermeyr*, 216–17: cf. above, p. 264). Probably now as later each tribe was to provide ten πρόκριτοι; perhaps it was now that the secretary to the thesmothetae was added to the nine archons to make up a college of ten (cf. on 55. i), and in the allotment one of the ten had to be picked from each tribe. Subsequently πρόκρισις was replaced by προκλήρωσις (8. i, cf. 55. i), but we are not told when.

This reform undoubtedly played a part in the change between the mid sixth century and the mid fifth by which the generals became the principal officers of the state and the archons became routine officials with duties which any loyal citizen could be trusted to perform, but the precise significance of this reform within the whole process is harder to determine. F. J. Frost (*CSCA* i 1968, 114–15) and E. Badian (*op. cit.*, 1–34) have argued that before it the archonship was already an unimportant post held by men beginning their political career: if the polemarch was already appointed to that particular post by lot, and was only titular commander-in-chief of the army, that would support their view, but the archonship ought still to have been important when Isagoras as a contender for supremacy was elected for 508/7, and we know too little about the men who held the office at the turn of the century to be sure of its significance. The reform may as well be a response to a decline in the archonship that had already begun as a revolutionary move intended to bring about a decline: at any rate there is no evidence that the reform is the work of Themistocles, far-sightedly preparing the way for the attack on the Areopagus which Ephialtes was to make a generation later (variations on that theme are surveyed by R. J. Buck, *CP* lx 1965, 96–101; they are treated with the scepticism they deserve by Badian).

I have written in this note of the reform of 487/6. That the reform was enacted in this year is the natural interpretation of what *A.P.* says, but it is possible that he has been careless and that 487/6 is the first year whose archons were appointed under the new procedure, enacted in the previous year (cf. 26. ii, where successive clauses have opposite implications).

δημοτ(ῶν): This is the reading of the London papyrus: the Berlin papyrus reads δήμων, which is suspect as the *facilior lectio* but has been preferred by Kaibel & Wilamowitz³, Thalheim and Oppermann.

καὶ ὠστρακίσθη Μεγακλῆς Ἱπποκράτους Ἀλωπεκῆθεν: Apparently the leading member of the Alcmaeonid family, his father being a younger brother of Cleisthenes (Kirchner, *P.A.* 9695, Davies, *A.P.F.*, 379); his sister was married to Xanthippus (cf. on §vi). 4,662 ostraca bearing his name have been found, more than for any other man (Themistocles comes next, with 2,264); and other Alcmaeonids too figure in Agora deposits which can be dated securely to the 480's: most prominent are Callixenus Ἀριστωνύμου Ξυπεταίων (265 ostraca known, one identifying him as [Ἀλκ]μεον[ιδῶν] and one calling him [ho πρ]οδότες: both quoted in M&L 21), whose father was probably another brother of Cleisthenes (*A.P.F.*, 376), Hippocrates Ἀλκμεωνίδου Ἀλωπεκῆθεν (127 or more ostraca known), perhaps a cousin of Cleisthenes (*A.P.F.*, 372-3); and some who voted against Xanthippus may have been influenced by his Alcmaeonid connections (cf. on §vi). The Alcmaeonids were accused of colluding with the Persians at Marathon, and Herodotus makes an unconvicing attempt to rebut the charge (vi. 121-4): in the light of the ostraca and of *A.P.*'s comment that the first three victims were τοὺς τῶν τυράννων φίλους it should be accepted that the charge was contemporary and that the Alcmaeonids had at any rate not been conspicuously loyal; the ostracism of Hipparchus and the votes against Alcmaeonids show that the first use of ostracism was against those who after Marathon were under suspicion but (presumably) could not be proved to be traitors.

According to Lys. xiv. *Alc. i.* 39, [And.] iv. *Alc.* 34 (as emended by Markland), Megacles was ostracised twice. Otherwise we are told nothing about him after his ostracism in 486, and so his second ostracism has been widely disbelieved; most think that all Megacles' ostraca and those associated with them belong to the ostracism of 487/6 (and H. B. Mattingly has remarked that the more informative ostraca against Megacles fail to support the view of the first ostracisms which I have given in the previous paragraph: *U. Leeds R.* xiv 1971, 281-3). However, most of Megacles' ostraca come from the major deposit found in the Ceramicus in 1965-7, and the other ostraca associated with them include some against men whom we should be surprised to find attracting votes as early as 486, notably Cimon; so it has been suggested that the story of Megacles' second ostracism should be taken seriously and this deposit should be dated to the 470's (D. M. Lewis, *ZPE* xiv 1974, 1-4, P. J. Bicknell, *AC* xliv 1975, 172-5; G. M. E. Williams, *ZPE* xxxi 1978, 103-13, attempts a defence of the earlier dating, but his reconstruction of the 480's is open to a number of objections). Lewis acknowledges that neither dating is without its difficulties; with the Ceramicus ostraca still unpublished, the question is best left open.

22. vi. ἐπὶ μὲν οὖν ἔτη γ' τοὺς τῶν τυράννων φίλους ὠστράκιζον: For the third year, 486/5, *A.P.* names neither the archon nor the victim.

Very probably he could have named both, but the name of the third victim meant nothing to him and he preferred to avoid the monotony of an annalistic list (cf. Wilamowitz, *A.u.A.*, i. 123, and above, pp. 42-4, 267; but G. V. Sumner believes that he omitted archons where he lacked good authority for them [*CQ*² xi 1961, 46] and Mattingly argues that our text of *A.P.* is defective and the third victim was named [*op. cit.*, 282]).

On the orthodox view of the major Ceramicus deposit (cf. previous note) the third victim is likely to be Callias Κρατίου Ἀλωπεκῆθεν (763 ostraca known, all but three from the Ceramicus; eleven label him ὁ Μῆδος or ἐκ Μέδον and a twelfth has a drawing of a man in Persian costume: G. Daux, *BCH* xcii 1968, 732, Mattingly, *op. cit.*, 282, Vanderpool, *Lectures* ... L. T. *Semple* ii 1966-70, 235-6); but if the doubts mentioned above are justified there is no obvious third victim and Callias will have been a serious candidate in the 470's (in which case, Lewis suggests, Μῆδος may be a nickname rather than an accusation of disloyalty). This Callias is probably related to Callias Ἱππονίκου Ἀλωπεκῆθεν, of the Κήρυκες, against whom there are twelve Ceramicus ostraca (see Davies, *A.P.F.*, 258-61, 598); but Bicknell tries to make him an Alcmaeonid (*Hist.* Einz. xix 1972, 64-71, cf. *Hist.* xxiii 1974, 147-50).

ὧν χάριν ὁ νόμος ἐτέθη: Cf. pp. 269-70.

μετὰ δὲ ταῦτα τῷ τετάρτῳ ἔτει: 485/4. Philocrates was archon for that year (or, less probably, the year before): *Marm. Par.* 239 A 50 with T. J. Cadoux, *JHS* lxviii 1948, 118, A. E. Samuel, *Greek and Roman Chronology*, 205.

καὶ πρῶτος ὠστρακίσθη τῶν ἄπωθεν τῆς τυραννίδος Ξάνθιππος ὁ Ἀρίφρονος: Sc. Χολαργεύς. Xanthippus married Agariste, daughter of the Alcmaeonid Hippocrates (cf. pp. 274-5), c. 500-496 (Davies, *A.P.F.*, 379, 455-6); in 489 he successfully prosecuted Miltiades, the hero of Marathon, for ἀπάτη in connection with his campaign against Paros (H. vi. 136). The success of that prosecution at that time makes it almost certain that in the 480's Xanthippus was not generally regarded as belonging to the 'Alcmaeonid set', and that *A.P.* is right to distinguish him from the first three victims of ostracism (cf. W. G. Forrest, *CQ*² x 1960, 233-4, contr. Bicknell, *Hist.* Einz. xix 1972, 73-4, 81-2). Twenty-three ostraca against Xanthippus are known, one of them bearing an elegiac couplet:

Χσάνθ[ιππον ?τόδε] φεσὶν ἀλειτερον πρυτανειον
τόστρακ[ον Ἀρρί]φρονος παῖδα μάλιστ' ἀδικεν.

Tantalisingly, several interpretations are grammatically possible. Raubitschek, who first published the text, preferred '... the accursed Xanthippus particularly wrongs the prytaneum' (*AJA*² li 1947, 257-62, cf. H. Schaefer, *RE*, ixA [1961/7], 1345); but the interpretation which has found most favour is that of A. Wilhelm, '... Xanthippus most of all the accursed prytanes is a wrongdoer' (*Anz. Wien* lxxxvi 1949, 237–43, cf. M&L, p. 42); for other suggestions see O. Broneer, *AJA*² lii 1948, 341–3, E. Schweigert, *AJA*² liii 1949, 266–8, R. Merkelbach, *ZPE* iv 1969, 201–2. Although Xanthippus was not generally regarded as tainted with the Alcmaeonid curse he may have been so regarded by some voters, and I suspect that he was so regarded by this voter and that Raubitschek's interpretation is correct.

Alcmaeonids were still attracting votes and being described as traitors in the later 480's, but ostracism was probably now being used more as Cleisthenes had envisaged, to eliminate the less popular of rival political leaders. Xanthippus, labelled προστάτης τοῦ δήμου in opposition to Miltiades in the list in 28. ii (cf. *ad loc.*), was one such man; Aristides, ostracised two years later (§vii), was another; another, who attracted votes in the 480's but was not ostracised until after the Persian Wars, was Themistocles (cf. on §vii). In the politics of the 480's Themistocles is clearly to be regarded as a successful rival of Xanthippus and Aristides—which is not to say that he was the man behind the whole series of ostracisms in this decade (alleged by Hignett, *H.A.C.*, 188–9, and others).

22. vii. ἔτει δὲ τρίτῳ μετὰ ταῦτα Νικοδήμου ἄρχοντος: 483/2 (cf. D.H. *A.R.* VIII. 83. i with Cadoux, *JHS* lxviii 1948, 118 n. 257, Samuel, *Greek and Roman Chronology*, 205). The Berlin papyrus agrees with D.H. in calling him Nicodemus, and that should be correct. The London papyrus calls him Nicomedes: Badian prefers that, identifying him with Themistocles' son-in-law (*Antichthon* v 1971, 2–3 n. 3, 33), and Raubitschek improbably places Nicodemus in 483/2 and Nicomedes in 482/1 (*Hist.* viii 1959, 127–8).

ὡς ἐφάνη τὰ μέταλλα ... ἐν Σαλαμῖνι πρὸς τοὺς βαρβάρους: The story it told also by H. VII. 144. i–ii, Pl. *Them.* 4. i–iii, Aristid. XLVI. *Quatt.* (ii. 250–1 Dindorf), cf. T. I. 14. iii, Nep. II. *Them.* 2. ii, viii, Just. II. 12. xii, Liban. *Decl.* x. 27; Polyaen. I. 30. vi is clearly derived from *A.P.* That the surplus money came from the silver mines, and that Themistocles was responsible for the decision not to distribute it among the citizens (as the Siphnians were said to have done with the profits of their mines in the sixth century: H. III. 57. ii)[26] but to spend it on shipbuilding, are agreed facts; but in the other versions Themistocles publicly proposed that the money should

---

[26] For a distribution of confiscated property in fourth-century Athens see [Pl.] *X. Or.* 843 D–E; and on the principle of distributing the city's surplus wealth among the citizens see K. Latte, *Nachr. Göttingen* 1946/7, 64–75 = *Kleine Schriften*, 294–312, S. C. Humphreys, *ASNP*² xxxix 1970, 11–12 = *Anthropology and the Greeks*, 145.

be spent on ships, giving as his reason the war with Aegina, and that is surely correct. *A.P.*'s story that the money was lent to rich citizens on trust, with no publicly declared purpose, fails to carry conviction, if only because nothing would be gained by secrecy (and our confidence is lessened by the ascription of similar secrecy to other plans of Themistocles in D.S. XI. 42, Pl. *Them.* 20. i–ii, *Arist.* 22. ii–iii, Cic. *Off.* III. 49, V.M. VI. v. ext. 2); but the story may have a true foundation, that a number of rich citizens were each made responsible for the building of one ship (e.g. A. R. Burn, *Persia and the Greeks*, 292, G. S. Maridakis, *Studi . . . B. Biondi*, ii. 207–18). Herodotus implies that the surplus was 50 talents (cf. v. 97. ii: but he may well have been unconscious of the implication), and states that 200 ships were built; in *A.P.* the surplus is 100 talents, and in *A.P.* and Plutarch 100 ships are built; Nepos envisages two separate consignments each of 100 ships: the sum of one talent as the cost of a trireme has seemed plausible to students of the early Delian League (see esp. S. K. Eddy, *CP* lxiii 1968, 189–95, D. J. Blackman, *GR&BS* x 1969, 184 with n. 16). In fact Athens had a fleet of 70 ships in 489 (H. VI. 132 cf. 89) and 200 in 480 (H. VIII. 1. i–ii, 14. i): Herodotus' mistake is easily understood; *A.P.*'s figure is possibly accurate (30 ships could have been added to the fleet before 483/2) but more probably an approximation. J. Labarbe, *La Loi navale de Thémistocle*, 21–51, tries to believe all the evidence by supposing that the two regions of Laurium and Maronea each provided 100 talents for 100 ships.

ἐφάνη τὰ μέταλλα τὰ ἐν Μαρωνείᾳ: For the Attic Maronea cf. D. XXXVII. *Pant.* 4, *L.S.* 279. 32, Harp. *s.v.* E. Ardaillon placed Maronea east of the modern Kamareza (*Les Mines du Laurion dans l'antiquité*, 138–40 with map, cf. R. J. Hopper, *BSA* lxiii 1968, 299–300, 313, 316–17, reproducing Ardaillon's map as pl. 65); but the evidence is flimsy, and Labarbe makes Maronea in a broad sense a strip running southwards from the region of Kamareza, with Maronea in a narrower sense about 3 km. slightly east of south from Kamareza (*op. cit.*, 24–37 with map on p. 27). The name is presumably borrowed from the Thracian Maronea, on the coast between the mouths of the Nestus and the Hebrus, and not itself particularly associated with mining (S. Casson, *Macedonia, Thrace and Illyria*, 90–3, *A.T.L.*, i. 517; H. VII. 109. i is mistaken in his siting of the town); and there are other names found both in Thrace and in the area of Laurium, perhaps reflecting the migration of workmen (cf. J. H. Young, *Hesp.* x 1941, 182, Hopper, *op. cit.*, 313 n. 160).

X. *Vect.* iv. 2 refers to the Attic mines as πάνυ πάλαι ἐνεργά; but it is usually said that Themistocles' shipbuilding programme was made possible by a sudden increase in yield, made perhaps when miners broke through from the 'first contact' to the 'third contact' seams (e.g. Hopper, *locc. citt.*, modifying Ardaillon). W. P. Wallace has stressed that the richer seams must actually have been discovered some years earlier (*NC*[7] ii 1962, 28–33). The mines were state property, worked by contractors (for their administration in the fourth century see 47. ii with commentary): perhaps for some years the state had been coining more silver than it needed to issue, and in 483/2 the question of what should be done with the surplus was raised.

τάλαντα ἑκατὸν ἐκ τῶν ἔργων: This is the word order of the London papyrus: the Berlin papyrus has ἐκ τῶν [ἔ]ργων ἑκατ[ὸν τάλαντα].

Θεμιστοκλῆς: *Sc. Νεοκλέους Φρεάρριος*, of the junior branch of the γένος Λυκομίδαι, and of a deme in south-eastern Attica (it is located north-west of the mining area by E. Vanderpool, *Hesp.* xxxix 1970, 47–53, cf. J. S. Traill, *Hesp.* Supp. xiv 1975, 45; E. Kirsten, *ap.* A. Philippson, *Die griechischen Landschaften*, I. iii. 850 n. 2, placed it farther east, near Plaka), but with a house in Melite, in the city, west of the Agora (Pl. *Them.* 22. ii; location Traill, *op. cit.*, 50). Accounts of his background are collected in Pl. *Them.* 1; his mother was probably not Athenian; Herodotus, the friend of the Alcmaeonids, represented him as ἀνὴρ ἐς πρώτους νεωστὶ παριών in 481 (VII. 143. i), and Pl. *Them.* knows nothing that would contradict that; but the battle of Sepeia also (*c.* 494) could be dated νεωστί in 481 (H. VII. 148. ii), and it must be this Themistocles who was archon in 493/2 (D.H. *A.R.* VI. 34. i), and his archonship to which Thucydides assigns the beginning of work at the Piraeus (I. 93. iii with D. M. Lewis, *Hist.* xxii 1973, 757–8, W. W. Dickie, *ibid.* 758–9, contr. A. A. Mosshammer, *Hermes* ciii 1975, 222–34). 'The general impression one receives is of a family of *domi nobiles*, whose irruption into metropolitan and Panhellenic politics is a sufficiently notable change of key to justify the modern description of Themistocles as a *novus homo*' (Davies, *A.P.F.*, 213). With 2,264 ostraca against him known he stands second only to Megacles (cf. §v with commentary): he was certainly attracting votes in the later 480's, and if the orthodox interpretation of the major Ceramicus deposit is correct he was already attracting votes in 487/6 (cf. p. 275): he was a candidate for political supremacy, more successful at this time than Xanthippus and Aristides (cf. p. 277).

τὴν δαπάνην: Inserted by a corrector in the London papyrus: the text can be punctuated to make sense without it (and this was preferred by Herwerden & Leeuwen and others: Polyaenus seems to have used a text from which it was missing), but the words must be restored in the Berlin papyrus and should be retained. Cf. Gomme, *CR* xlii 1928, 225.

αἷς ἐναυμάχησαν ἐν Σαλαμῖνι πρὸς τοὺς βαρβάρους: Cf. T. I. 14. iii ('Ἀθηναίους... ἔπεισεν Αἰγινήταις πολεμοῦντας, καὶ ἅμα τοῦ βαρβάρου προσδοκίμου ὄντος, τὰς ναῦς ποιήσασθαι αἷσπερ καὶ ἐναυμάχησαν).

Themistocles had used the war with Aegina as his pretext for urging that the surplus should be spent on shipbuilding; but when the Persians invaded in 480 Athens was able to contribute more than half of the Greek fleet. No doubt it was this timely provision of ships, and his interpretation of the 'wooden walls' oracle (H. vii. 141. iii–iv) that won Themistocles his reputation for far-sightedness (e.g. T. I. 138. iii).

ὠστρακίσθη δ' ἐν τούτοις τοῖς καιροῖς Ἀριστείδης ὁ Λυσιμάχου: Sc. Ἀλωπεκῆθεν. Cf. Pl. Arist. 7, which attaches a general account of the institution to the story of Aristides' ostracism. Aristides was probably a cousin of Callias 'Ἱππονίκου Ἀλωπεκῆθεν, of the Κήρυκες (Pl. Arist. 25. iv–viii with Davies, A.P.F., 48–9, 256–7); there was a widespread but apparently false tradition of his poverty (e.g. Pl. Arist. 1, with A.P.F., 48–53). Plutarch makes him a general at Marathon (Arist. 5. i–vi), but this was unknown to Nep. III. Arist. and is at best doubtful (cf. p. 686 n. 58); an Aristides, believed by Plutarch to be this man, was archon in 489/8 (Pl. Arist. 1. ii–viii, 5. ix–x, citing Dem. Phal. 228 FF 43–4, cf. M&L 6, d, Marm. Par. 239 A 49), and the identification is very probably to be accepted, though another Aristides, son of Xenophilus (P.A. 1687), was active at the time and is preferred by those who are reluctant to see the most important Athenians holding the archonship in the early fifth century (see Bicknell, AC xxxix 1970, 433–6, Davies, A.P.F., 48; contr. Badian, Antichthon v 1971, 11–13, Bicknell, RFIC c = ³1 1972, 164–72). He is usually but not always represented as the opponent and rival of Themistocles, 'aristocratic' whereas Themistocles was 'democratic', δίκαιος whereas Themistocles was cunning, opposing Themistocles' proposals simply because they were his (H. VIII. 79, Pl. Them. 3. i–iii, Arist. 2–3; cf. A.P. 28. ii but contr. 23. iii): in and after 480 they are better seen as partners than as opponents (cf. on 23. iii), but earlier they clearly were rivals, though we are not obliged to regard one as 'aristocratic' and the other as 'democratic', or to suppose that there were only two 'sides' in Athenian politics in the 480's. Although it is a commonplace of modern books that Themistocles' shipbuilding proposal was the issue which led to Aristides' ostracism (first suggested by Beloch, G.G.², II. ii. 142), it is stated in no ancient text and should not be regarded as certain. 114 ostraca against him are known, including one that wrongly places him in the deme Κοιλή: a puzzling pair call him Ἀριστ[είδεν] | τὸν Δά[τιδος] | ἀδελφ[όν] and perhaps [Ἀριστείδες | ho Λυσιμ]άχο | [hὸς τὸ]s hικέτας | [ἀπέοσ]εν (Raubitschek, Charites . . . [E. Langlotz gewidmet], 234–42), and the former reminds us of the tradition that he was a ἑταῖρος of his fellow-demesman Cleisthenes (Pl. Arist. 2. i, An Seni, 790 F: Davies, A.P.F., 48, suspects that it was a malicious invention at the time of his ostracism).

Pace Samuel, *Greek and Roman Chronology*, 206, ἐν τούτοις τοῖς καιροῖς must surely be another way of saying 'in this year', i.e. 483/2, used for variety's sake. Hieron. 108 Helm dates Aristides' ostracism to 484/3, but his dates are not trustworthy enough for that to disturb us.

22. viii. τετάρτῳ δ' ἔτει ... ἄρχοντος Ὑψιχίδου: This archon is not attested elsewhere: in the London papyrus Ὑψηχίδου was originally written but has been corrected to the likelier Ὑψιχίδου; in the Berlin papyrus the beginning of the name is not preserved. The 4th year after 483/2 is 480/79, but that is securely occupied by Calliades (D.S. XI. 1. ii, *Marm. Par.* 239 A 51), and Hypsichides must be assigned to 481/0 (e.g. Cadoux, *JHS* lxviii 1948, 118-19, Hignett, *H.A.C.*, 336-7, Samuel, *op. cit.*, 205-6). It is most improbable that we should save τετάρτῳ by reckoning the 4th year after 485/4, i.e. 482/1 (J. Carcopino, *L'Ostracisme athénien*², 153-7, M. H. Chambers, *Philol.* cxi 1967, 163-5; Raubitschek, *Hist.* viii 1959, 127-8, and G. Maddoli, *Cronologia e storia*, esp. 91-107, combine this with other eccentricities). G. V. Sumner, *CQ*² xi 1961, 33-5, suggests that *A.P.* is dating not the decree (of 481/0) ordering the return but the actual return (in 480/79), and that ἄρχοντος Ὑψιχίδου is to be deleted as a gloss inserted by someone who misunderstood him; but it is far likelier that *A.P.* or a copyist has made a simple mistake (the numeral is not preserved in the Berlin papyrus).

H. VIII. 79. i at first sight implies that Aristides did not return until shortly before Salamis, but many have followed J. B. Bury, *CR* x 1896, 414-18, in rejecting that implication and supposing that he returned in time to be elected general for 480/79; an order to the ostracised to go to Salamis is the last item in the inscribed Decree of Themistocles (M&L 23, 44 sqq.), but even if the individual items are substantially authentic an editor may have combined in a single text decrees of different dates (first suggested by I. Hahn, *A. Ant. Hung.* xiii 1965, 33-4); Nep. III. *Arist.* 1. v places Aristides' return *sexto anno*, clearly wrongly; Pl. *Arist.* 8. i dates the recall τρίτῳ ἔτει but adds Ξέρξου διὰ Θετταλίας καὶ Βοιωτίας ἐλαύνοντος ἐπὶ τὴν Ἀττικήν (which we should not press to yield the following year; nor should chronology be extracted from *Them.* 11. i). It need not be doubted that the recall of the ostracised was voted, whether on the proposal of Themistocles or of another, in 481/0.

Aristides and Xanthippus returned and played an active part in the resistance to Persia, both serving as generals in 479 (H. IX. 28. vi, VIII. 131. iii). Megacles must have returned too: except in the texts which say that he was ostracised twice (cf. p. 275) nothing more is heard of him, but his son Megacles survived in Athens to be secretary to the treasurers of Athena in 428/7 (*IG* i² 237-9, 261-3).

COMMENTARY ON THE *ATH. POL.*

Hipparchus son of Charmus did not appear to answer a charge of προδοσία, but in his absence was sentenced to death (Lyc. *Leocr.* 117 with Harp. Ἵππαρχος): very probably like his grandfather Hippias he had joined the Persians, and he failed to return in 480 and was condemned for that (but Raubitschek, *C&M* xix 1958, 107–8, and J. H. Schreiner, *SO* Supp. xxi 1968, 51–2, regard this story as a 'doublet' of that of his ostracism; and M. H. Hansen, *Eisangelia*, 70, and A. J. Holladay, *G&R*² xxv 1978, 189–90, press the wording of Lyc. to argue that he did return).

στρατείαν: In the sense 'expedition', 'campaign', στρατεία and στρατιά were interchangeable at the time of *A.P.* (while στρατιά is the regular form for 'army': Meisterhans & Schwyzer, *G.a.I.*, 55, LSJ *s.vv.*), so we should follow Blass in retaining the papyrus' στρατιάν. Cf. 27. ii, 37. i.

καὶ τὸ λοιπὸν ὥρισαν ... ἢ ἀτίμους εἶναι καθάπαξ: Geraestus is the cape at the south-east corner of Euboea (cf. H. VIII. 7. i); Scyllaeum is the cape at the eastern extremity of the Argolid (cf. T. v. 53). Some have accepted this text (the Berlin papyrus seems to have agreed with the London), supposing that these are points south-east of which the ostracised were not to go: that is, they were to keep well clear of Persian territory (Wilamowitz, *A.u.A.*, i. 114, R. Goossens, *CE* xx 1945, 125–33, Tovar, *REC* iii 1948, 163–4, Raubitschek, *C&M* xix 1958, 103–5, cf. Kenyon, Berlin and earlier edd.). Others think it necessary to emend, either substituting ἐκτός for ἐντός (W. Wyse, *CR* v 1891, 112, cf. 274) or inserting μή before κατοικεῖν (Kaibel, *Stil und Text*, 177, Kenyon, O.C.T.), and supposing that the ostracised were required to go at least as far from Athens as these two points (cf. Hignett, *H.A.C.*, 163–4, supposing the requirement to have been in the law from the beginning). Against the first interpretation are the facts that Cimon went to the Chersonese (And. III. *Pace* 3—if that is a fact) and that Hyperbolus went to Samos (T. VIII. 73. ii–iii), and against the second, that Thucydides the son of Melesias went to Aegina (Anon. *Vit. Thuc.* 7—if that is a fact); but we do not know how long the law remained in force. The account of ostracism in Phil. 328 F 30 includes ... μὴ ἐπιβαίνοντα ἐντὸς Γεραιστοῦ τοῦ Εὐβοίας ἀκρωτηρίου (*v.l.* ἐντὸς πέρα τῆς Εὐβοίας): probably Philochorus said the same as *A.P.*, appending to his general account of ostracism ἄρχοντος Ὑψιχίδου ἐψηφίσαντο ... *vel simile quid*; the quotation in the lexica, naming only one point, is clearly defective, and cannot be used to correct *A.P.* In the circumstances of 481/0 it is likelier that the ostracised should be ordered to keep their distance from Persia than that they should be ordered to keep their distance from Athens, and *A.P.*'s text should not be emended.†

ἀτίμους ... καθάπαξ is no doubt being used in the older, 'untamed' sense of ἀτιμία (cf. on 8. v, 16. x), so that offenders would become outlaws, denied any protection under Athenian law, and καθάπαξ may have been added either by the author of the decree or by a later writer reporting it in order to emphasise that fact; but in D. xxi. *Mid.* 32, 87, [D.] xxv. *Aristog. i.* 30, καθάπαξ is used to distinguish total from partial 'tamed' ἀτιμία (see Harrison, *L.A.*, ii. 176, and cf. And. 1. *Myst.* 75, where the adverb used is παντάπασιν).

H. *The Mid Fifth Century* (23–8)

This section comes as a disappointment to the reader who has enjoyed the 'pure gold' of *A.P.*'s earlier chapters. It contains a good deal of politically biased anecdote and comment, and comparatively little solid material; and in abbreviating from his sources and changing from one source to another the author has produced an account of the period which is far from coherent. I have discussed some of the problems in *LCM* i 1976, 147–54.

In 23. i–ii[a] we are told that after the Persian Wars the growth of the democracy was halted and the Areopagus was predominant. Then comes an abrupt change: no more is said of obstacles to democracy, but in 23. ii[b]–24 Aristides and Themistocles are introduced as joint προστάται τοῦ δήμου, and we read of Aristides' organisation of the Delian League, the conversion of the League into an empire, and the maintenance of large numbers of citizens on the revenue from the empire. The two themes are similarly juxtaposed in Arist. *Pol.* v. 1304 A 17–24: that passage comes dangerously close to saying that as a result of the Persian Wars the Athenian constitution changed in two opposite directions at the same time; in *A.P.* direct conflict has been avoided but the implicit contradiction remains. 23. i–ii[a] and 23. ii[b]–24 represent different views of the period following the Persian Wars, the first with an aristocratic bias, and the second (I argue) with a democratic bias. Ch. 25 opens first with a clause summarising the second theme, and secondly with a clause reverting to the first (necessary because what is to follow is Ephialtes' attack on the Areopagus); the account of Ephialtes and his reform which follows has more in common with 23. ii[b]–24 than with 23. i–ii[a], and gives us the viewpoint of the reformers. 25. iii–iv tells a story of Themistocles' involvement with Ephialtes in the attack on the Areopagus: almost certainly the story is chronologically impossible; there is no other trace of it except in the *hypothesis* to Is. vii. *Areop.*, and it seems very likely that the story was absent from the version of *A.P.* used by Plutarch. Here, as with the 'Draconian constitution' in ch. 4 (cf. pp. 84–7), we may detect a late addition to the text of *A.P.*, probably a deliberate revision made in the Aristotelian school rather than an interpolation made by a later reader in his own copy; at the end of the chapter an abrupt move to the murder of Ephialtes is perhaps a sign of the insertion.

26. i, after a sentence on demagogues which anticipates 27–8, belatedly introduces Cimon, known from other sources to have been an opponent of Themistocles in the 470's and of Ephialtes in the 460's, and does so in language more appropriate to his entry into politics *c*. 480 than to the period after Ephialtes' death; this leads to a difficult passage on the weakness of the opponents of the democracy, which perhaps reflects the opponents' apologies for not halting the advance of the democracy rather than the democrats' criticisms of their opponents. 26. ii begins with a statement reminiscent of Arist. *Pol.*, that the Athenians did not keep to the laws as they had done previously; but the remainder of the chapter reports three constitutional changes, the opening of the archonship to the ζευγῖται, the reintroduction of the δικασταὶ κατὰ δήμους and Pericles' law on the qualifications for citizenship, assigning each to an archontic year in the manner of ch. 22. Ch. 27 is centred on the supremacy of Pericles, and is chronologically wide-ranging: it begins with his prosecution of Cimon (before the reform of Ephialtes) and an attack on the Areopagus (probably to be identified with the reform of Ephialtes); it then turns to the growth of Athens' naval power, and looks ahead to the growing power of the δῆμος in the Peloponnesian War; §§iii–iv deal with Pericles' introduction of payment for jurors, representing it as a political manoeuvre against Cimon and as the brainchild of Damon; it ends by saying that this paved the way for the bribery of jurors, and mentions what is claimed to be the first instance of δεκάζειν (in 409); the chapter as a whole is clearly hostile to Pericles. Nevertheless, we read in 28, while Pericles was leader things were not too bad, but after his death they became much worse, for the leaders of the δῆμος were no longer men of the upper class. To illustrate this, there follows in 28. ii–iii a list of leaders, beginning with Solon and Pisistratus as προστάται τοῦ δήμου and continuing with paired προστάται τοῦ δήμου and τῶν γνωρίμων to the end of the fifth century: no earlier lists are known in which opposing leaders are paired in this way, but the opposition of δῆμος and γνώριμοι has a long history, and discrepancies between this list and *A.P.*'s main narrative suggest that it is not his own compilation but has been taken over from elsewhere. The point made at the beginning of the chapter, that things became worse after Pericles' death, is not mentioned again; instead the chapter ends with praise of the last three προστάται τῶν γνωρίμων, Thucydides, Nicias and Theramenes: on the first two πάντες σχεδὸν ὁμολογοῦσιν, but the favourable verdict on Theramenes is admitted to be controversial and is defended.

A.P. does not name his sources, and in these chapters he does not use any source which we can directly identify; but at any rate several separate strands can be distinguished. (a) 23. i–ii[a] gives the Areopagite view of Salamis and its consequences, 27 is hostile to Periclean Athens, and 28. i asserts that the democratic leaders who followed Pericles were worse: the attitude of all these passages is anti-democratic. (b) 28. ii–v also is anti-democratic: the list of leaders is in itself neutral, but the comment on Cleophon's successors with which it ends is hostile, and the praise of the last προστάται τῶν γνωρίμων which follows arises from the list, and is probably a judgment which A.P. took over with the list rather than his own original comment on it. (c) On the other hand, 23. ii[b]–24 seems to give a pro-democratic view of Athens' development after the Persian Wars, and 25. i–ii gives a pro-democratic view of Ephialtes' attack on the Areopagus. (d) 26. i is hostile to Cimon, but perhaps in the spirit of an aristocratic apologist rather than of a democratic opponent. (e) 26. ii–vi notes and dates three institutional changes, briefly, without anecdotes or obvious bias. (f) The story of Themistocles and Ephialtes in 25. iii–iv seems to be a late insertion in A.P., and so was presumably unknown to the author when he wrote the original text. It would be rash to claim that each of these six strands must be attributed to a separate source consulted by A.P., since earlier writers may have made some attempt to reconcile conflicting traditions, but the complexity of the material in these chapters seems undeniable.

It cannot have been easy for A.P. to fill the gap between 480 and 411. Herodotus ended his history at the end of the Persian Wars; Thucydides tells us disappointingly little about the internal history of Athens, though A.P. could have obtained from him, but did not, material for a favourable view of Pericles; and τοῖς πρὸ ἐμοῦ ἅπασιν ἐκλιπὲς τοῦτο ἦν τὸ χωρίον (sc. the Pentecontaetia) καὶ ἢ τὰ πρὸ τῶν Μηδικῶν Ἑλληνικὰ ξυνετίθεσαν ἢ αὐτὰ τὰ Μηδικά (T. I. 97. ii). The attack on the Areopagus was the only major formal change in the constitution during this period, comparable to the seizure of power by Pisistratus or the legislation of Solon or Cleisthenes, and the laws of Ephialtes and Archestratus about the Areopagites were destroyed by the Thirty (35. ii). It must have been hard for fourth-century writers to reconstruct the history of fifth-century Athens, and harder for A.P. to find material that could be used in a history of the πολιτεία. For one of the six strands we can at least identify the kind of source used: the dated list of institutional changes in 26. ii–iv is very likely to come from an *Atthis*, and since we have reason to ascribe the similar list in ch. 22 to Androtion (cf. pp. 240–1) we may guess that Androtion was used here too. Much of the other material will have been taken from less sober sources: for instance, echoes of old comedy can be found in the list of τρεφόμενοι in 24. iii and the list of προστάται in 28. ii–iii (cf. pp. 302; 345–6, 354–5), but we should expect to find clearer signs if *A.P.* had made direct use of the plays himself. It has been suggested that in those passages and in 27. iii–iv on Pericles' introduction of jury pay *A.P.*'s immediate source was Theopompus: it is not certain that Theopompus' *Philippica* was written early enough for this, but it is plausible that a work of that kind was used. In other passages we should perhaps think of partisan literature written in Athens, for instance the Areopagite account of Athens after the Persian Wars in 23. i–ii[a] and the democratic account of Ephialtes' reform in 25. i–ii.

A.P. has not succeeded in welding into a coherent whole the material which he found in his different sources. The ascendancy of the Areopagus and the προστασία of Aristides and Themistocles represent alternative views of the same period; Aristides and Themistocles are partners in 23. iii but (I argue) opponents in 28. ii; Cimon is introduced after Ephialtes' death in 26. i but is Ephialtes' opponent in 28. ii; the reform of the Areopagus is ascribed to Ephialtes in 25 but to Pericles in 27. i. Also there are signs of fairly drastic excerpting and condensation of the material: in particular 24. ii–iii, 26. i and 28. ii–iii contain difficulties which seem to have arisen in this way.

23. i. τότε μὲν οὖν μέχρι τούτου: *A.P.* sums up a period of democracy and progress before contrasting it with a reversal of the movement towards full democracy (πάλιν) in the ascendancy of the Areopagus: cf. H. I. 4. i (μέχρι μὲν ὧν τούτου ... τὸ δὲ ἀπὸ τούτου ...). τότε is surprising in a sentence concerned with a process rather than an event, but is probably to be accepted: E. Poste, *CR* v 1891, 226, suggested τό, but that use of a redundant τό to provide a hook on which μέν or δέ may be hung is most characteristic of the earliest Greek prose (e.g. τὸ δέ in H., *loc. cit.*).

The summary in 41. ii shows that *A.P.* viewed Athens' constitutional history as a development from the original monarchy to the 'final' democracy of his own day, marked by a series of μεταβολαί or μεταστάσεις, of which some take Athens further towards the goal while others are setbacks which interrupt the development (cf. *ad loc.*, and Introduction, pp. 7–9). The opening words of this chapter will refer to the fifth μεταβολή, the reforms of Cleisthenes (20–1) and the further matters dealt with in ch. 22 (where §iii associates the use of ostracism with the confidence of the δῆμος). The sixth μεταβολή is the change to the ascendancy of the Areopagus, and πάλιν here and ὑποφερομένη in 25. i make it clear that this like the tyranny is one of the interruptions of Athens' development towards full democracy (on the view of Day & Chambers that this régime is the 'third democracy' of Arist. *Pol.* see pp. 10–12).

κατὰ μικρὸν αὐξανομένη: Some have followed H. Richards, CR v 1891, 180, in emending to αὐξανομένῃ, but διέμεινεν ἡ πολιτεία . . . καίπερ ὑποφερομένη κατὰ μικρόν in 25. i shows this to be unnecessary. The metaphorical use of αὐξάνεσθαι is common: for its application to a πόλις cf. H. v. 78, Is. vi. *Archid.* 87, xv. *Antid.* 316, Arist. *Pol.* iv. 1297 B 22; in *Pol.* vi. 1319 B 21–2 we read of Cleisthenes βουλόμενος αὐξῆσαι τὴν δημοκρατίαν. There is no need to suppose, with Day & Chambers (*A.H.A.D.*, 33–4), that *A.P.* is thinking of a literal increase in the citizen population: that is something which he represents as occurring not κατὰ μικρόν but suddenly, when Cleisthenes enfranchised the νεοπολῖται (cf. Introduction, p. 12).

πάλιν ἴσχυσεν ἡ ἐν Ἀρείῳ πάγῳ βουλὴ: In 8. ii Solon's law on the appointment of magistrates is said to have supplanted a system in which appointments were made by the Areopagus; and his creation of the boule of four hundred, in 8. iv, may also have been seen as a derogation from the power of the Areopagus.

καὶ διῴκει τὴν πόλιν: Cf. 3. vi, 4. iv ('Draconian constitution') and 8. iv on the Areopagus in early Athens; also 14. iii and 16. ii on the rule of Pisistratus.

οὐδενὶ δόγματι λαβοῦσα τὴν ἡγεμονίαν: This prepares us for the view, expressed in 25. ii, that the powers of which Ephialtes deprived the Areopagus were ἐπίθετα, powers which had been improperly added to those which it originally possessed (cf. *ad loc.*); W. L. Newman, *CR* v 1891, 163–4, saw a deliberate contrast with the formal institution of the Four Hundred (29. i) and the Thirty (34. iii), which I doubt. Nothing is said to explain how this ἡγεμονία, based on *auctoritas* rather than on formally conferred *potestas*, was exercised, and it is suspicious that 'the Areopagus is said to have done exactly what the fourth-century theorists wished it could have done in their own day' (Moore, 246). It seems in fact to be the case that in this period the Areopagus was active as a lawcourt and gave verdicts which favoured Cimon and his supporters (cf. p. 317, and commentary on 25. iii, 27. i), it may also have offered recommendations to the assembly and advice to the magistrates, and in 480 it will have consisted largely of men who between 510 and 488 had gained their archonships by election, unhelped by the influence of a tyrant (cf. on 22. v), and so was in a suitable position to extend its influence; but most probably the tradition of a period of Areopagite supremacy arose later to explain why Ephialtes had had to attack the Areopagus to bring in a fuller democracy.

γενέσθαι τῆς περὶ Σαλαμῖνα ναυμαχίας αἰτία: Cf. Pl. *Them.* 10. vi–vii, citing *A.P.* for this story and then repeating from Clidemus (323 F 21) an alternative version in which the provision of the money resulted from a decree of Themistocles, who invented an excuse for searching men's luggage during the evacuation of Athens and confiscated sums of money that he found. Arist. *Pol.* v. 1304 A 17–24 says that a success or increase of one element in the πόλις can cause a change towards oligarchy or democracy or πολιτεία:

οἷον ἡ ἐν Ἀρείῳ πάγῳ βουλὴ εὐδοκιμήσασα ἐν τοῖς Μηδικοῖς ἔδοξε συντονωτέραν[27] ποιῆσαι τὴν πολιτείαν, καὶ πάλιν ὁ ναυτικὸς ὄχλος γενόμενος αἴτιος τῆς περὶ Σαλαμῖνα νίκης καὶ διὰ ταύτης τῆς ἡγεμονίας διὰ τὴν κατὰ θάλατταν δύναμιν τὴν δημοκρατίαν ἰσχυροτέραν ἐποίησεν

(and four non-Athenian examples follow); the second Athenian example is found also in II. 1274 A 12–15. The alleged success of the Areopagus can only be that it was 'responsible for the battle of Salamis'—so in *Pol.* v the first example refers to *A.P.*'s version of the story and the second refers to another form or another part of the alternative version of the same story: we can best make sense of this by supposing that Aristotle presented these stories as alternatives, either of which would serve to illustrate his point (rather than that he represented the move towards oligarchy as a short-term effect of the Persian Wars and that towards democracy as a long-term effect, as in Barker's translation). *A.P.*, while in 23. i–ii[a] he gives the 'Areopagite' version of the story, in 23. ii[b]–24 proceeds to write of Aristides and Themistocles as προστάται τοῦ δήμου, the organisation of the Delian League, the development of the League into an empire, and the maintenance of large numbers of citizens on the revenue from the empire. This is not overtly connected with the 'democratic' version of the Salamis story, but it yields the same consequences without the cause. *A.P.* like Aristotle in the *Politics* is aware of both versions, and (as Barker thinks was done in the *Politics*) he resolves the conflict by making the move towards oligarchy an immediate effect of Salamis and the growth of Athens' naval power and democracy a long-term effect (with the relevant version of the Salamis story suppressed). There is an echo of the debate in Cic. *Off.* 1. 75.

It is not implausible that, when the citizens were to be taken from their normal means of livelihood, and it would have been foolish to leave money behind for the Persians to take, what was in the treasury should have been distributed among the citizens (cf. p. 277 with n. 26), so it may be that in *A.P.*'s version the story is true: A. R. Burn, *Persia and the Greeks*, 429–30, is charitable to both versions, and M. B. Wallace, *Phoen.* xxviii 1974, 27 with n. 16, points out that 8 drachmae would be a suitable maintenance allowance for sailors on duty for 24 days at Salamis. But both versions have their place in a series of propaganda battles between Cimon and Themistocles after the Persian Wars, and our suspicions are in-

---

[27] On 'tautness' and 'slackness' in constitutions see 26. i with commentary.

evitably aroused. New statues of Harmodius and Aristogiton were set up in 477/6 to replace those taken by the Persians (*Marm. Par.* 239 A 54), and rival claims to the credit for liberating Athens were advanced on behalf of them, in an epigram by Themistocles' friend Simonides, and of the Alcmaeonids, who had provided Cimon with his wife (cf. A. J. Podlecki, *Hist.* xv 1966, 129–41, and above, p. 230);[28] perhaps in 476/5, Cimon conquered Scyros and brought back to Athens the bones of Theseus in response to a Delphic oracle (cf. p. 77), and it has been suggested that this was his reply to Themistocles' interpretation of the Delphic oracle concerning the 'wooden walls' (Podlecki, *JHS* xci 1971, 141–3); it was debated whether Athens and the Greeks owed their salvation in the Persian Wars primarily to Marathon, the hoplites and Cimon's father Miltiades or to Salamis, the fleet and Themistocles (cf. M&L 26 with commentary, Plat. *Legg.* IV. 707 B 4–C 7, and C. W. Fornara, *JHS* lxxxvi 1966, 51–3; also Aeschylus' *Persae*, on which see below, p. 312); stories were told in which Cimon appeared cleverer than the wily Themistocles (Pl. *Cim.* 5. i; 9 = Ion, 392 F 13). The story given in different versions by Clidemus and *A.P.* appears to be a part of this contest (cf. Wilamowitz, *A.u.A.*, i. 138–40, Jacoby, *Atthis*, 75, commentary on Clid.; contr. P. E. Harding, *Hist.* xxvi 1977, 153–4, but I agree with him that *A.P.*'s version is not necessarily from Androtion). Probably *A.P.*'s is the older version, an attempt to detract from the glory derived from the battle of Salamis by Themistocles, and Clidemus' version is a reply to it (Jacoby *ad loc.*, Hignett, *Xerxes' Invasion of Greece*, 199–200; but E. M. Walker, *C.A.H.*, v[1]. 472–4, supposed Clidemus' version to be the older, and G. L. Huxley, *GR&BS* ix 1968, 312–18, suggests that Clidemus reported the Decree of Themistocles and the Themistoclean version of this story and *A.P.* deliberately rejected both).

τῶν γὰρ στρατηγῶν ἐξαπορησάντων: ἐξαπορεῖν is used by Polybius (τοῖς δὲ λογισμοῖς ἐξηπόρουν, I. 62. i; ἐξαπορεῖν ὑπό, IV. 34. i), and LSJ cites an inscription and a papyrus of the third century (*SIG*[3] 495, 12, *P. Eleph.* ii. (501), 10, both referring to financial straits), but other instances of the word are late. Themistocles was one of the generals, and that is the point of these words; but, having been archon in 493/2 (cf. p. 279), he was also a member of the Areopagus.

κηρυξάντων σῴ[ζ]ειν ἕκαστον ἑαυτόν: Cf. H. VIII. 41. i (after

---

[28] For a suggestion that the pose of the new statues of the tyrannicides was copied in the murals of Cimon's Theseum see J. P. Barron, *JHS* xcii 1972, 20–45, esp. 39–40; K. H. Kinzl, *Gymnasium* lxxxv 1978, 125–6 with Taf. II, publishes a red-figure crater of *c.* 470, attributed to the Copenhagen Painter, which parodies this pose. Hyp. II. *Phil.* 3 cites a law which forbids the maligning of Harmodius and Aristogiton, μήτ' ἄσα[ι ἐ]πὶ τὰ κακίονα, which presumably was enacted because such attacks were being made.

23. i] COMMENTARY ON THE *ATH. POL.*

Thermopylae and Artemisium κήρυγμα ἐποιήσαντο, Ἀθηναίων τῇ τις δύναται σῴζειν τέκνα τε καὶ τοὺς οἰκέτας); Pl. *Them.* 10. iv assigns similar words to a decree moved by Themistocles, but there is no similar expression in the inscribed Decree of Themistocles, M&L 23, 4-12.

23. ii. παρεχώρουν αὐτῆς τῷ ἀξιώματι: 'Yielded to its reputation' (Sandys). The papyrus has αὐτ(ὴν): αὐτῆς, suggested by W. G. Rutherford, *CR* v 1891, 112 (omitting τῷ), and Blass, *LZB* 1891, 304, has won general acceptance (cf. Kaibel, *Stil und Text*, 178).

καὶ ἐπολιτεύθησαν ... τούτους τοὺς καιρούς: Cf. 33. ii, echoing the judgment of T. VIII. 97. ii on the intermediate régime of 411/0 (δοκοῦσι δὲ καλῶς πολιτευθῆναι κατὰ τούτους τοὺς καιρούς); also, on individual politicians, 28. v and 40. ii. It is of course uncontroversial that in the respects indicated in the following sentence Athens prospered in the period after the Persian Wars; but although this may be included in *A.P.*'s meaning ἐπολιτεύθησαν should refer primarily to the condition of the πολιτεία.

Hitherto *A.P.* has rarely expressed an opinion on the merits of the different régimes through which Athens passed. Ch. 9, like Arist. *Pol.*, defends Solon against the charge of being the founder of the classical democracy; 14. iii and 16. ii repeat the common view that Pisistratus ruled πολιτικῶς μᾶλλον ἢ τυραννικῶς, and 16. vii adds that Pisistratus' rule was compared with the age of Cronus; 19. i repeats the view that the tyranny became πολλῷ τραχυτέραν after the murder of Hipparchus. Here we are told more directly that this was a good régime. In 28. v we shall read that Nicias, Thucydides and Theramenes were the best of the more recent politicians, and this is a judgment which *A.P.* probably took over with the list of προστάται and repeated with his own approval; in 33. ii *A.P.*'s praise of the intermediate régime is certainly repeated from Thucydides: similarly here I suspect that *A.P.* praises the Areopagite régime because his source did so before him. This is not to say that *A.P.* had no views of his own—he evidently found most congenial a 'moderate' democracy or oligarchy, as we should expect of a member of the Aristotelian school (cf. Introduction, pp. 9-10)—but when we find a direct expression of opinion like this it is more likely to be a comment which he repeated from his source because he found himself in agreement with it than his own spontaneous comment on material which he found in his source as bare fact. Exceptionally, the comment in 40. ii, with its reference to γῆς ἀναδασμός in other democracies, was probably not first made as early as the near-contemporary source used by *A.P.* on the events of 404-402 (cf. *ad loc.*).

[[καὶ]] κατὰ τούτους τοὺς καιρούς: καί was queried by Kenyon[1-3],

COMMENTARY ON THE *ATH. POL.* [23. ii

deleted by Kaibel & Wilamowitz and by Kenyon in his Berlin ed. and O.C.T.; Herwerden & Leeuwen, Blass and Sandys are among editors who have retained it. Some defenders see a reference to the period before Solon's reforms (e.g. W. L. Newman *ap.* Sandys; but the period of democratic growth referred to at the beginning of this chapter began only with Cleisthenes' reforms [cf. *ad loc.*]), others to the intermediate régime of 411/0, praised in similar words in 33. ii (e.g. Herwerden & Leeuwen); but more probably a copyist has been careless and the word should be deleted.

περὶ τὸν χρόνον τοῦτον: The scribe originally wrote κ(ατὰ); πε[ρὶ] has been written above as a correction; and although κατὰ has occasionally been preferred (e.g. Kenyon[1-3], Thalheim) κατὰ τούτους τοὺς καιρούς before and after makes περὶ to κατὰ the likelier corruption. There is no need to follow Kaibel & Wilamowitz in deleting the whole phrase.

τά τε εἰς τὸν πόλεμον ... ἡγεμονίαν λαβεῖν: συνέβη γὰρ links this to what has been said above of the Areopagus' supremacy, and reminds us of the view often expressed by Isocrates that at this time political σωφροσύνη was combined with military activity which made the Athenians τοῖς μὲν Ἕλλησι πιστούς, τοῖς δὲ βαρβάροις φοβερούς, and enabled them to gain the mastery at sea (IV. *Paneg.* 75–109, VII. *Areop.* 50–5, 78–84, VIII. *Pace*, 36–56, 74–94, XII. *Panath.* 143–52: I quote VII. *Areop.* 51). However, as the new theme is developed it becomes clear that *A.P.* is no longer thinking of the ascendancy of the Areopagus but of the connection between Athens' naval power and the democracy. We have seen that *A.P.* tries to combine two incompatible views of Athens after the Persian Wars, and has at least avoided a direct conflict (cf. p. 288): this sentence eases the transition from the first to the second.

ἀκόντων Λακεδαιμονίων: T. I. 95. vii says that the Spartans were content to let Athens take over the leadership at sea (cf. X. *H.* VI. v. 34, Pl. *Arist.* 23. vii); in D.S. XI. 50 the Spartans debate whether to try to recover the leadership, and unexpectedly decide not to make the attempt; H. VIII. 3. ii perhaps implies that Sparta was displaced against her will. Many have thought that Spartan unwillingness is inappropriate to this context, or that *A.P.* ought to agree with Thucydides: ἑκόντων was suggested by J. E. B. Mayor, *CR* v 1891, 112, εἰκόντων by S. A. Naber *ap.* Herwerden & Leeuwen, ⟨οὐκ⟩ ἀκόντων by W. Vollgraff, *Mnem.*[2] 1 1922, 293–4; a few have retained the papyrus' text but have interpreted it to mean 'the Spartans being unwilling to keep the leadership' (Gomme, *Hist. Comm. Thuc.*, i. 270; *A.T.L.*, iii. 192 n. 30); but I see no need to doubt that ἀκόντων is correct and that according to *A.P.* Sparta was unwilling to yield the leadership to Athens (which a fourth-century writer could believe without censuring the Delian League or Athens' leadership

291

of it). There may, as Diodorus indicates, have been disagreement within Sparta; but it is clear that essentially Thucydides is right and that Athens and Sparta remained on good terms as long as Cimon was in the ascendant at Athens.

23. iii. ἦσαν δὲ προστάται τοῦ δήμου: Here we have the first clear sign that *A.P.* has changed to the second view of Athens after the Persian Wars: having told us that this was a period in which Athens was dominated by the Areopagus he turns to the achievements of two προστάται τοῦ δήμου and says no more about the Areopagus, except in the résumé in 25. i, until he comes to Ephialtes' attack on it. We need not suppose, with F. J. Frost, *CSCA*, i 1968, 111, that the Areopagus is to be thought of as filling the opposing role of προστάτης τῶν γνωρίμων.

Ἀριστείδης ὁ Λυσιμάχου καὶ Θεμιστοκλῆς ὁ Νεοκλέους: For Aristides and Themistocles before 480 see 22. vii with commentary, where I argue that they were two among several rival political leaders (Themistocles, not ostracised in the 480's, being the more successful) but are not necessarily to be viewed as representatives of distinctive political programmes. On their relations after 480 there are conflicting traditions. The view found more often is that Aristides was a mild and honest man and a believer in aristocracy, and at all times an opponent of the wily demagogue Themistocles; in due course Themistocles was succeeded by Ephialtes and Aristides by the gentlemanly Cimon (Pl. *Them.*, *Arist.*, *Cim.*, *passim*). That, I argue (*ad loc.*), is the view followed by *A.P.* 28. ii; but here Aristides and Themistocles are placed unequivocally on the same side, as προστάται τοῦ δήμου (καίπερ διαφερόμενοι πρὸς ἀλλήλους: §iv). This view of Aristides recurs in 41. ii, and there are other traces of it: he showed how τροφή could be provided for the masses (24. iii); after the Persian Wars he saw that the Athenians wanted and deserved democracy, and γράφει ψήφισμα κοινὴν εἶναι τὴν πολιτείαν καὶ τοὺς ἄρχοντας ἐξ Ἀθηναίων πάντων αἱρεῖσθαι (Pl. *Arist.* 22. i: there are no other references to this decree); though Themistocles was responsible for Aristides' ostracism, Aristides did not join in the attack on him (Pl. *Arist.* 25. x, contr. *Cim.* 5. v–vi, 10. viii); and in the rebuilding of the walls (§iv with commentary) and other stories of Themistocles' ingenuity (D.S. xi. 42, Pl. *Them.* 20. i–ii, *Arist.* 22. ii–iii, Cic. *Off.* iii. 49, V. M. vi. v. ext. 2) Aristides cooperates with him or is invited to comment on his schemes; there is also a story, which more probably belongs to the tradition of Aristides the aristocrat, that he discovered an oligarchic plot in the Athenian forces at Plataea and dealt with it tactfully (Pl. *Arist.* 13). The discussions of Aristides by Jacoby, *Supp.* ii. 95–6 n. 104, and C. W. Fornara, *JHS* lxxxvi 1966, 53–4, fail to consider the possibility that

A.P. here and in 28. ii used different sources which took different views of him.

Themistocles, the architect of the Athenian navy, is not found on any campaign after 480; stories of his political activity in the 470's all involve conflict with Sparta (to the references above add Pl. *Them.* 20. iii–iv); in due course he was ostracised, and after that condemned in absence for medism (cf. p. 320). Aristides unlike Themistocles was a general in 479 (H. IX. 28. vi); in 478/7 he played a prominent part in the organisation of the Delian League (§§iv–v with commentary); but thereafter no further activities of his are reported; he is a supporter or confidant of Themistocles in his anti-Spartan schemes. Cimon, notoriously, was well disposed towards Sparta, and gave the name Lacedaemonius to a son born probably in the 470's (Davies, *A.P.F.*, 305); Aristides is said to be the author of a decree by which Cimon and two others were sent on a deputation to Sparta in 479 (Pl. *Arist.* 10. x); down to the siege of Thasos, in all the campaigns of Athens and the League whose commander we know, that commander was Cimon (e.g. T. I. 98–100). We have already seen that there was a propaganda battle between Cimon and Themistocles in the 470's (pp. 288–9): clearly the two men differed also in their attitudes to Sparta; and such evidence as we have suggests that Aristides was more probably an associate of Themistocles than of Cimon. When the issue of how Athens ought to be governed arose, in the 460's, friends of Themistocles favoured democracy and Cimon opposed it (cf. p. 312 and commentary on 26. i, 27. i). By then Aristides must have been dead (though Davies, *A.P.F.*, 49–50, is too precise): we cannot tell what his attitude to the reforms of Ephialtes would have been.

ὁ μὲν τὰ πολέμια ... ὁ δὲ τὰ πολιτικὰ ... : This distinction between Themistocles and Aristides recurs (in the context of 480) in Pl. *Arist.* 8. iii. Arist. *Pol.* v. 1309 A 33–B 14 discusses the problem of choosing officers of state when loyalty, ability and justice are not found together in the same man, and it has been suggested that a reference to Themistocles and Aristides is intended (W. L. Newman, *CR* v 1891, 161, cf. *ad loc.*); Isocrates thought it a fault of fourth-century Athens that she looked to different men for wise counsel and for carrying out policies, and did not use the same men as στρατηγοί and σύμβουλοι (VIII. *Pace*, 49–56, XII. *Panath.* 138–43). Themistocles was more commonly admired for sharpness of intellect than for ability as a general (e.g. T. I. 138. iii), but to emphasise his cleverness here would give a poorer contrast with Aristides: 'Who, if not Themistocles, was τὰ πολιτικὰ δεινός?' (Gomme, *Hist. Comm. Thuc.*, i. 271).

πολέμια has been doubted and πολεμικὰ proposed by Blass, *LZB* 1891, 304, H. Richards and E. S. Thompson, *CR* v 1891, 227 (since

Aristotle normally uses the latter word, e.g. *Pol.* III. 1285 B 18, V. 1305 A 14, and the papyrus has πολεμικά in error for πολιτικά below); but πολέμια is frequently used in the nominative and accusative as an alternative to πολιτικά (e.g. H. III. 4. i [*v.l.* πολεμικά], V. 78, 111. i, T. I. 18. iii: cf. Kaibel, *Stil und Text*, 119), and may be retained both here and in 3. ii. δοκῶν ⟨ἀσκεῖν⟩ was suggested by Kenyon[3] and adopted in his Berlin ed. and O.C.T. The papyrus reads ἀσκῶν: originally he retained that and inserted δοκῶν after δεινὸς εἶναι; H. Richards and E. S. Thompson suggested that ἀσκῶν should be emended to δοκῶν (*loc. cit.*: followed by Herwerden & Leeuwen, Blass and others); but Kenyon's later solution is the best.

καὶ δικαιοσύνῃ τῶν καθ' ἑαυτὸν διαφέρειν: Cf. H. VIII. 79. i, 95. i, and many later texts: the one dissentient comment surviving is that found in [Them.] *Ep.* iv (743 Hercher), ὥσπερ ποτὲ ἔφη Κάλλαισχρος ἐπ' αὐτόν, μᾶλλον τῷ τρόπῳ Ἀλωπεκῆθεν ἢ τῷ δήμῳ, 'fox by deme and fox by nature' (R. Meiggs, *The Athenian Empire*, 42 with nn. 3–4, suggesting that Herodotus' insistence on the uprightness of Aristides is polemical; see also p. 280, on the ostraca cast against him in the 480's). Cf. 25. i with commentary, on the uprightness of Ephialtes.

23. iv. τὴν μὲν οὖν τῶν τειχῶν ἀνοικοδόμησιν κοινῇ διῴκησαν: The story is told in T. I. 90–3 and was repeated many times: Sparta wished to leave Athens unfortified after the Persian Wars; Themistocles had himself sent on an embassy to Sparta, where he prevaricated while the Athenians rebuilt their walls as rapidly as possible; when the walls had reached a sufficient height Habronichus and Aristides joined him and they admitted to what had been done. The story was rejected by Beloch (*G.G.*[2], II. ii. 149–54) and others, but the authenticity of its core is effectively defended by Gomme, *Hist. Comm. Thuc.*, i. 267–70.

καίπερ διαφερόμενοι πρὸς ἀλλήλους: The main tradition, that Themistocles and Aristides were opponents (already firmly asserted by H. VIII. 79. ii), has here been allowed to contaminate the alternative.

τὴν ἀπόστασιν τὴν τῶν Ἰώνων: For the naval campaign of 478, which led to Sparta's loss of hegemony, see T. I. 94–96. i *init.*, 128. iii–130, D.S. XI. 44–6, Pl. *Arist.* 23, *Cim.* 6. i–iii. According to Thucydides the allies took the initiative in offering the leadership to Athens; but according to H. VIII. 3. ii, Diodorus and Plutarch the Athenians took the initiative, and *A.P.* seems to favour that view; for Sparta's reaction see §ii with commentary. Thucydides does not name any Athenian involved in the campaign; but Diodorus and Just. II. 15. xvi name Aristides as Athens' commander and (in agreement with *A.P.*) the man responsible for winning the allegiance of the Greeks (cf. also Timocreon, fr. 1 Page, *ap.* Pl. *Them.* 21. iv), while Plutarch makes Aristides and Cimon commanders. Since Aristides undertook the assessment of tribute it is very likely that he was involved in the campaign of 478; Cimon was commander on many subsequent occasions, and Plutarch is probably mistaken in making him a general in 478 (Cimon's generalship is rejected by *A.T.L.*, iii. 159–60, hesitantly accepted by C. W. Fornara, *Hist.* Einz. xvi 1971, 42–3; N. G. L. Hammond, *JHS* lxxxvii 1967, 47, *CQ*² xix 1969, 135, 137 = *Studies*, 321–2, 380–1, 385, believes that from the time of the war against Xerxes the Athenians had an office which may be styled στρατηγὸς ἐξ ἁπάντων, and that Aristides held that office in 478, but see above, pp. 265–6).

In writing of 'Ionians' *A.P.* follows our earlier sources (H. ix. 104, T. 1. 89. ii, 95. i). It is a matter for dispute whether the word is to be interpreted strictly, as referring to the twelve states sharing in the Πανιώνιον and pointing to a Delian League whose beginnings were small (e.g. B. R. I. Sealey, *Ancient Society and Institutions: Studies . . . V. Ehrenberg*, 243–4; Hammond, *JHS* lxxxvii 1967, 43–7 = *Studies*, 315–21), or more broadly, as referring to the Asiatic Greeks in general and pointing to a Delian League whose membership was widespread from the beginning (e.g. Gomme, *Hist. Comm. Thuc.*, i. 257, 271–2; *A.T.L.*, iii. 202, 227 n. 9): I favour the latter view.

The origins of the Delian League are beset by many problems, of which I can discuss here only those to which *A.P.* is relevant. R. Meiggs, *The Athenian Empire*, 42–67, 459–64, provides a convenient survey.

διὰ Παυσανίαν: The Spartan regent Pausanias commanded the Greeks in the naval campaign of 478: he offended the allies by his high-handed behaviour (but *pace* Thucydides was probably not at that time guilty of medism: see C. W. Fornara, *Hist.* xv 1966, 261–7, Rhodes, *Hist.* xix 1970, 387–90) and was recalled to Sparta; the Athenians then took over the leadership, and when Dorcis arrived from Sparta to succeed Pausanias he was not accepted as commander.

23. v. τοὺς φόρους οὗτος ἦν ὁ τάξας: On the original organisation of the Delian League see T. 1. 96–97. i, D.S. xi. 47, Pl. *Arist.* 24–25. iii. The account in T. 1 does not name Aristides or any other Athenian, but τὸν φόρον τὸν ἐπ' Ἀριστείδου was mentioned in 421 in the terms of the Peace of Nicias (T. v. 18. v).

ἔτει τρίτῳ . . . ἐπὶ Τιμοσθένους ἄρχοντος: Salamis was fought in 480/79 (which recurs as a base date in 27. ii, but 479/8 is used in 25. i: cf. *ad locc.*), and this year is 478/7 (cf. D.S. xi. 38. i), confirming what the reader of Thucydides would naturally assume, that Pausanias' naval campaign was in 478. Diodorus narrates Pausanias' campaign and the organisation of the League under 477/6, and

Gomme was at pains to show how by equating Athenian and Roman years Diodorus could according to his own lights be correct (*Hist. Comm. Thuc.*, i. 272), but I doubt whether Diodorus' narrative dates deserve such generosity (cf. Rhodes, *Hist.* xix 1970, 396-7).

καὶ τοὺς ὅρκους ὤμοσεν τοῖς Ἴωσ[ιν]: Cf. Pl. *Arist.* 25. i (ὁ δ' Ἀριστείδης ὥρκισε μὲν τοὺς Ἕλληνας καὶ ὤμοσεν ὑπὲρ τῶν Ἀθηναίων); Hammond, who believes that 'Ionians' is used in its stricter sense, supposes that the two texts report distinct stages in the formation of the League (*JHS* lxxxvii 1967, 49-52 = *Studies*, 325-30), but this seems perverse.

ὥστε τὸν αὐτὸν ἐχθρὸν εἶναι καὶ φίλον: Given only by *A.P.*, this is the standard formula for a full offensive and defensive alliance (T. I. 44. i, cf. *SEG* x 86, 20, M&L 87, 17, and F. E. Adcock & D. J. Mosley, *Diplomacy in Ancient Greece*, 189), and goes far beyond what other texts tell us of the objectives of the League. T. 1. 96. i says πρόσχημα γὰρ ἦν ἀμύνεσθαι ὧν ἔπαθον δῃοῦντας τὴν βασιλέως χώραν, and in two speeches Thucydides mentions the further aim of liberating Greeks from Persian rule (III. 10. iii, quoted p. 298, VI. 76. iii-iv); D.S. XI. 47. i refers to the collection of tribute πρὸς . . . τὸν ἀπὸ τῶν Περσῶν ὑποπτευόμενον πόλεμον; in H. VIII. 132. i envoys come from the Ionians after Salamis asking the Spartans to liberate Ionia, and after Mycale a Peloponnesian plan to transport the Ionians to Greece is overruled and islanders join the Greek alliance and are bound by oaths ἐμμενέειν τε καὶ μὴ ἀποστήσεσθαι (H. IX. 106. ii-iv). Hammond supposes that *A.P.* correctly reports the terms of Athens' alliance with the Ionians, strictly interpreted (cf. previous note); probably there is no conflict between *A.P.* and the other sources but the Athenians announced that the purpose of the League was to continue the war against Persia and bound its members in an offensive and defensive alliance.

ἐφ' οἷς καὶ τοὺς μύδρους ἐν τῷ πελάγει καθεῖσαν: Cf. Pl. *Arist.* 25. i (μύδρους ἐμβαλὼν ἐπὶ ταῖς ἀραῖς εἰς τὴν θάλατταν). The act apparently signified that the alliance was to last until the lumps of metal rose to the surface, i.e. indefinitely: cf. H. I. 165. iii (but see H. Jacobson, *Philol.* cxix 1975, 256-8, suggesting that this need not have implied permanence). The declared objectives of the alliance must therefore have extended beyond revenge, which can hardly have been envisaged as an unending activity (*pace* Sealey, *Ancient Society and Institutions: Studies . . . V. Ehrenberg*, 237-42).

24. i. θαρρούσης ἤδη τῆς πόλεως: Cf. 22. iii (θαρροῦντος ἤδη τοῦ δήμου after Marathon), 27. i (θαρρήσαντας τοὺς πολλοὺς after Pericles προὔτρεψεν τὴν πόλιν ἐπὶ τὴν ναυτικὴν δύναμιν). In Arist. *Pol.* II. 1274 A 12-15, cf. VIII. 1341 A 30, we read that as a result of the Persian Wars the δῆμος ἐφρονηματίσθη.

ἠθροισμένων πολλῶν: The papyrus gives these words in the reverse order, but with β and α noted above them: rightly, the correction has been accepted by most editors. A present participle would be more appropriate (cf. Kaibel & Wilamowitz[1-2], Kaibel, *Stil und Text*, 179) but I doubt if we are justified in emending.

συνεβούλευεν ἀντιλαμβάνεσθαι τῆς ἡγεμονίας: The subject is still Aristides. He has in fact already acquired the hegemony for Athens by securing τὴν ἀπόστασιν τὴν τῶν Ἰώνων ἀπὸ τῆς τῶν Λακεδαιμονίων συμμαχίας (23. iv) and organising the Delian League (23. v): 24 like the latter part of 23 features Aristides as προστάτης τοῦ δήμου, and the awkwardness here is to be attributed not to another change of source but to *A.P.*'s careless excerpting of his material. In the middle ἀντιλαμβάνεσθαι normally means simply 'take hold of', and the implication 'in place of Sparta' need not be present.

καὶ καταβάντας ἐκ τῶν ἀγρῶν οἰκεῖν ἐν τῷ ἄστει: Contrast T. II. 14. ii, 16, on the Athenians' migration into the city in 431 (χαλεπῶς δὲ αὐτοῖς διὰ τὸ αἰεὶ εἰωθέναι τοὺς πολλοὺς ἐν τοῖς ἀγροῖς διαιτᾶσθαι ἡ ἀνάστασις ἐγίγνετο). Thucydides should be right on the fifth-century pattern of settlement, and it must therefore be a result of later theorising that Aristides and δημοσία τροφή are said to have encouraged the growth of an urban proletariat. Sandys notices the contrast with the policy of keeping the citizens away from the city, busy working their land in the country, which is ascribed to Pisistratus in 16. iii.

τροφὴν γὰρ ἔσεσθαι πᾶσι: The League and the revenue from it would provide for the maintenance of all the citizens, so they would not need to continue working their own land. For attempts to assess how, and to what extent, the Athenians benefited economically from the League see Meiggs, *The Athenian Empire*, 255-72, M. I. Finley in P. D. A. Garnsey & C. R. Whittaker (edd.), *Imperialism in the Ancient World*, 103-26.

τοῖς δὲ τὰ κοινὰ πράττουσι: For the expression cf. Arist. *Pol.* VII. 1324 B 1. The allusion is to the salaries paid for the discharge of a citizen's civilian duties, of which the earliest instance appears to be jury pay, introduced by Pericles probably in the 450's (27. iii–iv with commentary).

οὕτω κατασχήσειν: The implication seems to be that revenue from the League would enable the Athenians to devote themselves fully to the military and civilian tasks of administering the League, and this in turn would enable them to maintain their control of the League—as the Spartiates lived on the proceeds of the land worked by the helots, and so could devote themselves fully to soldiering and to maintaining their mastery of the helots.

24. ii. λαβόντες τὴν ἀρχήν: In §i *A.P.* has written of ἀντιλαμβάνεσθαι

COMMENTARY ON THE *ATH. POL.*

τῆς ἡγεμονίας and κατασχήσειν τὴν ἡγεμονίαν; but in this section ἡγεμονία suddenly gives way to ἀρχή, the word which came regularly to be applied to what became an Athenian empire (e.g. T. I. 75. i, II. 63. i, III. 37. ii). The change in the way in which the Athenians thought of the League is reflected in the language of their inscriptions, from M&L 40, 31, via M&L 45, §§1, 3, 46, 6–7, 12, to *SEG* x 19, 14–15, 23, 8–9: cf. Meiggs, *The Athenian Empire*, 171–2 with 425–7. Probably the source from which *A.P.* is excerpting went into some detail on the change from alliance to empire.

δεσποτικωτέρως: The comparative has not been found elsewhere, either in this form or as δεσποτικώτερον; the positive form of the adverb is used both by Isocrates (IV. *Paneg.* 104, claiming that Athens treated the members of the Delian League συμμαχικῶς ἀλλ' οὐ δεσποτικῶς; VIII. *Pace*, 134) and by Aristotle (*Pol.* IV. 1295 A 16).

πλὴν Χίων καὶ Λεσβίων καὶ Σαμίων: Arist. *Pol.* III. 1284 A 38–41 remarks that ἐπεὶ ... θᾶττον ἐγκράτως ἔσχον τὴν ἀρχήν the Athenians humbled Samos, Chios and Lesbos παρὰ τὰς συνθήκας. Samos lost her fleet and her old independence after the war of 440–439 (T. I. 117. iii), and Thucydides writes of what happened before the Peloponnesian War Ἀθηναῖοι ναῦς τε τῶν πόλεων τῷ χρόνῳ παραλαβόντες πλὴν Χίων καὶ Λεσβίων, καὶ χρήματα τοῖς πᾶσι τάξαντες φέρειν (I. 19 cf. II. 9. v); he represents the Mytilenaeans as saying in 428 οἱ ξύμμαχοι ἐδουλώθησαν πλὴν ἡμῶν καὶ Χίων· ἡμεῖς δὲ αὐτόνομοι δὴ ὄντες καὶ ἐλεύθεροι τῷ ὀνόματι ξυνεστρατεύσαμεν (III. 10. v); Mytilene and the Lesbian cities which joined her in revolt were deprived of their ships and their freedom (III. 50), but Methymna, which stayed loyal, retained her ships (VI. 85. ii); Chios in winter 424/3 was required to demolish a new wall and (ποιεῖν) πρὸς Ἀθηναίους πίστεις καὶ βεβαιότητα ἐκ τῶν δυνατῶν μηδὲν περὶ σφᾶς νεώτερον βουλεύσειν (IV. 51), but she retained her ships (VI. 43, 85. ii), and her revolt in 412 (VIII. 5. iv) was therefore of particular value to Sparta. It was rightly seen as a sign of independence that a member of the League should contribute ships rather than pay tribute in cash, since a state which contributed ships could refuse to take part in a campaign of which she disapproved and retained the means to resist in the event of a dispute with Athens (cf. T. I. 99. ii–iii). There were, of course, different degrees of independence, and the Athenians could claim that they left all their allies αὐτόνομοι (cf. Gomme, *Hist. Comm. Thuc.*, i. 225–6).†

τούτους δὲ φύλακας εἶχον τῆς ἀρχῆς: The Mytilenaeans in 428 protest ξύμμαχοι μέντοι ἐγενόμεθα οὐκ ἐπὶ καταδουλώσει τῶν Ἑλλήνων Ἀθηναίοις, ἀλλ' ἐπ' ἐλευθερώσει ἀπὸ τοῦ Μήδου τοῖς Ἕλλησιν, and allege that they were left independent for the sake of appearances and because it suited Athens to put pressure on her weaker allies first (T. III. 10. iii, 11. iii–vi).

ἐῶντες τάς τε πολιτείας παρ' αὐτοῖς: When Chios revolted in 412 this was the work of οἱ ὀλίγοι, while οἱ πολλοί were οὐκ εἰδότες τὰ πρασσόμενα (T. VIII. 9. iii), the decision to revolt seems to have been taken at a meeting of the boule (VIII. 14. ii), and Thucydides admired the constitution (VIII. 24. iv: for his taste in constitutions see on 33. ii); an oligarchic (or a more narrowly oligarchic) régime was established by the Spartan Pedaritus (VIII. 38. iii): probably the old régime in Chios was a moderate oligarchy (cf. W. G. Forrest, *BSA* lv 1960, 180–1, T. J. Quinn, *Hist.* xviii 1969, 22–6). In Mytilene and the cities which revolted with her it seems likely that Athens tolerated oligarchies before the revolt (T. III. 27. ii–iii, 39. vi, 47. iii, cf. R. P. Legon, *Phoen.* xxii 1968, 200) but imposed democracies afterwards (cf. the restoration of *A.T.L.*, ii, D 22, 6–7; but Quinn, *Hist.* xx 1971, 405–17, believes that oligarchies continued). In Samos Athens established a democracy and so provoked revolt in 440 (T. I. 115. iii), so there too she must previously have tolerated an oligarchy; Thucydides does not say what happened after the revolt, but according to D.S. XII. 28. iv a democracy was once more imposed, and that is probably correct (e.g. Meiggs, *The Athenian Empire*, 183–4, 348, 357–8, Legon, *Hist.* xxi 1972, 145–58, contr. E. Will, *REA* lxxi 1969, 305–19); in 412 an oligarchy was overthrown or an attempt to establish one was frustrated (T. VIII. 21, *SEG* xiv 9).

The propaganda of the Peloponnesian War associated Athens with democracy and Sparta with oligarchy (cf. T. III. 82. i, and on Sparta's encouragement of oligarchy in the Peloponnese I. 19), and it was often said that Athens imposed democratic constitutions throughout her empire (e.g. Is. IV. *Paneg.* 104–6, VIII. *Pace*, 79, XII. *Panath.* 54, 68, Arist. *Pol.* v. 1307 B 22–4, cf. [X.] *A.P.* i. 14, 16); when the Second Athenian League was formed in the fourth century the Athenians specifically undertook not to interfere with the constitutions of the member states (Tod 123, 20–1). It is not clear how many exceptions there were to that generalisation: [X.] *A.P.* iii. 10–11 cites as unsuccessful experiments support for oligarchy in Boeotia and Miletus; Potidaea was allowed to receive magistrates from Corinth, and was probably oligarchic, until Athens sent an ultimatum in 433 (T. I. 56. ii); in 411 the Athenian oligarchs decided to change to oligarchy in the allied states as well as in Athens (T. VIII. 64. i, 65, i, cf. 48. v); but in 407 Selymbria seems to have been guaranteed constitutional freedom (M&L 87, 10–12). It seems unlikely that there was ever a time when all the ship-providing allies, but no others, had escaped constitutional interference. (For general discussions see *A.T.L.*, iii. 149–54, Meiggs, *op. cit.*, 208–10, neither work citing this passage from *A.P.*).

καὶ ἄρχειν ὧν ἔτυχον ἄρχοντες: We have little detailed information, but enough to show that deprivation of subject territory was one way in which Athens interfered with the independence of her allies: this happened to Thasos in 463/2 (T. I. 101. iii); the Samian War of 440–439 originated in Athens' supporting Miletus against Samos in a dispute 'concerning Priene' (T. I. 115. ii, cf. Gomme *ad loc.* and Meiggs, *op. cit.*, 428); in 427 Mytilene was deprived of the 'Actaean cities' on the Asiatic mainland (T. III. 50. iii cf. IV. 52. ii–iii: the assessment lists show that these cities stretched from Ophryneum on the Hellespont to Antandrus on the gulf of Adramyttium, and were assessed in 425 at over 45 talents [*A.T.L.*, ii, A 9, iii. 124–41, A 10, iv. 14–27, with vol. i. 467]). Atarneus was acquired by Chios in the sixth century (H. I. 160. iv), and H. VIII. 106. i mentions Chios' possession of it in the present tense; it is not named in the tribute lists or by Thucydides; it was occupied by Chian exiles from 409 (D.S. XIII. 65. iii) until 398 (X. *H.* III. ii. 11): so very probably Athens left that in the possession of Chios.

There is much in the language of §ii to offend the purist: the τε before συμμάχοις has no correlative, and while Blass[2-4] and Sandys[1] merely deleted it Kaibel & Wilamowitz were encouraged to add after ἄρχοντες ⟨αὐτοῖς ἐπιτρέποντες, καὶ ...⟩, supposing that τούτους δὲ φύλακας ... ἐπιτρέποντες is a parenthesis and that a remark on the cleruchies is to be supplied in the following lacuna (in their 3rd ed. αὐτοῖς ἐπιτρέποντες disappears but καὶ and the lacuna remain); they also added τὰς after πολιτείας (cf. Kaibel, *Stil und Text*, 179–80), and H. Richards, disturbed to find ἐῶντες governing both an accusative without a verb and an infinitive without an accusative, restored ⟨τὰς⟩ παρ' αὐτοῖς ⟨ἔχειν⟩ (*CR* v 1891, 334). But there are many passages in *A.P.* where the grammatical and logical coherence are imperfect, especially when as here (cf. other notes on §§i–ii) the author is condensing or excerpting, and we should probably attribute the imperfections to the author and leave the text unemended.

24. iii. ὥσπερ Ἀριστείδης εἰσηγήσατο: This takes up the second theme announced in §i.

ἀπὸ τῶν φόρων καὶ τῶν τελῶν καὶ τῶν συμμάχων: καὶ τῶν συμμάχων reads oddly as the third member of this trio, after φόρος (paid by most member states of the League) and τέλη (taxes, paid [by Athenians and] by foreigners in Attica, whether citizens of allied states or not). L. Whibley, *CR* v 1891, 180, proposed εἰσφορῶν for φόρων, but the context requires a source of income from abroad, not a tax imposed on residents; Kaibel & Wilamowitz[1-2] deleted καὶ τῶν συμμάχων (cf. Kaibel, *Stil und Text*, 180), and Herwerden & Leeuwen proposed to delete καὶ τῶν τελῶν καὶ; Hude printed [[καὶ]] τῶν ⟨ἀπὸ τῶν⟩ συμμάχων, and one could make a simpler correction on the same lines, to . . . τελῶν ἀπὸ τῶν συμμάχων. *A.P.*'s source can hardly have said what we find in the London papyrus, but there is so much carelessness in this chapter that it would be rash to insist that the fault must lie with a copyist and not with *A.P.* himself.†

πλείους ἢ δισμυρίους ἄνδρας τρέφεσθαι: The list of τρεφόμενοι 'shows considerable, if perverted, learning, and strong political bias; it is based on genuine fifth-century evidence, but it is collected from isolated statements by fifth-century authors, of various dates and not all of equal value; some at least come from comedy. I suspect the collector to have been Theopompus' (Gomme, *CR* xl 1926, 8; cf. *Hist. Comm. Thuc.*, i. 47–8, suggesting that Theopompus in turn used Stesimbrotus). I doubt whether the collector can be reliably identified; on Stesimbrotus and Theopompus cf. Introduction, pp. 22–3.

I also doubt whether it can be assumed that the man who collected these details was hostile to the fifth-century democracy as Stesimbrotus and Theopompus were, although this assumption is almost always made (most recently by Moore, 247–8, cf. Mathieu, *Aristote, Constitution d'Athènes*, 59–60, 119, though he is more willing than most to see democratic influences in *A.P.*, but contrast J. H. Schreiner, *SO* Supp. xxi 1968, 60, 72). On Athens' treatment of the League §§i–ii are not apologetic, but if her rule could be described as a tyranny by men who did not disapprove of that rule (Pericles *ap.* T. II. 63. ii, Cleon *ap.* T. III. 37. ii, Ar. *Eq.* 1111–14) what is said here need not be critical of Athens: we need not suppose that the criticism of Is. VIII. *Pace*, 61–105, and the whitewashing of Lys. II. *Epit.* 55–6, Is. IV. *Paneg.* 103–9, were the only attitudes available to fourth-century commentators. Migration from the country to the city was indeed regarded by Aristotle as conducive to a worse kind of democracy (cf. *Pol.* VI. 1318 B 6–1319 A 39, cited by Moore), and the author of *A.P.* certainly had the same dislike of extreme democracy as we find in Arist. *Pol.*; but demagogues who wished to hold sway in an assembly attended by large numbers of lower-class citizens would presumably regard migration to the city as desirable, and I find nothing pejorative in the language used of migration in §i. Again, *A.P.* disliked as did Aristotle in the *Politics* the kind of democracy in which revenue and leisure allow the poor to play as active a part as the rich (cf. IV. 1291 B 30–1292 A 38, 1292 B 22–1293 A 10, VI. 1318 B 6–1319 A 39), but supporters of democracy approved of μισθοφορία and will have had few scruples if the allies helped to pay the μισθοί (in Ar. *Vesp.* 655–724 the only criticism seems to be that the money finds its way into the wrong pockets): any exaggeration in the suggestion that large numbers of citizens could be permanently maintained at the allies' expense could as easily have been made by a supporter of the practice as by a critic, and again I find nothing obviously hostile in the language of §iii. Contrast ch. 27, where the presentation of Pericles and his introduction of jury pay undoubtedly is hostile. What is at issue is not *A.P.*'s own attitude to the material assembled here but the attitude of his source. 23. ii^b–24 seems to me to form a unit, marred though it is by *A.P.*'s compression, and in it Aristides and the 'democratic' policies attributed to him are presented in terms that need not be regarded as hostile so long as we recognise that an Athenian could speak of ruling over the allies and of τροφή without necessarily implying disapproval.

On the whole list see Wilamowitz, *A.u.A.*, i. 153–61, ii. 201–7. T. vi. 24. iii mentions the hope of ἀΐδιον μισθοφορὰν as one reason why ordinary citizens enthusiastically supported the Sicilian expedition of 415. [X.] *A.P.* i. 15 says τοῖς δὲ δημοτικοῖς δοκεῖ μεῖζον ἀγαθὸν εἶναι τὰ τῶν συμμάχων χρήματα ἕνα ἕκαστον Ἀθηναίων ἔχειν, and i. 16–18 enumerates the economic benefits derived from requiring the allies to bring their lawsuits to Athens; iii. 4 seems to be derived from the same ultimate source as *A.P.*'s list (cf. p. 309). In Ar. *Vesp.* 707–11 it is said that Athens has 1,000 tribute-paying allies, who could provide maintenance for 20,000 Athenians: this is not to be taken as sober fact (before the Peloponnesian War the numbers of members paying tribute from year to year range between 140 and 175; the actual or potential members found in the quota lists and assessment lists total slightly under 350) but we may suspect that this is, or is derived from, the ultimate source of the 'fact' in *A.P.*, as Ar. *Pax*, 605–11 gave rise to the view of the origins of the Peloponnesian War adopted by Ephorus and found in D.S. xii. 38–41. i *init.* (cf. Gomme, *CR* xliv 1930, 66). The individual items in the list are discussed separately below: some of the figures are unverifiable, and it is unlikely that there was ever a time when all those listed, and no others, qualified for δημοσία τροφή; if with Kenyon we allow 4,000 men for the twenty νῆες φρουρίδες, and if we do not follow Kaibel & Wilamowitz in assuming a substantial lacuna in the following clause, we obtain a total of 19,750 men without the πρυτανεῖον καὶ ὀρφανοὶ καὶ δεσμωτῶν φύλακες. It must be remembered that many of the men listed, such as jurors and bouleutae, were paid only for the days when they actually served.

δικασταί . . . ἑξακισχίλιοι: Cf. Ar. *Vesp.* 662, Suid. (Π 2996) πρυτανεία; also And. 1. *Myst.* 17, claiming that one trial was held ἐν ἑξακισχιλίοις Ἀθηναίων; and compare the rules governing ostracism and other νόμοι ἐπ' ἀνδρί, according to which six thousand votes had to be cast (cf. p. 270). Gomme doubted whether the figure was ever more than a rhetorical approximation (*CR* xliv 1930, 66), but what we learn from the πινάκια about the enrolment of jurors in the fourth century suggests that even then there was a fixed quota of jurors (cf.

on 63. iii). On Pericles' introduction of payment for jurors see 27. iii–iv with commentary; on the rate of pay see 62. ii with commentary.

τοξόται δ' ἑξακόσιοι καὶ χίλιοι: This is the figure given by T. II. 13. viii for 431 (And. III. *Pace*, 7 has χιλίους τε καὶ διακοσίους ἱππέας καὶ τοξότας τοσούτους ἑτέρους, probably a careless error); it is likely that the archers were a regiment whose paper strength remained constant. They were presumably paid, we do not know how much, while on active service. These citizen archers are not to be confused with the regiment of Scythian archers maintained in the fifth century to keep order in the city (e.g. Ar. *Ach.* 54 with schol., *Eq.* 665: see Gilbert, *C.A.S.A.*, 173–4, Busolt & Swoboda, *G.S.*, ii. 979–80).

ἱππεῖς χίλιοι καὶ διακόσιοι: Again the same figure is found in T. II. 13. viii, where it is said to include the ἱπποτοξόται (and this time And. III. *Pace*, 7 agrees): the ἱππεῖς proper then numbered 1,000 (Ar. *Eq.* 225), and that number was maintained in the fourth century (X. *Hipparch.* ix. 3, suggesting that the number was hard to maintain; D. XIV. *Symm.* 13). Schol. Ar. *Eq.* 627 states that at one time the cavalry numbered 600 but later the number was increased to 1,200; And. III. *Pace*, 5, followed by A. II. *F.L.* 173, claims that (in the course of the Pentecontaetia) Athens acquired 300 cavalry; Phil. 328 F 39 (from book IV, which included the Periclean era) said πότε κατεστάθησαν χίλιοι· διάφορα γὰρ ἦν ἱππέων πλήθη κατὰ χρόνον Ἀθηναίοις, but further details are not preserved. On the size of the force in the Hellenistic period see *SEG* xxi 525 with J. Threpsiades & E. Vanderpool, *AΔ* xviii 1963, μελ. 106, J. H. Kroll, *Hesp.* xlvi 1977, 95–7. It is clear from the cup published by Cahn in *RA* 1973 (cf. below, p. 564) and the story in Pl. *Cim.* 5. ii–iii that Athens had cavalry in the late sixth and early fifth centuries, but the history of the Persian Wars does not suggest that they were a large or important force. When the force was enlarged has been inconclusively discussed: see A. Martin, *Les Cavaliers athéniens*, 121–34 (447–438), B. Keil, *Anonymus Argentinensis*, 139–42 (*c.* 450), W. Helbig, *Les ἱππεῖς athéniens*, 231–41 (470's).

Possibly the ἱππεῖς like other soldiers received a stipend when on active service (Ar. *Eq.* 576–7 suggests that they served without pay, but for the fourth century see D. IV. *Phil.* i. 28 with Kroll, *op. cit.*, 97–8 n. 36). They received a fodder grant for their horses, presumably paid throughout the year (cf. 49. i with commentary): we know from a papyrus fragment of Lysias that after the restoration of democracy in 403 the daily μισθός of the ἱππεῖς was reduced from 1 drachma to 4 obols, but that of the ἱπποτοξόται was increased from 2 obols to 8 obols (*P. Hib.* i 14 = Lys. fr. vi Gernet & Bizos, lines 70–82); 4 obols a day for 1,000 men will yield the 40 talents a year of X. *Hipparch.* i. 19 (cf. Kroll, *loc. cit.*; but earlier writers interpreted it as 1 drachma a day for a reduced force, e.g. Martin, *op. cit.*, 350–4, Busolt & Swoboda, *G.S.*, ii. 1186 n. 4). A capital sum, κατάστασις, was paid to those who joined the force, and certainly could be and probably regularly was reclaimed from those who left it (Lys. XVI. *Mant.* 6–7; Harp., Phot., Suid. [*K* 788] *s.v.*, quoting Eupolis, fr. 268 Kock, cf. Plat. Com. fr. 165 Kock: see Martin, *op. cit.*, 335–45, P. Cloché, *La Restauration démocratique à Athènes en 403 avant J.-C.*, 368–73). Two Hellenistic inscriptions refer to τιμήσεις τῶν ἵππων (*SEG* xxi 525, 14–15 [282/1], 435, 27–8 [187/6]), and recently hoards of lead tablets have been found recording the colour, brand and value of cavalrymen's horses (K. A. I. Braun, *AM* lxxxv 1970, 129–32, 198–269, Kroll, *Hesp.* xlvi 1977, 83–140): Kroll, *op. cit.*, 97–100, suggests that these values were registered because the state would pay the value of a horse killed in action (up to a limit of 1,200 drachmae). W. K. Pritchett in his study of military pay (*U. Calif. Pub. Cl. Stud.* vii 1971 = *The Greek State at War*, i, 3–29) does not deal with the cavalry.†

For the πρόδρομοι who succeeded the ἱπποτοξόται see 49. i with commentary.

βουλὴ δὲ πεντακόσιοι: This was the size of the boule from its remodelling by Cleisthenes (21. iii) until the creation of two additional tribes in 307/6. Payment to bouleutae was being made in 412/1 (T. VIII. 69. iv), and is likely to have been instituted before rather than after the outbreak of the Peloponnesian War; for the rate of pay see 62. ii with commentary.

φρουροὶ νεωρίων πεντακόσιοι: These may be identical with the φρουροί of 62. i, appointed by lot in the demes (cf. Sandys *ad loc.*); otherwise nothing is known about them. The identification is accepted and they are attributed to Aristides by B. Jordan, *U. Calif. Pub. Cl. Stud.* xiii 1975, 60–1.

ἐν τῇ πόλει φρουροὶ ν′: πόλει here probably denotes the Acropolis (rather than the city in contrast to the Piraeus); there is no need to follow Kaibel & Wilamowitz[2–3] and Blass in deleting τῇ. Little is known about these guards: πυλωροί and ἀκροφύλακες are attested in the Roman period (*IG* ii² 2292–2310); W. Wyse *ap.* Sandys cites *IG* i² 44, 14–17, where reference to τές φυλές τές πρυτανευόσες proves that the three men serving as φύλακες are citizens, but they are also described as τοξόται, and it may be that they (or indeed the whole contingent of Acropolis guards) belonged to the regiment of archers mentioned above.

ἀρχαὶ δ' ἔνδημοι μὲν εἰς ἑπτακοσίους ἄνδρας: For the contrast between ἔνδημοι and ὑπερόριοι ἀρχαί, those within and those beyond the frontiers of the state, cf. Arist. *Pol.* III. 1285 B 13–14, 18, and a law *ap.* A. 1. *Tim.* 19; see also next note. It is hard to imagine what the basis for *A.P.*'s figures may be: Wilamowitz, *A.u.A.*, ii. 202–4, lists a variety of candidates for inclusion in this category and has no difficulty in exceeding 700; if we reckon up the (by no means complete) list of fourth-century officials given in *A.P.* 43. i, 47. i–56. i, 60–1, excluding the διαιτηταί, whose numbers varied, and officials who already received a stipend as members of the boule, we reach a total of 305, a small number of them ὑπερόριοι.†

ὑπερόριοι δ' εἰς †ἑπτακοσίους†: Inscriptions make it clear that Athenian ἄρχοντες, ἐπίσκοποι, garrisons and garrison commanders were frequently sent to the allied cities (cf. Meiggs, *The Athenian Empire*, 211–15, J. M. Balcer, *Hist.* xxv 1976, 257–87; *IG* i² 56, 5–7, refers to ℎοίτινες Ἀθεναίον ἄρχοσι ἐν τῆι ℎυπερορίαι, and [X.] *A.P.* i. 19 refers to τὰς ἀρχὰς τὰς εἰς τὴν ὑπερορίαν; cf. also X. *Anab.* VII. i. 27). There were also Athenian colonies and cleruchies, some of which may have had to receive officials from Athens (cf. the study of Athenian overseas settlements by P. A. Brunt, *Ancient Society and Institutions: Studies . . . V. Ehrenberg*, 71–92) as the cleruchies of the fourth century did (62. ii); and there will also have been an ἄρχων εἰς Σαλαμῖνα (62. ii, cf. M&L 14, 11–12); but we cannot begin to estimate how many Athenian officials with postings abroad there may have been at any time during the existence of the Delian League. The language is not what we should expect with the same number of ἔνδημοι and of ὑπερόριοι ἀρχαί (cf. Kaibel, *Stil und Text*, 181, Wilamowitz, *A.u.A.*, ii. 202–3); here it is more likely that the error is due to a scribe's careless repetition than that a second ἑπτακοσίους was written by *A.P.*

ἐπεὶ συνεστήσαντο τὸν πόλεμον ὕστερον: The early commentators' objections to this as a piece of Greek (e.g. Leeuwen, *Mnem.* xix 1891, 187, H. Richards, *CR* v 1891, 334; contr. Kaibel, *Stil und Text*, 181) were unnecessary: cf. Is. x. *Hel.* 49, Polyb. II. 1. i, III. 25. i, also T. I. 15. ii. More serious doubts have been raised about the sense: if the text is right, τὸν πόλεμον without qualification must be the Peloponnesian War, and the figures for hoplites and sailors that follow ought to be those for Athens' total forces, perhaps at the beginning of the war (easily obtainable from T. II. 13. vi–viii); but the figures which we are given are much smaller, and can only be justified (there is no other evidence against which we can check them) on the assumption that they represent regular peace-time quotas of some kind. Some care has been devoted to the compilation of these figures, and it is incredible that what follows was intended to represent the strength of Athens' forces in the Peloponnesian War. Gomme accordingly suggested that we should combine the συνέστησαν of Leeuwen, *loc. cit.*, with the ⟨τὰ εἰς⟩ τὸν πόλεμον suggested by Kaibel & Wilamowitz¹⁻² and see in the passage a reference to the standing forces maintained before the outbreak of the Peloponnesian War (*CR* xl 1926, 9, cf. Wilamowitz, *A.u.A.*, 204): so much is unsatisfactory in this chapter that it is hard to be sure that a correction is not an improvement on *A.P.* rather than a restoration of the original text, but here the corruption is easily explained and emendation seems justified.

Ulpian's *hypothesis* to D. XIII. *Synt.* (222 Dindorf) ascribes military pay to Pericles: we do not know the authority for this. It is not clear when Athens introduced payment for service in the army and navy, but this could well be earlier than payment for performance of a citizen's civilian duties: W. K. Pritchett, *U. Calif. Pub. Cl. Stud.* vii 1971 = *The Greek State at War*, i, 7–14, collects and discusses the evidence.

ὁπλῖται μὲν δισχίλιοι καὶ πεντακόσιοι: T. II. 13. vi cf. 31. ii gives as the number of Athenian and metic hoplites in 431 13,000 combat troops + 16,000 on garrison duties; D.S. XII. 40. iv divides the same total into 12,000 + 17,000; and other figures for fifth-century Athens are compatible with these (cf. Gomme, *Population of Athens*, passim, *Hist. Comm. Thuc.*, ii. 34–9). Wilamowitz was the first to make the plausible but unverifiable suggestion that *A.P.*'s figure represents the peace-time quota of garrison troops needed by Athens in Attica and the League (*loc. cit.*). Thucydides tells us that the hoplites engaged in the siege of Potidaea were paid 2 drachmae a day, 1 drachma for themselves and 1 drachma for an attendant (III. 17. iv: many editors have regarded the chapter as an interpolator's concoction, and Gomme accepted the chapter but regarded this as an unusually high rate, but neither need be the case); in Ar. *Ach.* 159 the Odomantians demand 2 drachmae a day, but it is not clear how outrageous this is intended to be; in 413 Thracian mercenaries were expensive at 1 drachma a day (T. VII. 27. ii). Pritchett, *op. cit.*, 14–24, reviews the evidence and suggests that in fifth-century Athens 3 obols was the standard rate both for hoplites and for oarsmen but higher rates could be paid when necessary in special circumstances; but more probably a higher rate was normal until after the Sicilian expedition.

νῆες δὲ φρουρίδες εἴκοσι: There is no other evidence for a regular squadron of guard ships, except perhaps Pl. *Per.* 11. iv (each year sixty ships were sent out for eight months); the only other references to Athenian νῆες φρουρίδες in those words are to two at Miletus in 450/49 (*A.T.L.*, D 11, 87) and to the squadron based on Naupactus in the 420's (T. IV. 13. ii). The normal complement of a trireme was 200 men (H. VII. 184. i, VIII. 17, X. *H.* I. v. 4–7, Plat. *Critias*, 119 A–B), so *A.P.*'s twenty ships will have required 4,000 men (cf. Kenyon[3]). Athens perhaps paid her oarsmen 1 drachma a day until the Sicilian disaster, thereafter 3 obols (T. III. 17. iv, VI. 8. i, 31. iii, VIII. 45. ii, with Dover on VI. 31. iii, B. Jordan, *U. Calif. Pub. Cl. Stud.* xiii 1975, 112–16; contr. Gomme on III. 17. iv, Pritchett, *loc.*

cit., believing that the standard rate was always 3 obols). Not all the oarsmen were citizens: cf. p. 327.

νῆες αἱ τοὺς φόρους ἄγουσαι ... δισχιλίους ἄνδρας: Kenyon confidently prints the papyrus' text, with no hint in the *apparatus* of his Berlin ed. or O.C.T. that doubts have been expressed; but few have felt able to share his confidence. The clause is unsatisfactory in syntax, with the accusative τοὺς ... δισχιλίους ἄνδρας unattached, and in sense, because it was normally the duty of the allies to send their tribute to Athens (M&L 46, 68)—though when a state defaulted Athens might send men to exact the money (M&L 68, 15–17) and there may have been occasions when a commander found it convenient to collect tribute directly for the expenses of his own expedition (cf. Gomme, *Hist. Comm. Thuc.*, i. 277–8, A. French, *Hist.* xxi 1972, 1–20). ἀργυρολόγοι νῆες are mentioned in T. III. 19. i (428); IV. 50. i (425/4), 75. i (424); cf. II. 69 (430/29)—in each case, it seems, shortly after a reassessment of the tribute (cf. B. D. Meritt, *Athenian Financial Documents*, 19–20; *A.T.L.*, iii. 69–70). Elsewhere, however, ἀργυρολογεῖν is used not of tribute-collecting but of special exactions, by Theramenes and Thrasybulus in 411/0 (X. *H.* I. i. 8–12) and by Alcibiades at the time of Notium (Pl. *Alc.* 35. v), so Meiggs more plausibly suggests that Thucydides' allusions also are to special exactions in addition to the tribute (*The Athenian Empire*, 254, cf. Ar. *Eq.* 1070–1, Aristid. xiv. *Rom.* [i. 340 Dindorf]).

Gomme usefully reviewed the three ways in which scholars have tried to solve the problem (*CR* xl 1926, 9–10; but in *CR* xlii 1928, 225, he seems to repent of his own solution). (*a*) Blass substituted φρουροὺς for φόρους (*LZB* 1891, 304), and many have followed him (e.g. Kaibel, *Stil und Text*, 182; Sandys; Gomme, who to emphasise that the 2,000 are the crews of the transport ships addded ⟨ἐς⟩ δισχιλίους), but it is hard to believe that ships and crews were set aside in this way for the transport of garrisons (cf. Wilamowitz, *A.u.A.*, ii. 205 n. 7). (*b*) Many have made a minimal correction to rectify the syntax (e.g. ⟨ἐπὶ⟩ τοὺς φόρους, J. B. Mayor, *CR* v 1891, 112; φορολόγους, R. Y. Tyrrell, *ibid.*, 180; ἄγουσαι ⟨φέρουσαι⟩, G. Colin *ap.* Mathieu & Haussoullier; ἄγουσαι ⟨καὶ⟩, Mathieu & Haussoullier), while leaving the sense unchanged. (*c*) More boldly, Wilamowitz assumed that there is a larger lacuna after ἄγουσαι and that in the papyrus' text the beginning of one clause leads directly to the end of another (*A.u.A.*, ii. 205–6, cf. Kaibel & Wilamowitz), and like the champions of minimal emendation was prepared to accept the existence of ships sent to collect the tribute. It is hard to believe that the text of the papyrus is what *A.P.* wrote, but none of these solutions is wholly convincing: φόρους should be retained in preference to φρουρούς, since the change does not give a clearly better sense; Wilamowitz' larger lacuna has no intrinsic advantage over the simpler corrections of others, but there is ample evidence in this chapter that *A.P.* has been carelessly condensing his material, and Wilamowitz may be right with reference to *A.P.*'s source if not with reference to *A.P.*

IG i² 97 has been revised and related to this passage by B. D. Meritt, *Studies . . . D. M. Robinson*, ii. 298–303, cf. *SEG* xii 26 and *A.T.L.*, iii, p. xi: it concerns tribute and a naval squadron which includes some men appointed by lot. In *A.P.* Meritt accepts φόρους and a lacuna after ἄγουσαι: the 2,000 men could be used for tribute-collecting or for other purposes (*op. cit.*, 302–3).

ἔτι δὲ πρυτανεῖον: *A.P.*'s language becomes yet more condensed. The allusion must be to those who were entitled to the honour of σίτησις ἐν πρυτανείῳ. An inscription (*IG* i² 77, revised and discussed by W. E. Thompson, *AJP* xcii 1971, 226–37) contains part of a fifth-century decree regulating the honour, which was to be conferred on the priests of Demeter and Core (lines 4–5), on the senior living descendants of Harmodius and Aristogiton (5–9, cf. Isae. v. *Her. Dic.* 47, Din. I. *Dem.* 101; other distinguished Athenians and their descendants came to be similarly honoured), on certain men designated by Apollo (9–11), and on Athenians who won certain victories in the great games (11 sqq., cf. Plat. *Apol.* 36 D 5–9); others invited to dine in the prytaneum included the athlothetae at the time of the Panathenaea (62. ii with commentary), χρησμολόγοι (schol. Ar. *Pax*, 1084), distinguished foreign visitors, and Athenians returned from missions abroad (see evidence assembled by R. E. Wycherley, *The Athenian Agora*, iii, pp. 173–4). Hes. πρυτανεῖον refers to three συσσίτια at Athens: the other two should be the θεσμοθετεῖον, where the archons dined (schol. Plat. *Phaedr.* 235 D: see 3. v with commentary), and the θόλος, where the prytanes (43. iii with commentary) and the state secretaries dined (D. xix. *F.L.* 249 with schol., 314); see Wycherley, *op. cit.*, 168. If both ceremonial and working heads of state dined elsewhere, we may wonder who presided at the dinner in the prytaneum. For the prytaneum see commentary on 3. v; for the religious aspect of the meal there see N. D. Fustel de Coulanges, *La Cité antique*, liv. iii, ch. vii, §1 (179–83, ed. of 1916).

ὀρφανοί: Sons of citizens who fell in war were maintained at state expense until they came of age: cf. T. ii. 46. i, Plat. *Menex.* 248 E 6–8, Arist. *Pol.* ii. 1268 A 8–11, A. iii. *Ctes.* 154; also *SEG* x 6, 121–5, [X.] *A.P.* iii. 4; D.L. I. 55 ascribes the institution to Solon. According to Arist. *Pol.* the institution was devised for Miletus by Hippodamus, ὡς οὔπω τοῦτο παρ' ἄλλοις νενομοθετημένον (ἔστι δὲ καὶ ἐν Ἀθήναις οὗτος ὁ νόμος νῦν καὶ ἐν ἑτέραις τῶν πόλεων): this is regularly and perhaps correctly rendered 'as if . . . (but in fact . . .)', but the evidence that we have does not exclude the possibility that the

Milesian institution (2nd qr c5?) is indeed the earliest. See the discussion of R. S. Stroud, *Hesp.* xl 1971, 288–90, who unwisely regards this passage in *A.P.* as evidence for the time before Ephialtes' reforms.†

δεσμωτῶν φύλακες: Since *A.P.* is concerned with citizens the reference must be to the Eleven (52. i with commentary: 35. i refers to τοῦ δεσμωτηρίου φύλακες ἕνδεκα under the régime of the Thirty, and they are designated δεσμοφύλακες in schol. D. xxii. *Andr.* 26, schol. D. xxiv. *Tim.* 80, schol. Ar. *Vesp.* 1108 [corrupted to θεσμοφύλακες] and Poll. viii. 102 [confused with the νομοφύλακες]), rather than to the δημόσιοι who served under them. The same expression is found in [X.] *A.P.* iii. 4 (apparently regarding their appointment as a function of the δικαστήρια, though Wilamowitz, *A.u.A.*, ii. 206 n. 10, thought the boule was intended), and there too the reference is more probably to the Eleven than to their δημόσιοι.

The combination of these with the war orphans and the men entertained in the prytaneum is surprising (Wilamowitz, *A.u.A.*, ii. 206, remarked that invalids awarded a subsistence grant [49. iv] might more appropriately be added). The same surprising combination is found in [Xenophon]'s list of matters that keep the Athenians busy ([X.] *A.P.* iii. 4: . . . καὶ ὀρφανοὺς δοκιμάσαι καὶ φύλακας δεσμωτῶν καταστῆσαι), and it is hard to resist the conclusion that he and *A.P.* derived this from a common source.

ἡ διοίκησις: διοικεῖν in *A.P.* normally refers to the administration of the state's affairs (e.g. 3. vi, 14. iii, 16. ii, 23. i), and in 43. i τὴν ἐγκύκλιον διοίκησιν is the day-to-day, civilian administration of the state (cf. *ad loc.*); but the original meaning of διοικεῖν is 'to keep house', and it is a short step from that to the use of διοίκησις to mean 'maintenance'. D. xxiv. *Tim.* 97 uses διοικεῖν and διοίκησις of the state's regular expenditure; cf. διοικεῖν in Str. 659. xiv. ii. 24; also the decree *ap.* D. xxiv. *Tim.* 27, D. xlv. *Steph. i.* 32, Ath. ii. 46 E (doubtful reading).

25. i. ἡ μὲν οὖν τροφή . . . ἐγίγνετο: On the structure of these chapters cf. Introduction, pp. 48–9. Here *A.P.* sums up first his section on τροφή, which is said to be the result of Aristides' organisation of the Delian League after the Persian Wars, and is derived from a source which held that victory over the Persians led to the development of the democracy (23. ii[b]–24) . . .

ἔτη δὲ ἑπτακαίδεκα . . . ὑποφερομένη κατὰ μικρόν: . . . and then the previous section, which represented the post-war period as one of domination by the Areopagus, which was due to the Areopagus' assistance in the evacuation of Athens before Salamis (23. i–ii[a]). He is about to write of Ephialtes' reform, by which the Areopagus was deprived of τὰ ἐπίθετα δι' ὧν ἦν ἡ τῆς πολιτείας φυλακή (§ii), and the resumption of his first theme serves both to round off chs 23-4 and to prepare the way for his account of Ephialtes. Jacoby in his commentary on Phil. 328 F 117 argued that schol. Ar. *Lys*. 1144 is derived from Philochorus, irresponsibly emended a dating of the Spartan earthquake and the outbreak of the Third Messenian War from the 12th year after Plataea = 468/7 to the 18th year = 462/1, and deduced from this that Androtion (reflected in *A.P.*) and Philochorus both regarded the period of the Areopagus' supremacy as a distinct era in Athenian history.

ἔτη δὲ ἑπτακαίδεκα μάλιστα: This is followed by a statement that Ephialtes' reform was enacted in 462/1 (§ii), which could be described as 'the eighteenth year' (cf. p. 193): the 17 years are therefore from 479/8 (the year after Salamis, with which the Areopagus' ascendancy is associated in 23. i) to 463/2 inclusive. 480/79 was used as a base date in 23. v, and is to be used again in 27. ii (cf. G. V. Sumner, *CQ*² xi 1961, 32); the last battles of the war, Plataea and Mycale, were not fought until 479/8; but it would have been more natural to count from the year of Salamis here too, and we may wonder if *A.P.* has miscalculated or a scribe has miscopied.

προεστῶτ(ων) τ(ῶν) Ἀρεοπαγιτῶν: τ(ῶν) is reported as doubtful in Kenyon's Berlin ed., as absent by Wilcken and by M. H. Chambers, *TAPA* cii 1971, 44; but the article is needed even if the scribe omitted it.

ὑποφερομένη κατὰ μικρόν: The same metaphor is used in 36. i: τῆς πόλεως ὑποφερομένης under the régime of the Thirty, Theramenes is annoyed and urges them μεταδοῦναι ... τῶν πραγμάτων τοῖς βελτίστοις. Here the gradual 'decline' of the city under Areopagite domination is contrasted with its gradual 'growth' ἅμα τῇ δημοκρατίᾳ in the previous period (23. i with commentary). This use of ὑποφέρεσθαι seems originally to be medical (LSJ cites instances only from Hippocrates and from late writers, especially Plutarch; the two passages in *A.P.* are noticed in the 1968 Supplement); cf. Kaibel, *Stil und Text*, 48.

αὐξανομένου δὲ τοῦ πλήθους: This contrasts sharply with the words immediately preceding. It is not clear how such 'growth' could have taken place in a period of 'decline' and Areopagite domination; but it is easy to see how it could have taken place during the growth of the Delian League and the development of τροφή as outlined in 23. ii^b-24, and we are reminded of προῆλθεν ἡ πόλις ... κατὰ μικρὸν αὐξανομένη in the summary at the beginning of 23. i, and of the remarks on the confidence of the δῆμος or the city in 22. iii, 24. i and 27. i. In the next phrase Ephialtes is presented as τοῦ δήμου προστάτης, as were Aristides and Themistocles in 23. iii; Ephialtes like Aristides is said to be δίκαιος; and the account of Ephialtes' reform in §ii takes a democratic view of the Areopagus. Here as in 23. ii[b]–24 *A.P.* is following a pro-democratic source; the transition at this point is not handled as neatly as that in 23. ii.

In point of fact, as the prestige of the Areopagus was likely to be high in 480 because most of its members were men who had become archons by election but after the fall of the tyranny (cf. p. 287), by 462/1 its prestige is likely to have declined as an increasing number of its members were men who had become archons by lot.

τοῦ δήμου προστάτης: As in 23. iii we are given the 'democratic' leader but not his opponent; in 26. i, which purports to describe the situation after Ephialtes' reform, Cimon is προστάτης but not ἡγεμών of the ἐπιεικέστεροι. In 28. ii, however, Ephialtes and Cimon form an opposing pair.

Ἐφιάλτης ὁ Σοφωνίδου: We know nothing about Sophonides and very little about Ephialtes. Apparently after the battle of the Eurymedon, Ephialtes commanded a naval expedition which went beyond the Chelidonian Islands (Callisth. 124 F 16 *ap.* Pl. *Cim.* 13. iv, cf. Meiggs, *The Athenian Empire*, 79, 91); he unsuccessfully opposed Cimon's proposal to help Sparta in the Third Messenian War (Pl. *Cim.* 16. viii–ix); he is included in a list of leading statesmen who were not rich (Ael. *V.H.* II. 43, XI. 9, XIII. 39; III. 17 describes him as a philosopher); and he was assassinated shortly after enacting his reform (§iv *fin.* with commentary).

The reform of the Areopagus is ascribed here to Ephialtes and in §§iii–iv to Ephialtes and Themistocles; in 27. i a subsequent attack on the Areopagus is ascribed to Pericles (who is associated with Ephialtes' attack on the Areopagus by Pl. *Cim.* 15. ii, *Per.* 9. v, 10. vii); in 35. ii we read that in 404 the Thirty annulled the laws of Ephialtes and an unidentifiable Archestratus περὶ τῶν Ἀρεοπαγιτῶν; and in the list of μεταβολαί or μεταστάσεις in 41. ii Ephialtes achieves what Aristides had pointed out. Arist. *Pol.* II. 1274 A 7–8 mentions the 'pruning' of the Areopagus by Ephialtes and Pericles in language which would be compatible either with the two successive reforms of *A.P.* or with the joint reform of Plutarch (there is no justification for deleting καὶ Περικλῆς, with De Sanctis, *Ἀτθίς*[2], 410 n. 1, Hignett, *H.A.C.*, 197 n. 3). Ephialtes' reform was probably enacted while Cimon was in Messenia, and it was probably the success of this known opponent of Sparta which led the Spartans to fear their Athenian allies and dismiss them (cf. T. I. 102. iii, Pl. *Cim.* 15. ii–iii, with Busolt, *G.G.*, III. i. 261 and n. 1, Hignett, *H.A.C.*, 196, 337–41, J. R. Cole, *GR&BS* XV 1974, 369–85; contr. E. M. Walker, *C.A.H.*, v[1]. 71, 467–8, Jacoby, *Supp.* ii. 369–70 n. 17); on his return Cimon tried to upset the reform but failed and was ostracised (Pl. *Cim.* 15. iii, 17. iii, *Per.* 9. v). A link between the various opponents of Cimon is provided by Aeschylus, whose *Persae* focuses attention primarily on the achievement of the Athenians at Salamis, including that of Aristides and the hoplites on Psyttalea (cf. R. Lattimore, *Classical Studies ... W. A. Oldfather*, 82–93), but must in 472 also have served to glorify Themistocles (cf. above, p. 289), whose choregus on that occasion was Pericles (*hypothesis* with *IG* ii² 2318, 9–11), and who on the occasion when Cimon and his fellow generals replaced the regular judges forfeited the first prize to Sophocles (Pl. *Cim.* 8. viii–ix). Almost certainly there was one occasion when the Areopagus' powers were reduced, in 462/1: Themistocles, though he had been an associate of the reformers, was no longer in Athens (cf. on §iii); Pericles was one of the prosecutors of Cimon after his reduction of Thasos (27. i with commentary), but he was a supporter of Ephialtes rather than a principal actor, and the ascription to him in 27. i of a later attack on the Areopagus 'looks like a desperate attempt to reconcile conflicting traditions' (Hignett, *H.A.C.*, 197; on Sealey's view of the young Pericles see below, p. 336); Archestratus probably was an associate of Ephialtes and the author of some of the laws by which the Areopagus' powers were reduced, and since we know so little about Ephialtes it need cause no surprise that we know nothing about Archestratus (cf. Hignett, *H.A.C.*, 198). In the notes that follow I shall for convenience attribute the reform simply to Ephialtes.

There is no need for the commentator on *A.P.* to write an essay on the political views of Aeschylus. His connections with the opponents of Cimon are clear enough; in his *Supplices*, perhaps to be dated 463, he displays a sympathetic preoccupation with the idea that the will of the δῆμος is all-important (cf. A. J. Podlecki, *The Political Background of Aeschylean Tragedy*, 42–62); his *Eumenides*, produced in 458, centres on the institution of the Areopagus as a court to try Orestes for homicide (esp. lines 681–710). The significance of Athena's speech in the *Eumenides* has been disputed: it points to the good that will be done by the Areopagus in the role of which Ephialtes did not deprive it, as long as there are no innovations or defilements (the text of 693 is uncertain) in the laws; I find it easier to believe that Aeschylus is not expressing enthusiasm for the reform but after the event felt regret at what had happened or at any rate fear that in the future the democrats might go too far (cf. E. R. Dodds, *CQ*² iii 1953, 19–20, *PCPS*² vi 1960, 19–31 = *The Ancient Concept of Progress*, 45–63; but see also K. J. Dover, *JHS* lxxvii 1957, 230–7, esp. 234–6). Cf. below, p. 322.†

After Σοφωνίδου the text of *A.P.* is interrupted by 1½ columns of *hypothesis* to and commentary on D. XXI. *Mid.*, begun on the verso of the papyrus but abandoned before the text of *A.P.* was written there. Cf. Introduction, p. 4.

δοκῶν καὶ ἀδωροδόκητος εἶναι καὶ δίκαιος πρὸς τὴν πολιτείαν: The papyrus has κ(αὶ) δοκῶν, which Blass[1-3] and some others retained; others deleted καί (e.g. Kaibel & Wilamowitz[1-2]); but Kaibel's transposition (*Stil und Text*, 182) is the best solution. πρὸς τὴν πολιτείαν is probably to be understood with δίκαιος alone: W. L. Newman, *CR* v 1891, 160, compared Arist. *Pol.* v. 1309 A 36–7 (δικαιοσύνην . . . τὴν πρὸς τὴν πολιτείαν).

Ephialtes is honest as well as poor in Ael. *V.H.* xi. 9, xiii. 39; Aristides, represented in 41. ii as his predecessor, is credited with his notorious δικαιοσύνη in 23. ii (again with δοκῶν), and both are singled out as honest in Pl. *Cim.* 10. viii. Earlier *A.P.* has agreed with the δημοτικοί in rejecting as implausible the story that Solon contrived to profit from his σεισάχθεια (6. iii–iv); however in 27. iii–iv Pericles is not similarly upright but introduces payment for jurors as a manoeuvre to counter Cimon's generosity (T. ii. 65. viii cf. 60. v and Is. viii. *Pace*, 126 insist on Pericles' incorruptibility —polemically, since Plat. *Gorg.* 516 A 1–2 and Pl. *Per.* 32. iii–iv show that he had been charged with embezzlement; cf. T. ii. 21. i, Ar. *Nub.* 859 with schol., Pl. *Per.* 23. i–ii, on the suspicion that in 446 he bribed the Spartan king Pleistoanax). Nothing is said in criticism of the democrats in 23. ii[b]–25. ii, and we need not follow R. W. Wallace, *GR&BS* xv 1974, 259–60 n. 4, in asserting that there is no trace of democratic sources in *A.P.* and δοκῶν must be intended to cast doubt on Ephialtes' incorruptibility and justice. It should not surprise us that the man who prosecuted Areopagites περὶ τῶν διῳκημένων (cf. below) should himself have claimed or have been claimed to be conspicuously honest: whether the claim was justified we cannot tell.

τῇ βουλῇ: The Areopagus was the older council in Athens, and must for some time after Solon's institution of the council of four hundred have remained The Boule *par excellence*; in the time of Lysias the correct form of address to the Areopagus was still ὦ βουλή (Lys. iii. *Sim.* i, iv. *Vuln. Praemed.* i, vii. *Ol.* i). It is perhaps a sign of the comparative antiquity of *A.P.*'s ultimate source that here and in §ii ἡ βουλή *tout court* is used of the Areopagus and in §ii the council of five hundred is identified by number; if, as I suspect, the powers of the five hundred were at first limited to προβούλευσις and the discipline of their own members (cf. p. 260 and commentary on 8. iv), the older usage may well have persisted until after the time of Ephialtes.

25. ii. ἀγῶνας ἐπιφέρων περὶ τῶν διῳκημένων: It is hard to see why individual Areopagites should be prosecuted for their part in the official activities of the Areopagus. More probably they were prosecuted for their conduct as magistrates (cf. Wilamowitz, *A.u.A.*, ii. 94), in particular, in the εὔθυναι which they had to undergo on retirement from the archonship (cf. Wade-Gery, *BSA* xxxvii 1936/7, 269 = *Essays*, 177), and in this way Ephialtes was enabled to discredit the Areopagus, the council which these retired archons would join automatically unless sentenced to ἀτιμία. Pl. *Per.* 10. viii represents Ephialtes as φοβερὸν ὄντα τοῖς ὀλιγαρχικοῖς καὶ περὶ τὰς εὐθύνας καὶ διώξεις τῶν τὸν δῆμον ἀδικούντων ἀπαραίτητον.

ἐπὶ Κόνωνος ἄρχοντος: 462/1 (D.S. XI. 74. i). Diodorus' brief treatment of Ephialtes comes later, under 460/59 (XI. 77. vi), but his narrative dates are unreliable and *A.P.*'s dating need not be doubted (cf. pp. 295–6).

ἅπαντα περιείλε<το> τὰ ἐπίθετα: The middle form, restored in Kenyon's later editions, was championed by H. Richards, *CR* v 1891, 227, and Kaibel & Wilamowitz; champions of the papyrus' active form include Blass[2-4], Thalheim, Oppermann and Tovar (cf. *REC* iii 1948, 159–61). Here, as in 15. iv, the active is defensible and should therefore be retained (contrast §iv, below, where the middle is preferable).

In 3. iii ἐπίθετα are contrasted with πάτρια as 'additional', more recent (cf. *ad loc.*). According to Pl. *Cim.* 15. ii the many, led by Ephialtes, overturned τὸν καθεστῶτα τῆς πολιτείας κόσμον τά ⟨τε⟩ πάτρια νόμιμα οἷς ἐχρῶντο πρότερον (cf. D.S. XI. 77. vi, Paus. I. 29. xv, both clearly hostile to Ephialtes); Lysias wrote of ἐπίθετα . . . ὁπόσα μὴ πάτρια ὄντα ἡ ἐξ Ἀρείου πάγου βουλὴ ἐδίκαζεν (fr. 178 Sauppe). In these accounts of the powers exercised by the Areopagus before the reform, accretions or part of the established order, we very probably have the rival campaigning slogans of Ephialtes and his opponents. On the significance of ἐπίθετα cf. Wilamowitz, *A.u.A.*, ii. 186–7, Mathieu, *Aristote, Constitution d'Athènes*, 64–6, Hignett, *H.A.C.*, 195, Dover, *JHS* lxxvii 1957, 234; J. K. Davies, *Democracy and Classical Greece*, 69–70, compares the definition of what are πάτρια for the Praxiergidae in *SEG* xiv 3 (*c*. 450's); but Jacoby, *Supp.* ii. 106–7 n. 20, supposed that as in 3. iii the word is used in a purely historical sense, without political bias, and Sealey, overlooking the fragment of Lysias, supposed that in this language we have a debate of the fourth century projected back to the fifth (*CP* lix 1964, 13 = *Essays*, 45). Contemporary debate may be reflected also in the allegation that Cimon on his return to Athens tried τὴν ἐπὶ Κλεισθένους ἐγείρειν ἀριστοκρατίαν (Pl. *Cim.* 15. iii: cf. p. 261); and there is a very distorted reflection in D. XXIII. *Arist.* 205, where it is alleged that Cimon was fined ὅτι τὴν πάτριον μετεκίνησε πολιτείαν. *A.P.*, in describing the powers taken from the Areopagus as ἐπίθετα, gives us the democrats' view of Ephialtes' reform (cf. Mathieu, *loc. cit.*, 116, J. H. Schreiner, *SO* Supp. xxi 1968, 63); it is a view which it is hard to reconcile with the view of the pre-Draconian Areopagus given in 3. vi (noticed by Wilamowitz, *loc. cit.*, Mathieu, *op. cit.*, 10).†

COMMENTARY ON THE *ATH. POL.* [25. ii

The laws by which this reform was accomplished were presumably enacted by decrees of the assembly (cf. p. 248, on Cleisthenes): their text was published on the Areopagus, to be taken down in 404 by the Thirty (35. ii), as in 337/6 a law directed against the Areopagus was published on two stelae, τὴμ μὲν ἐπὶ τῆς εἰσόδου τῆς εἰς Ἄρειον πάγον τῆς εἰς τὸ βουλευτήριον εἰσιόντι, τὴν δὲ ἐν τῆι ἐκκλησίαι (*SEG* xii 87, 22–7).

δι' ὧν ἦν ἡ τῆς πολιτείας φυλακή: Before the legislation of Draco the Areopagus τὴν ... τάξιν εἶχε τοῦ διατηρεῖν τοὺς νόμους (3. vi); in the 'Draconian constitution' it φύλαξ ἦν τῶν νόμων καὶ διετήρει τὰς ἀρχὰς ὅπως κατὰ τοὺς νόμους ἄρχωσιν (4. iv); and Solon appointed it ἐπὶ τὸ νομοφυλακεῖν, ὥσπερ ὑπῆρχεν καὶ πρότερον ἐπίσκοπος οὖσα τῆς πολιτείας (8. iv). Aesch. *Eum.* 704–6 may be cited as evidence that the Areopagus' position as guardian of the state was discussed at this time:

> κερδῶν ἄθικτον τοῦτο βουλευτήριον,
> αἰδοῖον, ὀξύθυμον, εὑδόντων ὕπερ
> ἐγρηγορὸς φρούρημα γῆς καθίσταμαι.

The decree ordering a revision of the law code in 403 prescribed ἐπιμελείσθω ἡ βουλὴ ἡ ἐξ Ἀρείου πάγου τῶν νόμων, ὅπως ἂν αἱ ἀρχαὶ τοῖς κειμένοις νόμοις χρῶνται (*ap.* And. I. *Myst.* 84); later, apparently shortly before 323, a board of seven νομοφύλακες was instituted, who τὰς ἀρχὰς ἐπηνάγκαζον τοῖς νόμοις χρῆσθαι (Phil. 328 F 64 with Jacoby's commentary: the νομοφύλακες are not mentioned in *A.P.*; F 64b[a] ascribes them to Ephialtes, the most plausible attempt to uphold this is that of W. S. Ferguson, *Klio* xi 1911, 265–76, but in the absence of confirmatory evidence it must be rejected).

Unfortunately neither *A.P.* nor any other source states in concrete terms what powers were involved in the Areopagus' guardianship of the state and were taken away by Ephialtes. *A.P.*'s only hint is that Ephialtes distributed these powers among the boule of five hundred, the δῆμος and the δικαστήρια; in Pl. *Cim.* 15. ii–iii, *Per.* 9. v, the Areopagus is deprived of almost all its κρίσεις and the many make themselves masters of the δικαστήρια, and Cimon attempts πάλιν ἄνω τὰς δίκας ἀνακαλεῖσθαι; the fragment ascribing the νομοφύλακες to Ephialtes says that he μόνα κατέλιπε τῇ ἐξ Ἀρείου πάγου βουλῇ τὰ ὑπὲρ τοῦ σώματος, and in fact the Areopagus' judicial powers seem subsequently to have been limited to certain cases of homicide and wounding, certain religious offences, and arson (Lys. VII. *O.* 22, D. XXIII. *Arist.* 22, [D.] LIX. *Neaer.* 79–80, *A.P.* 57. iii, 60. ii, with commentary). Some have thought guardianship of the laws to be a power of overruling the assembly if it passed an illegal or otherwise undesirable resolution, as later this could be done by means of the γραφαὶ παρανόμων (apart from a possibly anachronistic allusion in a speech in T. III. 43. iv–v, first attested in 415, in And. I. *Myst.* 17; cf. [Pl.] *X. Or.* 833 D, Ant. frs 8–14, 47, Sauppe) and νόμον μὴ ἐπιτήδειον θεῖναι (attested in the fourth century) (for these γραφαί cf. 45. iv, 59. ii, with commentary): champions of this view include De Sanctis, *Ἀτθίς*, ¹349 = ²356, ²439 n. 2, Wade-Gery, *CQ* xxv 1931, 140, xxvii 1933, 24 with n. 3 = *Essays*, 130–1, 146–7 with 146 n. 4; for a later date for the institution of the γραφὴ παρανόμων see H. J. Wolff, *Sb. Heidelberg* 1970, ii. 15–22. Others believe this guardianship to be not a specific power but a convenient summary of the various powers possessed by the Areopagus which enabled it to enforce respect for the laws (e.g. Hignett, *H.A.C.*, 90–1, 127–8, 208–9). I have suggested as a refinement on this second view that the Areopagus' status was so described very early, at the time of Draco's codification or before, and that as circumstances changed the Areopagus used this description and the prestige of the ex-archons who were its members to justify it in new ways of enforcing the law, and that law-enforcing functions assumed in this way rather than conferred by law could easily be represented as accretions by reformers and as part of the established order by conservatives (*Essays . . . C. M. Bowra*, 41–2, *A.B.*, 203).†

Two areas of activity can be identified in which it is likely that the Areopagus exercised its guardianship of the state before the reforms. First, there is the process of εἰσαγγελία for charges of a treasonable nature and perhaps also for ἄγραφα δημόσια ἀδικήματα: εἰσαγγελίαι were directed to the Areopagus by Solon (8. iv), but in the late fifth and fourth centuries were heard by the boule, assembly and δικαστήρια (cf. on 43. iv), and Ephialtes' reform provides the obvious occasion for the transfer. Secondly, there were various judicial or quasi-judicial procedures concerned with the oversight of public officials which in classical Athens were handled by democratic organs but may earlier have been the preserve of the Areopagus (cf. Lipsius, *A.R.*, 37): the δοκιμασία undergone by officials before taking up an office to which they had been appointed (cf. Wilamowitz, *A.u.A.*, ii. 188–9, De Sanctis, *Ἀτθίς*, ¹146–7 = ²150, ²435, and commentary on 55. ii, but contr. Hignett, *H.A.C.*, 91, 205–8); the charge of νόμοις μὴ χρῆσθαι to which officials were liable during their term of office (cf. Hignett, *H.A.C.*, 90–1: on this see 45. ii with commentary); and the εὔθυναι in which their conduct was examined on retirement from office (cf. Hignett, *H.A.C.*, 203–5, Sealey, *CP* lix 1964, 18–20 = *Essays*, 52–4: on this examination see 48, iv–v, 54. ii, with commentary).[29] εἰσαγγελίαι and the oversight of officials would give the Areopagus an opportunity for great political influence; the

---

[29] On the claim of Arist. *Pol.* II. 1274 A 15–18, III. 1281 B 32–4, that Solon gave the right τὰς ἀρχὰς εὐθύνειν to the δῆμος, cf. p. 155.

archons from whom the Areopagus was recruited were now men appointed by lot to a routine office (cf. on 22. v), and a generation's experience of working Cleisthenes' political machinery (cf. p. 256) will have encouraged the Athenians to question the right of such a collection of men to important powers; it may be conjectured that the Areopagus had offended Ephialtes and his associates by condemning Themistocles for medism on an εἰσαγγελία (cf. §iii with commentary) and by acquitting Cimon in his εὔθυναι of taking bribes from Macedon (cf. 27. i with commentary); and I suspect that these are the activities of the Areopagus to which Ephialtes wished to put an end. In addition, if I am right in thinking that the guardianship of the state had become a pretext for the Areopagus' exercise of insecurely-based powers, the Areopagus' right to that title must have been attacked: a purely negative measure is unlikely (cf. Wilamowitz, *A.u.A.*, ii. 188), and I am inclined to think of a formal transfer of guardianship to the boule of five hundred and the assembly. I argue for the view of the Areopagus' powers taken here in *Essays . . . C. M. Bowra*, 39–49, *A.B.*, 201–6; see also Wilamowitz, *A.u.A.*, ii. 186–200, Hignett, *H.A.C.*, 193–213, Sealey, *CP* lix 1964, 11–22 = *Essays*, 42–58, R. W. Wallace, *GR&BS* xv 1974, 259–69, J. Martin, *Chiron* iv 1974, 29–42.†

τὰ μὲν τοῖς πεντακοσίοις: In the structure of the sentence the boule is distinguished from the δῆμος-and-lawcourts: it is a sufficient explanation that the lawcourts were regarded as meetings of the δῆμος, able to pronounce the will of the δῆμος as the boule was not (cf. below).

In post-Ephialtic Athens the boule was involved in the hearing of εἰσαγγελίαι for major offences against the state (cf. on 43. iv) and against magistrates on charges of νόμοις μὴ χρῆσθαι (45. ii), in some δοκιμασίαι, of which at any rate that of the archons was probably acquired from the Areopagus (45. iii, 55. ii–iv), in the interim examination of magistrates' accounts each prytany (48. iii), and in one side of the process of εὔθυναι (48. iv–v, contr. 54. ii). In 47. i and 49. v it is stressed that the boule συνδιοικεῖ . . . ταῖς ἄλλαις ἀρχαῖς τὰ πλεῖστα. If the powers of Cleisthenes' boule, like those of Solon's boule, were limited to προβούλευσις and the discipline of its own members, Ephialtes' transfer of the oversight of officials from the Areopagus to the boule will mark the beginning of the boule's development as the most important body in the administration of Athens (cf. Rhodes, *Essays . . . C. M. Bowra*, 49, *A.B.*, 201–6, 209–13); I have tentatively suggested that before Ephialtes' reform the boule was not busy enough to need a standing committee, and that it may have been Ephialtes rather than Cleisthenes who first divided it into prytanies (*A.B.*, 17–19).

τὰ δὲ τῷ δήμῳ: Here, as often, δῆμος denotes the meeting of the citizen body in the assembly (cf. M. H. Hansen, *GR&BS* xix 1978, 127–46): in post-Ephialtic Athens the assembly was involved in the hearing of εἰσαγγελίαι for major offences against the state (43. iv), and each prytany it held a vote of confidence in the ἀρχαί (*ibid.*, cf. 61. ii).

καὶ τοῖς δικαστηρίοις: The δικαστήρια of post-Ephialtic Athens were involved in almost all the procedures mentioned above: εἰσαγγελίαι for major public offences (cf. on 43. iv) and on charges of νόμοις μὴ χρῆσθαι (45. ii), δοκιμασίαι (45. iii, 55. ii–iv), trials of men deposed in a vote of confidence (61. ii), and εὔθυναι (48. iv–v, 54. ii).

Solon had provided for the assembly, as the heliaea, to try lawsuits referred to it from the verdict of an individual magistrate by the ἔφεσις of a dissatisfied party (9. i with commentary); in the late fifth and fourth centuries the archons and some other magistrates remained competent to impose fines or settle disputes up to a fairly low limit (cf. 52. iii with commentary), but otherwise the magistrate within whose purview a case fell would hold a preliminary enquiry to check that the case was in order, a survival of his old independent jurisdiction (cf. 56. vi with commentary), and the case would then be referred automatically to one of the δικαστήρια into which the heliaea was divided, in which that magistrate would preside. Although Hansen, *op. cit.*, stresses that the word δῆμος is not used of the δικαστήρια as it is used of the assembly, the δικαστήρια were thought of as a cross-section of the δῆμος, able to pronounce the will of the δῆμος on the litigants before them: there was no appeal against their decisions, and no limit to the penalties which they might impose in cases where the penalty was not fixed by law.

The manner and date of this change are disputed. Wade-Gery argued for an abrupt reform by Ephialtes, and believed that the older procedure can be detected in the Athenian decree for Phaselis (M&L 31) and that the newer is reflected in the trial of Orestes (for homicide, by the Areopagus) in Aeschylus' *Eumenides* (*BSA* xxxvii 1936/7, 236–70 = *Essays*, 171–9; *Essays*, 180–200; cf. earlier Wilamowitz, *A.u.A.* ii. 333–4, 341: the newer procedure is said to be characteristic of ἡ τελευταία δημοκρατία in Arist. *Pol.* IV. 1298 A 30–2). Sealey prefers to think of a gradual development, in which as the Athenians grew in political consciousness and confidence they made increasing use of their right of ἔφεσις, until ἔφεσις became automatic except in trivial cases (*CP* lix 1964, 14–18 = *Essays*, 46–52), and D. M. MacDowell is not sure that magistrates were ever forbidden to give verdicts in non-trivial cases (*The Law in Classical Athens*, 33). I agree with Sealey that gradual development is more likely than abrupt reform, but (as he admits) the division of the heliaea into separate δικαστήρια will have required legislation, and I suspect that in the end there was a law which standardised what had become normal practice. It is possible but not necessary that Ephialtes was responsible for some of this legislation; at any rate, to deal with the business taken from the Areopagus, he will probably have had to subdivide the heliaea if that had not already been done (cf. Rhodes, *Essays* . . . *C. M. Bowra*, 46–7, *A.B.*, 204 n. 1).

25. iii. ἔπρα[ξ]ε: Kenyon[1-3] claimed to read ἔπραττε, and the imperfect was championed by Kaibel, *Stil und Text*, 182; Blass and Wilcken claimed to read ἔπραξε. Either tense can be defended, but it appears that the scribe wrote the aorist.

συναιτίου γενομένου Θεμιστοκλέους: The only other text in which Themistocles is associated with Ephialtes' attack on the Areopagus is the *hypothesis* to Is. VII. *Areop.*, which cites *A.P.* but gives a different motive for the attack, that both men were in debt to the state. This silence is surprising: Plutarch wrote a life of Themistocles and included *A.P.* among his sources (*Them.* 10. vi cites *A.P.* 23. i; the last sentence of *A.P.* 25. iv is cited in *Per.* 10. viii, and 27. iv is cited in *Per.* 9. ii), and we might have expected him to mention the anecdote if only to rule it out as impossible. Plutarch may of course have been careless or have decided not to mention the anecdote, but probably as in the case of the 'Draconian constitution' in ch. 4 we should conclude from the silence of him and of other writers that the edition in which *A.P.* circulated most widely in antiquity did not include it; on the other hand, the appearance of the story with a reference to *A.P.* in the *hypothesis* indicates that this is not merely the interpolation of a note made by a reader in his private copy some centuries later. The way in which the story is appended suggests that it does not come from the same source as §§i–ii, and the abrupt transition from it to the last sentence of the chapter supports this explanation (cf. below). Cf. Introduction, pp. 53–5: this view of the story was first suggested by T. Reinach, *REG* iv 1891, 143–58, esp. 149–51, but not many have accepted it; Mathieu, *Aristote, Constitution d'Athènes*, 64–6, 119–20, attributed it to the 'oligarchic pamphleteer' whom he regarded as one of *A.P.*'s three principal sources, and J. H. Schreiner, *SO* Supp. xxi 1968, 63–77, *LCM* iii 1978, 213–14, attributes 25. i–ii to Clidemus and 25. iii–iv (with an earlier date for the reform) to Androtion, but neither explains the lack of other references to the story.

Themistocles was ostracised; on accusations from Sparta after he had left Athens he was convicted of medism, and he fled to the Persian court: the story is told in T. I. 135–8 and was often repeated; Pl. *Them.* 22–31 notes several variations; Crat. 342 F 11 names his prosecutor as Leobotes Ἀλκμέωνος Ἀγρυλῆθεν, an Alcmaeonid with a name borrowed from Sparta. The dating of his downfall has been frequently but inconclusively discussed (for maximum scepticism see Rhodes, *Hist.* xix 1970, 392-9), but almost all are agreed that he was condemned several years before 462/1; there is a unique allusion to his return, expunged by some editors, in Cic. *Ep. Fam.* v. 12. v. (Sandys cites early attempts to save the anecdote, to which may be added P. N. Ure, *JHS* xli 1921, 165-78, M. L. Lang, *GR&BS* viii 1967, 273, cf. Schreiner, *locc. citt.*) He belonged to the same circle as Ephialtes and Pericles (cf. p. 312), but he cannot have tried to avert his condemnation by assisting in the attack on the Areopagus, and it is more likely that his condemnation helped to provoke that attack (cf. p. 317). The 'fable' is firmly disposed of by Wilamowitz, *A.u.A.*, i. 140-2.

For the absolute use of συναίτιος cf. Arist. *De An.* II. 416 A 14, *Met.* Δ. 1015 A 21, also Plat. *Polit.* 287 B 7.

ὃς ἦν μὲν τῶν Ἀρεοπαγιτῶν: Having been archon in 493/2 (cf. p. 279).

ἔμελλε δὲ κρίνεσθαι μηδισμοῦ: Medism would be an appropriate charge for an εἰσαγγελία, and it is likely that that procedure was used and that the Areopagus was the body which condemned Themistocles (cf. Rhodes, *A.B.*, 199-201, *JHS* xcix 1979, 105, but Wilamowitz, *A.u.A.*, i. 140, went too far in proclaiming this as a 'notorious' fact: Reinach believed the story to be legally impossible and used this as a further argument for its being an interpolation, and Hansen, *Eisangelia*, 70, believes that Themistocles was charged before the assembly): Crat. 342 F 11a (*ap. L.R.C.* εἰσαγγελία) cites the case as an instance of εἰσαγγελία, while Pl. *Them.* 23. i (= F 11b) represents the prosecutor as γραψάμενος αὐτὸν προδοσίας. There are traces of a proposal that Themistocles should be tried by the Greeks as a whole (D.S. XI. 55. iv, Pl. *Them.* 23. vi: presumably, in view of Sparta's involvement, 'the Greeks' are those who united to resist Xerxes), and of a first accusation, against which he defended himself (D.S. XI. 54. ii-v, 55. vii-viii, Pl. *Them.* 23. iv-v, [Them.] *Ep.* xviii [757 Hercher], cf. Longin. *Inv.* [Walz, *Rhet. Graec.*, ix. 548-9]): there may be some truth behind them, but they more probably derive from an elaboration of the legend.

τὴν βουλήν: Although the anecdote is probably a late insertion in the text of *A.P.*, it shares with §i-ii the practice of using βουλή *tout court* to refer to the Areopagus, and of identifying the five hundred by their number.

πρὸς μὲν τὸν Ἐφιάλτην ... πρὸς δὲ τοὺς Ἀρεοπαγίτας ... : The story is at least *ben trovato*: the wily Themistocles wins the confidence both of Ephialtes and of the Areopagus, retaining as long as he can the possibility of supporting either against the other. Moore, 252, detects 'something of an echo of the way in which Pisistratus first got the tyranny'.

συνισταμένους ἐπὶ καταλύσει τῆς πολιτείας: For the language cf.

8. iv (εἰσαγγελία allowed against τοὺς ἐπὶ καταλύσει τοῦ δήμου συνισταμένους) and other νόμοι περὶ τῶν τυράννων quoted on pp. 220–1. In Athens καταλύειν is normally used of the δῆμος or the δημοκρατία, and Tod 144, 29–32, distinguishes between [τόν] δῆμον καταλύε[ι τὸν Φλειασίων] and [τὴν πολιτεία]ν τὴν Ἀχαιῶν ... [... καταλύηι ἢ] μεθιστῆι, but the verb can equally well be used of dissolving any kind of régime: in 28. v Theramenes is defended against the charge of πάσας τὰς πολιτείας καταλύειν, and in 36. i the extremists among the Thirty fear that he may (καταλύειν) τὴν δυναστείαν (cf. Plat. *Legg*. IX. 864 D 2–3, 'decree of Demosthenes' *ap*. D. XVIII. *Cor*. 182).

τοὺς [[ἀφ]]αιρεθέντας: The compound gives an unacceptable sense, and the correction to the simple verb (by Kenyon[1]) is generally accepted; there is no need to insert ὑπό (suggested by H. Richards, *CR* v 1891, 227). Sandys compares Lys. XIII. *Agor*. 23 (οἱ διαιρεθέντες τῶν βουλευτῶν codd., αἱρεθέντες Reiske). The reference here is to a group of men chosen (by and) from the Areopagus.

οὗ διέτριβεν ὁ Ἐφιάλτης: 'Where Ephialtes was': in this context the reference cannot be to Ephialtes' house (*pace* Kenyon's Oxford Translation).

μονοχίτων: This is the earliest known instance of the word, which recurs in Pythaen. 299 F 3, Polyb. XIV. 11. ii and writers of the Roman period; the Homeric equivalent is οἰοχίτων (*Od*. XIV. 489). The meaning is 'wearing the χίτων (undergarment) only, and not also the ἱμάτιον', and this was presumably thought to contribute to the self-abasement appropriate to the act of supplication (on which see J. P. A. Gould, *JHS* xciii 1973, 74–103).

ἐπὶ τὸν βῶμον: The precise reference, presupposed by the article, is not explained, but if *A.P.* is abbreviating from a more detailed source this need cause no alarm.

25. iv. συναθροισθείσης τῆς βουλῆς τῶν πεντακοσίων ... καὶ πάλιν ἐν τῷ δήμῳ: The Areopagus' powers will have been reduced by one or more decrees of the assembly, and before the assembly could vote on them the boule must at any rate have been persuaded to put the matter on the assembly's agenda (45. iv with commentary). It may also be relevant that after Ephialtes' reform a charge of συνίστασθαι ἐπὶ καταλύσει τῆς πολιτείας would be presented in an εἰσαγγελία to the boule and assembly (cf. on 43. iv).

περιείλοντο: The papyrus has περειλον, with το added above, and Kenyon's περιείλοντο should be accepted, though Herwerden & Leeuwen preferred παρείλοντο and Blass[4] παρεῖλον. The contrast between the middle here and the active in §ii is defended by Tovar, *REC* iii 1948, 159–61.

καὶ * * * ἀνῃρέθη δὲ καὶ ὁ Ἐφιάλτης: Themistocles disappears from the story, and we pass by an abrupt transition to the fate of

Ephialtes: Kaibel & Wilamowitz[1] were the first to postulate a lacuna from which the fate of Themistocles is missing (cf. Kaibel, *Stil und Text*, 182–3); a few have followed J. B. Mayor (*CR* v 1891, 112) and Blass (*LZB* 1891, 304) in simply deleting the first καί. The abruptness may be explained if the preceding anecdote is a late insertion in the text of *A.P.* (cf. p. 319), and the duplication of the καί may be a piece of carelessness perpetrated when the insertion was made.

δι' Ἀριστοδίκου τοῦ Ταναγραίου: 'Through the agency of . . .'; a man from Boeotia would be presumed to be the agent of an Athenian citizen. Cf. Pl. *Per.* 10. viii, citing *A.P.*; *Per.* 10. vii quotes and rejects the view of Idomeneus (338 F 8) that Pericles killed Ephialtes out of envy; Ant. v. *Caed. Her.* 68 says that the killers were never found; cf. also D.S. XI. 77. vi, [Plat.] *Axioch.* 368 D 6. That the mystery was solved between the time of Antiphon and the time of *A.P.* is extremely unlikely; Antiphon's argument requires an unsolved crime but he presumably had no need to invent one; either *A.P.* is repeating a rumour that was not substantiated or Aristodicus was known to be the actual killer but it was never discovered whose agent he was. The Ephialtic reform clearly aroused strong feelings: in addition to the ostracism of Cimon and the murder of Ephialtes we may note the fears of civil war in Aesch. *Eum.* 858–66, 976–87, and the rumour of an oligarchic plot at the time of Tanagra (T. 1. 107. iv, vi, cf. Pl. *Cim.* 17. iv–vii, *Per.* 10, i–iii).†

26. i. ἡ μὲν οὖν . . . τῆς ἐπιμελείας: A sentence of summary, rounding off the account of Ephialtes' reform before *A.P.* moves on to his next topic.

συνέβαινεν ἀνίεσθαι μᾶλλον τὴν πολιτείαν: 'The constitution became slacker.' ἀνιέναι means 'let go' (cf. its use by Solon, fr. 6 West *ap.* 12. ii); in one special sense it is used with the strings of a bow or a musical instrument as object (e.g. H. III. 22. i, Plat. *Lys.* 209 B 6), and in music some ἁρμονίαι were σύντονοι ('taut', apparently high-pitched) while others were ἀνειμέναι ('slack') or μαλακαί ('soft'). The different ἁρμονίαι were thought to have different moral qualities (cf. Plat. *Rep.* III. 398 C 1–399 E 4, Arist. *Pol.* VIII. 1339 B 40–1340 B 19, 1341 B 19–end), and came naturally to be compared with different political constitutions (e.g. Arist. *Pol.* IV. 1290 A 13–29, V. 1301 B 13–17, *Rhet.* I. 1360 A 19–30, also *E.E.* VII. 1241 B 27–30; cf. *Pol.* V. 1304 A 20–1, where the less democratic régime dominated by the Areopagus is συντονωτέραν [see 23. i with commentary]): probably this special sense is intended here. In Aristotelian usage the doctrine of the mean applies, and to be too taut and too slack are equally imperfect states; on the other hand, the association of manliness with tautness and of effeminacy with slackness led some to prefer the taut to the slack (cf. Plat. *Rep.*, *loc. cit.*, with the criticism of Arist. *Pol.* VIII. 1341 B 19–end). Whether ἀνιέναι is used here in its specialised or in a more general sense, whether (in the former case) the slackness is to be thought of as a departure from desirable tautness or from the mean, the description is clearly derogatory: the relaxation occurs διὰ τοὺς προθύμως δημαγωγοῦντας, at a time when the ἐπιεικεῖς have no ἡγεμών and under aristocratic but incompetent generals are suffering losses in war, and in this state of slackness the Athenians οὐχ ὁμοίως καὶ πρότερον τοῖς νόμοις (προσέχουσι).

On συμβαίνειν here and elsewhere in *A.P.* see Introduction, pp. 12–13: I am not persuaded by Day & Chambers that it is used of happenings that are 'accidental' in a philosophically significant sense.

διὰ τοὺς προθύμως δημαγωγοῦντας: The use of δημαγωγός and δημαγωγεῖν by Aristotle and earlier writers is studied by R. Zoepffel, *Chiron* iv 1974, 69–90 (cf. also W. R. Connor, *The New Politicians of Fifth-Century Athens*, 109–10). The older word for a political leader was προστάτης (cf. on 2. ii), and that is the term regularly used by Herodotus. [δημ]αγωγός is found in P. Heid. 182, *a* 4 (cf. M. Gigante, *Maia* ix 1957, 68–74, esp. 71, and Introduction, pp. 21–2); and it is used by Aristophanes of the leadership which is practised by Cleon and is to be taken over by the sausage-seller (*Eq.* 191–3, 213–22, cf. *Ran.* 416–21 [420–5 in some edd.]). Thucydides and Xenophon's *Hellenica* normally use προστάτης, but each twice uses δημαγωγός or a cognate (T. IV. 21. iii, of Cleon; T. VIII. 65. ii, of Androcles; X. *H.* II. iii. 27, of opponents of the Thirty; X. *H.* v. ii. 7, of the leaders in Mantinea whose power was broken when Sparta split the city into its component villages). In fourth-century writing Zoepffel distinguishes between orators, who use the word occasionally, without evaluative implications, as a synonym of ῥήτωρ or πολιτευόμενος (e.g. Lys. xxv. *Reip. Del. Defens.* 9, of δημοτικοί who changed to oligarchy in 411, XXVII. *Epicr.* 10), and historical and political writers, who use it of the great political leaders (e.g. Is. VIII. *Pace*, 126, XV. *Antid.* 234, cf. II. *Nic.* 16, X. *Hel.* 37, but the use of δημαγωγός of Pisistratus in XII. *Panath.* 148 is pejorative; he also uses προστάτης in the manner of Herodotus and Thucydides, e.g. XII. *Panath.* 15, 143, 151). Plato does not use δημαγωγός at all (in *Rep.* VIII. 565 A 6–566 A 4, describing the development of the democratic leader into the tyrant, he uses προστάτης). Aristotle differs from his predecessors in applying the word to a particular kind of leader, of whom he disapproves (a pejorative adjective is added only in *Pol.* II. 1274 A 14 and V. 1304 B 26, but the implication is always present: IV. 1292 A 4–37, associating δημαγωγοί with the extreme democracy in which the δῆμος considers itself above the laws, is fundamental).

A.P. uses δημαγωγεῖν here, in 27. i and in 28. i; in 27. iii Pericles in introducing jury pay is ἀντιδημαγωγῶν πρὸς τὴν Κίμωνος εὐπορίαν; δημαγωγία is used in 28. iv; δημαγωγός in 22. iii and 41. ii. In all seven passages the allusion is to a democratic kind of leadership: here and in 27. iii and 41. ii the implications are clearly hostile, and in 22. iii and 28. iv δημαγωγία is formally equivalent to προστασία τοῦ δήμου but has hostile undertones, but it is not obvious that δημαγωγεῖν is pejorative in 27. i or 28. i.

A.P.'s argument in 26–28. i is: after Ephialtes' reform, helped by the weakness of the opposition (26. i), the democracy made further progress (26. ii–iv); Pericles' introduction of jury pay had a corrupting effect (27); and after his death the leadership of the democracy fell into worse hands (28. i).

μηδ' ἡγεμόνα ἔχειν τοὺς ἐπιεικεστέρους, ἀλλ' αὐτῶν προεστάναι: What is said of Cimon in this section presents many difficulties. *A.P.* frequently identifies politicians as προστάται τοῦ δήμου or (in ch. 28) τῶν γνωρίμων, but here we are told that Cimon was προστάτης but not ἡγεμών, and however we explain or emend the text of this sentence (cf. below) the author's intention is clearly to disparage him. The distinction is a fine one, and various suggestions have been made for the insertion of an adjective before or after ἔχειν (σπουδαῖον, A. Gennadios, *CR* v 1891, 274; ἔμπειρον or πολιτικόν, H. Richards, *CR* v 1891, 227, 334, vii 1893, 212–13; ἱκανὸν, Sandys); Kaibel, *Stil und Text*, 183, defended the papyrus' text and contrasted 20. iv, where Cleisthenes is ἡγεμὼν . . . καὶ τοῦ δήμου προστάτης, and most editors print the papyrus' text with no sign of doubt. The addition of an adjective would certainly improve the sentence, but I doubt if *A.P.* used an adjective here.

Although *A.P.* labels Cimon as a προστάτης τῶν γνωρίμων, albeit unworthy, and Plutarch similarly places him on the aristocratic side, there were some who stressed his similarity to Pericles, the one achieving with his own wealth what the other was to achieve with the state's resources (cf. 27. iii–iv with commentary), and schol. Aristid. xlvi. *Quatt.* (iii. 446 Dindorf: revised text W. R. Connor, *Theopompus and Fifth-Century Athens*, 36) startlingly contrasts Cimon the προστάτης τῶν δημοτικῶν with Pericles the προστάτης τῶν ὀλιγαρχικῶν. Here ἐπιεικής is used as one of *A.P.*'s counterparts to δῆμος or πλῆθος, to denote a member of the upper classes (cf. 28. i, 36. ii, Arist. *Pol.* iii. 1282 a 25–7, v. 1308 b 27–8, with H. Richards, *CR* v 1891, 184), but at the end of this section he uses it of the 'respectable' men to be found in both the upper and the lower classes (cf. below).

Κίμωνα τὸν Μιλτιάδου: Sc. Λακιάδης; his mother was Hegesipyle, the daughter of Olorus of Thrace (Pl. *Cim.* 4. i cf. H. vi. 39. ii). Athenian politics immediately after the Persian Wars are best explained in terms of opposition between Themistocles and Cimon, in which

Cimon prevailed: the Delian League was organised by Aristides, but in all the early campaigns of Athens and the League whose commander is known the commander was Cimon (cf. pp. 288–9, 292–3); on his return from the siege of Thasos Cimon was prosecuted but acquitted (27. i with commentary); his proposal to help Sparta against the Messenians was unsuccessfully opposed by Ephialtes, and it is likely that Ephialtes' reform was enacted while he was in Messenia, and provoked the Spartans to dismiss the Athenian army; on returning from the Peloponnese Cimon tried to upset the reform but failed and was ostracised (cf. pp. 311–12). Surprisingly, *A.P.* has not mentioned him at all in the preceding chapters: the Delian League and all that followed from it are attributed to Aristides (23. iv–24), and no opponent of Ephialtes is named except the man from Tanagra who killed him (25. iv *fin.*). Now Cimon makes a belated and inauspicious appearance: the time to which *A.P.* seems to refer is that after Ephialtes' reform, when ostracism had removed Cimon from Athens and he was no longer available to lead the ἐπιεικέστεροι; but for much of the 470's and 460's he had occupied a position in which he could be represented as προστάτης τῶν ἐπιεικεστέρων, and it is likely that *A.P.* is using a source which (without flattering him) gave Cimon a prominent position in Athenian history after the Persian Wars, but either misdated Cimon's prominence or was so unclear that *A.P.* was led to misdate his prominence. By contrast, in 28. ii Ephialtes succeeds Themistocles as προστάτης τοῦ δήμου, and Cimon succeeds Aristides as προστάτης τῶν γνωρίμων (cf. *ad. loc.*).

†νεώτερον ὄντα† καὶ πρὸς τὴν πόλιν ὀψὲ προσελθόντα: 'Was rather young and had only recently entered public life' (Moore). The two things said of Cimon cohere well enough (*pace* H. Richards, *CR* v 1891, 334, and others), but are palpably untrue of him after Ephialtes' reform: he was born *c.* 510 (Davies, *A.P.F.*, 302), served on a deputation to Sparta in 479 (Pl. *Arist.* 10. x), and commanded the forces of Athens and the Delian League thereafter. At the beginning of his public career he was a little over thirty (the age at which an Athenian became eligible for office); and he may be compared with Pericles, who was νέος in his early thirties, when he prosecuted Cimon (27. i with commentary), or with Alcibiades, who was described as young in his early and middle thirties (T. v. 43. ii, vi. 12. ii, the latter in a speech of Nicias, about twenty-five years his senior). Earlier, Cimon had paid the fine imposed on his father Miltiades after his failure to take Paros in 490 or 489, and Plutarch says that he was then μειράκιον παντάπασιν and τὸν πρῶτον ἠδόξει χρόνον ἐν τῇ πόλει (H. vi. 136; Pl. *Cim.* 4. iv); he was said to resemble his grandfather Cimon Κοάλεμος in stupidity (Pl., *loc. cit.*), and according to Arsitid. XLVI. *Quatt.* (ii. 203 Dindorf) his guardians

did not allow him to manage his property μέχρι πόρρω τῆς ἡλικίας; in an anecdote told of 480 Pl. *Cim.* 5. i–ii turns his youth to his advantage (ἀμήχανον ὅσον ἐν ταῖς πολιτικαῖς ὑπερβαλέσθαι [*sc.* καὶ τὸν Μιλτιάδην καὶ τὸν Θεμιστοκλέα] νέος ὢν ἔτι καὶ πολέμων ἄπειρος). The major deposit of ostraca found in the Ceramicus includes 490 against Cimon, three of them joining ostraca against Megacles (R. Thomsen, *The Origin of Ostracism*, 93, 100, D. M. Lewis, *ZPE* xiv 1974, 2–3): on the orthodox view of this deposit Cimon appears to be a serious candidate for ostracism in 486, and may in that case have been a more prominent figure in the 480's than our other evidence suggests; but it may be that the ostraca against Cimon should be regarded as fatal to the orthodox view (cf. p. 275). In any case, Cimon was too young to hold office before *c.* 480; he could have been described as νεώτερον ὄντα καὶ πρὸς τὴν πόλιν ὀψὲ προσελθόντα in the 470's: probably the text is sound, and *A.P.* is misapplying this description of Cimon to the period after Ephialtes' reform (cf. previous note, and J. H. Schreiner, *SO* Supp. xxi 1968, 76–7).

However, νεώτερον has been almost universally condemned: of the many suggestions made by early commentators (conveniently reviewed by Sandys[2]) νωθρότερον ('rather sluggish': Κ. Σ. Κόντος, *Ἀθ.* iv 1892, 36, cf. Arist. *Rhet.* II. 1390 B 30) and ἐνεώτερον ('rather stupid': H. Weil, *JS* 1891, 212, cf. Pl. *Cim.* 4. iv–v, Plat. *Alc. ii.* 140 D 1) were the most plausible; R. Anastasi suggested ⟨οὐ⟩ νεώτερον, to be contrasted with the νέος Pericles in 27. i (*Sic. Gymn.* ix 1956, 101–3); R. D. Scott suggested νεωτερίζοντα or νεωτεροποιοῦντα, as an allusion to Cimon's dismissal from Sparta, and supposed the next phrase to mean that he returned to Athens too late to stop Ephialtes (*CP* lxix 1974, 117–18); G. Radet defended νεώτερον, but supposed it to mean 'rather inexperienced' as in Plat. *Phileb.* 13 D 6 (*REG* xxxii 1919, 429–32).†

With πρὸς τὴν πόλιν ... προσελθόντα compare 27. i (πρὸς τὸ δημαγωγεῖν ἐλθόντος). πρὸς τὴν πόλιν προσελθών is found in [D.] LVIII. *Theocr.* 30, and similar expressions occur in Is. XII. *Panath.* 140, Plat. *Ep.* vii. 324 B 9–C 1, D. XVIII. *Cor.* 257: cf. Kaibel, *Stil und Text*, 183.

ἐφθάρθαι τοὺς πολλοὺς κατὰ πόλεμον: To make sense in its context this must mean 'a great many of them (*sc.* οἱ ἐπιεικέστεροι) had perished in war' (Fritz & Kapp, cf. Poste, Mathieu & Haussoullier), not 'the masses had been decimated in war' (Moore, cf. Kenyon's translations, Rackham); compare the allusion to hoplite service that follows. However, the Delian League was notoriously a naval alliance (though Eurymedon at least was a land battle as well as a sea battle: e.g. T. I. 100. i); the fleet was manned by the poorer citizens (and non-citizens: cf. next note), and the claim that the wars of the League occasioned deaths particularly among the upper classes is implausible. Perhaps *A.P.* himself realised and was embarrassed by this, since at the end of §i he uses ἐπιεικής in a different sense and says ἀναλίσκεσθαι τοὺς ἐπιεικεῖς καὶ τοῦ δήμου καὶ τῶν εὐπόρων (cf. below).

τῆς γὰρ στρατείας γιγνομένης ἐν τοῖς τότε χρόνοις ἐκ καταλόγου: Cf. Arist. *Pol.*¹ v. 1303 a 8–10 (ἐν Ἀθήναις ἀτυχούντων πεζῇ οἱ γνώριμοι ἐλάττους ἐγένοντο διὰ τὸ ἐκ καταλόγου στρατεύεσθαι ὑπὸ τὸν Λακωνικὸν πόλεμον —that is, the Peloponnesian War). Editors have supposed the contrast to be between the citizen armies of the fifth century and the mercenary armies on which Athens (and other cities) increasingly relied in the fourth, a contrast frequently made by the orators (e.g. Is. VIII. *Pace*, 41–8, D. IV. *Phil. i.* 19–27), since citizen hoplite service was always ἐκ καταλόγου in the sense that it was based on the register of men who were of the hoplite class and had come of age (Ar. *Eq.* 1369–71, T. VI. 43, VII. 16. i, X. *M.* III. iv. 1, D. XIII. *Synt.* 4). Service in the fleet was already on a mercenary basis in the fifth century, and both citizens and non-citizens served (e.g. T. I. 121. iii, 143. i, VII. 13. ii, 63. iii–iv, cf. R. Meiggs, *The Athenian Empire*, 439–41). Hoplites were sometimes required to row ships (e.g. T. III. 16. i, 18. iii–iv), and before the battle of Arginusae the Athenians freed and accepted as citizens slaves who were willing to row (X. *H.* I. vi. 24, schol. Ar. *Ran.* 33, *Ran.* 693–4 with schol. 694 = Hellan. 4 F 171 = 323a F 25), but there is no evidence for the conscription of thetes as oarsmen until the fourth century (e.g. [D.] L. *Poly.* 6, Is. VIII. *Pace*, 48, D. III. *Ol. iii.* 4; D. XXI. *Mid.* 154–5 suggests that in the middle of the century conscription was a novelty).

In the time of *A.P.* a partial levy of hoplites was made by calling up a specified age range (53. vii with commentary), but a reference in A. II. *F.L.* 168 to service ἐν τοῖς μέρεσι points to a different system earlier, which in theory required the generals to conscript all in turn but in fact gave an opportunity for volunteers and men with experience to be used more than the reluctant and inexperienced (T. VI. 26. ii, 31. iii, Lys. IX. *Mil.* 4, 15: see A. Andrewes, in a volume presented to M. F. McGregor, cf. earlier Jones, *A.D.*, 163). It is better to see in *A.P.* and *Pol.* a contrast between this system and that of the second half of the fourth century for levying citizen hoplites: this earlier system is one which would lead to heavier casualties among the 'better' soldiers.†

στρατηγῶν ἐφισταμένων ἀπείρων μὲν ... τιμωμένων δὲ ...: Down to and including the generation of Pericles the Athenians who rose to the top tended still to be men from the aristocratic families which had dominated the state in the archaic period, but thereafter new families displaced the old aristocracy (cf. 28. i with commentary): it was certainly true of Cimon and doubtless true of many of his fellow generals that they were τιμωμένων διὰ τὰς πατρικὰς δόξας, and this will have given a hostile writer the opportunity to insinuate that they did not live up to their forebears' reputations. Generals were elected by the assembly, both in the time of Cimon and in the time of *A.P.* (22. ii, 61. i, with commentary), and we have no reason to suppose that the men elected were either more or less experienced in the earlier period than in the later. With πατρικὰς δόξας cf. T. vii. 69. ii (πατρικὰς ἀρετάς).

αἰεὶ συνέβαινεν τῶν ἐξιόντων ἀνὰ δισχιλίους ἢ τρισχιλίους ἀπόλλυσθαι: W. L. Newman, *CR* v 1891, 160, compared Is. viii. *Pace*, 87–8 (referring to deaths κατὰ χιλίους καὶ δισχιλίους in Athens' fifth-century wars). Far too little survives from the annually published casualty lists (see D. W. Bradeen, *CQ*[2] xix 1969, 145–59, *The Athenian Agora*, xvii, nos. 1–16) to enable us to say how many men died in war year by year in this period; but the mere existence of annual casualty lists from the period may have given rise to the idea that Athens' expansionist wars were prodigal of Athenian lives. We should expect the heaviest losses to be those in Egypt in 454 (T. i. 104, 109–10, defended against Ctes. 688 F 14, §§36–9 [32–6] by R. Meiggs, *The Athenian Empire*, 104–8, 473–6).

τοὺς ἐπιεικεῖς καὶ τοῦ δήμου καὶ τῶν εὐπόρων: Earlier in this section *A.P.* used τοὺς ἐπιεικεστέρους of the upper classes; but it was not plausible that the casualties in the wars of the Delian League should have occurred only or principally among the upper classes, and here ἐπιεικεῖς is used not in a political but in a moral sense, to denote the better sort of men in the lower and upper classes, who would under the system of selective call-up be the more likely to serve on campaigns and to risk their lives. The word is used in a moral sense regularly in Aristotle's *Ethics*, and sometimes in the *Politics* and the *Rhetoric* (e.g. *Pol.* II. 1267 B 5–9, 1273 B 3–7); cf. also 27. iv with commentary. εὔποροι as a counterpart of δῆμος or πλῆθος recurs in 28. ii.

This section is one of the passages in *A.P.* which Gomme thought was derived from Stesimbrotus by way of Theopompus (*Hist. Comm. Thuc.*, i. 48 n. 1). That is unlikely, as Theopompus may have written too late to be available to *A.P.* and Stesimbrotus probably did not write in this disparaging way about the upper classes in Athens (cf. Introduction, pp. 22–3). Although this passage is unflattering to Cimon and the aristocrats, however, it is hardly enthusiastic about demagogues and the democrats: the effect is to apologise for the weakness of the aristocrats and their leaders, as a result of which the advance of the democracy could not be prevented. I should guess that the source of this is a political pamphlet written in oligarchic circles in Athens, in the same spirit as [X.] *A.P.*

26. ii. οὐχ ὁμοίως καὶ πρότερον τοῖς νόμοις προσέχοντες: On attitudes to νόμος in classical Greece see in general J. de Romilly, *La Loi dans la pensée grecque des origines à Aristote*. One strand in the thinking of the late fifth and fourth centuries contrasted νόμος unfavourably with φύσις, as human convention in opposition to unfettered nature (e.g. P. *Oxy*. xi 1364, 6–63 = Antiph. Soph. 87 B 44, A. i. 6–ii. 30 Diels & Kranz, Hippias of Elis in Plat. *Protag*. 337 D 1–3, Callicles in Plat. *Gorg*. 482 E 4); but another, recognising the conventionality of human enactments but wanting to save the concept of universally valid laws, contrasted νόμοι favourably with ψηφίσματα, as 'laws', which transcend the will of individuals at a particular time and place, in opposition to 'decrees' of an assembly or council. In accordance with the latter distinction fourth-century Athens had separate mechanisms for the enactment of νόμοι and ψηφίσματα (cf. pp. 512–13). In T. II. 37 Pericles speaks of Athens' adherence to the laws, and in T. III. 37. iii–iv Cleon urges obedience to the laws even if they are imperfect. In the fourth century the contrast between νόμοι and ψηφίσματα is a commonplace (e.g. D. XX. *Lept*. 90–2, XXII. *Andr*. 49, XXIII. *Arist*. 86–7, 218, XXIV. *Tim*. 29–30, [D.] LIX. *Neaer*. 88, A. I. *Tim*. 177 [reading ⟨τὰ⟩ τῆς πόλεως, with Sauppe], Hyp. III. *Ath*. 22, Arist. *E.N.* V. 1137 B 11–29, [Plat.] *Def*. 415 B 8–11); the νόμος published by R. S. Stroud in *Hesp*. xliii 1974, 157–88, in lines 55–6 orders the demolition of any ψηφίσματα which may be found to conflict with it. Aristotle regarded it as a characteristic of extreme democracy that ψηφίσματα prevail over the νόμοι (*Pol*. IV. 1292 A 4–7, 23–5, 32–7, cf. III. 1282 B 1–6, IV. 1293 A 30–4, 1298 A 28–33); in 41. ii *fin*. *A.P.* states as the end product of Athens' constitutional development ἁπάντων γὰρ αὐτὸς αὑτὸν πεποίηκεν ὁ δῆμος κύριον, καὶ πάντα διοικεῖται ψηφίσμασιν καὶ δικαστηρίοις, ἐν οἷς ὁ δῆμός ἐστιν ὁ κρατῶν.

A.P. is moving from a strongly biased passage to one in which three laws of the 450's are baldly chronicled. They are not laws which take Athens a great deal further in the direction of radical democracy; even if they were, they would not be evidence for the Athenians' lack of respect for the laws unless they had been enacted in an unlawful manner; but this Aristotelian passage serves to mark the transition from the alleged military disasters of §i to the changes in the law of §§ii–iv.

τὴν δὲ τῶν ἐννέα ἀρχόντων αἵρεσιν οὐκ ἐκίνουν: Last changed, to κλήρωσις ἐκ προκρίτων, in 487/6 (22. v with commentary); αἵρεσιν here need mean nothing more specific than 'appointment' (cf. 13. ii with commentary). After the first part of the sentence *A.P.*'s point must be that although in other respects the Athenian democrats did not keep to the laws they did keep to the law about the method of appointment to the archonship (but even here they made a smaller change, in the qualification for the office). For κινεῖν cf. on 29. i.

ἀλλ' ἕκτῳ ἔτει μετὰ τὸν 'Εφιάλτου θάνατον ... πρῶτος ἦρξεν ἐξ αὐτῶν Μνησιθείδης: 25. iv does not make it clear whether Ephialtes' murder, like his reform of the Areopagus, fell in 462/1, but that must be the year of which *A.P.* is thinking here. The 6th year after 462/1 is 457/6; but that is the year in which Mnesithides was archon (D.S. XI. 81. i), so if he was the first archon appointed under the new dispensation the new dispensation must have been enacted in 458/7, or even at the end of 459/8 (cf. on 22. v). We have no way of determining whether Mnesithides was the archon when the new rules were adopted or was the first archon appointed under those rules; if the latter is true, the further implication, that he was a ζευγίτης himself and could not have been appointed under the old rules, may be based on good evidence but may be a further product of *A.P.*'s or his source's carelessness.

οἱ δὲ πρὸ τούτου πάντες ἐξ ἱππέων καὶ πεντακοσιομεδίμνων ἦσαν: *A.P.* nowhere states, and modern scholars have disputed, whether the archonship was open to the highest two classes from the time of Solon or was limited at first to the πεντακοσιομέδιμνοι: see p. 148, where I indicate a preference for the former view. Another topic of dispute is the application of Solon's classification in the fifth and fourth centuries (cf. pp. 142-3, 146): a cash valuation of property may have replaced produce, but we have no evidence for it; the decision to admit ζευγῖται but not θῆτες to the archonship indicates that in the 450's a meaningful distinction between the classes could still be made (cf. M&L 49, 39-42 [*c.* 445 or slightly later], where an amendment stipulates that the settlers at Brea are to be from the ζευγῖται and the θῆτες).

οἱ ‹δὲ› ζευγῖται τὰς ἐγκυκλίους ἦρχον: ἐγκύκλιος means 'recurring', and so 'regular' or 'ordinary' (cf. Is. III. *Nic.* 22, VIII. *Pace*, 87, Arist. *Pol.* I. 1255 B 25, II. 1263 A 21, 1269 B 35): here the ἐγκύκλιοι ἀρχαί are contrasted with the major offices (such as the archonship and the treasurership of Athena) from which the ζευγῖται had been excluded, but in 43. i the (ἀρχαὶ) περὶ τὴν ἐγκύκλιον διοίκησιν seem to be the civilian as opposed to the military offices (cf. *ad loc.*).

εἰ μή τι παρεωρᾶτο τῶν ἐν τοῖς νόμοις: After παρεωρᾶτο the papyrus has ὑπὸ τ(ῶν) δήμων, deleted: the text is clearly better without these words, but it is not clear how the scribe came to write them here.

The possibility that legal restrictions were disregarded accords with *A.P.*'s view that at this time the Athenians did not comply with the laws as they had earlier (cf. above); it accords also with his observation that in his own day the exclusion of the θῆτες from the archonship was not enforced (7. iv with commentary). We do not know how strictly these laws were enforced in the fifth century, but the decision to modify the qualification for the office, rather than to do without any qualification, suggests that at this time the restrictions were still taken seriously.

26. iii. ἔτει δὲ πέμπτῳ μετὰ ταῦτα ἐπὶ Λυσικράτους ἄρχοντος: 453/2 (cf. D.S. xi. 88. i).
οἱ τριάκοντα δικασταὶ κατέστησαν πάλιν οἱ καλούμενοι κατὰ δήμους: Cf. 16. v with commentary, on the institution of (not necessarily thirty) δικασταὶ κατὰ δήμους by Pisistratus: as an institution of the tyranny they were presumably abolished after Hippias' expulsion (cf. p. 257). Perhaps the extra business directed to the δικαστήρια by Ephialtes' reform (cf. pp. 318–19) and by the growing complexity of Athenian administration was now overburdening the δικαστήρια; certainly it was inconvenient to neighbours involved in small disputes to take their disputes to Athens; and so local justices were once more appointed. Their number, thirty, suggests that one may have been assigned to each of Cleisthenes' thirty trittyes. In the fourth century, when the oligarchy of 404/3 had made thirty an inauspicious number, they numbered forty and conducted their hearings in the city: they handled private suits against defendants of a tribe other than their own, being empowered to give a decision in suits for sums up to 10 drachmae and playing an administrative part in more serious suits (53. i–iii with commentary, cf. 48. v); likewise in the fifth century the thirty may have decided private suits for sums up to 10 drachmae.

26. iv. καὶ τρίτῳ μετὰ τοῦτον ἐπὶ Ἀντιδότου: 451/0 (cf. D.S. xi. 91. i).
διὰ τὸ πλῆθος τῶν πολιτῶν . . . μὴ ἐξ ἀμφοῖν ἀστοῖν ᾖ γεγονώς: Athenian laws on mixed marriages and νόθοι are usefully assembled by Harrison, *L.A.*, i. 24–8, 61–8. For the fact of Pericles' law cf. Pl. *Per.* 37. iii, Ael. *V.H.* vi. 10, xiii. 24, fr. 68 = Suid. (Δ 451) δημοποίητος. The law was still in force in 414 (Ar. *Av.* 1649–52), but in the last years of the Peloponnesian War it was either annulled or ignored (the contrary argument of W. E. Thompson, *SO* xlii 1968, 65–8, is based on a misunderstanding of the law *ap.* And. i. *Myst.* 83), and in addition Athenians were allowed to keep a concubine ἐπ' ἐλευθέροις παισίν (homicide law *ap.* D. xxiii. *Arist.* 53, Gell. xv. 20. vi, Ath. xiii. 556 A, D.L. ii. 26, with Harrison, *L.A.*, i. 13–17, MacDowell, *The Law in Classical Athens*, 89–90). At the end of the fifth century the law was reenacted with a clause exempting those born before 403/2 (D. lvii. *Eub.* 30, Eum. 77 F 2, Caryst. fr. 11 Müller *ap.* Ath. xiii. 577 B–C), and later the law was strengthened, to inflict penalties on the partners in a mixed marriage and on any citizen who fraudulently gave a foreign woman in marriage to a citizen ([D.] lix. *Neaer.* 16, 52: contr. H. vi. 130. ii, where in the sixth century Megacles marries Agariste of Sicyon by ἐγγύη, νομοῖσι τοῖσι Ἀθηναίων). Ar.

Vesp. 715–18 refers to a narrow escape in a γραφὴ ξενίας in connection with distributions of corn, and schol. 718 cites Philochorus (328 F 119) for an episode in 445/4, when Psammetichus of Egypt sent a consignment of corn to the Athenian δῆμος and 4,760 men were found to be παρέγγραφοι, while Pl. *Per.* 37. iv links that episode with Pericles' law. Plutarch notes also that after the death of his legitimate sons Pericles persuaded the Athenians to accept his son by Aspasia as a citizen (*Per.* 37. ii, v, cf. Ael., *locc. citt.*).†

Before Pericles' law was enacted, any son of an Athenian father by a lawfully wedded wife (whether or not she was an Athenian) was a γνήσιος, a legitimate son who would be acknowledged as a citizen when he came of age and who could inherit his father's property. A son not born by a lawfully wedded wife was a νόθος, his right of inheritance was severely limited (cf. Ar. *Av.* 1655–66, and, for the fourth century, Isae. VI. *Her.* Phil. 47, [D.] XLIII. *Mac.* 51), and he was excluded from the phratries (Ar. *Av.* 1668–70) and, it seems likely, from Athenian citizenship (cf. on 42. i). I assume that a foreign man could not become a citizen, acquire property in Attica or beget citizen sons, by marrying an Athenian woman. Three examples may be cited of μητρόξενοι who became prominent citizens under the old dispensation and whose right to citizenship was never, as far as we know, challenged: Cleisthenes (cf. p. 234), Themistocles (cf. p. 279), and Cimon (cf. p. 324). Under Pericles' law μητρόξενοι were denied citizenship (with all that citizenship entailed, including the right to inherit property in Attica from a citizen father), however formal the union between their parents: if this law did not for the future ban marriage between an Athenian man and a non-Athenian woman it will at least have made such marriages extremely unattractive; and mixed marriages certainly were illegal by the mid fourth century. Pericles' law thus limited the class of γνήσιοι who could succeed to their father's position in the community, and those affected by the limitation became νόθοι (the word is used of μητρόξενοι in Ath. XIII. 577 B; cf. *L.S.* 274. 21, Suid. [*K* 2721] Κυνόσαργες): doubtless it is the post-Periclean state of the law which leads H. V. 94. i to describe one of Pisistratus' sons by his Argive wife as νόθος and T. VI. 55. i–ii to omit the sons by that marriage from the roster of γνήσιοι (cf. on 17. iii). Pericles' law cannot have been retrospective, since Cimon ended his life, as an Athenian general, shortly after its enactment (e.g. Gomme, *Hist. Comm. Thuc.*, i. 395–6, Hignett, *H.A.C.*, 255, 346–7; but R. Meiggs, *HSCP* lxvii 1963, 13, prefers to date Cimon's last expedition before Pericles' law). Possibly, as S. C. Humphreys suggests, the law applied to all registrations of 18-year-olds after its enactment (*JHS* xciv 1974, 92–3), but when the law was reenacted at the end of the fifth century it applied to those born in or after 403/2 (D. LVII. *Eub.* 30).

Many have been attracted by the connection made by Plutarch between Pericles' law and the removal of unqualified citizens on the occasion of Psammetichus' gift of corn six years later, and have supposed that the law was first enforced, or was made retrospective, in 445/4 (e.g. Lipsius, *A.R.*, 412–14, E. M. Walker, *C.A.H.*, v[1]. 102, F. E. Adcock, *ibid.* 167–8). Such views provoked an angry response from Jacoby (commentary on Phil. 328 F 119, cf. earlier Busolt, *G.G.*, III. i. 337–9, 500–2, Hignett, *H.A.C.*, 345), and he is surely right in his contention that Pericles' law is irrelevant to the vetting of those who claimed a share in the Egyptian corn six years later, and that it is wholly implausible that as many as 4,760 were deprived of citizenship or exposed as non-citizens on either occasion.

A.P. is the only text to offer a motivation for Pericles' law: διὰ τὸ πλῆθος τῶν πολιτῶν (cf. Arist. *Pol.* III. 1278 A 26–34, arguing that cities define their citizenship generously when short of men, strictly when citizens are plentiful; but VI. 1319 B 6–11 argues that the leaders of democracies are generous in order to enlarge and strengthen the δῆμος), an explanation which accords ill with the view of 26. i that the period after Ephialtes' reform was one of heavy losses in war. Most commonly modern scholars have either written of a jealous desire to ensure that the increasingly valuable privileges of Athenian citizenship, and especially μισθοφορία, were not shared too widely (e.g. Walker, *C.A.H.*, v[1]. 102–3), or else have rejected *A.P.*'s explanation and have seen in the law an attempt to preserve the racial purity of the citizen body (e.g. Busolt, *G.G.*, III. i. 337–9, Hignett, *H.A.C.*, 255, 346); more eccentrically, Jacoby saw a 'party political' threat to Pericles' opponents in general and to Cimon in particular (*Supp.* i. 477–81). In the second half of the fourth century Aristotle could write (*Pol.* III. 1275 B 22–4):

> ὁρίζονται πρὸς τὴν χρῆσιν πολίτην τὸν ἐξ ἀμφοτέρων πολιτῶν καὶ μὴ θατέρου μόνον, οἷον πατρὸς ἢ μητρός, οἱ δὲ καὶ τοῦτ' ἐπὶ πλέον ζητοῦσιν, οἷον ἐπὶ πάππους δύο ἢ τρεῖς ἢ πλείους,

and [D.] LIX. *Neaer.* 75–6 reports an old law, inscribed ἀμυδροῖς γράμμασιν Ἀττικοῖς, that the wife of the basileus must be an ἀστή, but we need not doubt that pre-Periclean law corresponded to pre-Periclean opinion and mixed marriages had been generally acceptable.†

Jacoby's explanation of Pericles' change in the law may be ruled out in the absence of any evidence of a threat to Cimon and other known μητρόξενοι. We may also rule out, if it is true that all νόθοι were excluded from citizenship and that Pericles' law was not retrospective, *A.P.*'s διὰ τὸ πλῆθος τῶν πολιτῶν and modern applications of it, since the law would limit citizens in their choice of wives but would not reduce the number of sons born in wedlock to citizen fathers (cf. Gomme, *JHS* l 1930, 106 n. 1 = *Essays*, 87 n. 1, Hignett, *H.A.C.*, 346); such an explanation is even more inappropriate to the reenactment of the law at the end of the fifth century, after the losses of the Peloponnesian War. Pericles must have been concerned with the quality of the citizen body, not with its size, and I do not find it incredible that the proud Athenian to whom the funeral oration in T. II. 35–46 was ascribed should have insisted on the Athenian-ness of the Athenian people and the desirability of limiting membership of the Athenian community to those who were fully entitled to it (cf. M. F. McGregor, *Lectures . . . L. T. Semple* ii 1966–70, 64–6). While it will have been the rich rather than the poor who had the opportunity to bring foreign women back to Athens as their wives (cf. Gomme, *opp. citt.*, 106 = 87), the daughters of metics living in Athens will have been as accessible to the poor as to the rich (cf. Hignett, *H.A.C.*, 346): though unable to adduce statistics I should guess that the Pentecontaetia was the time when Athens' metic population grew most rapidly, and that mixed marriages were becoming more frequent and were therefore beginning to cause alarm.

Pericles was born about the mid 490's to Xanthippus and the Alcmaeonid Agariste (cf. p. 276). The law on citizenship is the earliest dated measure attributed to him (but the introduction of jury pay may be earlier [cf. pp. 339–40]; we learn from Pl. *Per.* 8. vii that a collection of his decrees was made). He was Aeschylus' choregus in 473/2 (p. 312); he was one of Cimon's prosecutors in 463/2 (27. i with commentary) and a supporter of Ephialtes in his attack on the Areopagus (pp. 311–12, cf. 27. i); the story was told that *c.* 457, at the battle of Tanagra, Cimon attempted to return prematurely from ostracism, and in one version Pericles fought bravely in the battle and after it was author of a decree recalling him (Pl. *Per.* 10. i–v, *Cim.* 17. iv–ix, cf. Thp. 115 F 88, And. III. *Pace*, 3, Nep. v. *Cim.* 3. iii, where the author of the decree is not named; cf. p. 339); Pericles commanded one expedition perhaps in the late 460's (Callisth. 124 F 16 *ap.* Pl. *Cim.* 13. iv with R. Meiggs, *The Athenian Empire*, 79, 91, but Wade-Gery, *HSCP* Supp. i 1940, 123 n. 2 = *Essays*, 203 n. 2, suspected that the reference is to 440), and at any rate one in the 450's (T. I. 111. ii–iii). *A.P.*'s view of Pericles as the successor of Ephialtes, and Plutarch's remark that after the ostracism of Thucydides (cf. on 28. ii) Pericles was elected general every year until his death (*Per.* 16. iii), have led the incautious to assume that every policy pursued by Athens between the death of Ephialtes and the death of Pericles was Pericles' policy (for protests see Gomme, *Hist. Comm. Thuc.*, i. 306–7, G. E. M. de Ste. Croix, *The Origins of the Peloponnesian War*, 315–17; according to Plutarch Pericles was one leader among many until the ostracism of Thucydides). But although we do not always know whether Pericles was the author of an Athenian policy or was in agreement with it, we may safely assume that Ephialtes' supporter approved of the two unattributed reforms of §§ii–iii, the opening of the archonship to the ζευγῖται and the revival of the δικασταὶ κατὰ δήμους.

μὴ μετέχειν τῆς πόλεως: Cf. 8. v and commentary, where in the report of Solon's law against neutrality the phrase is used as a gloss on ἄτιμον εἶναι. Here it may be quoted from Pericles' law.

27. i. μετὰ δὲ ταῦτα: The reference is unclear. Strictly these words here should imply that δημοτικωτέραν ἔτι συνέβη γενέσθαι τὴν πολιτείαν after the enactment of Pericles' citizenship law in 451/0. However, *A.P.* next digresses to mention Pericles' prosecution of Cimon, which preceded not only the laws of 26. ii–iv but also the reform of Ephialtes (25); and it is likely that the reference to an attack on the Areopagus which follows is to be explained as a misunderstanding of a text which attributed to Pericles a share in Ephialtes' reform; the chapter then looks ahead to the development of the democracy in the Peloponnesian War; it returns to the lifetime of Cimon for the introduction of jury pay; and from that it looks ahead again to what is said to be the first instance of δεκάζειν, in 409. 26. ii–iv gave us a sober chronicle of laws, with no obvious bias; this chapter, by contrast, is rambling and anecdotal, and hostile to Pericles. μετὰ δὲ ταῦτα has no genuine chronological reference, but merely serves to link a new block of material to the one preceding it.

πρὸς τὸ δημαγωγεῖν ἐλθόντος: 'Became one of the leaders of the people' (Moore): although in general this chapter is anti-Periclean, this use of δημαγωγεῖν is not necessarily hostile (cf. pp. 323–4).

πρῶτον εὐδοκιμήσαντος ... νέος ὤν: Prosecution of Cimon for his conduct as στρατηγός must be connected either with his expedition to Ithome or with an earlier expedition. The episode is placed in acceptable context by Pl. *Cim.* 14. iii–v, cf. *Per.* 10. vi, derived from Stesimbrotus (107 F 5): after the siege of Thasos (465/4–463/2: Gomme, *Hist. Comm. Thuc.*, i. 390–1) Cimon was accused of taking bribes to spare Macedon; Pericles was one of the prosecutors, ὑπὸ τοῦ δήμου προβεβλημένος according to *Per.*; according to Stesimbrotus Cimon's sister Elpinice tried to win over Pericles, and after that Pericles was very gentle in his attack; Cimon was acquitted. The charge should be authentic, and Pericles' mildness may be, even if Elpinice's intervention is mere rumour; Pericles will at that time have been a little over thirty, which accords well enough with νέος ὤν (cf. p. 325). *A.P.* alone says that Cimon was attacked in his εὔθυναι: we cannot tell whether this is based on information or on guesswork, but it is not improbable, and an acquittal of Cimon in his εὔθυναι by the Areopagus (whether deservedly or not) may well have been the last straw to Ephialtes and his supporters (cf. p. 317). The story of Pericles and Elpinice provides one of the pegs on which Sealey hangs a theory that at the beginning of his career Pericles was closer to Cimon than is commonly assumed (*Hermes* lxxxiv 1956, 234-47 = *Essays*, 59-74); but I am not persuaded that the usual view of Pericles as a supporter of Ephialtes is wrong.

The papyrus reads πρώτου: W. G. Rutherford and others (*CR* v 1891) and Blass (*LZB* 1891, 304) proposed πρῶτον, which is generally accepted; H. Jackson (*CR* v 1891, 112) proposed πρὸ τοῦ, and Leeuwen (*Mnem.* xix 1891, 176, cf. Herwerden & Leeuwen) proposed that or πρότερον. The prosecution must be earlier than the events recorded in 25-6, and the alternative correction has the advantage of showing that *A.P.* was aware of that fact; but the usual πρῶτον, noting this as Pericles' first success, is likelier.

δημοτικωτέραν ἔτι συνέβη γενέσθαι τὴν πολιτείαν: Compare *A.P.*'s judgment on Cleisthenes' reforms (22. i).

καὶ γὰρ τῶν Ἀρεοπαγιτῶν ἔνια παρείλετο: Arist. *Pol.* II. 1274 A 7-9 mentions the 'pruning' of the Areopagus by Ephialtes and Pericles (in language which would be compatible either with a joint reform or with successive reforms), and then the introduction of jury pay by Pericles (on which see 27. iii-iv with commentary). *A.P.* does not say what powers were left to the Areopagus by Ephialtes and removed by Pericles, and since this chapter lacks a firm chronological basis it is very likely that here he is misusing an attribution to Pericles of a share in Ephialtes' reform of the Areopagus (cf. p. 312). G. Smith suggested that Pericles discontinued the appointment of ἐφέται for the homicide courts from the Areopagus (*CP* xix 1924, 353-8), but see on 57. iv.

Kaibel & Wilamowitz preferred περιείλετο (cf. 25. ii, iv), but no change is necessary.

μάλιστα προύτρεψεν τὴν πόλιν ἐπὶ τὴν ναυτικὴν δύναμιν: Cf. 23. iv-24, stating that Aristides founded the Delian League and advised the Athenians to migrate into the city, where they could be maintained at the allies' expense; in the summary in 41. ii πλεῖστα συνέβη τὴν πόλιν διὰ τοὺς δημαγωγοὺς ἁμαρτάνειν διὰ τὴν τῆς θαλάττης ἀρχήν during the régime inaugurated by Ephialtes' reform. In T. I. 93. iii-iv, vii, Pl. *Them.* 19. iii-vii (on which see A. E. Raubitschek, *WS* lxxi 1958, 112-15), the policy of concentrating on naval power is attributed to Themistocles. It is not clear what Pericles' own contribution was supposed to be, but the importance of naval power to Athens in his time was and is notorious: it will be sufficient to cite [X.] *A.P.* i. 2, on democracy and the ναυτικὸς ὄχλος, ii. 2-16 on the advantages of Athens' rule of the sea; T. II. 13. ii, 62. ii-iii, 65. vii, on Pericles' appreciation of these advantages in his strategy for the Peloponnesian War; Is. VIII. *Pace*, 64, 74-5, 95, 126, on naval power and democracy; Arist. *Pol.* II. 1274 A 12-15, V. 1304 A 21-4, passing directly from Salamis to naval hegemony and democracy (cf. p. 288, where the latter passage is quoted), VI. 1321 A 5-14, VII. 1327 A 40-B 15, on naval power and democracy.

θαρρήσαντας τοὺς πολλούς: Cf. 22. iii (θαρροῦντος ἤδη τοῦ δήμου after Marathon, ostracism was first used), 24. i (θαρρούσης ἤδη τῆς πόλεως after the foundation of the Delian League, Aristides advised the Athenians ἀντιλαμβάνεσθαι τῆς ἡγεμονίας); also the 'increases' of 23. i and 25. i.

27. ii. μετὰ δὲ τὴν ἐν Σαλαμῖνι ναυμαχίαν ... ἐπὶ Πυθοδώρου ἄρχοντος: 432/1 (D.S. XII. 37. i; cf. T. II. 2. i, naming Pythodorus and dating the outbreak of the war to spring 431). 480/79, the year of Salamis, has already been used as a base date in 23. v, but in 25. i (if the text is sound) 479/8 is used (cf. *ad locc.*).

κατακλεισθεὶς ὁ δῆμος ἐν τῷ ἄστει: Cf. T. II. 13. ii, 14-17, also 52. i-ii, VII. 27. ii-28.

συνεθισθεὶς ἐν ταῖς στρατείαις μισθοφορεῖν: We should follow Blass[2-4] in retaining the papyrus' στρατιαῖς (cf. 22. viii with commentary, 37. i). On the payment of soldiers and sailors cf. p. 306: both were, of course, paid before the war, but the war greatly increased the amount of service required and therefore the amount of μισθοφορία.

τὰ μὲν ἑκὼν τὰ δὲ ἄκων ... διοικεῖν αὐτός: For the view that the δῆμος took affairs into its own hands during the Peloponnesian War cf. 28. i, iii, where it is said that the government of Athens became much worse after Pericles' death and Cleon initiated a new style of leadership; in 41. ii *fin.* cf. i the final result of Athens' constitutional development is said to be ἁπάντων γὰρ αὐτὸς αὑτὸν πεποίηκεν ὁ δῆμος κύριον, καὶ πάντα διοικεῖται ψηφίσμασιν καὶ δικαστηρίοις, ἐν οἷς ὁ δῆμός ἐστιν ὁ κρατῶν. For the changed style of leadership see pp. 344-5, 351-4: leaders like Cleon will doubtless have encouraged the δῆμος to think δεινὸν εἶναι εἰ μή τις ἐάσει τὸν δῆμον πράττειν ὃ ἂν βούληται (X. *H.* I. vii. 12, of the trial of the generals after Arginusae). To establish a direct connection between the Peloponnesian War and the advance of democracy is difficult: as Athens championed democracy and Sparta championed oligarchy there was a tendency for political attitudes to polarise (cf. p. 299); citizens cooped up in the city could more easily attend the assembly than citizens busy on their farms, but citizens serving on a campaign could not attend the assembly at all, and the scanty evidence we have suggests that attendances during the war were not good (Ar. *Ach.* 19-22, T. VIII. 72. i; cf. 41. iii with commentary); the war will have provided increased opportunities for the δῆμος to punish a politician who 'misled the people' by advising a venture which turned out unsuccessfully, or a general who failed to achieve the successes expected of him.

27. iii. ἐποίησε δὲ καὶ μισθοφόρα τὰ δικαστήρια Περικλῆς πρῶτος: Cf. Plat. *Gorg.* 515 E 2-7, Arist. *Pol.* II. 1274 A 8-9, Pl. *Per.* 9. ii–iii (citing *A.P.*, but suggesting that the provision of μισθοφορία paved the way for the attack of Ephialtes and Pericles on the Areopagus), Aristid. XLVI. *Quatt.* (ii. 192 Dindorf). On the date of this reform see next note; the way in which payment for jury service is emphasised in the sources suggests that this was the first instance of payment for the performance of a citizen's civic (as opposed to military) duties; a salary for the Eleusinian epistatae is mentioned in *SEG* x 24, 9-10, of *c*. 450/49 (date R. Meiggs, *JHS* lxxxvi 1966, 94, 96).

Such payment was necessary if Athens' democratic machinery was to work in a democratic manner: after the downgrading of the archons' jurisdiction into a preliminary enquiry, the division of the heliaea into separate δικαστήρια, and Ephialtes' increase in the business handled by the δικαστήρια (cf. pp. 318-19), jurors, in the large numbers favoured by the Athenians, will have been needed more frequently than ordinary citizens could afford to abandon their day-to-day business; and so, if ordinary citizens were to play their part in the working of the judicial machine, compensation for loss of earnings had to be provided. Such payments came to be seen as characteristic of democracies, while oligarchies in which political power was restricted to the rich did not need them and sometimes imposed fines for the non-performance of civic duties (cf. p. 117; Arist. *Pol.* IV. 1293 A 4-9 suggests that in a salaried democracy the poor, with fewer other claims on their time, may become more active in public affairs than the rich). There is little evidence for state salaries outside Athens, but Arist. *Pol.* V. 1304 B 27-31 cites an instance from Rhodes (cf. G. E. M. de Ste. Croix, *CQ*² xxv 1975, 48-52). The payments were never lavish: for jury service the rate was 2 obols a day at first, raised to 3 obols by Cleon in the 420's (Ar. *Eq.* 797-800, schol. *Vesp.* 88 [emended], 300), and unlike other stipends not increased between that time and the 320's (62. ii with commentary).†

ἀντιδημαγωγῶν πρὸς τὴν Κίμωνος εὐπορίαν: The only other text which makes this allegation is Pl. *Per.* 9. ii, but Cimon's generosity was notorious: cf. Thp. 115 F 89, Thph. *ap.* Cic. *Off.* II. 64, Nep. v. *Cim.* 4. i–iii, Pl. *Cim.* 10 (citing *A.P.*, Cratinus, Gorgias and Critias), schol. Aristid. XLVI. *Quatt.* (iii. 446, 517, Dindorf; revised text of the first, which places Pericles with the ὀλιγαρχικοί and Cimon with the δημοτικοί, W. R. Connor, *Theopompus and Fifth-Century Athens*, 36 [cf. above, p. 324]). There are discussions centred on the fragment of Theopompus by Wade-Gery, *AJP* lix 1938, 131-4 = *Essays*, 235-8, and Connor, *op. cit.*, 30-7 cf. 108-10. Theopompus seems to be the main source of Nepos, of both accounts by Plutarch (though both cite *A.P.* on points of detail) and of the first scholium on Aristides, while Theophrastus and the second scholium on Aristides agree with *A.P.* against Theopompus (cf. below). Theopompus claimed that as a result of his generosity Cimon ηὐδοκίμει καὶ πρῶτος ἦν τῶν πολιτῶν, that is, 'what Kimon achieved by personal liberality, his successors had to achieve by *misthos*': he too will have regarded Pericles' introduction of salaries as a gambit to counter Cimon's generosity, and so Wade-Gery suggested that this explanation derives from a source common to Theopompus and *A.P.*, perhaps Critias. In *A.P.*'s presentation of the material ἀντιδημαγωγῶν is clearly pejorative (cf. pp. 332–4; the only other citation of the word in LSJ is from Pl. *C.G.* 8. iv).

Cimon's generosity should be accepted as a fact; if the fine which he paid on the death of Miltiades was indeed of 50 talents (H. VI. 136. iii) the family must have been extremely rich by the standards of fifth-century Athens; other evidence for the family's wealth is discussed by Davies, *A.P.F.*, 310–12, with the suggestion that in order to maintain his political position against the challenge of the democrats Cimon made substantial inroads into his capital. Pericles too was rich, though doubtless far less so than Cimon and unable to rival him in expenditure of that kind (cf. Davies, *A.P.F.*, 459–60; for his efficient but uninterested attitude to his family estate see Pl. *Per.* 16): although it is probably a later slander that his generosity with the state's money was intended to counter Cimon's generosity with his own, there is a measure of truth in it, in that the democrats (including democratic leaders from the aristocracy, like Pericles) were opposed to the kind of aristocratic patronage and predominance which Cimon by his generosity was trying to maintain.

Whether the slander can be exploited for chronological purposes is disputed. If it goes back to a contemporary or near-contemporary source we may assume that jury pay was introduced at any rate in Cimon's lifetime, and indeed it is unlikely that the democrats would have waited more than ten years after Ephialtes' reform to introduce the payments which enabled the poorer citizens to sit on juries. But Cimon was ostracised when he tried to upset Ephialtes' reform, probably in 462/1 (cf. p. 311); Theopompus claimed that he was recalled after Tanagra, *c.* 457, but Athens' foreign policy shows no change at that point and Cimon's ostracism more probably ran its full ten years (the evidence is cited above, p. 334; for a recent discussion see R. Meiggs, *The Athenian Empire*, 111, 422–3; Meiggs suggests that Cimon was recalled one year early, but if he attempted to return at Tanagra and was positively invited or summoned to return when the ten years had expired our sources' statements will be sufficiently explained). This leaves little opportunity for rivalry between Cimon and Pericles after Ephialtes' reform, and Wade-Gery argued from the order of events in Pl. *Cim.* and *Per.* that

Theopompus placed the introduction of jury pay before Ephialtes' reform (*locc. citt.*, cf. *Essays*, 197). As a reconstruction of Theopompus that may be correct; but although I doubt whether the story would have arisen if jury pay had not been introduced in Cimon's lifetime I think it could still have arisen if jury pay was introduced while Cimon was away from Athens and the memory of his generosity was fresh. A date after 462/1 is likelier than a date before, and I should guess that the democrats did not wait until Cimon's return (cf. Hignett, *H.A.C.*, 342–3).†

τυραννικὴν ἔχων οὐσίαν: Ath. XII. 532 F–533 C cites Thp. 115 F 135 on Pisistratus' generosity immediately before F 89 on Cimon's generosity: F 89 comes from book x of the *Philippica* and F 135 from book XXI, but it is as likely that Athenaeus found the comparison in Theopompus as that he made it himself, and we may guess that it was made by the common source of Theopompus and *A.P.* and has been reduced to a generalisation by *A.P.* (cf. W. R. Connor, *Theopompus and Fifth-Century Athens*, 32 with 152 n. 29).

τὰς κοινὰς λῃτουργίας ἐλῃτούργει λαμπρῶς: On the public services called λῃτουργίαι, which Athens required of her richer citizens, see 56. iii, 61. i, with commentary: these provided some scope for meanness or generosity, and litigants seeking to win the favour of a jury often claimed to have performed more liturgies more generously than they need have done (e.g. Lys. XIX. *Bon. Arist.* 29, 42–3, 57–9, XXI. *Pec. Acc.* 1–5). We happen not to know of any liturgies, in the strict sense of the word, performed by Cimon; public buildings paid for from his family fortune or from booty are listed by W. Judeich, *Topographie von Athen*[2], 73–4.

τῶν δημοτῶν ἔτρεφε πολλούς: Theopompus and those who follow him extend the freedom of Cimon's estate not merely to his fellow demesmen but to all citizens. *A.P.*'s more precise and limited generosity is the more likely to be right; Davies remarks that Theopompus 'blurs the political point of the distinction between Kimon and Perikles as that between local dynast and national politician' (*A.P.F.*, 311).

ἔχειν τὰ μέτρια: Cf. 16. iii with commentary.

τὰ χωρία πάντα ἄφρακτα ἦν: Cf. Pl. *Cim.* 10. i, *Per.* 9. ii, stating more positively that he removed the fences so as to allow the Athenians access to his land.

τὰς ὀπώρας: The noun recurs in the account in Pl. *Cim.* 10. i, the verb ὀπωρίζειν in Thp. 115 F 89 and Pl. *Per.* 9. ii.

27. iv. ταύτην τὴν χορηγίαν: Strictly a χορηγία is the liturgy of undertaking the responsibility for a chorus in a festival; but the meaning could be extended to the civilian liturgies in general, of which the χορηγίαι were typical (Lys. XIX. *Bon. Arist.* 57 is a possible instance, D. xx. *Lept.* 19 a probable); here by a further extension Cimon's making his own resources available to his fellow demesmen is seen as a kind of liturgy.

ἐπιλειπόμενος ... τῇ οὐσίᾳ: Cf. 20. ii with commentary: there is no need for doubt or emendation.

συμβουλεύσαντος αὐτῷ Δαμωνίδου τοῦ Οἴηθεν: Cf. Pl. *Per.* 9. ii: συμβουλεύσαντος αὐτῷ Δημωνίδου τοῦ Οἴηθεν, ὡς Ἀριστοτέλης ἱστόρηκε (Οἴηθεν appears from Sintenis to be the reading of most MSS, and is said by G. Wentzel, *ap.* Kenyon's Berlin ed., to be the reading of **S**; Ziegler and the Budé editors are unclear). Many other texts refer to Δάμων as a musician and the teacher of Pericles (e.g. Is. xv. *Antid.* 235, Pl. *Arist.* 1. vii, *Per.* 4. i–iv; but Arist. fr. 401 Teubner, from Pl. *Per.* 4. i and Olymp. *ad.* Plat. *Alc. i.* 118 C 5, says that Pericles' teacher of μουσική was Pythoclides); he is named frequently by Plato, and was the author of an *Areopagitic* (37 B 1–10 Diels & Kranz); while *A.P.* says that Damonides was ostracised, Pl. *Arist.* 1. vii, *Per.* 4. iii, *Nic.* 7. i, says that Damon was ostracised. Nearly all have thought that the two men are one and the same (argued by Wilamowitz, *Hermes* xiv 1879, 318–20, *A.u.A.*, i. 134–5, cf. Kirchner, *P.A.* 3143): if so, his name must be Damon, since the one ostracon against him that has been found calls him Δάμον Δαμονίδο (*IG* i² 912), and Steph. Byz. Ὄα (= 37 A 1 Diels & Kranz) writes ὁ μέντοι δημότης Ὄαθεν λέγεται, Δάμων Δαμωνίδου Ὄαθεν; on his deme Plutarch, who followed *A.P.*, has no independent authority, and we should prefer the assignment to Oa of Stephanus, who was specifically interested in the deme (contrast S. Dow, *AJP* lxxxiv 1963, 180–1, who follows *A.P.* but prefers a properispomenon accentuation). For the orthodox view of his date and identity see the discussion of Davies, *A.P.F.*, 383 with bibliography p. 369, accepting it as possible that he was concerned with the introduction of jury pay. Against the consensus A. E. Raubitschek has argued, largely from Plato, that Damon was active and was ostracised in the last third of the century and his father Damonides was an adviser of the younger Pericles and was the deviser of jury pay; *A.P.* mistakenly confuses the two (*C&M* xvi 1955, 78–83). Most recently K. Meister has accepted that Damon was active and was ostracised in the last third of the century, but has returned (surely rightly) to the view that *A.P.* must here have been referring to Damon (*RSA* iii 1973, 29–45). Damon was a famous man, and one is tempted to say that *A.P.* should not have been mistaken but probably wrote ⟨Δάμωνος τοῦ⟩ Δαμωνίδου τοῦ Ὄαθεν, but Δάμωνος τοῦ was lost—which would be particularly easy in a genitive construction—and Ὄαθεν corrupted at an early stage (cf. W. Wyse, *CR* v 1891, 227, Kaibel, *Stil und Text*, 183–4). However, it would be surprising if the same corruption occurred in the early edition of *A.P.* apparently used by Plutarch and in the revised edition represented by the London papyrus, so more probably the errors were made earlier, by *A.P.* or his source (cf. Introduction, p. 56 with n. 278: Meister, *op. cit.*, 37, prefers the first explanation but thinks the second possible).

ὃς ἐδόκει τῶν πολλῶν εἰσηγητὴς εἶναι τῷ Περικλεῖ: For εἰσηγητής ('proposer', 'author') cf. T. III. 48. vi, A. I. *Tim.* 172, Hyp. VI. *Epit.* 3. For the *motif* of an adviser cf. the story that Themistocles was shown by Mnesiphilus that the Greek fleet needed to stay and fight at Salamis (H. VIII. 57–8, Pl. *Her. Mal.* 869 D–F, cf. *An Seni*, 795 C, *Them.* 2. vi). Probably, if not certainly, the purpose of the mention of (Damon) is malicious: the demagogue Pericles was not even capable of devising his own demagoguic manoeuvres. In contrast to this, Thucydides stresses the ability both of Themistocles and of Pericles (I. 138. iii; II. 60. v, 65. viii). The only other traces of the allegation are in Pl. *Per.* 4. ii (ὁ δὲ Δάμων ἔοικεν ἄκρος ὢν σοφιστὴς καταδύεσθαι μὲν εἰς τὸ τῆς μουσικῆς ὄνομα πρὸς τοὺς πολλοὺς ἐπικρυπτόμενος τὴν δεινότητα, τῷ δὲ Περικλεῖ συνῆν καθάπερ ἀθλητῇ τῶν πολιτικῶν ἀλείπτης καὶ διδάσκαλος), and in Plutarch's accounts of Damon's ostracism (cf. next note).

διὸ καὶ ὠστράκισαν αὐτὸν ὕστερον: Some have disbelieved in this and other little-attested ostracisms (e.g. H. B. Mattingly, *U. Leeds R.* xiv 1971, 287; for a list of certain or possible ostracisms later than 480 see above, p. 271); but one ostracon against Damon has been found (cf. above), and doubt is unnecessary. The ostracon has been dated after 450 on archaeological grounds (A. Brueckner, *AM* xl 1915, 20–1): most have thought in terms of the mid 440's (cf. A. Rosenberg, *NJA* xviii 1915, 205–12), but a few have preferred a later date (e.g. Beloch, *G.G.*², II. i. 313 n. 1, Meister, *RSA* iii 1973, 31–2; Raubitschek's distinction between father and son would require a later date for the son who was the victim of ostracism).†

διδόναι τοῖς πολλοῖς τὰ αὐτῶν: Kaibel, *Stil und Text*, 184, compares And. II. *Red.* 17.

τοῖς δικασταῖς· ἀφ' ὧν αἰτιῶνταί τινες χείρω γενέσθαι: Kenyon retains the papyrus' text; but many have either changed δικασταῖς to δικαστηρίοις, noting that δικαστήρια are mentioned in §iii (Blass, *LZB* 1891, 304; H. Richards, *CR* v 1891, 227, also proposing ἀφ' οὗ), or changed χείρω to χείρους, suspecting the influence of χείρω in 28. i (e.g. W. L. Newman, *CR* v 1891, 160, Kaibel, *Stil und Text*, 184), or made an insertion, e.g. τὰ πράγματα, after γενέσθαι (cf. J. B. Mayor and others, *CR* v 1891, 113, 180). Kaibel insists that it must be the jurors, not the courts, that 'became worse', which has some force; but it is probably best to keep the papyrus' text and suppose that *A.P.* made the easy transition from δικασταί to (understood) δικαστήρια. Newman, *loc. cit.*, suspected in τινες an allusion to Plat. *Gorg.* 515 E 2–7, but the opinion must have been expressed by many.

κληρουμένων ἐπιμελῶς: '... who took care to ensure that their names were included in the ballot for places on the juries' (Moore). There seems to have been a fixed quota of jurors, in the fifth century 6,000 (cf. on 24. iii, 63. iii), and whenever more than 6,000 applied for registration some applicants would have to be eliminated.

μᾶλλον τῶν τυχόντων ἢ τῶν ἐπιεικῶν ἀνθρώπων: ἐπιεικής was used to mean both 'of the upper classes' and 'of the better sort (from any class in society)' in the course of 26. i (cf. *ad locc.*). Here the meaning 'of the better sort' must be uppermost in the writer's mind, but no doubt one of his objections to οἱ τυχόντες is that they tend not to be members of the upper classes.

27. v. τὸ δεκάζειν: The word is not common, but it is found with the meaning 'bribe', in particular with jurors as object, often enough in the orators (e.g. Lys. XXIX. *Phil.* 12, Is. VIII. *Pace,* 50, A. 1. *Tim.* 87); possibly a particular form of bribery is denoted. The incident which is cited is to be dated to 409, or perhaps 410 (cf. next note), and we may wonder whether it is true that this was the earliest instance of a jury's being bribed: Athenian juries were large, and to bribe enough jurors to influence a verdict will have been difficult, but in the fifth century it could be discovered with a small margin of error which jurors would decide a given case (cf. Harrison, *L.A.*, ii. 239–40), and the possibility of bribing juries was familiar to [X.] *A.P.*, probably to be dated 431–424 (iii. 7, reading συνδεκάσαι). The interval of about fifty years makes nonsense of *A.P.*'s implication (ἤρξατο ... μετὰ ταῦτα) that it was the introduction of jury pay which was responsible for corruption in the courts.

Ἀνύτου μετὰ τὴν ἐν Πύλῳ στρατηγίαν: The papyrus reads αὐτοῦ, but Anytus' name can be supplied (and was supplied by Kenyon[1]) from Harp. δεκάζων, which cites *A.P.* and names Anytus. The same story is told of Anytus in D.S. XIII. 64. v–vii, Pl. *Coriol.* 14. vi, *L.S.* 211. 31, schol. A. 1. *Tim.* 87; in *L.S.* 236. 3, *E.M.* (254. 28) δεκάσαι, the offender's name becomes Μέλης (presumably corrupted from Meletus, who like Anytus was a prosecutor of Socrates: e.g. Plat. *Apol.* 23 E 3–24 A 1); all the texts repeat that this was the first instance of the offence.[30] The allegation is dismissed as a later invention by F. Kiechle, *Der Kleine Pauly*, i. 417.

Anytus Ἀνθεμίωνος Εὐωνυμεύς (for the demotic see Davies, *A.P.F.*, 41) was one of the *nouveaux riches* who rose to prominence in Athens in the last third of the fifth century, having inherited a tannery from his father (X. *Apol.* 29, Areth. schol. Plat. *Apol.* 18 B, 23 E). He may have been a member of the boule in 413/2 or 412/1 (the year before

---

[30] The third of Socrates' prosecutors, Lycon, is said to have betrayed Naupactus to the Spartans at the end of the Peloponnesian War (Metag. fr. 10 Kock).

Ar. *Thesm.*), involved in some corrupt practice (Ἄνυτος is perhaps to be read for αὑτὸς in *Thesm.* 809: P. Maas *ap.* Budé ed. of V. Coulon). In the episode alluded to here the Spartans attacked the Athenian fort at Pylos and Anytus was sent with thirty ships to relieve it, bad weather prevented him from reaching Pylos, on returning to Athens he was charged with προδοσία but managed to secure an acquittal: this apparently occurred in 409 (D.S., *loc. cit.*, and X. *H.* 1. ii. 18 both mention it after Thrasyllus' Aegean campaign; D.S.'s nominal date is 409/8, but in §vii he says that the Athenians occupied Pylos for fifteen years; confirmation depends on W. S. Ferguson's dating of *IG* i² 301 to 409/8 [*Treasurers of Athena*, 38–45 with 16–27], but D. M. Lewis doubts that and wonders if this episode occurred in 410 [*Sparta and Persia*, 126 n. 112]). For Anytus' later career see 34. iii with commentary; for W. Aly's conjecture, possible but not certain, that his father was the Anthemion of 7. iv, see *ad loc.*

28. i. ἕως μὲν οὖν Περικλῆς προειστήκει τοῦ δήμου ... τελευτήσαντος δὲ Περικλέους ...: The same opinion, that Pericles was the last of Athens' good leaders, was expressed by Is. VIII. *Pace*, 124–8, XV. *Antid.* 230–6 cf. 111, 306–9; cf. earlier Lys. XXX. *Nic.* 28; the germ of the idea may be found in T. II. 65. v–xiii. Is. VIII. *Pace*, 75 contrasts Aristides, Themistocles and Miltiades with Hyperbolus and Cleophon, saying nothing of the intervening generation, and schol. Ar. *Pax*, 681 (probably from Theopompus) makes Hyperbolus the first of the inferior leaders: see W. R. Connor, *Theopompus and Fifth-Century Athens*, 62–3 with 161–2 nn. 38–40. Pl. *Cim.* 19. iii says that after Cimon's death no general of the Greeks accomplished anything distinguished against the barbarians, ἀλλὰ τραπέντες ὑπὸ δημαγωγῶν καὶ πολεμοποιῶν ἐπ' ἀλλήλους ... συνερράγησαν εἰς τὸν πόλεμον.

οὐκ εὐδοκιμοῦντα παρὰ τοῖς ἐπιεικέσιν: 'Not in good repute with the upper classes', shown by the next clause to be a periphrasis for 'not a member of the upper classes'; ἐπιεικής is used here in its social and political rather than its moral sense (cf. the first occurrence of the word in 26. i, with commentary).

It was a commonplace that Pericles' death marked the end of an era for the Athenian ruling class: for contemporary comment on the post-Periclean leaders see Ar. *Eq.* 180–222, Eupolis, fr. 117 Kock; for a modern view of the change see W. R. Connor, *The New Politicians of Fifth-Century Athens*, with the qualifications of J. K. Davies, *Gnomon* xlvii 1975, 374–8. A glance through the list of προστάται in this chapter shows that, of those in Pericles' generation or earlier, all except Themistocles (of the lesser aristocracy) and presumably Ephialtes (of unknown family) were themselves of the great families of the archaic period or were capable of forming marriage alliances with those families; of those that follow, Nicias, Cleon and Theramenes were of families which achieved greatness only in the fifth century, and Cleophon and Callicrates have not earned inclusion in *A.P.F.* (though their absence may be due to defective evidence rather than lack of wealth, and lack of wealth does not prove lack of aristocratic ancestors); among the men prominent between Pericles' death and the end of the fifth century the old aristocracy is represented only by Alcibiades and Critias (with Conon as a rather doubtful candidate).[31] We need not be surprised at the time-lag between the creation of democratic institutions and the rise of men of the δῆμος to positions of political importance, but the disappearance of the old aristocracy from such positions is strikingly abrupt.

28. ii. ἐξ ἀρχῆς μὲν γὰρ καὶ πρῶτος ἐγένετο προστάτης τοῦ δήμου Σόλων: δῆμος, here as often, denotes the mass of the unprivileged, in whatever sense is appropriate to the occasion (cf. on 2. i); *A.P.* has frequently labelled political leaders as προστάται τοῦ δήμου (2. ii, 20. iv, 23. ii, 25. i, cf. 36. i: see especially p. 97), an expression first used of leaders of a democratic party by Thucydides (III. 75. ii, 82. i, IV. 46. iv, 66. iii, VI. 35. ii, VIII. 89. iv, cf. VI. 89. iv). Here we have a list: Solon and Pisistratus head it, as προστάται τοῦ δήμου, and thereafter we have pairs of opposed democratic and aristocratic leaders. It is not the earliest list of προστάται: Is. XV. *Antid.* 230–6 names Solon, Cleisthenes, Themistocles and Pericles as laudable προστάται τοῦ δήμου; and in Plat. *Gorg.* 503 C 1–3 cf. 515 C 4–D 1 Callicles names Themistocles, Cimon, Miltiades and Pericles as leaders who have 'made the Athenians better'; Theopompus in book X of his *Philippica* wrote a digression περὶ τῶν Ἀθήνησι δημαγωγῶν (Ath. IV. 166 D = 115 F 100: see FF 85–100), in which the 'demagogues' studied appear to be Themistocles, Cimon, Thucydides son of Melesias, Pericles, Cleon, Hyperbolus, and, in the fourth century, Callistratus and Eubulus (he perhaps assigned to each in turn a number of years of supremacy: see A. E. Raubitschek, *Phoen.* ix 1955, 125–6, W. R. Connor, *Theopompus and Fifth-Century Athens*, 61–2 with 160–1 nn. 36–7); and in the fifth century Stesimbrotus had written περὶ Θεμιστοκλέους καὶ Θουκυδίδου καὶ Περικλέους (Ath. XIII. 589 E = 107 F 10a: see FF 1–11). The ultimate model for these lists of προστάται may be Stesimbrotus' work, or, as suggested by Connor (*op. cit.*, 165–6 n. 69), Eupolis' *Demes* (produced in 412: for a reconstruction see D. L. Page, *Greek Literary Papyri: Poetry* [Loeb],

---

[31] None of these is mentioned in *A.P.*: it seems to be Platonic influence that is responsible for the absence of Critias (cf. p. 430), and this may explain Alcibiades' absence too.

202–17, fr. 40; text revised C. F. L. Austin, *Com. Gr. Frag. Pap.*, 84–92, fr. 92). Such lists became common: D. ix. *Phil. iii.* 23 divides fifth- and fourth-century Greek history into a series of hegemonies (applying the same word, προστάτης, to the leading cities, and assigning a number of years of supremacy to each); earlier Greek history was made to yield a list of 'thalassocracies', known to us from D.S. vii. 11, but based on an idea which goes back at least to Thucydides (1. 13–15. i, cf. W. G. Forrest, CQ^2 xix 1969, 95–6); and Theophrastus drew up a succession of philosophers (cf. J. B. McDiarmid, *HSCP* lxi 1953, 132).

Callicles names Themistocles and his opponent Cimon in the same breath; Theopompus' list of 'demagogues' includes Themistocles and Cimon, Pericles and Thucydides; Isocrates' four are all men regarded by *A.P.* as προστάται τοῦ δήμου, but he does not contrast them with aristocratic opponents: the succession not simply of leaders but of pairs of opposing leaders is first found in this chapter of *A.P.* F. J. Frost in a study of Themistocles has insisted that in all texts prior to *A.P.* Themistocles is not a partisan politician but a great statesman, the hero of Athens' finest hour; it was 'Aristotle' who conceived the idea of opposing democratic and aristocratic leaders, forced an interpretation of the facts to fit his theories, and established the pattern which was to be followed by later writers (*CSCA* i 1968, 109–12 cf. 123–4). This is unlikely: προστάται of the γνώριμοι in opposition to the δῆμος are absent not only from other writers but also from Arist. *Pol.*, and except in this chapter and in the difficult account of Cimon in 26. i προστάται τῶν γνωρίμων are absent also from *A.P.*; on the other hand, anyone who was familiar with Thucydides' treatments of στάσις and his party-political use of προστάτης τοῦ δήμου could without great originality have assumed that the γνώριμοι too had προστάται and have constructed a list of this kind.

The list here is a bare one, with a few details attached to some of the names; it is terse sometimes to the point of obscurity; it does not explicitly justify the statement about Pericles and his successors to which it is attached, and it corresponds by no means perfectly to the fuller account of Athens' political history in the rest of the first part of *A.P.* (cf. below, on individual entries). Probably the list is not *A.P.*'s own compilation, but he is summarising what he found at greater length in an earlier work (it was suggested by Gomme, *Hist. Comm. Thuc.*, i. 48 n. 1, and A. E. Raubitschek, *Phoen.* ix 1955, 125, xiv 1960, 82–3, that the list is derived from Theopompus: cf. Introduction, p. 23). The list is, of course, naïvely over-simple in its assumption of a permanent opposition between γνώριμοι and πλῆθος, with each party acquiring a new leader at the same time; but although over-simple it is not wholly wrong: inevitably it comes closer to the truth at some points than at others. Each pairing seems to be based on one notorious occasion of conflict.

Solon has already been described as πρῶτος ... τοῦ δήμου προστάτης in 2. ii; and ch. 9 emphasises the δημοτικώτατα elements in his reforms; similarly he is the first of the προστάται τοῦ δήμου in Isocrates' list. The fifth-century democracy regarded Cleisthenes a its founding hero, but at the end of the century oligarchs tried to distinguish between Cleisthenes' dispensation and the full democracy (29. iii with commentary), and thereafter there was much debate as to who was the founder of the democracy and what sort of democracy he founded (cf. 9. i, 22. i, with commentary). In 9. ii *A.P.* has repeated the judgment of Arist. *Pol.* that Solon is not to be held responsible for the democracy that has been built on his foundations; and the poems quoted in ch. 12 make it clear that Solon had a view of what was due to the δῆμος which would not have been considered democratic in the fifth and fourth centuries.

δεύτερος δὲ Πεισίστρατος: Cf. 13. iv–v, where Pisistratus is δημοτικώτατος εἶναι δοκῶν.

τῶν εὐγενῶν καὶ γνωρίμων: If the text is sound or requires only the insertion of a participle (ὤν, H. Richards, *CR* v 1891, 227; ὄντες, T. Gomperz, *DLZ* xii 1891, 1639–40), *A.P.* has chosen to emphasise that Solon and Pisistratus, though προστάται τοῦ δήμου, were not like the later demagogues but were themselves of good families (cf. §i, and perhaps the remark below, that Cleisthenes was τοῦ γένους ὢν τῶν Ἀλκμεωνιδῶν). Kaibel & Wilamowitz deleted the phrase as an interpolation (cf. Kaibel, *Stil und Text*, 184–5): Kaibel notes that the opponents of the δῆμος are not elsewhere labelled εὐγενεῖς, but in this list *A.P.* seems to be deliberately varying his presentation as far as the material allows (cf. Introduction, pp. 42–3), and the word need not arouse our suspicion. Poland believed that the list of opposed pairs of leaders should begin in the generation of Pisistratus, and suggested ⟨προεστηκότων Λυκούργου καὶ Μεγακλέους⟩ τῶν εὐγενῶν; and with the same interpretation Gomme proposed τῶν ⟨δὲ⟩ εὐγενῶν καὶ γνωρίμων ⟨Λυκοῦργος⟩ or ... ⟨Λυκοῦργος καὶ Μεγακλῆς⟩ or τῶν εὐγενῶν ⟨ὄντες, τῶν δὲ⟩ γνωρίμων ⟨Λυκοῦργος καὶ Μεγακλῆς⟩ (*HSCP* Supp. i 1940, 238 n. 2 = *More Essays*, 62–3 n. 44). Solon is widely represented as a mediator accepted by all, but Pisistratus was an opponent of Lycurgus and (at times) of Megacles (cf. 13. iv–v, 14. iv–15. i); the remark that Cleisthenes had no opponent will make more sense if his predecessor has been assigned one or more opponents. I therefore find the approach of Poland and Gomme attractive: since in the presentation of the list *A.P.* has been careful to avoid verbal monotony but less careful to avoid obscurity we cannot hope to restore the original text with certainty, but of the suggestions noted here Gomme's first seems the best; it would be in keeping with the list if Pisistratus was given a single opponent. See also next note.

καταλυθείσης δὲ τῆς τυραννίδος Κλεισθένης ... οἱ περὶ τὸν Ἰσαγόραν: The conflict between Cleisthenes and Isagoras is narrated in 20. i–iii, and §iv comments that κατασχόντος δὲ τοῦ δήμου τὰ πράγματα Κλεισθένης ἡγεμὼν ἦν καὶ τοῦ δήμου προστάτης; 22. i states as the result of Cleisthenes' reforms that δημοτικωτέρα πολὺ τῆς Σόλωνος ἐγένετο ἡ πολιτεία. For the fate of Isagoras and his supporters see 20. iii with commentary: Isagoras remained available for the Spartans to make a subsequent attempt to reinstate him.

If the suggestion of Poland and Gomme discussed above is rejected we can easily understand ἐγένετο προστάτης τοῦ δήμου of Cleisthenes. If, as I suspect, δεύτερος δὲ ... καὶ γνωρίμων should be expanded to include Pisistratus' opponent(s), what is being asserted of Cleisthenes becomes less obvious; but the obscurity is no greater here than on Themistocles and Aristides, below, and this objection to the expansion need not be fatal. Against the expansion, the note that Cleisthenes was an Alcmaeonid might be seen as a further reminder that the earlier democratic leaders were not themselves of the δῆμος, but more probably it is a simple biographical note like those attached to the names of Thucydides and Nicias.

μετὰ δὲ ταῦτα ... Ξάνθιππος ... Μιλτιάδης: This is one of the least satisfactory pairs in the list: there is no evidence that in the 490's and 480's Athenian politics were in a state that could be represented, with however much over-simplification, as a conflict between δῆμος and γνώριμοι, or that Xanthippus and Miltiades stood at the head of conflicting parties of any kind. Xanthippus prosecuted Miltiades after his failure to capture Paros in 490 or 489 (cf. on 22. vi); that, and the appearance of their respective sons Pericles and Cimon on the democratic and the aristocratic side later, were no doubt considered a sufficient basis for making these men a pair of leaders to fill the gap between Cleisthenes and Isagoras and Themistocles and Aristides. Miltiades is not mentioned elsewhere in *A.P.* except in 26. i, as Cimon's father.

ἔπειτα Θεμιστοκλῆς καὶ Ἀριστείδης: In 23. iii both are said to be προστάται τοῦ δήμου, and in 24 and 41. ii Aristides' political stance is represented as democratic, but in Plutarch's lives of the two men and elsewhere they are generally represented as opponents. In fact, in the 480's the two were political rivals but not the heads of rival parties (cf. on 22. vi–vii: I imagine that the tradition of their rivalry at that time, culminating in the ostracism of Aristides, provided the basis for this pairing); in the 470's there is clear evidence of opposition between Themistocles and Cimon, but it seems that Aristides is to be associated with Themistocles rather than with Cimon (cf. pp. 288–9, 292–3). Almost all commentators have assumed that here as in

23. iii *A.P.* is labelling both Themistocles and Aristides as προστάται τοῦ δήμου, but Gomme was surely right to see in this chapter's pattern of opposed pairs a better guide to the meaning of this abrupt item: Themistocles is leader of the δῆμος and Aristides of the γνώριμοι, 'according to the conventional picture; that this is inconsistent with 23. iii and 24. iii (as well as with the facts) is not, unfortunately, proof that it is not the correct interpretation' (*HSCP* Supp. i 1940, 238 n. 2 = *More Essays*, 62–3 n. 49, cf. Mathieu, *Aristote, Constitution d'Athènes*, 59, Jacoby, *Supp.* ii. 95 n. 104). The obscurity results from *A.P.*'s attempt to avoid monotony: we need not suppose with J. H. Schreiner, *SO* Supp. xxi 1968, 61–2, that he was embarrassed by two different views of Aristides and for that reason took refuge in ambiguity. Like Xanthippus and Miltiades, Themistocles and Aristides were προστάται at a time when the contrast between δῆμος and γνώριμοι was not important in Athenian politics; but Themistocles has links with men who were on the side of the δῆμος when the contrast did become important (cf. pp. 311–12).

μετὰ δὲ τούτους Ἐφιάλτης ... Κίμων ... : In his narrative *A.P.* perversely delayed the introduction of Cimon until after Ephialtes' death (26. i with commentary), and made no mention of Cimon's opposition to Ephialtes (for which see p. 311). In this list Cimon is given his due, and this is one of the better pairings: the two men had clashed publicly on the question of whether Athens should help Sparta against the Messenians; Ephialtes was a champion of the δῆμος, deliberately moving Athens in the direction of democracy, while Cimon was opposed to that move and tried to reverse it. τῶν εὐπόρων is used here simply as an equivalent of τῶν γνωρίμων (cf. 26. i *fin.*), but it is particularly appropriate when used in connection with the man who was said in 27. iii to have had τυραννικὴν ... οὐσίαν.

εἶτα Περικλῆς ... Θουκυδίδης ... : Pericles was a supporter of Ephialtes (cf. pp. 311–12), and in the course of the thirty years after Ephialtes' death attained to a position which prompted the historian Thucydides to write ἐγίγνετο ... λόγῳ μὲν δημοκρατία, ἔργῳ δὲ ὑπὸ τοῦ πρώτου ἀνδρὸς ἀρχή (ii. 65. ix); *A.P.* 27. i writes that when he was leader δημοτικωτέραν ἔτι συνέβη γενέσθαι τὴν πολιτείαν. Despite T. ii. 65. ix and Pl. *Per.* 16. iii, Pericles was not unopposed as leader of Athens either before or after the ostracism of Thucydides. Thucydides Μελησίου Ἀλωπεκῆθεν is mentioned by *A.P.* only here and in §v. His father was probably the wrestling-master known from Pind. *Ol.* viii, *Nem.* iv, vi (Wade-Gery, *JHS* lii 1932, 208–10 = *Essays*, 243–6, Davies, *A.P.F.*, 231). It is agreed that Thucydides was a κηδεστής of Cimon (connection by marriage: Pl. *Per.* 11. i uses the same word, schol. Aristid. XLVI. *Quatt.* [iii. 446 Dindorf] uses γαμβρός): the precise relationship is uncertain (cf. Davies, *A.P.F.*, 232–6), but it is an attractive conjecture that he married a sister of Cimon, that they had a daughter Hegesipyle who married Olorus, the son of another sister of Cimon, and that these two were the parents of Thucydides the historian (E. Cavaignac, *RPh*³ iii 1929, 281–5, Wade-Gery, *opp. citt.*, 210–1 = 246–7, relying on Marc. *Vit. Thuc.* 2).

The opposition between the elder Thucydides and Pericles is known to us principally from Pl. *Per.* 11–14 (cf. 6. ii, 8. v = *Praec. Ger. Reip.* 802 C, 16. iii, *Nic.* 2. i–ii): Thucydides succeeded to the leadership of the ἀριστοκρατικοί on the death of Cimon (*c.* 450); he was a politician rather than a soldier, encouraged his supporters to sit together in the assembly, and was responsible for the use of δῆμος and ὀλίγοι as party labels; opposition to Pericles crystallised around the building programme of the 440's, financed partly from the allies' tribute; the conflict was won by Pericles, and Thucydides was ostracised; after that Pericles was supreme, and was elected general each year οὐκ ἐλάττω τῶν πεντεκαίδεκα ἐτῶν (Pl. *Per.* 16. iii). Much of this is highly implausible as an account of fifth-century Athens (see in general A. Andrewes, *JHS* xcviii 1978, 1–5; W. R. Connor, *The New Politicians of Fifth-Century Athens*, 63 n. 54, suggests that it is 'approximately correct' that the use of δῆμος and ὀλίγοι as a pair of opposed terms began about this time); it has become customary to reckon the fifteen years from Pericles' death in 429/8 and assume that Thucydides was ostracised in 444/3 (e.g. Wade-Gery, *opp. citt.*, 206 = 240–1), but it is dangerous to build theories, as Wade-Gery did, on the assumption that that is the precise year and that Pericles was not general that year. See also schol. Ar. *Vesp.* 947, citing Idom. 338 F 1, Phil. 328 F 120, Ammon. 350 F 1, Thp. 115 F 91, Andr. 324 F 37; Aristid. XLVI. *Quatt.* with schol. (ii. 159–60, iii. 446–7, Dindorf). 64 ostraca against Thucydides are known, only 3 against Pericles; the ostracism of Callias Διδυμίου, and perhaps that of Damon, are to be dated about the same time (cf. pp. 271, 341–2). Thucydides will have returned to Athens *c.* 433, and it is apparently he who was prosecuted and convicted shortly before spring 425 (Ar. *Ach.* 676–718 with schol. 703, *Vesp.* 946–8 with schol. 947, cf. Wade-Gery, *opp. citt.*, 209 = 244, Davies, *A.P.F.*, 232); but the attacks on Pericles of Pl. *Per.* 31–2 are probably to be dated to the early 430's and attributed to δημαγωγοί like Cleon (F. J. Frost, *Hist.* xiii 1964, 385–99, *JHS* lxxxiv 1964, 69–72, against Wade-Gery, *opp. citt.*, 219–21 = 258–60).

Thucydides is one of the fifth-century politicians included in the title of Stesimbrotus' work (cf. p. 345: no surviving fragment deals with Thucydides). He is mentioned with Aristides in Plat. *Lach.* 179 A 1–8, and in Plat. *Meno*, 94 B 8–D 2 he is mentioned (with Themistocles, Aristides and Pericles) as a man unable to teach his sons virtue; but he is not much mentioned by fourth-century

Athenians. Theopompus, in the tradition of Stesimbrotus, makes Thucydides one of his δημαγωγοί (A. E. Raubitschek, *Phoen.* xiv 1960, 81–95, tried to derive from Theopompus all references to him later than Plato, but his arguments are insecure).

Here *A.P.* appears to have exhausted his list of synonyms, and he labels both Thucydides and Theramenes (below) as προστάται τῶν ἑτέρων. ἐσθλῶν was suggested in both places by W. Wyse, *CR* v 1891, 113; ἐπιεικῶν by J. E. B. Mayor, *ibid.*; εὐπόρων by H. Richards, *CR* v 1891, 227 (cf. Γ. Α. Παπαβασίλειος, Ἀθ. iii 1891, 282: Theramenes only). The scribe who spelled Cleon's patronymic Κλαιενέτου could have written ἑτέρων for ἑταίρων: to emend to that would in the case of Theramenes produce a clash with 34. iii (noticed by E. S. Thompson, *CR* v 1891, 227, Blass[2]); since there are other clashes between this list and the rest of *A.P.* that is not a fatal objection, but ἑταῖροι is very far from being a synonym for γνώριμοι, and it is better to retain the papyrus' text.

28. iii. Περικλέους δὲ τελευτήσαντος ... Νικίας ... Κλέων ... : The clash on which this pairing is based must be that of 425, when Nicias as general gave Cleon the opportunity to go to Pylos in his place (T. IV. 26–8; according to IV. 27. v they were already ἐχθροί). Thucydides in some sense admired Nicias (cf. VII. 86. v with Dover *ad loc.*, also A. W. H. Adkins, *GR&BS* xvi 1975, 379–92), and he detested Cleon (cf. III. 36. vi, IV. 28. v, V. 16. i); in the fourth century Nicias' reputation seems to have been good (he is favourably portrayed in Plat. *Lach.*, and D. III. *Ol. iii.* 21 mentions him with Aristides, Demosthenes and Pericles as a man who is praised but not imitated), while Cleon is rarely mentioned (in [D.] XL. *Boe. Dot.* he is mentioned with firm approval; D.S. XII. 74. i–ii suggests that he was treated more generously by Ephorus than by Thucydides). *A.P.* 28. v singles out Nicias for favourable mention along with the elder Thucydides and Theramenes, and states that Nicias like Thucydides was a καλὸς κἀγαθός; Plutarch begins his *Nicias* with this judgment of *A.P.* (*Nic.* 2. i), and proceeds to say that on Pericles' death Nicias εὐθὺς εἰς τὸ πρωτεύειν προήχθη, μάλιστα μὲν ὑπὸ τῶν πλουσίων καὶ γνωρίμων, ἀντίταγμα ποιουμένων αὐτὸν πρὸς τὴν Κλέωνος βδελυρίαν καὶ τόλμαν, οὐ μὴν ἀλλὰ καὶ τὸν δῆμον εἶχεν εὔνουν καὶ συμφιλοτιμούμενον (*Nic.* 2. ii).

The interpretation of Athenian politics in the 420's has been much discussed, too often with the use of unsatisfactory party labels. Beloch exaggerated a genuine difference in temperament and strategy to place Nicias at the head of a 'peace party' and Cleon at the head of a 'war party' (*Die attische Politik seit Perikles*, 19–46), and some have considered Nicias a champion not only of peace but of oligarchy (e.g. M. Croiset, *Aristophane et les partis à Athènes*, 26–7, trans. *Aristophanes and the Political Parties at Athens*, 16). A. B. West argued that in the 420's pacifists and oligarchs were few and unimportant; Nicias was the leader of the peasant farmers or conservative democrats, and the true heir of Pericles, while Cleon was the leader of a breakaway radical wing (*CP* xix 1924, 124–46, 201–28). Gomme, limiting his scope to imperial and military policy, regarded Cleon as Pericles' heir and Nicias as one of the ἀπράγμονες condemned by Pericles in T. II. 63. ii–iii (*JHS* lxxi 1951, 74–80 = *More Essays*, 101–11). More recent studies have emphasised that Cleon and Nicias came from very similar backgrounds: Cleon Κλεαινέτου Κυδαθηναιεύς inherited a tannery from his father (Ar. *Eq.* 44 with schol.), Nicias Νικηράτου Κυδαντίδης derived his wealth from the mines (Pl. *Nic.* 4. ii, X. *M.* II. v. 2, *Vect.* iv. 14). In each case the father became rich and the son was the first from his family to challenge the political predominance of the landed aristocracy; an attempt was made to give Nicias an ancestor who was important in the time of Solon (D.L. I. 110), but almost certainly this is an invention and *A.P.* is wrong to class Nicias with Thucydides as a καλὸς κἀγαθός (cf. W. R. Connor, *The New Politicians of Fifth-Century Athens*, 151–63, Davies, *A.P.F.*, 318, 403–4, D. Kagan, *The Archidamian War*, 129–31).

Cleon had more adventurous views than Nicias, and probably more adventurous view than Pericles, on how Athens ought to fight the Peloponnesian War. As for internal politics, Nicias at any rate acquiesced in the democracy, and the difference between the two men is best seen as one of style. Cleon was the δημαγωγός *par excellence* (he is one of the two men of whom Thucydides uses the word: IV. 21. iii, cf. p. 323), who paraded his attachment to the Athenian δῆμος rather than to any circle of friends (Pl. *Praec. Ger. Reip.* 806 F–807 A with Connor, *op. cit.*, 91–4; cf. what is said of Pericles, Pl. *Per.* 7 with Connor, *op. cit.*, 121–2, 127–8), who opposed those with intellectual or other claims to be better than their fellows (cf. T. III. 37–40 with Connor, *op. cit.*, 94–6), who based his supremacy not on regular office-holding but on his position as ῥήτωρ, a man able to make persuasive speeches in the assembly (cf. next two notes; T. III. 36. vi cf. IV. 21. iii describes him as τῷ ... δήμῳ παρὰ πολὺ ἐν τῷ τότε πιθανώτατος). In contrast to him Nicias, though a newcomer to politics, approached political life more in the traditional manner, frequently performing liturgies (whereas Cleon is not known to have performed any, though one is attested for his father: Davies, *A.P.F.*, 318–19, 403–4, cf. Pl. *Nic.* 3), frequently holding office as general (though not early in his life); but he like Pericles is said to have avoided dinner parties and social distractions (Pl. *Nic.* 5. i–ii). Although Nicias was not born among the γνώριμοι, unlike Cleon he was acceptable to them, at a time when they themselves were perhaps becoming disenchanted with politics (cf. Connor, *op. cit.*, 175–94, Adkins, *op. cit.*, esp. 385–9).

This time the opponents of the δῆμος are styled ἐπιφανεῖς: the usage is most clearly parallelled by H. II. 172. ii (δημότην τὸ πρὶν ἐόντα καὶ οἰκίης οὐκ ἐπιφανέος); cf. also H. II. 89. i, VII. 114. ii, VIII. 125. i. **ὃς δοκεῖ μάλιστα διαφθεῖραι τὸν δῆμον ταῖς ὁρμαῖς**: Neither 'by his wild undertakings' (Kenyon, Oxford Translation) nor 'by his violence' (Moore) is quite right. ὁρμή is used by Homer of the rage of fire (*Il.* XI. 157) or the shock of a wave (*Od.* V. 320); in T. III. 36. ii the fact that the Peloponnesians had sent ships to support Mytilene in its revolt contributed to the ὁρμή of the Athenians to punish Mytilene savagely; after the last battle in the bay at Syracuse the Athenians on land ἀπὸ μιᾶς ὁρμῆς gave themselves up to lamentation (T. VII. 71. vi); in Arist. *E.N.* I. 1102 B 21 the ὁρμαί of the undisciplined man carry him in the opposite direction to that which he intended; Themistocles was inconsistent and unstable in the first ὁρμαί of youth (Pl. *Them.* 2. vii), while Pericles did not give in to the ὁρμαί of the citizens (Pl. *Per.* 20. iii). Here I should translate as 'by his violent impulses': Thucydides describes Cleon as βιαιότατος τῶν πολιτῶν (III. 36. vi), and the ῥήτωρ caricatured by Aristophanes was a man given to making wild promises and wild accusations, of which the promise that he would finish the affair of Pylos in twenty days was typical (T. IV. 28. iv); it will be this tendency to extravagance and exaggeration which corrupted the δῆμος. This gives a reasonable sense, and there is no need to doubt the text; but J. B. Mayor proposed to insert a phrase indicating that Cleon ministered to the ὁρμαί of the δῆμος, and, noticing that in A. II. *F.L.* 76 Cleophon is described as διεφθαρκὼς νόμῃ χρημάτων τὸν δῆμον, Sandys suggested διανομαῖς and Thalheim νομαῖς.

A.P. omits to draw the reader's attention to the fact that what is said here bears out the point made at the beginning of the chapter, that after Pericles' death things became much worse (cf. p. 346).

καὶ πρῶτος ἐπὶ τοῦ βήματος ... ἐν κόσμῳ λεγόντων: Cf. Pl. *Nic.* 8. vi (τὸν ἐπὶ τοῦ βήματος κόσμον ἀνελὼν καὶ πρῶτος ἐν τῷ δημηγορεῖν ἀνακραγὼν καὶ περισπάσας τὸ ἱμάτιον καὶ μηρὸν πατάξας καὶ δρόμῳ μετὰ τοῦ λέγειν ἅμα χρησάμενος), *T.G.* 2. ii (using very similar language of Ti. Gracchus, with a reference to Cleon), Quint. XI. iii. 123, schol. Lucian, *Tim.* 30 = Thp. 115 F 92 + Phil. 328 F 128b (ὃς πρῶτος δημηγορῶν ἀνέκραγεν ἐπὶ βήματος καὶ ἐλοιδορήσατο. ... Ἀριστοτέλης δὲ ἐν Πολιτείᾳ καὶ περιζωσάμενον αὐτὸν λέγει δημηγορῆσαι). A. I. *Tim.* 25–6 says οὕτως ἦσαν σώφρονες οἱ ἀρχαῖοι ἐκεῖνοι ῥήτορες ... ὥστε ὃ νυνὶ πάντες ἐν ἔθει πράττομεν, τὸ τὴν χεῖρα ἔξω ἔχοντες λέγειν, τότε τοῦτο θρασύ τι ἐδόκει εἶναι, καὶ εὐλαβοῦντο αὐτὸ πράττειν, and cites a statue of Solon ἐντὸς τὴν χεῖρα ἔχων; D. XIX. *F.L.* 251 objected that the statue was less than fifty years old; and schol. A. I. *Tim.* 25 says that Solon stood like that to recite his elegies, notes Demosthenes' objection, and adds λέγεται δὲ Κλέων ὁ δημαγωγὸς παραβὰς τὸ ἐξ ἔθους σχῆμα περιζωσάμενος δημηγορῆσαι. Pl. *Praec. Ger. Reip.* 800 c says that it was Pericles' habit τὴν χεῖρα συνέχειν ἐντὸς τῆς περιβολῆς, and on Pericles' austere manner cf. Pl. *Per.* 5. Cleon, then, was the first ῥήτωρ to shout (ἀνακράζειν), to hurl abuse (λοιδορεῖσθαι) and to speak 'girt about' (περιζώννυσθαι): the last is presumably to be connected with Aeschines' 'having the hand outside' and Plutarch's 'pulling away his ἱμάτιον', and must mean that he fastened his clothes so as to be free to gesticulate with one or both hands. For his love of shouting and abuse cf. Ar. *Ach.* 377–82, *Eq.* 137, 217–18, 626–9, *Vesp.* 596, 1034, *Pax*, 757.

Gomme, *Hist. Comm. Thuc.*, i. 48 n. 1, suggested that this passage comes from Theopompus (as, he thought, does the whole list: cf. above, p. 346); Connor, *The New Politicians of Fifth-Century Athens*, 48–9, suggests that the first clause which I quote from schol. Lucian, though resembling *A.P.*, is derived not from *A.P.* but from Theopompus, and he believes that *A.P.* and Theopompus had a common source (*op. cit.*, 108–10). ἀνακράζειν is a favourite word of Aristophanes, which prompts the suggestion that the descriptions of Cleon in which it is found are derived ultimately from comedy; *Vesp.* 36 describes Cleon's voice as that of an enraged sow.

εἶτα μετὰ τούτους ... Θηραμένης ... Κλεοφῶν ... : The need to provide pairs of προστάται has led the compiler of the list to omit Alcibiades, his celebrated clashes with Nicias over the preservation of peace with Sparta (T. v. 43–6) and the expedition to Sicily (T. vi. 8–26), and the ostracism proposed by Hyperbolus, which resulted in the banishment not of Nicias or of Alcibiades but of himself (T. viii. 73. iii, Thp. 115 F 96, Pl. *Nic.* 11. i–viii, *Alc.* 13. iv–ix, cf. p. 271). No less strikingly, *A.P.* makes no mention of Alcibiades in his chapters on the revolutions of 411 (cf. pp. 371–2).

Theramenes Ἅγνωνος Στειριεύς was an opponent of democracy, who was prominent in setting up the oligarchic régimes of 411 (32. ii) and 404 (34. iii) but each time fell out with the extremists (33. ii, 36–7). His father Hagnon had a distinguished public career in the last decade of Pericles' life, swore to the Peace of Nicias, and was a πρόβουλος from 413 to 411: in Cratinus' *Plutus* one speaker describes Hagnon as ἀρχαιόπλουτος and another comments that his father Nicias was a φορτηγός (D. L. Page, *Greek Literary Papyri: Poetry* [Loeb], 200–1, fr. 38b, 32–7 = C. F. L. Austin, *Com. Gr. Frag. Pap.*, 39–44, fr. 73, 70–5), and it has been suggested that the first word is intended to mean not 'of ancient wealth' but 'rich from office-holding' (R. Goossens, *REA* xxxvii 1935, 410–12; Davies, *A.P.F.*, 227–8, is non-committal). Cleophon Κλεινπίδου Ἀχαρνεύς, frequently referred to as ὁ λυροποιός (e.g. And. 1. *Myst.* 146, A. 11. *F.L.* 76), was said to be of low or foreign origin (Plat. Com. *Cleophon*, fr. 60 Kock, Ar. *Ran.* 678–82 with schol. 678, schol. 1504, schol. 1532, A. II. *F.L.* 76, Ael. *V.H.* XII. 43), but is now known from the ostraca cast against him in Athens' last ostracism to be the son of a man who was general in 428 (T. III. 3. ii) and himself a candidate for ostracism in the 440's (E. Vanderpool, *Hesp.* xxi 1952, 114–15, xxxvii 1968, 120, xliii 1974, 192); he is said to have died a poor man (Lys. XIX. *Bon. Arist.* 48), and Davies gives him no entry in *A.P.F.* He was a δημαγωγός after the manner of Cleon and Hyperbolus, prominent between 410 and 404 as a strong opponent of peace with Sparta (cf. 34. i with commentary); after Aegospotami he was still opposed to peace and had to be eliminated before Theramenes could complete the negotiations with Sparta, and it is no doubt that conflict that is the basis of the pairing of Theramenes and Cleophon (no such conflict between Cleophon and the extreme oligarchs is recorded).

On the use of ἑτέρων for the opponents of the δῆμος see p. 351. ὃς καὶ τὴν διωβελίαν ἐπόρισε πρῶτος: The records of the treasurers of Athena include many advances to the Hellenotamiae (now presiding over an amalgamated treasury of the Athenian state and the Delian League: cf. on 30. ii) ἐς τὲν διοβελίαν between the third prytany of 410/09 (*IG* i² 304, *a* = M&L 84, 10) and 407/6 (*IG* i² 304, *b* 63 = Tod 92, 23), a reduction to 1 obol late in 407/6 and a return to 2 obols early in 406/5 (*IG* i² 304, *b* 75, 90, with B. D. Meritt, *Mélanges helléniques ... G. Daux*, 257, 262–3; but W. K. Pritchett, *Anc. Soc.* viii 1977, 45–6, prefers to interpret the 1 obol as a separate grant to war orphans); in 406/5 Archedemus ὁ γλάμων was ὁ τοῦ δήμου τότε προεστηκὼς ἐν Ἀθήναις καὶ τῆς διωβελίας ἐπιμελόμενος (X. *H.* I. vii. 2: διωκελ(ε)ίας codd., διωβελίας Dindorf); in 405/4 the treasurers of Athena made substantial distributions of corn, which may have taken the place of cash payments (*IG* ii² 1686, *B*, with W. S. Ferguson, *Treasurers of Athena*, 82–4, but see the cautionary note of A. M. Woodward, *Hesp.* xxv 1956, 116–17). Woodward has reconstructed a text of 404/3 to show payments still being made to the Hellenotamiae for the διωβελία in that year (*Hesp.* xxxii 1963, 144–55, no. 1, *Aa* 10–11, *Ba* 1 = *SEG* xxi 80, *Aa* and *Ab*: see especially his 150 with n. 10): this part of his reconstruction is speculative, and it would be startling if it were correct; the Hellenotamiae are mentioned in an inscription of 403 or later, but the context is lost and may have been an allusion to earlier practice (*Hesp.* xl 7, 18, with R. S. Stroud's commentary, pp. 292–5); P. Krentz, *Hesp.* xlviii 1979, 60, eliminates both the Hellenotamiae and the διωβελία from Woodward's text. A. II. *F.L.* 76 describes Cleophon as διεφθαρκὼς νόμῃ χρημάτων τὸν δῆμον.

What this 2-obol payment was remains uncertain. Payment to jurors was raised to 3 obols by Cleon (cf. on 27. iii); payment for attending the assembly was not introduced until after the democratic restoration of 403/2 (41. iii with commentary); the institution of the theoric fund is best attributed to Eubulus and Diophantus and dated to the 350's (cf. on 43. i). The best review of the evidence and of modern theories on the διωβελία is given by J. J. Buchanan, *Theorika*, 35–48: Sandys and other early commentators on *A.P.* supposed that the διωβελία was the theoric grant (cf. Gilbert, *C.A.S.A.*, 245); Beloch argued from Ar. *Ran.* 138–41 with schol. 140 that after the fall of the intermediate régime in 410 jury pay was restored but at the reduced rate of 2 obols (RM^2 xxxix 1884, 239–44, cf. $G.G.^2$, II. i. 398 n. 1, B. R. I. Sealey, *CSCA* viii 1975, 287, Pritchett, *op. cit.*, 41–5); Wilamowitz suggested that the διωβελία was a grant to citizens reduced to poverty by the Peloponnesian War (*A.u.A.*, ii. 212–16). Wilamowitz' view is probably right: the διωβελία should be regarded as a subsistence grant available to citizens not otherwise in receipt of money from the state.

ἐπόρισε calls to mind the office of ποριστής ('provider', 'deviser', *sc.* of funds), attested between 419 (Ant. VI. *Chor.* 49) and 405 (Ar. *Ran.* 1505): Cleophon is mentioned in *Ran.* 1504 (not as a ποριστής), and Beloch used And. II. *Red.* 17 and Lys. XIX. *Bon. Arist.* 48 to argue that the office was held by Cleophon (RM^2 xxxix 1884, 255–8, cf. $G.G.^2$, II. i. 397–8). That is likely enough, but we cannot say when he was ποριστής.

καὶ χρόνον μέν τινα διεδίδοτο: 'It continued to be paid.' The papyrus has the active form διεδίδου, which was retained by Kenyon[1-2], Blass and others, and defended by L. Whibley, *CR* v 1891, 168–9, Tovar, *REC* iii 1948, 161. διεδίδοτο was suggested by W. Wyse and W. G. Rutherford, *CR* v 1891, 113 (but Rutherford, *op. cit.*, 180, thought the passage totally corrupt); Wyse *ap.* Sandys cited schol. Ar. *Vesp.* 88 (on the δικαστικόν), 684 (citing Ἀριστοτέλης ἐν Πολιτείαις [= fr. 461 Teubner] and perhaps confusing the δικαστικόν with the διωβελία; cf. also Kaibel, *Stil und Text*, 185. For other suggestions see A. Gennadios and E. S. Thompson, *CR* v 1891, 274 and 277. Cleophon is said to have devised the διωβελία, not to have superintended its payment, so the passive is needed.

μετὰ δὲ ταῦτα κατέλυσε Καλλικράτης Παιανιεὺς πρῶτος ὑποσχόμενος . . . ἄλλον ὀβολόν: For κατέλυσε κατηύξησε was suggested by L. Whibley, *CR* v 1891, 168–9, κατήνυσε by A. Gennadios, *op. cit.*, 274, κατέλυσε⟨ν αὐτόν⟩ by E. S. Thompson, *op. cit.*, 277. No change is needed there, but we should follow Leeuwen in correcting πρῶτος to πρῶτον: Callicrates 'abolished it (possibly substituting the corn distributions of *IG* ii² 1686, *B*: cf. above), having first promised . . .' Pritchett, *op. cit.*, 45, comments, 'The promise was never carried out. The people realized the threat to financial solvency and abolished the entire fund' (but Gomme, *Hist. Comm. Thuc.*, i. 48 n. 1, thought he abolished the διωβελία by changing it to a τριωβελία, and suggested that this 'excellent rhetoric' comes from Theopompus: cf. above, p. 346). Nothing else is known of this Callicrates; there may be a confused recollection of this passage in schol. Ar. *Vesp.* 684 (cf. previous note), and there is another in various late texts which cite *A.P.* and state that Callicrates πρῶτον τοὺς δικαστικοὺς μισθοὺς εἰς ὑπερβολὴν αὐξῆσαι (e.g. Zenob. vi. 29, Phot., Suid. [*Y* 365] ὑπὲρ τὰ Καλλικράτους); cf. also Com. Adesp. fr. 384 Meineke (= 697 Kock), with Meineke's discussion, iv. 700–1, Wilamowitz, *A.u.A.*, ii. 214 n. 3, Kirchner, *P.A.* 7975. In Arist. *Pol.* II. 1267 B 1–3 we read ἡ πονηρία τῶν ἀνθρώπων ἄπληστον, καὶ τὸ πρῶτον μὲν ἱκανὸν διωβελία μόνον, ὅταν δ' ἤδη τοῦτ' ᾖ πάτριον, ἀεὶ δέονται τοῦ πλείονος, ἕως εἰς ἄπειρον ἔλθωσιν: some have thought a reference is intended to this grant and the proposal to increase it (e.g. Sandys; cf. Newman *ad loc.*), but Aristotle may have had no particular instance in mind.

θάνατον κατέγνωσαν ὕστερον: For the condemnation of Cleophon in 405/4 when after Aegospotami he was still opposed to peace with Sparta see on 34. i: the only charge specified is ὅτι οὐκ ἦλθεν εἰς τὰ ὅπλα ἀναπαυσόμενος (Lys. XIII. *Agor.* 12), but he was probably condemned as a traitor (cf. Rhodes, *A.B.*, 183 n. 4). Nothing is known about the fate of Callicrates.

εἴωθεν γὰρ ... τῶν μὴ καλῶς ἐχόντων: The fickleness of the Athenian assembly is a commonplace in writers who are not enthusiastic supporters of democracy: see, for example, T. II. 59. i–ii, 61. ii–iii, 65. iii–iv, III. 36. iv, 38. i, VIII. 1. i, [X.] *A.P.* ii. 17, X. *H.* I. vii. 35. W. L. Newman *ap.* Sandys suspected a reference here to the condemnation of Socrates (cf. D.S. XIV. 37. vii, D.L. II. 43), but I doubt if any specific reference is intended. The appearance, in Cleon and his successors, of the politician as ῥήτωρ rather than office-holder (subject to εὔθυναι and other checks on his conduct) made it harder for the δῆμος to deal with those who had led it astray, but various procedures were devised which could be used against the authors of unsuccessful policies: the γραφαὶ παρανόμων and νόμον μὴ ἐπιτήδειον θεῖναι (cf. 45. iv, 59. ii, with commentary); the δοκιμασία ῥητόρων (A. I. *Tim.* 28–30); the inclusion in the fourth-century νόμος εἰσαγγελτικός of the clause ἢ ῥήτωρ ὢν μὴ λέγῃ τὰ ἄριστα τῷ δήμῳ τῷ Ἀθηναίων χρήματα λαμβάνων καὶ δωρεὰς παρὰ τῶν τἀναντία πραττόντων τῷ δήμῳ (Hyp. IV. *Eux.* 8, Poll. VIII. 51, *L.R.C.* εἰσαγγελία). See S. Perlman, *Ath.*[2] xli 1963, 327–55, esp. 353–4.

28. iv. ἀπὸ δὲ Κλεοφῶντος: The politicians of the fourth century are dismissed collectively and anonymously: cf. Is. VIII. *Pace*, 75, contrasting Aristides, Themistocles and Miltiades with Hyperbolus, Cleophon καὶ τῶν νῦν δημηγορούντων (in the light of which it would be dangerous to insist that this list must have been compiled early in

the fourth century). Theopompus' δημαγωγοί included at any rate two from the fourth century, Callistratus and Eubulus (cf. p. 345). **ἤδη διεδέχοντο συνεχῶς τὴν δημαγωγίαν**: W. Wyse *ap.* Sandys compares schol. Ar. *Pax*, 681 (Hyperbolus μετὰ τὴν τοῦ Κλέωνος δυναστείαν διεδέξατο τὴν δημαγωγίαν); the verb reflects the idea that there was a continuous succession of προστάται. Here δημαγωγία is formally equivalent to προστασία τοῦ δήμου, but the context gives the word hostile undertones (cf. pp. 323-4).
οἱ μάλιστα βουλόμενοι θρασύνεσθαι καὶ χαρίζεσθαι τοῖς πολλοῖς: Cf. Is. xii. *Panath.* 132-3.
πρὸς τὰ παραυτίκα βλέποντες: τά was read by Kenyon[1], and defended by Kaibel (*Stil und Text*, 185) as referring to the various occasions of θρασύνεσθαι and χαρίζεσθαι; τό was preferred by A. Gennadios (*CR* v 1891, 274) and Κ. Σ. Κόντος (*Ἀθ*. iv 1892, 46), and claimed as the reading of the papyrus by Blass; but Wilcken read τά, and Kenyon in his Berlin ed. remarked *lectio non omnino certa, sed videtur a esse*. Though unusual, the plural is not objectionable.

28. v. δοκοῦσι δὲ βέλτιστοι . . . Νικίας καὶ Θουκυδίδης καὶ Θηραμένης: The last three of the προστάται τῶν γνωρίμων from the list in §§ii–iii. It is surprising to find these men singled out for special praise: Nicias' reputation was good in the fourth century (cf. on §iii), but although he was a cautious yet successful general he consented to go to Sicily as commander of an expedition of which he disapproved, and by his obstinacy made disaster certain when it might have been avoided; Thucydides opposed Pericles but was ostracised, and as an old man was prosecuted and convicted, but he is rarely mentioned in the fourth century and no positive achievements are known to his credit (cf. on §ii); Theramenes is the only man praised whose choice *A.P.* regards as controversial (cf. below). These are said to be the best μετὰ τοὺς ἀρχαίους: it is not clear where the line is to be drawn, but more commonly the modern era is said to begin after the death of Pericles or even the death of Cleon (cf. §i with commentary). Pl. *Nic.* 2. i cites *A.P.* and repeats but slightly distorts this judgment (τρεῖς ἐγένοντο βέλτιστοι τῶν πολιτῶν . . . ἧττον δ' οὗτος [*sc.* Θηραμένης] ἢ ἐκεῖνοι).

P. E. Harding writes of 'the clear indications that the judgement . . . is Aristotle's own' (*Phoen.* xxviii 1974, 110–11, referring to δοκεῖ, τοῖς μὴ παρέργως ἀποφαινομένοις and ὅπερ ἐστὶν ἀγαθοῦ πολίτου ἔργον). On these 'indications' see below; the men praised are men of whom we should expect *A.P.* to approve, but what he says makes it clear that he is conscious of the judgments of others on them, and I believe that in praising these men he is not producing a spontaneous comment of his own but is repeating with his approval a comment which he found attached to the list of προστάται.

Ἀθήνησι: Corrected by Kaibel & Wilamowitz[1] and Herwerden & Leeuwen from the papyrus' Ἀθήνησι. No instance of that spelling is known from an inscription: in the one exception noted by Meisterhans & Schwyzer, *G.a.I.*, 146 with n. 1260, now *IG* ii[2] 505, 11, Ἀθήνησιν was a false reading of Bursian.

καλοὺς κἀγαθούς: Cf. on §§ii, iii. Thucydides, as son of Melesias and relative by marriage of Cimon, was a καλὸς κἀγαθός; Nicias, as a first-generation politician and a second-generation rich man, was not one of the καλοὶ κἀγαθοί but made himself acceptable to them.

πολιτικοὺς καὶ τῇ πόλει πάσῃ πατρικῶς χρωμένους: Reproduced by Pl. *Nic.* 2. i as πατρικὴν ἔχοντες εὔνοιαν καὶ φιλίαν πρὸς τὸν δῆμον; in the papyrus καλῶς has been inserted above πατρικῶς, but we need not doubt that πατρικῶς is correct. The word means 'like a father': cf. Arist. *E.N.* VIII. 1160 B 26–7, *Pol.* V. 1315 A 20–2. Aristid. XLVI. *Quatt.* (ii. 161 Dindorf) described Pericles as ἐν πατρὸς ὢν τάξει τῷ δήμῳ.

Θηραμένους: Cf. on §iii. Pl. *Nic.* 2. i says καὶ γὰρ εἰς δυσγένειαν ὡς ξένος ἐκ Κέω λελοιδόρηται, καὶ διὰ τὸ μὴ μόνιμον ἀλλὰ καὶ ἐπαμφοτερίζον ἀεὶ τῇ προαιρέσει τῆς πολιτείας ἐπεκλήθη Κόθορνος. For Theramenes the κόθορνος (a boot capable of fitting either foot) cf. X. *H.* II. iii. 31, 47, also Ar. *Ran.* 534–41; T. VIII. 68. iv, having said that he was a leader of those who overthrew the democracy in 411, describes him as οὔτε εἰπεῖν οὔτε γνῶναι ἀδύνατος (cf. the praise of Themistocles, I. 138. iii, and Pericles, II. 65. viii); in Ar. *Ran.* he is not unkindly handled, and is represented as ὁ κομψός, ... σοφός γ' ἀνὴρ καὶ δεινὸς ἐς τὰ πάντα (967–8). The harshest ancient treatment of him is in Lys. XII. *Erat.* 62–78, arguing that it is not enough for Eratosthenes to say that in 404–403 he was a supporter of Theramenes rather than of Critias (the final verdict in §78 is δὶς γὰρ ὑμᾶς κατεδουλώσατο, τῶν μὲν παρόντων καταφρονῶν, τῶν δὲ ἀπόντων ἐπιθυμῶν; cf. also XIII. *Agor.* 9–17); P. Mich. 5982 (on which see Introduction, p. 22 with n. 132) seems to be part of a defence of Theramenes, written early in the fourth century by a man who knew those two speeches; Diodorus is generally favourable to him, and XIV. 3. v–vii, from an apologetic source, represents him as opposing the institution of the Thirty (see 34. iii with commentary). According to Arist. *Pol.* IV. 1296 A 38–40 εἷς ... ἀνὴρ συνεπείσθη μόνος τῶν πρότερον ἐφ' ἡγεμονίᾳ γενομένων ταύτην ἀποδοῦναι τὴν τάξιν (sc. τὴν πολιτείαν): some have thought that Theramenes was the man (e.g. Newman *ad loc.*), but this is very far from certain.

Nineteenth-century judgments on Theramenes were largely unfavourable (e.g. Grote, *H.G.* [1869–84], viii. 45–6); a rehabilitation was attempted by J. B. Bury, *H.G.* [1]496 = [4]320, and in detail by B. Perrin, *AHR* ix 1903/4, 649–69; twentieth-century opinion has remained largely unenthusiastic, but N. G. L. Hammond writes of him with approval (*H.G.*, 444). He may sincerely have held the 'moderate' political views ascribed to him in X. *H.* II. iii. 18–19, 48–9. The weakest point in his career is his willingness to risk a second period of oligarchy in 404 after he had seen and disliked what the extremists had made of oligarchy in 411: in 411 he had triumphed over the extremists, and we must assume that in 404 he hoped that, with the memory of 411 still fresh in the Athenians' minds, he would be able to do so again.

τὸ συμβῆναι κατ' αὐτὸν ταραχώδεις τὰς πολιτείας: '. . . when public affairs were in a turmoil' (Fritz & Kapp). On πολιτεία in *A.P.* see pp. 89–90; here the meaning must be that in the time of Theramenes there was confusion as to how the state was to be governed, as Athens alternated between democracy and oligarchy. ταραχωδής is a favourite word of Isocrates (e.g. IV. *Paneg.* 48, VII. *Areop.* 43, VIII. *Pace*, 9, XII. *Panath.* 15, 74), and is also used by Aristotle (e.g. *Pol.* II. 1268 B 11, VIII. 1337 A 40).

ἀμφισβήτησις τῆς κρίσεως: For ἀμφισβήτησις and its cognates in *A.P.* cf. 3. iv, 5. ii, 9. ii, 35. ii; in Arist. *Pol.* III. 1283 B 4–5 we find ἀναμφισβήτητος ἡ κρίσις.

μέν‹τοι› τοῖς: The papyrus reads μ(ὲν) τοῖς, but there is no corresponding δέ: Kenyon[1] corrected to μέν‹τοι› τοῖς, and Kaibel & Wilamowitz to μέντοι (cf. Kaibel, *Stil und Text*, 185–6); Blass[1] to δὲ τοῖς, and Blass[4] to μὴν τοῖς. There is no other instance of μέντοι in *A.P.* (cf. Introduction, p. 40), but Kenyon's is nevertheless the best solution.

τοῖς μὴ παρέργως ἀποφαινομένοις: 'To those who do not judge superficially': as often, γνώμην or a similar word must be understood as object of ἀποφαίνεσθαι (cf. Arist. *Pol.* I. 1260 B 23, IV. 1288 B 35; but the usage is not distinctively Aristotelian). παρέργως, again, is used by Aristotle (e.g. *Pol.* VII. 1330 B 11) but by other writers also. I have suggested that *A.P.* took over the praise of Nicias, Thucydides and Theramenes with the list of προστάται (cf. p. 358); but he knew that different verdicts on Theramenes were current, and so in his case the praise had to be justified. For P. E. Harding (*Phoen.* xxviii 1974, 110–11) the final comment on Theramenes is the author's own, and these words are 'a neat rhetorical device . . . that is used by a writer when he intends to introduce a new interpretation of his own and wishes to discredit existing ones'. Lys. XII. *Erat.* and P. Mich. 5982 (cf. above) show that Theramenes' part in the upheavals of the end of the fifth century was being debated not long after his death, and A. Andrewes plausibly suggests that for *A.P.* those who do judge superficially are the authors of such polemical works (*ZPE* vi 1970, 37–8). What is said in Theramenes' defence has no parallel in Aristotle's *Politics*, and I suspect that it is not *A.P.*'s original judgment but was found in one of his more sober sources.

ὥσπερ αὐτὸν διαβάλλουσι: For allegations of this kind cf. Critias' speech *ap.* X. *H.* II. iii. 30–1; also Lys. XII. *Erat.* 78.

πάσας προάγειν: For this an Aristotelian parallel can be adduced, in *Pol.* II. 1274 A 9–11 (τοῦτον δὴ τὸν τρόπον ἕκαστος τῶν δημαγωγῶν προήγαγεν [*sc.* τὴν πολιτείαν] αὔξων εἰς τὴν νῦν δημοκρατίαν).

ἕως μηδὲν παρανομοῖεν... παρανομούσαις δὲ...: In the classification of constitutions in Plat. *Polit.* 302 C 1–303 B 7 the correct forms are those which rule according to law and the incorrect are those which rule unlawfully; but in the similar classification in Arist. *Pol.* III. 1279 A 22–B 10 the correct are those which seek the common interest and the incorrect are those which seek the ruler's interest (the same criterion is employed in *E.N.* VIII. 1160 A 31–B 21).

In 411 the Four Hundred executed some, imprisoned others and expelled others (T. VIII. 70. ii); schol. Ar. *Ran.* 541 claims that Theramenes devised these three forms of penalty, and this does indeed seem to be the regular interpretation of the saying, τὰ τρία Θηραμένους (cf. Ar. fr. 549 Kock, Polyzelus, fr. 3 Kock). One lexicographer's note on this saying, Hes. τῶν τριῶν ἕν, reads Θηραμένης ἐψηφίσατο τρεῖς τιμωρίας κατὰ τῶν παράνομόν τι δρώντων, and this is cited by Sandys—but παράνομον and παρανομεῖν are not found in other notes on the saying, and there is no justification for supposing that the word is particularly to be associated with Theramenes' attacks on his opponents. As a defence of Theramenes this fails to convince: he may well have objected to the 'illegality' of the Four Hundred and the Thirty, and perhaps also to the 'illegality' of the democracy after Aegospotami (though such irregularities as the condemnation of Cleophon and, earlier, of the generals of Arginusae, worked to his advantage), but it is hard to apply a charge of illegality to the democracy overthrown in 411.

πολιτεύεσθαι: This can mean simply 'be a citizen' (e.g. And. II. *Red.* 10, Lys. XII. *Erat.* 20) or more positively 'take part in politics' (e.g. A. I. *Tim.* 195): the stronger meaning is clearly intended here.

ὅπερ ἐστὶν ἀγαθοῦ πολίτου ἔργον: Described as a 'blatantly Aristotelian aside' by P. E. Harding, *Phoen.* xxviii 1974, 111: however, Aristotle in his discussion of what makes a good citizen (*Pol.* III. 1276 B 16–1278 B 5, cf. 1283 B 42–1284 A 2, IV. 1293 B 1–7, VII. 1333 A 11–16) does not suggest that adaptability to different régimes is a desirable quality, but is more concerned with the different qualities required by ruler and subject. [X.] *A.P.* ii. 20 has hard words to say of any one who μὴ ὢν τοῦ δήμου εἵλετο ἐν δημοκρατουμένῃ πόλει οἰκεῖν μᾶλλον ἢ ἐν ὀλιγαρχουμένῃ; J. J. Keaney, *CJ* lxxv 1979/80, 40–1, detects echoes of Plat. *Apol.* on Socrates in this defence of Theramenes.

I. *The Four Hundred and the Five Thousand* (29–34. i. *init.*)

On the Athenian revolutions of 411 we have two detailed sources, book VIII of Thucydides and *A.P.* Thucydides wrote very shortly after the events, and as an exile was free from involvement in the events but dependent on what others told him about them: he sets the overthrow of the democracy in an atmosphere of intrigue, intimidation and distrust, and frequently contrasts the motives which the actors in the drama publicly professed with those by which he believes they were 'really' activated (for some instances see Rhodes, *JHS* xcii 1972, 115–16 with n. 4; on the subjectivity of his account see H. D. Westlake, *BRL* lvi 1973/4, 193–217). By contrast, *A.P.*'s account is devoted largely to technical details and the formalities of the constitutional changes: the effect is to give a version more favourable to the oligarchs, but *A.P.* probably chose to use this material because of the details which it offered rather than because of its political slant.†

After briefly relating the overthrow of the democracy to Athens' fortunes in the Peloponnesian War (29. i), *A.P.* records the motion of Pythodorus for the appointment of συγγραφεῖς, the fact that Melobius spoke, and a rider proposed by Clitophon (29. i–iii); then follow the recommendation of the συγγραφεῖς that the usual safeguards against rash legislation should be suspended (29. iv), a positive proposal that civilian salaries should be abolished and the state entrusted to a body of five thousand (29. v–30. i *init.*), and two constitutional schemes, said to be the work of a drafting committee appointed by the Five Thousand and to have been ratified by the πλῆθος when Aristomachus was in the chair (30. i–32. i). Next we are given dates: the boule of 412/1 was dissolved on 14 Thargelion (xi), the Four Hundred 'entered' on 22 Thargelion, and the new bouleutic year was due to begin on 14 Scirophorion (xii); the democracy was overthrown a hundred years after the fall of the Pisistratid tyranny (32. i–ii). After this there is a short passage of narrative, naming the leaders of the revolution, remarking that the Five Thousand were chosen λόγῳ μόνον and that Athens was in fact ruled by the Four Hundred, and reporting an unsuccessful attempt to make peace with Sparta (32. ii–iii). The Four Hundred ruled for four months; after the first two months of 411/0 their archon, Mnasilochus, was replaced by Theopompus; their fall was provoked by Athens' defeat in a sea battle off Eretria and the defection of Euboea, and power was then transferred to the Five Thousand (33. i: I shall refer to this régime established in autumn 411 as the intermediate régime). The leaders of this second revolution are named, and it is said that they were displeased at the Four Hundred's failure to refer business to the Five Thousand; *A.P.* expresses approval of the intermediate régime (33. ii). His account of the revolutions ends with the cryptic remark that the δῆμος quickly τούτους ... ἀφείλετο τὴν πολιτείαν (34. i init.).

Although their approaches are fundamentally different, and on one factual detail they directly disagree (the number of the συγγραφεῖς: T. VIII. 67. i contr. *A.P.* 29. ii), it is clear that *A.P.* must have used Thucydides' account (e.g. Wilamowitz, *A.u.A.*, i. 99–100 with n. 2, Sandys[2], lxvi). He repeats Thucydides' remark that the Four Hundred came to power a hundred years after the fall of the tyranny, in a passage in which the leaders of the revolution are named and are said to be men of σύνεσις and γνώμη (32. ii cf. T. VIII. 68: in *A.P.*'s list Phrynichus has been omitted, probably through a copyist's error); the two writers describe in very similar words the defection of Euboea except Oreus and the importance of Euboea to Athens, unimportant though this is for *A.P.*'s study of the πολιτεία (33. i cf. T. VIII. 95. vii–96. ii); they again correspond closely in their reports of the setting up of the intermediate régime and in their praise of that régime (33. i–ii cf. T. VIII. 97. i–ii); and they agree in making no distinction between Theramenes and Aristocrates as leaders of the extremists, though Thucydides detects a 'real' motive which *A.P.* omits (33. ii cf. T. VIII. 89, contr. Lys. XII. *Erat.* 66–7). *A.P.*'s brief attempts to set the revolutions in context are compatible with Thucydides' much fuller narrative: the overthrow of the democracy followed Sparta's alliance with Persia, and was undertaken in the hope that Persian support could be diverted to the Athenian side (29. i); once established, the Four Hundred in fact tried to negotiate peace with Sparta but failed (32. iii: but *A.P.*'s account of the failure conflicts with the implications of Thucydides' account); the fall of the Four Hundred was precipitated by the defeat off Eretria and the defection of Euboea (33. i).

It ought therefore not to be difficult to combine the accounts of Thucydides and *A.P.* (though there are problems, on which much ingenuity has been expended). Table 3 shows how the two are to be fitted together; italics and reference marks are used for passages which correspond to passages at a different point in the other column.

Items 2–4 have occasioned difficulty. There are serious differences between the two accounts of the positive proposals which followed the συγγραφεῖς' recommendations (3(*b*): see on 29. v), and a drastic solution has been advocated by Miss M. L. Lang (*AJP* lxix 1948, 272–89, lxxxviii 1967, 176–87): she believes that the thirty συγγραφεῖς of *A.P.* 29. i–iii were appointed during Pisander's first visit to Athens (T. VIII. 49, 53–4) and the assembly at which they reported (29. iv–v) was held between Pisander's first visit and his second, whereas the ten συγγραφεῖς of T. VIII. 67 were appointed and reported, as

[29-34. i] COMMENTARY ON THE *ATH. POL.*

Table 3

T. VIII	A.P.
1. Detailed account of preliminary moves by Alcibiades, and in Samos and Athens. (45–54, 56, 63–6)	After disaster in Sicily and Spartan alliance with Persia Athenians overthrow democracy in hope of Persian support. (29. i)
2. Appointment of συγγραφεῖς. (67. i)	Appointment of συγγραφεῖς. (29. i–iii)
3. Assembly at Colonus: (*a*) συγγραφεῖς suspend safeguards; (67. ii) (*b*) proposal to abolish stipends, and appoint Four Hundred, who may convene Five Thousand; (67. iii) (*c*) * *proposal made by Pisander supported by Antiphon, Phrynichus, Theramenes; 100 years after fall of tyranny;* (68) (*d*) ratified without opposition. (69. i)	(*a*) συγγραφεῖς suspend safeguards; (29. iv) (*b*) 'they' abolish stipends, entrust state to Five Thousand, appoint καταλογεῖς; (29. v) (*d*) when this is ratified, Five Thousand appoint ἀναγραφεῖς. (30. i)
4.	The ἀναγραφεῖς produce: (*a*) constitution for future; (30. ii–31. i *init.*) (*b*) constitution for immediate crisis; (31. i–iii) (*c*) order to distribute Four Hundred through four λήξεις; (31. iii *fin.*) (*d*) —and πλῆθος ratifies. (32. i *init.*)
5. (*a*) Four Hundred occupy bouleuterium, pay off old boule, inaugurate régime, . . . (*c*) . . . rule city; (69. i–70. ii) (*d*) try to come to terms with Sparta. (70. ii–71 cf. 86. ix)	(*a*) Old boule dissolved early, Four Hundred inaugurated (dates); (32. i) (*b*) * *100 years after fall of tyranny; work of Pisander, Antiphon, Theramenes;* (32. ii) (*c*) Four Hundred enter bouleuterium, rule city. (32. iii) (*d*) [cf. 7(*b*)]
6. Athens and Samos. (72–7, 81–2, 86, 89. i)	
7. (*a*) Discontent in Athens, † *headed by Theramenes and Aristocrates, who claim to want ἰσαιτέρα πολιτεία with participation of Five Thousand;* (89. ii–iv)	

364

Table 3—cont.

T. VIII	A.P.
(b) extremists fortify Eetionea, fail to reach settlement with Sparta; (90–91. i)	(b) Oligarchs make unsuccessful attempt to reach settlement with Sparta; (32. iii)
	(c) Four Hundred last 4 months: two of 412/1 and two of 411/0; (33. i)
(d) crises provoked by approach of ships from Peloponnese and by victory of these ships off Eretria and defection of Euboea. (91. ii–96)	(d) Athenians are defeated in sea battle off Eretria, Euboea defects. (33. i)
8. (a) Assembly on Pnyx deposes Four Hundred, hands over affairs to Five Thousand, abolishes stipends; many subsequent assemblies; (97. i–ii)	(a) They depose Four Hundred, hand over affairs to Five Thousand, abolish stipends; (33. i)
	(b) † work of Theramenes and Aristocrates, displeased at non-participation of Five Thousand; (33. ii)
(c) praise of this régime; (97. ii)	(c) praise of this régime. (33. ii)
(d) consequences of change; end of ὀλιγαρχία and στάσις. (97. ii–98)	
9.	Soon dispossessed by δῆμος. (34. i init.)

Thucydides states, after Pisander's second arrival in Athens (14 Thargelion, the earliest of the dates in *A.P.* 32. i, being the day when they reported); thus Thucydides and *A.P.* each report correctly the episodes known to them. This view has found little favour, and rightly so (for a brief but effective reply see Hignett, *H.A.C.*, 362–4): there was no need to suspend the safeguards against rash legislation twice, and it is more likely, and more creditable to our two authors, that each has reported the same episodes not wholly accurately than that each has omitted whole episodes which the other reports. A second problem concerns the ἀναγραφεῖς and their documents, found only in *A.P.* (3(d)–4): despite various attempts to place them elsewhere in the order of events, or to reject them as a fiction, I prefer to accept that these documents were drawn up and promulgated shortly after the assembly at Colonus, while admitting that they were not commissioned by the Five Thousand or approved by the πλῆθος and that the 'future' constitution was never brought into effect (see on 30. i).

Thucydides provides *A.P.*'s narrative background, and on the establishment of the intermediate régime *A.P.* tells us nothing that is not in Thucydides except the change of archon. On the establishment of the Four Hundred the points of detail on which *A.P.* supplements Thucydides or diverges from him appear to be derived from a series of documents. How accessible the documents of the revolution will have been is unclear: all decisions pertaining to the oligarchy were afterwards annulled, and the democrats might well have marked their annulment by cancelling the public texts of them (cf. 35. ii with commentary); but there are some documents published under the oligarchy which have survived. The Four Hundred appointed treasurers of Athena, who probably entered office regularly, on 28 Hecatombaeon (i) 411/0 (or else slightly earlier, on 1 Hecatombaeon); these were replaced under the intermediate régime, and were ignored in the dedication at the end of the quadrennium (*IG* ii² 1498, 6–8) and the prescripts of the quadrennium's inventories (*IG* i² 248, 210, 272, 151), but the inventories and accounts for their short period of office were published and allowed to stand (*IG* i² 251 + 252 + A. M. Woodward, *JHS* xlviii 1928, 165–7 [*SEG* x 188]; *SEG* xxii 30–4; *IG* i² 298 = M&L 81: see W. S. Ferguson, *Treasurers of Athena*, 100–1, 145–7); the treasurers of the intermediate régime presumably served until 28 Hecatombaeon 410/09, and there is no sign of an attempt to cast doubt on their legitimacy. An honorific decree set up probably by the Four Hundred survived to have a further decree inscribed after it in 399/8 (M&L 80). A decree of the boule under the intermediate régime, ordering the trial of Antiphon and others, survived with a record of the judgment to be included in Craterus' collection (342 F 5b *ap.* [Pl.] *X. Or.* 833 D–834 B). However, it should cause no surprise that the financial records of the oligarchic period were preserved, and there was no particular need for the restored democracy to suppress the honours for Pythophanes (loyal to Athens over a long period) or the condemnation of Antiphon. We do not know to what extent the constitutional acts of the oligarchs were published: it is likely that any such texts that were published were afterwards destroyed, but it may be that some texts remained in the archives, to be found by those who were willing to search for them (cf. on 29. iii: the possibility is assumed to be a certainty by Fritz & Kapp, 24–6, doubted by Moore, 258–9), or that copies were kept in private hands by men who hoped to make use of them. The question was first asked by W. Judeich, *RM*² lxii 1907, 306, and is discussed by A. Andrewes, *PCPS*² xxii 1976, 14–17.

There are signs that the documents cited by *A.P.* were known to him not from direct research but from an earlier narrative which made use of them: in particular his report not only of Pythodorus' motion and Clitophon's rider to it but also of Melobius as the principal speaker (29. i–iii with commentary). Such a narrative might have been found in a speech or a political pamphlet. As evidence of the use which could be made of speeches we have the 'Theramenes papyrus', P. Mich. 5982, which shows knowledge of Lys. XII. *Erat.* and XIII. *Agor.* (on the events of 404) and seems to come from a defence of Theramenes written early in the fourth century (cf. Introduction, p. 22 with n. 132); what survives of the *corpus Lysiacum* contains one speech (or, rather, parts of two speeches: Wilamowitz, *A.u.A.*, ii. 363–4, Andrewes in Gomme *et al.*, *Hist. Comm. Thuc.*, v. 201), xx. *Poly.*, which is concerned with the events of 411 (cf. p. 384), and there must have been other relevant speeches which have not survived. Antiphon, tried and condemned under the intermediate régime, made a speech in his own defence which was known to and admired by Thucydides and others; the fragments assigned to this speech include a Geneva papyrus which must belong, if not to the defence of Antiphon, to the defence of one of the other extremists of 411 (cf. Introduction, p. 22 with nn. 133–4). Either Antiphon or another oligarch on trial may have seen fit to quote the official documents, in which the oligarchs tried to make their revolution look as regular constitutionally, and as little different from the democracy, as they could (cf. pp. 372, 376), and will have been able to add from his first-hand knowledge information which was not in the documents, as the fact of Melobius' speech may not have been. For Antiphon as a possible source see especially J. Kriegel, *Der Staatsreich der Vierhundert in Athen, 411 v. Chr.*, 38, Wade-Gery, *CQ* xxvii 1933, 20–1 with 20 nn. 5–6 = *Essays*, 141 with nn. 3–4; contr. Jacoby, *Supp.* ii. 100, Andrewes, *PCPS*[2] xxii 1976, 19–20.

Another route by which information may have reached *A.P.* has often been mentioned. Androtion, whose *Atthis* was used by *A.P.* at any rate in ch. 22 and perhaps elsewhere (cf. pp. 241, 267–9, 285, and Introduction, p. 21), was the son of Andron, probably the man who under the intermediate régime proposed the trial of Antiphon and others (cf. Introduction, p. 19 with n. 110), and so may have had access through his father to material on the revolutions. Whereas T. VIII. 67. i makes the συγγραφεῖς who paved the way for the establishment of the Four Hundred ten in number, Androtion made them thirty and probably included among them the ten πρόβουλοι (324 F 43), and *A.P.* 29. ii agrees with Androtion: this latter version appears to be correct (cf. *ad loc.*), and agreement on it does not prove that Androtion was *A.P.*'s source; but the chronological information in 32. i and 33. i may point to an *Atthis* rather than a work of polemic. For the claims of Androtion to be *A.P.*'s immediate source see especially Busolt, *G.S.*, i. 69, 95–6, Jacoby, *Atthis*, 384 n. 30 cf. 382 n. 24, *Supp.* ii. 91–2, 100, Andrewes, *PCPS*[2] xxii 1976, 14–25, esp. 16–17 [but notice also 21–2]).

The account of the revolutions in D.S. xiii is presumably derived from Ephorus; but it is so brief that little use can be made of it. In xiii. 34. i–iii Athens' failure in Sicily and the revolt of the allies lead the δῆμος to accept the rule of the Four Hundred ἑκουσίως; after στάσις within the oligarchy the Athenians sail to Oropus and are defeated; in xiii. 36 this material is repeated, but with the defection of the allies placed after the naval battle, and it is most likely that Diodorus has carelessly made two independent extracts from the same passage in his source (cf. Andrewes, *Hist. Comm. Thuc.*, v. 208); xiii. 38. i–ii reports the overthrow of the Four Hundred and the establishment of the intermediate régime, ascribing this to Theramenes and making him the one man to advocate the recall of Alcibiades. There are two references to these events in Arist. *Pol.* v: 1304 B 7–15 cites the Four Hundred as an instance of a régime established by deceit (the promise of Persian support) and maintained by force, and 1305 B 22–7 alludes to the demagoguic methods employed by Phrynichus and his supporters within the Four Hundred.

I conclude with two negative points. First, the political controversies of the end of the fifth century must have generated a great deal of polemical writing—see, for instance, the 'Draconian constitution' in ch. 4 with pp. 84–7 and commentary *ad loc.*, the 'Theramenes papyrus' mentioned above, the *Athenaion Politeia* of [Xenophon], and P. Heid. 182 as interpreted by M. Gigante, *Maia* ix 1957, 68–74, and cf. Introduction, pp. 21–2—and, although it is possible that *A.P.* derived the non-Thucydidean material in these chapters from Antiphon's speech or Androtion's *Atthis* or from the first through the second, it is no less possible that he used a work not known to us at all. Secondly, although 28. v expresses admiration for Theramenes (probably repeated, though with *A.P.*'s agreement and in the knowledge that it was controversial, from the source which supplied the list of προστάται in that chapter), and although in Aristotelian thinking the best practicable form of constitution was one intermediate between a full democracy and a narrow oligarchy, there is nothing particularly 'Theramenean' about these chapters of *A.P.*: the documents are the public pronouncements made by the oligarchs when the régime of the Four Hundred was set up; on Theramenes' intermediate régime *A.P.* adds nothing to what he found in Thucydides; and the judgments on the principal actors in 32. ii and on the intermediate régime in 33. ii are derived not from a lost work but from Thucydides. For an attack on 'the Theramenes myth' see P. E. Harding, *Phoen.* xxviii 1974, 101–11; but his argument that there was no praise of Theramenes as a 'moderate' before *A.P.* falls short of proof (cf. on 34. iii).

Much has been written on the revolutions of 411; most recently

Andrewes has incorporated in *Hist. Comm. Thuc.*, v, not only a commentary on T. VIII but a study of other sources for the revolutions and (pp. 212-40) a commentary on *A.P.* 29-33. I cite here only those discussions which are most important for the elucidation of *A.P.*

29. i. ἕως μὲν οὖν ἰσόρροπα τὰ πράγματα: *A.P.* plunges abruptly into the new topic: ch. 27 was devoted to the ascendancy of Pericles (and 27. ii contains *A.P.*'s only previous allusion to the Peloponnesian War); the remark that Pericles was the last tolerable leader of the δῆμος led to the list of προστάται in 28. ἰσόρροπος, literally 'in equilibrium', is often used metaphorically: T. I. 105 v and Eur. *Suppl.* 706 use it of a battle.

μετὰ τὴν ἐν Σικελίᾳ γενομένην συμφοράν: Cf. schol. Ar. *Lys.* 421, Suid. (Π 2355) πρόβουλοι, probably derived from *A.P.*; also T. VIII. 24. v, Is. XVI. *Big.* 15, D. XX. *Lept.* 42: Blass[4] was certainly wrong to reinstate the papyrus' δ(ια)φοράν. Until she squandered her resources in the expedition of 415-413, Athens' ability to withstand the Peloponnesians' attack should never have been in doubt; but that episode left Athens seriously short of men and money, made it easier for the Spartans to establish their raiding post at Decelea, and suggested to members of the Delian League that defiance of Athens might yet succeed.

διὰ τὴν πρὸς βασιλέα συμμαχίαν: Sparta negotiated a first treaty with Tissaphernes in summer 412 (T. VIII. 17. iv-18) and a second in winter 412/1 (T. VIII. 36. ii-37); Lichas was dissatisfied with both (T. VIII. 43. ii-iv), and Alcibiades encouraged the Athenians to hope that Tissaphernes' support might be diverted to them; but nothing was achieved by the Athenians (T. VIII. 45-56), and at the end of winter 412/1 (but in Darius' thirteenth year, and so on or after 29 March: first noticed by D. M. Lewis, *Hist.* vii 1958, 392; defended against W. K. Pritchett, *CP* lx 1965, 259-61, by B. D. Meritt, *CP* lxi 1966, 182-4) the Spartans negotiated a third agreement with the Persians (T. VIII. 57-8). As the failure in Sicily reduced Athens' capacity to endure a long war, Persian help enabled Sparta to persist in the war and challenge the Athenians at sea.

ἠναγκάσθησαν: Contrast D.S. XIII. 34. ii (ὁ δῆμος ἀθυμήσας ἐξεχώρησεν ἑκουσίως τῆς δημοκρατίας)—but ἀθυμήσας shows that this is a difference of emphasis rather than a fundamental disagreement. For this exculpation of the δῆμος cf. *A.P.* 34. i, where the δῆμος is twice deceived, and 34. iii, where in 404 καταπλαγεὶς ὁ δῆμος ἠναγκάσθη χειροτονεῖν τὴν ὀλιγαρχίαν; here *A.P.* does not say, as Arist. *Pol.* does (cf. below), that the oligarchs were deceitful. The *motif* of the δῆμος' being deceived or compelled to do things which turned out badly is not likely to come from a source of oligarchic bias, and what we have in these passages may be an apologia commonly resorted to in the fourth century: in X. *H.* II. iii. 45 Theramenes emphasises that τὴν... ἐπὶ τῶν τετρακοσίων πολιτείαν καὶ αὐτὸς ὁ δῆμος ἐψηφίσατο (cf. Lys. xx. *Poly.* 16, quoted p. 382). This passage is overlooked in the remark of H. D. Westlake that *A.P.* 'creates the impression that the majority of Athenian citizens willingly consented to the measures for constitutional reform' (*BRL* lvi 1973/4, 197).

κι[νήσα]ντες: Strictly, κε[ινήσα]ντες. For this use of κινεῖν cf. 26. ii, Plat. *Hipp. Mai.* 284 B 6–7, Arist. *Pol.* II. 1268 B 28, 30, 34, and the use of ἀκίνητος in Cleon's speech *ap.* T. III. 37. iii.

εἰπόντος τὸν μὲν πρὸ τοῦ ψηφίσματος λόγον Μηλοβίου: πρό is not synonymous with ὑπέρ, and the phrase must mean 'the speech introducing the resolution' (Moore): cf. Kaibel, *Stil und Text*, 186. (W. Wyse, *CR* v 1891, 113, suggested περί, but the change is unnecessary.) This record of a proposal's being introduced by a man other than its nominal author is without parallel, and is a strong indication that *A.P.* found his documents not in the archives but incorporated in the narrative of a man with direct knowledge of what had happened (Wilamowitz, *A.u.A.*, i. 106, Busolt, *G.G.*, III. ii, 608 n., Andrewes, *PCPS*[2] xxii 1976, 17; cf. above, pp. 366–7). Melobius is very probably to be identified with the Melobius who was a member of the Thirty in 404/3 (Lys. XII. *Erat.* 12, 19, X. *H.* II. iii. 2, Hyp. fr. 65 Sauppe, from Harp. Μηλόβιος: identification accepted by Kirchner, *P.A.* 10102), but there is another Melobius who appears in a casualty list of 409 (*The Athenian Agora*, xvii 23, 271). The reason for the decree's having one man as author but another as principal advocate may be that Pythodorus was a member of the boule in 412/1 but Melobius was not (cf. p. 375).

τὴν δὲ γνώμην γράψαντος Πυθοδώρου το[ῦ Ἀναφλ]υ[σ]τίου: Read and restored by Blass, *NJPhP* cxlv (xxxviii) 1892, 573, and approved by Wilcken and by Kenyon in his Berlin ed. and O.C.T.; other suggestions were το[ῦ Ἐπι]ζ[ήλ]ου, Kaibel & Wilamowitz[1-2], cf. *IG* i[2] 770a with A. Brückner, *AM* xiv 1891, 398–408; το[ῦ Προσπαλ]-τίου, Herwerden, *BPW* xi 1891, 611; το[ῦ Πολυζήλ]ου, F. Poland, *NJPhP* cxliii (xxxvii) 1891, 262, Herwerden & Leeuwen, cf. D.L. IX. 54. Pythodorus is a fairly common name: the Pythodorus of *IG* i[2] 770a may be ruled out, since his deme was Halae Araphenides (cf. Kaibel, *Stil und Text*, 186, Davies, *A.P.F.*, 481, on *P.A.* 12402 = 12410); the member of the Four Hundred who had prosecuted Protagoras (D.L.) may be identical with this Pythodorus (thus Kirchner, *P.A.* 12412), but Kaibel suspected that in D.L. Πολυζήλου should be emended to Ἐπιζήλου to yield the Pythodorus of *IG* i[2] 770a; a man called Pythodorus was archon under the Thirty in 404/3 (35. i with commentary).

COMMENTARY ON THE *ATH. POL.* [29. i

γνώμην (or νόμον or ψήφισμα) γράφειν is common literary usage (e.g. Ar. *Nub.* 1429, X. *H.* i. vii. 34, Din. i. *Dem.* 70), but in the prescripts of published Athenian decrees and laws the regular formula is ὁ δεῖνα εἶπεν, and T. VIII. 67. i writes at this point εἶπον γνώμην (cf. VIII. 67. ii, 68. i). Drafts produced by συγγραφεῖς like those appointed under this decree are introduced by τάδε οἱ συγγραφεῖς συνέγραψαν (*A.T.L.*, D 11, 3, M & L 73, 3–4) or γνώμη τῶν συγγραφῶν (*A.T.L.*, D 9, 8, *SEG* x 123, 4); two decrees sponsored by the whole board of generals use the formula γνώμη στρατηγῶν (*SEG* x 86, 47 with *apparatus*, *IG* ii² 27, 5); one decree and a rider to it have γνώμη Κλεοσόφο καὶ συνπρυτάνεων (M & L 94, 6–7, 32). In published decrees of the fifth century proposers are not identified by patronymic or demotic even when they bear a name as common as Callias (M & L 58 A, 2, B, 2); *A.P.* again gives the proposer's demotic in 34. iii.

διὰ τὸ νομίζειν βασιλέα μᾶ[λ]λον ἑαυτοῖς συμπολεμήσειν: Cf. the account of Alcibiades' intrigues and the hopes of the Athenians in T. VIII. 45–56, esp. 48. i–iii (Samos), 53–54. i (Pisander's first visit to Athens); Arist. *Pol.* v 1304 B 7–15. By the time the oligarchic régime was set up it should have been public knowledge that Tissaphernes had not made an alliance with Athens but had entered into a revised alliance with Sparta (more than two months may have elapsed between that alliance and the assembly at Colonus: see pp. 369, 405). However, the hope of Persian support had been an avowed motive of those who were working for a change to oligarchy, and some may still have entertained that hope (cf. T. VIII. 82. ii–iii, 87–8, 108. i–iii, on Alcibiades and Tissaphernes in summer 411). Arist. *Pol.* suggests that the oligarchs were deceitful in holding out the hope of Persian support, which Thucydides does not claim (and the fact that after they had failed to gain Persian support and had broken with Alcibiades some tried to negotiate peace with Sparta does not mean that they were insincere in trying to gain Persian support against Sparta while that seemed possible). Here *A.P.* probably does not mean to imply that at the time of Pythodorus' motion there was still a general hope of Persian support or that the oligarchs concealed the failure of the negotiations from the citizens in Athens, but is giving a condensed account of the background to the revolution without too much thought for the implications which might be read into his words.

Other motives for revolution in 411 can be divined, and no doubt different men were swayed by different combinations of them. Some, including himself, hoped that under an oligarchic régime Alcibiades, exiled in 415, could return to Athens (e.g. T. VIII. 47: *A.P.*'s account, concentrating on what happened in Athens, makes no mention of him, and he is also strikingly absent from the list of προστάται in ch. 28 [cf. p. 354]; here, as in the case of Critias and the Thirty [cf. pp. 429–30], the Aristotelian school may have inherited a tactful silence from the Platonic); on the other hand, Phrynichus supported oligarchy once he was satisfied that the oligarchy would not favour Alcibiades (T. VIII. 68. ii). Some will have hoped to save money by abolishing the payment of salaries for the performance of civic duties (cf. 29. v, 30. ii, iv, 33. i, with commentary; T. VIII. 1. iii shows that the need for economy was acknowledged at the end of summer 413). Some, after the democracy's failure in Sicily, hoped that a change of government would lead to the more successful conduct of the war; but others hoped or came to hope that an oligarchic government could put an end to the war (cf. 32. iii with commentary; X. *H.* II. iii. 45 represents Theramenes as saying in 404 that the δῆμος voted for the constitution of the Four Hundred διδασκόμενος ὡς οἱ Λακεδαιμόνιοι πάσῃ πολιτείᾳ μᾶλλον ἂν ἢ δημοκρατίᾳ πιστεύσειαν). Some, pupils of the sophists, believed that democracy was a bad form of government (e.g. [X.] *A.P.*, *passim*); others, perhaps also pupils of the sophists, wanted to seize power for themselves (e.g. T. VIII. 66. i, cf. pp. 407–8 on Pisander).

ἐὰν δι' ὀλίγων ποιήσωνται τὴν πολιτείαν: Thucydides (how accurately we cannot tell) reports Alcibiades as saying εἰ μὴ δημοκρατοῖντο (VIII. 48. i), Pisander as saying first μὴ τὸν αὐτὸν τρόπον δημοκρατουμένοις and finally εἰ μὴ πολιτεύσομέν τε σωφρονέστερον καὶ ἐς ὀλίγους μᾶλλον τὰς ἀρχὰς ποιήσομεν (VIII. 53. i, iii).

At the end of §i the first roll of the papyrus ends; but the first scribe continues for the first column of the second roll. See Introduction, p. 3.

29. ii. τοῦ Πυθοδώρου: Blass[2], comparing 40. ii, preferred τό, and some have followed him; but τοῦ is not objectionable.

τοιόνδε: Contrast the stronger promises of τάδε (30. i), ταύτην ... τήνδε (31. i). What we are given is close to the language of a decree, but shows some signs of editing: cf. following notes.

μετὰ τῶν προϋπαρχόντων δέκα προβούλων: Despite the doubts of A. E. Raubitschek, *Chiron* iv 1974, 101–2, the usual translation must be correct: 'The people shall elect, in addition to the already existing (πρόβουλοι), twenty others' Fritz & Kapp). The πρόβουλοι are not previously mentioned or subsequently explained in *A.P.* T. VIII. 1. iii writes ἐδόκει ... ἀρχήν τινα πρεσβυτέρων ἀνδρῶν ἑλέσθαι, οἵτινες περὶ τῶν παρόντων ὡς ἂν καιρὸς ᾖ προβουλεύσωσιν (end of summer 413), and Ar. *Lys.* (411: usually assigned to the Lenaea) represents the πρόβουλοι as having taken over some of the functions of the prytanes and boule; D.S. XII. 75. iv has been thought to misdate their appointment to 421/0, but more probably the parallel Athenian and Spartan committees were appointed to help in the negotiation of the Peace of Nicias (A. Andrewes and D. M. Lewis,

JHS lxxvii 1957, 177). Probably the men had to be over forty, as in Pythodorus' motion (the same requirement is found for the καταλογεῖς in §v; M & L 65, 16–18, requires men over fifty to be sent to Perdiccas of Macedon *c*. 430; for other occasions when men over forty were needed see 42. ii, 56. iii); their appointment was presumably of indefinite duration, as there is no indication of another election between late summer 413 and early summer 411 (but this presumption is doubted by H. C. Avery, *Hist*. xxii 1973, 513–14). Two πρόβουλοι are known to us, both of them men well over forty: Hagnon, the father of Theramenes, born before 470 (Lys. xii. *Erat*. 65: see Kirchner, *P.A*. 171, Davies, *A.P.F*., 227–8), and the tragedian Sophocles, born *c*. 496 (Arist. *Rhet*. iii. 1419 a 26–30; see Kirchner, *P.A*. 12834, M. H. Jameson, *Hist*. xx 1971, 541–6, P. Karavites, *Klio* lviii 1976, 359–65; against the identification, Avery, *op. cit*., 510–4). The two texts cited confirm the involvement of the πρόβουλοι in the overthrow of the democracy.

προϋπαρχόντων betrays the later viewpoint of a narrator making use of Pythodorus' motion: Pythodorus more probably used τῶν ὑπαρχόντων or τῶν νῦν ὄντων.

ἄλλους εἴκοσι: Cf. Andr. 324 F 43, Phil. 328 F 136; also schol. Ar. *Lys*. 421, Suid. (Π 2355) πρόβουλοι, probably derived from *A.P*. T. viii. 67. i, quoted below and confirmed by Harp. συγγραφεῖς, makes the συγγραφεῖς ten in all. M. L. Lang, trying to believe both major sources, has argued that there were two distinct boards appointed at different times (cf. above, pp. 363–5); but most have agreed that the same board is referred to, and (since there is no propaganda value to the oligarchs in *A.P*.'s version, and the involvement of the πρόβουλοι is confirmed) that on this point of detail *A.P*. is right. The non-Thucydidean material in these chapters may be derived from Androtion, but agreement on this detail is not enough to prove it (cf. pp. 366–8).

ἐκ τῶν ὑπὲρ τετταράκοντα ἔτη γεγονότων: The text should mean that the fortieth birthday must have been reached (cf. on 42. i).

ὀμόσαντες . . . βέλτιστα εἶναι τῇ πόλει: They were to swear an oath of allegiance, comparable to those sworn by bouleutae (22. ii), archons (55. v) and others. Later an oath was imposed on the καταλογεῖς (§v with commentary), and the 'immediate' constitution invites the Four Hundred to concern themselves with an oath (31. i with commentary).

ἦ μὴν συγγράψειν . . . συγγράψουσι περὶ τῆς σωτηρίας: Cf. T. viii. 67. i (πρῶτον μὲν τὸν δῆμον ξυλλέξαντες εἶπον γνώμην δέκα ἄνδρας ἑλέσθαι ξυγγραφέας αὐτοκράτορας, τούτους δὲ ξυγγράψαντας γνώμην ἐσενεγκεῖν ἐς τὸν δῆμον ἐς ἡμέραν ῥητὴν καθ' ὅτι ἄριστα ἡ πόλις οἰκήσεται). It was common practice in the fifth century to appoint an *ad hoc* board of συγγραφεῖς to draft proposals when an elaborate bill was needed (references given on p. 371), and such boards were naturally appointed both in 411 and in 404 (cf. on 34. iii). But the fact that two boards of συγγραφεῖς led to the installation of an oligarchy discredited the practice (cf. Is. VII. *Areop.* 58), and in the fourth century matters which needed more consideration before the assembly could pronounce on them were referred to the boule (e.g. Tod 154, 6–9: cf. 45. iv with commentary).

περὶ τῆς σωτηρίας recurs in the recommendation of the συγγραφεῖς (§iv); cf. the oligarchs' message to Samos in T. VIII. 72. i, 86. iii. Its literal meaning is not here inappropriate—the Athenians were in 411 concerned for the safety of their city—but the phrase does seem to have become a recognised formula for an open debate, analogous to the Romans' *de re publica* (e.g. Livy, XXII. 1. v, Varro *ap.* Gellius, XIV. 7. ix): cf. Ar. *Eccl.* 394–402, and see Wilamowitz, *A.u.A.*, i. 102 n. 7, Rhodes, *A.B.*, 231–5. Similarly Thucydides may mean by αὐτοκράτορας that the συγγραφεῖς could make recommendations of whatever kind they thought appropriate (for the significance of that word see p. 402); but some have supposed it to mean that the boule was obliged to put their proposals to the assembly, as with Lampon's proposal in M&L 73, 59–61 (cf. Andrewes, *Hist. Comm. Thuc.*, v. 165).

ἐξεῖναι δὲ καὶ τῶν ἄλλων τῷ βουλομένῳ γράφειν: Cf. *IG* i² 88, 5–6, as revised in *IG* i³ 64 ([τὸν δ]ὲ [βο]λόμενον γράφσαντα ἀποδ[εῖχσαι τεῖ βολεῖ]: *c*. 435), and the decree of Tisamenus, ordering a revision of the laws on the restoration of the democracy in 403/2 (*ap.* And. 1. *Myst.* 83–4): a board of νομοθέται was to draw up proposals and publish them σκοπεῖν τῷ βουλομένῳ; the boule and another board of νομοθέται were to pronounce on the proposals; ἐξεῖναι δὲ καὶ ἰδιώτῃ τῷ βουλομένῳ εἰσιόντι εἰς τὴν βουλὴν συμβουλεύειν ὅ τι ἂν ἀγαθὸν ἔχῃ περὶ τῶν νόμων. Cf. also the invitations to ὁ βουλόμενος in the decree of 352/1 concerning the ἱερὰ ὀργάς (*IG* ii² 204, 16–23, 23–54). Thus the oligarchs in formally inviting any Athenian to submit his suggestions were conforming to democratic practice.

ἵν': ἵνα, ὅπως and ὅπως ἄν are interchangeable as final conjunctions, but ὅπως ἄν is used regularly in inscribed Athenian decrees of the fifth and fourth centuries: Meisterhans & Schwyzer, *G.a.I.*, 253–5 with n. 1980, knew only two instances of ἵνα earlier than the third century (M&L 69, 41, 46, cf. restoration of lines 20, 39); LSJ, *s.v.* ὅπως, remarks that in early Attic inscriptions only ὅπως ἄν is used, but ὅπως without ἄν is found once in the fourth century (Tod 173, 44) and later becomes prevalent; most Greek prose writers show a preference for ἵνα, but ὅπως is commoner in Thucydides and Xenophon (W. W. Goodwin, *Greek Grammar*², 291, cf. E. Schwyzer, *Griechische Grammatik*, ii. 665). *A.P.* uses both ἵνα and ὅπως as final conjunctions; in his material from documents of 411 ἵνα recurs in 31.

iii, ὅπως is used in 29. iii, ὅπως ἄν in 29. iv and 30. iv: this may betray some rephrasing of the original texts, but it is hard to be certain; Athenian documentary language never became completely standardised, and there was less standardisation in the fifth century than later.

29. iii. Κλειτοφῶν: Probably Clitophon Ἀριστωνύμου (Kirchner, *P.A.* 8546), a disciple of Socrates (Plato's *Clitophon* is named after him, and he also appears in *Rep.* I. 328 B 7, 340 A 3–B 8), a man mentioned with Theramenes in Ar. *Ran.* 967, and with Theramenes and others as aiming for the πάτριος πολιτεία in *A.P.* 34. iii (cf. *ad loc.*). See Wilamowitz, *A.u.A.*, i. 102 n. 8.

τὰ μὲν ἄλλα καθάπερ Πυθόδωρος εἶπεν: In inscriptions there are two formulae for introducing riders to decrees: ὁ δεῖνα εἶπεν· τὰ μὲν ἄλλα καθάπερ ὁ δεῖνα . . . (e.g. M & L 68, 26–7); ὁ δεῖνα εἶπεν· τὰ μὲν ἄλλα καθάπερ τῇ βουλῇ . . . (e.g. M & L 69, 51). The second, which is by far the commoner, is used when what is amended is a προβούλευμα presented to the assembly for ratification; the first is used either when what is amended is a motion before the assembly other than a προβούλευμα or in a second rider (which takes the form of a rider to the previous rider) to any motion before the assembly: see Rhodes, *A.B.*, 71–4. Here τὰ μὲν ἄλλα καθάπερ points to a documentary original, but the placing of εἶπεν (whose subject I take to be Κλειτοφῶν), and the insertion of ἔγραψεν after αἱρεθέντας, show that what we read in *A.P.* is not an unedited transcription of the original text. If the original motion stood in the name of Pythodorus but the speech introducing it was made by Melobius, it may be that Pythodorus was a member of the boule in 412/1 and so well placed to take the initiative but Melobius was not (cf. p. 370), but in that case we should expect to find καθάπερ τῇ βουλῇ: the distinction which I have drawn between the two formulae may sometimes have been overlooked even in official texts, but here it is possible that *A.P.* or his source has substituted for an original reference to the boule a formula which makes more sense in his narrative. The suggestion that Pythodorus was a member of the boule and Melobius was not need not be ruled out.

προσαναζητῆσαι: This is the only instance recorded in LSJ and the 1968 Supplement of the double compound προσαναζητεῖν. The implications of the word for the knowledge of Cleisthenes' laws in the late fifth century have been disputed: some translate it as 'also search for' (e.g. Jacoby, *Atthis*, 206, A. Fuks, *The Ancestral Constitution*, 5–6, 13: ζητεῖν has this implication in M & L 58 A, 11); others think that the existence of Cleisthenes' laws in the archives is assumed and that the word means 'also consult' (e.g. Andrewes, *Hist. Comm. Thuc.*, v. 214–15, citing ἀναζητεῖν in H. I. 137. ii, T. II. 8. iii, VIII. 33. iv; cf.

Wade-Gery, *CQ* xxvii 1933, 19–20 = *Essays*, 139–40). I suspect that in itself the word may bear either meaning. However, the events of 411–410 showed that the laws of Athens were confused and uncertain, and in 410/09 a process of revision and republication was begun which proved to be a lengthy one (cf. pp. 441–2: see especially Lys. xxx. *Nic.* 2–4): I am therefore inclined to think that in 411 it was probably not known whether Cleisthenes' laws existed, and that the first interpretation is likelier. Whether Cleisthenes' laws actually did exist in 411 is uncertain: cf. p. 241.

καὶ τοὺς πατρίους νόμους οὓς Κλεισθένης ἔθηκεν ὅτε καθίστη τὴν δημοκρατίαν: The appeal to the πάτριος πολιτεία in Athens at this time has been discussed by Fuks, *op. cit.*, and provides the starting point for the study of appeals to the past in political propaganda by M. I. Finley, *The Ancestral Constitution = The Use and Abuse of History*, 34–59 with 217–24. Clitophon's appeal to the constitution of Cleisthenes, which he calls democracy, accords with the tendency of the revolutionaries to make their revolution seem as respectable as possible by the standards of the democrats, by suggesting that their aim was not so much an oligarchy as a purified form of the now degenerate democracy (cf. p. 367 and the passages quoted on p. 372).[32] To the democrats the πάτριος πολιτεία was the democratic constitution under which they were still living (see Fuks, *op. cit.*, 33–51, K. R. Walters, *AJAH* i 1976, 129–44; according to T. viii. 76. vi the extreme oligarchs were accused by the Athenians on Samos as τοὺς πατρίους νόμους καταλύσαντας). Hitherto they had thought of theirs as the régime set up on the overthrow of the tyranny, and had regarded Cleisthenes as their founding hero; but from the late fifth century, as the government of Athens became a controversial matter, they looked increasingly far into the past for the origins of the democracy (cf. pp. 159, 261, and Finley, *opp. citt.*, esp. 13 = 40: one product of this concern with the past survives in ch. 4 as the 'Draconian constitution', drawn up *c.* 411 or later by a man who disapproved of the extreme democracy; Walters, *op. cit.*, 136–7 with 139 n. 40, suggests that Pythodorus' motion included a reference to the laws of Draco and Solon, and that this explains Clitophon's προσ-αναζητῆσαι and καί). In appealing to the democracy of Cleisthenes Clitophon may have been sincere, believing that that had been a good constitution and that subsequent changes had been for the worse (e.g. Fuks, *op. cit.*, 1–32), or he may have

---

[32] In *CQ* xxvii 1933, 19–25 = *Essays*, 139–48, Wade-Gery suggested that Clitophon's concern was not with the substance of Cleisthenes' laws but with the procedure by which he carried them through the assembly; but the explanatory phrase at the end of the sentence supposes it to be the substance that matters, and this is surely right. Fuks, *op. cit.*, 2–3 with 25 n. 2, reports that Wade-Gery later abandoned this theory.

been insincere, interested only in the propaganda value of his appeal to the hero of the democracy (e.g. Hignett, *H.A.C.*, 130): it is the thesis of Fuks that appeal to the πάτριος πολιτεία was particularly the hallmark of Theramenes and the 'moderates' (cf. 34. iii, where Clitophon is named as one of the group centred on Theramenes in 404 whose objective was the πάτριος πολιτεία), and Clitophon did at any rate survive the upheavals of 411–410 to become involved in those of 404–403; but the difference between the 'moderates' and the extreme oligarchs seems not to have become apparent until they had the opportunity to put their views into practice, and Clitophon was not necessarily by proposing this rider proclaiming himself a 'moderate'.†

ὅπως: Kaibel & Wilamowitz, followed by many editors (including Kenyon, Berlin ed.), inserted ὅπως ⟨ἂν⟩ to accord with epigraphic usage; Kenyon in the *corrigenda* of his Berlin ed. and his O.C.T. abandoned the insertion on the grounds that *mavult constructionem sine ἂν Arist*. ὅπως ἂν is indeed normal epigraphic usage, but it is not uniformly followed in the documents in these chapters and is not used at all by *A.P.* except in these documents (cf. pp. 374–5): it should not be restored here.

ὡς οὐ δημοτικὴν . . . τῇ Σόλωνος: This is not documentary in style (cf. Andrewes, *PCPS*[2] xxii 1976, 17), and it has often been recognised that the phrase is not a part of Clitophon's rider but an explanation of how he came to advocate any form of δημοκρατία. Wilamowitz, pointing out that Clitophon's views will have been known to the Platonic school, saw it as 'Aristotle's' own comment (*A.u.A.*, i. 102 with n. 8); Wade-Gery attributed the explanation to Antiphon's defence (*CQ* xxvii 1933, 19–20 = *Essays*, 139–41), and Jacoby attributed it to Androtion (*Atthis*, 384 n. 30, *Supp.* ii. 91). Whoever was the author of the explanation, he was ascribing a view of Cleisthenes' constitution to Clitophon, not asserting his own belief in that view—and, with the proviso that Clitophon may or may not have been sincere in professing that view, he was surely right: the point of Clitophon's rider was that the 'democracy' of Cleisthenes was better than the democracy of the late fifth century. For *A.P.*'s own view of Solon and Cleisthenes see especially 9 and 22. i with commentary.

29. iv. οἱ δ' αἱρεθέντες πρῶτον μὲν . . . ἔπειτα . . . : The assembly at which the συγγραφεῖς reported is the assembly held at Colonus, recounted in T. VIII. 67. ii–68. i *init*. (for the belief of Miss Lang that Thucydides and *A.P.* are writing of different boards, which reported on different occasions, see pp. 363–5). The holding of the assembly at Colonus, rather than in the city, may have deterred those without arms from attending (but Andrewes, *op. cit.*, 24 n. 18, is not eager to make much of this), but some more innocent reason for the choice must have been publicly stated.

πρῶτον μὲν ἔγραψαν ... ἐπιψηφίζειν: Cf. T. VIII. 67. ii (καὶ ἐσήνεγκαν οἱ ξυγγραφῆς ἄλλο μὲν οὐδέν, αὐτὸ δὲ τοῦτο, ἐξεῖναι μὲν Ἀθηναίων ἀνατεὶ εἰπεῖν γνώμην ἣν ἄν τις βούληται: ἀνατεὶ εἰπεῖν Sauppe, ἀνατρέπειν or ἀνειπεῖν codd.). The two texts are complementary: any citizen was to be free to make any proposal (as earlier any had been free to draft proposals: §ii), and any proposal was to be put to the vote. *A.P.*'s account, though couched in narrative form (ἔγραψαν ... ἀνεῖλον), has a documentary flavour: the adverb ἐπάναγκες is found particularly in documents (e.g. M&L 73, 61); for the phrase περὶ τῆς σωτηρίας cf. §ii with commentary; ἐπιψηφίζειν is the regular word for 'put to the vote', and although it is used also by narrative writers (e.g. T. VI. 14) it is inevitably found frequently in documents (e.g. 30. v, decree *ap*. And. I. *Myst*. 77; also the formula used in and after the 370's, τῶν προέδρων ἐπεψήφιζεν ὁ δεῖνα, e.g. Tod 124, 6).

ἔπειτα τὰς τῶν παρανόμων γραφὰς ... ἀνεῖλον: Cf. T. VIII. 67. ii (ἣν δέ τις τὸν εἰπόντα ἢ γράψηται παρανόμων ἢ ἄλλῳ τῳ τρόπῳ βλάψῃ, μεγάλας ζημίας ἐπέθεσαν). In the γραφὴ παρανόμων, apparently at this date a recent institution, a speaker could be prosecuted for making an illegal proposal (cf. 45. iv, 59. ii, with commentary: the abolition of this safeguard is associated with the overthrow of democracy by D. XXIV. *Tim*. 154; A. III. *Ctes*. 190–200, esp. 191, suggesting that the safeguard was abolished in 404 [cf. p. 434]); εἰσαγγελία is relevant both in the major sense of that word (charges of a treasonable nature: cf. 8. iv, 43. iv, with commentary) and in one of its other senses (the prytanes if they put an improper proposal to the vote would normally be vulnerable to an εἰσαγγελία μὴ χρῆσθαι τοῖς νόμοις: cf. 45. ii with commentary); πρόσκλησις is the prosecutor's summons to a defendant to appear before the relevant magistrate (cf. προσκαλεῖσθαι in 16. viii; see Lipsius, *A.R.*, 804–15, Harrison, *L.A.*, ii. 85–8: the papyrus' προκλήσεις was seen to be inappropriate by W. Wyse, *CR* v 1891, 113, Blass, *LZB* 1891, 304). In addition to the general restrictions, some particular decrees contained 'entrenchment-clauses', making it harder or legally impossible to reverse the provisions of those decrees; and ἐὰν δέ τις τούτων ... below may be described as 'an entrenchment-clause against entrenchment-clauses' (D. M. Lewis, Φόρος ... *B. D. Meritt*, 81–9). The actual report of the συγγραφεῖς no doubt intended to suspend all the impediments by which the assembly's freedom of decision was normally restricted; but the Athenians could be inefficient in such matters, as I suspect Patroclides was in the decree *ap*. And. I. *Myst*. 77–9. If any loopholes were left on this occasion they were not exploited.

ὅπως ἂν οἱ ἐθέλοντες: This time the final clause is introduced by ὅπως

COMMENTARY ON THE *ATH. POL.* [29. iv

ἄν, as in inscribed decrees (contrast §§ii, iii, with commentary; ὅπως ἄν recurs in 30. iv). οἱ ἐθέλοντες, however, is not normal in decrees, and Blass[1] suggested that it is an imitation of old-fashioned Greek: in decrees of the fifth century (ἐ)θέλειν is used normally in conditional or indefinite clauses (cf. M&L 91, 13–14: [περὶ τὸ μ]ὲ ἐθέλοντος ἀπι-[έναι]), but ὁ (ἐ)θέλων is found sometimes in literary texts (e.g. Soph. *Phil.* 619, *Aj.* 1146, Plat. *Gorg.* 508 c 9, *Legg.* IV. 707 E 2–3).

περὶ τῶν προκειμένων: τὰ προκείμενα are the matters set before the assembly or any other body for discussion (cf. H. I. 207. iii [τοῦ προκειμένου πρήγματος], Plat. *Gorg.* 457 D 4–5, *Lach.* 184 c 8; in Ar. *Eccl.* 401 we have the genitive absolute περὶ σωτηρίας προκειμένου); no instance is listed in the index to *IG* i².

τούτων χάριν: I.e. for an offence against any of the regulations now being suspended. Meisterhans & Schwyzer, *G.a.I.*, 222 with nn. 1769–70, knew no prepositional use of χάριν in prose inscriptions earlier than 50 B.C.; but it is used several times by Plato (e.g. *Phaedr.* 241 c 8, *Rep.* V. 475 A 4), very frequently by Aristotle (Bonitz, *Index Aristotelicus, s.v.*: H. Richards, *CR* V 1891, 273, remarks that Aristotle regularly uses it prospectively rather than retrospectively), and in four other passages by *A.P.* (16. iii, 18. vi, 22. vi, 35. iii).

ἢ ζημιοῖ ἢ προσκαλῆται ἢ εἰσάγῃ [[ἢ]] εἰς δικαστήριον: The prytanes, as chairmen of the assembly, responsible for the maintenance of order, could probably impose modest fines on the spot (cf. the laws, of the time when the πρόεδροι presided, inserted in A. I. *Tim.* 35: they do not prove Aeschines' point, but they may be authentic laws); a private prosecutor, doing his patriotic duty as ὁ βουλόμενος, would προσκαλεῖσθαι an offender (cf. above); a magistrate, accepting the prosecutor's suit, would εἰσάγειν εἰς τὸ δικαστήριον (cf. 56. vi, 57. iv, 58. iii, 59. ii, iv, v, and Wade-Gery, *BSA* xxxvii 1936/7, 270 = *Essays*, 178–9).

ἔνδειξιν αὐτοῦ εἶναι ... ζημιῶσαι: ἔνδειξις and ἀπαγωγή were procedures by which a man guilty of certain offences and caught *in flagrante delicto* could be denounced to the authorities, either by their being brought to him (ἔνδειξις) or by his being haled before them (ἀπαγωγή): cf. on 52. i. Under the democracy the generals had judicial responsibilities only in connection with military offences (Lipsius, *A.R.*, 110–13, Harrison, *L.A.*, ii. 31–4): their use here perhaps reflects the oligarchs' dislike of salaried civilian officials, perhaps is intended to heighten the sense of crisis. The Eleven were gaolers and executioners, empowered to put to death without formal trial κακοῦργοι who were delivered into their hands by the procedures named here and who confessed their guilt (cf. 52. i with commentary).

29. v. μετὰ δὲ ταῦτα τὴν πόλιν διέταξαν: The last main clause was οἱ δ' αἱρεθέντες πρῶτον μὲν ἔγραψαν (§iv *init.*), the next is οἱ μὲν οὖν αἱρεθέντες ταῦτα συνέγραψαν. κυρωθέντων δὲ τούτων ... (30. i *init.*); but διατάττειν should denote a decision by the person or body empowered to decide rather than a recommendation to that body: *A.P.* uses διατάττειν τὴν πολιτείαν twice of Solon, in 7. ii (cf. *ad loc.*) and 11. i; he also uses διατάττειν in 8. ii and 61. i, of the making of appointments by the body competent to do so. Here we must suppose either that he intended οἱ Ἀθηναῖοι as the subject of this sentence, and failed to take account of the change when writing the first sentence of 30 (e.g. Andrewes, *Hist. Comm. Thuc.*, v. 217, cf. J. Kriegel, *Der Staatsreich der Vierhundert in Athen, 411 v. Chr.*, 50, T. Lenschau, *RM*² lxviii 1913, 204–5) or that he has used διέταξαν loosely, in a way not paralleled by the texts cited in LSJ, of the συγγραφεῖς who recommended the constitutional changes to the assembly (e.g. E. Meyer, *Forschungen*, ii. 419; implied by the discussions of Wilamowitz, *A.u.A.*, i. 102–3, and others). T. VIII. 67. ii says emphatically of the withdrawal of constitutional safeguards ἐσήνεγκαν οἱ ξυγγραφῆς ἄλλο μὲν οὐδέν, αὐτὸ δὲ τοῦτο, and 68. i *init.* ascribes the positive proposals which followed to Pisander.

In their account of the positive proposals Thucydides and *A.P.* have little in common (which encouraged Miss Lang in her view that they report different proposals, put to different assemblies). T. VIII. 67. iii gives the abolition of existing offices and stipends; the appointment of five πρόεδροι, to appoint a hundred men, who will coopt a further three hundred; the constitution of these four hundred as a boule, to rule αὐτοκράτορας and convene 'the Five Thousand' when they see fit. *A.P.* 29. v reports the abolition of almost all non-military stipends for the duration of the war; the entrusting of the state to a body of five thousand or more, empowered to make treaties; and the appointment of a hundred men to register the Five Thousand; 30. i reports the appointment of another hundred, τοὺς ἀναγράψοντας τὴν πολιτείαν. Most probably the two texts do refer to the same occasion but both are incomplete: the assembly at Colonus resolved to base the constitution on a powerful boule of Four Hundred and a residual assembly of 'Five Thousand'. Thucydides concentrates on realities, and omits the appointment of the Five Thousand, because he has already mentioned them in his account of the oligarchs' programme (VIII. 65. iii) and their 'appointment' on this occasion did not take effect (VIII. 92. xi, 93. ii, cf. 89. ii); *A.P.* concentrates on formalities, and includes the 'appointment' of the Five Thousand in its place but omits the immediate appointment of the Four Hundred, which seemed to conflict with the constitution for the immediate crisis that he reports in 31 (cf. the similar but not identical explanation of Hignett, *H.A.C.*, 360–2, and Andrewes, *PCPS*² xxii 1976, 18–19). E. Meyer supposed that Pisander was one of the συγγραφεῖς and introduced the positive proposals on their behalf (*Forschungen*, ii. 419); Busolt was prepared to accept that interpretation of the material in *A.P.*, but thought that the material which is peculiar to Thucydides, yet presupposes the institution of the Five Thousand, represents a supplementary proposal of more extreme tendency made personally by Pisander (*G.G.*, III. ii. 1479–82, cf. the more elaborate theories of *G.S.*, i. 71–7, Wilcken, *Sb. Berlin* 1935, 35–47); Wade-Gery believed that *A.P.* followed Antiphon in ascribing the positive proposals to the συγγραφεῖς, and that the emphatic language of T. VIII. 67. ii is a deliberate denial of that ascription (*CQ* xxvii 1933, 20 n. 5 = *Essays* 141 n. 2, cf. Lenschau, *op. cit.*, 205, Hignett, *H.A.C.*, 275, 361–2).†

Clearly, even if their authors were the same, the withdrawal of safeguards and the positive proposals were presented to the assembly as distinct recommendations: the safeguards were withdrawn, proposals were invited, and Pisander was ready with proposals. Thucydides' informants may have suggested that the συγγραφεῖς did nothing but withdraw the safeguards, even if later the positive proposals were presented in their name; oligarchs on trial may have sought to lessen their guilt by attributing the authorship of the oligarchic constitution to the συγγραφεῖς, even if the συγγραφεῖς had not unanimously approved of the constitution (cf. the attempt of Eratosthenes to pass to the Thirty the responsibility for his acts in 404, countered in Lys. XII. *Erat.* 25–34); while any of the συγγραφεῖς who did not approve (either at the time or later) will have been anxious to deny their responsibility. I believe that *A.P.* does use διέταξαν loosely and attribute responsibility for the positive proposals to the συγγραφεῖς: probably Pisander was one of the συγγραφεῖς (contr. Busolt, *G.S.*, i. 71 with n. 2, D. Flach, *Chiron* vii 1977, 20 with n. 68; but Arist. *Rhet.* III. 1419 A 26–30 does not prove that he was not, and as a man who held office in 421/0 [cf. p. 407] he should now have been over forty and therefore eligible), and in introducing these proposals stated or implied that he had their support; how far he did have their support may never have been known. The appointment of the Four Hundred will have taken place now, as stated by Thucydides (the oligarchs were no doubt ready with names), and was perhaps alleged to be a provisional appointment, pending the working out of the details of the new constitution (cf. below): the registration of the Five Thousand, whom the extreme oligarchs intended to ignore, could be delayed, but if the revolution was to succeed the Four Hundred had to be brought into existence quickly.

τὰ μὲν χρήματα ⟨τὰ⟩ προσιόντα: Instead of adding τὰ (Kenyon[1]), H. Richards deleted χρήματα, comparing 39. ii (*CR* v 1891, 228), but there is no need to enforce uniformity.

μὴ ἐξεῖναι ... εἰς τὸν πόλεμον: Cf. the account of the oligarchs' programme in T. VIII. 65. iii (οὔτε μισθοφορητέον εἴη ἄλλους ἢ τοὺς στρατευομένους): military stipends are unaffected by the ban which follows. One reason for the overthrow of the democracy was that the state could no longer afford the μισθοφορία which it demanded: cf. p. 372.

ἄλλοσε: The word is cited by LSJ from early verse, T. VII. 51. i (also 1. 53. ii), X. *H.* VI. i. 11, and Plato, always with reference to place; we should have expected εἰς ἄλλο τι here.

τὰς δ' ἀρχὰς ... οἳ ἂν ὦσιν: Cf. T. VIII. 67. iii (μήτε ἀρχὴν ἄρχειν μηδεμίαν ἔτι ἐκ τοῦ αὐτοῦ κόσμου μήτε μισθοφορεῖν). The qualifications added by *A.P.* are no doubt an authentic part of what was formally resolved at Colonus: the abolition of stipends was said to be an emergency measure for the duration of the war (cf. the remark attributed to Pisander on his first visit to Athens in T. VIII. 53. iii: ὕστερον γὰρ ἐξέσται ἡμῖν καὶ μεταθέσθαι, ἢν μή τι ἀρέσκῃ); the nine archons were the nominal heads of state (and had been more important in the past to which some oligarchs were appealing: this probably counts for more than the expensive ceremonial obligations mentioned by Moore), and negative evidence suggests that those of 412/1 were left in office until the end of the year (cf. pp. 405, 410); 'whatever prytanes there might be' would be the effective heads of state, the men on full-time duty (cf. Moore).

τρεῖς ὀβολούς: This was the current rate for jurors (cf. p. 338), and perhaps for other civilian officials; hoplites and oarsmen had at any rate on some occasions been paid more, but now oarsmen too were paid 3 obols a day (cf. pp. 306–7). For payments to the nine archons (4 obols εἰς σίτησιν) and the prytanes (5 obols as bouleutae, and 1 obol εἰς σίτησιν) in the 320's see 62. ii with commentary.

τὴν δ' ἄλλην πολιτείαν ἐπιτρέψαι πᾶσαν ... ὁ πόλεμος ᾖ: Again the representation of the change as an emergency measure for the duration of the war is no doubt authentic. That a resolution on these lines was adopted at this time, though Thucydides makes no direct mention of it, is confirmed by Lys. xx. *Poly.* 13 (ὑμῶν ψηφισαμένων πεντακισχιλίοις παραδοῦναι τὰ πράγματα), 16 (ὑμεῖς αὐτοὶ πεισθέντες ὑπὸ τούτων παρέδοτε τοῖς πεντακισχιλίοις). It has normally and rightly been assumed that this language refers to the constitution of the Five Thousand as the assembly, the residual sovereign body in the state; that has been doubted for the intermediate régime (33. i with commentary) by G. E. M. de Ste. Croix, *Hist.* v 1956, 1–23, and for the whole of 411 by B. R. I. Sealey, *Essays*, 111–32, *CSCA* viii 1975, 271–95, but I have attempted to answer them in *JHS* xcii 1972, 115–27 (cf. also below, pp. 413–14, 448).†

τοῖς δυνατωτάτοις καὶ τοῖς σώμασιν καὶ τοῖς χρήμασιν λῃτουργεῖν: Cf. the account of the oligarchs' programme in T. VIII. 65. iii (οἳ ἂν μάλιστα τοῖς τε χρήμασι καὶ τοῖς σώμασιν ὠφελεῖν οἷοί τε ὦσιν); also T. I. 13. v (χρήμασί τε δυνατοὶ ἦσαν, of the Corinthians as a whole), X.

Hipparch. i. 9 (τοὺς μὲν τοίνυν ἱππέας ... καθιστάναι δεῖ ... τοὺς δυνατωτάτους καὶ χρήμασι καὶ σώμασιν) and *A.P.* 49. ii, *IG* ix (i) 694, 45 (Corcyra, c2), D.H. *A.R.* II. 8. ii; and contrast H. II. 88 (τοὺς χρήμασι ἀσθενεστέρους); but in T. VIII. 47. ii, 48. i, cited by Sandys, οἱ δυνατώτατοι are the most influential men. On the public services called λητουργίαι which Athens required of her richer citizens see 27. iii, 56. iii, 61. i, with commentary. For 'serving the state with one's body' cf. D. x. *Phil.* iv. 28 (ἃ δεῖ τοῖς σώμασι καὶ ταῖς οὐσίαις λητουργῆσαι ἕκαστον), XXI. *Mid.* 165 (τοῖς σώμασιν ... λητουργεῖν); also XIV. *Symm.* 16-17.

Here and in T. VIII. 65. iii the reference must be to men of hoplite status and above: notice the part played by the hoplites in T. VIII. 92-3, and compare what is said of the Five Thousand under the intermediate régime in T. VIII. 97. i (εἶναι δὲ αὐτῶν ὁπόσοι καὶ ὅπλα παρέχονται) and *A.P.* 33. i (τοῖς πεντακισχιλίοις τοῖς ἐκ τῶν ὅπλων); also the 'Draconian constitution' in 4. ii (ἀπεδέδοτο μὲν ἡ πολιτεία τοῖς ὅπλα παρεχομένοις); X. *H.* II. iii. 48 uses τοῖς δυναμένοις καὶ μεθ' ἵππων καὶ μετ' ἀσπίδων ὠφελεῖν (in a speech of Theramenes) to denote men of cavalry and of hoplite status. There are general discussions of 'hoplite franchise' in Arist. *Pol.* III. 1279 A 37-B 4, IV. 1297 B 1-34, and in the second passage it is noted that the Malians included in the citizen body men too old to fight but did not allow them to hold office. It is not clear what the oligarchs' attitude to older men was in 411: the problem may have been left unresolved at Colonus, but the intermediate régime must have come to a decision (cf. on 33. i).

μὴ ἔλαττον ἢ πεντακισχιλίοις: In the papyrus a corrector has written ων above πεντακισχιλίοις (but has not deleted ἤ): Kenyon and most other editors have retained the original reading, but ἔλαττον πεντακισχιλίων was preferred by Kaibel & Wilamowitz and Blass[3-4]. *A.P.* more often uses the construction with ἤ, but the genitive construction is used in 3. iv, and in the 'Draconian constitution' both are used within 4. ii. In documentary material, such as we have here, it is in any case unwise to insist on conformity to *A.P.*'s normal usage, and since there would be no need to alter ἔλαττον ἢ πεντακισχιλίοις unless that was not the reading of the text being copied the genitive construction is the more likely to be right.†

T. VIII. 65. iii includes in the oligarchs' programme οὔτε μεθεκτέον τῶν πραγμάτων πλέοσιν ἢ πεντακισχιλίοις: no doubt his use of five thousand as a maximum correctly reflects the oligarchs' ambitions, *A.P.*'s use of it as a minimum correctly reflects the formal proposal presented to the assembly at Colonus. The oligarchs alleged that attendance at assemblies was never as high as five thousand (T. VIII. 72. i), but even if that was true it will not have been true that all who attended were of hoplite status and above. In 431 Athens had

13,000 + 16,000 hoplites, including at least 4,000 metics, and 1,200 cavalry (T. II. 13. vi–viii cf. 31. ii); 4,400 of the 13,000 died in the plague (III. 87. iii); 1,500 Athenian hoplites went to Sicily in 415, and an unknown number in 413 (T. VI. 43, VII. 42. i). How many men were killed elsewhere and how many young men came of age we do not know, but it seems unlikely that there were as few as five thousand citizens of hoplite status and above in 411.

κυρίους δ' εἶναι ... ἐθέλωσιν: Some may still have been hoping to secure Persian support (though it should have been public knowledge by this time that Tissaphernes had renewed his alliance with Sparta: cf. p. 371); others may already have been thinking of negotiating a peace settlement with Sparta (cf. 32. iii with commentary). If this is an authentic part of what was resolved at Colonus (which I see no reason to doubt) it confirms that the Five Thousand were intended to function as an assembly, with residual sovereign powers (cf. p. 382): even where little business was referred to the sovereign body, that business regularly included the right to make peace or declare war, and to enter into alliances (cf. *IG* i² 114, 36 [35, Wade-Gery, *BSA* xxxiii 1932/3, 113–22, and *IG* i³ 105], Arist. *Pol.* IV. 1298 B 5–8, and Y. Garlan, *La Guerre dans l'antiquité*, 26, trans. *War in the Ancient World*, 43). In fifth-century Athenian decrees we find αὐτοκράτωρ rather than κύριος (G. E. M. de Ste. Croix, *CQ*² xiii 1963, 115 n. 2 = S. Perlman [ed.], *Philip and Athens*, 41 n. 2).

ἑλέσθαι δ(ὲ) κ(αὶ): The reading of the papyrus is retained by Kenyon and most editors; but δ' (ἐ)κ was suggested by Herwerden and adopted by Blass, Kaibel & Wilamowitz³ and others (cf. Kaibel, *Stil und Text*, 187). However, δὲ καί (on which see J. D. Denniston, *The Greek Particles*², 305–6) is not objectionable: after the principles of the new constitution have been outlined, the appointment of men who will bring it into effect marks a further stage; *A.P.* uses ἀπό in similar contexts in 43. i, 61. i, ἐκ in 44. ii, 47. i, ii, 53. i, cf. 62. i, genitive without preposition in 48. iv, 61. iii, v, and this last construction is found also in M&L 52, 66–7.

τῆς φυλῆς ἑκάστης δέκα ... καταλέξουσι τοὺς πεντακισχιλίους: In Lys. XX. *Poly.* we have parts of two speeches (cf. p. 367) in defence of a man who was a member of the Four Hundred and was also one of the hundred καταλογεῖς: the text claims that he was appointed, apparently to membership of the Four Hundred, ὑπὸ τῶν φυλετῶν (§2); that as καταλογεύς he registered as many as nine thousand, having agreed to serve only under pressure (§§13–14); that after eight days as a member of the Four Hundred he went to Eretria, and did not return until after the fall of the Four Hundred (§§14–16). It is thus confirmed that καταλογεῖς existed at the beginning of the régime of the Four Hundred: *A.P.* says that ten were appointed from each tribe, and *pace* Sandys and others does not say how they were appointed; but we may guess that, like the Four Hundred, they were appointed on the spot at Colonus. Altogether we read of three groups of 100 men in 411: the nucleus of the Four Hundred (whose appointment *A.P.* omits at this point: see T. VIII. 67. iii and pp. 380–1); the καταλογεῖς; and the ἀναγραφεῖς (30. i with commentary, 32. i): Polystratus belonged to the Four Hundred and to the καταλογεῖς, and some have argued that the first two groups of 100 (Wilamowitz, *A.u.A.*, ii. 357) or even all three (E. Meyer, *Forschungen*, ii. 428, 433, Busolt, *G.G.*, III. ii. 1481–2 n. 1, 1486) were identical. ὑπὸ τῶν φυλετῶν in Lys. should not be pressed: the speaker will have sought to confer on Polystratus as much democratic respectability as possible; what he says may be untrue, or may be a grave distortion of the truth (he may deliberately confuse Polystratus' two appointments; or it may be that the hundred who formed the nucleus of the Four Hundred were ten from each tribe, that each coopted further members of his own tribe, and that Polystratus was thus coopted and in that sense was chosen ὑπὸ τῶν φυλετῶν). I suspect that the three groups of 100 were not identical but overlapped to a large extent; if the five πρόεδροι of T. VIII. 67. iii had the function which he assigns to them (which not all have believed) they may have nominated each of the three groups for the assembly's approval.

A minimum age of forty had been prescribed earlier, probably for the πρόβουλοι and certainly for the twenty who joined them as συγγραφεῖς: see §ii with commentary.

ὀμόσαντες καθ' ἱερῶν τελείων: 'An oath taken on unblemished sacrificial victims' (Moore). Cf. the opening words of ch. 1 (omitting τελείων); also M & L 73, 39, *Hesp.* xi 55, 15, 16; T. v. 47. iii, And. I. *Myst.* 97 (both quoting documents), [D.] LIX. *Neaer.* 60. Earlier an oath had been imposed on the συγγραφεῖς (§ii with commentary), and we may guess that an oath was imposed on the ἀναγραφεῖς of 30. i; the duties assigned to the Four Hundred in 31. i include some kind of responsibility for an oath (cf. *ad loc.*). Lys. xx. *Poly.* 14 does not make it clear whether the oath which Polystratus was obliged to take concerned his membership of the καταλογεῖς or of the Four Hundred.

30. i. οἱ μὲν οὖν αἱρεθέντες ταῦτα συνέγραψαν: It is implied that the positive proposals, as well as the removal of safeguards, were the work of the συγγραφεῖς: see pp. 379–81.

κυρωθέντων δὲ τούτων . . . ἑκατὸν ἄνδρας: Cf. 32. i *init*. This has been a major stumbling-block in the interpretation of *A.P.*'s account of 411. According to T. VIII. 69–70. i the proposals made at Colonus were ratified without opposition, and ὕστερον the Four Hundred contrived to take over the bouleuterium without opposition; later he makes it clear that under the régime of the Four Hundred the list of the Five Thousand was not completed or published (VIII. 92. xi, 93. ii, cf. 89. ii). It is alleged that Polystratus registered as many as nine thousand qualified citizens (Lys. xx. *Poly.* 13), and Nicomachus' prosecutor claims not to have been registered among the Five Thousand (Lys. xxx. *Nic.* 8, emended but certain): but the first passage is certainly compatible with the register's having been begun but not completed, and I should not like to insist that the second is not. *A.P.* 32. iii says οἱ μὲν πεντακισχίλιοι λόγῳ μόνον ᾑρέθησαν; and in 33. ii the complaint against the extremists, οὐδὲν ἐπαναφέροντες τοῖς πεντακισχιλίοις, does not prove that the Five Thousand existed: those remarks are compatible either with the view that they did not exist or with the view that they existed but were not allowed to function. *Pace* Wilamowitz (*A.u.A.*, i. 103–5, ii. 357–8) it should be accepted that Thucydides is right and under the régime of the Four Hundred the Five Thousand did not exist. Yet here *A.P.* asserts that the Five Thousand appointed a body of ἀναγραφεῖς (as we may style them); he outlines their proposals; and in 32. i he claims that these proposals were ratified by the πλῆθος.

Some wholly reject the ἀναγραφεῖς and their documents (cf. following note); various solutions have been attempted by those who prefer to be less drastic. Kenyon[1] suggested that those of hoplite status and above deemed themselves to be the Five Thousand, until the definitive list should be published (cf. W. S. Ferguson, *C.A.H.*, v[1]. 331). Others have thought that the existence of the Five Thousand was a mistaken inference made by *A.P.* or his source from the constitutional documents in 30–1 (e.g. E. Meyer, *Forschungen*, ii. 431–3, Busolt, *G.G.*, III. ii. 1483–4 n., cf. *G.S.*, i. 73–4). Others have resorted to chronological devices to save *A.P.* Beloch assigned the appointment of the ἀναγραφεῖς and the documents of 30–1 to the intermediate régime established on the fall of the Four Hundred (*G.G.*[2], II. ii. 311–24); M. Cary once suggested that the documents were produced towards the end of the rule of the Four Hundred, hurriedly, in response to the growing discontent with their rule (*ap.* G. H. Stevenson, *JHS* lvi 1936, 57 n.; but in *JHS* lxxii 1952, 57–61, he accepted Beloch's dating). However, the 'immediate' constitution of 31 can hardly be a constitution contemplated in the autumn of 411. If the documents are at all authentic there are two serious possibilities, neither without difficulty: either the documents were presented to the Colonus assembly, in which case it is hard to find any occasion for the appointment of the ἀναγραφεῖς and the references to οἱ ἑκατὸν ἄνδρες in 30. iii and 31. iii are embarrassing, or the ἀναγραφεῖς were appointed by the Colonus assembly and produced their documents shortly afterwards, in which case Thucydides' narrative is an obstacle to the view that their recommendations were adopted by a meeting of the πλῆθος as stated in 32. i (champions of the first view include T. Lenschau, *RM*² lxviii 1913, 210–13, Busolt, *G.S.*, i. 75–7, Wilcken, *Sb. Berlin* 1935, 44; of the second, E. Meyer, *Forschungen*, ii. 432–5, Busolt, *G.G.*, III. ii. 1486, also M. L. Lang, *AJP* lxix 1948, 282–6). The second view seems preferable: the Colonus assembly will have decided in principle that the constitution should be based on a powerful boule of Four Hundred and a residual assembly of 'Five Thousand', and as it appointed the καταλογεῖς to register the Five Thousand it appointed the ἀναγραφεῖς to work out the details of the new constitution. Either at the time or later it was supposed that the assembly which appointed the ἀναγραφεῖς was an assembly of the Five Thousand: I think it more likely that this supposition was made officially, either at the Colonus assembly or very soon after, than that it is merely a mistaken inference by *A.P.* or his source. Almost certainly, however, *A.P.* is wrong to say that the recommendations of the ἀναγραφεῖς were adopted by the πλῆθος: probably the assembly at which Aristomachus presided was the Colonus assembly, and the documents were published later but were not ratified by any body larger than the Four Hundred (see 32. i with commentary).

The choice of title for these men is surprising: ἀναγραφεύς and ἀναγράφειν are normally used of the recording of what has already been decided (e.g. M&L 85, 21–2, 28–9, And. I. *Myst.* 82, 84; M&L 86, 5–6, Lys. xxx. *Nic.* 2, 4, of the ἀναγραφεῖς appointed in 410/09), and we should expect these drafters like the thirty of 29. ii to be styled συγγραφεῖς.

οἱ δ' αἱρεθέντες ἀνέγραψαν καὶ ἐξήνεγκαν τάδε: The difficulties of 30–32. i *init.* are such that some have rejected this account altogether, believing with Thucydides that after the Colonus assembly the Four Hundred simply seized power and ruled by force, and supposing that the documents in these chapters, together with the ἀναγραφεῖς who drafted them and the meeting of the πλῆθος which ratified them, are a fraud which was perpetrated in or soon after 411 to help legitimise the oligarchy and which deceived *A.P.* (e.g. U. Kahrstedt, *Forschungen zur Geschichte des ausgehenden V. und des IV. Jahrhunderts*, 250–5; Andrewes, *PCPS*² xxii 1976, 20–1, *Hist. Comm. Thuc.*, v. 242–6 [fraud put about officially by the Four Hundred]). There is not a sharp line between believers and unbelievers: unbelievers may like Andrewes accept that the fraud was put into circulation in 411 with the blessing of the Four Hundred; while none except those who believe that it was the constitution of the intermediate régime (cf. below) have thought that the 'future' constitution of 30 was ever put into effect, and the 'immediate' constitution of 31, even if officially issued at the beginning of the rule of the Four Hundred, may embody their propaganda rather than their intentions. The documents as we read them in *A.P.* are incoherent and, one is tempted to say, incomplete (for instance, nothing is said of the administration of justice: in fact And. II. *Red.* 13–15 confirms that, as we might expect, the Four Hundred themselves acted as a court of law). Some incoherencies may have been imported by *A.P.* as he condensed what he found in his source, but others may have been present in the original documents. Consequently it is hazardous to attempt a reconstruction of the two constitutions outlined here: what seems to be the most plausible interpretation of the text may not always be what was intended by the author(s) of the documents.

The 'immediate' constitution may be accepted as a document issued officially at the beginning of the rule of the Four Hundred: it would not suffice as a complete instrument of government, but it would be adequate as an announcement to the Athenians of how the state was to be administered in the immediate crisis—essentially, by giving full power to the boule and generals (cf. E. Meyer, *Forschungen*, ii. 434). On the appointment of officials it distinguishes between 'now' and 'the future', 'the future' apparently being identical with 'next year'; but only one method for the appointment of the boule is given, and appointments for 'the future' are dependent on that. This makes sense in a document issued late in 412/1: a provisional boule of Four Hundred already exists, and the document authorises the appointment (by whom, it does not say) of provisional boards of generals and others; for 411/0 (and if necessary for subsequent years) a boule of Four Hundred is to be appointed from tribal πρόκριτοι, and it will appoint the generals and others; it is pretended that generals can now be chosen from the Five Thousand, as it was pretended that the ἀναγραφεῖς were appointed by the Five Thousand. Cf. Fritz & Kapp, 178–9 n. 103.

Beloch thought that the two documents together embodied the constitution of the intermediate régime (cf. previous note); V. L. Ehrenberg thought that the 'immediate' constitution was Pisander's proposal at Colonus and the 'future' constitution of 30 was put into effect by the intermediate régime (*Hermes* lvii 1922, 613–20 = *Polis und Imperium*, 315–21, cf. W. S. Ferguson, *CP* xxi 1926, 72–5, *Mélanges Glotz*, i. 349–66), and his view of the 'future' constitution won considerable support for some time. More recently the objections to Ehrenberg's theory have been stressed: what little evidence we have for the intermediate régime does not suggest that it divided its citizen body into four βουλαί; of the details on which this document diverges from the democratic practice of before 411, the amalgamation of the city and Delian League funds under an enlarged board of Hellenotamiae occurred in or before 411/0, but the amalgamation of the two major boards of sacred treasurers did not occur until 406 (see in general Fritz & Kapp, 25, 181–2 n. 117, Hignett, *H.A.C.*, 376–8, G. E. M. de Ste. Croix, *Hist.* v 1956, 14–20). This document is a theorist's sketch, which owes something to the constitutions of the Boeotian cities: it was never put into practice, but it could have been issued as a 'future' constitution in the summer of 411. (D. Flach, *Chiron* vii 1977, 28–9 suggests that the oligarchs' message to Samos [T. VIII. 72. i, 86. iii] presupposes the issue of the 'future' constitution, but this is not conclusive.)†

The presentation of the two constitutions together has caused difficulty. Beloch (cf. above) and Miss Lang (*AJP* lxix 1948, 286–8, lxxxviii 1967, 183–7) thought that the two should be combined as a single constitution with some provisional clauses; M. Cary attempted major surgery to separate 'immediate' from 'future' provisions (*JHS* lxxii 1952, 57–8). I suggest that 30. ii–vi and 31. i–iii (βουλεύειν μὲν τετρακοσίους . . . ἄρξαι τὴν αὐτὴν ἀρχήν) are two distinct drafts, envisaged as 'future' and 'immediate' constitutions as stated in 31. i *init.*; the last sentence of 31. iii (εἰς δὲ τὸν ἄλλον χρόνον . . . οἱ ἑκατὸν ἄνδρες) refers not to the 'immediate' but to the 'future' constitution, and its occurrence at the end may point the way to an explanation. When the ἀναγραφεῖς met, a division between 'moderate' and extreme oligarchs emerged, and led to the production of the two constitutions quoted by *A.P.* (extremists could allow the publication of the 'future' constitution as a document valuable for propaganda purposes, though they had no intention of bringing it into effect): this last sentence represents an amendment added by one of the 'moderate' ἀναγραφεῖς, calling on the καταλογεῖς to include in their registration a division of the Four Hundred into the four sections of 30, in order to facilitate the introduction of the 'future' constitution in due course (cf. *ad loc.*, and Rhodes, *JHS* xcii 1972, 117 n. 20).

30. ii. βουλεύειν μὲν κατ' ἐνιαυτὸν: This needs to be read with §iii, βουλὰς δὲ ποιῆσαι τέτταρας . . . καὶ εἰς ἐνιαυτὸν βουλεύειν; the end of §ii shows that there are to be men eligible for minor offices who will not be members of the current boule. I believe that this sentence is concerned with eligibility for membership of the boule, as the next (τούτων δ᾽ εἶναι . . .) is concerned with eligibility for the various offices; we advance from eligibility to appointment at αἱρεῖσθαι δὲ πάντας τούτους. The confusion, if I have interpreted it aright, will have been made easier by the fact that all who were eligible were to serve in the boule, though not all in the same year.

A.P. plunges *in medias res*, with no indication that the draft in this chapter is of a constitution for the future. It is not stated, but must have been assumed, that men other than the Five Thousand would be excluded from the boule and all offices.

τοὺς ὑπὲρ τριάκοντα ἔτη γεγονότας: The same minimum age is attested for jurors under the democracy (63. iii with commentary) and for bouleutae under the Thirty (X. *M.* i. ii. 35; for the democracy, D. xxii. *Andr.*, *hyp.* i. 1 refers to τῶν τὴν βουλευτικὴν ἡλικίαν ἀγόντων); it appears also in 4. iii ('Draconian constitution') and 31. i. Probably this requirement applied to office-holding, in the widest sense, under the democracy and under Athens' various oligarchic régimes whenever no higher minimum was stipulated (cf. p. 510); contrast 29. ii with commentary, on the συγγραφεῖς.

ἄνευ μισθοφορᾶς: Contrast 29. v, where the abolition of civilian stipends is said to be for the duration of the war.

τούτων: Since the previous sentence fails to distinguish between those eligible to serve in the boule and those actually serving in a particular year it is not immediately clear to which of these categories τούτων refers. However, we read later in §ii that the officials listed are to be chosen from the boule currently in office, while other officials are to be appointed from outside the boule, so τούτων must be the men currently serving (contr. T. Nicklin, *CR* v 1891, 228).

τοὺς στρατηγούς: It is stated below that the archons will still number nine; it is not stated, but was probably intended, that the generals should still number ten. As members of the current one of the four βουλαί (§iii), men could not have served as generals or other major officers more than one year in four: this would not make for the efficient waging of war, but it is defended as an application of the principle of equality within the oligarchy by J. A. O. Larsen, *Representative Government in Greek and Roman History*, 197 n. 30 (and cf. the ban on iteration in the Spartan navarchy, below, p. 696).

τὸν ἱερομνήμονα: This was the title of the voting representative sent by Athens, as one of two from the Ionians, to the council of the Delphic Amphictyony (Ar. *Nub.* 623–4 with schol., D. xviii. *Cor.* 148–9, A. iii. *Ctes.* 115: see Busolt & Swoboda, *G.S.*, ii. 1303–8 cf. 1102 with n. 2). Arist. *Pol.* vi. 1321 b 34–40 notes that the title is given in some cities to a legal official, but there is no evidence that this was ever true of Athens.

τοὺς ταξιάρχους καὶ ἱππάρχους καὶ φυλάρχους: Respectively, the ten commanders of the tribal regiments of hoplites, the commanders-in-chief of the cavalry, and the ten commanders of the tribal regiments of cavalry (61. iii–v). Here there is a plurality of hipparchs but the number is not specified; in 31. iii there is only one; there were three in the mid fifth century, two in the fourth (61. iv with commentary).

ἄρχοντας εἰς τὰ φρούρια: Attica was at this time overrun by Agis and the Spartans, and Athens can have had garrisons only in the fortified area of Athens and the Piraeus and in allied states (for a garrison on the Acropolis see 24. iii with commentary). If these garrison commanders numbered eight and the hipparchs two, the major officials listed here would reach a total of 100, which may well have been intended (cf. Sandys[2], 130).

ταμίας τῶν ἱερῶν χρημάτων τῇ θε[ῷ] καὶ τοῖς ἄλλοις θεοῖς δέκα: Restored thus by Kenyon[1] (Athena is regularly ἡ θεός: *IG* i², index, p. 356); Wilcken read θεᾷ, and Dr. J. D. Thomas finds that slightly more likely, but Kenyon in his Berlin ed. commented *vestigia litterae tertiae ω vel α aeque apta sunt*. Athens had a long-established board of treasurers of Athena (cf. 8. i with commentary), in the fifth century usually designated ℎοι ταμίαι ℎοι τὰ τε̑ς θεο̑ ἐταμίευον (e.g. *IG* i² 340, 44–5) or ℎοι ταμίαι το̑ν ℎιερο̑ν χρεμάτον τε̑ς Ἀθεναίας (e.g. *IG* i² 237, 54. or simply ℎοι ταμίαι (e.g. *IG* i² 3, 18; 355 = M & L 54 A [2], 8–9; cf. 4. ii, 7. iii, 8. i); in M & L 55, 9–10, they are ταμι]ὸν ἐ[κ πόλεο]ς) Very probably in 434/3, other temple treasuries were amalgamated and entrusted to a board of treasurers of the Other Gods (M & L 58 A, 13 sqq.). The further amalgamation of these two boards, foreshadowed here, seems actually to have occurred at the beginning of 406/5 (W. S. Ferguson, *Treasurers of Athena*, 104–6, cf. W. E. Thompson, *Hesp.* xxxix 1970, 61–3); the title of the joint board was usually οἱ ταμίαι τῶν ἱερῶν χρημάτων τῆς Ἀθηναίας καὶ τῶν ἄλλων θεῶν. (*IG* ii² 1370, 1–2) or οἱ ταμίαι τῆς θεοῦ καὶ τῶν ἄλλων θεῶν (decree *apv* And. 1. *Myst.* 77), but we once find simply ταμίαι τῶν τῆς θεο̑ (*IG* ii² 1391, 5). At the beginning of 385/4 the two separate boards were restored (Ferguson, *op. cit.*, 14); for their further history see 47. i with commentary.†

ἑλληνοταμίας καὶ τῶν ἄλλων ὁσίων χρημάτων ἁπάντων εἴκοσιν οἳ διαχειριοῦσιν: I.e. τῶν Ἑλληνικῶν ταμίας καὶ τῶν ἄλλων . . ., a board of twenty who were to have charge of the funds both of the Delian League and of the Athenian state (Kaibel, *Stil und Text*, 187–8, Sandys[2]). This gives an acceptable sense, though many have thought the text corrupt (e.g. Kaibel & Wilamowitz, cf. Wilamowitz, *A.u.A.*, ii. 117 n. 12; H. Richards, *CR* v 1891, 181, vii 1893, 211; E. S. Thompson, *CR* v 1891, 277). If anything is amiss it is the appearance of the redundant οἳ διαχειριοῦσιν (thus Wilamowitz): the closest parallel is ℎοὶ νῦν διαχερίζο[σι]ν used in M & L 58 A, 19–20, of the treasurers and other sacred officials who are to hand over their treasures to the new treasurers of the Other Gods, which suggests that the words may be defended as a (condensed) allusion to the new duties of the new, combined board of secular treasurers. Hitherto ten Hellenotamiae had been responsible both for receiving and for disbursing the funds of the Delian League, ten apodectae (48. i–ii with commentary) had received and ten colacretae (7. iii with commentary) had disbursed the funds of the Athenian state: the apodectae survive into the fourth century, but the colacretae are last attested in 418/7 or perhaps 416/5 (*IG* i² 94, 28; M & L 73, 51–2 [date disputed]), and in and after 410 the Hellenotamiae do number twenty and make payments which earlier would have been made by the colacretae (e.g. M & L 84), so it is likely that the imperial and city treasuries were amalgamated about this time. Whether the amalgamation had already occurred or is making its first appearance in this draft must remain uncertain. See Rhodes, *A.B.*, 98–102, esp. 99 n. 4.

ἱεροποιοὺς καὶ ἐπιμελητὰς δέκα ἑκατέρους: On titles borne by religious officials see in general Arist. *Pol.* VI. 1322 B 19–25. Boards of hieropoei, usually ten in number and often appointed from the boule of five hundred, cooperated with priests in the administration of various festivals; two such boards are listed in 54. vi–vii (cf. *ad. loc.*, and see Rhodes, *A.B.*, 127–30). Epimeletes is a title borne by various officials with religious duties, including the four epimeletae of the Mysteries (57. i with commentary) and the ten of the Dionysia (56. iv with commentary), and religious officials are presumably intended here; the title is also borne by secular officials, such as the epimeletae of the market (51. iv). Wilamowitz, *A.u.A.*, ii. 120, suggested that it would accord with the centralising tendency of this document if it was intended that there should be only one board of hieropoei and one of epimeletae.

αἱρεῖσθαι δὲ πάντας τούτους ἐκ προκρίτων: Since it is stated below that minor offices are to be sortitive, αἱρεῖσθαι here should mean not merely 'appoint' but specifically 'elect': the procedure envisaged is election from an elected short list.

ἐκ τῶν ἀεὶ βουλευόντων πλείους προκρίνοντας: The incompleteness of this provision probably betrays the theoretical nature of this document rather than abbreviation by *A.P.* (but there is a similar incompleteness in the 'immediate' constitution, 31. i): the size of the short lists is not specified; and, *pace* Fritz & Kapp ('The Council was to appoint . . . candidates selected by it . . .'), it is not stated whether nominations, προκρίσεις and appointments are to be made by the boule from which these officials will be drawn or the previous year's boule or the whole body of qualified citizens (but no assemblies of all qualified citizens are envisaged in this text: cf. §iv with commentary); see Wilamowitz, *A.u.A.*, ii. 116–17 n. 11. These major officials are to be appointed from the men currently serving as bouleutae, a quarter of the whole body of qualified citizens, whereas minor officials are to be appointed from the remaining three quarters; but this division of the citizen body into quarters is not expounded until §iii.

τοὺς δὲ ἑλληνοταμίας. . . μὴ συμβουλεύειν: This is one of the most difficult sentences in the constitutional documents: the Hellenotamiae are among the major officials, to be appointed by election from the current boule; yet they, or some of them, may not συμβουλεύειν—presumably, may not 'sit in the *Boule*' (Moore). Interpreters have been divided between those who suppose οἳ ἂν διαχειρίζωσι τὰ χρήματα to describe the whole board (e.g. Kahrstedt,

Forschungen zur Geschichte des ausgehenden V. und des IV. Jahrhunderts, 251, Ferguson, *C.A.H.*, v[1]. 339) and those who suppose it to define a smaller group within the whole (e.g. Wilamowitz, *A.u.A.*, ii. 117 n. 12, Kaibel, *Stil und Text*, 187-8, N. J. Krom, *Mnem.*[2] xxxvii 1909, 156-61, M. Giffler, *RM*[2] lxxxix 1940, 62-4); but if the text is sound, and *A.P.* wrote both οἳ διαχειριοῦσιν above and οἳ ἂν διαχειρίζωσι here, the verb ought to have the same meaning in both places and here describe the whole board of Hellenotamiae. I do not know why the author(s) of this draft should have wished to exclude the Hellenotamiae, but not other major officials, from the boule from whose ranks they were appointed: possibly, but not necessarily, what was said of the Hellenotamiae was clearer in the original draft than in *A.P.*'s report of it.

The papyrus reads οἳ ἐὰν διαχειρίζωσι: rightly, most editors have corrected to οἳ ἂν (the same error is found elsewhere, e.g. 31. ii *init.*), but Hude suggested ὅταν and Thalheim ⟨καὶ⟩ οἳ ἂν. This sentence is alluded to in Harp. Ἑλληνοταμίαι (taking the disputed clause to be descriptive of the whole board): ὅτι ἀρχή τις ἦν οἱ Ἑλληνοταμίαι, οἳ διεχείριζον τὰ χρήματα, καὶ Ἀριστοτέλης δηλοῖ ἐν τῇ Ἀθηναίων Πολιτείᾳ.

30. iii. βουλὰς δὲ ποιῆσαι τέτταρας ... τὸ λαχὸν μέρος βουλεύειν: Those who are divided into four βουλαί should be all qualified citizens (i.e. members of the Five Thousand) who have reached the age of thirty (§ii *init.*): there is no need to suppose, as some have done (e.g. Kenyon[1], Sandys, cf. the elaborate interpretation of Beloch, *G.G.*[2], II. ii. 316-18: see the reply of Hignett, *H.A.C.*, 368-9), that the four βουλαί were either each or together to comprise four hundred men. This fourfold division seems to be copied from the individual cities of Boeotia, in which ἦσαν καθεστηκυῖαι βουλαὶ ... τέττα[ρες], to one of which each citizen possessed of a certain property qualification was assigned; each of the four took it in turn to act as the probouleutic body, while the four met together as a sovereign assembly (*H.O.* 16. ii). Similarly in the federal organisation of Boeotia in the late fifth and early fourth centuries there was a sovereign council of 660, in which it seems that one quarter acted as a probouleutic body (*H.O.* 16. iv with T. v. 38. ii–iv: the debt to Boeotia was first noticed by U. Koehler, *Sb. Berlin* 1895, 455-7). The words εἰς τὸν λοιπὸν χρόνον should be redundant, since the whole constitution outlined in 30 is intended εἰς τὸν μέλλοντα χρόνον (31. i *init.*), but in *A.P.*'s text they are the first indication of that fact which the reader encounters: I imagine that they are used here to confirm that the form of government just established, based on a boule of Four Hundred and a citizen body of 'Five Thousand', is not to be abolished immediately.

νεῖμαι δὲ καὶ τοὺς ἄλλους πρὸς τὴν λῆξιν ἑκάστην: Another difficult clause. λῆξις can denote either the process of allotment (e.g. Plat. *Critias*, 113 B 8, *Legg*. VI. 765 D 1) or what is allotted (e.g. Plat. *Critias*, 113 C 1, *Legg*. V. 740 A 3, 747 E 4): Fritz & Kapp, 177 n. 97, accordingly argue that here it must mean the term of office allotted to one of the four divisions. However, we obtain a far better sense both here and in 31. iii if we may suppose that the word is used in an unparallelled way and denotes the four divisions themselves (e.g. Wilamowitz, *A.u.A.*, ii. 116, E. Meyer, *Forschungen*, ii. 435). It is not clear who τοὺς ἄλλους are: those who believe that the four βουλαί each or together comprise four hundred men (cf. previous note) suppose that they are the remainder of the Five Thousand; if, as is more likely, the four βουλαί comprise all of the Five Thousand who are over thirty, the best interpretation that can be suggested is that τοὺς ἄλλους are those of the Five Thousand who are under thirty and who will become members of the βουλαί when they reach thirty (cf. Wilamowitz, *A.u.A.*, ii. 116 n. 10, Busolt, *G.G.*, III. ii. 1487 with n. 1: presumably young men under eighteen, or perhaps under twenty [cf. p. 495], were not included among the Five Thousand). In the following sentence τοὺς ἄλλους is used in contrast to τοὺς ... ἑκατὸν ἄνδρας.

τοὺς δ' ἑκατὸν ἄνδρας ... τέτταρα μέρη ὡς ἰσαίτατα: The hundred men are presumably the καταλογεῖς of 29. v (e.g. Wilamowitz, *A.u.A.*, ii. 116) rather than the ἀναγραφεῖς of 30. i (e.g. Moore, 262); and τοὺς ἄλλους should be not whatever group is denoted by those words in the previous sentence but all the Five Thousand except the καταλογεῖς themselves (this awkwardness may be due either to the author(s) of the original draft or to *A.P.*). Here the καταλογεῖς are to divide into four sections themselves and the rest of the Five Thousand; in 31. iii they are to subdivide the Four Hundred (presumably in order to provide a measure of continuity between the 'immediate' and the 'future' constitution: cf. *ad loc.*). ὡς ἰσαίτατα may mean, literally, 'as nearly equally as possible' (e.g. Fritz & Kapp, Moore), or it may mean, more generally, 'as fairly as possible', by criteria which are not stated. ὡς ἰσαίτατα is found also in Plat. *Legg*. V. 744 C 2–3, but *SIG*[3] 531, 29–30 (Dyme, c3), has διακλαρωσάν[τω αἱ συναρ]χίαι ὡς ἰσότατα ἐπὶ τὰς φυλάς.

καὶ διακληρῶσαι: For the verb cf. T. VIII. 30. i, the Decree of Themistocles, M&L 23, 26, and the inscription quoted above. Here the purpose of the allotment must be not to assign men to one or other of the four divisions (e.g. Fritz & Kapp) but to determine the order in which the divisions are to hold office (cf. τὸ λαχὸν μέρος above: e.g. Busolt, *G.G.*, III. ii. 1487, Sandys): it is not stated who is to be responsible for drawing lots. The sentence is best punctuated with one comma after ἰσαίτατα and another after διακληρῶσαι.

καὶ εἰς ἐνιαυτὸν βουλεύειν: Each of the four βουλαί in turn is to hold office for a year (e.g. Busolt, *G.G.*, III. ii. 1487; Beloch, *G.G.*², II. ii. 318, thought that each would serve for a quarter of the year, but then generals and other officials would have to be appointed four times a year, which is unlikely). Kaibel & Wilamowitz, followed by Blass¹⁻³, added τοὺς λαχόντας at the end of the sentence: this makes the sense clearer, but I am not convinced that it restores what *A.P.* wrote; more probably he did not supply a subject either for διακληρῶσαι or for βουλεύειν.

30. iv. ‹βουλεύεσθαι› δὲ: The papyrus' text is clearly defective, and most have sought to cure it by making an insertion before δὲ ᾗ ἂν δοκῇ. Kenyon¹⁻³ suggested ... ⟨βουλεύειν⟩. βουλεύειν; Kaibel & Wilamowitz (cf. Kaibel, *Stil und Text*, 188, and see previous note) βουλεύειν ⟨τοὺς λαχόντας. πράττειν⟩; Blass ¹⁻³ βουλεύειν ⟨τοὺς λαχόντας. βουλεύεσθαι⟩; and Sandys βουλεύειν. ⟨βουλεύεσθαι⟩. Some editors have preferred to put the major break at διακληρῶσαι, followed by καὶ εἰς ἐνιαυτὸν βουλεύεσθαι [[δὲ]] ᾗ ἂν δοκῇ (perhaps intended by the laconic note of H. Richards, *CR* V 1891, 228; Leeuwen; Thalheim). The first approach is better than the second, and more recent editors (including Kenyon in his Berlin ed. and O.C.T., Mathieu & Haussoullier, Oppermann) have rightly judged Sandys' reconstruction to be the most convincing.

περί τε τῶν χρημάτων: One reason for the overthrow of the democracy was that the state could no longer afford the stipends needed if the poorer citizens were to hold office: cf. p. 372 and 29. v with commentary.

ὅπως ἂν: Here as in 29. iv we have the final construction which is standard in Athenian inscriptions of the fifth and fourth centuries: contrast 29. ii with commentary, 29. iii, 31. iii.

σῷα: The papyrus reads σῶα, and that form should be retained. Athenian inscriptions offer σᾶ and σῶα as alternative forms of the neuter plural (Meisterhans & Schwyzer, *G.a.I.*, 66 with n. 580, 149 with n. 1288); see also Eur. fr. 762 Nauck² (σᾶ: quoted by Eustathius as an instance of that spelling), Plat. *Critias*, 111 C 7 (MSS divided between σᾶ and σῶα). However, σῷος and its cases are found in some MSS of Athenian writers (e.g. D. IX. *Phil. iii.* 70, XVIII. *Cor.* 49, XXIV. *Tim.* 106); *E.M.* (741. 38) σωτηρία cites the arguments of Didymus for including iota and of Herodian for omitting it; and Kaibel & Wilamowitz printed σῷα here, to be followed by Kenyon (Berlin ed. and O.C.T.) and most other editors.

εἰς τὸ δέον: It was alleged that in 446 Pericles paid a bribe of 10 talents to induce Plistoanax and the Spartan army to withdraw from Attica, and entered this item in his accounts under the heading εἰς τὸ δέον (Ar. *Nub.* 859 with schol., Pl. *Per.* 23. i–ii, cf. T. II. 21. i: cf. p. 313). Here the meaning is that the boule should ensure that money is spent on what is necessary and is not wasted on what is unnecessary.

κἄν τι θέλωσιν βουλεύσασθαι μετὰ πλειόνων: Provision is made here for meetings of an enlarged boule, in which each current member coopts one man from the remaining three quarters of the qualified citizen body. There is no provision (unless it has been omitted in *A.P.*'s condensation of his material: but on so important a matter he should be given the benefit of the doubt) for assemblies of all of the Five Thousand, or of all of them who are over thirty and so qualified for bouleutic service. Whereas it is arguable that the provision for enlarged meetings of the boule would render assemblies unnecessary, a constitution which made no provision for assemblies of the whole body of men possessed of political rights would be most unusual in a single Greek city (but in federal organisations, like that of Boeotia, sovereign power might be entrusted to a representative body).

The papyrus reads ἐάν τι: to supply a link with the previous sentence Kenyon[1] suggested κἄν, J. B. Mayor (*CR* v 1891, 113) ἐὰν ⟨δέ⟩; one or the other is needed, and the latter has been the more popular.

ἐπεισκαλεῖν ... ἐπείσκλητον: No other instance is known either of the verb or of the adjective in this sense, 'invite(d) in addition'; in *I. v. Magnesia*, 44, 10 (Hellenistic), ἡ ἐπείσκλητος is an extraordinary assembly.

ἐκ τῆς αὐτῆς ἡλικίας: Probably 'with the same age qualification', i.e. over thirty (cf. §ii: e.g. Kenyon, Oxford Translation); 'of the same age(-class) as himself' (e.g. Fritz & Kapp, Moore) is possible but less likely.

τὰς δ' ἕδρας ... ἐὰν μὴ δέωνται πλειόνων: Meetings were to be 'every fifth day': probably the counting is inclusive and this is 'every fourth day' as we should reckon it. In X. *H.* VII. i. 14 κατὰ πενθήμερον is used of an alternation of command between Athens and Sparta every fifth day; in *SIG*[3] 364, 8–9 (Ephesus, early c3), καθ' ἑκάστην πενθήμερον is used of men to be appointed every five days. In the fourth century and probably also in the late fifth the boule met daily except on public holidays (43. iii with commentary) and the assembly had forty regular meetings a year (43. iii–vi with commentary): this body, intermediate in size between the democratic boule and assembly, is to be intermediate in the frequency of its meetings. Nothing is said of a smaller committee which could meet more frequently and so be available to deal with urgent business. This passage must be the source of the note in Hes. (*E* 503) ἕδραι βουλῆς that the boule met κατὰ πεντάημερον.

30. v. κληροῦν δὲ τὴν βουλὴν τοὺς ἐννέα ἄρχοντας: (Kenyon's O.C.T. begins §v at this point: in the original section division of Kaibel &

Wilamowitz, followed in Kenyon's Berlin ed. and many other editions, §v begins at κληροῦν δὲ τοὺς λαχόντας, below.) The boule does not allot the archons, who are appointed by double election (§ii; but D. Flach, *Chiron* vii 1977, 31–2, suggests that the boule is to allot particular offices to particular members of the college); the archons do not allot the boule (whose members are assigned to their division by the καταλογεῖς: §iii), unless it is they who conduct the allotment to determine which division will hold office in which year (as believed by Fritz & Kapp, 178 n. 100). It is therefore highly probable, if not certain, that the text here is corrupt. H. Weil, *REG* iv 1891, 407, suggested πληροῦν, with the meaning 'cause to assemble': the verb is found with meeting-place as object (e.g. Aesch. *Eum.* 570), or, in the passive, of a meeting (e.g. Ar. *Eccl.* 89, cf. πλήρης in 95–6); in D. xxiv. *Tim.* 92 we read δικαστήρια πληροῦτε with the Athenian citizens as subject; and πληροῦν δικαστήρια with the thesmothetae as subject is found in *IG* ii² 466, *b* 33–5, cf. παρα-[πλ]ηρῶσαι δικαστήρια in *IG* ii² 1629 = Tod 200, 206–7, and the passive in 63. ii *fin.* πληροῦν may very well be right; or, as Kaibel pointed out (*Stil und Text*, 188–9), κληροῦν may have been imported here from the beginning of the next sentence and have displaced some other verb.

In the democracy, meetings of the boule and assembly were convened by the prytanes (43. iii with commentary). Here no standing committee is mentioned (cf. previous note), and the archons are given a duty which they may well have had in early Athens (cf. Hignett, *H.A.C.*, 92, 98–9).

τὰς δὲ χειροτονίας κρίνειν . . . τὸν ἐπιψηφιοῦντα: τὰς . . . χειροτονίας κρίνειν means 'to determine (the results of) the voting': the same expression recurs in the description of the duties of the proedri in 44. iii; cf. A. III. *Ctes.* 3. In early Athens the archons probably presided over the meetings which they had summoned. In the democracy meetings of the boule and assembly were held until the early fourth century under the presidency of the fifty prytanes, thereafter of the nine proedri; each board had an ἐπιστάτης picked by lot for a single day (43. iii, 44. i–iii, with commentary); most but not all resolutions of the boule and assembly were decided by show of hands (cf. p. 492), and in these votes, in the assembly if not in the boule, it is likely that no precise count was taken but the presiding officers had to recognise a majority or order a second vote (cf. M. H. Hansen, *GR&BS* xviii 1977, 123–37). The appearance of five proedri (as the nucleus of the Four Hundred) in T. VIII. 67. iii, and of five men here who discharge the function of the fourth-century proedri, had led the unwary to suppose that πρόεδροι was the title of the five men here and of the five men named as presiding officials in M&L 80; but no title is used here, and if we are to rely on Thucydides' language we must notice that according to VIII. 70. i the Four Hundred πρυτάνεις ἑαυτῶν ἀπεκλήρωσαν (see Rhodes, *A.B.*, 28–9). Here the ἐπιστάτης serves for a single day; no term of office is specified for the five.

Blass printed καθ' ἑκάστην ⟨τὴν⟩ ἡμέραν, and that is regular documentary usage in the classical period (cf. Kaibel, *Stil und Text*, 189–90, Meisterhans & Schwyzer, *G.a.I.*, 232 with nn. 1824–5). Nevertheless it is unwise to insist on regularity here: cf. the variety of final conjunctions used in 29. ii (with commentary), iii, iv, 30. iv, 31. iii.

κληροῦν ... τοὺς ἐθέλοντας προσελθεῖν ἐναντίον τῆς βουλῆς: It may seem surprising to us, but would not necessarily seem surprising to an Athenian, that topics for debate should be picked by lot (and in fact in the House of Commons of the United Kingdom private members draw lots for the right to introduce bills). 43. vi records a quota of so many topics of certain kinds for debate at certain meetings of the assembly, and there too the lot may have been used, or the topics may have been chosen by προχειροτονία (cf. *ad loc.*).

πρῶτον μὲν ἱερῶν ... τέταρτον τῶν ἄλλων: The papyrus' πρεσβεῖαι was corrected to the dative plural by W. Wyse, *CR* v 1891, 113. The same order of priorities, with the fourth item labelled ὁσίων, is found in A. I. *Tim.* 23; the same as in Aeschines, except that κήρυξιν and πρεσβείαις are (perhaps wrongly) conflated as a single item, in *A.P.* 43. vi. (Poll. VIII. 96 assigns heralds and embassies to one assembly and sacred and profane business to another: Sandys in his note on this passage quotes a text of Aeschines transposed by Benseler to yield Pollux' pairs.) In each of the three passages the first and fourth items appear in the genitive but the second and third appear in the dative: presumably all three owe this distinction ultimately to the phraseology of the democratic law, which was perhaps echoed in a formula recited at meetings of the assembly; cf. the collection of laws about the boule, *IG* i² 114, 48–9, where Wade-Gery restored [... πρῶτον ἱερ]ά, δεύτερον πρεσβείαν, τρίτον δεμόσ[ια χρέματα ...] (*BSA* xxxiii 1932/3, 121: lines 47–8 in his text and *IG* i³ 105).

τὰ δὲ τοῦ πολέμου ... χρηματίζεσθαι: In [X.] *A.P.* iii. 2 (written, I believe, between 431 and 424: cf. W. G. Forrest, *Klio* lii 1970, 107–16) περὶ τοῦ πολέμου heads the list of topics debated by the boule; two lists of major topics of debate given by Aristotle include περὶ πολέμου καὶ εἰρήνης, without the article (*Pol.* IV. 1298 A 3–7, *Rhet.* I. 1359 B 21–3). Some have thought that this 'future' constitution envisages a time when the Peloponnesian War is over, and that τὰ ... τοῦ πολέμου is to be understood generally (e.g. Moore; Andrewes, *Hist. Comm. Thuc.*, v. 226); but more probably a reference to the Peloponnesian War is intended both here and in [Xenophon]. There is some evidence that during the Peloponnesian War the generals enjoyed a privileged position *vis-à-vis* the boule and assembly (see Rhodes, *A.B.*, 43–6: *SEG* x 86 is dated to the end of Perdiccas' reign, shortly before 413, by C. F. Edson, Ἀρχαία Μακεδονία, [i.] 35, cf. J. W. Cole, *GR&BS* xviii 1977, 29–32 [423/2 or later], to 431 by R. J. Hoffmann, *GR&BS* xvi 1975, 359–77): in this régime they would in any case be members of the boule, but the requirement is that they should be brought before the meeting to speak to it. For ἀκληρωτὶ cf. Lys. xvi. *Mant.* 16, *CIG* 2880, 6 (Miletus).

χρηματίζεσθαι: The active is normally used (χρηματίζειν περὶ τοῦ δεῖνα) both of the raising of a question at a meeting by its presiding officers and of the discussion of a question by a meeting (e.g. 43. iii, iv, 44. iii, M&L 65, 52 cf. 55, 69, 35, *SEG* x 86, 13). χρηματίζειν was preferred here by Kaibel & Wilamowitz[3] and Blass[4], and should be the correct form.

30. vi. τὸν δὲ μὴ ἰόντα εἰς τὸ βουλευτήριον: Cf. the 'Draconian constitution', 4. iii, with commentary. Whereas democracies tended to pay salaries to encourage the poorer citizens to attend, oligarchies tended to impose fines to deter the richer citizens from non-attendance. Neither the Old Bouleuterium, built in the first half of the fifth century (cf. p. 522), nor the New, built *c.* 400, could easily accommodate a boule of about 1,000 members (see Rhodes, *A.B.*, 30–1).

τὴν ὥραν: 'The time' in general; not necessarily 'the hour' or 'the time of day' (*pace* Moore).

εὑρισκόμενος ἄφεσιν: This use of the present is unparalleled, and R. Y. Tyrrell and H. Richards suggested εὑρόμενος (*CR* v 1891, 181), but the present is defended by Wilamowitz, *A.u.A.*, ii. 118 n. 17, who supposed that the member sent his application for leave and departed, and the boule probably considered his application in his absence. We are not told by what mechanism, if any, Polystratus obtained leave of absence from the boule of Four Hundred after eight days (Lys. xx. *Poly.* 14, 16): he held an ἀρχή (§17), and perhaps needed no special permission. ἄφεσις can mean 'release' in a variety of contexts: the closest parallel cited by LSJ is στρατείας . . . ἄφεσιν in Pl. *Ages.* 24. iii; in *A.P.* 43. iii a day when there is no meeting of the boule is termed ἀφέσιμος; cf. also D. xxiv. *Tim.* 26 (ἀφειμένης τῆς βουλῆς).

31. i. ταύτην μὲν οὖν . . . τήνδε: The beginning of ch. 31 coincides with the beginning of col. xiii of the papyrus, and the beginning of the second scribe's work; he continues to the middle of col. xx (41. ii). See Introduction, p. 3.

The two draft constitutions are separated by a sentence cast in narrative form. If, as I suspect, the two were published together, there must have been some formula at this point in the original text to separate the 'future' from the 'immediate' constitution: e.g. ταύτῃ μὲν τῇ πολιτείᾳ χρῆσθαι Ἀθηναίους ἐν τῷ μέλλοντι χρόνῳ, ἐν δὲ τῷ παρόντι καιρῷ τῇδε.

βουλεύειν μὲν τετρακοσίους κατὰ τὰ πάτρια: A boule of four hundred had been instituted by Solon (though many modern scholars have denied it: see 8. iv with commentary). This will have been known, to some if not to all, in the late fifth century, and κατὰ τὰ πάτρια is a piece of the oligarchs' propaganda: their changes were represented as a restoration of institutions from a past that was better than the present.

τετταράκοντα ἐξ ἑκάστης φυλῆς: Cleisthenes' ten tribes were too firmly rooted to be abolished; Solon's boule had comprised a hundred men from each of the four Ionian tribes.

ἐκ προκρίτων . . . ὑπὲρ τριάκοντα ἔτη γεγονότων: For appointment to the boule here and for appointment to the boule and magistracies in the 'future' constitution there is the same minimum age, thirty; and in each case we are not told how many the πρόκριτοι are to be or who is to make the final choice from among them (cf. 30. ii with commentary). The φυλέται who make the πρόκρισις are presumably to be limited to members of the Five Thousand over eighteen or twenty, or over thirty. It was perhaps envisaged that this procedure should first operate for the election of the boule of 411/0; but it seems clear that there was in fact only one boule of Four Hundred, which held office from late 412/1 to early 411/0 (for the dates see 32. i, 33. i, with commentary). Perhaps the Four Hundred formally reappointed themselves for the new year (though it is unlikely that any men other than the Four Hundred themselves would have been involved in the charade); more probably by the new year they were less interested in maintaining a show of legitimacy.

τάς τε ἀρχὰς καταστῆσαι: Only the generals and other military officials are dealt with in §§ii–iii.

περὶ τοῦ ὅρκου ὅντινα χρὴ ὀμόσαι γράψαι: Presumably the oath is to be taken by the ἀρχαί (Kaibel, *Stil und Text*, 190). Justifiably, Kaibel found περὶ τοῦ ὅρκου . . . γράψαι obscure: it can hardly mean 'propose' in a sentence which entrusts full powers to the Four Hundred; 'draw up the oath' should be τὸν ὅρκον (συγ)γράψαι. Kaibel & Wilamowitz[1] suggested that this clause should be governed by πράττειν in the next, and that the correct ending of this clause might be ὅντινα χρὴ ὀμόσαντας ἄρξαι; Wilcken, *Sb. Berlin* 1935, 42–3, proposed to delete γράψαι and read ὅντινα . . . τῶν ἄλλων as a clause indicating the matters to be covered by the oath—in which case this sentence would not after all entrust full powers to the Four Hundred (but see F. Taeger, *Gnomon* xiii 1937, 352, F. Sartori,

COMMENTARY ON THE *ATH. POL.* [31. i

La crisi del 411 a.C. nell'Athenaion Politeia di Aristotele, 90–1). I wonder whether περὶ has been wrongly inserted and this clause should read καὶ τὸν ὅρκον ὅντινα χρὴ ὀμόσαι γράψαι.

<καὶ> περὶ τῶν νόμων: καὶ, added by Kenyon[1], is necessary unless we accept Wilcken's proposal (cf. previous note).

πράττειν ᾗ ἂν ἡγῶνται συμφέρειν: This sentence confers full powers on the Four Hundred, and it is not accidental that there is no mention of assemblies of the Five Thousand (contr. 30. iv with commentary).

31. ii. τοῖς δὲ νόμοις ... μηδ' ἑτέρους θέσθαι: The subject of χρῆσθαι and the other verbs should be τοὺς Ἀθηναίους (Sartori, *La crisi del 411 a.C.*, 92–3; for (τι)θέσθαι νόμον cf. 45. i). The indefinite οἳ ἂν τεθῶσιν should cover not only such laws as have already been enacted but also any further laws that may be enacted; in view of the μὴ ἐξεῖναι μετακινεῖν μηδὲ ἑτέρους θέσθαι which follows, the 'further' laws are perhaps to be envisaged as supplementary, not modificatory. περὶ τῶν πολιτικῶν, if the papyrus' text is right, must mean not 'about public affairs' but, more narrowly, constitutional laws, laws about the working of the πολιτεία (e.g. Fritz & Kapp, Moore), a usage which is not unthinkable but seems to be without parallel (σχῆμα πολιτικὸν τοῦ λόγου in T. VIII. 89. iii is perhaps closest). It was claimed both in the resolutions at Colonus (cf. 29. v with commentary) and in the publication of the 'immediate' and 'future' constitutions together that the régime of the Four Hundred was an emergency régime, not intended to last for ever; yet the ban on constitutional change which seems to be envisaged here would make peaceful transition to any other form of constitution impossible.

τῶν δὲ στρατηγῶν τὸ νῦν εἶναι ... τῶν πεντακισχιλίων: For τὸ νῦν εἶναι as a fossilised expression with purely adverbial force cf. X. *Cyr.* v. iii. 42, Plat. *Rep.* VI. 506 E 1. I imagine the contrast to be between immediate arrangements made in a hurry for the remainder of 412/1 (Athens was at war and could not manage without military commanders) and arrangements to be made in due course for 411/0 and, if necessary, thereafter (cf. Fritz & Kapp, 178–9 n. 103, Moore, 263–4); but Andrewes notes the emphatic position of ἐξ ἁπάντων and prefers to see a contrast between the time of the 'immediate' and that of the 'future' constitution (*Hist. Comm. Thuc.*, v. 230–1, cf. M. L. Lang, *AJP* lxxxviii 1967, 186). As with the Four Hundred themselves, we may doubt whether even the formality of a fresh appointment for 411/0 was observed. It is not stated who is to make the immediate choice: perhaps it was in fact made by the inner caucus of the revolutionaries and in due course was ratified by the Four Hundred. If the text is to be taken at its face value, men aged under thirty are not in this régime to be excluded from the generalship (contr. 30. ii with commentary).

401

τὴν δὲ βουλὴν ἐπειδὰν καταστῇ: The Four Hundred were probably appointed on the spot at Colonus (T. VIII. 67. iii, cf. pp. 380–1): they occupied the bouleuterium ὕστερον (T. VIII. 69. i); according to A.P. 32. i the old boule was dismissed on 14 Thargelion (xi) but the new 'entered' on 22 Thargelion. Probably 14 Thargelion was the day when the old boule was dismissed by the Four Hundred and 22 Thargelion was the day when the Four Hundred formally inaugurated their rule (cf. on 32. i); and probably the ἀναγραφεῖς drafted their constitutions between the Colonus assembly and 22 Thargelion and so could refer to the 'establishment' of the boule of Four Hundred as an event still in the future.

ἐξέτασιν <ἐν> ὅπλοις: ἐν was added by W. Wyse, CR v 1891, 113, Blass, LZB 1891, 304, cf. X. Cyr. II. iv. 1, Anab. v. iii. 3 (v.l. σὺν); that is a better correction than ἐξέτασιν ὅπλων, suggested by W. G. Rutherford, CR v 1891, 113, cf. T. IV. 74. iii, VI. 45.

γραμματέα: There is no evidence for a secretary to the generals in democratic Athens.

τὸν εἰσιόντα ἐνιαυτὸν: I take that to be 411/0 (cf. Dover, Hist. Comm. Thuc., iv. 276); there is no need for emendation.

αὐτοκράτορας: When individuals or boards in Athens were made αὐτοκράτορες (or, in the fourth century, κύριοι) they were given a free hand to do a particular job with less interference or need to secure approval of their actions than they would otherwise be subject to, but precisely how far and in what respects they were to be free tends not to be specified (cf. Rhodes, A.B., 171 n. 1, 180 n. 4, 186–8). The following clause, stating that the generals are to ask the Four Hundred for anything that they need, does nothing to resolve the problem.

καὶ ἄν: Kenyon retains the reading of the papyrus, which is possible but unlikely (Meisterhans & Schwyzer, G.a.I., 255–6 with nn. 1988–9, regard ἄν = ἐάν as 'gänzlich fremd ... der attischen Inschriften', but nevertheless cite a few examples): Herwerden (BPW xix 1891, 611, cf. Herwerden & Leeuwen) preferred καὶ ἐάν, which is the easiest correction; Sandys κἄν.†

31. iii. ἑλέσθαι δὲ καὶ ἵππαρχον ἕνα καὶ φυλάρχους δέκα: The commander-in-chief of the cavalry (always two or more under other régimes: see 30. ii with commentary) and the commanders of the tribal regiments of cavalry. It is surprising to find no mention of the taxiarchs, the commanders of the tribal regiments of hoplites, who appear with the hipparchs and phylarchs in 30. ii and 61. iii–v: the omission may be due to A.P. or to a copyist, and Wilamowitz proposed to insert after ἵππαρχον ἕνα ⟨καὶ ταξιάρχους δέκα⟩ (A.u.A., ii. 115 n. 9, Kaibel & Wilamowitz³).

τὸ δὲ λοιπὸν ... κατὰ τὰ γεγραμμένα: Presumably, as in the case of the generals, there is to be an immediate appointment for the remainder of 412/1, followed by a more regular appointment for 411/0 (but Andrewes punctuates not before but after τὸ δὲ λοιπόν, making the contrast that between the new régime and the democracy: *Hist. Comm. Thuc.*, v. 231–2). τὰ γεγραμμένα will be the procedure laid down in §ii for the future election of generals (Sartori, *La crisi del 411 a.C.*, 97–8).

τῶν δ' ἄλλων ἀρχῶν ... πλέον ἢ ἅπαξ ἄρξαι τὴν αὐτὴν ἀρχήν: In the fourth century a man could serve twice in the boule, and as often as the people were willing to elect him in military offices, but otherwise only once (62. iii with commentary); in the 'Draconian constitution' repetition is forbidden πρὸ τοῦ πάντας ἐξελθεῖν (4. iii with commentary); in the 'future' constitution no restriction is directly mentioned, but appointment of major officials from the current boule will prevent any one from holding office more than one year in four (30. ii with commentary). A ban on repetition was not peculiar to democracies, but might be adopted whenever it was thought that offices should be shared equally among those who were equally eligible.

μήτε τούτοις μήτε ἄλλῳ μηδενί: I find this totally obscure. Fritz & Kapp, 179 n. 108, suggest that the purpose of the tortuous phraseology is to make it clear that neither the present bouleutae and generals nor any one else may repeat any office except that of bouleutes or general; but if that was its purpose it must be judged a failure. Possibly the original text was clearer and *A.P.* in condensing has lost the meaning.

εἰς δέ τὸν ἄλλον χρόνον: This sentence, with its reference to the four λήξεις of 30. iii, looks ahead not to 411/0 but to the 'future' constitution (cf. M. Cary, *JHS* lxxii 1952, 57): I have suggested that it represents a rider added by one of the 'moderate' ἀναγραφεῖς, calling on the καταλογεῖς to include in their registration a division of the Four Hundred into the four λήξεις, to facilitate the introduction of the 'future' constitution in due course (cf. p. 389).

ἵνα νεμηθῶσιν οἱ τετρακόσιοι εἰς τὰς τέτταρας λήξεις: For the variety of final conjunctions in the documents of chs 29–31 cf. 29. ii (with commentary), iii, iv, 30. iv. Extremists intended the rule of the Four Hundred, and indeed of the present Four Hundred, to continue indefinitely; according to the theory embodied in the 'immediate' constitution the present Four Hundred would be succeeded by other councils of four hundred as long as 'the immediate crisis' lasted; 'moderate' oligarchs no doubt hoped that the present Four Hundred would soon be replaced by a régime more to their taste. If the constitution of 31 were to be succeeded by the constitution of 30 it might be thought desirable, either for the sake of continuity or to split the Four Hundred, to distribute the Four Hundred through all four λήξεις; and I imagine that the purpose of this clause is to take that preparatory measure for the transition to the constitution of 30.

ὅταν τοῖς ἀστοῖς γίγνηται μετὰ τῶν ἄλλων βουλεύειν: It seems clear that ἀστοῖς is the reading of the papyrus, but the city was not separated from the Piraeus in 411 as it was in 404-403, and it is hard to give an acceptable sense to it: Wilamowitz, *A.u.A.*, ii. 120-1 cf. 116, supposed the ἀστοί to be contrasted with the Athenians in the fleet at Samos (accepted by Hignett, *H.A.C.*, 370); Fritz & Kapp, 179 n. 109, suppose them to be 'the ordinary citizens', men who are members of the Five Thousand but not of the Four Hundred. T. Nicklin and E. Poste, *CR* v 1891, 228, proposed drastically to rewrite the text of this sentence; R. Y. Tyrrell, *op. cit.*, 181, suggested τοῖς αὐτοῖς, and Sandys [[τοῖς]] αὐτοῖς, to make this clause refer to the time when 'they' (i.e. the Four Hundred) can join 'the rest' (of the Five Thousand) in deliberation, the meaning which Fritz & Kapp extract more awkwardly from the papyrus' text. Sandys' text should be accepted. Gomme, *CR* xlii 1928, 225 (accepting τοῖς αὐτοῖς), proposed to substitute for the present subjunctive the aorist γένηται, but the present may be retained.

διανειμάντων: The change from the infinitive of *oratio obliqua* to the imperative of *oratio recta* may confirm (but is not striking enough to prove) that this sentence is an addition to the pair of constitutional documents.

οἱ ἑκατὸν ἄνδρες: The καταλογεῖς of 29. v: cf. 30. iii with commentary.

32. i. οἱ μὲν οὖν ἑκατὸν ... ταύτην ἀνέγραψαν τὴν πολιτείαν: Cf. 30. i with commentary.

ἐπικυρωθέντων δὲ τούτων ὑπὸ τοῦ πλήθους, ἐπιψηφίσαντος Ἀριστομάχου: For a discussion of when, if at all, these documents were approved and published see pp. 385-9, where I argue that the ἀναγραφεῖς were appointed at the Colonus assembly and did their work before the formal inauguration of the Four Hundred. There can have been no assembly theoretically open to all whom the democracy regarded as citizens later than that held at Colonus (and so Lenschau and his followers thought that the ἀναγραφεῖς did their work before the Colonus assembly and their drafts were approved at that assembly); subsequently an assembly of 'citizens' would be an assembly of the Five Thousand, and *A.P.* with his reference to the Five Thousand in the previous sentence is clearly thinking of such a meeting, but although it is not impossible that the word πλῆθος should be so used (cf. Andrewes, *PCPS*[2] xxii 1976, 22) it is very hard in the light of Thucydides' narrative to believe that such a meeting was held (*pace* Busolt, *G.G.*, III. ii. 1490 cf. 1484 n.). Beloch's moving of the ἀναγραφεῖς and their documents to the period after the fall of the Four Hundred has at least the merit of providing a possible occasion for this meeting of the πλῆθος. Yet the naming of the ἐπιστάτης, and the dates that follow, suggest that *A.P.*'s statement has documentary backing (though in contemporary documents the formula naming the ἐπιστάτης is regularly ὁ δεῖνα ἐπεστάτει): if they are to be salvaged the least difficult explanation is that Aristomachus was in fact ἐπιστάτης at the Colonus assembly and that the documents of the ἀναγραφεῖς were not approved by any larger body than the Four Hundred (cf. E. Meyer, *Forschungen*, ii. 432: it may be relevant that T. VIII. 69. i *init*. concludes his account of the Colonus assembly κυρώσασα ταῦτα διελύθη); another possibility is that he presided in the meeting of the Four Hundred which approved these documents. Aristomachus is a common name, and this bearer of it cannot be identified.

ἡ μὲν βουλὴ ⟨ἡ⟩ ἐπὶ Καλλίου: I.e. the boule of 412/1. We are probably justified in concluding *e silentio* that Callias was left in office for the remainder of the year, as the treasurers of Athena were left in office (cf. p. 366): cf. 33. i with commentary. Another Callias was archon in 406/5 (34. i with commentary): the Callias of 412/1 (*P.A.* 7887) was sometimes distinguished as Σκαμβωνίδης (*IG* ii² 4960, 38–9) or ὁ μετὰ Κλεόκριτον (Ar. *Lys.*, *hyp*. i, [Pl.] *X. Or.* 835 D, E); *A.P.*'s failure to distinguish him from the later Callias may be adduced in support of those who believe him to be using a source written very shortly after the events, such as the defence of Antiphon (cf. p. 367).

πρὶν διαβουλεῦσαι: 'Before completing its term of office.' This use of the active is unique; the middle is found, in the sense 'debate to the end', in T. II. 5. v, VII. 50. iv, And. II. *Red.* 19.

κατελύθη μηνὸς Θαργηλιῶνος τετράδι ἐπὶ δέκα: How this was done is recounted in T. VIII. 69–70. i. The Colonus assembly ended, and ὕστερον the Four Hundred occupied the bouleuterium, as follows: τῇ ... ἡμέρᾳ ἐκείνῃ the oligarchs allowed those not in the plot to go away as usual, while they themselves waited; the Four Hundred with weapons and a gang of young supporters went to the bouleuterium and dismissed the old boule, giving it its pay for the remainder of the year, and this dismissal met with no resistance; the Four Hundred then occupied the bouleuterium, drew lots to appoint prytanes, and inaugurated their rule. Thucydides' narrative is not wholly unambiguous, but probably the dismissal of the old boule did not take place on the same day as the Colonus assembly (Andrewes, *PCPS*² xxii 1976, 22–3 with 25 n. 22, against Hignett, *H.A.C.*, 360): 14 Thargelion (xi) (9 June: see next note and tables in B. D. Meritt, *The Athenian Year*, 218, *P. A. Philos. S.* cxv 1971, 114) will be the date of the democratic boule's actual dismissal, and the Colonus assembly will have been held a very few days before. There is no reason why the date should be fictitious.

οἱ δὲ τετρακόσιοι εἰσῄεσαν ἐνάτῃ φθίνοντος Θαργηλιῶνος: On this later date the Four Hundred 'entered' (as the democratic boule of 411/0 was due to 'enter' on 14 Scirophorion: cf. below). It is of course inconceivable that Athens was left without any form of government for a week after the democracy was overthrown and its boule dismissed; but T. VIII. 70. i states that the Four Hundred formally inaugurated their rule with prayers and sacrifices, and these inaugural ceremonies (known as εἰσιτητήρια: D. XIX. *F.L.* 90, XXI. *Mid.* 114) may well have been delayed for a week; most probably it was during this week that the ἀναγραφεῖς completed their work, and the formal inauguration of the new régime was accompanied by the publication of the constitutional documents (cf. E. Meyer, *Forschungen*, ii. 425–6, 435, Hignett, *H.A.C.*, 359–60, 373; this is preferable to the suggestion of D. Flach, *Chiron* vii 1977, 23–5, that 14 Thargelion was the date of the Colonus assembly and 22 Thargelion that of the dismissal of the old boule and the inauguration of the Four Hundred).

The Athenian calendar used a backward count for the last decade of the month (see now B. D. Meritt, *Mnem.*[4] xxx 1977, 218–20): if, as W. K. Pritchett believes (most recently *CSCA* ix 1976, 181–95, *ZPE* xxxii 1978, 281–5), the day omitted in a 'hollow', 29-day month was δευτέρα φθίνοντος, the 22nd must always have been ἐνάτῃ φθίνοντος; if, as Meritt believes (most recently *AAA* ix 1976, 193–7, *Mnem.*[4] xxx 1977, 217–42), the omitted day was never δευτέρα φθίνοντος and at this date was ἐνάτῃ φθίνοντος, in full months the 22nd will have been ἐνάτῃ φθίνοντος, and in hollow the 22nd will have been ὀγδόῃ φθίνοντος and there will have been no ἐνάτῃ. Meritt's view seems likelier, and entails that the month is a full one and *A.P.*'s date is 22 Thargelion: the Julian date will be 17 June (cf. *The Athenian Year*, 218, *P. A. Philos. S.* cxv 1971, 114).†

ἔδει δὲ τὴν εἰληχυῖαν τῷ κυάμῳ βουλὴν ... Σκιροφοριῶνος: The democratic boule is similarly characterised in T. VIII. 66. i, 69. iv, and in the decree of Demophantus enacted at the beginning of 410/09 (*ap.* And. I. *Myst.* 96). This passage is one of the texts which led B. Keil to the discovery that at any rate in the second half of the fifth century the boule's year of office was not the archontic year of twelve or thirteen lunar months but an independent solar year (*Hermes* xxix 1894, 32–81, 321–72, esp. 38–9; the authenticity of this detail in *A.P.* was denied, unnecessarily, by W. B. Dinsmoor, *Archons of Athens*, 328–9). When this separate bouleutic year was instituted is unknown; it was abandoned in 407 (see Rhodes, *A.B.*, 224–5; to the discussions listed there add G. Donnay, *RBPh* xli 1963, 136, and W. K. Pritchett's acceptance of Meritt's terminal date of 407 in *U. Calif. Pub. Cl. Stud.* v 1970, 34). On Meritt's reckoning 14 Scirophorion (xii) 412/1 will have fallen on 9 July, 1 Hecatombaeon (i) 411/0 on 25 July (*The Athenian Year*, 218, *P. A. Philos. S.* cxv 1971, 114).

32. ii. ἔτεσιν δ' ὕστερον ... μάλιστα ἑκατόν: Cf. T. viii. 68. iv (ἐπ' ἔτει ἑκατοστῷ μάλιστα ἐπειδὴ οἱ τύραννοι κατελύθησαν). The tyranny was ended in 511/0 (cf. p. 195), so by the inclusive reckoning appropriate to Thucydides' ordinal numeral 412/1 is precisely the 100th year after: *A.P.* has retained Thucydides' μάλιστα while changing to a cardinal numeral.

αἰτίων μάλιστα γενομένων ... διαφέρειν: Cf. T. viii. 68, placed at the end of his account of the Colonus assembly (and ending with the chronological note quoted above): Pisander is named first, as the author of the positive proposals made at that assembly (cf. pp. 380–1); next Antiphon, as the most important man behind the scenes; then Phrynichus and Theramenes. Antiphon is described as ἀρετῇ τε οὐδενὸς ὕστερος καὶ κράτιστος ἐνθυμηθῆναι γενόμενος καὶ ἃ γνοίη εἰπεῖν (§i), Theramenes as οὔτε εἰπεῖν οὔτε γνῶναι ἀδύνατος (§iv; cf. also D.S. xiii. 38. ii), and in summing up Thucydides says that the revolution was the work of ἀνδρῶν πολλῶν καὶ ξυνετῶν. Thucydides does not say that the leaders of the revolution were γεγενημένων εὖ (I suspect that this may be a guess by *A.P.*; Hignett, *H.A.C.*, 272, suggests that the supporters of the extreme oligarchy were mainly the aristocratic ἱππεῖς): in fact, of these four, Theramenes was the son of a father who had achieved prominence, while none of the others is known to have belonged to a rich or aristocratic family.

Pisander Ἀχαρνεύς (since the name is rare he is presumably to be identified with the Πείσανδρος Γλαυκέτο Ἀχαρ[ν]εύς who was ἐπιστάτης ἀγαλματοῖν in 421/0 [*IG* i² 370, 1–3, with A. D. J. Makkink, commentary on And. i. *Myst.* 27]; his father may be the Glaucetes who was a butt of the comic poets, *P.A.* 2944 [A. G. Woodhead, *AJP* lxxv 1954, 133 with n. 7]) was attracting the attention of the comedians in the 420's, and is probably the author of *IG* i² 93 (425–412). In 416/5 he was a member of the boule (And. i. *Myst.* 43 with Dover, *Hist. Comm. Thuc.*, iv. 273–6; but many have followed B. Keil, *Hermes* xxix 1894, 354–5 n. 1, in preferring 415/4), and in 415 he played a prominent part in the investigation of the hermocopid scandal, serving on the board of ζητηταί: he is one of two ζητηταί described in And. i. *Myst.* 36 as δοκοῦντες ἐν ἐκείνῳ τῷ χρόνῳ εὐνούστατοι εἶναι τῷ δήμῳ, who insisted that the damage to the hermae had been done ἐπὶ τῇ τοῦ δήμου καταλύσει (for his colleague Charicles see p. 430). In Ar. *Lys.* 490–1 nothing except the imperfect tense suggests that he is not the politician he was (see A. H. Sommerstein, *JHS* xcvii 1977, 113–16, accepting the normal assignment of the play to the Lenaea and suggesting that Aristophanes revised the passage after Pisander's first visit to Athens); but in Thucydides' narrative he is the leader of the men who travelled between Samos and Athens and organised the oligarchic revolution, and in Lys. xxv. *Reip. Del. Defens.* 9 Phrynichus and he are the principal of the δημαγωγοί who changed sides and set up the oligarchy. As a member of the Four Hundred he opposed the attempt of Andocides to return to Athens (And. II. *Red.* 14); on their fall he fled to the Spartans at Decelea (T. VIII. 98. i) and his property was confiscated (Lys. VII. *Ol.* 4 cf. Lyc. *Leocr.* 120–1: M. H. Jameson, *Hist.* xx 1971, 541–68, conjectures that Sophocles made or contributed to an εἰσαγγελία against Pisander, who did not await his trial). Most have regarded him as an opportunist; Woodhead, *op. cit.*, 131–46, tries to present a more favourable picture of him and suggests that he was led to oligarchy through support for Alcibiades, but I am not persuaded; it can at least be said that accusations of cowardice appear unfounded (e.g. Ar. *Av.* 1553–64, X. *Symp.* ii. 14: see Grote, *H.G.* [1869–84], vii. 250 n. 1).

Antiphon Σοφίλου ‘Ραμνούσιος (*P.A.* 1304) was Athens' first professional orator (cf. [Pl.] *X. Or.* 832 c–e); Antiphon the sophist (*P.A.* 1278) is probably rightly distinguished from him (see conveniently W. K. C. Guthrie, *History of Greek Philosophy*, iii. 292–4). His father was a sophist ([Pl.] *X. Or.* 832 c); his grandfather was perhaps one of the tyrants' δορυφόροι (Ant. fr. 1 Sauppe *ap.* Harp. στασιώτης). According to Thucydides Pisander was the most conspicuous of the revolutionaries, but Antiphon was ὁ ... ἅπαν τὸ πρᾶγμα ξυνθεὶς ὅτῳ τρόπῳ κατέστη ἐς τοῦτο καὶ ἐκ πλείστου ἐπιμεληθείς, a man ἐς μὲν δῆμον οὐ παριὼν οὐδ᾽ ἐς ἄλλον ἀγῶνα ἑκούσιος οὐδένα, ἀλλ᾽ ὑπόπτως τῷ πλήθει διὰ δόξαν δεινότητος διακείμενος; in Ar. *Vesp.* 1301–2 he is included in a list of men which ends with οἱ περὶ Φρύνιχον; at some time he attacked Alcibiades (Ant. frs 68–9, from Pl. *Alc.* 3, Ath. XII. 525 B). In the summer of 411 he and Phrynichus were the most prominent of those who attempted to negotiate peace with Sparta (T. VIII. 90. ii); on the fall of the Four Hundred he stayed in Athens but was brought to trial, condemned and executed (Crat. 342 F 5 *ap.* Harp. Ἄνδρων, [Pl.] *X. Or.* 833 D–834 B); the speech which he made at his trial was admired by Thucydides and others, and may be the ultimate source of some of *A.P.*'s non-Thucydidean material (cf. pp. 367–8).†

Phrynichus Στρατωνίδου Δειραδιώτης is omitted by our text of *A.P.* (but here *A.P.* seems to be basing himself on Thucydides, and there is no obvious reason why he should omit Phrynichus—as there is an obvious reason why he should omit Critias from his account of the Thirty: cf. pp. 429–30—so the omission may well be due to a copyist). He is alleged to have come from a poor family and to have become a συκοφάντης (Lys. xx. *Poly.* 11–12); it is probably this Phrynichus whom Ar. *Vesp.* links with Antiphon, and Lys. xxv. *Reip. Del. Defens.* regards him like Pisander as a man who changed sides (cf. above). We know nothing specific about his earlier career, though Lys. xx suggests that he was a contemporary of Polystratus, born *c.* 480 (§10). In 412/1 he was one of Athens' generals, and his intrigues to prevent a revolution and Alcibiades' return led to his deposition (T. VIII. 48–51, 54. iii); T. VIII. 68. iii says that he now supported the oligarchy, thinking that it would not favour the return of Alcibiades; Arist. *Pol.* v. 1305 B 22–7 alludes to the demagoguic methods practised by him and his supporters within the Four Hundred, which is hard to fit in with what we know from other sources. With Antiphon and others he attempted to negotiate peace with Sparta (T. VIII. 90. ii); after the failure of that attempt he was murdered, but later he was judged to be a traitor and those involved in his murder were honoured (T. VIII. 92. ii, Lys. XIII. *Agor.* 71–6 cf. VII. *Ol.* 4, M&L 85, Lyc. *Leocr.* 112–15).

On Theramenes Ἁγνωνος Στειριεύς see pp. 359–60: his father had a distinguished public career ending with service as a πρόβουλος (cf. p. 373), but his grandfather Nicias was alleged to have been a φορτηγός. Though his aims were different from those of the extremists, and he helped to overthrow the régime which he had helped to set up (cf. 33. ii with commentary), it seems clear that the difference between them did not become apparent until after the régime of the Four Hundred had come into being.

32. iii. οἱ μὲν πεντακισχίλιοι λόγῳ μόνον ᾑρέθησαν: T. VIII. 92. xi, 93. ii, cf. 89. ii (τοὺς πεντακισχιλίους ἔργῳ καὶ μὴ ὀνόματι χρῆναι ἀποδεικνύναι), makes it clear that the list of the Five Thousand was not completed or published; this passage and 33. ii, and Lys. xx. *Poly.* 13, xxx. *Nic.* 8, are consistent with that; but 30. i and 32. i allege that the ἀναγραφεῖς who drafted the constitutional documents of 30–1 were appointed by the Five Thousand. For a discussion see on 30. i: I believe that it was supposed either officially at the time or (less probably) afterwards by *A.P.* or his source that the body which appointed the ἀναγραφεῖς, in fact the Colonus assembly, had been a (provisional) assembly of the Five Thousand, and that *A.P.* did not regard that as incompatible with the fact that there were no further assemblies of the Five Thousand and the definitive list was never produced. Andrewes, however, doubts whether *A.P.* involved himself in this contradiction, and suggests that *A.P.* wrongly believed that the Five Thousand did exist and did not intend by λόγῳ μόνον here to deny their existence (*Hist. Comm. Thuc.*, v. 238–9, comparing T. II. 65. ix, VI. 78. iii, Lys. IX. *Mil.* 21, Is. v. *Phil.* 6).

μετὰ τῶν δέκα τῶν αὐτοκρατόρων: The generals, who are described as αὐτοκράτορες in the 'immediate' constitution, 31. ii. (But Gomme, *CR* xl 1926, 10, perversely supposed them to be the ten συγγραφεῖς of T. VIII. 67. i.)

εἰσελθόντες εἰς τὸ βουλευτήριον ἦρχον τῆς πόλεως: Cf. T. VIII. 70. i (οἱ τετρακόσιοι ἐσελθόντες ἐς τὸ βουλευτήριον ... ὕστερον δὲ πολὺ μεταλλάξαντες τῆς τοῦ δήμου διοικήσεως ... τά τε ἄλλα ἔνεμον κατὰ κράτος τὴν πόλιν).

καὶ πρὸς Λακεδαιμονίους πρεσβευσάμενοι: Thucydides gives a detailed account. The oligarchs first approached Agis at Decelea, but he reacted by summoning reinforcements to take advantage of Athens' disarray; later they approached Agis again, and with his encouragement sent envoys to Sparta (VIII. 70. ii–71), but the crew of their ship handed over the envoys to the Argives (VIII. 86. ix); when opposition to the extremists was mounting, Antiphon, Phrynichus and others were sent to Sparta κατὰ τάχος, but failed to achieve anything (VIII. 90. ii, 91. i).

ἐφ' οἷς ἑκάτεροι τυγχάνουσιν ἔχοντες ... καὶ τὴν ἀρχὴν τῆς θαλάττης ἀφήσουσιν: Athens' proposal and Sparta's demand are not given by Thucydides, who says in VIII. 90. ii ἐπιστείλαντες παντὶ τρόπῳ ὅστις καὶ ὁπωσοῦν ἀνεκτὸς ξυναλλαγῆναι πρὸς τοὺς Λακεδαιμονίους, and in VIII. 91. iii (as an instance of what was 'really' the case: cf. p. 362) that the extremists were willing καὶ τοὺς πολεμίους ἐσαγαγόμενοι ἄνευ τειχῶν καὶ νεῶν ξυμβῆναι καὶ ὁπωσοῦν τὰ τῆς πόλεως ἔχειν, εἰ τοῖς γε σώμασι σφῶν ἄδεια ἔσται. Phrynichus after his death (Lyc. *Leocr.* 112), Antiphon and others (Crat. 342 F 5b *ap.* [Pl.] *X. Or.* 833 E) were accused of betraying the interests of the city in their negotiations with Sparta, and those who were brought to trial will no doubt have insisted in their defence (whether truthfully or not) that they would not have accepted terms detrimental to Athens. Moore, 265, suggests that the negotiations in fact failed because the oligarchs could not answer for the fleet at Samos. The stage in the negotiations which *A.P.* reports, though not in Thucydides, may well be authentic.

33. i. μῆνας μὲν οὖν ἴσως τέτταρας: Repeated by Harp. τετρακόσιοι, citing *A.P.* The Four Hundred had seized power in the middle of Thargelion (xi) 412/1 (32. i); we are now told that their archon Mnasilochus held office for the first two months of 411/0; if he held office for no more than two months *A.P.* has rounded up, perhaps because the rule of the Four Hundred spanned four calendar months. The use of ἴσως (rather than μάλιστα) to qualify a numeral is cited by LSJ only from comedy (Ar. *Plut.* 1058, Damoxenus, fr. 3, 2 Kock).

ἦρξεν ἐξ αὐτῶν Μνασίλοχος δίμηνον ἐπὶ Θεοπόμπου ἄρχοντος: Callias, the democrats' archon for 412/1, was apparently allowed to serve his full year (32. i with commentary); but the fall of the Four Hundred was marked by the appointment of a new archon for the remainder of 411/0, and *A.P.*'s language shows that Theopompus came to be officially regarded as the archon of that year (cf. D.S. xiii. 38. i). Mnasilochus (the papyrus has Μνασίμαχος with λο written above; M & L 81, 2, now has [Μνασιλ]όχου) is presumably to be identified with the Mnesilochus who was one of the Thirty in 404/3 (X. *H.* ii. iii. 2: thus Kirchner, *P.A.* 10324). Kaibel and Wilamowitz printed Μνησίλοχος, but the Doric form of the name is defended by B. Keil, *Hermes* xxix 1894, 39 n. 1.

ἡττηθέντες δὲ τῇ περὶ Ἐρέτριαν ναυμαχίᾳ: T. viii. 91. ii-96 gives a detailed account. Forty-two ships from the Peloponnese came close to Athens and caused great alarm; when they sailed on to Oropus the Athenians hurriedly dispatched ships to join a squadron based on Eretria; the Athenians with thirty-six ships were forced to fight a battle unprepared and were defeated: the approach of the Peloponnesian ships had encouraged fears that the extremists were planning to betray the city to the Spartans, and news of the battle precipitated the overthrow of the Four Hundred. οἱ Ἀθηναῖοι was added after ἡττηθέντες by Herwerden (*BPW* xi 1891, 323, cf. Herwerden & Leeuwen) and H. Richards (*CR* v 1891, 181); but although the change of subject is awkward it is not incredible that *A.P.* in summarising Thucydides should have perpetrated this piece of awkwardness.

τῆς Εὐβοίας ἀποστάσης ὅλης πλὴν Ὠρεοῦ: Cf. T. viii. 95. vii (καὶ ὕστερον οὐ πολλῷ Εὔβοιαν ἅπασαν ἀποστήσαντες πλὴν Ὠρεοῦ· ταύτην δὲ αὐτοὶ Ἀθηναῖοι εἶχον).

χαλεπῶς ἐνεγκόντες ἐπὶ τῇ συμφορᾷ μάλιστα τῶν προγεγενημένων: Cf. T. viii. 96. i (ἔκπληξις μεγίστη δὴ τῶν πρὶν παρέστη. οὔτε γὰρ ἡ ἐν Σικελίᾳ ξυμφορά . . . οὔτε ἄλλο οὐδέν πω οὕτως ἐφόβησεν). Kaibel, *Stil und Text*, 191, was inclined to see a deliberate echo of ἀξιολογώτατον τῶν προγεγενημένων in T. i. 1. i. The addition of ταύτῃ before τῇ συμφορᾷ (Hude, cf. Γ. *A.* Παπαβασίλειος, *Ἀθ.* iii 1891, 283, Kaibel, *Stil und Text*, 190-1) is an improvement but not a necessity.

πλείω γὰρ ἐκ τῆς Εὐβοίας ἢ τῆς Ἀττικῆς ἐτύγχανον ὠφελούμενοι: Cf. T. viii. 96. ii (Εὔβοιαν ἀπωλωλέκεσαν, ἐξ ἧς πλείω ἢ τῆς Ἀττικῆς ὠφελοῦντο). Agis' occupation of Decelea, in 413, had made Athens more dependent than ever on friendly territory which could be reached by sea; the importance of Euboea is stressed also in T. ii. 14, vii. 28. i.

κατέλυσαν τοὺς τετρακοσίους . . . ἐκ τῶν ὅπλων: Cf. T. viii. 97. i: the Athenians held an assembly on the Pnyx (as under the democracy), ἐν ᾗπερ καὶ τοὺς τετρακοσίους καταπαύσαντες τοῖς πεντακισχιλίοις ἐψηφίσαντο τὰ πράγματα παραδοῦναι (εἶναι δὲ αὐτῶν ὁπόσοι καὶ ὅπλα παρέχονται). For the Five Thousand as those of hoplite status and above see 29. v with commentary; the convenient contraction ἐκ τῶν ὅπλων is found twice in this chapter but nowhere else (4. ii uses τοῖς ὅπλα παρεχομένοις). A decision must have been taken now, whether or not one had been taken earlier, on the part to be played in the state by men who had been of hoplite status but were now too old to fight (cf. p. 383).

T. VIII. 97. ii goes on to say ἐγίγνοντο δὲ καὶ ἄλλαι πυκναὶ ἐκκλησίαι, ἀφ' ὧν καὶ νομοθέτας καὶ τἆλλα ἐψηφίσαντο ἐς τὴν πολιτείαν; but he gives no more indication than *A.P.* of how the state was organised under the intermediate régime of 411/0. D.S. XIII. 38. i is no more informative: Ἀθηναῖοι τὴν ἐκ τῶν τετρακοσίων ὀλιγαρχίαν κατέλυσαν καὶ τὸ σύστημα τῆς πολιτείας ἐκ τῶν ὁπλιτῶν συνεστήσαντο (ὁπλιτῶν Krüger: πολιτῶν codd.). The documents of Crat. 342 F 5b *ap.* [Pl.] *X. Or.* 833 D–834 B are evidence for a boule divided into prytanies and equipped with a secretary and an ἐπιστάτης who might come from the same tribe (as they might not under the democracy until the creation of the proedri: see on 54. iii), and for generals, a δικαστήριον and thesmothetae to organise it, the Eleven, and demarchs. The decree of 410/09 *ap.* And. I. *Myst.* 96 describes the boule of the restored democracy as ἡ βουλὴ οἱ πεντακόσιοι οἱ λαχόντες τῷ κυάμῳ, and we may guess that the boule of the intermediate régime numbered five hundred (T. VIII. 86. vi is not enough to prove this, but four hundred was now an inauspicious number, and the Four Hundred are referred to in terms suggesting that there was only one boule of that size at this time) but was elected. These meagre indications point to a constitution closer in structure to that of the democracy than that of the 'future' constitution of 30, and there is no good reason to suppose that that constitution was now brought into effect.

It has normally been assumed that τὰ πράγματα παρέδωκαν means that an assembly of the Five Thousand became the effective sovereign body in the state, and I believe this to be correct; G. E. M. de Ste. Croix argued in *Hist.* v 1956, 1–23, that the assembly and lawcourts of the democracy were restored but the right to hold office was restricted to the Five Thousand (cf. B. R. I. Sealey, *CSCA* viii 1975, 271–95); I have attempted to answer his arguments in *JHS* xcii 1972, 115–27. *A.P.* uses τὴν ... πολιτείαν ἐπιτρέψαι in 29. v, μεταδιδόναι τῶν πραγμάτων and τῆς πολιτείας in 36. i (cf. 40. ii, 42. i); I would stress that, as shown by 7. iii–8. i, 26. ii, the thetes were legally debarred from holding office even under the democracy (see esp. 7. iv with commentary). The rule of the Four Hundred had proved unsatisfactory not because they came from a limited class but because they seized unlimited power for themselves, and we should expect that to be the aspect of oligarchy which the intermediate régime was most concerned to avoid (but the boule of the intermediate régime may have been slightly more powerful than that of the democracy: see Rhodes, *A.B.*, 166, 182–90).

ψηφισάμενοι μηδεμίαν ἀρχὴν εἶναι μισθοφόρον: Cf. T. VIII. 97. i (καὶ μισθὸν μηδένα φέρειν μηδεμιᾷ ἀρχῇ). This is a reiteration of one of the decisions taken at the Colonus assembly (29. v with commentary).

33. ii. αἰτιώτατοι δ' ἐγένοντο τῆς καταλύσεως Ἀριστοκράτης καὶ Θηραμένης: Cf. T. VIII. 89. ii, 91–2, naming the leaders of the opposition to the extremists as Theramenes, Aristocrates and others; Lys. XII. *Erat.* 66–7, in a passage whose object is to blacken Theramenes, alleges that ἕως μὲν ἐτιμᾶτο Theramenes was loyal (to the oligarchy), but when he saw Pisander, Callaeschrus and others gaining an advantage over him but losing the ear of the πλῆθος he decided to cooperate with Aristocrates; D.S. XIII. 38. ii names only Theramenes, and says that he was the one man to advocate recalling Alcibiades. Aristocrates Σκελλίου came from a family which, if not demonstrably of the old aristocracy, was prominent in Athens for several generations (cf. Davies, *A.P.F.*, 56–7; but IG^2 772 has been rediscovered and republished as *Hesp.* xlii 1, and the letters other than sigma do not suggest a date before *c.* 450): apart from that inscription, he first appears as one of the men who swore to the Peace of Nicias and the alliance with Sparta in 421 (T. V. 19. ii, 24, with A. Andrewes & D. M. Lewis, *JHS* lxxvii 1957, 179); he served as general in 413/2 (T. VIII. 9. ii), and as taxiarch under the Four Hundred (T. VIII. 92. iv); like Theramenes (D.S. XIII. 47. vi–iii, 49–51) he served as general with the fleet in and after 410 (M&L 84, 35); unlike Theramenes he was also general after Alcibiades' return to Athens, in 407/6 and 406/5, which suggests that he may have been less closely connected with the oligarchs than Theramenes (X. *H.* I. iv. 21, v. 16); and he was one of the generals condemned after Arginusae (X. *H.* I. vii. 2: cf. on 34. i).

A.P. does not name the leaders of the extremists. T. VIII. 90. i names Phrynichus, Aristarchus (*P.A.* 1663: Davies, *A.P.F.*, 48, thinks it impossible to decide whether the choregus of 422/1 is identical with the oligarch of 411), Pisander and Antiphon; X. *H.* II. iii. 46 names Aristoteles (*P.A.* 2057: a member of the Thirty in 404/3), Melanthius (otherwise unknown) and Aristarchus.

οὐ συναρεσκόμενοι . . . οὐδὲν ἐπαναφέροντες τοῖς πεντακισχιλίοις: According to Thucydides they expressed alarm over Alcibiades and the fleet, and over the attempt to come to terms with Sparta, and insisted τοὺς πεντακισχιλίους ἔργῳ καὶ μὴ ὀνόματι χρῆναι ἀποδεικνύναι καὶ τὴν πολιτείαν ἰσαιτέραν καθιστάναι, but really they were motivated by personal ambition and their belief that the extreme oligarchy was doomed to failure (VIII. 89. ii–iv); their agitation led to a mutiny in response to which the extremists offered to hold constitutional talks, but in the greater alarm inspired by the approach of the Peloponnesian fleet (cf. 33. i, 37. i, with commentary) those talks were not held (VIII. 90–4). X. *H.* II. iii. 45–6 represents Theramenes as saying in 404 that he turned against the Four Hundred when it had become clear that the change to oligarchy had not lessened Sparta's hostility to Athens but some of the oligarchs were preparing to betray Athens to Sparta. For the distinction drawn by Lysias between Theramenes and Aristocrates see previous note. *A.P.*'s acceptance of their avowed reason for dissatisfaction with the régime of the Four Hundred need not imply conscious disagreement with Thucydides, nor need his expression οὐδὲν ἐπαναφέροντες τοῖς πεντακισχιλίοις imply a belief that the registration of the Five Thousand had been accomplished (see on 30. i, 32. iii).

This is the earliest occurrence by several centuries of the passive of συναρέσκειν (noticed in the 1968 Supplement to LSJ); but the impersonal active is found in X. *H.* II. iii. 42 and D. XIX. *F.L.* 202, and the passive of the simple verb ἀρέσκειν is reasonably common in this construction (e.g. H. III. 34. v, T. I. 129. iii, II. 68. iii).

γιγνομένοις: LSJ and the 1968 Supplement cite no instance of γίγνεσθαι ὑπό + genitive. The text appears to be sound (Dr J. D. Thomas confirms ὑπό): *A.P.* has used γιγνομένοις as πραττομένοις would normally be used.†

δοκοῦσι δὲ καλῶς πολιτευθῆναι ... τῆς πολιτείας οὔσης: Cf. T. VIII. 97. ii (καὶ οὐχ ἥκιστα δὴ τὸν πρῶτον χρόνον ἐπί γε ἐμοῦ Ἀθηναῖοι φαίνονται εὖ πολιτεύσαντες· μετρία γὰρ ἥ τε ἐς τοὺς ὀλίγους καὶ τοὺς πολλοὺς ξύγκρασις ἐγένετο καὶ ἐκ πονηρῶν τῶν πραγμάτων γενομένων τοῦτο πρῶτον ἀνήνεγκε τὴν πόλιν). Here, as in 23. ii, 28. v and 40. ii (cf. *ad locc.*), the favourable verdict is not original to *A.P.* but is repeated (though with a different slant) from a source with which he found himself in agreement. In II. 65. viii-x Thucydides expressed his approval of the democracy as led by Pericles and his disapproval of the rivalry between demagogues which followed Pericles' death; in I. 18. i he referred to Spartan εὐνομία; and in VIII. 24. iv we read Χῖοι γὰρ μόνοι μετὰ Λακεδαιμονίους ὧν ἐγὼ ᾐσθόμην ηὐδαιμόνησάν τε ἅμα καὶ ἐσωφρόνησαν. The meaning of his μετρία ξύγκρασις need not be discussed here (see, briefly, Rhodes, *JHS* xcii 1972, 122-3); *A.P.*'s explanatory comment is clear enough: it was good to limit political rights to men of hoplite status and above in time of war, when the safety of the state depended on its soldiers (the continuing importance of the fleet is conveniently ignored) and no money could be spared for civilian stipends. There is no need for the ⟨καίπερ⟩ πολέμου suggested by Herwerden & Leeuwen, but the πολέμου γε of J. B. Bury *ap.* Sandys may be right.

34. i. τούτους μὲν οὖν ἀφείλετο τὴν πολιτείαν ὁ δῆμος διὰ τάχους: 'Took away their control of the state.' This should be an allusion to the ending of the intermediate régime and the restoration of the democracy, of which *A.P.* otherwise says nothing: formally τούτους will refer to the Five Thousand (or, less probably, to the authors of this régime, Aristocrates and Theramenes). However, Fritz & Kapp argue (partly from the use of μὲν οὖν) that the reference is not to the ending of the intermediate régime, which *A.P.* like the historians omits, but to ch. 33's account of the fall of the Four Hundred, rounding that off before a new subject is introduced with ἔτει ἑβδόμῳ (180–2 n. 117; cf. Ste. Croix, *Hist.* v 1956, 22–3, almost persuaded; Sealey, *CSCA* viii 1975, 277–9, proposes to make this conclusion more obvious by deleting the last sentence of 33 as an interpolation, which I am sure is wrong; on *A.P.*'s use of resumptive expressions cf. Introduction, pp. 44–9). *A.P.*'s résumé of changes in the constitution, in 41. ii, is too brief at this point to be of help (cf. *ad loc.*). But there are other passages in *A.P.* where a clause with μὲν οὖν adds further information about one period before a clause with δέ proceeds to what happened afterwards (17. i [with a digression before the δέ in §iii], 22. vi, 28. i, 29. i, 33. i, 35. ii [δέ in §iv]), and we may retain the normal interpretation and regard this as another instance of that usage. The sentence is strikingly laconic, but in view of the silence of our other surviving texts we should not be surprised if *A.P.* could discover no more about the restoration of the democracy.

The restoration seems in fact to have occurred in the summer of 410, perhaps in response to the success of the fleet at Cyzicus (B. D. Meritt, *Athenian Financial Documents*, 105–7, *P. A. Philos. S.* cxv 1971, 106 with n. 11, 114–15; J. Hatzfeld argued unconvincingly for an earlier date, in *REA* xl 1938, 113–24; see also Sealey, *op. cit.*, 273–7), but Thucydides' narrative ends in the autumn of 411 and there is no word of the democratic restoration in X. H. or D.S. Our best evidence for the change is the decree of Demophantus against the overthrow of the democracy, dated to the first prytany of 410/09, *ap.* And. I. *Myst.* 96–8 (on the democratic restoration see in general Rhodes, *JHS* xcii 1972, 125–6, against Ste. Croix, *op. cit.*, 10–13). M&L 84, 5–6, has a payment for the Great Panathenaea in the second prytany: Meritt believes that such payments precede the festival, which would imply that the bouleutic year 410/09 began earlier than the archontic; but probably it was also possible for payments to be made shortly after the festival, to balance the books (cf. p. 669 n. 55), and if that happened in 410 the bouleutic year need not have begun before the archontic.

J. *The Thirty and the Ten* (34–41. i)

Between the ending of the intermediate régime of 411/0 and the institution of the Thirty *A.P.* offers very little: a brief and inaccurate allusion to the condemnation of the generals after Arginusae (34. i); the rejection of a Spartan peace offer at the instance of Cleophon, again inaccurately reported (34. i); and, as the event which led to the institution of the Thirty, Athens' final defeat at Aegospotami (34. ii). Moore, 266, suggests that the two episodes in 34. i 'are no doubt selected as illustrations of the workings of the democracy, and are intended to be taken as typical'; it is noticeable that both are represented as episodes in which the δῆμος was deceived. One topic which could very properly have been included in the history of the πολιτεία, but is not, is the compilation of a revised code of laws, begun in 410, interrupted by the Thirty and completed in 399 (cf. pp. 441–2: similarly the second part of *A.P.* is silent on the process of νομοθεσία by which in the fourth century alterations to that code were enacted [cf. pp. 512–13]). The bare facts reported in 34. i–ii will have been common knowledge in the fourth century; the attachment of archontic dates to Arginusae and Aegospotami may point to the use of an *Atthis*, but these two dates may themselves have been common knowledge, and for this material *A.P.* may not have consulted any written source.

On the Thirty, the Ten who replaced them and the reconciliation arranged by Pausanias, we have some information in speeches (especially Lys. XII. *Erat.*, XIII. *Agor.*, Is. XVIII. *Call.*), one allusion in Arist. *Pol.* (V. 1305 B 22–7: see p. 430), and four narrative accounts: X. *H.* II. iii. 11–iv. 43, D.S. XIV. 3–6, 32–3, Just. V. 8. v–10. xi, and *A.P.* 34. ii–41. i. The four narratives are compared in Table 4: I use italics and reference marks for items reported by Diodorus, Justin or *A.P.* at a different point in the narrative from Xenophon; in the left-hand column I use the letters A–T as in Hignett, *H.A.C.*, 384–9.

Table 4

X. *H.* II	D.S. XIV	Just. V	*A.P.*
Θ πάτριος πολιτεία not among peace terms. (ii. 20)	πάτριος πολιτεία among peace terms; dispute over constitution; oligarchy opposed by Theramenes but required by Lysander. (3. ii–vii)	Oligarchy among peace terms. (8. v)	πάτριος πολιτεία among peace terms; oligarchs, Theramenists, democrats; Theramenists want πάτριος πολιτεία but oligarchy required by Lysander. (34. ii–iii)

COMMENTARY ON THE *ATH. POL.* [34–41. i

Table 4—*contd.*

	X. *H.* II	D.S. XIV	Just. V	A.P.
A	Thirty appointed; delay legislation; set up government; execute sycophants. (iii. 11–12)	Thirty appointed; delay legislation; set up government; execute scoundrels. (3. vii–4. ii)	Thirty appointed; become tyrants; appoint guard (cf. p. 439). (8. viii–x)	Thirty appointed; delay legislation; set up government; revise laws; execute sycophants. (35. i–iii)
B	Thirty send to Sparta, obtain Callibius and garrison. (13–14)	Thirty send to Sparta, obtain Callibius and garrison. (4. iii–iv)	Thirty obtain garrison from Sparta. (8. xi)	‡ See below.
C	First reign of terror. (14)			Reign of terror. (35. iv)
D	Theramenes objects, wants broader régime. (15–17)			Theramenes objects, wants broader régime. (36. i)
E	Three Thousand selected. (18)			Three Thousand selected. (36. ii)
F	Theramenes again objects. (19)	Reign of terror: Theramenes objects. (4. iv–v)	Reign of terror: Theramenes objects. (9. i–ii)	Theramenes again objects. (36. ii)
				* *Thrasybulus occupies Phyle, defeats oligarchs.* (37. i)
G	Unprivileged citizens disarmed. (20)			† See below.
H	Second reign of terror. (21)			
J	Attack on metics: Theramenes objects. (21–2)	* See below.		
K	Theramenes clashes with Critias (speeches); is deleted from Three Thousand, condemned; supplicates in vain; is executed. (23–56)	Theramenes clashes with Critias; is arrested; supplicates in vain; forbids Socrates to attempt rescue; is executed. (4. v–5. iv)	Theramenes executed. (9. ii)	Two laws enable Theramenes to be deleted from Three Thousand, executed. (37. i)
	–			† *Unprivileged citizens disarmed.* (37. ii)
	–			‡ *Thirty send to Sparta, obtain Callibius and garrison.* (37. ii)

417

Table 4—contd.

	X. *H.* II	D.S. XIV	Just. v	*A.P.*
L	Thirty free to rule tyrannically. (iv. 1)	Reign of terror. (5. v–vi)		
	–	* Attack on metics. (5. vi)		
	–	Athenians flee, are harboured despite Spartan ban. (5. vi–6. iii cf. 32. i)	Athenians flee, are harboured despite Spartan ban. (9. iii–v)	
M	Unprivileged expelled from city. (1)	† *See below.*	† *See below.*	
N	Thrasybulus occupies Phyle. (2)	Thrasybulus occupies Phyle. (32. i)	Thrasybulus occupies Phyle. (9. vi)	⎫
	–		Thrasybulus supported by Ismenias and Lysias. (9. vii–ix)	⎪
O	Snowstorm frustrates attack on Thrasybulus. (3)	Snowstorm frustrates attack on Thrasybulus. (32. ii–iii)	Oligarchs defeated (* *cf. below*) (9. x–xi)	⎬ * *See above.*
	–	† *Unprivileged sent from city to Piraeus.* (32. iv)	† *Unprivileged sent from city to walls.* (9. xii)	⎪
P	Oligarchs defeated in battle near Phyle. (4–7)	‡ *See below.*	* *Cf. above.*	⎭
Q	Thirty arrest Eleusinians. (8)	⎫		
R	Three Thousand condemn Eleusinians. (9–10)	⎬ Eleusinians and Salaminians condemned. (32. iv) ⎭		
	–	Thirty fail to corrupt Thrasybulus; appeal to Sparta. (32. v–vi)	Thirty fail to corrupt Thrasybulus; appeal to Sparta. (9. xiii–xiv)	
	–	‡ *Oligarchs defeated in battle at Acharnae.* (32. vi–33. i)		
S	Thrasybulus to Piraeus; battle of Munichia; speech by herald. (10–22)	Thrasybulus to Piraeus; battle(s) of Munichia. (33. ii–iii)	Thrasybulus to Piraeus; battle of Munichia; speech by Thrasybulus. (9. xiv–10. iii)	Thrasybulus to Piraeus; battle of Munichia. (38. i)
	–	§ *Democrats grow in strength.* (33. iv)		

COMMENTARY ON THE *ATH. POL.* [34-41. i

Table 4—*contd.*

	X. *H.* II	D.S. XIV	Just. v	*A.P.*
T	Thirty deposed; replaced by Ten; retire to Eleusis. (23-4)	Thirty deposed; replaced by Ten to make peace. (33. v)	Thirty sent to Eleusis; replaced by Ten. (10. iv–v)	Thirty deposed; replaced by Ten to make peace. (38. i)
	–			§ *Ten neglect peace, appeal to Sparta.* (38. i)
	–			Demaretus killed. (38. ii)
U	Democrats grow in strength. (24-7)	§ *See above.*		Democrats grow in strength. (38. iii)
V	Ten appeal to Sparta; Lysander comes. (28-9)	Ten appeal to Sparta; Lysander comes. (33. v)		§ *See above.*
	–			Ten superseded by second Ten, who negotiate. (38. iii)
W	Pausanias follows; battle against Piraeus. (29-34)	Pausanias follows. (33. vi)	Pausanias sent from Sparta. (10. vi)	
X	Pausanias and committee from Sparta arrange reconciliation; speech by Thrasybulus. (35-42)	Pausanias arranges reconciliation. (33. vi)	Pausanias arranges reconciliation. (10. vii)	Pausanias and committee from Sparta arrange reconciliation; terms summarised. (38. iv–39)
	–			Moderation of restored democracy. (40. i–iii)
Y	Final clash and settlement with Eleusis. (43)		Final clash and settlement with Eleusis. (10. viii–xi)	Final settlement with Eleusis. (40. iv)

Differences in content and arrangement show that the four accounts are independent of one another. Xenophon writes from first-hand knowledge of the events (and, in particular, may have fought against Thrasybulus at Phyle: see E. Schwartz, *RM*² xliv 1889, 165, on X. *H.* II. iv. 2-7; E. Delebecque, *Essai sur la vie de Xénophon*, 61-2); Diodorus' account is presumably derived from Ephorus (but this version, in which history is seriously distorted to the advantage of Theramenes, is not to be blamed on the *Hellenica Oxyrhynchia*: see A. Andrewes, *Phoen.* xxviii 1974, 119-20); Justin's brief summary of

Pompeius Trogus contains material that is not in Diodorus, but nowhere seriously disagrees with Diodorus, so here we probably have a second account derived from Ephorus (cf. Busolt, *Hermes* xxxiii 1898, 75–6, *G.S.*, i. 79, seeing in Nep. VIII. *Thras.* 1–3 yet another descendant of Ephorus). *A.P.* agrees with Diodorus and Justin against Xenophon, that the peace terms with Sparta required Athens to be governed according to the πάτριος πολιτεία; he agrees with Xenophon on the objections of Theramenes to the first reign of terror, the recognition of the Three Thousand privileged citizens in response to those objections, and (especially) Theramenes' further objections; he disagrees with the consensus of the others on the order in which four major events occurred (the arrival of Callibius with the Spartan garrison, the disarming of the unprivileged [omitted by Diodorus and Justin], the killing of Theramenes, Thrasybulus' occupation of Phyle); and he includes, especially on the terms of the reconciliation and their implementation, a good deal of material that is not found in the other narratives.†

Some of the material peculiar to *A.P.* (as on the revolutions of 411: cf. pp. 366–7) appears to be derived ultimately from official documents (cf. Wilamowitz, *A.u.A.*, i. 122): he reports the author of the decree under which the Thirty were appointed (34. iii *fin.*); the name of the Thirty's archon of 404/3 (35. i *init.*); the two laws which were used as an excuse for the elimination of Theramenes (37. i: not reported in conspicuously documentary language); the details of the terms of reconciliation arranged in 403 (39: again with an archontic date, but one which could not have been attached to the terms at the time); and documents may also underlie what is said of the mild beginning of the Thirty's rule (35. i–ii). But much that we read in *A.P.*'s account is clearly tendentious: most flagrant is the (false) claim that there were two successive boards of Ten after the deposition of the Thirty, the second board and in particular Rhinon being well disposed towards the δῆμος and not incurring the hostility either of the surviving oligarchs or of the democrats (38); in 40. i–iii the policies of the restored democracy in general and of Archinus in particular are praised. Earlier, 34. iii distinguishes between 'oligarchs', who with Lysander's support were able to prevail, and the laudable men whose aim was the πάτριος πολιτεία, Theramenes and his supporters; of these supporters four are named, and we find that none were members of the Thirty and two were with Thrasybulus at Phyle; the fact that Theramenes was a member of the Thirty is passed over in silence, while in 36 his objections to extreme oligarchy are clearly stated; the chronological distortion in *A.P.*'s account was originally made to Theramenes' advantage, though it is not so used by *A.P.* (cf. pp. 422, 454–5). It is remarkable that, whereas more men are named in *A.P.*'s account than in the

COMMENTARY ON THE *ATH. POL.* [34–41. i

others (if we disregard the complete list of the Thirty interpolated in X. *H.* II. iii. 2), the name of Critias is wholly absent: this may well be due to the Platonic school's desire to protect Critias' reputation (cf. pp. 429–30).

Some have thought that *A.P.* made use of Xenophon (e.g. Busolt, *Hermes* xxxiii 1898, 71–3, *G.S.*, i. 79 [ch. 36 only]; Fritz & Kapp, 182–3 [35–6]); but close agreement between the two is limited to Theramenes' objections to the rule of the Thirty, and it is more likely that both had access to a defence of Theramenes, either by himself when he was attacked by Critias or by a supporter not long after his death (Lys. xII. *Erat.* 77 alludes to Theramenes' defence, and the 'Theramenes papyrus', P. Mich. 5982 [on which see Introduction, p. 22 with n. 132], purports to quote a speech of Theramenes). Wilamowitz, *A.u.A.*, i. 165–7[–85], argued that *A.P.* made extensive use of a pamphlet by Theramenes, and, so that the pamphlet could serve as the source of *A.P.*'s material on 404–403, O. Seeck and A. von Mess adapted this theory and thought in terms of a work written *c.* 390 by a supporter of Theramenes (see Introduction, pp. 15–16, 18; and on the fourth-century controversy over Theramenes pp. 359–61, 368). Busolt, *opp. citt.*, 71–86, 78–80, claimed that *A.P.* agrees closely with Diodorus at those points where Diodorus disagrees with Xenophon, and suggested that *A.P.* and Diodorus are derived from a common source (originally, that Androtion was used by Ephorus and by *A.P.* [cf. A. Fuks, *The Ancestral Constitution*, 62–3, G. Adeleye, *Mus. Afr.* v 1976, 12]; in *G.S.*, that Theopompus was used by Ephorus and by Androtion): *A.P.*'s agreement with Diodorus (xiv. 3, but contrast xiii. 107) and Justin against Xenophon on a constitutional requirement in the peace terms is significant, but some of Busolt's other agreements are trivial and there are important disagreements to set against them, so it is not likely that *A.P.* and Diodorus have a common source. We have hardly any fragments from the Atthidographers' accounts of 404–403, and none which confirms that *A.P.* made use of Androtion here: 324 F 10 alludes to 'the Ten and what happened afterwards' (not 'the Ten and the following ⟨Ten⟩': see p. 459); and the men named in *A.P.*'s account do not include Molpis, named as one of the Piraeus Ten in F 11. In spite of the amnesty of 403, what a man had done in 404–403 was a topic regularly raised in the lawsuits of the next twenty years (cf. p. 472): many speeches allude to these events, and no doubt there were many political pamphlets which alluded to them also (cf. p. 368); there was probably ample material available to *A.P.* His narrative contains no inconsistencies which might betray an uneasy amalgamation of material from different sources, except that after the claim in ch. 38 that there were two boards of Ten the document quoted in 39 mentions only one (§vi), and that the summary in 41. i is at odds with the narrative which precedes it. There is nothing in his account which could not have been transmitted by one of the 'moderate' leaders of the restored democracy (and notice the comment of Rudberg on the last sentence of 38, cited *ad loc.*).

On the chronological conflict between *A.P.* and the other sources most scholars have judged *A.P.* to be in the wrong, and that is surely the correct verdict (e.g. Beloch, *G.G.*[2], III. i. 5 n. 3, P. Cloché, *La Restauration démocratique à Athènes en 403 avant J.-C.*, 4–7, E. Meyer, *G.d.A.*, v[4]. 17 n. 1, Hignett, *H.A.C.*, 384–9, contr. Wilamowitz, *A.u.A.*, i. 166, Busolt, *Hermes* xxxiii 1898, 71–86, G. Colin, *Xénophon historien*, 41–5, 57–61): it is highly implausible that the Thirty should first have eliminated Theramenes, next disarmed the unprivileged, and only after that obtained the support of a Spartan garrison (but it is arguable that the other sources date Thrasybulus' occupation of Phyle too late: see on 37. i). The effect of *A.P.*'s distortion (lost in his own account, which does not admit that Theramenes was one of the Thirty) is that most of the outrages of the Thirty are placed after Theramenes' death, and he therefore cannot be made to share the blame for them.

34. i. τούτους μὲν οὖν ἀφείλετο τὴν πολιτείαν ὁ δῆμος διὰ τάχους: For commentary on the first sentence of ch. 34 see pp. 414–15.

ἔτει δ' ἑβδόμῳ ... ἐπὶ Καλλίου τοῦ Ἀγγελῆθεν ἄρχοντος: Callias is given his demotic to distinguish him from the archon of 412/1 (32. i with commentary): in *IG* i[2] 124, 3, he is similarly distinguished; in D.H. *A.R.* VII. 1. v, Ar. *Ran.*, hyp. i (cf. schol. 694), he is distinguished in the later manner, as Callias τοῦ μετὰ Ἀντιγένη; in *Marm. Par.* 239 A 64 τοῦ προτέρου is probably to be corrected, with le Paulmier, to τοῦ δευτέρου. The Four Hundred were deposed in 411/0 (33. i with commentary); Callias was archon (cf. D.S. XIII. 80. i, *Marm. Par.*, *loc. cit.*), and the battle of Arginusae was fought (cf. Ath. v. 218 A; Ar. *Ran.*, produced in that year, contains many allusions to the battle), in 406/5, the sixth year from 411/0 by inclusive counting. Numerals are easily corrupted, and many blame a copyist for the error and emend to ἕκτῳ (ϛ' for ζ': Kaibel & Wilamowitz[2], cf. Wilamowitz, *A.u.A.*, i. 8 n. 11, G. V. Sumner, *CQ*[2] xi 1961, 31–3); Kaibel & Wilamowitz[1] emended κατάλυσιν to κατάστασιν, which is less likely; but the short and inaccurate note on the condemnation of the generals which follows may well have been written from memory, and the error may be *A.P.*'s own (cf. pp. 415–16).

γενομένης τῆς ἐν Ἀργινούσσαις ναυμαχίας: The papyrus has Ἀργινούσας with σαις written above: since Blass[1] editors have regularly printed Ἀργινούσσαις, but it is certain that the name was normally spelled with one sigma, and the corrector of the papyrus need not have intended to spell it with two. For the battle, in which an Athenian reserve fleet forced the Spartan Callicratidas to divide his fleet and defeated him, but owing to bad weather did not afterwards pick up corpses or shipwrecked survivors, see X. *H*. I. vi. 25-38, D.S. XIII. 98-100, and for the reaction of the Athenians and the condemnation of the generals see X. *H*. I. vii, D.S. XIII. 101-103. ii; the fact that Socrates was one of the prytanes who tried without success to enforce a lawful procedure in the assembly added to the notoriety of the episode, and there are many other allusions to it. The most helpful modern discussions are by P. Cloché, *RH* cxxx 1919, 5-68, A. Andrewes, *Phoen.* xxviii 1974, 112-22.

πρῶτον μὲν τοὺς δέκα στρατηγοὺς ... ἐπ' ἀλλοτρίας νεὼς σωθέντας: Of the generals of 406/5, listed in X. *H*. I. v. 16, D.S. XIII. 74. i, Conon and Archestratus were with the first Athenian fleet, blockaded in Mytilene, and Archestratus died there (Lys. xxi. *Pec. Acc.* 8); Leon must either have remained in Mytilene with Conon or have sailed out on the ship which was captured by the Spartans (X. *H*. I. vi. 16-22); eight generals, one apparently a suffect, fought at Arginusae, and of them six returned to Athens and were put to death while the remaining two did not return and were condemned in absence. The generals who did not take part in the battle were not condemned; the suffect Lysias had his own ship sunk but survived the battle (D.S. XIII. 99. iii cf. X. *H*. I. vii. 32). Sandys takes exception also to *A.P.*'s use of μιᾷ χειροτονίᾳ, whereas in X. *H*. the first, procedural votes were taken by show of hands but the actual condemnation was voted by ballot (I. vii. 34 cf. 9), but I suspect that in using χειροτονίᾳ *A.P.* does not intend a more precise meaning than 'vote' (cf. 41. iii with commentary; but D. M. MacDowell, *JHS* xcv 1975, 70, claims that ψηφίζεσθαι is not limited to voting by ballot but χειροτονεῖν is limited to voting by show of hands). *A.P.* is preceded in his erroneous statement that all ten generals were condemned by Plat. *Apol.* 32 B 2-3, and the error is found also in [Plat.] *Axioch.* 368 D 6-7 and some later texts.

τοὺς τῇ ναυμαχίᾳ νικῶντας: τοὺς τῇ ναυμαχίᾳ νικῶντας ... τοὺς μὲν οὐδὲ συνναυμαχήσαντας is clumsy, and H. Richards deleted this first phrase as a gloss (*CR* v 1891, 228), but I am not persuaded that *A.P.* did not write it.

ἐξαπατηθέντος τοῦ δήμου διὰ τοὺς παροργίσαντας: The active παροργίζειν is otherwise known to LSJ only from Philo, *Somn.* II. 177, the Septuagint and the New Testament, but occurrences of the passive include Thph. *H.P.* IX. 16. vi: J. B. Bury, unnecessarily, proposed to emend (*CR* v 1891, 181).

In Xenophon's account the condemnation of the generals results from a malicious attack by Theramenes; in Diodorus the conflict arises from a more innocent misunderstanding, and Andrewes has shown that Diodorus' version is to be preferred (*Phoen.* xxviii 1974,

112–22). After the people's wave of anger had passed, Callixenus (the author of the motion under which the generals were condemned) and four others were charged with ἀπάτη and arrested, but in the greater troubles which followed they escaped without being brought to trial (X. *H.* I. vii. 35, D.S. XIII. 103. i–ii, Suid. [*E* 1136] ἐνάυειν). In both episodes treated in this section the δῆμος acts wrongly because it is deceived; similarly in 29. i and 34. iii the δῆμος is 'compelled' to set up the régimes of the Four Hundred and the Thirty. Oligarchs defending themselves stressed that the oligarchies had been instituted by resolutions of the δῆμος, and no doubt it was commonly said in the fourth century that the δῆμος only went astray because it was led astray (cf. on 29. i).

βουλομένων Λακεδαιμονίων ἐκ Δεκελείας ἀπιέναι: Peace offers by Sparta in the last phase of the Peloponnesian War are recorded after Cyzicus by D.S. XIII. 52–3 and in 411/0 by Phil. 328 F 139, both texts assigning to Cleophon the responsibility for the rejection of the offer; in 408/7 by Andr. 324 F 44 (cf. Busolt, *G.G.*, III. ii. 1565, Jacoby *ad loc.*, D. M. Lewis, *Sparta and Persia*, 114 n. 47, 126–7, against V. L. Ehrenberg, *RE* xv [1931/2], 329: on this occasion an exchange of prisoners was arranged); the peace offer after Arginusae is found also in schol. Ar. *Ran.* 1532 (avowedly derived from *A.P.*); A. II. *F.L.* 76 mentions the rejection of a peace offer and Cleophon's responsibility for its rejection, but gives no indication of date (Wilamowitz and Busolt refer this to the aftermath of Aegospotami, but see below). Many have believed that at any rate the two peace offers after Cyzicus and Arginusae should be reduced to one (e.g. Grote, *H.G.* [1869–84], viii. 1 with n. 1, Wilamowitz, *A.u.A.*, i. 130–1, Busolt, *G.G.*, III. ii. 1535 n. 1); and Day & Chambers, *A.H.A.D.*, 149, consider also the evidence of Lys. XIII. *Agor.* 5–12, cf. xxx. *Nic.* 10–13, for Cleophon's opposition to peace after Aegospotami, and argue that this last was the only occasion when Cleophon prevented the making of peace with Sparta. That Cleophon was opposed to peace after Aegospotami, and peace could not be made until he had been brought to trial and condemned, seems certain; there is no reason why Sparta should not have offered peace earlier, but there should not be too many such occasions. *A.P.*'s peace offer after Arginusae is suspiciously like the offer after Cyzicus: Cyzicus was a greater shock to Sparta than Arginusae, and after his treatment of the condemnation of the generals *A.P.*'s unsupported placing of the offer at this point is unlikely to be right against Philochorus and Diodorus; Aeschines seems to combine an inaccurate version of terms appropriate to this earlier occasion (cf. next note) with an attitude of Cleophon more appropriate after Aegospotami; the peace offer of 408, which had some result, is an independent episode. Day & Chambers suggest that *A.P.* has chosen the version best suited to illustrate the collapse of Athenian democracy, but I suspect there is no conscious choice here: rather, before proceeding to the peace finally made with Sparta, the author without checking his facts wrote what he thought he knew; I do not imagine that Androtion had a different date from Philochorus for this offer.

For Sparta's occupation of Decelea from 413 to the end of the war see T. VII. 19. i–ii, X. *H.* II. iii. 3, and for its effects on Athens see T. VII. 27–8, *H.O.* 17. iii–v. Decelea lay near the modern Tatoi, slightly east of north from Athens, at the southern end of the easternmost of the passes through Parnes; the Spartan fort was probably on the hill called Palaiokastro (J. R. McCredie, *Hesp.* Supp. xi 1966, 56–8, J. S. Traill, *Hesp.* Supp. xiv 1975, 52).

καὶ ἐφ' οἷς ἔχουσιν ἑκάτεροι εἰρήνην ἄγειν: Thus Kenyon, not acknowledging in his Berlin ed. or O.C.T. that the papyrus differs; in the papyrus ἰρήνην precedes ἑκάτεροι; schol. Ar. *Ran.* 1532 earlier reverses βουλομένων Λακεδαιμονίων, here has ἐφ' οἷς ἔχουσιν ἑκάτεροι καὶ εἰρήνην ἄγειν, then paraphrases, and returns to direct quotation at ἐλθών. Kaibel & Wilamowitz and Blass[1–3] preferred the scholiast's word order (cf. Kaibel, *Stil und Text*, 191), and T. Gomperz placed ἑκάτεροι after ἄγειν (*DLZ* xii 1891, 1641), but Kenyon's correction is sufficient.

D.S. XIII. 52. iii gives the proposed terms as τὰς μὲν πόλεις ἔχειν ἃς ἑκάτεροι κρατοῦμεν, τὰ δὲ φρούρια τὰ παρ' ἀλλήλοις καταλῦσαι, τῶν δ' αἰχμαλώτων λυτροῦντες ἀνθ' ἑνὸς Ἀθηναίου λαβεῖν ἕνα Λάκωνα (the φρούρια are presumably Pylos and Decelea: Athens still possessed Pylos at the time of Cyzicus but not at the time of Arginusae; cf. 27. v with commentary). A. II. *F.L.* 76, less plausibly, gives ἔχοντας πρὸς τῇ Ἀττικῇ Λῆμνον καὶ Ἴμβρον καὶ Σκῦρον (an issue probably first raised in 392/1: cf. And. III. *Pace*, 12, 14) καὶ δημοκρατουμένους κατὰ τοὺς νόμους (which is likely to have been invented after the eventual peace led to the overthrow of the democracy).

ἐσπούδαζον: Kaibel, *Stil und Text*, 42–3, remarks that this absolute usage is otherwise confined to later Greek (e.g. Pl. *Crass.* 12. ii); but the verb is used absolutely by Aristophanes (*Vesp.* 694, *Ran.* 813, *Plut.* 557, cf. [perf. part.] *Thesm.* 572, X. *Symp.* ii. 17).

τὸ δὲ πλῆθος οὐχ ὑπήκουσεν ἐξαπατηθέντες ὑπὸ Κλεοφῶντος: This change from singular to plural is natural and common enough, and there is no need for the proposed emendations of early commentators. On Cleophon see 28. iii with commentary. On the claim that the δῆμος was deceived cf. above; this time the same claim was made in D.S. XIII. 53. iii.

ἐλθὼν εἰς τὴν ἐκκλησίαν μεθύων καὶ θώρακα ἐνδεδυκώς: The verb θωρήσσεσθαι is often used to mean 'fortify oneself with drink' (LSJ, sense II), and Aristophanes twice plays on its two meanings (*Ach.* 1134–5, *Pax*, 1286). J. J. Hartman (*ap.* Herwerden & Leeuwen, who were not persuaded) thought that θώρακ' ἔχων in *Vesp.* 1195 has this sense, and that what *A.P.* says here derives from a misunderstanding of a comedian's account of the incident: MacDowell *ad loc.* denies that θώρακ' ἔχων ever has this sense; the possibility that θωρήσσεσθαι has been misunderstood remains, but the literal sense is not inappropriate here (cf. Solon's display of arms when Pisistratus was trying to seize power: 14. ii with commentary). Wilamowitz, *A.u.A.*, i. 130 n. 15, thought that *A.P.* was reproducing an eye-witness's account, but Cleophon's appearance in military garb could easily be a later embellishment (cf. next note). This allegation is found only in *A.P.*: according to D.S. XIII. 53. ii(–iv) Cleophon πολλὰ πρὸς τὴν ὑπόθεσιν οἰκείως διαλεχθεὶς ἐμετεώρισε τὸν δῆμον, τὸ μέγεθος τῶν εὐημερημάτων προφερόμενος; in A. II. *F.L.* 76 he ἀποκόψειν ἠπείλει μαχαίρᾳ τὸν τράχηλον εἴ τις εἰρήνης μνησθήσεται (an attitude more appropriate in 405/4 than in 410 or 406: cf. above).

ἐὰν μὴ πάσας ἀφιῶσι Λακεδαιμόνιοι τὰς πόλεις: This demand is not appropriate before Aegospotami, when the cities under Sparta's command were, at any rate in theory, supporting of their own free will a leader who proposed to free the Greeks from Athenian domination: like Aeschines, *A.P.* gives an anachronistic account. Schol. Ar. (cf. above) reads ἀφῶσι, which some have preferred (H. Richards, *CR* v 1891, 228, S. A. Naber *ap.* Herwerden & Leeuwen), but the present may stand.

34. ii. οὐ χρησάμενοι δὲ καλῶς ... ἔγνωσαν τὴν ἁμαρτίαν: The same obvious point is made by D.S. XIII. 53. iii–iv, A. II. *F.L.* 76–7.

τῷ γὰρ ὕστερον ἔτει ἐπ' Ἀλεξίου ἄρχοντος: 405/4 (cf. D.S. XIII. 104. i). ἠτύχησαν τὴν ἐν Αἰγὸς ποταμοῖς ναυμαχίαν: See X. *H.* II. i. 20–32, D.S. XIII. 105. ii–106. vii, Pl. *Alc.* 36. vi–37. v, *Lys.* 9. vi–11(–13), Nep. VII. *Alc.* 8; and, in defence of Diodorus' version, C. T. H. R. Ehrhardt, *Phoen.* xxiv 1970, 225–8, cf. J. Hatzfeld, *Alcibiade*, 334–7. ἠτύχησαν τὴν ... ναυμαχίαν seems to be an unparalleled usage, but is only a short step beyond τὴν μάχην ἡττήθησαν (Is. v. *Phil.* 47); D.H. 551. *Isoc.* 9 writes ἠτύχητο ... ἡ ... περὶ Λεῦκτρα μάχη, and in the fourth century A.D. Eunapius, *V.S.* 469. VI. 8. iii writes πάντες δὲ τὸ ... ἀγαθὸν ⟨οὐδὲν⟩ ἀτυχήσουσι.

κύριον γενόμενον τῆς πόλεως Λύσανδρον: After Athens had accepted Sparta's peace terms Lysander entered the city (X. *H.* II. iii. 22–3, Lys. XIII. *Agor.* 34: Pl. *Lys.* 15. i dates his entry to 16 Munichion [x], about 25 or 26 April according to the tables of B. D. Meritt, *The Athenian Year*, 218, *P. A. Philos. S.* cxv 1971, 114). Earlier he had been on Samos (D.S. XIII. 106. viii, P. Mich. 5982 [for which see Introduction, p. 22 with n. 132]); he may have returned there after entering Athens (Lys. XII. *Erat.* 71–2, D.S. XIV. 3. iv: cf. E. Meyer, *G.d.A.*, v⁴. 16 with n. 3, Hignett, *H.A.C.*, 381), but if so he later came to Athens again, since he was present at the assembly which instituted the Thirty (§iii with commentary).

34. iii. τῆς εἰρήνης γενομένης αὐτοῖς ἐφ' ᾧ τε πολιτεύσονται τὴν πάτριον πολιτείαν: For the accusative after πολιτεύεσθαι Kaibel, *Stil und Text*, 191, compares A. I. *Tim.* 5, Plat. *Legg.* III. 676 c 1–2. In our most detailed accounts of the peace terms there is no mention of a constitutional requirement (X. *H.* II. ii. 20, D.S. XIII. 107. iv, And. III. *Pace*, 11–12, Pl. *Lys.* 14. viii), but *A.P.* has the support of D.S. XIV. 3. ii cf. vi and of Just. v. 8. v (*reique publicae ex semet ipsis xxx rectores acciperent*); the complaint in Lys. XII. *Erat.* 70 that Theramenes in his negotiations with Sparta offered to demolish the Piraeus walls and τὴν ὑπάρχουσαν πολιτείαν καταλῦσαι does not prove that there was a requirement in the peace treaty (*pace* Busolt & Swoboda, *G.S.*, ii. 911 n. 1, A. Fuks, *The Ancestral Constitution*, 62). After the democratic régime had exhausted Athens' funds and had lost the war, and peace had been negotiated by Theramenes, it was of course very likely that the democracy would collapse, and Theramenes may indeed have promised that he would help to bring about its collapse; in due course Lysander was present at and influenced the assembly which instituted the Thirty; and so it could easily have been supposed that there had been a constitutional requirement in the peace terms. We should accept that there was no such formal requirement (e.g. Hignett, *H.A.C.*, 285, Fuks, *op. cit.*, 52–8; contr. W. J. McCoy, *YCS* xxiv 1975, 133–41). However, the different interpretations placed upon πάτριος πολιτεία by *A.P.* and Diodorus point to a contemporary dispute (cf. next note), and as Fuks suggests the peace treaty may very well have contained a clause such as Ἀθηναίους εἶναι αὐτονόμους κατὰ τὰ πάτρια (cf. the clause on the autonomy of the Peloponnesian cities in the short-lived treaty of 418/7 between Sparta and Argos, T. v. 77. v), which was not intended to refer to the constitution but could have been misinterpreted as applying to the constitution by men seeking a pretext for overthrowing the democracy (*op. cit.*, 58–63 with 80 n. 16; K. R. Walters, *AJAH* i 1976, 129–44, blames the misinterpretation not on the oligarchs in 404 but on Androtion in the fourth century).†

οἱ μὲν δημοτικοί . . . τῶν δὲ γνωρίμων οἱ μὲν . . . οἱ δ' ἐν ἑταιρείᾳ μὲν οὐδεμιᾷ . . . : For *A.P.*'s use of the opposition between δῆμος or πλῆθος and γνώριμοι see especially 2. i, 28. ii–iii, with commentary. D.S. XIV. 3. iii has a twofold division, in which each party declares its objective to be a form of πάτριος πολιτεία: οἱ γὰρ τῆς ὀλιγαρχίας ὀρεγόμενοι τὴν παλαιὰν κατάστασιν ἔφασαν δεῖν ἀνανεοῦσθαι, καθ' ἣν παντελῶς ὀλίγοι τῶν ὅλων προεϊστήκεισαν· οἱ δὲ πλεῖστοι δημοκρατίας ὄντες ἐπιθυμηταὶ τὴν τῶν πατέρων πολιτείαν προεφέροντο, καὶ ταύτην ἀπέφηναν ὁμολογουμένως οὖσαν δημοκρατίαν (cf. Theramenes in §vi,

COMMENTARY ON THE *ATH. POL.*

Thrasybulus in 32. vi; also Thrasybulus in X. *H.* II. iv. 42, and schol. A. I. *Tim.* 39 [quoted p. 440]). The interpolator of X. *H.* II. iii. 2 (as I believe him to be) writes of τριάκοντα ἄνδρες ... οἳ τοὺς πατρίους νόμους συγγράψουσι. *A.P.* subdivides the γνώριμοι to produce a threefold division, in which the πάτριος πολιτεία is the constitution wanted by Theramenes and his supporters, intermediate between democracy and oligarchy. Another text which points to a threefold division is Lys. XII. *Erat.*: δημοκρατίας ἔτι οὔσης the oligarchic ἑταιρεῖαι appointed five 'ephors' (§§43–7: cf. below); and when the Thirty were appointed they comprised ten nominated by Theramenes, ten nominated by the ephors and ten ἐκ τῶν παρόντων (the last perhaps falsely alleged to represent the democrats: §§75–6 with Fuks, *op. cit.*, 73).†

If the phrase κατὰ τὰ πάτρια did occur in some context in the peace treaty, extreme or moderate oligarchs will have taken the lead in claiming that Athens was thereby required to abandon the democracy, and the democrats will have replied, as they are made to reply by Diodorus, that in Athens the πάτριος πολιτεία was democracy (cf. πολιτεύεσθαι Ἀθηναίους κατὰ τὰ πάτρια in the decree of Tisamenus enacted after the reconciliation in 403, *ap.* And I. *Myst.* 83). Similarly in 411 the oligarchs had represented their revolution as a return to the πάτριοι νόμοι of the past, and the democrats had accused the oligarchs of undoing the πάτριοι νόμοι; and for further confirmation that the πάτριος πολιτεία was disputed in Athens at the end of the fifth century cf. Thrasymachus, 85 B 1 *fin.* Diels & Kranz, *ap.* D.H. 961. *Dem.* 3 (σκέψασθε γὰρ ἐξ ἀρχῆς ἃ ζητοῦσιν ἑκάτεροι. πρῶτον μὲν ἡ πάτριος πολιτεία ταραχὴν αὐτοῖς παρέχει, ῥᾴστη γνωσθῆναι καὶ κοινοτάτη τοῖς πολίταις οὖσα πᾶσιν). On the appeal to the past by both sides see M. I. Finley, *The Ancestral Constitution*, 11–14 = *The Use and Abuse of History*, 39–40.

οἱ μὲν δημοτικοὶ διασῴζειν ἐπειρῶντο τὸν δῆμον: Lys. XIII. *Agor.*, esp. 15–43, reports but tries to misdate a democratic conspiracy, betrayed by Agoratus: the plot in fact began after the peace terms had been accepted in principle; it was betrayed and the plotters were arrested before the overthrow of the democracy; but the plotters were condemned to death by the boule of the Thirty (cf. Grote, *H.G.* [1869–84], viii. 26 n. 1, Busolt, *G.G.*, III. ii. 1637 n. 1).

A.P. is about to name five leading 'moderates' (cf. below), but he does not name any leaders of the 'democrats' or 'oligarchs'. We may regard as prominent democrats the more distinguished of the men put to death by the Thirty while Theramenes was still of their number (cf. p. 446); *A.P.* does not say what policy was favoured by Thrasybulus (37. i with commentary) at this stage, but he places in Theramenes' party some of the men who were to join Thrasybulus at Phyle (cf. below).

COMMENTARY ON THE *ATH. POL.* [34. iii

οἱ μὲν ἐν ταῖς ἑταιρείαις ὄντες: Cf. Lys. XII. *Erat.* 43–4: δημοκρατίας ἔτι οὔσης ... πέντε ἄνδρας ἔφοροι κατέστησαν ὑπὸ τῶν καλουμένων ἑταίρων, to act as political agents and see that the democratic machinery worked as the ἑταῖροι wished. Andocides in 415 had given information that the mutilation of the hermae was the work of οἷς ... ἐχρῶ καὶ οἷς συνῇσθα ἄνευ ἡμῶν τῶν συγγενῶν (I. *Myst.* 49), his ἑταῖροι (§54), an act proposed at a drinking-party but carried out subsequently (§§61–2) and capable of being regarded as a πίστις (§67). Pisander on his first visit to Athens in 411 encouraged τὰς ... ξυνωμοσίας αἵπερ ἐτύγχανον πρότερον ἐν τῇ πόλει οὖσαι ἐπὶ δίκαις καὶ ἀρχαῖς ... ὅπως ξυστραφέντες καὶ κοινῇ βουλευσάμενοι καταλύσουσι τὸν δῆμον. The standard modern discussion of the ἑταιρεῖαι is G. M. Calhoun, *Athenian Clubs in Politics and Litigation*; see also F. Sartori, *Le eterie nella vita politica ateniese del VI e V secolo a.C.*, with the review of A. E. Raubitschek, *AJP* lxxx 1959, 81–8. We need not suppose that every ἑταιρεία of political significance was opposed to the democracy, still less that every one was in favour of extreme rather than moderate oligarchy (cf. Calhoun, *op. cit.*, 21–3); but both ἑταιρεῖαι and oligarchy will have appealed particularly to the younger and richer Athenians, and we need not doubt that most of the ἑταιρεῖαι were in favour of oligarchy.

In Xenophon's and Diodorus' accounts the leader of the extreme oligarchs is Critias Καλλαίσχρου, tenuously related to Solon (Plat. *Charm.* 155 A 2–3, 157 E 4–158 A 1, *Tim.* 20 E 1–3: cf. p. 123), and cousin on his father's side to the mother of Plato and on his mother's side to the father of Andocides. There is no good evidence for his involvement in the régime of the Four Hundred ([D.] LVIII. *Theocr.* 67 is not good evidence [see pp. 453–4]; that he was one of the Four Hundred is denied by H. C. Avery, *CP* lviii 1963, 165–7, asserted by G. Adeleye, *TAPA* civ 1974, 1–9). Either under the intermediate régime or under the restored democracy he was the author of a motion leading to the posthumous trial of Phrynichus (Lyc. *Leocr.* 113); either on the restoration of the democracy or in 408/7 he was the author of a motion recalling Alcibiades (Pl. *Alc.* 33. i: earlier date Wade-Gery, *CQ* xxxix 1945, 24 with n. 3 = *Essays*, 279 with n. 2; later date Andrewes, *JHS* lxxii 1953, 3 n. 7). When Alcibiades withdrew into exile after Notium Critias was exiled on the prosecution of Cleophon, went to Thessaly, and δημοκρατίαν κατεσκεύαζε καὶ τοὺς πενέστας ὥπλιζεν ἐπὶ τοὺς δεσπότας (X. *H.* II. iii. 36 cf. *M.* I. ii. 24: he is associated with the Larissan constitution of Arist. *Pol.* III. 1275 B 26–30 by Wade-Gery, *opp. citt.*, 25–6 = 280–1, with the tyranny of Lycophron of Pherae by C. Mossé, *CH* vi 1961, 354–5 n. 6, *La Tyrannie dans la Grèce antique*, 122 n. 3; date Wade-Gery, *opp. citt.*, 33 n. 1 = 292 n. 1); when the exiles returned to Athens in 404 (cf. next note) he was among them, and he was among the five 'ephors' appointed by the oligarchic ἑταιρεῖαι (Lys. xii. *Erat.* 43). He is named among the Thirty in X. *H.* ii. iii. 2, and notoriously came into conflict with Theramenes (37. i with commentary); he was killed in the battle briefly reported in 38. i (cf. *ad. loc.*); his cousin Charmides was one of the Piraeus Ten (35. i with commentary), and was killed in the same battle. That Critias the overthrower of the democracy was a pupil of Socrates was widely remembered (e.g. X. *M.* i. ii. 12, A. i. *Tim.* 173), but *A.P.* does not mention Critias at all, and the only allusion to the Thirty in Arist. *Pol.* (v. 1305 B 22–7) states that Charicles used demagoguic methods within the Thirty as Phrynichus had used demagoguic methods within the Four Hundred. Charicles Ἀπολλοδώρου was a democrat and a ζητητής with Pisander in 415 (And. i. *Myst.* 36: cf. p. 407), and a general in 414/3 (T. vii. 20. i, 26. i); probably he was a member of the Four Hundred and went into exile after their downfall (Is. xvi. *Big.* 42 with MacDowell on And. i. *Myst.* 36; but ἅπαντες in Lys. xiii. *Agor.* 74 cannot be true [cf. p. 435]). He is named among the Thirty in X. *H.* ii. iii. 2; Lys. xii. *Erat.* 55 describes some of the more moderate oligarchs as οἱ δοκοῦντες εἶναι ἐναντιώτατοι Χαρικλεῖ καὶ Κριτίᾳ καὶ τῇ ἐκείνων ἑταιρείᾳ; cf. also D. xxiv. *Tim.* 90.

For Plato's hopes and disillusionment in 404–403 see Plat. *Ep.* vii. 324 B 8–325 A 7: the Platonic school will not have wished to emphasise the misdeeds of Critias, and may have focused attention on Charicles in his place; and the appearance of Charicles in Arist. *Pol.* and the absence of Critias from *A.P.* may well be due to Platonic influence (cf. E. Meyer, *G.d.A.*, v[4] [13–]14 n. 1, Davies, *A.P.F.*, 503). One other extremist deserves mention, Satyrus Κηφισιεύς: he was a bouleutes in 405/4 and played a leading part in the elimination of Cleophon (Lys. xxx. *Nic.* 10, 14); in 404/3 he was not one of the Thirty, but was one of the Eleven (X. *H.* ii. iii. 2, 54–6, contr. Lys. xxx. *Nic.* 12).

καὶ τῶν φυγάδων οἱ μετὰ τὴν εἰρήνην κατελθόντες: At the beginning of 405 Aristophanes had urged the restoration of the ἄτιμοι (*Ran.* 686–705: for the 'tamed' ἀτιμία of the classical period, which involved the loss of political and judicial rights but not outlawry, see on 8. v); in the autumn of 405, after Aegospotami, this was done (And. i. *Myst.* 73–9, quoting in 77–9 the decree of Patroclides; cf. 109, X. *H.* ii. ii. 10–11, Lys. xxv. *Reip. Del. Defens.* 27); the return of exiles (φυγάδες) was stipulated in the peace terms of 404 (X. *H.* ii. ii. 20, Pl. *Lys.* 14. viii, And. iii. *Pace*, 12, cf. i. *Myst.* 80, 109, Lys. xxv. *Reip. Del. Defens.* 27; Dem. Phal. 228 F 3 = Phil. 328 F 137 *ap.* Marc. *Vit. Thuc.* 32 may be relevant, but Jacoby refused to delete the reference to Sicily). The ἄτιμοι included members of the Four Hundred and men involved in τῶν ἐν τῇ ὀλιγαρχίᾳ πραχθέντων (And. i. *Myst.* 78); others of the Four Hundred had gone into exile

(T. VIII. 98, Lys. XIII. *Agor.* 74); the exiles also included Critias, who was to become the leader of the extremists (cf. previous note).

οἱ δ' ἐν ἑταιρείᾳ μὲν οὐδεμιᾷ συγκαθεστῶτες: J. J. Keaney compares the claim of Socrates that he took no part in συνωμοσιῶν καὶ στάσεων τῶν ἐν τῇ πόλει γιγνομένων (Plat. *Apol.* 36 B 8–9: cf. above, p. 361). As stated above, it is unlikely that every ἑταιρεία was in favour of extreme oligarchy; but Lys. XII. *Erat.* 43–7 with 76 confirms that the ἑταιρεῖαι were particularly associated with the extremists (or were thought to be), and so the attempt to make a clear distinction between Theramenes and the extremists leads to the assertion that Theramenes and his supporters were not members of the ἑταιρεῖαι. P. E. Harding, *Phoen.* xxviii 1974, 101–11, argues that no one before *A.P.* defended Theramenes as a 'moderate', but this use of a threefold division to defend Theramenes was surely found by *A.P.* in his source.

[ἄ]λλως δὲ δοκοῦντες οὐδενὸς ἐπιλείπεσθαι τῶν πολιτῶν: 'And in other respects seeming inferior to none of the citizens', ἐπιλείπεσθαι being equivalent to ἥττονες εἶναι (as in T. II. 60. V). ἐπιλείπεσθαι is a favourite expression of *A.P.*, found also in 20. ii and 27. iv, and there is no need to change to ἀπολείπεσθαι or ὑπολείπεσθαι: cf. Kaibel, *Stil und Text*, 43, 171. We are not told in what respects these men seemed inferior to none: ἄλλως if pressed would imply 'in addition to the merit of not belonging to the ἑταιρεῖαι'; Kenyon in his Oxford Translation offers 'though in other respects they considered themselves as good as any other citizens'.

τὴν πάτριον πολιτείαν ἐζήτουν: See pp. 427–8.

'Αρχῖνος: ἐκ Κοιλῆς. At some time before 405 he combined with Agyrrhius (41. iii with commentary) to reduce the payment made to comic poets competing at the Dionysia and Lenaea (Ar. *Ran.* 367 with schol., cf. *Eccl.* 102 with schol.); he was not a member of the Thirty (X. *H.* II. iii. 2), but was with Thrasybulus at Phyle (D. XXIV. *Tim.* 135, A. III. *Ctes.* 187, 195, cf. Aristid. XXXIV. *Leuctr. ii.* [i. 661 Dindorf]). In 40. i–ii he is praised for his moderation in the conduct of affairs after the restoration of the democracy (cf. D. XXIV. *Tim.* 135, A. II. *F.L.* 176); he disappears from history as abruptly as he appeared (but Demosthenes says ἐστρατηγηκότος πολλάκις). It is surprising to find a man remembered in the fourth century as one of the principal heroes of Phyle praised as an associate of Theramenes: cf. below.

"Ανυτος: Said in 27. v to be the first Athenian to secure acquittal by bribing a jury (in 409: cf. *ad loc.*). Like Archinus he was not a member of the Thirty (X. *H.* II. iii. 2) but was with Thrasybulus at Phyle (X. *H.* II. iii. 42, 44, Lys. XIII. *Agor.* 78, 82, Pl. *Glor. Ath.* 345 D–E: according to Lysias he showed moderation in preventing the killing of Agoratus at Phyle), and like Archinus he was influential at the restoration of the democracy (Is. XVIII. *Call.* 23, Plat. *Men.* 90 B 2–3, cf. X. *Apol.* 29). He was a defender of Andocides in 400 (And. I. *Myst.* 150), and a prosecutor of Socrates in 399 (e.g. Plat. *Apol.* 23 E 3–24 A 1); associated with Thrasybulus and Aesimus in a desire to avoid trouble with Sparta in 396 (*H.O.* 6. ii); but the Anytus of 388/7 (Lys. XXII. *Frum.* 8) need not be the same man (thus Kirchner, *P.A.* 1322). He ended his life as an exile in Heraclea Pontica, where he was stoned to death (D.L. II. 43, Themist. XX. *Patr.* 239 C: the facts may be correct, even if the alleged reason, a change of heart by the Athenians after their condemnation of Socrates, is rendered unlikely by a date after 396; but in X. *Apol.* 31 it is only because of the bibulous habits of his son that Anytus has a bad reputation after his death).

Κλειτοφῶν: Named in 29. iii as author of the rider instructing the συγγραφεῖς of 411 to examine or search for τοὺς πατρίους νόμους οὓς Κλεισθένης ἔθηκεν ὅτε καθίστη τὴν δημοκρατίαν (cf. *ad loc.*). Like the other men said here to have been associates of Theramenes, he was not a member of the Thirty (X. *H.* II. iii. 2); nothing further is heard of him.

Φορμίσιος: In Ar. *Ran.* 964–7 he is named (perhaps simply on grounds of personal appearance) as a disciple of Aeschylus, in contrast to Theramenes and Clitophon, the disciples of Euripides: schol. 965 says δραστικὸς ἦν καὶ τὴν κόμην τρέφων καὶ φοβερὸς δοκῶν εἶναι (cf. schol. *Eccl.* 97). He was not a member of the Thirty (X. *H.* II. iii. 2); he was τις τῶν συγκατελθόντων μετὰ τοῦ δήμου (D.H. 526. *Lys.* 32 = Lys. XXXIV. *Rep. Patr.*, *hyp.*), but is not said to have been at Phyle; after the restoration he proposed that exiles should return but citizenship should be limited to those who owned land in Attica (*ibid.*), Lys. XXXIV was written in opposition, and the proposal failed (cf. p. 472). About 393 he and Epicrates (*P.A.* 4859; a man who had not been eager to avoid trouble with Sparta in 396: *H.O.* 7. ii cf. Paus. III. 9. viii) served on an embassy to Persia and were accused of taking bribes (Plat. Com. Πρέσβεις, frs. 119–22 Kock [cf. I. A. F. Bruce, *Hist.* xv 1966, 277–8, but on the play see K. J. Dover, *CR* lxiv 1950, 5–6], Hegesander *ap.* Ath. VI. 251 A–B, Pl. *Pelop.* 30. xii, Aristid. XIII. *Panath.* with schol. [i. 283, iii. 277, Dindorf]); at the time of the Spartan occupation of Thebes he supported the Thebans (Din. I. *Dem.* 38–40).

The alleged supporters of Theramenes are an interesting set of men (cf. E. Meyer, *G.d.A.*, v[4]. [13–]14 n. 1): none were members of the Thirty, though ten of the Thirty are said to have been nominated by Theramenes (Lys. XII. *Erat.* 76: cf. pp. 428, 435); Archinus and Anytus are among the most prominent of the men of Phyle, though Archinus is shown by his actions after the restoration and Anytus is shown by his treatment of Agoratus not to have been vindictively anti-oligarchic; Clitophon was author of the rider invoking the πάτριοι νόμοι of Cleisthenes in 411; Phormisius was with the democrats at the Piraeus, but was no lover of extreme democracy. It is by no means impossible that these men should have been supporters of Theramenes in summer 404; afterwards, of course, it would be in their interest not to draw attention to that, but to stress that they did not stay in Athens under the rule of the Thirty; but defenders of Theramenes at the beginning of the fourth century might have thought it useful to link him with men who honourably survived 404-403. The defence of Theramenes in X. *H.* includes the claim, ἐπεί γε μὴν πολλοὺς ἑώρων ἐν τῇ πόλει τῇ ἀρχῇ τῇδε δυσμενεῖς, πολλοὺς δὲ φυγάδας γιγνομένους, οὐκ αὖ ἐδόκει μοι οὔτε Θρασύβουλον οὔτε Ἄνυτον οὔτε Ἀλκιβιάδην φυγαδεύειν (II. iii. 42). It would be particularly interesting to know whether this information on Theramenes' supporters is true, and, whether or not it is true, where *A.P.* obtained it.

Θηραμένης: Cf. 28. iii, v (Theramenes is the last in the list of προστάται τῶν γνωρίμων, and is singled out for praise), 32. ii, 33. ii (he was active in 411 both in the overthrow of the democracy and in the overthrow of the Four Hundred), and commentary *ad locc.* In fact, in 404 as in 411, he helped to overthrow the democracy only to find that the oligarchy which resulted was too extreme for his tastes; but *A.P.* by distinguishing between oligarchs and men whose aim was the πάτριος πολιτεία exculpates him from the charge of helping to overthrow the democracy and set up the régime of the Thirty in 404 (cf. next note). Lys. XII. *Erat.* 76 states that ten of the Thirty were nominated by him (cf. above); X. *H.* II. iii. 2 includes him in the list of the Thirty, and D.S. XIV. 4. i alleges that he was elected to counteract the influence of the oligarchs; but *A.P.* nowhere mentions that Theramenes was one of the Thirty.

Λυσάνδρου δὲ προσθεμένου τοῖς ὀλιγαρχικοῖς ... χειροτονεῖν τὴν ὀλιγαρχίαν: X. *H.* II. iii. 11 makes no mention of Lysander's intervention, and states laconically οἱ δὲ τριάκοντα ᾑρέθησαν μὲν ἐπεὶ τάχιστα τὰ μακρὰ τείχη καὶ τὰ περὶ τὸν Πειραιᾶ καθῃρέθη (cf. §28, in Critias' speech, and §38, in Theramenes' speech); §15 adds τῷ μὲν οὖν πρώτῳ χρόνῳ ὁ Κριτίας τῷ Θηραμένει ὁμογνώμων τε καὶ φίλος ἦν. D.S., with his twofold division between oligarchs and democrats, places Theramenes on the democratic side: as the dispute over the πάτριος πολιτεία progressed the oligarchs summoned Lysander from Samos; Lysander called an assembly at which he spoke in favour of oligarchy and Theramenes spoke against; Lysander pointed out that by not demolishing their fortifications within the time specified the Athenians were in breach of the peace treaty; διόπερ ὅ τε Θηραμένης καὶ ὁ δῆμος καταπλαγεὶς ἠναγκάζετο χειροτονίᾳ καταλῦσαι τὴν δημοκρατίαν (XIV. 3. ii–vii). Another account is given by Lysias: Theramenes summoned Lysander from Samos; an assembly was held at which

433

Lysander and his colleagues were present; Theramenes spoke in favour of oligarchy, Lysander supported him and pointed out that the Athenians had broken the peace treaty, opponents of oligarchy left the meeting or remained quiet; and so the Thirty were appointed (XII. *Erat.* 71–6: the charge of breaking the peace treaty is found also in Pl. *Lys.* 15. ii–v). Lysias, who claims that his account is supported by Theramenes' own defence (§77), is not of course unbiased—he attacks Theramenes in order to show that a man who supported Theramenes rather than Critias was still a supporter of the oligarchy—but all that we know of Theramenes suggests that Lysias' account of his part in the setting up of the Thirty is correct, and that Diodorus and *A.P.* have in different ways distorted the truth to conceal his guilt. (P. Salmon, *AC* xxxviii 1969, 497–500, cf. W. J. McCoy, *YCS* xxiv 1975, 141–4, tries to combine Diodorus and Lysias and suggests that Theramenes did oppose the proposals for an oligarchy until Lysander insisted that they must be accepted; but I am not persuaded.)

The reader who proceeds to 35. ii finds to his surprise that although the 'oligarchs' triumphed over the champions of the πάτριος πολιτεία the Thirty at first προσεποιοῦντο διώκειν τὴν πάτριον πολιτείαν: cf. *ad loc.*

καταπλαγεὶς ὁ δῆμος ἠναγκάσθη χειροτονεῖν τὴν ὀλιγαρχίαν: D.S. XIV. 3. vii, after a different account of how it came about, uses very similar language (quoted in previous note); cf. also *A.P.* 29. i (ἠναγκάσθησαν κινήσαντες τὴν δημοκρατίαν καταστῆσαι τὴν ἐπὶ τῶν τετρακοσίων πολιτείαν), and the statements in 34. i that the δῆμος condemned the generals after Arginusae and rejected Sparta's peace offer because it was deceived, with commentary *ad locc.* Probably now as in 411 such safeguards as the γραφὴ παρανόμων were suspended: cf. 29. iv with commentary.

ἔγραψε τὸ ψήφισμα Δρακοντίδης Ἀφιδναῖος: Cited by schol. Ar. *Vesp.* 157. Kirchner was not necessarily right to identify him with the Dracontides of Ar. *Vesp.* 157, Plat. Com., fr. 139 Kock (*P.A.* 4546); but we may safely identify the author of the decree with the member of the Thirty (X. *H.* II. iii. 2, Hyp. fr. 67 Sauppe ap. Harp. Δρακοντίδης). As in 29. i *A.P.* gives the proposer's demotic, although published fifth-century decrees do not.

According to Lys. XII. *Erat.* 73 Theramenes ἐκέλευσεν ὑμᾶς τριάκοντα ἀνδράσιν ἐπιτρέψαι τὴν πόλιν καὶ τῇ πολιτείᾳ χρῆσθαι ἣν Δρακοντίδης ἀπέφαινεν. Presumably Dracontides proposed that the assembly should appoint a board of Thirty for a stated purpose. According to X. *H.* II. iii. 11 the Thirty were appointed ἐφ' ᾧτε συγγράψαι νόμους καθ' οὕστινας πολιτεύσοιντο (cf. the interpolated §2: τριάκοντα ἄνδρας ἑλέσθαι, οἳ τοὺς πατρίους νόμους συγγράψουσι, καθ' οὓς πολιτεύσουσι); according to D.S. XIV. 3. vii–4. i the Thirty were οἱ διοικήσοντες τὰ κοινὰ τῆς πόλεως, ἁρμόζοντες μὲν τῷ λόγῳ, τύραννοι δὲ τοῖς πράγμασιν. . . . ἔδει δὲ τοὺς ᾑρημένους βουλήν τε καὶ τὰς ἄλλας ἀρχὰς καταστῆσαι, καὶ νόμους συγγράψαι καθ' οὓς ἔμελλον πολιτεύεσθαι; A.P. 35. i says τὰ μὲν ἄλλα τὰ δόξαντα περὶ τῆς πολιτείας παρεώρων, πεντακοσίους δὲ βουλευτὰς καὶ τὰς ἄλλας ἀρχὰς καταστήσαντες . . .; Plat. *Ep.* vii. 324 D 4–5 says ᾠήθην γὰρ αὐτοὺς ἔκ τινος ἀδίκου βίου ἐπὶ δίκαιον τρόπον ἄγοντας διοικήσειν δὴ τὴν πόλιν; Lys. XII. *Erat.* 71–6 equates the appointment of the Thirty with the setting aside of the democracy, but since the Thirty did in fact make themselves the rulers of Athens that does not help us to determine their formal terms of reference. Probably Diodorus is right, and the Thirty were given a double task (cf. Hignett, *H.A.C.*, 383, G. Adeleye, *Mus. Afr.* v 1976, 13–16): to act as συγγραφεῖς, drawing up new laws (cf. the συγγραφεῖς of 411: 29. ii), in which capacity they superseded the ἀναγραφεῖς of the democracy (see on 35. ii); and also to act as a provisional government, and bring a new constitution into being, after which their own work would be complete (cf. the provisional government of Twenty appointed after the reconciliation in 403: p. 441).

The Thirty are listed in X. *H.* II. iii. 2 (which, though interpolated, does not appear to be inaccurate): Lys. XIII. *Agor.* 74 alleges that all were τῶν τετρακοσίων τῶν φυγόντων, which is clearly wrong in the case of Theramenes, to pursue the matter no further. R. Loeper, *JM(R)I* cccv. v–vi May–June 1896, *Otd. kl. Fil.* 90–6, 97–101, remarked that they appear to be three from each tribe and one from each trittys, listed in official tribal order:[33] that they are three from each tribe, in official tribal order, remains compatible with all the information that we now have, but if one was from each trittys the trittyes were not taken in the same order in each tribe. (On Erasistratus [*P.A.* 5028] see Davies, *A.P.F.*, 523; and on the problems of identifying the Thirty see the cautionary note of W. E. Thompson, Φόρος . . . *B. D. Meritt*, 148–9.) Lys. XII. *Erat.* 76 writes παρήγγελτο αὐτοῖς (*sc.* τοῖς Ἀθηναίοις) δέκα μὲν οὓς Θηραμένης ἀπέδειξε χειροτονῆσαι, δέκα δὲ οὓς οἱ καθεστηκότες ἔφοροι κελεύοιεν, δέκα δ' ἐκ τῶν παρόντων· . . . πρότερον ᾔδεσαν (*sc.* οἱ ὀλιγαρχικοί) τὰ μέλλοντα ἐν τῇ ἐκκλησίᾳ πραχθήσεσθαι (on the significance of the three tens see p. 428): this suggests that the three tens were not a part of Dracontides' formal proposal. If he proposed ἑλέσθαι τριάκοντα ἄνδρας αὐτίκα μάλα, ἐξ ἑκάστης φυλῆς τρεῖς, this method of arriving at the three men from each tribe may have been suggested from the floor of the house by men who had already drawn up lists of suitable candidates; I doubt if they restricted themselves by requiring one from each trittys.†

---

[33] I owe my knowledge of the contents of this article to Dr. D. M. Lewis.

35. i. οἱ μὲν οὖν τριάκοντα τοῦτον τὸν τρόπον κατέστησαν: This sentence rounds off the passage introduced by Λύσανδρον καταστῆσαι τοὺς τριάκοντα τρόπῳ τοιῷδε (34. ii); but in fact *A.P.* has said nothing directly about the Thirty. The omission may be due simply to *A.P.*'s condensation of his material; or perhaps his source was more concerned to explain how the Thirty came into being than to explain (what readers could be expected to know) what they were.

ἐπὶ Πυθοδώρου ἄρχοντος: 404/3. Pythodorus is used also for dating purposes in 41. i and Lys. vii. *Ol.* 9, and is to be restored in *IG* ii² 1498, 21–2, *SEG* xxi 80, 1, and possibly Tod 100, 2 (but there the archon of 401/0 is likelier: cf. pp. 476–7). The interpolator in X. *H.* ii. iii. 1 writes Πυθοδώρου δ' ἐν Ἀθήναις ἄρχοντος, ὃν Ἀθηναῖοι, ὅτι ἐν ὀλιγαρχίᾳ ᾑρέθη, οὐκ ὀνομάζουσιν, ἀλλ' ἀναρχίαν τὸν ἐνιαυτὸν καλοῦσιν, and D.S. xiv. 3. i writes ἀναρχίας γὰρ οὔσης Ἀθήνησι.

The chronological implications of X. *H.* ii. iii. 1 and *A.P.* have been much discussed. If, as I believe, the whole of ii. iii. 1–3 is among the passages in X. *H.* which are interpolated, Xenophon did not mention the Thirty until he had finished with the Peloponnesian War, when he said that they were appointed ἐπεὶ τάχιστα τὰ μακρὰ τείχη καὶ τὰ περὶ τὸν Πειραιᾶ καθῃρέθη (ii. iii. 11: O. Blank, *Die Einsetzung der Dreissig zu Athen im Jahre 404 v. Chr.*, 1–18, Beloch, *G.G.*², iii. ii. 204–6, Hignett, *H.A.C.*, 379–80). Lysander was able to claim that the Athenians did not demolish the walls within the time stipulated (Lys. xii. *Erat.* 74, D.S. xiv. 3. vi, Pl. *Lys.* 15. ii), but we are not told how long that time was. Our one firm date is that of Lysander's (first) entry into Athens, after the acceptance of the peace terms, on 16 Munichion (x) (Pl. *Lys.* 15. i: cf. p. 426), which would allow the appointment of the Thirty to fall either at the very end of 405/4 or early in 404/3 (Hignett, *H.A.C.*, 381–2, cf. A. G. Roos, *Klio* xvii 1920, 1–11 [accepting X. *H.* ii. iii. 1–3 as authentic]; Blank, *op. cit.*, 32–4 cf. 77–80, and G. Colin, *Xénophon historien*, 31–4, would delay the appointment of the Thirty until autumn 404, but their arguments are not cogent). It cannot be true both that the Thirty were appointed when Pythodorus was archon and that Pythodorus was appointed under the oligarchy (as Xenophon's interpolator suggests); and there is no other text which would require us to date the appointment of the Thirty before the end of 405/4 (despite the arguments of Beloch, *G.G.*², iii. ii. 204–9). If their appointment is to be dated early in 404/3, two explanations are possible: either Pythodorus was indeed appointed by the Thirty, and in the uncertainty of early 404 the democratic régime had made no appointment but prolonged the archonship of Alexias beyond the end of 405/4, so that early 404/3 could only be assigned to Alexias at the time but might come to be assigned to Pythodorus after he had been appointed; or Pythodorus was appointed by the democratic régime and took office on 1 Hecatombaeon (i) 404/3, but was retained in office by the Thirty and (although the archon was not personally responsible for the acts of his year) came to be closely enough associated with the Thirty to suffer *damnatio memoriae* on the restoration of the democracy. We have enough evidence for the institution of the Thirty to argue confidently *e silentio* against a third possibility, that the year began with new archons and other officials of the democracy, who were dispossessed by the Thirty. The first explanation is normally adopted, that Pythodorus was appointed after the beginning of 404/3 but came to be regarded as the archon of the whole year, just as Euclides was appointed after the beginning of 403/2 but came to be regarded as the archon of the whole year (cf. pp. 462–3) (e.g. Blank, *op. cit.*, 28, Roos, *op. cit.*, 2, Hignett, *H.A.C.*, 381–2). We are told that the Thirty appointed a boule καὶ τὰς ἄλλας ἀρχάς (cf. below), and it is natural to suppose that these ἀρχαί included the eponymous archon.

Pythodorus is a common name: it is possible but by no means necessary that this man is the author of the proposal to appoint συγγραφεῖς in 411 (see on 29. i).

τὰ μὲν ἄλλα τὰ δόξαντα περὶ τῆς πολιτείας παρεώρων: For the Thirty's formal terms of reference see pp. 434–5. According to X. *H.* II. iii. 11 τούτους μὲν (sc. τοὺς νόμους, καθ᾽ οὕστινας πολιτεύσοιντο) ἀεὶ ἔμελλον συγγράφειν τε καὶ ἀποδεικνύναι . . .; similarly D.S. XIV. 4. ii says τὰ μὲν οὖν περὶ τῆς νομοθεσίας ἀνεβάλοντο, προφάσεις εὐλόγους ἀεὶ ποριζόμενοι . . . They do seem to have brought in a rule under which laws were to be approved by the boule: see 37. i with commentary.

πεντακοσίους δὲ βουλευτὰς καὶ τὰς ἄλλας ἀρχὰς καταστήσαντες: Cf. X. *H.* II. iii. 11 (. . . βουλὴν δὲ καὶ τὰς ἄλλας ἀρχὰς κατέστησαν ὡς ἐδόκει αὐτοῖς), 38, D.S. XIV. 4. ii (. . . βουλὴν δὲ καὶ τὰς ἄλλας ἀρχὰς ἐκ τῶν ἰδίων φίλων κατέστησαν, ὥστε τούτους καλεῖσθαι μὲν ἄρχοντας, εἶναι δ᾽ ὑπηρέτας τῶν τριάκοντα). No other text states that the Cleisthenic size of five hundred for the boule was retained, but we need not doubt it. Lys. XIII. *Agor.* 20 says ἡ δὲ βουλὴ ἡ πρὸ τῶν τριάκοντα βουλεύουσα διέφθαρτο καὶ ὀλιγαρχίας ἐπεθύμει, ὡς ἴστε, μάλιστα. τεκμήριον δέ· οἱ γὰρ πολλοὶ ⟨οἱ⟩ ἐξ ἐκείνης τῆς βουλῆς τὴν ὑστέραν βουλὴν ⟨τὴν⟩ ἐπὶ τῶν τριάκοντα ἐβούλευον (ὑστέραν Taylor: ὑμετέραν codd.): there is no sign that in 404 as in 411 a boule appointed under the democracy was dismissed from office (32. i with commentary), so presumably the 'corrupt' boule was that of 405/4 (whose year was now the archontic year: see on 32. i), which served until democratic institutions were suspended on the appointment of the Thirty, probably early in 404/3 (cf. above). We do not know how many men were bouleutae both in 405/4 and in 404/3 (the Thirty need not, of course, have considered themselves bound by the rule of 62.

iii): Chremon was a bouleutes in 405/4 and a member of the Thirty (*P.A.* 15570: Lys. xxx. *Nic.* 12, 14, X. *H.* ii. iii. 2), and Satyrus was a bouleutes in 405/4 and a member of the Eleven under the Thirty (cf. p. 430); the allegation in Lys. xiii. *Agor.* 74 that the Thirty and their boule αὐτοὶ ἦσαν ἅπαντες τῶν τετρακοσίων τῶν φυγόντων cannot be accurate, on mathematical grounds (and cf. p. 435), and the men of whom it is true will not have returned to Athens in time to be bouleutae in 405/4 (cf. p. 430). The other ἀρχαί appointed by the Thirty probably included the nine archons (cf. above: for Patroclides as basileus see Is. xviii. *Call.* 5); the officials of most importance were the Piraeus Ten and the Eleven, mentioned below.

ἐκ προκρίτων ἐκ τῶν χιλίων: The πρόκριτοι are not mentioned elsewhere, and the papyrus' text is hard to accept: the article presupposes a well-known body of 1,000 or a previous mention of them (it is not likely that they are the 1,000 cavalry [cf. p. 303], as suggested by W. L. Newman, *CR* v 1891, 164; we know all too little about the 1,000 who are said by Lys. fr. 146 Sauppe, Isae. fr. 106 Sauppe, ap. Harp. χίλιοι διακόσιοι to have preceded the 1,200 λῃτουργοῦντες); and unless the 1,000 are a preliminary body from whom the πρόκριτοι are to be chosen, for which purpose we should expect a larger number, the second ἐκ is redundant. E. S. Thompson (*CR* v 1891, 277) and Leeuwen emended to ἐκ τῶν πεντακισχιλίων, and Kaibel & Wilamowitz tentatively suggested ἐκ προκρίτων πεντακισχιλίων (cf. Kaibel, *Stil und Text*, 191–2); but there is no other evidence to suggest that the concept of the Five Thousand, employed in 411 (cf. 29. v, 33. i, with commentary), was revived in 404. Hude proposed ἐκ τῶν φυλῶν (*NTF*² x 1890–2, 251, cf. Moore, 268); J. Raeder, *NTF*³ vii 1898/9, 194, ἐκ τῶν ἰδίων ?φίλων (cf. D.S. xiv. 4. ii, quoted above); G. E. Marindin, *CR* v 1891, 181, deleted ἐκ τῶν χιλίων, but it would be surprising if a copyist had invented the phrase *ex nihilo* (cf. Kaibel, *loc. cit.*). Herwerden's deletion of ἐκ τῶν, leaving 1,000 as the number of the πρόκριτοι, has won some support and seems to be the best solution of the problem.

τοῦ Πειραιέως ἄρχοντας δέκα: Cf. Plat. *Ep.* vii. 324 c 3–5, Pl. *Lys.* 15. i, *L.S.* 235. 31; also Andr. 324 F 11 (Androtion certainly named one of them, Molpis, and may have named all); they included Charmides Γλαύκωνος, cousin of Critias and uncle of Plato (Plat. *Charm.* 154 B 1–2, X. *H.* ii. iv. 19: Kirchner, *P.A.* 15512, Davies, *A.P.F.*, 330–1); these are among the men most implicated in the oligarchy who in 39. vi are excluded from the amnesty of 403 unless they submit to a process of εὔθυναι. No equivalent of this office is known to have existed under the democracy (except that the demarch of the Piraeus was a state appointment, not a local one: 54. viii with commentary): these Ten seem to have been the deputies of the Thirty in the Piraeus; Plato regards them as comparable to the Eleven in Athens, and says rather surprisingly of both περί τε ἀγορὰν ἑκάτεροι τούτων ὅσα τ' ἐν τοῖς ἄστεσι διοικεῖν ἔδει—which makes us think of the ἀγορανόμοι, of whom in the fourth century there were five in the city and five in the Piraeus (51. i with commentary).

The normal Greek spelling of Piraeus is Πειραιεύς (Πειραιέα, &c.); in the fourth century the αι on several occasions becomes α in this and similar names (Meisterhans & Schwyzer, *G.a.I.*, 30–3 with 32 n. 173, 33 n. 175); in the accusative and genitive the ending is usually contracted in the fifth century (Πειραιᾶ, Πειραιῶς), equally often contracted or uncontracted in the fourth, and increasingly rarely contracted thereafter, while the dative is regularly Πειραιεῖ (*op. cit.*, 140–2). Here the papyrus has Πιραιῶς, corrected to Πιραιέως; elsewhere many epsilons are omitted and some are added above the line; it seems best to do as Kenyon and most editors have done and print the fullest forms *passim* (cf. Kaibel & Wilamowitz, [1-2]xiii = [3]xv).

καὶ τοῦ δεσμωτηρίου φύλακας ἕνδεκα: Cf. X. *H.* II. iii. 54, Plat. *Ep.* vii. 324 C 3–5: the Eleven were afterwards seen not as underlings but, like the Piraeus Ten, as men so far implicated in the oligarchy that they too were excluded from the amnesty of 403 unless they submitted to εὔθυναι (39. vi); Xenophon describes their leader, Satyrus (cf. p. 430), as τοῦ θρασυτάτου τε καὶ ἀναιδεστάτου. The Eleven, gaolers and executioners, existed also under the democracy: cf. 24. iii, 52. i, with commentary.

καὶ μαστιγοφόρους τριακοσίους ὑπηρέτας: These are the ὑπηρέται who took Theramenes to his death (X. *H.* II. iii. 23, 54–5 [armed on that occasion with daggers], D.S. XIV. 5. i [but στρατιῶται in 4. vi]); and the *tria milia . . . satellitum* of Just. V. 8. x–xi are perhaps these rather than the three thousand privileged citizens (cf. Hignett, *H.A.C.*, 385). We are not told what was their standing or where they were recruited. The word ὑπηρέτης was sometimes used of public slaves, and B. Jordan, *CSCA* ii 1969, 190–3 = *U. Calif. Pub. Cl. Stud.* xiii 1975, 247–9, supposes that it was always so used, but see Y. Garlan, *Actes du colloque 1972 sur l'esclavage*, 26–7. μαστιγοφόρος is used in T. IV. 47. iii with reference to Corcyra; other instances cited by LSJ are late.

35. ii. τὸ μὲν οὖν πρῶτον μέτριοι τοῖς πολίταις ἦσαν: Cf. D.S. XIV. 4. ii (καὶ μέχρι τούτου τοῖς ἐπιεικεστάτοις τῶν πολιτῶν εὐαρέστει τὰ γινόμενα); and the texts cited on §iii, below, imply that at first the rule of the Thirty was tolerable to 'respectable' citizens.

καὶ προσεποιοῦντο διοικεῖν τὴν πάτριον πολιτείαν: διώκειν was suggested by M. C. Gertz, *NTF*[2] x 1890–2, 254, K. Σ. Κόντος, *Ἀθ.* iv 1892, 72 (cf. 13. iv, where Megacles and his supporters ἐδόκουν μάλιστα διώκειν τὴν μέσην πολιτείαν), and adopted by many editors; Kenyon retained διοικεῖν, in his Berlin ed. and O.C.T. comparing 27. ii (ὁ δῆμος ... προῃρεῖτο τὴν πολιτείαν διοικεῖν αὐτός) and remarking *non petere sed habere antiquam civitatem prae se ferebant.* However, there is no close parallel to διοικεῖν τὴν πάτριον πολιτείαν, and διώκειν is likelier.

Schol. A. I. *Tim.* 39 says οἱ λ' τύραννοι ... τὴν πάτριον πολιτείαν τῶν Ἀθηναίων καταλύσαντες ... (cf. below). Fritz & Kapp, 182–3, remark that the claim made in *A.P.* is hardly reconcilable with the Thirty's neglect of part of their terms of reference (§i). More serious is the fact that, whereas in 34. iii the 'oligarchs' and the champions of the πάτριος πολιτεία are distinct groups and with Lysander's support the 'oligarchs' prevail, here we are told that the extremists at first 'pretended' to seek the πάτριος πολιτεία. *A.P.*'s source attempted to minimise Theramenes' involvement in the régime of the Thirty by drawing a distinction between 'moderates' and extremists from the beginning (cf. pp. 420, 422, and commentary on 34. iii): since he could not suppress the mild beginning of the Thirty's rule he represented this mildness as a pretence (cf. Fuks, *The Ancestral Constitution*, 77–9).

καὶ τούς τ' Ἐφιάλτου καὶ Ἀρχεστράτου νόμους ... καθεῖλον ἐξ Ἀρείου πάγο[υ]: *A.P.* has written of an attack on the Areopagus' powers by Ephialtes, culminating in 462/1 (25), and of an attack by Pericles, probably to be identified with Ephialtes' attack (27. i: see *ad loc.*); apart from the stories linking Themistocles with Ephialtes in 25. iii–iv and Is. VII. *Areop., hyp.*, no other text names any one except these two as an attacker of the Areopagus. Gomme, *CR* xl 1926, 11, wrote 'we are very near the limit (*sc.* of improbability) here', and wanted to read Ἐφιάλτου καὶ Περικλέους and insert at the end of the clause Ἀρχεστράτου γράψαντος τὴν γνώμην; but since we have so little information on the reduction of the Areopagus' powers (cf. pp. 311, 315) this is altogether too drastic, and we should accept what *A.P.*'s text tells us: Archestratus cannot be reliably identified (a possible candidate is Archestratus Λυκομήδους, *P.A.* 2411: Wilamowitz, *A.u.A.*, i. 68 n. 40, Busolt, *G.G.*, III. i. 270 n. 1), but was presumably a collaborator of Ephialtes. The laws were annulled by the physical removal from the Areopagus of the stelae on which they were inscribed (for the destruction of published texts cf. e.g., decree *ap.* And. I. *Myst.* 79, Tod 123, 31–5); the law of 337/6, threatening the Areopagus with suspension if the democracy was overthrown, was published ἐπὶ τῆς εἰσόδου τῆς εἰς Ἄρειον πάγον τῆς εἰς τὸ βουλευτήριον εἰσιόντι and in the ecclesia (*SEG* xii 87, 22–7).†

καὶ τῶν Σόλωνος θεσμῶν ὅσοι διαμφισβητήσεις εἶχον: Schol. A. I. *Tim.* 39, from a source of democratic complexion (cf. above), says ... ἐλυμήναντο τοὺς Δράκοντος καὶ Σόλωνος νόμους. Cf. 9. ii with commentary, where *A.P.* cites the law of inheritance as an example of an obscure law, but does not explain. For the use of θεσμός for

Solon's laws see 12. iv with commentary. On ἀμφισβητεῖν and its cognates in *A.P.* see 3. iv with commentary (διαμφισβήτησις is found in Arist. *Pol.* I. 1256 A 14). The scribe writes διαμφιζβητήσεις and (below) ἀναμφιζβήτητον, and Meisterhans & Schwyzer, *G.a.I.*, 88 with n. 766, cite examples of ζ added to or replacing σ from the last third of the fourth century (*IG* ii² 448, 39, 1672, 308–9), but in 3. iv, 5. ii and 9. ii the first scribe did not use ζ, so we may confidently attribute the spelling with ζ to this scribe. The ἄξονες on which Solon's laws were inscribed were housed in the Stoa of the Basileus (7. i with commentary), not on the Areopagus: Sandys considered deleting τ' before 'Εφιάλτου; but it is better to follow Gomme, *CR* xl 1926, 11, in regarding τ' as linking 'Εφιάλτου and Ἀρχεστράτου, and to punctuate with a comma after πάγου and none after εἶχον (so that Solon's laws will be the object of κατέλυσαν). Although the laws of Ephialtes and Archestratus were physically demolished, it is unlikely that the Thirty dared to tamper with the ἄξονες.

Revision of the laws was a task inherited by the Thirty from the democracy. The upheavals of 411–410 had presumably exposed or emphasised the fact that the laws of Athens were in confusion, and so in 410/09 a commission of ἀναγραφεῖς had been appointed, to republish 'the laws of Solon and the homicide law of Draco' (which seems to have meant 'the laws currently in force'); the task proved complicated, and was unfinished when the Thirty came to power (Lys. xxx. *Nic.* 2–3, cf. M&L 86, 3–8). After the reconciliation of 403 a board of Twenty was appointed to act as a provisional government under 'the laws of Solon and Draco' and bring a more lasting régime into being (And. 1. *Myst.* 81, schol. A. 1. *Tim.* 39); a procedure for revising the laws was then instituted (And. 1. *Myst.* 82–4, quoting the decree of Tisamenus) and the commission of ἀναγραφεῖς was reappointed; the revised code was completed and published in the Stoa in 400/399 (Lys. xxx. *Nic.* 4, And. 1. *Myst.* 85). From the first phase of this work we possess the republication of the part of Draco's homicide law that was still in force (M&L 86, discussed above, pp. 111–12), and a more fragmentary text which seems to be a collection of laws concerning the boule (*IG* i² 114, discussed by Rhodes, *A.B.*, 195–9). For the epigraphic fragments belonging to the later phases see especially S. Dow, *Proc. Mass. Hist. Soc.* lxxi 1953–7, 3–24, *Hesp.* xxx 1961, 58–73, A. Fingarette, *Hesp.* xl 1971, 330–5: Miss Fingarette suggests that before 404 the ἀναγραφεῖς began their sacred calendar on one side of the wall to be erected in the Stoa and overflowed on to the reverse; the Thirty began to prepare for their code by erasing the text on the main face; the ἀναγραφεῖς when they were reappointed started again on the main face, and the wall was finally set up in a position where the undeleted reverse could not be seen (for an alternative view of the 'wall', which need not invalidate this as a history of the inscribed texts, see above, pp. 134–5). We have no inscribed text of new laws published by the Thirty; but two laws are mentioned in 37. i as providing a legal basis for the killing of Theramenes, and in X. *H.* 11. iii. 51 Critias mentions one of them as ἐν τοῖς καινοῖς νόμοις.

καὶ τὸ κῦρος ὃ ἦν ἐν τοῖς δικασταῖς κατέλυσαν: Probably this refers simply to the removal of ambiguities from the laws of Solon (but for other ways in which the Thirty may have weakened juries see R. J. Bonner, *CP* xxi 1926, 212–17): 9. i remarks (of ἔφεσις εἰς τὸ δικαστήριον) κύριος γὰρ ὢν ὁ δῆμος τῆς ψήφου κύριος γίγνεται τῆς πολιτείας; 9. ii regards as a consequence of the ambiguities πάντα βραβεύειν καὶ τὰ κοινὰ καὶ τὰ ἴδια τὸ δικαστήριον, and criticises those who believe that Solon was deliberately ambiguous ὅπως ᾖ τῆς κρίσεως ὁ δῆμος κύριος; in 41. ii *fin.* the result of the growth of democracy is said to be ἁπάντων γὰρ αὐτὸς αὑτὸν πεποίηκεν ὁ δῆμος κύριον, καὶ πάντα διοικεῖται ψηφίσμασιν καὶ δικαστηρίοις, ἐν οἷς ὁ δῆμός ἐστιν ὁ κρατῶν. Fourth-century theorists shared the Thirty's dislike of leaving matters to the discretion of jurors: see p. 162.

ἀναμφισβήτητον: Like other words from the same root this is an Aristotelian word (e.g. *Pol.* III. 1283 B 4–5, VII. 1332 B 20–1), but it is found also in T. 1. 132. v, Lys. 11. *Epit.* 43, X. *Cyr.* VIII. v. 6, cf. ἀναμφισβητήτως in Is. IV. *Paneg.* 21. For the spelling (with ζ in the papyrus) see above.

οἷον περὶ τοῦ δοῦναι τὰ ἑαυτοῦ ᾧ ἂν ἐθέλῃ: Pl. *Sol.* 19. iii states that previously there had been no freedom of bequest, but Solon granted it in cases where there were no children: part of the law is quoted, with a reference to the situation obtaining ὅτε Σόλων εἰσῄει τὴν ἀρχήν, in [D.] XLVI. *Steph. ii.* 14 (τὰ ἑαυτοῦ διαθέσθαι εἶναι ὅπως ἂν ἐθέλῃ, ἂν μὴ παῖδες ὦσι γνήσιοι ἄρρενες, . . .: Sandys wrongly inserts the requirement of legitimacy in his quotation from Plutarch); cf. also Isae. II. *Her. Men.* 13, VI. *Her. Phil.* 9, 28, D. xx. *Lept.* 102. What was to be done when there were legitimate daughters but not sons was laid down in the clauses περὶ ἐπικλήρων (cf. 9. ii with commentary): any one who received property under the will had to marry a daughter, and would hold the inherited property in trust for the sons of this marriage (Isae. III. *Her. Pyrrh.* 42, 68, x. *Her. Arist.* 12–13). Probably what later came to be regarded as freedom of bequest was originally freedom for a man with no legitimate sons to adopt an heir (who if there were daughters would have to marry one of them); such adoption would preclude the right and duty of the next of kin to inherit the property (Ar. *Av.* 1660–6) and marry the daughters ([D.] XLVI. *Steph. ii.* 22–3) in order to prevent the extinction of the οἶκος: see L. Gernet, *REG* xxxiii 1920, 123–68, 249–90 = *Droit et société dans la Grèce ancienne,* 121–49, Harrison, *L.A.,* i. 82–4, 149–50. By the fourth century there was some freedom of bequest not tied to adoption and marriage: see Harrison, *L.A.*, i. 131–2. In Plat. *Legg.* xi. 922 A sqq. the Athenian claims that earlier lawgivers had granted complete freedom of bequest, and recommends regulations under which a childless man will have free disposal of one tenth of ἡ ἐπίκτητος but must adopt an heir and leave the rest of the property to him.

In the interests of grammatical coherence Kaibel & Wilamowitz (cf. Kaibel, *Stil und Text*, 192) inserted ⟨τὸν⟩ περὶ and emended to κύριον ἐποίησαν below, and Herwerden added ἄν ⟨τις⟩; but *A.P.* is perfectly capable of this kind of irregularity.

κύριον ποιήσαντες καθάπαξ: 'Absolutely', in the sense that the qualifications mentioned below are withdrawn; we need not wonder, with Sandys, whether the limitation of this freedom to cases where there were no legitimate sons was withdrawn also. It is clear from the fourth-century orators that the qualifications were restored after the restoration of the democracy: cf. below.

τὰς δὲ προσούσας δυσκολίας: 'The attached difficulties.' δυσκολία is another Aristotelian word, sometimes simply equivalent to ἀπορία (e.g. *Phys.* vi. 239 b 11), sometimes implying unpleasant disagreement over an ἀπορία (e.g. *Pol.* ii. 1263 a 11); that implication is strongly present in D. xxxix. *Boe. Nom.* 11; the point here is that difficulties of interpretation give rise to (undesirable) lawsuits and exercise of discretion by jurors.

'**ἐὰν μὴ μανιῶν ἢ γηρῶν ἢ γυναικὶ πιθόμενος**': Cf. the quotation of the law in [D.] xlvi. *Steph. ii.* 14 (... ἂν μὴ μανιῶν ἢ γήρως ἢ φαρμάκων ἢ νόσου ἕνεκα, ἢ γυναικὶ πειθόμενος, ὑπὸ τούτων του παρανοῶν, ἢ ὑπ᾽ ἀνάγκης ἢ ὑπὸ δεσμοῦ καταληφθείς: ἕνεκα Rennie, ἕνεκεν codd.; παρανοῶν Wesseling, παρανόμων codd.), and the paraphrases *ibid.* 16, Lys. fr. 230 Sauppe, Isae. iv. *Her. Nic.* 16, vi. *Her. Phil.* 9, 21, Hyp. iii. *Ath.* 17, Pl. *Sol.* 21. iv, *Q.R.* 265 E, which show that in repeating this clause writers could be selective and could make small verbal changes. Kaibel, *Stil und Text*, 192–4, argued that *A.P.* is more likely than the orators to have consulted the law and reproduced it accurately; he defended μανιῶν and γηρῶν as participles (but the plural μανίαι, which he condemned as meaningless, occurs several times in early verse and in Plat. *Legg.* ix. 869 A 3, 881 B 4, and the verb μανιᾶν is found elsewhere only in Jos. *B.J.* i. 150) and restored γηρῶν in [D.] xlvi. 14 in contrast to the ὑπὸ / ἕνεκα γήρως ἢ μανιῶν of the paraphrases; similarly he accepted the aorist πιθόμενος, and presumably would have restored that too in [D.] xlvi. 14. Others have emended and supplemented *A.P.* to bring it into line with [D.] xlvi. 14: most drastically Poland (*NJPhP* cxliii [xxxvii] 1891, 260–1) and Herwerden (*BPW* xi 1891, 418, 611, cf. Herwerden & Leeuwen). However, we should be wary of enforcing too much conformity (and the reader of *A.P.* should not allow the inverted commas of Kenyon and other editors to raise his hopes too high): the frequent allusions of the orators show that this clause was notorious, and I doubt if *A.P.* or his source thought it necessary to consult the law in order to report the Thirty's modification of it. I think it very probable that in [D.] XLVI. 14 μανιῶν and γήρως are to be retained as genitives dependent on ἕνεκα, and probable that in *A.P.* we should read either μανιῶν ἢ γήρως with Blass, *LZB* 1891, 304, E. Ruschenbusch, *Hist.* Einz. ix 1966, 87 (F 49d), or, more coherently, μανιῶν ἢ γήρως ⟨ἕνεκα⟩ with W. Wyse, *CR* v 1891, 114, Blass[1-4]. Believers in πιθόμενος (e.g. Kaibel & Wilamowitz) can cite πεισθείς in Lys., *loc. cit.*, Isae. II. *Her. Men.* 20; those who prefer πειθόμενος (e.g. Wyse, Poland, Ruschenbusch, *locc. citt.*) can cite [D.] XLVI. 16, Hyp., *loc. cit.*, Pl., *locc. citt.*: corruption either way would be easy, but the aorist is perhaps more appropriate and the aorist καταληφθείς is regularly used, so I am inclined to restore πιθόμενος in [D.] XLVI. 14 and retain it in *A.P.* (but not necessarily to restore it in all paraphrases of the law where the present is found).

For another law on insanity see 56. vi with commentary; for the view that men who are old and close to death are not fit to dispose of their property cf. Plat. *Legg.* XI. 922 B 2–923 C 4. Solon's law 'contained disputes' in that it inevitably left to a jury, meeting after a man's death, the decision whether he had been mad, senile or otherwise unfit when he made his will: the removal of these qualifications would indeed remove the possibility of dispute, but it is not obvious that it would lead to greater justice in matters of inheritance. More generally, the ambition to produce a code of laws so clear and complete that it will apply to all eventualities without needing to be interpreted is unrealisable: see Plat. *Polit.* 294 A 6–295 B 2, Arist. *Pol.* II. 1269 A 9–12, and, for a modern discussion of the problem, J. R. Lucas, *The Principles of Politics*, 25–6, 135–43.

ὅπως μὴ ᾖ τοῖς συκοφάνταις ἔφοδος: Kaibel, *Stil und Text*, 11, remarks that this is the only instance in the first part of *A.P.* of hiatus after μή; there are three instances in the second part (42. i, 52. ii, 57. iv). συκοφάντης ('[contraband-] fig-revealer') is applied frequently by Aristophanes and later Athenian writers to the men who took advantage of the laws allowing prosecution by ὁ βουλόμενος on 'public' charges (cf. 9. i with commentary) to make a profession of prosecuting, in order to obtain the rewards offered to successful prosecutors or payments from the victims or their enemies: this abuse of the law was a recognised evil, and various attempts were made to discourage the συκοφάνται without discouraging the genuinely public-spirited (cf. §iii, 43. v, 59. iii, with commentary; Ar. *Ach.* 860–958, *Plut.* 850–958, and for a defence of prosecutors Lyc. *Leocr.* 3–4; with J. O. Lofberg, *Sycophancy in Athens*, Bonner & Smith, *Administration of Justice*, ii. 39–74, D. M. MacDowell, *The*

Law in Classical Athens, 62-6). In Theramenes' speech in X. *H.* ii. iii. 38 we read μέχρι μὲν τοῦ ... τοὺς ὁμολογουμένως συκοφάντας ὑπάγεσθαι πάντες ταὐτὰ ἐγιγνώσκομεν.

ἐπὶ τῶν ἄλλων: We do not know in what other ways the Thirty simplified the law.

35. iii. κατ' ἀρχὰς μὲν οὖν ... καὶ πονηροὺς ἀνῄρουν: Cf. X. *H.* ii. iii. 12 (πρῶτον μὲν οὓς πάντες ᾔδεσαν ἐν τῇ δημοκρατίᾳ ἀπὸ συκοφαντίας ζῶντας καὶ τοῖς καλοῖς κἀγαθοῖς βαρεῖς ὄντας συλλαβόντες ὑπῆγον θανάτου ...), 38, D.S. xiv. 4. ii (καὶ τὸ μὲν πρῶτον παραδιδόντες κρίσει τοὺς πονηροτάτους τῶν ἐν τῇ πόλει κατεδίκαζον θανάτῳ ...), Lys. xii. *Erat.* 5 (after describing the Thirty instead of their victims as πονηροὶ καὶ συκοφάνται: φάσκοντες χρῆναι τῶν ἀδίκων καθαρὰν ποιῆσαι τὴν πόλιν καὶ τοὺς λοιποὺς πολίτας ἐπ' ἀρετὴν καὶ δικαιοσύνην τράπεσθαι), xxv. *Reip. Del. Defens.* 19 (ἐν τῇ προτέρᾳ δημοκρατίᾳ τῶν τὰ τῆς πόλεως πραττόντων πολλοὶ μὲν τὰ δημόσια ἔκλεπτον, ἔνιοι δ' ἐπὶ τοῖς ὑμετέροις ἐδωροδόκουν, οἱ δὲ συκοφαντοῦντες τοὺς συμμάχους ἀφίστασαν. καὶ εἰ μὲν οἱ τριάκοντα τούτους μόνους ἐτιμωροῦντο, ἄνδρας ἀγαθοὺς καὶ ὑμεῖς ἂν αὐτοὺς ἡγεῖσθε), Plat. *Ep.* vii. 324 D 3-6, Sall. *Cat.* 51. xxix-xxx, Pl. *Soll. An.* 959 D, *Es. Carn.* ii. 998 B.

τοὺς τῷ δήμῳ πρὸς χάριν ὁμιλοῦντας παρὰ τὸ βέλτιστον: Cf. Arist. *E.N.* x. 1173 B 33-4 (ὁ μὲν γὰρ [*sc.* φίλος] πρὸς τἀγαθὸν ὁμιλεῖν δοκεῖ, ὁ δὲ [*sc.* κόλαξ] πρὸς ἡδονήν). πρὸς χάριν ὁμιλεῖν is found in Is. ii. *Nic.* 4, xv. *Antid.* 133, and πρὸς χάριν ὁμιλεῖσθαι in Philod. *Lib.*, col. xxiii (62 Olivieri); λέγειν πρὸς χάριν is frequent (e.g. Eur. *Hec.* 257, X. *H.* vi. iii. 7 cf. *M.* iv. iv. 4); and in D. viii. *Chers.* 1 we read ποιεῖσθαι λόγον μηδένα μήτε πρὸς χάριν, ἀλλ' ὃ βέλτιστον ἕκαστος ἡγεῖτο τοῦτ' ἀποφαίνεσθαι. In X. *H.* ii. iii. 15 Theramenes says to Critias καὶ ἐγώ ... καὶ σὺ πολλὰ δὴ τοῦ ἀρέσκειν ἕνεκα τῇ πόλει καὶ εἴπομεν καὶ ἐπράξαμεν. T. ii. 65. viii, x, writes of Pericles τὸ μὴ κτώμενος ἐξ οὐ προσηκόντων τὴν δύναμιν πρὸς ἡδονήν τι λέγειν, but the politicians after his death ἐτράποντο καθ' ἡδονὰς τῷ δήμῳ καὶ τὰ πράγματα ἐνδιδόναι.

καὶ κακοπράγμονας ὄντας: Cf. Is. xv. *Antid.* 224, 225 (both in conjunction with συκοφάνται), 236, X. *H.* v. ii. 36. We need not follow Kaibel & Wilamowitz (cf. Kaibel, *Stil und Text*, 194) in deleting καί.

ἐφ' οἷς ἔχαιρον ἡ πόλις γιγνομένοις: Cf. X. *H.* ii. iii. 12 (... καὶ ἥ τε βουλὴ ἡδέως αὐτῶν κατεψηφίζετο οἵ τε ἄλλοι ὅσοι συνῄδεσαν ἑαυτοῖς μὴ ὄντες τοιοῦτοι οὐδὲν ἤχθοντο), D.S. xiv. 4. ii (... καὶ μέχρι τούτου τοῖς ἐπιεικεστάτοις τῶν πολιτῶν εὐαρέστει τὰ γινόμενα), Sall. *Cat.* 51. xxix: notice that Xenophon and Diodorus both (but differently) specify who within the πόλις took pleasure in these condemnations. ἔχαιρον was corrected to ἔχαιρεν by A. Sidgwick and W. G. Rutherford, *CR* v 1891, 114, and that is probably right notwithstanding the plural ἡγούμενοι which follows (cf. T. viii. 21).

35. iv. ἐπεὶ δὲ τὴν πόλιν ἐγκρατέστερον ἔσχον: X. *H.* II. iii. 13–14, D.S. XIV. 4. iii–iv, Just. v. 8. xi and Pl. *Lys.* 15. vi all place at this point the Thirty's obtaining a garrison from Sparta, which *A.P.* defers until 37. ii: see pp. 420, 422, and commentary *ad loc.*

οὐδενὸς ἀπείχοντο τῶν πολιτῶν, ἀλλ' ἀπέκτειναν τοὺς ... προέχοντας: Cf. X. *H.* II. iii. 14, 15, 17 (where the victims are potential opponents of the Thirty), 21 (after the selection of the Three Thousand πολλοὺς μὲν ἔχθρας ἕνεκα ἀπέκτεινον, πολλοὺς δὲ χρημάτων), 38, D.S. XIV. 4. iv (where the victims are the rich). The victims of Agoratus' disclosures, among them Strombichides (Lys. XIII. *Agor.* 13, 30, XXX. *Nic.* 14: *P.A.* 13016, Davies, *A.P.F.*, 161) and other generals and taxiarchs of 405/4, were probably dealt with during the 'mild' period (Lys. XIII. *Agor.* 35–8): in this later period we may place the deaths of Leon the Salaminian (X. *H.* II. iii. 39, Plat. *Apol.* 32 C 4–E 1), Eucrates and Niceratus, the brother and son of Nicias (X. *H.* II. iii. 39, D.S. XIV. 5. v–vi [after Theramenes' death], Lys. XVIII. *Nic. Frat.* 5–8, Pl. *Es. Carn.* II. 998 B), Antiphon Λυσωνίδου (X. *H.* II. iii. 40, material in [Pl.] *X. Or.* 832 F–833 B [Cratin. fr. 74 Kock, Lys. fr. 25 Sauppe, Thp. 115 F 120]: *P.A.* 1283, Davies, *A.P.F.*, 327–8), Lycurgus Λυκομήδους Βουτάδης, grandfather of the orator Lycurgus ([Pl.] *X. Or.* 841 B, 843 E, decree *ap.* 852 A: *P.A.* 9249, Davies, *A.P.F.*, 349–50), and Autolycus Λύκωνος Θορίκιος (D.S. XIV. 5. vii, Pl. *Lys.* 15. viii, Paus. IX. 32. viii [ascribing his condemnation to Lysander]: *P.A.* 2748). Later we hear of an attack on rich metics, whose principal motive is said to be financial: X. *H.* II. iii. 21–2, 41 (after the selection of the Three Thousand but before the killing of Theramenes), D.S. XIV. 5. vi (in the reign of terror after Theramenes' death), Lys. XII. *Erat.* 6–7, cf. *P. Oxy.* xiii 1606, 1–238 = Lys. fr. i Gernet & Bizos. No doubt the Thirty were motivated both by the need for money and by the desire to rid themselves of actual or potential opponents, as *A.P.* claims in the two phrases which end this sentence.

Many have followed Blass, *LZB* 1891, 304, and Κ. Σ. Κόντος, Ἀθ. iv 1892, 82, in printing ἀπέκτεινον, but the aorist may stand, as in T. VIII. 70. ii.

ὑπεξαιρούμενοί τε τὸν φόβον: 'Cunningly removing all whom they had reason to fear' (Sandys): the Thirty would remove their fear by removing the men of whom they were afraid.

χρόνον διαπεσόντος βραχέος: This use of διαπίπτειν is without parallel: Kaibel, *Stil und Text*, 42, cites H. III. 71. v (ἢν ὑπερπέσῃ ἡ νῦν ἡμέρη), Eur. *H.F.* 506–7 (ὡς ἐλπίδας μὲν ὁ χρόνος οὐκ ἐπίσταται | σῴζειν τὸ δ' αὑτοῦ σπουδάσας διέπτατο), and the use of παραπίπτειν with καιρός (T. IV. 23. ii, X. *Hipparch.* vii. 4, D. I. *Ol. i.* 8). J. B. Mayor, *CR* v 1891, 114, suggested διαλιπόντος, and Herwerden, *BPW* xi 1891, 611, cf. Herwerden & Leeuwen, διελθόντος, but there is no need to emend.

οὐκ ἐλάττους ἀνῃρήκεσαν ἢ χιλίους πεντακοσίους: The papyrus' figure is confirmed by *Epit. Heracl.* 7, and the same figure for men killed by the Thirty is found in Is. VII. *Areop.* 67, xx. *Lochit.* 11, A. III. *Ctes.* 235; schol. A. 1. *Tim.* 39 gives this as the figure of ἔνιοι, 2,500 as the figure of Lysias. The figure is probably intended to represent the total number put to death by the Thirty, rather than the number put to death during a particular period.

36. i. οὕτως δὲ τῆς πόλεως ὑποφερομένης: Cf. 25. i with commentary: the πολιτεία was ὑποφερομένη κατὰ μικρόν under the ascendancy of the Areopagus.

Θηραμένης ἀγανακτῶν ἐπὶ τοῖς γιγνομένοις: Cf. X. *H.* II. iii. 15 (τῷ μὲν οὖν πρώτῳ χρόνῳ ὁ Κριτίας τῷ Θηραμένει ὁμογνώμων τε καὶ φίλος ἦν· ἐπεὶ δὲ αὐτὸς μὲν προπετὴς ἦν ἐπὶ τὸ πολλοὺς ἀποκτείνειν ... ὁ δὲ Θηραμένης ἀντέκοπτε), D.S. XIV. 4. v, Just. V. 9. ii.

τῆς μὲν ἀσελγείας: Arist. *Pol.* v. 1304 B 21 writes of τὴν τῶν δημαγωγῶν ἀσέλγειαν; it is also an orators' word.

μεταδοῦναι δὲ τῶν πραγμάτων τοῖς βελτίστοις: Cf. X. *H.* II. iii. 17 (ἐπεὶ δέ, ἀποθνησκόντων πολλῶν καὶ ἀδίκως, πολλοὶ δῆλοι ἦσαν συνιστάμενοί τε καὶ θαυμάζοντες τί ἔσοιτο ἡ πολιτεία, πάλιν ἔλεγεν ὁ Θηραμένης ὅτι εἰ μή τις κοινωνοὺς ἱκανοὺς λήψοιτο τῶν πραγμάτων ἀδύνατον ἔσοιτο τὴν ὀλιγαρχίαν διαμένειν). On the objections of Theramenes, the selection of the Three Thousand, and (especially) the further objections of Theramenes, *A.P.* is very close to Xenophon: since elsewhere his account is very different from that of Xenophon it is most unlikely that he has used Xenophon for this one part of his narrative; more probably both had access to a defence of Theramenes by himself or by one of his supporters (cf. p. 421).

οἱ δὲ πρῶτον ἐναντιωθέντες: This is not stated by Xenophon, but we may be sure that the extremists did not immediately give way to Theramenes.

ἐπεὶ διεσπάρησαν οἱ λόγοι πρὸς τὸ πλῆθος ... φοβηθέντες: X. *H.* II. iii. 18 says ἐκ τούτου μέντοι Κριτίας καὶ οἱ ἄλλοι τριάκοντα, ἤδη φοβούμενοι καὶ οὐχ ἥκιστα τὸν Θηραμένην, μὴ συρρυείησαν πρὸς αὐτὸν οἱ πολῖται ... For διασπείρειν of λόγοι cf. X. *H.* v. i. 25.

μὴ προστάτης γενόμενος τοῦ δήμου καταλύσῃ τὴν δυναστείαν: Cf. T. VIII. 89. iv, where in autumn 411 among the men in Athens opposed to the Four Hundred ἠγωνίζετο ... εἷς ἕκαστος αὐτὸς πρῶτος προστάτης τοῦ δήμου γενέσθαι. The extremists are afraid that Theramenes, still a member of the ruling oligarchy (though *A.P.* never admits this) if now a discontented one, will help to overthrow the régime which he has helped to set up, as he had done in 411. Here we have *A.P.*'s last use of προστάτης τοῦ δήμου to denote a democratic leader: see especially 2. ii, 28. ii, with commentary. This passage contains the only instance of δυναστεία in *A.P.*: occasionally

36. i] COMMENTARY ON THE *ATH. POL.*

the word serves as a general term for oligarchy (e.g. Plat. *Polit.* 291 D 1–292 A 4, where δυναστεῖαι are subdivided into [lawful] ἀριστοκρατίαι and [lawless] ὀλιγαρχίαι); but more commonly δυναστεία is the despotic rule of a small clique, οὔτε κατ᾽ ὀλιγαρχίαν ἰσόνομον πολιτεύουσα οὔτε κατὰ δημοκρατίαν· ὅπερ δέ ἐστι νόμοις μὲν καὶ τῷ σωφρονεστάτῳ ἐναντιώτατον, ἐγγυτάτω δὲ τυράννου, δυναστεία ὀλίγων ἀνδρῶν (T. III. 62. iii, cf. IV. 78. iii, 126. ii, Arist. *Pol.* II. 1272 B 1–11, IV. 1292 A 39–B 10, 1293 A 10–34, VI. 1320 B 18–1321 A 4).

καταλέγουσιν τῶν πολιτῶν τρισχιλίους ὡς μεταδώσοντες τῆς πολιτείας: Cf. X. *H.* II. iii. 18 (... καταλέγουσι τρισχιλίους τοὺς μεθέξοντας δὴ τῶν πραγμάτων). μεταδιδόναι/μεθέχειν τῶν πραγμάτων, used by *A.P.* above and by Xenophon at this point, is an expression familiar from the language used in 411 (cf. 33. i with commentary), where it referred to those who were to be full citizens with political rights; and τὴν ... πολιτείαν ἐπιτρέψαι in 29. v and μεταδιδόναι τῆς πολιτείας here should have the same force (cf. 40. ii, 42. i, using μεταδιδόναι/ μετέχειν τῆς πολιτείας, Lys. xxx. *Nic.* 15, where those not among the Three Thousand are οὐ μετασχόντας τῆς πολιτείας; but in Lys. XVI. *Mant.* 3 οὐδὲ μέτεσχον τῆς τότε πολιτείας means rather 'and I did not play a part in that régime'). τῆς πόλεως μετέχειν is used in 8. v in a gloss on ἄτιμον εἶναι, and in 26. iv of the exclusion from citizenship of those who do not satisfy the requirements of Pericles' law; cf. also the language used in 37. For a discussion of such expressions see C. Mossé, *La Fin de la démocratie athénienne*, 141–4, cf. 243 with n. 1, 359).†

In fact in 404/3 the right to a trial before the boule was limited to the Three Thousand, and men other than the Three Thousand were disarmed and later expelled from the city (37 with commentary); the Three Thousand were used as a jury or assembly to condemn the men of Eleusis, and presumably those of Salamis (X. *H.* II. iv. 9–10: cf. p. 452); but the laws which made Theramenes' condemnation possible are said to have been passed by the boule (37. i with commentary).

36. ii. πρῶτον μὲν ... τῆς ἀρετῆς ὡρισμένης: Cf. X. *H.* II. iii. 19 (ἔλεγεν ὅτι ἄτοπον δοκοίη ἑαυτῷ γε εἶναι τὸ πρῶτον μὲν βουλομένους τοὺς βελτίστους τῶν πολιτῶν κοινωνοὺς ποιήσασθαι τρισχιλίους, ὥσπερ τὸν ἀριθμὸν τοῦτον ἔχοντά τινα ἀνάγκην καλοὺς καὶ ἀγαθοὺς εἶναι, καὶ οὔτ᾽ ἔξω τούτων σπουδαίους οὔτ᾽ ἐντὸς τούτων πονηροὺς οἷόν τε εἴη γενέσθαι ... (where καταλέξαι *vel sim.* needs to be added after τρισχιλίους); in II. iii. 49, at the end of his speech, Theramenes challenges Critias to show ὅπου ἐγὼ σὺν τοῖς δημοτικοῖς ἢ τυραννικοῖς τοὺς καλούς τε κἀγαθοὺς ἀποστερεῖν πολιτείας ἐπεχείρησα. ἐπιεικής, like other similar words, can be used either with connotations of social class or to express approval of a man irrespective of his position in society (see 26. i with commentary): we are not told by what criteria the Three

Thousand were chosen, but they must have been in some sense the upper-class Athenians, so that Theramenes could object that this class did not have a monopoly of virtue.

ἔπειθ' ὅτι δύο ... κατασκευάζοντες: Cf. X. *H.* ii. iii. 19 (... ἔπειτα δ' ἔφη, ὁρῶ ἔγωγε δύο ἡμᾶς τὰ ἐναντιώτατα πράττοντας, βιαίαν τε τὴν ἀρχὴν καὶ ἥττονα τῶν ἀρχομένων κατασκευαζομένους). ἥττω must mean not 'fewer' but 'weaker': there is no incompatibility between rule by a minority and rule by force. For πρῶτον μὲν ... ἔπειτα (without δέ) ... see J. D. Denniston, *The Greek Particles*², 377.

οἱ δὲ τούτων μὲν ὠλιγώρησαν: X. *H.* has nothing corresponding to the remainder of this section, but in ii. iii. 20 proceeds directly to the disarming of men outside the Three Thousand (delayed by *A.P.* until 37. ii, after the death of Theramenes: cf. *ad loc.*), which could not be done until the identity of the Three Thousand was public knowledge. There may be some truth in what *A.P.* says, but we should also consider the possibility that the history of the Three Thousand in 404/3 has been contaminated by the history of the Five Thousand in 411, on which see pp. 385–6.

τὸν δὲ κατάλογον τῶν τρισχιλίων: Cf. X. *H.* ii. iii. 51, 52, iv. 1. There was also a κατάλογος ὁ μετὰ Λυσάνδρου of men disliked by the Thirty: Is. XVIII. *Call.* 16, XXI. *Euth.* 2, Lys. XXV. *Reip. Del. Defens.* 16.

παρ' αὑτοῖς ἐφύλαττον τοὺς ἐγνωσμένους: 'Kept to themselves (*sc.* the names of) those whom they had decided upon.'

ὅτε δὲ καὶ δόξειεν αὑτοῖς ἐκφέρειν: 'And every time they did decide to publish it they proceeded to ...' (Kenyon, Oxford Translation). Leeuwen, doubting the logic of this, suggested συμφέρειν and Hude emended to ὅτε δὲ καὶ ἔδοξεν ... ἐξήλειψαν ... ἀντενέγραψαν (answered by Kaibel, *Stil und Text*, 194); but the papyrus' text should be retained. We are not told when, or why, the Thirty overcame their hesitations and published the list.

τοὺς μὲν ἐξήλειφον τῶν <ἐγ>γεγραμμένων: For ἐξαλείφειν of deleting a man's name from a register cf. X. *H.* ii. iii. 51, 52 (Critias' deletion of Theramenes), Is. XVIII. *Call.* 16, XXI. *Euth.* 2, *A.P.* 49. ii; also *A.P.* 40. iii, Ar. *Eq.* 877, *Pax*, 1181, T. III. 57. ii, Lys. XXX. *Nic.* 5, [D.] XXV. *Aristog.* i. 73; *A.P.* 47. v–48. i uses ἀπαλείφειν but προεξαλείφειν of contracts (cf. *ad locc.*). The compound verb ἐγγράφειν, restored here by Herwerden (*BPW* xi 1891, 323, cf. Herwerden & Leeuwen) is used in 42. i, 49. ii, and (of defaulting contractors) 48. i: cf. *ad locc.*

τοὺς δ' ἀντενέγραφον: The only parallel cited by LSJ is [D.] XXV. *Aristog.* i. 73 (ἂν ἔλῃ τὸν Ἀρίστωνα τῆς βουλεύσεως, τί ἔσται; ἐξαλειφθήσεται νὴ Δία, ὁ δ' ἀντεγγραφήσεται).

37. i. ἤδη δὲ τοῦ χειμῶνος ἐνεστῶτος: 'When it was already winter' (Moore) is a fairer translation than 'At the beginning of winter'

(Fritz & Kapp). This is the first and only indication of season given in *A.P.*'s account: Hignett, *H.A.C.*, 385, 386–7, regards it as simply a deduction from Xenophon's reference to the snowstorm (but the snowstorm appears also in Diodorus [cf. p. 451] and must have been common knowledge); but there is no reason why the detail should not be authentic, and unless we insist that the beginning of winter is meant it need cause no chronological difficulties (cf. p. 462). καταλαβόντος Θρασυβούλου μετὰ τῶν φυγάδων Φυλήν: Thrasybulus Λύκου Στειριεύς first appears as a trierarch with the Athenian fleet at Samos in 412/1 (T. VIII. 73. iv), prominent in the return to democracy there (T. VIII. 75. ii) and elected general after the return to democracy (T. VIII. 76. ii), but in the naval campaigns of the next few years cooperating with Alcibiades and Theramenes rather than the extreme democrats (A. Andrewes, *JHS* lxxiii 1953, 3–4); together with Theramenes he was a trierarch at Arginusae and was made responsible for collecting bodies and survivors after the battle (X. *H.* I. vi. 35, vii. 5, D.S. XIII. 101. ii). When the Thirty came to power he went into exile (cf. X. *H.* II. iii. 42, 44, D.S. XIV. 32. i), and set out from Thebes to occupy Phyle (X. *H.* II. iv. 2, D.S. XIV. 32. i, Pl. *Lys.* 27. v–vii, cf. Just. v. 9. viii, *H.O.* 17. i). After successfully leading the returning democrats he was prominent in Athenian politics until *c.* 390, when he was killed while in command of an expedition to Asia Minor (X. *H.* IV. viii. 25–30, D.S. XIV. 94, 99. iv), thereby escaping a trial for peculation (Lys. XXVIII. *Erg.* 4–8).

Hitherto *A.P.* has mentioned executions but not exiles. In X. *H.* the first reference to exiles is in Theramenes' defence (II. iii. 42, 44, naming Thrasybulus and others); after the execution of Theramenes those outside the Three Thousand are excluded from the city, and many withdraw into exile (II. iv. 1); after that the occupation of Phyle is mentioned (II. iv. 2). Diodorus writes of Athenians fleeing after the death of Theramenes (XIV. 5. vi–6 cf. 32. i); next he reports the occupation of Phyle, and the attack on it frustrated by a snowstorm (XIV. 32. i–iii); then follows the exclusion from the city of the unprivileged (XIV. 32. iv). Justin like Diodorus writes of exiles after the death of Theramenes (v. 9. iii–v); next the occupation of Phyle, and the failure of the only attack on it which he mentions (v. 9. vi–xi); and then the expulsion of *omnes Athenienses* from the city (v. 9. xii). *A.P.* does not mention the exclusion of the unprivileged, but places their disarming (which should precede their exclusion) after the death of Theramenes, and that after the occupation of Phyle.

Most now agree that *A.P.* is wrong in placing the execution of Theramenes after the occupation of Phyle (e.g. E. Meyer, *G.d.A.*, v[4]. 21, 32–3, Hignett, *H.A.C.*, 386–7, cf. Cloché, *La Restauration démocratique à Athènes en 403 avant J.-C.*, 4–6; champions of *A.P.* have included Busolt, *Hermes* xxxiii 1898, 77–86, O. Armbruster, *Über die Herrschaft der Dreissig zu Athen, 404/3 v. Chr.*, 18–22 cf. 5). However, although in general Xenophon's chronology is to be preferred (cf. p. 422), the suggestion of Armbruster that for tidiness' sake he has narrated together all that happened at Phyle, and that the occupation of Phyle may have occurred earlier than he implies, is not self-evidently wrong and does not deserve the ridicule with which it was rejected by Hignett: X. *H.* II. iii. 44, in Theramenes' defence, could be read as an allusion to a democratic movement that has already begun. On the exclusion of the unprivileged Diodorus and Justin diverge from Xenophon, and in each account the exclusion is given a reason appropriate to its chronological position; references by Lysias and Isocrates to the exclusion do not help to date it. Xenophon is defended confidently by Hignett, *H.A.C.*, 386, less confidently by E. Meyer, *G.d.A.*, v[4]. 33 n. 1; the alternative version was preferred by A. Boerner, *De Rebus a Graecis 410–403 Gestis*, 56–8, Armbruster, *locc. citt.*, W. S. Ferguson, *C.A.H.*, v[1]. 369–70; Cloché, *REG* xxiv 1911, 63–76, accepted both and believed in two distinct exclusions. In favour of Xenophon it may be said that considerations of tidiness would not have led him to place this episode where he does; and we may wonder whether it would have seemed wise to the Thirty, after the occupation of Phyle had become a threat to be taken seriously, to drive out men who might then support Thrasybulus.

Phyle lay on the south side of Mount Parnes, due north of the Piraeus, on 'quite the worst of the routes from Attica' to Boeotia (A. R. Burn, *Persia and the Greeks*, 511): see J. Wiesner, *RE* xx (1941/50), 1011–13, cf. A. Philippson ed. H. Lehmann & E. Kirsten, *Die griechischen Landschaften*, I. ii. 538, J. S. Traill, *Hesp.* Supp. xiv 1975, 50.

καὶ κατὰ τὴν στρατιὰν ... κακῶς ἀποχωρήσαντες: The expression is awkward but not impossible: Kaibel & Wilamowitz[1-2] deleted καί, but in their 3rd ed. they retained it (cf. Kaibel, *Stil und Text*, 194–5); Kaibel & Wilamowitz preferred στρατείαν (cf. Kaibel, *loc. cit.*), but in the time of *A.P.*, although the two words were interchangeable in the sense 'expedition', στρατιά was the regular form for 'army', and that is needed here as the object of ἐξήγαγον (cf. 22. viii, 27. ii, with commentary); οἱ τριάκοντα was placed before ἔγνωσαν by J. B. Mayor, deleted as a gloss by H. Richards (*CR* v 1891, 114, 228), but it may be left in place.

Xenophon and Diodorus mention two failures of the Thirty against Phyle: one in which a snowstorm prevented them from setting up a blockade (X. *H.* II. iv. 2–3, D.S. XIV. 32. ii–iii); and a second, when Thrasybulus attacked the oligarchs' camp, placed by Xenophon about 15 stades from Phyle and by Diodorus near Acharnae (X. *H.* II. iv. 4–7, D.S. XIV. 32. vi–33. i: Cloché, *La*

Restauration démocratique, 26 n. 2, argued that the two locations are compatible). Just. v. 9. x, like A.P., condenses and reports only one battle. An unsuccessful attempt to corrupt Thrasybulus is reported by D.S. xiv. 32. v–vi and Just. v. 9. xii–xiv, but omitted by Xenophon and A.P. (cf. p. 472); the killing by the Thirty of the men of Eleusis and Salamis, in case either place should be needed as a safe retreat, is reported by X. H. ii. iv. 8–10 (Eleusis only), D.S. xiv. 32. iv, Lys. xii. Erat. 52, xiii. Agor. 44, but omitted by Justin and A.P. (cf. p. 448).

τῶν μὲν ἄλλων τὰ ὅπλα παρελέσθαι: Cf. §ii with commentary: 'the others' would appear in this sentence to be those other than Theramenes, but we see below that they are the unprivileged, those not included in the register of the Three Thousand.

Θηραμένην δὲ διαφθεῖραι τόνδε <τὸν> τρόπον: On the condemnation and execution of Theramenes cf. X. H. ii. iii. 23–56, D.S. xiv. 4. v–5. iv, Just. v. 9. ii. Xenophon and Diodorus both write of a clash between Critias and Theramenes in the boule, with Theramenes winning the support of the bouleutae and taking refuge at the ἑστία but nevertheless being dragged away to his death: A.P. says nothing of this, but reports what the Thirty presumably wished to be known, that two laws had the effect of excluding Theramenes from the Three Thousand and from the right to a public trial (one of these laws is incorporated in Xenophon's account: cf. below). A.P. omits Critias not only from this episode but from the whole of his account of 404–403: cf. pp. 420–1, 429–30.

νόμους εἰσήνεγκαν εἰς τὴν βουλὴν δύο: It is no doubt true that these laws served as a formal justification for the condemnation of Theramenes. A.P. reports them not as he reports the acts of 411 but as devices designed to lead to Theramenes' condemnation: in the case of the second law he is surely right, and that law was forced on the boule either at the meeting at which Critias attacked Theramenes (Kenyon) or subsequently to provide a retrospective justification for what had not been achieved by lawful means (Hignett, H.A.C., 389); but the first law may have been enacted when the Three Thousand were set apart from the unprivileged, with no *ad hominem* intent (Hignett, H.A.C., 289). The Thirty had not produced a constitution, as they were required to do (34. iii–35. i with commentary); but it was apparently decided at some stage by the Thirty that new laws were to be approved by the boule.

ἐπιχειροτονεῖν: This can mean 'put to the vote', like ἐπιψηφίζειν (e.g. law *ap*. D. xxiv. Tim. 39, misunderstood by LSJ); but it more commonly means 'vote in approval of', and that is surely its meaning here: Fritz & Kapp, 183, are too cautious. For its more specialised use, of confirming a decision already taken, see 43. iv, 55. vi, 61. ii, with commentary.

COMMENTARY ON THE *ATH. POL.* [37. i

ὁ μὲν εἷς ... τοῦ καταλόγου μετέχοντας τῶν τρισχιλίων: Cf. X. *H.* II. iii. 51: after Theramenes' defence had won the favour of the boule, Critias discussed the matter with the remainder of the Thirty and said to the boule, ἔστι δὲ ἐν τοῖς καινοῖς νόμοις τῶν μὲν ἐν τοῖς τρισχιλίοις ὄντων μηδένα ἀποθνῄσκειν ἄνευ τῆς ὑμετέρας ψήφου, τῶν δ' ἔξω τοῦ καταλόγου κυρίους εἶναι τοὺς τριάκοντα θανατοῦν. Xenophon and *A.P.* report what is directly relevant; probably the law laid down in more general terms that (whenever a penalty above a certain level was in question?) the Three Thousand were entitled to a trial before the boule but the unprivileged were not. Xenophon must be right in including a clause which gives the right of trial to the Three Thousand; but a law enacted at this date is more likely to have used *A.P.*'s αὐτοκράτορας than Xenophon's κυρίους (cf. p. 384).

ὁ δ' ἕτερος ἐκώλυε κοινωνεῖν τῆς παρούσης πολιτείας: κοινωνεῖν τῆς πολιτείας is found in Plato (e.g. *Legg.* VI. 753 A 6: ἐκοινωσάτην ἡμῖν τῆς πολιτείας) and Aristotle (e.g. *Pol.* II. 1268 A 18); but the text of the law will more probably have read μὴ μετέχειν τῆς πόλεως (cf. 8. v, 26. iv, 36. i, with commentary, Eum. 77 F 2), or perhaps μὴ εἶναι τῶν τρισχιλίων. This second law is not mentioned in X. *H.* II. iii. 51, where Critias says ἐγὼ οὖν ... Θηραμένην τουτονὶ ἐξαλείφω ἐκ τοῦ καταλόγου, συνδοκοῦν ἅπασιν ἡμῖν.

ὅσοι τυγχάνουσιν τὸ ἐν Ἡετιωνείᾳ τεῖχος κατασκάψαντες: Eetionea, χηλή ... τοῦ Πειραιῶς (T. VIII. 90. iv), lay on the north side of the main, westward-facing harbour, known in antiquity as Κάνθαρος (cf. Harp. Ἡετιωνεία). In 411, when a split had occurred between extreme and 'moderate' oligarchs, the extremists began to add to the fortifications there, allegedly to keep out the fleet if it should sail on Athens from Samos; on the approach of a fleet from the Peloponnese the 'moderates' led a mutiny of the men working on the fortifications, and they began to demolish the walls; Theramenes had objected to the fortifications, and gave his approval to their demolition (T. VIII. 90–2; for the context see *A.P.* 33 with commentary). *A.P.* did not mention Eetionea in his account of 411, but here he alludes to the fortress as if no further explanation were needed.

ἢ τοῖς τετρακοσίοις ... [[ἢ]] τοῖς κατασκευάσασι τὴν προτέραν ὀλιγαρχίαν: The second ἢ was retained by Kenyon[1-3] but deleted by Hude (*NTF*[2] x 1890–2, 251), Herwerden (*BPW* xi 1891, 323, cf. Herwerden & Leeuwen) and most editors; Blass[4] deleted ἢ τοῖς; Blass[4] and Sandys[2] inserted ἢ after ὅσοι τυγχάνουσιν, which might be right. The régime of the Four Hundred was ἡ προτέρα ὀλιγαρχία (cf. Kaibel, *Stil und Text*, 195, citing Lys. XII. *Erat.* 65). [D.] LVIII.

Theocr. 67 ascribes the fortification of Eetionea to οἱ περὶ Κριτίαν, but Critias' career in the years following 411 makes that unlikely, and it

453

is probably a mistake inspired by this episode (cf. Wade-Gery, *CQ* xxxix 1945, 24 n. 3 = *Essays*, 179 n. 2, and above, p. 429). For the use of κατασκευάζειν cf. X. *H.* II. iii. 36 (Critias δημοκρατίαν κατεσκεύαζε in Thessaly).

ἔξω τε γίγνεσθαι τῆς πολιτείας αὐτὸν: Cf. τῶν ἐν τῇ πολιτείᾳ in 38. ii, τοὺς λαχόντας ἐκ τῆς πολιτείας in 4. iii ('Draconian constitution'); Arist. *Pol.* VI. 1321 A 30–1 writes of τῶν ἐν τῷ πολιτεύματι καὶ τῶν ἔξωθεν.

κυρίους εἶναι θανατοῦντας: For the participle cf. T. v. 34. ii, VIII. 51. i, Plat. *Legg.* IX. 878 E 3, Polyb. III. 85. ii, and LSJ s.v. κύριος, A. I. 4.

37. ii. τά τε ὅπλα παρείλοντο πάντων πλὴν τῶν τρισχιλίων: Cf. X. *H.* II. iii. 20: after the Three Thousand had been selected and Theramenes had objected, the Thirty ordered separate parades of the Three Thousand and the others, instructed the men to leave their arms (this must be the meaning, but it cannot be extracted from the transmitted text), and τὰ ὅπλα πάντων πλὴν τῶν τρισχιλίων παρείλοντο, καὶ ἀνακομίσαντες εἰς τὴν ἀκρόπολιν συνέθηκαν ἐν τῷ ναῷ; also II. iii. 41. Xenophon's version, in which Theramenes is not eliminated until after the unprivileged have been disarmed and both events take place after the arrival of the Spartan garrison, makes far better sense (though some have thought otherwise): *A.P.*'s source presumably ante-dated the execution of Theramenes to free him as far as possible from responsibility for the acts of the Thirty (cf. below and pp. 422, 450–1). I doubt if any chronological implication should be seen in the brief preliminary allusion to the disarming in §i, and I doubt if this distortion of the chronology has contributed to the omission of the disarming in the Ephorus-based narratives of Diodorus and Justin (but see Hignett, *H.A.C.*, 388). For the disarming of the people by Pisistratus or his sons see 15. iv–v with commentary.

καὶ ἐν τοῖς ἄλλοις πολὺ πρὸς ὠμότητα καὶ πονηρίαν ἐπέδοσαν: For ἐπιδιδόναι πρός cf. Is. III. *Nic.* 32, Plat. *Legg.* XI. 913 B 5–6; Thalheim suggested ἐπεδίδοσαν, but the aorist may stand. This general condemnation of the extremists' wickedness contrasts strikingly with the more specific account of their misdeeds which *A.P.* has given hitherto.

πρέσβεις ‹δὲ› πέμψαντες εἰς Λακεδαίμονα: All have found the asyndeton of the papyrus' text intolerably harsh, and some have thought this second half of §ii misplaced. ⟨δέ⟩, suggested by J. B. Mayor and A. Sidgwick, *CR* v 1891, 114, Blass, *LZB* 1891, 304, and others, is the simplest and most popular correction; ⟨καὶ⟩ πρέσβεις was suggested by K. Ziegler *ap*. Oppermann. Leeuwen and Kaibel & Wilamowitz[1-2] (cf. Kaibel, *Stil und Text*, 195–6) proposed to move πρέσβεις πέμψαντες ... ἐλθόντες ἐφρούρουν to the end of 36, and

Kaibel & Wilamowitz[1-3] postulated a lacuna after πονηρίαν ἐπέδοσαν: the transposition would place Callibius' arrival before the occupation of Phyle, the condemnation of Theramenes and the disarming of the unprivileged, but still later than it is placed by Xenophon, Diodorus and Justin (cf. Boerner, *De Rebus a Graecis 410–403 Gestis*, 59). H. J. Polak (cited by Sandys) moved this passage to the middle of 37. i, after τόνδε ⟨τὸν⟩ τρόπον, which would place Callibius' arrival after the occupation of Phyle but before the condemnation of Theramenes and the disarming of the unprivileged. However, implausible though the late arrival of Callibius in *A.P.*'s text may be, it is not implausible that *A.P.*'s source should have placed it late in the interests of defending Theramenes (cf. p. 422), and we may content ourselves with inserting δέ.

τοῦ τε Θηραμένους κατηγόρουν: Sandys remarks that 'it is too late to accuse Theramenes when he is already executed'; but after his large part in the peace negotiations at the end of the war Theramenes will have been well known to the Spartans, and the extremists may have felt it desirable to justify his execution. An embassy to Sparta on this topic may be authentic.

βοηθεῖν αὐτοῖς ἠξίουν: D.S. XIV. 32. vi mentions an appeal to Sparta before the battle of XIV. 32. vi–33. i (pp. 451–2), and Just. v. 9. xiv mentions an appeal before the battle of Munichia (cf. below): again there may be some truth behind *A.P.*'s version (cf. Boerner, *De Rebus a Graecis 410–403 Gestis*, 60, contr. Hignett, *H.A.C.*, 387–8).

οἱ Λακεδαιμόνιοι Καλλίβιον ἀπέστειλαν: Cf. X. *H.* II. iii. 13–14 (Aeschines and Aristoteles, two of the Thirty [II. iii. 2], were sent to Lysander), D.S. XIV. 4. iii–iv, Just. v. 8. xi, Pl. *Lys.* 15. vi. All place Callibius' arrival early in the rule of the Thirty, and that is surely right.

ἁρμοστὴν: The word is used by Xenophon and Plutarch also: it was the title given to a Spartan citizen placed in command of a city garrison or of an army which did not include regular Spartiate soldiers (see U. Kahrstedt, *Griechisches Staatsrecht*, i. 229–31, H. W. Parke, *JHS* lii 1932, 42–6, and for an exhaustive survey G. Bockisch, *Klio* xlvi 1965, 129–239 [on Athens in 404–403, 186–92]). When Lysander returned to Attica in 403 he went as harmost (X. *H.* II. iv. 28).

καὶ στρατιώτας ὡς ἑπτακοσίους: The number is given by Justin also.

τὴν ἀκρόπολιν: This detail is given by Plutarch also, and is confirmed by Lys. XII. *Erat.* 94, XIII. *Agor.* 46.

38. i. καταλαβόντων τῶν ἀπὸ Φυλῆς τὴν Μουνιχίαν: Cf. X. *H.* II. iv. 10 (the move was made by night, and the next day was the fifth [§13] from the battle of §§4–7 [cf. pp. 451–2]), D.S. XIV. 33. ii, Nep. VIII. *Thras.* 2. v. Munichia, the hill on the east side of the Piraeus,

38. i] COMMENTARY ON THE *ATH. POL.*

facing towards Phalerum Bay, had been fortified by Hippias after his brother's murder (19. ii with commentary) and garrisoned by the Four Hundred in 411 (T. VIII. 92. v: it may have been the normal station of some of the περίπολοι). The move from Phyle was made possible by the demolition of the Long Walls and the Piraeus walls on the conclusion of peace in 404 (e.g. X. *H.* II. iii. 20).

καὶ νικησάντων μάχῃ τοὺς μετὰ τῶν τριάκοντα βοηθήσαντας: Cf. X. *H.* II. iv. 10–19, D.S. XIV. 33. ii–iii, Just. v. 9. xv–10. i, Nep. VIII. *Thras.* 2. v–vi (Diodorus and Nepos make two battles of this). The dead included Critias and one other of the Thirty, and Charmides of the Piraeus Ten; after the battle Xenophon reports a truce under which the oligarchs collected their dead; and then a speech to the oligarchs is ascribed to the herald Cleocritus by X. *H.* II. iv. 20–2 (cf. p. 465), to Thrasybulus by Just. v. 10. i–iii (presumably Xenophon is right).

ἐπαναχωρήσαντες ... τῇ ὑστεραίᾳ: According to X. *H.* II. iv. 22–3, on the next day the Thirty sat alone ἐν τῷ συνεδρίῳ while the members of the Three Thousand debated the matter wherever they were; how a meeting of the Three Thousand came to be held is not stated. D.S. XIV. 33. iv writes (probably mistakenly: see p. 458) of many from the city as well as many exiles joining Thrasybulus.

τοὺς μὲν τριάκοντα κατέλυσαν ... ἐπὶ τὴν τοῦ πολέμου κατάλυσιν: Cf. X. *H.* II. iv. 23–24 *init.*, D.S. XIV. 33. v, Just. v. 10. iv, Lys. XII. *Erat.* 54–5; also *L.S.* 235. 31, Harp., Suid. (*Δ* 171), δέκα καὶ δεκαδοῦχος. The surviving members of the Thirty retired to Eleusis (Xenophon, Justin), with the exception of Pheidon and Eratosthenes (Lysias). The Ten were one from each tribe (Xenophon), including Pheidon and others οἱ δοκοῦντες εἶναι ἐναντιώτατοι Χαρικλεῖ καὶ Κριτίᾳ καὶ τῇ ἐκείνων ἑταιρείᾳ (Lysias); Xenophon and Justin say only that they superseded the Thirty, but Diodorus like *A.P.* regards them as αὐτοκράτορας, εἰ δύναιντο, μάλιστα φιλικῶς διαλύεσθαι τὸν πόλεμον, and Lysias suggests that negotiation with the democrats began before the Thirty were deposed (§53) and that the Ten were expected to work for peace (cf. §58; also Is. XVIII. *Call.* 17). That the Ten were given such a mandate was accepted by E. Meyer, *G.d.A.*, v[4]. 35 with n. 3, and this view was developed by A. Fuks, *Mnem.*[4] vi 1953, 198–207; but Cloché argued against it at length (*La Restauration démocratique*, 61–136). It does appear that the Three Thousand were not yet ready for peace, but this view of the Ten may have arisen because the men with Thrasybulus expected the change of government to betoken a change of attitude in the city and were disappointed when it did not.

ἐφ' οἷς μὲν ᾑρέθησαν οὐκ ἔπραττον: Cf. D.S. XIV. 33. v (οὗτοι δὲ παραλαβόντες τὴν ἀρχὴν τούτων μὲν ἠμέλησαν ...), Lys. XII. *Erat.* 55 sqq.

ἔπεμπον δ' εἰς Λακεδαίμονα: Cf. D.S. xiv. 33. v (... ἑαυτοὺς δὲ τυράννους ἀποδείξαντες ἀπὸ Λακεδαίμονος τετταράκοντα ναῦς μετεπέμποντο καὶ στρατιώτας χιλίους, ὧν ἦρχε Λύσανδρος); Just. v. 10. vi omits Lysander and places after the appointment of the Ten a war *ad quod comprimendum Pausanias rex mittitur*; in Pl. *Lys.* 21. iii–iv after the victory of the men of Phyle Lysander has himself sent to support the Thirty. However, in Xenophon's detailed account we read of a period in which the men at the Piraeus grew in confidence, after which both the Thirty and the men in the city sent envoys to Sparta, and Lysander arranged for himself and his brother Libys to be sent with hoplites and ships (X. *H.* ii. iv. 24–9); and in Lys. xii. *Erat.* 55–60 the Ten first made war both on the Thirty and on Thrasybulus, and later (it seems) Pheidon went to Sparta and gained the assistance of Lysander. This second version is defended by Cloché, *La Restauration démocratique*, 186–8; the accounts of our other sources are probably condensed rather than deliberately distorted.

Kenyon originally restored ἐ[πρέσβευ]σ[αν]; Leeuwen suggested the shorter ἔ[πεμψαν]; ἔπεμπον, due to Blass[2], is printed without any comment of Wilcken by Kaibel & Wilamowitz[3], is accepted in Kenyon's Berlin ed. and O.C.T. as *lectio non certa sed probabilis*, and is confirmed by Dr J. D. Thomas. As Kenyon and Leeuwen saw, we should expect an aorist rather than an imperfect: possibly ἔπεμψαν has been corrupted to the imperfect under the influence of the preceding ἔπραττον.

χρήματα δανειζόμενοι: Cf. X. *H.* ii. iv. 28, Lys. xii. *Erat.* 59, Is. vii. *Areop.* 68, Pl. *Lys.* 21. iv, all giving the amount as 100 talents. Debts incurred by both sides are alluded to in the terms of reconciliation, 39. vi *fin.*, cf. 40. iii.

38. ii. χαλεπῶς δὲ φερόντων ἐπὶ τούτοις: *A.P.*'s story is consistent: the majority of the men in the city wanted peace, and were displeased when the Ten attempted to continue the war.

τῶν ἐν τῇ πολιτείᾳ: 'Those in the citizen body', i.e. the Three Thousand. For the expression cf. ἔξω ... τῆς πολιτείας in 37. i, τοὺς λαχόντας ἐκ τῆς πολιτείας in 4. iii ('Draconian constitution').

φοβούμενοι: The subject must be the Ten.

καταλύθωσιν τῆς ἀρχῆς: Cf. H. i. 104. ii, vi. 9. ii, X. *Cyr.* viii. v. 24.

συλλαβόντες [Δ]ημάρετον ... ἀπέκτειναν: The restoration is due to Blass, *LZB* 1891, 304; Wilcken claimed to read every letter of the name; according to Dr J. D. Thomas there is only an unhelpful trace of the first letter but the rest is virtually certain. H. Richards, *CR* v 1891, 228, proposed to insert ἀρετῇ after the name, which is possible but not necessary. Nothing else is known of Demaretus and his execution; the name is rare but not unique in Athens.

ἐνίων τῶν ἐν τοῖς ἱππεῦσι: The cavalry had fought actively for the Thirty (X. *H*. II. iv. 2, 4, 8, 10); after the battle of Munichia they spent the night in the Odeum with their horses and shields, expecting an attack from the Piraeus (II. iv. 24); in the days that followed they were involved in skirmishing (§§26–7); later they joined Pausanias in his attack on the Piraeus (§§31–2). As indicated in *A.P.*'s next sentence, the cavalry were thought to be more deeply implicated in the oligarchy than the remainder of the Three Thousand. In autumn 400, when the Spartans sent Thibron to fight against the Persians in Asia Minor, he asked Athens for three hundred cavalry; οἱ δ' ἔπεμψαν τῶν ἐπὶ τῶν τριάκοντα ἱππευσάντων, νομίζοντες κέρδος τῷ δήμῳ εἰ ἀποδημοῖεν καὶ ἐναπόλοιντο (X. *H*. III. i. 4). Mantitheus, defended in Lys. XVI. *Mant.*, was charged with having served in the cavalry under the oligarchy, and replied that he was away from Athens when the Thirty came to power (but returned while they were in power), that the σανίδιον of those who served under the Thirty was inaccurate and his name was not included in the list of cavalrymen from whom the restored democracy voted to recover their κατάστασις (cf. p. 304), and that many who served under the Thirty had subsequently continued their careers in public life (§§3–8). Cf. also Lys. XXVI. *Evand.* 10 (claiming that a cavalryman appointed to the boule would be rejected at the δοκιμασία without an accuser), *P. Hib.* i 14, fr. *c* = Lys. fr. vi. 3 Gernet & Bizos.†

38. iii. ἀποστάντος ἅπαντος τοῦ δήμου πρὸς αὐτούς: D.S. XIV. 33. iv writes that immediately after the battle of Munichia πολλοὶ μὲν ἐκ τῆς πόλεως ἐπιθυμοῦντες ἀπαλλαγῆναι τῆς τυραννίδος συνέρρεον εἰς τὸν Πειραιᾶ, πάντες δ' οἱ κατὰ τὰς πόλεις διερριμμένοι φυγάδες ἀκούοντες τὰ προτερήματα τῶν περὶ Θρασύβουλον ἧκον εἰς Πειραιᾶ. That members of the Three Thousand deserted to the opposing party in significant numbers, either immediately after the battle or later, is unlikely; but Thrasybulus was continually receiving reinforcements of the men who had fled from Attica, and perhaps also of those of the unprivileged who had risked staying in Attica: cf. Cloché, *La Restauration démocratique*, 56 n. 2. It is not clear whether, in using δήμου, *A.P.* like Diodorus envisaged defections from the Three Thousand (he does not use this word of them elsewhere, and δῆμος later in this section is not the Three Thousand), but if he did it would be consistent with the general tendency of this part of his narrative.

ἐπεκράτουν τῷ πολέμῳ: *A.P.*'s chronology is unclear: the Ten's appeal to Sparta was mentioned in §i; the arrival of Lysander and Libys is not mentioned at all; Pausanias' intervention is to be mentioned below. In X. *H*. II. iv. 24–8 the successes of Thrasybulus precede the appeal to Sparta; Lysander and Libys on their arrival mount a blockade of the Piraeus, enabling the oligarchs to gain the upper hand once more (§29). Cloché, *op. cit.*, 186–8 cf. 170–1, uses Xenophon to prove that Lysander's arrival should be thought of as occurring after this point in *A.P.*'s narrative; I would rather say that Lysander arrived before this point, but is suppressed so that in this tendentious narrative Thrasybulus' successes may lead to the (fictitious) change to a second board of Ten, to whom rather than Pausanias the credit will be given for the reconciliation.

τότε καταλύσαντες τοὺς δέκα. ... βελτίστους εἶναι δοκοῦντας: No other text supports *A.P.*'s claim that the original Ten were deposed and replaced by a second board of Ten, while many passages, including the terms of reconciliation in 39. vi, refer to 'the Ten' as if there was only one such board: in Andr. 324 F 10 περὶ τῶν μετὰ τὴν κατάλυσιν τῶν λ' Ἀθήνησιν χειροτονηθέντων ἀνδρῶν ι' καὶ τῶν ἑξῆς should mean not '... the Ten and the following ⟨Ten⟩' (which tempted Boerner, *De Rebus a Graecis 410–403 Gestis*, 62–3, and others; cf. Fritz & Kapp, 184) but '... the Ten and ⟨what happened⟩ afterwards' (e.g. Boerner, *loc. cit.*, Busolt, *G.S.*, i. 80 n. 2, Jacoby *ad loc.*; Cloché, *op. cit.*, 173–5, thought either rendering possible); the reference to ἄνδρας ἀγαθούς in Lys. XII. *Erat.* 60 is too vague to prove anything. The authenticity of *A.P.*'s second board of Ten was first doubted by Boerner, *op. cit.*, 62–5; Cloché, *op. cit.*, 170–85, reviewed the arguments for and against and decided against, not so much because of the silence of our other sources—though that is surely significant—as because the desire for peace on the part of the Three Thousand which is essential to *A.P.*'s account seems not to have existed (cf. p. 456, and notice especially the attitude of τὸ κοινόν in X. *H.* II. iv. 37), and more particularly because Rhinon, placed by *A.P.* in the second Ten but certainly a member of the Ten who succeeded the Thirty (cf. below), appears to have acquiesced in the acts of the original Ten. The second Ten are defended, but unconvincingly, by A. von Mess, *RM*[2] lxvi 1911, 383, A. P. Dorjahn, *Philos. Q.* xxiii 1944, 289–96, cf. *Political Forgiveness in Old Athens*, 17 n. 5; A. Fuks, *Mnem.*[4] vi 1953, 198–9, agreed with Cloché in rejecting the second Ten. Moore, 270–1, in an obscure note seems to regard the appointment of *A.P.*'s first Ten as 'the seizure of power by a group within the Thirty' and *A.P.*'s second Ten as the well-attested board, 'manifestly different from the Thirty', and suggests that the (first) Ten's appeal to Sparta went unanswered; Beloch tried to save the second Ten by placing their appointment later, as a change arranged by Pausanias (*G.G.*[2], III. i. 12, cf. J. B. Bury, *H.G.*, [1]512 = [4]321).

The change to a second board of Ten may be ruled out, whether at the point where *A.P.* places it or later. If the second Ten have any basis in fact—and in a matter of this kind distortion is more likely than outright invention—we should look for them in the provisional government of Twenty appointed after the reconciliation

(And. I. *Myst.* 81, cf. Poll. VIII. 112, schol. A. I. *Tim.* 39: Fuks, *op. cit.*, 199), who may well have comprised ten men from the city and ten from the Piraeus (Wilamowitz, *A.u.A.*, ii. 223, Busolt & Swoboda, *G.S.*, ii. 918; contr. Cloché, *op. cit.*, 409).†

ἐφ' ὧν: 'In whose term of office'.

συναγωνιζομένων καὶ προθυμουμένων τούτων: The reference must be to the second board of Ten: 'While these men were in power and were sincerely doing whatever they could to help' (Fritz & Kapp).

'Ρίνων τε ὁ Παιανιεύς: Sc. Χαρικλέους. We meet Rhinon first as πάρεδρος of the Hellenotamiae in 417/6 (M&L 77, 26-7, giving his patronymic); he was probably the eponym of the *Rhinon* of Aeschines Socraticus (D.L. II. 61, Poll. VII. 103) and of Archippus (frs 40-2 Kock). In Is. XVIII. *Call.* 5-8 he appears as one of οἱ δέκα οἱ μετὰ τοὺς τριάκοντα καταστάντες, not at odds with his colleagues; but the fact that he was acceptable to the restored democracy supports the claim that he showed himself amenable to the men of the Piraeus at some time before the reconciliation was arranged (cf. below).

Φάϋλλος ὁ Ἀχερδούσιος: Phayllus' son Ariston was a victor at the Thargelia, probably with boys' chorus, in 359/8 (*ΑΔ* XXV 1970, μελ. 146, 5), and was trierarch in the 330's (*IG* ii² 1624, 71-2). The Phayllus of *Hesp.* XXXII 1963, 156-63, 2*b*, 6, may be the same man (cf. A. M. Woodward's commentary, p. 162); he may be related to Thucydides Ἀριστ⟨ί?⟩ωνος Ἀχερδούσιος (Andr. 324 F 57 *ap.* Marc. *Vit. Thuc.* 28), who was treasurer of Athena in 424/3 (e.g. M&L 72, 25) and who may be the author of the rider to M&L 70 if that too is to be dated to 424/3. See Davies, *A.P.F.*, 53-4.

πρὶν [[ἢ]] ⟨τε⟩ Παυσανίαν [[τ']] ἀφικέσθαι διεπέμποντο πρὸς τοὺς ἐν Πειραιεῖ: From our other evidence this seems unlikely to be true. *A.P.* omitted Lysander's intervention altogether (cf. pp. 458-9); he mentions Pausanias, but in such a way that most of the credit for the reconciliation is given to Rhinon and Phayllus. According to X. *H.* II. iv. 29-37 the Spartan king Pausanias, jealous of Lysander, gained the support of three out of five ephors and took an army of Spartans and allies to Athens; he first attacked the Piraeus, but afterwards encouraged both the men of the Piraeus and those of the city to seek a settlement; a deputation from the Piraeus and ἰδιῶται from the city went to Sparta, and then a separate delegation from τὸ κοινόν in the city offered to surrender to the Spartans. Other accounts are much briefer: Lys. XII. *Erat.* 60 regards the arrival of the Spartans and their allies, like the arrival of Lysander, as a response to the appeal of the Ten; D.S. XIV. 33. vi gives Pausanias two motives, jealousy of Lysander and a care for Sparta's reputation; Just. V. 10. vii gives as his reason for the reconciliation pity for the exiles; Pl. *Lys.* 21. iv-vii makes Pausanias' intervention the policy of both kings, inspired by fear of Lysander. Paus. III. 5. i-ii says that

COMMENTARY ON THE *ATH. POL.* [38. iii

Pausanias came to Attica τῷ λόγῳ an enemy to Thrasybulus and the Athenians, and in order to confirm the tyranny set up by Lysander, that he won a battle against the Piraeus but then returned home rather than strengthen the tyranny, and that for this he was brought to trial but acquitted, though king Agis was among those voting for condemnation (if what is said of Agis is correct this trial must have followed shortly after the events; but these events were alluded to also in the trial which followed the battle of Haliartus in 395 [X. *H.* III. v. 25, cf. Pl. *Lys.* 21. vii with 30. i]). For a discussion see Cloché, *La Restauration démocratique*, 200–13: *pace* Lysias we may accept that Pausanias was jealous of Lysander (Cloché compares the rivalry of Plistoanax and Brasidas earlier) and would not wish to maintain the oligarchy with which Lysander was closely associated, but there is no need to suppose that he was completely in sympathy with the men at the Piraeus (*op. cit.*, 225–6, 233); he will no doubt have thought of Sparta's interests, and perhaps also of her honour, at a time when Thebes and others were supporting the men at the Piraeus; the pity attributed to Pausanias by Justin is less likely (but Cloché too readily dismisses Lys. XVIII. *Nic. Frat.* 10–12 as an explanation of his change of attitude: *op. cit.*, 214–20).†

38. iv. ἐπὶ πέρας γὰρ ἤγαγε τὴν εἰρήνην καὶ τὰς διαλύσεις: Aristotle uses both πέρας and ἄγειν ἐπί, and πέρας ἔχειν is common, but the only other instance of ἐπὶ πέρας ἄγειν seems to be Phil. Byz. *Synt. Mech.* IV. 3 (50. 29 Thevenot = 8 Diels & Schramm, *Abh. Berlin* 1918, xvi). Kaibel, *Stil und Text*, 39, compares ἐπὶ τέλος ἄγειν in Anon. Iambl. 89 fr. 2. vii Diels & Kranz *ap.* Iambl. *Protr.* 20, Polybius (frequently, e.g. III. 5. vii, viii), *P. Teb.* i 14, 8. For εἰρήνη and διαλύσεις see p. 463.

μετὰ τῶν δέκα διαλλακτῶν . . . ἐκ Λακεδαίμονος: According to X. *H.* II. iv. 38 the Spartans in response to the deputations sent to them ἐξέπεμψαν πεντεκαίδεκα ἄνδρας εἰς Ἀθήνας, καὶ ἐπέταξαν σὺν Παυσανίᾳ διαλλάξαι ὅπῃ δύναιντο κάλλιστα. In view of the proliferation of boards of ten in this chapter of *A.P.*, Xenophon's fifteen is more likely to be correct (cf. B. Keil, *Hermes* xxxii 1897, 406 with n. 1, remarking that fifteen is often found in Dorian states); but I am not sure that we should follow the suggestion of Kaibel & Wilamowitz[3] and emend *A.P.*'s text.

τὴν εὔνοιαν τὴν εἰς τὸν δῆμον: Cf. above.

καὶ λαβόντες . . . τὰς εὐθύνας ἔδοσαν ἐν δημοκρατίᾳ: The contrast ἐν ὀλιγαρχίᾳ . . . ἐν δημοκρατίᾳ . . . became a common one: Kaibel, *Stil und Text*, 196, cites Lys. XII. *Erat.* 78, And. I. *Myst.* 99, Is. XV. *Antid.* 27. The terms of reconciliation provided that the Thirty, the Ten, the Eleven and the Piraeus Ten, the men most responsible for the acts of the oligarchic régimes, were to be excluded from the general amnesty unless they submitted to a process of εὔθυναι (39. vi with commentary). Rhinon, who subsequently held office, must as *A.P.* says have undergone his εὔθυναι successfully; Cloché, *La Restauration démocratique*, 344–5, suggests that all of the Ten did so.

στρατηγὸς εὐθὺς ᾑρέθη 'Ρίνων: This appointment is unconfirmed; but Rhinon is probably to be restored among the treasurers of Athena for 402/1 in *IG* ii² 1370 + 1371, 10 (fasc. ii. 2, p. 797; cf. *SEG* xxiii 81).

G. Rudberg, *Eranos* xxii 1924, 217–19, remarks that this last sentence is a fine piece of rhetoric, Gorgiastic rather than Isocratean in manner, perhaps derived from a speech or decree of 403 ⟨or shortly afterwards⟩; at any rate we may allow that it points to a source nearer to the events than to the time of *A.P.* Cf. Introduction, p. 41, and pp. 421–2.

39. i. ἐγένοντο δ' αἱ διαλύσεις ἐπ' Εὐκλείδου ἄρχοντος: Euclides was the archon of 403/2 (e.g. D.S. xiv. 12. i); but 41. i places the institution of τὴν νῦν οὖσαν πολιτείαν in the archonship of Pythodorus, 404/3. The Thirty came to power in the summer of 404, probably early in the year 404/3 (35. i with commentary); the first attempt to dislodge Thrasybulus from Phyle was frustrated by a snowstorm (cf. pp. 450, 451); the battle of Munichia was fought on the fifth day from the second battle near Phyle (cf. p. 455), and in the days immediately following men from the Piraeus gathered ὀπώρα, 'fruit', which should point to early June (X. *H.* ii. iv. 25, cf. G. Colin, *Xénophon historien*, 66 with n. 3, Hignett, *H.A.C.*, 383); but on the day of the battle of Munichia it was said that the Thirty had killed more Athenians in eight months than the Peloponnesians had killed in ten years of war (X. *H.* ii. iv. 21); Pl. *Glor. Ath.* 349 F dates the return of οἱ ἀπὸ Φυλῆς to 12 Boedromion (iii). To avoid the embarrassment of ὀπώρα Busolt & Swoboda, *G.S.*, ii. 912 n. 7, proposed to read ὄσπρια, 'pulse'; Beloch, *G.G.*², iii. ii. 209, believed that ὀπώρα included olives and could be gathered in December; A. G. Roos, *Klio* xvii 1921, 11–15, suggested that ὀπώρα was gathered but not immediately after the battle of Munichia. Hignett, *H.A.C.*, 383, after dating the appointment of the Thirty early in 404/3, accepted ὀπώρα with its implications and supposed that the eight months were reckoned from the beginning of the reign of terror rather than from the appointment of the Thirty, and that is the easiest solution: Thrasybulus' occupation of Phyle need not be placed as early as the beginning of winter (cf. on 37. i); probably the reconciliation was arranged late in the summer of 403, and 12 Boedromion 403/2 may be accepted as the date of the return procession of X. *H.* ii. iv. 39 and Lys. xiii. *Agor.* 80 (cf. Cloché, *La Restauration démocratique*, 247 with n. 1). When the last day of Scirophorion (xii) 404/3 was reached,

Pythodorus' year as archon should have ended; certainly Euclides will not have been appointed until after the reconciliation had taken effect. If Pythodorus was retained in office after the end of 404/3, that will explain 41. i (cf. Kaibel, *Stil und Text*, 201, D. Hereward, *BSA* xlvii 1952, 112, and commentary *ad loc.*); but the restored democracy did not recognise his archonship, and if it officially regarded Euclides as archon for the whole of 403/2 that will explain this passage: cf. the problem of the archonship under which the Thirty were appointed, discussed on pp. 436–7.

A.P. writes of διαλύσεις here and in 38. iv, 40. i, and D.H. 525–6. *Lys.* 32 uses διαλύσασθαι; X. *H.* II. iv. 38 writes οἱ δὲ διήλλαξαν..., D.S. XIV. 33. i writes Παυσανίας ... διήλλαξε, and we find διαλλάσσειν or διαλλαγαί in Lys. VI. *And.* 39, XIII. *Agor.* 80, And. I. *Myst.* 90, Tod 100, 8; συνθῆκαι, used by *A.P.* of the terms of the reconciliation, reappears in Lys. VI. *And.* 39, 45, XIII. *Agor.* 88, XXV. *Reip. Del. Defens.* 23, Is. XVIII. *Call.* 19–21 cf. 23 (in each case combined with ὅρκοι: Isocrates cites the συνθῆκαι and the ὅρκοι as distinct documents); and there are further references to ὅρκοι in And. I. *Myst.* 90–1 (quoting from an oath taken by all citizens and from the bouleutic and dicastic oaths), *A.P.* 39. iv, X. *H.* II. iv. 42, A. II. *F.L.* 176; finally, we read of a further reconciliation and oaths in the settlement of 401/0 with Eleusis (X. *H.* II. iv. 43, Just. v. 10. x–xi: cf. p. 480). Xenophon begins his account of the terms οἱ δὲ διήλλαξαν ἐφ' ᾧτε εἰρήνην μὲν ἔχειν ὡς πρὸς ἀλλήλους; *A.P.*, who omits that clause from his account of the terms, writes in 38. iv of τὴν εἰρήνην καὶ τὰς διαλύσεις; and this led Cloché to suppose that there was a peace agreement followed by a separate agreement on the terms of reconciliation (*op. cit.*, 242–4); but I am not persuaded that *A.P.* 'distingue formellement la paix (εἰρήνη) des διαλύσεις' (cf. G. Colin, *Xénophon historien*, 84–5).

We cannot always be sure whether an omission is due to the drafter(s) of the document or to *A.P.* or his source, but it is clear that *A.P.* does not give a complete transcription: a fragment of Lysias quotes a clause on property which *A.P.* omits (cf. p. 465), and it appears from Is. XVIII. *Call.* 20 that the clause stipulating μηδενὶ πρὸς μηδένα μνησικακεῖν ἐξεῖναι (§vi) included a reference to τοὺς ἐνδείξαντας ἢ φήναντας ἢ τῶν ἄλλων τι τῶν τοιούτων πράξαντας. In the text presented by *A.P.* we are told that those who wish to join the community at Eleusis must register within ten days, but we are not told how or with whom they are to register (§iv with commentary); and the arrangements for εὔθυναι are extremely obscure (§vi with commentary). *A.P.*'s ultimate source is the official text of the settlement (cf. p. 420), but his archontic date could not have been attached to the document at the time, and probably he did not consult the original document himself. The document could have been quoted in speeches and pamphlets attacking μνησικακοῦντες and defending the moderation of the settlement; much of it will have lost its relevance after Eleusis was reabsorbed into the Athenian state in 401/0 (40. iv); for this document as for his narrative in general *A.P.*'s immediate source is probably a polemical work written not long after the settlement.

τοὺς βουλομένους Ἀθηναίων ... ἔχειν Ἐλευσῖνα: Ἀθηναίων is added above the line; Kenyon originally printed it after τῶν; Kaibel & Wilamowitz and Herwerden & Leeuwen deleted it; but it is best inserted before τῶν, as by Blass, *LZB* 1891, 304 (cf. Kaibel, *Stil und Text*, 196, Kenyon's 3rd and later edd.).

Cf. X. *H.* ii. iv. 38 (εἰ δέ τινες φοβοῖντο τῶν ἐξ ἄστεως, ἔδοξεν αὐτοῖς Ἐλευσῖνα κατοικεῖν), D.S. xiv. 33. vi (τοῖς δ' εὐλαβουμένοις, μή τι πάθωσι διὰ τὰ γενόμενα κατὰ τὸ συνεχὲς αὐτῶν ἀδικήματα, τὴν Ἐλευσῖνα κατοικεῖν συνεχώρησαν); Just. v. 10. vii writes *decem tyrannos ex urbe Eleusina emigrare ad ceteros iubet*, but see §vi with commentary, below; cf. also Lys. vi. *And.* 45, xxv. *Reip. Del. Defens.* 9. The Thirty had occupied Eleusis (cf. pp. 448, 452) and some of their supporters may have joined them there, and as far as we know these men were not a party to the reconciliation between those of the Piraeus and those of the city (cf. Lys. vi. *And.* 37–41, xiii. *Agor.* 88–90, trying to exploit the fact that the reconciliation was between these two groups; according to Lys. xviii. *Nic. Frat.* 12 Pausanias rejected the ξένια sent him by the Thirty): it was simplest to leave them in possession of Eleusis and to allow any of their partisans who so wished to join them. In *A.P.*'s text the right of migration is offered to those who had stayed in the city under the oligarchy: those who had left Athens, whether voluntarily or under compulsion, would hardly be interested in joining this community of their enemies; but contrast §iv, where there are provisions both for men in Athens and for men away from Athens to register for membership of this community.

ἐξοικεῖν: Cf. Lys. xxxi. *Phil.* 9, D. xxix. *Aphob. iii.* 3, Hyp. iii. *Ath.* 29 (in each case, to a specified place); also Hyp. iii. *Ath.* 33, and ἐξοίκησις in Plat. *Legg.* iv. 704 c 5–6, viii. 850 B 8–c 1 (without specifying destination).

ἐπιτίμους ὄντας ... καὶ τὰ αὐτῶν καρπουμένους: See Cloché, *La Restauration démocratique*, 251–3: those who migrate to Eleusis remain ἐπιτίμους, in possession of their rights as Athenian citizens (subject to certain limitations, stated in the clauses that follow); κυρίους καὶ αὐτοκράτορας ἑαυτῶν, with full power and authority over themselves, so that the authorities in Athens cannot legislate for the internal affairs of the community at Eleusis or impose taxes on it; καὶ τὰ αὐτῶν καρπουμένους, (in possession of and) entitled to draw the revenues from their own property. The last clause is too succinct: there would be no difficulty in leaving to the oligarchs property which was already theirs before the institution of the Thirty, but disputes could all too easily arise as to the legitimacy of more recent transactions. One aspect of the problem was solved by a ruling that judicial decisions given under the democracy were to be upheld as valid but those given under the Thirty were to be invalid (And. I. *Myst.* 87 [first clause only], D. xxiv. *Tim.* 56); *P. Oxy.* xiii 1606 = Lys. fr. i Gernet & Bizos, lines 38–48, quotes a further ruling from the συνθῆκαι, that land and houses, and unsold movable property, were to revert to their original owners, but sales of movable property under the oligarchy were to be valid; but it might not always be clear how or when an oligarch had acquired what he had acquired. For the working of the amnesty as it affected property see pp. 471–2, and for property at Eleusis see §iii with commentary.

39. ii. τὸ δ' ἱερὸν εἶναι κοινὸν ἀμφοτέρων: The community at Eleusis was to be autonomous but not totally independent of Athens; and for the purposes of the Eleusinian cult this split in the state was to be ignored (cf. Cloché, *op. cit.*, 253–5).

ἐπιμελεῖσθαι δὲ Κήρυκας καὶ Εὐμολπίδας κατὰ τὰ πάτρια: The two γένη in which the principal offices of the Eleusinian cult were hereditary (cf. 57. i with commentary). On the occasion of Pisander's first visit to Athens, early in 411, these clans had objected on religious grounds to the proposal to recall to Athens Alcibiades, the profaner of the Mysteries (T. viii. 53. ii), but otherwise their views in 411–410 are not known; in 404–403 one member of the Κήρυκες was found on the democratic side, Cleocritus ὁ τῶν μυστῶν κῆρυξ, who after the battle of Munichia made a speech on behalf of Thrasybulus' supporters to the men of the city (X. *H.* ii. iv. 20: cf. p. 456).

μὴ ἐξεῖναι ... Ἐλευσινάδε ἰέναι: Without some such principle of isolation, extreme oligarchs and extreme democrats might come into conflict, notwithstanding the provisions of the amnesty. The men of Eleusis are excluded only from the city of Athens: they were presumably free to travel in the remainder of Attica at their own risk; if they had property there they could attempt to draw the revenue from it (cf. above), but if they had property in the city they would be cut off from that unless a friend could act as agent.

There is a marginal note, δ εισιεν|ετει, interpreted by Kenyon as a gloss, δ' εἰσὶ ἐν ἔτει (sc. μυστήρια); by Kaibel & Wilamowitz[3] as a correction to Ἐλευσινάδ' εἰσιέναι, which they print as their text (but they make no sense of the ετει).

πλὴν μυστηρίοις ἑκατέρους: 'Except that at the Mysteries those of Eleusis may go to the city and those of the city may go to Eleusis': since the sacred objects were taken from Eleusis to Athens, there were then ceremonies in Athens, next the great procession went from Athens to Eleusis, and finally there were rites at Eleusis, it was necessary to break the principle of isolation if the Mysteries were to be celebrated and members of both communities were to be free to participate. We should not emend to ἑκατέροις and see in the word a reference to the Greater and Lesser Mysteries (H. Jackson, *CR* v 1891, 114; Hude); Sandys suggests that the purpose of the change to accusative at the end of the sentence was to avoid that misunderstanding.

συντελεῖν ... εἰς τὸ συμμαχικὸν καθάπερ τοὺς ἄλλους 'Αθηναίους: *Sc.* τοὺς 'Ελευσῖνι κατοικοῦντας; for συντελεῖν cf. D. xx. *Lept.* 28 (συντελοῦσιν εἰς τὸν πόλεμον); D. Lotze, *Abh. Leipzig* LVII. i 1964, 63-4, suggests that the Spartans attempted, without much success, to use συντέλεια rather than φόρος as the term for the money which they levied from their allies after the Peloponnesian War. By the peace treaty of 404 Athens became a subordinate ally of Sparta (X. *H.* II. ii. 20, D.S. XIII. 107. iv): this alliance remained in force (e.g. X. *H.* III. ii. 25), and for the purposes of the alliance as for those of the Eleusinian cult the split in the Athenian state was to be ignored. *A.P.* has not previously mentioned the alliance, and this clause would puzzle a reader who knew no account of 404-403 except that of *A.P.*

39. iii. ἐὰν δέ τινες τῶν ἀπιόντων ... συμπείθειν τὸν κεκτημένον: 'If any of those departing (to Eleusis) take a house at Eleusis, they are to persuade the owner.' As it stands this provision is perfectly sensible—those who go to Eleusis may not expropriate property there but must negotiate with the owners—but after the Thirty's massacre of the inhabitants of Eleusis (cf. p. 448) there must have been many houses for which it would be difficult to find a legitimate owner from whom they might be bought or rented (cf. Cloché, *La Restauration démocratique*, 256).

τιμητάς: If this word was used in the original document, it will be our earliest instance of it; it is not noted in LSJ or the 1968 Supplement.

'Ελευσινίων δὲ συνοικεῖν οὓς ἂν οὗτοι βούλωνται: αὐτοί was suggested by H. Richards (*CR* v 1891, 228) and Herwerden, but we should retain οὗτοι (cf. Kaibel, *Stil und Text*, 197). The meaning will be: 'Those of the people of Eleusis whom the new settlers are willing to accept are to be allowed to stay and live together with them' (Fritz & Kapp, restored to present tense). Cloché, *op. cit.*, 256-8, followed Haussoullier in referring συνοικεῖν to joint occupation of a house, but the reference is surely to residence at Eleusis: any of the old inhabitants who wish to do so may remain at Eleusis if permitted by the oligarchs who are settling there. It is not clear how many of the old inhabitants had survived the Thirty's massacre, but the account of X. *H.* II. iv. 8 may indicate that only men of military age were killed, and some men marked out for death may in fact have escaped.

39. iv. τὴν δ' ἀπογραφὴν: Those who wish to join the community at Eleusis are to register their names (cf. Lys. xxv. *Reip. Del. Defens.* 9): if they are already in Athens they must register within ten days of taking the oath (to the reconciliation: cf. p. 463) and must go within twenty days (either of taking the oath or of registering their names or of the end of the period of registration: cf. Cloché, *op. cit.*, 258); if they are not already in Athens the periods are to be reckoned from the time of their return. The following sentence shows that provision was made for any who had gone to Eleusis to cancel their registration and return to Athens; for Archinus' foreclosing on the time allowed for registration see 40. i with commentary. The Thirty, already at Eleusis, seem not to have participated formally in the reconciliation (cf. p. 464), and unless they could do so at Eleusis are not likely to have registered themselves as members of the separate community: perhaps men known to have gone to Eleusis were registered *in absentia*. In addition to giving an inadequate definition of the period of twenty days, this text does not state how or with whom registrations are to be made: perhaps the omissions are due to abbreviation by *A.P.* or his source, but they are not outside the range of Athenian documentary incompetence (cf. p. 463: for a similar omission in an inscribed text see M&L 49, 26–7).

δ[έκ]α ἡμερῶν: Suggested by Kaibel & Wilamowitz[1] and Leeuwen, read thus by Wilcken and by Kenyon in his Berlin ed.; M. H. Chambers, *TAPA* xcvi 1965, 36, reads δέκα.

39. v. μὴ ἐξεῖναι δὲ ἄρχειν μηδεμίαν ἀρχὴν ... τὸν Ἐλευσῖνι κατοικοῦντα: Those who migrate to Eleusis retain their rights in private law as Athenian citizens, but are members of an autonomous community (§i) and are excluded from the city of Athens (§ii): it is therefore natural that they should be debarred from holding any office in the Athenian state.

πρὶν ἂν ἀπογράψηται πάλιν ἐν τῷ ἄστει κατοικεῖν: Here, even more than in §iv, the text is excessively concise. It is clear from §i that there was an absolute right to register for migration to Eleusis; but although from this clause it seems to be the case it has not been directly stated that anyone who had exercised this right was free to re-register and return to the city. According to Lys. xxv. *Reip. Del. Defens.* 9 some men who had registered for Eleusis (remained in or returned to the city and) in 401/0 joined in the attack on their fellow oligarchs (cf. 40. iv with commentary). For a law of the early fifth century dealing with the right of colonists to return home, not a parallel situation, see M&L 20.

τὰς δὲ δίκας τοῦ φόνου εἶναι κατὰ τὰ πάτρια: There would be no special point in stipulating that for homicide trials traditional procedure was to be followed, and presumably the purpose of this sentence is to state an exception to the rule laid down in the following sentence, μηδενὶ πρὸς μηδένα μνησικακεῖν ἐξεῖναι: the amnesty is not to apply to cases of homicide or of wounding covered by the homicide law (cf. 57. iii with commentary) in which a man is accused not merely of arresting or of procuring a condemnation (that is, of helping to implement the policies of the Thirty) but of doing the deed in person. Cf. Cloché, *Le Restauration démocratique*, 259–61; R. J. Bonner, *CP* xix 1924, 175–6, who remarks that the amnesty could not wipe out the pollution associated with murder.

αὐτοχειρίᾳ ἔκτεινεν ἢ ἔτρωσεν: The papyrus reads αυτοχιραεκτισιοτρωσασ, with ε inserted above the first ι, ε inserted above the second ι, and οτ deleted and ιε inserted above. Kenyon[1-2] read αὐτοχειρὶ ⟨ἀπέκτονεν⟩ ἐκτίσει ἱερώσας, and Kenyon[3] read †αὐτόχειρα ἐκτίσει ἱερώσας†. Kaibel & Wilamowitz and Herwerden & Leeuwen (after earlier conjectures of Herwerden, *BPW* xi 1891, 323, 611) emended to αὐτοχειρίᾳ ἔκτεινεν ἢ ἔτρωσεν, which is accepted by Kenyon in his Berlin ed. and O.C.T., and by Mathieu & Haussoullier and Oppermann, and is at any rate on the right lines (cf. Kaibel, *Stil und Text*, 197–8); others have preferred αὐτόχειρ . . . (Leeuwen, Blass[1-3] [αὐτόχειρ ἀπέκτεινεν], Sandys [cf. *CR* vii 1893, 448–9]), or . . . τρώσας (W. Wyse, *CR* v 1891, 114, Thalheim, *BPW* xxix 1909, 703 [. . . ἐκτείσατο τρώσας, referring to acts of revenge committed after the amnesty]). αὐτόχειρ in agreement with the subject of (ἀπο)κτείνειν is used by Plat. *Legg.* ix. 865 B 4–5, 866 D 5, 867 C 4–5, 871 A 2–3, 871 E 8–872 A 2, 872 B 4–5, and the word is found in Is. iv. *Paneg.* 111, D. xviii. *Cor.* 287, xxi. *Mid.* 106, 116, as well as in verse: we should read either the usual αὐτοχειρίᾳ ἔκτεινεν or Blass' αὐτόχειρ ἀπέκτεινεν. ἢ ἔτρωσεν is to be preferred to ἢ τρώσας, though further from the papyrus' text: cf. ἀποκτείνῃ ἢ τρώσῃ in 57. iii.

39. vi. τῶν δὲ παρεληλυθότων μηδενὶ πρὸς μηδένα μνησικακεῖν ἐξεῖναι: In 40. ii the papyrus reads ἐπεί τις ἤρξατο τῶν κατεληλυθότων μνησικακεῖν. In each case either παρεληλυθότων ('past events') or κατεληλυθότων ('the men who have returned') will give an acceptable sense: H. Richards, *CR* v 1891, 228, proposed to emend to κατεληλυθότων here, while Π. Ν. Παπαγεώργιος, 'Αθ. iv 1892, 569, hinted at a change to παρεληλυθότων in 40. ii; but the papyrus' text should be retained in both places.

μὴ μνησικακεῖν, easy to understand but hard to translate into English, is the regular formula for an amnesty (cf. T. iv. 74. ii, Tod 68, 15–16). X. *H.* ii. iv. 43 writes of oaths ἦ μὴν μὴ μνησικακήσειν after the final settlement with Eleusis (cf. 40. iv with commentary); his equivalent in 403 (II. iv. 38) is ἀπιέναι δὲ ἐπὶ τὰ ἑαυτῶν πλήν ... Just. v. 10. xi (again after the final settlement with Eleusis) writes *ne qua dissensio ex ante actis nasceretur, omnes iure iurando obstringuntur discordiarum oblivionem fore*; and Nep. VIII. *Thras.* 3. ii writes that Thrasybulus *legem tulit, ne quis ante actarum rerum accusaretur neve multaretur, eamque illi oblivionis appellarunt.* And. I. *Myst.* 90-1 quotes from the oath taken by all citizens, and from the bouleutic and dicastic oaths, to which undertakings to respect the amnesty were added (the first and third contain the words οὐ μνησικακήσω). D.S. XIV. 33. vi says nothing of this, but in 34. iii-vi (under 401/0, the same year as chs 32-3) he reports στάσις in Cyrene, at the end of which διηλλάγησαν ... ὀρκωμοτήσαντες μὴ μνησικακήσειν: one reconciliation may have affected his report of the other, but there is no need to follow A. P. Dorjahn, *Political Forgiveness in Old Athens*, 11 n. 12, in doubting the episode in Cyrene.

The full text of the συνθῆκαι went into further detail (cf. p. 463): Is. XVIII. *Call.* 20 shows that there was a reference to τοὺς ἐνδείξαντας ἢ φήναντας ἢ τῶν ἄλλων τι τοιούτων πράξαντας, and this is confirmed by a reference to ἔνδειξις and ἀπαγωγή in Andocides' quotation from the bouleutic oath.

πλὴν πρὸς τοὺς τριάκοντα ... καὶ τοὺς τοῦ Πειραιέως ἄρξαντας: Cf. X. *H.* II. iv. 38 (omitting the Ten), And. I. *Myst.* 90 (omitting both the Ten and the Piraeus Ten). With Cloché, *La Restauration démocratique*, 259-62, and Hignett, *H.A.C.*, 294, I accept *A.P.*'s list of exclusions: the Eleven and the Piraeus Ten had been the principal agents of the Thirty (cf. on 35. i), and the Ten had continued the war against Thrasybulus and his supporters (cf. on 38. i). τοὺς δέκα, without further qualification, conflicts with the claim of 38. iii-iv that there had been two successive boards of Ten; but the reference to Rhinon's εὔθυναι in 38. iv confirms that the Ten were among those excluded from the full amnesty, and that Moore is wrong to delete them here. Thalheim was embarrassed by the relationship between the exclusions in this sentence and the exception in the previous sentence (τὰς δὲ δίκας ... ἢ ἔτρωσεν): in *BPW* xxix 1909, 703, he emended that sentence to make it refer to acts of revenge committed after the amnesty (cf. *ad loc.*); on another occasion he argued that not even those excluded by this sentence might be prosecuted for murder or wounding unless they were charged with doing the deed in person; but the right combination was obtained by Cloché, *op. cit.*, 261-2, that any Athenian might be prosecuted for murder or wounding by his own deed, and in addition members of these four boards might be prosecuted on any other charge.[34] A member who joined the

---

[34] I have not been able to penetrate Cloché's reference to the second suggestion of Thalheim.

community at Eleusis would, however, be protected by the fact that he was not obliged to leave Eleusis and face an Athenian court. For evidence that property was confiscated from some of the oligarchs cf. pp. 477, 556.

μηδὲ πρὸς τούτους, ἐὰν διδῶσιν εὐθύνας: Cf. And. I. *Myst.* 90. The amnesty will be extended to these men if they submit to a procedure of εὔθυναι (cf. the εὔθυναι undergone by magistrates retiring from any office: 48. iv–v, 54. ii, with commentary) and are cleared of guilt, whereas if they are not cleared of guilt they will be liable to punishment: this obvious point was made by Grote, *H.G.* (1869–84), viii. 94.

εὐθύνας δὲ δοῦναι τοὺς μὲν ἐν Πειραιεῖ ἄρξαντας ... τοὺς δ' ἐν τῷ ἄστει ... : See Cloché, *La Restauration démocratique*, 268–72. In *A.P.*'s text, if not in the document from which it is derived, this clause is condensed to the point of obscurity. That the Piraeus Ten should render their accounts to the men domiciled at (or perhaps, to the demesmen of) the Piraeus is clear enough; but it is not clear whether the other oligarchs were to be judged by the men of the city demes or by the whole citizen body; and it would be surprising if the property qualification imposed on the jury (cf. below) was to apply only to cases heard in the city (as the transmitted text states) and not also to cases heard in the Piraeus. It is easier to decide what procedure would have been most just than to demonstrate what procedure must have been intended. The rule of the Piraeus Ten impinged only on men living at the Piraeus, whereas the rule of the other boards had impinged directly or indirectly on all inhabitants of Attica (except that the Eleven may not have impinged on those living at the Piraeus); so it would be reasonable if the Piraeus Ten were judged by those domiciled at the Piraeus and the others were judged by the whole citizen body, including those domiciled at the Piraeus.

τοῖς τὰ τιμήματα παρεχομένοις is an unparalleled expression (but Arist. *Pol.* VI. 1321 A 28 writes of τοῖς τὸ τίμημα κτωμένοις): some have sought a reference to guarantors (Reinach), or to assessment of penalties (considered by Kenyon[1-2]; adopted by some early translators, including Haussoullier, but abandoned by Mathieu & Haussoullier); but most have agreed that the reference should be to men possessed of a property qualification, perhaps men in the upper three of Solon's four property classes (e.g. Kenyon, Sandys, Wilamowitz, *A.u.A.*, ii. 217–18): cf. τῶν ὅπλα παρεχομένων in the 'Draconian constitution', 4. ii, and T. VIII. 97. i; for the use of τίμημα in connection with Solon's property classes cf. 7. iii, 8. i, with commentary. Normally there was no property qualification for jury service in Athens (7. iii, 63. iii, with commentary): if, as seems to be the case, a property qualification was imposed here, its purpose will presumably have been to prevent the use of juries too strongly biased against the oligarchs (cf. Cloché, *op. cit.*, 312–13). We should expect the same qualification to apply to juries in the Piraeus as in the city: Kenyon[1-3] therefore proposed ἐν τοῖς ⟨ἐν τῷ ἄστει⟩ τὰ τιμήματα; M. C. Gertz, *NTF*[2] x 1890–2, 254, suggested either ἐν τοῖς ⟨ἐν τῷ ἄστει⟩ [[τὰ]] τιμήματα or ἐν τοῖς τὰ ⟨αὐτὰ⟩ τιμήματα; but the defect in the text transmitted to us may as well be due to carelessness in the drafting or the reporting of the document as to carelessness by a copyist of *A.P.* One other question is left unresolved by our text: I have written of juries, but it is not clear whether these cases were to be heard by juries of a predetermined size or by assemblies of as many of those eligible as cared to attend (Lys. XII. *Erat.*, written for the εὔθυναι of Eratosthenes, is addressed to ἄνδρες δικασταί, but this is not enough to solve the problem).

εἶθ' οὕτως ἐξοικεῖν τοὺς ἐθέλοντας: (The scribe's original text is read as ειουτως by Kenyon in his Berlin ed., as ειθυτως by M. H. Chambers, *TAPA* xcvi 1965, 32.) 'Then, after satisfying all these legal requirements, those who wish may emigrate' (Fritz & Kapp, restored to the present tense, after Sandys). However, Eleusis was recognised as a semi-independent community for oligarchs unwilling to live under the restored democracy, and as far as we know only oligarchs who did wish to remain in Athens submitted to εὔθυναι. Blass[1] proposed τοὺς ἁλόντας, which can hardly be right; but in his 3rd and 4th edd. he suggested εἶθ' . . . τοὺς ⟨μὴ⟩ ἐθέλοντας ('sive qui nolunt emigranto, ut supra scriptum est'), and I suspect that that is right (Cloché, *op. cit.*, 272, quotes the text thus emended at the end of a paragraph which implies acceptance of the orthodox text).

τὰ δὲ χρήματα . . . ἑκατέρους ἀποδοῦναι χωρίς: 40. iii and D. xx. *Lept.* 11 allude to money borrowed by the Thirty, and for money borrowed by the Ten cf. 38. i with commentary; for money borrowed by Thrasybulus and his supporters see Lys. xxx. *Nic.* 22, D. xx. *Lept.* 149. *A.P.* 40. iii repeats this clause and remarks that in fact the restored democracy undertook the responsibility for the debts of both sides: cf. *ad loc.*

How far the terms of the amnesty were observed is discussed at length by Cloché, *op. cit.*, 296–404, and by A. P. Dorjahn, *Political Forgiveness in Old Athens*, 24–53. Some court cases were brought in defiance of the amnesty, and measures were taken to hinder this (cf. 40. ii with commentary), but as far as we know no one was convicted on a charge on which the amnesty ought to have protected him (no δίκαι, private suits, were tried until 401/0: Lys. XVII. *Bon. Erat.* 3, Is. XXI. *Euth.* 7, emphasised by D. M. MacDowell, *RIDA*[3] xviii 1971, 267). Questions of property were bound to present problems (cf. pp. 464–5): Is. XVIII. *Call.* 23 claims that Thrasybulus and Anytus endured the loss of their property rather than bring lawsuits to recover it, and *A.P.* 40. iii contrasts the generosity of the restored democracy at Athens with democracies elsewhere, which indulge in γῆς ἀναδασμός; *P. Oxy.* xiii 1606, 1–238 = Lys. fr. i Gernet & Bizos shows Lysias trying to recover property worth 70(?) talents; but in general we may suspect that fear of breaking the amnesty left oligarchs in possession of property to which their right was doubtful. Phormisius' proposal to limit Athenian citizenship to men possessed of a property qualification was supported by Sparta but successfully opposed by Lysias (xxxiv. *Rep. Patr., ap.* D.H. 525–33. *Lys.* 32–3), but *A.P.* 40 is to mention various matters on which the restored democracy did not go to extremes. However, there is one respect in which the amnesty could not change the habits of the Athenians: in speeches in the lawcourts, irrespective of the question formally at issue, the whole career of a man tended to be adduced to show that he was or was not a good citizen, deserving or undeserving of the jury's sympathy, and so we frequently find membership of the democratic party in 404–403 cited in a man's favour and membership of the oligarchic party cited against a man or excused by him; as late as 343 Aeschines is careful to point out that his father had been on the democratic side (II. *F.L.* 78, 147). As a special instance of this we find that what a man had done in 404–403 was inevitably cited at his δοκιμασία if he was appointed to any office under the restored democracy; but if the Evander against whom Lys. xxvi. *Evand.* was written was the man who served as archon in 382/1 it was not automatically a fatal objection that a man had been on the oligarchic side.

Nothing is said in *A.P.*'s text of how the state was to be governed after the reconciliation, but it is hard to believe that there was no agreement at all on this. Between the first and the second battle near Phyle Ephorus reported an attempt by the Thirty to win over Thrasybulus, to which Thrasybulus had replied τὸν πόλεμον οὐ καταλύσειν εἰ μὴ πάντες οἱ πολῖται κατέλθωσι καὶ τὴν πάτριον πολιτείαν ὁ δῆμος ἀπολάβῃ (D.S. xiv. 32. v–vi, cf. Just. v. 9. xiii–xiv: cf. p. 452); in X. *H.* II. iv. 40–43 *init.* the return procession from the Piraeus (cf. p. 462) is followed by a speech by Thrasybulus, reproaching the oligarchs and urging them to keep the oaths, and claiming ὅτι οὐδὲν δέοι ταράττεσθαι, ἀλλὰ τοῖς νόμοις τοῖς ἀρχαίοις χρῆσθαι. . . . καὶ τότε μὲν ἀρχὰς καταστήσαντες ἐπολιτεύοντο. Phormisius' proposal to limit the citizenship (cf. above) was evidently rejected; an interim government of Twenty was followed by a restoration of the democracy, and the task of revising and codifying the laws was resumed and completed (cf. pp. 441–2).

40. i. φοβουμένων ὅσοι μετὰ τῶν τριάκοντα συνεπολέμησαν: There must at first have been considerable uncertainty as to how effective the amnesty would be; and men who had been on the oligarchic side might well fear that they would have to emigrate to Eleusis to ensure their own safety, but delay the decision in the hope that it might after all prove safe to stay in Athens. Cloché, *La Restauration démocratique*, 249, uses this passage to confirm that the majority of the Three Thousand had remained hostile to the democrats (cf. above, pp. 456, 459), but what *A.P.* says does not guarantee the conclusion.

πολλῶν μὲν ἐπινοούντων ἐξοικεῖν ἀναβαλλομένων δὲ τὴν ἀπογραφήν: Blass, *LZB* 1891, 304, placed μέν after ἐπινοούντων, and some editors followed him, but although logically better this is not required by Greek usage (cf. Kaibel, *Stil und Text*, 199-200, J. D. Denniston, *The Greek Particles*[2], 371-3). In Plat. *Legg.* VIII. 850 A 6–D 2 metics are normally to be required to leave after twenty years, but they may apply for τινα ἀναβολὴν τῆς ἐξοικήσεως (B 8–C 1).

ὅπερ εἰώθασιν ποιεῖν ἅπαντες: This comment on human nature is unusual in *A.P.*; Aristotle commonly uses εἴωθα with verbs of speaking (e.g. *Pol.* III. 1276 A 37), but notice *Pol.* IV. 1297 B 10–12: the poor εἰώθασι δέ, ὅταν πόλεμος ᾖ, ὀκνεῖν, ἂν μὴ λαμβάνωσι τροφήν, ἄποροι δὲ ὦσιν· ἐὰν δὲ πορίζῃ τις τροφήν, βούλονται πολεμεῖν.

Ἀρχῖνος: Cf. 34. iii with commentary. In addition to the three 'moderate' acts recorded in this chapter, he instituted late in 401/0 the procedure of παραγραφή, by which a defendant who believed that a case brought against him infringed the amnesty could first call for a decision as to whether the case was admissible (subsequently pleas that a case was inadmissible on other grounds could be made by παραγραφή, but it is probable that Archinus introduced a totally new procedure): see Is. XVIII. *Call.* 1-3, schol. A. 1. *Tim.* 163, and on παραγραφαί in general Poll. VIII. 57, Phot., Suid. (Π 319), παραγραφή, with Lipsius, *A.R.*, 846-58, H. J. Wolff, *Die attische Paragraphe*, Harrison, *L.A.*, ii. 106-24, S. Isager & M. H. Hansen, *Aspects of Athenian Society in the Fourth Century B.C.*, 123-37, and on the date D. M. MacDowell, *RIDA*[3] xviii 1971, 267-73. Isager & Hansen, *op. cit.*, 129-30, suggest that παραγραφαί may have been available only in private suits. It was on the motion of Archinus also that the Athenians officially adopted the Ionic alphabet as from 403/2 (Thp. 115 F 155; schol. Vat. Dion. Thr. *ap.* A. Hilgard, *Grammatici Graeci*, I. iii. 183. 16-20; but in fact Ionic spellings begin to appear in inscriptions of the second half of the fifth century and some Attic spellings persist in the first half of the fourth); for his interest in linguistic matters cf. Thph. *ap.* Syr. *ad* Arist. *Met.*, *Comm. Arist. Gr.*, VI. i. 191. 29 sqq.

συνιδὼν τὸ πλῆθος καὶ βουλόμενος κατασχεῖν αὐτούς: 'Seeing the number (*sc.* of men thinking of migrating to Eleusis) . . .': the existence of this semi-independent state would cause less danger and embarrassment to the Athenian state if it comprised only a small minority of the citizens.

ὑφεῖλε τὰς ὑπολοίπους ἡμέρας τῆς ἀναγραφῆς: For the period within which registration for membership of the community at Eleusis was allowed see 39. iv with commentary. We are not told how Archinus cut short the period: perhaps he carried a resolution in the assembly, or perhaps he persuaded whoever was in charge of registration to accept no more names; but it must have been contrary to the terms of reconciliation, even if it was approved by a majority of the citizens. L. Taran, *ap.* B. D. Meritt, *The Athenian Year*, 206–7 n. 11, suggests that Archinus subtracted days from the calendar; but I doubt if the period allowed for registration was defined in terms of calendar dates.

ἕως ἐθάρρησαν: That is, until they realised that the amnesty was being respected and they were safe under the restored democracy.

40. ii. καὶ δοκεῖ τοῦτό τε πολιτεύσασθαι καλῶς: Cf. the similar expressions of approval in 23. ii, 28. v and 33. ii, with commentary *ad locc.* This approval of 'moderate' acts is what we should expect of *A.P.* and of the Aristotelian school, but I suspect that here as elsewhere *A.P.* is repeating with his own agreement praise which he found in his source, rather than commenting spontaneously on what he found presented as bare fact: cf. D. xxiv. *Tim.* 135, where the praise of Archinus τοῦ καταλαβόντος Φυλὴν καὶ μετά γε τοὺς θεοὺς αἰτιωτάτου ὄντος τῆς καθόδου τῷ δήμῳ includes the phrase καλὰ πεπολιτευμένου. Contrast, however, §iii with commentary. It is not obvious why Archinus, of the leaders of the returning democrats, should be singled out for particular commendation.

καὶ μετὰ ταῦτα γραψάμενος τὸ ψήφισμα τὸ Θρασυβούλου παρανόμων: References to rewards for those who had supported Thrasybulus are plentiful but hard to fit together:

(*a*) After the battle of Munichia the democrats promised ἰσοτέλεια to any ξένοι who would join them in the struggle (X. *H.* ii. iv. 25).

(*b*) Thrasybulus proposed, and Archinus attacked in a γραφὴ παρανόμων, a measure to give Athenian citizenship to all who 'joined in the return from the Piraeus' (*A.P.* 40. ii).

(*c*) ἐπ' ἀναρχίας τῆς πρὸ Εὐκλείδου Thrasybulus proposed to give citizenship to the orator Lysias, and the proposal was approved by the assembly but successfully attacked in a γραφὴ παρανόμων by Archinus διὰ τὸ ἀπροβούλευτον εἶναι; for the remainder of his life Lysias had ἰσοτέλεια ([Pl.] *X. Or.* 835 F–836 A; cf. schol. A. III. *Ctes.* 195 [in the second line in the edition of F. Schultz read ⟨Λυσίᾳ τῷ⟩ Κεφάλου for Κεφάλῳ, with W. Wyse], Planudes *ad* Hermog. στάσεις [C. Walz, *Rhetores Graeci*, v. 343, quoted

Sandys[2], 154: here the reason for the decree's being ἀπροβούλευτον is said to be οὐ γὰρ ἦν πω καταστᾶσα ἡ βουλή]).
(d) There are two other allusions to Archinus' attacking Thrasybulus in a γραφὴ παρανόμων: *P. Oxy.* xv 1800, frs 6–7 (restored with a plurality of beneficiaries; the decree was ἀ[προβου]λεύτου); A. III. *Ctes.* 195.
(e) By a decree of Archinus those who could demonstrate that they ἐπὶ Φυλῇ ἐπολιορκήθησαν ὅτε Λακεδαιμόνιοι καὶ οἱ τριάκοντα προσέβαλλον were awarded an olive crown and a sum of money for a sacrifice and dedications (A. III. *Ctes.* 187–90 [rather more than 100 men]; A. E. Raubitschek, *Hesp.* x 1941, 284–95, 78 [comprising a heading, a list arranged by tribes, which he reconstructs as naming at most 58 citizens, the epigram quoted by Aeschines, and the beginning of a decree: in the list Archinus heads the men of Hippothontis, in line 55, and Thrasybulus may be restored at the head of the men of Pandionis, in line 24]).
(f) By a decree of Theozotides (*P.A.* 6913 = 6914; Davies, *A.P.F.*, 222–3), unsuccessfully attacked in a speech of Lysias for its restriction to γνήσιοι, the legitimate sons of ὁπόσοι Ἀθηναίων ἀ[πέθαν]ον [β]ιαίωι θανάτωι ἐν τῆι ὀλιγ[αρχίαι β]ο[ηθ]όντες τῆι δημοκρατίαι became like war-orphans (24. iii with commentary) the responsibility of the state and were to be paid a grant of 1 obol a day (*P. Hib.* i 14, frs *a–b* = Lys. fr. vi Gernet & Bizos; R. S. Stroud, *Hesp.* xl 1971, 280–301, 7, from which I quote lines 4–6).
(g) Non-citizens who died fighting for the democrats at the Piraeus were given a public funeral and ἔχειν αὐτοῖς τὸν ἅπαντα χρόνον τὰς αὐτὰς τιμὰς τοῖς ἀστοῖς (Lys. II. *Epit.* 66).
(h) Another inscription contains a decree enacted under an archon ending –ος (i.e. Pythodorus, 404/3, or Xenaenetus, 401/0: there is no other such archon until 395/4) which seems to refer to –οι ὅσοι συνκατῆλθον ἀπὸ Φυλῆς and those who συνεμάχησαν δὲ τὴμ μάχην τὴμ Μουνιχίασιν as distinct categories, and to confer something less than full citizenship on at any rate the second category (Tod accepted the restorations of Wilhelm, according to which the first category received citizenship and the second ἰσοτέλεια); there is a list of names, many of them strikingly non-Athenian, in which the men are arranged by tribes and described by occupation; among the new fragments of the list a third category has been detected, οἵδε παρέμ[ενον τῶι] ἐμ Πειραιεῖ δ[ήμωι] (Tod 100, discussed with new fragments by D. Hereward, *BSA* xlvii 1952, 102–17 [cf. *SEG* xii 84]; Miss Hereward's contribution was apparently unknown to T. Alfieri, *RIL* civ 1970, 154–61).

40. ii] COMMENTARY ON THE *ATH. POL.*

Miss Hereward believes that after failing with his more general proposal (*b*) Thrasybulus made a proposal specifically for Lysias, and failed with that too (*c*: *op. cit.*, 112 with n. 23); but Lysias was far more distinguished than most of the men who would have become citizens under *b*, and more probably a general proposal was remembered by some as a proposal for Lysias, and the texts cited under *b*, *c* and *d* should all be seen as references to that general proposal (commonly accepted; argued by C. D. Adams, *Lysias*: *Selected Speeches*, 21 n. 3). Procedural irregularity was, of course, simply an excuse for invalidating the decree: in *A.B.*, 62, I doubted the explanation that at that time there was no boule (it would be too easy to reply that all resolutions taken by the assembly before a new boule was appointed were equally invalid—including, perhaps, one proposed by Archinus to forbid further registrations for migration to Eleusis: cf. p. 474), but [Pl.] *X. Or.* dates the proposal ἐπ' ἀναρχίας τῆς πρὸ Εὐκλείδου, when we should expect no boule to exist; Thrasybulus' rewards were presumably proposed earlier than the less generous rewards actually conferred by Tod 100, but for that document I incline to the later date, 401/0 (cf. below); Archinus' γραφὴ παρανόμων cannot have been tried until the democratic machinery, including the lawcourts, was working again, but γραφαὶ παρανόμων did not have to be presented as soon as a bill was carried. I am still not sure that Planudes' explanation is right—[Plutarch] may represent the same false tradition—but I am no longer confident that it is wrong. *e*, *f* and *g* are three independent but compatible measures.†

The greatest difficulty has been occasioned by *h*. Since some if not all of its beneficiaries are rewarded with less than full citizenship, we should not identify it either with *e*, which gives formal honours to a group of men among whom citizens are prominent (E. Ziebarth, *AM* xxiii 1898, 30–2, H. von Prott, *AM* xxv 1900, 36–7), or with *bcd* (A. E. Raubitschek, *Hesp.* x 1941, 286), but should regard it as a fourth measure together with *e*, *f* and *g*. A. Wilhelm, *JŒAI* xxi–xxii 1922–4, 159–71 (cf. *SEG* iii 70), reconstructed a preamble requiring a proposer of seven letters, and postulated Archinus; of which it can only be said that Archinus is possible, and if the later date is adopted Wilhelm's preamble is possible. The principal argument for restoring [Πυθόδωρ]ος (referring to the early part of 403/2, before Euclides was appointed [cf. p. 463]: e.g. Prott, *op. cit.*, 37–8, Hereward, *op. cit.*, 112) is that it is unlikely that the matter should have remained unresolved until 401/0; those who believe that some beneficiaries received Athenian citizenship doubt if Athens would have been so generous after reenacting Pericles' citizenship law (cf. p. 331: I am not sure that I share their doubts). More scholars have preferred [Ξεναίνετ]ος (e.g. Ziebarth, *op. cit.*, 32, A. Koerte,

AM xxv 1900, 394-6, Wilhelm, *op. cit.*, 159, Tod): it is theoretically possible that the decree should have been enacted early in 403/2, in the prolongation of Pythodorus' archonship, but I find it very hard to believe that the claimants should have been vetted and the stele inscribed before Euclides took office, or that (careless though the Athenians could be in documentary matters) Pythodorus' name should have been used for the early part of 403/2 on a stele inscribed after Euclides had taken office. Archinus' decree *e*, which need be no later than *h*, assumes the existence of a boule to vet claimants to honours; and if there was disagreement as to how generous Athens ought to be it need not surprise us if *h* was not enacted until 401/0. I understand that an unpublished inscription from the Agora, which mentions the Thirty and is probably concerned with the confiscation of their property (cf. D. M. Lewis, *Ancient Society and Institutions . . . V. Ehrenberg*, 179) contains the formula [ἐπὶ Μ]ίκωνος ἄρ[χοντος] (402/1).†

μετεδίδου τῆς πολιτείας: Cf. 36. i with commentary; *P. Oxy.* xv 1800, frs 6-7, has μεταδιδοὺς [αὐτοῖς?] τῆς πολιτείας.

ὧν ἔνιοι φανερῶς ἦσαν δοῦλοι: See Hereward, *BSA* xlvii 1952, 113-17, on the names and occupations of the men rewarded in Tod 100. In 117 n. 139 she says, 'The word φανερῶς may even suggest that the author saw the stone', but I do not think this need be so.

καὶ τρίτον . . . ἀπαγαγὼν τοῦτον ἐπὶ τὴν βουλὴν καὶ πείσας ἄκριτον ἀποκτεῖναι: We need not change κατεληλυθότων to παρεληλυθότων with Π. Ν. Παπαγεώργιος: cf. p. 468. ἀπαγωγή was the technical term for haling before the authorities certain kinds of offender caught in the act (cf. 52. i with commentary): here ἀπαγαγὼν is used in a natural sense very close to the technical (but M. H. Hansen, *Eisangelia*, 41, *Apagoge, Endeixis and Ephegesis*, 126-7, believes that this is an instance of the technical usage).

In the time of *A.P.* the boule was not competent to inflict the death penalty on Athenian citizens: many have believed that earlier the boule had unlimited judicial powers, but I think it more likely that its judicial competence was always limited (cf. 45. i with commentary). Here *A.P.* uses the word ἄκριτον, 'without a proper trial': this might simply be an anachronism, but I suspect that at the time this condemnation was illegal or at best of doubtful legality (in the months immediately following the reconciliation it might have been argued that it was not yet certain what was lawful); Archinus' action on registrations for migration to Eleusis (§i) shows that he was not prepared to let legality stand in the way of what he considered a wise decision. Though it lacks the names of the actors other than Archinus the story is vividly told. Is. xviii. *Call.* 1-3 reports a more prosaic way in which Archinus ensured that no one should μνησικακεῖν, by the institution of the παραγραφή (cf. p. 473). I should guess that both are true, and that after securing the summary execution of *A.P.*'s story Archinus instituted the legal procedure so that any future attempt to break the amnesty could be frustrated; *A.P.*'s οὐδεὶς πώποτε ὕστερον ἐμνησικάκησεν will be due as much to the availability of the παραγραφή as to this παράδειγμα. According to Nep. VIII. *Thras.* 3. iii Thrasybulus *cum quidam ex iis qui simul cum eo in exilio fuerant caedem facere eorum vellent cum quibus in gratiam reditum erat publice, prohibuit et id quod pollicitus erat praestitit*: this may be a vaguer version of what *A.P.* says of Archinus.

οὐδεὶς πώποτε ὕστερον ἐμνησικάκησεν: Or, at any rate, no one succeeded in obtaining a verdict in breach of the amnesty from a lawcourt: cf. p. 471.

40. iii. ἀλλὰ δοκοῦσιν κάλλιστα δὴ ... ταῖς προγεγενημέναις συμφοραῖς: This is the only instance in *A.P.* in which ἀλλά does not follow a negative. Oppermann removes the exception by punctuating with a comma after ἐμνησικάκησεν and taking ἀλλὰ δοκοῦσιν ... closely with what precedes (and begins §iii at οὐ γὰρ μόνον), but Kenyon's punctuation is to be preferred.

A.P. has already praised the acts of Archinus; this is his most fulsome expression of praise and, with its contrast between the behaviour of the democrats in Athens and the behaviour of democrats elsewhere, it is unlike his others. The comment on γῆς ἀναδασμός is likely to have been made nearer to the time of *A.P.* than to the beginning of the century, and here if anywhere we might expect to find an Aristotelian judgment; but several non-Aristotelian usages are found in this section (cf. following notes).

κάλλιστα δὴ καὶ πολιτικώτατα: δή is said not to be used after a superlative by Aristotle (R. Eucken, *De Aristotelis Dicendi Ratione*, i. *Observationes de Particularum Usu*, 49). The superlative πολιτικώτατος is cited by LSJ only from X. *Lac. Pol.* iv. 5 (adjective); Aristotle uses the comparative in *H.A.* VIII. 589 A 2 (adverb), *Pol.* II. 1273 B 12, V. 1305 B 10, *Rhet.* I. 1354 B 24 (adjective).

καὶ ἰδίᾳ καὶ κοινῇ: Cf. X. *H.* I. ii. 10, *M.* II. i. 12 (καὶ κοινῇ καὶ ἰδίᾳ); also T. III. 45. iii, Plat. *Apol.* 30 B 4 (καὶ ἰδίᾳ καὶ δημοσίᾳ), T. I. 141. iii (οὔτε ἰδίᾳ οὔτ' ἐν τῷ κοινῷ χρήματα); Aristotle uses various forms of the contrast between ἴδιος and κοινός, and in *Pol.* V. 1304 B 22–4 τὰ μὲν γὰρ ἰδίᾳ ... τὰ δὲ κοινῇ ... (cf. *Pol.* III. 1278 B 23–4: καὶ κοινῇ πᾶσι καὶ χωρίς); *A.P.* 9. ii uses καὶ τὰ κοινὰ καὶ τὰ ἴδια.

τὰς περὶ τῶν πρότερον αἰτίας ἐξήλειψαν: The verb is used in its fully literal sense in 36. ii, 49. ii; here it is used in a sense very close to the literal, as in Lys. I. *Caed. Erat.* 48, D. XXXVII. *Pant.* 34.

τὰ χρήματα Λακεδαιμονίοις ... καὶ τοὺς ἐκ τοῦ Πειραιέως: Cf. 39. vi *fin.* with commentary. This act of generosity by the restored democracy is mentioned also by Is. VII. *Areop.* 67–9 (κοινὴν ποιήσασθαι τὴν ἀπόδοσιν, §68) and D. xx. *Lept.* 11-12 (κοινῇ διαλῦσαι τὰ χρήματα, §12; A. Boerner, *De Rebus a Graecis 410-403 Gestis*, 66-7, notices the similarity of wording between *A.P.* and Demosthenes and suggests a common source): both refer to a debate, and Demosthenes states that the debate was provoked by an embassy from Sparta asking for the money due from the oligarchs, an embassy alluded to also by Lys. xxx. *Nic.* 22 (who makes the Spartans utter threats). In rejecting Phormisius' proposal to restrict the citizenship the Athenians had defied Sparta (cf. p. 472): if they were to succeed in asserting their full independence it was important that they should give the Spartans no excuse for interfering again. Schol. D. xx. *Lept.* 11 denies that the δῆμος paid under compulsion; and Cloché, *La Restauration démocratique*, 379-83, makes heavy weather of rejecting the view that the δῆμος yielded to Spartan pressure. Arist. *Pol.* III. 1276 A 6-B 15 poses but does not answer the question whether obligations undertaken by one régime are binding on a second régime which supplants the first.

ἀποδιδόναι: 39. vi has ἀποδοῦναι, but we need not follow Γ. Α. Παπαβασίλειος, Ἀθ. iii 1891, 283-4, in changing to the aorist here.

ἡγούμενοι τοῦτο πρῶτον ἄρχειν δεῖν τῆς ὁμονοίας: Cf. Is. VII. *Areop.* 69 (διὰ ταύτην τὴν γνώμην εἰς τοιαύτην ἡμᾶς ὁμόνοιαν κατέστησαν), D. xx. *Lept.* 12 (τῶν δὲ τοῦτο πρῶτον ὑπάρξαι τῆς ὁμονοίας σημεῖον ἀξιούντων).

ἐν δὲ ταῖς ἄλλαις πόλεσιν ... τὴν χώραν ἀνάδαστο[ν] ποιοῦσιν: Cf. the generalisations in Plat. *Rep.* VIII. 565 E 3-566 A 4, *Legg.* III. 684 D 1-E 5, Arist. *Pol.* V. 1305 A 3-7, 1309 A 14-20, the undertakings quoted from the heliastic oath in D. XXIV. *Tim.* 149 and from the treaty with Macedon in [D.] XVII. *Foed. Alex.* 15, and the allusions to Sparta in Is. XII. *Panath.* 259, Arist. *Pol.* V. 1306 B 39-1307 A 2. At the beginning of the sixth century Solon had resisted demands for γῆς ἀναδασμός (see 11. ii and Sol. fr. 34. 8-9 West *ap.* 12. iii, with commentary). From the middle of the fourth century in Greece demands for social revolution including γῆς καὶ οἰκιῶν ἀναδασμός became frequent, after the comparative stability of the fifth and early fourth centuries, but Athens remained conspicuously free from such demands (see D. Asheri, *Distribuzioni di terre nell'antica Grecia*, 60-119, A. Fuks, *PP* xxi 1966, 437-48, P. E. Harding, *Phoen.* xxviii 1974, 285-6). While it is not impossible that this comment should first have been made by the defender of Theramenes who seems to be *A.P.*'s main source for this period (cf. pp. 419-22), it is more likely that it originated near or after the middle of the fourth century.

οὐχ οἷον ... ἀλλὰ καὶ ...: The earliest user of οὐχ οἷον cited by LSJ is Polybius (who uses it frequently: e.g. I. 20. xii, xiii). Aristotle uses οὐχ ὅτι ... ἀλλὰ καὶ ... in *Pol.* VII. 1331 A 11-12, *Poet.* 1448 B 35, and οὐχ ὅτι ... ἀλλὰ ... elsewhere.

ἔτι προστιθέασιν τῶν οἰκείων: 'Pay additional sums out of their own

property' (Sandys). Kenyon's text is probably right, but A. Gennadios (*CR* v 1891, 274) and Kaibel & Wilamowitz[1-2] preferred ἐπιπροστιθέασιν, J. B. Mayor (*CR* v 1891, 115) οὐχ [[οἷον]] ὅτι (cf. previous note) and Blass[4] οἷόν τι προστιθέασιν.

οἱ δημοκρατήσαντες: The papyrus' text, retained by Kenyon and Blass (who compared μοναρχήσαντες); others have preferred δῆμοι κρατήσαντες (Leeuwen ['*cum vicerunt populares*'], Hude and others: cf. Kaibel, *Stil und Text*, 200); Gennadios (*loc. cit.*) suggested δήμῳ κρατήσαντες. LSJ and the 1968 Supplement know only the passive δημοκρατεῖσθαι, so it is better to emend to δῆμοι κρατήσαντες.

40. iv. διελύθησαν δὲ καὶ πρὸς τοὺς ἐν Ἐλευσῖνι [κατο]ικήσαντας: ἐν is 'added above the line, and perhaps would be better away' (Kenyon[3]). Herwerden & Leeuwen and Sandys[1] deleted it, and the text will conform to normal classical usage without it; but since the first instance of ἐν Ἐλευσῖνι known to Meisterhans & Schwyzer, *G.a.I.*, 208 with nn. 1680–1, is dated *c.* 315/4 (*IG* ii[2] 2971, 2) the ἐν may be authentic.

According to X. *H.* II. iv. 43, ὕστερον δὲ χρόνῳ the Athenians heard that the men at Eleusis were hiring mercenaries, and marched out against them in full force; they killed the generals of the community at Eleusis when they came to negotiate, and sending friends and relatives to the others ἔπεισαν συναλλαγῆναι· καὶ ὀμόσαντες ὅρκους ἦ μὴν μὴ μνησικακήσειν, ἔτι καὶ νῦν ὁμοῦ τε πολιτεύονται καὶ τοῖς ὅρκοις ἐμμένει ὁ δῆμος. Just. v. 10. viii–xi says that *interiectis diebus repente* the oligarchs were angry at being exiled and attacked Athens; on going to negotiate they were tricked and killed; the people were recalled to the city, and an oath was taken *discordiarum oblivionem fore*. Cf. also Lys. xxv. *Reip. Del. Defens.* 9, cited on p. 467. Probably the amnesty of 403 was extended to those who had been at Eleusis, and members of the Thirty, the Ten, the Eleven and the Piraeus Ten were required to submit to εὔθυναι or go into exile.

ἔτει τρίτῳ μετὰ τὴν ἐξοίκησιν, ἐπὶ Ξε[ναι]νέτου ἄρχοντος: In 401/0 (D.S. xiv. 19. i, giving the name as Ἐξαίνετος; Ξεναίνετος is confirmed by Lys. xvii. *Bon. Erat.* 3, D.L. ii. 55), the third year by inclusive counting from 403/2, to which year the reconciliation is dated in 39. i. *A.P.* is the only text to date the final clash and reconciliation with Eleusis: D.S. xiv. 32–3 narrates the events from the occupation of Phyle to the first reconciliation under 401/0 (and says nothing of the final episode), but I fear that it is by accident that he has picked a relevant year. The date is confirmed by the fact that in 400/399 the treasurers of Athena and the Other Gods took charge of objects [Ἐλευσ]ινόθ[εν]: *IG* ii[2] 1375, 28, with A. B. West & A. M. Woodward, *JHS* lviii 1938, 70, R. S. Stroud, *Hesp.* xli 1972, 422–3, Acr. 54

(new fragment), D. M. Lewis & A. M. Woodward, *BSA* lxx 1975, 183-9.

41. i. ταῦτα μὲν οὖν . . . καιροῖς: The reference is to the final settlement with Eleusis, in 40. iv; *A.P.* now returns to the original restoration of the democracy.

τότε δὲ κύριος ὁ δῆμος γενόμενος τῶν πραγμάτων: In the terms of reconciliation as presented in ch. 39 nothing is said of how the state is to be governed (though it is hard to believe that the reconciliation was achieved without any agreement on this matter: cf. p. 472); 40. i-iii has shown that the restored democracy did not flaunt its victory; and 40. iv again refers not to victory but to reconciliation. In 41. i the atmosphere is different. The author is now looking ahead to the summary which is to be given in §ii of Athens' constitutional development, where τὴν ἀπὸ Φυλῆς καὶ ἐκ Πειραιέως κάθοδον is followed by the eleventh and last μετάστασις, . . . ἀεὶ προσεπιλαμβάνουσα τῷ πλήθει τὴν ἐξουσίαν. ἁπάντων γὰρ αὐτὸς αὑτὸν πεποίηκεν ὁ δῆμος κύριον. Whatever the correct text of this section (cf. below), *A.P.*'s purpose here is to represent what happened in 403 as the triumph of the δῆμος; he is no longer following the 'Theramenist' bias of the source which he used for his narrative (cf. below, on the date).

ἐνεστήσατο τὴν [νῦν] οὖσαν πολιτείαν: νῦν was restored by Kenyon[1], and is still bracketed in his Berlin ed. and O.C.T.; Wilcken claimed to read it; Dr. J. D. Thomas sees traces of the first letter. ἐνστήσασθαι τὸ πρᾶγμα is found in Ar. *Lys.* 268, D. x. *Phil. iv.* 21, Arist. *Probl.* xxix. 13. 951 A 28; otherwise Aristotle uses only the intransitive forms of ἐνιστάναι, but συνιστάναι τὴν πόλιν/πολιτείαν is used in *Pol.* II. 1266 A 23-4, III. 1284 B 18, 1288 A 40-1, VI. 1319 B 33-4.

ἐπὶ Πυθοδώρου ἄρχοντος: The reconciliation was dated to the archonship of Euclides explicitly in 39. i and implicitly in 40. iv. It is indeed likely that the early part of 403/2, in which the reconciliation took place, was at the time regarded as an extension of Pythodorus' archonship (cf. p. 463), but if the text here is sound *A.P.* must when he wrote this sentence have been unconscious of what he wrote earlier (cf. above, on the attitude expressed towards the restoration of the democracy). Blass expected to find Euclides, and in his 4th ed. restored him to the text, but it is unlikely that a copyist would have corrupted the text in this way; Kaibel & Wilamowitz postulated a lacuna after ἄρχοντος, in which the removal of Pythodorus on the appointment of Euclides was mentioned as the removal of Mnasilochus is mentioned in 33. i (cf. Kaibel, *Stil und Text*, 200-1, Gomme, *CR* xlii 1928, 225, Fritz & Kapp, 185, Moore, 272); Thalheim, *BPW* xxviii 1908, 978, inserted ἄρχοντος ⟨καταλυθέντες⟩. In view of the difference in atmosphere between this section and the preceding chapters, I do not find it incredible that *A.P.* should have stated here that the democracy was restored in the archonship of Pythodorus.

†δοκοῦντος δὲ δικαίως ... δι' αὐτοῦ τὸν δῆμον†: Kenyon[1-3] printed δι' αὐτόν; δι' αὐτοῦ was suggested by J. B. Mayor, *CR* v 1891, 115, and seems to be what the corrector of the papyrus intended. The other difficulties are less easy to solve: the δῆμος appears too often, and there is no grammatical justification for the genitive δοκοῦντος ... τοῦ δήμου in a sentence which began with ὁ δῆμος in the nominative. Kenyon[1-3] suggested Θρασυβούλου for τοῦ δήμου; Kaibel & Wilamowitz could allow their lacuna (cf. previous note) to explain the genitive, and deleted τὸν δῆμον at the end of the sentence; Hude emended to δοκοῦσι and deleted τοῦ δήμου; Thalheim, having inserted καταλυθέντες (cf. above), continued δοκοῦντες δὲ δικαίως τότε ἀναλαβεῖν τὴν πολιτείαν; E. Drerup, *Mnem.*[3] x 1942, 3–4, deleted ἐπὶ Πυθοδώρου ... τὸν δῆμον as an editor's interpolation. The correct text is irrecoverable, but the meaning is clear: the downfall of the oligarchy and the restoration of the democracy was the δῆμος' own achievement (here *A.P.* is consistent with what he has said before: in 39. iii–iv the part played by Pausanias is minimised), and the maintenance of the democracy is thus justified.

K. *Conclusion to First Part* (41. ii–iii)

A.P. ends his historical survey at the end of the fifth century. 41. i described the restored democracy of 403 as τὴν νῦν οὖσαν πολιτείαν; §ii offers as a résumé a list of (originally) eleven changes in the πολιτεία from the time of Ion to the restoration of 403/2, adding that from this last change the power of the δῆμος has continually increased and ἁπάντων ... αὐτὸς αὑτὸν πεποίηκεν ὁ δῆμος κύριον; as a postscript to that §iii notes the introduction of and increases in payment for attending the assembly, in the years after 403. The comments which end §ii form one of the most strikingly Aristotelian passages in *A.P.* (cf. Introduction, p. 10). Whereas the list of προστάται in 28. ii–iii seems to be an imported list, compiled by someone other than *A.P.* and not wholly compatible with *A.P.*'s main exposition (cf. p. 284 and commentary *ad loc.*), this list may be accepted as *A.P.*'s own summary of what has preceded (the only surprises are the omission of any specific reference to the intermediate régime of 411/0, and the reference to a single board of Ten after the Thirty, on which see below); a reference to Draco was added to the original list when the 'Draconian constitution' was added in ch. 4. Earlier *A.P.* has written of the πολιτεία's becoming more democratic (22. i, 27. i, cf. 9), of its increasing (23. i) and declining (25. i), and of its becoming slacker (26. i): here he summarises Athens' constitutional history in terms of a series of changes, some towards democracy (each of these taking Athens further than the previous such change) and some away from it, by which Athens developed from the original monarchy to the complete democracy of the fourth century (cf. Introduction, pp. 7–9). The reason for his ending where he does is not that he relied heavily on a source written not long after 403/2 but that, although there were many piecemeal changes in the working of the state during the fourth century, there were no major changes like those chronicled here until the suppression of the democracy by Macedon in 321 (cf. p. 9).

41. ii. αὕτη: 'This' is the restoration of the democracy in 403, to which *A.P.* returned in 41. i after noting in 40. iv the final settlement with the oligarchs at Eleusis in 401/0.

μετά‹σ›τασις τῶν ἐξ ἀρχῆς: 'Modification of the original constitution' (Moore). Kenyon[1-3] restored [ἡ κ]ατάστασις (cf. Kaibel, *Stil und Text*, 201–2) and Blass[1-2] [κα]τάστασις; μετά⟨σ⟩τασις was first read by Wilcken, and gives a much better sense with τῶν ἐξ ἀρχῆς; M. H. Chambers, *TAPA* cii 1971, 44, reads μετά⟨σ⟩τασις, and Dr. J. D. Thomas concurs. μεταβολή, used in the previous sentence, is a general word for 'change', used frequently in Arist. *Pol.* (e.g. III. 1275 B 35); in *Poet.* 1449 A 9–15 Aristotle writes that tragedy, πολλὰς μεταβολὰς μεταβαλοῦσα, stopped when it had reached its own φύσις; μετάστασις is used more specifically of a change of political constitution in Lys. xxx. *Nic.* 10, Plat. *Legg.* IX. 856 C 4–5, cf. T. IV. 74. iv.

Ἴωνος καὶ τῶν μετ' αὐτοῦ συνοικησάντων: 'When Ion and those with him settled.' Kenyon originally read συνοικισάντων, and reaffirmed this in his 3rd ed.; συνοικησάντων (Blass, *LZB* 1891, 304, Kaibel & Wilamowitz, Herwerden & Leeuwen) is accepted in Kenyon's Berlin ed. and O.C.T. (without comment; his Oxford Translation mistakenly retains the meaning of συνοικισάντων, 'brought the people together into a community') and by most editors; Dr. J. D. Thomas regards ι as the more obvious reading but does not rule out η; συνοικησάντων should be what *A.P.* wrote. Cf. fr. 1 (sometimes similarly misinterpreted) with pp. 66–7, and 3. ii with commentary. Ion, son of king Xuthus of the Peloponnese and Erechtheus' daughter Creusa, commanded the Athenians and enabled them to defeat an attack of Eleusis and the Thracians under Eumolpus; he then settled in Athens.

τότε γὰρ πρῶτον εἰς τὰς τέτταρας συνενεμήθησαν φυλάς: For the four 'Ionian' tribes, said to be named after Ion's sons, see frs 1, 3, with pp. 66–73.

καὶ τοὺς φυλοβασιλέας κατέστησαν: Cf. 8. iii, 57. iv, with commentary.

δευτέρα δὲ καὶ πρώτη μετὰ ταύτη[ν], ἔχουσα πολιτείας τάξιν: The papyrus reads μετὰ ταῦτα (corrected to η[ν]) ἔχουσαι (with the ι deleted) πολιτείαν τάξιν. Kenyon[1-2] printed μετὰ ταῦτα [ἐξ]έχουσα πολιτείας τάξις; a number of supplements for the supposed gap in the papyrus were proposed; πολιτείαν τάξις was suggested by W. G. Rutherford, *CR* v 1891, 115, and πολιτείας τάξιν by W. Wyse, *ibid.*, Kaibel & Wilamowitz[1-2] and others. In his 3rd and later edd. Kenyon printed the text as in my lemma (no comma in 3rd ed.), believing it to mean 'first after this, having now some semblance of a constitution' (Oxford Translation). Kaibel, *Stil und Text*, 202, writing when κατάστασις was still read above), followed by Sandys[2], Fritz & Kapp and Moore, quoted the text of Kenyon[3] but understood πρώτη with ἔχουσα πολιτείας τάξιν ('τῇ μὲν τάξει δευτέρα, πρώτη δὲ πολιτεία οὖσα'); he regarded μετὰ ταύτην as unsatisfactory but could suggest no explanation or cure. Kaibel & Wilamowitz[3] cited Arist. *Pol.* ΙΙ. 1272 Β 9–11 (ἔχει τι πολιτείας ἡ τάξις [*sc.* the Cretan constitution], ἀλλ' οὐ πολιτεία ἐστὶν ἀλλὰ δυναστεία μᾶλλον), and restored μετὰ ταύτην ἔχουσά [τι] πολιτείας τάξις; but μετάστασις had by then been read above, and so soon after it *A.P.* ought not to have forgotten that he was listing changes of constitution rather than constitutions (cf. next note); and πολιτεία is not used elsewhere in *A.P.*, as it is sometimes used in Arist. *Pol.* (e.g. *loc. cit.*), of a particular kind of constitution, the form of which 'democracy' is a perversion. Other suggested emendations are noted by Sandys[2]; none seems to me to be preferable to ἔχουσα πολιτείας τάξιν.

The reading μετάστασις above gives this statement the very clumsy meaning that Theseus' change was second but first after Ion's: after it we read of Draco's change, without number, and then of Solon's change, numbered third. The 'Draconian constitution' in ch. 4 is a late addition to *A.P.*, and the unnumbered reference to Draco in this list will have been added at the same time (cf. pp. 84–7 and commentary on 4): our difficulties here may be connected with the addition of Draco. If the revised text had said simply that Theseus' change was second, Draco's was next, and Solon's was third, the addition would have been all too obvious; I suspect that καὶ πρώτη μετὰ ταύτην was added when Draco was added, in order to make the interruption of the original sequence less obvious. The puzzling ἔχουσα πολιτείας τάξιν may belong to this revision also: ch. 3 purports to set out ἡ τάξις τῆς ἀρχαίας πολιτείας, and in the sentence containing those words (3. i) the reviser added τῆς πρὸ Δράκοντος (cf. pp. 85, 86, and commentary *ad loc.*); he used the word τάξις again in the sentence introducing the 'Draconian constitution' (4. i *fin.*); and perhaps in order to mask the insertion of Draco into this list he decided to make a second beginning with Theseus on the grounds that he was the first to deviate from pure monarchy and give Athens 'a form of constitution' (cf. Wilcken, *Apophoreton* [1903], 87–90, O. Seeck, *Klio* iv 1904, 272 n. 2, De Sanctis, *Ἀτθίς*, ¹164 = ²163, E. Drerup, *Mnem.*³ x 1942, 2–3).

ἡ ἐπὶ Θησέως ... παρεγκλίνουσα τῆς βασιλικῆς: With τῆς βασιλικῆς we must understand πολιτείας vel simile quid, but there is no reason why the subject to be understood should not still be μετάστασις. On Theseus cf. *Epit. Heracl.* 1 and *A.P.* fr. 2, with pp. 74–6: he was credited with the synoecism of Attica, and with a lessening of the power of the monarchy, perhaps to be connected with the recognition of the εὐπατρίδαι as an aristocratic caste in the state.

μετὰ δὲ ταύτην ἡ ἐπὶ Δράκοντος, ἐν ᾗ καὶ νόμους ἀνέγραψαν πρῶτον: The original numbered list passed directly from Theseus to Solon, though we might have expected the abolition of the monarchy to be chronicled as one of the changes in the πολιτεία; the reference to Draco will have been added here when the 'Draconian constitution' was added in ch. 4 (cf. above). A sentence in 4. i, which probably belongs to the original version of *A.P.*, reports that Draco τοὺς θεσμοὺς ἔθηκεν (the terminology normally used of Draco's laws); the 'constitution' added in 4. ii–iv may have displaced further detail on Draco's laws. The point which the reviser has singled out to characterise Draco's change (but, surprisingly, has predicated of the Athenians, if the text is sound) is authentic: Draco did give Athens her first written laws.

ἡ μετὰ τὴν στάσιν: Cf. 2. i (στασιάσαι τούς τε γνωρίμους καὶ τὸ πλῆθος πολὺν χρόνον) and 5. i–ii (ἀντέστη τοῖς γνωρίμοις ὁ δῆμος. ἰσχυρᾶς δὲ τῆς στάσεως οὔσης καὶ πολὺν χρόνον ἀντικαθημένων ...).

ἡ ἐπὶ Σόλωνος, ἀφ' ἧς ἀρχὴ δημοκρατίας ἐγένετο: Cf. 5–12 with commentary. Ch. 9 draws attention to the three δημοτικώτατα features of Solon's πολιτεία, but argues that Solon did not intend to create the full democracy which developed from his dispensation. Here and with Draco the subject may still be μετάστασις.

ἡ ἐπὶ Πεισιστράτου τυραννίς: Cf. 13–17 with commentary.

μετὰ ⟨τὴν⟩ τῶν τυράννων κατάλυσιν: For the ending of the tyranny cf. 17–19 with commentary.

ἡ Κλεισθένους, δημοτικωτέρα τῆς Σόλωνος: Cf. 20–2 with commentary: 22. i states that as a result of Cleisthenes' reforms δημοτικωτέρα πολὺ τῆς Σόλωνος ἐγένετο ἡ πολιτεία, and 23. i *init.* states that until after the Persian Wars προῆλθεν ἡ πόλις ἅμα τῇ δημοκρατίᾳ κατὰ μικρὸν αὐξανομένη. The noun to be understood with δημοτικωτέρα here must be πολιτεία, not μετάστασις: τυραννίς above eases the change.

ἡ μετὰ τὰ Μηδικά, τῆς ἐξ Ἀρείου πάγου βουλῆς ἐπιστατούσης: Cf. 23. i–ii[a] with commentary.

ἑβδόμη δὲ καὶ μετὰ ταύτην: An odd expression: J. B. Mayor, *CR* v 1891, 115, substituted ἡ for καί (cf. Kaibel, *Stil und Text*, 202–3), Blass[2-3] deleted καί, Blass[4] deleted καὶ μετὰ ταύτην. But here as in

485

other places where he presents a list (22, 28. ii–iii: cf. Introduction, pp. 42–3) *A.P.* tries to vary his forms of expression; there is another unusual expression in connection with the ninth change (cf. below); I am not persuaded that either is corrupt.

ἦν 'Αριστείδης μὲν ὑπέδειξεν: For Aristides the democrat cf. 23. ii^b–24 with commentary. ὑποδεικνύναι is to indicate by marking out (e.g. H. I. 189. iii), and so to point the way or set an example (e.g. Arist. *Rhet.* III. 1404 B 25, *Poet.* 1448 B 36–7).

'Εφιάλτης δ' ἐπετέλεσεν καταλύσας τὴν 'Αρεοπαγῖτιν βουλήν: Cf. 25 with commentary. Here *A.P.* exaggerates: Ephialtes did not dissolve the Areopagus but took away those of its powers which were of political significance. The only other instance of the adjective noted by LSJ is Alciphron, IV. 18. vi: the papyrus has Ἀρεοπαγῖδιν with τ written above; Blass[4] deleted the word (cf. the references to the Areopagus as ἡ βουλή in 25), but I doubt if he was right to do so. J. J. Keaney, *HSCP* lxvii 1963, 115–46, esp. 131–6, makes much of the fact that Ephialtes' reform of the Areopagus occupies the middle position in this list, but see Introduction, p. 14.

ἐν ᾗ πλεῖστα συνέβη ... διὰ τὴν τῆς θαλάττης ἀρχήν: Cf. 26–7 with commentary: after Ephialtes' reform συνέβαινεν ἀνίεσθαι μᾶλλον τὴν πολιτείαν διὰ τοὺς προθύμως δημαγωγοῦντας (26. i); πρὸς τὸ δημαγωγεῖν ἐλθόντος Περικλέους (but this probably means no more than προστάτου τοῦ δήμου γενομένου) Pericles μάλιστα προύτρεψεν τὴν πόλιν ἐπὶ τὴν ναυτικὴν δύναμιν (27. i). Although in that section he claims that under Pericles δημοτικωτέραν ἔτι συνέβη γενέσθαι τὴν πολιτείαν, *A.P.* does not here attribute a separate μετάστασις to Pericles. In this clause the double διά has aroused suspicion: Leeuwen suggested ἁμαρτάνειν ⟨καὶ⟩ διά, Π. Ν. Παπαγεώργιος διά ⟨τε⟩ ... ⟨καὶ⟩ διά (*Ἀθ.* iv 1892, 574), H. Richards ἁμαρτάνειν κατά (*CR* v 1891, 229), Kaibel & Wilamowitz ἁμαρτάνειν ⟨θαρρήσασαν ?⟩ (from 27. i: cf. Kaibel, *Stil und Text*, 203); but I hesitate to improve the text.

The work of the second scribe ends (in the middle of col. xx of the papyrus, and in the middle of a sentence) with συνέβη, and the third begins with τὴν πόλιν; he writes to the end of col. xxiv (46. i: ... βουλῆς λαμβάνουσιν) and resumes at the beginning of col. xxxi (64). See Introduction, pp. 3–4.

ἡ τῶν τετρακοσίων κατάστασις: Cf. 29–32 with commentary.

καὶ μετὰ ταύτην, ἐνάτη δέ, δημοκρατία πάλιν: 'And after this, ninth, democracy again': this translates easily into informal English, but is a startling piece of Greek. Ch. 33 records the fall of the Four Hundred and the institution of the intermediate régime of the Five Thousand (which is singled out for praise); 34. i begins with a curt reference to the supplanting of 'these' (probably the Five Thousand, but some have believed in a reference to the Four Hundred: cf.

ad loc.) by the δῆμος—but here, if the text is sound, there is no mention of the intermediate régime (though below the Ten are mentioned as well as the Thirty), and scholars have disputed whether that is to be thought of as subsumed under the oligarchy of the Four Hundred or under the restored democracy. Some sought to improve the Greek by deleting δέ (e.g. J. B. Mayor, *CR* v 1891, 115, Blass, *LZB* 1891, 304, Kaibel & Wilamowitz[1-2], cf. Kaibel, *Stil und Text*, 202-3); Wilcken read and Kaibel & Wilamowitz[3] deleted δὲ ἡ (Kenyon in his Berlin ed. thought the reading possible, and M. H. Chambers, *TAPA* cii 1971, 44, and Dr. J. D. Thomas confirm it); Blass[4] deleted καὶ μετὰ ταύτην. Wilcken in *Apophoreton*, 89 n. 1, thought it incredible that *A.P.* should have omitted to mention the intermediate régime, and proposed ... κατάστασις καὶ μετὰ ταύτην ⟨ἡ τῶν πεντακισχιλίων⟩, ἐνάτη δὲ ...; K. Ziegler *ap.* Oppermann achieves the same result with ... καὶ ⟨ἡ⟩ μετὰ ταύτην, ἐνάτη δὲ [[ἡ]] ...; G. Vlastos, *AJP* lxxiii 1952, 191-5, refuses to emend and assumes that the intermediate régime was subsumed under the restored democracy. We should read δέ, ἡ; and here as with the seventh change I am not persuaded that the text of the papyrus is wrong: I suspect that in summarising his previous narrative the author thought of 411-410 in terms of an oligarchic revolution and a return to democracy without deliberately subsuming the intermediate régime under one head or the other.

ἡ τῶν τριάκοντα καὶ ἡ τῶν δέκα τυραννίς: (Kaibel & Wilamowitz deleted the second ἡ, perhaps rightly: cf. Kaibel, *Stil und Text*, 203). Cf. 34-8 with commentary. Here, in agreement with our other sources but in disagreement with 38. iii, *A.P.*'s language implies that there was only one board of Ten after the deposition of the Thirty. Except in this summary, the earliest direct reference to the Thirty as tyrants is in D.S. xiv. 2. i, but X. *H.* ii. iii. 16, 49, comes close to making Critias and Theramenes describe the régime as a tyranny; contrast τὴν ἐπὶ τῶν τριάκοντα ὀλιγαρχίαν in *A.P.* 53. i, cf. *Hesp.* xl 7, 5. Neither of these points need imply that this list is an importation rather than *A.P.*'s own summary of what he has written above, though the summary will not be a product of the same spell of work as the detailed account of 404-403 (cf. on §i, above).

ἡ μετὰ τὴν ἀπὸ Φυλῆς καὶ ἐκ Πειραιέως κάθοδον: Cf. 37-40 with commentary.

ἀφ' ἧς διαγεγένηται μέχρι τῆς νῦν: Kaibel, *Stil und Text*, 203-4 (when κατάστασις was still read in conjunction with Ion: cf. above) understood this as ἀφ' ἧς (καθόδου) διαγεγένηται (ἡ κατάστασις) μέχρι τῆς νῦν (καταστάσεως); Sandys[2] offered ἧς (καθόδου) ... τῆς νῦν (πολιτείας); with μετάστασις above the correct interpretation might be ἀφ' ἧς (μεταστάσεως) διαγεγένηται (ἡ πολιτεία) μέχρι τῆς νῦν (πολιτείας); but in the course of the list *A.P.*'s attention has shifted from changes of constitution to constitutions (contrast the notes above on the second change and on Cleisthenes), and more probably the early commentators were right to understand καθόδου with ἧς; ἡ πολιτεία may be understood as subject of διαγεγένηται. There is no need to change to τοῦ νῦν with Herwerden & Leeuwen: cf. τὴν νῦν οὖσαν πολιτείαν in §i.

ἀεὶ προσεπιλαμβάνουσα τῷ πλήθει τὴν ἐξουσίαν: If the text is sound the meaning must be 'always increasing the power of the mass of the people' (cf. LSJ s.v. προσεπιλαμβάνω, I. 3, treating this as a distinct sense of the word). Many emendations have been suggested: ἡ ἐξουσία by Kaibel & Wilamowitz[1]; προσεπιβάλλουσα by Π. Ν. Παπαγεώργιος, Ἀθ. iv 1892, 574–5; προσεπαυξάνουσα by Thalheim, BPW xxviii 1908, 978; more drastically, Κ. Σ. Κόντος, Ἀθ. iv 1892, 105–6, proposed προσεπιλαμβάνον τὸ πλῆθος τῆς ἐξουσίας; Kaibel, Stil und Text, 203–4, had little faith either in the papyrus' text or in any of these emendations. A.P.'s sense is clear, if the language in which he expressed it is not: the democratic restoration of 403 was the last abrupt μετάστασις (or: the restored democracy of 403 was the last distinctly new constitution), but since then the power of the δῆμος has continued to increase, as it continued to increase in the generation after Cleisthenes' reforms and in the period after Ephialtes' reform (cf. above). It is because no later μετάστασις can be identified that the historical survey ends here (cf. p. 483).

It is by no means obvious that the power of the δῆμος did continually increase from the end of the fifth century to the time of A.P. The introduction of payment for attending the assembly, to which A.P. proceeds in §iii, may be regarded as completing the fifth century's progress towards full democracy, and other constitutional changes at the beginning of the fourth century, such as the institution of the διαιτηταί (54. ii–vi with commentary), are consistent with democracy as it was understood in the fifth century. Changes made later in the fourth century, however, such as the entrusting of considerable power first to the controllers of the theoric fund and afterwards to ὁ ἐπὶ τῇ διοικήσει (43. i, 47. ii, with commentary), will have made the administration of the state more efficient but will not have made it more democratic as that term had earlier been understood. I hope to discuss the nature of fourth-century Athenian democracy elsewhere.†

The complete democracy whose achievement is set out here was certainly disliked by Aristotle, and by A.P., and I do not wish to deny that the author's tone here is disapproving (cf. 27–8 but contrast 23. ii[b]–24: notice especially here πάντα διοικεῖται ψηφίσμασιν καὶ δικαστηρίοις . . ., and the fact that the transfer of the boule's κρίσεις to the δῆμος is thought to require justification). However, the comment of Moore, 273, that 'Aristotle breaks into a violent denunciation of the constitution under which he lived at Athens', is unfair: the disapproval is implicit, not explicit.

αὐτὸς αὑτὸν πεποίηκεν: Cf. §i, where it is claimed that the δῆμος' resumption of control is justified because the δῆμος was itself responsible for its return.

καὶ πάντα διοικεῖται ψηφίσμασιν καὶ δικαστηρίοις... ὁ κρατῶν: It was commonly believed in fourth-century Athens that νόμοι were or ought to be of higher status and of more general application than ψηφίσματα, and Aristotle regarded it as a characteristic of extreme democracy that the δῆμος and its ψηφίσματα prevailed over the νόμοι (cf. p. 329, on 26. ii *init.*, where the Athenians are criticised for not keeping to the νόμοι); after the revision of the laws completed in 400/399 (cf. pp. 441-2) Athens had a code of νόμοι which it tried to keep distinct from the ψηφίσματα of the boule and ecclesia (cf. pp. 512-13). For the part played by jury-courts in keeping power in the hands of the δῆμος see 9 and 35. ii with commentary: ch. 9, to explain why ἡ εἰς τὸ δικαστήριον ἔφεσις was one of the δημοτικώτατα features of Solon's reforms, comments κύριος γὰρ ὢν ὁ δῆμος τῆς ψήφου κύριος γίγνεται τῆς πολιτείας and πάντα βραβεύειν καὶ τὰ κοινὰ καὶ τὰ ἴδια τὸ δικαστήριον, and 35. ii remarks that the Thirty τὸ κῦρος ὃ ἦν ἐν τοῖς δικασταῖς κατέλυσαν. *A.P.* in those two passages concentrates on the power of the courts to interpret unclear laws; in addition the courts derived political importance from the power to try a commander or politician on charges of betraying the interests of Athens (cf. on εἰσαγγελίαι in 43. iv), and to quash in a γραφὴ παρανόμων or νόμον μὴ ἐπιτήδειον θεῖναι (cf. 45. iv, 59. ii, with commentary) the enactments of the boule and ecclesia or the nomothetae: the way in which these powers made the courts rather than the ecclesia the final sovereign body in the state is explored by M. H. Hansen, *The Sovereignty of the People's Court in Athens* (but despite his reply to his critics, in *GR&BS* xix 1978, 127-46, I am not persuaded that the Athenians thought of their courts as a source of authority distinct from and superior to the δῆμος).

καὶ γὰρ αἱ τῆς βουλῆς κρίσεις... ἐληλύθασιν: Cf. 45. i with commentary (where I argue that the boule of five hundred never had the unlimited judicial power of which *A.P.* says it was deprived); and 45. iii and 49. iii on specific decisions which have been taken from the boule. Arist. *Pol.* IV. 1299 B 38-1300 A I remarks καταλύεται δὲ καὶ τῆς βουλῆς ἡ δύναμις ἐν ταῖς τοιαύταις δημοκρατίαις ἐν αἷς αὐτὸς συνιὼν ὁ δῆμος χρηματίζει περὶ πάντων (cf. VI. 1317 B 30-5: τῶν δ' ἀρχῶν δημοτικώτατον βουλή, ὅπου μὴ μισθοῦ εὐπορία πᾶσιν· ἐνταῦθα γὰρ ἀφαιροῦνται καὶ ταύτης τῆς ἀρχῆς τὴν δύναμιν· εἰς αὐτὸν γὰρ ἀνάγει τὰς κρίσεις πάσας ὁ δῆμος εὐπορῶν μισθοῦ, καθάπερ εἴρηται πρότερον ἐν τῇ μεθόδῳ τῇ πρὸ ταύτης). In each case mentioned by *A.P.* the body which has gained the final right of decision is not the ecclesia but a δικαστήριον, and there are no clear indications that in the fourth century there was any reduction in the power of the boule vis-à-vis the ecclesia (see Rhodes, *A.B.*, 218–21, with discussions of particular problems cited there; on δῆμος and δικαστήρια cf. previous note). By κρίσεις *A.P.* means primarily if not solely judicial and quasi-judicial decisions, though Arist. *Pol.* III. 1286 A 26–7 seems to use κρίνειν and κρίσις to cover both judicial and deliberative decisions.

καὶ τοῦτο δοκοῦσι ποιεῖν ὀρθῶς: This kind of comment on a particular feature of the constitution is most reminiscent of [X.] *A.P.*, who likewise claims to judge on its own terms a régime which is not to his taste (e.g. iii. 10: δοκοῦσι δὲ Ἀθηναῖοι καὶ τοῦτό μοι [?] οὐκ ὀρθῶς βουλεύεσθαι), but cf. also the critique of the Spartan, Cretan and Carthaginian constitutions in Arist. *Pol.* II (e.g. 1270 A 18–20: τοῦτο δὲ καὶ διὰ τῶν νόμων τέτακται φαύλως· ὠνεῖσθαι μὲν γάρ, ἢ πωλεῖν τὴν ὑπάρχουσαν, ἐποίησεν οὐ καλόν, ὀρθῶς ποιήσας).

εὐδιαφθορώτεροι γὰρ ‹οἱ› ὀλίγοι τῶν πολλῶν εἰσιν: What this justifies is the transfer of κρίσεις from the boule to the δῆμος: cf. Arist. *Pol.* III. 1286 A 26–35, on the entrusting of judicial and other decisions to an assembly (again τὸ πλῆθος τῶν ὀλίγων ἀδιαφθορώτερον). The view that the many are best at judging, but not specifically because it is harder to corrupt them, is expressed at *Pol.* III. 1281 A 39–B 21 (with reservations), and also by Athenagoras in T. VI. 39. i; their incorruptibility is asserted by D. XXIV. *Tim.* 37. Kaibel, *Stil und Text*, 204, contrasts the discovery of Aristagoras of Miletus that it was easier to mislead 30,000 Athenians than Cleomenes of Sparta (H. V. 97. ii), and with that we may compare H. III. 81. i–ii, Eur. *Suppl.* 410–18.

καὶ κέρδει καὶ χάρισιν: 'Whether by money or by favours.' If the support of individuals has to be bought, the fewer the individuals the easier the task; but the author overlooks the fact that a mass of people can be corrupted *en masse*, for example by a promise of benefits for the many to be financed from taxes paid by or property confiscated from the few (e.g. Ar. *Eq.* 773–6, 1357–61, Lys. XIX. *Bon. Arist.* 11, XXVII. *Epicr.* 1, XXX. *Nic.* 22, and *A.P.*'s own exposition of the financial benefits to the Athenians of the Delian League [24] and of the introduction of jury pay as a gambit to counter Cimon's generosity [27. iii–iv]).

41. iii. μισθοφόρον δ' ἐκκλησίαν: (We need not emend to δὲ ⟨τὴν⟩ with Kaibel & Wilamowitz.) Arist. *Pol.* IV, quoted on p. 489, goes on to say that power tends particularly to be transferred from the boule to the ecclesia ὅταν εὐπορία τις ᾖ μισθοῦ τοῖς ἐκκλησιάζουσιν (1300 A 1–3; cf. *Pol.* VI, quoted above).

τὸ μὲν πρῶτον: In the fifth century, when stipends were provided for jurors (27. iii–iv with commentary), bouleutae (commentary on 32. i) and various officials (24. iii with commentary). This sentence takes up the theme ἁπάντων γὰρ αὐτὸς αὑτὸν πεποίηκεν ὁ δῆμος κύριον, καὶ πάντα διοικεῖται . . ., from §ii.

οὐ συλλεγομένων . . . σοφιζομένων τῶν πρυτάνεων: Herwerden & Leeuwen objected that καίπερ would be more appropriate than ἀλλὰ with σοφιζομένων: other editors have been unworried, probably rightly, but the objection could be met by reading ἄλλα. Aristophanes tells us of one device that was tried: citizens were herded from the Agora to the Pnyx by men carrying a rope dipped in red dye, and any absent from the assembly but marked with the dye were fined (*Ach.* 21–2 with schol., Poll. VIII. 104; but *Eccl.* 376–82 probably indicates that the red dye served a different purpose in the early fourth century, *pace* schol. 378 [see Ussher *ad loc.*]). συλλεγομένων reminds us that in the fourth century there was a board of συλλογεῖς τοῦ δήμου, probably three from each tribe; but their only attested duties concern religion (Rhodes, *A.B.*, 21, 129–30) and offences against a law on the vetting of silver coins (*Hesp.* xliii 1974, 157–88, lines 13–16, 19–20).

The number of adult male citizens has been estimated at 35,000–40,000 *c.* 432, 20,000–25,000 *c.* 400, 28,000–30,000 *c.* 360 (V. L. Ehrenberg, *The Greek State*[2], 31). In 411 the oligarchs alleged that attendance never exceeded 5,000 (T. VIII. 72. i: cf. p. 383); after the revision of the laws at the end of the fifth century (and probably before then also) a quorum of 6,000 was required to approve various kinds of decision affecting named individuals (laws *ap.* And. I. *Myst.* 87, D. XXIV. *Tim.* 59, cf. XXIII. *Arist.* 86, [D.] XLVI. *Steph. ii.* 12; D. XXIV. *Tim.* 45; [D.] LIX. *Neaer.* 89–90; in the fifth century a quorum of 6,000 was required for an ostracism [cf. p. 270]), and M. H. Hansen has argued that in the fourth century, since citizenship awards were frequently confirmed at other assemblies as well as ἐκκλησίαι κύριαι, attendances must normally have exceeded 6,000 (*GR&BS* xvii 1976, 115–34, esp. 127–30). When the Pnyx was remodelled *c.* 400 its capacity was at any rate slightly and perhaps appreciably increased (K. Kouroniotes & H. A. Thompson, *Hesp.* i 1932, 90–217, esp. 113–28, cf. Travlos, *Pictorial Dictionary*, 466–76; for an appreciable increase W. B. Dinsmoor, *AJA*[2] xxxvii 1933, 181, W. A. McDonald, *The Political Meeting Places of the Greeks*, 70–6), and Hansen suggests that it held about 6,000 before the remodelling, and (6,500 or) 8,000 after (*op. cit.*, 130–2). Hansen believes that the larger attendances which he thinks were achieved in the fourth century were due largely to the introduction of payment (*op. cit.*, 132–3); in addition it is likely that not all who migrated to the city at the beginning of the Peloponnesian War (cf. T. II. 14–16) or after Sparta's occupation of Decelea returned to their old homes after the war, and that in the fourth century a higher proportion of the population lived within easy reach of the city.

προσιστῆται: The closest parallels cited by LSJ are Aesch. *Pers.* 203 (βωμὸν προσέστην) and A. 1. *Tim.* 117 (προσεστηκότας πρὸς τῷ δικαστηρίῳ).

πρὸς τὴν ἐπικύρωσιν τῆς χειροτονίας: 'For the ratification of the voting': the only other instances of ἐπικύρωσις cited by LSJ are D.H. *A.R.* IX. 51. iii, Justinian, *Nov.* XLII. 1. i. As in 34. i χειροτονία presumably means 'voting' in general, not specifically 'voting by show of hands': the assembly normally voted by show of hands (cf. Gilbert, *C.A.S.A.*, 297, Busolt & Swoboda, *G.S.*, ii. 1000 with n. 3, E. S. Staveley, *Greek and Roman Voting and Elections*, 83–7), but business which required a quorum of 6,000 required also a secret ballot (cf. texts cited above).

πρῶτον μὲν Ἀγύρριος: *Sc. Κολλυτεύς.* At some time before 405 he combined with Archinus to reduce the payments made to comic poets (cf. on 34. iii); from the silence of And. 1. *Myst.* 133–6 we may assume that he was on the democratic side in 404–403; he was one of the secretaries in the first year of the restored democracy, 403/2 (*IG* ii[2] 1, 41–2 = Tod 97, 1–2; *IG* ii[2] 2, 1; *Hesp.* x 78, 77: cf. p. 603), and as head of a tax-collecting syndicate he came into collision with Andocides in 401 (And. 1. *Myst.* 133–6: on the date, MacDowell's ed., p. 205); *c.* 390 he succeeded Thrasybulus as Athens' commander in the Aegean (X. *H.* IV. viii. 31, D.S. XIV. 99. v: cf. p. 450); subsequently he spent a long time in prison until he had repaid money which he was said to have embezzled, and his nephew, the politician Callistratus, did not take advantage of his position to save him (D. XXIV. *Tim.* 134–5, describing him as ἄνδρα χρηστὸν καὶ δημοτικὸν καὶ περὶ τὸ πλῆθος τὸ ὑμέτερον πολλὰ σπουδάσαντα). The creation of the theoric fund is ascribed to him by Harp. θεωρικά, and many believe that it was either created by him or created by Pericles and modified by him; but Aristophanes and other contemporaries are suspiciously silent on the theoric fund in the late fifth and early fourth centuries, and I prefer to believe that the fund was created by Diophantus and Eubulus in the 350's (cf. on 43. i).

The level of assembly pay had reached 3 obols by the time of Aristophanes' *Ecclesiazusae* (cf. below): the introduction of payment must be dated soon after the democratic restoration, but I know no justification for the precise date of 399 given by C. Mossé, *La Fin de la démocratie athénienne*, 303. It is clear from *Eccl.* 186–8, 289–93, that payment was not given to all who attended but to the first so many to arrive (perhaps the first 6,000?).

Ἡρακλείδης ὁ Κλαζομένιος ὁ βασιλεὺς ἐπικαλούμενος: For Athens' (conferment of citizenship on him and subsequent) election of him as general cf. Plat. *Ion*, 541 D 1–4, Ath. XI. 560 A, Ael. *V.H.* XIV. 5.

Kirchner (*P.A.* 6489) and most others have accepted the view of U. Koehler, *Hermes* xxvii 1892, 68–78, that it is he to whom citizenship was probably granted in the first decree of M & L 70 and lesser honours (for helping to bring about the 'Peace of Epilycus' with Persia *c.* 423: cf. And. III. *Pace*, 29) were granted in the second decree; but P. Foucart, *BCH* xii 1888, 163–9, believed the beneficiary to be a different Heraclides, honoured early in the fourth century. In support of Koehler see Wade-Gery, *HSCP* Supp. i 1940, 127–32 = *Essays*, 207–11, A. Andrewes, *Hist.* x 1961, 1–7, D. M. Lewis, *Sparta and Persia*, 70–7; in support of Foucart see D. L. Stockton, *Hist.* viii 1959, 74–9, H. B. Mattingly, *Philol.* cxix 1975, 48–51; for a non-committal summary see J. Pečírka, *The Formula for the Grant of Enktesis*, 22–5: I fear I am not quite persuaded that there was a Peace of Epilycus. If Koehler's identification is right, the connection with the Persian king will explain Heraclides' nickname.†

πάλιν δ' 'Αγύρριος τριώβολον: This level of payment had been reached by the time of Ar. *Eccl.* (lines 289–311, 392), i.e. some time between 393 (ed. of R. G. Ussher, pp. xx–xxv) and 390 (R. J. Seager, *JHS* lxxxvii 1967, 107 with n. 110). By the time of *A.P.* there had been a further increase, to 1½ drachmae at the κυρία ἐκκλησία of each prytany and 1 drachma at other meetings (62. ii).

L. *Beginning of Second Part: Registration and Training of Citizens* (42)

Having in his first part outlined the history of the πολιτεία to its last μετάστασις, at the end of the fifth century, in his second part *A.P.* sets out ἡ νῦν κατάστασις τῆς πολιτείας (42. i *init.*). For the organisation of this second part of his work, and its derivation from the laws of Athens, see Introduction, pp. 30–7. Many entries in lexica and scholia are derived from the second part of *A.P.*, often avowedly so: the fullest collection of these (by G. Wentzel) is to be found in Kenyon's Berlin ed.; I shall refer to significant divergences from *A.P.* and to points at which these derivatives help us to reconstruct *A.P.*'s text.

Ch. 42 is devoted to the citizenship: the basic requirement of citizen parentage on both sides; the δοκιμασία and registration of citizens at their coming of age; and their two years of training as ἔφηβοι. *A.P.*'s summary has left open to dispute various questions which will be discussed below: whether citizens had to be born in wedlock (pp. 496–7, 499–500); whether in fact (as *A.P.* states) in the δοκιμασία the courts were concerned only with the criterion of freedom and the boule was concerned only with the criterion of age (pp. 500, 502); and whether two years of hoplite training were given to all newly registered citizens or only to those belonging to the three higher Solonian classes (p. 503).

This is not one of the chapters in which *A.P.* contrasts what happened πρότερον μέν with what happens νῦν δέ (cf. Introduction, pp. 34–5); but we do find such a contrast in connection with the ephebi in 53. iv, and it seems clear that the ἐφηβεία as described here is an institution of *c*. 335/4. Lyc. fr. 25 Sauppe *ap.* Harp. Ἐπικράτης refers to an Epicrates of whom a bronze statue was set up διὰ τὸν νόμον τὸν περὶ τῶν ἐφήβων; we have perhaps nine inscriptions concerned with ephebi registered in the years 334/3 and 333/2, and a continuing series thereafter (the fourth-century inscriptions are collected by O. W. Reinmuth, *Mnem.* Supp. xiv 1971, and in the commentary on this chapter I shall cite them as Reinmuth 1, etc.), but no earlier inscriptions deal with ephebi[35] and some literary texts suggest that earlier a newly-registered citizen was not necessarily taken out of normal life for two years (e.g. Ant. fr. 69 Sauppe: for further evidence see A. A. Bryant, *HSCP* xviii 1907, 74–88). On the other hand, although Wilamowitz believed that the ἐφηβεία of the 330's was a totally new institution (*A.u.A.*, i. 193–4), there are signs that something of the kind existed earlier: most strikingly, A. II. *F.L.* 167 (in 343) claims

ἐκ παίδων μὲν γὰρ ἀπαλλαγεὶς περίπολος τῆς χώρας ἐγενόμην δύ' ἔτη, καὶ τούτων ὑμῖν τοὺς συνεφήβους καὶ τοὺς ἄρχοντας ἡμῶν μάρτυρας παρέξομαι

(ἄρχοντας Bekker: συνάρχοντας *codd.*), and the counter-claim of D. XVIII. *Cor.* 261 that Aeschines became a secretary immediately on registration, even if true, does not undermine the significance for our present purpose of what Aeschines says. The ephebic oath, inscribed on stone in the fourth century (Tod 204, 5–20) and summarised by Lycurgus (*Leocr.* 76; cf. also Poll. VIII. 105–6, Stob. XLIII. 48, and see p. 506), is agreed to be an ancient oath (for an attempt to detect echoes of it in fifth-century literature see P. Siewert, *JHS* xcvii 1977, 102–11), and is already referred to as the oath of the ephebi in D. XIX. *F.L.* 303 (in 343), while the δοκιμασία of young citizens is at least as old as Ar. *Vesp.* 578. Both in the 450's and at the beginning of the Peloponnesian War the νεώτατοι are attested as a separate category in the Athenian army (T. I. 105. iv, II. 13. vii). [D.] XLIV. *Leoch.* 35 indicates that the demes kept an ἐκκλησιαστικὸς πίναξ distinct from their ληξιαρχικὸν γραμματεῖον, and X. *M.* III. vi. 1 (while confirming that a newly-registered

---

[35] Reinmuth connects his no. 1 with the ephebi of 361/0, but see D. M. Lewis, *CR*² xxiii 1973, 254–5, F. W. Mitchel, *ZPE* xix 1975, 231–43 (suggesting 333/2). The restoration of ephebi in an inscription of 421/0, *IG* i² 84, 31–2, is wisely abandoned by F. Sokolowski, *Lois sacrées des cités grecques*, 13, *IG* i³ 82.

citizen did not find his time so occupied that he could not attend the assembly) suggests that it was irregular for Glaucon to speak when he was under twenty; and that distinction may help to explain Poll. VIII. 105, which places registration on the ληξιαρχικὸν γραμματεῖον and the taking of the oath at the end of the ἐφηβεία. The word ἔφηβος belongs to the series of words for age-classes found throughout the Greek world (see pp. 502–3, and cf. κοῦροι πρωθῆβαι in Hom. Od. VIII. 262–3; for other words formed from this root see Ch. Pélékidis, Histoire de l'éphébie attique, 59–61) and best known to us from the Spartan ἀγωγή. We should accept that the δοκιμασία of young citizens and the imposition of an oath on them were ancient institutions, that it was an ancient practice to give the title ἔφηβος to young citizens in their first two years after the δοκιμασία and to treat them differently from citizens over twenty, and that (as in the case of Aeschines) it was at any rate possible for ἔφηβοι to be given garrison duties; but it was Epicrates in the 330's who converted the ἐφηβεία into a period of full-time national service for all young citizens (except the unfit and the thetes: cf. p. 503). For this view of the ἐφηβεία see Reinmuth, TAPA lxxxiii 1952, 34–50, cf. Mnem. Supp. xiv 1971, 123–38 (vitiated by his dating of inscription 1: cf. p. 494 n. 35), Pélékidis, op. cit., 7–79; for the significance of Epicrates' reform in Athens after Chaeronea see F. W. Mitchel, G&R² xii 1965, 189–204, or Lectures ... L. T. Semple ii 1966–70, 163–214. Plat. Legg. VI. 760 B 2–763 C 2 has a scheme of national service for men between twenty-five and thirty.†

A further change was made in the ἐφηβεία towards the end of the fourth century. IG ii² 478 = Reinmuth 17 (enacted in 305/4) is restored in line 10 with a formula indicating that the ephebi honoured had been registered in the previous year, and so had served not for two years but for one; and the size of the list appended to that decree suggests that perhaps already, as was certainly the case later, ephebic service had ceased to be compulsory (see Reinmuth's commentary, 101–15). The military importance of the ἐφηβεία then inevitably declined.‡

The fact that this account of the ἐφηβεία appears in the text with no signs of strain suggests that this part of A.P. was written after the mid 330's (cf. commentary on 53. iv, and Introduction, pp. 51–2).

42. i. ἔχει δ' ἡ νῦν κατάστασις τῆς πολιτείας τόνδε τὸν τρόπον: This sentence introduces the second part of A.P.; there is no resumptive sentence corresponding to it at the end of the work (on A.P.'s use of introductory and resumptive expressions cf. Introduction, pp. 44–5; the principal such expressions in the second part are noted in the analysis of this part, pp. 30–2). Sandys compares Plat. Legg. VIII. 832 D 4–5 (ἡ τοιαύτη κατάστασις πολιτείας); cf. also κατάστασις in H. v. 92.

β. i, T. iv. 55. i; earlier *A.P.* has used τάξις τῆς πολιτείας (3. i, 5. i, cf. 41. ii, and 4. i *fin.* [introducing the 'Draconian constitution']).

μετέχουσιν μὲν τῆς πολιτείας: *A.P.* embarks immediately on the topic of citizenship: the qualifications for citizenship lead him to the registration of citizens, and that in turn leads to the training undergone by newly-registered citizens in their two years as ephebi. Similarly in the closing chapters of Arist. *Pol.* IV the discussion of the best form of constitution begins with the citizen body (1296 B 13–1297 B 34). On μετέχειν τῆς πολιτείας and similar expressions see on 8. v, 36. i.

οἱ ἐξ ἀμφοτέρων γεγονότες ἀστῶν: That a citizen must be of citizen descent on his mother's side as well as his father's was first required by Pericles' law of 451/0; in the last years of the Peloponnesian War this rule was either annulled or ignored; at the end of the fifth century it was reenacted; and later the law was strengthened, to inflict penalties on the partners in a mixed marriage and on any citizen who fraudulently gave a foreign woman in marriage to a citizen (see 26. iv with commentary). Women could thus transmit citizenship, as they could transmit property; but in Athens as elsewhere in the Greek world they could not be citizens, and *A.P.* does not think it necessary to state this fact. He also does not state whether there was a requirement that citizens must have been born in wedlock; but in this case he is not silent because only one answer was conceivable, since it is clear from Arist. *Pol.* III. 1278 A 26–34, VI. 1319 B 8–10, that neither the admission of bastards to citizenship nor their exclusion was unthinkable in the Greek world. Whether bastards were entitled to Athenian citizenship is disputed: it is argued that they were by Harrison, *L.A.*, i. 63–5, and D. M. MacDowell, *CQ*[2] xxvi 1976, 88–91; that they were not by W. K. Lacey, *The Family in Classical Greece*, 282 n. 15, S. C. Humphreys, *JHS* xciv 1974, 88–95, and Rhodes, *CQ*[2] xxviii 1978, 89–92. MacDowell bases one of his arguments on *A.P.*'s failure to mention a requirement of legitimate birth; but there are very many omissions in the second part of *A.P.*, and I do not believe that a strong case can be based on this (cf. also below, pp. 499–500). It is generally accepted that bastards were not entitled to membership of a phratry (cf. *IG* ii[2] 1237, 109–11), and that before Cleisthenes' reforms a man had to belong to a phratry to be an Athenian citizen (cf. pp. 69, 253): bastards were therefore not entitled to citizenship before Cleisthenes' reforms, and the onus of proof must rest with those who believe that they were entitled to Athenian citizenship subsequently.[36] The sons of naturalised Athenians, if unlike their fathers they were to have full rights including the right to be archon or priest, had to be born ἐκ γυναικὸς

---

[36] On concubines kept ἐπ' ἐλευθέροις παισίν see p. 331.

ἀστῆς καὶ ἐγγυητῆς κατὰ τὸν νόμον ([D.] LIX. *Neaer.* 92, 106: cf. pp. 510–11); but this is not enough to prove my case, as legitimate birth might have been required only for these appointments. For further signs of the political importance of legitimate birth in Athens cf. 4. ii on military officers ('Draconian constitution') and texts cited *ad loc.*, and *P. Hib.* i. 14, frs *a–b* = Lys. fr. vi. 1–2 Gernet & Bizos.†

ἐγγράφονται δ' εἰς τοὺς δημότας: ἐγγράφειν is the technical term: cf. Isae. VII. *Her. Apoll.* 28, D. LVII *Eub.* 61, Lyc. *Leocr.* 76, *IG* ii² 1237, 97–8 (admission to phratry), 1156 = Reinmuth 2, 53. There was no central register of all citizens (but there was a central register of citizens qualified by age and property for military service: 53. iv–v, vii, with commentary): each deme kept the ληξιαρχικὸν γραμματεῖον of its members, and those who were registered as members of demes were Athenian citizens. There must also have been a register of metics, since they like citizens had financial and military obligations: in the Decree of Themistocles they are registered with the polemarch (M&L 23, 29–31); other inscriptions show that they like citizens were regarded as attached to a deme (Κηφισοδόρο μετοίκο ἐμ Πειρα[ι-εῖ ?οἰκῶντος], *IG* i² 329, 14 = M&L 79 A, 33, with commentary, p. 245; Τεῦκρος ἐν Κυδαθ[εναίοι h]οικῶν, *IG* i² 374, 14–15, is the usual formulation: see D. Whitehead, *PCPS* Supp. iv 1977, 31–2, 152), and it is likely that each deme kept a register of its metics (the registration of metics is alluded to by schol. Ar. *Av.* 1669, *Ran.* 416, Poll. III. 57, cf. Plat. *Legg.* VIII. 850 A 5–D 2). We should not, however, follow Wilamowitz (*Hermes* xxii 1887, 107–28, 211–59 = *Kleine Schriften*, v. i. 272–342) in regarding the metics as virtually members of their demes (see P. Gauthier, *Symbola*, 111–16, Whitehead, *op. cit.*, 72–4, and 58. ii with commentary).

ὀκτωκαίδεκα ἔτη γεγονότες: There was in fact an annual ceremony of δοκιμασία and registration, probably early in the new year (cf. Lys. XXI. *Pec. Acc.* 1: D. XXX. *Onet.* i. 15 is not sufficient to place the registration late in the old year). Pélékidis, *Histoire de l'éphébie attique*, 174–5, 205, notes that decrees honouring ephebi at the end of their service were normally enacted in the month Boedromion (iii); on pp. 219–20 he notes that the first festival in which their participation is recorded is that of Artemis Ἀγροτέρα, on 6 Boedromion (date L. Deubner, *Attische Feste*, 209, J. D. Mikalson, *The Sacred and Civil Calendar of the Athenian Year*, 50); we have no fourth-century evidence, but there are no grounds for supposing that the ephebic year was subsequently changed.

It has been disputed whether men were registered at the new year after reaching their eighteenth birthday (and entering on the nineteenth year of their life) or after (reaching their seventeenth birthday and) entering on the eighteenth year of their life. B. R. I. Sealey, *CR*² vii 1957, 195–7, argued for registration after the seventeenth birthday from D. xxvii. *Aphob. i* (cf. A. Schaefer, *Demosthenes und seine Zeit*, III. ii. 19–57, written before the discovery of *A.P.*), and J. M. Carter, *BICS* xiv 1967, 51–7, argued that this is what ὀκτωκαίδεκα ἔτη γεγονότες should mean; A. Hoeck, *Hermes* xxx 1895, 347–54, argued for registration after the eighteenth birthday from *A.P.*; D. Welsh, *Cl. News & Views* xxi 1977, 77–85, suggested that after Demosthenes had come of age the rules were changed. *A.P.* uses two different kinds of expression to indicate age: in this chapter men are registered when ὀκτωκαίδεκα ἔτη γεγονότες, and a man is to be rejected if νεώτερος ὀκτωκαίδεκ' ἐτῶν; in 53. iv the διαιτηταί are men οἷς ἂν ἑξηκοστὸν ἔτος ᾖ, and *A.P.* goes on to explain that men serve as διαιτηταί in the forty-second year after their registration: if these details are all correct it must be the case that men were registered after reaching their eighteenth birthday (and entering on the nineteenth year of their life), and served as διαιτηταί in the sixtieth year of their life (i.e. the official year in which their sixtieth birthday fell). In *A.P.*'s usage, as in modern English usage, two systems of reckoning are possible: service as διαιτητής, a year-long process, is placed in the sixtieth year of a man's life; but registration, an event, is placed after the eighteenth birthday. Men were not allowed to hold office (cf. p. 510) or to sit on juries (63. iii cf. oath *ap.* D. xxiv. *Tim.* 151) until ὑπὲρ τριάκοντα ἔτη γεγονότες; probably the πρόβουλοι of 413–411 and certainly the additional συγγραφεῖς of 411, the supervisors of ephebi and the choregi of boys' choruses had to be ὑπὲρ τετταράκοντα ἔτη γεγονότες (29. ii with commentary, 42. ii, 56. iii); the trierarchs in the Decree of Themistocles, the men sent to proclaim Pericles' congress decree, the envoys sent to Perdiccas of Macedon in 430 and, according to some of the lexica, the ephetae had to be ὑπὲρ πεντήκοντα ἔτη γεγονότες, and the first opportunity to speak in the assembly was offered to men over fifty (M&L 23, 22; Pl. *Per.* 17. ii; M&L 65, 16–18; lexica cited p. 647; A. I. *Tim.* 23): in all these cases the intention should be that the stated birthday must have been passed. *A.P.*'s different forms of expression, and the circumstantial detail of the forty-two ἐπώνυμοι in ch. 53, seem to guarantee his account. That the age of majority was changed seems unlikely, and I assume that what Demosthenes says of himself is misleading: possibly those who reached eighteen in the previous year were supposed to be registered, and the status of those with birthdays between 1 Hecatombaeon (i) and the day of registration was ambiguous (cf. the similar suggestion of M. Golden, *Phoen.* xxxiii 1979, 25–38). Cf. Rhodes, *A.B.*, 172; for a similar dispute on the reckoning of ages in Sparta see Pl. *Lyc.* 17. iv with K. M. T. Chrimes, *Ancient Sparta*, 89–90, against M. P. Nilsson, *Klio* xii 1912, 310.

διαψηφίζονται ... ὁμόσαντες οἱ δημόται: There was a tendency in

Athens to use ψηφίζειν and χειροτονεῖν of different kinds of decision rather than of different methods of voting (cf. Rhodes, *A.B.*, 39, where the reference to black and white ψῆφοι is an aberration; also commentary on 34. i, 41. iii), and (δια)ψηφίζειν is regularly used of the decision to accept or reject a citizen (cf. διαψηφισμόν in 13. v, and 55. iv on the δοκιμασία of the archons); but the assembly voted by ballot on various questions affecting a named individual (cf. on 41. iii), and D. LVII. *Eub.* 13–14 cf. 61 makes it clear that the demes voted by ballot in the review with which that speech is concerned, so we need not doubt the appropriateness of the verb. For the oath cf. Isae. VII. *Her. Apoll.* 28, D. LVII. *Eub.* 26, 61, 64; §64 records one clause of the oath, (ψηφιοῦμαι) γνώμῃ τῇ δικαιοτάτῃ καὶ οὔτε χάριτος ἕνεκ᾽ οὔτ᾽ ἔχθρας. An oath was required perhaps because the demesmen were engaging in a quasi-judicial activity.

A. Diller, *TAPA* lxiii 1932, 193–205, suggested that the procedures for δοκιμασία and appeal were revised and standardised at the time of the review of 346/5, but his arguments are not cogent: see Gomme, *CP* xxxix 1934, 123–30 = *Essays*, 67–75.

εἰ δοκοῦσι γεγονέναι τὴν ἡλικίαν: Since Athenians were not registered at birth there might be no good evidence of a man's age (cf. the uncertainty in Plat. *Lys.* 207 B 8–C 2); but many Athenians would have been enrolled in their father's phratry when young (though not at a fixed age: Gilbert, *C.A.S.A.*, 191–2 with 192 n. 1, Busolt & Swoboda, *G.S.*, ii. 960–2), and evidence of that enrolment might provide a measure of confirmation. Physical maturity might also be considered, as in Ar. *Vesp.* 578.

ἀπέρχονται πάλιν εἰς παῖδας: The demesmen may be penalised if they accept a young man as being of age but the boule rejects him (§ii), but nothing is said here of penalising the father or the guardian if he wrongly claims that the candidate is of age: sponsors risk fines in the 'Demotionid decrees', *IG* ii² 1237, and I imagine that they risked fines in presenting candidates for this δοκιμασία.

εἰ ἐλεύθερός ἐστι: 'Whether he is free (i.e. not a slave) . . .' There are texts in which ἐλεύθερος seems to denote not merely a free man but one possessed of citizenship, and it has been suggested that this clause should mean, 'Whether he is of citizen birth' (see W. L. Newman, ed. of Arist. *Pol.*, i. 248 n. 1 cf. iv. 173–4, W. Wyse, ed. of Isaeus, 281; also Sandys², Fritz & Kapp and Moore on this passage); but the requirement of citizen birth should be covered by the following clause (cf. next note), and the fact that a candidate judged not to be ἐλεύθερος was sold as a slave may be regarded as confirmation that ἐλεύθερος has its normal meaning here (but see pp. 501–2).

καὶ γέγονε κατὰ τοὺς νόμους: '. . . and was born in accordance with the laws.' The significance of this and the previous clause have been debated in connection with the question whether bastards were entitled to Athenian citizenship (cf. pp. 496–7). εἰ ἐλεύθερός ἐστι need mean no more than it says (cf. previous note); this clause refers not to being born in wedlock (Gilbert, *C.A.S.A.*, 191 n. 1, MacDowell, *CQ*² xxvi 1976, 89, rightly, against W. Wyse, ed. of Isaeus, 281) but generally to being born in accordance with the laws which state the requirements for Athenian citizenship: the requirement that both parents must be Athenians has been stated above; but unlike Gilbert and MacDowell I do not find *A.P.*'s failure to state that there was a further requirement, of birth from parents lawfully married, sufficient to prove that there was no such requirement.

ἂν μὲν ἀποψηφίσωνται μὴ εἶναι ἐλεύθερον: The papyrus has ἐπιψηφίσωνται, but the correction is certain: cf. *IG* ii² 1237, 31 etc., D. LVII. *Eub.* 11, 56, etc. (verb used absolutely), xix. *F.L.* 174 (ἀπεψηφίσαντο μὴ πέμπειν); also various passages in the lexica dealing with men who are ἀπεψηφισμένοι (listed by A. Diller, *TAPA* lxiii 1932, 202). Since there is no corresponding δέ, this μὲν was deleted by Π. Ν. Παπαγεώργιος, *Ἀθ.* iv 1892, 576; but cf. 48. v with commentary.

If *A.P.*'s text gives a complete and accurate account of the procedure, an appeal lay to a δικαστήριον if the deme judged a candidate not to be ἐλεύθερος, all candidates approved by the deme were then reviewed by the boule on the criterion of age, but no further check was made on the criterion of birth in accordance with the laws. Athenian law is not renowned for its tidiness, but this is improbably haphazard: Ar. *Vesp.* 578, if pressed, would indicate that a δικαστήριον might also consider the criterion of age (but any involvement of the jurors in the vetting of young citizens would provide Aristophanes with a sufficient excuse for this remark); and we may guess that on all criteria a candidate rejected by the deme could appeal to a δικαστήριον, and (in case the deme had erred in the direction of generosity) candidates accepted by the deme, or rejected by the deme but reinstated by a court, were reviewed on all criteria by the boule (cf. Moore, 275). In the general review of 346/5 Euphiletus, rejected as a ξένος by the deme of Erchia, and Euxitheus, rejected as a ξένος by the deme of Halimus, appealed to a δικαστήριον against their rejection (Isae. xii. *Euph.*, D. LVII. *Eub.*): Euphiletus' case went first to the διαιτηταί, perhaps because there were so many appeals that it was necessary to spread the burden (Wyse, ed. of Isaeus, 716–17).[37] On that general review see also A. 1. *Tim.* 77 with

---

[37] Differences between D. LVII and Isae. xii are discussed also by A. Diller, *TAPA* lxiii 1932, 201–2, Gomme, *CP* xxix 1934, 125–8 = *Essays*, 69–72. L. Gernet, *Mélanges A.-M. Desrousseaux*, 171–80, was sufficiently impressed by the anomalies to regard Isae. xii as spurious; D. M. MacDowell, *The Law in Classical Athens*, 207,

schol., 86, 114, 11. *F.L.* 182, D.H. 655. *Din.* 11, with M. J. Osborne, *BSA* lxvi 1971, 329 n. 32.

ὃ μὲν ἐφίησιν: Until he has been registered as an adult citizen a man cannot initiate proceedings in the courts: presumably the appeal was made by the candidate's father or guardian. The thesmothetae were the εἰσάγουσα ἀρχή (59. iv).

οἱ δὲ δημόται κατηγόρους αἱροῦνται πέντε [ἄν]δρας: The κατήγοροι are accusers, who in opposition to the candidate will state the deme's case for rejecting him. Sandys cites *IG* ii² 1237, 30–8, but fails to bring out the difference: there any candidates rejected by the Decelean phratry may appeal to the γένος of the Demotionidae, and the phratry will choose five συνήγοροι to sit and vote with the Demotionidae (on the Deceleans and the Demotionidae see Wade-Gery, *CQ* xxv 1931, 129–43 = *Essays*, 116–34, A. Andrewes, *JHS* lxxxi 1961, 3–5, W. E. Thompson, *SO* xlii 1968, 52–6; Thompson supposes that only members of the γένος were admitted under the law of the Demotionidae and could appeal to the γένος, which I doubt). A. 1. *Tim.* 114 suggests that in the general review of 346/5 as here κατήγοροι were elected to oppose men who appealed against their rejection. κατήγοροι elected by a deme, possibly in a case of this kind, are praised in *IG* ii² 1205 = *SIG*³ 916.

κἂν μὲν μὴ δόξῃ ... πωλεῖ τοῦτον ἡ πόλις: Moore, 275, believing that ἐλεύθερος denotes not merely freedom but citizen birth, comments: 'The penalty was fitting for the son of slaves, who was a slave unless specifically freed, and it is this class which Aristotle has in mind in discussing the sale into slavery of those rejected. To treat the sons of foreigners in this way would have been monstrously unjust.' If, as I suggest above, ἐλεύθερος here denotes no more than freedom, the Athenians can more easily be saved from the imputation of monstrous injustice: it can then be claimed that this sentence refers only to those who are judged not to be free, and that those who are judged to be free but not to have been 'born according to the laws' are perhaps registered as metics (cf. the impassioned discussion of Gomme, *CP* xxix 1934, 130–40 = *Essays*, 75–85, also Jacoby, *Supp.* i. 463). However, other texts suggest a modification of this explanation. In *IG* ii² 1237 a man who introduces an unqualified candidate to the Decelean phratry is to be fined 100 drachmae (lines 20–2), but if on rejection he appeals to the Demotionidae and they concur in the rejection the fine is to be 1,000 drachmae (lines 38–40); under Nicodemus' rider the θίασος is to hold a preliminary enquiry, and if a candidate is accepted by the θίασος but rejected by the phratry

---

suggests that an appeal by a young man rejected in the regular δοκιμασία was an instance of ἔφεσις but Euphiletus entered a δίκη against his deme (he does not discuss the difference between the case of Euxitheus and that of Euphiletus).

the fine is to be levied not on the sponsor but on the θίασος (lines 78–106: cf. Wade-Gery, *opp. citt.*, 136–7 = 125–6). In the review of 346/5 men rejected by the deme who accepted the deme's judgment were to be registered as metics, but men who appealed to a δικαστήριον and had their rejection confirmed there were to have their property confiscated and to be sold as slaves (Isae. XII. *Euph.*, *hyp.* = D.H. 617–18. *Isae.* 16; D. LVII. *Eub.*, *hyp.*: Gomme thought that the *hypothesis*-writers were misled by *A.P.*'s compression, but there is no foundation in *A.P.* for the registration as metics of those who accept their rejection [*hyp.* D.]). I suspect that in the regular δοκιμασία a man found to be a slave would be sold even if he accepted the deme's judgment, while a man found to be free but foreign would be registered as a metic if he accepted that judgment but sold as a slave if he appealed and the rejection was upheld; it would of course be open to the sponsor to buy the man and free him: the Athenians tried by threatening heavy penalties to discourage frivolous litigation, and this threat may not have seemed to them to be monstrously unjust (cf. G. Daviero Rocchi, *Acme* xxviii 1975, 257–79, who suggests that only adult male citizens were considered to have an absolute right to liberty). If my interpretation is correct, this sentence will not confirm that ἐλεύθερος here means no more than 'free', though I still believe that to be so (cf. p. 499).†

42. ii. δ[οκ]ιμάζει τοὺς ἐγγραφέντας ἡ βουλή: A candidate rejected by the deme might appeal against rejection, but if the demesmen conspired to accept an unqualified candidate no one might be willing to appeal; so δοκιμασία in the deme was followed by compulsory reference to the boule. For a double vetting of candidates cf. Nicodemus' amendment to the procedures of the Decelean phratry (*IG* ii[2] 1237, discussed above), and the δοκιμασία of [bouleutae and] archons (45. iii, 55. ii–iv, with commentary).

κἄν τις δόξ[ῃ] νεώτερος ὀκτωκαίδεκ' ἐτῶν εἶναι: We may guess that both the δικαστήρια and the boule were in fact entitled to take note of all criteria: cf. p. 500.

ζημιοῖ τ[ο]ὺς δημότας τοὺς ἐγγράψαντας: Cf. *IG* ii[2] 1237, 88–94, where the θίασος is to be fined if it accepts a candidate subsequently rejected by the Decelean phratry—but members of the θίασος who opposed acceptance are not required to contribute to the fine.

ἐπὰν δὲ δοκιμασθῶσιν οἱ ἔφηβοι: This is the earliest instance cited in LSJ of the form ἐπάν: it is not found in inscriptions until the third century (Meisterhans & Schwyzer, *G.a.I.*, 252 with n. 1969), and Herwerden emended to ἐπειδάν, but the word is found also in Arist. *E.N.* v. 1132 A 32, Thph. *Char.* 24. x and may be retained here. Cf. 56. i, and probably 48. v (see *ad loc.*).

A.P. has not hitherto used the word ἔφηβος. It belongs to the series of words for age-classes found throughout the Greek world (cf. p. 495): an Athenian was a παῖς until he came of age (cf. §i: ἀπέρχονται πάλιν εἰς παῖδας); various texts use the archaic expression ἐπὶ διετὲς ἡβῆσαι to refer to the completion of two years after reaching puberty (e.g. law *ap.* [D.] XLVI. *Steph. ii.* 20, cf. p. 509), which seems in classical Athens to have been applied to the last two years before coming of age, as in Hyp. fr. 223 Sauppe, *L.S.* 255. 15, but Harp. ἐπὶ διετὲς ἡβῆσαι and schol. A. III. *Ctes.* 122 report the view of Didymus that the age of puberty was fourteen and the two years referred to are those from fourteen to sixteen (see J. Labarbe, *La Loi navale de Thémistocle*, 67–8 with 68–9 n. 1); and it is likely that the two years of ἐφηβεία which in classical Athens followed coming of age have been retained and adapted from a more extensive system of age-classes (see Pélékidis, *Histoire de l'éphébie attique*, 51–70). W. K. Lacey, *The Family in Classical Greece*, 294 n. 28, notes that Plato regularly uses not ἔφηβος but μειράκιον, and thinks that the adoption of the word ἔφηβος may belong to the reform of the 330's, but A. II. *F.L.* 167 (referring to Aeschines' own youth) and D. XIX *F.L.* 303 both write of ἔφηβοι in 343.†

A.P. implies that all newly registered citizens became ephebi and underwent the two years of training set out in the remainder of this chapter (cf. Lyc. *Leocr.* 76, and *A.P.*'s similar implication for the διαιτηταί in 53. iv–v). A small exception must be made for those who were physically unfit for military service (cf. Pélékidis, *op. cit.*, 97 with n. 5, suggesting that their exemption would be granted by the boule). Many have believed, and I join them in believing, that despite the silence of *A.P.* and Lycurgus there was a larger exception: the training given to the ephebi was training primarily in hoplite warfare, and they were presented with a shield and a spear by the state (§§iii–iv); evidence for their taking part in boat races is not found until the late second century (e.g. *IG* ii² 1006, 30: Pélékidis, *op. cit.*, 247–9, 272); it is surely improbable that the thetes were required to take part in this course of training, although they as well as the richer citizens must have been registered in the ληξιαρχικὰ γραμματεῖα (cf. Beloch, *G.G.*², III. ii. 402, Gomme, *Population of Athens*, 11, Reinmuth, *Mnem.* Supp. xiv 1971, 106; contr. Pélékidis, *op. cit.*, 113–14, Lacey, *op. cit.*, 94–5, Reinmuth, *op. cit.*, 127).‡

For the compilation of annual lists of ephebi see 53. iv–v with commentary.

συλλεγέντες οἱ πατέρες αὐτῶν: No other text directly mentions these tribal meetings of the fathers (and presumably, where relevant, guardians) of the newly registered ephebi; but in *IG* ii² 1159 = Reinmuth 19, 11–14, we read that the fathers of one contingent of ephebi have reported to the tribe their satisfaction with the σωφρονιστής.

αἱροῦνται τρεῖς ἐκ τῶν φυλετῶν τῶν ὑπὲρ τετταράκοντα ἔτη γεγονότων: To reduce the risk of corrupting the young, those chosen must have passed their fortieth birthday (cf. p. 498): the same age was required of choregi for boys' choruses (56. iii). The supervision of ephebi was presumably considered to demand skill or moral fitness as well as loyalty to the state, and could also be regarded as a quasi-military duty: hence the supervisors and instructors, like all military officials (43. i, 61), were appointed not by lot but by election.

οὓς ἂν ἡγῶνται βελτίστους καὶ ἐπιτηδειοτάτους ἐπιμελεῖσθαι τῶν ἐφήβων: Cf. *IG* ii² 1006, 56, of 122/1 (... δι' ἣν αἰτίαν καὶ κοσμή[τ]ην καθίστησα[ιν ἐκ] τῶν ἄριστα βε[βι]ωκότων [*sc.* ὁ δῆμος]).

ὁ δῆμος ἕνα τῆς φυλῆς ἑκάστης χειροτονεῖ σωφρονιστήν: A σωφρονιστής is one who makes σώφρων, especially by chastising those who fail to display σωφροσύνη (cf. T. III. 65. iii, VI. 87. iii, VIII. 48. vi, Plat. *Rep.* V. 471 A 6–7, D. XIX. *F.L.* 285); an inscription of the second century A.D. has above it a relief representing three σωφρονισταί armed with withes (*IG* ii² 2122: photograph P. Graindor, *Album d'inscriptions attiques d'époque impériale*, pl. lxiii. 79): nothing concrete can be added to what §iii says of their duties (and of the fact that the teaching of specific military skills was the responsibility not of them and of the κοσμητής but of specialist instructors). σωφρονισταί are found in the ephebic inscriptions of the late fourth century (*IG* ii² 1156 = Reinmuth 2, 28–9, etc., of the ephebi registered in 334/3, to *IG* ii² 1159 = Reinmuth 19, of those registered in 303/2); they then disappear; the title reappears in the second century A.D. (beginning with *IG* ii² 2044, 2–9, of those registered in 139/40: see Reinmuth, *Mnem.* Supp. xiv 1971, 120). It is not clear whether the σωφρονισταί and κοσμητής served for two years, with responsibility for one set of ephebi throughout their two years' service, or for one year, with responsibility for both first-year and second-year ephebi, or for one year, with responsibility for first-year ephebi only: the last solution has often been adopted (e.g. Gomme, *Population of Athens*, 67–8, Pélékidis, *Histoire de l'éphébie attique*, 104), but should be ruled out by the fact that in *IG* ii² 1156 = Reinmuth 2, 45–51, and *IG* ii² 1189 = Reinmuth 3, the deme of Eleusis praises the ephebi of two tribes and their σωφρονισταί for guard duties performed there, which according to §iv should have fallen in their second year (cf. Reinmuth, *op. cit.*, 77, but contrast *ibid.* 9); Reinmuth prefers the second solution (*op. cit.*, 81); I find the first more probable.

καὶ κοσμητὴν ἐκ τῶν ἄλλων Ἀθηναίων ἐπὶ πάντας: κόσμος, 'orderliness', was a virtue associated more with Sparta (e.g. H. I. 65. iv) and with Crete (where there were magistrates known as κοσμοί: e.g. Arist. *Pol.* II. 1272 A 6), but it is not wholly alien to fourth-century Athens: the proedri were responsible for εὐκοσμία at meetings of the boule and assembly (44. iii), decrees of the second half of the fourth century praise those who have secured the εὐκοσμία of the theatre (*IG* ii² 223 B, 7–8, cf. C, 11, 354, 16–17), and κόσμος is a fitting companion for σωφροσύνη; κοσμητῆρα μάχης and κοσμητὰς πολέμου appear in an epigram quoted by Aeschines, allegedly commemorating the capture of Eion by Cimon *c.* 476/5 (III. *Ctes.* 185: discussions of these epigrams are reviewed by R. E. Wycherley, *The Athenian Agora*, iii, p. 104); see also on ἀκοσμοῦντας in 3. vi. The title κοσμητής is given to the principal supervisor of all the ephebi (ἐπὶ πάντας: reading confirmed by Dr J. D. Thomas) throughout the history of the ἐφηβεία: ἐκ τῶν ἄλλων Ἀθηναίων should mean that the appointment was made from the citizen body as a whole, not from the short list of thirty from whom the ten σωφρονισταί were chosen. We are not told whether a minimum age of forty was required: since it was required of the σωφρονισταί it was probably required of the κοσμητής too; Pélékidis remarks that in the second century A.D. we find Archelaus Ἀπολλωνίου Πειραιεύς serving as ἔφηβος in 125/6 and as κοσμητής in 139/40 (*IG* ii² 2037, 23, 2044, 10: *op. cit.*, 105 with n. 2), but for this and other reasons S. Follet prefers to date 2037 *c.* 110 (*Athènes au II*e *et au III*e *siècle*, 188–91). As with the σωφρονισταί, it has been disputed whether the κοσμητής served for one year or for two (cf. previous note). As Pélékidis remarks (*op. cit.*, 106), the relative responsibilities of the ephebi's officers and the Athenian generals are not made clear: Reinmuth (*op. cit.*, 79–80) suggests that the generals were responsible for the strictly military duties of the ephebi and the κοσμητής and σωφρονισταί for their gymnastic and patriotic training.

Inscriptions show that some of the ephebi themselves secured 'cadet' appointments as ταξίαρχοι and λοχαγοί (e.g. *Hesp.* ix 8 = Reinmuth 9, i. 20–31: see F. W. Mitchel, *TAPA* xcii 1961, 347–57, and for those offices in the regular army see 61. iii with commentary).

42. iii. συλλαβόντες δ᾽ οὗτοι: *Sc.* the κοσμητής and the σωφρονισταί. **πρῶτον μὲν τὰ ἱερὰ περιῆλθον**: The aorist in the middle of the presents is surprising: Sandys, *CR* v 1891, 115, suggested περιίασιν.

The purpose of this tour of the temples was presumably to instil in the ephebi a sense of devotion to the cults of Athens: cf. the possibility that the ephebi took part in the revived quadrennial festival at the sanctuary of Amphiaraus at Oropus (Ἀρχ. Ἐφ. 1918, 73–100, 95–7 = Reinmuth 15, as interpreted by Reinmuth in *Acta of the Fifth International Congress of Greek and Latin Epigraphy, 1967*, 50; on his discussion in *Mnem.* Supp. xiv 1971 see D. M. Lewis, *CR*² xxiii 1973, 255; on the Amphiarea see below, p. 610), and the long programme of festivals in which the ephebi of later centuries participated (e.g. *IG* ii² 1006, 8–16). Later inscriptions record inaugural sacrifices at the beginning of the period of service (e.g. *IG* ii² 1006, 6-8).

It seems to be at this stage, before beginning their military training, that the ephebi took their oath (on which see p. 494): it was taken in the sanctuary of Aglaurus (D. xix. *F.L.* 303: for the site see pp. 103, 211), and Aglaurus is the first deity invoked in the inscribed oath (Tod 204, 17). It is thought that the swearing of the oath is depicted on a black-figure vase and (with greater probability) a red-figure vase published by A. Conze, *Ann. Inst. Corr. Arch.* xl 1868, 264-7 with pls H, 1 (Hermitage, Leningrad, 59 Stephani = C. H. E. Haspels, *Attic Black-Figured Lekythoi*, i. 239, Diosphos Painter no. 141; private collection = Beazley, *A.R.V.*², ii. 1069, Thomson Painter no. 1).

εἶτ' εἰς Πειραιέα . . . τὴν Ἀκτήν: Cf. 61. i, where of the five generals with regular duties there are δύο δ' ἐπὶ τὸν Πειραιέα, τὸν μὲν εἰς τὴν Μουνιχίαν, τὸν δ' εἰς τὴν Ἀκτήν, οἳ τῆς φυλακῆς ἐπιμελοῦνται τῶν ἐν Πειραιεῖ. Munichia is the hill on the east side of the Piraeus, facing towards Phalerum Bay (cf. 19. ii, 38. i, with commentary); Acte is the peninsula to the south of the main, westward-facing harbour known as Κάνθαρος (cf. p. 453). [τῶι γυμνασί]ωι τῶν ἐφήβων is restored in *IG* ii² 478 = Reinmuth 17, 30, found at the Piraeus; περίπολοι (cf. p. 508) at Munichia are mentioned in T. viii. 92. v.

παιδοτρίβας αὐτοῖς δύο: Gymnastic trainers (Ant. iii. *Tetr. ii. γ*. 6). Later there was only one of these: e.g. *IG* ii² 478 = Reinmuth 17, 26 (of 305/4), *IG* ii² 585, 10, 665, 25. I have suggested above (p. 504) that the κοσμητής and σωφρονισταί were responsible for one set of ephebi for both of their years of service; if *A.P.*'s arrangement of material may be pressed (which is not certain) the instructors mentioned here will have taught the ephebi in their first year only, but Gomme thought that the κοσμητής had dealings with the ephebi in their first year only and the instructors in both years (*Population of Athens*, 68).

καὶ διδασκάλους: *A.P.* does not say how many they were (cf. next note), but enumerates four skills to be taught: hoplite-fighting (for the verb cf. Is. xv. *Antid.* 232), archery, javelin-throwing and catapult-firing. Later inscriptions attest the employment of separate instructors styled ὁπλομάχης, τοξότης, ἀκοντιστής and (καταπαλτ)-αφετής: cf. Pélékidis, *Histoire de l'éphébie attique*, 179-80. In the fourth century no such instructors of the whole *corps* are attested: *Hesp.* ix 8 = Reinmuth 9, i. 33-6, praises two [δ]ιδ[ασκάλου]ς τῆς φυλῆ[ς] (*sc.* Λεωντίδος), one of them a non-Athenian and the other not a member of Leontis, while (*IG* ii² 2976 =) *AJP* lxvi 1945, 234-9 = Reinmuth 8, 11-13, of the same year, names four men, none of them known to be members of the tribe, who are thought to be the διδάσκαλοι of Pandionis; one or two διδάσκαλοι are found in the inscription of Pandionis, J. Pouilloux, *La Forteresse de Rhamnonte*, 107-10, 2 = Reinmuth 10, 7-8; and one in the inscription of Leontis, *Ἀρχ. Ἐφ.* 1918, 73-100, 96 = Reinmuth 15, l.h.s. 7-10.

οἵτινες ὁπλομαχεῖν: Kaibel & Wilamowitz[1-2] suggested τ[ἐτ]τ[α]ρας ⟨οἱ⟩, but οἵτινες seems secure (cf. Kaibel, *Stil und Text*, 204). On training in ὁπλομαχεῖν cf. Plat. *Lach.* 178 A 1-185 C 4.

καταπάλτην: This, restored by Kaibel & Wilamowitz[1], is the fourth-century spelling (cf. Meisterhans & Schwyzer, *G.a.I.*, 14-15 with n. 64), but although Herwerden claimed to read it in the papyrus (*BPW* xi 1891, 611, cf. Herwerden & Leeuwen) it seems established that the corrector wrote απελτην.

διδάσκουσιν: The future, διδάξουσιν, was suggested by W. G. Rutherford, *CR* v 1891, 115, cf. Herwerden, Kaibel, *Stil und Text*, 204, comparing 29, ii, v *fin.*: the present is more appropriate to *A.P.*'s indicative account of the working of the constitution (cf. Introduction, p. 34), and should be retained, but the law which lies behind his account probably read χειροτονεῖν ... οἵτινες διδάξουσιν.

δίδωσι δὲ καὶ εἰς τροφ[ὴν]: For contemporary state stipends see 62. ii with commentary. The instructors, not necessarily Athenian citizens, were presumably paid a salary higher than these maintenance grants (cf. Pélékidis, *Histoire de l'éphébie attique*, 108, citing *SIG*[3] 578, 7-34 [Teos, C2]).

τὰ δὲ τῶν φυλετῶν ... (συσσιτοῦσι γὰρ κατὰ φυλάς): Ephebic service in the time of *A.P.* was a full-time occupation (and eating together by tribes was perhaps a conscious imitation of the more extensive Spartan ἀγωγή); but before the reform of the 330's the ἐφηβεία was not, or at any rate was not necessarily, a full-time occupation (cf. pp. 494-5).

καὶ τῶν ἄλλων ἐπιμελεῖται πάντων: *A.P.* is disappointingly vague. Apart from visiting temples and taking part in festivals (cf. p. 505), learning the military skills taught them by specialists, and eating together, we are not told what was involved in the training of the fourth-century ephebi.

42. iv. τὸν δ' ὕστερον: This passage is repeated with verbal changes by Harp., Suid. (Π 1259), περίπολος, schol. A. II. *F.L.* 167. Kaibel & Wilamowitz substituted τὸν δὲ δεύτερον from the derivative texts, but no change is needed.

ἐκκλησίας ἐν τῷ θεάτρῳ γενομένης ... τὰ περὶ τὰς τάξεις: The theatre of Dionysus, to the south of the eastern half of the Acropolis, was rebuilt in the time of Lycurgus (cf. A. W. Pickard-Cambridge, *The Theatre of Dionysus in Athens*, 134-74, Travlos, *Pictorial Dictionary*, 537-52): presumably this was used in preference to the Pnyx (also remodelled in the time of Lycurgus: cf. H. A. Thompson [& R. L.

42. iv] COMMENTARY ON THE *ATH. POL.*

Scranton], *Hesp.* xii 1943, 269–301, esp. 297–301, Travlos, *op. cit.*, 466–76) because its orchestra was convenient for the display of the ephebi's prowess. In later centuries the ἀπόδειξις was made not to the assembly but to the boule (first in *Hesp.* vii 20, 17–18, of 258/7).†

τὰ περὶ τὰς τάξεις: 'Their military skill' (Fritz & Kapp); 'Their knowledge of warfare' (Moore); but we probably need something more specific. Plat. *Lach.* 182 B 6–7 cf. A 7–8 and X. *Anab.* II. i. 7 distinguish περὶ τὰς τάξεις from ἐν ὅπλοις μάχεσθαι; cf. also X. *Cyr.* II. ii. 6–7 and τάττειν in *M.* III. i: the reference here should be to their skill at manoeuvring in formation.

λαβόντες ἀσπίδα καὶ δόρυ παρὰ τῆς πόλεως: (The derivative texts [cf. above] read παρὰ τοῦ δήμου, but no change is needed.) Ephebi performing military duties must always have been suitably armed, and the ἔφηβος on the red-figure vase cited on p. 506 is equipped with a shield and a spear, but the presentation of a shield and spear to all ephebi is presumably an innovation of the 330's; earlier the state had presented arms to the sons of men killed in war (Plat. *Menex.* 248 E 6–249 B 2).

περιπολοῦσι τὴν χώραν . . . ἐν τοῖς φυλακτηρίοις: Cf. A. II. *F.L.* 167, quoted on p. 494; περίπολοι are mentioned in T. IV. 67. ii, and in T. VIII. 92. v (cf. p. 506). There is epigraphic evidence for the presence of ephebi in the fourth century at Eleusis (e.g. *IG* ii^2 1156 = Reinmuth 2, 45–51, *IG* ii^2 1189 = Reinmuth 3); at Phyle, north-west of Athens (cf. on 37. i) (e.g. Pouilloux, *La Forteresse de Rhamnonte*, 2 = Reinmuth 10, 9–10); and at Rhamnus (e.g. Pouilloux, *op. cit.*, 2 = Reinmuth 10, 9–10). While on these garrison duties they were under the command of the στρατηγὸς ἐπὶ τῇ χώρᾳ (e.g. *Hesp.* ix 8 = Reinmuth 9, ii. 10–12: cf. 61. i with commentary). Presumably, as argued by Pélékidis, *Histoire de l'éphébie attique*, 48, they might in exceptional circumstances be required to fight outside Attica (in the First Peloponnesian War the oldest and youngest were sent out to the Megarid: T. I. 105. iv).

42. v. χλαμύδας ἔχοντες: The χλαμύς is a short cloak, worn originally by horsemen (cf. X. *Anab.* VII. iv. 4) in Thessaly (Poll. x. 124) or Macedon (Arist. fr. 500 Teubner = Phyl. 81 F 62), and adopted as the uniform of ephebi both in Athens and elsewhere (cf. Pl. *Amat.* 752 F, *IGRR* iv 360, 25, 35 [Pergamum, C2 A.D.]). According to Philemon I, fr. 34 Kock ap. Poll. VIII. 164, the ephebi also wore the broad-brimmed hat known as the πέτασος. On the red-figure vase cited on p. 506 the ἔφηβος wears a χλαμύς and Νίκη holds a helmet for him. The χλαμύδες of the Athenian ephebi were black for an unknown period until A.D. 165/6, when white ones were provided at the expense of Herodes Atticus (Philostr. 550. *V.S.* II. I. v, *IG* ii^2 2090, 5–11).‡

καὶ ἀτελεῖς εἰσι πάντων: ἀτέλεια πάντων is a common expression (cf. Busolt, *G.S.*, i. 300–1), but it is not clear what burdens the ephebi were exempted from apart from liability to prosecution. In Lys. XXXII. *Diog.* 24 ἀτέλεια is represented as a privilege from which orphaned minors can benefit, and as different from exemption from liturgies (granted for one year after the δοκιμασία to the sons of men who fell in the Peloponnesian War); the speaker of Lys. XXI. *Pec. Acc.* claims to have served as choregus in the year of his δοκιμασία (§1), and Demosthenes claims to have served as trierarch εὐθὺς ἐκ παίδων ἐξελθών (XXI. *Mid.* 154), while exemption from the trierarchy was granted to τῶν ἐπικλήρων καὶ τῶν ὀρφανῶν καὶ τῶν κληρουχικῶν καὶ τῶν κοινωνικῶν καὶ εἴ τις ἀδύνατος (D. XIV. *Symm.* 16); D. XX. *Lept.* 18 claims that ἀτέλεια traditionally does not include exemption from εἰσφοραί and the trierarchy (but Leptines' law, while drastically reducing the number of ἀτελεῖς, extended the exemption of those who remained), and Demosthenes' speeches against his guardians make it clear that εἰσφορά was a burden which could fall on an orphaned minor (e.g. XXVII. *Aphob. i.* 7). Clearly ephebi were not exempted from military service; it is possible that in the time of *A.P.* they were exempted from festival liturgies, or from all liturgies, and it is possible that they were exempted from εἰσφοραί and from any other direct taxes. Exemption from liturgies will have been justified by the fact that the reorganised ἐφηβεία was a full-time occupation and would not leave the ephebi the leisure which was needed for the conscientious performance of a liturgy.

For ἀτέλεια conferred on non-citizens see p. 653.

περὶ κλήρου: When a man was registered as a citizen he became κύριος ... τῆς οὐσίας (A. I. *Tim.* 103): thus Demosthenes prosecuted his guardians immediately after his δοκιμασία (e.g. XXX. *Onet. i.* 15). Exemption from other lawsuits may be an innovation of the 330's, and so the fact that the speaker of Lys. X. *Theomn. i* attacked the Thirty ἐπειδὴ τάχιστα ἐδοκιμάσθην (§31) does not prove that *A.P.*'s list of exceptions is incomplete (as suggested by Sandys).

καὶ ἐπικλή[ρου]: The son of an ἐπίκληρος (the daughter of a man who had no legitimate sons: cf. 9. ii with commentary) became κύριος of the property, but perhaps not of the ἐπίκληρος herself, when he came of age: see the law *ap.* [D.] XLVI. *Steph. ii.* 20, with Harrison, *L.A.*, i. 113 and n. 2, and on the phrase ἐπὶ διετὲς ἡβῆσαι see above, p. 503.

κἂν τ[ι]νι κατὰ τὸ γένος ἱερωσύνη γένηται: This is presumably an exception to ἵνα μὴ πρόφασις ᾖ τοῦ ἀπιέναι rather than to exemption from lawsuits. For the spelling of ἱερωσύνας see on 21. vi: here the papyrus has —ο—.

διε[ξ]ελθό[[ι]]ντων τῶν δυεῖν ἐτῶν: Kaibel & Wilamowitz[1,3] retain δυεῖν, *pace* Sandys' *apparatus*, but in their 2nd ed. they emended to δυοῖν; Kaibel, *Stil und Text*, 204, was not sure which form the author had used. The London papyrus has δυοῖν in 16. iii, τοῖν δυοῖν ὀβολοῖν in 28. iii, δυεῖν δραχμαῖς in 50. ii, δυοῖν φυλαῖν in 52. ii and δυεῖν φυλαῖν in 56. iii. According to Meisterhans & Schwyzer, *G.a.I.*, 199–201 cf. 157 with nn. 1356–7, the dual gradually gave way to the plural; and δυοῖν was used until 329 but δυεῖν for the following hundred years, the latter form never being used with the dual (in *IG* ii² 1672, of 329/8, line 101 has δυοῖν προτανείαιν but 286 has τῶν ἑξήκοντα καὶ δυεῖν μεδίμνω[ν]). In 56. iii we should certainly correct to δυοῖν, and in 50. ii we should expect both the law from which the text is derived and *A.P.*'s text to use δυοῖν δραχμαῖν: that would leave this passage as the only instance in *A.P.* of δυεῖν, and probably we should follow Kaibel & Wilamowitz² in correcting to τῶν δυοῖν ἐτῶν.

M. *Officials, Sortitive and Elective: The Boule* (43–9)

The longest section of *A.P.*'s second part is devoted to a survey of Athenian ἀρχαί (43–62), within which there are recognisable subsections on the boule (43. ii–49) and the archons (55–9): cf. Introduction, pp. 30–2.

In 43. i we are given an introductory note on officials, stating that the civilian officials are appointed by lot but the military officials and a few others are elected; and in 62 we are given further information on officials in general; but there are matters on which we should welcome information but are given none. Naturally, candidates for office had to be Athenian citizens; they had to belong to one of the three higher Solonian property-classes, or, in the case of the treasurers of Athena, to the highest class (but in *A.P.*'s time this requirement was no longer taken seriously: see 7. iii–8. i, 47. i, with commentary); probably, whenever no higher minimum is stipulated, they had to have passed their thirtieth birthday (see on 30. ii, 63. iii, but it is possible that younger men could hold military office: in the case of generals doubts are hinted at by W. K. Pritchett, *The Greek State at War*, ii. 63 n. 17, and men under thirty may not have been excluded in the 'immediate' constitution of 411 [31. ii with commentary]; and in Men. *Sam.* 15 Moschion claims to have served as phylarch while young). In addition, there are signs of stricter requirements for some offices. After the destruction of Plataea in 427 Athens granted citizenship to the surviving Plataeans, stipulating that these men could not themselves hold any of the archonships or priesthoods, but their sons could do so ἂν ὦσιν ἐξ ἀστῆς γυναικὸς καὶ ἐγγυητῆς κατὰ τὸν νόμον ([D.] LIX. *Neaer.* 104–6: on the requirement of being born in wedlock see pp. 496–7); earlier in the same speech (§92) this limitation of the rights of naturalised citizens is quoted as a general rule, still in force in the mid fourth century, and the questions asked at the δοκιμασία of the archons included a check on their ancestry as far back as both grandfathers (55. iii with commentary) (cf. Gilbert, *C.A.S.A.*, 186–7, De Sanctis, *RFIC* li = ³i 1923, 294–5 = *Scritti Minori*, i. 127, Mathieu, *REG* xl 1927, 65–116, esp. 72–82, 113–15, M. J. Osborne, *Anc. Soc.* vii 1976, 113 with n. 22).[38] Prospective archons were also asked at their δοκιμασία questions about household cults which imply a requirement of phratry membership (55. iii with commentary), whereas it was probably not necessary for a citizen to belong to a phratry in post-Cleisthenic Athens although most did (cf. p. 70). Din. i. *Dem.* 71 claims

> τοὺς μὲν νόμους προλέγειν τῷ ῥήτορι καὶ τῷ στρατηγῷ, ⟨τῷ⟩ τὴν παρὰ τοῦ δήμου πίστιν ἀξιοῦντι λαμβάνειν, παιδοποιεῖσθαι κατὰ τοὺς νόμους, γῆν ἐντὸς ὅρων κεκτῆσθαι, πάσας τὰς δικαίας πίστεις παρακαταθέμενον οὕτως ἀξιοῦν προεστάναι τοῦ δήμου,

and there are two other texts mentioning a requirement that certain officials should have a stake in Athens by owning property and begetting children, the 'Draconian constitution' (4. ii with commentary: generals and hipparchs required to have legitimate children) and the Decree of Themistocles (M&L 23, 18–22: trierarchs required to have land, house and legitimate children), while the doctrine is expounded in Pericles' funeral oration, T. II. 44. iii (cf. Nep. xv. *Epam.* 5. v, where Epaminondas of Thebes is reproached for his lack of wife and children). These requirements are probably survivals from the archaic state (though a law concerning ῥήτορες is not likely to be earlier than the end of the fifth century); probably they were enforced in classical Athens only when a man realised that an enemy of his could be excluded from office if the law were to be enforced in his case. For the sake of the ritual marriage mentioned in 3. v the basileus had to be married to an Athenian woman who had not previously been married to any one else ([D.] LIX. *Neaer.* 75).

Another question about appointments which *A.P.* does not answer is whether a man formally became a candidate for office by offering himself, or by being nominated by one or more of his fellow citizens. X. *M.* III. iv shows us a disappointed candidate for the generalship, but does not reveal how he became a candidate; voluntary candidacy is suggested by Lys. VI. *And.* 4, XXXI. *Phil.* 33 (κληρωσόμενος ἰέναι), Is. XV. *Antid.* 150, Harp. ἐπιλαχών; M. Piérart, *BCH* xcviii 1974, 125–46, believes that candidates had to be nomina-

---

[38] For requirements of citizen ancestry in Roman Athens cf. p. 617 n. 49.

ted, and in 141 n. 7 cites Pl. *Phoc.* 8. ii, but §i may be thought to indicate that it was possible to volunteer, though Phocion did not do so. Compulsion may have been possible if there were too few volunteers (cf. E. S. Staveley, *Greek and Roman Voting and Elections*, 39–40, 51), but appointments by κληρωτήριον (cf. pp. 704, 606–9) could not be made without the candidates' consenting and supplying their πινάκια.†

A.P. begins his discussion of the boule with its organisation (the ten prytanies, and the daily changing ἐπιστάτης), and to this he attaches what he has to say about the meetings of the boule and assembly (in connection with which he introduces the proedri and their ἐπιστάτης) (43. ii–44). Chs 45–9 are devoted to the various powers of the boule: limitations on its jurisdiction (45. i–iii); προβούλευσις (45. iv); its duties in connection with the navy (46. i), and with public works (46. ii); its supervision of various financial officials (the treasurers of Athena, the poletae and the apodectae; the logistae who check officials' accounts each prytany, after whom follow the εὔθυνοι, who like them are members of the boule) (47–8); and, finally, the δοκιμασίαι conducted by the boule (49). Chs 47–9 are presented as a sub-section which begins and ends with the remark that the boule συνδιοικεῖ δὲ καὶ ταῖς ἄλλαις ἀρχαῖς τὰ πλεῖστα; but although in its δοκιμασίαι the boule did have to work with other officials the concluding sentence would be better placed at the end of 48.

The boule was involved in policy-making and legislation, and in administration, and in jurisdiction. *A.P.* does not treat these separately as separate activities, but (probably following the organisation of Athens' laws: cf. Introduction, pp. 33–4) subdivides the activities of the Athenian state by ἀρχαί. Laws concerning the boule formed one principal section of the Athenian code (law *ap.* D. XXIV. *Tim.* 20), and so the boule occupies a principal section of *A.P.*'s survey of the ἀρχαί, and the meetings of the assembly (dependent on the προβουλεύματα of the boule) and the activities of the financial officials who were directly supervised by the boule are both included in the section on the boule. It is perhaps because of this principle of arrangement that *A.P.* says nothing of the mechanism by which laws were enacted in the fourth century (for a different explanation, which I reject, see Introduction, p. 35 with n. 184). The doctrine was accepted that νόμοι were or ought to be of higher status and of more general application than ψηφίσματα of the boule and assembly (cf. p. 329: this underlies criticism of the democracy in 26. ii and 41. ii); after the revision of the laws completed in 400/399 Athens had a code of νόμοι, approved by the boule and (not the assembly but) a specially appointed board of νομοθέται (cf. pp. 441–2); and for the next three quarters of a century she tried to observe the distinction between νόμοι and ψηφίσματα. The repeal of old νόμοι and the enactment of new were entrusted to boards of νομοθέται, and the boule and assembly were normally involved only in setting the procedure in motion: earlier discussions of the procedure are superseded by D. M. MacDowell, *JHS* xcv 1975, 62–74; the extent to which the theoretical distinction between νόμοι and ψηφίσματα was observed is discussed by M. H. Hansen, *GR&BS* xx 1979, 27–53.

43. i. τὰ μὲν οὖν ... τοῦτον ἔχει τὸν τρόπον: *A.P.* summarises the two topics treated in ch. 42 ...

τὰς δ' ἀρχὰς τὰς περὶ τὴν ἐγκύκλιον διοίκησιν: ... and introduces the theme of chs 43–62 or, perhaps better, 43–60. διοικεῖν in *A.P.* normally refers to the administration of the state's affairs (e.g. 3. vi, 14. iii, 16. ii, 23. i); the word was associated particularly with financial administration (cf. the official ἐπὶ τῇ διοικήσει, discussed on pp. 515–16), and in 24. iii the financial associations of διοίκησις have led to its being used to mean 'maintenance', but its sense is not limited to finance here. ἐγκύκλιος means 'recurring', and so 'regular' or 'ordinary': in 26. ii the ἐγκύκλιοι ἀρχαί are the routine as opposed to the major offices of state, but here ἡ ἐγκύκλιος διοίκησις is the day-to-day administration of the state, and seems to be used to mark the distinction between civilian and military officials (cf. Is. III. *Nic.* 22, Arist. *Pol.* II. 1269 B 35). *A.P.* deals with civilian officials to the end of ch. 60, and then devotes 61 to military officials before ending his treatment of the ἀρχαί in 62.

ἁπάσας ποιοῦσι κληρωτάς: Kaibel, *Stil und Text*, 205, expected κληροῦσιν, to balance χειροτονοῦσιν below, but *A.P.*'s interest in the balance of his sentences is only intermittent (cf. Introduction, p. 41). In ch. 42 *A.P.* wrote of ὁ δῆμος (§§ii–iv); here he reverts to plural verbs with which we must understand οἱ Ἀθηναῖοι. Appointment by lot was used, especially but not only by democracies, to ensure that offices which were thought to require loyalty rather than skill were fairly distributed among those equally eligible rather than awarded to the best or the most popular candidates: cf. on 4. iii. For elected civilian officials other than those mentioned below see 54. iii–v with commentary.

πλὴν ταμίου στρατιωτικῶν: The budgeting procedure of the fourth century (cf. 48. ii with commentary) recognised a plurality of spending authorities: the stratiotic fund, τὰ στρατιωτικά, existed certainly by 373 ([D.] XLIX. *Timoth*. 12, 16) and perhaps earlier; its treasurer is first attested in 344/3 (*IG* ii² 1443, 12–13), but there is no reason why he should not be as old as the fund (G. L. Cawkwell, *Mnem.*⁴ xv 1962, 377–83, cf. Rhodes, *A.B.*, 105 with n. 3, against G. Glotz, *RH* clxx 1932, 385–97). If that is right, this is the earliest of the fourth-century elected treasurers (cf. next note): I should guess that the post was made elective because it was thought of as quasi-military (cf. the καταλογεῖς of the cavalry, 49. ii with commentary). The involvement of this treasurer in the work of the old financial boards supervised by the boule (together with οἱ ἐπὶ τὸ θεωρικόν: 47. ii with commentary) and in the preparation of prizes for the Panathenaea (49. iii with commentary) I suspect to be a result of the moves in the 330's to reduce the power of the controllers of the theoric fund.

καὶ τῶν ἐπὶ τὸ θεωρικὸν: The ostensible purpose of the theoric fund was to pay grants to citizens at the time of major festivals, to cover the cost of their theatre tickets (Harp. θεωρικά, cf. Suid. [Θ 219] θεωρικά, quoting Philochorus [328 F 33] and Philinus [fr. 3 Sauppe]; D. I. Ol. i, hyp. 4, cf. Phot. θεωρικά, θεωρικὸν καὶ θεωρική, Suid. [Θ 218] θεωρικά, [Θ 220] θεωρικὸν καὶ θεωρική, E.M. [448. 47] θεωρικὸν ἀργύριον). Theoric distributions are ascribed to Pericles in very general passages in Pl. Per. 9. i, 34. ii (cf. schol. D. I. Ol. i. 1, A. III. Ctes. 24: accepted by Busolt & Swoboda, G.S., ii. 899, Jacoby, Supp. i. 318–20, A. W. Pickard-Cambridge rev. J. P. A. Gould & D. M. Lewis, *The Dramatic Festivals of Athens*, 266–8), but there is no contemporary evidence to support a fifth-century date. The institution is ascribed to Agyrrhius (who at the beginning of the fourth century instituted payment for attending the assembly: 41. iii with commentary) by Harp. θεωρικά, and other texts claim that ἐπὶ Διοφάντου τὸ θεωρικὸν ἐγένετο δραχμή (Hes. [Δ 2351], Suid. [Δ 1491], δραχμὴ χαλαζῶσα, Zenob. III. 27: a Diophantus, P.A. 4417, was archon in 395/4): this is accepted by J. J. Buchanan, *Theorika*, 29–34, 48–60, and (as evidence of an adjustment) by those who believe the attribution to Pericles, but again there is a striking lack of contemporary confirmation; Aristophanes and others are suspiciously silent on the theoric fund both in the late fifth century and in the 390's. I therefore prefer the third explanation that has been canvassed, that Diophantus is Δ. Σφήττιος (P.A. 4438), an associate of Eubulus in the 350's and 340's, and that the institution was created by these men, probably soon after 355: the references to Pericles will be a careless extension of the fact that he instituted the first state payments to civilians (27. iii–iv with commentary), and Harpocration will have confused theoric grants with assembly pay (cf. Just. VI. 9. i–v, schol. A. III. Ctes. 24, with J. van Ooteghem, *LEC* i 1932, 388–407, G. L. Cawkwell, *JHS* lxxxiii 1963, 55 n. 53).†

It is certainly through Eubulus that the controllers of the theoric fund became reponsible for a great deal more than small payments to the citizens at festivals:

διὰ δὲ τὴν πρὸς Εὔβουλον γενομένην πίστιν ὑμῖν οἱ ἐπὶ τὸ θεωρικὸν κεχειροτονημένοι ἦρχον μέν, πρίν ἢ τὸν Ἡγήμονος νόμον γενέσθαι, τὴν τοῦ ἀντιγραφέως ἀρχήν, ἦρχον δὲ τὴν τῶν ἀποδεκτῶν, καὶ ⟨ἦρχον τὴν?⟩ νεωρίων ἀρχήν, καὶ σκευοθήκην ᾠκοδόμουν, ἦσαν δὲ ὁδοποιοί, καὶ σχεδὸν τὴν ὅλην διοίκησιν εἶχον τῆς πόλεως

(A. III. *Ctes*. 25, which may exaggerate but must have a factual basis). Previously it had been prescribed that when Athens was at war any surplus money in the state's hands was to be allocated to the stratiotic funds, but in 349/8 surpluses were paid to the theoric fund even though Athens was at war (D. I. *Ol. i.* 19–20 with *hyp*. 4–5, III. *Ol. iii.* 10–13, 31, [D.] LIX. *Neaer*. 4–6: on this I am not dissuaded by M. H. Hansen, *GR&BS* xvii 1976, 235–46, but I agree with him that both funds are likely to have received allocations in the μερισμός and that the allocation to one fund could be increased at the expense of the other). There may have been some officials who were supplanted by the controllers of the theoric fund (this is probably true of the ἀντιγραφεύς: cf. p. 601), but I have suggested that these officials became important in two ways: (*a*) their fund contained whatever surplus money there might be in Athens, on which the state would have to depend for any non-routine expenditure; and (*b*) by being involved in the work of other financial boards (47. ii with commentary) they even more than the boule (which was a large body, appointed by lot, in which a man might serve only twice in his life) were able to acquire a comprehensive knowledge of Athens' financial affairs: see Rhodes, *A.B.*, 105–7, 237–40.

In *A.P.* τῶν ἐπὶ τὸ θεωρικόν, after the singular ταμίου στρατιωτικῶν, clearly denotes a board (presumably of ten men, one from each tribe), and nothing is said to suggest that earlier practice was different. In A. III. *Ctes*. 25 οἱ ἐπὶ τὸ θεωρικὸν κεχειροτονημένοι might refer either to a board or to a succession of individual controllers, and I have argued from the appearance of one man ἐπὶ τὸ θεωρικόν in *IG* ii² 223 c, 5–6, of 343/2, that in the time of Eubulus the fund was controlled not by a board but by a single official (*A.B.*, 235). The post was elective, probably by analogy with the treasurership of the stratiotic fund (cf. above); the elective offices in classical Athens were so nearly coextensive with the military that I doubt if 62. iii justifies the conclusion that reelection was forbidden; Lycurgus was hampered by a law μὴ πλείω πέντε ἐτῶν διέπειν τὸν χειροτονηθέντα ἐπὶ τὰ δημόσια χρήματα ([Pl.] *X. Or*. 841 c: cf. below), and Dr D. M. Lewis in an unpublished essay has suggested that originally there was no limit on tenure but Hegemon's law limited the tenure of this and (presumably) comparable offices.

Something must be said about the position held in the 330's and 320's by Lycurgus: for τρεῖς πενταετηρίδας ([Pl.] *X. Or*. 841 B cf.

decree *ap.* 852 B, D.S. XVI. 88. i) he controlled Athenian finance, at first in person and subsequently through his friends ([Pl.] *X. Or.* 841 c). Presumably he was not simply one among the members of the theoric board; the treasurership of the stratiotic fund was probably held by Demades during Lycurgus' first quadrennium (*IG* ii² 1493/4/5 with F. W. Mitchel, *TAPA* xciii 1962, 213–29, esp. 219–25: I assume that Lycurgus' twelve years did not begin as early as 338); but *A.P.*, though writing in the time of Lycurgus, mentions no other office that could fit him. The principal financial officials of Hellenistic Athens were the treasurer of the stratiotic fund and ὁ or οἱ (according to the complexion of the régime) ἐπὶ τῇ διοικήσει: Hyp. fr. 139 Sauppe describes Lycurgus as ταχθείς . . . ἐπὶ τῇ διοικήσει τῶν χρημάτων, and an inscription probably of the Lycurgan period honours Xenocles, appointed [ἐπ]ὶ τῆι διοι[κήσει τῆς π]όλεως (*Hesp.* xxix 3 = *SEG* xix 119, 7–9), while A. III. *Ctes.* 25 says of the theoric officials in the time of Eubulus that they σχεδὸν τὴν ὅλην διοίκησιν εἶχον τῆς πόλεως, and I should guess that Aeschines' brother Aphobetus, elected ἐπὶ τὴν κοινὴν διοίκησιν (A. II. *F.L.* 149), was ἐπὶ τὸ θεωρικόν (cf. Hyp. v. *Dem.*, col. xxviii, with D. M. Lewis *ap.* G. L. Cawkwell, *JHS* lxxxiii 1963, 58 n. 68). Before the discovery of *A.P.* most scholars dated the creation of ὁ ἐπὶ τῇ διοικήσει between 378 and 338 (cf. A. Motzki, *Eubulos von Probalinthos und seine Finanzpolitik*, 18 with n. 2): *A.P.*'s omission of the office was quickly noticed (e.g. J. W. Headlam, *CR* v 1891, 115: cf. next note), and not all have thought that his silence proves that the office did not yet exist (e.g. Motzki, *op. cit.*, 18–48, Rhodes, *A.B.*, 107–10; for the view of V. von Schoeffer that the first version of *A.P.* must have been written *c.* 350 see Introduction, p. 53): if a single title must be found for the position held by Lycurgus it should probably be ὁ ἐπὶ τῇ διοικήσει. The office may perhaps have been created for Lycurgus not by νόμος but by ψήφισμα, and this may help to explain the silence of *A.P.*, whose account was based on the νόμοι (cf. B. Keil, *BPW* xi 1891, 614–15: 'sicher noch nicht als offizielles Amt bestand').

καὶ τοῦ τῶν κρηνῶν ἐπιμελητοῦ: Two inscriptions from the third quarter of the fourth century honour men elected ἐπι[μελεῖσθαι τῶν κρηνῶν] (*IG* ii² 215) or ἐπὶ τὰς κρήνας (*IG* ii² 338); κρηνῶν ἐπιμεληταί are found in Plat. *Legg* VI. 758 E 5–6, Arist. *Pol.* VI. 1321 B 26, among the officials needed by a city; various titles are found in Hes. (*K* 4066) κρηνάγγη (κρηναρχίη Latte), (*K* 4072) κρηνοφύλαξ, Phot. κρηνοφύλαξ, Poll. VIII. 113. The man honoured in *IG* ii² 338 had built a new fountain-house by the sanctuary of Ammon and had repaired that in the sanctuary of Amphiaraus; according to Pl. *Them.* 31. i Themistocles had been ὑδάτων ἐπιστάτης, catching men who diverted the water for their own use: but neither of those duties makes it clear why this should have been singled out as an elective office. We should not, however, follow J. W. Headlam, *Election by Lot at Athens*, 186–7, and Herwerden & Leeuwen in emending to κοινῶν and seeing a reference to ὁ ἐπὶ τῇ διοικήσει: cf. last paragraph of previous note.

ἄρχουσιν ἐκ Παναθηναίων εἰς Παναθήναια: Early commentators supposed this to mean that these officials held office for a quadrennium, from Great Panathenaea to Great Panathenaea. W. S. Ferguson argued that they served for a single year and that the phrase defines their year of office as the Panathenaic, beginning on 28 Hecatombaeon (i), rather than the archontic (*Hellenistic Athens*, 474–5); the older interpretation has been championed by F. W. Mitchel, *TAPA* xciii 1962, 220–1, cf. J. A. Davison, *JHS* lxxviii 1958, 23, 31–3 = *From Archilochus to Pindar*, 28–9, 43–7. There are contexts in which the phrase seems to denote the quadrennium from Great Panathenaea to Great Panathenaea (e.g. *IG* i² 232, 1–2, M&L 72, 1–2, where a quadrennium is specified), but it is hard to maintain that Παναθήναια without qualification always refers to the major festival (especially in M&L 58 A, 24–9, 77, 67); epigraphic references to the treasurer of the stratiotic fund and the κρηνῶν ἐπιμελητής make it likelier that they served for one year than for four, and in the absence of decisive evidence Ferguson's interpretation should be accepted (cf. Rhodes, *A.B.*, 236–7). By 305 the Panathenaic year had been abandoned for the treasurer of the stratiotic fund (*IG* ii² 1492, 118–24 with 124–38). The boule's year of office had by the end of the fifth century been made conterminous with the archontic year (cf. pp. 406–7, 519), and for most officials that was presumably their year of office (for the generals see p. 537); but there were officials other than those mentioned here who served for the Panathenaic year (cf. Rhodes, *A.B.*, 236–7).†

These civilian elective officials receive only incidental mention in the chapters that follow. Some have supposed that a section in which they were treated at length has been lost before ch. 61, but more probably *A.P.* omitted to deal directly with them (cf. p. 677). [χ]ειροτονοῦσι δὲ καὶ τὰς πρὸς τὸν πόλεμον ἁπάσας: Cf. ch. 61 with commentary and, on their election, 44. iv with commentary. A. III. *Ctes.* 13 writes of sortitive ἀρχαί and ἃς ὁ δῆμος χειροτονεῖ ἐν ἀρχαιρεσίαις, στρατηγοὺς καὶ ἱππάρχους καὶ τὰς μετὰ τούτων ἀρχάς.

43. ii. βουλὴ δὲ κληροῦται φ΄, ν΄ ἀπὸ φυλῆς ἑκάστης: There is no need to follow Blass in inserting ⟨τῆς⟩ φυλῆς: on the variety which *A.P.* allows himself in expressions of this kind see Introduction, pp. 42–3 with n. 213.

The practice of appointing fifty men from each of the ten tribes goes back to Cleisthenes (21. iii with commentary); appointment by lot may have been introduced later, but presumably not later than the 450's, when Athens imposed a sortitive boule on Erythrae (M&L 40, 8–9). In the various tribal changes of later Athens the appointment of fifty bouleutae from each tribe was retained until the reform of Hadrian, when the number was reduced to about forty (cf. Rhodes, *A.B.*, 1, 241, B. D. Meritt & J. S. Traill, *The Athenian Agora*, xv, pp. 21–2). Nothing is said here of the composition of the tribal contingents, but we read in 62. ii that, whereas most appointments used to be allocated to individual demes, now all are made by the tribe as a whole except for the bouleutae and φρουροί, who are still appointed by the demes. In all but a few late instances, inscriptions listing bouleutae group them by tribes and demes: it is clear that at any time between *c.* 400 and *c.* 200 B.C. there were 'normal' quotas for the representation of the individual demes within the tribal contingents, but that there were on occasions either *ad hoc* adjustments or reallocations of one or two seats within tribes; before *c.* 400 there is hardly any evidence, but we may assume that there were quotas, not necessarily the same as the fourth-century quotas; after *c.* 200 the system of regular quotas broke down. The inscriptions are collected by Meritt & Traill, *op. cit.*, and discussed by Traill, *Hesp.* Supp. xiv 1975; see also Rhodes, *A.B.*, 8–12, *Phoen.* xxx 1976, 194–204.†

A.P. says nothing of the reserves, ἐπιλαχόντες, attested occasionally in the late fifth and fourth centuries (e.g. schol. Ar. *Thesm.* 808, citing Plat. Com. frs 166–7 Kock; A. III. *Ctes.* 62 with schol.: cf. Rhodes, *A.B.*, 7–8).

πρυτανεύει: In the earliest texts cited by LSJ πρύτανις and πρυτανεύειν are used of a ruler or chief; in *IG* i² 4, 21–5, of 485/4, there is an official restored as ὁ πρύτανις, who does not look like a member of a tribal prytany; in classical and post-classical Athenian practice the prytany played the same role with regard to the boule as did the boule with regard to the assembly (cf. below).

ἐν μέρει ... καθ' ὅ τι ἂν λάχωσιν: Inscriptions show that it was not known during any except the penultimate prytany of the year which tribe would hold the next prytany (the clearest instance is *IG* ii² 553, 16–17: τοὺς π[ρ]υτάνει[ς οἳ ἂν τυγχάνω]σι πρυτανεύοντες μετὰ τ[ὴ]ν Οἰνη[ΐδα φυλὴν]): there must therefore have been nine separate sortitions in the course of each year to determine the order of prytanies (W. S. Ferguson, *The Athenian Secretaries*, 19–27, cf. Rhodes, *A.B.*, 19–20).

αἱ μὲν πρῶται τέτταρες ... ἄγουσιν τὸ[ν] ἐνιαυτόν: For κατὰ σελήνην ... ἄγουσιν cf. Ar. *Nub.* 626, D.L. I. 59: the clause appears also in the note on πρυτάνεων in schol. Plat. *Legg.* XII. 953 C.

A.P.'s meaning is clear, but this sentence has given rise to much dispute. For most purposes Athens used a year of twelve or thirteen lunar months, each of 29 or 30 days, making c. 354 or c. 384 days in all; if the calendar was to remain as nearly as possible correct by the sun, about three years in eight should have been 'intercalary' years, with the thirteenth month added. Probably an alternation between 'hollow' and 'full' months was normal, but could be modified for a variety of reasons, astronomical, political or other (e.g. B. D. Meritt, *The Athenian Year*, 16–37; regular lunar observation to determine the beginning of the month was postulated by W. K. Pritchett & O. Neugebauer, *Calendars of Athens*, 10–14). Only a very irregular year will have comprised a number of days divisible by ten, and so some prytanies must have been longer than others, 36 or 35 days (as stated by *A.P.*) in a twelve-month year, 39 or 38 days in a thirteen-month year. Pritchett accepts *A.P.*'s statement as an invariable rule, applicable to both ordinary and intercalary years, that the first four prytanies were the longer ones (and an adjustment was made in the last prytany if observation required a year one day shorter or one day longer than the norm: e.g. Pritchett & Neugebauer, *op. cit.*, 36); Meritt believes that the lengths of prytanies did not vary more than necessary, but *A.P.*'s placing of the longer prytanies at the beginning of the year is merely an illustration and was not followed every year (e.g. *op. cit.*, 10–15, 72; the most recent version of his views, *GR&BS* xvii 1976, 147–52). From some time before the middle of the fifth century until 407 (cf. 32. i with commentary: for the concluding date see most recently Meritt, *Mélanges helléniques . . . G. Daux*, 259, Pritchett, *BCH* ci 1977, 28) the boule used a separate solar year of 365 or 366 days (Meritt, *TAPA* xcv 1964, 200: invariably 366 days, Pritchett & Neugebauer, *op. cit.*, 94–7): this again cannot be equally divided into ten prytanies, and Pritchett postulated a rule similar to that stated here, that in this bouleutic year there were six prytanies of 37 days followed by four of 36 (e.g. Pritchett & Neugebauer, *op. cit.*, 94–7). Most of our evidence comes from inscriptions giving equations between calendar dates and prytany dates, many of them fragmentary and capable of being restored in more than one way: there is no text which cannot be made compatible with Pritchett's reliance on and extension of what we read in *A.P.*, while detailed and uncontroversial information for a number of years would be needed to cast doubt on Meritt's more flexible approach. Nevertheless I believe that Pritchett's faith in *A.P.* is unfounded: there are a great many matters on which the second part of *A.P.* does not tell the whole truth; nothing is said here about years of other than 354 days; it is agreed that there must have been errors and irregularities in the application of other calendar rules, and it is most unwise to make this one rule sacrosanct because it happens to be stated by *A.P.* However, I should not rule out the possibility that what *A.P.* states is what the law stated for years of 354 days, but that the law was not always adhered to.

43. iii. οἱ δὲ πρυτανεύοντες αὐτῶν: Sc. τῶν βουλευτῶν.
πρῶτον μὲν συσσιτοῦσιν ἐν τῇ θόλῳ: Cf. D. xix. F.L. 190 (πάντες οἱ πρυτάνεις . . . συνδειπνοῦσιν ἀλλήλοις). The Tholos, a circular building (not particularly appropriate for its purpose), was built on the west side of the Agora, to the south of the βουλευτήριον, in the second quarter of the fifth century (I should guess, after the tribal contingents of bouleutae had been constituted as prytanies by Ephialtes: cf. p. 317): see H. A. Thompson, *Hesp.* Supp. iv 1940, R. E. Wycherley, *The Athenian Agora*, iii, pp. 179–84, Travlos, *Pictorial Dictionary*, 553–61, Thompson & Wycherley, *The Athenian Agora*, xiv. 41–6, Rhodes, *A.B.*, 17–19, 32, *Agora Guide*[3], 54–7, S. G. Miller, *The Prytaneion*, 54–65. The state secretaries dined with the prytanes in the Tholos (D. xix. F.L. 249 with schol., 314; these ἀείσιτοι are appended to some lists of bouleutae); the archons dined together in the θεσμοθετεῖον (schol. Plat. *Phaedr.* 235 D: see 3. v, 62. ii, with commentary); men whom the state wished to honour dined in the πρυτανεῖον (24. iii *fin.* with commentary).

Here we have a clear instance of *A.P.*'s using πρῶτον . . . ἔπειτα . . . with no temporal implications: see on 22. ii.

λαμβάνοντες ἀργύριον παρὰ τῆς πόλεως: Cf. 62. ii with commentary: in the time of *A.P.* each member received 1 obol a day, in addition to the 5 obols which he was paid as a bouleutes.

ἔπειτα συνάγουσιν καὶ τὴν βουλὴν καὶ τὸν δῆμον: The significance of συνάγουσιν is explained in what follows: they announce when and where meetings are to be held and what business is to be transacted. In the fourth century there was a board of three bouleutae from each tribe known as συλλογεῖς τοῦ δήμου, found performing religious duties (Rhodes, *A.B.*, 192–30) and taking an interest in the enforcement of a law on the vetting of silver coins (*Hesp.* xliii 1974, 157–88, lines 13–16, 19–20) but not as yet found convening the δῆμος; in the Hellenistic period the activities for which the prytanes are honoured include taking care of the συλλογὴ τῆς βουλῆς καὶ τοῦ δήμου (first in *Hesp.* xxxviii 1 = *The Athenian Agora*, xv 89, 15–16, of 254/3). Until the early fourth century the prytanes had also presided at meetings (e.g. T. vi. 14, X. *H.* i. vii. 14–15), but that duty then passed to a new board of proedri: cf. 44. ii–iii with commentary.

τὴν μὲν οὖν βουλὴν . . . ἐάν τις ἀφέσιμος ᾖ: οὖν is omitted by the quotation of this passage in Harp. κυρία ἐκκλησία, and was deleted by Kaibel & Wilamowitz and others, but unnecessarily (this is the 'transitional' usage of J. D. Denniston, *The Greek Particles*[2], 470–3). ὁσημέραι (to which Kenyon originally emended) is left uncontracted as ὅσαι ἡμέραι also in Hesp. xliii 1974, 157–88, line 6, Hyp. III. *Ath.* 19; cf. [X.] *A.P.* iii. 4 (ὅσα ἔτη), D. XXIV. *Tim.* 142 (ὅσοι μῆνες). The only parallel to this use of ἀφέσιμος (*sc.* ἡμέρα), 'day of exemption', is Aristid. XXVI. *Sacr. Serm. iv* (i. 530 Dindorf), but the 'future' constitution in 30. vi uses εὑρισκόμενος ἄφεσιν of a man applying for leave of absence, and in D. XXIV. *Tim.* 26 we read ἀφειμένης τῆς βουλῆς; in 44. iii ἀφεῖναι is used of closing a meeting. The days of exemption comprised holidays and days of ill omen (cf. Lucian, *Pseudol.* 12): for the courts they are said to have amounted to about sixty a year (Ar. *Vesp.* 660–3 with schol. 663); J. D. Mikalson, *The Sacred and Civil Calendar of the Athenian Year*, 196–7 with 198, concludes that the boule was released from meetings on annual festival days (numbering about sixty) but not on monthly festival days. Days specifically mentioned as free from meetings are the Plynteria (Pl. *Alc.* 34. i–ii), the Μέση of the Thesmophoria (Ar. *Thesm.* 78–80) and the Cronia (D. XXIV. *Tim.* 26); Ath. IV. 171 E records a fourth-century decree in which the boule votes itself five days' holiday for the Apaturia; and four decrees from the second century reveal that the boule was given a καθέσιμον, or attendance fee, by the ἀγωνοθέτης of the Thesea (*IG* ii² 956, 14, with commentary, 957, 9–10, 958, 12, 959, 11–12). I imagine that before Ephialtes' reform added to the duties of the boule (cf. p. 317) meetings were less frequent: cf. D. W. Bradeen, *TAPA* lxxxvi 1955, 27.†

τὸν δὲ δῆμον τετράκις τῆς πρυτανείας ἑκάστης: One of the four was designated κυρία, and different business was assigned to different meetings among the four: cf. below. We may guess that earlier the κυρία ἐκκλησία was the only regular meeting each prytany, and that the likeliest time for an increase in the number of regular meetings is the half-century following Ephialtes' reform (cf. G. T. Griffith, *Ancient Society and Institutions* ... *V. Ehrenberg*, 124 with 136 n. 43). Many ancient commentators say that there were three assemblies a month, and that all these were called κυρίαι (schol. Ar. *Ach.* 19, A. 1. *Tim.* 60, III. *Ctes.* 24, D. XXIV. *Tim.* 20, Phot. κυρία ἐκκλησία): this yields about the same annual total as four assemblies a prytany, and in later Athens, when at different times there were twelve or thirteen tribes, there may have been three assemblies a prytany; but it is clear from the evidence of inscriptions that this use of κυρία is wrong.

It is normally assumed that there were four regular assemblies each prytany but additional meetings (σύγκλητοι in some Hellenistic inscriptions, e.g. *IG* ii² 945, 5) could be summoned if necessary. M. H. Hansen, *GR&BS* xviii 1977, 43–70, accepts that before *c.* 355 the frequent trial of εἰσαγγελίαι by the assembly is incompatible with a limit to the number of meetings; but he argues from D. XIX. *F.L.* 122–3, A. II. *F.L.* 72 and the events of 347/6 that between *c.* 355

and 307/6 there were only four meetings a prytany and σύγκλητος denoted not an additional meeting but one not summoned at five days' notice in the normal way; in *GR&BS* xx 1979, 149–56, he argues that in the Hellenistic period, when there were three regular meetings a prytany, an ἐκκλησία σύγκλητος was again not an extra meeting but one summoned at short notice. I am not persuaded.†

καὶ ὅσα δεῖ χρηματίζειν ... ἐν ἑκάστῃ τῇ ἡμέρᾳ: That is, the prytany performs a probouleutic function with regard to the whole boule: cf. M&L 46, 31–41, 69, 26–31, D. xviii. *Cor.* 169–70.

καὶ ὅπου καθίζειν: The boule's permanent headquarters was the βουλευτήριον, on the west side of the Agora: the Old Bouleuterium, replacing buildings which may have been used by Solon's boule, has usually been dated c. 500, but on account of the reused material in it Prof. H. A. Thompson now prefers a date in the second quarter of the fifth century; a New Bouleuterium was built to the west of the Old c. 400. See Thompson, *Hesp.* vi 1937, 115–224, R. E. Wycherley, *The Athenian Agora*, iii, pp. 128–37, Travlos, *Pictorial Dictionary*, 191–5, Thompson & Wycherley, *The Athenian Agora*, xiv. 25–38, Rhodes, *A.B.*, 30–5, *Agora Guide*³, 63–7; Thompson's revised date for the Old Bouleuterium was announced in a lecture given to the Archaeological Institute of America in Washington, D.C., 20 October 1978. Meetings of the boule in many other places are attested, especially to give attention to business which could be transacted only in a particular place (such as the transfer of sacred treasures, on the Acropolis: 47. i, M&L 58 A, 18–21): see Rhodes, *A.B.*, 35–6.‡

προγράφουσι: προγράφειν is a technical term for publicly announcing things that are to happen: cf. Ar. *Av.* 448–50 (τοὺς ὁπλίτας ... σκοπεῖν δ' ὅ τι ἂν προγράφωμεν ἐν τοῖς πινακίοις), [D.] xlvii. *Ev. & Mnes.* 42 (τοὺς πρυτάνεις προγράφειν αὐτῷ τὴν κρίσιν), A. ii. *F.L.* 60 (προγράψαι τοὺς πρυτάνεις ἐκκλησίας δύο κατὰ τὸν νόμον), *IG* ii² 120, 9–11 ([ἀ]νειπεῖν δὲ καὶ τὸγ κήρυ[κ]α τῆς βου[λῆ]ς παρ[εῖναι τὰ]ς ἀρχὰς ταύτας εἰς τὴν ἡμέραν ἣν ἂ[ν] πρ[ο]γράψω[σιν οἱ] πρυτάνεις). Cf. also D. xix. *F.L.* 185. The written announcement was a πρόγραμμα (44. ii).

43. iv. προγράφουσι δὲ καὶ τὰς ἐκκλησίας οὗτοι: According to *L.S.* 296 8, Phot. πρόπεμπτα, five days' notice was normally given. The prytanes drew up the πρόγραμμα on the basis of the rules on regular business which follow and of the προβουλεύματα resolved by the boule as a whole (45. iv).

μίαν μὲν κυρίαν: On the use of the term cf. above. In the schedule which follows the most essential regular business is assigned to the κυρία ἐκκλησία; in the time of *A.P.* a higher payment was given for attendance at this than at other meetings. From the middle 330's the terms ἐκκλησία (first in *IG* ii² 330, 49) or ἐκκλησία κυρία (first in

IG ii² 336, 4-5) are sometimes included in the prescripts of decrees. They show that the κυρία ἐκκλησία was not necessarily held early in the prytany: *IG* vii 4253 = *SIG*³ 287, 5-7, records a κυρία ἐκκλησία on the 23rd day of the prytany in 332/1 (no letters missing): *IG* ii² 352 records a κυρία ἐκκλησία on the 32nd of the prytany in 330/29 (restored, but] καὶ τριακοσ[τῆι survives, and [κυρία] need not be doubted). The assembly did not meet either on monthly or on annual festival days, and at some times in the year there will not have been many days when it could meet (cf. Mikalson, *The Sacred and Civil Calendar of the Athenian Year*, 182-204).

A.P.'s list of regular agenda is not complete: each year there was to be an ἐπιχειροτονία τῶν νόμων at an assembly on the eleventh day of the first prytany, and each year the thesmothetae were to search ἐν τῷ δήμῳ for any inconsistencies in the νόμοι (law *ap.* D. XXIV. *Tim.* 20-3, A. III. *Ctes.* 38-9: cf. D. M. MacDowell, *JHS* xcv 1975, 62-74); προβολαί were allowed after certain major festivals, in addition to those mentioned in §v; at a specified assembly the archon allocated pipers to dithyrambic choruses and their choregi (D. XXI. *Mid.* 13); nothing is said at this point of the election of military and other officials (44. iv with commentary). As in the modern state not all business or all important business was regular business: in 339 it seems to have been an extraordinary assembly that authorised Demosthenes to negotiate an alliance with Thebes (D. XVIII. *Cor.* 169-79).

τὰς ἀρχὰς ἐπιχειροτονεῖν εἰ δοκοῦσι καλῶς ἄρχειν: ἐπιχειροτονεῖν commonly means 'vote in approval of' (37. i with commentary); sometimes, as here, it is used specifically of confirming a decision already taken (cf. ἐπιχειροτονία in 55. iv, D. XXIV. *Tim.* 20). Presumably there was a general vote of confidence in the ἀρχαί, preceded by a debate in which objections could be raised to the conduct of particular officials. Harp. καταχειροτονία, derived from Theophrastus' *Νόμοι* (fr. 7 Hager, *JP* vi 1876, 1-27), combines this vote of confidence in the ἀρχαί with συκοφαντῶν προβολαί (§v, below). *A.P.* gives further detail with reference to the generals in 61. ii; see also p. 659. For an occasion when the thesmothetae were deposed in the ἐπιχειροτονία see [D.] LVIII. *Theocr.* 27.

περὶ σίτου: Athens was heavily dependent on imported corn, and the corn supply was therefore a subject of the greatest importance: for the officials appointed to regulate the corn trade see 51. iii-iv with commentary. The corn supply is one of the subjects on which Socrates exposes Glaucon's ignorance in X. *M.* III. vi. 1-13; but it is not explicitly mentioned in the lists of major topics of deliberation in Arist. *Pol.* IV. 1298 A 3-7, *Rhet.* I. 1359 B 21-3 (though in *Rhet.* one topic is περὶ ... τῶν εἰσαγομένων καὶ ἐξαγομένων, discussed in 1360 A 12-17 under the heading περὶ τροφῆς).

περὶ φυλακῆς τῆς χώρας: There is no reason why this should not mean what it says, and presumably it originally did: when regular duties were assigned to the generals one general was designated ἐπὶ τὴν χώραν, ὃς φυλάττει ... (61. i with commentary); φυλακὴ τῆς χώρας is included among the topics on which Socrates examines Glaucon in X. *M*. III. vi. 1–13, and in Arist. *Rhet*. I. 1359 B 21–3 cf. 1360 A 6–11, but not in *Pol*. IV. 1298 A 3–7 (one topic in that list is περὶ πολέμου καὶ εἰρήνης); the list of the boule's concerns in [X.] *A.P*. iii. 2 begins with περὶ τοῦ πολέμου (I believe that this was written during the Archidamian War and refers specifically to that). However, three Athenian decrees from the time of *A.P*. (*IG* ii² 435, 13, 1629 = Tod 200, 270–1, 1631, 401–3), and some later decrees from Athens and elsewhere, are not conspicuously relevant to the defence of the country but contain the clause ταῦτα δ᾿ εἶναι ἅπαντα εἰς φυλακὴν τῆς χώρας *vel simile quid*: clearly by this time εἰς φυλακὴν τῆς χώρας had become a privileged category, into which it was worthwhile to insert a decree; but except that it could be debated at a κυρία ἐκκλησία we do not know what privileges were conferred (*IG* ii² 791 = *Hesp*. xi 56 has a prescript including the formula ἐκκλησία, not ἐκκλησία κυρία). See Rhodes, *A.B*., 231–5.

καὶ τὰς εἰσαγγελίας ... τοὺς βουλομένους ποιεῖσθαι: Harp., Suid. (*EI* 222), εἰσαγγελία distinguishes three technical uses of the word: (*a*) charges of major public offences, for which πρὸς τὴν βουλὴν ἢ τὸν δῆμον ἡ πρώτη κατάστασις γίνεται; (*b*) for maltreatment of parents and wards, for which the εἰσαγγελία is submitted to the archon; (*c*) for misconduct in office by a διαιτητής, for which the εἰσαγγελία is submitted (according to this note) to the δικασταί. For the second category see 56. vi with commentary; for the third see 53. vi with commentary; εἰσαγγελία to the boule for misconduct in office by magistrates (45. ii with commentary) I regard as a fourth category but one which came to influence procedure in the first; the first, εἰσαγγελία for major public offences, is our concern here. For recent discussions of this procedure see Harrison, *L.A*., ii. 50–9, Rhodes, *A.B*., 162–71, M. H. Hansen, *Eisangelia*, Rhodes, *JHS* xcix 1979, 106–14 (on points on which I differ from Hansen).†

A.P. first mentions εἰσαγγελία as a procedure for major public offences in 8. iv: Solon allowed εἰσαγγελία to the Areopagus against τοὺς ἐπὶ τοῦ δήμου συνισταμένους (cf. *ad loc*.: this is probably a later formulation, but there is no reason why *A.P*. should not be substantially correct). In classical Athens εἰσαγγελίαι were heard not by the Areopagus but by the boule, assembly and δικαστήρια: in 462/1 Ephialtes took from the Areopagus powers, at least partly judicial, which gave it ἡ τῆς πολιτείας φυλακή, and I believe this to be the occasion when εἰσαγγελίαι were transferred from the Areopagus to bodies more representative of the δῆμος (cf. 25. ii with commentary).

In the fourth century there was a consolidated νόμος εἰσαγγελτικός which specified the major public offences to which this procedure was appropriate; extracts are quoted by Hyp. IV. *Eux.* 7–8, 29, 39, and may be added to from Theophrastus as quoted by the lexicographers (fr. 6 Hager, *JP* vi 1876, 1–27). The offences fall under three main heads: attempting to overthrow the democracy, treason, and being a ῥήτωρ and taking bribes to speak otherwise than in the interests of Athens; deceiving the people by false promises ([D.] XLIX. *Timoth.* 67: for προβολαί on this charge see §v with commentary) may be added, to the specification of the third offence or as a fourth. The lexicographers claim that εἰσαγγελία was available ἐπὶ τῶν ἀγράφων δημοσίων ἀδικημάτων (Poll. VIII. 51), ἐφ' οἷς μήτε ἀρχὴ καθέστηκε μήτε νόμοι κεῖνται τοῖς ἄρχουσιν καθ' οὓς εἰσάξουσιν (Harp., Suid., *loc. cit.*); according to L.R.C. εἰσαγγελία (= Phil. 328 F 199) this was the view of Caecilius: no instance is preserved of a prosecutor's relying on a clause of this kind, and it may be that the offences specified in the law came to be so generously interpreted that Caecilius was misled, but I am not yet persuaded that this open clause did not exist. As A. III. *Ctes.* 191–2 complains that the γραφὴ παρανόμων is no longer treated with proper seriousness Hyp. IV. *Eux.* 1–3 complains that εἰσαγγελία is now used for trivial offences.

As for the procedure, I believe that after Ephialtes' reform it was stipulated that εἰσαγγελίαι were to be submitted εἰς τὴν βουλὴν καὶ τὸν δῆμον. In accordance with the principle of προβούλευσις (cf. 45. iv) the assembly could not decide any matter that had not first been considered by the boule: under this provision for the presentation of εἰσαγγελίαι at κύριαι ἐκκλησίαι it may have been possible to bring an εἰσαγγελία to the assembly without giving prior notice to the boule (after which the charge would be referred to the boule for further consideration), but I imagine that many εἰσαγγέλλοντες did give prior notice to the boule. The final hearing of a case initiated by εἰσαγγελία took place either in the assembly or in a δικαστήριον (but after 362 no final hearings in the assembly are attested and the assembly may have lost its right to the final hearing: cf. Hansen, *op. cit.*, 51–7): I suspect that Ephialtes' intention was that εἰσαγγελίαι should be heard by the boule and assembly, but that the tendency to regard the δικαστήρια as fully representative of the δῆμος, and the analogy of the procedure for εἰσαγγελίαι against magistrates, led to the increasing use of the δικαστήρια to try εἰσαγγελίαι for major public offences.

καὶ τὰς ἀπογραφὰς τῶν δημευομένων ἀναγιγνώσκειν: Cf. 47. ii, iii, 52. i: when property was confiscated by the state, the poletae made a list of the property on the basis of a report by the man's demarch or of ἀπογραφαί by private individuals, and sold it in the presence of the boule. The purpose of this reading of the list was presumably to enable any one who knew of property wrongly omitted or included to draw attention to it; the reading presumably preceded the judgment in the court of the Eleven (52. i).

καὶ τὰς λήξεις τῶν κλήρων καὶ τῶν ἐπικλήρων [[ἀναγινώσκειν]]: 'And claims to inheritances and heiresses.' The repeated ἀναγινώσκειν, first deleted by A. Gennadios, *CR* v 1891, 274, is absent from the passages in the lexica derived from this. Any claimants to an estate except direct descendants of or men adopted by the deceased had to register their claim with the archon (cf. 56. vi *fin.*): see Lipsius, *A.R.*, 579–85, Harrison, *L.A.*, i. 10–11, 158–62, D. M. MacDowell, *The Law in Classical Athens*, 102–8, and on the law of succession 9. ii, 35. ii, with commentary.

ὅπως μηδένα λάθῃ μηδὲν ἔρημον γενόμενον: 'So that nothing should escape any one and go unclaimed'; LSJ distinguishes from the normal legal sense of ἔρημος, 'abandoned', of actions one party to which does not appear (III. 1), a second, 'unclaimed' (III. 2), found also in Isae. III. *Her. Pyrrh.* 61, Plat. *Legg.* XI. 927 C 2 cf. 925 C 7, Arist. *E.N.* IV. 1125 B 17. Again the object of the exercise is publicity, so that a man with a weak claim to property shall not succeed through the ignorance of a man with a stronger claim. In addition, claims were published on the archon's σανίς (cf. Is. XV. *Antid.* 237); and when the archon's court had decided the claim a herald made a proclamation ([D.] XLIII. *Mac.* 5).

43. v. πρὸς τοῖς εἰρημένοις: *A.P.* is still listing the regular agenda of a κυρία ἐκκλησία, and now mentions business that comes up only once a year.

καὶ περὶ τῆς ὀστρακοφορίας ... ποιεῖν ἢ μή: For the institution and procedure of ostracism see 22. iii with commentary. If the assembly voted to hold an ostracism, it took place in the eighth prytany (Phil 328 F 30 with Jacoby's commentary). There had not in fact been an ostracism since that of Hyperbolus, 417–415 (Pl. *Nic.* 11. viii): presumably the institution was not formally abolished, and the assembly voted each year not to hold an ostracism.

The papyrus' ἐπιχειροτονίαν is confirmed by *L.R.C.* κυρία ἐκκλησία (= Dem. Phal. 228 F 4); Kaibel & Wilamowitz, cf. Kaibel, *Stil und Text*, 206, emended to προχειροτονίαν from *L.R.C.* ὀστρακισμοῦ τρόπος (= Phil. 328 F 30), schol. Ar. *Eq.* 855, but the προ- is appropriate specifically to that context and is not required here; I should rather have expected διαχειροτονίαν as in 49. ii (in inscriptions διαχειροτονεῖν is the verb regularly used of deciding between alternatives, e.g. M&L 65, 5; contrast the use of ἐπιχειροτονίαν in §iv, above).

καὶ συκοφαντῶν προβολὰς ... μέχρι τριῶν ἑκατέρων: There is no obvious reason why these accusations should be admitted once a year, in the sixth prytany: Gilbert, *C.A.S.A.*, 303 n. 3, suggested

526

that in spite of the impression given by *A.P.*'s arrangement of his material these προβολαί could in fact be presented at any κυρία ἐκκλησία, and this may be right. *A.P.* mentions προβολαί against sycophants (cf. Is. xv. *Antid.* 313–14, A. ii. *F.L.* 145; on sycophants see 35. ii with commentary) and for deceiving the people by false promises; προβολαί were also allowed, immediately after the event, for offences connected with certain major festivals (D. xxi. *Mid.* 1–2, 8–11, cf. *L.S.* 288, 18, Poll. viii. 46). προβολή was unusual among the means of initiating judicial proceedings in that it secured a vote of the assembly whose force was purely advisory: if the assembly condemned (καταχειροτονεῖν: e.g. D. xxi. *Mid.* 1–2), the complainant might still decline to proceed further; if it acquitted (ἀποχειροτονεῖν: e.g. D. xxi. *Mid.* 214), the complainant was not forbidden to proceed further: see *L.S., loc. cit., E.M.* (699. 30) προβάλλεσθαι, Poll. *loc. cit.*, and Lipsius, *A.R.*, 211–19, Harrison, *L.A.*, ii. 59–64, MacDowell, *The Law in Classical Athens*, 194–7. The thesmothetae were the εἰσάγουσα ἀρχή both for trials following προβολαί of the kind mentioned by *A.P.* and for trials of charges concerning festivals (59. ii with commentary: contr. Harrison, *op. cit.*, 14, 62, who thought that charges concerning festivals were handled by the basileus).

As with εἰσαγγελίαι, we are not told how the rule of προβούλευσις was applied. Complainants did not have to be Athenian citizens (cf. D. xxi. *Mid.* 175), but a non-citizen would require special permission to address the assembly. *A.P.* reports a limitation to three προβολαί against citizens and three against metics (for the expression cf. μέχρι δυοῖν in Plat. *Legg.* vi. 756 B 4; in most γραφαί non-citizens could not prosecute, and it is surprising that there should have been as many opportunities for accusing metics as citizens [cf. p. 655]): we are not told how the προβολαί to be presented to the assembly were chosen if too many were submitted (cf. on §vi, below), but the fact of the limitation suggests that it was normal to give notice to the boule of intention to make a προβολή; Harrison, *op. cit.*, 59, says that written notice had to be given to the prytanes.

κἄν τ[ι]ς ὑποσχόμενός τι μὴ ποιήσῃ τῷ δήμῳ: This is another charge on which προβολαί might be made at the κυρία ἐκκλησία of the sixth prytany (or perhaps, of any prytany). For the offence of failing to keep a promise as a form of ἀπάτη cf. H. vi. 136 on Miltiades after Marathon, and the law *ap.* D. xx. *Lept.* 100, 135, [D.] xlix. *Timoth.* 67; this charge could be the subject of an εἰσαγγελία.

43. vi. ἑτέραν δὲ: That is, at one of the other regular assemblies in each prytany: cf. μίαν μὲν in §iv.

ταῖς ἱκετηρίαις ... διαλέξεται πρὸς τὸν δῆμον: On ἱκετεία, 'supplication', as a religious and social institution see J. P. A. Gould, *JHS* xciii 1973, 74–103. Here we have a version of the original act which has been tamed and set in a political framework (cf. Gould, *op. cit.*, 101): a petitioner places a suppliant branch (θείς ... ἱκετηρίαν— an olive branch bound with wool: Aesch. *Suppl.* 22 191–2) on the altar, as a sign that he is not claiming a right but asking a favour, and then sets forth his plea (cf. And. I. *Myst.* 110–16, A. I. *Tim.* 104, II. *F.L.* 15, D. XVIII. *Cor.* 107, XXIV. *Tim.* 12, 53, all referring to citizens). A number of decrees of the middle or late fourth century —all, as far as we know, granting requests to non-citizens—contain the formula περὶ ὧν ὁ δεῖνα ἔδοξεν ἐν τῶι δήμωι / τῆι βουλῆι ἔννομα ἱκετεύειν: *IG* ii² 192, 1–2, [211 = Tod 166, 1–3, wildly restored], 218, 7–9, 23–5, 276, 3–5, 336, *b* 14–16, 337 = Tod 189, 33–8, 404, 4, 502, 12–14 (cf. Rhodes, *A.B.*, 72–3, where there are two misprints in the references). As with εἰσαγγελίαι and προβολαί, the rule of προβούλευσις may have been so applied as to permit but not require supplication without prior notice to the boule; and supplications might also be made to the boule (e.g. A. I. *Tim.* 104: if they concerned a matter within the boule's competence they need not be referred to the assembly). As Wilamowitz remarked (*A.u.A.*, ii. 252–3), supplications would not necessarily be made every prytany, and this meeting would then be free for other business.

[ὑπὲρ] ὧν: ὑπέρ was suggested by Leeuwen; περί by Κ. Σ. Κόντος, *Ἀθ.* iv 1892, 114, M. C. Gertz, *NTF*² x 1890–2, 254, and adopted by Kaibel & Wilamowitz. Herwerden & Leeuwen had observed that between ἱκετηρίαν and ὧν there is space for one or two letters, so (as the third scribe is not known to have abbreviated περί: Kenyon, Berlin ed., ix, Sandys², xlv) what is missing must be ὑ(πέρ); Kenyon in his O.C.T., Mathieu & Haussoullier and Oppermann print ὑπέρ unbracketed, but it is not clear from the comments of Kenyon and Oppermann that this is based on a positive decipherment; Dr J. D. Thomas reports that before ὧν there could be just a space or one letter only.

αἱ δὲ δύο: Poll. VIII. 96 divides these, assigning heralds and embassies to the third assembly and sacred and profane business to the fourth: A. Reusch, *De Diebus Contionum Ordinarium apud Athenienses*, 71–9, written before the discovery of *A.P.*, conjectured that *A.P.* had not assigned separate matters to the second, third and fourth assemblies of the prytany; he was wrong about supplication but right about business for the third and fourth assemblies. P. Foucart, *RPh*² xviii 1894, 245, noticed that πρεσβεῖς appeared before two assemblies in the seventh prytany of 368/7 (Tod 131, 1–9, 135, 1–7): these are Athenian πρεσβεῖς reporting at the end of a mission, and it is not clear whether this rubric was intended to cover them as well as πρεσβεῖς of other cities. Some decisions of particular importance involving πρεσβεῖς had two consecutive days assigned to them (e.g.

COMMENTARY ON THE *ATH. POL.* [43. vi

on Corcyra and Corinth in 433, T. I. 44. i; on peace with Philip of Macedon in 346, A. II. *F.L.* 61, 65).

κελεύουσιν οἱ νόμοι: *A.P.*'s normal manner in his second part is to describe what does happen rather than prescribe what ought to happen; but this is the first of a number of passages in which he states that the laws prescribe something (cf. Introduction, p. 34).

τρία μὲν ἱερῶν . . . κήρυξιν καὶ πρεσβείαις . . . ὁσίων: Cf. 30. v with commentary, and A. I. *Tim.* 23, where the same items (but with τῶν ἄλλων for ὁσίων in *A.P.* 30) appear in the same order and with the same mixture of cases; Poll. VIII. 96 assigns heralds and embassies to the third assembly and sacred and profane business to the fourth (cf. above), and before the discovery of *A.P.* editors of Aeschines transposed his text to obtain Pollux' pairs. *A.P.* 30 and Aeschines do not conflate heralds and embassies into a single item: it is possible that *A.P.* or a copyist has been careless here, but D. XIX. *F.L.* 185 (ὅταν ᾖ κήρυξι καὶ πρεσβείαις προγεγραμμένον, in the boule) may be cited in support of the conflation.

Priority was given to sacred business, ἱερά: in inscriptions we read frequently that a man is to have access or a matter is to be raised πρῶτον μετὰ τὰ ἱερά (e.g. *IG* ii² 107 = Tod 131, 15–16, 212 = 167, 55–7); less often that a matter is to be raised ἐν ἱεροῖς (e.g. *IG* ii² 772, 16). On the difference between heralds (κήρυκες) and ambassadors (πρεσβεῖς) see F. E. Adcock & D. J. Mosley, *Diplomacy in Ancient Greece*, 152–5, Y. Garlan, *La Guerre dans l'antiquité*, 27–8, trans. *War in the Ancient World*, 44–5: heralds were regarded as men under divine protection, and were used for the most formal kinds of business.

χρηματίζειν: The word is used both of the raising of a question at a meeting by its presiding officers and of the discussion of a question by a meeting (cf. p. 399): either τοὺς προέδρους (on whom see 44. ii–iii) or τὸν δῆμον might be understood here.

τρία δὲ ὁσίων: Above this a corrector has written συρακοσιων: Kaibel & Wilamowitz[1–2] wondered if this represents an attempt to correct τρία to τέτταρα (cf. Wilamowitz, *A.u.A.*, ii. 254 n. 2, but contr. Kaibel, *Stil und Text*, 206–7). τρία should be accepted; but at the assembly ἐν Διονύσου on 19 Elaphebolion (ix) 332/1 decrees were enacted for at least four honorands (*IG* ii² 345, 346, 347, *Hesp.* viii 6).

χρηματίζουσιν δ' ἐνίοτε καὶ ἄνευ προχειροτονίας: After stating that three items may be dealt with in each category, *A.P.* passes abruptly to the remark that sometimes they transact business without a 'preliminary vote'. Two surviving fourth-century speeches allude to the προχειροτονία: A. I. *Tim.* 23, quoting the laws on procedure in the assembly, says that after the opening religious ceremonies the proedri are required to προχειροτονεῖν . . . περὶ ἱερῶν τῶν πατρίων καὶ κήρυξι καὶ πρεσβείαις καὶ ὁσίων (cf. above), and after that the herald invites members to speak; D. xxiv. *Tim.* 11–12 reports that when Euctemon wished to give information against men in possession of public money he went to the boule, a προβούλευμα was produced, μετὰ ταῦτα γενομένης ἐκκλησίας προὐχειροτόνησεν ὁ δῆμος, and then he stood up and spoke. Harp., Phot., Suid. (Π 2933), προχειροτονία (the last two omitting the final sentence) give an account derived from a lost speech of Lysias (= fr. 181 Sauppe):

> ἔοικεν Ἀθήνησι τοιοῦτό τι γίγνεσθαι, ὁπόταν τῆς βουλῆς προβουλευσάσης εἰσφέρεται εἰς τὸν δῆμον ἡ γνώμη· πρότερον γίνεται χειροτονία ἐν τῇ ἐκκλησίᾳ πότερον δοκεῖ περὶ τῶν προβουλευθέντων σκέψασθαι τὸν δῆμον, ἢ ἀρκεῖ τὸ προβούλευμα. ταῦτα δ' ὑποσημαίνεται ἐν τῷ Λυσίου πρὸς τὴν Μιξιδήμου γραφήν.

A.P.'s abrupt transition can best be explained by the assumption that when more topics in any category were suggested for debate than the law allowed to be debated the assembly decided by προχειροτονία which of these topics it would debate and in what order (cf. Wilamowitz, *A.u.A.*, ii. 254–6, H. Swoboda, *JAW* cxxiv [Supp.] 1905, 255). Wilamowitz rejected the lexicographers' explanation as *unsinnig*; Gilbert, *C.A.S.A.*, 293–4, and Busolt & Swoboda, *G.S.*, ii. 996, accepted it; Lipsius, *LSKP* xvii 1896, 405–12, thinking acceptance without debate incredible, supposed that the προχειροτονία involved a choice between debate and outright rejection (he was mistaken to argue from the debate on whether to hold an ostracism, on which see §v with commentary). B. Keil, *Hermes* xxxiv 1899, 196–202, attempted a different kind of explanation: the compulsory business outlined in §§iv–vi took priority over other business which might be raised at a meeting, and προχειροτονία denotes the prior transaction of that compulsory business. Acceptance of a προβούλευμα without debate, in the lexicographers' explanation, would of course be possible only when the προβούλευμα incorporated a positive proposal, as it did not always do (cf. on 45. iv). Wilamowitz' explanation is attractive, but not certain, since we are not told how the three questions in each of the separate categories were to be selected, and it might have been the responsibility of the boule and the prytanes not to place on the πρόγραμμα of any meeting more questions than were allowed; but προβολαί for sycophancy were likewise limited in number, and if they could be presented at a κυρία ἐκκλησία without prior notice some form of selection at the meeting must have been used when too many were presented. Jones, *A.D.*, 108 with 156 n. 77, did not mention προχειροτονία and supposed that in the democracy as in the 'future' constitution of 411 (30. v: cf. *ad loc.*) questions for debate were picked by lot; but Wilamowitz may well be right to see here a difference between the oligarchs' draft and democratic practice.†

Whatever the method used to pick questions for debate, *A.P.*'s text, which mentions προχειροτονία only to state that sometimes it is not used, is clearly over-condensed. Some have tried to fill the gap: Π. Ν. Παπαγεώργιος, Άθ. iv 1892. 578, inserted προχειροτονία before τρία μὲν; Thalheim suggested προχειροτονεῖν for χρηματίζειν; A. A. Sakellarios, *Untersuchung des Textes der A.Π. des Aristoteles*, 14–15, inserted χρηματίζουσι δ' οἱ πρυτάνεις περὶ τούτων προχειροτονίαν διδόντες after ὁσίων. More probably, however, the compression is *A.P.*'s own work, and there is a further sign of it in χρηματίζουσιν δ' ἐνίοτε where the laws must have specified in what circumstances προχειροτονία was not required (cf. 52. i *fin.*, on ἔνδειξις, and Introduction, p. 35).

προσέρχονται ... τούτοις ἀποδιδόασι: Since the prytanes draw up the agenda for the boule and the boule draws up the agenda for the assembly, all kinds of messages and deputations must first be brought to the prytanes: cf. D. xviii. *Cor*. 169–70, on the receipt in 339 of the news that Philip had occupied Elatea. It appears from D. xix. *F.L.* 185 that in the boule as in the assembly particular meetings were set aside for the reception of heralds and embassies.

44. i. ἔστι δ' ἐπιστάτης τῶν πρυτάνεων ... τὸν αὐτὸν γενέσθαι: In the fifth and early fourth centuries, when the prytanes presided in the boule and assembly, this was the ἐπιστάτης named in the prescripts of decrees (e.g. M & L 31, 3–4, 37, 3, 40, 2, cf. p. 534 and schol. Plat. *Gorg.* 473 E, *s.v.* ἐπιψηφίζειν). Limitation to one day, so that in the course of the year about three quarters of the bouleutae would hold the post, is a special instance of the rule stated in 62. iii, that men might serve twice in the boule but only once in any other civilian office. With the ἐπιστάτης of the proedri the limit is one day in the year (§iii); the different language used here suggests that with the ἐπιστάτης of the prytanes the limit was one day in a man's life (F. Groh, *LF* xxv 1898, 444–5 [in Czech], *Charisteria A. Rzach ... dargebracht*, 56), but, if many men took advantage of the opportunity to serve twice in the boule, we may wonder whether precautions were taken to ensure that enough men were appointed as bouleutae each year who had not held this appointment. Under the Roman Empire a single ἐπιστάτης seems to have served for the whole prytany (P. Graindor, *Athènes de Tibère à Trajan*, 68 n. 2, D. J. Geagan, *Hesp.* Supp. xii 1967, 102–3).‡

τηρεῖ δ' οὗτος τάς τε κλεῖς ... τῇ πόλει: Cf. D. xxii. *Andr., hyp.* ii. 7 (αὐτὸς τὰς κλεῖς τῆς ἀκροπόλεως ἐπιστεύετο καὶ πάντα τὰ χρήματα τῆς πόλεως), in the course of a mixture of good and bad information on the boule. Treasures were kept in various sacred buildings. Three parts of the Parthenon had separate inventories until 386/5: the east porch, πρόνεως (*IG* i² 232–55), the east cella, ἑκατόμπεδος νεώς (*IG* i² 256–75), and the west cella, παρθενών (*IG* i² 276–92). Another religious building used as a treasury was the ὀπισθόδομος, perhaps the rebuilt west end of the old temple of Athena between the Erechtheum and the Parthenon (W. B. Dinsmoor, *AJA*² li 1947, 127–40, cf. R. J. Hopper, *The Acropolis*, 114–15, Travlos, *Pictorial Dictionary*, 143), where in 434/3 the treasury of Athena was already housed and a new, consolidated treasury of the Other Gods was to be housed (M&L 58 A, 15–18, B, 23–5, D. xxiv. *Tim.* 136 with schol., cf. M&L 72, 20, *IG* i² 139, 17, 305, 13, 313, 178, 314, 14, D. xiii. *Synt.* 13): we read in the first text cited that the treasurers of Athena and those of the Other Gods were together to unlock and lock the doors of the ὀπισθόδομος, presumably obtaining the keys from and returning them to the ἐπιστάτης. It is very probable if not certain that *A.P.* includes these sacred funds in 'the city's money': there were also funds directly in the possession of the Athenian state, in the fifth century kept in a central treasury but in the fourth divided between different spending authorities (cf. on 48. i–ii); we have no evidence as to where these funds were kept, but presumably in the fourth century officials who had a building of their own kept their money there. Official records were no doubt kept in various places, but one building in particular came to be used for the purpose: the Old Bouleuterium, left standing after the building of a New Bouleuterium *c.* 400, known as the Μητρῷον from about the middle of the fourth century, and replaced by a new Metroum in the third quarter of the second century. See R. E. Wycherley, *The Athenian Agora*, iii, pp. 150–60, Travlos, *Pictorial Dictionary*, 352–6, H. A. Thompson & R. E. Wycherley, *The Athenian Agora*, xiv. 29–38, Rhodes, *A.B.*, 31–2, *Agora Guide*³, 63–7; and, on the date of the establishment of a central archive, A. L. Boegehold, *AJA*² lxxvi 1972, 23–30, A. Andrewes, *PCPS*² xxii 1976, 24 n. 5.

καὶ τὴν δημοσίαν σφραγῖδα: He is called on to use it in *IG* ii² 204, 39–40 (352/1); but in A.D. 38/9 (?) the public seal is used by the herald of the Areopagus (*IG* iv² (i) 83 = *SIG*³ 796 B, 17–19). X. *Vect.* iv. 21 refers to slaves σεσημασμένα τῷ δημοσίῳ σημάντρῳ. There is a note on the public seal by W. P. Wallace, *Phoen.* iii 1949, 70–3, suggesting that it was introduced shortly before the mid fourth century; but D. M. Lewis, *Phoen.* ix 1955, 32–4, shows that the seal is attested earlier, in 397 (*IG* ii² 1408, 12–13).

καὶ μένειν ἀναγκαῖον ἐν τῇ θόλῳ τοῦτόν ἐστιν: Kaibel & Wilamowitz added τοῦτον ⟨τ'⟩, and Π. Ν. Παπαγεώργιος, Ἀθ. iv 1892, 579, ⟨καὶ⟩ τοῦτον (cf. Kaibel, *Stil und Text*, 207); but the papyrus' text may be retained. Until the institution of the proedri the official duties of this ἐπιστάτης would not allow him to spend the whole twenty-four hours in the Tholos (on which see 43. iii with commentary); but probably the requirement was that he should be in the Tholos when his duties did not take him elsewhere.

καὶ τριττὺν τῶν πρυτάνεων ἣν ἂν οὗτος κελεύῃ: Whatever from its form the word ought to have meant, in Athenian usage τριττύς denoted a third part of a tribe (cf. p. 68). Neither 50 nor 49 is divisible by 3, so the τριττύς τῶν πρυτάνεων cannot have been a mathematical third; many have thought that it comprised the bouleutae of one Cleisthenic trittys, who might be as few as nine or as many as twenty-seven (for the most up-to-date figures see the tables of J. S. Traill, *Hesp.* Supp. xiv 1975). It was first suggested by A. Milchhöfer that published lists of prytanes were arranged by Cleisthenic trittyes (*Sb. Berlin* 1887, iv. 43, elaborated by him, *Abh. Berlin* 1892, 10–11, 12, etc., and by R. Loeper, *AM* xvii 1892, 336–40, etc.); W. E. Thompson has detected in the fourth-century lists of some tribes a regular adaptation of the Cleisthenic division to yield more nearly equal thirds, and plausibly suggests that these modified trittyes are the τριττύες τῶν πρυτάνεων alluded to here, but it cannot be demonstrated that this modification took place in every tribe (*Hist.* xv 1966, 1–10, *Mnem.*[4] xxii 1969, 137–52, cf. Rhodes, *Hist.* xx 1971, 385–404, *A.B.*, 24–5, Traill, *Hesp.* xlvii 1978, 89–109,[39] but contr. C. W. J. Eliot, *Phoen.* xxi 1967, 79–84). S. Dow, *Essays . . . O. J. Brendel*, 72–9, suggests that the ἐπιστάτης was free to choose about a third of the prytanes, which I think less likely. In D. xiv. *Symm.* 22–3 (cited by B. Jordan, *U. Calif. Pub. Cl. Stud.* xiii 1975, 228 n. 60) the argument requires that trittyes should be approximately equal thirds of a tribe, but Demosthenes may have been thinking of Cleisthenic trittyes and have been careless in his argument. *A.P.*'s wording perhaps implies that the ἐπιστάτης was free to decide at any rate which of the three trittyes should remain on duty with him.

44. ii. καὶ ἐπειδὰν συναγάγωσιν . . . ἢ τὸν δῆμον: Cf. 43. iii with commentary.

οὗτος κληροῖ προέδρους ἐννέα . . . πλὴν τῆς πρυτανευούσης: That is, a board of proedri was appointed on each day when there was to be a meeting of the boule or assembly. What *A.P.* says is repeated in many later texts and confirmed by inscriptions (in particular, a number of decrees from the late fourth to the late third century list all the proedri: S. Dow, *Hesp.* xxxii 1963, 335–65); but other late texts give an incorrect account, that the proedri were ten members of the tribe in prytany, given full presidency of the state for seven days (schol. A. III. *Ctes.* 3, 4, D. XXII. *Andr., hyp.* ii. 7, cf. *E.M.* [364. 48] ἐπιστάται), or were a board of ten, one man from each tribe,

---

[39] I doubt Traill's suggestion that what I have called the modified trittyes are in fact the original Cleisthenic trittyes (*op. cit.*, 109).†

among whom the presidency rotated (schol. D. xxii. *Andr.* 5, *s.v.* ἐπήρετο). In later Athens the number of the proedri remained one fewer than the number of the tribes (e.g. eleven in *IG* ii² 502, 5-11). The nomothetae of the fourth century (cf. p. 512) had their own proedri and ἐπιστάτης: see law *ap.* D. xxiv. *Tim.* 71, *IG* ii² 222, 48-52, with Rhodes, *A.B.*, 28, D. M. MacDowell, *JHS* xcv 1975, 63, M. H. Hansen, *C&M* xxxii 1971-80, 103 n. 17 (contr. *ZPE* xxx 1978, 151-7).

καὶ πάλιν ἐκ τούτων ἐπιστάτην ἕνα: Decrees down to 403/2 include in their prescript the formula ὁ δεῖνα ἐπεστάτει, and the man thus designated is a member of the tribe in prytany and must therefore be the ἐπιστάτης of the prytanes (*IG* ii² 1, 42 = Tod 97, 2, *IG* ii² 2, 7, *Hesp.* x 78, 78, of 403/2). From 379/8 decrees include in their prescript either ὁ δεῖνα ἐπεστάτει (not after 343/2) or τῶν προέδρων ἐπεψήφιζεν ὁ δεῖνα, and the man thus designated (even when the older formula is used) is not a member of the tribe in prytany and so must be the ἐπιστάτης of the proedri; and the 'probouleumatic formula' found in many decrees embodies instructions from the boule to the proedri to raise a matter in the assembly (W. K. Pritchett, *CSCA* v 1972, 164-9, 2, 9-11, of 379/8; *IG* ii² 43 = Tod 123, 6, 44 = 124, 6-7, of 378/7). Between 403/2 and 379/8 only the older prescript-formula is found, and there is no case in which we can determine which ἐπιστάτης is named: the institution of the proedri must have occurred during this period; indications that it has not yet occurred may be seen probably in Lys. xiii. *Agor.* 37, of 399, and possibly in Ar. *Eccl.* 86-7, of the late 390's. Some have seen in the creation of a new presiding committee an attempt to reduce the power of the prytanes, but more probably its object was to lessen the burdens of the prytany and to share out the work more fairly among the bouleutae. I doubt if there is much point in the suggestion of J. H. Thiel, *Med. Kon. Ned. Akad.*² xxviii 1965, 431-41 (in Dutch), that an additional purpose of the change was to make bouleutae more attentive to the boule's debates, since under the new system almost any member might find himself called on to preside when a topic debated by the boule went forward to the assembly. Both ἐπιστάται appear in *IG* ii² 204, 30-41. See G. Glotz, *REG* xxxiv 1921, 1-19, S. B. Smith, *CP* xxv 1930, 250-76, D. M. Lewis, *BSA* xlix 1954, 31-4, Rhodes, *A.B.*, 26-7.

καὶ παραδίδωσι τὸ πρόγραμμα αὐτοῖς: Cf. προγράφουσι in 43. iii (with commentary), iv. The word is used also in [D.] xxv. *Aristog. i.* 9; it is restored, to refer to the instructions for the payment of jurors' stipends, in 66. iii.

44. iii. οἱ δὲ: Kaibel & Wilamowitz and others print οἵ, but the article is preferable.

τῆς τ' εὐκοσμίας ἐπιμελοῦνται: Cf. Ar. *Thesm.* 853-4, 920-46, [D.] xxv. *Aristog. i.* 9; also the law inserted into A. i. *Tim.* 35, revised or enacted after the institution of the proedri, laying down rules for conduct at meetings and authorising the proedri to impose fines, A. iii. *Ctes.* 4, on the ἀκοσμία of contemporary Athens; also (not referring to the assembly) Is. vii. *Areop.* 37, Arist. *Pol.* iv. 1299 B 14-20, vi. 1321 B 12-23. For the importance attached to κόσμος in fourth-century Athens cf. 42. ii with commentary, on the κοσμητής of the ephebi.

καὶ ὑπὲρ ὧν δεῖ χρηματίζειν προτιθέασιν: (A corrector has added δεῖ κ(αί) after χρηματίζειν, whence Kaibel & Wilamowitz preferred χρηματίζειν δεῖ.) 'Put forward topics for discussion' (Moore): cf. *IG* iv² (i) 68, 80 (Epidaurus, 302), xii (ii) 526, *a* 21 = Tod 191, 21 (Eresus, end c4), 645, *b* 35-6 (Nesus, end c4), *AΔ* vii-ix 1922-5, *παρ.* 52-4, line 2 (Eresus, end c3); also H. 1. 206. iii, viii. 59, T. i. 139. iii, vi. 14, Is. viii. *Pace*, 15, D. iv. *Phil. i.* 1, A. ii. *F.L.* 65-6.

καὶ τὰς χειροτονίας κρίνουσιν: 'Determine the results of the voting': cf. the 'future' constitution of 411, 30. v, with commentary. The verb has added point if, as M. H. Hansen suggests (*GR&BS* xviii 1977, 123-37), votes were not precisely counted when taken by show of hands. I believe he is right; but contr. A. L. Boegehold, *Hesp.* xxxii 1963, 372-4, E. S. Staveley, *Greek and Roman Voting and Elections*, 81-7, esp. 86 (suggesting that at any rate when there was not an obvious majority a count was taken).

καὶ τοῦ [[τ']] ἀφεῖναι κύριοί εἰσιν: The meaning is presumably not 'cancel' (cf. ἀφέσιμος, 43. iii with commentary) but 'close' the meeting, equivalent to λῦσαι: in Ar. *Ach.* 169-73, cf. *Eq.* 674, before the institution of the proedri, we read οἱ ... πρυτάνεις λύουσι τὴν ἐκκλησίαν; τὰ δικαστήρι' ἀφεῖναι is found in *Vesp.* 595.

καὶ ἐπιστατῆσαι ... τῆς πρυτανείας ἑκάστης: Cf. §i with commentary, on the ἐπιστάτης of the prytanes. If proedri were needed on three hundred days in the year, a man could expect to serve as πρόεδρος five or six times, and three fifths of the bouleutae would be called on to serve as ἐπιστάτης of the proedri; in the course of the year some men would have to spend one day as ἐπιστάτης of the proedri and also one as ἐπιστάτης of the prytanes.

44. iv. ποιοῦσι δὲ καὶ [[δεκ]] ἀρχαιρεσίας: For the election of military officers cf. 43. i, 61, with commentary; also X. *M.* iii. iv. 1, D. xxiii. *Arist.* 171, A. iii. *Ctes.* 13, Pl. *Phoc.* 8. i-ii; we are not told whether the civilian officials mentioned with them in 43. i were elected on the same occasion. This section is oddly placed: we should expect to find it in the latter part of 43, where the regular business of the assembly is set out.

καθ' ὅ τι ἂν τῷ δήμῳ δοκῇ: 'In whatever way the people see fit'

(Fritz & Kapp). The law will have specified that ten generals should be elected ἐξ ἁπάντων Ἀθηναίων and five of them assigned to particular posts (61. i), that one taxiarch and one phylarch should be elected from each tribe (61. iii, v), and so on; it may have specified a minimum age and other qualifications (cf. pp. 510–11). *A.P.*'s statement should mean that the assembly had some discretion as to the actual procedure of election, which could be exercised by acceptance, modification or rejection of the προβούλευμα (cf. below). Procedure has most often been discussed with reference to the election of the ten generals on a modified tribal basis in the second half of the fifth century (cf. pp. 265–6). Wade-Gery saw in this clause a reference to the modification of the tribal basis and restored a similar clause in *IG* i² 114, 43–4 (his 42–3: *CQ* xxiv 1930, 38, 117–18, *BSA* xxxiii 1932/3, 121–2), and C. W. Fornara sees a reference to the assignment of particular posts to particular generals (*Hist.* Einz. xvi 1971, 18 n. 23), but we need an interpretation applicable to the other officers as well as to the generals. M. Piérart suggests that the reference is to the assembly's freedom to receive nominations at the meeting and to choose between candidates thus nominated, rather than having to vote on a list presented to it (*BCH* xcviii 1974, 140), but this is perhaps to make too little of the clause.

ποιοῦσι δ'... εὐσημία γένηται: 'They are elected by the (*sc.* first) prytany after the sixth in whose term of office there are good omens' (cf. B. D. Meritt, *Klio* lii 1970, 277–8): '... there are signs of fair weather', preferred by Sandys, would not be more appropriate to electoral than to other assemblies; for an allegation that thunder, lightning and an eclipse did not prevent the election of Cleon see Ar. *Nub.* 579–87. εὐσημία is cited by LSJ from this passage, Hippocr. *Epid.* VI. ii. 17 and a papyrus of the sixth century A.D.; εὔσημος is found in tragedy and later, usually with the meaning 'clear', 'distinct', but notice Eur. *I.A.* 252 (εὐσημόν γε φάσμα ναυβάταις); εὐσήμως is found in Arist. *Meteor.* II. 363 A 27 ('distinctly'). Other business has been assigned to a particular occasion in the prytany, or in the year; but great importance was attached to obtaining good omens before embarking on any military venture (cf. Y. Garlan, *La Guerre dans l'antiquité*, 25–6, trans. *War in the Ancient World*, 42–3, W. K. Pritchett, *U. Calif. Pub. Cl. Stud.* vii 1971 = *The Greek State at War*, i, 109–26), and it is perhaps for that reason that the election of military officers was made subject to good omens in this way. *A.P.* does not make it clear whether the elections were placed on the agenda of one of the regular assemblies or had a separate assembly devoted to them. Meritt dated to 188/7 three decrees which include in their prescript the formula ἐκκλησία ἀρχαιρεσίαι κατὰ τὴν μαντείαν τοῦ θεοῦ (*IG* ii² 892, 954, 955, dated 29 Munichion [x] and 29th day of tenth prytany, equivalent to the middle of the ninth prytany in the time of the ten tribes: Meritt, *op. cit.*, 278–80), and suggested that the business additional to the elections included making Pausanias an Athenian citizen so that he could be elected general (*op. cit.*, 282). That year is certain for *IG* ii² 892; but S. V. Tracy joins *IG* ii² 954, fr. *a*, and *SEG* xxv 124 to obtain for that text a prescript with the same date in the year but requiring an archon with a shorter name than that of 188/7 (*Hesp.* xli 1972, 46–9). At any rate these texts show that in the second century other business could be transacted at electoral assemblies. D. xxii. *Andr.*, *hyp.* ii. 6, wrongly places the ἀρχαιρεσίαι in the last four days of the year.

The tragedian Sophocles was general in 441/0 (*Andr.* 324 F 38), and it is alleged that he obtained τῆς ἐν Σάμῳ στρατηγίας as a result of his success with *Antigone* (Soph. *Ant.*, *hyp.* i). In the second half of the fifth century the archontic and bouleutic years were not conterminous (cf. pp. 406–7, 519); the first day when the assembly could meet after the Dionysia was 18 Elaphebolion (ix) (J. D. Mikalson, *The Sacred and Civil Calendar of the Athenian Year*, 137), about the 254th day of a twelve-month year or the 284th day of a thirteen-month year. If in fact the archontic and bouleutic years had in that instance begun together the 254th day would have occurred about the end of the seventh prytany or the 284th late in the eighth; but the years need not have begun together and the rule stated by *A.P.* need not then have been in force. No conclusion about the timing of elections in the fifth century can be drawn from T. ii. 65. ii–iv.

These men's year of office was presumably the archontic year, beginning in mid summer (cf. p. 517): the Athenians evidently did not find it intolerably inconvenient that new military commanders should enter office in the middle of the campaigning season. H. B. Mayor, *JHS* lix 1939, 45–64, supposed that it must have been intolerable and that generals took office as soon as they were elected, but he was answered by Pritchett, *AJP* lxi 1940, 469–74. Wade-Gery, *CQ* xxvii 1933, 28 = *Essays*, 153, guessed that in the period of the separate bouleutic year that was the generals' year of office, but this depends not on direct evidence but on his understanding of Cleisthenes' reforms.†

δεῖ δὲ καὶ προβούλευμα γενέσθαι καὶ περὶ τούτων: *A.P.* must again be condensing, since he has not hitherto said anything about προβουλεύματα, the preliminary resolutions of the boule which were required before the assembly could reach a decision on any matter (45. iv with commentary). A προβούλευμα for an election may have taken the form, ἑλέσθαι τὸν δῆμον αὐτίκα μάλα ταξιάρχους δέκα, ἕνα τῆς φυλῆς ἑκάστης, ἐξ Ἀθηναίων οἷς ἔξεστιν.

45. i. ἡ δὲ βουλὴ πρότερον . . . καὶ ἀποκτεῖναι: On this section see especially P. Cloché, *REG* xxxiii 1920, 1–50, Rhodes, *A.B.*, 179–207. It has proved difficult to find a time when the boule had the absolute power to fine, imprison or put to death which is here claimed for it: Wilamowitz, *A.u.A.*, ii. 195–7, believed that it possessed this power until some time between 386 and 352; Cloché thought that the power was lost when the boule had an oath imposed on it (in 501/0: 22. ii with commentary), recovered after the fall of the Thirty, but lost again before 386; C. Mossé, *La Fin de la démocratie athénienne*, 263–4, suggests that the boule's powers were reduced piecemeal from the early fourth century. I can find no instance when the boule exercised such a power over citizens and was clearly entitled to do so, and have therefore suggested that *A.P.* is mistaken and the boule never possessed this absolute power. Before the middle of the fifth century there is no evidence of the boule's discharging judicial functions, and I suspect that it first acquired judicial powers (apart from the δοκιμασία and discipline of its own members) as a result of Ephialtes' attack on the Areopagus (25. i–ii with commentary), and that these powers were limited from the start (cf. pp. 616–17, on the δοκιμασία of the archons). Cloché and others have supposed that when the oath was imposed on it the boule swore not to do things which previously it had been allowed to do: although I do not accept this argument, it may have appealed to fourth-century Athenians as well as to modern scholars, and the anecdote of Eumelides and Lysimachus may have been invented or misapplied to illustrate a fictitious reduction in the power of the boule.

This is the first of many passages in the second part of *A.P.* which contrast earlier with current practice (cf. Introduction, pp. 34–5), but the anecdote is unique in the second part. The present state of the law is reported (incompletely: cf. below) after νόμον ἔθετο, with the infinitive used as in the texts of laws and decrees, in contrast to *A.P.*'s normal practice of stating what is done, in the indicative; but what precedes cannot have been found in the laws.

καὶ Λυσίμαχον: Kaibel & Wilamowitz supposed that there is a lacuna before this sentence (cf. Kaibel, *Stil und Text*, 207–8); but this awkward transition could be the work of *A.P.* Lysimachus is a common name in Athens, and we cannot tell who is intended here.

ὡς τὸν δήμιον: For ὁ δήμιος (*sc.* δοῦλος) as the public executioner, acting under the orders of the Eleven (52. i with commentary) cf. Lys. XIII. *Agor.* 56 (emended by Schott), Ar. *Eccl.* 81, A. II. *F.L.* 126 (some MSS).

καθήμενον ἤδη μέλλοντα ἀποθνῄσκειν: Attempts to improve on this phrase are unnecessary (cf. Kaibel, *Stil und Text*, 208). Lysimachus was to be killed by ἀποτυμπανισμός: cf. below. For the execution of the death sentence see Gilbert, *C.A.S.A.*, 414, Lipsius, *A.R.*, 76–7, Bonner & Smith, *Administration of Justice*, ii. 276–87; the administration of the hemlock to Socrates is recounted in Plat. *Phaed.* 116 A 2–end (where the man who brings the hemlock is ὁ τῶν ἕνδεκα ὑπηρέτης: 116 B 8); in Pl. *Phoc.* 35–6 ὑπηρέται administer torture, ὁ δημόσιος the hemlock. Sitting is not the most obvious posture for a man about to be put to death by ἀποτυμπανισμός: L. Gernet wondered whether to emend to καθη⟨λω⟩μένον, but decided to accept A.P.'s text (*AC* v 1936, 333–4, cf. *REG* xxxvii 1924, 267 n. 1 = *Anthropologie de la Grèce antique*, 295–6, cf. 307 n. 23).

Εὐμηλίδης ὁ Ἀλωπεκῆθεν: The detail of the demotic suggests that a known person is intended, even if the story has been invented or misapplied. Eumelides is not an uncommon name in Athens, but this passage is our only reference to a Eumelides of Alopece.

οὐ φάσκων ... ἀποθνῄσκειν: Even if the story is true, it is unlikely that Eumelides maintained that no citizen should be put to death unless sentenced by a δικαστήριον: murderers could be condemned to death by the Areopagus (57. iii with commentary); men prosecuted in an εἰσαγγελία, by the assembly (43. iv with commentary, cf. D. xx. *Lept.* 100, 135, with [D.] XLIX. *Timoth.* 67); κακοῦργοι who did not deny their guilt, by the Eleven (52. i with commentary); adulterers caught in the act could be killed by the husband whom they wronged (57. iii with commentary, Lys. I. *Caed. Erat.* 25–31). Eumelides is claiming not that only a δικαστήριον should sentence to death but that the boule should not sentence to death.

κρίσεως ἐν δικαστηρίῳ γενομένης: It is not clear what mechanism will have been invoked after Eumelides had forcibly prevented Lysimachus' execution, but presumably the procedure will have been similar to that used in the fifth and fourth centuries when the boule wanted a penalty beyond its competence (cf. below): the hearing in court will have been a fresh trial, and either the original prosecutor will have prosecuted again or someone will have prosecuted on behalf of the boule. δικαστηρίῳ without the article recurs in 46. ii, 55. ii (twice): no insertion is needed.

ἐπωνυμίαν ἔσχεν ὁ ἀπὸ τοῦ τυπάνου: ἐπωνυμία is the regular word for a derived name. ὁ ἀπὸ τοῦ τυπάνου is 'the man who came back from the garrotte', the man who escaped execution by the brutal method known as ἀποτυμπανισμός. Modern interpretations of this are based on findings of A. Δ. Κεραμοπούλλος, Ὁ Ἀποτυμπανισμός (attacked by A. Σ. Ἀρβανιτοπούλος, Μέθοδος πρὸς ἔρευναν τοῦ Ἀττικοῦ ποινικοῦ δικαίου, but accepted by Gernet, *REG* xxxvii 1924, 261–93 = *Anthropologie de la Grèce antique*, 302–29, Bonner & Smith, *Administration of Justice*, ii. 279–87): a collection of skeletons found at Phalerum suggests that the victims were fastened to a plank and perhaps slowly strangled by a collar round the neck. According to *L.S.* 438. 12 τύμπανον δέ ἐστι ξύλον ὥσπερ σκύταλον, and so it used to be thought that the victims were clubbed to death (e.g. Lipsius, *A.R.*, 77 n.

101): D. M. MacDowell, *Athenian Homicide Law*, 111-12, suggests that *L.S.* may mean no more than that the τύμπανον was of wood; more probably *L.S.* is simply wrong. For an instance of ἀποτυμπανισμός cf. p. 683.†

ὁ δὲ δῆμος ἀφείλετο ... χρήμασιν ζημιοῦν: As late as the 350's the boule was κυρία to impose fines of up to 500 drachmae ([D.] XLVII. *Ev. & Mnes.* 43, cf. earlier *Hesp.* xliii 1974, 157-88, lines 32-6) and to order precautionary, but as far as we know not penal, imprisonment (D. XXIV. *Tim.* 63; 144, 147-8). *A.P.* implies that all penalties imposed by the boule had to be confirmed by a δικαστήριον: that seems clearly wrong; some have believed that penalties within the boule's competence were subject to appeal (Lipsius, *A.R.*, 196-8, M. H. Hansen, *Eisangelia*, 24-5); but more probably the boule like other authorities had an absolute right to impose fines up to the limit stated but was required to refer a case to a δικαστήριον for penalties beyond this limit (cf. Bonner & Smith, *op. cit.*, ii. 240-3, Rhodes, *A.B.*, 147; on ἐπιβολαί imposed by magistrates Harrison, *L.A.*, ii. 4-7, and 56. vii, 61. ii, also 52. iii, 53. ii, with commentary). Similar problems arise in §§ii, iii, 46. ii.

νόμον ἔθετο: The active is used of legislators (e.g. 4. i, 6. i); the middle is used of the δῆμος or bodies representative of the δῆμος (cf. 31. ii). What follows, though over-simplified (cf. above), is worded as the actual law might have been worded.

ἄν τινος ἀδικεῖν ἡ βουλὴ καταγνῷ: Cf. M&L 46, 38, A. 1. *Tim.* 111; also law *ap.* D. XXIV. *Tim.* 63 (κατάγνωσις).

τὰς καταγνώσεις ... εἰς τὸ δικαστήριον: Cf. 59. iv (εἰσάγουσιν [*sc.* οἱ θεσμοθέται] ... τὰς καταγνώσεις τὰς ἐκ τῆς βουλῆς). ἐπιζημίωσις is not found elsewhere: W. Wyse (*CR* v 1891, 116) and Herwerden proposed ζημιώσεις, but that too is cited only once by LSJ, from Arist. *Pol.* IV. 1300 B 22. In ἐπιζημιοῦν (X. *H.* v. ii. 22) and ἐπιζήμιον (Plat. *Legg.* VI. 784 E 4, VII. 788 B 5) no special shade of meaning seems to be imported by the prefix, and I doubt Wilamowitz' view (*A.u.A.*, ii. 196) that ἐπιζημιώσεις here specifically denotes fines beyond the boule's competence.

καὶ ὅ τι ἂν ... κύριον εἶναι: When a case was referred from the boule to a δικαστήριον the hearing in court took the form of a new trial, with verdict as well as sentence to be decided: the defendant would be prosecuted as if the final hearing were the only hearing.

45. ii. κρίνει δὲ τὰς ἀρχάς ... ὅσαι χρήματα διαχειρίζουσιν: That is, officials accused of misconduct in office, and particularly of misappropriating public money, were tried by the boule. The boule's jurisdiction over officials accompanied its administrative supervision of them (cf. 47. i, 49. v: συνδιοικεῖ δὲ καὶ ταῖς ἄλλαις ἀρχαῖς τὰ πλεῖστα): a committee of the boule examined officials' accounts each prytany (48. iii); the boule was less involved in the financial examination at the end of the year (54. ii), but the εὔθυνοι, who received general complaints against retired officials, were bouleutae (48. iv). A. III. *Ctes*. 14, arguing about what constitutes an accountable ἀρχή, quotes a law referring to πάντας ὅσοι διαχειρίζουσί τι τῶν τῆς πόλεως πλέον ἢ τριάκονθ' ἡμέρας; and it appears that for the purposes of this section ἀρχή covers not only those whom we should regard as 'officials' or 'magistrates' but also private individuals with public duties to perform, such as trierarchs or men who contracted to collect a tax (cf. M. Piérart, *AC* xl 1971, 550–1, Rhodes, *A.B.*, 147, M. H. Hansen, *Eisangelia*, 27). For the suggestion that the boule acquired this oversight of officials through the reform of Ephialtes, see pp. 316–17.

οὐ κυρία ... εἰς τὸ δικαστήριον: As with the conclusion of §i, the question arises whether this statement is accurate (and, if so, whether ἐφέσιμος indicates that a dissatisfied litigant had the right of appeal, as in 53. ii, or that the boule was bound to refer cases to a δικαστήριον irrespective of the wishes of the litigants, as in 55. ii) or the boule had an absolute power to impose penalties within its own competence but was bound to refer cases to a δικαστήριον if it wanted a heavier penalty: I believe the latter alternative to be more likely. Most citations of ἐφέσιμος in LSJ are late, but ἐφέσιμον ... γνῶσιν is found in [D.] VII. *Halon*. 9.

ἔξεστι δὲ καὶ τοῖς ἰδιώταις: The καί, repeated in what is said of ἔφεσις below but ignored in Moore's translation, is important: the trial of an official might arise either from the boule's own work of supervision (cf. 47–8) or from an accusation by a private citizen. The speaker of Ant. VI. *Chor*. made a private accusation of this kind in 420/19 (§35), and uncovered further malpractices as a bouleutes and member of the first prytany of 419/8 (§§49 with 45).

εἰσαγγέλλειν ... μὴ χρῆσθαι τοῖς νόμοις: Cf. Ant. VI. *Chor*. 35 (εἰσήγγειλα εἰς τὴν βουλήν); also lines 32–6 of the law published by R. S. Stroud, *Hesp*. xliii 1974, 157–88, where in line 33 'εἰσαγ[γελλέτω] might seem to be an attractive restoration but spatial considerations seem to favor εἰσαγ[αγέτω αὐτὸ]ν' (p. 182). Although the same word is used, and some offences might fall into either category, εἰσαγγελίαι to the boule on a charge of misconduct in office ought strictly to be distinguished from εἰσαγγελίαι to the boule and δῆμος for major offences against the state (43. iv with commentary; contr. M. H. Hansen, *Eisangelia*, esp. 21–8, who bases his analysis on the body to which the εἰσαγγελία was made rather than the offence which gave rise to the εἰσαγγελία). See also p. 546.†

ἔφεσις δὲ καὶ τούτοις ... ἡ βουλὴ καταγνῷ: This time it is stated that the boule's judgment is subject to ἔφεσις if the boule votes for condemnation, which lends support to the view that we are dealing here not with a right of appeal (which we should expect to be available to the prosecutor as well as the defendant) but with compulsory reference (in cases where the boule wanted a penalty beyond its own competence).

45. iii. δοκιμάζει δὲ καὶ ... βουλεύσοντας: It was standard practice in Athens for officials to be subjected to a vetting process, δοκιμασία, between their appointment and their entry into office: formally the purpose of this was to check their qualifications for the office (cf. the questions asked of the archons, 55. iii), but in practice the officials might find themselves under pressure more generally to justify their career and demonstrate that they were satisfactory citizens (cf. p. 472). In classical Athens most δοκιμασίαι took place in the δικαστήρια (55. ii), but the institution seems to be an ancient one, and in early Athens the δοκιμασίαι of the most important officials may have been conducted by the Areopagus (cf. p. 316); but it may always have been the responsibility of the boule to vet the following year's bouleutae (cf. Rhodes, *A.B.*, 178). Lys. XVI. *Mant.*, XXXI. *Phil.*, were written for the δοκιμασίαι of bouleutae. For other δοκιμασίαι conducted by the boule (in which its decisions were not subject to ἔφεσις) see ch. 49.

καὶ τοὺς ἐννέα ἄρχοντας: Cf. 55. ii–iv with commentary, where the δοκιμασία of the archons is treated in detail. The duplication may be explained on the supposition that the δοκιμασία of the bouleutae was dealt with in the laws about the boule but that of the archons in the laws about the archons, but *A.P.* adds a reference to that of the archons at this point because it was a δοκιμασία conducted by the boule and subject to ἔφεσις.

καὶ πρότερον ... εἰς τὸ δικαστήριον: Cf. 55. ii (καὶ πρότερον μὲν οὐκ ἦρχεν ὅντιν' ἀποδοκιμάσειεν ἡ βουλή, νῦν δ' ἔφεσίς ἐστιν εἰς τὸ δικαστήριον, καὶ τοῦτο κύριόν ἐστι τῆς δοκιμασίας). In these two sentences *A.P.*'s text implies that ἔφεσις took place only when the boule rejected a candidate, but it appears from the whole of the more detailed account in 55. ii–iv that in the case of the archons there was in *A.P.*'s time compulsory reference to a δικαστήριον whether the boule accepted a candidate or rejected him (cf. on 55. ii). But ch. 55 deals only with the δοκιμασία of the archons: it is hard to believe that the cumbersome procedure of a double δοκιμασία was undertaken for five hundred bouleutae each year. Since what links the topics covered in §§i–iii is that in these the boule was ἄκυρος (§iv *init.*: cf. below), we should accept that there was some possibility of ἔφεσις in the δοκιμασία of bouleutae; 55. iv expresses a fear of conspiracy to pass unworthy candidates, but with bouleutae I imagine ἔφεσις is likely to have applied (whether as an optional appeal or as an automatic reference) only in cases where the boule rejected a candidate. Cf. Rhodes, *A.B.*, 178.

A.P. does not state when the change took place. For the δοκιμασία of the archons see on 55. ii; on the bouleutae Kahrstedt, *U.M.A.*, 62, noted that in the constitution imposed on Erythrae in the late 450's the δοκιμασία of bouleutae appears to be held in the boule alone (M&L 40, 8-12: M&L do not restore a continuous text).

νῦν δὲ τούτοις: Kaibel & Wilamowitz inserted ⟨καὶ⟩ τούτοις, comparing §ii, but we cannot be sure that *A.P.* was as consistent as that.

45. iv. τούτων μὲν οὖν ἄκυρός ἐστιν ἡ βουλή: ἄκυρος here is very strictly the opposite of κύριος: in these matters the boule has a right to make a decision, but (in certain circumstances) this decision is not final but may be reversed by a δικαστήριον. With μὲν οὖν ... δὲ ... we might expect a transition to an area in which the boule's right of decision was absolute (cf. J. D. Denniston, *The Greek Particles*², 472); but in fact §iv deals with a phenomenon comparable to ἔφεσις, the boule's submission of προβουλεύματα to provide a basis for debate and final decision in the assembly.

προβουλεύει ... ψηφίσασθαι τῷ δήμῳ: In Pl. *Sol.* 19. i (but not in *A.P.* 8. iv) we read of Solon's boule of four hundred ... οὓς προβουλεύειν ἔταξε τοῦ δήμου καὶ μηδὲν ἐᾶν ἀπροβούλευτον εἰς ἐκκλησίαν εἰσφέρεσθαι. On the principle of προβούλευσις, prior consideration by a small body of a matter on which the final decision was to be taken by a larger body, see A. Andrewes, *Probouleusis*; on the application of this principle in Athens see Rhodes, *A.B.*, 52-81, R. A. de Laix, *Probouleusis at Athens*, 3-139, Rhodes, *JHS* xciv 1974, 232-3 (reviewing de Laix). As far as we can tell the rule was normally observed, in the sense that a decision in the assembly was preceded by a debate in the boule, resulting in the submission of a προβούλευμα, which might either embody a positive recommendation or simply invite the assembly to make up its own mind; in the assembly recommendations of the boule might be accepted unchanged, or accepted with riders, or revised, or rejected in favour of an alternative motion from the floor of the house. Other cities interpreted the same principle more strictly: it will be sufficient here to cite the remark of Arist. *Pol.* II. 1273 A 6-13, that in Carthage the δῆμος is entitled not only to listen to but to κρίνειν the proposals of the kings and γέροντες, and ὁ βουλόμενος may ἀντειπεῖν, but these rights do not exist in Crete and Sparta.

In the fifth century *ad hoc* committees of συγγραφεῖς were appointed to draft some complicated measures, and in M&L 73, 59-61, Lampon has himself appointed to συγγράφειν and the boule required to submit his draft to the assembly; but the συγγραφεῖς who prepared the way for the régime of the Four Hundred in 411 (29. ii with commentary), and the Thirty in 404/3 (34. iii with commentary) discredited the institution of συγγραφεῖς. After 403 we find instead that the boule may be commissioned by the assembly to consider a matter and submit a προβούλευμα to a subsequent meeting (e.g. Tod 154, 6–9). For the application of the principle of προβούλευσις to εἰσαγγελίαι, προβολαί and ἱκετηρίαι see 43. iv–vi with commentary; for the interaction of προβούλευσις and προχειροτονία see 43. vi with commentary. Three occasions are known when the proposer of a motion was prosecuted because his motion was ἀπροβούλευτον: the proposal by Thrasybulus after the restoration of the democracy in 403 to confer citizenship on all who 'joined in the return from the Piraeus' (cf. pp. 474–7); Androtion's proposal to honour the boule in which he served his second term of office (D. xxii. *Andr.* 5–6 cf. *hyp.* i. 2, ii. 9; p. 547 and Rhodes, *A.B.*, 62: Androtion claimed that the question of honouring the boule had by law to be put to the assembly each year, and that a προβούλευμα was unnecessary and was regularly omitted; he was apparently acquitted); and Aristogiton's proposal for the execution or trial of Hierocles, where it is not clear that the charge was justified ([D.] xxv. *Aristog. i, hyp.* 1–2: cf. Rhodes, *A.B.*, 53). Moore, 282, suggests that after Philip's occupation of Elatea in 339 there was no time for the boule to issue a προβούλευμα, but I conclude from D. xviii. *Cor.* 169–70 that the boule did hurriedly agree on an (open) προβούλευμα (cf. Rhodes, *A.B.*, 59, 234; A. iii. *Ctes.* 140–51 does not accuse Demosthenes of breaking this rule).

ὅ τι ἂν μὴ προγράψωσιν οἱ πρυτάνεις: When the boule had resolved on its προβούλευμα it was the duty of the prytanes to include the matter in the agenda (πρόγραμμα) for the assembly: cf. 43. iv with commentary, 44. ii.

κατ' αὐτὰ γὰρ ταῦτα: 'For in this respect (as also in others) . . .': cf. D. xx. *Lept.* 96 (κατ' αὐτὸ τοῦτ' ἔνοχον εἶναι τῇ γραφῇ).

ἔνοχός: Used with γραφῇ also by X. *M.* i. ii. 64, and by D. xx. *Lept.* 96 (cf. above).

ὁ νικήσας: 'The man who carried the motion': in this sense the verb is often used impersonally (e.g. H. vi. 101. ii: ἐνίκα μὴ ἐκλιπεῖν τὴν πόλιν) or with the proposal as subject (e.g. H. v. 36. iv: αὕτη μὲν δὴ οὐκ ἐνίκα ἡ γνώμη): for this usage, with personal subject, cf. H. i. 61. iii, iii. 82. iii, P. *Hib.* i 14 = Lys. fr. vi Gernet & Bizos, 79–81, A. iii. *Ctes.* 63, 68. Here ὁ εἰπών or ὁ γράψας would have been more appropriate, since a γραφὴ παρανόμων could be initiated before the vote was taken (e.g. D. xxiv. *Tim.* 11–14), or probably could in theory be undertaken against the proposer of a motion that had been defeated (though little purpose would be served by this and we know no instance of it); but I am not attracted by the κινήσας of Σ. Ν. Δραγούμης, *Ἀθ.* xviii 1906, 41–4. If more than a year had elapsed from the proposal of the decree (or perhaps, if the year in which the decree was proposed had ended) a γραφή παρανόμων was still possible against the decree but the proposer could no longer be penalised (cf. D. xx. *Lept.* 144 [γραφὴ νόμον μὴ ἐπιτήδειον θεῖναι] with *hyp.* ii. 3: A. III. *Ctes.* 210 was still able to threaten Ctesiphon in 330 for his proposal of 336, probably because he had initiated proceedings within the year).

γραφῇ παρανόμων: Listed (together with the similar γραφὴ νόμον μὴ ἐπιτήδειον θεῖναι) among the lawsuits of the thesmothetae in 59. ii. The γραφὴ παρανόμων, first clearly attested in 415 (but some attribute it to Ephialtes: cf. pp. 315-16), and suspended in 411 and in 404 to facilitate the overthrow of the democracy (cf. 29. iv with commentary, and p. 434), was a prosecution for illegally proposing a ψήφισμα of the boule or δῆμος; by analogy with it the γραφὴ νόμον μὴ ἐπιτήδειον θεῖναι was created after the revision of the νόμοι at the end of the fifth century, for illegally proposing a νόμος; despite the titles, questions both of legality and of expediency could be raised in both suits. As Hyp. IV. *Eux.* 1-3 complains of the use of εἰσαγγελία for trivial offences, A. III. *Ctes.* 191-2 complains that the γραφὴ παρανόμων is no longer treated with proper seriousness. See especially H. J. Wolff, *Sb. Heidelberg* 1970, ii, cf. M. H. Hansen, *GR&BS* xix 1978, 325-9; in *The Sovereignty of the People's Court in Athens* Hansen collects the evidence for instances of these γραφαί and argues that the courts rather than the assembly were the ultimate sovereign body of Athens—but the Athenians regarded both courts and assembly as representative in their own way of the δῆμος, and were probably not conscious of this opposition.†

46. i. ἐπιμελεῖται δὲ καὶ . . . τῶν νεωσοίκων: Cf. [X.] *A.P.* iii. 2, where νεωρίων ἐπιμεληθῆναι is among the responsibilities of the boule. Strictly νεώρια are docks or dockyards (where the boule could meet: M&L 65, 53-4) and νεώσοικοι are ship-sheds, 'in which ships might be built, repaired or laid up in winter' (LSJ *s.vv.*), but the distinction is not always rigidly observed (cf. D. J. Blackman *ap.* J. S. Morrison & R. T. Williams, *Greek Oared Ships, 900-322 B.C.*, 181 n. *, and notice Lys. XII. *Erat.* 99, XIII. *Agor.* 46 with xxx. *Nic.* 22). *A.P.* 24. iii writes of φρουροὶ νεωρίων.

The dockyards and their contents were directly controlled by the ἐπιμεληταὶ τῶν νεωρίων (not mentioned in *A.P.*), best known for the records which they published in the second and third quarters of the fourth century (*IG* ii² 1604-32): this title is not found in the fifth century (the ἐπιμεληταί of *SEG* x 142, 5, 6, are probably not this board), but we do in the fifth century meet the titles [ηοι ἐπιμε]-λόμενοι τὸ νεορίο (*IG* i² 73, 19) and νεωροί (*IG* i² 74 with *SEG* x 41 [but Lewis reads a dual in line 16], *IG* ii² 1 = M&L 94, 30); various titles are found also in fourth-century inscriptions, and similarity of

545

duties suggests that all these are different titles for the same board (B. Jordan, *U. Calif. Pub. Cl. Stud.* xiii 1975, 30–46, accepted with qualifications by D. M. Lewis, *CP* lxxiii 1978, 70–1). Decisions as to what should be done with the ships and equipment in the dockyards were normally taken by the boule, but some decisions, apparently no more fundamental, were taken by the assembly; routine lawsuits concerning naval matters were tried by the δικαστήρια, but some cases came to the boule, and εἰσαγγελίαι could be made to the boule ἐάν τις ἀδικεῖ περὶ τὰ ἐν τοῖς νεωρίοις (*IG* ii² 1631, 398–401; this was probably intended as an instance of μὴ χρῆσθαι τοῖς νόμοις, as in 45. ii, but an offence concerning the dockyards might easily be interpreted as treason, and made the subject of an εἰσαγγελία as in 43. iv). See Rhodes, *A.B.*, 115–21, 153–8, Jordan, *op. cit.*, 21–30, 93–6.

καὶ ποιεῖται καινὰς [[δὲ]]: δέ was first deleted by Kenyon[1], whom most editors follow; but B. Keil, *Anonymus Argentinensis*, 209–10, suggested δ' (four), and W. Kolbe, *AM* xxvi 1907, 398–407, δέκα. D.S. XI. 43. iii credits Themistocles with a target of twenty ships a year after the Persian Wars, and the Anonymus Argentinensis is commonly but insecurely restored with a decision of the boule or an order to the boule to build ten ships a year (P. Strasb. 84, ᵛ10–11: e.g. Wilcken, *Hermes* xlii 1907, 399–400: see Rhodes, *A.B.*, 115–16, Jordan, *op. cit.*, 26–8, with references to earlier discussions): D. XXII. *Andr.*, *hyp.* i. 1 and ii. 8, conspicuously fail to give a figure, and the evidence is not sufficient to justify us in seeing a regular quota of ships here. On the size of the fleet from 387 to 378 see R. K. Sinclair, *Chiron* viii 1978, 49–52. In 357/6 Athens had 283 ships, in 353/2 349, in 330/29 410 and in 325/4 412; but we do not know how many new ships were built and how many old were lost or scrapped, except that quadriremes and quinqueremes were added to the fleet in the 330's and 320's while between 330/29 and 326/5 the number of triremes fell from 392 to 360 (*IG* ii² 1611, 9, 1613, 302, 1627, 266–9, 275–8, 1628, 481–94, 1629, 783–812, and see next note: cf. Kolbe, *op. cit.*, 377–418). D. J. Blackman, *GR&BS* x 1969, 202–16, discusses the evidence for shipbuilding programmes: he is not eager to restore a numeral here, but thinks the use of ὁποτέρας rather than ὁπόσας implies that there was a fixed quota (204 with n. 74).

τριήρεις ἢ τετρήρεις ... χειροτονήσῃ: At the beginning of the sentence and again below *A.P.* refers simply to triremes; here he refers to triremes or quadriremes; he makes no mention of quinqueremes. In the list of 330/29 18 quadriremes appear, in that of 326/5 an uncertain number of quadriremes and still no quinqueremes, and in that of 325/4 50 quadriremes and 2 quinqueremes (*IG* ii² 1627, 275–8, 1628, 495–7, 1629, 808–12; on the last see N. G. Ashton, *GR&BS* xx 1979, 237–42). This is one of the passages from which we must conclude that our text of *A.P.* was completed *c.* 328–325, but the fact that quadriremes are mentioned here but not above suggests that they have been inserted in a text originally written without them (Tovar, *REC* iii 1948, 153–9 cf. Tovar, 27–31, J. J. Keaney, *Hist.* xix 1970, 326–36; cf. Introduction, pp. 51–6).†

καὶ σκεύη ταύταις καὶ νεωσοίκους: νεωσοίκους is to be taken strictly here, even if it includes νεώρια (or νεώρια are to be understood in addition) above. The boule of 335/4 provided 256 ὑποζώματα (braces used to strengthen the hull: *IG* ii² 1627, 49–51, cf. later lists). From 347/6 to 323/2 a special εἰσφορά ... εἰς τὰ δέκα τάλαντα was levied on metics towards the building of the νεώσοικοι needed for Athens' growing fleet and the σκευοθήκη (*IG* ii² 505, 7–17: συγγραφαί for the σκευοθήκη, *IG* ii² 1668); A. III. *Ctes.* 25 refers to the building of the σκευοθήκη as one of the achievements of the controllers of the theoric fund; in 339/8 on account of the war with Philip work on the νεώσοικοι and the σκευοθήκη was suspended (Phil. 328 F 56a); the building programme of Lycurgus in the 330's and 320's is said to have included νεώρια and λιμένας (Hyp. fr. 139 Sauppe), and the decree honouring him claims ἡμίεργα παραλαβὼν τούς τε νεωσοίκους καὶ τὴν σκευοθήκην ... ἐξειργάσατο ([Pl.] *X. Or.* 852 C cf. *IG* ii² 457, *b* 5–8).

χειροτονεῖ δ' ἀρχιτεκτόνας ὁ δῆμος ἐπὶ τὰς ναῦς: In the fourth-century lists ships are commonly identified as τοῦ δεῖνα ἔργον (e.g. *IG* ii² 1612, 100–213); in one list the word ἀρχιτέκτων is used of the man responsible for repairing a ship, as opposed to the original designer (*IG* ii² 1612, 151–213: Jordan, *U. Calif. Pub. Cl. Stud.* xiii 1975, 53, regards the man whose ἔργον the ship is not as the original designer but as ναυπηγός, but see D. M. Lewis, *CP* lxxiii 1978, 72). It is not clear whether the architects had to be reengaged for each year's shipbuilding.

ἂν δὲ μὴ παραδῶσιν ... τὴν δωρεὰν οὐκ ἔστιν αὐτοῖς λαβεῖν: Cf. the remark in 60. iii that the archon may not 'go up to the Areopagus' until he has handed to the treasurers of Athena the olive oil which he is required to collect for the Panathenaea. Androtion proposed that the boule in which he had served his second term of office (possibly 359/8: D. M. Lewis, *BSA* xlix 1954, 43–4, cf. E. Schweigert, *Hesp.* viii 1939, 12–17; more probably 356/5: B. R. I. Sealey, *REG* lxviii 1955, 89–92, G. L. Cawkwell, *C&M* xxiii 1962, 50–5) should be rewarded, although it had not satisfied its shipbuilding requirement, and on this and on other counts he was prosecuted, apparently unsuccessfully, in a γραφὴ παρανόμων (D. XXII. *Andr.* 8–20, cf. *hyp.* i, ii. 8, 10: cf. p. 544). The δωρεά took the form of a gold crown (A. I. *Tim.* 111–12, D. XXII. *Andr.* 36, 38–9: see Rhodes, *A.B.*, 15).

ἐπὶ γὰρ τῆς ὕστερον βουλῆς λαμβάνουσιν: The law had changed between the prosecution of Androtion and the time of *A.P.*: earlier the boule put the proposal of a reward on the assembly's agenda late in its own year of office (αἰτῆσαι, D. XXII. *Andr.* 8); the boule of 343/2 was certainly honoured during its year of office for successful management of the Dionysia, and may also have received its general reward before the end of the year (*IG* ii² 223 B, 5–6, 7–8; A, 1–3). A. III. *Ctes.* 9–12, in 330, claims that in the case of individual honorands there used to be no restriction, but when it was found that votes of thanks were prejudicing the εὔθυναι a law was passed forbidding the honouring of men who were still ὑπεύθυνοι. Provisional honours, to be conferred on a man ἐπειδὰν λόγον καὶ εὐθύνας τῆς ἀρχῆς δῷ, are found in inscriptions from the late 340's to the early 320's, and I have suggested that these provisional honours may have resulted from an enactment after the prosecution of Androtion, and that this loophole in the law was closed in the early 320's (*A.B.* 15–16).

The third scribe ceases work with λαμβάνουσιν, in mid-line, and in the middle of col. xxiv of the papyrus; the fourth begins with ποιεῖται, at the beginning of col. xxv, and writes to the end of col. xxx (63 *fin.*); after that the third scribe resumes. See Introduction, pp. 3–4.

ποιεῖται δὲ τὰς τριήρεις ... τριηροποιούς: Inscriptions of the late fifth century mention ναυπηγοί, the shipwrights who did the work, and τριηροποιοί, a subcommittee of bouleutae who administered the funds and supervised the work (*SEG* x 226, 11 sqq., 131, 8–13, M & L 91, 4–16: cf. Poll. I. 84, Jordan, *U. Calif. Pub. Cl. Stud.* xiii 1975, 46–53). D. XXII. *Andr.* 17–20 refers to a ταμίας τῶν τριηροποιϊκῶν, who absconded with 2½ talents, and alleges that the boule had broken the law by electing him (τριηροποιϊκῶν H. Weil, cf. c4 inscriptions: τριηροποιῶν codd.): on the allegation see Rhodes, *A.B.*, 121–3. A. III. *Ctes.* 30 refers to the building of triremes as a task assigned to the tribes νῦν: the significance of this is not clear; it is disbelieved by W. Kolbe, *Philol.* lviii = ²xii 1899, 525.

46. ii. ἐξετάζει δὲ καὶ τὰ οἰκοδομήματα τὰ δημόσια πάντα: According to the previous section the boule was responsible both for the provision of new ships and equipment and for the safe keeping of those already in existence: here *A.P.* does not make it clear whether the boule is responsible for new buildings, buildings already standing or both. There is no evidence to confirm the boule's responsibility for buildings already standing (apart from those actually used by the boule). In the fifth century the immediate supervision of new buildings was entrusted to boards of ἐπιστάται, probably elected by the δῆμος (attested for the Eleusinian epistatae: *SEG* x 24, 7–13); the financial responsibilities of the epistatae will have brought them under the eye of the boule. In the fourth century elected epistatae of public building projects are clearly attested (*IG* ii² 244, 28–9, cf. A. III *Ctes.* 14), and so too is the involvement of the boule (*IG* ii² 244, 26–7, 36–7, 38–40). See also 49. iii with commentary, on the boule and παραδείγματα.

κἄν τις ἀδικεῖν ... καταγνόντος παραδίδωσι δικαστηρίῳ: We should expect the same kind of procedure as in other areas where the boule had jurisdiction (45. i–iii with commentary), a first hearing in the boule, followed by reference to a δικαστήριον—reference occurring either if a right to appeal was exercised or automatically; if automatically, probably only when the boule wanted a penalty beyond its own competence. One special use of ἀποφαίνειν in the time of *A.P.* was for reports which the Areopagus after holding an enquiry made to the assembly; in the light of these reports the assembly decided whether to prosecute in a δικαστήριον (cf. p. 659). The papyrus reads καταγνοῦσα, which will mean that the boule holds a first hearing and if it finds the accused guilty refers the case to a δικαστήριον; the submission of a report to the assembly will then (unlike the ἀποφάσεις of the Areopagus) be an additional requirement, outside the course of the judicial proceedings. Kaibel & Wilamowitz emended to καταγνόντος (*sc. τοῦ δήμου*), so that the boule holds the first hearing and like the Areopagus reports to the assembly, and the assembly holds a second hearing, and if the assembly finds the accused guilty the boule (not the assembly) refers the case to a δικαστήριον: many editors have been persuaded, but I find this procedurally more difficult than the papyrus' text. See, for the emendation, B. Keil, *AM* xx 1895, 46–7 n. 2, Kenyon, Oxford Translation, Moore; against it P. Foucart, *RPh*² xviii 1894, 247–8, Lipsius, *A.R.*, 197 n. 61, Kahrstedt, *U.M.A.*, 207 n. 2, Fritz & Kapp. In A. 1. *Tim.* 111 we read ἐὰν μὲν ἡ βουλὴ καταγνοῦσα τουτουὶ (not on a charge connected with public buildings) καὶ ἐκφυλλοφορήσασα δικαστηρίῳ παραδῷ ...

47. i. συνδιοικεῖ δὲ καὶ ταῖς ἄλλαις ἀρχαῖς τὰ πλεῖστα: This sentence introduces a subsection which is concluded by συνδιοικεῖ δὲ καὶ ταῖς ἄλλαις ἀρχαῖς τὰ πλεῖσθ', ὡς ἔπος εἰπεῖν, in 49. v. Chs 47–8 are devoted to financial officials, and 49 to δοκιμασίαι conducted by the boule; the concluding sentence would be better placed at the end of 48. Cf. also 45. ii: κρίνει δὲ τὰς ἀρχὰς ἡ βουλὴ τὰς πλείστας, καὶ μάλισθ' ὅσαι χρήματα διαχειρίζουσιν.

οἱ ταμίαι τῆς Ἀθηνᾶς: For the history of the treasurers of Athena and the treasurers of the Other Gods to 385/4 (when an amalgamated board gave way to two separate boards) see p. 391. The boards were amalgamated again about 342–341 or a little earlier (cf. W. S. Ferguson, *Treasurers of Athena*, 104–5, 118; A. M. Woodward, *HSCP* Supp. i 1940, 404–6, suggesting 346): this time the Other

Gods disappear from their title and they are called ταμίαι (τῶν) τῆς θεοῦ (e.g. *IG* ii² 244, 38 [337/6 or earlier], 1458, 0–1, 1493, 2 [334/3], 1484, 1 [307/6], [1477 =] *Hesp.* xl 1971, 448–57, line 3 [304/3]) or simply ταμίαι (e.g. *IG* ii² 1457, 20–2 [I understand from Dr D. M. Lewis that 1458 joins the bottom of 1457], 1462, 16, 1468, 1 [321/0]). Treasurers of Athena are not attested after 299/8 (Ferguson, *op. cit.*, 126, citing *IG* ii² 1264; S. M. Burstein, *ZPE* xxxi 1978, 181–5, reconsidering *IG* ii² 1485, *A*); there is an unpublished third-century text which refers to treasurers of the Other Gods (cf. T. Linders, *Studies in the Treasure Records of Artemis Brauronia*, 74 with n. 57). The goddess, known earlier as Ἀθηναία or occasionally Ἀθηνάα, is by the time of *A.P.* regularly Ἀθηνᾶ (cf. Meisterhans & Schwyzer, *G.a.I.*, 31 with n. 157).

The affairs of the gods were a part of the concerns of the Athenian state: it was by a decree of the assembly, for instance, that the treasurers of the Other Gods were created after the model of the treasurers of Athena in 434/3 (M&L 58 A, 13 sqq.). The treasury of Athena, with or without that of the Other Gods, was the richest treasury in Athens: owing to the diversion into it of money from the Delian League, it contained about 6,000 talents in 431 and earlier (if the orthodox text of Thucydides is sound, of which I am not confident) had contained nearly 10,000 (T. II. 13. iii); during the Peloponnesian War the state borrowed from Athena and from the Other Gods (e.g. M&L 72), and towards the end of the war non-monetary dedications had to be melted down to supply the state's needs (cf. schol. Ar. *Ran.* 720 = Phil. 328 F 141a). In the fourth century the stock of dedications was again built up, but we have only casual references to money in the treasury of Athena (e.g. *IG* ii² 1414, 51: text revised by Woodward, *op. cit.*, 391–2); early in the century the treasurers controlled the fund for casual expenditure by the assembly which was later administered by the treasurer of the δῆμος (cf. W. B. Dinsmoor, *AJA*² xxxvi 1932, 158–9), but otherwise it was only on exceptional occasions that the state now used the treasury of Athena as a bank: see Ferguson, *op. cit.*, 128–40.

εἰσὶ μὲν δέκα: They presumably became a board of ten at or after Cleisthenes' creation of the ten tribes: there were probably eight in the sixth-century inscription, *IG* i² 393.

κλη[ροῦτα]ι δ' εἰς ἐκ τῆς φυλῆς: Restored by M. C. Gertz, *NTF*² x 1890–2, 254; M. H. Chambers, *TAPA* cii 1971, 44, reads κλ[ηρο]ῦται. W. Wyse, *CR* v 1891, 116, suggested ἐξ ⟨ἑκάσ⟩της φυλῆς, and J. B. Bury, *ibid.* 181, ἐκ τῆς φυλῆς ⟨ἑκάστης⟩, but *A.P.* varies his expression and it would be wrong to enforce uniformity (cf. 43. ii with commentary, and Introduction, pp. 42–3).

ἐκ πεντακοσιομεδίμνων ... κύριός ἐστιν): Cf. 8. i with commentary.

The only other cross-reference from the second part of *A.P.* to the first is in 55. i, on the appointment of the archons (cf. Introduction, p. 39).

ἄρχει δ' ὁ λαχὼν κἂν πάνυ πένης ᾖ: This may be for either or both of two reasons: that the assignment of citizens to Solonian classes was now wholly unrealistic and a poor man might be a πεντακοσιομέδιμνος (whereas in the 450's it must have seemed reasonable to admit zeugitae but not thetes to the archonship: 26. ii with commentary), or that the law was only nominally observed, and anyone who wished to be treasurer would claim to be a πεντακοσιομέδιμνος and his claim would not be questioned, so that the office might fall to a poor man who was not in fact a πεντακοσιομέδιμνος (cf. 7. iv *fin.* with commentary). A fragment of Theophrastus (MS Vat. Gr. 2306, в 17–36, published by J. J. Keaney & A. Szegedy-Maszak, *TAPA* cvi 1976, 227–40, and J. H. Oliver, *GR&BS* xviii 1977, 326–9) remarks δοκεῖ γοῦν ὡς ἐπὶ τὸ πᾶν ἀρχαικώτερος ὁ τῶν τιμημάτων νόμος εἶναι διὰ τὸ κωλύειν ἂν πολλάκεις τοὺς ἀληθεινοὺς ἡγεμόνας, and names various Athenians and others who it claims would have been excluded from office if a property qualification had been enforced.

παραλαμβάνου[σι] δὲ ... ἐναντίον τῆς βουλῆς: The statue that was made by Phidias between 447/6 and 438/7 (cf. Phil. 328 F 121, M&L 54): in 431 Pericles included the gold plates on it among the treasures on which Athens could rely for emergency funds (T. II. 13. v), but this gold was not used in the Peloponnesian War, and the statue survived intact until the gold was removed in 296/5 (*P. Oxy.* xvii 2082. iv = *F.G.H.* 257a F 4, 1–16): it is mentioned in some of the fourth-century παραδόσεις (e.g. *IG* ii² 1443, 10–11). Several gold Νῖκαι were dedicated in the second half of the fifth century: all but one were melted down for currency in and after 407/6 (schol. Ar. *Ran.*, 720, cited above); one was replaced in 374/3 (*IG* ii² *Add.* 1424a, 50); in the 330's and 320's Lycurgus was responsible for the making of other new Νῖκαι ([Pl.] *X. Or.* 841 D, 852 B, Paus. I. 29. xvi, cf. *IG* ii² 1493–7: see Ferguson, *Treasurers of Athena*, 89–95, 118 n. 1, 122 n. 2, D. B. Thompson, *Hesp.* xiii 1944, 173–209, H. B. Mattingly, Φόρος ... B. D. Meritt, 94–7, P. Krentz, *Hesp.* xlviii 1979, 61–3), the work being supervised by the boule and the ταμίας τῶν στρατιωτικῶν (49. iii); like the statue of Athena the new Νῖκαι were destroyed in 296/5. τὸν ἄλλον κόσμον will include other items dedicated to the gods, and also the vessels and other equipment needed for religious ceremonies; τὰ χρ[ήματ]α will be money.

The boule met on the Acropolis to witness the transfer (cf. M&L 58 A, 18–21); the παραδόσεις, records of what each successive board received from its predecessors and handed on to its successors, were inscribed on stone (*IG* i² 232–92, ii² 1370–1513).

47. ii] COMMENTARY ON THE *ATH. POL.*

47. ii. οἱ πωληταί: The 'sellers', makers of state contracts of all kinds: they are mentioned among the Solonian magistrates in 7. iii, and are attested epigraphically from the mid fifth century (e.g. M&L 44, 7). Like the treasurers of Athena (§i) they probably became ten in number at or after Cleisthenes' reforms. They had their own office, the πωλητήριον, probably in the south-western part of the Agora ([D.] xxv. *Aristog. i.* 57, Harp., Phot., Suid. [Π 2160], πωληταί καί πωλητήριον: cf. R. E. Wycherley, *The Athenian Agora*, iii, p. 165, H. A. Thompson & R. E. Wycherley, *The Athenian Agora*, xiv. 73, *Agora Guide*[3], 58–9). A dedication by two of the poletae of 324/3 is published in Ἀρχ. Ἐφ. 1973, 175–6 no. 1.

[μ]ισθοῦσι δὲ καὶ τὰ μισθώματα πάντα: 'They let out all lettings': in its most general sense the word μίσθωμα is applicable to all contracts by which an individual agrees to make a payment to the state in return for the right to pursue some activity for a stated period, including the two kinds of contract mentioned in the next clause, for working mines and collecting taxes; and also contracts by which the state agrees to make a payment to men who will do a job of work for it (e.g. the law published in *Hesp.* xliii 1974, 157–88, lines 47–9: ὁ δὲ γραμματε[ὺ]ς [ὁ] τῆς βολῆς παραγγειλάτω μίσθωμα τοῖς πωλ[ηταῖς]· οἱ δὲ πωληταὶ ἐσενεγκόντων ἐς τὴμ βολήν, for the inscription of a stele).

καὶ τὰ μέταλλα πωλοῦσι καὶ τὰ τέλη: πωλεῖν was regularly used in connection with tax-collecting contracts (cf. A. 1. *Tim.* 119, quoted below; also And. 1. *Myst.* 133–4): in this connection it denotes letting, for a fixed period; but later in this same section, when used of confiscated goods, it denotes selling.

μετὰ τοῦ ταμίου τῶν στρατιωτικῶν καὶ τῶν ἐπὶ τὸ θεωρικὸν ᾑρημένων: For these financial officials see 43. i with commentary. I have guessed that one way in which the (originally single) controller of the theoric fund became influential is that he in addition to the boule was allowed to cooperate in the work of the old ten-man financial committees; in the 330's Hegemon's law substituted a board for a single controller, and that law or another allowed the treasurer of the stratiotic fund to share in this work (see *A.B.*, 105–7, 237–40, and cf. on 48. i). In 307/6 ὁ ἐπὶ τῇ διοικήσει is found working with the poletae (*IG* ii[2] 463, 36).

ἐναντίον τῆς [βουλῆς]: Thus A. 1. *Tim.* 119 can state that καθ' ἕκαστον ἐνιαυτὸν ἡ βουλὴ πωλεῖ τὸ πορνικὸν τέλος; Andocides went εἰς τὴν βουλὴν to outbid Agyrrhius for a tax contract (And. 1. *Myst.* 134).

καὶ κυροῦσιν, ὅτῳ ἂν ἡ βουλὴ χειροτονήσῃ: Kenyon[1] read κατακυροῦσιν (making that, not πωλοῦσι, the verb governing τὰ τέλη): Π. Ν. Παπαγεώργιος, Ἀθ. iv 1892, 583–4, suggested [... καὶ] κατακυροῦσιν (cf. P. Foucart, *RPh*[2] xviii 1894, 248–9); κ(αὶ) κυροῦσιν is given as the reading of the papyrus by Wilcken and by Kenyon in his

Berlin ed. (confirmed by Dr J. D. Thomas), but Kaibel & Wilamowitz[3] and Blass[3-4] still preferred καὶ ⟨κατα⟩κυροῦσιν. The compound is unnecessary. If the arrangement of the papyrus' text is sound, this remark applies specifically to mine leases. We should expect the same to be true of all contracts, that the poletae did the detailed work and the boule formally awarded the contract (in most cases, to the highest bidder; but most of the mining concessions seem to have been let at fixed rates [cf. below], and there some other principle must have been used to determine which applicant should have which mine): it has therefore been suggested that καὶ τὰ πραθέντα ... [ι'] ἔτη πεπραμένα should be placed after οἱ θ' ἄρχοντες and that καὶ κυροῦσιν ... χειροτονήσῃ should be understood with what precedes (A. A. Sakellarios, *Untersuchung des Textes der A.Π. des Aristoteles*, 18–19, A. Rehm, *Philol.* lxxxvi = ²xl 1930/1, 118–19, cf. Fritz & Kapp). I am not convinced that the text as we have it is not what *A.P.* wrote: if mining contracts were not awarded to the highest bidder a vote of the boule may for these have been particularly important; there is a particularly strong link with the boule in the case of mine leases, in that these bear a prytany date (*Hesp.* x 1 = xix 1 = *SEG* xii 100, 40) whereas sales of confiscated property bear calendar dates (e.g. *Hesp.* v 10, 11–12, 115–16).

The law published in *Hesp.* xliii 1974 mentions the poletae and the boule for the making of a contract for a stele (cf. above); but from the second half of the fourth century two inscriptions concerning public works refer to the placing of a contract in a δικαστήριον (*IG* ii² 1669, 8, 21, etc., 1678, *aA* 27–8).

τὰ πραθέντα μέταλλα: For recent studies of the Athenian silver mines see R. J. Hopper, *BSA* xlviii 1953, 200–54 (dealing in detail with the fourth century), *G&R*² viii 1961, 138–51, *BSA* lxiii 1968, 293–326; C. Macdonald, *G&R*² viii 1961, 19–21, C. J. K. Cunningham, *G&R* xiv 1967, 145–56 (on the techniques). Fragments of the poletae's records of mine leases, dating from 367/6 to 307/6, are published by M. Crosby, *Hesp.* xix 1950, 189–312, xxvi 1957, 1–23; E. Ardaillon, *Les Mines du Laurion dans l'antiquité*, is still important; there is some useful material in J. Labarbe, *La Loi navale de Thémistocle*. The legal status of the silver mines has been much disputed, but it now seems clear that the state claimed an interest in all mining, and would let out the mining rights, while at least some and perhaps most of the land beneath which the silver was mined remained in private ownership (Hopper, *BSA* xlviii 1953, 205–9, 227–8): the lessee paid in accordance with his contract for the mining rights; he was presumably free to dispose of the silver that he mined, the state's mint being an obvious but not the only purchaser.†

τά τ' ἐργάσιμα ... τὰ συγκεχωρημένα τὰ εἰς [ι'] ἔτη πεπραμένα: The fourth-century leases use three categories, ἐργάσιμα, καινοτομίαι, and ἀνασάξιμα (in some instances παλαιὰ ἀνασάξιμα). ἐργάσιμα are obviously mines which are going concerns when the contract is made; καινοτομίαι, equally obviously, are new cuttings, which may not prove worth developing (it is perhaps a sign of condensation that *A.P.* omits this category); συγκεχωρημένα '(conceded'; συγκεχωσμένα ['heaped up', 'filled in'], suggested by Poland, is improbable) are probably to be identified with ἀνασάξιμα and referred to mines which have been given up by a previous lessee in which a fresh attempt is now to be made (see Kaibel, *Stil und Text*, 210, Hopper, *BSA* xlviii 1953, 201–3). The mine leases point to a mixture of fixed prices and prices reached by auction, the figures perhaps representing sums due each prytany; the standard charge of $\frac{1}{24}$ of the yield (Suid. [*A* 345] ἀγράφου μετάλλου δίκη) was perhaps levied after the time of *A.P.*, in a period of declining activity (Hopper, *op. cit.*, 224–39).

τά τ', due to Kaibel & Wilamowitz[1] and retained in their 3rd ed. after Wilcken's examination of the papyrus, is accepted in Kenyon's Berlin ed. and O.C.T. but as *lectio incerta*; Dr J. D. Thomas judges it possible. The numeral with συγκεχωρημένα is not clear: the first verdict, by Kenyon[3], was that 'it most resembles γ', cf. Wilcken, M. H. Chambers, *TAPA* xcvi 1965, 36–7, and Dr Thomas concurs; but in his Berlin ed. Kenyon hesitated between γ' and ι', and in his O.C.T. he preferred ι' *e re ipsa*. *A.P.* is not likely to have written τά τ'... εἰς τρία ἔτη πεπραμένα καὶ τὰ ... εἰς τρία ἔτη πεπραμένα; the surviving documents suggest that the longer leases were for seven years (cf. Crosby, *Hesp.* xix 1950, 199–200, Hopper, *op. cit.*, 237: we should expect this longer period to apply to καινοτομίαι as well as to συγκεχωρημένα/ἀνασάξιμα); most probably *A.P.* wrote ζ' and a scribe carelessly repeated γ' from the ἐργάσιμα.

καὶ τὰς οὐσίας ... τῶν ἄλλων ἐναν[τίον τῆς] βουλῆς πωλοῦσιν: There were various early guesses; αλλ was read by Blass[1], ἄλλων conjectured by Π. Ν. Παπαγεώργιος (*Ἀθ.* iv 1892, 586) and Kaibel (*Stil und Text*, 210–11) and accepted by Blass[2]; ἐναντίον τῆς was conjectured by Kenyon[1] and confirmed by his reexamination of the papyrus for the Berlin ed.; Wilcken read τῶν ..... ἐπ[ὶ] τῆς; M. H. Chambers (*TAPA* cii 1971, 44) reads αλλ['] εναντ[ι° τ'] βου^λ, and Dr J. D. Thomas finds Chambers' text acceptable with 'a lot of faith' and cannot see Wilcken's ἐπί.

Here πωλοῦσιν means 'sell' (contrast its use above); it is not clear why 'exiles from the Areopagus', who had not waited for the result of their trial for homicide (cf. D. XXIII. Arist. 45, 69) should be distinguished from 'the other men' whose property had been confiscated. The earliest published documents of the poletae are 'the Attic stelae', recording the sales of property of men condemned for involvement in the scandals of 415 (W. K. Pritchett, *Hesp.* xxii

1953, 223–99, xxv 1956, 178–328, D. A. Amyx, xxvii 1958, 163–310, Pritchett, xxx 1961, 23–9; cf. *SEG* xiii 12–22, xix 23–5; excerpts M & L 79): permanent and public records were presumably thought desirable to protect the purchasers' right to what they bought (cf. the reading of the inventories at an ἐκκλησία κυρία: 43. iv with commentary).

κατακυροῦσι δ' οἱ θ' ἄρχοντες: What this amounted to is not clear; perhaps the archon had to confirm that the property was confiscated and that the poletae were authorised to sell it (but it was not an archon's court but the court of the Eleven which passed judgment on ἀπογραφαί: cf. 52. i with commentary). In *Hesp.* v 9, 4–5, 14, ratification by (an archon) καὶ σύμβο(υ)λοι is very doubtfully restored, but in *Hesp.* v 10 (e.g. 13, 117) we meet only a κυρωτὴς παρὰ πρυτάνεων; in *Hesp.* xxix 33 = *SEG* xix 133, 1–2, we find ἐννέ' ἄρχοντε[ς ἔφηναν κυρώσα]ντε[ς ἐ]ν τῆι βουλῆι τοῖς πεντακοσ[ίοις].

τὰ τέλη τὰ εἰς ἐνιαυτ[ὸ]ν πεπραμένα: Such as the πεντηκοστή of And. i. *Myst.* 133–4: Agyrrhius' syndicate bought the right to collect the tax in 402/1, and Andocides' syndicate outbid them in 401/0. In *Hesp.* v 10, 125–7, we read of a man μετασχόντα τέλους μετοικίου ἐπὶ Πυθοδότου ἄρχοντος, but this designation by archontic year appears to be unique.

ἀναγράψαντες εἰς λελευκωμένα γραμματεῖα: Whitened boards, on which the text was written in charcoal, were the normal medium for temporary notices (cf. §iv, 53. iv; 48. iv uses πινάκιον λελευκωμένον; 48. ii uses σανίς; sometimes the noun λεύκωμα is used, as in Lys. ix. *Mil.* 6, D. xxiv. *Tim.* 23). An official record was needed of who had contracted to collect a particular tax, and how much he had contracted to pay (cf. the words that follow); a separate document was produced for each payment that would be required (§iii); once the tax had been collected and the agreed sum had been paid the record was cancelled (48. i) and the transaction was complete: the poletae did not publish permanent records of tax contracts.

[ὅσου]: ὅ[σο]υ was read by Kaibel & Wilamowitz[1-2]. The reading of the papyrus is [ὅσ]α (Wilcken, Kenyon's Berlin ed., M. H. Chambers, *TAPA* xcvi 1965, 37, Dr J. D. Thomas): that was retained by Blass[2-4], but Kaibel's argument (*Stil und Text*, 211–12) that the sense requires ὅσου remains strong (cf. *IG* i² 94, 23–4: τὸν δὲ μισθοσάμενον τὸ τέμενος καὶ ὁπόσο ἂν μισθόσεται ἀντενγραφσάτο ὁ βασιλεύς).

τῇ βουλῇ παραδιδόασιν: Cf. 47. v–48. i.

47. iii. ἀναγράφουσιν δὲ χωρὶς ... [ἐπ]ὶ τῆς ἐνάτης πρυτανείας: We do not know how it was decided whether the sum due on a contract should be paid in ten instalments, or in three, or in a lump sum towards the end of the year: Hopper, *BSA* xlviii 1953, 224–39,

47. iii] COMMENTARY ON THE *ATH. POL.*

argues that the sums mentioned in the fourth-century mine leases are to be regarded as sums due each prytany (cf. above). καταβάλλειν and καταβολή are regularly used of such payments: cf. D. xxiv. *Tim.* 98, [D.] lix. *Neaer.* 27, Hesp. v 10, 117-53 (payments due each prytany). D. xxiv. *Tim.* 98 confirms that much of the state's revenue from τέλη was not received until περὶ λήγοντα τὸν ἐνιαυτὸν (schol. §40 wrongly suggests that all payments on tax contracts were due in the ninth prytany), and complains that Timocrates' law would worsen this situation by allowing certain categories of state debtor to defer payment until the ninth prytany (cf. Rhodes, *A.B.*, 149-51).

ἀναγράφουσι δὲ καὶ . . . οὗτοι πωλ[οῦσιν: This return to the subject of confiscated property (cf. §ii), with the note that follows on how purchasers are to make their payments, suggests that *A.P.* is relying here on clauses in the law which stipulated on what terms payments were to be made and what records were to be made by the poletae. **ἐστὶ] δὲ τῶν μὲν οἰκιῶν . . . ἐν δέκα:** Cf. *SEG* xii 100, 36; also *IG* ii² 1579 + *Hesp.* xv 31 (*SEG* xvi 120) + *Hesp.* xvi 38, and *Hesp.* v 9 (associated by D. M. Lewis, *Ancient Society and Institutions . . . V. Ehrenberg*, 179, with the aftermath of 404-403), with B. D. Meritt, *Hesp.* iv 1935, 570-1.†

47. iv. εἰσφέρει δὲ καὶ ὁ βασιλεὺς τὰς μισθώσεις τῶν τεμενῶν: εἰσφέρει sc. εἰς τὴν βουλήν: cf. §v, and the law quoted on p. 552. *A.P.* does not state that the poletae had to cooperate with the basileus in the leasing of sacred land, but we should expect this to be the case, and it is confirmed by *IG* i² 94, of 418/7, where the poletae are to let the contract for the fencing of the shrine (5-6) and the basileus and the poletae together are to rent out the τέμενος (11-12). *IG* ii² 1672, 242-6, refers to lettings made by ὁ βασιλεὺς καὶ οἱ πάρεδροι καὶ οἱ ἐπιστάται Ἐλευσινόθεν καὶ οἱ ἐπιμεληταὶ τῶν μυστηρίων. A list of property of Athena Πολιάς leased in 343/2 (*IG* ii² 1590) begins without any mention of the officials involved.

καὶ τούτων: The last reference in *A.P.*'s text to a ten-year period is in §iii *fin.*, where purchasers of confiscated land pay in ten annual instalments. This is not a very good parallel to a ten-year lease, and we may wonder if the reference is to a better parallel which preceded this item in the law on which *A.P.*'s account is based but which *A.P.* has omitted.

εἰς ἔτη δέκα, καταβάλλεται δ' ἐπὶ τῆς [θ'] πρυτανείας: The τέμενος which is the subject of *IG* i² 94 was let for twenty years (lines 13, 37-8); payment was to be made in the ninth prytany of the year (15-16). Ten-year leases are found for land on Delos and Rhenea (M&L 62, 16, 21: 430's), for the Νέα in the 330's (*SEG* xviii 13, 9, restored), for τεμένη at the Piraeus in 321/0 (*IG* ii² 2498, 17-21:

payment in two instalments, 13–15) and for phratry land in 300/299 (*IG* ii² 1241, 9, 25–9).

διὸ καὶ πλεῖστα χρήματα ἐπὶ ταύτης συλλέγεται τῆς πρυ[τ]ανείας: Cf. D. xxiv. *Tim.* 98, cited above. This clause, beginning with an inferential διό, will not have been found in the laws but is an observation added by *A.P.*: such comments are rarer in the second part of *A.P.* than in the first, but compare 54. iii with commentary (and Introduction, p. 37).

47. v. εἰσφέρεται μὲν οὖν εἰς τὴν βουλὴν ... τηρεῖ δ' ὁ δημόσιος: The poletae made the record when the contract was entered into, the apodectae cancelled it when payment was made (48. i); meanwhile the records were in the custody of a public slave attached to the boule. In the fourth century, after the building of the New Bouleuterium, the Old was used as a record office: see p. 532.

κ[ατὰ] τὰς καταβολὰς ἀναγεγραμμένα: 'Written out according to the times of payment' (reading confirmed by Dr J. D. Thomas).

ὅταν δ' ᾖ χρημάτων [κατα]βολή: M. H. Chambers, *TAPA* cii 1971, 44–5, reads χρημάτ[.'] κ̣'.βολη; the same expression is found in the law published in *Hesp.* xliii 1974, 157–88, line 7 (quoted p. 558). It was presumably part of the duty of the prytanes to name a day when the boule would meet to witness καταβολαί (cf. 43. iii).

τοῖς ἀποδέκταις: Cf. 48. i–ii with commentary.

αὐτὰ ταῦτα: The γραμματεῖα.

καθελ[ὼν] ἀπ[ὸ τῶν] ἐπιστυλίων: The ἐπιστύλια are evidently objects serving the purpose of pigeon-holes, in which can be stored or to which can be attached the different γραμματεῖα relevant to the different occasions on which payments are due: the normal meaning of ἐπιστύλιον is 'architrave', as in *IG* i² 372, 33–9, Pl. *Per.* 13. vii, Vitruv. iv. 3. iv.

ὧν ἐν ταύτῃ τῇ ἡμέρᾳ: Probably ὧν is masculine, and refers to the men who are due to make payments (as in the translations of Rackham and Moore).

ἀ]παλειφθῆναι: Cf. 48. i. In 36. ii and 49. ii *A.P.* uses ἐξαλείφειν of deleting a man's name from a register. Ath. ix. 407 C (using διαλείφειν) tells the story of Alcibiades' going to the Metroum (an anachronistic detail) and destroying the record of an impending trial: it is to be hoped that such improper deletion of records was not easy or frequent.

ἵνα μὴ προεξαλει[φθῇ]: Records of payments due later are kept separately so that they shall not be cancelled until the relevant payments are made. This is the only instance of the double compound cited by LSJ; προαπαλείφειν is cited only from D.C. XLIII. 21. iv.

48. i. ἀποδέκται: 'Receivers' of state revenue of all kinds, including

48. i] COMMENTARY ON THE *ATH. POL.*

revenue destined for the temple treasuries. Androtion thought, or was believed by Harpocration to have thought, that the apodectae were created by Cleisthenes to replace the colacretae (324 F 5, from Harp. ἀποδέκται); but the apodectae are first attested in *IG* i² 94, 15–18 (418/7), receiving money due to the Other Gods, while the colacretae, mentioned in 7. iii as Solonian officials and attested in the fifth century not as receiving but as paying officers, make their last dated appearance in the same inscription (line 28; they appear also in M&L 73, 51–2, which some date 416/5 but others date slightly earlier) and have ceased to exist by 410 (cf. pp. 391–2 and Rhodes, *A.B.*, 98–102, esp. 99 n. 4). On the involvement of the apodectae in Androtion's collection of arrears of εἰσφορά see D. XXIV. *Tim.* 162, 197; in addition to what is said of them here the apodectae acted as εἰσάγουσα ἀρχή for lawsuits concerning tax-collecting (52. iii with commentary). On revenue officers in general see Arist. *Pol.* VI. 1321 B 31–3.

A. III *Ctes.* 25 claims that in the time of Eubulus the controllers of the theoric fund ἦρχον ... τὴν τῶν ἀποδεκτῶν (*sc.* ἀρχήν): I imagine that this refers to supervision rather than supersession, and is to be compared with their working with the poletae (47. ii with commentary; see also 54. i with commentary, on the ὁδοποιοί).

παραλαβόντες τὰ [γρα]μματεῖα: The records made by the poletae and kept by a δημόσιος on behalf of the boule: 47. ii–v.

ἀπαλείφουσι τὰ καταβαλλόμενα χρήματα: For ἀπαλείφειν cf. 47. v with commentary; for καταβάλλειν cf. 47. iii with commentary.

ἐναντίον τ[ῆς βουλῆς] ἐν τῷ βουλευτηρίῳ: As the poletae made contracts in the presence of the boule (47. ii, v) the apodectae collected revenue in the presence of the boule: cf. the law published in *Hesp.* xliii 1974, 157–88, lines 4–8, by which the δοκιμαστής who tests coins is to sit daily με[ταξὺ τῶν τρ]απεζῶν ... [πλὴν] ὅταν ἦ[ι] χρημάτων καταβολή, τότε δὲ ἐ[ν τῶι βολευτ]ηρίωι. Payments noted in the navy lists are sometimes described as εἰς βουλευτήριον (e.g. *IG* ii² 1622, 524–5, 570–1), sometimes as payments to the apodectae (e.g. *IG* ii² 1627, 215, 232).

καὶ πάλιν ἀποδιδόασιν τὰ γραμματεῖα: If any payments were outstanding, the records obviously had to be kept until the money was received; but when payment was made the transaction was closed. We do not know how long, if at all, the records were kept after this; but records kept not on papyrus but on λελευκωμένα γραμματεῖα will have occupied considerable space (and the result of wiping out all the entries will have been a blank tablet), so we should not expect them to be kept longer than was necessary.

κἄν τις ἐλλίπῃ καταβολήν: For this use of ἐλλείπειν cf. D. XXIV. *Tim.* 172, Polyb. IV. 60. ii.

ἐνταῦθ' ἐγγέγραπται: 'There stands his name entered.' For the use of ἐγγράφειν cf. 42. i, 49. ii, and (for the registration of debtors) [D.] xxv. *Aristog. i.* 4, XLIII. *Mac.* 71; for this 'future' use of the perfect cf. the perfects in 49. i *fin.*, with Schwyzer, *Griechische Grammatik*, ii. 287 (§1), Goodwin, *Syntax of the Moods and Tenses of the Greek Verb*[3], 15 (§51).

καὶ διπλά[σιον... καταβάλλειν ἢ δεδέσθαι: For διπλάσιον, rather than the more usual διπλοῦν, cf. And. 1. *Myst.* 73. On the law governing public debts see Rhodes, *A.B.*, 148–51. In the first half of the fourth century those who became public debtors by entering into a contract had to provide guarantors when the contract was made; if they defaulted on a payment the debt was doubled and they became ἄτιμοι until it was discharged, and to secure the discharge of the debt the boule was entitled to imprison them and confiscate their guarantors' property; men from whom immediate payment could be demanded (such as those who had incurred fines) were treated as contractual debtors already in default; some instances of doubled debts may be seen in *Hesp.* v 10, 145–6, 165–6. Under the law proposed by Timocrates in the 350's, which is attacked in D. XXIV. *Tim.*, men in the second category were given a respite by being treated as if they were under contract to pay by the ninth prytany; 54. ii reports that men convicted in a γραφὴ ἀδικίου had their penalty doubled if they failed to pay by the ninth prytany.

καὶ ταῦτα εἰσπράτ[τειν... κατὰ τοὺς νόμους ἐστίν: The boule did its exacting through another board of ten, not mentioned by *A.P.*, the πράκτορες: cf. laws *ap.* And. 1. *Myst.* 77–9, [D.] XLIII. *Mac.* 71, A. 1. *Tim.* 35.

48. ii. τῇ μὲν οὖν προτεραίᾳ: Since on some contracts an instalment was due each prytany (47. iii with commentary), a pair of days was presumably assigned in each prytany to the receipt and distribution of revenue.

τὰς π[άσα]ς: Conjectured by Kaibel & Wilamowitz[3] after Wilcken had read the first letter of the doubtful word as π or τ; Kenyon in his Berlin ed. and O.C.T. judged the reading possible and accepted the conjecture. Earlier Kaibel, *Stil und Text*, 213, had suggested τὰς [κ(ατα)βολὰ]s, and that must be the noun to be understood with πάσας.

μερίζουσι ταῖς ἀρχαῖς: In the fifth century Athens had a central treasury; in the fourth she attempted to budget for expenditure and made regular allocations (for which μερίζειν, μερισμός are technical terms) to separate spending authorities: this system is first attested in Tod 116, 18–22, of 386 (see Rhodes, *A.B.*, 99–101). The discussion of the revenue officer in Arist. *Pol.* VI. 1321 B 31–3 reflects fourth-century Athenian practice: ἄλλη δ' ἀρχὴ πρὸς ἣν αἱ πρόσοδοι τῶν κοινῶν ἀναφέρονται, παρ' ὧν φυλαττόντων μερίζονται πρὸς ἑκάστην διοίκησιν.

τῇ δ' ὑστεραίᾳ . . . εἰσ[φέρου]σι γράψαντες ἐν σανίδι: 'And on the second day they bring in (*sc*. an account of) the Allocation written on a board.' For εἰσφέρουσι cf. 47. iv, v; there seems to be no difference in meaning between σανίς and (λελευκωμένον) γραμματεῖον. What has to be checked is that the apodectae have distributed the revenue they have collected in accordance with the μερισμός, not giving too much or too little to any recipient and not keeping any money for themselves; the recipients will need at their accounting to show how much money they have received and how they have spent it. Nothing is said here of receipts which would assist the memory of the bouleutae and enable them to check that the payments listed on the second day corresponded to those actually made on the first day, and which could be used later as evidence that the various authorities had actually received the sums which they claimed to have received.

καταλέγουσιν ἐν τῷ βουλευτηρίῳ: To make it easier for the boule to consider the μερισμός and uncover any malpractices, the document is read to the members: cf. 43. iv, 54. v, with commentary (where ἀναγιγνώσκειν is used).

καὶ προ[τιθ]έασιν ἐν τῇ βουλῇ: The verb means 'put forward for debate', as in 44. iii; we should expect the proedri to be the subject both of this and of γνώμας ἐπιψηφίζουσιν ('put proposals to the vote'), and it is probably owing to *A.P.*'s condensation of his material that they are not mentioned here.

48. iii. κ]ληροῦσι δὲ καὶ λογιστάς . . . κατὰ τὴν πρυτανείαν ἑκάστην: These 'reckoners', appointed from the boule to make an interim check on officials' accounts each prytany, are not to be confused with the annual logistae, appointed from the whole citizen body to make a final check on officials' accounts on their retirement (on whom see 54. ii with commentary). Presumably on this board as on others one man was appointed from each tribe; but despite the formulation of this clause (κληροῦσι δὲ καὶ . . .) *A.P.* has not said above, and we have no reason to believe, that the treasurers of Athena, the poletae and the apodectae were appointed from the ranks of the boule.

We know from inscriptions of logistae of another kind, accountants, attested in the fifth century but not the fourth (e.g. *A.T.L.*, list 1, 2, M&L 58 A, 7–9, 72, 1); logistae of the fourth-century kind are not found before 403, and there will have been more need for them after the institution of the μερισμός, but Lys. xxx. *Nic*. 5 refers to the interim check, in 399, without implying that this was something new, and I believe that it was a long-established practice to make some check on the conduct of an official at his retirement (cf.

pp. 115, 316). For detailed studies of λογισταί and εὔθυνοι in Athens see Wilamowitz, *A.u.A.*, ii. 231–51, M. Piérart, *AC* xl 1971, 526–73; Rhodes, *A.B.*, 111, is wrong in stating that logistae are not found after *A.P.*

48. iv. κληροῦσι δὲ καὶ εὐθύνους ... καὶ παρέδρους β' ... : Cf. p. 155 on the meaning of εὐθύνειν. The final examination of an official's conduct comprised a financial part (λόγος), treated in 54. ii, and a general part (εὔθυναι), treated here; but the separate senses of the two words are not always distinguished, and εὔθυναι is often used of the taking of the λόγος to court (cf. below).[40] We might have expected the two parts of the examination to be treated together, in the laws of Athens and in *A.P.*; but the εὔθυνοι (presumably: *A.P.* does not openly say so) and the interim logistae were subcommittees of the boule, while the annual logistae were appointed from the whole citizen body and the boule was not involved in their work.

A πάρεδρος is one who sits beside, and so an assistant or adviser (cf. Pind. *Ol.* ii. 76, viii. 22, H. VII. 147. ii): in Athens we know of πάρεδροι to the three senior archons (56. i with commentary), the hellenotamiae (M&L 77, 4) and the generals (*ibid.* 50); the annual logistae were assisted by συνήγοροι, on whom see 54. ii with commentary. The πάρεδροι of the εὔθυνοι are found in *IG* i² 127, 19, decree *ap*. And. I. *Myst.* 78, *IG* ii² 1629, 238–9; in a decree of the deme Halae we find a εὔθυνος and his πάρεδροι, examining accounts (*IG* ii² 1174); but in a decree of Myrrhinus there are separate officials styled λογιστής and εὔθυνος, and the εὔθυνος is assisted by an elected committee of ten, from whose condemnation an appeal lies to the deme assembly (*IG* ii² 1183, 13–22).

ταῖς ἀ[γορ]αῖς: Restored by Kenyon[1], and accepted *faute de mieux* by most editors: this was interpreted by Kenyon (and Kaibel, *Stil und Text*, 213–14) as 'on the occasions of the tribal assemblies'; by Wilamowitz (*A.u.A.*, ii. 235 with n. 15), more plausibly, as 'in market hours'. Wilcken read αγ ... λαις (or ϙαις), of which M. H. Chambers, *TAPA* cii 1971, 45, prefers the former; Kenyon in his Berlin ed. printed α ..... αις, remarking that there is a vertical stroke after the first α and a letter which might be λ before the second, and wondering if a longer word than ἀγοραῖς is needed; Dr J. D. Thomas reads ạ.[....]αις. Σ. Ν. Δραγούμης, *Ἀθ.* xxxi 1920, 159–72, has suggested ἀ[πογραφ]αῖς, and A. Rehm, *Philol.* lxxxvi = ²xl 1930/1, 119–22, ἀν[ατο]λαῖς ('at daybreak'). Some indication of time is needed, since the place is specified in what follows. Not every retired magistrate would have his accounts passed by a court on the same

---

[40] In a deme decree, *IG* ii² 1174, officials of the deme are to place their λόγος in a box each month, and are to undergo εὔθυναι on the λόγοι in the box and not on any others at the beginning of the following year.

day, and if the period within which general complaints might be made was thirty days (cf. below) attending every day to receive complaints would take these bouleutae away from their other duties for a long time. Dr D. M. Lewis has suggested to me νουμηνίαις: this gives an attractive sense, but it seems impossible that it is what the scribe wrote.

κατὰ τὸν ἐπώνυμον τὸν τῆς φυλῆς ἑκάστης: By the time of *A.P.* the statues of the tribal ἐπώνυμοι stood opposite the Old Bouleuterium, by the road running along the west side of the Agora (see p. 259). Presumably each team sat by the ἐπώνυμος of one tribe (perhaps being assigned to a tribe other than its own: cf. 53. ii *fin.* with commentary), to receive complaints against officials from that tribe. This passage is not included in R. E. Wycherley, *The Athenian Agora,* iii, *s.v.* eponymoi, nor mentioned by Thompson & Wycherley, *The Athenian Agora,* xiv. 41.

τινι τῶν τὰς εὐθύνας ἐν τῷ δικαστηρίῳ δεδωκότων: According to *A.P.* the εὔθυνοι and their assistants receive complaints from individuals after a process that has already taken place in court; he does not say that they were involved in that process, and if they were involved in it this will be a particularly careless piece of condensation. Probably they were not, and the process in question is the presentation of the financial account (54. ii, where we read that the annual logistae are the officials τοῖς ὑπευθύνοις λογιζόμενοι καὶ τὰς εὐθύνας εἰς τὸ δικαστήριον εἰσάγοντες: cf. Wilamowitz, *A.u.A.,* ii. 234–5, Harrison, *L.A.,* ii. 30); but λογιστηρίῳ, suggested by Π. Σ. Φωτιάδης, Ἀθ. xi 1899, 361–77, is unnecessary.

ἐντὸς γ' ἡ[μερῶν ἀφ'] ἧς: Read and restored thus by Kenyon[1] and most editors. Wilcken read τ' (300), of which Kenyon rightly remarked in his Berlin ed. *incredible est;* there Kenyon thought λ' (30) possible, Dr J. D. Thomas finds it acceptable, and some have preferred it (Lipsius, *A.R.,* 105 n. 208, Φωτιάδης, Ἀθ. xiii 1901, 57 with n. 1, Rehm, *Philol.* lxxxvi = ²xl 1930/1, 119 n. 2). Since retired officials were allowed thirty days within which to present their λόγος (cf. on 54. ii), it is more probable that a further thirty days were allowed for complaints to the εὔθυνοι (see also above, on ἀ[γορ]αῖς).

εὔθυναν ἄν τ' ἰδίαν ἄν τε δ[η]μο[σί]α[ν] ἐμβαλέσθαι: For ἐάν τε ... ἐάν τε ... cf. X. *Cyr.* I. i. 5, Plat. *Lys.* 212 E 7, with Schwyzer, *Griechische Grammatik,* ii. 633. I know no other instance of εὔθυναν ἐμβάλλεσθαι, but ἐμβάλλεσθαι is used of submitting a document in various legal contexts (e.g. 53. ii, iii, [D.] XL. *Boe. Dot.* 21, D. XLV. *Steph. i.* 8, [D.] XLIX. *Timoth.* 65).

γράψας εἰς πινάκιον λελευκωμένον ... ὅ τι ἂν ἐγκαλῇ: For πινάκιον λελευκωμένον cf. M&L 46, 44–5, *IG* ii² 1237, 62–3. Efficiently enough, the complainant is required to state his own name, the defendant's name and the alleged offence, and to add (cf. next note) a recommended penalty. Notices of γραφαί were similarly written out, and posted by the tribal ἐπώνυμοι (D. xxi. Mid. 103, Liban. Decl. 1. Apol. Socr. 43).

τίμημα ἐ[πιγραψ]άμενος: Cf. Ar. Plut. 480, A. 1. Tim. 16; also Poll. viii. 47 (ἐν γραμματείῳ γράψαντες). A τίμημα is a valuation: in 7. iii, 8. i, 39. vi, a valuation of property for political purposes; here and in 53. ii an assessment of a sum at issue or a penalty for judicial purposes (so that lawsuits could be classified τιμητοί or ἀτίμητοι according to whether the penalty or damages were subject to assessment or fixed: cf. pp. 722–3 and 69. ii with commentary).

48. v. ἀν[αγνού]ς: Suggested by Blass (*LZB* 1891, 304) and Kaibel & Wilamowitz[1]; W. Wayte (*CR* v 1891, 116) suggested ἀνακρίνας, which has been preferred by Lipsius (*A.R.*, 82 n. 115), Harrison (*L.A.*, ii. 30, 210) and some editors. What the εὔθυνος does here is not quite comparable to the ἀνάκρισις performed by the εἰσάγουσα ἀρχή (56. vi with commentary), since he apparently has the right to acquit, and he does not act as εἰσάγουσα ἀρχή if he does pass the case on (cf. Harrison, *L.A.*, ii. 210–11), so ἀναγνούς is perhaps the better restoration.

ἐὰν μὲν καταγνῷ: Kaibel & Wilamowitz deleted μέν, but this is not the only instance in *A.P.* of μέν not answered by δέ (cf. ἂν μὲν ἀποψηφίσωνται in 42. i, with commentary), and it may be retained: cf. Kaibel, *Stil und Text*, 214–15, J. D. Denniston, *The Greek Particles*[2], 380–2.

τὰ μὲν ἴδια τοῖς δικασταῖς τοῖς κατὰ δήμ[ους τοῖς] τὴν φυλὴν ταύτην εἰσάγουσιν: For the δικασταὶ κατὰ δημούς cf. 16. v, 26. iii, 53. i–ii, with commentary. This is their first appearance in the second part of *A.P.*, and when they are treated in detail they are introduced as the Forty: the older term, which is used here, was presumably used in the law on which *A.P.*'s account is based. In place of εἰσάγουσιν, δικάζουσιν was suggested by H. Richards and E. S. Thompson (*CR* v 1891, 229) and Kaibel & Wilamowitz (cf. Kaibel, *Stil und Text*, 215), comparing 53. ii, 58. ii: δικάζουσιν is certainly the more appropriate verb, since εἰσάγειν applies only to cases which are brought before a δικαστήριον and ought not to have τὴν φυλὴν as object; εἰσάγουσιν is used correctly in the following sentence, and I am inclined to suspect a scribal error and restore δικάζουσιν here.

τοῖς θεσμοθέτα[ις ἀ]ναγράφει: Restored by Kenyon[1]. Various alternative guesses were rendered obsolete by the readings of Wilcken and of Kenyon's Berlin ed.; Wilcken read θεσμοθέταις συναναγράφει, Kenyon in his Berlin ed. and O.C.T. thought the space sufficient but could not read συν, M. H. Chambers, *TAPA* cii

T 563

1971, 45, reads θεσμοθέταις ς[υν]αναγράφει. The passive of συναναγράφειν is found in A. ii. F.L. 83, and the active in D.S. xvii. 1. ii, in neither case with the meaning 'report' which the verb must have here. With παραδίδωσιν preceding τὰ μὲν ἴδια another verb is strictly not required, but there is no cause for alarm.

A.P. omits to mention that the εὔθυνοι could themselves impose fines for misconduct in office: see *IG* i² 127, 18–20, ii² 1629 = Tod 200, 233–42, with Wilamowitz, *A.u.A.*, ii. 237 n. 22, M. Piérart, *AC* xl 1971, 529–30, 549–51. 59. ii mentions στρατηγοῖς εὐθύνας among the cases for which the thesmothetae are the εἰσάγουσα ἀρχή. When a major offence against the state was alleged, or when an offence was interpreted as μὴ χρῆσθαι τοῖς νόμοις, an accusation to the εὔθυνοι could lead to a trial in the form appropriate to these εἰσαγγελίαι (cf. M. H. Hansen, *Eisangelia*, 45–7, Rhodes, *JHS* xcix 1979, 110).

ἐὰν παραλάβωσιν: The εὔθυνος in deciding to pass on the complaint has already judged that there is a *prima facie* case (ἐὰν μὲν καταγνῷ, above): it is not clear what discretion the thesmothetae had in the matter, and to remove the implication that they had any ἐπὰν was suggested by Κ. Σ. Κόντος, *Ἀθ.* iv 1892, 133, and ἐπειδὰν by A. A. Σακελλάριος, *Ἀθ.* xi 1899, 522–3; ἐπὰν (cf. 42. ii, 56. i) may well be right.

εἰσάγουσιν [ταύτ(ην) τ(ὴν)] εὔθυναν: Kenyon[1] restored [τὴν]; Blass[2] thought the space required ταύτην τὴν, and has been generally followed; M. H. Chambers, *TAPA* cii 1971, 45, reverts to εἰσάγουσιν [τὴ]ν.

δικαστ[αί, τοῦτο κύ]ριόν: Restored by Leeuwen, Kaibel & Wilamowitz: cf. 45. i *fin*.

49. i. δοκιμάζει δὲ καὶ τοὺς ἵππους: i.e. The horses of the cavalry: cf. X. *Oec.* ix. 15, *Hipparch.* i. 13; also *Hipparch.* i. 8, iii. 9–14, *SEG* xxi 525, 14–15 (282/1), 435, 29–30 (187/6). On the δοκιμασίαι of the cavalry cf. Rhodes, *A.B.*, 174–5. To the name-vase of the δοκιμασία Painter (cited there, but to be dated *c.* 480–470) a similar illustration on a cup about thirty years earlier has been added by H. A. Cahn, *RA* 1973, 3–22, who adduces other vases depicting young men with horses. There was also a valuation of the horses, mentioned in the inscriptions cited here, for which see above, p. 304.

For other δοκιμασίαι conducted by the boule (grouped with matters in which the boule is not κυρία) see 45. iii.

καλ[ὸν ἵππον ἔχ]ων: Proposed by Kaibel & Wilamowitz[1] and accepted by most editors; Blass[3] suggested καλ[ὸ]ν [δύνατο]ς ὤν; Kenyon in his Berlin ed. thought the letter before ων either χ, σ or μ; M. H. Chambers, *TAPA* cii 1971, 45, considers Blass' reconstruction 'perhaps the least unsatisfactory'; Dr J. D. Thomas regards χ as possible but σ as easier, but accepts Kaibel & Wilamowitz' text as there is not room for δύνατο]ς.

ζημιοῖ τῷ σίτῳ: The cavalry received a fodder grant for their horses, presumably paid throughout the year (cf. schol. D. xxiv. *Tim*. 101: X. *Hipparch*. i. 19 puts the state's expenditure on the cavalry at 40 talents a year); it is possible but not certain that the ἱππεῖς themselves received a stipend when on active service; certainly before and during the oligarchic régime of the Thirty those who joined the cavalry received a κατάστασις which could be reclaimed from them when they left the force (cf. pp. 304, 458). Payment towards σῖτος for the cavalry is attested in M & L 84, 4, *IG* ii² 1264, 5–8.

τοῖς δὲ μὴ δυναμ[ένοις ἀκολ]ουθεῖν ... μένειν ἀλλ' ἀνάγουσι: 'Which cannot keep up, or will not remain in line but run away' (Moore). δυναμένοις ἀκολούθειν, suggested by W. Wyse (*CR* v 1891, 116: cf. X. *M*. III. iii. 4) is generally accepted. Kenyon¹ printed μένειν ἀνάγουσι, remarking that a corrector has written λγ over the να of ἀνάγουσι; Blass¹ read the correction as λλ and printed ἀλλ' ἀνάγουσι (this reading is confirmed by Dr J. D. Thomas); Kaibel & Wilamowitz³ preferred Kenyon's original text, but Kenyon in his Berlin ed. and O.C.T. followed Blass (cf. Gomme, *CR* xl 1928, 225); Leeuwen suggested μένειν ἀναγ⟨ώγοις⟩ οὖσι ('ill-trained', 'unmanageable': cf. X., *loc. cit*.), and Thalheim ἀναβαίνουσι; Kaibel, *Stil und Text*, 215–18, discussed the problem inconclusively. No instance of ἀνάγειν in a sense which is at all appropriate is cited by LSJ, while ἀνάγωγος is used also of dogs in X. *M*. iv. i. 3: μένειν ἀναγ⟨ώγοις⟩ οὖσι is to be preferred here.

τροχὸν ἐπὶ τὴν γνάθ[ο]ν [ἐπιβ]άλλει: 'It (*sc.* the boule) brands on the jaw with the sign of a wheel.' From Hes. τρυσίππιον, Phot. ἱππότροχος, Eust. 1517. 8 *ad Od*. iv. 762, Zenob. iv. 41 (citing Crates, fr. 30 Kock), cf. Poll. vii. 186, R. D. Hicks (*CR* v 1891, 116) suggested γνάθον ἐμβάλλουσιν and Blass¹ ἐπιβάλλει; Blass' text is supported by an additional fragment of the London papyrus, first cited in Kenyon's Berlin ed. Kaibel & Wilamowitz suggest that the lexicographers' notes derive from schol. Eup. *Taxiarchi*, which in turn derives from *A.P.*

καὶ ὁ τοῦτο παθὼν ἀδόκιμός ἐστι: Restored by Kenyon¹, and confirmed by the additional fragment. One who is ἀδόκιμος is one rejected in the δοκιμασία: cf. with reference to ships' equipment δόκιμα καὶ ἐντελῆ (*SEG* x 353–5), ἀδόκιμα ([D.] L. *Poly*. 36); and the use of ἀδόκιμος of coins in Plat. *Legg*. v. 742 A 6.

δοκιμάζει δὲ καὶ τοὺς προ[δ]ρ[όμους οἵ]τινες ἄν... : The text as now printed is established by the additional fragment. The πρόδρομοι are mentioned also by X. *Hipparch*. i. 25, Phil. 328 F 71 (from Harp. ἄμιπποι): in Herodotus (e.g. vii. 206. ii) the word denotes any advance force, but in Athens in the later fourth century it denotes a special body of light-armed cavalry, apparently the successors of the two hundred ἱπποτοξόται of the fifth and early fourth centuries (cf. Gilbert, *C.A.S.A.*, 324 n. 3, Jacoby, commentary on 328 F 71, A. F. Pauli, *RE*, xxiii (1957/9), 102–4, W. K. Pritchett, *U. Calif. Pub. Cl. Stud.* vii 1971 = *The Greek State at War*, i, 130–1, *The Greek State at War*, ii. 188–9, and on the ἱπποτοξόται see above, pp. 303–4). No other instance of the verb προδρομεύειν is recorded in LSJ or the 1968 Supplement.†

καταβέβηκεν: 'He has dismounted', and so ceased to belong to the *corps*: the closest parallel is [D.] XLII. *Phaen.* 24. For the tense cf. ἐγγέγραπται in 48. i and πέπαυται below, with commentary.

τοὺς ἀμίππους: The papyrus reads ανιππους: it was corrected by W. Wyse and W. L. Newman, *CR* v 1891, 116–17, Blass, *LZB* 1891, 304, from Harp. ἄμιπποι. These men, light infantry who fought with the cavalry, are best known from the Boeotian army (T. v. 57. ii, X. *H.* VII. v. 24; in these texts also the MSS read ἄνιπποι); in 362 the army in which the Athenians fought at Mantinea contained no ἄμιπποι (X. *H.* VII. v. 23); their use is recommended by X. *Hipparch.* v. 13. See Phil. 328 F 71 (from Harp. ἄμιπποι) with Jacoby's commentary. Harp. also cites Isaeus (= fr. 125 Sauppe), so the Athenian ἄμιπποι may have been instituted between 362 and his death *c*. 350.

πέπαυται: For this 'future' use of the perfect cf. ἐγγέγραπται in 48. i, with commentary, and καταβέβηκεν above. It is found especially with παύειν in official contexts: cf. the law published in *Hesp.* xliii 1974, 157–88, line 35, D. XVIII. *Cor.* 266, [D.] XXVI. *Aristog. ii.* 5, with H. Wankel, *ZPE* xxi 1976, 149–51.

49. ii. τοὺς δ' ἱππέας: A force of 1,000: see pp. 303–4.

οἱ καταλογεῖς ... χειροτονήσῃ δέκα ἄνδρας: Cf. *SEG* xxi 435, 26–7 (187/6). Probably one man was appointed from each tribe: they were appointed by election rather than by lot, perhaps in extension of the principle that military appointments were elective (cf. the ταμίας στρατιωτικῶν: 43. i with commentary). κατάλογος and καταλέγειν are found elsewhere in connection with the cavalry (e.g. Lys. XVI. *Mant.* 13), but these καταλογεῖς are not mentioned elsewhere. Their instructions were presumably to list those whom they thought qualified for cavalry service who were not already members of the cavalry: cf. below.

τοῖς ἱππάρχοις καὶ φυλάρχοις: Cf. *SEG* xxi 525, 6–7 (282/1), 435, 6–7 (187/6: honouring a hipparch). The hipparchs are the commanders-in-chief of the cavalry and the phylarchs the commanders of the tribal regiments: cf. 61. iv–v with commentary.

τὸν πίνακ' ἀνοίξαντες: Kaibel, *Stil und Text*, 219, makes clear the distinction between the sealed πίναξ of the πρότερον ἐγγεγραμμένοι, those who had served in the previous year, and the κατάλογος of those newly registered for cavalry service by the καταλογεῖς (cf. the use of πίναξ at the end of this section). Sandys notes that the register of those who served under the Thirty was drawn up on a σανίδιον (Lys. XVI. *Mant.* 6) or σανίδες (Lys. XXVI. *Evand.* 10); whereas a κατάλογος is a list, and a σανίς is a tablet on which a list may be written, πίναξ, strictly another word for 'board' or 'tablet', tends also to be used of a list written on a tablet (cf. ἐκκλησιαστικὸς πίναξ: [D.] XLIV. *Leoch.* 35).

κατασεσημασμένα: After the primary meaning of the verb, 'cause to be sealed up' (cf. 53. ii), LSJ lists a secondary meaning, 'cause to be noted down', citing Plat. *Legg.* VI. 756 C 5, E 2–3, and this passage; but in this passage the primary meaning is appropriate, since the πίναξ has to be opened (I am supported by Kenyon's Oxford Translation and Fritz & Kapp, but not by Moore), and it seems to me to be appropriate also in *Legg.*, in the contrast between (doing this) on the first four days to the names of men elected to the short list and bringing them out for all the citizens to see on the fifth day (Prof. T. J. Saunders tells me that I am supported by the translations of J. Grou [1769], A. Cassarà [²1947], L. Robin [1950] and A. Zadro [1952], and that he now accepts this interpretation). There is no need for LSJ's secondary meaning.

τοὺς μὲν ἐξομνυμένους: The verb is used regularly of refusing or denying on oath. *A.P.* gives no indication that a cavalryman's claim of inability would be checked: perhaps a claim made on oath was accepted unless ὁ βουλόμενος challenged it. Cavalrymen had to be capable of serving 'with their body and their property' (cf. below): although *A.P.* does not say so, it ought to have been possible for a man whose property had been seriously diminished to plead inability on that score; but I doubt if Π. Ν. Παπαγεώργιος, Ἀθ. iv 1892, 590, was right to add σώμασιν ⟨ἢ ταῖς οὐσίαις⟩; more probably the omission is due to *A.P.*

ἐγγεγραμμένων: Cf. 36. ii, 42. i.
ἐξαλείφουσι: Cf. 36. ii with commentary.
τοὺς δὲ κατειλεγμένους: Those newly listed by the καταλογεῖς.
ἐξομόσηται: The papyrus reads εξομησηται: Kenyon[1] corrected to the regular aorist form; Kaibel & Wilamowitz and some others have preferred the present subjunctive, ἐξομνύηται, but I doubt if they are right.

μὴ δύνασθαι τῷ σώματι ἱππεύειν ἢ τῇ οὐσίᾳ: Cf. the reference to τὴν τῶν σωμάτων δοκιμασίαν in *SEG* xxi 525, 15–18. The double requirement of health and wealth for the cavalry is mentioned also by X. *Hipparch.* i. 9: wealth was necessary because the cavalryman had to provide his own horse (though when first enrolled he was assisted with a κατάστασις, and a fodder grant was paid). Cf. the formulation of the requirement for membership of the Five Thousand, in 411, where the reference is to men of hoplite status and above (29. v with commentary).

διαχειροτονοῦσιν οἱ βουλευταί . . . ἱππεύειν ἢ οὔ: If there was a quota of 1,000 cavalry the boule will have needed, after first taking account of deaths and exempting some of the men who had served in the previous year, to approve a particular number of men from the κατάλογος. διαχειροτονεῖν is the verb regularly used in inscriptions when the assembly is called on to decide between alternatives (cf. p. 526): χειροτονεῖν is not always restricted to voting by show of hands (cf. 34. i, 41. iii, with commentary), but that method was probably used here.

49. iii. ἔκρινεν δέ ποτε καὶ τὰ παραδείγματα καὶ τὸν πέπλον: The significance of παραδείγματα in this context has been disputed. The word can denote models or plans for buildings, sculpture, painting or other works of skill (e.g. H. v. 62. iii, Plat. *Rep.* vi. 500 E 3–4, *IG* i² 374, 248–54, ii² 1668, 95): most have supposed the reference to be to public works in general (e.g. Wilamowitz, *A.u.A.*, i. 212–13 with n. 50, Rhodes, *A.B.*, 122), but some have thought of patterns for the πέπλος (Blass[1], reading παραδείγματα τὰ εἰς τὸν, Kaibel, *Stil und Text*, 220, P. Foucart, *RPh*² xix 1895, 24–6).

In decrees of the fifth century many matters of detail with regard to public works are decided by the assembly (e.g. *IG* i² 81; 88, 1–5), so if Wilamowitz' interpretation is right there must have been two changes, one by which such matters were transferred to the boule, and a second, after accusations of corruption had been made, by which the boule gave way to a court (cf. Rhodes, *loc. cit.*). The πέπλος is the robe taken in procession at the Great Panathenaea (Plat. *Euthyphr.* 6 c 2–3, Harp. πέπλος; schol. Ar. *Eq.* 566 combines a statement that this was done quadrennially with one that it was done annually: T. L. Shear, jr, *Hesp.* Supp. xvii 1978, 36 with n. 89, reviews the evidence and concludes that the offering of a new πέπλος was still quadrennial in the early third century[41]) and handed to the priestess of Athena to clothe the old cult statue of the goddess; in the procession it was taken as the sail of a ship-like vehicle (Harp. τοπεῖον = Strattis, fr. 30 Kock, lines 66–7 of the inscription published by Shear, *op. cit.*, *IG* ii² 657, 14–16, 968, 48–9, Phot. ἱστὸς καὶ κεραία).[42] Nine months before, at the Χαλκεῖα, the priestesses and

---

[41] By the end of the second century, if we date *IG* ii² 1036 in 108/7 and 1034 in 103/2 (agreed by A. E. Samuel, *Greek and Roman Chronology*, 221, B. D. Meritt, *Hist.* xxvi 1977, 187), it was annual.

[42] Shear, *op. cit.*, 39–44, notes that the epigraphic texts do not explicitly mention a 'ship', and suggests that a single vehicle was used for this and for other processional purposes.

the ἀρρηφόροι set up the warp for the new robe (Suid. [X 35] Χαλκεῖα, E.M. [805. 43] Χάλκεια), and two of the four ἀρρηφόροι then directed the weaving of the robe (Harp. ἀρρηφορεῖν, L.S. 446. 18 cf. 202. 3, E.M. [149. 18] ἀρρηφορεῖν: cf. p. 639) under the supervision of the athlothetae (60. i); the ἐργαστῖναι (Hes. [E 5653] s.v.) who did the work are honoured and listed in IG ii² 1034 and 1036 and listed in 1942, 1943 (c. 100 B.C.).[43] See L. Deubner, *Attische Feste*, 11, 29-31, 35-6, J. A. Davison, *JHS* lxxviii 1958, 25-6 = From *Archilochus to Pindar*, 33-4, H. W. Parke, *Festivals of the Athenians*, 38-43, and 60. i with commentary; J. Boardman, *Festschrift für F. Brommer*, 40-1, suggests that the east frieze of the Parthenon included the loom on which the πέπλος was woven and the handing over of the πέπλος by one of the ἀρρηφόροι. Blass and his followers supposed that the boule had to approve a design for the πέπλος; Kenyon and Sandys that it had to appoint the ἐργαστῖναι or the two ἀρρηφόροι (which is not what the text states); Fritz & Kapp confess uncertainty and wonder if the text is corrupt.

No other evidence is available to make a definitive solution possible. Since most public works were at least partly of religious significance, I do not find it unacceptable that public works and the πέπλος should be mentioned together in this section; on the other hand, it is likely that a design or designer had to be approved for each πέπλος (I do not imagine that the ἀρρηφόροι were responsible for the design). I am now inclined to favour Blass' interpretation and emendation, but without confidence.†

τὸ δικαστήριον τὸ λαχόν: *A.P.* continues to be tantalisingly brief. We are not told which of the archons acted as εἰσάγουσα ἀρχή.

καὶ τῆς ποιήσεως τῶν Νικῶν: Cf. 47. i with commentary: Lycurgus was responsible for the making of new Νῖκαι in the 330's and 320's. The decisions in the first sentence of this section are presumably, from their location in this chapter, regarded as analogous to δοκιμασίαι: in this second sentence *A.P.* proceeds to the boule's responsibility for other religious objects.

καὶ τῶν ἄθλων τῶν εἰς τὰ Παναθήναια: Cf. 60. i with commentary, where among the duties of the athlothetae we find τοὺς ἀμφορεῖς ποιοῦνται μετὰ τῆς βουλῆς.

συνεπιμελεῖται μετὰ τοῦ ταμίου τῶν στρατιωτικῶν: For the treasurer of the stratiotic fund see 43. i with commentary; and for the influence gained by this and other elected treasurers through cooperating in the work of other boards see 47. ii with commentary. His involvement in the making of the new dedications of the Lycurgan period is confirmed by *IG* ii² 1493, cf. also 1672, 40, vii 4252, 20-3.

---

[43] P. MacKendrick, *TAPA* lxx 1939, xxxix-xl, suggested that *IG* ii² 1034 and 1943 belong to the same stele, but he does not repeat the suggestion in *The Athenian Aristocracy, 399 to 31 B.C.*, 89 n. 47.

49. iv. δοκιμάζει δὲ καὶ τοὺς ἀδυνάτους: After his digression on religious objects *A.P.* reverts to the main theme of this chapter, the boule's δοκιμασίαι.

τοὺς ἐντὸς τριῶν μνῶν ... μηδὲν ἔργον ἐργάζεσθαι: Cf. Lys. XXIV. *Pens. Inv.* (an invalid's reply, delivered before the boule, to objections that he should not receive the grant), A. 1. *Tim.* 103–4 with schol.; information from *A.P.* is combined with information from elsewhere in Harp., Suid. (*A* 540), ἀδύνατοι (= Phil. 328 F 197a), *L.S.* 345. 15, Phot. ἀδύνατοι (= 328 F 197b). Grants to war invalids are said to have been instituted by Solon or Pisistratus (Pl. *Sol.* 31. iii–iv), and it may be true that some distinguished invalids received grants or σίτησις ἐν πρυτανείῳ in the sixth century; by 431 the sons of citizens who fell in war were maintained at the state's expense until they came of age, and that institution is ascribed to Solon by D.L. 1. 55 (cf. 24. iii *fin.* with commentary); this institution is ascribed to Solon by schol. A. 1. *Tim.* 103 but must be a creation of the Periclean or post-Periclean democracy. The speaker of Lys. XXIV seeks to show both that he is in need of support and that he is physically incapacitated.

The estates of the rich are, inevitably, better documented than the possessions of the poor: under a law of 357 the richest 1,200 of the citizens, about 4% of the whole, were made liable to the trierarchy (Rhodes, *A.B.*, 5–6); before liability was redefined in this way a man seems to have been liable if his property was worth more than about 3–4 talents (Davies, *A.P.F.*, xxiii–xxiv), 60–75 times the sum stipulated here.

δύο ὀβολοὺς ἑκάστῳ τῆς ἡμέρας: Earlier in the fourth century the grant was 1 obol a day (Lys. XXIV. *Pens. Inv.* 13, 26); it may be that in 361 one instalment was paid each prytany (A. 1. *Tim.* 104, date §109; but alternatively the point may be that ἱκετηρίαι to the boule as to the assembly [43. vi] were allowed once a prytany); *A.P.*'s figure of 2 obols is given also by Hes. (*A* 1217) ἀδύνατοι; Phil. 328 F 197a gives a figure of 9 drachmae a month, which probably represents a commutation made in the twelve-tribe period when there were as many prytanies as months (cf. Jacoby *ad loc.*). The grant was at all times less than the wage which an unskilled but ablebodied citizen could earn: cf. on 62. ii.

καὶ ταμίας ἐστὶν αὐτοῖς κληρωτός: Kaibel supposed the reference to be to a special treasurer of the invalids' fund (*Stil und Text*, 25–6, cf. Sandys[2] and most editors and translators), Wilamowitz to the treasurer of the boule (*A.u.A.*, i. 214, cf. Sandys[1]). After a sentence which has mentioned the boule in the singular (as always) and the invalids in the plural, Kaibel's is the more natural interpretation of the Greek, but we have no other evidence for the existence of a separate fund with its own treasurer, and the fact that this δοκιμασία was conducted by the boule rather than a δικαστήριον may support the view that the invalids' grants were paid from the boule's expense account. In that case this sentence is better regarded as a separate paragraph, to which *A.P.* has been led by his mention of an item which involves the boule in expenditure, rather than as simply the conclusion of the note on invalids. He has no systematic treatment of the spending authorities which received allocations of money in the μερισμός (on which see 48. i–ii with commentary), but it would be a serious omission (though not an impossible one) if his detailed treatment of the boule did not mention that it had funds and a treasurer to disburse them.

On the history of the treasurer of the boule see Rhodes, *A.B.*, 141 with nn. 3–4. There is a plurality of treasurers in *IG* ii² 120, 20–2 (353/2), and there are two in *IG* ii² 223 c, 7–9 (343/2); in 335/4 we find a ταμίας τῆι βουλῆι and a ταμίας τῶν εἰς τὸ ἀνάθημα (*IG* ii² 1700, 218–19 = *The Athenian Agora*, xv 43, 232–3), and thereafter there is regularly a single treasurer. There had thus been a change from two treasurers to one not long before *A.P.* wrote.

49. v. συνδιοικεῖ δὲ καὶ ταῖς ἄλλαις ἀρχαῖς τὰ πλεῖσθ᾽, ὡς ἔπος εἰπεῖν: Cf. 47. i, which uses the same words without ὡς ἔπος εἰπεῖν. Herwerden found this sentence embarrassingly superfluous and deleted it (cf. Kaibel, *Stil und Text*, 26, Blass⁴); Wilamowitz regarded it as a stylised *und so weiter* (*A.u.A.*, i. 214–15). *A.P.* is willing enough to use the expository device of beginning and ending a subsection with the same or similar phrases (cf. Introduction, pp. 30–2, 44–5); but it is clumsy to use two concluding expressions as consecutive sentences in 49. v–50. i, and, although a case can be made for the placing of the sentence here, a more obvious position for it would be at the end of ch. 48 (cf. on 47. i). However, successive copyists did not have our chapter divisions and there is no reason why they should have moved the sentence: clumsiness is more likely than corruption.

N. *Sortitive Officials* (50–4)

Three of the four sections into which the laws of Athens are divided in a law *ap.* D. xxiv. *Tim.* 20 are τῶν βουλευτικῶν, οἳ κεῖνται τοῖς ἐννέα ἄρχουσι and τῶν ἄλλων ἀρχῶν: *A.P.* has dealt in his chapters on the boule with officials directly supervised by the boule (47–8); he deals with a further selection of sortitive officials in 50–4, between his chapters on the boule and those on the archons; after his chapters on the archons, in 60–2, he deals with the athlothetae and elective military officials, and adds a concluding note on officials in general (cf. Introduction, pp. 30–2). Of the officials treated in these chapters, those in 50–1 are concerned with city facilities; those in 52–3 are concerned with the administration of justice (but *A.P.* is led from the Forty to the διαιτηταί, who were not appointed by lot, and from the use of the forty-two year-classes in the appointment of the διαιτηταί to the use of the year-classes in the army); in 54 we find the ὁδοποιοί (who would have been better placed in 50–1), the λογισταί (treated separately from the εὔθυνοι, who were dealt with as a sub-committee of the boule, in 48. iv–v), three secretaries (of whom the first had earlier been and the third was still elected), two boards of ἱεροποιοί (with a note on Athens' quadrennial festivals), and two other officials mentioned for their organisation of festivals.

'Ein solches chaos gibt Aristoteles statt einer ordnung.' Wilamowitz, *A.u.A.*, i. 233–4, sought to explain the whole of *A.P.*'s arrangement as based on methods of appointment: the boule was treated first, as a body appointed from the individual demes; in 50–1 decemviral boards appointed on a tribal basis; the Eleven end the first series of sortitive officials; and then from the εἰσαγωγεῖς (52. ii) to the end of 54 Wilamowitz saw a second series, of officials who were new or whose method of appointment had been changed (in particular he interpreted κληροῦσι δὲ καὶ τάσδε τὰς ἀρχάς, at the beginning of 54, as introducing additions to the original list). I am not sure that this is the answer: the purpose of the sentence quoted may rather be to mark the return to *A.P.*'s theme of sortitive officials, after his digression to the διαιτηταί and the forty-two year-classes, and only the placing of the ὁδοποιοί is palpably in need of explanation. I am more disturbed by *A.P.*'s selectivity: in 54. iii–v he mentions three secretaries out of the six attested in contemporary inscriptions (in particular, he mentions the ἐπὶ τοὺς νόμους but not the apparently parallel ἐπὶ τὰ ψηφίσματα); and in 54. vi–vii he mentions two of Athens' many boards of ἱεροποιοί. On the other hand, the reader may think that 53 gives disproportionate attention to the διαιτηταί, the procedures which they follow, and their appointment from the forty-second year-class (as chs 63–9 give disproportionate attention to the mechanical details of the working of the δικαστήρια: cf. p. 697): I imagine that the Athenians were proud of and interested in the elaborate devices by which they sought to secure fairness in the running of the courts, and that *A.P.*'s detailed treatment reflects this interest.

50. i. τὰ μὲν οὖν ὑπὸ τῆς βουλῆς διοικούμενα ταῦτ' ἐστίν: This sentence rounds off the section on the boule which began in 43. ii.
κληροῦνται δὲ καὶ ἱερῶν ἐπισκευασταί: Found elsewhere in a law *ap.* Ath. VI. 235 D. Sandys suggested that they are to be identified with the ναοποιοί of Arist. *Rhet.* I. 1374 B 27 (a word familiar at Delphi

COMMENTARY ON THE *ATH. POL.* [50. i

and elsewhere; the only ναοποιοί found in Athenian documents are those appointed to supervise work on Delos (*IG* ii² 1678 = *I. de Délos* 104-4, *aA* 20, *bA* 14 [where the Attic spelling of *IG* is wrong], cf. *I. de Délos* 104-5, *A* 35, 104-6, 22 [restored], 104-23, 104-24: see J. Coupry, *Atti del 3° Congresso Internazionale di Epigrafia Greca e Latina, 1957*, 60–1). In Arist. *Pol.* VI. 1322 B 19–22 men responsible for the maintenance of sacred buildings are designated ἐπιμεληταὶ τῶν περὶ τὰ ἱερά.†

In Greek thinking the affairs of the gods were not distinct from the affairs of the state; and so in Athens the repairers of the temples, like the treasurers of Athena (47. i), were officials of the δῆμος, and they received an annual allocation of funds in the μερισμός (cf. below).

δέκα ἄνδρες: Presumably this board and the other sortitive decemviral boards, like those treated in 47–8, consisted of one man from each tribe.

λαμβάνοντες τριάκοντα μνᾶς παρὰ τῶν ἀποδεκτῶν: That is, in accordance with fourth-century financial practice, they received an annual allowance of 30 minas (½ talent) as part of the μερισμός of the state's revenue to different spending authorities (cf. 48. i–ii with commentary). This allowance would cover only the most elementary repairs: the second decree of Callias, enacted in 434/3 as the Periclean building programme was brought to a premature halt before the Peloponnesian War, seems to have authorised expenditure on ἐπι[σκευά]ζεν up to 10 talents a year (M&L 58 B, 5–12). In Hellenistic Athens we find the στρατηγὸς ἐπὶ τὴν παρασκευήν and the ἀρχιτέκτων ἐπὶ τὰ ἱερά responsible for temples and their contents: cf. Rhodes, *A.B.*, 125–6.

50. ii. καὶ ἀστυνόμοι δέκα: As set out by *A.P.*, their duties concern the hire of entertainers, and the cleanliness and safety of the streets; the latter duty is referred to by schol. D. XXIV. *Tim.* 112, which adds ὅν (*sc.* τὸν ἀστυνόμον) καλοῦσί τινες πατέρα τῆς πόλεως. Concern with entertainers is an instance of their duty to enforce whatever sumptuary legislation there may be, as they are said to have punished the Cynic Crates about the end of the century for wearing linen (D.L. VI. 90). In particular they had to ensure that sanctuaries and roads along which processions passed were in a fit state (cf. *IG* ii² 380 [320/19], recording the transfer of their duties, at any rate in the Piraeus, to the ἀγορανόμοι; 659 [283/2], showing them still or again at work in the city). On offices of this kind see in general Plat. *Legg.* VI. 759 A 2–7, 763 C 3–764 C 4, 779 B 7–C 7; Arist. *Pol.* VI. 1321 B 18–27, VII. 1331 B 6–13; also *OGIS* 483 (reedited by G. Klaffenbach, *Abh. Berlin* 1953, vi; date pp. 19–25), a Hellenistic law published in the second century A.D. which sets out the duties of the ἀστυνόμοι of

50. ii] COMMENTARY ON THE *ATH. POL.*

Pergamum (lines 29-35 require them to see that those who have property adjoining a road keep the road clean).

τούτων δὲ ε'... πέντε δ' ἐν ἄστει: This division between Athens and the Piraeus recurs with the ἀγορανόμοι (51. i), μετρονόμοι (51. ii) and σιτοφύλακες (51. iii); similarly a law of 375/4 presupposes the existence of a (slave) δοκιμαστής of silver coins ἐν ἄστει and provides for the appointment of one ἐμ Πειραιεῖ (*Hesp.* xliii 1974, 157-88). Here, in that law, and in *IG* ii² 380, 13-14 (ἀγορανόμοι), the preposition used is ἐν; in all instances in ch. 51 it is εἰς (in a different construction).

τάς τε αὐλητρίδας καὶ τὰς ψαλτρίας καὶ τὰς κιθαριστρίας: Girls who play the αὐλοι (reed-pipes), ψαλτήριον (harp) and κιθάρα (lyre): no doubt they might also be called on to provide sexual entertainment. Plat. *Prot.* 347 C 3-E 1 remarks that the symposia of commonplace men force up the price of αὐλητρίδες, but at the symposia of καλοὶ κἀγαθοί and πεπαιδευμένοι you will not find αὐλητρίδες, ὀρχηστρίδες or ψαλτρίαι; but Xenophon's *Symposium*, though a gathering of καλοὶ κἀγαθοί (i. 1), was entertained by an αὐλητρίς, an ὀρχηστρίς and a boy who played the lyre and danced, for whom their Syracusan owner gained a large sum (ii. 1). We should expect ὀρχηστρίδες as well as musicians to be covered by the law, and probably *A.P.*'s list is incomplete.

σκοποῦσιν ὅπως μὴ πλείονος ἢ δυεῖν δραχμαῖς μισθωθήσονται: Kenyon retains the reading of the papyrus, but it is very likely that the law will have used and *A.P.* will have repeated the older form, δυοῖν δραχμαῖν, and we should follow Herwerden & Leeuwen and Kaibel & Wilamowitz[2] in emending. Cf. 42. v with commentary.

Hyp. IV. *Eux.* 3 mentions that men have been prosecuted (in an εἰσαγγελία) ὡς πλέονος μισθοῦντες τὰς αὐλητρίδας ἢ ὁ νόμος κελεύει; and Suid. (Δ 528) διάγραμμα writes διέγραφον γὰρ οἱ ἀγορανόμοι (*sic*) ὅσον ἔδει λαμβάνειν τὴν ἑταίραν ἑκάστην. As Moore remarks, the richest citizens presumably had entertainers permanently attached or regularly available to their households (cf. previous note); the entertainers dealt with here were those available for casual hire by the not-so-rich. The sale of bread (51. iii) and the hire of entertainers are the two trades which the state saw fit to regulate.

κἂν πλείους τὴν αὐτὴν σπουδάσωσι... μισθοῦσιν: Many have followed Blass[2] in substituting for the aorist subjunctive the present, σπουδάζωσι, and that is probably right. This provision for the allocation of entertainers among rival customers competing for their services implies that there must have been fixed times and places for hiring.

καὶ ὅπως τῶν κοπρολόγων μηδεὶς... ἐπιμελοῦνται: For dung-collectors cf. Ar. *Vesp.* 1184, *Pax*, 9, Poll. VII. 134 (with further quotations from comedy); in *IG* ii² 380, 25-8, 34 sqq., those who throw out χοῦς into the processional streets are to be obliged to remove it in whatever way they can, and for the future the throwing out of rubbish and dung is to be forbidden. Cf. also the law of Pergamum, *OGIS* 483, 36–47; and Wilamowitz, *A.u.A.*, i. 217 n. 57.†

καὶ τὰς ὁδοὺς κωλύουσι κατοικοδομεῖν: '... building to encroach on the streets.' [X.] *A.P.* iii. 4 lists among the affairs with which the Athenian state busies itself διαδικάζειν εἴ τις ... κατοικοδομεῖ τι δημόσιον.

καὶ δρυφάκτους ὑπὲρ τῶν ὁδῶν ὑπερτείνειν: Elsewhere δρύφακτοι are railings or barriers (see Rhodes, *A.B.*, 33–4, G. Roux, *BCH* c 1976, 475–83): here the word must denote wooden balconies projecting from the walls of houses (cf. schol. Ar. *Eq.* 675, *Vesp.* 386, offering as synonyms ταβλωτά, ταβλώματα, words found only in these scholia and presumably of Latin origin). It is said of the tyrant Hippias by [Arist.] *Oec.* II. 1347 A 4–8 and of Iphicrates by Polyaen. III. 9. xxx that the one announced and the other persuaded the Athenians that such projections should be broken off or (confiscated and) sold, and rich houseowners paid large sums to save their houses.

καὶ ὀχετοὺς μετεώρους ... ποιεῖν: 'Overhead drain-pipes.' Cf. *OGIS* 483, 60–78.

καὶ τὰς θυρίδας εἰς τὴν ὁδὸν ἀνοίγειν: θύρα means 'door'; of the diminutive forms θύριον and θυρίδιον mean 'small door', but θυρίς regularly means 'window' (cf. Ar. *Vesp.* 379, *Thesm.* 797, Plat. *Rep.* II. 359 D 6, Ar. *De An.* I. 404 A 4, *Probl.* XV. 13. 913 A 10, and Sandys on this passage): the reference should therefore be to (overhead) outward-opening window-shutters, which if not secured might fall down into the street. Kenyon, however, citing Pl. *Public.* 20. iii–iv, [Arist.] *Oec.* II. 1347 A 6, supposed that here the word means 'door' and the danger was that which threatened passers-by if doors were suddenly opened outwards.

καὶ τοὺς ἐν ταῖς ὁδοῖς ἀπογιγνομένους ἀναιροῦσιν: '... take up for burial': cf. Ar. *Vesp.* 386, X. *Anab.* VI. iv. 9, *IG* ii² 1672, 119.

51. i. κληροῦνται δὲ καὶ ἀγορανόμοι <ι′ >: The numeral was inserted by Π. Ν. Παπαγεώργιος, *Ἀθ.* iv 1892, 590–1: cf. 50. ii, and §§ii, iii, below; I doubt the inference of D. M. MacDowell (commentary on Ar. *Vesp.* 1407) from Ar. *Ach.* 723–4 that in the fifth century there were only six. ἀγορανόμοι are already well-established officials in Aristophanes: they maintained order in the Agora (*Ach.* 968); they collected market dues (schol. Hom. *Il.* XXI. 203 [καὶ ἐν τῷ ἀγορανομικῷ δὲ νόμῳ Ἀθηναίων διέσταλται ἰχθύων καὶ ἐγχελύων τέλη][44] cf. schol. Ar. *Ach.* 896 with 723), and probably the additional tax paid by foreign traders (D. LVII. *Eub.* 31, 34). They had powers of corporal punish-

---

[44] However, D. M. MacDowell, *The Law in Classical Athens*, 157, refers this not to taxes but to prices.

COMMENTARY ON THE *ATH. POL.*

ment over non-citizens (cf. Ar. *Ach.* 724, Cratin. fr. 115 Kock *ap.* Poll. x. 177, *IG* ii² 380, 40 sqq.), and probably could fine citizens a small sum or prosecute them in court for a heavier penalty; surprisingly, in the law published in *Hesp.* xliii 1974, 157–88, lines 13–23, it is not they but the συλλογεῖς τοῦ δήμου (on whom see above, p. 520) who discipline the city δοκιμαστής and receive notice of offences in the Agora and the rest of the city. They had an office, the ἀγορανόμιον (ἀγορανόμιον in the Piraeus, *IG* ii² 380, 10–12; ἀγορανόμιον dedicated to Antoninus Pius, *IG* ii² 3391 with Travlos, *Pictorial Dictionary*, 37–41); for lead tokens which they issued, perhaps as receipts for market dues, see A. Engel, *BCH* viii 1884, 6–7 with pl. i nos. 23–6, *I. N. Σβορῶνος, JIAN* iii 1900, 332–3 nos. 159–66 (pl. ιθ' nos. 4–9), [M. L. Lang &] M. Crosby, *The Athenian Agora*, x. 79 with n. 11, 80–1, with 102 no. L 170, 105 no. L 194. On ἀγορανόμοι in general see Plat. *Legg.* VI. 759 A 2–7, 763 C 3–764 C 4, XI. 917 A 9–918 A 1; Arist. *Pol.* IV. 1299 B 14–18, VI. 1321 B 12–18, VII. 1331 B 6–13.

τῶν ὠνίων ἐπιμελεῖσθαι πάντων, ὅπως ... πωλήσεται: That is, they had to ensure that goods were in an acceptable condition and that there was no fraud; a law prescribing ἀψευδεῖν ἐν τῇ ἀγορᾷ is cited by D. xx. *Lept.* 9, Hyp. III. *Ath.* 14. Earlier their responsibilities had included bread (X. *Symp.* ii. 20) but not corn (Lys. XXII. *Frum.* 16); but §§iii–iv make the σιτοφύλακες responsible for the retail trade in both bread and corn, and the ἐμπορίου ἐπιμεληταί responsible for the wholesale trade in corn: cf. below.

The papyrus has the present subjunctive πωλῆται here, and the inappropriate aorist subjunctive χρήσωνται in §ii, but the future indicatives ἔσται and πωλήσουσιν in §iii and μισθωθήσονται and καταβαλεῖ in 50. ii (cf. Meisterhans & Schwyzer, *G.a.I.*, 253–5): editors have rightly followed Kaibel, *Stil und Text*, 220–1 cf. 76 n. 1, in emending to πωλήσεται here, and A. Sidgwick and W. G. Rutherford, *CR* v 1891, 117, in emending to χρήσονται in §ii.

ἀκίβδηλα: 'Unadulterated.' κίβδηλος is frequently used of adulterated coins, in which the metal is not of the expected purity (R. S. Stroud, *Hesp.* xliii 1974, 171, is too generous in suggesting that in lines 10–13 of the law which he publishes it may refer to 'any other kind of falsification' apart from the use of a core of base metal); ἀκίβδηλος is used of coinage in Plat. *Legg.* XI. 916 D 3.

51. ii. κληροῦνται δὲ καὶ μετρονόμοι <ι'>: The number is specified in the lexicographers' notes on μετρονόμοι (in Harp. *s.v.*, . . . ι', ε' εἰς . . . has been corrupted into . . ., ιε' εἰς . . .), and was inserted here by Π. Ν. Παπαγεώργιος, *Ἀθ.* iv 1892, 590–1: cf. §§i, iii, 50. ii. For Athenian standard measures and weights see ch. 10 with commentary; there is a lengthy decree of the late second century on the enforcement of standards (*IG* ii² 1013, cf. *Hesp.* vii 27), where the officials concerned are referred to not as μετρονόμοι but simply as ἄρχοντες (e.g. line 12), and the boule has an overriding responsibility (6–7, 16–18). There is a list of μετρονόμοι, their secretaries and the measures and weights which they handed over to their successors, in *Hesp.* xxxvii 1 (222/1); cf. also *Hesp.* vi 2, and perhaps *IG* ii² 1710, 1711. There was an official called προμετρητής, ὁ τοὺς πιπρασκομένους πυροὺς ἐν τῇ ἀγορᾷ καὶ τῶν ἄλλων σπερμάτων ἕκαστον διαμετρῶν (*L.S.* 290. 33, Harp., Phot., Suid. [Π 2504], *s.v.*; provision for his μισθός is found in *IG* ii² 1672, 291, 299), who may have been a ὑπηρέτης of the μετρονόμοι (cf. Gilbert, *C.A.S.A.*, 260 with n. 2, Busolt & Swoboda, *G.S.*, ii. 1059 with n. 2).

χρήσονται: Cf. on §i *fin*.

51. iii. ἦσαν δὲ καὶ σιτοφύλακες κληρωτοὶ <ι´ > . . . νῦν δ´ . . . : Again the number is specified in the lexica (and in Harp. and Phot. *s.v.* we have the same corruption as in Harp. μετρονόμοι) : it was inserted here by Kaibel & Wilamowitz[1] (cf. Kaibel, *Stil und Text*, 221); cf. §§i, ii, 50. ii. This is one of the places where *A.P.* distinguishes between earlier and current practice (cf. Introduction, pp. 34–5): he does not say when this change was made, but B. D. Meritt has plausibly connected it with the corn shortage which affected Athens and the rest of Greece in the reign of Alexander (*Hesp.* xiii 1944, 245); in Lys. xxii. *Frum.* 8, where the MSS read δύο (defended, as implying that in the early fourth century *A.P.*'s earlier practice had not yet been instituted, by W. Göz, *Klio* xvi 1919–20, 187–90), and T. Bergk suggested δ´ (compatible with *A.P.*'s earlier practice if half the board is referred to), Thalheim's νῦν is to be preferred (cf. R. J. Seager, *Hist.* xv 1966, 174 with n. 23). In the third century the twelve tribes supplied ten σιτοφύλακες and two secretaries: see *Hesp.* vi 2, xiii 8, xxx 23, with commentaries. J. J. Keaney, *Hist.* xix 1970, 330–2, notes that Harpocration in retailing what he found in *A.P.* gives only the earlier number of σιτοφύλακες, and argues that the record of the increase is a late addition to the text of *A.P.* and that Harpocration used an edition of *A.P.* from which this and other additions were absent; on the other hand, Photius has a corrupt version of the revised text (giving the later number as 30 + 5): see Introduction, pp. 55–6.

At any rate from the beginning of the sixth century, Athens had relied on imported corn to supplement the local crop (cf. pp. 95–6, 127), and to ensure that the citizens should be fed the state was led to take a special interest in the corn trade. For an early non-Athenian instance see M & L 30 A, 6–12 (Teos, *c.* 470); Arist. *Pol.* iv. 1299 A 23 mentions σιτομέτραι as commonly found economic officials. In Athens Solon forbade the export of natural products other than olive oil (Pl. *Sol.* 24. i–ii); in the time of the Delian League it was by a special privilege that Methone was allowed to buy corn directly from Byzantium rather than through Athens (M&L 65, 34–41); in the fourth century both citizens and metics were forbidden to transport corn, or to lend money for the transport of corn, to any destination outside Attica (e.g. [D.] xxxiv. Phorm. 37, xxxv. *Lacr.* 50–1, Lyc. *Leocr.* 27: cf. on §iv, below); in the 380's σιτοπῶλαι, retail corn dealers, were forbidden to build up a stock of more than 50 φορμοί of corn (Lys. xxii. *Frum.* 5 with Seager, *op. cit.*, 173–7: W. K. Pritchett, *Hesp.* xxv 1956, 194–8, suggests that the φορμός was identical with the μέδιμνος), or to make a profit of more than 1 obol, perhaps per μέδιμνος (*ibid.* 8). D. xx. *Lept.* 32 shows that the σιτοφύλακες kept records of the amounts of corn imported; [D.] lix. *Neaer.* 27 shows that the 2% harbour tax was levied separately on corn. περὶ σίτου was one of the items prescribed for the agenda of the κυρίαι ἐκκλησίαι (43. iv with commentary); other indications of the state's attempts to control the corn trade are given here and in §iv; for the duties of the σιτοφύλακες under the currency law of 375/4 see on §iv.†

νῦν δ' εἴκοσι μὲν εἰς ἄστυ, πεντεκαίδεκα δ' εἰς Πειραιέα: Wilamowitz found a total of 35 implausible, and suggested εἰσὶ ιε' μὲν ... (Kaibel & Wilamowitz[1]) or εἰσὶ λ', ιε' μὲν ... (*A.u.A.*, i. 219 n. 64), but Kaibel & Wilamowitz[3] accepted the papyrus' text (cf. Kaibel, *Stil und Text,* 221). Probably a scheme was devised by which each year half the tribes supplied four men and half three (cf. occasions when five men had to be appointed: 52. ii [εἰσαγωγεῖς], 54. i [ὁδοποιοί], 56. iii [choregi for the Thargelia], 62. ii [amphictyons for Delos], with commentary).

ἀργός: 'Unground': cf. πυροὺς ... ἀργούς in Hippocr. *V.M.* 13. Wilamowitz' suggestion (*A.u.A.*, i. 219 n. 63) that the word order ὁ ἐν ἀγορᾷ σῖτος ἀργός is derived from the law is likely enough, but there are parallels in Arist. *E.N.* vi. 1140 a 3–5, *Pol.* i. 1252 b 27–8.

ἔπειθ' ὅπως οἵ τε μυλωθροὶ ... πωλήσουσιν: 'That the millers sell the meal in accordance with the price (which they paid) for the barleycorns', and do not take a greater profit than they are allowed. Cf. the law cited above which set a limit to the profits of the σιτοπῶλαι. **καὶ οἱ ἀρτοπῶλαι πρὸς τὰς τιμὰς τῶν πυρῶν τοὺς ἄρτους:** 'And that the bread-sellers sell the loaves in accordance with the price (which they paid) for the wheat.' Female ἀρτοπωλίδες are found in Ar. *Vesp.* 238, *Ran.* 858; ἀρτοπῶλαι, cited by LSJ only from Poll. vii. 21 and an inscription of the third century A.D., are found also in *SEG* xviii 36, B 6 (320's) and are a possible expansion of αρτοπ in Tod 100, back, 23, and *SEG* xii 84, B 82 (401/0?).

καὶ τὸν σταθμὸν ἄγοντας ὅσον ἂν οὗτοι τάξουσιν: Sc. οἱ σιτοφύλακες.

COMMENTARY ON THE *ATH. POL.* [51. iii

Loaves of bread were to be of a standard weight, so that it would be easy to ensure that the bakers were not taking an excessive profit.

51. iv ἐμπορίου δ' ἐπιμελητὰς δέκα κληροῦσιν: *A.P.* began his catalogue of officials with the passive κληροῦνται (50. i, 51. i, ii); in 51. iii he used ἦσαν ... κληρωτοί; now he turns to κληροῦσιν (*sc.* οἱ Ἀθηναῖοι), which remains his standard expression to the end of 54 except in 54. v–vii. For these officials *A.P.* mentions only one duty more specific than τῶν ... ἐμπορίων ἐπιμελεῖσθαι, that of ensuring that two thirds of all imported corn were sent to the city. They were also responsible for enforcing the law which forbade the transport of corn to destinations outside Attica ([D.] xxxv. *Lacr.* 51, LVIII. *Theocr.* 8–9 with *hyp.*: cf. on §iii, above). Until recently there was no evidence for their existence before the middle of the fourth century (cf. Wilamowitz, *A.u.A.*, i. 221); but the currency law of 375/4 stipulates that charges are to be laid, of offences

τὰ μὲν ἐν [τ]ῶι σί[τωι πρὸς]
τὸς σιτοφύλακας, τὰ δὲ ἐν τῆι ἀγορᾶι κ[α]ὶ [ἐν τῶι ἄλ]-
λωι ἄστει πρὸς τοὺς τὸ δήμο συλλογέ[ας], τὰ [δὲ ἐν τῶ]-
ι ἐμπορίωι καὶ τῶι Πει[ρ]αιεῖ πρὸς τοὺ[ς ἐπιμελητ]-
ὰς τοῦ ἐμπορίο πλὴν τὰ ἐν τῶι σίτωι, τὰ δὲ [ἐν τῶι σί]-
τωι πρὸς τοὺς σιτοφύλακας

(*Hesp.* xliii 1974, 157–88, lines 18–23): see Stroud's commentary, pp. 180–1 with n. 92. It appears that in the course of the fourth century there were changes in the boundaries drawn between the responsibilities of the σιτοφύλακες and of other officials (cf. p. 576), and this text suggests that in the 370's the σιτοφύλακες controlled the wholesale as well as the retail trade in corn.

εἰς τὸ σιτικὸν ἐμπόριον: None of the entries in the lexica which are derived from this passage has σιτικὸν: most have ἀστικὸν, which was proposed in the text of *A.P.* by Sandys, *CR* v 1891, 117, and accepted by Blass[1]; others have Ἀττικὸν, which was proposed by C. Torr, *ibid.*, and accepted by Sandys[1]; but most editors have retained σιτικὸν (cf. Kaibel, *Stil und Text*, 221–3). That they were right to do so is shown by the currency law of 375/4, which refers to places designated σῖτος/ν both in the city and in the Piraeus (*tit. cit.*, 18, 22–3 [quoted above], with Stroud's commentary, p. 180). This, the earliest instance of σιτικός, is omitted from LSJ but included in the 1968 Supplement.

τὰ δύο μέρη ... εἰς τὸ ἄστυ κομίζειν: That is, the importers were not free to sell their corn wherever they could get the highest price for it.

52. i. καθ[ισ]τᾶσι δὲ καὶ τοὺς ἕνδεκα κλήρῳ: Kenyon[1-3] printed κληρωτούς, after which τοὺς was inserted by W. G. Rutherford, *CR* v 1891, 91, and Herwerden (cf. τοὺς ἐπιμελησομένους in *Epit. Heracl.* 8); the neater solution, κλήρῳ τούς, is due to Kaibel, *Stil und Text*, 223; Kenyon adopted this in his Berlin ed., changed back to κληρωτούς, ἐπιμελησομένους in the *corrigenda*, changed again to κλήρῳ τούς in his O.C.T. On the Eleven see Lipsius, *A.R.*, 74–81, Harrison, *L.A.*, ii. 17–18. Why they should number eleven is not clear, but they presumably ante-date Cleisthenes' creation of the ten tribes, and are in fact mentioned in connection with Solon in 7. iii (cf. *ad loc.*, and Wilamowitz, *A.u.A.*, i. 222 n. 70). They were gaolers and executioners: in early Athens they may, as Wilamowitz suggested, have had powers of jurisdiction; those who served under the Thirty were regarded as sufficiently involved in that régime to be excluded from the amnesty of 403 (35. i, 39. i, with commentary). According to Poll. VIII. 102, Areth. schol. Plat. *Phaed.* 59 E, and perhaps schol. Ar. *Vesp.* 1108, they were renamed νομοφύλακες by Demetrius of Phalerum; but on the νομοφύλακες of the late fourth century see p. 315. The Eleven are mentioned by Arist. *Pol.* VI. 1322 A 19–20, in the course of a discussion of the unpopular but necessary office which has to enforce judicial decisions (1321 B 40–1322 A 29).

τοὺς ἐπιμελησομένους τῶν ἐν τῷ δεσμωτηρ[ί]ῳ: The Athenians undoubtedly used imprisonment as a precautionary measure for certain men awaiting trial, men with outstanding fines or other debts to the state, and men awaiting the death sentence (e.g. bouleutic oath *ap.* D. XXIV. *Tim.* 144; proposed law *ap.* §§39–40 with schol.; Plat. *Phaed.* 58 C 4–5); that they also used imprisonment as a form of punishment has been denied (e.g. Gilbert, *C.A.S.A.*, 414, Busolt & Swoboda, *G.S.*, ii. 1109, cf. E. E. Cohen, *Ancient Athenian Maritime Courts*, 79 with n. 185) but should nevertheless be accepted (I. Barkan, *CP* xxxi 1936, 338–41, cf. Bonner & Smith, *Administration of Justice*, ii. 275–6, Harrison, *L.A.*, ii. 177). It does not appear that Athens had more than one prison (the evidence is collected and discussed by R. E. Wycherley, *The Athenian Agora*, iii, pp. 149–50, H. A. Thompson & R. E. Wycherley, *The Athenian Agora*, xiv. 125 n. 48); it is now believed that the prison was the 'Poros Building' of M. Crosby, *Hesp.* xx 1951, 168–87, Thompson & Wycherley, *op. cit.*, 74 (see *Agora Guide*³, 172–5, E. Vanderpool, Penn. U. Mus. Pap. i 1980, 17–31). The Eleven must have had subordinates, whether slave or free, to keep the prison for them (cf. ὁ τοῦ δεσμωτηρίου φύλαξ in Plat. *Crit.* 43 A 5–6, and pp. 439 on the ὑπηρέται of the Thirty, 539 on those who administered the hemlock to men sentenced to death). According to Isae. IV. *Her. Nic.* 28 all the members of one board were condemned for letting prisoners go free.

καὶ τοὺς ἀπαγομένους . . . εἰ δὲ μή, τότε θανατώσοντας: On the procedures referred to in this section see Lipsius, *A.R.*, 317–38, Harrison, *L.A.*, ii. 221–32, M. H. Hansen, *Apagoge, Endeixis and*

Ephegesis against Kakourgoi, Atimoi and Pheugontes. The procedure known as ἀπαγωγή was available (*a*) against the kind of offenders referred to in Greek as κακοῦργοι and in English as 'common criminals' (the three terms used by *A.P.*, 'thieves', 'kidnappers' and 'clothes-stealers' [highwaymen] are frequently encountered and were presumably used in the law; the procedure came to be employed for other offences regarded as comparable), who had in theory to be caught ἐπ' αὐτοφώρῳ (but this requirement came to be interpreted so generously that it ceased to be significant); and (*b*) against ἄτιμοι and exiles who exercised rights to which they were not entitled (this second category is omitted in *A.P.*'s summary, but for a special instance of it see 63. iii with commentary). The distinctive characteristics of this procedure are that the prosecutor began it not by filing an accusation but by physically haling the accused before the authorities, and that offenders who admitted their guilt could be executed summarily, without trial; by the similar ἐφήγησις the prosecutor brought the authorities to the accused and required them to arrest him; for ἔνδειξις see below. On the jurisdiction of the Eleven cf. [D.] xxxv. *Lacr.* 47.†

The text as we read it in the papyrus is not perfectly logical: ἀπαγομένους ought to apply to all three of the nouns which follow, but if the wording is strictly interpreted it will apply to κλέπτας only. Kaibel & Wilamowitz inserted ἀπαγομένους ⟨κακούργους, τούς τε⟩ κλέπτας (cf. Kaibel, *Stil und Text*, 223, citing *L.S.* 250. 4, *E.M.* [338. 31] ἕνδεκα); Herwerden deleted τοὺς before ἀνδραποδιστὰς and λωποδύτας; but the papyrus' illogicality is probably authentic.

ἂν μὲν [ὁμολογῶ]σι: Restored by Kenyon[1] from *L.S.* 310. 4, Poll. VIII. 102: the fact is confirmed by A. 1. *Tim.* 113, D. XXIV. *Tim.* 65. **εἰσάξοντας εἰς τὸ δι[κ]αστήριον:** εἰσάξοντας is technical: the Eleven are the εἰσάγουσα ἀρχή, and preside in the court. For the court of the Eleven cf. Ar. *Vesp.* 1108, Ant. fr. 43 Sauppe *ap.* Harp. παράβυστον, and Wycherley, *The Athenian Agora*, iii, pp. 146–8, Thompson & Wycherley, *The Athenian Agora*, xiv. 59.

καὶ τὰ ἀπογραφόμενα χωρία καὶ οἰκίας εἰσάξοντας εἰς τὸ δικαστήριον: If a man's property was forfeit (whether by sentence of a court or automatically, if for instance he defaulted on a debt to the state), in some cases it was the responsibility of his demarch ([Pl.] *X. Or.* 834 A, *L.S.* 199. 4, 237. 8, Harp. δήμαρχος), in others it was left to individual citizens to ἀπογράφειν the items which the state was entitled to seize (for instances of ἀπογραφαί see *Hesp.* v 10, 118–19, 1153–4, 85–6). This quasi-prosecution was taken to court, and a man who claimed that an item belonged to him and was not liable to forfeiture would enter a defence; if there was no defence within a stated period (which should have included a κυρία ἐκκλησία at which the ἀπογραφή was read out: 43. iv with commentary), the

52. i] COMMENTARY ON THE *ATH. POL.*

Eleven could probably accept the ἀπογραφή without more ado. Cf. Lipsius, *A.R.*, 299–308, Harrison, *L.A.*, ii. 211–17.

In various places the author has sought to avoid linguistic monotony, as in his variations on the theme of ten men appointed one from each tribe; but he has conspicuously not done so here, where it would have been easy to interrupt the string of future participles and make a fresh start with εἰσάγουσι δὲ καί . . . (cf. Kaibel, *Stil und Text*, 26, and Introduction, pp. 42–4).

παραδώσοντας τοῖς πωληταῖς: Cf. 47. ii–iii with commentary.

καὶ τὰς ἐνδείξεις εἰσάξοντας: ἔνδειξις was available for the same offences as ἀπαγωγή and ἐφήγησις, but in this the prosecutor initiated the proceedings by denouncing the offender to the authorities. As a corollary of this distinction, it was not stipulated that κακοῦργοι against whom an ἔνδειξις was made should have been caught ἐπ' αὐτοφώρῳ; whereas the arrest of the offender was an essential element of ἀπαγωγή and ἐφήγησις, a man accused by ἔνδειξις could be but did not have to be placed under arrest (cf. M. H. Hansen, *Apagoge, Endeixis and Ephegesis*, 11–17).

καὶ γὰρ ταύτας εἰσάγουσιν οἱ ἕνδεκα: Qualified by the following sentence.

εἰσάγουσι δὲ καὶ τῶν ἐνδείξεών τινας καὶ οἱ θεσμοθέται: As in 43. vi, on προχειροτονία, *A.P.* generalises where the laws must have specified which kinds of ἔνδειξις were an exception to the general rule (cf. Introduction, p. 35 with n. 182). ἔνδειξις is not mentioned among the kinds of lawsuit handled by the thesmothetae in ch. 59 (cf. p. 661); ἔνδειξις to the thesmothetae against public debtors (who failed to comply with their ἀτιμία) is mentioned in a law *ap.* D. XXIV. *Tim.* 22. Hansen, *op. cit.*, 20–1, plausibly suggests that the Eleven acted as εἰσάγουσα ἀρχή for ἐνδείξεις when the accused had been placed under arrest but the thesmothetae when he had not.

52. ii. κληροῦσι δὲ καὶ εἰσαγωγέας ε' ἄνδρας . . . δυοῖν φυλαῖν ἕκαστος: Kaibel, *Stil und Text*, 223, insisted that the words δυοῖν φυλαῖν ἕκαστος, placed at the end of the sentence, must belong to the relative clause and mean that each εἰσαγωγεύς was responsible for the lawsuits of two tribes (that is, for suits against defendants of two tribes: cf. 53. ii *fin.* with commentary). However, it may also be true that the tribes were grouped in pairs for the purpose of appointing εἰσαγωγεῖς (perhaps by a separate sortition each year, or perhaps I and II together, and so on, in official tribal order) and that *A.P.* is thinking of the appointment of the εἰσαγωγεῖς as well as of the distribution of lawsuits among them. For other occasions when five men had to be appointed see 54. i (ὁδοποιοί), 56. iii (choregi for the Thargelia) and 62. ii (amphictyons for Delos), also 51. iii (thirty-five σιτοφύλακες), with commentary.

An εἰσαγωγεύς is an εἰσάγουσα ἀρχή, an official who brings a case to court and presides in the court (cf. D. xxxvii. *Pant.* 33-4). As the title of particular officials it is found in the decree of 425/4 ordering a reassessment of the Delian League's tribute (M&L 69, 7, 12, 13), used of the chairmen of the special courts set up to hear appeals against assessments. The fourth-century εἰσαγωγεῖς are known only from this passage and Poll. viii. 101 (quoted below): the usage of D. xxxvii. *Pant.* 33-4 makes it probable that they were instituted after the mid 340's, when that speech was delivered (L. Gernet, *REG* li 1938, 5 = *Droit et société dans la Grèce ancienne*, 175-6, cf. Harrison, *L.A.*, ii. 21 with n. 3). The earliest δίκαι ἔμμηνοι were presumably instituted at the same time as, or earlier than, the εἰσαγωγεῖς (cf. Gernet, *opp. citt.*, 2-9 = 174-8).

οἳ τὰς ἐμμήνους εἰσάγουσι δίκας: (Kaibel, *Stil und Text*, 223-5, wanted to rearrange the words to yield οἳ ἐμμήνους εἰσάγουσι τὰς δίκας δυοῖν . . .: cf. below, pp. 585-6.) It has normally been assumed that these lawsuits were 'monthly' in the sense that a decision was promised within a month, if not always actually given within a month (e.g. Lipsius, *A.R.*, 901, Harrison, *L.A.*, ii. 16, 21, 154). However, it is argued convincingly by E. E. Cohen, *Ancient Athenian Maritime Courts*, 9-59, that although prompt decisions were a feature of these suits (achieved in part by not following the rule of 53. ii and first sending them to διαιτηταί: Lipsius, *A.R.*, 228 with n. 32, Cohen, *op. cit.*, 35 with n. 75, against T. D. Goodell, *AJP* xii 1891, 323-5) the term δίκαι ἔμμηνοι means 'suits where there is an opportunity to institute proceedings every month'. Notice particularly ἐμπορικαὶ δίκαι . . . ἀκριβεῖς, αἱ κατὰ μῆνα in [D.] vii. *Halon.* 12, and the provision for prosecution on the last day of the month in Crat. 342 F 4a; in M&L 68, 47, of 426/5, ἔμμηνα will be equivalent to κατὰ μῆνα, not to ἐντὸς ἑνὸς μηνός; in [D.] xxxiii. *Apat.* 23 αἱ δὲ λήξεις τοῖς ἐμπόροις τῶν δικῶν ἔμμηνοί εἰσιν ἀπὸ τοῦ Βοηδρομιῶνος (iii) μέχρι τοῦ Μουνιχιῶνος (x), ἵνα παραχρῆμα τῶν δικαίων τυχόντες ἀνάγωνται will mean that there was an opportunity to institute a δίκη ἐμπορική each month during the winter, so that cases could be settled outside the sailing season and traders would be free to sail at the beginning of summer (contr. U. E. Paoli, *ZSS* xlix 1928, 473-7, Italian trans. *Studi sul Processo Attico*, 175-86, who emended to obtain trials during the summer). A Thasian law of the late fourth century, including among days when ἔνδειξις and ἀπαγωγή are not permitted μηδὲ ὅταν τὰ δικαστήρια τὰ ἔμμηνα δικάζηι μηδὲ ἐν ταῖς ἀντωμοσίαις τῶν ἐμμήνων (*SEG* xvii 415, 4), tends to support Cohen. The fact that in Athens and elsewhere provisions are found for bringing certain categories of suit to court within a stated period (e.g. D. xxiv. *Tim.* 63; Tod 162, 16-18 [Ceos, 350's]) does not undermine this conclusion. Cf. D. M. MacDowell, *The Law in Classical Athens*, 232.

COMMENTARY ON THE *ATH. POL.* [52 ii

εἰσὶ δ' ἔμμηνοι: (For Kaibel's deletion of these words see below, p. 586.) In Poll. VIII. 101 we read εἰσαγωγεῖς οἱ τὰς ἐμμήνους δίκας εἰσάγοντες· ἦσαν δὲ προικός, ἐρανικαί, ἐμπορικαί. Pollux' first two categories are included in *A.P.*'s longer list; but ἐμπορικαί (and μεταλλικαί, another category of 'monthly' suit) are assigned by *A.P.* 59. v and Poll. VIII. 88 to the thesmothetae, and *pace* Blass[1] should not be inserted here. That *A.P.*'s assignment of δίκαι ἐμπορικαί is correct for his own time is confirmed by [D.] XXXIII. *Apat.* 1, XXXIV. *Phorm.* 45. It is commonly believed that Pollux is simply mistaken (e.g. Gernet, *REG* li 1938, 11 n. 3 = *Droit et société dans la Grèce ancienne*, 179 n. 5, cf. Harrison, *L.A.*, ii. 16); Cohen, *op. cit.*, 158–98, suggests that δίκαι ἐμπορικαί came within the purview of the εἰσαγωγεῖς when they were first made ἔμμηνοι, but were transferred to the thesmothetae *c.* 330. We have no contemporary evidence which directly supports Pollux; the suggestion of a change is supported by δίκαι αἰκείας, which fell to the εἰσαγωγεῖς in the time of *A.P.* but (though *A.P.* does not say so) to the Forty earlier; but against a change as late as *c.* 330 may be set the fact that there is no sign of disruption in *A.P.*'s text here comparable to that at the end of 54. vii (cf. *ad loc.*, and Introduction, p. 57). Probably the usual explanation is correct and Pollux is mistaken.

It is not clear why this particular set of charges, but not others, was felt to require 'monthly' procedure: some, but not all, can be explained by military or commercial needs for haste; probably 'monthly' procedure was instituted for some of these charges and the others were added piecemeal (cf. p. 585, and Cohen, *op. cit.*, 10–22).

προικός, ἐάν τις ὀφείλων μὴ ἀποδῷ: 'For a dowry . . .' (some have followed Blass, *LZB* 1891, 304, in emending to ἀπο⟨δί⟩δῳ, but the aorist may stand). This procedure was certainly available to the κύριος to whom a woman returned, against the husband who divorced her or the heirs of a husband who predeceased her (Isae. III. *Her. Pyrrh.* 9, 78, D. XXVII. *Aphob. i.* 17, [D.] LIX. *Neaer.* 52), or to the head of a woman's own family if she predeceased her husband and left no children (Isae. III. *Her. Pyrrh.* 36, 38). Some have argued that it was available also to a husband who had not received the dowry promised him, against the head of his wife's family; if this procedure was not available to him we do not know what procedure was available (for, Lipsius, *A.R.*, 496–7; against, H. J. Wolff, *RE*, xxiii [1957/9], 144–5; Harrison, *L.A.*, i. 50–2, is non-committal). The cases at issue in [D.] XL. *Boe. Dot.* (*c.* 348–347: L. Gernet, Budé ed. of D.'s *Plaidoyers civils*, ii. 32) and D. XLI. *Spud.* had been to διαιτηταί (§§16–17; 12): presumably it is after these cases that the δίκη προικός was made ἔμμηνος and the responsibility of the εἰσαγωγεῖς (cf. p. 583).

COMMENTARY ON THE *ATH. POL.* [52. ii

κἄν τις ἐπὶ δραχμῇ δανεισάμενος ἀποστερῇ: 'If any one borrows at a rate of 1 drachma (in the mina per month: 1% per month, or 12% per annum) and defaults.' This was regarded as a reasonable rate of interest (cf. D. xxvii. *Aphob. i.* 23, 35, A. iii. *Ctes.* 104). Higher rates were sometimes charged, but presumably lacked the protection of this category of δίκη ἔμμηνος: a rate of 1½% per month on dowries due for return to the wife's κύριος was laid down by law (D. xxvii. *Aphob. i.* 17, [D.] lix. *Neaer.* 52: cf. previous note), and the same rate is found in A. i. *Tim.* 107; interest of 16⅔% is found in [D.] xxxiv. *Phorm.* 23–4, of 33⅓% in Isae. fr. 79 Sauppe.

κἄν τις ἐν ἀγορᾷ ... ἀφορμήν: 'If any one wishing to ply his trade in the Agora borrows capital from someone (and defaults).' In this case there was presumably no limit to the rate of interest. D. xxxvi. *Phorm.* is said by *hyp.* 2 to be concerned with a δίκη ἀφορμῆς, but this classification is rejected by Gernet (Budé ed. of D.'s *Plaidoyers civils*, i. 201–2).†

ἔτι δ' αἰκείας: 'Also for battery' (the papyrus' spelling is the normal Attic form: cf. Lipsius, *A.R.*, 643 n. 25); there was a more serious charge of τραῦμα ('wounding'), which was tried by the Areopagus under the homicide laws (57. iii with commentary). According to D. xxxvii. *Pant.* 33 (mid 340's) charges of αἰκεία had to be made to the Forty, and the case at issue in D. liv. *Con.* had been to a διαιτητής (§§26–9); the institution of the εἰσαγωγεῖς is probably later than those speeches (cf. p. 583); these suits must have been transferred to the εἰσαγωγεῖς (and probably at the same time made ἔμμηνοι) between the 340's and the writing of *A.P.*, either when the εἰσαγωγεῖς were first instituted or subsequently. Sandys perhaps supposed that the change was subsequent to the institution of the εἰσαγωγεῖς and δίκαι ἔμμηνοι, and that ἔτι here serves to distinguish the additions from the original list of δίκαι ἔμμηνοι: certainly it is possible that additions were made to the original list (cf. p. 584), but ἔτι could simply be a sign that *A.P.* is deciding not to explain what is at issue in each charge on the list; there is no need to suppose that the charges following ἔτι were added in a revision of *A.P.*'s original text (cf. Introduction, p. 52 n. 249).

καὶ ἐρανικαί: Commentators have suggested 'for the recovery of friendly loans' or 'concerning disputes between members of a friendly association' or both: the two uses of ἔρανος are discussed by Lipsius, *A.R.*, 729–30, M. I. Finley, *Studies in Land and Credit*, 100–6, and Finley makes it clear that there is no evidence for 'friendly associations' before the middle of the third century; the reference here must be to 'friendly loans' (made by a plurality of people, without interest, and repaid in regular instalments).

The papyrus reads ἐρανικὰς καὶ κοινωνικὰς ... καὶ τριηραρχίας καὶ τραπεζιτικάς, though the sentence begins εἰσὶ δ' ἔμμηνοι ... The

52. ii] COMMENTARY ON THE *ATH. POL.*

nominatives were restored by J. B. Bury, *CR* v 1891, 182; Kaibel preferred ... οἳ ἐμμήνους εἰσάγουσι τὰς δίκας δυοῖν φυλαῖν ἕκαστος [[εἰσὶ δ' ἔμμηνοι]], προικός ... καὶ ἐρανικὰς καὶ κοινωνικὰς ... καὶ τριηραρχι⟨κ⟩ὰς καὶ τραπεζιτικάς (*Stil und Text*, 223–5; cf. Kaibel & Wilamowitz[3], Oppermann, who retain the accusatives but do not emend above); but it is more likely that a scribe mentally supplied a verb such as εἰσάγουσι and that we should restore the nominatives.

καὶ κοινωνικαί: 'Concerning associations.' This is sometimes interpreted to mean suits entered by or against associations (e.g. Lipsius, *A.R.*, 771), but it is not certain that Athenian law regarded an association as a person, capable of suing and being sued (cf. Harrison, *L.A.*, i. 242, ii. 22). D. xiv. *Symm.* 16 includes τῶν κοινωνικῶν among those able to claim exemption from trierarchic liability (perhaps in cases where the total property was sufficient to qualify but the individual partners' shares were not).

καὶ ἀνδραπόδων καὶ ὑποζυγίων: 'Concerning slaves and yoke-animals' (perhaps domestic animals generally). What is at issue here may be damage done by or to slaves and animals, rather than property in them (Harrison, *L.A.*, ii. 22 n. 10, cf. Lys. x. *Theomn.* i. 19, Pl. *Sol.* 24. iii, against Lipsius, *A.R.*, 640, 682, 745).

καὶ τριηραρχι⟨κ⟩αί: Presumably not suits concerning claims of the state against trierarchs or disputes as to who should be trierarchs, for which other procedures were available, but private suits entered by or against trierarchs (cf. Gernet, *REG* li 1938, 7–8 = *Droit et société dans la Grèce ancienne*, 177, Harrison, *L.A.*, ii. 22 n. 9). If [D.] L. *Poly.*, of 358, was written for a δίκη τριηραρχική, it was after that date that these δίκαι became ἔμμηνοι (cf. Gernet, Budé ed. of D.'s *Plaidoyers civils*, iii. 36–7; but he notes that the terminology does not point to a δίκη τριηραρχική, and prefers a δίκη βλάβης).

καὶ τραπεζιτικαί: 'Concerning banking': suits entered by bankers, or against bankers, or both (cf. Gernet, *REG* li 1938, 6 n. 1 = *Droit et société*, 176 n. 2, Harrison, *L.A.*, ii. 22 n. 7). The actions concerning Pasion's bank in the 360's seem not to have been ἔμμηνοι.

52. iii. δικάζουσιν: Here the verb is used of the officials who preside at the trial and, presumably, are responsible for the declaration of the verdict (cf. 57. iv, of the basileus); but more commonly it is used of the men, whether magistrates or jurors, who actually decide the verdict (e.g. 53. i–ii, 63. iii; cf. καταδικάζειν in M&L 31, 18–19, with Wade-Gery, *Essays*, 182–5, Rhodes, *A.B.*, 204 n. 1). Presumably the word was used of magistrates in the days when they habitually did decide verdicts, but its use here cannot be explained simply as a survival from that period, since the εἰσαγωγεῖς were a recent creation; this is still a live usage. The original meaning of the word may have been 'state the right'. See H. J. Wolff, *Traditio* iv

586

1946, 75-6, D. M. MacDowell, *Athenian Homicide Law*, 37-8, Harrison, *L.A.*, ii. 38 n. 1; and cf. on διαδικάζει in 57. ii.

οἱ δ' ἀποδέκται τοῖς τελώναις καὶ κατὰ τῶν τελωνῶν: '... suits entered by and against tax-collectors.' For the letting of tax-collecting rights see 47. ii with commentary; for the apodectae see 48. i-ii with commentary.

τὰ μὲν μέχρι δέκα δραχμῶν ὄντες κύρι[οι]: Cf. 53. ii *init.*, where we read that the Forty are competent to decide cases up to 10 drachmae, and the same limit is found in the law published in *Hesp.* xliii 1974, 157-88, lines 23-6; cf. also 56. vii, 61. ii, with commentary, on the power of magistrates to impose ἐπιβολαί; but in 45. i-iii, 46. ii, *A.P.* does not distinguish clearly between sentences which were and sentences which were not within the competence of the boule. Neither *A.P.* nor any other text suggests that there was a right of appeal against decisions given by a magistrate on a case within his competence, and we must assume that such decisions were final. Arist. *Pol.* IV. 1300 B 32-5 remarks of small disputes, ὅσα δραχμιαῖα καὶ πεντάδραχμα, that δεῖ μὲν γὰρ καὶ περὶ τούτων γίνεσθαι κρίσιν, οὐκ ἐμπίπτει δὲ εἰς δικαστῶν πλῆθος.

εἰσάγοντες ἔμμηνα: 'Accepting monthly for presentation to a court': cf. p. 583.

53. i. κληροῦσι δὲ καὶ <τοὺς> τετταράκοντα, τέτταρας ἐκ τῆς φυλῆς ἑκάστης: Like the Eleven (52. i) the Forty were known by their number (e.g. D. XXXVII. *Pant.* 33, Is. XV. *Antid.* 237), so τοὺς, inserted by Kaibel & Wilamowitz[1] (cf. Kaibel, *Stil und Text*, 225-6), is necessary.

πρὸς οὓς τὰς ἄλλας δίκας λαγχάνουσιν: Sc. οἱ διώκοντες: the plaintiff summons the defendant to appear before the appropriate authority, and the authority allots a day for the preliminary hearing: by this procedure the authority κληροῖ and the plaintiff λαγχάνει δίκην (cf. Lipsius, *A.R.*, 817-18, Harrison, *L.A.*, ii. 88-9). τὰς ἄλλας δίκας, handled by the Forty and the διαιτηταί, will be private suits other than those mentioned in 52. ii-iii—but in saying this *A.P.* is simplifying: for δίκαι which fell to the archon see 56. vi, to the basileus 57. ii-iv, to the polemarch 58. iii and to the thesmothetae 59. v-vi; cases which if they concerned only citizens fell to the Forty and the διαιτηταί if they concerned metics or other privileged foreigners went first to the polemarch, but otherwise there is no need to believe that δίκαι handled by other magistrates came also to the Forty and the διαιτηταί (cf. R. J. Bonner, *CP* ii 1907, 407-18, Bonner & Smith, *Administration of Justice*, ii. 97-116, against Lipsius, *A.R.*, 82 n. 116, 226-8, 981-2, Busolt & Swoboda, *G.S.*, ii. 1111 n. 4, who accepted this statement of *A.P.* as true without qualification). δίκαι which arose in the course of a retired official's εὔθυναι were referred to the

COMMENTARY ON THE *ATH. POL.*

Forty if they were the proper magistrates for the suits in question (48. v with commentary).

Here *A.P.* says nothing of how the work was divided among the Forty: later it appears that four were allocated to each tribe (not their own) and that cases were handled by the judges allocated to the tribe of the defendant (§ii *fin.* with commentary).

οἳ πρότερ[ον] μὲν ... τετταράκοντα γεγόνασιν: δικασταί κατὰ δήμους were instituted by Pisistratus (16. v), abolished presumably on the fall of the tyranny (cf. p. 257) and revived in 453/2 (26. iii): thirty was a convenient number for Cleisthenes' system of tribes and trittyes, and presumably was chosen in 453/2; but, as *A.P.* indicates, after the régime of the Thirty this seemed an inauspicious number. This is one of several places where *A.P.* contrasts earlier with current practice (cf. Introduction, pp. 34–5): here he gives a date and a reason for the change. The Forty were still sometimes referred to by the old title, δικασταὶ κατὰ δήμους (e.g. 48. v, D. xxiv. *Tim.* 122). We are not told when or why they ceased to travel on circuit, but may guess that administrative convenience came to outweigh the convenience of litigants: Lys. xxiii. *Panc.* 2 implies that the change was an accomplished fact when the hearing of δίκαι was resumed in 401/0, after the democratic restoration (cf. D. M. MacDowell, *RIDA*³ xviii 1971, 270, against L. Gernet, *REG* lii 1939, 395 n. 2 = *Droit et société dans la Grèce ancienne*, 107 n. 2); probably the judges discontinued their travels in the last period of the Peloponnesian War, when Decelea was occupied by the Spartans and the citizens were confined to Athens and the Piraeus, and after the war it was decided that they should continue to work in the city (Gernet, *opp. citt.*, 392–4 = 105–6, suggests that their number and duties were changed simultaneously, in conjunction with the institution of the διαιτηταί, but MacDowell, *op. cit.*, 267–73, shows that the first διαιτηταί did not serve until 399/8).

περιόντες: Emended by Kenyon[1-3] and some others to περι⟨ι⟩όντες (cf. Harp. κατὰ δήμους δικασταί, Poll. viii. 100); the contracted form was defended by Kaibel & Wilamowitz[2-3], Blass[1-3] (cf. Hyp. i. *Lyc.* 2, v. *Dem.*, col. xiii) and accepted by Kenyon in his Berlin ed. and O.C.T., and may be retained.

ἐπὶ τῶν τριάκοντα: ἐπὶ was omitted by the scribe and has been added above the line, is absent from Poll. viii. 100, and was deleted by Blass[4] and Thalheim (cf. 41. ii), but it should be retained.

53. ii. καὶ τὰ μὲν μέχρι δέκα δραχμῶν αὐτοτελεῖς εἰσι δ[ικά]ζε[ι]ν: δ[ικά]ζε[ι]ν was read by Wilcken; Dr. J. D. Thomas reads δ[ι]κάζειν; and [δικ]άζειν is found in a (modified) quotation of §§ii *init.*–iv *init.* and v *med.*–vi *fin.* in a fragment of a lexicon to D. xxi. *Mid.* published by C. Wessely, *Stud. Pal. u. Pap.* iv 1905, 111–13, and cited in Kenyon's O.C.T. and Mathieu & Haussoullier. αὐτοτελής is used with the infinitive, in conjunction with κύριος, in 3. v; here it is used as a synonym for κύριος. The apodectae had the same right to pronounce judgment on δίκαι brought to them in which the sum at issue did not exceed 10 drachmae (52. iii with commentary). In the case of the Forty, the limit may have been inherited from the jurisdiction of the travelling judges, who are not likely to have had unlimited authority to decide δίκαι.

τὰ δ' ὑπὲρ τοῦτο τὸ τίμημα: For the judicial use of τίμημα cf. 48. iv with commentary.

τοῖς διαιτηταῖς: Cf. §§iv–vi with commentary, below.

παραλαβόντες: Wessely's fragment (cf. above) reads λαβόντε[ς]. When they accepted a case the διαιτηταί took an oath on the λίθος in front of the Stoa of the Basileus (55. v with commentary).

[ἐ]ὰν μὴ δύνωνται διαλῦσαι, γιγνώσκουσι: The public arbitrators were not technically an ἀρχή but were similar to the private individuals to whose arbitration men might agree to refer a dispute (cf. Lipsius, *A.R.*, 220–33, Harrison, *L.A.*, ii. 64–8): it is perhaps for this reason that they were required first to try to bring the disputants to an agreed settlement, and only if they failed in that to pronounce judgment (cf. Isae. v. *Her. Dic.* 32, and the formal records in [D.] LIX. *Neaer.* 47, 71, *IG* ii² 1289, *Hesp.* vii 1, 2, with W. S. Ferguson's commentary, pp. 48–9, all referring to private arbitrations). γιγνώσκειν and γνῶσις are regularly used of arbitrators' judgments (e.g. D. XXI. *Mid.* 92, of a public arbitrator; [D.] XXXIII. *Apat.* 31–3, LIX. *Neaer.* 47, of private); we also encounter ἀποφαίνεσθαι (e.g. 55. v, [D.] XXXIII. *Apat.* 19, 20) and ἀπόφασις (e.g. [D.] XXXIII. *Apat.* 34).

κἂν μὲν ἀμφοτέροις ἀρέσκῃ . . . ἂν δ' ὁ ἕτερος ἐφῇ . . .: The arbitrator's judgment is final if both parties accept it, but either party may appeal against it. Contrast 45. i–ii, 46. ii, with commentary (with ἐφέσιμος and ἔφεσις in 45. ii), where I argue that the boule's judgment was final if it imposed fines up to 500 drachmae but subject to compulsory reference to a court if it wanted a more severe penalty, 45. iii and 55. ii with commentary (with ἔφεσις), where at any rate in the case of the archons' δοκιμασία we are dealing with compulsory reference to a court. E. E. Cohen, *Ancient Athenian Maritime Courts*, 150 n. 116 (citing [D.] XL. *Boe. Dot.* 31), claims that 'Virtually all cases decided by public arbitrators were appealed'; but we have not the evidence to decide whether that was so.

ἐμμένωσιν: An appeal must be made promptly after the announcement of the judgment, since otherwise there is no guarantee that the necessary documents will still be available, so Dr D. M. Lewis suggests to me that we should correct to ἐμμεν⟨εῖν ὁμολογ⟩ῶσιν; but the compression of thought in the papyrus' ἐμμένωσιν is not impossible.

53. ii] COMMENTARY ON THE *ATH. POL.*

ἐμβαλόντες ... εἰς ἐχίνους: Wessely's fragment (cf. above) reads εἰς τοὺς ἐχ[ί]νους. Moore takes the subject to be οἱ διαιτηταί, but with τὴν γνῶσιν τοῦ διαιτητοῦ appearing later in the sentence it is more probably οἱ ἀντίδικοι. In the jars the litigants place their testimony from witnesses, their challenges to their opponents and the laws which they cite—that is, all their evidence in the broadest sense of the word. *A.P.* might also have mentioned agreements, tortures and oaths (cf. Arist. *Rhet.* I. 1375 A 22–1377 B 12, with Harrison, *L.A.*, ii. 133–4). Evidence in all lawsuits had to be submitted in writing from about the 370's (cf. R. J. Bonner, *Evidence in Athenian Courts*, 46–7; G. M. Calhoun, *TAPA* l 1919, 177–93, arguing for 378/7); challenges (cf. Harrison, *L.A.*, ii. 153) are mentioned in conjunction with evidence in [D.] XLVII. *Ev. & Mnes.* 1–17. Gernet argued that challenges, oaths and the like were more decisive in an arbitration than in a trial in a δικαστήριον (*REG* lii 1939, 395–404 = *Droit et société dans la Grèce ancienne*, 107–12). ἐχῖνοι are frequently referred to by the orators (e.g. [D.] XLVII. *Ev. & Mnes.* 16), apparently always in connection with arbitration (W. Wyse *ap.* Sandys); a fragment of an ἐχῖνος lid is to be published by Prof. A. L. Boegehold.†

καὶ τούτους κατασημηνάμενοι: References to the sealing of the ἐχῖνοι are again frequent (e.g. [D.], *loc. cit.*).

καὶ τὴν γνῶσιν τοῦ διαιτητοῦ ... προσαρτήσαντες: Presumably the tablet on which the judgment was written was fastened to both jars. Kaibel & Wilamowitz claimed to read τὴν τοῦ, and this survived in the text of their 3rd ed., and is included in the restoration of the missing left-hand part of Wessely's fragment, but Kenyon in his Berlin ed. states firmly that the additional τὴν is not present in the London papyrus.

παραδιδόασι το[ῖ]ς δ' ... δικάζουσιν: Wessely's fragment reads [παραδιδόασι προσ]αρτήσαντες τηρεῖν τέταρσι. The four will be the four members of the Forty who acted for the defendant's tribe. Sandys comments, 'Probably those ... who belonged to the same tribe as the defendant' (cf. Harrison, *L.A.*, i. 194 n. 2, ii. 19), but the fact that *A.P.* says not τοῖς τῆς φυλῆς τοῦ φεύγοντος but τοῖς τὴν φυλὴν τοῦ φεύγοντος δικάζουσιν (corrected from the papyrus' τ(ῆς) φυλ(ῆς) by W. Wyse, *CR* v 1891, 117) suggests rather that the judges were assigned to a tribe other than their own (cf. pp. 582 on the εἰσαγωγεῖς, 594 on the διαιτηταί; for the expression cf. 48. v, where δικάζουσιν is to be substituted for εἰσάγουσιν, 58. ii, Lys. XXIII. *Panc.* 2). I do not share the view of Harrison, *L.A.*, i. 194 n. 2, that cases 'were divided tribe-wise only after a decision by an arbitrator had been given and rejected by one or other party': he seems to have abandoned that view at ii. 19.

COMMENTARY ON THE *ATH. POL.* [53. iii

53. iii. τὰ μὲν ἐντὸς χιλίων ... τὰ δ' ὑπὲρ χιλίας ... : *Sc.* δραχμῶν, δραχμάς; this passage is omitted by Wessely's fragment. For the sizes of juries cf. 67. vi–68. i with commentary: *A.P.* does not in his chapters on the δικαστήρια repeat this information on the sizes of juries in δίκαι; for the different time allowances for δίκαι with different sums at issue see 67. ii with commentary.

οὐκ ἔξεστι δ' ... εἰς τοὺς ἐχίνους ἐμβεβλημέναις: In other instances of ἔφεσις the final hearing was a completely fresh trial (cf. p. 540), but in this there is the restriction that the court has presented to it the material presented to the διαιτητής and is not allowed to consider any other material (in D. xxxix. *Boe. Nom.* 17 a fact is mentioned which is not formally admissible as evidence because it was not presented to the διαιτητής; in D. xlv. *Steph. i.* 57–60 it is alleged that a vital piece of evidence was excluded from the ἐχῖνος). D. M. MacDowell, *The Law in Classical Athens*, 209, suggests that the object of this was to prevent litigants from relying on the possibility of appeal to a jury and not taking trouble over the presentation of their case to the διαιτητής. It is possible that more latitude was allowed to the διαιτηταί than to the courts in arriving at their judgment (cf. Arist. *Rhet.* I. 1374 B 20–2, *Pol.* II. 1268 B 4–22, and see Harrison, *L.A.*, ii. 73–4; for Gernet's suggestion that more account was taken of oaths and the like by διαιτηταί than by the δικαστήρια see above, p. 590). Wessely's fragment reads προβεβλημέναις.

ἀλλ' ἢ ταῖς ... χρῆσθαι: Wessely's fragment reads ἄλλαις χρήσασθαι ἢ ταῖς.

53. iv. διαιτηταὶ δ' εἰσὶν οἷς ἂν ἑξηκοστὸν ἔτος ᾖ: Poll. VIII. 126 says ἐκ τῶν ὑπὲρ ἑξήκοντα ἔτη γεγονότων; schol. D. xxi. *Mid.* 83, *L.S.* 186. 1, Suid. (Δ 887) διαιτηταί, give the age as ὑπὲρ πεντήκοντα ἔτη, and it has been suggested that the age was lowered by Demetrius of Phalerum (cf. 228 F 13: Kahrstedt, *U.M.A.*, 19, Harrison, *L.A.*, ii. 67 n. 1), but more probably the lexica are wrong and the διαιτηταί were abolished after 322/1 (cf. Wilamowitz, *A.u.A.*, i. 224). The age requirement must mean men 'in their sixtieth year', whose sixtieth birthday falls during the year in which they serve as διαιτηταί (cf. next note, and 42. i with commentary). As *A.P.* does not state in ch. 42 that the thetes were excluded from the ἐφηβεία, so here he does not state that they did not serve as διαιτηταί; but I believe that they did not serve in either capacity (cf. p. 503).†

The first board of διαιτηταί served in 399/8 (cf. p. 588). If the Forty already and before them the thirty δικασταὶ κατὰ δήμους had jurisdiction only in matters of up to 10 drachmae (cf. p. 589), the institution of these public arbitrators will have extended the range of lawsuits which could be decided cheaply without having to be brought before a jury.

COMMENTARY ON THE *ATH. POL.*

τοῦτο δὲ δῆλον ἐκ τῶν ἀρχόντων καὶ τῶν ἐπωνύμων: That is, from the facts that there are forty-two year-classes, and that men are registered after their eighteenth birthday so that their nineteenth birthday falls during the first of their forty-two years of liability for service, it follows that their sixtieth birthday will fall in the last of their forty-two years.

εἰσὶ γὰρ ἐπώνυμοι δέκα μὲν οἱ τῶν φυλῶν: For the eponymous heroes of the ten tribes see 21. vi with commentary: they are not relevant here except in the final words of §iv, but are mentioned to distinguish them from the forty-two ἐπώνυμοι of the year-classes. Wilamowitz, *A.u.A.*, i. 225–6, compared the notes of Harp., *E.M.* (369. 15) and other lexica *s.v.* ἐπώνυμοι, noted that Harp. στρατεία ἐν τοῖς ἐπωνύμοις cites Philochorus (328 F 38), and suggested that here as in his first part *A.P.* has made use of an Atthidographer; but a man living in fourth-century Athens will not have needed to consult any book to obtain the facts which *A.P.* reports here (on Wilamowitz' theory of an earlier analysis of the constitution see Introduction, pp. 33–5).

τῶν ἡλικιῶν: 'Of the age-classes': the men registered in each year formed a separate ἡλικία.

οἱ δὲ ἔφηβοι ἐγγραφόμενοι πρότερον μὲν ... νῦν δ' ... : Blass, *LZB* 1891, 304, inserted ⟨οἱ⟩ ἐγγραφόμενοι, but the οἱ is absent also from Harp. στρατεία ἐν τοῖς ἐπωνύμοις, and I am not convinced that *A.P.* must have included it. For the δοκιμασία and registration of eighteen-year-olds see 42. i–ii with commentary. *A.P.* does not date the change which he mentions, but we may plausibly associate it with the reorganisation of the ἐφηβεία *c.* 335/4 (cf. pp. 494–5). Harp., *loc. cit.*, quotes this passage and §vii: J. J. Keaney notes that Harpocration used an unrevised text of 51. iii (cf. *ad loc.*), and concludes that this passage was already present in the earlier version of *A.P.* and that the earlier version must therefore have been written after the reorganisation of the ἐφηβεία (*Hist.* xix 1970, 330–6: cf. above, pp. 494–5, and Introduction, p. 56).

λελευκωμένα γραμματεῖα: Whitewashed boards: cf. 47. ii with commentary.

καὶ ἐπεγράφοντο ... τῷ προτέρῳ ἔτει δεδιαιτηκώς: Kaibel & Wilamowitz emended to πρότερον, but προτέρῳ is confirmed by Harp. στρατεία ἐν τοῖς ἐπωνύμοις and should be retained. Sandys notes that elsewhere in Attic the perfect of διαιτᾶν normally has the double augment, δεδιῃτ—.

Notice the imperfect ἐπεγράφοντο: the system of the forty-two ἐπώνυμοι was older than the reorganised ἐφηβεία. (How much older, we do not know: for extravagant chronological speculation applying 42-year cycles to the sixth century see M. Miller, *Klio* xxxvii 1959, 49–52, xli 1963, 86–7.) To identify the year-classes forty-two eponymous heroes were used in rotation, so that the ἐπώνυμος of the men who were διαιτηταί in 336/5 was used again for the men who were registered as eighteen-year-olds at the beginning of 335/4; to provide an absolute date a note was added to each list of the archontic year in which its members were registered (cf. §vii); presumably not all who were registered as citizens but only those of hoplite class and above who became ephebi were listed in the year-classes (cf. above). The forty-two ἐπώνυμοι were not entirely ornamental: in a world in which years were not numbered they provided a simple way of ensuring that men were exempted from further liability for service after completing their forty-two years.

νῦν δ' εἰς στήλην χαλκῆν ἀναγράφονται: Harp., *loc. cit.*, omits the last part of this sentence and ends his quotation νῦν δ' εἰς τὴν βουλὴν ἀναγράφονται. None of these bronze stelae has been found; but we have inscriptions on stone concerning the ephebi and the διαιτηταί. The ephebic inscriptions comprise decrees, dedications and lists (those of the fourth century are collected by O. W. Reinmuth, *Mnem*. Supp. xiv 1971): each document concerns the ephebi of a single year-class; since some have been found in the frontier demes where the ephebi spent their second year, while none earlier than the reduction of the ἐφηβεία to one year (cf. p. 495) has been found at the Piraeus, where they spent their first year (42. iii–iv), the inscriptions must have been set up after the completion of the second year (cf. Reinmuth, *op. cit.*, 106). The names of the forty-two ἐπώνυμοι are not used to identify the years (but Munichus, to whom a dedication is recorded in *AM* lxxvi 1961, 143–6, 2 = Reinmuth 6, may be the ἐπώνυμος of the ephebi who made that dedication); the ephebi are normally identified as οἱ ἔφηβοι οἱ ἐπὶ —— ἄρχοντος (e.g. *IG* ii² 1156 = Reinmuth 2, 26–7), but once we find the fuller formula . . . οἱ ἐπὶ —— ἄρχοντος ἐνγραφέντες (*ibid*. 52–3), so we may assume that the shorter formula was regularly used to identify the year at the beginning of which the ephebi were registered (cf. previous note, and F. W. Mitchel, *TAPA* xcii 1961, 348 n. 3). Some boards of διαιτηταί set up a list with a simple heading, in which the members are identified as διαιτηταὶ οἱ ἐπὶ —— ἄρχοντος: we have fragments of the lists of 330/29 and 329/8, and the list of 325/4 (*IG* ii² 1924 + 2409 [D. M. Lewis, *BSA* l 1955, 27–36], 1925, 1926); for other lists which have been suggested as lists of διαιτηταί see Gomme, *Population of Athens*, 70–3; in *IG* ii² 143 + *Hesp*. vii 13 + *IG* ii² 2813 a board of διαιτηταί is praised and praises its secretaries (cf. A. M. Woodward, *BSA* l 1955, 271–4; *SEG* xv 89); *IG* ii² 2834 is a dedication by a board.

πρὸ τοῦ βουλευτηρίου παρὰ τοὺς ἐπωνύμους: That is, by the statues of the ten tribal heroes, which since the middle of the fourth century had stood opposite the Old Bouleuterium, by the road running along the west side of the Agora, and whose base served as a state notice board (cf. p. 259). Limestone bases for triangular bronze stelae have been found near this site: see R. S. Stroud, *Hesp.* xxxii 1963, 143, *U. Calif. Pub. Cl. Stud.* xix 1979, 49–57, cf. R. E. Wycherley, *The Athenian Agora*, iii, p. 87, H. A. Thompson & R. E. Wycherley, *The Athenian Agora*, xiv. 39 n. 83.†

53. v. τὸν δὲ τελευταῖον ... ἃς ἕκαστος διαιτήσει: Here again the reference is to the ἐπώνυμοι of the forty-two year-classes. Nothing is said explicitly about the allocation of particular arbitrators to defendants of particular tribes, as four of the Forty were allocated to each tribe (§ii *fin.*), but evidently that was done, as we read in [D.] XLVII. *Ev. & Mnes.* 12 that οἱ ... τὴν Οἰνῇδα καὶ τὴν 'Ερεχθῇδα διαιτῶντες sit in the heliaea. Normally different numbers of διαιτηταί will have belonged to different tribes (in *IG* ii² 1926 the tribal contingents vary between 3 and 16), but presumably in this allocation they were distributed as nearly equally as possible: comparison with the Forty leads us to expect that they will have been assigned to a tribe other than their own, and this is confirmed by the example of Strato of Aiantis, who gave judgment when Demosthenes of Pandionis sued Midias of Erechtheis (D. XXI. *Mid.* 83 cf. 68). There were therefore two operations, an allocation of arbitrators to tribes, and an allocation of particular cases to particular arbitrators (noticed already by T. D. Goodell, *AJP* xii 1891, 322); of what is said here διανέμουσιν αὐτοῖς τὰς διαίτας should refer to the first of these operations.‡

καὶ ἀναγκαῖον ... διαίτας ἐκδιαιτᾶν: Having taken a case a διαιτητής must complete it, perhaps even if it runs on after the end of his year of service: cf. the paraphrase of this passage by Greg. Cor. (A. Walz, *Rhetores Graeci*, VII. ii. 1284, quoted by Sandys²), and ἐκδικάζειν in 67. i and passages cited *ad loc.* It may be that arbitrators were required to complete their cases within the year, and were not allowed to take new cases so late in the year that there was no possibility of this (cf. Wyse, ed. of Isaeus, 721–2, H. C. Harrell, *Public Arbitration in Athenian Law*, 15).

τῆς ἡλικίας αὐτῷ καθηκούσης: 'When his age has come', that is, when the time has come for his year-class to serve.

ἄτιμον εἶναι: For ἀτιμία cf. on 8. v, 16. x. Sandys supposes that here 'the severer form of ἀτιμία is probably meant' (that is, outlawry); but in a law which cannot have been enacted before the fourth century the word more probably denotes, as it usually does in the laws of the classical period, deprivation of civic rights only. That ἄτιμον has this weaker sense here is confirmed by D. XXI. *Mid.* 83–102, which represents Strato (made ἄτιμος by the procedure mentioned in §vi) as still in Athens and capable of being exhibited, but not of giving evidence, in court.

πλὴν ἐὰν τύχῃ ἀρχήν . . . ἀτελεῖς εἰσὶ μόνοι: Exemption of men who hold some office is straightforward enough, but exemption of those who are away from Attica calls for further refinement. For how long a period did a man have to be absent to qualify for exemption? Did the absence have to be 'for good cause', or could any man evade this duty by going on his travels? It is natural enough that no mention should be made at this point of the exemption of the thetes, who will not have been included in the lists of year-classes (cf. pp. 591, 593).

ἢ ἀποδημῶν: Wessely's fragment (cf. p. 588) omits ἢ, and after ἀποδημῶν continues οὐκ ἀτελεῖς [ἔστιν δὲ καὶ . . .].

53. vi. ἔστιν δὲ καὶ εἰσαγγέλλειν εἰς τοὺς διαιτητάς: For other procedures known as εἰσαγγελίαι see 43. iv, 45. ii, 56. vi, with commentary. This procedure is noted also by Harp., Suid. (*EI* 222), εἰσαγγελία, but according to them the εἰσαγγελία is presented πρὸς τοὺς δικαστάς. If δικαστάς were right the ἔφεσις which may follow would be very hard to explain (cf. W. R. Hardie, *CR* v 1891, 164), so most scholars have rightly accepted *A.P.*'s version (it is confirmed by Wessely's fragment, and before the discovery of *A.P.* Bergk had proposed to emend to διαιτητάς in the lexica; the same corruption is found in the report of the first sentence of §ii in *L.S.* 306. 15); but Kenyon[1-2] emended to δικαστάς in *A.P.*, and was followed by Kahrstedt, *U.M.A.*, 110 n. 4, 148 n. 2, cf. Harrison, *L.A.*, ii. 68. The inscriptions cited above (p. 593) confirm that the διαιτηταί could be thought of as a board.

We learn more about this procedure from D. xxi. *Mid.* 83–102. The διαιτηταί reported their judgments to the archons (§85). The 'last day of the arbitrators', apparently the last day on which an appeal could be made to the whole board, was the last day of the archontic year (§86, cf. schol. [586. 8–10 Dindorf]; the words τὴν τοῦ Θαργηλιῶνος ἢ τοῦ Σκιροφοριῶνος should be deleted, with G. H. Schaefer, Lipsius, *A.R.*, 232 n. 46); at the hearing of that appeal one διαιτητής served as ὁ πρυτανεύων to δοῦναι τὴν ψῆφον (§87, cf. Lipsius, *A.R.*, 232, Busolt & Swoboda, *G.S.*, ii. 1113; but Kahrstedt, *U.M.A.*, 164 n. 2, Harrison, *L.A.*, ii. 68 n. 1, supposed that the relevant member of the Forty is ὁ πρυτανεύων). Possibly if the arbitration was completed after the end of the arbitrator's year (but see above) an εἰσαγγελία could be made to the new board.

ἀτιμοῦσθαι: Cf. on §v, above. Wessely's fragment reads ἀτίμους εἶναι.

ἔφεσις δ' ἔστι καὶ τούτοις: In the missing left-hand half of Wessely's fragment there should be about 22 letters between οἱ νόμοι and ἔφεσις. Probably here as in §ii (cf. *ad loc.*) ἔφεσις denotes an appeal by a dissatisfied litigant, from the decision of the board of διαιτηταί to a δικαστήριον. T. D. Goodell, *AJP* xii 1891, 322, suggests that the law must have been changed after the disfranchisement of Strato (cf. above); but others argue from D. XXI. *Mid.* 91 that Strato appealed and his condemnation was upheld by the court (cf. Goodwin *ad loc.*), or it is possible that Strato was entitled to appeal but did not dare to exercise his right against the powerful Midias.

53. vii. χρῶνται δὲ τοῖς ἐπωνύμοις καὶ πρὸς τὰς στρατείας: The Forty led *A.P.* to digress from his theme of sortitive officials to the διαιτηταί and the way in which they were appointed; he now digresses further to explain the military use made of the forty-two year-classes.

ὅταν ἡλικίαν ἐκπέμπωσι: 'When they send an age-group on campaign' (Moore), not 'When men liable to military service are sent on an expedition' (Fritz & Kapp). Cf. M&L 23, 23–5 (Decree of Themistocles: ἐπιβάται to be between twenty and thirty), D. III. *Ol. iii.* 4 (ἐψηφίσασθε ... καὶ τοὺς μέχρι πέντε καὶ τετταράκοντα ἐτῶν αὐτοὺς ἐμβαίνειν), A. II. *F.L.* 133 (ψηφισαμένων ὑμῶν ... τοὺς μέχρι τριάκοντα [*v.l.* τετταράκοντα] ἔτη γεγονότας ἐξιέναι). We also find a reference in A. II. *F.L.* 168 to service ἐν τοῖς μέρεσιν: A. Andrewes argues that this is a different and older principle of enlistment, taking no account of age, according to which all men liable for service were in theory called up in turn (cf. above, p. 327).

ἀπὸ τίνος ἄρχοντος καὶ ἐπωνύμ[ου] μέχρι τίνων: A year-class was identified both by the archontic year in which it was registered and by its ἐπώνυμος: cf. §iv.

54. i. κληροῦσι δὲ καὶ τάσδε τὰς ἀρχάς: This sentence marks *A.P.*'s return from his digression on the διαιτηταί and the year-classes to the main theme of chs 50–4 (but Wilamowitz saw it as introducing a supplementary list of officials whose method of appointment had been altered: cf. p. 572).

ὁδοποιοὺς πέντε ... τὰς ὁδοὺς ἐπισκευάζειν: Perhaps for the purpose of appointing roadbuilders the tribes were grouped in pairs; for other occasions when five men had to be appointed from the ten tribes see 52. ii (εἰσαγωγεῖς), 56. iii (choregi for the Thargelia), 62. ii (amphictyons for Delos), also 51, iii (thirty-five σιτοφύλακες), with commentary. Arist. *Pol.* VI. 1321 B 18–27 includes ὁδῶν ... διόρθωσις among the duties of ἀστυνόμοι (adding that in the larger cities there are several offices in this general field), and schol. A. III. *Ctes.* 25 supposes that the ὁδοποιοί were οἱ ἐπιμελούμενοι τῆς καθαρότητος τῶν ὁδῶν τῆς πόλεως, which in Athens seems rather to have been the duty of the ἀστυνόμοι (50. ii with commentary); but there is no need to follow those who suggest that the ἀστυνόμοι were active inside and the ὁδοποιοί outside the city (e.g. Wilamowitz, *A.u.A.*, i. 226 n. 80: the right explanation is given by Busolt & Swoboda, *G.S.*, ii. 1116). A. III. *Ctes.* 25, claiming that the controllers of the theoric fund ἦσαν δὲ καὶ ὁδοποιοί, means that they provided funds for road-building, and probably worked with the ὁδοποιοί, not that they supplanted them: cf. 47. ii, 48. i, with commentary. The second-century law on the ἀστυνόμοι of Pergamum specifies minimum widths for streets (*OGIS* 483, 23-9).

We should expect to find the ὁδοποιοί included in chs 50-1, where other officials concerned with city facilities are treated: I know no convincing explanation of this displacement.

δημοσίους ἐργάτας: State-owned slave labourers.

54. ii. καὶ λογιστὰς δέκα καὶ συνηγόρους τούτοις δέκα ... λόγον ἀπενεγκεῖν: These are the auditors who examined the accounts of officials after the end of the year (cf. A. III. *Ctes.* 17-24: we read in §22 that any official who had handled no public funds had to make a declaration to that effect). *A.P.* has mentioned earlier a committee of bouleutae styled λογισταί, who conducted an interim examination each prytany (48. iii with commentary), and a committee of bouleutae styled εὔθυνοι, who received general complaints after the final examination of accounts (48. iv-v with commentary). The final examination is thus divided between two passages in *A.P.*, presumably because the εὔθυνοι were bouleutae but these logistae were not.†

The συνήγοροι are usually translated 'assistants' (e.g. Kenyon's Oxford Translation, Fritz & Kapp, Moore), and *L.R.C.* λογισταὶ καὶ συνήγοροι, which claims to cite *A.P.* but does not closely resemble *A.P.* (cf. Introduction, p. 57), says that the συνήγοροι συνανακρίνουσι (i.e. join in the preliminary examination made by the logistae), but assistants to other officials are styled πάρεδροι (cf. 48. iv, 56. i); Arist. *Pol.* VI. 1322 B 7-12 includes συνήγοροι among the different titles given to examining officials. In Athens συνήγοροι were normally advocates; Pericles was one of the accusers of Cimon in his εὔθυναι on his return from Thasos (27. i with commentary), and according to Pl. *Per.* 10. vi he was εἷς τῶν κατηγόρων ὑπὸ τοῦ δήμου προβεβλημένος; an inscription of the deme Myrrhinus mentions a logistes who swears λογιεῖσθαι ἃ ἄν μοι δοκεῖ ἀν[ηλ]ωκέναι, and συνήγοροι who swear συνηγορήσειν τῶι δήμωι τ[ὰ δ]ίκαια καὶ ψ[ηφ]ιεῖσθαι ἃ ἄν μοι δοκεῖ δικαιότατα εἶναι (*IG* ii² 1183, 13-16). It is plausibly suggested that the συνήγοροι mentioned by *A.P.* acted as public prosecutors when the λόγος was taken to court (LSJ *s.v.* συνήγορος, Kahrstedt, *U.M.A.*, 234, D. M. MacDowell, *The Law in Classical Athens*, 61). In the 420's such συνήγοροι were paid 1 drachma a day (Ar. *Vesp.* 691 with MacDowell *ad loc.*). It was possible also for private citizens to prosecute on their own initiative: D. XVIII. *Cor.* 117, A. III. *Ctes.* 23.

οὗτοι γάρ εἰσι μόνοι <οἱ> ... εἰσάγοντες: Strictly the financial account submitted to the logistae was the λόγος, and the receipt of general complaints by the εὔθυνοι was the εὔθυναι, but this distinction was not always observed, and εὔθυναι is often used of the taking of the λόγος to court (cf. 48. iv with commentary): the εἰσάγουσαι ἀρχαί for εὔθυναι in the strict sense were the Forty for private suits and the thesmothetae for public (48. v), and in this sentence *A.P.* must still be referring to the λόγος (cf. τῶν τὰς εὐθύνας ἐν τῷ δικαστηρίῳ δεδωκότων in 48. iv). It appears that the λόγος had to be produced in court even if no objections were raised: cf. D. XVIII. *Cor.* 117, XIX. *F.L.* 211, *L.R.C.* λογισταὶ καὶ συνήγοροι, and *IG* ii² 847, 27–30 (C3: περὶ τούτων ἁπάντων τούς τε λόγους ἀ[π]ενηνόχασιν πρὸς τοὺς λογιστὰς καὶ εἰς [τὸ] Μητρῶιον καὶ τὰς εὐθύνας δεδώκασιν ἐν τῶι δικαστηρίωι κατὰ τοὺς νόμους). Logistae of this kind are not attested before the fourth century, though accounts were certainly examined before then (cf. Rhodes, *A.B.*, 111).

οἱ was added by J. B. Mayor, *CR* v 1891, 117 (cf. Kaibel, *Stil und Text*, 226); to avoid the hiatus Blass²⁻³ and Kaibel & Wilamowitz³ preferred εἰσι⟨ν οἱ⟩; but οὗτοι γὰρ εἰσι μόνοι is oddly emphatic, and I know no reason why this emphasis should have been thought appropriate. Perhaps we should correct to [[μον]]οἱ. In Ar. *Vesp.* 836–1008 one of the thesmothetae (935) is represented as presiding in a trial in which the charge is probably to be thought of as κλοπὴ δημοσίων καὶ ἱερῶν χρημάτων (896 with MacDowell *ad loc.*), and 59. iii includes the γραφὴ δώρων among suits handled by the thesmothetae: probably the explanation is that these charges could arise at the examination of the λόγος or at other times, and were handled by the logistae only when they arose at the examination of the λόγος.

κἂν μέν τινα κλέπτοντ' ἐξελέγξωσι, κλοπὴν οἱ δικασταὶ καταγιγνώσκουσι: 'If they (logically, the prosecutors) demonstrate that anyone is an embezzler, the jurors convict him of embezzlement': in contrast to *A.P.*'s normal practice of paraphrasing the texts of the laws, this is very much the language of narrative (cf. Introduction, p. 34). *A.P.* distinguishes three charges which could arise from the λόγος, the γραφαὶ κλοπῆς (*sc.* δημοσίων καὶ ἱερῶν χρημάτων: 'embezzlement'), δώρων ('bribery') and ἀδικίου ('misdemeanour': see below). The same three charges are mentioned in Pl. *Per.* 32. iv in connection with Hagnon's modification of the prosecution of Pericles; Hyp. v. *Dem.*, col. xxiv, contrasts the penalties for ἀδικίου and δώρων (cf. Din. I. *Dem.* 60: see below). This list is commonly accepted as exhaustive (e.g. Lipsius, *A.R.*, 104–5, Bonner & Smith, *Administration of Justice*, ii. 257): it may well be so, but the fact that *A.P.* mentions three charges is not enough to prove that only those three charges were possible. For the γραφὴ κλοπῆς cf. Ar. *Vesp., loc. cit.*, Ant. II. *Tetr.* i. a. 6, β. 9, D. XIX. *F.L.* 293, XXIV. *Tim.* 112, 127.

καὶ τὸ γνωσθὲν ἀποτίνεται δεκαπλοῦν: The offender has to repay ten times the amount he is found to have taken (cf. D. xxiv. *Tim.* 112, 127). There is no need for the ⟨κατα⟩γνωσθέν of Kaibel & Wilamowitz and Blass[1]: cf. διατίθησιν ... τίθησι, in 57. i, and the instances of compound verb followed by simple cited by Sandys.

ἐὰν δέ τινα δῶρα λαβόντα ἐπιδείξωσιν ... καὶ τοῦτο δεκαπλοῦν: For a tenfold penalty in cases of bribery cf. Din. 1. *Dem.* 60, 11. *Aristog.* 17, Hyp. v. *Dem.*, col. xxiv. In the first passage cited Dinarchus remarks that bribery may be punished either with death or with a tenfold payment: in Athenian law the same wrongful act could often be dealt with by different procedures, leading to different penalties; and in the case of bribery the death penalty could be obtained by means of an εἰσαγγελία, whereas tenfold payment was prescribed for conviction in a γραφὴ δώρων. ἐπιδεικνύναι is used of proving a man guilty of taking bribes in Ar. *Eq.* 832–5.

ἂν δ' ἀδικεῖν καταγνῶσιν ... τοῦθ' ἁπλοῦν: In this third case *A.P.*'s language is different: 'If they condemn him for ... they punish him for ...' The γραφὴ ἀδικίου is alluded to in Pl. *Per.* 32. iv, Hyp. v. *Dem.*, col. xxiv (which confirms that the penalty was simple repayment); Din. 1. *Dem.* 60 contrasts with the heavy penalty for bribery διπλῆν τὴν βλάβην for τῶν ἄλλων ἀδικημάτων τῶν εἰς ἀργυρίου λόγον ἀνηκόντων, but we need not doubt that what *A.P.* and Hyperides say of the penalty is correct (for the doubling of overdue debts cf. 48. i with commentary). No text makes it clear what wrongs were covered by the γραφὴ ἀδικίου: as Bonner & Smith point out, the minimal penalty suggests that they were not serious wrongs (*Administration of Justice*, ii. 257 n. 2), so I translate ἀδίκιον as 'misdemeanour'; perhaps they were accounting errors in connection with which no intention to defraud was alleged (cf. MacDowell, *The Law in Classical Athens*, 171).

ἐὰν πρὸ τῆς θ' πρυτανείας ἐκτ⟨ε⟩ίση τις: If he pays by the ninth prytany (*sc.* of the year in which he is condemned): for the significance of the the ninth prytany of the year in Athenian finance see 47. iii with commentary. This provision is in accordance with the law of Timocrates attacked in D. xxiv. *Tim.*, by which men from whom the state could demand immediate payment were not to be treated as defaulting debtors unless they failed to pay by the ninth prytany: it seems generous treatment for a man who has after all done wrong, but the amount of money lost through a magistrate's negligence might be a large sum for an individual to raise.

τὸ ⟨δὲ⟩ δεκαπλοῦν οὐ διπλοῦται: No other text states this fact.

54. iii. κληροῦσι δὲ καὶ γραμματέα τὸν κατὰ πρυτανείαν καλούμενον: On the Athenian state secretaries see Rhodes, *A.B.*, 134–41 (where earlier studies are cited). *A.P.* mentions only three secretaries; there was also a secretary ἐπὶ τὰ ψηφίσματα, presumably parallel to the ἐπὶ τοὺς νόμους (cf. on §iv); and various other secretaries are known, of whom the ἀντιγραφεύς (cf. p. 601) and the ἀναγραφεύς are found in fourth-century lists of the ἀείσιτοι who dined with the prytanes in the Tholos (see on 43. iii). The first secretary mentioned by *A.P.* was the most important, and the third had a special importance; with the exception of these two we do not know how the work was distributed among the various secretaries, nor why *A.P.* should have singled out one of the others for inclusion here.

The γραμματεὺς κατὰ πρυτανείαν was the principal secretary of the Athenian state: it is he who is named as secretary in the prescripts of decrees (*IG* ii² 223 c, 1–2, with 224, 2, 225, 4–5), and who is ordered to publish both decrees (e.g. *IG* ii² 222, 27–8) and laws (e.g. *IG* ii² 140, 31–5, using the older title γραμματεὺς τῆς βουλῆς). The title of this secretary used to be restored as τὸ κ[ατὰ πρυτανείαν γραμμ]ατέος τὲς βουλὲς in *IG* i² 115 = M&L 86, 6–7, but that restoration is ruled out by R. S. Stroud's new readings, and γραμματεὺς τῆς βουλῆς is now the only title securely attested for the fifth and early fourth centuries. Between 363/2 and 322/1 γραμματεὺς τῆς βουλῆς and γραμματεὺς κατὰ πρυτανείαν are alternative titles for the same official (*SEG* xix 129, 13–14, with *IG* ii² 138, 3, 139, 3–4; in *IG* ii² 120, 11–19 [quoted below], the two titles are used within four lines: see W. K. Pritchett & B. D. Meritt, *The Chronology of Hellenistic Athens*, 2 n. 6, Rhodes, *A.B.*, 136–7); in the turbulence of the next half-century there were two short periods when the title ἀναγραφεύς was applied to the chief secretary, but otherwise the title γραμματεὺς κατὰ πρυτανείαν became standard (until in the second century A.D. it gave way to a new title, περὶ τὸ βῆμα). The reason for the change is obscure: there is no evidence for a separate secretary of the boule whose existence would make the old title inappropriate; until the 360's this secretary held office for one prytany, but the title γραμματεὺς κατὰ πρυτανείαν was used only after the office had been made annual (cf. pp. 601–2).†

ὃς τῶν γραμμάτων ἐστὶ κύριος: The τ' which follows γραμμάτων in most MSS of Harp. γραμματεύς, though favoured by Blass and Kaibel & Wilamowitz³, is not needed (cf. Kaibel, *Stil und Text*, 227–8). This secretary was responsible for the publication of documents (cf. above), and presumably had general responsibility for the state's records, for which in the fourth century there was a central depository, the Old Bouleuterium or Μητρῷον (cf. p. 532).

καὶ τὰ ψηφίσματα τὰ γιγνόμενα φυλάττει: This presumably means that he was responsible for keeping an official copy of the text, whether or not publication on stone was ordered (cf. the reference to τὸ . . . βιβλίον [τοῦ ψηφίσματος] in Tod 97, 22–3); in the law published in *Hesp.* xliii 1974, 157–88, lines 55–6, it is this secretary who is to demolish any inscribed ψηφίσματα that may conflict with the law.

Since this same secretary was responsible for the publication of laws (cf. above), he was presumably required also to keep an official text of them.

καὶ τἄλλα πάντα ἀντιγράφεται: 'And checks the recording of everything else', the actual writing probably being done by a δημόσιος. In *IG* ii² 120, 11–19, Eucles the δημόσιος is summoned to the Acropolis γρα[ψόμ]ενον τ[ὰ] ἐν τῆι χαλκοθήκει, ... ἀντιγράφεσθαι δὲ τὸγ γραμματέα τὸν κατὰ [πρ]υτανείαν καὶ τοὺς ἄλλους γραμματ{τε}έας τοὺς ἐπὶ τοῖ[ς δ]ημοσίοις γράμμασιν, ... τὸγ γραμματέα τῆς βυολῆς ἀναγράψαντα [ἐν] στήληι λιθίνηι στῆσαι ἔμπροσθεν τῆς χαλκοθήκη[ς]. According to A. III. *Ctes*. 25 there used to be an elected ἀντιγραφεύς, ... ὃς καθ' ἑκάστην πρυτανείαν ἀπελογίζετο τὰς προσόδους τῷ δήμῳ, but in the time of Eubulus the controllers of the theoric fund ἦρχον ... τὴν τοῦ ἀντιγραφέως ἀρχήν; the γραμματεὺς τῆς βουλῆς καὶ τοῦ δήμου and an ἀντιγραφεύς are listed at the end of *IG* ii² 1740 = *The Athenian Agora*, xv 12 (400–350), and an ἀντιγραφεύς is included in longer lists of ἀείσιτοι in *IG* ii² 1700, 217 = *Agora* xv 43, 231 (335/4), [*Hesp.* Supp. i 1, 79 cf. 83 =] *Agora* xv 58, 80 (305/4), *Hesp.* xxxvii 1968, 1–24, line 298 = *Agora* xv 62, 233 (303/2). Harp. ἀντιγραφεύς (cf. Poll. VIII. 98: πρότερον μὲν αἱρετός, αὖθις δὲ κληρωτὸς ἦν) cites D. XXII. *Andr*. 38, 70, A. III. *Ctes*. 25, and claims διττοὶ δὲ ἦσαν ἀντιγραφεῖς, ὁ μὲν τῆς διοικήσεως, ὥς φησι Φιλόχορος (= 328 F 198), ὁ δὲ τῆς βουλῆς, ὡς Ἀριστοτέλης ἐν Ἀθηναίων Πολιτείᾳ (= fr. 439 Teubner). Most probably the revenue clerk existed in the first half of the fourth century but was abolished or made a subordinate official in the time of Eubulus; either immediately or after a lapse of time in which there was no ἀντιγραφεύς the title was given to a secretary working under the γραμματεὺς κατὰ πρυτανείαν; and Harpocration is wrong in referring to *A.P.* for this later ἀντιγραφεύς. LSJ *s.v.* ἀντιγράφω, II. 2, gives the meaning here as 'keep a counter-reckoning of money paid or received', but there is no reason why the word should have financial implications in this passage.

καὶ παρακάθηται τῇ βουλῇ: 'And attends meetings of the *Boule*' (Moore). He must also have attended meetings of the assembly and of the nomothetae; and when matters were referred from any of these bodies to a court it was his job to give the relevant documents to the εἰσάγουσα ἀρχή (cf. M&L 69, 51–4, D. XXIV. *Tim*. 63). In Ar. *Thesm*. 383–432 a speaker outlines her general plan for dealing with Euripides, and ends by offering to work out the details in conjunction with the secretary. For the verb cf. T. VI. 13. i (of one citizen sitting beside another in the assembly), Ar. *Ran*. 1492.

πρότερον μὲν οὖν οὗτος ἦν χειροτονητός ... νῦν δὲ γέγονε κληρωτός: No other text mentions the change to which *A.P.* alludes, but the epigraphic evidence allows us to identify and date two other changes which are probably to be associated with it. (*a*) Until 368/7 or

54. iii]   COMMENTARY ON THE *ATH. POL.*

slightly later the secretary served for one prytany only, and was appointed in such a way that all tribes were represented in the course of the year and the secretary was never a member of the tribe in prytany (W. S. Ferguson, *The Athenian Secretaries*, 14–27), whereas from 363/2 or slightly earlier one secretary served for the whole year (Tod 134, and 131, 135, 136, from two prytanies of 368/7; *IG* ii² 109, Tod 142, 143, from three prytanies of 363/2), and from 356/5 (but with interruptions) the office rotated among the tribes in their official order (Ferguson, *op. cit.*, 32–8, *Klio* xiv 1914–15, 393–7).[45] (*b*) Before the change the secretary certainly could be and probably had to be a member of the boule (Tod 97, 2, 12, 16–17: Rhodes, *A.B.*, 135 n. 2), whereas after the change he certainly could be and probably normally was a non-member (*IG* ii² 1749, 63–5, with 228, 5–6, 229, 3–4). The introduction of the new title for this secretary (cf. above) seems to have accompanied the changes.†

καὶ τοὺς ἐνδοξοτάτους ... οὗτος ἀναγράφεται: The argument is: they used to elect the most distinguished and trustworthy men to this office; this can be seen from the men named as secretaries in the headings of stelae on which alliances, proxenies and citizenship grants are inscribed. Secretaries were regularly named both before and after the change in the prescripts of decrees (the introductory formulae which identified the text as a resolution of the boule and/or δῆμος and specified the archontic year, the prytany, the chairman and the proposer); above the prescript we often find a heading in larger letters (inscribed primarily for purposes of identification), and in the fifth century and the first half of the fourth, but not subsequently, the secretary was often named in this heading (e.g. *IG* i² 87, alliance; 82, proxeny; *IG* ii² 1 = M&L 94, citizenship; *IG* ii² 127 = Tod 157 [356/5] is the latest instance[46]); archons too had disappeared from headings by the time of *A.P.*, but they had come to be featured emphatically at the beginning of the prescript; the reduced prominence of the secretary will reflect not so much his reduced importance as the fact that when the archon and secretary had the same term of office the secretary was less useful as an eponymous magistrate (cf. A. S. Henry, *Mnem.* Supp. xlix 1977, 20–4, 34–7). Alliances with other states, awards of proxeny to men who would represent the interests of Athens in their own state, and awards of Athenian citizenship—the last two becoming increasingly

---

[45] Ferguson's suggestion that annual secretaries began in 366/5 and each tribe took one of the first ten years in a random order remains neither proved nor disproved, but in favour of it see W. B. Dinsmoor, *Archons of Athens*, 351 with n. 4.

[46] I doubt the suggestion of A. S. Henry, *Mnem.* Supp. xlix 1977, 21, that on this occasion the secretary was celebrating the introduction of tribal cycles for the appointment of the secretaries.

frequent and increasingly honorary from the fourth century—are cited as three kinds of resolution of the Athenian δῆμος which were regularly inscribed on stone, to secure publicity for the ally or honorand.

A.P. may be thinking of the fact that in his own day secretaries were no longer named in headings, but his main point seems to be that the post was now held by less distinguished men than in the past. The change in the method of appointment should have led to a change in the kind of man appointed: a secretary elected for one prytany from one tribe in the boule will have been a politician; a secretary appointed for a year by lot from volunteers in one tribe of the whole citizen body will have been a man who found this kind of work attractive. In fact, of the earlier secretaries known to us, two of the men who served in 403/2 are important (Agyrrhius [41. iii with commentary] and Cephisophon [Davies, *A.P.F.*, 148]), but the others do not rank among the men known to be prominent citizens. None of the secretaries from 363/2 to 322/1 appears to be a man of distinction. Arguments are found less often in the second part of *A.P.* than in the first, but cf. the remark on the ninth prytany in 47. iv.

54. iv. κληροῦσι δὲ καὶ ἐπὶ τοὺς νόμους ἕτερον: The statement of Poll. VIII. 98 that this secretary was ὑπὸ τῆς βουλῆς χειροτονούμενος is presumably wrong. This is our earliest mention of the secretary ἐπὶ τοὺς νόμους: he is included in lists in *Hesp.* x 11, 21 = *Agora* xv 53, 19 (324/3), [*Hesp.* Supp. i 1, 77 =] *Agora* xv 58, 78 (305/4), *Hesp.* xxxvii 1968, 1–24, line 300 = *Agora* xv 62, 235 (303/2). The parallel ἐπὶ τὰ ψηφίσματα, not mentioned by *A.P.*, is found in *IG* ii² 223 c = *Agora* xv 34, 3 (343/2), *IG* ii² 1700, 216 = *Agora* xv 43, 230 (335/4: a long list from which ἐπὶ τοὺς νόμους is definitely absent), *Hesp.* Supp. i 1, 81 = *Agora* xv 58, 82 (305/4), *Hesp.* xxxvii 1968, 1–24, line 293 = *Agora* xv 62, 200 (303/2). That these and the γραμματεὺς κατὰ πρυτανείαν were three distinct secretaries was established with the publication of *Hesp.* x 11, whereas the text of *A.P.* wrongly suggests that this secretary was responsible for laws and the γραμματεὺς κατὰ πρυτανείαν for decrees. The inscriptions cited indicate that ἐπὶ τοὺς νόμους was a very recent creation when *A.P.* was written: there would be no incoherence if §iv were removed from the text, but there is no positive indication that it was not present in the original version of *A.P.*, and the verbal echo of §iii without νῦν or any other sign of an addition suggests that it was already present in the original version (cf. Introduction, p. 52).

ὃς παρακάθηται τῇ βουλῇ, καὶ ἀντιγράφεται καὶ οὗτος πάντας: Sc. τοὺς νόμους. Since νόμοι were enacted not by the boule, which merely helped to set the machinery in motion, but by the nomothetae (cf.

COMMENTARY ON THE *ATH. POL.*

pp. 512–13), he will not have needed to attend meetings of the boule, as will the γραμματεύς κατὰ πρυτανείαν (§iii) and, we may assume, the ἐπὶ τὰ ψηφίσματα. It is clear from *IG* ii² 120 (quoted p. 601) that ἀντιγράφεσθαι could be done jointly by several secretaries; *A.P.* has omitted the ἐπὶ τὰ ψηφίσματα, and it is possible that despite their contrasting titles both men assisted the γραμματεύς κατὰ πρυτανείαν at both decree-making and law-making. (In the University of Durham meetings of the Senate are attended by the Chief Clerk [the δημόσιος] and by the Registrar and all his graduate deputies and assistants [the γραμματεῖς ἐπὶ τοῖς δημοσίοις γράμμασιν].)†

54. v. χειροτονεῖ δὲ καὶ ... ἀναγνωσόμενον αὐτῷ καὶ τῇ βουλῇ: This is clearly the γραμματεύς τῆς πόλεως who παρελθὼν ἀνέγνω τοῖς Ἀθηναίοις the letter which Nicias sent from Syracuse to Athens in 414/3 (T. vii. 10; cf. also D. xx. *Lept.* 94). He is most economically identified with the epigraphically attested γραμματεύς (τῆς βουλῆς καὶ) τοῦ δήμου/(τῆι βουλῆι καὶ) τῶι δήμωι, found in *IG* ii² 1740 = *Agora* xv 12, 64 (400–350) and subsequent lists of ἀείσιτοι; but in *IG* ii² 223 A, 10, τῶι δήμωι may as easily be indirect object as part of his title (cf. Rhodes, *A.B.*, 136 with n. 3). Before the invention of printing and other devices for producing multiple copies of texts it was impossible to supply documents to men attending a meeting, and so essential documents were read out at the meeting; cf. the employment of a secretary to read documents in each of the δικαστήρια (67. iii). Not every citizen could do this audibly and intelligibly, so for this office election was appropriate; but it seems nevertheless to have been subject to the normal rule that appointment was for one year and reappointment was forbidden (62. iii: cf. B. D. Meritt & J. S. Traill, *The Athenian Agora*, xv. 15). [Pl.] *X. Or.* 841 F cites a law of Lycurgus requiring τὸν τῆς πόλεως γραμματέα παραναγινώσκειν τοῖς ὑποκρινουμένοις the official texts of the plays of Aeschylus, Sophocles and Euripides.

καὶ οὗτος οὐδενός ἐστι κύ[ρι]ος ἀλλὰ τοῦ ἀναγνῶναι: ἀλλ' ⟨ἢ⟩ was suggested by Blass, *LZB* 1891, 304, H. Richards, *CR* v 1891, 182, and others (cf. Suid. [Γ 418] γραμματεύς). That would be the more normal construction (and the construction normally used by Aristotle: H. Bonitz, *Index Aristotelicus*, 33), but the use of ἀλλά alone is an established phenomenon and we need not emend (see LSJ *s.v.* ἀλλά, I. 3: ἀλλά alone is found in the MSS' text of Arist. *E.N.* VII. 1152 B 30, X. 1176 A 22, *Rhet.* II. 1402 A 27).

This statement is emphatic, and I assume that it means what it says: the sole duty of this man was to read aloud. Kaibel, *Stil und Text*, 3, saw in this the underlining of the fact that the man who (merely) read out documents was elected whereas the principal secretary of the state, though formerly elected and an officer of distinction, was in *A.P.*'s day appointed by lot; but I doubt if the Athenians would have shared Kaibel's view of the reading of documents, and am not sure that this criticism was intended. Some have supposed that the actual reading was done by the herald on the secretary's instructions, and that the secretaryship was an important political office, but this view too seems unjustified (cf. Rhodes, *A.B.*, 136 with n. 3, against M. Brillant, *Les Secrétaires athéniens*, 110–1, 122, S. Dow, *Hesp.* Supp. i 1937, 16).

54. vi. κληροῖ δὲ καὶ ἱεροποιοὺς: From 51. iv *A.P.* has written κληροῦσι (*sc.* οἱ Ἀθηναῖοι); but χειροτονεῖ δὲ καὶ ὁ δῆμος was used in §v, and *A.P.* continues to use the singular in §§vi–vii before reverting to the plural in §viii.

The different kinds of religious officials that a state may need are reviewed by Arist. *Pol.* vi. 1322 b 18–19: there are priests and ἐπιμεληταί of sacred buildings; in small cities one man can combine the various duties, but elsewhere in addition to priests there are officials such as ἱεροποιοί, ναοφύλακες and sacred treasurers; finally there is the official responsible for those state sacrifices which are not assigned to the priests, who may be styled archon or basileus or πρύτανις. There were large numbers of hieropoei in Athens, usually boards of ten and often appointed from the boule, who cooperated with the relevant priests in the administration of festivals: those attested earliest are the hieropoei who are found in the first half of the fifth century making sacrifices before the Eleusinia and exacting dues from initiates (*IG* i² 5, *SEG* x 6, 89–92); several boards are recorded (together with other functionaries) in *IG* ii² 1496, col. iv, as paying to the treasury of Athena the proceeds of the sale of sacrificial victims; in *IG* ii² 1749, 80–4, we find ten hieropoei τοὺς τὰ μυστήρια ἱεροποιήσαντας, all from one tribe in the boule; and in the course of an Eleusinian document, *IG* ii² 1672, we meet ἱεροποιοὶ κατ' ἐνιαυτὸν (251) and ἱεροποιοὶ ἐγ βουλῆς (280). See in general J. Oehler, *RE*, viii (1913), 1583–8, Rhodes, *A.B.*, 127–30. Why *A.P.* should have singled out the two boards which he mentions is unclear.†

δέκα, τοὺς ἐπὶ τὰ ἐκθύματα καλουμένους: '... in charge of expiatory sacrifices', as appears from what follows (but Kaibel, *Stil und Text*, 228, preferred 'extraordinary sacrifices'). These hieropoei are not attested elsewhere. ἔκθυμα is found in the medical writers, with the meaning 'pustule' (e.g. Hippocr. *Epid.* iii. 7), and in a fragmentary inscription, where its meaning is unclear (*I. of Cos* 27 = F. Sokolowski, *Lois sacrées des cités grecques* 166, 36); ἐκθύειν means 'sacrifice' in Soph. *El.* 572, Eur. *Cycl.* 371, *I. of Cos* 382 = *SIG*³ 1107, 10, and other inscriptions of Cos; ἐκθύεσθαι 'expiate' in H. vi. 91. i, Eur. fr. 912. 12 Nauck², Thph. *H.P.* v. 9. viii, and 'sacrifice' or 'complete the sacrifice' in *I. of Cos* 36, *b* 27–8 = *SIG*³ 1106, 65–6 = Sokolowski 177, 65–6. The precise significance of ἐπιθύσιμα (*IG* ii² 1672, 295), cited by Sandys, is not clear (K. Kunst, *BPW* xxxix 1919, 499, cited in *IG*, suggests *Nachopfer*; LSJ renders 'sacrificial victims').

[οἳ] τά τε μ[αν]τευτὰ ἱερὰ θύουσιν: 'Who make the sacrifices ordered by oracles' when some misfortune has befallen Athens and the advice of an oracle has been sought. For μαντευτός cf. Eur. *Ion*, 1209, X. *Anab.* VI. i. 22. *L.S.* 265. 22, Phot. ἱεροποιοί, have οἵ τά τε μαντεύματα ἱεροθυτοῦσι, *Lex. Patm. ad* D. IV. *Phil. i.* 26 (*BCH* i 1877, 11 = K. Latte & H. Erbse, *Lexica Graeca Minora*, 141) οἳ τὰ μεμαντευμένα ἱερὰ θύουσιν.

κἄν τι καλλιερῆσαι δέῃ: 'And if it should be necessary to seek good omens' before going to war, founding a colony or embarking on any other major undertaking. For καλλιερεῖν cf. M&L 49, 5, X. *Cyr.* VI. iv. 12, *Vect.* vi. 3.

μετὰ τῶν μάντε[ων]: For μάντεις, 'soothsayers', in Athens cf. M&L 33, 129, T. VIII. 1. i.

54. vii. κληροῖ δὲ καὶ ἑτέρους δέκα, τοὺς κατ' ἐνιαυτὸν καλουμένους ... πλὴν Παναθηναίων: ἱεροποιοὶ κατ' ἐνιαυτόν are mentioned in an Eleusinian document, *IG* ii² 1672, 251 (cf. above); in 410/09 ἱεροποιοὶ κατ' ἐνιαυτόν received money from the treasurers of Athena for a hecatomb at the Great Panathenaea (M&L 84, 6–7), but *A.P.* excludes the Panathenaea from the responsibilities of his 'annual' hieropoei. About 335 a decree provided for the administration of the Lesser Panathenaea by τοὺς ἱεροποιοὺς τοὺς διοικοῦντας τὰ Παναθήναια τὰ κατ' ἐνιαυτόν (*IG* ii² 334, esp. 31–2; cf. 1496, 98–9, 129). We must assume that from the 330's if not earlier a separate board of hieropoei, not mentioned by *A.P.*, was responsible for the Panathenaea.

ε[ἰσὶ δ]ὲ πεντετηρίδες μία μ[ὲν ἡ εἰ]ς Δῆλον: Inclusive counting was used for compounds in —ετηρίς: as we reckon, these festivals were held every fourth year.

The ancient Ionian festival of Apollo on Delos was revived by the Athenians after their 'purification' of the island in winter 426/5 (T. III. 104). The festival was celebrated in the month Ἱερός, normally equivalent to the Athenian Anthesterion (viii), presumably at first in the third year of each Olympiad, beginning 426/5, but there were interruptions after the Peloponnesian War and probably after the Peace of Antalcidas, and in the fourth century the festival fell in the second year (month, *IG* xi (ii) 203, *A* 31–2, 32–57, with T. Homolle, *BCH* v 1881, 25–30, C. Robert, *Hermes* xxi 1886, 161–9, A. B. West, *AJA*² xxxviii 1934, 2; fourth-century festivals, *IG* ii² 1635 = *I. de Délos* 98, 31–40, 1640 = 104-12, 9–10, *IG* xi (ii) 161, *B* 105–14, with

Homolle, *BCH* xv 1891, 149–55, V. von Schoeffer, *De Deli Insulae Rebus*, 59–61, J. Coupry, *Atti del 3° Congresso Internazionale di Epigrafia Greca e Latina, 1957*, 55–8, J. K. Davies, *JHS* lxxxvii 1967, 38, M. J. Osborne, *Eranos* lxxii 1974, 180 n. 26[47]). For Athens' control of Delos, and the amphictyons, see 62. ii with commentary; for what is known of the festival see 56. iii *fin.* with commentary, T. III. 104, Pl. *Nic.* 3. v–viii, Lucian, *Salt.* 16, and the discussions of W. A. Laidlaw, *A History of Delos*, 45–50, I. R. Arnold, *AJA*² xxxvii 1933, 452–5, and, on the festival in the archaic period, E. Bethe, *Antike* xiv 1938, 105–18.

ἔστι δὲ καὶ ἐπ[τ]ετηρὶς ἐνταῦθα: The word is cited in LSJ from this passage only; it occurs also (as ἑπταετηρίς) in Dion. Alex. *ap.* Euseb. *H.E.* VII. 23. iv. The text should mean that there existed both a quadrennial and a sexennial Delian festival (as there existed both a biennial and a quadrennial Eleusinian festival: cf. below); a sexennial festival is not mentioned elsewhere, and to explain the number of crowns in *IG* xi (ii) 161 it has been suggested that after 330 the one festival, formerly quadrennial, was made sexennial, and that this passage was written after it had been decided that the next festival should be held not in 326 but in 324 (C. Torr, *CR* v 1891, 277: cf. Introduction, p. 52 n. 252); but it is far from certain that the natural interpretation of the text is wrong.

δευτέρα δὲ Βραυρώνια: This was a festival of Artemis *Βραυρωνία*, of Brauron, in eastern Attica (H. VI. 138. i: cf. p. 187); there was also a *Βραυρώνιον* on the Acropolis, on which the south side of the Propylaea abutted (cf. Paus. I. 23. vii: see R. J. Hopper, *The Acropolis*, 55, 141, Travlos, *Pictorial Dictionary*, 124–5); the cult may well have been adopted by the Athenian state in the time of Pisistratus, whose family home was at Brauron. The festival incorporated a procession from Athens to Brauron (Ar. *Pax*, 874, misunderstood by schol.); ten-year-old girls 'shed their robes' as 'bears' (Ar. *Lys.* 643–5 with schol. and C. Sourvinou, *CQ*² xxi 1971, 339–42, T. C. W. Stinton, *CQ*² xxvi 1976, 11–13; L. Ghali-Kahil, *AK* viii 1965, 20–33). Dresses of women who had given birth (schol. Call. *Hymn.* i. *Jov.* 77) or who died in childbirth (Eur. *I.T.* 1464–7) were dedicated to Brauronian Artemis, and these dresses are included in inventories published on the Acropolis (J. J. E. Hondius, *Novae Inscriptiones Atticae*, nos. x, xi, *IG* ii² 1514–31, cf. T. Linders, *Studies in the Treasure Records of Artemis Brauronia found in Athens*). A priestess of Brauronian Artemis is mentioned in Din. II. *Aristog.* 12, [D.] xxv. *Aristog. i, hyp.* 1, and hieropoei are mentioned in connection with her in *IG* ii² 1480, 12–16. Dr D. M. Lewis suggests to me that *IG* ii² 1480, 1–2,

---

[47] This change from the third to the second year of the Olympiad was disbelieved by A. Mommsen, *Philol.* lxvi = ²xx 1907, 451, F. Courby, *BCH* xlv 1921, 180.

records a transfer by ταμίαι οἱ ἐπὶ] Θε[οφράστου to ταμίαις τοῖς ἐπὶ Πολέ]μωνος, dating a celebration of the festival to 313/2, the fourth year of an Olympiad. See in general Hondius, *op. cit.*, 64–8, L. Deubner, *Attische Feste*, 207–8, *I. Κοντής*, *ΑΔ* xxii 1967, μελ. 156–206, H. W. Parke, *Festivals of the Athenians*, 139–40 (wrongly stating that this festival was managed by the same hieropoei as the Panathenaea).†

τρίτη [δ' Ἡράκλε]ια: Restored by Kenyon[1] from Poll. VIII. 107: Wilcken read ..... τα, but Kenyon in his Berlin ed. was not dissuaded and thought traces of the ε might be made out before ια; Dr J. D. Thomas reads, very hesitantly, [δ]'η[ρ]α[κλ]εια. Harp. Ἡράκλεια remarks that there were many local festivals of Heracles, the most important being at Marathon (for this festival cf. schol. Pind. *Ol.* ix. 134d, 137a) and Cynosarges; D. xix. *F.L.* 125 says that in the summer of 346 fear of an invasion by Philip of Macedon led to the celebration of the Heraclea in the city. Cynosarges lay only a short distance outside the city wall (on the left bank of the Ilissus: Travlos, *Pictorial Dictionary*, 340–1 with 291 fig. 379), so Deubner, *op. cit.*, 226–7, supposed that both Demosthenes and *A.P.* refer to the Marathonian festival. That festival he dated to the beginning of Hecatombaeon (i) (from Demosthenes: cf. A. Mommsen, *Feste der Stadt Athen im Altertum*, 161–2); the festival at Cynosarges he dated to Metageitnion (ii) (from the calendar frieze of Hag. Eleutherios: *op. cit.*, 248–54 with Taf. 34–40, cf. Mommsen, *op. cit.*, 160–1). If Demosthenes' festival in 346 is the same as *A.P.*'s, the year must in either case be the third of the Olympiad. See also Parke, *op. cit.*, 51–2.‡

τετάρτη [δ'] Ἐλευσ[ίν]ια: *IG* ii² 1672, 258–62, refers to offerings εἰς τὴν τριετηρίδα τῶν Ἐλευσινίων and εἰς τὴν πεντετηρίδα, both being accompanied by games, and 1304, 25, refers to τῆς πανη[γύρε]ως τῶν Ἐλευσ[ι]νίω[ν] τῶμ μεγάλων, presumably the quadrennial festival: see Deubner, *op. cit.*, 91–2. The festival was held at Eleusis, probably in mid Metageitnion (ii); in the Hellenistic period the quadrennial festival fell in the second year of the Olympiad (cf. *IG* ii² 1304, 17–27, 847, 23–5; Kirchner's dates, 219/8, 215/4, 211/0, are upheld by A. E. Samuel, *Greek and Roman Chronology*, 216, B. D. Meritt, *Hist.* xxvi 1977, 178) and the biennial festival in the first and third years (cf. J. D. Mikalson, *The Sacred and Civil Calendar of the Athenian Year*, 46; R. M. Simms, *GR&BS* xvi 1975, 269–70, with a 'plain' festival in the fourth year). However, *IG* ii² 1672 seems to envisage only one festival of each kind in four years, i.e. a biennial Eleusinia of which alternate (quadrennial) celebrations will have been Great, and our only fourth-century evidence places a celebration of the Eleusinia in 332/1, the first year of an Olympiad (*IG* ii² 1496, 126–30). Probably, then, in the time of *A.P.* the Eleusinia was celebrated in the first and third years of the Olympiad and after the upheavals of the late fourth and early third centuries the timetable was changed, and it will be easier to make sense of what *A.P.* says below if the first year was the year of the Great Eleusinia (but K. Clinton, *AJP* c 1979, 9–12, believes that in the fourth century as later the Great Eleusinia fell in the second year, and so places the biennial festival in the fourth year and 'plain' festivals in the first and third).

ε΄ δὲ Πα[ν]αθήναια: ε΄ was first suggested by W. Wyse, *CR* v 1891, 335, and was confirmed by Wilcken and by Kenyon in his Berlin ed.; Gomme, *CR* xl 1926, 11–12, suggested τὰ δὲ Παναθήναια ⟨ὑπὸ τῶν ἀθλοθετῶν διοικεῖται⟩, but the papyrus' list of five quadrennial festivals after τὰς πεντετηρίδας ἁπάσας διοικοῦσιν πλὴν Παναθηναίων and before καὶ τούτων οὐδεμία ... ἐγγίγνεται, though inelegant, is not impossible (see also next note). The Great Panathenaea was celebrated in the city, in Hecatombaeon (i), in the third year of each Olympiad, and the Lesser Panathenaea in the other years (date 62. ii with commentary; year Lys. XXI. *Pec. Acc.* 1 [410/09], *IG* ii² 3023 [338/7]). Cf. ch. 60 with commentary.

καὶ τούτων οὐδεμία ἐν τῷ αὐτῷ ἐγγίγνε[ται: The papyrus is said to read οὐδ(ε)αμια, and γινετ[αι] with εν inserted above the line (Kenyon, Berlin ed., cf. M. H. Chambers, *TAPA* cii 1971, 45–6; Herwerden & Leeuwen claimed to read οὐδ(ὲ) τρία, but have found no support; Dr J. D. Thomas doubts Kenyon's first α and thinks οὐδ(ὲ) ἡ μία would be possible). If this text is correct, it should mean 'None of these festivals occurs in the same place' (Moore), which is not the most obvious of comments but is in fact true (cf. above, on the individual festivals). J. B. Mayor (*CR* v 1891, 117) proposed ἐν τῷ αὐτῷ ἔτει γίνεται, and Blass (*LZB* 1891, 304, cf. Gomme, *CR* xl 1926, 11–12) ... ἐνιαυτῷ γίγνεται: this would be a more reasonable comment; it cannot be true of five quadrennial festivals, but it might be true of the four administered by the ἱεροποιοὶ κατ' ἐνιαυτόν (with εἰσὶ δὲ πεντετηρίδες ... ἡ δὲ Παναθήναια regarded as a parenthesis; or, more drastically but unnecessarily, as suggested by Blass[1] and J. A. Davison, *JHS* lxxviii 1958, 31 n. 13 = *From Archilochus to Pindar*, 43 n. 1, ε΄ δὲ Παναθήναια deleted [cf. previous note]). We have seen that in the fourth century the Delia fell in the second year of the Olympiad, the Heraclea (and the Panathenaea) in the third and the Brauronia in the fourth; there was a celebration of Eleusinia in the first year, and it is possible that at this time the Great and the Lesser Eleusinia together provided a biennial festival. It thus seems a serious possibility that each of the four quadrennial festivals apart from the Panathenaea did fall in a different year. On the other hand, the suggestion of Kaibel & Wilamowitz[1–2], [τ]ὰ δὲ Πα[ν]αθήναια [[καὶ]] τούτων οὐδεμιᾷ ἐν τῷ αὐτῷ ἐν[ιαυτῷ] γίν[εται] (cf. Kaibel, *Stil und Text*, 228–9, Wilamowitz, *A.u.A.*, i. 229–30 n. 89), now appears to be untrue. On the evidence now available it is best to follow Blass in restoring... ἐν τῷ αὐτῷ ἐν⟨ιαυτῷ⟩ γίγνεται.

[νῦν] δὲ πρόσκειται [καὶ 'Η]φαίσ[τια] ἐπὶ Κηφισοφῶντος ἄρχοντος: This restoration is due to Blass[2]; Wilcken and Kenyon in his Berlin ed. agreed on the reading of the papyrus, and Kenyon added *vestigia cum τια congruunt*. Cephisophon was archon in 329/8: this is the latest date mentioned in *A.P.* (and the only date mentioned in the second part), and this clause reads clearly as a late addition to a text originally written without it; Poll. VIII. 107, which omits the additional festival, may but need not be derived from an edition of *A.P.* which did not contain it (as argued by J. J. Keaney, *Hist.* xix 1970, 332-3: cf. Introduction, pp. 55-6). The Hephaestia fits the traces on the papyrus, and is known to be a festival with which hieropoei were concerned (*IG* i[2] 84, 19-25, of 421/0); but we have no other evidence for a quadrennial festival, and no reason is apparent for the institution of one in 329/8. We do know from inscriptions that the quadrennial Amphiarea at Oropus was revived by Athens in 329/8 (*IG* vii 4253 = *SIG*[3] 287, 12-13; 4254 = 298; cf. next note):[48] it has been suggested by P. Foucart (*RPh*[2] xix 1895, 27-30: [ἕκτῃ] δὲ ...) and others that Ἀμφιάραια should be restored here, but it seems clear that this is not compatible with the traces on the papyrus (Dr J. D. Thomas reports that φα is certain; Ἀμ]φ⟨ι⟩άρα[ι]α could be restored, but this is not as easy a reading as]φαισ[); it remains possible that Ἀμφιάραια was written but was quickly corrupted and the corruption misguidedly emended by our scribe or a predecessor to a name which made sense to him. *A.P.* does not make it clear whether the additional festival was added simply to the roster of quadrennial festivals, or to the responsibilities of the ἱεροποιοὶ κατ' ἐνιαυτόν.

54. viii. κληροῦσι δὲ καὶ εἰς Σαλαμῖνα ἄρχοντα: Although in the possession of Athens continuously from the sixth century, Salamis was never absorbed into Attica but was ruled as subject territory (cf. p. 253): hence the Athenians appointed a governor of Salamis, as they appointed officials to govern their other Aegean possessions (cf. 62. ii with commentary). Similarly the territory of Oropus (on the east coast, between Attica and Boeotia) was ruled as subject

---

[48] T. Klee, *Zur Geschichte der gymnischen Agone an griechischen Festen*, 29-32, 58-9, distinguished between a quadrennial festival in 331/0, to which he assigned *IG* vii 414, and the celebration of 329/8. E. Preuner, *Hermes* lvii 1922, 80-106, combined with that text *IG* ii[1] (v) 978b (*SEG* i 126), accepted Klee's distinction and noticed that in *SEG* i 126, 44, there is a ἱ]εροπο[ι]ός but *SIG*[3] 298, 12, 15, points to ἐπιμεληταί, and assigned *SEG* i 126 to a first quadrennial festival in 335/4 (esp. pp. 83-9). However, Klee's evidence for the dates of the quadrennial festivals is from the first century, and there is no reason why ἱεροποιοί and ἐπιμεληταί should not have parts to play in the same festival.

territory when it was in Athenian hands: it was transferred from Boeotia to Athens in 338/7 as part of the territorial adjustments made by Philip after Chaeronea (Paus. I. 34. i, schol. D. XVIII. *Cor.* 99, [Demad.] *XII. Ann.* 9, cf. D.S. XVIII. 56. vi, Hyp. IV. *Eux.* 16–17), and lost again, probably immediately after the Lamian War (cf. D.S., *loc. cit.*). Despite the silence of *A.P.* both here and in 62. ii we should expect Athens to appoint one or more civilian administrators of Oropus (as she certainly took charge of the cult of Amphiaraus: cf. previous note); in *IG* ii² 1672, 272–3, we do in fact encounter a δήμαρχος handing over first-fruits ἐκ τῆς ἐπ' Ἀμφιαράου.†

καὶ εἰς Πει[ραι]έα δήμαρχον: The δήμαρχοι of the other demes were appointed by their demes (in the fourth century, presumably by lot [attested for Eleusis *c.* 300: *IG* ii² 1194, 3], but they may earlier have been elected [cf. 21. v with commentary]); but the Piraeus, as the harbour town of Athens, was not merely one deme among many and its demarch was a state appointment. Similarly the Thirty had appointed ten τοῦ Πειραιέως ἄρχοντες (35. i, 39. vi). As noticed by Wilamowitz, *A.u.A.*, i. 232, we are not told whether the demarch had to be a demesman of the Piraeus: we have no other evidence to decide the question. We encounter this demarch in *IG* ii² 1176, 1214 (cf. next note); 1177; 2498, 1.

οἳ τά τε Διονύσια ποιοῦσιν . . . καθιστᾶσιν: Dionysia κατ' ἀγρούς are attested in several demes; the festival was celebrated in the month Posideon (vi), and at any rate in some demes included dramatic performances: as the financing of performances at the state festivals was a state liturgy (cf. 56. iii with commentary) the financing of performances at the rural Dionysia was a deme liturgy. See in general L. Deubner, *Attische Feste*, 134–8, A. W. Pickard-Cambridge rev. J. P. A. Gould & D. M. Lewis, *The Dramatic Festivals of Athens*, 42–56. At the Piraeus there was a theatre before the end of the fifth century (T. VIII. 93. i, Lys. XIII. *Agor.* 32, X. *H.* II. iv. 32), and several texts attest the interest of the Athenian state in the Dionysia there (law *ap.* D. XXI. *Mid.* 10, *IG* ii² 1496, 70–1, 144–5, 380, 456, 32–3); men whom the deme wished to honour had reserved seats in the theatre and were escorted to them by the demarch (cf. *IG* ii² 1176, 2–9, 1214, 19–25). From Salamis we have a dedication of the early fourth century recording a dithyrambic victory and naming the ἄρχων (*IG* ii² 3093), and evidence from the second century for tragedies, and for ἐπιμεληταί of the Dionysia (*IG* ii² 1227, 30–7, 1008, 82–3, 1011, 58–9).†

The demarch of the Piraeus and the ἄρχων of Salamis will of course have had secular reponsibilities as well as religious; but it is no doubt because of their religious responsibilities that they are mentioned (whether in the laws or simply on *A.P.*'s initiative) at this point, after the hieropoei.

54. viii] COMMENTARY ON THE *ATH. POL.*

ἐν Σαλαμ[ῖνι] δὲ καὶ τοὔ[ν]ομα τοῦ ἄρχοντος ἀναγράφεται: Fritz & Kapp translate: 'In Salamis the name of the Archon is added in public documents' (cf. Sandys², Mathieu & Haussoullier). That was indeed the case (e.g. *IG* ii² 1227, 1, 3093, 5), as in the regular demes of Attica the demarch was the eponymous officer (e.g. *IG* ii² 2498, 1, from Piraeus; 1191, 1, from Eleusis; but in most surviving deme decrees the prescript names only the proposer), and that is the meaning of ἀναγράφεται in §iii above; but (with all due allowance for *A.P.*'s habit of condensation) this sentence ought to state something that is true of Salamis but not of the Piraeus, and the allusion may rather be to a published list of ἄρχοντες.

O. *The Archons* (55–9)

οἳ κεῖνται τοῖς ἐννέα ἄρχουσιν is one of the four categories of laws distinguished in the law on νομοθεσία ap. D. XXIV. *Tim.* 20, and the nine archons occupy an extensive section in *A.P.*'s survey of the constitution (cf. Introduction, pp. 30–4). 55–56. i deals with the appointment of the archons, the secretary to the thesmothetae and the πάρεδροι of the three senior archons, and at some length with the archons' δοκιμασία (which has already been mentioned briefly in 45. iii, in connection with the duties of the boule). Lys. XXVI. *Evand.* 11–12 claims that the Athenians should be stricter in the δοκιμασία of the archons than in the other δοκιμασίαι; certainly they used a more elaborate procedure for the archons, and in ceremony if not in power the archons remained the principal magistrates of the Athenian state, and it may be for this reason that *A.P.* has chosen to give a detailed account of the archons' δοκιμασία. In the later fifth and fourth centuries the main duties of the archons were religious and judicial, and *A.P.* surveys in turn the duties of the archon (56. ii–vii), the basileus (57), the polemarch (58) and the thesmothetae (59. i–vi), ending with a duty shared by the whole college, the allocation of jurors to courts (59. vii, treated in more detail in 63–5).

These chapters enable us to see most clearly the relationship between *A.P.* and the laws of Athens (cf. pp. 33–5). [D.] XLIII. *Mac.* 75 quotes the law requiring the archon to care for orphans and others which lies behind 56. vii, and D. XXIII. *Arist.* 22 with 24, 53, 77, quotes parts of the homicide law which similarly lie behind 57. iii. *A.P.* summarises and rephrases, but his text is sufficiently close to the text of the laws to justify the claim that no intermediary need be postulated but *A.P.* was working directly from the laws.

COMMENTARY ON THE ATH. POL. [55. i

55. i. αὖται μὲν οὖν αἱ ἀρχαὶ κληρωταί τε . . . εἰ[ρη]μένων [πάντ]ων εἰσίν: This sentence rounds off *A.P.*'s section on sortitive officials, begun in ch. 50. Kenyon originally restored [πραγμάτ]ων; Kaibel & Wilamowitz[3] [πράξε]ων (cf. Kaibel, *Stil und Text*, 229; Blass[4] and subsequent Teubner edd.); *Π. Ν. Παπαγεώργιος* (*Ἀθ*. iv 1892, 598) [ἁπάντ]ων, and Kenyon in his Berlin ed. and O.C.T. [πάντ]ων, which is preferable to [πράξε]ων as a short supplement. E. Neustadt in the index to Kenyon's Berlin ed., 148, *s.v.* τε, suggested τε ⟨πᾶσαι⟩ (cf. 43. i), but I doubt if that is right.

οἱ δὲ καλούμενοι ἐννέα ἄρχοντες: The 'nine archons' are thus distinguished from the (eponymous) ἄρχων, and from ἄρχοντες in the broader sense (as in §ii).

τὸ μὲν ἐξ ἀρχῆς . . . [εἴρ]ηται: Blass[2-4] and Kaibel & Wilamowitz[3] restored [προε]ίρητα[ι] (cf. Kaibel, *Stil und Text*, 229–30), but Kenyon in his Berlin ed. and O.C.T. insisted that there is not room for the compound verb. *A.P.* has dealt with the institution of the nine archons in 3. ii–iv, with their manner of appointment under Solon in 8. i (citing the practice of his own time), with the reintroduction of κλήρωσις ἐκ προκρίτων in 487/6 in 22. v, and with the opening of the archonship to ζευγῖται in 457/6 in 26. ii. In several passages in his second part he contrasts earlier with current practice (cf. Introduction, pp. 34–5): this time for earlier practice we are referred to his first part; the only other cross-reference from the second part to the first is in 47. i, on the appointment of the treasurers of Athena and the Solonian property-classes (cf. p. 37).

[νῦν] δὲ κληροῦσιν . . . κατὰ μέρος ἐξ ἑκάστης φυλῆς: The secretary to the thesmothetae, making with the nine archons a college of ten, has not been mentioned before; neither has the distribution of the offices among the ten tribes; *A.P.* has said in 8. i but does not repeat here that the κλήρωσις ἐκ προκρίτων reintroduced in 487/6 had by his own day given way to a two-stage sortition, the first stage yielding the ten candidates in each tribe (we may wonder if ten or more candidates were forthcoming in each tribe each year: cf. p. 512). In *Hesp.* ii 1 = *IG* ii[2] 2811 the archon of 394/3 has one πάρεδρος and a secretary (cf. p. 621); our only allusion to the secretary to the thesmothetae outside *A.P.* is Poll. viii. 92 (προσαιροῦνται δὲ καὶ γραμματέα, ὃς ἐννόμῳ δικαστηρίῳ κρίνεται: this follows a note on the πάρεδροι of the senior archons, and the senior archons are the apparent but perhaps not the intended subject of προσαιροῦνται). The secretary's existence made possible the appointment of one member of the college from each tribe, and the superintendence of each tribe by one member of the college in the complicated fourth-century procedure for allocating jurors to courts (59. vii, 63. i, with commentary). We do not know when the post was created (it is presumably not earlier than Cleisthenes' creation of the ten tribes;

613

it is perhaps to be dated 487/6 [22. v with commentary], but for a consideration favouring a later date see p. 615); nor why the holder should be designated secretary to the thesmothetae rather than to all nine archons, unless it is relevant that the senior archons were assisted by πάρεδροι (56. i with commentary) but the thesmothetae were not (in his account of the δικαστήρια *A.P.* three times mentions a θεσμοθέτης where the reference appears to be to any member of the college of ten: 63. v, 64. i, 66. i, with commentary).

κατὰ μέρος (ignored in Kenyon's translations) should mean that different posts within the college went to different tribes in rotation, either by tribal order or by lot over a ten-year period (cf. N. G. L. Hammond, *CQ*² xix 1969, 131 = *Studies*, 375–6): for most years we know the eponymous archon by personal name only and the other members of the college not at all, so we can neither discover at what date the rotation was introduced nor, assuming that it continued in the Hellenistic period, make use of it in reconstructing the archon list. No kind of regularity is apparent from the instances in which we do know an archon's tribe: 412/1 Σκαμβωνίδης (Leontis = IV; 32. i with commentary), 408/7 Κυδαθήναιος or Κυθήρριος (Pandionis = III; Andr. 324 F 44 as emended by Usener), 406/5 Ἀγγελῆθεν (Pandionis = III; 34. i), 370/69 Φλυεύς (Cecropis = VII; *SEG* xix 133, 2–3), 349/8 Περγασῆθεν (Erechtheis = I; Phil. 328 F 49), 340/39 Ἁλαιεύς (Aegeis = II or Cecropis = VII; Phil. 328 F 54), 339/8 Ἀχαρνεύς (Oeneis = VI; Phil. 328 F 56); for the polemarch we have 371/0 Κειριάδης (Hippothontis = VIII; [D.] LIX. *Neaer.* 40), 370/69 Aegeis = II or Aiantis = IX (by elimination in *SEG* xix 133, 2–6); the basileus in 370/69 was Χολλείδης (Leontis = IV; *SEG* xix 133, 3). In the inscription cited the archon is listed first, then (it is to be assumed) the basileus and the polemarch, and then the thesmothetae in tribal order. Beloch in *NJPhP* cxxix (xxx) 1884, 481–8 (written before the discovery of *A.P.*), had observed that this is the order followed in a list of archons of the 220's (*IG* ii² 1706, reedited by S. Dow, *Hesp.* ii 1933, 418–46, new fragment added *Hesp.* xxiii 17 = *SEG* xiv 87) and suggested that although no two thesmothetae might come from the same tribe there might be tribal overlaps between them and the three senior archons: there now seem to be no instances of that exception to *A.P.*'s rule earlier than the first century B.C. (*IG* ii² 1714, 1717), and no more regularity can be detected later than in the fifth and fourth centuries.

55. ii. δοκιμάζονται δὲ οὗτοι . . . ἔν τε τῇ βουλῇ καὶ πάλιν ἐν δικαστηρίῳ: Cf. 45. iii on the boule's δοκιμασία of bouleutae and archons; the double δοκιμασία of the thesmothetae is mentioned by D. xx. *Lept.* 90. Lys. xxvi. *Evand.* was written for the δοκιμασία of a prospective archon (a man appointed as substitute after another had failed his δοκιμασία); probably the defendant is the Evander who held office as archon in 382/1: §§11–12 claim that, because the archonship leads to life membership of the Areopagus, the Athenians should be stricter in the δοκιμασία for this than for other offices. δοκιμασίαι in the δικαστήρια were handled by the thesmothetae (59. iv with commentary).

πλὴν τοῦ γραμματέως ... οἱ ἄλλοι ἄρχοντ[ες]: Cf. Poll. VIII. 92, quoted above; the difference in δοκιμασία may indicate that this post was not created until it had become normal for officials to undergo their δοκιμασία in a δικαστήριον (but see also above).

πάντες γὰρ ... δοκιμασθέντες ἄρχουσιν: (H. Diels, *GGA* 1894, 304 n. 3, cf. Blass[2-4] and Wilcken, claimed to read ἅπαντες, but Kenyon in his Berlin ed. doubted the reading and judged the space insufficient, and Dr J. D. Thomas agrees.) Cf. A. III. *Ctes.* 14–15, Poll. VIII. 44. ὥσπερ οἱ ἄλλοι ἄρχοντες may well have been said of the secretary to the thesmothetae in the law which dealt with this post and prescribed the δοκιμασία for it, but this parenthesis is *A.P.*'s own comment, noting a fact which he has not had occasion to mention elsewhere.

καὶ πρότερον μὲν ... κύριόν ἐστι τῆς δοκιμ[α]σίας: Cf. 45. iii (καὶ πρότερον μὲν ἦν ἀποδοκιμάσαι κυρία [*sc.* ἡ βουλή], νῦν δὲ τούτοις ἔφεσίς ἐστιν εἰς τὸ δικαστήριον). In 53. ii and probably 53. vi ἔφεσις and ἐφιέναι are used of appeals by a dissatisfied litigant; in 45. i–ii and 46. ii I believe the words are used of compulsory reference from the boule to a δικαστήριον (cf. *ad locc.*). Here and in 45. iii *A.P.*'s text seems to imply that ἔφεσις takes place only when the boule has rejected a candidate, but πρῶτον ... πάλιν ..., the provisions in §iv which envisage a situation in which no one wishes to accuse a candidate before the court, and D. xx. *Lept.* 90 suggest that in the time of *A.P.* all archons had to be vetted both by the boule and by a court. Often *A.P.* contrasts earlier with current practice (cf. Introduction, pp. 34–5); here there has been much dispute as to what the earlier and the current practice were.

Many accept that the later practice required all candidates to be considered by a court as well as by the boule (e.g. Gilbert, *C.A.S.A.*, 219 with n. 1, Busolt & Swoboda, *G.S.*, ii. 1045 with n. 2, J. D. Ralph, *Ephesis in Athenian Litigation*, 17–19, Bonner & Smith, *Administration of Justice*, ii. 243–4); Kahrstedt believed that earlier the boule's decision was final but later candidates rejected by the boule were granted the right of appeal to a court (*U.M.A.*, 62, cf. M. Just, *Hist.* xix 1970, 132–40), and Lipsius believed that both rejected candidates and defeated accusers were granted the right of appeal (*A.R.*, 271 with n. 8); Wade-Gery argued that originally the boule's rejection was final but candidates passed by the boule had also to be considered by a court, but later candidates rejected by the boule were allowed to appeal to a court (and it was only to these appeals that the word ἔφεσις was appropriate) (*Essays*, 194-5). A second contrast between earlier and current practice, on the hearing in court, is made in §iv: previously when there was no accuser one man gave a formal vote in favour of the candidate, but now, in case a candidate should have eliminated potential accusers by bribery, the court votes seriously on every candidate. This confirms that ἔφεσις denotes automatic reference in all cases, since provision for cases with no accuser ought not to have been necessary if the courts heard only contested cases which went to them on appeal. Although both here and in 45. iii *A.P.* refers to the boule's right to reject candidates, I do not think it is safe to infer that the boule had never had the final right to accept candidates, and I am not attracted by Wade-Gery's suggestion that in the earlier procedure the boule's rejection was final but its acceptance required confirmation. I believe that originally the boule's decision was final in all cases (but see the end of this note); later its vote was a pointer (like a προβολή in the assembly: 43. v, 59. ii, with commentary) but, unless a candidate rejected by the boule accepted his defeat and withdrew, the real decision was taken by a court. Cf. Nicodemus' amendment to the admission procedures of the Decelean phratry, by which the θίασος votes first but all candidates are then considered by the phratry unless they have been rejected by the θίασος and have withdrawn (*IG* ii² 1237, 78-103); less straightforwardly, candidates for registration as citizens are first examined by the deme, if the deme rejects them they may appeal to a court, if the deme accepts them ⟨or if a court overrules its rejection⟩ they are examined again by the boule (42. i-ii with commentary). 45. iii implies that the same double procedure was used for the δοκιμασία of archons and of bouleutae, but I am not confident that there was automatic ἔφεσις for the five hundred bouleutae (cf. *ad loc.*).

A.P. seems to envisage three stages in the development of this δοκιμασία: a first, in which the boule's was the only hearing; a second, in which the Athenians were primarily afraid of unjust rejection, and so two hearings were required but the hearing in court was a formality when there was no accuser; and a third, when they realised that there was also a danger of unjust acceptance, and so two serious hearings were required. It would be surprising, however, if a reformer simultaneously required ἔφεσις in all cases but made the ἔφεσις a formality in some of those cases, and if *A.P.*'s account is correct the second stage perhaps represents a reform weakened by an opponent's amendment. An alternative explanation is possible (which I advance only as a guess), that *A.P.* is wrong to locate the formal vote in a court and it belongs to an earlier stage in the history of this δοκιμασία (cf. Rhodes, *A.B.*, 176-8). I have suggested that until 462/1 the δοκιμασία of the archons was conducted by the Areopagus (p. 316), and that when the boule began to acquire judicial powers, in 462/1, its sentences were from the beginning made subject to automatic ἔφεσις whenever they were more severe than a 500-drachmae fine (p. 538): possibly these δοκιμασίαι were transferred by Ephialtes from the absolute decision of the Areopagus to the boule, the boule's decision was from the beginning subject to automatic ἔφεσις, and it was in the Areopagus before 462/1 that a purely formal vote was taken when no one wished to accuse.

55. iii. ἐπερωτῶσιν: For the questions asked at the δοκιμασία cf. Poll. VIII. 85–6 (ἐπερώτα δ' ἡ βουλή), *L.R.C.* θεσμοθετῶν ἀνάκρισις (ἐρωτώμενοι); also X. *M.* II. ii. 13, D. LVII. *Eub.* 66–70, Din. II. *Aristog.* 17–18. The questions asked suggested that the δοκιμασία was an ancient institution, though in the archaic state, where the candidates came from a restricted class and were likely to be well known to their examiners, the examination is likely to have been a matter of formal confirmation rather than genuine enquiry (cf. Rhodes, *A.B.*, 178 n. 4).

τίς σοι πατήρ . . . καὶ τίς μητρὸς πατὴρ καὶ πόθεν τῶν δήμων: Cf. D. LVII. *Eub.* 66 (ὦ ἄνθρωπε, τίς ἦν σοι πατήρ;). The nine archons had to be not only citizens but the sons of citizens by lawful marriage to citizen wives ([D.] LIX. *Neaer.* 92, 104–6, with pp. 496–7, 510–11; εἰ Ἀθηναῖοί εἰσιν ἐκ τριγονίας, in Poll. VIII. 85, should be seen not as a sign of a stricter requirement of third-generation Athenian citizenship but as an inaccurate summary of the questions about ancestry listed by *A.P.* [cf. Gilbert, *C.A.S.A.*, 186 n. 3, Busolt & Swoboda, *G.S.*, ii. 947 n. 4][49]). The proof that a man was a citizen was that his name was entered on the register of his deme (cf. p. 497); women were not registered, and the proof that a woman was a πολῖτις was that her father was registered as a citizen. Thus candidates were asked their father's name, deme and paternity (the last was not strictly necessary, but despite the intention attributed to Cleisthenes in 21. iv the patronymic remained part of a man's full designation), and their mother's name, paternity and her father's deme.†

εἰ ἔστιν αὐτῷ Ἀπόλλων πατρῷος . . . τὰ ἱερά ἐστιν: Cf. D. LVII. *Eub.* 54, 67; Harp. ἕρκειος Ζεύς, citing Din. fr. (2) xxvii Sauppe, Hyp. fr. 100 Sauppe, Dem. Phal. 228 F 6; Crat. Jun. fr. 9. 4–5 Kock, *ap.* Ath. XI. 460 F; on Din. II. *Aristog.* 17 see next note. It was a further confirmation that a man was an Athenian that he had in Athenian

---

[49] J. H. Oliver publishes in *Hesp.* Supp. xiii 1970 an inscription of Marcus Aurelius, revealing that by his time 'good birth' for three generations (ἀπὸ τῆς τριγονίας) was required for membership of the Areopagus, and for two generations for membership of the boule (col. ii, 59–79; 79–81, 96–103).

territory household cults of Apollo πατρῷος (so styled because through Ion Apollo was regarded as the common ancestor of all the Athenians: cf. p. 66, and, for a guess that the cult was instituted by Solon, Jacoby, *CQ* xxxviii 1944, 72–3 = *Abhandlungen*, 254–5) and Zeus ἕρκειος ('of the courtyard': e.g. Hom. *Od.* xxii. 334–5, H. vi. 68. i; see N. D. Fustel de Coulanges, *La Cité antique*, liv. ii, ch. vi [65 with n. 2, ed. of 1916]). A. Andrewes, *JHS* lxxxi 1961, 7–8, suggests that strictly the cults were in the custody of the γένη but all members of the phratry associated with each γένος were regarded as having a share in its cult; if this is right, and if this examination was taken seriously, the effect will have been to exclude from the archonship any citizen who did not belong to a phratry (cf. p. 511).

εἶτα ἠρία εἰ ἔστιν καὶ ποῦ ταῦτα: An ἠρίον is a mound (e.g. Hom. *Il.* xxiii. 126), and by extension any kind of tomb: to provide further confirmation that he is a true Athenian the candidate is asked whether and where he has family tombs. Cf. X. *M.* ii. ii. 13, D. lvii. *Eub.* 67; in Din. ii. *Aristog.* 17 the MSS read εἰ ἱερὰ πατρῷά ἐστιν, but the reference in §18 to the death of Aristigiton's father supports Valesius' emendation to ἠρία.

ἔπειτα γονέας εἰ εὖ ποιεῖ: Cf. X. *M.* ii. ii. 13, D. lvii. *Eub.* 70, Din. ii. *Aristog.* 17–18. The laws of Solon required Athenians to support their fathers (*sc.* in old age): Ar. *Av.* 1353–7, Liban. *Decl.* xi. *Cim.* 14, Ael. *N.A.* ix. 1, cf. A. 1. *Tim.* 13, Pl. *Sol.* 22. i, iv. A man who failed to support his parents or grandparents was liable to prosecution (cf. 56. vi with commentary).

[καὶ] τὰ τέλη <εἰ> τελεῖ: εἰ was inserted by Kaibel & Wilamowitz[1] (cf. Kaibel, *Stil und Text*, 230); cf. Crat. Jun. fr. 9. 5 Kock *ap.* Ath. xi. 460 f, Din. ii. *Aristog.* 17 with 18, *L.R.C.* θεσμοθετῶν ἀνάκρισις. Poll. viii. 86 has καὶ εἰ τὸ τίμημα ἔστιν αὐτοῖς (καὶ τί, E. Koch, *RE*, v [1903/5], 1271), so he or an intermediary must have seen here a reference not to payment of taxes but to membership of a Solonian property-class, and this was accepted by Gilbert, *C.A.S.A.*, 219 with n. 2. Membership of a Solonian class other than the lowest was legally required (26. ii with commentary; p. 510); candidates were asked which class they belonged to before the lots were drawn (7. iv *fin.*), and we should expect a check to be made at the δοκιμασία; but it is clear from Cratinus and Dinarchus that this question did refer to payment of taxes.

καὶ τὰς στρατείας εἰ ἐστράτευται: Cf. Din. ii. *Aristog.* 17–18. For the importance in δοκιμασίαι of a man's record of military service cf. Lys. xvi. *Mant.* 12–18; also D. xxi. *Mid.* 160–74.

ἀνερωτήσας: §iii began with the third person plural verbs ἐπερωτῶσιν, δοκιμάζωσιν; it ends with the singular ἀνερωτήσας, φησίν (cf. §iv): the subject is presumably the ἐπιστάτης in the boule or the presiding magistrate in a δικαστήριον.

'κ[ά]λει', φησίν, 'τούτων τοὺς μάρτυρας': Cf. D. LVII. *Eub*. 67 (οἰκεῖοί τινες εἶναι μαρτυροῦσιν αὐτῷ;). In judicial proceedings written depositions replaced spoken testimony from about the 370's (cf. p. 590), but the witnesses still had to appear in court to acknowledge their testimony (cf. on §v): in, for example, D. LVII. *Eub*. the older καλεῖ τοὺς μάρτυρας (§§21, 23, 27, 38, 39, etc.) alternates with the newer λάβε τὰς μαρτυρίας (§§19, 22, 23, 25, 28, etc.). Cf. R. J. Bonner, *Evidence in Athenian Courts*, 46–7.

55. iv. ἐπειδὰν δὲ παράσχηται τοὺς μάρτυρας: *Sc*. the candidate.
'τούτου βούλεταί τις κατηγορεῖν;' The δοκιμασία began with the formal interrogation of the candidate and the presentation of his supporting testimony, and in this first stage he was as it were a defendant without an accuser; then an opportunity to object to the candidate was provided, and if any one did object the candidate was allowed to reply (e.g. Lys. XXVI. *Evand*. 3). The invitation was presumably extended to members of the citizen body as a whole, who must have been able to hear the interrogation and to come within the κιγκλίς to raise objections: in Lys. XVI. *Mant*., XXV. *Reip. Del. Defens*., XXVI. *Evand*., we have prepared speeches of defence and accusation; it ought to have been possible for a man to decide on hearing the interrogation that he would raise an objection, but we do not know if this was so.
οὕτω δίδωσιν ἐν μὲν τῇ βουλῇ ... εὐθὺς δίδωσι τὴν ψῆφον: In the boule, which normally voted by show of hands, *A.P*.'s word for the vote is ἐπιχειροτονία (cf. 43. iv, 61. ii, iv, on the assembly's confirmation in office of the ἀρχαί each prytany); in the court, which voted by ballot, his word is ψῆφος. Presumably in both bodies the vote was taken immediately after the invitation to objectors if no one responded, otherwise after the objector had spoken and the candidate had replied, and the appearance of ψῆφον alone in the second half of the sentence is due simply to condensation.
καὶ πρότερον μὲν εἷς ... ἐπὶ τοῖς δικασταῖς γένηται τοῦτον ἀπ[ο]δοκιμάσαι: Here *A.P*. refers explicitly to the δικασταί, and the casting of a token vote is appropriate to a body which votes by ballot but inappropriate to one which votes by show of hands. For discussion of this change see pp. 615–17.
διαψηφίζεσθαι: Cf. the use of this word in the δοκιμασία of eighteen-year-old citizens (42. i with commentary).

55. v. δοκιμασθέν<τες>: Due to W. G. Rutherford and H. Richards, *CR* v 1891, 117: Kenyon[1-3] retained the papyrus' δοκιμασθέν, and in his Berlin ed. commented *quod nescio an retinendum sit*; an accusative absolute is not impossible, but the nominative plural is more

COMMENTARY ON THE *ATH. POL.*

probably right. For the timing of the oath-taking see the last note on this chapter, p. 621.

βαδίζουσι πρός τόν λίθον: Cf. 7. i with commentary (οἱ δ' ἐννέα ἄρχοντες ὀμνύντες πρὸς τῷ λίθῳ): the stone has now been found, in front of the Stoa of the Basileus, near the north wing.

ἐφ' ο[ὗ] τὰ τόμι' ἐστίν: This text is due to Leeuwen (*Mnem.*² xix 1891, 180–1, cf. Herwerden & Leeuwen: cf. Bergk's correction of Poll. VIII. 86, Ar. *Lys.* 186–7, D. XXIII. *Arist.* 68; also Ant. v. *Caed. Her.* 88, A. II. *F.L.* 87). M. C. Gertz, *NTF*² x 1890–2, 254, and Kaibel & Wilamowitz[1-2] preferred ὑφ' ᾧ (cf. Wilamowitz, *A.u.A.*, i. 46–7 n. 9), and Blass and Kaibel & Wilamowitz[3] (supported by Wilcken's reading of the papyrus: cf. Kaibel, *Stil und Text*, 230–1) ἐφ' ᾧ, but Kenyon in his 3rd and Berlin edd. confirmed Leeuwen's text, and Dr J. D. Thomas reports that φο is certain and ε acceptable. τόμια are victims cut up for sacrifice: the prosecutor in a homicide trial before the Areopagus swore ἐπὶ τῶν τομίων κάπρου καὶ κριοῦ καὶ ταύρου (D. XXIII. *Arist.* 68).

ἐφ' οὗ καὶ οἱ διαιτηταὶ ὀμόσαντες ἀποφαίνονται τὰς διαίτας: Cf. 53. ii–vi with commentary (where *A.P.* does not mention this fact), and Isae. v. *Her. Dic.* 32 (of private arbitrators). The oath was probably a promissory oath sworn on accepting a case, rather than a confirmatory oath sworn when pronouncing judgment (Bonner & Smith, *Administration of Justice*, ii. 156–7).

καὶ οἱ μάρτυρες ἐξόμνυνται τὰς μαρτυρίας: 'Witnesses swear in denial of their evidence.' From the 370's written statements of evidence were taken in advance of the hearing of a lawsuit; but witnesses had to be present at the hearing to acknowledge their evidence or deny it on oath, and a man who had refused to give evidence could be summoned to acknowledge a statement drawn up by one of the litigants or deny that on oath (cf. Isae. IX. *Her. Ast.* 18, A. I. *Tim.* 45–7, 67, D. XIX. *F.L.* 176, Lyc. *Leocr.* 20, Poll. VIII. 37, 55; also Plat. *Legg.* XI. 936 E 6–937 A 3; and Lipsius, *A.R.*, 976–82, Bonner & Smith, *Administration of Justice*, ii. 136–44, 163–4, Harrison, *L.A.*, ii. 139–45). Some have taken this to mean 'Witnesses swear to their testimony' (Kenyon's translations, Moore); but for that meaning of ἐξομνύναι LSJ cites only a papyrus of the third century A.D., and our evidence suggests that except in homicide trials witnesses could swear to the truth of their testimony but were not bound to do so (Lipsius, *A.R.*, 884–5, Bonner & Smith, *op. cit.*, 172–4).

ἀναβάντες δ' ἐπὶ τοῦτον: The stone was *c.* 0·4 m. high, with a surface *c.* 1 m. × 3 m.

ὀμνύουσιν ... τῆς ἀρχῆς ἕνεκα: Members of the boule swore κατὰ τοὺς νόμους βουλεύσειν (X. *M.* I. i. 18); τὰ βέλτιστα βουλεύσειν τῇ πόλει/τῷ δήμῳ τῷ Ἀθηναίων (Lys. XXXI. *Phil.* 1 cf. XXX. *Nic.* 10, [D.] LIX. *Neaer.* 4). Jurors swore ψηφιοῦμαι κατὰ τοὺς νόμους καὶ τὰ

COMMENTARY ON THE *ATH. POL.* [55. v

ψηφίσματα τοῦ δήμου τοῦ Ἀθηναίων καὶ τῆς βουλῆς τῶν πεντακοσίων (oath *ap.* D. xxiv. *Tim.* 149 cf. D. xx. *Lept.* 118, xxi. *Mid.* 42, A. iii. *Ctes.* 6); γνώμῃ τῇ δικαιοτάτῃ δικάσειν (D. xxxix. *Boe. Nom.* 40, lvii. *Eub.* 63); οὐδὲ δῶρα δέξομαι τῆς ἡλιάσεως ἕνεκα οὔτ' αὐτὸς ἐγὼ οὔτ' ἄλλος ἐμοὶ οὔτ' ἄλλη εἰδότος ἐμοῦ, οὔτε τέχνῃ οὔτε μηχανῇ οὐδεμιᾷ (oath *ap.* D. xxiv. *Tim.* 150 cf. [D.] xlvi. *Steph. ii.* 26).

κἄν τι λάβωσι ἀνδριάντα ἀναθήσειν χρυσοῦν: Cf. 7. i with commentary (ἀναθήσειν ἀνδριάντα χρυσοῦν, ἐάν τινα παραβῶσι τῶν νόμων). This passage, linking the dedication with bribe-taking, is the more likely to be correct.

εἰς ἀκρόπολιν βαδίζουσιν καὶ πάλιν ἐκεῖ ταὐτὰ ὀμνύουσι: No other text mentions this, and we do not know where on the Acropolis the archons repeated their oath. E. Will, *RPh*³ xlii 1968, 135, suggested that originally the oath was sworn on the Acropolis alone, where the laws were published, and this is supported by the discovery of the Stoa of the Basileus and its post-Solonian date (cf. on 7. i).

καὶ μετὰ ταῦτ': There must have been an appreciable lapse of time either between the completion of the δοκιμασία and the swearing of the oath or between the swearing of the oath and entry into office at the beginning of the new year or at both points: I should guess that more probably the archons' oath immediately preceded their entry into office.

56. i. λαμβάνουσι δὲ καὶ παρέδρους ... οὓς ἂν βούληται: Cf. 48. iv with commentary, on the πάρεδροι of the εὔθυνοι; schol. A. 1. *Tim.* 158 wrongly states that a πάρεδρος was appointed ἑκάστῳ ἄρχοντι. In *Hesp.* ii 1 = *IG* ii² 2811 the archon of 394/3 is joined in a dedication by one πάρεδρος and a secretary (cf. p. 613): Meritt in his commentary (p. 150) suggests that the number of πάρεδροι was subsequently increased, but it is possible that this archon had two πάρεδροι, but only one shared in the dedication. It used to be thought that the two men listed in *IG* ii² 1696 with each of the (eponymous) archons of the 350's were their πάρεδροι, but S. Dow on rereading the stone has found that one man served for three successive years, which makes that interpretation improbable. Two πάρεδροι are listed in each of two dedications of a basileus, *Hesp.* xl 5 (end c4: one is his son), 6 (mid c2: one is his brother); *Hesp.* vii 18 and *IG* ii² 668 honour the archons of 283/2 and 282/1 and the two πάρεδροι of each, and Dow identifies as an archon and his πάρεδροι the men honoured in the first decree of *SEG* xxiii 78 = O. W. Reinmuth, *Mnem.* Supp. xiv 1971, no. 1 (361/0). It is not clear from [D.] lviii. *Theocr.* 27 how official a position Theocrines held with respect to the thesmothetae of 344/3. D. xxi. *Mid.* 178–9 mentions a man who served as πάρεδρος to his son and incurred a hostile vote in a προβολή; in [D.] lix. *Neaer.* 72 a basileus marries the alleged daughter of one of his

621

πάρεδροι, but in §83 he dismisses the πάρεδρος for deceiving him; [D.] LVIII. *Theocr.* 32 shows a πάρεδρος formally accepting one of the archon's lawsuits; *IG* ii² 1230 honours a man who as πάρεδρος of the basileus helped in the administration of the Eleusinian Mysteries. It is striking that the three senior archons were allowed to choose their own assistants; this may be a survival from the archaic state (cf. Moore, 293); but having been appointed they were, at any rate in the classical state, subjected to the usual procedures of δοκιμασία and εὔθυναι. See Dow, *Essays* ... *O. J. Brendel*, 80–4.

56. ii. καὶ ὁ μὲν ἄρχων: Having dealt with the appointment of the board and its assistants, *A.P.* deals separately with the duties of the different archons, first their religious and then their judicial responsibilities. On the origins of the eponymous archon, believed by *A.P.* to be the most recent of the three senior archons, see 3. i, iii, with commentary; a religious duty of the archon mentioned not here but in 60. ii–iii is to collect the olive oil for the prizes at the Panathenaea.

πρῶτον μὲν κηρύττει ... μέχρι ἀρχῆς τέλους: Fritz & Kapp render 'proclaims through the public herald' (cf. Gilbert, *C.A.S.A.*, 251): there was a herald of the archon (62. ii with commentary), and it is likely that the proclamation was made by him. Most have thought that this proclamation guaranteeing the citizens in the secure possession of their property during the year must be a survival from the archaic state: in the classical period the archon had little power to enforce its observance (as pointed out by Moore, 293), or himself to break the undertaking. If this is so, Solon must instead have proclaimed his σεισάχθεια (Wilamowitz, *A.u.A.*, ii. 62, Busolt & Swoboda, *G.S.*, ii. 829); others have thought that the undertaking must be post-Solonian (W. J. Woodhouse, *Solon the Liberator*, 134–5 n. 30, M. Mühl, *RM*² xcviii 1955, 349–54; G. Glotz, *RH* cxxii 1916, 370, compared the heliastic oath *ap*. D. xxiv. *Tim.* 149 and dated the undertaking to 403/2). As noticed by Mühl, we have the peripatetics' resolution of the dilemma in Phaenias, fr. 20 Wehrli *ap.* Pl. *Sol.* 14. ii: Solon secretly promised τοῖς μὲν ἀπόροις γῆς νέμησιν, τοῖς δὲ χρηματικοῖς βεβαίωσιν τῶν συμβολαίων. I am inclined to believe that this proclamation was not instituted until the possibility of γῆς ἀναδασμός had arisen: perhaps Solon himself, having proclaimed his σεισάχθεια, enacted that future archons should proclaim the security of property.

ἔχειν καὶ κρατεῖν: Cf. *IG* ii² 2758, 3–4, 2759, 6 (Hellenistic).

56. iii. ἔπειτα χορηγοὺς τραγῳδοῖς ... τοὺς πλουσιωτάτους: On choregi see especially A. W. Pickard-Cambridge rev. J. P. A. Gould & D. M. Lewis, *The Dramatic Festivals of Athens*, 75–8, 86–93:

evidence supporting statements in this and the following notes for which I cite no authority will be found in that book.†

The χορηγία, the undertaking of financial and general responsibility for the performance of a chorus at one of the major festivals, was one of the ληιτουργίαι which the Athenian state imposed on its richer citizens (there were also liturgies at deme level: see 54. viii with commentary, on the rural Dionysia): for the range of festival liturgies see J. K. Davies, *JHS* lxxxvii 1967, 33–40; for a survey of the evidence for the cost of festival liturgies see Davies, *A.P.F.*, xxi–xxii; and for the level of wealth at which a man could be called on to perform liturgies see *A.P.F.*, xxiii–xxiv. It was possible for a man to volunteer as choregus (the speaker of Lys. XXI. *Pec. Acc.* 1–5 claims to have undertaken eight χορηγίαι in nine years; Demosthenes volunteered to undertake a dithyrambic chorus when the normal arrangements in his tribe had broken down [D. XXI. *Mid.* 13]). The archon's instructions were presumably to call on the richest of the men who were not temporarily or permanently exempt on the grounds stated below: a man who was called upon when a richer man had been passed over could attempt to have the burden transferred to him by the procedure of ἀντίδοσις (cf. below); in 406/5 the duties of choregus were divided between two men (schol. Ar. *Ran.* 404 with Pickard-Cambridge, *op. cit.*, 87 n. 2). Aristotle disliked the imposition of these burdens on the rich (*Pol.* v. 1305 A 4–5, 1309 A 14–20), and *c.* 316–315 festival liturgies were abolished by Demetrius of Phalerum: thereafter the people elected an ἀγωνοθέτης who was provided with public money but could add to it from his own pocket (cf. Pickard-Cambridge, *op. cit.*, 91–3). Three tragedians competed each year at the Great Dionysia (there was also a tragic competition at the Lenaea, in the fifth century between two contestants, but this was less important: cf. p. 638): it was also the responsibility of the archon to διδόναι χόρον to the poets whom he accepted as contestants.

If ἔπειτα may be pressed, to indicate that this was one of the first duties of the new archon, ample time for preparation was allowed: the Dionysia was held in Elaphebolion (ix).

πρότερον δὲ καὶ κωμῳδοῖς ... τούτοις αἱ φυλαὶ φέρουσιν: For τούτοις (*sc.* τοῖς κωμῳδοῖς) W. Wyse, *CR* v 1891, 117, suggested τούτους (*sc.* τοὺς χορηγούς), comparing D. xxxix. *Boe. Nom.* 7, where the verb φέρειν is again used of such appointments: some editors have been persuaded, but the papyrus' text is unobjectionable.

Both at the Lenaea and at the Great Dionysia five comedians competed (the number was reduced to three during the Peloponnesian War; for the Dionysia it was increased to six in the Hellenistic period, but for the Lenaea it was still five when we last have evidence, in 284: Pickard-Cambridge, *op. cit.*, 83). We do not know when the change in procedure was made, except that it appears to be earlier than 348/7 (D. xxxix. *Boe. Nom.* 7: see J. J. Keaney, *Hist.* xix 1970, 330 with n. 19); in spite of the change comic choruses remained, like tragic and unlike dithyrambic choruses, non-tribally organised. The tribal procedure for appointing choregi involved officials known as the ἐπιμεληταὶ τῆς φυλῆς (D. xxi. *Mid.* 13, for dithyrambs); there were three in each tribe (*IG* ii² 1151, 1152, 2818, *Hesp.* v 10, 167–70, *SEG* xxi 515).†

The Great Dionysia and the Thargelia were the responsibility of the archon (§§iv–v); but the Lenaea was among the responsibilities of the basileus, and it should be he who had charge of choregi for that festival (cf. [D.] xxxv. *Lacr.* 48, D. xxxix. *Boe. Nom.* 9).

ἔπειτα παραλαβὼν τοὺς χορηγοὺς τοὺς ἐνηνεγμένους ὑπὸ τῶν φυλῶν: The archon takes charge of the choregi appointed by the tribes for the festivals for which he is responsible; in addition to dealing with claims for exemption as set out by *A.P.*, he supervises the drawing of lots between choregi for poets and pipers (D. xxi. *Mid.* 13).

εἰς Διονύσια ἀνδράσιν καὶ παισὶν: That is, in the dithyrambic contests. (εἰσὶ δ' οἱ μὲν εἰς Διονύσια ... εἰς Θαργήλια <δὲ> δυοῖν φυλαῖν ...): The papyrus' δυεῖν φυλαῖν was retained by Kenyon¹ and Kaibel & Wilamowitz¹, ³, but we should certainly correct to δυοῖν φυλαῖν (which the papyrus has in 52. ii), with Herwerden & Leeuwen: see on 42. v.

In the dithyrambic competitions at the Dionysia each of the ten tribes competed both in the men's and in the boys' class, so two choregi will have been needed from each tribe (Davies, *JHS* lxxxvii 1967, 33, Pickard-Cambridge, *op. cit.*, 75 with n. 1: the epigraphic evidence makes this certain, but Pickard-Cambridge in his 1st ed. concluded from schol. A. I. *Tim.* 10 that only five choruses competed in each class). In Ant. vi. *Chor.* 11 we read ἐπειδὴ χορηγὸς κατεστάθην εἰς Θαργήλια καί ἔλαχον Παντακλέα διδάσκαλον καὶ Κεκροπίδα φυλὴν πρὸς τῇ ἐμαυτοῦ, which suggests that in the late fifth century the tribes which did not supply choregi for Thargelia were paired by lot for the one occasion with tribes which did. The epigraphic evidence indicates that there was a regular pairing (at any rate for boys' choruses) in and after 365/4 (*IG* ii² 3065–70 and the inscriptions published by Σ. Ν. Κουμανούδης, *ΑΔ* xxv 1970, μελ. 143–9) but that this pairing was not in force in and before 384/3 (*SEG* xviii 69 [=*IG* ii² 3064 + new fr.: men], *IG* ii² 3063 [boys]). For other occasions when five men had to be appointed from the ten tribes see 52. ii (εἰσαγωγεῖς), 54. i (ὁδοποιοί), 62. ii (amphictyons for Delos), also 51. iii (thirty-five σιτοφύλακες), with commentary.

τούτοις τὰς ἀντιδόσεις ποιεῖ: On ἀντιδόσεις see W. A. Goligher, *Hermath.* xiv 1906–7, 481–515, Lipsius, *A.R.*, 590–9, Harrison, *L.A.*, ii. 236–8, D. M. MacDowell, *The Law in Classical Athens*, 162–4. A man who was called on to perform a liturgy and claimed that another richer man had been passed over could challenge the other man either to perform the liturgy or to exchange property with him; if the man challenged would do neither, the case went to court as a διαδικασία, and the man found to be richer was required to perform the liturgy. Some have denied that in the fourth century an actual exchange of property was a serious possibility (e.g. L. Gernet, Budé ed. of D.'s *Plaidoyers civils*, ii. 72-5, C. Mossé, *La Fin de la démocratie athénienne*, 153 n. 6); but probably it remained theoretically available, even if most Athenians would have thought it too inconvenient to be worth resorting to. Cf. 61. i with commentary, on ἀντιδόσεις and διαδικασίαι for the trierarchy; and for an exchange of duties between two officials in the second century A.D. see *Hesp.* xlvii 28, 7-10, with the commentary of J. S. Traill.†

καὶ τὰς σκήψεις εἰσ[άγει: A σκῆψις (on which see Lipsius, *A.R.*, 588-90, Harrison, *L.A.*, ii. 232-6) was a claim that a man was legally exempt from a liturgy to which he had been appointed. *A.P.* proceeds to list three grounds of exemption (the second and third being temporary); in addition, hereditary exemption had been conferred on various distinguished Athenians, until Leptines proposed that except for the descendants of Harmodius and Aristogiton this exemption should be revoked, and none should in future be conferred (e.g. D. xx. *Lept.* 127, 160); it is probable that men with less than a stated amount of property were exempt (cf. D. xx. *Lept.* 19); and it is possible that in the time of *A.P.* the ephebi were exempt from festival liturgies (42. v with commentary). For the importance of such claims to exemption cf. [X.] *A.P.* iii. 4.

ἢ λελητουργη[κέ]ν[αι] φῇ πρότερον ταύτην τὴν λητουρ[γίαν: As a man could not hold any civilian magistracy more than once in his life (62. iii), so he could not be required to undertake any particular festival liturgy more than once; I do not know of an instance when any one did so.

ἢ ἀ]τέλης εἶναι ... μὴ ἐξεληλυθό[των: There was a general rule that, having performed a liturgy in one year, a man was exempt from liturgies in the following year (D. xx. *Lept.* 8); *a fortiori*, he was exempt from other liturgies in the same year ([D.] L. *Poly.* 9). Some expensive liturgies might be followed by a longer period of exemption: a man who had been trierarch (before Periander applied the symmory-organisation to the trierarchy: cf. on 61. i) was exempt certainly from the trierarchy and perhaps from other liturgies also for two years afterwards (Isae. VII. *Her. Apoll.* 38).

ἢ τὰ] ἔτη ... ὑπὲρ τεττaρά[κον]τα ἔτη γεγονέναι: For the requirement that choregi for boys' choruses must be over forty cf. A. I. *Tim.* 11, also Plat. *Legg.* VI. 764 E 6-765 A 1; the same age was required of the σωφρονισταί and probably the κοσμητής of the ephebi (42. ii

COMMENTARY ON THE *ATH. POL.*

with commentary). This rule was an innovation of the fourth century (cf. D. M. Lewis, *BSA* l 1955, 24, Pickard-Cambridge, *op. cit.*, 75 n. 4): in 406/5 there was a boys' choregus in his early twenties (Lys. xxi. *Pec. Acc.* 1–5), and Alcibiades served as boys' choregus when under forty (D. xxi. *Mid.* 147, Pl. *Alc.* 16. v, [And.] iv. *Alc.* 20–1, cf. Davies, *A.P.F.*, 18).

καθίστησι δὲ καὶ εἰς Δῆλον χορηγοὺς καὶ ἀρχ[ι]θέω[ρον τ]ῷ τριακοντορίῳ τοὺς ἠθέους ἄγοντι: (For bracketing see the *corrigenda* of Kenyon's Berlin ed.) For the quadrennial festival on Delos to which Athens sent θεωροί and choruses cf. 54. vii with commentary, and for the amphictyons who administered the temple property see 62. ii with commentary. A θεωρία was sent to Delos every year (cf. Plat. *Phaed.* 58 A 6–c 2: Socrates was tried in 400/399, the first year of an Olympiad [D.L. ii. 44, D.S. xiv. 37. vii], whereas the quadrennial festival was held at first in the third and later in the second year of the Olympiad [cf. on 54. vii]). According to *L.R.C.* ἐπώνυμος ἄρχων the archon was responsible for θεωρίαι both to Delos and elsewhere (θεωριῶν Lugebil: χορῶν codd.).

ἀρχιθέωρον was suggested by Lipsius, *Ber. Leipzig* xliii 1891, 49 n. 3, and M. Fränkel, *Deut. Zeitschr. Geschichtswissenschaft* v 1891, 166 n. 1, and has become the standard restoration; C. Torr, *CR* v 1891, 118, noticing that in 375/4 ⟨and 371/0⟩ there was a plurality of ἀρχιθέωροι, and of θεωροί and choruses (*IG* ii² 1635 = Tod 125 = *I. de Délos* 98, 34–5, ⟨*I. de Délos* 100, 41⟩), suggested ἀρχιθεώρους. X. *M.* iii. iii. 12 and Pl. *Nic.* 3. v–vi refer to the sending of a single chorus from Athens; there is no need to suppose that more than one of the ἀρχιθέωροι of the inscriptions was from Athens (cf. commentary on Tod 125, p. 80, but J. Coupry, *BCH* lxxxviii 1954, 285–90, was prepared to believe in a plurality of Athenian ἀρχιθέωροι; the usage would be unparalleled); and according to Kenyon's Berlin ed. the shorter, singular form fits the space in *A.P.* better (confirmed by Dr J. D. Thomas). For the diminutive τριακοντόριον cf. *IG* ii² 1627, 16, 1631, 426, and for this and other sacred ships see 61. vii with commentary. ἤθεοι (ἠίθεοι) are unmarried young men, the male equivalent of παρθένοι (cf. H. iii. 48. iii: χόρους παρθένων τε καὶ ἠϊθέων).

56. iv. πομπῶν δ' ἐπιμελεῖτ[αι τῆς τ]ε τῷ Ἀσκληπιῷ γιγνομένης, ὅταν οἰκουρῶσι μύσται: (Wilcken hesitated between τ(ῆς) τ]ε and τῇ]ς, but there is no sign of uncertainty in Kenyon's Berlin ed.; Dr Thomas judges ς an easier reading but τ(ῆς) τ]ε better for the space.) The procession for Asclepius, 'when the initiates stay indoors', was held on the day of the Epidauria, 18 Boedromion (iii), the day before the great procession from Athens to Eleusis for the Mysteries. The initiates spent the day in the temple of Asclepius (cf. Ar. *Plut.*

411, 621): LSJ translates οἰκουρῶσι 'keep watch' (sense 1), and Parke describes this as 'a suitable preparation for the spiritual experience of the two final days', which is better than Mylonas' view of it as a 'rest day'. See *IG* ii² 974, 12, Paus. II. 26. viii, Philostr. *Vit. Apoll.* IV. 18, and L. Deubner, *Attische Feste*, 73 with n. 3 (wrongly assigning this procession to the basileus), G. E. Mylonas, *Eleusis and the Eleusinian Mysteries*, 251, H. W. Parke, *Festivals of the Athenians*, 63.

3. iii *fin.* states that the archon administered only the more recent festivals (ἐπίθετα): Athens had revived the quadrennial festival on Delos in 426/5 (cf. on 54. vii); the cult of Asclepius was not introduced into Athens until 420 (*IG* ii² 4960, 10–13).

καὶ τῆς τῶν Διονυσίων τῶν μ[εγά]λων: The procession leading to the sacrifices in the precinct of Dionysus was held on the first day of the Great Dionysia proper, 10 Elaphebolion (ix), having been preceded by the προαγών and Asclepiea on the 8th, and the εἰσαγωγὴ ἀπὸ τῆς ἐσχάρας, a reenactment of the advent of Dionysus from Eleutherae, on the night of the 8/9th or 9/10th. See Deubner, *op. cit.*, 138–42 (accepting A. Mommsen's dating of the procession to the 9th, but against that see W. S. Ferguson, *Hesp.* xvii 1948, 133–5 n. 46, W. B. Dinsmoor, *Hesp.* xxiii 1954, 306–8 [on *Hesp.* xxiii 183 = *SEG* xiv 65]), Pickard-Cambridge, *op. cit.*, 59–66, J. D. Mikalson, *The Sacred and Civil Calendar of the Athenian Year*, 123–6, Parke, *op. cit.*, 127–8 (Parke's 132 dates the προαγών to the 9th, which is certainly wrong: see A. III. *Ctes.* 67).

This was generally regarded as one of the more recent festivals: it was a festival of Dionysus Ἐλευθερεύς, whose image was said to have been brought to Athens from Eleutherae, on the borders of Boeotia and Attica, by one Pegasus (cf. Paus. I. 2. v, 38. viii), allegedly in the time of Amphiction, third king of Athens after Cecrops I and Cranaus; but it was in the time of Pisistratus that the cult became important, and that may well be the time when it was brought to Athens (cf. Pickard-Cambridge, *op. cit.*, 57–8).†

μετὰ τῶν ἐπιμελητῶν, οὓς πρότερον μὲν ... ἑκατὸν μνᾶς: In *IG* ii² 668, 13–15, 22–31 (282/1), and 896, 29 sqq. (186/5), the epimeletae are among the men praised for the conduct of the festival (in the earlier inscription they number ten, in the later twenty-four, in neither case tribally based); for the fourth century cf. *IG* ii² 354, 15–19, referring to οἱ λαχόντες ἐπιμεληταὶ τῆς εὐκοσμίας τῆς περὶ τὸ θέατρον. The number confirms that they are not to be identified with the ἐπιμεληταὶ τῆς φυλῆς, three in each tribe, who were involved in the appointment of choregi (p. 624). In Thph. *Char.* 26. ii the oligarchic man objects to the appointment of democratic epimeletae to help the archon with the organisation of a procession.

This change took place not long before the time of *A.P.*: the epimeletae were still elected in the middle of the fourth century (D.

56. iv] COMMENTARY ON THE *ATH. POL.*

xxi. *Mid.* 15—not necessarily disproved by D. iv. *Phil. i.* 35, which refers to the appointment by lot of οἱ ... ἐπιμελούμενοι of the Panathenaea and the Dionysia). Originally the office was a form of liturgy, the elected epimeletae being expected to pay for the procession out of their own pockets, whereas in the time of *A.P.* the cost was borne by the state: we may guess that the change was a part of the reorganisation of Athens' festivals in the Lycurgan period (cf. the reorganisation of the lesser Panathenaea and the earmarking of particular items of revenue to pay for it, *c.* 335: *IG* ii² 334, law published by D. M. Lewis, *Hesp.* xxviii 1959, 239–47 = *SEG* xviii 13, with his comments, pp. 245–7, and F. W. Mitchel, *Lectures* ... *L. T. Semple* ii 1966–70, 197–8). As with the reorganisation of the ἐφηβεία (pp. 494–5, 592), the change will have been very recent indeed when *A.P.* was written but there is nothing to suggest that the original edition did not mention it (cf. Introduction, p. 52).

56. v. ἐπιμελ[εῖτα]ι δὲ καὶ τῆς εἰς Θαργήλια: *Sc.* πομπῆς. The Thargelia, a festival of Apollo, occupied 6 and 7 Thargelion (xi): on the 6th the city was purified by the driving out of two men as scapegoats (φαρμακοί); on the 7th first-fruits of unripe corn were offered, and there was a procession (mentioned also in the law *ap.* D. xxi. *Mid.* 10), together with dithyrambic contests for men's and boys' choruses. Parke points out that agriculture was not normally Apollo's concern, and suggests that this cult of Apollo was imported from Asia about the eighth century: that may be true with regard to Apollo, but the festival must have been well established when the Athenian months acquired their names and its name was used for one of them, and so it would be wrong to consider this like the archon's other festivals to be a comparatively recent addition to the calendar. See Deubner, *Attische Feste*, 179–98, Parke, *Festivals of the Athenians*, 146–9.

καὶ τῆς τῷ Διὶ τῷ Σωτῆρι: The Διισωτήρια was in fact a festival of Zeus Σωτήρ and Athena Σώτειρα, with which other deities also came to be associated: the festival was held in mid Scirophorion (xii), in the Piraeus (*IG* ii² 380, 19–21, 30–2, mentioning the procession); there was also a sacrifice to Zeus Σωτήρ on the last day of the year (Lys. xxvi. *Evand.* 6). We have no evidence on the antiquity of the festival; but Parke suggests that it was instituted not earlier than Themistocles' 'foundation' of the Piraeus in 493/2 (cf. above, p. 279), and possibly after the Persian Wars, when a festival of the Saviours might be thought appropriate. See Deubner, *op. cit.*, 174–6, Mikalson, *Sacred and Civil Calendar*, 180, Parke, *op. cit.*, 167–9.

διοικεῖ δὲ καὶ τὸν ἀγῶνα ... καὶ τῶν Θαργηλίων: On the change of construction see Kaibel, *Stil und Text*, 232–3. In addition to his responsibility for choregi (§iii) and for processions (§§iv–v), the archon was responsible for the actual contests for tragedies, comedies and dithyrambic choruses at the Dionysia and for dithyrambic choruses at the Thargelia.

ἑορτῶν μὲν οὖν ἐπιμελεῖται τούτων: *A.P.* rounds off the first, religious part of the archon's duties (cf. p. 622) . . .

56. vi. γραφαὶ δ[ὲ καὶ] δίκαι λαγχάνονται πρὸς αὐτόν: . . . and proceeds to the second, judicial part. For λαγχάνειν cf. 53. i with commentary.
ἃς ἀνακρίνας: Cf. [D.] XLVIII. *Olymp.* 31 (καὶ μετὰ ταῦτα ὁ ἄρχων ἀνέκρινε πᾶσιν ἡμῖν τοῖς ἀμφισβητοῦσιν, καὶ ἀνακρίνας εἰσήγαγεν εἰς τὸ δικαστήριον). The ἀνάκρισις was the preliminary enquiry conducted by the εἰσάγουσα ἀρχή, to check that the case submitted to him was technically in order and prepare it for presentation to the court. See Lipsius, *A.R.*, 829–44, Bonner & Smith, *Administration of Justice*, i. 283–93, Harrison, *L.A.*, ii. 94–105; the verb is used in the active of the magistrate, in the middle of the litigants and in the passive of the case (Harrison, *op. cit.*, 95 n. 1).†

εἰς τὸ δικαστήριον: τὸ was read by Wilcken; Kenyon printed it in his Berlin ed. but with the note *non certum*, and Blass[2-4] had doubts; Dr J. D. Thomas suggests that ειστοκασ may have been corrected to εισδικασ. It is needed, even if the scribe omitted it (cf. Kaibel, *Stil und Text*, 233).

[γο]νέων κακώσεως . . ., ὀρφανῶν . . ., ἐπικλήρου . . ., οἴκου ὀρφανικοῦ: *A.P.* begins his list with genitives dependent on γραφαὶ δὲ καὶ δίκαι; after παρανοίας we have three items introduced by εἰς (one εἰς . . . διαδικασίαν); then an accusative and infinitive; and finally the nominative ἐπι[δικασίαι]. Prosecution for maltreatment of one's parents, of orphans, of heiresses, or for mismanagement of an orphan's estate, could be referred to either as an εἰσαγγελία (Harp., Suid. [*EI* 222], *s.v.*) or as a γραφή; Isae. XI. *Her. Hagn.* uses both terms within the one speech (§§6, 15; 28, 31, 32, 35: the fact is noted by Harp., Suid., *loc. cit.*). *L.S.* 269. 1, Harp., Suid. (*K* 178), κακώσεως, use the term δίκη, but as Harp. states it was certainly open to ὁ βουλόμενος to prosecute. See Lipsius, *A.R.*, 342–53, Harrison, *L.A.*, i. 117–19; for other kinds of εἰσαγγελίαι see 43. iv, 45. ii, 53. vi, with commentary.

[γο]νέων κακώσεως: Athenians were required by law to care for their parents while alive and to give them a proper burial when they died: cf. the questions asked at the δοκιμασία of the archons (55. iii with commentary); and X. *M.* II. ii. 13, Lys. XIII. *Agor.* 91, Isae. VIII. *Her. Cir.* 32, A. I. *Tim.* 13 cf. 28, D. X. *Phil. iv.* 40, XXIV. *Tim.* 107 cf. law *ap.* 105, Hyp. IV. *Eux.* 6, D.L. I. 55. γονεῖς included grandparents (cf. Isae., *loc. cit.*); the offences included τύπτειν (Lys.), μὴ τρέφειν (X., A., D. XXIV. *Tim.* 107), μὴ παρέχειν οἴκησιν (A.), τοὺς τάφους μὴ κοσμεῖν (X.); Hyperides confirms that such cases fell to the archon.

56. vi] COMMENTARY ON THE *ATH. POL.*

(αὗται δ' εἰσὶν ἀζήμιοι τῷ βουλομένῳ δ[ι]ώκειν): *A.P.* notes the exception without stating the normal rule, which was that prosecutors in γραφαί who withdrew their charge or who failed to obtain one fifth of the votes were fined 1,000 drachmae and subjected to a form of ἀτιμία (Lipsius, *A.R.*, 449 with n. 10, Bonner & Smith, *Administration of Justice*, ii. 56–7, Harrison, *L.A.*, ii. 83 with n. 2). Originally, it seems, in εἰσαγγελίαι of all kinds prosecutors were free from this risk; but not long before 330, at any rate in the case of major public offences (43. iv), εἰσαγγέλλοντες were threatened with the fine but not with ἀτιμία (Hyp. I. *Lyc.* 8, 12, with Poll. VIII. 52–3, D. XVIII. *Cor.* 250: see Harrison, *L.A.*, ii. 51 with n. 3, M. H. Hansen, *Eisangelia*, 29–31 [arguing, unnecessarily, that εἰσαγγέλλοντες who withdrew their charge had always been liable to this fine]; contr. Bonner & Smith, *op. cit.*, i. 296–8). This exemption applies to all charges of κάκωσις, not only γονέων (it is mentioned in cases concerning ἐπίκληροι in Isae. III. *Her. Pyrrh.* 46, D. XXXVII. *Pant.* 46); unless *A.P.* has failed to bring this passage up to date (cf. Introduction, p. 57), the exemption remained complete for this kind of εἰσαγγελία.

ὀρφανῶν κακώσεως (αὗται . . . κατὰ τῶν ἐπιτρόπων): The procedures on behalf of orphans and heiresses were in fact available against any one who wronged them, not only against their legal guardians (e.g. D. XXXVII. *Pant.* 45: Lipsius, *A.R.*, 344, Harrison, *L.A.*, i. 118). A convicted guardian could be deprived of his guardianship (Isae. XI. *Her. Hagn.* 31).

ἐπικλήρου κακώσε[ως . . . . (αὗτ]αι . . . τῶν συνοικούντων): Restored, with no gap, by Kenyon[1]; Wilcken and others were untroubled, but in his Berlin ed. and O.C.T. Kenyon detected room for four letters after κακώσε[ως, *nisi litura fuit*; Dr J. D. Thomas estimates that there should be two or three letters there. On ἐπίκληροι, legitimate daughters of a man with no legitimate sons, cf. 9. ii, 35. ii, 42. v, 43. iv, with commentary. Offences include failure by the next of kin to marry the heiress himself or find her a husband, ὕβρις (laws *ap.* [D.] XLIII. *Mac.* 54, 75), and failure by the husband to have intercourse with her as prescribed by the law *ap.* Pl. *Sol.* 20. ii–iv (Poll. VIII. 53). συνοικεῖν is used of the fact of cohabitation, and came to be used of living together in wedlock (Harrison, *L.A.*, i. 2 with n. 4); the same verb is used in a 'law of Charondas' on heiresses said to be the same as Solon's law (D.S. XII. 18. iii); its use here points to the capacity in which the husband might fail the heiress. That such cases fell to the archon is confirmed by Isae. III. *Her. Pyrrh.* 46, 62, D. XXXVII. *Pant.* 46.

οἴκου ὀρφανικοῦ . . . [αὗται κατὰ τῶν] ἐπιτρό[π]ων): Charges under this head could also be made by φάσις (D. XXXVIII. *Naus. & Xen.* 23, entries in the lexica: see L. Beauchet, *L'Histoire du droit privé de la république athénienne*, ii. 294-303, Lipsius, *A.R.*, 310-11, Harrison, *L.A.*, i. 115-17; contr. O. Schulthess, *RE*, xv [1931/2], 2113, rejecting φάσις on the grounds of *A.P.*'s silence.

παρανοίας ... τὰ [ὑπάρχοντα ἀ]πολλύν[αι]: Kenyon[1-3] restored τὰ [ἑαυτοῦ χρήματα, but in his 3rd ed. he realised that a shorter supplement was needed; suggestions include τὰ πατρῷα or πατρῷαν οὐσίαν (W. Wyse, *CR* v 1891, 118), τ[ὸν οἶκον (Kaibel & Wilamowitz[1-2]), ἑαυτοῦ (*Π. Ν. Παπαγεώργιος, Ἀθ.* iv 1892, 601), ὑπάρχοντα (Blass: cf. τὴν ὑπάρχουσαν in Arist. *Pol.* ii. 1270 A 18-20), οἰκεῖα (Kaibel, *Stil und Text*, 233-4); Wilcken marked a lacuna of ten letters between τὰ and ἀ]πολλύναι, as did Kenyon in his Berlin ed., who remarked that ὑπάρχοντα would fit the space but not the traces of the first letter; Dr J. D. Thomas reports that the space would not rule out either ὑπάρχοντα or πατρῷια but the first letter does not look like υ or π. The sense is clear, and the existence of this lawsuit is confirmed by Ar. *Nub.* 844-6, X. *M.* i. ii. 49, A. iii. *Ctes.* 251, cf. Plat. *Legg.* xi. 928 E 2-3, 929 D 7-E 1; for another law on insanity see 35. ii with commentary. This suit was probably a γραφή (Lipsius, *A.R.*, 340, Harrison, *L.A.*, i. 80-1; contr. Beauchet, *op. cit.*, ii. 382-92).

εἰς δατητῶν αἵρεσιν, ἐάν τις μὴ θέλῃ κοινὰ [τὰ ὄντα νέμεσθαι]: Corrected (the papyrus has διαιτητ(ῶν), and the same corruption occurs in Poll. viii. 89 and elsewhere in the lexica) and restored by Kenyon[1] from *L.R.C.* εἰς δατητῶν ⟨αἵρεσιν⟩. Wilcken read θελητ.κοινα; Kenyon in his Berlin ed. stood by his reading of θελητι; but Blass[4] and Thalheim printed τ[ὰ] κοινὰ [ὄντα (cf. Harp. δατεῖσθαι, Suid. [Δ 88] δατεῖσθαι καὶ δατηταί), and M. H. Chambers, *TAPA* xcvi 1965, 37-8, reads θέληι [τὰ] κοινὰ [ὄντα νέμε]σ⟨θαι⟩; Dr Thomas thinks there was probably no τὰ before κοινὰ but otherwise confirms Chambers' reading. Neither κοινὰ τὰ ὄντα nor τὰ κοινὰ ὄντα is an easy expression, and Dr D. M. Lewis suggests to me that the correct text might be τὰ κοινωνικά.

A δατητής is a distributor (cited by LSJ only from Aesch. *S.c.T.* 944-5 and Athenian legal contexts): according to Harp. and Suid., if some members of a partnership wanted the partnership to be dissolved and others did not, those who did could sue for the appointment of liquidators. It has been suggested that the oldest use of δατηταί was in disputes over the division of an inheritance, and that only such family disputes were the responsibility of the archon (M. H. E. Meier *ap.* Meier & G. F. Schömann rev. J. H. Lipsius, *Das attische Prozess*, 483, cf. E. Caillemer, *D.A.*, ii. i. 27-8). See Beauchet, *op. cit.*, iii. 642-7, D. P. Pappulias, *ZSS* xxvi 1905, 550-2 (both rejecting Meier), Lipsius, *A.R.*, 576-7 (suit for family disputes only), Harrison, *L.A.*, i. 243 (originally for family disputes but later extended: this may well be right).

This and the suits which follow will have been δίκαι, in which only interested parties might sue.

εἰς ἐπι[τρ]οπῆς κατάστασιν, εἰς ἐπιτροπῆς διαδικασίαν: See Beauchet, *op. cit.*, ii. 182–3, W. Wyse, ed. of Isaeus, 190–2, Lipsius, *A.R.*, 524–7, Harrison, *L.A.*, i. 99–104. The first will be a suit for the appointment of a guardian to an orphaned minor (probably necessary to confirm the guardian's status even when a guardian was nominated in the dead man's will); the second will be a dispute between potential guardians, competing either to obtain what they regarded as an advantage or to evade what they regarded as a disadvantage. For διαδικασίαι cf. 57. ii, 61. i, 67. ii, with commentary.

εἰς [ἐμφανῶν κατάστασ]ιν: Restored by Kaibel & Wilamowitz[1] (cf. Kaibel, *Stil und Text*, 234–5) from Harp. *s.vv.*, which cites Isae. vi. *Her. Phil.* 31 and *A.P.* This is a suit to secure the production of an object, to enable the claimant to lay hands on it (cf. *L.S.* 246. 4, also Plat. *Legg.* xi. 914 c 3–e 1: see Wyse, *op. cit.*, 517–18, Lipsius, *A.R.*, 585–8, E. Rabel, *ZSS* xxxvi 1915, 381–5, M. Kaser, *ZSS* lxiv 1944, 151–8, Harrison, *L.A.*, i. 207–10). L. Gernet, I think wrongly, attached more importance to the fine which resulted from condemnation (Budé ed. of D.'s *Plaidoyers civils*, iii. 84–5, on [D.] liii. *Nic.* 14–15); L. Margetić, *Z. Ant.* xv 1965–6, 371–9, argues that by the fourth century the aim was to establish possession of the disputed object, not necessarily to secure the physical production of it. Lipsius, Sandys, and Moore, 295, regard this as another family suit; but Harrison, *L.A.*, i. 209 n. 1, thought that it came to the archon as protector of the rights of property (cf. Beauchet, *op. cit.*, iii. 409–17).

ἐπίτρ[οπ]ον αὐτὸν ἐγγράψαι: Thought by Kenyon[1] to form one phrase with the preceding words, the whole being explanatory of εἰς ἐπιτροπῆς διαδικασίαν (cf. above), and still thought to form one item with εἰς ἐμφανῶν κατάστασιν by Kaibel, *loc. cit.* (suggesting that other cases εἰς ἐμφανῶν κατάστασιν would fall to the thesmothetae), and Sandys[2]; obelised by Kaibel & Wilamowitz[1], Kenyon[3] and Sandys[1] (believing it to be a gloss on εἰς ἐπιτροπῆς διαδικασίαν); treated as a separate lawsuit by Beauchet, *op. cit.*, ii. 183–4, Kenyon's Oxford Translation, Mathieu & Haussoullier, Fritz & Kapp, Moore. Harrison, *L.A.*, i. 103, with index, 339. ii, suggests that this may have been a γραφή by which a man interested in a guardianship could intervene without making a claim.

κλήρων καὶ ἐπικλήρων ἐπι[δικασίαι: Restored by Kenyon[1] from Poll. viii. 89 (where the preceding item is another nominative, ἐπιτρόπων καταστάσεις); cf. [D.] xlvi. *Steph.* ii. 22. Any claimants to an estate except direct descendants of or men adopted by the deceased had to register their claim with the archon; so that they should not succeed to the estate through the ignorance of any one with a stronger claim, their claim had to be read out at a κυρία ἐκκλησία (43. iv with commentary), and any one who disputed the claim could then enter an ἐπιδικασία. See Lipsius, A.R., 579-85, Harrison, L.A., i. 10-11, 158-62.

56. vii. ἐπιμελεῖτ]αι δὲ καὶ . . . τελευτ[ήσαντος τοῦ ἀνδρ]ὸς σκή[πτω]νται κύειν: '. . . who on the death of their husband claim that they are pregnant.' Cf. law *ap*. [D.] XLIII. *Mac.* 75 (quoted below); also Lys. XXVI. *Evand.* 12, D. XXXVII. *Pant.* 46, [D.] XXXV. *Lacr.* 48, XLVI. *Steph. ii.* 22, A. I. *Tim.* 158. It is easy to understand that in archaic Athens the archon's obligation to care for those who had been bereft of their κύριος may have involved substantial executive duties; what duties he retained in the classical period beyond acting as εἰσάγουσα ἀρχή for lawsuits concerning them is not clear. According to the law as quoted in [D.] XLIII he was bound to protect them from ὕβρις; it is plausibly suggested that when no one was named as guardian by the deceased or claimed the right to act as guardian the archon had to nominate one (Harrison, L.A., i. 101-4); and cf. below, on the last clause in this chapter. X. *Vect.* ii. 7 mentions ὀρφανοφύλακες (to suggest that a similar body of μετοικοφύλακες should be appointed), perhaps guardians of those orphaned in war (J. H. Thiel, ed. of X. *Vect.*, 46-7, cf. LSJ *s.v.*, R. S. Stroud, *Hesp.* xl 1971, 289-90): cf. the references to ὀρφανισταί and χηρωσταί (who must be guardians of widows, though in Homer the word denotes distant relatives) collected by Lipsius, A.R., 344-5 n. 20. A widow who had sons could probably choose between staying in her husband's household and returning to her father's; if she had no children, and probably if she had only daughters, she would normally return to her father's household; she could remarry immediately (Harrison, L.A., i. 38-9).

In [D.] XLIII. *Mac.* 75 we have what purports to be (and may be accepted as) a *verbatim* quotation of the law whose substance *A.P.* gives here:

ὁ ἄρχων ἐπιμελείσθω τῶν ὀρφανῶν καὶ τῶν ἐπικλήρων καὶ τῶν οἴκων τῶν ἐξερημουμένων καὶ τῶν γυναικῶν ὅσαι μένουσιν ἐν τοῖς οἴκοις τῶν ἀνδρῶν τῶν τεθνηκότων φάσκουσαι κυεῖν. τούτων ἐπιμελείσθω καὶ μὴ ἐάτω ὑβρίζειν μηδένα περὶ τούτους. ἐὰν δέ τις ὑβρίζῃ ἢ ποιῇ τι παράνομον, κύριος ἔστω ἐπιβάλλειν κατὰ τὸ τέλος. ἐὰν δὲ μείζονος ζημίας δοκῇ ἄξιος εἶναι, προσκαλεσάμενος πρόπεμπτα καὶ τίμημα ἐπιγραψάμενος, ὅ τι ἂν δοκῇ αὐτῷ, εἰσαγέτω εἰς τὴν ἡλιαίαν. ἐὰν δ' ἁλῷ, τιμάτω ἡ ἡλιαία περὶ τοῦ ἁλόντος, ὅ τι χρὴ αὐτὸν παθεῖν ἢ ἀποτεῖσαι.

As remarked by Wilamowitz, *A.u.A.*, i. 258-9, we have here a test case for studying the relationship between the second part of *A.P.* and the laws of Athens. *A.P.* describes what happens where the law prescribes what should happen; he paraphrases (ὅσαι ἂν τελευτήσαντος τοῦ ἀνδρὸς σκήπτωνται κύειν for ὅσαι μένουσιν ἐν τοῖς οἴκοις τῶν ἀνδρῶν τῶν τεθνηκότων φάσκουσαι κυεῖν), sometimes substituting the normal fourth-century terminology for the terminology of the law (σκήπτεσθαι for φάσκειν, δικαστήριον for ἡλιαία); he abbreviates (the vague τοῖς ἀδικοῦσιν represents ἐὰν δέ τις ὑβρίζῃ ἢ ποιῇ τι παράνομον; and it is less clear in *A.P.* than in the law how the archon may proceed against offenders: cf. below). However, *A.P.*'s text is clearly derived from the law, and unlike Wilamowitz I see no reason to postulate an intermediary and to suppose that this account of the law was made by him rather than by *A.P.* Cf. 57. iii with commentary, and Introduction, pp. 33-5.

τοῖς ἀδικοῦσιν ἐπιβάλ[λειν ἢ εἰσάγειν εἰς] τὸ δικα[στή]ριον: The law (quoted above) is more specific, in stating that the archon is to proceed against those who commit ὕβρις or τι παράνομον, and in setting out the procedure. It was regular practice in Athens that magistrates should be entitled to impose limited ἐπιβολαί on men who committed offences within their jurisdiction, or to take them to court if they thought a heavier penalty was called for than they themselves could impose (cf. A. III. *Ctes.* 27: to the instances assembled by Harrison, *L.A.*, ii. 4 n. 1, add now *Hesp.* xlix 1980, 258–88); probably the man on whom the ἐπιβολή was imposed had no right of appeal as such, but in practice could gain a hearing in court by refusing to pay his fine (cf. the procedure with 'ticket' fines imposed by Traffic Wardens in the United Kingdom). The standard restoration of *A.P.*'s text is due to Lipsius, *Ber. Leipzig* xliii 1891, 50 n. 4: Kahrstedt, *U.M.A.*, 216, believing that in the fourth century ἐπιβολή denotes not a penalty within a magistrate's competence but one beyond his competence, imposed by a court on his recommendation, preferred καὶ εἰσάγειν (cf. Harrison, *L.A.*, ii. 5 n. 1); but the law distinguishes between ἐπιβάλλειν κατὰ τὸ τέλος, which surely means 'impose a penalty within his competence' (as in L. Gernet's Budé translation; but the usage is unparalleled, and Kahrstedt adopted R. Dareste's 'impose a penalty according to the Solonian class of the offender'), and ἐὰν δὲ μείζονος ζημίας δοκῇ ἄξιος εἶναι . . . εἰσαγέτω εἰς τὴν ἡλιαίαν. With the normal restoration of the law's distinction is preserved, though made less clear; with Kahrstedt's restoration this distinction would be obliterated: the normal restoration should stand. ἐπιβάλλειν in this sense is regularly transitive, but here the verb has no object expressed either in the law or in *A.P.*; it appears without object again in 61. ii *fin.*, but there ἐπιβολὴν ἐπιβάλλειν has been used immediately before. We do not know what special arrangements, if any, the Athenians made when a magistrate needed *ex officio* to prosecute for a penalty beyond his own competence in the court over which he presided (cf. D. M.

MacDowell, *The Law in Classical Athens*, 277). On ἐπιβολαί in general cf. Lipsius, *A.R.*, 53-4, Hignett, *H.A.C.*, 221-3, Harrison, *L.A.*, ii. 4-7; *A.P.* 45. i–iii, 46. ii, with commentary, on the jurisdiction of the boule; also 52. iii, 53. ii, on the jurisdiction of the apodectae and the Forty in δίκαι where the sum at issue was up to 10 drachmae.

μισθοῖ ... τῶν ἐπικλ[ήρων, ἕως ἄν τις τετταρ]ακαιδε[κέ]τις γένηται: The papyrus has]τεις with η written above; the standard reconstruction is due to Blass[1] (cf. Kaibel, *Stil und Text*, 235-6). A guardian might be directed by the testator, or in the absence of directions might choose, to put up the estate for auction to a lessee who would pay interest for the maintenance of the ward and surrender the property when the ward came of age: the auction took place in a court presided over by the archon (Isae. VI. *Her. Phil.* 36-7). See Beauchet, *L'Histoire du droit privé*, ii. 238-57, Lipsius, *A.R.*, 346-9, O. Schulthess, *RE*, XV (1931/2), 2111-14, J. V. A. Fine, *Hesp.* Supp. ix 1951, 96-115, M. I. Finley, *Studies in Land and Credit in Ancient Athens*, 38-44, Harrison, *L.A.*, i. 105-7.

τετταρακαιδεκέτις, if that is what *A.P.* wrote, is feminine and must refer specifically to ἐπίκληροι: presumably an orphaned girl with no legitimate brothers was to be treated as an orphan until she reached the age of fourteen, and as an ἐπίκληρος, who had to be found a husband, thereafter (cf. Lipsius, *A.R.*, 481; W. K. Lacey, *The Family in Classical Greece*, 297 n. 63). In *I. Cret.* iv 72 (=Gortyn Code), xii. 17-19, we find ὀπυίεθαι δέ (*sc.* τὰν πατροιôκον) δυοδεκαϝέτια ἢ πρείγονα (cf. R. F. Willetts, *Aristocratic Society in Ancient Crete*, 19, 78, *The Law Code of Gortyn*, 27, 79); in Plat. *Legg.* VIII. 833 D 2-4 thirteen is regarded as the minimum age for a girl to marry. Male orphans entered on their inheritance at eighteen (cf. 42. v with commentary).

καὶ τὰ ἀποτιμήματα λαμβάν[ει: The lessee of an orphan's estate had to provide land as security (which was marked as such by ὅροι, but remained in the lessee's possession), and the archon sent ἀποτιμηταί to value the security and ensure that it was sufficient: cf. Isae. VI. *Her. Phil.* 36, Harp. ἀποτιμηταί, and Fine, *loc. cit.*, Finley, *loc. cit.*, Harrison, *L.A.*, ii. 293-6.

καὶ τοὺς ἐπιτρόπους,] ἐὰν μὴ [δι]δῶσι ... εἰσπράττει: Restored by Kaibel & Wilamowitz[1] (cf. Harp., Suid. [Σ 502], σῖτος). Wards during their minority were not legally in a position to complain of injustice on the part of their guardians, so this may be a matter in which the archon had the right of initiative and was expected to see for himself that wards were not deprived of their due (cf. pp. 633-4): no doubt he would only exercise this initiative in particularly flagrant cases of injustice.

σῖτος is used of a fodder grant to the cavalry in 49. i; it is used as here of the maintenance due to orphans and ἐπίκληροι in D. XXVII. *Aphob. i.* 15, XXVIII. *Aphob. ii.* 11; in 62. ii the list of stipends for civilian officials begins μισθοφοροῦσι, but the later payments in the list are labelled εἰς σίτησιν (cf. *ad loc.*, and W. K. Pritchett, *U. Calif. Pub. Cl. Stud.* vii 1971 = *The Greek State at War*, i, 3–52, esp. 3–6, on 'wages' and 'maintenance' in military pay). The use of the article here suggests a recognised level of maintenance.

57. i. καὶ ὁ [μὲν ἄρχων ἐπιμελεῖτ]αι τούτ[ων: *A.P.* rounds off his chapter on the archon . . .

ὁ] δὲ βασιλεὺς πρῶτον μὲν μυστηρίων ἐπιμελεῖτ[αι: . . . and passes to the basileus, beginning in §i with his religious duties. For the evolution of an annual magistrate with this title, retaining the religious functions of the kings of early Athens, see 3. i–iii with commentary. For his responsibility for the Eleusinian Mysteries cf. Lys. vi. *And.* 4, *And.* i. *Myst.* 111; for modern treatments of the Mysteries see L. Deubner, *Attische Feste*, 69–91, G. E. Mylonas, *Eleusis and the Eleusinian Mysteries*, esp. 224–85, H. W. Parke, *Festivals of the Athenians*, 55–72.

μετὰ τῶν ἐπιμελητῶν ὧ]ν ὁ δῆμ[ος χ]ειροτονεῖ . . . **ἕνα δ' [ἐξ Εὐμολπιδῶν, ἕνα] δ' ἐκ Κηρ[ύκω]ν:** Cf. Harp., Suid. (*E* 2468), *E.M.* (362. 9), ἐπιμελητὴς τῶν μυστηρίων. Wilcken and Kenyon in his Berlin ed. both accept the ὧ]ν of Blass[2], but Kenyon labels the ν *non certum est*; Dr J. D. Thomas reports that the traces are compatible with ν. Kenyon[1] omitted ἐξ and ἐκ; M. C. Gertz, *NTF*[2] x 1890–2, 254, argued that the prepositions are needed; in his Berlin ed. Kenyon gives the papyrus' reading as δ(ὲ) Κηρ[ύκω]ν and doubts the claim of Kaibel, *Stil und Text*, 236, and Wilcken that κ has been inserted above.

Epimeletae of the Mysteries are not attested in the fifth century (for *IG* i[2] 185, 6, see the reconstructions of *SEG* x 60, 36, *IG* i[3] 58, 35). They are instituted, and are empowered to impose ἐπιβολαί on or to prosecute ἀκοσμόντας, in a law to be dated shortly before the middle of the fourth century (published by K. Clinton, *Hesp.* xlix 1980, 258–88, lines 29–37[50]), and they are mentioned in D. xxi. *Mid.* 171, *IG* ii[2] 1672, 243–6 (329/8). In the Hellenistic inscriptions which praise them there are only two epimeletae (*IG* ii[2] 661, 683, 807, 847); it was once thought that the two men named in *IG* ii[2] 1672, 244, are the epimeletae, and Dittenberger concluded that there must have been four earlier and that in this respect *A.P.* is out of date (note on *SIG*[3] 384 = *IG* ii[2] 661; for the correct interpretation of *IG* ii[2] 1672 see Kirchner *ad loc.*). The law published by Clinton agrees with *A.P.* (lines 30–1: προσαιρεῖσθαι δὲ [τ]ὸν δ[ῆμον ἐπιμελητὰς δύο περὶ τὴν] ἑορτὴν ἐξ Ἀθηναίων ἁπάντων ἐκ τῶν ὑ[πὲρ τριάκοντα] ἔτη γεγονότων καὶ Κηρύκων ἕνα καὶ [Εὐ]μολπιδ[ῶν ἕνα]),

---

[50] In line 29 I prefer ἱεροποιοὺ]ς to Clinton's ἐπιμελητὰ]ς.

and there is no good reason to suppose that a change had been made by the time of *A.P.* I doubt the suggestion of P. Foucart (*RPh*² xix 1895, 30–1, also using the mistaken interpretation of *IG* ii² 1672) that there was a division of labour within the college. Either there was a change to two epimeletae, but after the time of *A.P.*, as Dittenberger once thought (*Hermes* xx 1885, 30, cf. Clinton, *op. cit.*, 282), or in the Hellenistic period the two from the Εὐμολπίδαι and the Κήρυκες perhaps ceased to be elected by the δῆμος, and the δῆμος praised only the two whom it still did elect (Dittenberger's note on *SIG*¹ 386, Busolt & Swoboda, *G.S.*, ii. 1170 n. 4 *fin.*, contr. 1066 n. 1, which agrees with Foucart).

The principal offices of the Eleusinian cult were hereditary in the two γένη Εὐμολπίδαι and Κήρυκες (cf. 39. ii): the Εὐμολπίδαι claimed descent from Eumolpus, the Thracian leader who fought for the Eleusinians against Athens in the time of Erechtheus (cf. p. 100); the Κήρυκες from Ceryx, son of Hermes by one of the daughters of Cecrops (*IG* xiv 1389, 30–3; Paus. I. 38. iii; Poll. VIII. 103); the latter did not claim an Eleusinian origin, and their recognition as a clan with an interest in the cult is a sign of the cult's ceasing to concern the Eleusinians alone (cf. W. S. Ferguson, *Hesp.* vii 1938, 42; but Paus., *loc. cit.*, preferred a pedigree which made Ceryx a son of Eumolpus). The ἱεροφάντης, high priest of the cult, and the ἐξηγηταὶ Εὐμολπιδῶν, φαιδυντής and other priests were Εὐμολπίδαι; the δᾳδοῦχος, the ἱεροκῆρυξ and others were Κήρυκες (cf. Mylonas, *op. cit.*, 229–37, Clinton, *The Sacred Officials of the Eleusinian Mysteries*, *passim*). If the epimeletae were concerned with the ritual of the cult as well as with the more secular aspects of its administration, it will not be surprising that these two clans should have claimed two places in the college, alongside the two open to all citizens.†

ἔπειτα Διονυσίων τῶν ἐπὶ Ληναίῳ: For the papyrus' επιληναιων most have accepted ἐπὶ Ληναίῳ (suggested by J. E. B. Mayor and others, *CR* v 1891, 118, Blass, *LZB* 1891, 304: cf. *IG* ii² 1496, 74, 105; ἐπὶ Ληναίῳ is found also in Ar. *Ach.* 504, Plat. *Prot.* 327 D 4, and in D. XXI. *Mid.* 10, quoted below); P. Foucart, *RPh*² xix 1895, 31, and Kaibel & Wilamowitz³ preferred ἐπιληναίων (cf. ἐπιστάταις ἐπιλήναια εἰς Διονύσια, *IG* ii² 1672, 182; schol. Ar. *Ach.* 202), but the usual emendation is probably right. On the Dionysia at the Λήναιον, i.e. the Lenaea, held in mid Gamelion (vii), see Deubner, *Attische Feste*, 123–34, Pickard-Cambridge rev. Gould & Lewis, *The Dramatic Festivals of Athens*, 25–42, Parke, *Festivals of the Athenians*, 104–6. For attempts to locate the Λήναιον see Pickard-Cambridge, *op. cit.*, 37–40, R. E. Wycherley, *Hesp.* xxxiv 1965, 72–6; the word is probably derived from λῆναι, a term used of the maenads who worshipped Dionysus.

ταῦτα δέ ἐστι [πομπή τε καὶ ἀγών. τ]ὴν μὲν οὖν ... διατίθησιν ὁ

57. i] COMMENTARY ON THE *ATH. POL.*

βασιλεύς: A law *ap*. D. XXI. *Mid*. 10 refers to ἡ ἐπὶ Ληναίῳ πομπὴ καὶ οἱ τραγῳδοὶ καὶ οἱ κωμῳδοί. Kaibel & Wilamowitz[1] suggested [πομπὴ καὶ μουσικῆς ἀγών. τὴν], and Leeuwen (*Mnem*.[2] xix 1891, 182, cf. Herwerden & Leeuwen) [πομπὴ καὶ ἀγών. τὴν]; the restoration which has become standard, which fits the length of the lacuna better, is due to *Π. Ν. Παπαγεώργιος, Ἀθ*. iv 1892, 602, Kaibel, *Stil und Text*, 236. All these restorations yield an awkwardly abrupt sentence, but *A.P.* was capable of such abruptness and I have no improvement to offer.

At the Lenaea there were contests for comedy (five comedians each presented one play) and tragedy (in the fifth century two tragedians each presented two plays); comic and tragic victors are listed in a dedication of a basileus of the early fourth century (*Hesp.* xl 4); a third-century inscription attests a dithyrambic victory at the Lenaea (*IG* ii[2] 3779, 7–8), but no dithyrambic contest is mentioned in the law *ap*. D. XXI. That the epimeletae of the Mysteries should be involved in the Lenaea is surprising, and is presumably a comparatively late development; but *IG* ii[2] 1496, 74–5 (334/3), and 1672, 182, confirm their involvement, and we read in schol. Ar. *Ran*. 479 that at the Lenaea the δᾳδοῦχος led an invocation of Iacchus (cf. Pickard-Cambridge, *op. cit.*, 34–5).

τίθησι δὲ καὶ τοὺς τῶν λαμπάδων ἀγῶνας ἅπαντας: H. Richards, *CR* v 1891, 182, and some others preferred ⟨δια⟩τίθησι (cf. Kaibel, *Stil und Text*, 236), but cf. 54. ii with commentary (καταγιγνώσκουσι... τὸ γνωσθέν). On torch-races see J. Jüthner, *RE*, xii (1925), 569–77. Some texts claim that there were three torch-races in Athens, at the Panathenaea, the Hephaestea and the Promethea (Harp. λαμπάς; Suid. [Λ 88] λαμπάδος, citing Polemon; schol. Ar. *Ran*. 131, 1087); we also find another group of three, at the Hephaestea and the Promethea and to Pan (e.g. *L.S.* 228. 11, *Lex. Patm. ad* D. LVII. *Eub*. 43 [*BCH* i 1877, 11 = K. Latte & H. Erbse, *Lexica Graeca Minora*, 141]). In fact torch-races are attested at several festivals: the Aiantea (*IG* ii[2] 1011, 53–4: 106/5), the Anthesteria (*IG* ii[2] 3013 with Deubner, *Attische Feste*, 116, 239, 243: A.D. 165/6), the Apaturia (Istr. 334 F 2a *ap*. Harp. λαμπάς: not a race?), the Epitaphia (*IG* ii[2] 1011, 9–10: 106/5), the Hephaestea (H. VIII. 98. ii [κατά περ Ἕλλησι], *IG* i[2] 84, 32–3, ii[2] 3006), the Panathenaea (possibly the πεντετηρίς in *IG* i[2] 84, 32–3; ii[2] 2311, 77, 3019, 3023, Ar. *Ran.* 1087–98, schol. Plat. *Phaedr*. 231 E [265 Hermann: not in Greene]; cf. p. 671), the Promethea (Paus. I. 30. ii: perhaps the oldest of the torch-races, as suggested by Deubner, *op. cit.*, 211), the Thesea (*IG* ii[2] 956, 6–7: 161/0), to Pan (H. VI. 105. iii), and, on horseback, at the Bendidea (Plat. *Rep*. I. 328 A 1–5: on the date, J. Pečírka, *The Formula for the Grant of Enktesis*, 122–30).

Teams competing in the torch-races were entrusted to γυμνασίαρχοι, men performing a liturgy analogous to the χορηγία (e.g. And. 1. *Myst.* 132 [Hephaestea], Lys. xxi. *Pec. Acc.* 3 [Promethea], D. xx. *Lept.* 21), appointed by their tribes like the dithyrambic choregi (D. xxxix. *Boe. Nom.* 7; cf. 56. iii with commentary). The basileus was the εἰσάγουσα ἀρχή for ἀντιδόσεις and σκήψεις ([D.] xxxv. *Lacr.* 48; cf. 56. iii on choregi).

ὡς δ' ἔπος εἰπεῖν καὶ τὰς πατρίους θυσίας διοικεῖ οὗτος πάσας: Some have deleted καί (e.g. Kaibel & Wilamowitz[1-2]) or considered rearranging the words (cf. Kaibel, *Stil und Text*, 236–7), but the text may stand. For what is said cf. Plat. *Polit.* 290 E 6–8; *A.P.* 3. iii mentioned to confirm the modernity of the office of archon τὸ μηδὲν τῶν πατρίων τὸν ἄρχοντα διοικεῖν, ὥσπερ ὁ βασιλεὺς καὶ ὁ πολέμαρχος, ἀλλ' ἁπλῶς τὰ ἐπίθετα: see *ad loc.*, and on the festivals of the archon 56. iii–v with commentary, of the polemarch 58. i with commentary. The festivals assigned to the polemarch, like those assigned to the archon (except perhaps the Thargelia), appear not to be ancient, so of *A.P.*'s two pronouncements on the subject the one here is the more accurate. We know that the basileus presided over the drinking competition at the Χόες, the middle day of the Anthesteria (Ar. *Ach.* 1224–5 with schol. 1224); he designated the two ἀρρηφόροι who directed the weaving of the πέπλος (Suid. [*E* 2504] ἐπιώψατο: cf. p. 569); a sacrifice by the παράσιτοι of Acharnae was prescribed ἐν τοῖς τοῦ βασιλέως ... νόμοις (Ath. VI. 234 F); for the ἱερὸς γάμος of the basileus' wife with Dionysus see 3. v with commentary.

57. ii. γραφαὶ δὲ λαγχάνονται πρὸς αὐτὸν ἀσεβείας: Cf. Hyp. IV. *Eux.* 6 (ἀσεβεῖ τις περὶ τὰ ἱερά· γραφαὶ ἀσεβείας πρὸς τὸν βασιλέα), [D.] xxxv. *Lacr.* 48; D. xxii. *Andr.* 27 mentions a variety of procedures available in cases of ἀσέβεια (τῆς ἀσεβείας κατὰ ταῦτ' ἔστ' ἀπάγειν, γράφεσθαι, δικάζεσθαι πρὸς Εὐμολπίδας, φαίνειν πρὸς τὸν βασιλέα). The men accused of ἀσέβεια in 415 were prosecuted by εἰσαγγελία (And. I. *Myst.* 14, 27, Pl. *Alc.* 19. iii, 22. iv); Andocides in 400/399 was prosecuted by ἔνδειξις, apparently to the basileus, for non-compliance with the ἀτιμία which he had incurred for ἀσέβεια (And. I. *Myst.* 10, 111); Socrates later that year was prosecuted in a γραφὴ ἀσεβείας (Plat. *Euthyphr.*, init., cf. *Theaet.* 210 D 1–3). See Lipsius, *A.R.*, 358–68.

κἄν τις ἱερωσύνης ἀμφισβητῇ πρός τινα: The reference is presumably to rival claims to perform a hereditary priesthood.

διαδικάζει δὲ καὶ ... τὰς ὑπὲρ τῶν ἱερῶν ἀπάσας οὗτος: Kenyon[1] restored [τῶν γε]ρῶν from *L.S.* 219. 14; ἱερῶν was suggested by H. Richards, *CR* v 1891, 229, and read by Blass[1], and is found in Phot., Suid. (*H* 39), ἡγεμονία δικαστηρίου (where γερῶν has been conjectured) and *L.S.* 309. 33 (at 310. 8–9). γερῶν has had its champions (e.g. Kaibel, *Stil und Text*, 237, Mathieu & Haussoullier, Fritz & Kapp);

but there is another corruption in the quotation of *A.P.* in *L.S.* 219. 14 (προστιμᾷ for πρός τινα), and ἱερῶν is certainly to be preferred. The basileus 'had jurisdiction . . . where families [or, better, γένη in the technical sense of the word] or priests were at odds about cult matters' (Harrison, *L.A.*, ii. 8–9).

This is the only instance in *A.P.* of the compound διαδικάζειν: like the noun διαδικασία it is used of suits in which rival claimants seek to obtain a right or avoid a duty (cf. 56. vi with commentary; the middle of the verb is used in [Arist.] *Oec.* II. 1347 B 28). The active of the simple verb δικάζειν is used normally of a magistrate with a right to give a personal decision (e.g. 53. i–ii) or of jurors with a right of decision (e.g. 63. iii), but in 52. iii and in 57. iv (of the basileus) it is used of an εἰσάγουσα ἀρχή (cf. *ad locc.*); this sentence therefore does not necessarily imply that in διαδικασίαι ὑπὲρ τῶν ἱερῶν the basileus was empowered to give a personal ruling rather than to preside over a court.

λαγχάνονται δὲ καὶ αἱ τοῦ φόνου δίκαι πᾶσαι πρὸς τοῦτον: There were various forms of trial for homicide, according to the precise nature of the charge and the defence, as set out by *A.P.* in the remainder of this chapter; but in all cases the accusation had to be lodged with the basileus, who would make a proclamation against the accused (cf. below), and hold three προδικασίαι, in separate months, before bringing the case to its final trial in the fourth month (Ant. VI. *Chor.* 42, cf. Phot., Suid. [Π 2364], προδικασία). (See Lipsius, *A.R.*, 840, 845 with n. 2, D. M. MacDowell, *Athenian Homicide Law*, 34–7.) These trials for homicide are all δίκαι, private suits where only an interested party may prosecute; for λαγχάνειν cf. 53. i with commentary.

Athens' various homicide courts are reviewed by D. XXIII. *Arist.* 65–79, adding in 80–1 the procedure of ἀπαγωγή, and Paus. I. 28. v, viii–xi. Plat. *Legg.* IX. 865 A 1–874 D 1 begins with unintentional killing, treating as a subdivision of that some cases which Athenian law regarded as lawful killing (865 A 2–866 D 4); then follow three categories of deliberate killing, passionate and spontaneous, passionate but premeditated, and downright evil (866 D 5–873 D 1); he ends with suicide (873 C 2–D 8), killing by an animal or inanimate object (873 E 1–874 A 3), killing by a person unknown (874 A 4–B 5) and lawful killing (874 B 6–D 1). Arist. *Pol.* IV. 1300 B 24–30 distinguishes four different kinds of homicide courts, on Athenian lines: (*a*) περί τε τῶν ἐκ προνοίας, (*b*) καὶ περὶ τῶν ἀκουσίων, (*c*) καὶ ὅσα ὁμολογεῖται μέν, ἀμφισβεῖται δὲ περὶ τοῦ δικαίου, (*d*) τέταρτον δὲ ὅσα τοῖς φεύγουσι φόνου ἐπὶ καθόδῳ ἐπιφέρεται, οἷον Ἀθήνησι λέγεται καὶ τὸ ἐν Φρεαττοῖ δικαστήριον· συμβαίνει δὲ τὰ τοιαῦτα ἐν τῷ παντὶ χρόνῳ ὀλίγα καὶ ἐν ταῖς μεγάλαις πόλεσιν.†

καὶ ὁ προαγορεύων εἴργεσθαι τῶν νομίμων οὗτός ἐστιν: Cf. §iv, Poll.

viii. 90, L.S. 309. 33 (at 310. 6–7). Elsewhere we read of a similar proclamation made in the Agora by the relatives of the deceased—Ant. vi. Chor. 35 (πείσαντες δὲ τούτους ἀπογράφεσθαι καὶ προαγορεύειν ἐμοὶ εἴργεσθαι τῶν νομίμων), [D.] xlvii. Ev. & Mnes. 69 fin., cf. M & L 86, 20–1, law ap. [D.] xliii. Mac. 57—but it appears that the ban had legal force only when the charge had been lodged with the basileus and he had made his proclamation (Ant. vi. Chor. 36–8). εἴργεσθαι τῶν νομίμων means 'to be excluded from the things specified in the laws' (cf. J. H. Kells, CR^2 xv 1965, 206, MacDowell, The Law in Classical Athens, 111), not 'from sacred ceremonies' (Kenyon, Oxford Translation) or 'from legal things' (MacDowell, Athenian Homicide Law, 23, 25) or 'from customary ceremonies' (Moore); the same expression is used in Plat. Legg. ix. 871 A 3, 873 B 1–2. The effect of the ban is given in detail by D. xx. Lept. 158 (χέρνιβος εἴργεσθαι τὸν ἀνδροφόνον, σπονδῶν, κρατήρων, ἱερῶν, ἀγορᾶς, πάντα τἆλλα διελθὼν οἷς μάλιστ' ἄν τινας ᾤετ' ἐπισχεῖν τοῦ τοιοῦτόν τι ποιεῖν), cf. Plat. Legg. ix. 871 A 3–5 (μήτε ἱερὰ μήτε ἀγορὰν μήτε λιμένας μήτε ἄλλον κοινὸν σύλλογον μηδένα μιαίνων); §iv and Ant. v. Caed. Her. 10 mention exclusion from the Agora, and it is clear from Ant. vi. Chor. that a man awaiting trial for homicide was unable to take any other legal proceedings; according to Poll. viii. 90 the basileus' proclamation ordered the accused ἀπέχεσθαι μυστηρίων καὶ τῶν ἄλλων νομίμων. The killer was polluted, and would defile other Athenians by associating with them; the accused was presumed guilty of the killing unless and until proved innocent; and therefore the accused was placed under a ban pending his trial. See Lipsius, A.R., 810, MacDowell, Athenian Homicide Law, 3–5, 23–7. MacDowell, op. cit., 141–50, doubts the importance of the notion of pollution, citing D. xx. Lept. 158; but Soph. O.T. 236–43, Ant. ii. Tetr. i. a. 10, Plat. Legg. ix. 871 A 2–B 5, all mention pollution in connection with the ban; cf. Ant. v. Caed. Her. 11 on the reason for holding homicide trials out of doors.

57. iii. εἰσὶ δὲ φόν[ου] δίκαι καὶ τραύματος . . . καὶ πυρκαιᾶς: Cf. the law quoted ἐκ τῶν φονικῶν νόμων τῶν ἐξ Ἀρείου πάγου ap. D. xxiii. Arist. 22, repeated in D.'s text, §24: δικάζειν δὲ τὴν βουλὴν τὴν ἐν Ἀρείου πάγῳ φόνου καὶ τραύματος ἐκ προνοίας καὶ πυρκαιᾶς καὶ φαρμάκων, ἐάν τις ἀποκτείνῃ δούς. Here, as in 56. vii and below on cases tried at the Delphinium and ἐν Φρεάτου, we have what purports to be a direct quotation of the law to compare with A.P.'s account. As usual, A.P. has transposed the law's prescription of what is to happen into a statement of what does happen (εἰσὶ δὲ φόνου δίκαι is not the language of the law). In other respects he has this time improved on the law: it is clearer in his text than in the law that ἐκ προνοίας is to be understood both with φόνου and with τραύματος (and we read below that those accused of unintentional killing were tried at the Palladium); and he rearranges the three charges so that arson comes after the two homicide charges instead of between the two (Poll. VIII. 117 begins ἐδίκαζε δὲ φόνου ... and then repeats the text of the law; *L.S.* 311. 9 follows *A.P.*'s rearrangement). Cf. Introduction, p. 34.

The first charge of homicide covers intentional killing and 'intentional wounding'; the second, poisoning 'if one gives poison and kills'. By the time of Antiphon φόνος included killing by poisoning (1. *Noverc.* 3, 20, etc., VI. *Chor.* 36, 42, etc.); but in Homer φόνος may refer to shed blood as well as to violent killing (*Il.* x. 298, XVI. 162, XXIV. 610), and it is likely that in Athenian law φόνος was originally limited to killing by violence and bloodshed, and poisoning had to be mentioned separately for that reason (cf. J. H. Thiel, *Mnem.*² lvi 1928, 91–2, MacDowell, *op. cit.*, 45). There was a charge of αἰκεία (52. ii with commentary) for 'battery', wounding which did not kill and was not intended to kill, so that it is arguable that only wounding which was intended to kill should be prosecuted under the homicide law (cf. Lys. III. *Sim.* 41–2); but another speech suggests that τραῦμα was not necessarily limited to attempted homicide (D. LIV. *Con.* 17–19): see MacDowell, *The Law in Classical Athens*, 123–4. Whether the deed was done by violence or poison, the Areopagus was the proper court for the trial of the actual killer only, and if he was thought to be the agent of someone else that person would be charged with βούλευσις and tried at the Palladium (cf. below); but the word δούς used with φαρμάκων is probably not intended to emphasise the distinction between the agent and the planner (cf. MacDowell, *Athenian Homicide Law*, 44–5, against Lipsius, *A.R.*, 124). Whether a killer was tried by the Areopagus for intentional homicide or at the Palladium for unintentional homicide seems to have depended on the prosecutor: Arist. *M.M.* 1. 1188 B 29–38 mentions an instance of a woman prosecuted before the Areopagus and acquitted on the grounds that she had killed but not intentionally (contr. Harrison, *L.A.*, i. 168, thinking that the case went to the Palladium if the defendant admitted the act but pleaded lack of intent). Arson was perhaps included in the province of the Areopagus because of the danger to life; Lipsius suggests that arson which did not endanger life would be treated as βλάβη (*A.R.*, 123–4, 984), but MacDowell is sceptical (*The Law in Classical Athens*, 150). On trials before the Areopagus see in general Lipsius, *A.R.*, 121–7, 600–9, MacDowell, *Athenian Homicide Law*, 39–47; for trials in connection with the sacred olives, which were no longer held in the time of *A.P.*, see 60. ii with commentary.

τῶν δ' ἀκουσίων ... οἱ ἐπὶ Παλλαδίῳ: The court at the Palladium is thought to have occupied a site south-east of the Acropolis and west of the temple of Olympian Zeus, where a courtyard with a stoa certainly on the north side and perhaps on all four sides was built *c.* 300 to replace a building of the early fifth century (*A. Ἀνδρειομένου, ΑΔ* xxi 1966, χρον. 81–3; Travlos, *Pictorial Dictionary*, 412–16 with 291 fig. 379, 333 fig. 435, *Hesp.* xliii 1974, 500–11; cf. also *O. Ἀλεξανδρή, ΑΔ* xxvii 1972, χρον. 102–4). Three kinds of charge were tried there, each of them in some way less serious than the charges tried by the Areopagus: unintentional homicide; planning homicide, when some other person did the deed (for another use of the word βούλευσις see 59. iii with commentary); and killing someone other than an Athenian citizen or the wife or child of a citizen. See in general Lipsius, *A.R.*, 125–7, 129–33, 609–14, MacDowell, *Athenian Homicide Law*, 58–69.

That charges of unintentional homicide were tried at the Palladium is confirmed by Ar. fr. 585 Kock, D. xxiii. *Arist.* 71, Paus. i. 28. viii; Plat. *Legg.* ix. 865 B 4–866 D 4 treats unintentional killing as one category, within which he distinguishes the killing of slaves and of ἐλεύθεροι; Arist. *Pol.* iv. 1300 B 26 makes unintentional homicide the second of his four categories. In the inscribed law of Draco, M & L 86, no reference to the Palladium survives, but the text of the law begins καὶ ἐὰμ μὲ 'κ [π]ρονοί[α]ς [κ]τ[ένει τίς τινα . . .], and the trial procedure is said to be [δ]ικάζεν δὲ τὸς βασιλέας . . . τὸς δὲ ἐφέτας διαγν[ὸ]ν[α]ι (lines 11–13: for the βασιλεῖς see p. 649, and for the ἐφέται see §iv with commentary). Whether the killer was prosecuted for intentional or for unintentional homicide depended on the prosecutor (cf. previous note); a man found guilty of unintentional homicide was exiled unless or until pardoned by the deceased's family.†

A man would be charged with βούλευσις if he made a plan, carried out by someone else, which led either intentionally (e.g. Ant. I. *Noverc.* 26) or unintentionally (e.g. Ant. vi. *Chor.* 16 with 19) to a death; according to Harp., Suid. (B 429), βουλεύσεως, *L.S.* 220. 11, a charge was possible also in the event of a plan which failed to secure the victim's death. A law *ap.* And. i. *Myst.* 94 prescribes τὸν βουλεύσαντα ἐν τῷ αὐτῷ ἐνέχεσθαι καὶ τὸν τῇ χειρὶ ἐργασάμενον: Wilamowitz, *A.u.A.*, i. 252 n. 138, supposed *A.P.* to mean that βούλευσις of intentional homicide was tried by the Areopagus and only βούλευσις of unintentional homicide at the Palladium (cf. E. Grace, *Eirene* xi 1973, 23), and Lipsius, *A.R.*, 125–7, believed that Wilamowitz' distinction had been observed earlier but by the time of *A.P.* all charges of βούλευσις were tried at the Palladium. M & L 86, 11–13, deals with both killing and βούλευσις under the general heading of μὲ 'κ προνοίας, and says nothing of βούλευσις of intentional homicide; the only text alleging that βούλευσις of intentional homicide fell in the province of the Areopagus is Harp., Suid. (B 429), βουλεύσεως, saying that Isaeus (fr. 62 Sauppe) assigned this to the Palladium, Dinarchus (fr. xv. 2 Sauppe) to the Areopagus, and *A.P.* agrees with Isaeus—and since *A.P.* is said to agree with an earlier orator against a contemporary this provides only minimal support for Lipsius. More probably all charges of βούλευσις were tried at the Palladium, both earlier and in the time of *A.P.*, and Andocides' law refers not to the court but simply to the penalty (cf. MacDowell, *Athenian Homicide Law*, 64–9).

On the penalties for killing non-Athenians see MacDowell, *Athenian Homicide Law*, 126–7, *The Law in Classical Athens*, 120, and cf. below, p. 655. E. Grace, *Eirene* xi 1973, 5–30, argues that the recognition of killing non-Athenians as a separate charge meriting a separate procedure is a later addition to the Draconian scheme, and that the Draconian scheme was never extended to cover non-Athenian killers.

ἐὰν δ' ἀποκτεῖναι ... τούτ[ῳ] ἐπὶ Δελφινίῳ δικάζουσιν: The court at the Delphinium, and to the east of it the temple of Apollo Δελφίνιος, have been located south of the temple of Olympian Zeus, not far from the Palladium (cf. above); the court is an enclosure bounded on the north by a building of *c.* 500 (*I. Θρεψιάδης* & *I. Τραυλός, ΑΔ* xvii 1961/2, χρον. 9–14, R. E. Wycherley, *GR&BS* iv 1963, 167–8, Travlos, *Pictorial Dictionary*, 83–90 with 291–2 figs 379–80). For trials at the Delphinium cf. D. xxIII. *Arist.* 74, Paus. I. 28. x; Arist. *Pol.* IV. 1300 B 26–7 follows Athenian practice; Plat. *Legg.* IX treats killing in war, in the games and by doctors under the heading of unintentional killing (865 A 2–B 4), but killing in defence of self, family and property as lawful killing (869 C 6–E 4, 874 B 6–D 1). A man who agreed that an act of killing had been lawful ought not to prosecute (Plat. *Euthyphr.* 4 B 8–10); a trial at the Delphinium was appropriate when someone was accused of unlawful killing, whether intentional or unintentional, and in defence admitted the act but claimed that it was lawful (MacDowell, *Athenian Homicide Law*, 70–1, against Bonner & Smith, *Administration of Justice*, ii. 169–71). See in general Lipsius, *A.R.*, 129–33, 614–19, MacDowell, *op. cit.*, 70–81.

Another list of instances in which killing was lawful is to be found in a law *ap.* D. xxIII. *Arist.* 53: ἐάν τις ἀποκτείνῃ ἐν ἄθλοις ἄκων, ἢ ἐν ὁδῷ καθελών, ἢ ἐν πολέμῳ ἀγνοήσας, ἢ ἐπὶ μητρὶ ἢ ἐπ' ἀδελφῇ ἢ ἐπὶ θυγατρί, ἢ ἐπὶ παλλακῇ ἣν ἂν ἐπ' ἐλευθέροις παισὶν ἔχῃ, τούτων ἕνεκα μὴ φεύγειν κτείναντα. *A.P.* has rephrased the first of these four categories, omitted the second, repeated the third *verbatim* and summarised the fourth, and has reversed the order of the law (cf. 56. vii with commentary, other notes on this section, and Introduction, p. 34). In athletic contests it was only the unintentional killing of an opponent which was specifically exculpated (MacDowell, *op.*

cit., 73–4, citing Pl. *Per.* 36. v, Ant. III. *Tetr. ii*). In war what was exculpated was the killing of someone who was mistaken for an enemy. ἐν ὁδῷ καθελών refers to the killing of highwaymen (cf. Harp. ὁδός); it was also lawful to kill on the spot any one φέροντα ἢ ἄγοντα βίᾳ ἀδίκως one's own property (D. XXIII. *Arist.* 60–1, quoting law), or to kill any one stealing anything at night (D. XXIV. *Tim.* 113, quoting law of Timocrates); or, since the female members of an Athenian's family were analogous to his property, to kill a man caught in sexual intercourse with any of them (cf. Lys. I. *Caed. Erat.*, esp. 30–1).[51] It was also lawful to kill in self-defence against any attacker who was the first to strike (Ant. IV. *Tetr. iii. δ.* 3), but M. Gagarin distinguishes between 'simple self-defence' and the more specific kinds of self-defence listed above, and suggests that a killer who pleaded simple self-defence would not be tried at the Delphinium (*GR&BS* xix 1978, 111–20).

We know of other instances of lawful killing not mentioned in *A.P.* or in D. XXIII. *Arist.* 53. Any one could be killed with impunity if he had been exiled for homicide but was found in Athenian territory (D. XXIII. *Arist.* 28–36, quoting law; cf. M&L 86, 30–1, with R. S. Stroud, *U. Calif. Pub. Cl. Stud.* iii 1968, 54–6), or if he was ἄτιμος in the strong sense of 'outlawed', which made him equivalent to a πολέμιος (law *ap.* And. I. *Myst.* 96, *SEG* xii 87, 7–11, cf. 16. x with commentary). A doctor under whose care a patient died was absolved from guilt (Ant. IV. *Tetr. iii. γ.* 5, cf. Plat. *Legg.* IX. 865 B 2–4): presumably a patient who entrusted himself to a doctor, like a man who competed in the games, was deemed to have accepted the risk involved. A law is mentioned in Ant. III. *Tetr. ii. β.* 9, γ. 7, IV. *Tetr. iii. β.* 3, δ. 8, which prescribed μήτε δικαίως μήτε ἀδίκως ἀποκτείνειν: presumably we should distinguish between a broad category, δικαίως, and a narrower category within it, ἐννόμως (cf. MacDowell, *op. cit.*, 80–1), and M. Gagarin argues that the prohibition was not in fact a law but a moral observation on the law (*GR&BS* xix 1978, 291–306).†

57. iii–iv. ἐὰν δὲ φεύγων φυγὴν ὧν αἴδεσίς ... ἐν πλοίῳ: The papyrus has αἴδεσίς with ρ written above: ἄρεσίς was suggested by H. Weil, cf. Blass²⁻⁴, Kaibel, *Stil und Text*, 240; ἄφεσίς by Σ. Ν. *Δραγούμης, Ἀθ.* xviii 1906, 44–50. αἴδεσις appears in a relevant context in D. XXI. *Mid.* 43, cf. αἰδεῖσθαι in D. XXXVII. *Pant.* 59, XXXVIII. *Naus. & Xen.* 22, laws *ap.* D. XXIII. *Arist.* 72, 77, [D.] XLIII. *Mac.* 57 (the verb is restored in M&L 86, 13, 15–16), and the λίθος ἀναιδείας of Paus. I. 28. v; ἄρεσις is cited in LSJ only from a second-century inscription of Priene; ἄφεσις is used in Plat. *Legg.* IX. 869 D 7, E 1,

---

[51] On concubines kept ἐπ' ἐλευθέροις παισίν see p. 331.

and ἀφεῖναι with αἰδεῖσθαι in D. XXXVII. *Pant.* 58–60, XXXVIII. *Naus.* & *Xen.* 21–2; Kenyon in his Berlin ed. denied that the papyrus' corrector had marked the ι as well as the δ for deletion. αἴδεσις should be retained. The papyrus reads ἐν Φρεάτου: Kenyon[1-3] emended to Φρεαττοῖ, but Kaibel & Wilamowitz reverted to the papyrus' form, and Kenyon in his later editions was persuaded. The evidence for the name of the court is reviewed by Kaibel, *Stil und Text*, 240, MacDowell, *op. cit.*, 82–3: the connection with a hero named Φρέατος is at any rate as old as Theophrastus, and we should not emend.

The court is located at the Piraeus by Pausanias, and at Zea (the south-facing bay between Acte and Munichia, still known by that name) by *L.S.* 310. 28 (at 311. 17–19 [ἐν Ζέᾳ], cf. 20–2 [ἐν Φρεαττοῖ]). Its purpose was to try those who had been exiled for an act of killing which admitted of reconciliation (i.e. unintentional homicide: cf. texts cited in previous paragraph) and had not yet been reconciled, who were accused of another act of killing: so that they should not be brought back from exile prematurely they stood their trial in a boat moored off the shore. Cf. D. XXIII. *Arist.* 77–8 (quoting the protasis of the law which *A.P.* has summarised: ἐάν τις ἐπ' ἀκουσίῳ φόνῳ πεφευγώς, μήπω τῶν ἐκβαλλόντων αὐτὸν ᾐδεσμένων, αἰτίαν ἔχῃ ἑτέρου φόνου ἑκουσίου), Arist. *Pol.* IV. 1300 B 27–30 (commenting that such cases are rare), Paus. I. 28. xi (and II. 29. x). A. L. Boegehold, *CSCA* ix 1976, 14–17, argues from the discovery of well-worn ballots at Zea and the improbability that there were many trials of this kind that in the fourth century an ordinary δικαστήριον met at Zea and *L.S.* has confused the court ἐν Φρεάτου with that. See in general Lipsius, *A.R.*, 130–1, MacDowell, *op. cit.*, 82–4.†

ὁ δ' ἀπολογεῖται προσορμισάμενος ἐν πλοίῳ: D. XXIII. *Arist.* 87 (not at this point claiming to quote the law) says εἶθ' ὁ μὲν ἐν πλοίῳ προσπλεύσας λέγει τῆς γῆς οὐχ ἁπτόμενος, οἱ δ' ἀκροῶνται καὶ δικάζουσιν ἐν τῇ γῇ.

57. iv. δικάζουσι δ' οἱ λαχόντες ταῦ[τ' ἐφέται] πλὴν τῶν ἐν Ἀρείῳ πάγῳ γιγνομένων: τα[ῦτα ἐφέται] was restored by Kenyon[1] (from Harp. ἐφέται and other texts cited below); τα[ῦτα δικασταὶ] was suggested by W. R. Paton, *CR* v 1891, 182, and τα[ῦτα πάντα] by Lipsius, *Ber. Leipzig* xliii 1891, 51–2 (cf. Kaibel, *Stil und Text*, 240). Wilcken read and Kaibel & Wilamowitz[3] restored ταῦτ' ἄ[νδρε]ς; the reading was doubted by Kenyon in his Berlin ed. and O.C.T.; M. H. Chambers, *TAPA* xcvi 1965, 38–9, read ταῦτ' ἄν[δ]ρ[ε]ς, and his latest reading is quoted by A. L. Boegehold, *CSCA* ix 1976, 18 n. 12, as ταῦ[τ]α .[.].[.]ς; Dr J. D. Thomas reads ταυ 5 or 6 ς. The sense is much improved if we restore ταῦτ⟨α να'⟩ ἄνδρες, suggested by R. S. Stroud, *CP* lxiii 1968, 212 (for the number see below).

Kenyon[1] punctuated with a colon after (Φρεάτου) δικάζουσιν and a comma after ἐν πλοίῳ; but it is probably at the latter point that Kaibel & Wilamowitz[1] intended §iv to begin; Kenyon[3] printed a colon after δικάζουσιν and a full point after ἐν πλοίῳ, and began §iv at the latter point; Kaibel & Wilamowitz[3] began §iv at the latter point. The major break in the sense comes at the latter point, since the passage from δικάζουσι δ' οἱ λαχόντες to εἰσελθὼν ἀπολογεῖται concerns all trials of a named individual for homicide, not only trials ἐν Φρεάτου, but unfortunately in more recent editions the beginning of §iv has been moved to the former point; Kenyon in his Berlin ed. and O.C.T. uses no full point between the beginning of §iii and τὸν στέφανον.

Various texts indicate that the jury in homicide courts other than the Areopagus was a body of men styled ἐφέται (M & L 86, 13, 17 with law *ap.* [D.] XLIII. *Mac.* 57; Harp. ἐφέται, Phot., Suid. [*E* 3876-8], ἐφέται, Poll. VIII. 125, *L.S.* 188. 30). The ephetae, or rather those forming the jury on a particular occasion, numbered fifty-one (M & L 86, [D.], Poll., *locc. citt.*: fifty, in Tim. ἐφέται, is an approximation; eighty [π' ὄντες] in Suid. [*E* 3876], Zon., ἐφέται, is unconfirmed, and the corresponding entry in Phot. has περιόντες). According to Pollux they were ἀριστίνδην αἱρεθέντας, and according to Phot., Suid. (*E* 3877), ἐφέται, cf. *L.S.*, they were ἄνδρες ὑπὲρ πεντήκοντα ἔτη γεγονότες καὶ ἄριστα βεβιωκέναι ὑπόληψιν ἔχοντες; Andr. 324 F 4a = Phil. 328 F 20b has been thought to show that the ephetae were appointed from the Areopagus (J. W. Headlam, *CR* vi 1892, 252, Bonner & Smith, *Administration of Justice*, i. 99-100), and although it is hard to base any conclusion on that confused text it is perhaps more likely than not that the ephetae were Areopagites (cf. Harrison, *L.A.*, ii. 41-2; MacDowell, *op. cit.*, 51-2, is agnostic). It has commonly been believed that by the fourth century these courts were composed of ordinary jurors, though the use of the word ἐφέται persisted (e.g. Sandys; Lipsius, *A.R.*, 40-1; G. Smith, *CP* xix 1924, 353-8, cf. Bonner & Smith, *op. cit.*, 270-5, suggesting that this is the weakening of the Areopagus ascribed to Pericles in 27. i [but see *ad loc.*]). However, of the two passages thought to prove this change, Is. XVIII. *Call.* 54, mentioning a court of 700 jurors, may refer not to a homicide trial but to a subsequent trial ψευδομαρτυριῶν, and [D.] LIX. *Neaer.* 10 should be read as ὀλίγας ψήφους μεταλαβὼν ἐκ πεντακοσίων δραχμῶν, '... for the expenditure of 500 drachmae'; there is no need to suppose that any change was made in the appointment of the ephetae (MacDowell, *op. cit.*, 52-6, Harrison, *L.A.*, ii. 39-41; but see R. J. Seager, *JHS* xcv 1975, 246). οἱ λαχόντες ταῦτα refers to the allocation of particular cases to particular bodies of fifty-one ephetae, not to the appointment of men to the panel of ephetae (cf. T. J. Saunders, *JHS* lxxxv 1965, 225, suggesting 'take these cases for hearing in an order they determine by lot'). See in general MacDowell, *op. cit.*, 48–57, R. S. Stroud, *U. Calif. Pub. Cl. Stud.* iii 1968, 47–9, Harrison, *L.A.*, ii. 36–43.†

εἰσάγει δ' ὁ βασιλεύς: The basileus acts as εἰσάγουσα ἀρχή, as do his fellow archons in trials before the δικαστήρια. Cf. below.

καὶ δικάζο[υ]σιν ἐν ἱερ[ῷ] καὶ ὑπαίθριοι: Trials for homicide were held in a religious sanctuary but, because of the pollution with which a killer was tainted, out of doors: cf. Ant. v. *Caed. Her.* 11.

καὶ ὁ βασιλεὺς ὅταν δικάζῃ περιαιρεῖται τὸν στέφανον: Normally δικάζειν is used of the magistrate or jury which decides the verdict, but here it is clear from the two preceding clauses that the basileus acted simply as εἰσάγουσα ἀρχή and the Areopagus or the ephetae decided the verdict: for this use of the verb cf. 52. iii (δικάζουσιν ... εἰσάγοντες, of the εἰσαγωγεῖς), 57. ii (διαδικάζει, of the basileus), with commentary. All the archons wore a myrtle crown as a badge of office (e.g. Lys. xxvi. *Evand.* 8, A. I. *Tim.* 19 with schol.): removal of the crown when presiding over a homicide trial is probably again due to the pollution of the killer (cf. Wilamowitz, *A.u.A.*, i. 252–3 n. 139). A. III. *Ctes.* 77 regarded it as a great affront against decency that Demosthenes, on the seventh day from his daughter's death, should have appeared στεφανωσάμενος καὶ λευκὴν ἐσθῆτα λαβὼν to make thank-offerings for the death of Philip of Macedon.

ὁ δὲ τὴν αἰτίαν ἔχων ... εἰς τὸ ἱερὸν εἰσελθὼν ἀπολογεῖται: ν[όμος], proposed by Blass[2] and approved by Kaibel, *Stil und Text*, 241, is accepted with some hesitation by Wilcken, by Kenyon in his Berlin ed. and by Dr J. D. Thomas; originally Kenyon had proposed δ[ύναται], but in his Berlin ed. he acknowledged that that and other early supplements are too long. This sentence notes that to enable the trial to take place an exception has to be allowed to the ban proclaimed by the basileus (§ii with commentary). ὁ ... τὴν αἰτίαν ἔχων is 'the man under accusation', as often (H. v. 70 uses αἰτίη ἔχει τινά in §i, αἰτίην ἔχει τίς in §ii). ἐμβάλλειν εἰς τὴν ἀγοράν is often used of the 'invasion' of the Agora by a man who ought not to set foot in it: cf. A. I. *Tim.* 164, II. *F.L.* 148, D. xxiv. *Tim.* 103, 165, Lyc. *Leocr.* 5.

ὅταν δὲ μὴ εἰδῇ τὸν ποιήσαντα, τῷ δράσαντι λαγχάνει: Sc. ὁ διώκων. Π. Ν. Παπαγεώργιος, *Ἀθ.* iv 1892, 607–8, proposed εἰδῇ ⟨τις⟩ (cf. D. xxiii. *Arist.* 76): this may be right, but the concise style of the papyrus' text is by no means impossible for *A.P.* In the last two sentences of this chapter *A.P.* deals with charges of homicide which were brought before yet another court, at the prytaneum (cf. D., *loc. cit., Lex. Patm. ad loc.* [*BCH* i 1877, 138–9 = K. Latte & H. Erbse, *Lexica Graeca Minora*, 148–9], Paus. I. 28. x, Poll. VIII. 120). A lacuna in which a reference to the prytaneum is to be supplied was postulated after λαγχάνει by Kaibel & Wilamowitz[1-2], before τῷ δράσαντι by Thalheim; Kaibel & Wilamowitz[1-2] punctuated with a full point after φυλοβασιλεῖς, and required another lacuna after ζῴων (cf. Kaibel, *Stil und Text*, 242); but more probably we should accept the transmitted text as evidence of further condensation by *A.P.* For the prytaneum cf. 3. v with commentary; for charges against a person unknown cf. *Lex. Patm.*, Poll., *locc. citt.*, also Plat. *Legg.* IX. 874 A 4–B 5. See in general Lipsius, *A.R.*, 23–7, MacDowell, *Athenian Homicide Law*, 85–9, Harrison, *L.A.*, ii. 42–3.

δικάζει δ' ὁ βασιλεὺς καὶ οἱ φυλοβασιλεῖς: For the φυλοβασιλεῖς of the four old tribes cf. 8. iii with commentary, 41. ii. In the amnesty law *ap.* Pl. *Sol.* 19. iv ὅσοι ἐξ Ἀρείου πάγου ἢ ὅσοι ἐκ τῶν βασιλέων . . . ἔφευγον are excluded from the amnesty; in the decree of Patroclides *ap.* And. I. *Myst.* 78 ⟨οἷς ἢ⟩ ἐξ Ἀρείου πάγου ἢ τῶν ἐφετῶν ἢ ἐκ πρυτανείου ἢ Δελφινίου δικασθεῖσιν ὑπὸ τῶν βασιλέων . . . τίς ἐστι φυγὴ ἢ θάνατος κατεγνώσθη are excluded from the reinstatement of the ἄτιμοι: in each case it is easiest to believe that the Areopagus, the ephetae and the βασιλεῖς (i.e. the basileus and the φυλοβασιλεῖς) at the prytaneum are together intended to cover all homicide courts (the words ἢ Δελφινίου ought not to have been included by Patroclides, and I would follow Droysen and Lipsius in deleting them). Similarly in M&L 86, 12, in connection with unintentional homicide, τὸς βασιλέας probably refers to the basileus and φυλοβασιλεῖς currently in office (M&L, p. 266; contr. R. S. Stroud, *U. Calif. Pub. Cl. Stud.* iii 1968, 46, Harrison, *L.A.*, ii. 43, who believe that the reference is to successive βασιλεῖς). A jury might well be thought unnecessary in a 'trial' in which there was no defendant, and if my interpretation of them is right Solon's law and Patroclides' decree imply that the ephetae did not take part in trials at the prytaneum; but Harp. ἐφέται includes the prytaneum among the courts of the ephetae, and Poll. VIII. 125 refers to five courts (including both the Areopagus and the prytaneum?). Probably, despite προειστήκεσαν in Poll. VIII. 120, the court at the prytaneum comprised simply the basileus and the four φυλοβασιλεῖς.

καὶ τὰς τῶν ἀψύχων καὶ τῶν ἄλλων ζῴων: For the expression cf. Arist. *Rhet.* I. 1366 A 30 (καὶ ἄψυχα καὶ τῶν ἄλλων ζῴων τὸ τυχόν), and on this use of ἄλλος R. Kühner rev. B. Gerth, *Ausführliche Grammatik der griechischen Sprache*, II. i. 275, §405 (c), Anm. 1, LSJ *s.v.*, II. 8. For charges against inanimate objects and animals cf. D. XXIII. *Arist.* 76 and *Lex. Patm. ad loc.* (cf. above), Paus. I. 28. x, Poll. VIII. 90, 120; also Plat. *Legg.* IX. 873 E 1–874 A 3. An inanimate object (and probably an animal) if 'found guilty' was removed from Attica: A. III. *Ctes.* 244, Paus. VI. 11. vi, *Lex. Patm.*, Poll. VIII. 120. The first καί probably means 'in addition to charges against a person unknown' (but MacDowell, *Athenian Homicide Law*, 87, declines to choose between that and 'in addition to all other homi-

[57. iv] COMMENTARY ON THE *ATH. POL.*

cide cases', which would imply that the φυλοβασιλεῖς were associated with the basileus in all).

58. i. ὁ δὲ πολέμαρχος θύει μὲν θυσίας τήν τε τῇ Ἀρτέμιδι τῇ ἀγροτέρᾳ καὶ τῷ Ἐνυαλίῳ: To improve the balance of the sentence Kaibel & Wilamowitz substituted τῇ τε for τήν τε τῇ (cf. Kaibel, *Stil und Text*, 242–3), and Κ. Σ. Κόντος, Ἀθ. iv 1892, 170, inserted ⟨τὴν⟩ τῷ; but more probably *A.P.* wrote an unbalanced sentence. It is not in fact clear whether *A.P.* refers to two separate festivals (implied by Wilamowitz, *A.u.A.*, i. 250) or to a single festival of the two deities (as assumed by Deubner).

The Athenians vowed at Marathon that they would sacrifice a goat to Artemis ἀγροτέρα for every barbarian killed; but after the battle, in which H. vi. 117. i gives the number of Persian dead as 6,400, they resolved to sacrifice 500 each year (X. *Anab.* iii. ii. 12, Pl. *Her. Mal.* 862 B–C, Ael. *V.H.* ii. 25 [300], schol. Ar. *Eq.* 660 [oxen originally vowed, goats substituted]). The festival was celebrated on 6 Boedromion (iii) (Pl. *Glor. Ath.* 349 E cf. *Her. Mal.* 862 A [emended]; also *ibid.* 861 F, *Camill.* 19. v, dating the battle; but 6 Thargelion [xi], Ael., *loc. cit.*): very probably the battle was fought earlier in the year, and that date was chosen for the commemoration because the 6th of each month was a day sacred to Artemis (D.L. ii. 44, Procl. 200 D *ad* Plat. *Tim.* 35 B: J. D. Mikalson, *The Sacred and Civil Calendar of the Athenian Year*, 18) and 5 Boedromion was the day of the Genesia, a festival of the dead (*L.S.* 86. 20 = Phil. 328 F 168: L. Deubner, *Attische Feste*, 229–30, Jacoby, *CQ* xxxviii 1944, 65–75 = *Abhandlungen*, 243–59).[52] ἐνυάλιος, 'warlike', is found in Homer and later as an epithet of Ares (e.g. *Il.* ii. 651, xvii. 210–11); elsewhere Enyalius is a separate war-god (e.g. Ar. *Pax.* 457 with schol.). See Deubner, *op. cit.*, 209, H. W. Parke, *Festivals of the Athenians*, 54–5.†

διατίθησι δ' ἀγῶνα τὸν ἐπιτάφιον [[καὶ]] τοῖς τετελευτηκόσιν ἐν τῷ πολέμῳ: Kenyon follows Poll. viii. 91 and deletes καὶ; Kaibel & Wilamowitz retained καὶ, and punctuated after ἐπιτάφιον instead of after πολέμῳ (cf. Wilamowitz, *A.u.A.*, i. 249 with n. 130, and see following note); Π. Ν. Παπαγεώργιος, Ἀθ. iv 1892, 608–9, proposed to emend to ἐπὶ (cf. Philostr. 623. *Vit. Soph.* i.. 30). The emendation

---

[52] The argument for dating the battle to the middle of the previous month depends on the Spartans' delay, thought to be due to the Carnea, and cf. Jacoby, *JHS* lxiv 1944, 62 with n. 121 = *Abhandlungen*, 307 with n. 121; but W. K. Pritchett, *U. Calif. Pub. Cl. Stud.* vii 1971 = *The Greek State at War*, i, 116–20, rejects the link with the Carnea and believes that the Athenian calendar may have been out of step with the moon and 6 Boedromion may have been the day of the battle; and Parke suggests that 6 Boedromion was already the day of Artemis ἀγροτέρα and was the day when the Athenians took the decision to march out to Marathon.‡

should be accepted: it is supported by three bronze vases of the fifth century bearing the inscription Ἀθεναῖοι· ἆθλα ἐπὶ τοῖς ἐν τῶι πολέμοι (E. Vanderpool, *AΔ* xxiv 1969, μελ. 1–5, cf. P. Amandry, *BCH* xcv 1971, 602–9, and, on this use of ἐπί, R. Étienne & M. Piérart, *BCH* xcix 1975, 55).

Cf. Plat. *Menex.* 249 B 3–6, Lys. II. *Epit.* 80, Philostr., *loc. cit.* In the winter of 431/0 the Athenians τῷ πατρίῳ νόμῳ χρώμενοι δημοσίᾳ ταφὰς ἐποιήσαντο τῶν ἐν τῷδε τῷ πολέμῳ πρώτων ἀποθανόντων (T. II. 34. i), and in §v Thucydides states that the burial on the spot of those who fell at Marathon was the only exception to this practice (I am not persuaded by M. Ostwald, *Nomos and the Beginnings of the Athenian Democracy*, 175–6, that γε means that Marathon was not the only exception). In fact other exceptions are known, notably after Plataea (H. IX. 85. ii); no fragments of inscribed Athenian casualty lists are datable earlier than 464; and Paus. I. 29. iv asserts that those who died at Drabescus *c.* 464 were the first to be thus commemorated (but contr. §§vii, xiv). Jacoby therefore argued that Thucydides' πάτριος νόμος was enacted in 464 (*JHS* lxiv 1944, 37–66 = *Abhandlungen*, 260–315); but Pausanias' assertion is an insecure basis for argument, and it is hard to believe that Thucydides should have been wrong about a law enacted only ten years before he was born (cf. Gomme, *Hist. Comm. Thuc.*, ii. 94–100, D. W. Bradeen, *CQ*[2] xix 1969, 154–5). How old the custom was I do not pretend to know; D.S. XI. 33. iii dates the institution of the ἐπιτάφιος ἀγών and the oration in 479 (cf. D.H. *A.R.* v. 17. iv, not mentioning the ἀγών), and that, or a more general link with the Persian Wars, may be correct; R. Stupperich, *Staatsbegräbnis und Privatgrabmal im klassischen Athen*, 206–24, discusses possible early public funerary monuments and suggests that the πάτριος νόμος is to be linked with Cleisthenes' tribal reorganisation (cf. 33–53 on the oration, 54–6 on the ἀγών and the polemarch).†

Many have associated the institution with the Thesea, on 8 Pyanopsion (iv) (e.g. A. Mommsen, *Feste der Stadt Athen*, 298–307); Jacoby argued for a connection with the Genesia, on 5 Boedromion (iii) (*opp. citt.*, 61–2 = 305–8); but a date outside the campaigning season, towards the middle of the Athenian year, is more likely (e.g. Gomme, *op. cit.*, 100–1, Bradeen, *op. cit.*, 155). See also Deubner, *op. cit.*, 230–1, Parke, *op. cit.*, 54.

καὶ Ἁρμοδίῳ καὶ Ἀριστογείτονι ἐναγίσματα ποιεῖ: This is the earliest citation of the noun ἐνάγισμα in LSJ except Ar. fr. 488. 12 Kock; but ἐναγίζειν is found in Herodotus and elsewhere, and in H. II. 44. v we read τῷ μὲν ὡς ἀθανάτῳ ... θύουσι, τῷ δὲ ἑτέρῳ ὡς ἥρωι ἐναγίζουσι (cf. Paus. II. 10. i, 11. viii). According to D. XIX. *F.L.* 280 (Ἁρμόδιον) τιμᾶτ' ἐξ ἴσου τοῖς ἥρωσι καὶ τοῖς θεοῖς. As pointed out by I. Calabi Limentani, *Acme* xxix 1976, 9–27, the cult of Harmodius and Aristogiton was comparable to the honours of men who had died fighting for Athens; but apart from those who died at Marathon (*IG* ii² 1006, 26–7, 69–70, Paus. I. 32. iv) there is no evidence that those who fell in war were treated as heroes, as Harmodius and Aristogiton were. Unless we follow the punctuation of Kaibel & Wilamowitz, as I am not inclined to do (cf. above; it is accepted by Deubner, *op. cit.*, 230 with n. 8, rejected by Vanderpool, *op. cit.*, 4 n. 7), the cult of Harmodius and Aristogiton was distinct from the commemoration of those who had died in war.

For the cult of Harmodius and Aristogiton see pp. 230, 289, 308. This cannot have been instituted earlier than the expulsion of Hippias in 511/0; and so (as noticed by Wilamowitz, *A.u.A.*, i. 249–50), with the possible exception of Enyalius, it appears that all the religious observances assigned by *A.P.* to the polemarch were introduced at the end of the sixth century or later: (ὁ βασιλεὺς) τὰς πατρίους θυσίας διοικεῖ οὗτος πάσας (57. i) is therefore to be preferred to μηδὲν τῶν πατρίων τὸν ἄρχοντα ποιεῖν, ὥσπερ ὁ βασιλεὺς καὶ ὁ πολέμαρχος (3. iii).

58. ii. δίκαι δὲ λαγχάνονται πρὸς αὐτὸν ἴδιαι μόνον: The expression δίκαι ἴδιαι (emphasising that δίκη is being used in its narrower sense) recurs in 59. v. The papyrus has ἴδιαι μ(ὲν); but that would lead the reader to expect δημοσίαι δὲ, whereas *A.P.* does not suggest that the polemarch was the recipient of any γραφαί (cf. Kaibel, *Stil und Text*, 243: on the charge ἀπροστασίου see §iii with commentary): Kaibel & Wilamowitz therefore emended to μόνον, and this is accepted by Kenyon in his Berlin ed. and O.C.T., very probably rightly (but many editors retain μὲν). It appears that in the fifth century the polemarch handled all lawsuits in which metics and privileged foreigners were involved (except on homicide charges: cf. below), but in the fourth public suits were handled by the same magistrates as would handle them if both parties were citizens, and the polemarch handled private suits only (D. M. MacDowell, *The Law in Classical Athens*, 223; on 224 he guesses that private suits handled by the thesmothetae or by specialised magistrates were likewise in the fourth century still handled by them when metics were involved).

αἵ τε τοῖς μετοίκοις ... γιγνόμεναι: Owing to the position of τε, ⟨αἱ⟩ τοῖς προξένοις was inserted by Kaibel, *Stil und Text*, 243, Kaibel & Wilamowitz³, but that is probably an improvement rather than a correction.

μέτοικοι are non-citizens registered as residents in Attica, whether temporary or permanent (on their registration see p. 497). ἰσοτελεῖς and πρόξενοι are specially privileged non-citizens: ἰσοτελεῖς are those who are allowed to rank with the citizens in respect of certain obligations; πρόξενοι are strictly men appointed to represent

Athenian interests and look after visiting Athenians in their own cities, but in the fourth and later centuries such appointments became increasingly frequent and increasingly honorary, and could be conferred on men who lived in Attica and might want to appear before Athenian courts. ἰσοτέλεια is not found in inscriptions before the fourth century: in the fifth and early fourth centuries privileged foreigners were granted ἀτέλεια, exemption from obligations (cf. p. 509); and when ἰσοτέλεια came to be the more normal privilege the word ἀτέλεια survived for a consequence of ἰσοτέλεια, ἀτέλεια τοῦ μετοικίου (e.g. *IG* ii² 211 = Tod 166, 5, 8–9; restored in fifth-century inscriptions *IG* i² 106, 6–7, 106a, 3, but the restoration in 154, 14–15 is abandoned in *IG* i³ 164, 29). ἀτέλεια or ἰσοτέλεια is often found combined with προξενία: *IG* ii² 8 = M&L 70, 18–20, offers γῆς ἔγκτησιν κα[ὶ οἰκίας Ἀθήνησιν καὶ ἀ]τέλειαν καθάπ[ερ τοῖς ἄλλοις προξένο]ις (or, as suggested by D. Whitehead, *PCPS* Supp. iv 1977, 23 n. 58, καὶ μετοικίο ἀ]τέλειαν), and *IG* ii² 288, 5–7, is restored [εἶναι δ' αὐτοῖς καθά]πε[ρ] τοῖς ἄλλ[οις προξένοις καὶ ε]ὐε[ρ]γέταις [ἰσοτέλειαν Ἀθήνησι]; but not every proxeny decree mentions ἀτέλεια or ἰσοτέλεια (e.g. *IG* ii² 206, which does include οἰκίας ἔηκτησις).†

It has been disputed how large a package of privileges is denoted by the various words indicating a privileged status. Athenian honorific decrees show a considerable variety in the range of titles and privileges which they mention (cf. the table of J. Pečírka, *The Formula for the Grant of Enktesis*, 152–9), and do not make it clear whether a clause mentioning a privilege such as οἰκίας ἔγκτησις is to be regarded as explanatory of or as supplementary to a clause conferring such a status as ἰσοτέλεια. The minimum privilege which all ἰσοτελεῖς must enjoy is exemption from the μετοίκιον (cf. above) and any other tax that was levied on metics but not on citizens; equality with citizens in liability for εἰσφορά and other taxes, and for military service, mentioned in one inscription, may have been thought of as part of rather than as an addition to ἰσοτέλεια (*IG* ii² 287, 2–7: δ[εδόσθαι] αὐτοῖς ἰσοτέ[λε]ιαν οἰκο[ῦσιν Ἀ]θήνησιν [καὶ] τ[ὰς] εἰσφορὰς εἰσφέρειν καὶ τὰ τέλη τελεῖν καθάπερ Ἀθηναῖοι, καὶ τὰς στρατείας στρατ[εύ]εσθαι μετὰ Ἀθηναίων); οἰκίας ἔγκτησις is more likely to have been thought of as a further privilege granted with the status than as an essential part of the status (*IG* ii² 8, quoted above, implies that γῆς καὶ οἰκίας ἔγκτησις was a normal concomitant of proxeny, but some πρόξενοι were offered only οἰκίας ἔγκτησις, e.g. *IG* ii² 130). Undoubtedly the Athenians were haphazard either in the selection of privileges offered to different honorands or in the specification of the privileges attached to different statuses or in both: I hesitate to assume that no honorand had any privileges except those specifically mentioned in the decree in his favour. See most recently Whitehead, *op. cit.*, 7–14, with notes citing earlier discussions: he is

58. ii] COMMENTARY ON THE *ATH. POL.*

more convinced than I that clauses specifying particular privileges must be supplementary rather than explanatory. On the judicial standing of πρόξενοι cf. P. Gauthier, *Symbola*, 137–8 (Athens), 230–2 (elsewhere). *A.P.* suggests that recourse to the polemarch's court was the right of all metics, ἰσοτελεῖς and πρόξενοι. Some decrees make specific mention of the right to go to law in Athens: *IG* ii² 53, 4–5, reads [τὰς δίκας] ἔναι αὐτῶι πρὸς τὸν πολέμαρχον [καθάπ]ε[ρ] το[ῖ]ς ἄλλοις προξένοις, and *IG* ii² 237 = Tod 178, 26–7, reads διδόναι αὐτοὺς δίκα[ς καὶ λαμβάνειν κα]θ[άπε]ρ Ἀθηναῖοι, while some honorific decrees of the fifth century grant access to the polemarch's court with exemption from or limitation of court fees (*IG* i² 153, 5–9, *A.T.L.* D 23, 20–4; *SEG* x 23, 2–7). Wade-Gery argued that the polemarch's court was reserved for privileged foreigners, while other foreigners, if they had access to Athenian courts as a result of σύμβολα between their own city and Athens, had to go to the thesmothetae (as in 59. vi), and suggested that a privileged foreigner using the polemarch's court required no προστάτης (*Essays*, 188 n. 2, arguing from M & L 31, 6–11 with 11–14); G. E. M. de Ste. Croix suggests in addition that the polemarch's court was less busy and could give a quicker decision (*CQ*² xi 1961, 100–1). On the other hand, it is not obvious from speeches of the Demosthenic period that any foreigners had to be represented in court by a προστάτης (cf. on §iii), and Harrison believed that the privilege consisted simply of the right to go to law in Athens: δίκαι ἀπὸ συμβόλων went to the thesmothetae because it was they who ratified the σύμβολα (59. vi); non-citizens with a personal right of access to the Athenian courts took their cases to the polemarch (who may once have had a general duty to care for privileged foreigners, as the archon had a duty to care for orphans and ἐπίκληροι: 56. vii with commentary); in each case the relevant magistrate would vouch for the non-citizen's right to go to law (*L.A.*, i. 189–95, ii. 10–16, cf. Gauthier, *op. cit.*, 183–6). Harrison's explanation presupposes that foreigners who were neither registered as metics (or ἰσοτελεῖς or πρόξενοι) nor citizens of a state which had σύμβολα with Athens had no right of access to Athenian courts (except in δίκαι ἐμπορικαί, on which see 59. v with commentary). [D.] VII. *Halon.* 11–13 implies, whether rightly or wrongly, that in the past Macedonians had in fact been able to sue in Athenian courts without σύμβολα, which Ste. Croix regards as confirmation of 'what we should have surmised anyway' (Harrison, *CQ*² x 1960, 248–52, Ste. Croix, *op. cit.*, 111), and the killer of a ξένος could be brought to trial at the Palladium (57. iii with commentary); but probably if a foreigner's rights were not guaranteed by σύμβολα or by his personal status his access to the courts depended not on entitlement but on favour and his chances of obtaining justice in

Athens were far less good (MacDowell, *The Law in Classical Athens*, 222–4, suggests that foreigners with no right of access to the thesmothetae or the polemarch had to go to the ξενοδίκαι, on whom see below, p. 662). In M & L 31 it is clearly a privilege for the Phaselites that their δίκαι ἀπὸ συμβόλων are to be tried in the polemarch's court rather than by whatever procedure may have been agreed previously, and Ste. Croix's suggestion that the polemarch's court was able to give quicker decisions than other courts is for fifth-century procedure an attractive additional point.

Metics and privileged foreigners could appear either as plaintiffs or as defendants in Athenian courts (e.g. *IG* ii² 237, quoted above: cf. Gauthier, *op. cit.*, 137–8, Harrison, *L.A.*, i. 194 n. 2), though what follows suggests that *A.P.* is thinking of them primarily as defendants. The rule appears to have been that any case in which such a man was either plaintiff or defendant was handled by the polemarch; Lys. XXIII. *Panc.* is a reply to a defendant's claim that he should be treated not as a metic but as a citizen and so ought not to be indicted before the polemarch. *A.P.* refers specifically to δίκαι ... ἴδιαι μόνον (cf. above), and it seems that normally though not invariably non-citizens could not prosecute in γραφαί, where if necessary a citizen might prosecute on their behalf (cf. Harrison, *L.A.*, i. 195 n. 1, Whitehead, *op. cit.*, 94–5, and above, p. 527, on metic sycophants). Since there was more danger of a non-citizen's than of a citizen's absconding, non-citizen defendants in some or all δίκαι could be required by the plaintiff to provide guarantors (Is. XVII. *Trap.* 12, with Lipsius, *A.R.*, 811 and n. 28, Harrison, *L.A.*, i. 196 and n. 1, Gauthier, *op. cit.*, 138–41; cf. below on δίκαι ἐμπορικαί, pp. 664–5).

What is said in this chapter does not apply to homicide charges: we may guess that a metic killer would be tried by the same court as a citizen killer on the same charge (but there is no evidence, and see the doubts of E. Grace, *Eirene* xi 1973, 5–30); when a metic or ξένος was killed, his next of kin brought a charge to the basileus, and the trial was held at the Palladium, whether for intentional or for unintentional homicide (57. iii with commentary, [D.] XLVII. *Ev. & Mnes.* 68–73: see MacDowell, *Athenian Homicide Law*, 69, Harrison, *L.A.*, i. 196–9, Gauthier, *op. cit.*, 141–4, Whitehead, *op. cit.*, 93–4). Sometimes when a foreigner came to Athens in circumstances in which his murder was a serious possibility it was decided that his murder would be (tried and) punished in the same way as the murder of a citizen (e.g. *IG* ii² 226 = Tod 173, 36–42).

καὶ δεῖ τοῦτον λαβόντα ... τοῖς διαιτηταῖς ἀποδοῦναι: *Π. Ν. Παπαγεώργιος, Ἀθ.* iv 1892, 609, proposed παραδοῦναι (cf. 53. ii), which may be right. Most δίκαι between citizens went first to the members of the Forty acting for the defendant's tribe; if the sum at issue was more than 10 drachmae the case was remitted to one of the board of διαιτηταί acting for the defendant's tribe; an appeal lay from his judgment to a court presided over by one of the Forty (53. i–iii with commentary). Foreigners were not members of the tribes (though demes kept registers of metics living in their territory: cf. p. 497), so the procedure had to be adapted when a non-citizen appeared as defendant (but I should guess that in this respect normal procedure was followed when a non-citizen sued a citizen: cf. Gauthier, *op. cit.*, 136–8); and so the polemarch, in addition to vouching for the status of non-citizen defendants, would distribute suits against them equally among the tribal subdivisions of the Forty (τοὺς ... τὴν φυλὴν δικάζοντας). Thereafter the normal fourth-century procedure for δίκαι could be followed; and, though *A.P.* does not say so, I have no doubt that cases where the sum at issue was up to 10 drachmae were decided by one of the Forty, without reference to a διαιτητής. Cf. Harrison, *L.A.*, ii. 19–21 (better than i. 194 n. 2).

58. iii. αὐτὸς δ' εἰσάγει δίκας τάς τε τοῦ ἀπο[σ]τασίου: Where the London papyrus has αὐτὸς δ', Harp. ἀποστασίου has οὗτος δὲ and Harp. πολέμαρχος has αὐτός τε: οὗτος δ' would be *A.P.*'s normal usage, and is probably to be restored here (J. J. Keaney, *LCM* iv 1979, 17; if the papyrus' text were correct, αὐτὸς would be emphatic and resumptive after the mention of the Forty and the διαιτηταί). The article is unusual in the name of a lawsuit, and Kaibel & Wilamowitz deleted τοῦ (cf. Kaibel, *Stil und Text*, 243–4); it is present in both quotations of the passage by Harpocration; but even so we should probably delete.

Cf. [D.] xxxv. *Lacr.* 48. This was a suit against a freedman (and so, a metic) who deserted his former master for another προστάτης, or failed to comply with any conditions imposed at his manumission (cf. Harp. ἀποστασίου, *E.M.* [124. 53] ἀποστασίου, *L.S.* 201. 5, 434. 24; Poll. viii. 35; *L.R.C.* ἀποστασίου δίκη); Suid. (*A* 3546) ἀποστασίου, *L.S.* 184. 24, 434. 30, appear to be wrong in making this a suit by which a slave claimed to be free. See Lipsius, *A.R.*, 621–5, Harrison, *L.A.*, i. 165, 182.

καὶ <ἀ>προστασ[ί]ου: (Omitted by the original scribe but added by a corrector; the words are present in the quotations of this passage by Harp., *locc. citt.*). Cf. [D.] xxxv. *Lacr.* 48. This was a suit against a metic who had no προστάτης (cf. Harp. ἀπροστασίου, *L.S.* 201. 12); although *A.P.* has written of δίκαι ... ἴδιαι μόνον (§ii with commentary), and the other suits listed here were δίκαι, this must from the nature of the charge have been a γραφή in which ὁ βουλόμενος might prosecute (it is classified as δημοσία in Poll. viii. 35; see Lipsius, *A.R.*, 65 and n. 48 with 979). How far a metic needed a citizen προστάτης, not merely at his registration but thereafter, is disputed: cf. above, p. 654, and for recent discussions see Harrison,

L.A., i. 189–93, Gauthier, *Symbola*, 126–36, Whitehead, *PCPS* Supp. iv 1977, 89–92. MacDowell, *The Law in Classical Athens*, 78, suggests that this was a prosecution for failing to register as a metic.

καὶ κλήρων καὶ ἐπικλήρων τοῖς μετοίκοις: Cf. [D.] XLVI. *Steph. ii*. 22. In the suits mentioned above, a citizen would be suing a non-citizen. In inheritance suits, since a citizen could not marry a non-citizen (cf. 26. iv, 42. i, with commentary), one non-citizen would be suing another. For the archon's responsibility in such disputes between citizens see 56. vi–vii with commentary.

καὶ τἄλλ'... τοῖς μετοίκοις ὁ πολέμαρχος: The reference will be to such charges as γονέων κάκωσις: cf. 56. vi–vii with commentary. Among citizens such charges could be labelled γραφή or εἰσαγγελία; probably it was assumed that in the case of a metic family only a metic would wish to prosecute.

59. i. οἱ δὲ θεσμοθέται πρῶτον μὲν ... δοῦναι ταῖς ἀρχαῖς: The six thesmothetae prescribe the days on which the courts are to sit, and allocate courts to their presiding magistrates; the second point is made again in §v *fin.* (cf. *ad loc.*). The thesmothetae will not have had direct knowledge of all the judicial business that was pending, and the various officials entitled to preside over courts must have told them what their needs were: the thesmothetae will have told a particular magistrate that he was to have a court on a particular day, with a jury of a particular size (A. L. Boegehold, 'Aristotle and the Dikasteria', 18–23: cf. 66. i with commentary); how a particular jury was assigned to that court in the time of *A.P.* is expounded in chs 63–6. D. XXI. *Mid.* 47 quotes a law requiring the thesmothetae to bring charges of ὕβρις to trial within thirty days, ἐὰν μή τι δημόσιον κωλύῃ, εἰ δὲ μή, ὅταν ᾖ πρῶτον οἷόν τε (as noticed by Harrison, *L.A.*, ii. 13 n. 2, the thesmothetae are here both the appointers of the calendar and the εἰσάγουσα ἀρχή); cf. the law of Timocrates *ap.* D. XXIV. *Tim.* 63 (see on §iv, below). In the law published in *Hesp.* xliii 1974, 137–88, accusations where a sum of over 10 drachmae is at stake are to be brought to court by the officials to whom the accusation is made, οἱ δὲ θε[σμ]οθ[έται π]αρεχόντων αὐτοῖς ἐπικληρ-όντες δικα[στήριον ὅ]ταμ παραγγέλλωσιν, ἢ εὐθυνέσθω[ν —] δραχ[μαῖς] (lines 25–8); Tod 200, 204–17, orders the thesmothetae to provide the στρατηγὸς ἐπὶ τὰς συμμορίας with courts on two stated days to try σκήψεις by trierarchs (see on 61. i).

Ar. *Vesp.* 661–3 calculates the money paid to jurors on the assumption that all 6,000 were required on 300 days in the year. The courts sat throughout the year ([X.] *A.P.* iii. 6); they did not sit on festivals (*ibid.* 8: e.g. Ar. *Thesm.* 78–80, Lys. XXVI. *Evand.* 6) and days of ill omen (Lucian, *Pseudol.* 12), which occurred at fixed points in the calendar, nor on days when the assembly met (D.

XXIV. *Tim.* 80; Ar. *Vesp.* 594–5 does not prove that this was not so in the fifth century: see MacDowell *ad loc.*), which were appointed by the prytanes (43. iii with commentary). The Athenians were notorious for their love of litigation (T. 1. 77. i, Ar. *Vesp.*, *passim*), and we do not read of any occasions when the courts did not have to meet because there were no cases for them to try; but specified sizes of jury were used for different kinds of suit (53. iii, 68. i, with commentary), and on any day the Athenians could only employ as many jurors as they had cases for. See Lipsius, *A.R.*, 159–61.†

καθότι γὰρ ἂν οὗτοι δῶσιν, κατὰ τοῦτο χρῶνται: A loose sentence, which adds nothing to our knowledge—which is not to say that *A.P.* cannot have written it. For this absolute use of χρῆσθαι cf. X. *Cyr.* IV. iii. 23.

59. ii. ἔτι δὲ τὰς εἰσαγγελίας εἰσαγγέλλουσιν εἰς τὸν δῆμον: Repeated by Poll. VIII. 87 and (with εἰσήγγελλον for εἰσαγγέλλουσιν) Phot. θεσμοθέται; but schol. A. I. *Tim.* 16 reads τὰς εἰσαγγελίας εἰσάγειν εἰς τὸν δῆμον, and schol. Plat. *Phaedr.* 235 D reads καὶ τὰς εἰσαγγελίας εἰσῆγον (not specifying before whom). However, no other text suggests that the thesmothetae presided when εἰσαγγελίαι were submitted to the assembly (for this procedure see 43. iv with commentary); and elsewhere the subject of εἰσαγγέλλειν is regularly the prosecutor, not the presiding magistrate: what we should expect *A.P.* to say here is that the thesmothetae were the εἰσάγουσα ἀρχή when an εἰσαγγελία was referred to a δικαστήριον. Kaibel & Wilamowitz deleted εἰσαγγέλλουσιν εἰς τὸν δῆμον, so that εἰσαγγελίας like καταχειροτονίας and προβολὰς is included in the object of εἰσάγουσιν (cf. Wilamowitz, *A.u.A.*, i. 244 n. 117, Kaibel, *Stil und Text*, 245–6); T. Gomperz emended to εἰσάγουσιν, leaving εἰς τὸν δῆμον (*DLZ* xii 1891, 1640); Blass[3] suggested ⟨ἃς ἄν τινες⟩ εἰσαγγείλωσιν, and Blass[4] ⟨ἃς⟩ εἰσαγγέλλουσιν (cf. Lipsius, *A.R.*, 207 n. 99); Thalheim, *Hermes* xxxvii 1902, 350, retained the papyrus' text as a reference to the reporting of the boule's καταγνώσεις; Dr D. M. Lewis has suggested ⟨τοῖς⟩ εἰσαγγέλλουσιν (cf. Rhodes, *A.B.*, 166 n. 1). I am confident that in the sentence written by *A.P.* the verb governing εἰσαγγελίας was εἰσάγουσιν; the last-mentioned is the neatest emendation, but I am not sure that Kaibel & Wilamowitz were wrong to delete the offending words. (This sentence has not fared well at the hands of recent English translators: Fritz & Kapp ignore the later εἰσάγουσιν and treat all the accusatives in §ii as objects of εἰσαγγέλλουσιν εἰς τὸν δῆμον, while Moore takes both εἰσαγγελίας and καταχειροτονίας as objects of εἰσαγγέλλουσιν εἰς τὸν δῆμον; Kenyon's Oxford Translation mistranslates προβολὰς but otherwise accurately renders the transmitted text; Rackham is free from error.)

καὶ τὰς καταχειροτονίας: The lexica and scholia derived from this passage have τὰς χειροτονίας, but the papyrus' text fits the context better. However, it is not immediately clear what 'condemnations' are referred to. A confused note by Sandys begins, 'They bring forward all cases of "removal from office by the votes of the people" '; after citing D. XXI. *Mid.* 6, etc., where the word is used in connection with προβολαί, and LI. *Cor. Tri.* 8, where it is used of a hostile vote by the boule in an εἰσαγγελία referred to a δικαστήριον (M. H. Hansen, *Eisangelia*, 118, case 142 n. 2 [i], Rhodes, *JHS* xcix 1979, 109–10), he ends, 'In the text the reference is to sentences passed by the ἐκκλησία on the occasion of an εἰσαγγελία, and then referred to a court of law' (and cites Lipsius, *Ber. Leipzig* xliii 1891, 48). τὰς καταγνώσεις τὰς ἐκ τῆς βουλῆς appear in §iv, below, and it seems that what εἰσαγγελίαι, καταχειροτονίαι and προβολαί here have in common is that they are all matters which may come to a δικαστήριον after a debate in the assembly (cf. Wilamowitz, *A.u.A.*, i. 244). καταχειροτονίαι have usually been interpreted as at the beginning of Sandys' note, to refer to cases of deposition from office; but the standard word for these is ἀποχειροτονίαι, and *A.P.* probably subsumed them under εἰσαγγελίαι (cf. on 61. ii).

Recently an alternative explanation has been suggested. Harp. καταχειροτονία refers to κατὰ τῶν ἀρχόντων καὶ κατὰ τῶν συκοφαντῶν προβολάς, and cites D. XXI. *Mid.* (cf. above), Hyp. ὑπὲρ Χαιρεφίλου (frs 211–22 Sauppe; this passage is fr. 218) and Thph. *Νόμοι* (fr. 7 Hager, *JP* vi 1876, 1–27). We now know from a new fragment that the trial of Chaerephilus was an example of the procedure, found in the second half of the fourth century, by which the Areopagus reported in an ἀπόφασις to the assembly and the assembly if it wished to pursue the matter elected κατήγοροι to prosecute in a δικαστήριον (*P. Oxy.* xxxiv 2686; the procedure is best known from the Harpalus affair, on which see especially Din. I. *Dem.* 4, 61; 50–1, 58–9, II. *Aristog.* 6; and Lipsius, *A.R.*, 801–2, Harrison, *L.A.*, ii. 105, Hansen, *op. cit.*, 39–40). The term καταχειροτονία is used of the assembly's vote following an ἀπόφασις (Din. II. *Aristog.* 20, cf. Harp., *loc. cit.*): Hansen therefore argues, I believe correctly, that καταχειροτονίαι in this passage are cases referred by the assembly to a δικαστήριον after an ἀπόφασις (*op. cit.*, 44).†

καὶ τὰς προβολάς: On προβολαί see 43. v with commentary: these were charges debated in the assembly, on which the assembly's vote had a purely advisory force; whether the vote was in his favour or not, the complainant was free to proceed further but was not obliged to do so. It is therefore at first sight surprising to find separate mention here of the thesmothetae's bringing προβολαί into court (cf. Rhodes, *A.B.*, 166 n. 1): however, D. XXI. *Mid.* shows that Demosthenes began his proceedings against Midias with a προβολή ἀδικεῖν τοῦτον περὶ τὴν ἑορτήν (§1); the festival in question was the

Great Dionysia (*ibid.*), a responsibility of the archon (56. iv); but Demosthenes' speech presupposes a trial under the presidency of one of the thesmothetae (§32) and on a charge distinct from βλαβή, αἰκεία, ὕβρις (§35) or ἀσεβεία (which would be handled by the basileus: 57. ii); cf. Lipsius, *A.R.*, 213. We should therefore assume that distinct rules did govern the bringing to court of cases initiated by προβολή; and the case of Midias makes it clear that προβολαί on festival charges as well as on the charges mentioned in 43. v were handled by the thesmothetae (contr. Harrison, *L.A.*, ii. 14, 62).

καὶ γραφὰς παρανόμων καὶ νόμον μὴ ἐπιτήδειον θεῖναι: The γραφὴ παρανόμων was a prosecution for illegally proposing a ψήφισμα of the boule or δῆμος, the γραφὴ νόμον μὴ ἐπιτήδειον θεῖναι a prosecution for illegally proposing a νόμος. See 45. iv with commentary; and, for the suspension of the γραφὴ παρανόμων in 411 and 404, 29. iv with commentary and p. 434.

καὶ προεδρικὴν καὶ ἐπιστατικήν: Harp. ῥητορικὴ γραφή, *L.S.* 299. 21, give that name to a suit against ῥήτορες and compare it with the γραφαὶ πρυτανική and ἐπιστατική; no other text mentions the γραφὴ προεδρική. These charges presumably concern offences in connection with the presidency of the boule and assembly (and nomothetae?). Nicias *ap.* T. VI. 14 tells 'the πρύτανις' not to be afraid to break the laws by letting the Athenians vote again on the Sicilian expedition; in the assembly which condemned the generals after Arginusae (34. i with commentary) some of the prytanes refused to put Callimachus' proposal to the vote, but all except Socrates acquiesced when they were threatened with the same fate as the generals (X. *H.* I. vii. 14–15: Socrates was not punished for his resistance); Hyp. II. *Phil.* was written for the prosecution (in a γραφὴ παρανόμων) of a man who had proposed to honour the board of proedri under whose presidency honours had been decreed for certain Macedonians. We have no contemporary evidence for these γραφαί as separate lawsuits, and the offences to which they applied could also be made the subject of an εἰσαγγελία μὴ χρῆσθαι τοῖς νόμοις (45. ii with commentary); but there are many overlaps in Athenian judicial procedure and we need not doubt that these suits existed. If the γραφὴ πρυτανική was concerned specifically with the prytanes as presiding committee of the boule and assembly, it will have been superseded by the γραφὴ προεδρική when the proedri were instituted (44. ii with commentary). Cf. Lipsius, *A.R.*, 71, 397, Harrison, *L.A.*, ii. 14.[53]

[53] M. H. Hansen, *The Sovereignty of the People's Court in Athens*, 25, suggests that ῥητορικὴ γραφή was another name for the γραφὴ παρανόμων; but if the ῥητορικὴ γραφή is after all to be identified with another process known to us it is perhaps better to think of the δοκιμασία τῶν ῥητόρων, on which see A. I. *Tim.* 28–32, 81, 186, with Lipsius, *A.R.*, 278–82, Harrison, *L.A.*, ii. 204–5.

καὶ στρατηγοῖς εὐθύνας: On εὔθυναι, strictly the non-financial side of the calling to account of retired officials, see 48. iv–v with commentary. It is not clear why *A.P.* refers here specifically to the generals: 48. v states of εὔθυναι in general that if the εὔθυνος found the charges proved he referred private suits to the Forty and public to the thesmothetae.

59. iii. ὧν παράστασις τίθεται: 'Suits in which a prosecutor's deposit is paid.' In many δίκαι fees known as πρυτανεῖα were demanded from both plaintiff and defendant, and afterwards the losing party had to reimburse the winning (Lipsius, *A.R.*, 824–7; Harrison, *L.A.*, ii. 92–4); in property suits against the state and in some if not all inheritance suits there was a plaintiff's deposit called παρακαταβολή (Lipsius, *A.R.*, 933–7, Harrison, *L.A.*, ii. 179–83); in many γραφαί the prosecutor had to pay a παράστασις, and although it is not confirmed by any text it is likely that this was refunded if his prosecution succeeded (Lipsius, *A.R.*, 827–8, Harrison, *L.A.*, ii. 94). Isae. III. *Her. Pyrrh.* 47 states that εἰσαγγελίαι κακώσεως (56. vi with commentary) are not subject either to πρυτανεῖα or to παράστασις; And. 1. *Myst.* 120 uses παράστασις in a context where the correct technical term should be παρακαταβολή. The term παράστασις is used also of fees paid to the διαιτηταί by the litigants in δίκαι which they adjudicated (Lipsius, *A.R.*, 231, Harrison, *L.A.*, ii. 67).

A.P.'s list of γραφαί is incomplete. We know of various γραφαί handled by the thesmothetae which are not mentioned in this chapter: Lipsius, *A.R.*, 72, and Harrison, *L.A.*, ii. 15–16, list δεκασμοῦ, ὕβρεως, ἑταιρήσεως, ἀδίκως εἰρχθῆναι ὡς μοιχόν, κλοπῆς, and Harrison adds ἀναπογράφου μετάλλου and διαφθείρειν τὸ νόμισμα. There is no evidence that a παράστασις was demanded in any of these γραφαί not mentioned by *A.P.*, but it is not obvious why those which he names should attract a παράστασις and those which he omits should not, and it is easier to believe that he has left one category incomplete than that he has given one in full and wholly omitted another.

Another omission may be noted at this point. 52. i *fin.* states that some ἐνδείξεις were handled by the thesmothetae (cf. *ad loc.*), but there is no reference to ἐνδείξεις in this chapter.

ξενίας: *L.R.C. ξενίας γραφὴ καὶ δωροξενίας* gives the obvious explanation: ξενίας μὲν ἐάν τις κατηγόρηται ξένος εἶναι, sc. when posing as a citizen. Although this is not one of the passages in which *A.P.* draws attention to a change (cf. Introduction, pp. 34–5), it appears that in the fifth century this suit was handled by officials styled ναυτοδίκαι (Crat. 342 F 4 and Ar. fr. 225 Kock *ap.* Harp. *s.v.*, Hes. [*N* 159] *s.v.*, Poll. VIII. 126, cf. Cratin. fr. 233 Kock): they must have been instituted for a purpose to which their name would be appropriate, and they are not concerned with the γραφὴ ξενίας in *IG* i² 41, 4–6 (revised text *IG* i³ 41, 90–2). We also find references in fifth- and fourth-century inscriptions to ξενοδίκαι:[54] there is no evidence that they were ever concerned with the γραφὴ ξενίας (against A. Koerte, *Hermes* lxviii 1933, 238–40, see Kahrstedt, *Klio* xxxii 1939, 148–55, Jacoby, *Supp.* ii. 380–1 n. 29). See Lipsius, *A.R.*, 416–17, and, on the ναυτοδίκαι, 86–8, Harrison, *L.A.*, ii. 23–4, E. E. Cohen, *Ancient Athenian Maritime Courts*, 162–76; for the ναυτοδίκαι and δίκαι ἐμπορικαί in the early fourth century see on §v, below.

καὶ δωροξενίας, ἄν τις δῶρα δοὺς ἀποφύγῃ τὴν ξενίαν: That is, if any one charged in a γραφὴ ξενίας corruptly secures his acquittal.

καὶ συκοφαντίας: συκοφαντίας and δώρων are missing from the list in Harp. παράστασις but included in other lexicographers' lists. On sycophants see 35. ii with commentary, and for προβολαί against sycophants 43. v with commentary. Is. xv. *Antid.* 314 remarks that proceedings may be taken against sycophants by γραφή to the thesmothetae, by εἰσαγγελία to the boule or by προβολή in the assembly. On the γραφὴ συκοφαντίας see Lipsius, *A.R.*, 448–51.

καὶ δώρων: Bribery likewise could be dealt with by more than one procedure: by εἰσαγγελία for a major offence against the state (43. iv with commentary), perhaps by εἰσαγγελία μὴ χρῆσθαι τοῖς νόμοις (45. ii with commentary), in the λόγος submitted by an official on retirement from office (54. ii with commentary), or by γραφή, whether δωροξενίας (cf. above) or δεκασμοῦ (not mentioned by *A.P.*) or δώρων. According to Poll. viii. 42 the γραφὴ δώρων was aimed at receivers of bribes and the γραφὴ δεκασμοῦ at givers, which seems to be confirmed by the law *ap.* [D.] xlvi. *Steph. ii.* 26; according to *L.S.* 237. 3 the γραφὴ δώρων was aimed at both, which seems to be confirmed by D. xxi. *Mid.* 104–7. δεκάζειν is found particularly with jurors as object (cf. on 27. v), and the likeliest explanation is that after the institution of the γραφὴ δώρων a separate γραφὴ δεκασμοῦ was created with a more limited scope. See Lipsius, *A.R.*, 401–4.

καὶ ψευδεγγραφῆς: A charge of falsely entering a man's name on the list of public debtors (Harp. *s.v.*, Suid. [Ψ 46–7] *s.v.* and ψευδέγγραφος δίκη, Poll. viii. 43). See Lipsius, *A.R.*, 443–6, and cf. below on βουλεύσεως and ἀγραφίου.

καὶ ψευδοκλητείας: To initiate most kinds of lawsuit the prosecutor in the presence of witnesses summoned the defendant to appear before the relevant authority; the γραφὴ ψευδοκλητείας was a prosecution for falsely appearing as witness to such a summons (Poll. viii. 44; Harp. *s.v.* and *L.S.* 317. 3, misunderstanding [D.] liii. *Nicostr.* 15, wrongly limited it to cases concerning public debtors). See Lipsius, *A.R.*, 446–8, 804–7, Harrison, *L.A.*, ii. 85–6.

---

[54] It is arguable that all fourth-century instances are non-Athenian: LSJ ξενοδίκης, P. Gauthier, *Symbola*, 167, 192.

καὶ βουλεύσεως: This charge and the next, like ψευδεγγραφῆς (cf. above), are concerned with the registration of public debtors. This charge is one of failure to delete a discharged debtor from the list (*IG* ii[2] 1631, 385–98); Harp., Suid. (*B* 429), *s.v.*, *L.S.* 220. 11 and Poll. VIII. 43 apply the term to false registration, but have no support except in [D.] XXV. *Aristog. i.* 28, 71–3, a speech which is suspect partly because it includes unconfirmed details of this kind (cf., briefly, D. F. Jackson & G. O. Rowe, *Lustrum* xiv 1969, 74). See Lipsius, *A.R.*, 443–6.

It is not clear why this offence should be termed βούλευσις: in 57. iii the word is used of planning to kill when the deed is performed by someone other than the planner; in Hyp. III. *Ath.* 18 it is used of similar planning in relation to property.

καὶ ἀγραφίου: According to [D.] LVIII. *Theocr.* 51–2 this is the proper procedure in cases where a debtor has been registered but is deleted without having discharged the debt, whereas the proper procedure in cases where a debtor has not been registered is ἔνδειξις; but from its name we should expect this suit to be available in cases of the second kind, and Lipsius argues that it was available in cases of both kinds. See Lipsius, *A.R.*, 410–12.

καὶ μοιχείας: Before these words Harp. ἡγεμονία δικαστηρίου and some other entries in the lexica have καὶ ὕβρεως, which some scholars have wanted to insert here (e.g. Kaibel, *Stil und Text*, 246); but *A.P.*'s list of γραφαί is certainly incomplete (cf. above, p. 661), and I doubt if insertion is justified. μοιχεία was probably limited originally to violation of the marriage tie by having intercourse with a man's wife, but the concept was extended to cover intercourse with other free women in a man's household, including concubines kept for the purpose of bearing free children (on whom see p. 331). Such an adulterer might be killed ἐπ' αὐτοφώρῳ (cf. 57. iii with commentary), or the wronged *paterfamilias* could proceed in a γραφὴ μοιχείας, or in a γραφὴ ὕβρεως or a δίκη βιαίων (the second certainly not mentioned by *A.P.*). See Lipsius, *A.R.*, 429–34, Harrison, *L.A.*, i. 32–6.

59. iv. εἰσάγουσιν δὲ καὶ τὰς δοκιμασίας ταῖς ἀρχαῖς ἁπάσαις: The δοκιμασία of bouleutae was conducted in the boule, with ἔφεσις to a δικαστήριον (45. iii with commentary); the δοκιμασία of the archons was conducted in two stages, the first in the boule and the second in a δικαστήριον (45. iii, 55. ii–iv, with commentary); the δοκιμασίαι of other ἀρχαί were conducted in a δικαστήριον (cf. 55. ii). Various δοκιμασίαι other than those of the ἀρχαί were handled by the boule alone (49. i–iv with commentary).

καὶ τοὺς ἀπεψηφισμένους ὑπὸ τῶν δημοτῶν: Cf. 42. i with commentary.

καὶ τὰς καταγνώσεις τὰς ἐκ τῆς βουλῆς: M. H. Hansen, *Eisangelia*, 14–22, believes this to refer solely to 'εἰσαγγελίαι to the boule' (cf. on 45. ii). I believe that it refers to all cases remitted by the boule to a δικαστήριον for a penalty beyond its own competence: εἰσαγγελίαι on charges of major public offences when they came by that route to a δικαστήριον, εἰσαγγελίαι μὴ χρῆσθαι τοῖς νόμοις, and any other trials in which the boule acted as a court of first instance (see 43. iv, 45. i–ii, with commentary, and Rhodes, *JHS* xcix 1979, 107, 111 n. 73).

Timocrates' *habeas corpus* law *ap.* D. xxiv. *Tim.* 63 provides that if men have been imprisoned by the boule on an εἰσαγγελία and the secretary has not transmitted the boule's κατάγνωσις to the thesmothetae, the Eleven are to εἰσάγειν . . . εἰς τὸ δικαστήριον within thirty days of receiving them into custody. This passage in *A.P.*, and that law's assumption that the boule's καταγνώσεις are normally reported to the thesmothetae, lead us to expect that the thesmothetae would act as εἰσάγουσα ἀρχή: perhaps Timocrates' language is condensed, and he meant that, when the boule failed to initiate the process by which the thesmothetae brought the accused to a trial in court, the Eleven were to initiate the process instead.

59. v. δίκας ἰδίας, ἐμπορικάς: For the use of ἰδίας to emphasise that δίκας is being used in its narrower sense cf. 58. ii with commentary. δίκαι ἐμπορικαί were available τοῖς ναυκλήροις καὶ τοῖς ἐμπόροις τῶν Ἀθήναζε καὶ τῶν Ἀθήνηθεν συμβολαίων, καὶ περὶ ὧν ἂν ὦσι συγγραφαί (D. xxxii. *Zen.* 1, cf. [D.] xxxiii. *Apat.* 1, xxxiv. *Phorm.* 42): the suit must concern trade to or from Athens, and there must be a written contract (that both requirements must be satisfied is argued by E. E. Cohen, *Ancient Athenian Maritime Courts*, 100–14, I believe correctly; that one or other must be satisfied, by L. Gernet, *REG* li 1938, 22–4 = *Droit et société dans la Grèce ancienne*, 186–7); but probably it was assumed that whenever these conditions were satisfied at least one party to the suit would be a ναύκληρος or ἔμπορος, and there was not a separate requirement that one of the litigants must fit that description (Cohen, *op. cit.*, 114–29, contr. Gernet, *opp. citt.*, 20–1 = 185–6, S. Isager & M. H. Hansen, *Aspects of Athenian Society in the Fourth Century B.C.*, 86). Plaintiffs in such cases were not obliged to resort to Athenian law: if the defendant was domiciled elsewhere it might well be preferable to sue in the town where the dispute arose or in the defendant's home town, under the laws of that town, where the judgment could be executed more easily (cf. G. E. M. de Ste. Croix, CQ^2 xi 1961, 110). These suits were available to all men, whether citizens, metics or of no standing in Athens (e.g. D. xxi. *Mid.* 176); the plaintiff could require the defendant to present guarantors before the polemarch (e.g. D.

XXXII. *Zen.* 29: cf. p. 655), and defeated litigants could be kept under arrest until their debt was discharged, since they might have no property in Athens which could be taken as security (e.g. [D.] XXXIII. *Apat.* 1, xxxv. *Lacr.* 46–7). Cohen argues from the flattering remarks addressed to the jurors in a δίκη ἐμπορική in [D.] xxxv. *Lacr.* 43, 46, that jurors for these suits were not appointed by the random process described in *A.P.* 63–5 but were picked from men with relevant experience (*op. cit.*, 93–5, cf. Thalheim, *RE*, v [1905], 2531). We do find juries of Eleusinian initiates in And. 1. *Myst.* 28, 31, and of soldiers in Lys. XIV. *Alc. i.* 5, but here the orator's flattery is not unintelligible except on that assumption, and no other evidence suggests that in δίκαι ἐμπορικαί jurors were drawn from a special panel (cf. Lipsius, *A.R.*, 143 n. 31, Gernet, Budé ed. of D.'s *Plaidoyers civils*, i. 194 n. 2, P. Gauthier, *Symbola*, 190 with n. 44).

These were 'monthly' suits: [D.] XXXIII. *Apat.* 23 will mean that δίκαι ἐμπορικαί could be initiated each month during the winter, so that they could be settled outside the sailing season (cf. 52. ii with commentary, where [D.] is quoted, Cohen, *op. cit.*, 9–59). Early in the fourth century the ναυτοδίκαι (for whom cf. on §iii) had jurisdiction in some cases concerning ἔμποροι (Lys. XVII. *Publ. Ini.* 5). X. *Vect.* iii. 3 (*c.* 355) recommends the establishment of a rapid procedure for commercial suits, while the term δίκη ἐμπορική is found in D. XXI. *Mid.* 176 (?347/6, referring to the recent past), and [D.] VII. *Halon.* 12 (343/2) refers to a time when ἐμπορικαὶ δίκαι οὐκ ἦσαν, ὥσπερ νῦν, ἀκριβεῖς, αἱ κατὰ μῆνα: 'monthly' δίκαι ἐμπορικαί were therefore instituted between *c.* 355 and 343/2. In the second half of the fourth century most 'monthly' suits were handled by a board of five εἰσαγωγεῖς, and Poll. VIII. 101 includes δίκαι ἐμπορικαί in that category, but contemporary speeches show that at any rate for his own time *A.P.* is right to assign these suits to the thesmothetae: it is usually and probably rightly assumed that Pollux is simply mistaken, but Cohen argues that δίκαι ἐμπορικαί were for a short time the responsibility of the εἰσαγωγεῖς before being transferred to the thesmothetae (*op. cit.*, 158–98: see 52. ii with commentary).

καὶ μεταλλικάς: Our only other evidence for δίκαι μεταλλικαί is in D. XXXVII. *Pant.* The speech confirms that these suits fell to the thesmothetae (§34) and shows that they too were 'monthly' (§2), and specifies four wrongs which could be made the subject of a δίκη μεταλλική: ejection of a man from his concession, sending smoke into his concession, making an armed attack on it, or encroaching on it when mining another concession (§§35–6).

καὶ δούλων, ἄν τις τὸν ἐλεύθερον κακῶς λέγει: That is, δίκαι κακηγορίας in which a slave was charged with maligning a free man. Other δίκαι κακηγορίας followed the normal procedure for δίκαι (ch. 53 with commentary), and went to the Forty and the διαιτηταί (cf. D. XXI.

Mid. 81 with 83). Why the procedure should have been different in these cases is not clear: Wilamowitz suggested that it was a survival from the archaic state, due to the need to require a master to answer for his slaves (*A.u.A.*, i. 245), but that does not explain why a special procedure should have been used for this charge. See Lipsius, *A.R.*, 627–8.

καὶ ἐπικληροῦσι ... τὰ ἴδια καὶ τὰ δημόσια: (τά ⟨τ'⟩ ἴδια, first suggested by Kaibel, *Stil und Text*, 247, may be right.) Since the allocation of jurors to courts was presided over not by the thesmothetae alone but by the nine archons and the secretary to the thesmothetae, and is to be mentioned in §vii, this sentence is to be read as a reiteration of what was stated in §i, that the thesmothetae assign courts to particular officials on particular days, with the added information that they do so by a form of allotment. The sentence interrupts the list of δίκαι handled by the thesmothetae: Kaibel & Wilamowitz[1-2] deleted it; Kaibel, *Stil und Text*, 247–8, regarded it as a sign of *A.P.*'s unfinished state. I find this duplication more embarrassing than that of §vii (cf. *ad loc.*) and 63. i, and similar duplications, but there is no obvious reason why an interpolation should have been made here. *A.P.* specifies τὰ δικαστήρια τὰ ἴδια καὶ τὰ δήμοσια: the only procedural differences between δίκαι which came to a court and γραφαί are that γραφαί were tried by larger juries (53. iii, 68. i, with commentary), and that on any day only one of these two kinds of case was tried and a court would try only one γραφή in the day but several δίκαι (66. i, 67. i, with commentary).

59. vi. καὶ τὰ σύμβολα τὰ πρὸς τὰς πόλεις οὗτοι κυροῦσι: σύμβολα are the complementary parts of a tally retained by the parties to an agreement, and by extension the agreement itself, in particular one between states on the means of resolving disputes between their citizens (LSJ *s.v.*, II. 3: cf. Harp. *s.v.*). Such agreements need not be confined to trading matters (see especially *SEG* xvii 17–20 with G. E. M. de Ste. Croix, *CQ*[2] xi 1961, 101–4, 108–10); it appears from [D.] VII. *Halon.* 9, *IG* ii[2] 466, 32–5, that in Athens they had to be ratified in a δικαστήριον (under the presidency of one of the thesmothetae). See in general P. Gauthier, *Symbola*: in 62–104 he attempts to distinguish between the kinds of agreement denoted by συμβολαί and σύμβολα (but see D. M. Lewis, *CR*[2] xxv 1975, 262–3); in 157–205 he discusses Athenian συμβολαί and σύμβολα.

Arist. *Pol.* III. 1275 A 8–11 remarks that access to the courts of a city is not a sufficient criterion of citizenship; τοῦτο γὰρ ὑπάρχει καὶ τοῖς ἀπὸ συμβόλων κοινωνοῦσιν. 1280 A 34–B 5 points out that the existence of σύμβολα between states does not make them into a single state. Presumably when σύμβολα were made it was thought advantageous to the citizens of the participating states to make them; but although his rights were more secure if he was a metic or could rely on σύμβολα (and strictly he may not otherwise have had rights) it may not have been the case that otherwise a non-citizen would be refused access to Athenian courts (cf. pp. 654-5).

καὶ τὰς δίκας τὰς ἀπὸ τῶν συμβόλων εἰσάγουσι: The term presumably includes γραφαί as well as δίκαι ἴδιαι (cf. Ste. Croix, *op. cit.*, 94 with n. 3). Probably these cases were handled by the thesmothetae because they, as the officials responsible for ratifying σύμβολα, would be best placed to confirm that σύμβολα relevant to the intended lawsuit existed, as the polemarch handled the lawsuits concerning metics and privileged foreigners because he was best placed to confirm their legal standing (58. ii with commentary). Ste. Croix has argued that δίκαι ἀπὸ συμβόλων would be tried in Athens when the defendant was an Athenian citizen or metic, so that the judgment could easily be executed if the court found for the plaintiff (*op. cit.*, 105-6): but Gauthier has shown that a likelier principle is that the case should be tried in the city where the dispute arose (most commonly, in practice, the city where the defendant was resident: *Symbola*, 174-83, cf. R. J. Seager, *Hist.* xv 1966, 509-10).

There has been much discussion of a passage in Athens' fifth-century decree for Phaselis, which provides that 'whatever cause of action arises at Athens involving a Phaselite, the case shall be tried at Athens, in the polemarch's court; ... other cases shall be tried ἀπὸ ξυμβολῶν according to the existing ξυμβολαί with Phaselis' (M&L 31, 6-14), and of the Athenians' claim in a speech in Thucydides that they were ἐλασσούμενοι ... ἐν ταῖς ξυμβολαίαις πρὸς τοὺς ξυμμάχους δίκαις (i. 77. i). See especially Ste. Croix, *op. cit.*, 95-112: trial of the first category of Phaselite cases at the polemarch's court is a privilege, perhaps providing for quicker decisions (cf. above, p. 655); and the Athenians claimed to be ἐλασσούμενοι in that they submitted to judicial decisions which might go against them when they could simply have enforced their own will (*op. cit.*, 96-100).

The thesmothetae were involved likewise when a lawsuit was transferred to Athens from a member state of the Delian League (e.g. M&L 52, 71-6). In the fourth century the fragmentary agreement with Troezen, *IG* ii² 46, several times refers to the nine archons, always *in rasura* (A. G. Woodhead, *Hesp.* xxvi 1957, 225-9, D. M. Lewis, *Hesp.* xxviii 1959, 248-50), and in line 63 refers to the θε[σμοθετεῖον] (Lewis, *op. cit.*, 249, correcting *IG*); Tod 142 does not state which Athenian magistrates were involved when a lawsuit was transferred to Athens from Ceos; but the thesmothetae are mentioned in the fragmentary agreement with Naxos, *IG* ii² 179, *a* 10, 17.

καὶ τὰ ψευδομαρτύρια <τὰ> ἐξ Ἀρείου πάγου: Poll. viii. 88 reads καὶ τὰς τῶν ψευδομαρτυρίων τῶν ἐξ Ἀρείου πάγου. The papyrus' reading was retained by Kenyon[1-3], Thalheim and Oppermann; τὰ was inserted by Γ. Βερναδάκης ('Επιστολὴ περὶ τῆς Π. Α. τοῦ Ἀριστοτέλους), Kaibel & Wilamowitz and others, probably rightly; Κ. Σ. Κόντος, Ἀθ. iv 1892, 172, wanted to restore *A.P.* to complete conformity with Pollux, and Blass[4] printed τὰς ψευδομαρτυρίων ⟨τῶν⟩.

On the δίκη ψευδομαρτυρίων see Lipsius, *A.R.*, 778–83, Harrison, *L.A.*, ii. 127–31, 192–7, and 68. iv with commentary (there is no good Attic evidence for the feminine ψευδομαρτυρία). According to Arist. *Pol.* II. 1274 B 5–7 perjury was first treated as a ground for action by the Sicilian Charondas. Normally a charge of perjury would be handled by the same magistrate as the original lawsuit (but, as pointed out by Harrison, *L.A.*, ii. 46, it is hard to imagine that it could be tried by the same body of jurors as the original lawsuit unless the two trials were held on the same day, and that could hardly be contrived); there is no obvious reason why, when the original court was the Areopagus (and the εἰσάγουσα ἀρχή was the basileus), charges of perjury should have been handled by the thesmothetae.

59. vii. τοὺς δὲ δικαστὰς κληροῦσι πάντες ... τῆς αὐτοῦ φυλῆς ἕκαστος: Where subdivision by tribes is appropriate the secretary to the thesmothetae is combined with the nine archons to produce a standard college of ten. The fact stated here is repeated in 63. i, at the beginning of *A.P.*'s account of the organisation of the δικαστήρια (cf. *ad loc.*). Kaibel & Wilamowitz[1-2] deleted this section (cf. Kaibel, *Stil und Text*, 247–8); but I find this duplication less embarrassing than that of §§i and v above. Kaibel commented that here *A.P.* is concerned with the thesmothetae, not with the whole college of archons, but this is unfair: 55–56. i dealt with the appointment of the whole college, 56. ii–59. vi dealt with the different duties of the different archons, ending with the thesmothetae, and here *A.P.* concludes his account of the archons with a duty common to all of them; it is as natural that this should be mentioned in two contexts as that the δοκιμασία of the archons should be mentioned in connection with the boule's δοκιμασίαι in 45. iii and in connection with the archons in 55. ii–iv, or that ἐπιχειροτονίαι should be mentioned as part of the assembly's regular business in 43. vi and in connection with the generals in 61. ii. A text of *A.P.* which included this sentence seems to underlie schol. Ar. *Vesp.* 775 and, as noticed by Kaibel, Poll. VIII. 87.

P. *The Athlothetae* (60)

In 43. ii–59 *A.P.* has dealt with the boule (which was appointed by lot and served for a year), the nine archons (who were appointed by lot and served for a year) and other sortitive annual officials. Before concluding his section on the ἀρχαί he deals in this chapter with the athlothetae, who were appointed by lot but served for four years, and in the next with the military officials, who served for one year but were elected (on the omission of elected civilian officials see p. 677). In the course of his discussion of the athlothetae he digresses to deal with the collection and storage of the sacred olive oil, and from that to deal with the prizes awarded in the different contests at the Panathenaea.

60. i. τὰ μὲν οὖν ... τοῦτον ἔχει τὸν τρόπον: *A.P.* concludes the section on the archons, begun in 55. i, ...
κληροῦσι δὲ καὶ ἀθλοθέτας ... τῆς φυλῆς ἑκάστης: ... and moves on to deal with the athlothetae. The subject to be understood with κληροῦσι is οἱ Ἀθηναῖοι, as in 51. iv–54. iii, 54. viii; but Poll. VIII. 87 wrongly supposed *A.P.* to mean here that the archons appointed the athlothetae and in 61 that the archons appointed the military officials (cf. Wilamowitz, *A.u.A.*, i. 295–6, Kaibel, *Stil und Text*, 248 n. 1; but J. A. Davison, *JHS* lxxviii 1958, 31 = *From Archilochus to Pindar*, 44, was attracted by Pollux' interpretation).
οὗτοι δὲ δοκιμασθέντες ἄρχουσι τέτταρα ἔτη: All allotted and elected officials had to undergo a δοκιμασία before entering on their office (55. ii): no doubt here *A.P.* is transmitting a statement which he found in the law about the athlothetae. The Panathenaea was celebrated annually in Hecatombaeon (i) (cf. 62. ii), but more elaborately, as the Great Panathenaea, in the third year of each Olympiad (cf. on 54. vii). Since the principal responsibility of the athlothetae was for the Great Panathenaea (cf. below), we should expect that festival to fall towards the end of their term of office (cf. Davison, *locc. citt.*), but how their term of office was defined remains unknown. We are not much helped by payments ἀθλοθέταις ἐς Παναθέναια in the second prytany of 415/4 (M&L 77, 66–8: the suggestion of Davison, *opp. citt.*, 31–3 = 45–7, that this represents an advance payment towards the Great Panathenaea of 414/3, has not found favour), and ἀθλοθέταις ... ἐς Παναθέναια τὰ μεγάλα in the second prytany of 410/09 (M&L 84, 5–6).[55]
καὶ διοικοῦσι τήν τε πομπὴν τῶν Παναθηναίων: On the Panathenaea in general see A. Mommsen, *Feste der Stadt Athen*, 41–159 (contests

---

[55] It has commonly been assumed, e.g. by B. D. Meritt, *The Athenian Calendar*, 93–5, K. J. Dover in Gomme *et al.*, *Hist. Comm. Thuc.*, iv. 266, that payments for a festival were made before the festival; but W. K. Pritchett, *Hist.* xxvi 1977, 295–306, is surely right to suggest at any rate as an alternative possibility that payments were made shortly after the festival, to balance the books. On the implications of this for the restoration of the full democracy in 410 see p. 415.

60. i] COMMENTARY ON THE *ATH. POL.*

61–106), L. Deubner, *Attische Feste*, 22–35 (not discussing the contests), H. A. Thompson, *AA* 1961, 224–31, H. W. Parke, *Festivals of the Athenians*, 33–50. There was a procession at the Lesser Panathenaea as well as the Great, but at this time it was only at the Great that a new πέπλος was taken in procession and given to the priestess of Athena to clothe the cult statue (cf. Deubner, *op. cit.*, 25, and above, p. 568; the procession at the Lesser Panathenaea is mentioned in *IG* ii² 334, 2–5, 33–4). It is normally believed that it was the procession at the Great Panathenaea that was depicted on the frieze of the Parthenon; on the problems see most recently J. Boardman, *Festschrift für F. Brommer*, 39–49, who suggests that the frieze shows 'the fighters of Marathon celebrating the prime festival of their goddess' (44). The title of the athlothetae suggests that their original duty was to organise the contests (most of which took place at the Great Panathenaea only); when the Lesser Panathenaea was reorganised in the 330's the procession at that festival was the responsibility of ἱεροποιοί (*IG* ii² 334, 31–5); and we may guess that originally hieropoei had overall control of the Great Panathenaea, with the athlothetae responsible simply for the contests (cf. Davison, *opp. citt.*, 29–33 = 41–8; but if the payment in M&L 77 is for the Lesser Panathenaea an account is needed which allows the athlothetae some part in that festival). A. E. Raubitschek combined *IG* i² 463 + 475 as a commemoration of the hieropoei responsible for the first Great Panathenaea and its contests in 566/5 (*Dedications from the Athenian Akropolis*, 326, cf. L. H. Jeffery, *Local Scripts of Archaic Greece*, 72, 77, no. 18; cf. also *Dedications*, 327, 328). B. Nagy, *GR&BS* xix 1978, 307–13, notes that *IG* ii² 784, 7–11, and 1036 + 1060 show the athlothetae still existing, and performing the same duties (at both the Great and the Lesser Panathenaea) in the Hellenistic period.

καὶ τὸν ἀγῶνα τῆς μουσικῆς: Pl. *Per.* 13. ix–xi ascribes to Pericles the building of the Odeum (to the south-east of the Acropolis: Travlos, *Pictorial Dictionary*, 387–91), and the institution of musical contests at the Panathenaea, for which he prescribed the rules, ἀθλοθέτης αἱρεθείς. On the other hand, Vitruv. v. 9. i, which may be supported by Hes. ᾠδεῖον, Suid. (Π 2230) Πρατίνας, says that Themistocles 'roofed' the Odeum; and Panathenaic amphorae and literary texts suggest that musical contests were in fact held from *c.* 560 (cf. the texts which may indicate that the festival was organised in 566/5: Marc. *Vit. Thuc.* 2–4, Euseb. Arm. 188 Karst, Hieron. 102b Helm, discussed by T. J. Cadoux, *JHS* lxviii 1948, 104, Davison, *opp. citt.*, 26–9 = 35–41); but there is no evidence for the period from *c.* 470 to *c.* 450. This gap in the evidence might be fortuitous; but Davison suggests that musical contests were introduced and the first Odeum built in the sixth century; the Odeum was roofed by Themistocles shortly after the Persian Wars; soon after that the use of the Odeum, and perhaps the musical contests, were discontinued; and about the middle of the fifth century Pericles was responsible for the rebuilding of the Odeum and the revival of the musical contests in it (*opp. citt.*, 33–42 = 48–66, *JHS* lxxxii 1962, 141–2 = *From Archilochus to Pindar*, 66–9). Various kinds of musical contest and the prizes awarded for them are listed in *IG* ii² 2311, 1–22 (first half c4).

καὶ τὸν γυμνικὸν ἀγῶνα: The athletic contests are associated with the sixth-century organisation of the festival by Eusebius (*cit. supr.*), and attested by Panathenaic amphorae for the earliest of which a date *c.* 560 is acceptable (Davison, *opp. citt.*, 26–8 = 35–8, J. Boardman, *Athenian Black Figure Vases*, 167–8). These contests and their prizes are listed in *IG* ii² 2311, 23–50 (cf. 2312–17). Earlier they were held in the Agora (Thompson, *AA* 1961, 227); but in the time of *A.P.* they were held in the stadium east of the city, beyond the Ilissus (cf. Travlos, *Pictorial Dictionary*, 498–504), whose building is mentioned in a decree of Lycurgus, Tod 198 (330/29), and ascribed to Lycurgus by [Pl.] *X. Or.* 841 D, decree *ap.* 852 C = *IG* ii² 457, *b* 7–8. In the first half of the third century the honours conferred on Phaedrus Σφήττιος were to be proclaimed at the Dionysia and Παναθηναίων τῶν μεγάλων τῶι γυμνικῶι ἀγῶνι (*IG* ii² 682, 75–8).

καὶ τὴν ἱπποδρομίαν: Horse races at the Panathenaea are again attested by Panathenaic amphorae from *c.* 560 (cf. Davison and Boardman, *locc. citt.*), and are mentioned in X. *Symp.* i. 2. These races and their prizes are listed in *IG* ii² 2311, 51–70 (cf. 2313–17). The races were held at Echelidae, in the deme of Xypete at the mouth of the Cephisus (*E.M.* [340. 53] ἐν Ἐχελιδῶ⟨ν⟩, cf. W. Judeich, *Topographie von Athen*², 456, J. S. Traill, *Hesp.* Supp. xiv 1975, 87, 114; but S. Benton, *BSA* lxviii 1972, 13–19, argues that the hippodrome was north of the city, below and to the east of Colonus ἵππιος).

There were other contests at the Panathenaea, in addition to those mentioned here: one in εὐανδρία, mentioned at the end of this chapter (cf. *ad loc.*), three in the war-dance called πυρρίχη (*IG* ii² 2311, 72–4), a torch-race (*ibid.* 77: cf. on 57. i), and a contest for ships (*ibid.* 78); Lys. xxi. *Pec. Acc.* 2, 4, refers to χορηγίαι for a 'cyclic' chorus and the πυρρίχη at the Lesser Panathenaea. Since εὐανδρία appears in §iii some have inserted it here (before καὶ τὴν ἱπποδρομίαν, Π. Ν. Παπαγεώργιος, Ἀθ. iv 1892, 610; after μουσικῆς, A. A. Sakellarios, *Untersuchung des Textes der A. Π. des Aristoteles*, 25–6), but that would still not give us a complete list of contests, and we must accept that *A.P.* has been selective.

καὶ τὸν πέπλον ποιοῦνται: The actual weaving was done by ἐργαστῖναι under the direction of two of the four ἀρρηφόροι; παραδείγματα for the πέπλος had in the past been judged by the boule but in the time of

A.P. were judged by a δικαστήριον (49. iii with commentary). The athlothetae presumably supervised the work.

καὶ τοὺς ἀμφορεῖς ποιοῦνται μετὰ τῆς βουλῆς: Cf. 49. iii with commentary: the boule... τῶν ἄθλων τῶν εἰς τὰ Παναθήναια συνεπιμελεῖται μετὰ τοῦ ταμίου τῶν στρατιωτικῶν. Some have deleted the repeated ποιοῦνται (e.g. Kaibel & Wilamowitz, cf. Kaibel, *Stil und Text*, 205-6), but the repetition is necessary to make it clear that the boule shared in the responsibility for the amphorae but not for the πέπλος (Blass, disbelieved by Kaibel).

The prizes for the athletic and equestrian contests took the form of olive oil (§iii *fin.* with commentary), supplied in distinctive amphorae for which by *c.* 530 a particular shape and style of black-figure decoration had become standard, which persisted to the second century although for other purposes black-figure vase painting had long since been abandoned: one side of the vase features Athena between columns supporting cocks, and by the left-hand column is the inscription τῶν Ἀθένεθεν ἄθλον; the other side features an event from the games; there are also 'souvenir' vases which resemble but do not precisely follow the standard pattern (see Boardman, *Athenian Black Figure Vases*, 167-77). The contract for making the vases seems to have been awarded by competition (*IG* ii[2] 6320 with T. B. L. Webster, *Potter and Patron in Classical Athens*, 11).†

καὶ τὸ ἔλαιον τοῖς ἀθληταῖς ἀποδιδόασι: Presumably, they present the oil to the victorious contestants (cf. Mathieu & Haussoullier). The same fact is stated more clearly in §iii, at the end of the digression which starts at the beginning of §ii, in which *A.P.* explains how the oil finds its way to the athlothetae.

60. ii. συλλέγεται δὲ τὸ ἔλαιον ἀπὸ τῶν μοριῶν: The papyrus has σ(υλ)λέγεται τοδ' ἔλαιον· δὲ τό, suggested by H. Richards (*CR* v 1891, 229) and others, is generally accepted; τὸ δ' ἔλαιον συλλέγεται, suggested by R. D. Hicks (*CR* v 1891, 118), was preferred by Kaibel & Wilamowitz[2-3]; Kaibel, *Stil und Text*, 248, judged either acceptable, but Richards' is the neater solution. The sacred olives from which oil for the Panathenaea was taken were regularly known as μορίαι (cf. Ar. *Nub.* 1005 with schol., Lys. vii. *Ol.* 7, Suid. [*M* 1248] *s.v.*).

εἰσπράττει... τρί' ἡμικοτύλια ἀπὸ τοῦ στελέχους ἑκάστου: '... 1½ κοτύλαι from each root' (Kenyon[1] remarked that the papyrus has τρι, 'as if the writer intended to make one word of it, τριημικοτύλιον'; that form is found in *IG* i[2] 842, *D* = i[3] 246, 8-15 [in the British Museum], and Kaibel & Wilamowitz[1-2] emended to it). The Athenian κοτύλη was 267-300 c.c., about half an imperial pint (M. L. Lang [& M. Crosby], *The Athenian Agora*, x. 41-8). στέλεχος means 'root', and

COMMENTARY ON THE *ATH. POL.* [60. ii

so 'plant' as a whole (not brought out clearly in LSJ): cf. [D.] XLIII. *Mac.* 69. Olives which were designated sacred, supposed to be offshoots of the tree planted by Athena on the Acropolis, were to be found throughout Attica; whoever acquired the land on which the tree grew acquired with it the obligation attached to the tree, and dead stumps had to be preserved in case they might revive as the stump on the Acropolis was said to have revived in 480 (H. VIII. 55). We read below that in the time of *A.P.* the oil was not collected specifically from the sacred olives, but was a general charge on the estates where sacred olives grew. This duty of the archon was not mentioned among his religious responsibilities in 56. iii–v.†
πρότερον δ' ἐπώλει τὸν καρπὸν ἡ πόλις: The contrast between earlier and current practice which *A.P.* does make clear is that earlier the oil had to come specifically from the sacred olives but in his time it no longer did. This clause has normally been taken to mean that earlier, although the sacred olives grew on private ground, public officials collected the crop and sold whatever was surplus to the requirements of the Panathenaea (e.g. Kenyon); but it is better to take it as the counterpart of εἰσπράττει ... ὁ ἄρχων, meaning that earlier the right to collect the oil was farmed like a tax but in *A.P.*'s time the collection was made directly by the archon (Gernet & Bizos on τοὺς ἐωνημένους τοὺς καρποὺς τῶν μοριῶν, in Lys. VII. *Ol.* 2: cf. the use of πωλεῖν in 47. ii, with commentary). According to that speech, replying to an allegation of an offence committed in 397/6 (§11) and brought to trial some time afterwards (§42), the Areopagus ἐπιμελεῖται each month and sends ἐπιγνώμονες each year (§25, cf. §§7, 29; ἐπιγνώμονας Harp. *s.v.*, γνώμονας *codd.*); there is no sign of the archon's being involved in the collection of the olive oil.
καὶ εἴ τις ἐξορύξειεν ἐλαίαν μορίαν ... θαν[ά]τῳ τοῦτον ἐζημίουν: The verb used in the charge answered in Lys. VII. *Ol.* seems to have been ἀφανίζειν (§§2, 11, 22, 26, 29); in §26 ἐξορύττειν is used in a parenthesis by the speaker; in §11 ἐκκόπτειν is used. Herwerden & Leeuwen and Blass[4] preferred the spelling ἐλάαν (cf. Ar. *Ach.* 550, *Pax*, 578, Lys. VII. *Ol.* 7, 29, Plat. *Rep.* II. 372 C 5, D. XVIII. *Cor.* 262 [reading of S]; in Ar. *Av.* 617 and [D.] XLIII. *Mac.* 69–70 editors restore the form without iota): ἐλαίαν is found in Soph. *O.C.* 701; but ἐλάα is the normal form in Athenian inscriptions (Meisterhans & Schwyzer, *G.a.I.*, 31 with n. 158) and should be restored here. For the use together of ἐλάαν and μορίαν cf. Lys., *locc. citt.* It appears from Lys. VII. *Ol.* 3, 32, 41, that at the beginning of the fourth century the penalty was no longer death but exile and confiscation of property, and from §§25, 29, that there were lesser penalties for encroaching by cultivating the land too near to one of the sacred olives.

673

60. ii] COMMENTARY ON THE *ATH. POL.*

ἐξ οὗ δὲ τὸ ἔλαιον ... ἡ δὲ κρίσις καταλέλυται: 'Ever since the owner of the farm has been paying the olive oil as a tax, the law has nominally remained in force, but the trial [for its violation] has gone out of use' (Fritz & Kapp). *A.P.* often refers to the laws which he is summarising (cf. Introduction, p. 34): here he remarks that the law has become a dead letter; cf. 61. ii on the generals' right to fine, and what is implied but not directly stated in 7. iv *fin.*, on the exclusion of the thetes from office. These comments will, of course, come not from the laws but from *A.P.*'s own direct knowledge of current practice.

τὸ δὲ ἔλα[ιον] ἐκ τοῦ κτήματος ... τῇ πόλει: 'From the property.' Previously Athena's oil had been collected specifically from the sacred olives; but probably so many of the plants designated sacred had died that it had become impossible to collect enough oil by this means, and so the obligation was treated as a general levy on the property where sacred olives had been grown. In these changed circumstances no notice needed to be taken if a farmer dug up one of the sacred plants, as long as he continued to supply the oil due from his land.

60. iii. συλλέξας οὖν ὁ ἄρχων τὸ ἐφ' ἑαυ[τοῦ] γιγνόμενον: Some Panathenaic amphorae of the fourth century have the archon's name by the column to the right of Athena, balancing the official Panathenaic inscription by the other column (cf. above); the earliest firm instance is 375/4, but there is a possible instance of 392/1; surviving inscriptions all name archons of years in which the lesser festival was held, but there is no logical reason why oil should not have been collected in the year of the Great Panathenaea for the festival three and a half years later (for an attempt to give a reason see E. N. Gardiner, *JHS* xxxii 1912, 192). In the Hellenistic period the archon is replaced first by the ταμίας τῶν στρατιωτικῶν and later, in the mid second century, by an ἀγωνοθέτης (G. R. Edwards, *Hesp.* xxvi 1957, 320–49, esp. 331–6). Cf. Boardman, *Athenian Black Figure Vases,* 169–70; there is a catalogue of inscribed Panathenaic amphorae by A. Smets, *AC* v 1936, 87–104.†

τοῖς ταμίαις παραδίδωσιν εἰς ἀκρόπολιν: That is, to the treasurers of Athena (in the time of *A.P.*, to the single board of sacred treasurers using that title: cf. on 47. i).

καὶ οὐκ ἔστιν ἀναβῆναι ... παραδῷ τοῖς ταμίαις: Cf. the statement in 46. i that the boule cannot receive its δωρεά unless it has handed over to the following year's boule the new ships required of it: in that case we know of an instance when the requirement had not been satisfied, which may help to explain *A.P.*'s emphasis (cf. *ad loc.*); we do not know if there had been a recent instance of the archon's failing to collect the olive oil required of him. Satisfying this require-

COMMENTARY ON THE *ATH. POL.* [60. ii

ment was a necessary condition for 'going up to the Areopagus', not a sufficient condition: in the law *ap.* D. xxiv. *Tim.* 22 we read that a πρύτανις or πρόεδρος who fails to play his part in the annual ἐπιχειροτονία τῶν νόμων shall be liable to a fine and may be proceeded against by ἔνδειξις, οἱ δὲ θεσμοθέται τοὺς ἐνδειχθέντας εἰσαγόντων εἰς τὸ δικαστήριον κατὰ τὸν νόμον, ἢ μὴ ἀνιόντων εἰς Ἄρειον πάγον, ὡς καταλύοντες τὴν ἐπανόρθωσιν τῶν νόμων. Cf. also [D.] xxvi. *Aristog. ii.* 5, Hyp. fr. 164 Sauppe *ap.* Ath. xiii. 566 f. These passages make it clear that the archons did not join the ranks of the Areopagus until they had satisfactorily completed their year of office: cf. p. 107.†

Sandys cites also Is. vii. *Areop.* 38, [D.] lix. *Neaer.* 80(-3); but it is clear from the dismissal of the πάρεδρος Stephanus (cf. on 56. i) that in [D.] lix ἀναβαίνειν and καταβαίνειν are used of an appearance before the Areopagus of the nine archons during their year of office, and that is perhaps the meaning of Isocrates too.

ἀπομετροῦσι τοῖς ἀθλοθέταις: The verb suggests that the oil was stored in comparatively large containers and transferred to the prize amphorae at a later stage; but the use of archons' names on fourth-century amphorae suggests rather that the oil was placed in those amphorae in the year of its collection. P. E. Corbett, *Hesp.* xviii 1949, 306-8 no. 1, suggests that a vase of the late fifth century depicts the taking of the amphorae to the place where the prizes were awarded (Agora P 10554).

οἱ δ' ἀθλοθέται τοῖς νικῶσι τῶν ἀγωνιστῶν: Cf. §i *fin.* (καὶ τὸ ἔλαιον τοῖς ἀθληταῖς ἀποδιδόασι).

ἔστι γὰρ ἄθλα τοῖς μὲν τὴν μουσικὴν νικῶσιν ἀργύρια καὶ χρυσία: At first and, perhaps as an emergency measure, during the Peloponnesian War, the evidence of amphorae shows that olive oil was used for the musicians' prizes (cf. Davison, *JHS* lxxviii 1958, 36-8 = *From Archilochus to Pindar*, 54-8). For prizes in silver and gold cf. *IG* ii² 2311, 1-22: in the contest for κιθαρῳδοί the winner received a gilded olive crown worth 1,000 drachmae and 500 drachmae in cash, and there were cash prizes for the men placed second to fifth. The papyrus has ἀργύρια κ(αὶ) χρυσᾶ, which Kenyon[1-2] retained; the text of Kenyon's later editions is due to Herwerden (*BPW* xi 1891, 324, cf. Herwerden & Leeuwen); Kaibel & Wilamowitz preferred ἀργύριον καὶ χρυσᾶ (cf. Kaibel, *Stil und Text*, 249) and W. G. Rutherford ἀργυρᾶ καὶ χρυσᾶ (*CR* v 1891, 118). Since the silver took the form of cash but the gold did not, χρυσᾶ is probably correct (cf. the headings, e.g. τάδε χρυσᾶ, in *IG* ii² 1421-35), though χρυσία is not impossible (cf. D. xxvii. *Aphob. i.* 10, [D.] xlviii. *Olymp.* 55; and the singular χρυσίον καὶ ἀργύριον in Plat. *Alc. i.* 122 E 2); with ἄθλα preceding and another plural following, ἀργύριον could easily have been corrupted into the plural, and the best text is Kaibel & Wilamowitz' ἀργύριον καὶ χρυσᾶ.‡

675

60. iii]   COMMENTARY ON THE *ATH. POL.*

τοῖς δὲ τὴν εὐανδρίαν ἀσπίδες: εὐανδρία was omitted from the list of contests in §i (cf. p. 671): *IG* ii² 2311, 75 (first half c4), shows that it was a tribal competition, and there the prize is said to be an ox worth 100 drachmae (cf. W. K. Pritchett, *Hesp.* xxv 1956, 257). Dr D. M. Lewis points out to me that *IG* ii² 1461, 10–11, 18–20, appears to record ἀσπίδες from the Panathenaea of 346/5 and 330/29, perhaps unawarded prizes like the crown in *IG* ii² 1388, 36–7. Harp. εὐανδρία cites Dinarchus (= fr. xvi. 2 Sauppe), [And.] iv. *Alc.* 42 (suggesting that the financing of the teams was a liturgy) and Philochorus (= 328 F 102); *L.S.* 257. 13 states that the contest was not open to ξένοι; cf. also Ath. xiii. 565 F. The essence of the contest was military prowess: at the Thesea, in the second century, there were contests in εὐανδρία and εὐοπλία, for ἐπίλεκτοι, ἔθνη and ἱππεῖς (e.g. *IG* ii² 956, 48–60). Jacoby, on Phil., *loc. cit.*, cites contests in εὐεξία in Tralles (*SIG*³ 1060, 3: c4–3) and Samos (*SIG*³ 1061, 3, 16: c2), but these are not for teams but for individuals.

τοῖς δὲ τὸν γυμνικὸν ἀγῶνα καὶ τὴν ἱπποδρομίαν ἔλαιον: First and second prizes, in amphorae of olive oil, for various athletic and equestrian contests are listed in *IG* ii² 2311, 23–70; cf. *Anth. Pal.* xiii. xix. 3–4 with C. Blinkenberg, *Hermes* lxiv 1929, 272–4 (60 amphorae for the winner of the pentathlon).

Q. *Elective Military Officials* (61)

Appointment by lot was used for civilian offices which were thought to require loyalty rather than skill, so that they should be fairly distributed among those considered equally eligible (cf. 4. iii with commentary); but command of the army and navy was thought to require skill as well as loyalty, and so for the principal military offices election was used (cf. the cynical comment of [X.] *A.P.* i. 3). Our knowledge of the men elected as generals makes it clear that the term of office was a year and that there was no impediment to reelection: these facts are not stated here by *A.P.*, but the annual election is treated in 44. iv as an item of business brought regularly to the assembly. Inconvenient though it must have been for a change to take place in the middle of the campaigning season, it appears that for the military as for most civilian officials the year of office was the archontic year, beginning in mid summer (cf. p. 537). For the qualifications for office cf. pp. 510–11: MS Vat. Gr. 2306, B (a fragment from Theophrastus, accessible in J. J. Keaney & A. Szegedy-Maszak, *TAPA* cvi 1976, 227–40, and J. H. Oliver, *GR&BS* xviii 1977, 326–39), reports in lines 105–70 that Hagnon advised the Athenians to have a mixture of younger and older generals, which some smaller cities do; and in 172–83 repeats a remark made earlier, that men elected to the generalship ought previously to have been taxiarchs or phylarchs (but does not suggest that this rule was ever in force in Athens).

61. i. χειροτονοῦσι δὲ καὶ τὰς πρὸς τὸν πόλεμον ἀρχὰς ἁπάσας: Cf. 43. i *fin*. (χειροτονοῦσι δὲ καὶ τὰς πρὸς τὸν πόλεμον ἁπάσας). καὶ implies that other elective officials have been mentioned above, which is not the case here. Believing that the civilian elective officials who ἄρχουσιν ἐκ Παναθηναίων εἰς Παναθήναια held office for four years (43. i: cf. *ad loc.*), Kaibel & Wilamowitz postulated before this sentence a lacuna in which an account of those officials was to be supplied, so that *A.P.* would have treated annual sortitive officials (43–59), quadrennial sortitive officials (60), quadrennial elective officials (lacuna) and finally annual elective officials (61) (cf. H. Weil, *JS* 1891, 198 with n. 1, Wilamowitz, *A.u.A.*, i. 207–8, Kaibel, *Stil und Text*, 249–50): many have been persuaded. It is more probable that the civilian elective officials served for a single year, however, and there is no reference in 61 to the military officials' term of office, as we should expect if their one year was contrasted with the civilian officials' four; but it is true that 43. i leads us to expect a treatment of the civilian elective officials and that our expectation is not satisfied. Poll. VIII. 87 is based on a text of *A.P.* which proceeded directly from the athlothetae to the military officials (cf. p. 669), and I suspect that the absence of any treatment of the civilian officials is due to *A.P.*'s own remissness rather than to the loss of a section from a text which did contain it. Kenyon in his 3rd and later edd. suggested that if there is no lacuna at this point the καὶ should be deleted, and that is probably the right solution.

στρατηγοὺς δέκα, πρότερον μὲν ἀφ᾿ <ἑκάστης> φυλῆς ἕνα, νῦν δ᾿ ἐξ ἁπάντων: We learn from 22. ii that in 501/0 the Athenians began to elect ten generals, one from each tribe, and according to Pl. *Cim.* 8. viii there was one general from each tribe in 469/8; for 441/0 Andr. 324 F 38 gives a list in which Pericles has a colleague from his own tribe, and for 357/6 Tod 153, 20–4, lists seven or eight of the ten generals, representing six or seven of the ten tribes; but in 323/2 four of the six known generals belonged to one tribe, Acamantis (cf. J. Sundwall, *Klio* Bhft. iv 1906, 23–4, 25). Between 441/0 (or perhaps earlier) and the mid fourth century the evidence has suggested to most scholars that there was an intermediate stage, in which the appointment of generals was still based on the tribes but at any rate one exception to the tribal basis (and possibly more than one) was permitted; C. W. Fornara believes that the exceptions are too many to support that hypothesis and that there was a single change, from election based on the tribes to election irrespective of tribe, which he dates to the late 460's (*Hist.* Einz. xvi 1971, esp. 19–27), but he is too eager to adopt identifications which add to the list of exceptions, and the intermediate stage should be accepted. Cf. above, pp. 265–6. The tribal basis of election was abandoned between 357/6 and 323/2, and so the change will have been fairly recent when *A.P.* was written (cf. Introduction, p. 52). The original connection with the tribes was so far forgotten that, as far as we know, the number of generals remained ten throughout the various tribal changes of later Athens.†

44. iv tells us that the elections of generals and other military officials were held καθ' ὅ τι ἂν τῷ δήμῳ δοκῇ, in the first prytany after the sixth in which there were good omens: cf. *ad loc*. καὶ τούτους διατάττουσι τῇ χειροτονίᾳ, ἕνα μὲν ἐπὶ τοὺς ὁπλίτας ... ἂν ἐξίωσι: '... who leads the hoplites if they go out of Attica' (contrast what is said below of the στρατηγὸς ἐπὶ τὴν χώραν). The first clear evidence for the creation of regular postings for some of the generals shows that there was a στρατηγὸς ἐπὶ τὴν χώραν shortly before 350 (cf. next note), whereas in Tod 153, 20–4, seven or eight of the generals are listed with no indication that any had particular responsibilities, and in Tod 156, 7–15, it is prescribed that one of the generals, without further qualification, is to be appointed to take responsibility for Andros (both 357/6). There happen not to survive any epigraphic references to the στρατηγὸς ἐπὶ τὰ ὅπλα (as he is regularly entitled) earlier than the third century (*IG* ii² 682, 30–2, referring to 292/1),[56] and we do not know when this assignment was created; but W. S. Ferguson was probably right to suggest that the existence of this general is presupposed by that of the στρατηγὸς ἐπὶ τὴν χώραν (*Klio* ix 1909, 321–2), and there may be an allusion to this general in D. IV. *Phil. i.* 26 (*c*. 351; cf. Sandys *ad loc.*). I am not persuaded by N. G. L. Hammond that the partitioning of the generalship began shortly after the Persian Wars, that Lys. XXXII. *Diog.* 5 *ap.* D.H. 502. *Lys.* 25 gives this title to Thrasyllus in 410/09, and that Alcibiades held this appointment in 407 (*CQ*² xix 1969, 115–17, 142 = *Studies*, 353–5, 391–2); on the other hand, Θ. Χ. Σαρικάκης, *Ἀθ.* lvii 1953, 257–61, is excessively sceptical in doubting the existence of any regular postings before the 330's. In Roman Athens the στρατηγὸς ἐπὶ τὰ ὅπλα became one of the chief officers of state: cf. Sarikakis, *The Hoplite General in Athens* (introduction but not list published also in Greek in *Ἀθ.* lviii 1954, 119–32), D. J. Geagan, *Hesp.* Supp. xii 1967, 18–31. It is not clear whether generals were elected directly to particular posts or first elected generals and then by a separate vote assigned to

---

[56] In *IG* ii² 649, 23–5, the correct reading is [ἐ]πὶ τὸ [ν]αυτικόν (W. B. Dinsmoor, *Archons of Athens*, 7); this leaves as the only epigraphic instance of *A.P.*'s terminology κατασταθεὶς στ[ρατηγὸς ἐπὶ τοὺς] ὁπλίτας, in *IG* ii² 1281, 2–3 (mid C3). Cf. below on the other titles, and Introduction, pp. 38–9.

particular posts: *A.P.*'s use of the article, if pressed, would imply the former; on the other hand, as long as the tribal basis for elections was retained the latter is more likely, and that is supported by πάλιν [τε] ἐπὶ Πειθ⟨ι⟩δήμου ἄρχοντος, χειροτονήσαντος αὐτὸν στρατηγὸν τοῦ δήμου, κα[ὶ τάξαν]τος ἐπὶ τὴν χώραν τὴν παραλίαν (*SEG* xxiv 154, 4–6: 265/4, when the generals were no longer tribally based).

The generals had an office in the Agora, the στρατήγιον (testimonia, R. E. Wycherley, *The Athenian Agora*, iii, pp. 174–7): the excavators tentatively identify this with a building south-west of the Tholos (above, p. 520), erected soon after the middle of the fifth century (H. A. Thompson & R. E. Wycherley, *The Athenian Agora*, xiv. 73, *Agora Guide*³, 57–8).

ἕνα δ' ἐπὶ τὴν χώραν, ὃς φυλάττει ... πολεμεῖ οὗτος: This use of πολεμεῖ is startling: Kaibel & Wilamowitz proposed ἡγεῖται (cf. Kaibel, *Stil und Text*, 250–1), and Κ. Σ. Κόντος, *Ἀθ.* iv 1892, 174, πολεμαρχεῖ (but that verb would not be used of a στρατηγός). Other editors have accepted this startling usage (which is not noticed in LSJ or the 1968 Supplement), but Kaibel & Wilamowitz may well be right.

This general is first found in *IG* ii² 204, 19–20 (352/1: τὸν στρατηγὸν τὸν ἐπὶ τῆ[ν φυλ]ακῆ[ν τῆς χ]ώρας κεχειροτονημένον), and Phil. 328 F 155 (350/49: ᾽Εφιάλτου στρατηγοῦντος ἐπὶ τὴν χώραν); in O. W. Reinmuth, *Mnem.* Supp. xiv 1971, 5 (I understand), 7, 9, ii. 10–11, 15, l.h.s., the title is consistently ἐπὶ τεῖ χώραι. On φυλακὴ τῆς χώρας in Athenian decree-making see 43. iv with commentary.

δύο δ' ἐπὶ τὸν Πειραιέα ... τῆς φυλ⟨ακ⟩ῆς ἐπιμελοῦνται [[καὶ]] τῶν ἐν Πειραιεῖ: Kaibel & Wilamowitz[1] were probably right to delete καὶ when they adopted the correction φυλ⟨ακ⟩ῆς. For the separate postings of Munichia and Acte cf. 42. iii with commentary. I understand that Reinmuth, *op. cit.*, 5 mentions the στρατηγὸν τοῦ Πειραιῶς ... καὶ τὸν ἐπὶ τῆι χώραι; the same two generals appear in 7 (334/3 or 333/2) and in 9, ii. 9–11 (333/2); but in 15, l.h.s.–r.h.s. (325/4?), we have three, στρατηγὸν τὸν ἐπὶ τεῖ χώραι, στρατηγὸν ἐπ[ὶ] τῶι Πειραιεῖ, and στρατηγὸν ἐπὶ τεῖ Ἀκτεῖ. This suggests that at the time of the earliest ephebic inscriptions there was a single general for the Piraeus; by the mid 320's there were two, and the older, now no doubt in fact ἐπὶ τὴν Μουνιχίαν, retained the old title (a στρατηγός ... ἐπὶ τὴν Μουνιχίαν καὶ τὰ νεώρια κεχειροτονημένος in 325/4 is found in Din. III. *Phil.* 1); this passage in *A.P.* either was written after the change or was rewritten but in such a way as to leave no trace of the alteration (cf. Introduction, p. 52).

ἕνα δ' ἐπὶ τὰς συμμορίας ... τὰς διαδικασίας αὐτοῖς εἰσάγει: ([[αὐτοῖς]] εἰσάγει was deleted by Kaibel & Wilamowitz[2–3], but the repetition, though inelegant, is not impossible.) συμμορίαι were first created, as groups of men liable to εἰσφορά, in 378/7 (Phil. 328 F 41, cf. Clid.

679

323 F 8). The trierarchy, which by the time of [X.] *A.P.* i. 13, Ar. *Eq.* 912–18, if not earlier, involved not merely the command of a ship in the fleet but the liturgy of bearing the ship's running expenses for the year, was becoming an intolerable burden in the first half of the fourth century, both because the expenses of a ship were often too heavy even to be shared between two trierarchs and because the expenses of one ship in one year might be much heavier than those of another ship in another year or even in the same year. To remedy this a law of Periander, *c.* 357, shared the burden of the trierarchy each year among the 1,200 richest citizens, treated as equals and grouped in twenty συμμορίαι for the purpose ([D.] XLVII. *Ev. & Mnes.* 21–2 [the speaker was τριηραρχῶν καὶ ἐπιμελητὴς ὢν τῆς συμμορίας; §44 yields the date 357/6], D. XIV. *Symm.* 16–17, XVIII. *Cor.* 102–4, XXI. *Mid.* 154–5); a συντέλεια was formed of men responsible for each ship (Suid. [Σ 1631] συντελεῖς, *E.M.* [736. 11] συντελής; [D.] XLVII. *Ev. & Mnes.* 29); but both before and after Periander's law it was possible to make over one's responsibility to a professional contractor (D. XXI. *Mid.* 80, 155), and the new system still left room for volunteer trierarchs (D. XXI. *Mid.* 161, XVIII. *Cor.* 99). In the navy lists of the years following Periander's law we still find trierarchs assigned to ships, sometimes named individually (e.g. *IG* ii² 1613, 202–23), sometimes identified as one man's συμμορία (e.g. *IG* ii² 1617, 29–67). In 354/3 Demosthenes in XIV. *Symm.* proposed to extend the list of men liable to the trierarchy to 2,000 and to make them contribute in proportion to their wealth; some have concluded from Clid. 323 F 8 that the number of trierarchic συμμορίαι was increased to a hundred (e.g. Jacoby, *Supp.* i. 58) but probably, *pace* D. XV. *Lib. Rhod.* 6, no action resulted from that speech. Probably in 340, Demosthenes did reform the trierarchy: liability was now limited to the 300 richest citizens, and they were made to contribute in proportion to their wealth (D. XVIII. *Cor.* 102–9, A. III. *Ctes.* 222, Din. I. *Dem.* 42, Hyp. fr. 160 Sauppe, cf. schol. D. XXI. *Mid.* 155 [628. 7 Dindorf]); this reduced list was still divided into twenty συμμορίαι (Hyp. fr. 173 Sauppe). Demosthenes alleges that, apparently after Chaeronea, Aeschines accepted a bribe from the richest citizens to defile his law, by what kind of modification we do not know (D. XVIII. *Cor.* 312); in the later navy lists we find ships assigned to a single trierarch (e.g. *IG* ii² 1629, 64–7) or to a plurality (e.g. *IG* ii² 1629, 43–50); voluntary trierarchies remained possible (*IG* ii² 1623, 309–11). See in general A. Böckh, *Urkunden über das Seewesen des attischen Staates*, 166–94, Böckh rev. M. Fränkel, *Die Staatshaushaltung der Athener*, i. 628–69, M. Brilliant, *D.A.*, v. 442–65, Busolt & Swoboda, *G.S.*, ii. 1199–1210, B. Jordan, *U. Calif. Pub. Cl. Stud.* xiii 1975, 61–93. Most recently E. Ruschenbusch, *ZPE* xxxi 1978, 275–84, has argued that the same

συμμορίαι were used for εἰσφορά and after c. 357 (with some of their members exempted) for the trierarchy.†
  The στρατηγὸς ἐπὶ τὰς συμμορίας in the time of *A.P.* performs the same function with regard to the trierarchy as the relevant archon with regard to the festival liturgies (cf. 56. iii with commentary): he registers the men liable to the trierarchy, and presumably allocates particular ships to particular trierarchs; and he is responsible for challenges by a man who has been called on to serve, to another who has been passed over but whom the challenger believes to be richer (ἀντιδόσεις), and other claims to exemption. *A.P.* uses the same language here and in 56. iii except that there he uses and explains σκήψεις, here he uses διαδικασίας. Both words may be used in two ways in connection with the trierarchy: of suits in which exemption is claimed, and of suits arising from loss of or damage to ships and equipment (διαδικάζειν in both senses, [X.] *A.P.* iii. 4; σκήψεις in first sense, *IG* ii² 1629 = Tod 200, 204–17 [cf. below]; σκήπτεσθαι in second sense [not in LSJ, which misunderstands *IG* ii² 1629, 746–7], that passage and *IG* ii² 1631, 343–7). Here presumably the first sense is intended, as in *IG* ii² 1629, 204–17 (325/4), the thesmothetae are to provide courts for the στρατηγὸς ἐπὶ τὰς συμμορίας on two stated days for the hearing of σκήψεις before an expedition is sent out: contrast *IG* ii² 1623, 147–59 (334/3), where we read that οἱ στρατηγοὶ καὶ οἱ εἴκοσιν (the ἡγεμόνες or the ἐπιμεληταὶ τῶν συμμοριῶν) appointed one man to be syntrierarch with another, and the references in speeches to the appointment of trierarchs by 'the generals' (e.g. D. xxxix. *Boe. Nom.* 8, [D.] xxxv. *Lacr.* 48); so the institution of the στρατηγὸς ἐπὶ τὰς συμμορίας must have been very recent when *A.P.* was written, though there is nothing in the text to betray this (cf. Introduction, p. 52; but Jordan, *op. cit.*, believes that this appointment dates from the time of Periander's law).[57] In the inscribed Decree of Themistocles the generals are ordered to appoint trierarchs and allot ships to them (M&L 23, 18–23, cf. M. H. Jameson, *Hist.* xii 1963, 397). In 357/6 it was the ἀποστολεῖς and the ἐπιμεληταὶ τῶν νεωρίων (for whom see pp. 545–6) who εἰσῆγον τότε τὰς διαδικασίας . . . περὶ τῶν σκευῶν ([D.] xlvii. *Ev. & Mnes.* 26); the ἀποστολεῖς were an extraordinary appointment, so perhaps it is their involvement which is thought to require comment in [D.] xlvii, and σκήψεις of this second kind were regularly the responsibility of the epimeletae. Cf. Lipsius, *A.R.*, 456–9, Harrison, *L.A.*, ii. 235–6.

[57] [D.] xlii. *Phaen.* 5 (320's: L. Gernet, Budé ed. of D.'s *Plaidoyers civils*, ii. 76–7) refers to the generals as holding ἀντιδόσεις for 'the three hundred'; but in that speech 'the three hundred' are probably being considered as προεισφέροντες rather than as trierarchs (cf. §3 *fin.*), and the whole board of generals may have remained responsible for προεισφορά (cf. R. Thomsen, *Eisphora*, 210).

Exemption from the trierarchy was given more sparingly than exemption from festival liturgies (cf. D. xx. *Lept.* 18); but orphaned minors and some other categories of citizens were exempt (D. xiv. *Symm.* 16, quoted p. 509), and the nine archons (D. xx. *Lept.* 27-8) and perhaps other officials were exempt during their year of office. Before the συμμορίαι were instituted a man who had been trierarch was entitled to exemption for two years afterwards (Isae. vii. *Her. Apoll.* 38), but the entitlement was not always claimed (e.g. Lys. xxi. *Pec. Acc.* 2).

Athens lost most of her fleet in the battle near Abydus in 322 (D.S. xviii. 15. ix), and the classical trierarchy was probably abolished at the same time as the festival liturgies, by Demetrius of Phalerum (cf. p. 623); but the title τριήραρχος was still used of the man responsible for a ship (e.g. *IG* ii² 1491, *B, passim*). There will then have been no further need for a στρατηγὸς ἐπὶ τὰς συμμορίας; but a στρατηγὸς ἐπὶ τὸ ναυτικόν, whose job is not to organise the fleet but to command it, is first found in 321 (*IG* ii² 682, 4-7: cf. next note).

τοὺς δ' ἄλλους πρὸς τὰ παρόντα πράγματα ἐκπέμπουσιν: In the time of *A.P.* five of the generals had regular postings while the other five were available for *ad hoc* assignment as all ten had been earlier. In 321 there was a στρατηγὸς ἐπὶ τὸ ναυτικόν, but under Demetrius of Phalerum the στρατηγὸς ἐπὶ τὰς συμμορίας disappeared (cf. end of previous note). By 296/5 there was a στρατηγὸς ἐπὶ τὴν παρασκευήν, responsible for buildings and equipment, not only military (*IG* ii² 682, 21-3); during the first half of the third century ἐπὶ τὴν χώραν was divided into two postings, ἐπὶ τὴν χώραν τὴν ἐπ' Ἐλευσῖνος (e.g. *IG* ii² 1304, 12-24) and ἐπὶ (τὴν χώραν) τὴν παραλίαν (e.g. *IG* ii² 1302, 4-5). Probably before the end of the third century regular postings had been devised for all ten: ἐπὶ τὰ ὅπλα, two ἐπὶ τὴν χώραν, ἐπὶ τὴν παρασκευήν, three ἐπὶ τὸ ναυτικόν and three ἐπὶ τὸν Πειραιέα; other titles are found which may have been used for a time, such as ἐπὶ τοὺς ξένους in *IG* ii² 682, 25. Cf. W. S. Ferguson, *Klio* ix 1909, 314-23, Θ. Χ. Σαρικάκης, *Ἀθ.* lvii 1953, 254-61.

61. ii. ἐπιχειροτονία δ' αὐτῶν ... εἰ δοκοῦσιν καλῶς ἄρχειν: Cf. 43. iv, where the first item of business specified for the κυρία ἐκκλησία of each prytany is τὰς ἀρχὰς ἐπιχειροτονεῖν εἰ δοκοῦσι καλῶς ἄρχειν. Lipsius, *Ber. Leipzig* xliii 1891, 48-9, plausibly suggested that the procedure was instituted with special reference to military officials. It will have been mentioned here because it was included in the νόμος στρατηγικός, and also in 43. iv because, either when it was instituted for the generals or when it was extended to all ἀρχαί, a clause was included in that part of the νόμος βουλευτικός which dealt with the regular business of the assembly. We read in §iv that the hipparchs too were subject to ἐπιχειροτονία.

κἄν τινα ἀποχειροτονήσωσιν, κρίνουσιν ἐν τῷ δικαστηρίῳ: Presumably ἀποχειροτονία was regarded as comparable to the other instances in which a vote in the assembly preceded a trial in a δικαστήριον, and the thesmothetae acted as εἰσάγουσα ἀρχή (cf. 59. ii with commentary, where *A.P.* mentions εἰσαγγελίαι, καταχειροτονίαι [after an ἀπόφασις by the Areopagus to the assembly?] and προβολαί). Probably as in the case of προβολαί there were distinct rules for the procedure following an ἀποχειροτονία; but often the deposed man would be charged with a major offence against the state and would undergo an eisangeltic form of trial (cf. Harrison, *L.A.*, ii. 59, M. H. Hansen, *Eisangelia*, 41–4, Rhodes, *JHS* xcix 1979, 110 with n. 69), and this may explain, if an explanation is necessary, why ἀποχειροτονίαι are not mentioned separately in 59. ii. Earlier an eisangeltic trial following deposition might be held not in a δικαστήριον but in the assembly (as in the case of Timotheus in 373/2, [D.] XLIX. *Timoth.* 9–10), but soon after 362 trials in the assembly were discontinued (cf. p. 525). D. M. MacDowell, *The Law in Classical Athens*, 169, doubts whether trial was an automatic consequence of deposition, or reinstatement an automatic consequence of acquittal.

κἄν μὲν ἁλῷ, τιμῶσιν ὅ τι χρὴ παθεῖν ἢ ἀποτεῖσαι: That is, the trial following an ἀποχειροτονία was an ἀγὼν τιμητός, in which the penalty was not fixed but had to be assessed by the court. No doubt what *A.P.* says is correct of the distinct procedure for trial after ἀποχειροτονία; if the trial took an eisangeltic form it was possible for the penalty to be specified by the boule or assembly in referring the case to a δικαστήριον, and for some offences subject to εἰσαγγελία the law seems to have prescribed the death penalty ([D.] XLIX. *Timoth.* 67 with D. xx. *Lept.* 100, 135, on deceiving the people with false promises): see Harrison, *L.A.*, ii. 82, Hansen, *op. cit.*, 33–6. An example of the procedure specified by *A.P.* is the trial of Cephisodotus in 360/59 (D. XXIII. *Arist.* 167, where ψῆφοι points to a vote in court).

ἂν δ' ἀποφύγῃ, πάλι[ν] ἄρχει: That is, the assembly's deposition is provisional, pending the trial of the accused, and if he is acquitted he is reinstated in office; see above for MacDowell's doubt as to whether reinstatement was an automatic consequence of acquittal. The thesmothetae of 344/3 were deposed in an ἀποχειροτονία, acquitted and reinstated ([D.] LVIII. *Theocr.* 27–8).

κύριοι δέ εἰσιν ὅταν ἡγῶνται καὶ δῆσαι τὸν ἀτακτοῦντα: In [D.] L. *Poly.* 51 we find a trierarch afraid of being placed under arrest. Earlier, generals might be more drastic: in the course of the Sicilian expedition of 415–413 Lamachus put to death by ἀποτυμπανισμός (cf. pp. 539–40) a soldier caught signalling to the enemy (Lys. XIII. *Agor.* 67); in the Corinthian War Iphicrates killed on the spot a sentry found asleep at his post (Front. *Strat.* III. xii. 2—but his soldiers were mercenaries and he may not have been an Athenian στρατηγός). On military discipline see Kahrstedt, *U.M.A.*, 245–8; D. III. *Ol. iii.* 11 complains of laws περὶ τῶν στρατευομένων, which τοὺς ἀτακτοῦντας ἀθῴους καθιστᾶσιν (but the scholiast refers this to claims for exemption from service, not to disobedience while on service).

καὶ <ἐκ>κ[η]ρῦξαι: The compound verb was restored by Blass, *LZB* 1891, 304, cf. Kaibel, *Stil und Text*, 251: Lys. III. *Sim.* 45 states that this was done to one Simon in the Corinthian War, for assaulting a taxiarch (LSJ cites *A.P.* but not Lys.). The word has the general meaning 'banish by proclamation', and in these passages must mean 'cashier from the army'. Cf. Lys. XIII. *Agor.* 77–81, on the treatment of Agoratus when he tried to join the democrats in 403; according to Pl. *Cim.* 17. v the generals were ordered by the boule not to admit Cimon to the Athenian ranks at Tanagra, but contr. *Per.* 10. i.

καὶ ἐπιβολὴν ἐπιβάλλειν· οὐκ εἰώθασι δὲ ἐπιβάλλειν: H. Diels (*ap.* Kenyon, Berlin ed.) suggested ἐπιβολὴν ἐπιβαλεῖν, to match the preceding aorists, and that is probably right. For ἐπιβολαί, fines up to a stated limit which a magistrate could impose on his own authority, cf. 56. vii with commentary. Lys. IX. *Mil.* 6–12 complains that the generals fined the speaker for abusing them (but not while on service), did not attempt to collect the fine but reported it at the end of their year of office; the ταμίαι quashed the sentence; but now he is being prosecuted as a defaulter (on the procedure implied see M. Bizos in the Budé ed. of Lysias, i. 131–2). [Lys.] XV. *Alc. ii.* 5 suggests that in 395 the generals should have imposed an ἐπιβολή on the phylarch who expelled the young Alcibiades from his squadron. For this note of a point in the law which has become obsolete cf. 60. ii with commentary, on trials for destroying the sacred olives.

61. iii. χειροτονοῦσι δὲ καὶ ταξ[ι]άρχους δέκα ... ἡγεῖται τῶν φυλετῶν: These, and the cavalry officers to be treated below, are mentioned together with the generals in D. IV. *Phil. i.* 26. Taxiarchs are attested from the time of the Peloponnesian War (Ar. *Ach.* 569, T. IV. 4. i, VII. 60. ii [in council with generals], VIII. 92. iv [ταξιαρχῶν καὶ τὴν ἑαυτοῦ φυλὴν ἔχων]; cf. the 'future' constitution of 411, *A.P.* 30. ii). If from their institution in 501/0 the ten generals were commanders of the whole Athenian army (cf. on 22. ii), taxiarchs as commanders of the tribal contingents in the army should have been instituted at the same time; B. Jordan, *U. Calif. Pub. Cl. Stud.* xiii 1975, 240 with n. 79, notices Herodotus' untechnical use of the word and accepts the view of Wilamowitz, *A.u.A.*, ii. 88, 108, that in the Persian Wars the generals were the commanders of the tribal regiments and Athens had no taxiarchs, but ταξίαρχον is the correct reading in the inscribed Oath of Plataea, Tod 204, 25 (G. Daux, *RA*⁶ xvii 1941, 177–8). For taxiarchs with the fleet at Arginusae see X. *H.* i. vi. 29; the taxiarchs are sometimes coupled with the generals in religious matters (e.g. *IG* ii² 334, 13–14) and in swearing to treaties (e.g. Tod 144, 38–9). Cf. also D. xxxix. *Boe. Nom.* 17, A. ii. *F.L.* 169; and Jordan, *op. cit.*, 130–4.

As there were not necessarily two vacancies in the generalship when Menander and Euthydemus were elected as colleagues of Nicias (T. vii. 16. i with Dover *ad loc.*), similarly special appointments of taxiarchs could be made when necessary: cf. Dover on T. vii. 60. ii, and notice the two taxiarchs of Leontis in the casualty list published as *The Athenian Agora*, xvii 23, 111–14. We should have expected the number of taxiarchs, unlike the number of generals, to change with the number of tribes in the Hellenistic period (cf. W. S. Ferguson, *Hellenistic Athens*, 97–8), but an inscription of 271/0 makes it clear that at that time there were still only ten (*SEG* xiv 64).

καὶ λοχαγοὺς καθίστησιν: There is no indication in LSJ that the Athenian army had λόχοι and λοχαγοί (the word retains its Doric form in Athenian usage); the 1968 Supplement cites the 'cadet' λοχαγοί of the ephebi (cf. p. 505). λοχαγοί are mentioned in X. *M.* iii. i. 5, iv. 1, Isae. ix. *Her. Ast.* 14, Is. xv. *Antid.* 116; Athenian λόχοι are mentioned only in X. *H.* i. ii. 3, of Thrasyllus' army in 409, where the word may well be used untechnically. We have no further information on the division of the tribal regiments into λόχοι: P. J. Bicknell, *Hist.* Einz. xix 1972, 21 with n. 67, citing H. ix. 21. iii, T. vi. 100. i (whose relevance I doubt) and Plat. *Rep.* v. 475 A 9–10, suggests that in Cleisthenes' army each trittys provided a λόχος of 300 men, and as each tribe had a general and a taxiarch each trittys had a trittyarch and a λοχαγός. Ar. *Ach.* 575, 1073–4, does not help us.

61. iv. χειροτονοῦσι δὲ καὶ ἱππάρχους δύο ... οἱ στρατηγοὶ κατὰ τῶν ὁπλιτῶν: A dedication of the mid fifth century names three hipparchs (*IG* i² 400 with R. Meiggs, *JHS* lxxxvi 1966, 94–5); in 411 we find a plurality of hipparchs in the 'future' constitution but only one in the 'immediate' constitution (30. ii, 31. iii); for the fourth century the number is confirmed by D. iv. *Phil. i.* 26, and the assignment of five tribes to each by X. *Hipparch.* iii. 11. In Ar. *Av.* 79–89 the alleged upstart Diitrephes ᾑρέθη φύλαρχος, εἶθ' ἵππαρχος; cf. also Lys. xvi. *Mant.* 8, xxvi. *Evand.* 20. The parallel between generals and hipparchs is not as close as *A.P.* suggests: both had commanders of tribal regiments under them, but the generals were commanders in chief of all the Athenian forces, cavalry, infantry and navy, while the hipparchs were commanders of the cavalry alone. In the exceptional circumstances of Marathon, when the whole Athenian army went out to fight the Persians in Attica, it is likely that each general fought with his own tribe, even if the taxiarchs did already exist;[58] we do not know what was done when the Athenians invaded the Megarid πανδημεί in the Peloponnesian War (T. II. 31: §i names Pericles alone as commander in the invasion of autumn 431; commonly all ten generals will not have been available), or in other major battles at which more than one general was present.

For the involvement of the hipparchs and phylarchs in the registration of the cavalry cf. 49. ii with commentary. The hipparchs had an office, the ἱππαρχεῖον (SEG xxi 436, 6), which was possibly in the north-west of the Agora near the Stoa of the Herms (H. A. Thompson & R. E. Wycherley, *The Athenian Agora*, xiv. 73 n. 199).

ἐπιχειροτονία δὲ γίγνεται ‹καὶ› τούτων: The ἐπιχειροτονία is treated in §ii in connection with the generals, and briefly in 43. iv in connection with the regular business of the assembly: the additional reference to it here suggests that the taxiarchs and phylarchs may not have been subject to it.

61. v. χειροτονοῦσι δὲ καὶ φυλάρχους ‹ι′› . . . ‹τῶν ἱππέων› ὥσπερ οἱ ταξίαρχοι τῶν ὁπλιτῶν: (For the insertion of τῶν ἱππέων cf. Poll. VIII. 94) Cf. Ar. *Lys.* 561–2, Isae. XI. *Her. Hagn.* 41, Men. *Sam.* 15 (where Moschion is a very young phylarch: see Gomme & Sandbach on line 13). H. v. 69. ii states that as a result of Cleisthenes' tribal reform the number of phylarchs was raised from four to ten, but his reference can hardly be to cavalry officers (on the history of the Athenian cavalry see pp. 303–4).

61. vi. χειροτονοῦσι δὲ καὶ εἰς Λῆμνον ἵππαρχον: Lemnos was acquired for Athens by Miltiades, probably during the Ionian Revolt (H. VI. [137–]140), and Imbros, mentioned with Lemnos in 62. ii *fin.*, was probably acquired at the same time (cf. H. VI. 41, 104. i); Athens lost them, together with all her overseas possessions except Salamis, at the end of the Peloponnesian War (And. III. *Pace*, 12,cf. D.S. XIII. 107. iv, Pl. *Lys.* 14. viii); by 392 Lemnos, Imbros and Scyros were apparently in Athenian hands once more; in Sparta's first attempt at a common peace treaty it was proposed that all the islands and the cities on the European mainland should be autonomous (X. *H.* IV. viii. 14–15), but in winter 392/1 (And., *loc. cit.*) and in the Peace of

---

[58] Pl. *Arist.* 5. i says that Aristides was a general, but 5. iv does not say that Themistocles and Aristides were generals: A. R. Burn, *Persia and the Greeks*, 250, does claim that both were generals; C. Hignett, *Xerxes' Invasion of Greece*, suggests that they may have been generals in his index *s.nn.*, but not on p. 61.

COMMENTARY ON THE *ATH. POL.* [61. vi

Antalcidas (X. *H.* v. i. 31) Athens' claim to these three islands was allowed. A fragmentary inscription (*Hesp.* xl AGR. 23) refers to the Athenian cleruchs on Lemnos, and ἱππαρ]χόντος is a possible but not necessary restoration in line 5 (see the commentary of R. S. Stroud, 170 n. 24, who prefers ἄρ]χοντος); clay tablets have been found in the Athenian Agora with seals naming Pheidon, hipparch to Lemnos (T. L. Shear, jr, *Hesp.* xlii 1973, 178–9, cf. J. H. Kroll, *Hesp.* xlvi 1977, 84 with n. 5). Cf. also D. IV. *Phil. i.* 27, Hyp. I. *Lyc.* 17, *IG* ii² 672, 1224; strikingly, the hipparch is not named with the two generals and four others who sent firstfruits from the towns of Lemnos in 329/8 (*IG* ii² 1672, 276–8).†

61. vii. χειροτονοῦσι δὲ καὶ ... καὶ δίχα τῆς το[ῦ] Ἄμμωνος: Kenyon originally printed ἄλλον τῆς; Blass² and subsequent Teubner editions have printed ν[ῦν] τῆς (cf. Kaibel, *Stil und Text*, 252); Wilcken read §.. α, Kenyon in his Berlin ed. and O.C.T. prints δίχα as possible though not certain, M. H. Chambers *ap.* J. J. Keaney, *Hist.* xx 1970, 328 n. 9, reads δίχα, Dr J. D. Thomas regards δι as acceptable, χα as possible but not easy. τῆς (above an erasure) το[ῦ] is likewise not certain. On Ἄμμωνος see n. 59, below.

It is normally believed that in the fifth and fourth centuries Athens had two 'sacred' triremes, which were used to convey θεωρίαι and on formal state business; originally the two were named Πάραλος and Σαλαμινία (e.g. T. III. 77. iii, Ar. *Av.* 1204); shortly before *A.P.* was written the name Ἀμμωνιάς replaced Σαλαμινία;[59] in the Hellenistic period additional sacred ships were named Δημητριάς and Ἀντιγονίς (Phil. 328 F 48, *L.S.* 267. 21: according to schol. D. XXI. *Mid.* 171 the original two were called Σαλαμινία or Δηλία, and Πάραλος, and three further ships were called Ἀντιγονίς, Πτολεμαΐς and Ἀμμωνιάς). In the late 350's Philip of Macedon captured τὴν ἱερὰν ... τριήρη at Marathon (D. IV. *Phil. i.* 34): Harp. ἱερὰ τριήρης concluded from Andr. (= 324 F 24) and Phil. (= 328 F 47) that this was the Paralus; Phil. 328 F 75 does not justify the inference of Sandys on D., *loc. cit.*, that it was the ship carrying the state's θεωρία to Delos (Phot. Πάραλος says that the ship used for that purpose was the Paralus, but in fact the ship used was not a trireme but a triaconter: 56. iii *fin.*). Most have agreed with U. Koehler that ships with such names as Σαλαμινία in the navy

---

[59] The ship called Ἄμμωνος in the papyrus of *A.P.* is called Ἀμμωνίς by Harp. *s.v.* (adopted in Moore's translation), Ἀμμωνιάς by Phot. Πάραλος, *L.R.C.* Πάραλος καὶ Σαλαμινία (Ἀμοριάδα, *cod.*), schol. D. XXI. *Mid.* 171 (adopted in Kenyon's Oxford Translation); Ἄμμωνος recurs as a lemma in *Lex. Patm.* (*BCH* i 1877, 150 = K. Latte & H. Erbse, *Lexica Graeca Minora*, 160). Probably Ἀμμωνάς was the correct name of the ship, but I am not convinced that *A.P.* did not write the Ἄμμωνος of the papyrus. Cf. Introduction, pp. 38–9.

lists (e.g. *IG* ii² 1611, 95, 164) were ordinary warships and the sacred triremes were not reckoned as part of Athens' general fleet (*AM* viii 1883, 165–72, cf. Busolt & Swoboda, *G.S.*, ii. 1208 n. 2); B. Jordan, *U. Calif. Pub. Cl. Stud.* xiii 1975, 153–84, has argued that Athens had many sacred ships and has reverted to the view of A. Böckh that the sacred ships were included in the general fleet (*Urkunden über das Seewesen des attischen Staates*, 76–9), but it is clear from our sources that the Paralus and Salaminia were not merely two sacred ships among many, and Koehler's view should be retained. One other sacred ship is clearly attested, the triaconter sent to Delos (cf. above).

When the Athenians named one of the ships Ammonias is disputed. Some have dated it as late as 324, making this the latest reference in *A.P.* (H. Weil, *JS* 1891, 199–200, H. Nissen, *RM*² xlvii 1892, 197–8 [with a brief reversion to the name Salaminia after Alexander's death], cf. Tovar, 28 and *REC* iii 1948, 154 with 165 n. 3); most have thought that the Athenians might use this name at any time after Alexander's consultation of the oracle of Ammon in 332/1 (e.g. Busolt, *G.G.*, ii². 18 n., Day & Chambers, *A.H.A.D.*, 197 n. 19, R. J. Lane Fox, *Alexander the Great*, 224 with 526 [dating the ship 331/0]); but even that is not secure as a *terminus post quem*, since there was a φιάλη Ἄμμωνος in the temple treasures by 375/4 (*IG* ii² 1415, 6–7, 1421, 63, with W. S. Ferguson, *Treasurers of Athena*, 180, and A. M. Woodward, *BSA* lvii 1962, 5–13), and the oracle of Ammon is mentioned together with those of Delphi and Dodona in Ar. *Av.* 618–20, 716. *A.P.*'s is our earliest reference to the Ammonias, and (if δίχα, though not the most obvious word, is correct) is not among the passages in *A.P.* which refer to a change in practice or which betray signs of revision (cf. Introduction, p. 53). Our latest evidence for the Salaminia is X. *H.* vi. ii. 14 (373), and Philip's capture of a sacred trireme in the 350's (cf. above) provides as good an excuse as any for the building of a new one.

It is not clear how far these ships were financed by the state: Midias as treasurer of the Paralus in 357/6 had 12 talents to spend, half as much again as would be needed to pay two hundred men at the rate stated (D. xxi. *Mid.* 171–4); but these triremes were warships as well as sacred ships (Phot. Πάραλος: e.g. T. iii. 77. iii, X. *H.* vi. ii. 14, D., *loc. cit.*), and there are references also to a trierarch of the Paralus (*IG* ii² 2966, Isae. v. *Her. Dic.* 6). The treasurer of the Paralus is mentioned also in *IG* ii² 1623, 225, 1628, 8, 79; there is no contemporary reference to the treasurer of the Salaminia or Ammonias, but a treasurer of the Salaminia is mentioned also in Poll. viii. 116, *L.R.C.* Πάραλος καὶ Σαλαμινία.

R. *Concluding Note on Officials* (62)

A.P.'s discussion of the ἀρχαί, begun in ch. 43, is concluded with notes on the ἀρχαί in general: on the method of allotment used for sortitive appointments (§i), on civilian stipends paid by the state (§ii), and on repetition of office (§iii). *A.P.* then passes to the δικαστήρια, without any indication that a major subdivision of his second part ends at this point. The assembling of the material in this chapter is probably *A.P.*'s own work: the laws no doubt prescribed what stipends were to be paid to what officials, but it is unlikely that there was a single law which listed all state stipends together.

62. i. αἱ δὲ κληρωταὶ ἀρχαὶ πρότερον μὲν ... ἐκ τῆς φυλῆς ὅλης κληροῦσι: Previously, sortitive appointments could be divided into those for which lots were drawn among candidates (whether volunteered or nominated: cf. pp. 511–12) from a whole tribe, and those 'allotted in the Theseum' which were apportioned among the individual demes. The heliastic oath *ap.* D. xxiv. *Tim.* 149–51 includes in §150 an undertaking not to admit to any office a man who is currently ὑπεύθυνος for another, whether τῶν ἐννέα ἀρχόντων καὶ τοῦ ἱερομνήμονος καὶ ὅσοι μετὰ τῶν ἐννέα ἀρχόντων κυαμεύονται τῇ αὐτῇ (Reiske: ταύτῃ τῇ codd.) ἡμέρᾳ or (other kinds of office); A. iii. *Ctes.* 13 says that his opponents will regard as regular ἀρχαί only ἐκείνας ... ἃς οἱ θεσμοθέται ἀποκληροῦσιν ἐν τῷ Θησείῳ, κἀκείνας ἃς ὁ δῆμος χειροτονεῖ ἐν ἀρχαιρεσίαις, στρατηγοὺς καὶ ἱππάρχους καὶ τὰς μετὰ τούτων ἀρχάς.

We are not told which officials were appointed from the whole tribe and which were apportioned among the demes: it is likely that the first category comprised at any rate the more important offices, for which a higher property qualification was required (E. S. Staveley, *Greek and Roman Voting and Elections*, 48–9, but his 240 n. 76 mistranslates '... those to which appointment is now made in the Theseion ...'; on the regional distribution of the πεντακοσιομέδιμνοι see W. E. Thompson, *Klio* lii 1970, 437–51). Many (including Kenyon *ad loc.*, Wilamowitz, *A.u.A.*, i. 200–1) have believed that all the boards of ten were in the first category and the second was limited to jurors and officials appointed from the ranks of the jurors: however, it is unlikely that the demes were ever involved in the appointment of jurors, and a hoard of tokens to be discussed below may confirm that one board of ten, the poletae, was in the late fifth century appointed through the demes. *A.P.* gives no location for appointments of the first category, and places the second category in the Theseum (for which see 15. iv with commentary); Aeschines (in 330, when A.P.'s 'current' practice should have been in force) places all sortitive appointments in the Theseum. Wilamowitz, *A.u.A.*, i. 203–4, remarked that *L.S.* 310. 28 places ἀρχαιρεσίαι in the heliaea, supposed the lexicographer to refer to the first category of sortitive appointments (since ἀρχαιρεσίαι proper, elections, took place at meetings of the assembly: cf. 44. iv), and assumed that Aeschines was wrong; I do not know the basis for *L.S.*'s statement, but suspect that all sortitions were made in the Theseum and *A.P.* has been careless in his phrasing.

Although in his own day apportionment among the demes was a thing of the past, *A.P.* does not tell the reader how this was done. M. L. Lang, *Hist.* viii 1959, 80–7, like many earlier writers supposed that in proportion to their population, perhaps using the same quotas as for the appointment of bouleutae (cf. on 43. ii), the demes supplied a short list of men among whom lots were drawn to make the actual appointments; but Staveley, *op. cit.*, 48–51, 69–72, notes that under such a system the corruption mentioned by *A.P.* is hard to envisage, and suggests more attractively that the allotment in the Theseum was used to determine which deme should supply the tribe's member of a particular board. Miss Lang and Staveley both write in the light of a hoard of clay tokens, published by H. A. Thompson, *Hesp.* xx 1951, 51–2, each divided in two by a jig-saw cut, bearing on one side the abbreviated name of a tribe running across both halves, and on the other the name of a deme in one half and either ΠΟΛ or nothing in the other. Staveley suggests that first the tribe was marked on the tokens; then they were cut; then the deme was marked on one half of each (fifty tokens being distributed in accordance with bouleutic quotas); as many second halves were marked with an office as there were offices to be filled; and the halves were then rejoined to show which office fell to which deme: a man who wanted to become πωλητής might then be tempted to 'buy' the office from the deme to which it had fallen. This system will have been used before the introduction of the κληρωτήριον (for which see 63. ii, 64. ii–iii, with commentary).

We do not know when apportionment among the demes was abandoned, but a *terminus ante quem* may be suggested. Soon after 388 κληρωτήρια were used for the allocation of jurors to courts, and bronze πινάκια were issued to the men registered as jurors (cf. 63. iv with commentary); *c.* 370 the use of κληρωτήρια was extended to magisterial appointments, and the magisterial as well as the dicastic πινάκια show each tribe divided into ten sections lettered *A–K*, men being assigned for life to one of these sections (cf. J. H. Kroll, *Athenian Bronze Allotment Plates*, esp. 51–6, 91–4). Kroll shows that these sections were particularly appropriate to the appointment of the archons, where the sortition was conducted in two stages and the first stage had to yield ten candidates in each tribe (8. i); but we may guess that these sections were used for all magisterial appointments in which it was convenient to work with subdivided tribes, and that apportionment among the demes was discontinued not later than the introduction of this system.

πλὴν βουλευτῶν καὶ φρουρῶν· τούτους δ' εἰς τοὺς δήμους ἀποδιδόασι: For the allocation of seats in the boule to individual demes in accordance with their size, so that each tribe had fifty seats, see on 43. ii. The φρουροί may be the five hundred φρουροὶ νεωρίων of 24. iii (cf. *ad loc.*): it would be easy to use bouleutic quotas for five hundred (or for any multiple of five hundred).

62. ii. μισθοφοροῦσι δὲ πρῶτον ὁ δῆμος ... ἐννέα <ὀβολούς>: Fifth-century recipients of stipends, without rates of pay, are listed in 24. iii, from which assembly pay is correctly absent. On the introduction of assembly pay—first 1 obol, then 2, then 3, between the restoration of 403 and Aristophanes' *Ecclesiazusae*—see 41. iii with commentary; and on κύριαι and other ἐκκλησίαι see 43. iv–vi with commentary. In the Erechtheum accounts of 409–407 unskilled workers are paid 3 obols and skilled 1 drachma (*IG* i² 373–4, cf. Gomme, *Hist. Comm. Thuc.*, ii. 45), and in the accounts of the Eleusinian epistatae for 329/8 unskilled workers are paid 1½ drachmae and skilled 2 or 2½ drachmae (*IG* ii² 1672, cf. Jones, *A.D.*, 143–4 n. 86); so the increase in assembly pay between the 390's and the time of *A.P.* will roughly have kept pace with wage inflation.

For πρῶτον ... ἔπειτα ... εἶθ' ... (without μέν, δέ) Kenyon in his Berlin ed. compares Arist. *Part. Anim.* i. 640 A 14–16.

ἔπειτα τὰ δικαστήρια τρεῖς ὀβολούς: Jury pay was introduced by Pericles, perhaps in the early 450's: the rate was 2 obols at first, raised to 3 obols by Cleon (cf. 27. iii–iv with commentary)—and, strikingly, not raised again between the 420's and the 320's. By the time of *A.P.* jury pay was lower than any other stipend mentioned here, and inadequate as compensation for loss of earnings: jury service will presumably have appealed only to those rich enough not to be deterred by the loss of a day's earnings, and to those so poor that they would regard 3 obols as better than nothing at all (like Philocleon, otherwise dependent on his son, in Ar. *Vesp.*: Is. VII. *Areop.* 54 writes of men offering themselves for jury service because they need the money for the necessities of life; Jones, *A.D.*, 36–7, argues that fourth-century lawcourt speeches were not written with poor jurors in mind, but I doubt if this argument can be pressed far).

εἶθ' ἡ βουλὴ πέντε ὀβολούς: The boule was being paid in 411 (T. VIII. 69. iv), and is included in the list in 24. iii: as a civilian payment this is more likely to have been introduced before than after

COMMENTARY ON THE *ATH. POL.*

the outbreak of the Peloponnesian War. We may guess that payment was not automatic but dependent on attendance, and that the original rate was lower (cf. Rhodes, *A.B.*, 13). Hes. (*B* 931) βουλῆς λαχεῖν gives the rate as 1 drachma, probably by adding the prytanes' extra 1 obol to the bouleutae's 5 (thus Sandys).

τοῖς δὲ πρυτανεύουσιν εἰς σίτησιν ὀβολὸς προστίθεται [[δέκα προστίθενται]]: Blass, *LZB* 1891, 304, restored [ὀβολὸς π]ροστίθεται and deleted δέκα προστίθενται, suggesting that | προστίθεται had been misunderstood (cf. Kaibel, *Stil und Text*, 252-3); Kenyon in his Berlin ed. confirmed Blass' text with the aid of an additional fragment but, objecting to his explanation of the error that in papyri the abbreviation for 1 obol is -, suggested that a commentator had reckoned 10 obols for ten prytanies. Certainly the last two words should be deleted: P. Foucart, *RPh*² xlii 1918, 55-9, suggested ⟨τῷ δ' ἐπιστάτῃ⟩ δέκα προστίθενται, but by comparison with other payments that is far too generous.

This payment is said to be εἰς σίτησιν, and in the case of the prytanes the expression can be seen to be appropriate: for the corporate meals of the prytanes in the Tholos see 43. iii with commentary, and on the vocabulary of Athenian payments see pp. 635-6. Probably μισθός was paid only for the days on which it was earned while money εἰς σίτησιν was paid, to officials who ate together (cf. Arist. *Pol.* VI. 1317 B 38) or who had to spend some time away from Athens, every day (cf. M. H. Hansen, *SO* liv 1979, 7-10; I doubt the suggestion of E. Will, *Le Monde grec ... C. Préaux*, 433-4, that all the payments mentioned in this section should be regarded as εἰς σίτησιν). The συγγραφεῖς of 411 in abolishing civilian stipends made an exception of the nine archons and τῶν πρυτανέων οἳ ἂν ὦσιν, who were each to receive 3 obols a day (29. v with commentary).

ἔπειτ' εἰς σίτησιν λαμβάνουσιν ἐννέ' ἄρχοντες τέτταρας ὀβολοὺς ἕκαστος: As in the case of the prytanes, the payment to the archons is specifically εἰς σίτησιν. According to 3. v in the time of Solon all the nine archons took to using the thesmotheteum as their headquarters (cf. *ad loc.*): it appears from schol. Plat. *Phaedr.* 235 D cf. Hes. πρυτανεῖον that they dined in the thesmotheteum.

καὶ παρατρέφουσι κήρυκα καὶ αὐλητήν: Lists of archons of the Roman period include a κῆρυξ ἄρχοντος/ἄρχοντι and an αὐλητής (e.g. *IG* ii² 1717, 17-20, 1721, 16-19: other officials in these lists are the herald of the Areopagus and a λειτουργός); these functionaries are distinct from the κῆρυξ τῆς βουλῆς καὶ τοῦ δήμου and αὐλητής included among the ἀείσιτοι attached to the boule, who dined in the Tholos (cf. Rhodes, *A.B.*, 140-1, B. D. Meritt & J. S. Traill, *The Athenian Agora*, xv. 7-15, with lists of heralds corrected by M. Piérart, *BCH* c 1976, 443-7). We are left to guess whether the archons' allowance had to cover these men or an extra allowance was paid for them. παρατρέφειν is found also in fourth-century comedy (Timocl. fr. 9. 2 Kock); the passive is used in D. XIX. F.L. 200 to describe Aeschines as a hanger-on ἐπὶ τῷ τριταγωνιστεῖν; cf. P. Soc. It. vi 571, 15 (mid C3: of maintaining a secretary).

ἔπειτ' ἄρχων εἰς Σαλαμῖνα δραχμὴν τῆς ἡμέρας: For this appointment cf. 54. viii with commentary.

ἀθλοθέται δ' ἐν πρυτανείῳ ... ἀπὸ τῆς τετράδος ἱσταμένου: For the athlothetae and their responsibility for the Panathenaea see ch. 60 with commentary. The festival was held towards the end of Hecatombaeon (i): the athlothetae began dining in the prytaneum (cf. 3. v, 24. iii *fin.*, with commentary) on the 4th of the month ('fourteenth', in Kenyon's Oxford Translation, is a slip); the principal day of the Great Panathenaea, the day of the procession, was τρίτη φθίνοντος, the 27th or 28th of the month (Procl. 9 B *ad* Plat. *Tim.* 17 B, schol. Plat. *Rep.* I. 327 A; on the count of days in the last decade of the month see p. 406). Sandys suggests that *A.P.* is referring to the Great Panathenaea only, so that ὅταν ᾖ τὰ Παναθήναια will mean '(in the years) when the Great Panathenaea is celebrated'; but the athlothetae seem to have had some responsibility for the lesser festival also (cf. p. 670), so it is possible that they dined in the prytaneum every year and that ὅταν ᾖ τὰ Παναθήναια is explanatory of τὸν Ἑκατομβαιῶνα μῆνα (implied by Kenyon's Oxford Translation, Mathieu & Haussoullier).

It is surprising to find the dining rights of the athlothetae inserted into this list of cash payments (cf. next note); but I imagine that *A.P.* had to put together himself the material in this section (cf. p. 689), and has digressed from the prytanes and archons to mention another category of men who dined at the state's expense *ex officio*.

ἀμφικτύονες εἰς Δῆλον δραχμὴν τῆς ἡμέρας ἑκάστης ἐκ Δήλου <λαμβάνουσι>: The verb was inserted by Kenyon[1], probably rightly (cf. Kaibel, *Stil und Text*, 253); but Blass refused to insert, and Wilamowitz, *A.u.A.*, i. 195 n. 2, cf. Kaibel & Wilamowitz[3], suggested that the sentence on the athlothetae has been carelessly inserted here and that the amphictyons are part of the subject of ἔπειτ' εἰς σίτησιν λαμβάνουσιν, above.

On festivals at Delos see 54. vii, 56. iii *fin.*, with commentary. The amphictyons were the officials with financial responsibility for the sanctuary: 'in theory they were the deputies of the Ἰώνων τε καὶ περικτιόνων νησιωτῶν' (Sandys, quoting T. III. 104. iii). In the earliest relevant document, M&L 62 = *I. de Délos* 89 (434–432), the title of the officials is not preserved; *I. de Délos* 92 perhaps reflects the Athenian upheavals of 411; Tod 85 = *I. de Délos* 93 (410/09) shows a board of four Athenian amphictyons, and mentions also some Delian νεωκόροι; the accounts of *I. de Délos* 94 (408/7) were drawn up jointly by Athenian amphictyons and Delian [ἐ]π[ίσκ]οποι or [ἐ]π[ίτρ]οποι; Delos was freed from Athens after the Peloponnesian War (cf. Tod 99, with new fragment, *I. de Délos* 87), but was again in Athenian hands and administered by amphictyons before the end of the 390's (*IG* ii² 1634 = *I. de Délos* 97); it was probably made independent by the Peace of Antalcidas, but not for long; there were four Athenian amphictyons until 375/4, five and a secretary and also five Andrians from 374/3 (*IG* ii² 1635 = Tod 125 = *I. de Délos* 98); at that time the office was quinquennial, but in or shortly after 367 it was made annual and the Andrians disappeared (*I. de Délos* 100, 103, 104, with commentary). The amphictyons of 374/3 were from tribes VI–X in official order, and it has been plausibly suggested that the first five tribes would be represented on one board and the other five on the next (cf. W. S. Ferguson, *CR* xv 1901, 38–40): for other occasions when the Athenians had to appoint five men see 52. ii (εἰσαγωγεῖς), 54. i (ὁδοποιοί), 56. iii (choregi for Thargelia), also 51. iii (thirty-five σιτοφύλακες), with commentary. Payments from temple funds εἰς [τ]ἀπ[ι]τήδει[α] to the Athenian amphictyons, their secretary and their under-secretary, and to the Andrian amphictyons, are recorded in *IG* ii² 1635, 74–6. On the administrative changes cf. J. Coupry, *Atti del 3⁰ Congresso Internazionale di Epigrafia Greca e Latina, 1957*, 58–61.

About 345–343 the Delians protested to the Delphic amphictyony against Athenian control of their sanctuary; after the appointment of Aeschines had been quashed, Hyperides was chosen to state Athens' case; and the decision went in Athens' favour (D. XVIII. *Cor.* 134–6, cf. [Pl.] *X. Or.* 850 A, Hyp. frs 71–9 Sauppe: date discussed by M. J. Osborne, *Eranos* lxxii 1974, 176–7 n. 19). Osborne dates *c.* 334 the decree awarding both citizenship and a maintenance grant to Pisithides, who clearly had incurred hostility by following a pro-Athenian line in Delos, and remarks that 'the Athenian grip on Delos was clearly shaky after the late 330's' (*op. cit.*, 175–84, on *IG* ii² 222). For Athens' loss of Delos see next note.

λαμβάνουσι δὲ καὶ ... εἰς σίτησιν ἀργύριον: Samos fell into Athenian hands when it was besieged by Timotheus, in 366–365, in the course of his supporting the Persian rebel Ariobarzanes (D. XV. *Lib. Rhod.* 9, Is. XV. *Antid.* 111); the Samians were banished and Athenian cleruchs sent (Arist. *Rhet.* II. 1384 B 32–5, fr. 611. 35 Teubner [epit. of Σαμ. Πολ.], D.L. x. 1, Str. 638. XIV. i. 18; according to schol. A. I. *Tim.* 53 some were sent in 361/0); more cleruchs were sent in 352/1 (Phil. 328 F 154); the island was left in Athens' possession by Philip after Chaeronea (D.S. XVIII. 56. vii), but the Athenian cleruchy was threatened in 324 by Alexander's order for the return of exiles (D.S. XVIII. 8. vii cf. Pl. *Alex.* 28. ii: see R. M. Errington, *Chiron* v 1975, 51–7, K. Rosen, *Hist.* xxvii 1978, 20–39), and Samos was freed at the end of the Lamian War in 322 (D.S. XVIII. 18. ix; this is the *terminus ante quem* for the completion of *A.P.*: cf. Introduction, p. 52); but Athens recovered control, and Samos was to be returned to Athens according to the edict issued in the name of Philip Arrhidaeus by Polyperchon in 319 (D.S. xviii. 56. vii). Scyros was acquired for Athens by Cimon *c.* 476/5 (cf. p. 77); Lemnos and Imbros were acquired by Miltiades in the 490's; and all three were settled by Athenians and remained in Athens' hands except for a few years after the Peloponnesian War (cf. pp. 686–7). In 315 Antigonus proclaimed that all Greek cities were to be free and independent (D.S. xix. 61. iii); Lemnos rebelled against Athens in 314/3 (D.S. xix. 68. iii), and Imbros and Delos were lost at the same time (cf. W. S. Ferguson, *Hellenistic Athens*, 49–51); the autonomy of the Greek cities was reaffirmed in the peace of 311 (*Svt* 428: *OGIS* 5 = C. B. Welles, *Royal Correspondence in the Hellenistic Period*, 1, 53–6, cf. D. S. xix. 105. i, xx. 19. iii); there is no mention of Scyros in the sources for this period. The further history of the islands need not be pursued here. As for Athenian officials, we find a general on Scyros and two on Lemnos in 329/8 (*IG* ii² 1672, 275–7), and [τ]ὸν [σ]τρα[τ]ηγὸν [τ]ὸν τῶν Ἀθηναίων εἰΣάμον [κ]εχει[ρ]οτον[ημ]ένον in an inscription referred to early 321, with Athens' dispossession not yet complete, by C. Habicht, *AM* lxxii 1957, 156–64, no. 1 (= J. Pouilloux, *Choix d'inscriptions grecques*, 8), *A* 3–4 cf. 9–11, to summer 323 (better) by Errington, *loc. cit.* There are archons, probably appointed from the cleruchs, on Samos in the 330's and 320's (*SIG*³ 276, with new fragment, J. Bousquet, *BCH* lxxxiii 1959, 152–5), and on Imbros (J. Tréheux, *BCH* lxxx 1956, 465–6, on *IG* xii (viii) 51, 13–14).

I doubt whether the list of salaried officials which *A.P.* has put together is complete: in moving from the boule to the prytanes he moves from μισθός to σίτησις, and he then adds other instances of σίτησις and does not return to μισθός. Payments εἰς τροφήν to the ephebi and their σωφρονισταί (who ate together) are mentioned in 42. iii. 24. iii claims of fifth-century Athens that in addition to the armed forces, the jurors and the bouleutae, ἀρχαὶ δ' ἔνδημοι μὲν εἰς ἑπτακοσίους ἄνδρας, ὑπερόριοι δ' εἰς †ἑπτακοσίους† were paid (cf. *ad loc.*). If enough men were to be available to make possible the working of an administrative system which required a large number of board members, who could not hold any of these appointments more than once in their lives (§iii, below), we should expect payments to be made to the poletae, the apodectae and the various other functionaries listed in chs 50–4: there should have been a significant number of ἀρχαί deprived of their stipends in 411 (29. v with commentary), and these stipends ought to be provided in the fourth century no less than in the fifth (contr. M. H. Hansen, *SO* liv 1979, 5–22).†

62. iii] COMMENTARY ON THE *ATH. POL.*

62. iii. ἄρχειν δὲ τὰς μὲν κατὰ πόλεμον ἀρχὰς ἔξεστι πλεονάκις: Military offices were acknowledged to require ability, and therefore the appointments were made not by lot but by election (43. i, 61. i, with commentary) and reelection was permitted: that it occurred is confirmed by the careers of many generals (most notoriously, Phocion, Pl. *Phoc.* 8. i–ii, and Pericles, Pl. *Per.* 16. iv). We may note that not all Greek states were prepared to make this concession: we read in X. *H.* II. i. 7, D.S. XIII. 100. viii, Pl. *Lys.* 7. iii, that Spartan navarchs could not be reelected (but it is argued by B. R. I. Sealey, *Klio* lviii 1976, 340–9, that it was only *c.* 409 that the navarchy became an annual office). In Athens the elective offices and the military were so nearly coextensive that this sentence may not rule out the possibility that the other elected officials of 43. i could also be reelected; Hegemon's law of the 330's may then have set a maximum of four years to the tenure of those and similar offices (see above, p. 515, and Rhodes, *A.B.*, 235, after D. M. Lewis; cf. A. Motzki, *Eubulos von Probalinthos*, 36–8). Most have thought that in the fifth century the hellenotamiae were elected (e.g. Busolt & Swoboda, *G.S.*, ii. 1132, Hignett, *H.A.C.*, 244), and W. K. Pritchett believes on the basis of *IG* i^2 304, *b* + *c*, that they could be reelected (e.g. *U. Calif. Pub. Cl. Stud.* v 1970, 108–9, *Hist.* xxvi 1977, 295–7 cf. 306; contr. B. D. Meritt, *TAPA* xcv 1964, 205 with n. 22, *AJP* lxxxv 1964, 415, *P. A. Philos. S.* cxv 1971, 105–6, 120).

τῶν δ' ἄλλων οὐδεμίαν, πλὴν βουλεῦσαι δίς: Civilian offices were thought to require loyalty to the state but no special ability, and therefore to distribute the jobs fairly among those considered equally eligible appointment was made by lot and reappointment was forbidden. The effect of this rule on the efficiency of Athenian administration will have been mitigated by the fact that, in any particular year, though all office-holders will have been new to their current post, most will in previous years have acquired experience of public service in similar posts. That two years' service were allowed in the boule presumably indicates that if the normal rule had been applied Athens would not have had enough men eligible and willing to fill five hundred seats in the boule each year (cf. Rhodes, *A.B.*, 3–4, with 242–3, listing men known to have served twice in the fourth century). In the democratic constitution imposed on Erythrae in the late 450's service one year in four was allowed (M&L 40, 12). Presumably for the purposes of this rule the college of nine archons and a secretary was regarded as a single office (cf. pp. 243–4).†

The heliastic oath *ap.* D. xxiv. *Tim.* 150 includes an undertaking to enforce both this rule and a rule that a man may not hold two ἀρχαί in the same year (cf. διχόθεν μισθοφορῇ, §123): we may guess that in this connection there were arguments over what appointments counted as ἀρχαί (cf. A. III. *Ctes.* 13–16, 29–30); Demosthenes in 337/6 was simultaneously τειχοποιός and ἐπὶ τὸ θεωρικόν (*ibid.* 24); in 346/5 Eubulides was simultaneously a member of the boule and demarch of Halimus (D. LVII. *Eub.* 8).

S. *Jury-Courts* (63–9)

Having ended (without any expression of conclusion) in ch. 62 the treatment of the ἀρχαί which he began in 43, *A.P.* deals in this final section with certain aspects of the working of the δικαστήρια. He describes in 63–5 the complicated procedure by which jurors were assigned to courts; in 66. i the assignment of magistrates to courts; in 66. ii–iii the appointment of some of the jurors as courtroom officials; in 67 the timing of speeches in different categories of lawsuit; in 68. i the size of juries in public lawsuits; in 68. ii–69. i the voting procedure; and in 69. ii the provision for the second vote in ἀγῶνες τιμητοί, and the payment of the jurors at the end of the day. This is, of course, very far from being a complete account of Athenian judicial procedure: nothing is said about the preliminary stages which preceded the bringing of a case to a δικαστήριον, about the rules governing speeches by the litigants themselves and by their συνήγοροι, about the presentation of evidence, and so on. *A.P.* has concentrated on what we may regard as the mechanical side of the δικαστήρια: the elaborate allotment procedures designed to ensure that the jurors in each court should be a cross-section of the full body of registered jurors, and that no one could know in advance which jurors would try which case; the rules designed to ensure that suitable time should be devoted to different cases according to their importance, and that prosecutor and defendant should have an equal chance to be heard; the voting procedure, designed to ensure that each juror cast one vote and that his vote should be secret. The procedures as described by *A.P.* represent an advanced form of a system that had been growing in elaboration over the past century or more: much ingenuity had been expended in an effort to make it as impartial as possible, and I imagine that *A.P.*'s contemporaries took some pride in this achievement. Presumably *A.P.* himself was fascinated by the details of the system, and this is why he gives a disproportionately lengthy account of it in his survey of the Athenian state (cf. p. 572, on *A.P.*'s treatment of the διαιτηταί and the forty-two year-classes in ch. 53). (J. J. Keaney, *HSCP* lxvii 1963, 121–2, argued that the purpose of this lengthy treatment is to underline the point made in 41. ii *fin.*, καὶ γὰρ αἱ τῆς βουλῆς κρίσεις εἰς τὸν δῆμον ἐληλύθασιν, but see Introduction, p. 37; Prof. D. M. MacDowell suggests to me that, as elsewhere in his second part *A.P.* is concerned primarily with the appointment and functions of officials, here he is concerned primarily with the appointment and functions of jurors, and this explains his selection of topics for discussion.)

It is difficult to describe an elaborate procedure with which one is familiar in such a way that it will be readily understood by a reader who is not familiar with it: at several points *A.P.* has not hit on the best order of exposition, but makes a statement which cannot be understood on the basis of the material thus far presented, and then has to add the further material which the reader needs if he is to understand that statement (see 64. ii, iii, iv, 67. iii, with commentary). Having embarked on the allotment of jurors he adds in 63. iii a note on who may serve as jurors; while dealing with the allotment of jurors he says nothing of the size of juries, but the size of juries in public suits is dealt with in 68. i and the size of juries in private suits (having been mentioned in 53. iii) is not mentioned again here; the time allowance for τιμήσεις is mentioned in 69. ii instead of with other time allowances in 67; the payment of the jurors is baldly mentioned in the last sentence of the work, having been anticipated in 65. iv, 66. iii and 68. ii. There are points at which *A.P.* does not give the reader enough information: he does not say what purpose is served by the σύμβολον mentioned in 65. ii; he does not say (if indeed it was the case) that only one size of jury was used on any one day, that the time allowances of 67. ii were for private suits, probably those where the sum at issue exceeded 1,000 drachmae, that the διαμεμετρημένη ἡμέρα of 67. ii was used to time public suits, probably not only the more important but all, that the time allowance for τιμήσεις in 69. ii was for private suits; he does not say how secret voting was achieved in διαδικασίαι, where the jury might have to decide between more than two litigants. Cf. G. Colin, *REG* xxx 1917, 21–8.

In the preceding chapters of his second part, *A.P.* has often contrasted current with earlier practice. Here, except in the fragmentary end of ch. 67, where there is a clear imperfect ἔσπευδον probably preceded by πρότερον in §iv and perhaps an aorist ἐξεῖλε in §v, he confines himself to the elaborate procedure of his own day. Where earlier practice was different, I note the fact in the commentary; but a systematic discussion of earlier procedure would fall outside the scope of a commentary on *A.P.* (see especially H. Hommel, *Philol.* Supp. XIX. ii 1927, 109–35, Harrison, *L.A.*, ii. 239–41). The most recent of the changes whose result is incorportated in *A.P.*'s account is the introduction of a daily allotment of magistrates to courts, after the late 340's (66. i with commentary).†

I have argued that in his second part *A.P.* is summarising what he found in the laws of Athens (cf. Introduction, pp. 33–5). Here as earlier he uses language which does not prescribe what should happen but describes what happens; οὗτος δὲ καλεῖται ἐμπήκτης, in

64. ii, is unlikely to correspond to anything in the laws; we have references to the laws (as earlier) in 67. i and 69. ii; how fully and how clearly the laws will have expounded the complicated allotment procedures we cannot tell. If the author of this work was an Athenian citizen aged over thirty, he could have been familiar with the whole process from having participated in it himself; if he was Aristotle or a young or non-citizen pupil, he could have witnessed procedure in the courts and, if Dow's account of the court complex (cf. p. 700) is correct, he could also have witnessed the allotment procedures by which the courts were manned. The author will surely have consulted the laws on this as he consulted them on other aspects of the πολιτεία, and his report will no doubt have been influenced by his own knowledge of how things were done.

Columns xxxi–xxxv of the papyrus, containing 64–69. i, are incomplete and where they survive hard to read (especially col. xxxiv, containing 67. iii–68. ii), and we have comparatively few quotations and derivative passages in scholia and lexica to assist reconstruction of this part of the work. However, except in col. xxxiv, enough has been deciphered to make the general sense clear and, although we cannot always be sure of *A.P.*'s actual words, to leave few uncertainties which affect the meaning. Oppermann's Teubner ed. gives an up-to-date text arranged according to the lines of the papyrus from 64. i to the end. In my lemmata I continue to reproduce Kenyon's O.C.T. (but with more punctilious bracketing); I have been very selective in commenting on readings and restorations on which Kenyon's O.C.T., the Budé ed. of Mathieu & Haussoullier and the Teubner ed. of Oppermann are in agreement. In addition to the editors of the whole of *A.P.*, the following have made particularly important contributions to the reconstruction and elucidation of these chapters:

Π. Σ. ΦΩΤΙΑΔΗΣ περὶ κληρώσεως καὶ πληρώσεως τῶν ἡλιαστικῶν δικαστηρίων. *Ἀθ.* xiv 1902, 241–82.

—— περὶ τῆς τῶν ἡλιαστῶν μισθοφορᾶς καὶ τῶν δικαστικῶν συμβόλων. *Ἀθ.* xv 1903, 3–32.

—— περὶ τῆς διαμεμετρημένης ἡμέρας καὶ τῆς δικαστικῆς κλεψύδρας. *Ἀθ.* xvi 1904, 3–87.

G. COLIN 'Les Sept Derniers Chapitres de l' *Ἀθηναίων Πολιτεία.*' [Includes translation of whole, restoration of 67. iv–68. i.] *REG* xxx 1917, 20–87.

H. HOMMEL *Heliaia.* [Includes text and translation of whole.] *Philol.* Supp. XIX. ii 1927.

A. L. BOEGEHOLD 'Aristotle and the Dikasteria.' Harvard thesis, 1957 (cf. abstract, *HSCP* lxiii 1958, 526–8).

For S. Dow's explanation of the κληρωτήρια see on 63. ii. Throughout

COMMENTARY ON THE *ATH. POL.*

this last section of the commentary, references to Colin, *op. cit.*, and to Hommel, *op. cit.*, are to the works listed here.

63. i. τὰ δ(ὲ) [[τὰ]] δικαστήρια [κ]ληρ[οῦ]σ[ιν] ... τῆς] δεκάτης φυλῆς: Cf. 59. vii, where the same fact is stated at the end of *A.P.*'s account of the archons and their duties: we read there that each of the ten officials supervises the allotment for his own tribe. The allotment which is conducted by tribes is that described in detail in 63-5: it picks from the registered jurors who offer themselves for service each day which are to serve, and which of them are to serve in which court. 59. vii guarantees the κληροῦσιν of Kenyon[1] against the πληροῦσιν of R. Dareste, *JS* 1891, 266 with n. 2; but there is no need to insert ⟨ὁ⟩ τῶν, or ⟨τοὺς⟩ or ⟨τὰ⟩ τῆς, as some have done, to bring this passage linguistically into line with 59. vii. In this sentence δικαστήρια refers to the courts as collections of men, but in the next it refers to the courtooms.

63. ii. εἴσοδοι δέ εἰσιν ε[ἰς] τὰ δικαστ[ή]ρια δέκα: The theory that the κληρωτήρια were allotment-rooms (cf. next note) had led scholars to infer the existence of a court complex with ten entrances leading to twenty rooms, from which the jurors selected to serve proceeded through a κιγκλίς (65. i), across a courtyard or along a corridor, to their appointed courtrooms (cf. Hommel, *op. cit.*, 52-9 with 140 Abb. 1). Dow's identification of the κληρωτήρια allowed him to propose a simpler arrangement: the tribal entrances led directly to the courtyard or corridor which gave access to the courtrooms; the κιγκλίδες were the gates in these entrances; and the allotments were performed outside these tribal entrances, which is why we read at the beginning of 64. i that the κιβώτια are placed ἐν τῷ ἔμπροσθεν τῆς εἰσόδου, cf. πρὸ τῶν δικαστηρίων κληρουμένους in Is. VII. *Areop.* 54 (*HSCP* l 1939, 15-20, followed by Fritz & Kapp, 197-9 n. 192, but not by Moore, 306, 307). For buildings in the Agora which are throught to have served as lawcourts see R. E. Wycherley, *The Athenian Agora*, iii, pp. 144-9, H. A. Thompson & R. E. Wycherley, *The Athenian Agora*, xiv. 52-72, cf. *Agora Guide*[3], 58-60, 118-19, 166-8, 307-10, Wycherley, *The Stones of Athens*, 53-60. The excavators believe that none of these buildings can be the court complex required by *A.P.*'s account (Thompson & Wycherley, *op. cit.*, 61; Wycherley, *Stones*, 60, 'wonders whether such a degree of concentration and regularization ... was ever attained'). Certainly none would satisfy Hommel's requirements; it is possible, though not easy, to suppose that Dow's simpler requirements were briefly satisfied by the buildings under the northern half of the Stoa of Attalus (late c5-mid c4; replaced by the Square Peristyle, on which work began *c.* 325); Boegehold, 'Aristotle and the Dikasteria', 6-17, suggests that there was a gradual concentration of the courts towards the north-east of the Agora, and that at the beginning of each day when courts were to sit a suitable area was temporarily fenced off.[60] Other evidence does not confirm what we should conclude from *A.P.*, that all the courts were in a single complex: *IG* ii² 1641, 28–30 (mid c4) and 1670, 34–5 (*c.* 330) refer to courts meeting in the Stoa Poecile; trials in the Odeum are mentioned by Ar. *Vesp.* 1109 and [D.] LIX. *Neaer.* 52, 54 (suggesting that they were still held there in the late 340's: cf. on 66. i); for the heliaea cf. 68. i with commentary; for a survey of the names of Athenian courts see Andr. 324 F 59 with commentary. Boegehold has suggested that there was a δικαστήριον in the Piraeus, at Zea, whose jurors can hardly have been allotted by the process described by *A.P.* (cf. above, p. 646).†

καὶ κληρ[ωτήρι]α εἴκοσι, δ[ύο τ]ῇ φυλῇ ἑκάστῃ: Early interpreters were uncertain whether κληρωτήρια were vessels for holding lots (e.g. Reinach) or rooms in which allotments were made (Kaibel & Kiessling, and many others, to Hommel, *op. cit.*, 12, 53 with n. 129). The problem was solved when S. Dow identified blocks of stone with columns of slits in one face as Hellenistic versions of an 'allotment-machine', showed how they will have been used, and applied the term κληρωτήριον to these (*Hesp.* Supp. i 1937, 198–215, *HSCP* l 1939, 1–34, cf. *RE*, Supp. vii [1940], 322–8; refinements by J. D. Bishop, *JHS* xc 1970, 1–14; the correct meaning is given by the 1968 Supplement to LSJ, but the latest edition of Mathieu & Haussoullier still translates 'salles'). The word κληρωτήριον is first found in Ar. *Eccl.* 681, but the procedure for allotting jurors was simpler in the early fourth century than in the time of *A.P.* (Hommel, *op. cit.*, 115–26, Harrison, *L.A.*, ii. 240–1). For the use of these κληρωτήρια see 64. ii–iii with commentary. *A.P.* begins here a list of the equipment needed for the allotment of jurors to courts.‡

καὶ κιβώτια ἑκατόν, δέκα τῇ φυλῇ ἑκάστῃ: 100 boxes. Within each tribe members are divided into ten sections designated *A–K* (§iv): on arrival men drop their πινάκιον into the box by their tribal entrance which bears their section-letter (64. i).

καὶ ἕτερα κιβώτι[α, εἰς ἃ ἐ]μβάλλεται τῶν λαχόντων δικαστῶν τὰ πινάκια: The πινάκια (§iv with commentary) of the men selected for service are dropped into appropriately lettered boxes when the men have drawn lots for their courts; each tribe will have had as many boxes for this purpose as there were courts sitting that day (64. iv–v,

---

[60] We encounter in *Hesp.* v 10 (342/1) [δικαστήριον] πρῶτον τῶν καιν[ῶν] (lines 12–13) and δικαστήριον τὸ μέσ[ον τῶ]ν καινῶν (116–17), and in *Hesp.* xxxvii 50 = *SEG* xxv 180, 13–14 (320's) δικαστή[ρι]ον μέσον τῶν καινῶν: these expressions are best understood as references to the first and the middle courts in the new complex of courts, presumably in the north-east of the Agora (Dow, *HSCP* l 1939, 23, R. E. Wycherley, *The Athenian Agora*, iii, p. 147; but contr. B. D. Meritt, *Hesp.* v 1936, 408).

63. ii] COMMENTARY ON THE *ATH. POL.*

65. iv). In 66. ii we read that each courtroom is equipped with a κιβώτιον for the allotment of courtroom officials.

καὶ ὑδρίαι δύο: The water pots hold the lettered βάλανοι used to allot jurors to particular courts (below and 64. iv); it was desirable to use a narrow-topped vessel if the jurors were to pick their βάλανοι blindly. Presumably there are not two pots in all but two for each tribe: since there are ten entrances to the court complex, and the twenty κληρωτήρια are now known not to have been or to have required twenty rooms (cf. above), there is no obvious reason why one larger pot should not have been used (and D. M. MacDowell suggests that we should emend to δέκα, one pot for each tribe), but perhaps it was thought convenient to place one by each κληρωτήριον. Fritz & Kapp and Moore punctuate with a full point before rather than after these words, but that is not an improvement.

καὶ βακτηρίαι ... ὅσοιπερ οἱ δικασταί: Cf. D. xviii. *Cor.* 210. The staves bore the colours of the different courts, as many of each colour as there were needed jurors to man that court (65. i–iii). κατὰ τὴν ε[ἴσοδον] was restored by Kenyon[1]: Hommel objected that in the court complex which he envisaged the staves were needed not at the tribal entrances but at the κιγκλίδες, and restored ἔ[ξοδον] (*op. cit.*, 12, 56–8, accepted by Oppermann and by Gomme, *CR* xliv 1930, 64); but if Dow is right in locating the allotment of jurors outside the ten tribal entrances (cf. above) Kenyon's εἴσοδον will be correct.

καὶ βάλανοι ... ἴσαι ταῖς βακτηρίαις: Cf. above. The βάλανοι are acorns, or (by the time of *A.P.*, more probably) manufactured tokens resembling or replacing acorns.

ἐγ[γ]έγραπται δ' ... τὰ δικαστήρια πληρωθήσεσθαι: The courts are identified by distinctive letters as well as colours (§v), and jurors are allotted to courts by drawing a lettered βάλανος from a water pot; letters beginning with Λ are used to designate the courts, to avoid confusion with the letters Α–Κ used to designate sections of tribes. Π. Ν. Παπαγεώργιος, *Ἀθ.* iv 1892, 613, proposed ⟨γράμματα⟩ τῶν στοιχείων, but a subject can be supplied from ὅσαπερ. After στοιχείων in the papyrus, 'the words at first written appear to have been απο του ενδεκατου του τριακοστου. Then του τριακοστου is cancelled, and above the last syllable of ενδεκατου and the cancelled words is written του λ · τριακοστου ·. It is clear that the insertion of τριακοστου is a mistake', and that a copyist supposed λ here to denote 30 (Kenyon[1]). For πληροῦν δικαστήρια cf. p. 397.

63. iii. δικάζειν δ' ἔξεστιν ... ἢ ἄτιμοί εἰσιν: In the fifth century there was a panel of six thousand jurors (24. iii, and other texts cited *ad loc.*). *A.P.* has usually been supposed to mean by this sentence that in his own time all citizens over thirty were eligible to (register and

COMMENTARY ON THE *ATH. POL.* [63. iii

thereafter) offer themselves for jury service, without limit of numbers (e.g. Sandys; Hommel, *op. cit.*, 36–7, 49–50); but the heliastic oath was administered every year (Is. xv. *Antid.* 21) and, as argued by J. H. Kroll, life membership of the panel seems incompatible with the frequent reuse to which surviving πινάκια have been subjected: there must have been an annual registration, with men changing their πινάκιον whenever they became or ceased to be members of the panel, and the size of the panel may well have remained fixed (*Athenian Bronze Allotment Plates*, 69–86). If more than the prescribed number volunteered in any year, either the first to volunteer will have been accepted or perhaps lots will have been drawn (the second possibility was championed by Wilamowitz, *A.u.A.*, i. 200–4, Jones, *A.D.*, 123–4 with 159 n. 145: Kroll, *op. cit.*, 85–6, finds their arguments insufficient but still accepts the possibility); the problem of filling the panel if too few volunteered perhaps did not arise. *A.P.* says nothing of a fixed number or of annual registration, but for the dangers of assuming that he tells the whole truth in such matters cf. 42. i with commentary, 42. ii and 53. iv with commentary, and Introduction, p. 36.

Thirty was the normal age requirement for holding office in Athens (cf. p. 510), whereas citizens could attend the assembly from the age of eighteen or at any rate twenty (cf. pp. 494–5). Men in debt to the state were automatically ἄτιμοι until their debt was discharged (cf. Rhodes, *A.B.*, 150, M. H. Hansen, *Apagoge, Endeixis and Ephegesis*, 93–4), so the statement of disqualification should be translated 'as many of them as are not in debt to the state or otherwise deprived of rights' (cf. Colin, *op. cit.*, 30). For the minimum age cf. the heliastic oath *ap.* D. xxiv. *Tim.* 151, Poll. viii. 122; for the ban on public debtors cf. D. xxiv. *Tim.* 123.

Logically, this section might suitably have been placed at the beginning of the account of the δικαστήρια, but *A.P.* seems to have embarked on his treatment of the allotments and then to have decided that this information was necessary (cf. p. 698).

ἐὰν δέ τι[ς] δικάζῃ ... προστιμήσῃ τ[ὸ δικ]αστήριον: ἔνδειξις was a procedure initiated by the prosecutor's denouncing an offender to the authorities: it was available against κακοῦργοι, and against ἄτιμοι and exiles who exercised rights to which they were not entitled; this is an instance of the latter (cf. 52. i with commentary). *A.P.* describes this trial as an ἀγὼν τιμητός, for which the penalty was not fixed but had to be assessed by the court. The boule was entitled but not obliged to imprison defaulting public debtors (cf. Rhodes, Hansen, *locc. citt.*); but if a defaulting debtor incurred a further fine for attempting to serve on a jury while disqualified he had to be imprisoned. There is an instance of ἔνδειξις on this charge, leading to the death sentence, in D. xxi. *Mid.* 182.

63. iv] COMMENTARY ON THE *ATH. POL.*

63. iv. ἔχει δ' ἕκαστος δικαστὴς τὸ πινάκιον πύξινον ... ἐν ἑκάστῳ τῷ γράμ[μα]τι: Here, as elsewhere in his chapters on the jury-courts, *A.P.* describes current practice and says nothing of different earlier practice (cf. p. 698), but D. xxxix. *Boe. Nom.* 10-12 (*c.* 348) refers to bronze πινάκια (in connection with magisterial appointments). No boxwood πινάκια survive, but nearly two hundred bronze πινάκια answering to *A.P.*'s description of the boxwood πινάκια do survive, and many are stamped with the design used on the reverse of Athenian triobol coins, which has long been recognised as appropriate to jurors (O. Benndorf, *ZÖG* xxvi 1875, 601, S. Bruck, *Philol.* liv = ²viii 1895, 70: on the jurors' stipend of 3 obols see 62. ii with commentary). The bronze plates measure about 11 × 2 × 0.2 cm; some but not all include the patronymic; for an illustration see fig. 1. They are catalogued and discussed by J. H. Kroll, *Athenian Bronze Allotment Plates*, who argues:

(*a*) Soon after 388, bronze πινάκια with the 'triobol' stamp were first issued, for dicastic allotments.

(*b*) Subsequently the mechanism was applied to magisterial allotments, with πινάκια bearing a 'gorgoneum' stamp, and citizens eligible for dicastic as well as magisterial allotments were given a πινάκιον bearing both stamps.

(*c*) About 350, boxwood πινάκια replaced bronze for dicastic allotments; bronze πινάκια were retained for magisterial allotments but stamps were no longer used.

The πινάκια were needed for allotment by κληρωτήριον (64. i-iii). There were ten sections (μέρη) of each tribe, designated *A-K*, and Kroll has shown that citizens became members for life of whichever section they were assigned to.

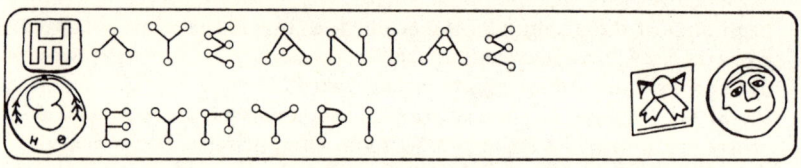

Fig. 1 A πινάκιον, validated for both dicastic and magisterial allotments (section letter and 'triobol' left, year stamp(?) and 'gorgoneum' right)

63. v. ἐπειδὰν δὲ ὁ θεσμοθέτης ... τὸ γράμμα τὸ λαχόν: The lot was used even to determine which court should be designated by which letter. This seems an unnecessary refinement (cf. p. 711). Presumably the colours of the different courts were assigned permanently (63. ii, 65. i-iii); but magistrates with the cases for which they were responsible were assigned to courts by lot (not by letter but by colour), after the allotment of jurors was completed (66. i); so, even if it were possible for a juror to exchange a prepared βάλανος for the one which he drew, permanent lettering would enable him to choose his courtroom but not his cases. However, the allotment of magistrates to courts seems to have been a recent innovation when *A.P.* wrote, and this allotment of court letters may be a survival from a time when it could be known in advance which magistrate would take his cases to the court of which colour. The medley of information and misinformation in schol. Ar. *Plut.* 277 includes a statement that πρὸ θυρῶν δὲ ἑκάστου δικαστηρίου ἐγέγραπτο πύρρῳ βάμματι τὸ στοιχεῖον, ᾧτινι τὸ δικαστήριον ὠνομάζετο.

Probably any of the 'ten archons' might perform this allotment, though *A.P.* says ὁ θεσμοθέτης (cf. 64. i, 66. i, with commentary, but contr. Colin, *op. cit.*, 54 with n. 1): by analogy with 66. i we may guess that he was himself picked by lot (Hommel, *op. cit.*, 59, considered both that and rotation possible). Gilbert (*C.A.S.A.*, 398 with n. 2) and Sandys are probably mistaken in referring specifically to this allotment the praise of a man who as thesmothetes ἐπιμελεῖται δὲ καὶ τῆς πληρώσεως τῶν δικαστ[ηρ]ίων (*IG* ii² 1163, 8–10). We encounter ὁ ὑπηρέτης here; ὁ ὑπηρέτης in each tribe in 64. i and 65. i; οἱ... ὑπηρέται οἱ δημόσιοι ἀπὸ τῆς φυλῆς ἑκάστης in 65. iv; a plurality of ὑπηρέται in each court in 69. i. It will be sufficient for all passages except the last if one public slave is assigned to each of the 'ten archons', and the man who makes the allotment described here is assisted by the slave assigned to him (cf. Colin, *op. cit.*, 61, believing that one ὑπηρέτης in each court would suffice; Hommel, *op. cit.*, 62, not mentioning 69. i); perhaps when the allotments were completed the ten ὑπηρέται were distributed among the courts that were sitting that day.

At the end of this chapter, almost at the bottom of a full-length column of the papyrus (col. xxx) but in the middle of a line, the work of the fourth scribe ends. The remainder of our text was written by the third scribe, on a fresh piece of papyrus, taken from an earlier section of the accounts whose reverse has been used hitherto (cf. Kenyon[1–3]). See p. 699 and Introduction, p. 4.

64. i. τὰ δὲ [κιβώ]τια τὰ δέ[κ]α ... πιν]άκιον ἕν: Kenyon, Mathieu & Haussoullier and Oppermann agree on α[ὐτ]ῷ τῶν στοιχείω[ν], proposed by Blass[3]; Hommel, *op. cit.*, 14 with n. 44, preferred ἀ[πὸ], proposed by Herwerden & Leeuwen but said to be impossible by Wilcken; Kaibel *ap.* Kaibel & Wilamowitz[3] read and deleted [[ἐστιν α[ὐτ]ὸ τῶν στοιχεί[ων ἕν]]]; Dr J. D. Thomas finds ω slightly preferable to o. [τότε] σείσαντος is restored by Kenyon in his Berlin ed. and O.C.T. and may well be right; Mathieu & Haussoullier and Oppermann prefer the [δια]σείσαντος of Haussoullier, *RPh*² xv

1891, 99; [ἀνασ]είσας is restored in *IG* ii² 204, 36, and that compound would be a better alternative to Kenyon's restoration here if one is needed; Gomme, *CR* xliv 1930, 65 n. 3, suggested εἰσενέγκαντος, but no such act is needed if we may locate the allotments outside the ten tribal entrances (cf. p. 700). The Homeric verb for shaking lots is πάλλειν (e.g. *Il*. III. 316), but the only prose author from whom this is cited by LSJ is Herodotus (III. 128. i). This refers to the first set of boxes mentioned in 63. ii. In front of each tribal entrance to the court complex there are ten boxes labelled *A–K*, and each man offering himself for jury service drops his πινάκιον into the box labelled with his section letter. At each entrance is a ὑπηρέτης (cf. 63. v with commentary), who after all the potential jurors have surrendered their πινάκια shakes each box; the archon from that tribe (ὁ θεσμοθέτης here, ὁ ἄρχων subsequently: cf. 63. v, 66. i, with commentary, and Hommel, *op. cit.*, 62–3) draws one πινάκιον from each box (for ἕλκειν cf. *IG* ii² 204, 36, not cited by LSJ or the 1968 Supplement), and the man whose πινάκιον is drawn serves as ἐμπήκτης (cf. next note).

64. ii. οὗτο[ς] δὲ καλεῖται ἐμ[πήκτ]ης ... ἐπὶ τοῦ [κιβωτίο]υ: ἐμπήκτης was first suggested by I. Bywater, *CR* v 1891, 119; the nominative plural (corrupted to ἐμπερηκται, corrected by Blass²) is preserved at the end of 65. iii. Hes. (*E* 2451) supposes the ἐμπήκτης to be a ὑπηρέτης; *L.S.* 258. 21 supposes him to be ὁ θεσμοθέτης: both are now seen to be wrong.

To understand this sentence we must look ahead to the last sentence in §ii. Each tribe has two allotment-machines (see illustration in fig. 2; these are the κληρωτήρια: 63. ii with commentary); each machine has five κανονίδες, columns of slots, labelled *A–E* and *Z–K* (in *Hesp.* Supp. i 1937, 214, Dow translated κανονίς as 'bar' and was unhappy at the thought of κανονίδες as vertical columns, but in *HSCP* l 1939, 5–8, he cited the 'door-frames' of *IG* ii² 1672, 155, and was reconciled to κανονίδες as columns); the man whose πινάκιον has been drawn from each box acts as 'inserter' (ἐμπηγνύναι is a reasonably common verb, but the noun is found only in this connection), and inserts the remaining πινάκια from his box in the slots of the appropriate column, presumably beginning at the top and working steadily downwards. (The 1968 Supplement to LSJ has the correct meaning of κληρωτήριον, but lacks the correct meanings of other technical terms used in connection with the κληρωτήρια.)

[κληροῦται δ'] οὗτος ... κακουργῇ: The ἐμπήκτης is chosen by lot: that is in keeping with the elaborate randomness of this system of allotting jurors, and in fact there is one departure from pure randomness in the system which he could exploit to his enemies' disadvantage. It is likely that more men will offer themselves for service in some of the ten sections than in others; as will be seen (§iii with commentary), men whose πινάκια are placed lower on the κληρωτήριον than the last πινάκιον in the shortest column have no chance of being picked for service that day; it may have been easier to see the πινάκια in the boxes than the βάλανοι in the water pots (cf. on 63. ii), and an unscrupulous ἐμπήκτης may have been able deliberately to leave until last his enemies' πινάκια.

εἰσὶ δὲ κανονίδες [πέντε ἐ]ν ἑκάστῳ τῶν κληρωτηρίων: Cf. above. Each tribe has two κληρωτήρια; the columns like the boxes are labelled A–K; the number to be supplied is therefore πέντε (Blass[3]).

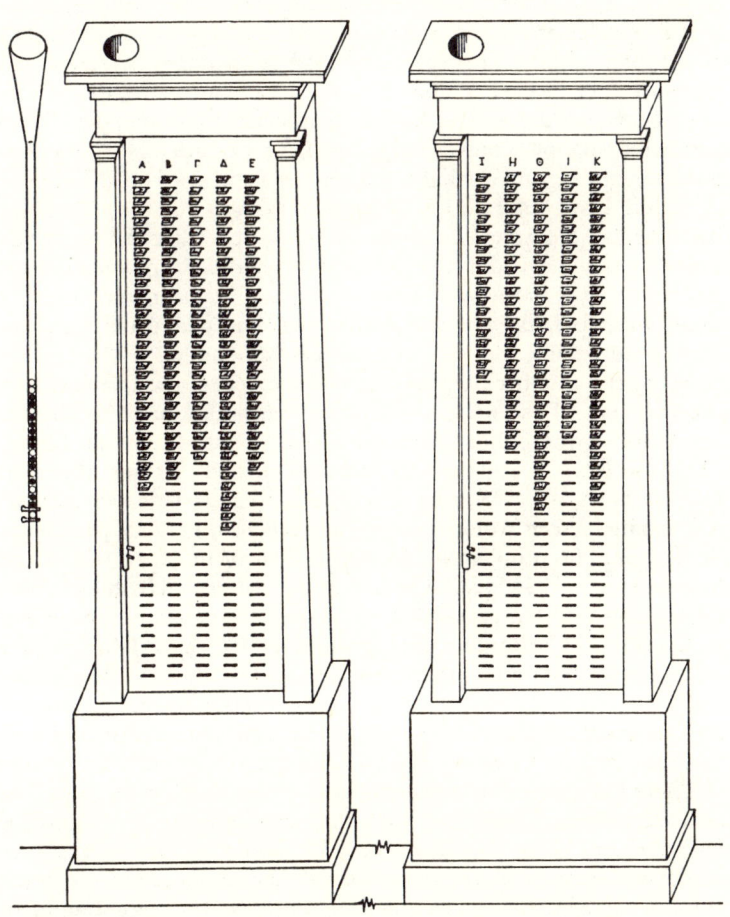

Fig. 2   A pair of κληρωτήρια, for dicastic allotments

707

64. iii. ὅ[ταν δὲ] ἐμβάλῃ ... τὸν αὐτὸν τρόπον: Haussoullier, *RPh*[2] xv 1891, 99, had restored [ἐπειδὰν δ']; ὅ[ταν δ'] was read by Wilcken; Kenyon in his Berlin ed. judged the reading doubtful but ὅταν δὲ a better-length supplement; M. H. Chambers, *TAPA* xcvi 1965, 39, prefers ἐ[πειδὰν δ'] and thinks the space sufficient for that; Dr Thomas finds ε a slightly preferable reading, but ὅ[ταν better for the space though ἐ[πιδὰν δ'] would just fit. Kaibel and Wilamowitz restored [εἰς τ]ὸ κληρωτήριον, but that presupposes a contorted word order and Kenyon in his Berlin ed. rejected the ο: the κατὰ of Blass[3] is rightly accepted in more recent editions. Kenyon and Oppermann punctuate before ὁ ἄρχων, Mathieu & Haussoullier and Hommel (*op. cit.*, 15) after: even with the former punctuation it will not be disputed that the archon is the subject of both verbs in this sentence.

A.P.'s order of exposition is again not ideal for the reader who is new to the subject. There was attached to each κληρωτήριον a tube with an open funnel at the top and a release mechanism at the bottom. When the πινάκια had been inserted into their slots, black and white ballots (called κύβοι by *A.P.*: presumably cubes were used originally, and probably cubes were still used in the time of *A.P.* [cf. Dow, *Hesp.* Supp. i 1937, 213–14], but the κληρωτήρια published by Dow were designed for cylindrical tubes, and spherical ballots in cylindrical tubes will have been most practical) were poured into the funnel, and fell into the tube in a random order. As many white ballots were used as there were needed jurors from each tribal section, and enough black ballots were added to yield a total equal to the number of πινάκια in the shortest of the five columns; the insertion of the πινάκια must have been completed before the black and white ballots were mixed and poured into the funnel. (The ἐμπῆκται were automatically reckoned among the men selected for jury service, so if two thousand jurors were needed in all a further nineteen would have to be picked from each section [cf. below]; for the problem of the odd one juror in excess of a round hundred see pp. 712, 729.) The sortition is performed by the member of the board of 'ten archons' who belongs to the tribe in question: he operates the release mechanism so that one ballot falls from the tube; that ballot applies to the five columns on the one κληρωτήριον, so if it is white the five men whose πινάκια occupy the first horizontal row are accepted, but if it is black they are rejected; and he continues with one ballot at a time until all have been released.

There must not be more ballots in all than there are πινάκια in the shortest column, since otherwise the late emergence of a white ballot will result in the acceptance of fewer than five jurors: men whose πινάκια were placed lower than the last πινάκιον in the shortest column therefore had no chance of acceptance. If different numbers of men offered themselves for service in various of the hundred tribal sections, the Athenians could not both select an equal number from each section and give each man an equal chance of being selected: it would probably have been thought fairer to draw lots separately for each section rather than to eliminate in advance some members of most sections, but that would have made the process much slower, and to draw lots for five sections at a time rather than for all ten together was presumably thought to be an acceptable compromise. It is of course possible that on days when many jurors were needed too few offered themselves for service, either too few in particular sections or too few in a whole tribe or altogether (cf. Hommel, *op. cit.*, 61). *A.P.* mentions no provision for these shortages: if there were too few men in some sections but too many in others, surplus πινάκια could be transferred from the longest column to the shortest; if there were too few altogether, either more jurors would have to be recruited or one or more courts would have to operate with a reduced jury or one or more courts would be unable to sit. (I imagine that the second of these possibilities would be considered the least acceptable: for a period in wartime when, owing to a shortage either of jurors or of money to pay them, the hearing of δίκαι was suspended and only γραφαί were tried, see D. XLV. *Steph. i.* 4.)

ἐπειδὰν δ' ἐ[ξέλῃ] ... ὁ κ[ῆρυξ]: Kenyon follows Haussoullier (*RPh*[2] xv 1891, 100) in restoring ἐξέλῃ; Hommel (*op. cit.*, 15) and Oppermann follow Blass in restoring ἐξαιρῇ (cf. Kaibel, *Stil und Text*, 260, arguing that τοὺς κύβους requires the present but τὸν κύβον or τῶν κύβων ἕκαστον would require the aorist). Colin, *op. cit.*, 31 n. 1, 52, argued for the aorist on the grounds that the summoning of the men selected could more conveniently be done when the allotment had been completed; but it seems unlikely that the κληρωτήρια contained a provision for retaining a display of the black and white ballots in the order in which they had emerged, so it is likelier that each time a ballot was released the five men to whose πινάκια it applied were forthwith declared accepted or rejected, and if accepted proceeded immediately to draw lots for their courts (cf. Dow, *HSCP* l 1939, 30). If that is correct, we should restore the present ἐξαιρῇ. There is a single herald of the archons in 62. ii; the courts require a herald for each tribe in the allotments, and a herald for each court during the hearings (68. iv–69. i, cf. 66. i with commentary).

ὑπάρχει δὲ καὶ ὁ ἐμπήκτης εἰς τὸν [ἀριθμό]ν: As first suggested by Lipsius, *A.R.*, 147, this means that each ἐμπήκτης is reckoned among the men picked for service from his section.

64. iv. ὁ δὲ κληθεὶς καὶ ὑπακ[ού]σας ... ἄνω ἔχ]ων τὸ γράμμα: The subject is ὁ εἰληχώς. ὑπακούσας was suggested by Blass[3] in his

COMMENTARY ON THE *ATH. POL.*

apparatus; the reading is far from certain but nothing preferable has been proposed; 'answering to the summons' (as in And. 1. *Myst.* 112) gives a very satisfactory sense. Sandys proposed ἀνέχ]ων, which Oppermann and Dr J. D. Thomas prefer; Kenyon in his Berlin ed. judged ἄνω ἔχ]ων more appropriate to the space. When a man is picked for service he goes to the water pot, one of which presumably stands near each κληρωτήριον (63. ii with commentary), draws out a βάλανος, and holds it up so as to show the letter on it. δ[εί]κνυσιν πρῶ[τον μὲν] ... οὓς ἂν βούληταί τις: Yet again the reader needs to look ahead, to §v: there are placed near the κληρωτήρια as many boxes for each tribe as there are courts to be manned, labelled with the letters designating the courts (these are the ἕτερα κιβώτια of 63. ii). Each juror, when he has drawn his βάλανος, first shows it to the archon, who takes his πινάκιον from the κληρωτήριον and drops it into the box bearing the same letter as his βάλανος; he then proceeds to the κιγκλίς and shows his βάλανος to the ὑπηρέτης (65. i). As a further measure to ensure that jurors go to the courts to which they are assigned, the boxes of πινάκια are taken to the appropriate courts, and the πινάκια are returned to their owners there when they are paid at the end of the day's business (65. iv, 66. iii, 69. ii).

64. v. πα[ράκει]ται δὲ τῷ ἄρχοντι ... ἑκάσ[του] εἰληχός: Cf. previous note. Kaibel & Wilamowitz[3] restored [ῇ] τοῦ δικαστηρίου; earlier Kaibel, *Stil und Text*, 262, had restored [ῇ τό], and that is preferred by Kenyon and others as more appropriate to the space (cf. Hommel, *op. cit.*, 16 n. 46).

65. i. αὐτ[ὸς δὲ δείξα]ς πάλιν τ[ῷ ὑ]πηρέτῃ εἶτ' ἐ[ντὸς εἰσέρχετ]αι τῆς κ[ι]γκλ[ί]δος: Reconstructed in Kenyon's Berlin ed.: there he printed Diels' εἰσέ[ρχεται, ἐντὸς ἰὼ]ν τῆς; his own εἶτ' ἐντὸς εἰσέρχεται, suggested in the *apparatus*, is adopted in his O.C.T. (εἰσέρχεται] τῆς) and by Mathieu & Haussoullier, Hommel (*op. cit.*, 16) and Oppermann; Dr J. D. Thomas reports that εἶ[τ]' ἐν[is acceptable. A κιγκλίς is a gate in a barrier: if Dow is right in locating the allotments outside the tribal entrances to the court complex (cf. p. 700), these κιγκλίδες will have been at the εἴσοδοι of 63. ii; men selected for jury service will thus have entered the court complex and gone to their separate courts. (Cf. on the κιγκλίδες of the boule Rhodes, *A.B.*, 33–4, G. Roux, *BCH* c 1976, 475–83). On the ὑπηρέται cf. 63. v with commentary.

ὁ δὲ ὑπηρέτης ... [τ]ῆς βακτηρίας: Reconstructed largely by Kaibel & Wilamowitz[1], cf. *L.S.* 220. 17, schol. Ar. *Vesp.* 1110. Kaibel & Wilamowitz restored ἕτερον εἰσ[ίῃ]; Kenyon in his Berlin ed. and O.C.T., cf. Mathieu & Haussoullier, Tovar, restored εἰ[σέ]λ[θῃ];

COMMENTARY ON THE *ATH. POL.* [65. i

Hommel (*op. cit.*, 17 with n. 47: εἰ[σ]ί[η]) and Oppermann revert to the present; according to Dr Thomas the aorist form fits the space better but neither really suits the traces on the papyrus. Hommel argues that a juror entering the wrong court will be exposed as he enters rather than after he has entered; but I am not sure that his meaning requires the present, and in any case if the jurors retain their staves until they vote (65. iii, 68. ii, with commentary; but Hommel rejects Kenyon's restorations) the aorist may be right here.

Once more the reader needs to look ahead: we find in §ii that each courtroom is designated by a colour; the staves have been mentioned but without reference to their colours, in 63. ii. Each court has a letter allotted to it for the day (63. v), and the jurors have drawn βάλανοι assigning them to their courts by letter (64. iv–v); at the κιγκλίς each juror is handed a staff of the colour which that day corresponds to the letter on his βάλανος, and a juror who tries to enter the wrong court will thus be easily detected. However, it should have been no more troublesome to check βάλανοι at the entrances to the courtrooms than to check βάλανοι and issue staves at the κιγκλίδες: once the magistrates were assigned to their courtrooms by lot the double designation of the courts by colour and by letter was superfluous, and trouble might arise if a careless ὑπηρέτης gave a juror a staff of the wrong colour (cf. pp. 704–5).

65. ii. τοῖ[ς γὰρ δι]καστηρίοις ... τῷ σφη[κ]ίσκῳ τῆς εἰσ[όδο]υ: Quoted by schol. Ar. *Plut.* 278: editors have preferred the scholiast's χρῶμα to the papyrus' χρώματα, the papyrus' ἑκάστῳ to the scholiast's ἐφ' ἑκάστῳ (for which there is no room), and in the next sentence the papyrus' τὸ δικαστήριον to the scholiast's δικαστήριον. σφηκίσκος (derived from σφήξ, 'wasp') denotes a pointed stake in Ar. *Plut.* 301; in building schedules it denotes a rafter (e.g. *IG* i² 372, 81: *pace* LSJ there is no reason why it should not have that meaning in *IG* i² 313, 108); here it is normally translated 'lintel' (for which the normal term is ὑπέρθυρον, as in H. I. 179. iii, *IG* i² 372, 201 = i³ 474, 200), and that seems to be the obvious interpretation.

Paus. I. 28. viii mentions among the Athenian courts βατραχιοῦν δὲ καὶ φοινικοῦν ἀπὸ χρωμάτων καὶ ἐς τόδε διαμεμένηκεν ὀνομάζεσθαι. Whereas the letters were allotted day by day, the designation of particular courtrooms by particular colours was permanent.

ἐπε[ιδὰν δ' εἰσ]έλθῃ ... ταύτη[ν] τὴν ἀ[ρχήν: We read here of a σύμβολον issued when the juror enters the court, which is therefore distinct from the σύμβολον issued when he casts his vote (68. ii): the two are confused by Fritz & Kapp, ch. 65 n. *b*, Moore, 306, but rightly distinguished by Fritz & Kapp, 199–200 n. 198. This will be the σύμβολον mentioned with the staff in D. XVIII. *Cor.* 210. On

Thalheim's reconstruction of 65. iii and 68. ii this σύμβολον was surrendered when the juror received his ballots and voted, but that is to be rejected in favour of the reconstruction of Φωτιάδης and Kenyon (cf. *ad locc.*), with the consequence that there is no further reference to this σύμβολον or indication of its purpose in *A.P. O.* Benndorf, *ZÖG* xxvi 1875, 601, suggested that these σύμβολα might be a series of lead tokens bearing the 'triobol' stamp (cf. p. 704) on one face and one of the letters *A–K* on the other (cf. Colin, *op. cit.*, 55–6, Hommel, *op. cit.*, 69–70). More recently A. L. Boegehold, *Hesp.* xxix 1960, 393–401, has proposed in their place two series of bronze tokens (series *B'a'* and *Γ"a'* of *I. N. Σβορῶνος, JAN* i 1898, 37–120, which he had suggested might be theatre tickets [p. 64]), bearing on one face a lion's head or a head of Athena and on the other one of the twenty-five letters *A–Ω* and **T**. Boegehold makes the attractive suggestion that the purpose of this σύμβολον was to assign jurors to particular sections of seating in the courtroom (cf. *Phil.* 328 F 140 on the requirement from 410/09 that members of the boule should sit ἐν τῷ γράμματι ᾧ ἂν λάχωσιν); the correspondence between the lettered σύμβολον and the lettered section of the court would explain the use of the word (P. Gauthier, *Symbola*, 74). It is not clear why the issue of this object, among the various objects issued to jurors in the course of the day, should have been thought particularly worthy of the adverb δημοσίᾳ. For the possibility that Benndorf's lead tokens are the σύμβολα of 68. ii cf. *ad loc.*

We are told no more of 'the man who has drawn this office by lot'. Colin, *op. cit.*, 39 with n. 1, 63–4, and Hommel, *op. cit.*, 69 n. 165, identify him with the similarly described man in 68. ii, which is plausible; and Boegehold, 'Aristotle and the Dikasteria', 50–2, suggests that this is the man who makes up the complement of a jury to one over the round hundred (cf. pp. 708, 729). Suid. (*B* 49) βακτηρία καὶ σύμβολον says that both were issued by slaves, which many including Colin and Hommel have believed, but if that were right we should not expect to find ἀρχήν (cf. Gomme, *CR* xliv 1930, 65) or appointment by lot. Kaibel, *Stil und Text*, 262–3, cf. Boegehold, *loc. cit.*, supposes that one of the jurors is meant: Boegehold's theory requires the selection of one juror for each court before the tribal allotments are made; otherwise the selection must be made from the successful candidates after the tribal allotments but before they begin to go to their courts. Whatever the solution, *A.P.* has failed to give us enough information on this point.

65. iii. ε]ῖτα τήν τε [β]άλαν[ον] καὶ τὴν βακτηρίαν <ἔχοντες καθίζουσιν> ... ε[ἰ]σελ[ηλυθό]τες: A verb must be supplied, to take τήν τε βάλανον καὶ τὴν βακτηρίαν as object: Kenyon in his Berlin ed. proposed the supplement which I print here, according to which the jurors retain their βάλανος and staff on entering the court, and surrender the staff when they receive their ballots (68. ii as restored by Φωτιάδης); Thalheim (*BPW* xxi 1909, 701–2, followed by Hommel, *op. cit.*, 17 with n. 48, 70 with n. 169, and by Oppermann) proposed ⟨ἀποτιθέασιν⟩, according to which the jurors surrender their βάλανος and staff when they receive their first σύμβολον on entering the court, and surrender that when they receive their ballots (68. ii as restored by Thalheim). Thalheim's reconstruction is undoubtedly the more elegant procedurally, since there is no need for the jurors to collect an accumulation of official symbols (cf. p. 735); but the statement in 69. ii, that the staves are reissued to the jurors if the ἀγών is τιμητός and a second vote is required, is decisive in favour of Φωτιάδης and Kenyon (cf. Gomme, *CR* xliv 1930, 65, K. K. Carroll, *Philol.* cxviii 1974, 274–6, and commentary on 68. ii, 69. ii). Colin, *op. cit.*, 33 with n. 2, accepted Kenyon's interpretation but suggested that the scribe had omitted a whole line and proposed ⟨καὶ τὸ σύμβολον ἔχοντες, καθίζουσι μὲν⟩.

τοῖς δ' ἀπολαγχάνουσ[ιν] ἀποδιδ[όασιν] οἱ ἐμπῆκται τὰ πινάκια: Having followed the men selected as jurors to their courts, we return to the place where the allotments are held. Probably as soon as their black κύβος has emerged, the unsuccessful applicants have their πινάκια returned to them and are dismissed. (Alternatively, it would be possible to leave the πινάκια of unsuccessful applicants in the κληρωτήριον until the allotment was completed and then dismiss all together: cf. Dow, *HSCP* l 1939, 30).

65. iv. οἱ δὲ ὑπη[ρέται] οἱ δημόσιοι ... ἐν ἑκάστῳ τῶν δικασ[τηρί]ων: (Kaibel & Wilamowitz[3] emended to [[ἑκάστῳ]] τῷ δικασ[τηρί]ῳ, but this is an improvement rather than a correction.) For the boxes cf. 63. ii, 64. iv–v, and for the ὑπηρέται, here most fully described, cf. 63. v with commentary. The boxes containing the jurors' πινάκια are taken to the appropriate courts independently of their owners: each tribe is represented in each jury, and the πινάκια are already sorted by tribes for the payment of the jurors (66. iii cf. 69. ii); to provide ten officials in each court, the presiding magistrate draws one πινάκιον from each of the ten boxes brought to his court (66. ii–iii).

παραδιδόασι δὲ τοῖς εἰληχό[σι] ... ἀπο[δι]δῶσι τὸν μισθόν: Blass[1–3] restored εἰληχ[όσιν ἀποδι]δόναι, but something longer is needed: Wilcken read τὸ πάλιν διδόναι; Kaibel & Wilamowitz[3] restored τόπ[ον δ]ιδόναι; Kenyon in his Berlin ed. hesitantly printed ταῦ[τ]α [ἀπο]διδόναι, which subsequent editors have accepted, M. H. Chambers, *TAPA* cii 1971, 46, reads τ]α[ῦτα ἀ[πο]διδόναι, and Dr J. D. Thomas thinks ταυτ[α] α[possible. ἀριθμῷ τὰ πινάκια makes no sense: Kaibel's proposal (*Stil und Text*, 263–4) to treat ἀριθμῷ as a synonym for δικαστηρίῳ and read [[δικαστηρίῳ]] ⟨τῷ⟩ ἀριθμῷ is most unlikely; Kenyon in his Berlin ed. suggested and Mathieu & Haussoullier printed ἀριθμῷ ⟨πέντε⟩ (this is the only way to save ἀριθμῷ: 66. iii tells us that in each court five jurors were picked for this purpose; Φωτιάδης, Ἀθ. xv 1903, 28–9, and Blass⁴ suggested πέντε ἀποδιδόναι above); τὰ πινάκια must be deleted as a gloss on ταῦτα. Hommel, *op. cit.*, 18 with n. 49, proposed ταῦ[τ]α ⟨τὰ πινάκια⟩ and ἀριθμῷ [[[τὰ]]] ⟨πέντε⟩, which is ingenious if not convincing.

66. i. ἐπειδὰν δὲ πάντα πλή[ρ]η ... τὰ [ὀ]νό[μ]ατα ἐπιγε[γ]ραμμένα: After the jurors have gone to their courts, it remains to assign magistrates (with the cases for which they are responsible) to their courts; the thesmothetae have already assigned particular dates to particular magistrates, and it is known which cases will be tried on which day (59. i, v, with commentary). This further allotment seems to have been a recent innovation: [D.] LIX. *Neaer.* 52 cf. 54 cites as still in force a law stipulating that δίκαι σίτου are to be tried in the Odeum (cf. D. M. MacDowell, *The Law in Classical Athens*, 40). So that there shall be witnesses to see fair play, this allotment is performed in 'the first' of the courts (i.e. the one designated Λ? Hommel, *op. cit.*, 71, mentions this and other possibilities; the way in which *A.P.* expresses this suggests that the same courtroom was not always used). In this process presiding magistrates are assigned to courts directly by colour, without the intermediary use of the letters employed in assigning jurors to courts: on a κληρωτήριον which could have been used for this allotment see J. D. Bishop, *JHS* xc 1970, 5–9.

With appropriate numbers of differently lettered βάλανοι it would have been possible to make up juries of varying sizes on any one day —of 201 or 401 for private suits (53. iii), or of 501, 1,001 or more for public suits (68. i with commentary)—but underlying this allotment is the assumption that any magistrate with his cases may be combined with any of the day's juries. *A.P.* has failed either to state that only one size of jury was used on any day or, if that was not the case, to explain how allowance was made for different sizes of jury in assigning magistrates to courts. Colin, *op. cit.*, 54 cf. 45, 47, believed that only one size of jury was used on any day; Hommel, *op. cit.*, 72–8, began with the distinction between days when private and days when public suits were tried (cf. ὅταν in 67. i), and suggested that only one size of jury was used on any day except that when public suits were tried there might exist one large jury in the heliaea (68. i with commentary) simultaneously with juries of 501 in other courts. We do not know how frequent different categories of lawsuit were, but presumably except at times when several men were charged with the same offence (and had to be tried separately, presumably on separate days) public suits requiring large juries were not very numerous. Colin's solution may have been logistically possible (and for an argument in favour of it see p. 730); but it would have the disadvantage, which the Athenians would surely have appreciated, of making the bribery of jurors particularly easy in the most important cases, since any one who wished to interfere with a major public suit would know that potential jurors to whom he offered bribes would hear his case or none at all. On Hommel's solution one greater case may coexist with several lesser ones, greater prospects of employment may encourage more potential jurors to offer themselves, and not all picked to serve will hear the same case. In the absence of further evidence, Hommel's solution is to be preferred.

Hommel, *op. cit.*, 83–4 n. 195, contrasts the first clause of this section ('when the assignment of jurors to courts has been completed') with the first clause of §ii ('when the jurors have taken their places'). I doubt if a distinction is intended: it is unlikely that the allotment described in this section would be performed in one of the courtrooms while the jurors were still taking their places.

λαχόντες [δὲ] τῶν θεσ[μ.]οθετῶν δύο ... ἑκάσ[τη, τούτῳ χρήσηται: To the end of col. xxxii (χρήσε[τα]ι [τ]ῷ π[ρ]ώτῳ), most of *A.P.*'s text is preserved and comparatively small supplements are required. Col. xxxiii is not in so bad a state of preservation as col. xxxiv but, especially in the upper part, it needs much more restoration than was needed earlier: most of the supplements are due to Blass.

Probably the two men who performed this allotment could be any two of the 'ten archons', not necessarily the thesmothetae (cf. 63. v, 64. i, with commentary, and Hommel, *op. cit.*, 72 with n. 174; but Colin believed that the thesmothetae are intended when that word is used). With unnecessary elaboration the Athenians use one κληρωτήριον to yield a random order of magistrates and a second to yield a random order of courts: first a magistrate is drawn, and the herald announces his name; then a court is drawn, presumably the herald announces that he is assigned to that court, and he thereupon goes to it. There is a herald in each court (68. iv, 69. i): probably these announcements are made by the herald of the court in which the allotment takes place.

66. ii. ἐπε]ιδὰ[ν δ' ἔλ]θωσιν ... λα[χόντας κληροῖ: Oppermann adopts δ[ιακληροῖ from Kaibel & Wilamowitz[3] (and Dr J. D. Thomas prefers this), while Mathieu & Haussoullier, Hommel (*op. cit.*, 20 with n. 50) and Tovar accept Kenyon's λα[χόντας κληροῖ; otherwise these editions are in full agreement with Kenyon: enough is preserved at the edges of the column to guarantee the sense. For ἐφεστηκυῖα (Kaibel & Wilamowitz[3]) cf. 64. iv; ἵνα γένωνται δέκα is an unnecessary piece of verbosity but fits the context; ε' and the following α' are guaranteed as factually correct by τέτταρας and π]έντε below, and by the reappearance of the one man in charge of the clock in 67. iii. Prof. D. M. MacDowell tells me that he is unhappy with ἔλ]θωσιν καὶ ν[ενεμημένοι ἐφ' ἕκαστον ὦ]σιν, since the second thing mentioned occurs before the first, and with Boegehold's interpretation of 65. ii in mind he suggests ἐπὶ τὰ ξύλα (cf. Ar. Vesp. 90) or ἐπὶ τὰ μέρη (cf. 69. ii).

Each courtroom now contains an equal number of jurors from each of the ten tribes, and a presiding magistrate. To pick ten men to undertake particular responsibilities in the court, the magistrate draws one πινάκιον from each of the ten tribal boxes (65. iv), and drops these into another box; the order in which he draws them from that box determines which man shall do which job. These ten men are included in the number of the jurors, and there is no reason why they should not vote and be paid with the others (Boegehold, 'Aristotle and the Dikasteria', 52–7, against Hommel, op. cit., 66 n. 156).

α' μὲν] ἐπ[ὶ τὸ ὔ]δωρ ... κα]κούρ[γημ]α μηδ[έ]ν: Hommel, op. cit., 20, and Oppermann after Blass[2] restore ἕνα rather than α': for the number cf. previous note. The omission of [μήτε] after παρασκε[νάζη]ι by Mathieu & Haussoullier is presumably a simple error. To prevent any dishonesty in the working of the water-clock, by which litigants' speeches are timed (67. ii–iv), and in the issue and counting of ballots (68. ii, 69. i), jurors are allotted to these tasks after arriving in court. Probably the man whose πινάκιον was drawn first was assigned to the clock and the next four were assigned to the ballots (cf. Colin, op. cit., 65, Hommel, op. cit., 84): probably the use of four for the latter task derives simply from a desire to employ ten selected jurors in all. There is one epigraphic reference to these functionaries: Hesp. xxxvii 50 = SEG xxv 180, 15–19, with the commentary of D. M. Lewis, p. 373.

66. iii. οἱ δὲ ἀπολαχόντ[ες π]έντε ... ἀλ]λήλοις ἐνοχλῶ[σι]ν: π]ρόγ[ραμμ]α (Blass[2]) and λ[ήψο]ντ[αι] (Kenyon, Berlin ed.) are reconstructed from doubtful readings: for the first Wilcken read τὸ γ̄, whence Φωτιάδης, Ἀθ. xv 1903, 29–31, suggested τὰ το[ῦ] γ' [σύμβολ]α καθ' ἃ [ἔστι λαβεῖν]; Dr J. D. Thomas reads ηργ̄, the second letter possibly ο with a stray descender. συγκλε[ισθέντες ἀλ]λήλοις (Blass[3]) is accepted by Kenyon (Berlin ed., O.C.T.) and other editors, but Kenyon judged it too long to fill the space if unabbreviated.

πρόγραμμα is used elsewhere of the assembly's agenda (44. ii with commentary), and in a judicial context we should expect the word to refer to the notice of which cases are to be tried on which day, in which magistrate's court, and in what order (cf. προγράψαι in 59. i, and the σανίδες in Ar. Vesp. 349, 848). This section is clearly concerned with the responsibility of the remaining five selected jurors for the payment of stipends at the end of the day's hearings: to prevent a crush, the jurors are grouped by tribes, and there is an element of sortition in the placing of the tribes in the courtroom (69. ii with commentary); the selected jurors take the tribal boxes of πινάκια and call the men by name to receive their pay (65. iv). Colin, op. cit., 64–5, and Hommel, op. cit., 84–5, are happy to apply the term πρόγραμμα both to the notice of cases to be tried and to the instructions for the payment of jurors, but I am not confident that πρόγραμμα is right here. On the other hand, Φωτιάδης' text does not lead naturally to what follows, and can hardly be right.

67. i. ταῦτα δὲ ποιήσ[αντες εἰ]σκαλοῦσι τοὺς ἀγῶνας: Fritz & Kapp, 199 n. 196, comment: 'This is another case which shows clearly that, with the initial words of a transition to something new, Aristotle refers back to the whole preceding section, not to its last part.' In fact, the allotment described in 66. ii–iii is the last thing to be done before the cases are called, and I doubt whether A.P. distinguished in his mind between this immediate and a more general reference.

It was known in advance which magistrates would hold courts, for which cases, on any particular day; it is not certain whether it was also known in advance in what order they would take their cases or whether that had to be determined at the beginning of the day and all litigants had to appear at that time; except for cases to be tried by a large jury in the heliaea (68. i) it was not known which cases would be tried in which courtroom. There must therefore have been an area where all litigants, συνήγοροι and witnesses due to appear in any court waited until they were called (cf. Hommel, loc. cit.). With εἰσκαλοῦσι τοὺς ἀγῶνας cf. καλεῖν δίκην/γραφήν in Ar. Vesp. 824–4, D. xxxvii. Pant. 42, [D.] lviii. Theocr. 43.

ὅταν μὲν τὰ ἴδια ... ἐκ τοῦ νόμο[υ]: τῷ ἀριθμῷ [ὃς ἄ]ν ᾖ [ἑκά]στων (Blass[2]) was supported by Wilcken and Colin (op. cit., 35 wih n. 2); Kenyon in his Berlin ed. and O.C.T. restored τῷ ἀριθμῷ δ' [ἐ]ξ [ἑκά]στων (cf. Mathieu & Haussoullier, Tovar); Hommel, op. cit., 21 with n. 52, 79–83, argued for τῷ ἀριθμῷ δ', [ἕνα ἐ]ξ [ἑκά]στων (cf. Oppermann, Gomme, CR xliv 1930, 64, Fritz & Kapp, Moore). The last gives the best sense (though Dr J. D. Thomas thinks there is insufficient space for it): the reference will be to the four categories of lawsuit in §ii, and if each court tries one suit in each of these categories (and there are only two parties to the διαδικασία) the time needed for speeches will be 3½ hours with a χοῦς lasting 3 minutes or 4 hours 40 minutes with a χοῦς lasting four minutes (cf. pp. 721, 726), plus a few more minutes when the ἀγῶνες are τιμητοί (69. ii); there would not be time to try four cases in each of these categories

67. i] COMMENTARY ON THE *ATH. POL.*

in a day. The procedure for allotting magistrates to courts presupposes that only one size of jury was used on any day (66. i with commentary); private suits were tried by juries of 201 if the sum at issue was up to 1,000 drachmae, of 401 if it was over 1,000 drachmae (53. iii): Hommel supposes that in this chapter *A.P.* is thinking of juries of 401, and juries of 201 would try more than four cases in a day, and he produces a reconstruction of §ii in which all four categories of lawsuit are suits where the sum at issue was over 1,000 drachmae. This is very neat, but one cannot help doubting whether suits in these four categories would regularly occur in equal numbers: perhaps what we read in *A.P.* represents the maximum that could be required of one court in any day. (Harrison, *L.A.*, ii. 156, contr. 47, suggests that the number of private suits tried by a court in one day 'was probably four on the average'; on p. 47 he says that juries 'would normally number 200'.)

In 53. i the private suits which are handled by the Forty and the διαιτηταί, and which come to a δικαστήριον only on appeal, are termed δίκαι; in 59. ii–iii, v, *A.P.* distinguishes between γραφαί and δίκαι ἴδιαι; here he distinguishes between δημόσιοι and ἴδιοι ἀγῶνες. The conventional distinction is between γραφαί as suits in which ὁ βουλόμενος might prosecute and δίκαι as suits in which only the injured party or his family might prosecute (there were also, of course, other forms of prosecution open to ὁ βουλόμενος, such as εἰσαγγελία and ἔνδειξις); D. xxi. *Mid.* 42–6 makes a distinction between public and private wrongs where public wrongs are those for which a penalty is due to the state in addition to any satisfaction that may be due to the injured party. Lipsius, *A.R.*, 238–46, treats both criteria as contributing to a single distinction between public and private suits, but Harrison, *L.A.*, ii. 75–8, regards them as criteria which in some cases might conflict (Demosthenes' first example of a public wrong is the δίκη βλάβης) and believes that it is Demosthenes' distinction which is intended in these chapters. Clearly Harrison is right in stating that the remedy for some of Demosthenes' public wrongs is a δίκη, but I think it likelier that the distinction intended in these chapters is that between γραφαί and δίκαι.

κ[α]ὶ δ[ιο]μνύ[ουσι]ν οἱ ἀντίδικοι εἰς αὐτὸ τὸ πρᾶγμ[α] ἐρεῖν: The speaker of D. LVII. *Eub.* frequently insists that he is speaking εἰς αὐτὸ τὸ πρᾶγμα (7, 33, 59, 60, 63, 66); the heliastic oath *ap.* D. xxiv. *Tim.* 151 includes an undertaking διαψηφιοῦμαι περὶ αὐτοῦ οὗ ἂν ἡ δίωξις ᾖ; according to Arist. *Rhet.* i. 1354 A 22–3 litigants before the Areopagus were forbidden ἔξω τοῦ πράγματος λέγειν.

The implication of *A.P.*'s including this clause at this point, that this oath was taken in private suits only, is regularly accepted (Lipsius, *A.R.*, 918–19, Hommel, *op. cit.*, 104, Bonner & Smith, *Administration of Justice*, ii. 162–3, Harrison, *L.A.*, ii. 163): many have supposed that this was made necessary by the shorter time allowed for private suits, but Harrison points out that the water clock should have been sufficient to keep speeches short and suggests that the oath is a survival from a time when the clock was not yet used. But, although it clearly is the implication of *A.P.*'s text, I am not confident that the oath was taken in private suits only: it is dangerous to rely on *A.P.*'s silences in such matters, and the distinction between public and private suits in these chapters is not clearly maintained. It is in any case abundantly clear from surviving speeches that the Athenians did not observe standards of relevance which would satisfy the modern critic, either in public or in private suits (but we should not follow Lipsius in concluding that the oath must have been instituted not long before *A.P.* was written).

[ὅταν] δὲ τὰ δ[η]μόσια . . . ἐ]κδικάζουσι: Cf. §iii with commentary, on the διαμεμετρημένη ἡμέρα. It appears to be the case, though there is no direct evidence for it, that any lawsuit had to be completed within the one day (cf. Harrison, *L.A.*, ii. 161 with n. 4): even if they wished to do so, the Athenians would have found it hard to ensure that all the members of a large jury reassembled on a second day. For ἐκδικάζειν, emphasizing the completion of a case, cf. Ar. *Eq.* 50, [X.] *A.P.* iii. 2, Lys. xvii. *Bon. Erat.* 5, and ἐκδιαιτᾶν in 53. v.†

67. ii. εἰσι δὲ κλεψύδ[ραι] . . . [λ]έγειν τὰς δίκας: The restoration of this section is due largely to Wilcken. For his αὐλ[ίσκους] ἔχουσαι ἔκρους Kenyon in his Berlin ed. and O.C.T. follows A. A. Sakellarios, *Untersuchung des Textes der A.Π. des Aristoteles*, 32–3, in preferring ἔχουσ[αι μι]κρούς, but M. H. Chambers, *TAPA* cii 1971, 47, agrees with Wilcken and dots only the αι; Sandys[2], excessively influenced by Empedocles' κλεψύδρα (below), proposed αὐλ[ούς τε] ἔχουσ[αι καὶ ἔ]κρους (sic); Diels *ap.* Oppermann suggested αὐλ[ώδεις], a word not recorded in LSJ or the 1968 Supplement. Probably Wilcken's text should be retained: αὐλίσκος, of the axles of ballots for voting, is preserved entire in 68. ii *init.*; ἔκροος is used by H. vii. 129. ii of the River Peneus' outlet to the sea through the pass of Tempe, and Arist. *Meteor.* i. 351 A 10 remarks that the Caspian has no visible ἔκρους; there is no instance of that compound as an adjective in LSJ but we have the adjectival use of ἀπόρρους in Antiphan. fr. 52. 8 Kock and of παράρους in *I. de Délos* 439, *b* 22, 442, *A* 226. Before τὰς δίκας, at the beginning of a line, Wilcken and Kenyon read but banished to the *apparatus* κ(αὶ); Hommel, *op. cit.*, 22 with n. 53, suggested [π](ερὶ), as in Plat. *Gorg.* 490 c 8, *Soph.* 232 b 2–3, which is accepted by Oppermann and is probably right.‡

The oldest description of a κλεψύδρα is in Empedocles, 31 b 100

Diels & Kranz *ap.* Arist. *Resp.* 473 B 8–474 A 7: this is a closed vessel with holes for water in the bottom and a pipe (αὐλός) for air at the top; when it is placed in water with the αὐλός uncovered it fills, and when the αὐλός is covered it can be lifted and will not lose the water inside; it thus 'steals water' (cf. Arist. *Probl.* XVI. 8. 914 B 9–915 A 24, II. 1. 866 B 11–13). The use of a κλεψύδρα as a water-clock in the courts is attested for the late fifth century by Ar. *Ach.* 693, *Vesp.* 93, 857–8. S. Young, *Hesp.* viii 1939, 274–84, published a κλεψύδρα of the late fifth century (cf. H. A. Thompson & R. E. Wycherley, *The Athenian Agora*, xiv. 55, *Agora Guide*[3], 248–9). This is an earthenware bowl with a hole near the rim (to ensure that it was always filled to the same level) and a bronze-lined hole at the foot through which the water flowed out (cf. schol. Ar. *Ach.* 693: ἀγγεῖόν ἐστιν ἔχον μικροτάτην ὀπὴν περὶ τὸν πυθμένα); it is an open bowl, so the flow could be stopped only by blocking the hole at the foot (Poll. x. 61 includes among σκεύη δικαστικά a ἡλίσκος ἐπικρούειν τὴν κλεψύδραν, and in schol. Lucian, *Pisc.* 28, we read ... κελεύοντες τὸν ῥήτορα λέγειν ἐν ἀρχῇ τῆς ἀφέσεως τοῦ κρουνίσκου; the angle of flow would indicate to an experienced observer how much water was left. This vessel is marked XX (= δίχους) and Ἀντιοχ[ίδος]; it holds 6·4 litres, and empties itself in 6 minutes. It is of course possible that by the time of *A.P.* more sophisticated κλεψύδραι were used, and (independently of that possibility) that the time taken by that quantity of water to pass through the κλεψύδραι then used was different (cf. pp. 726–7).

The provisions which follow, in the second half of this section and the first half of §iii, relate to private suits; *A.P.* then turns to the tripartite division of the day, which was used for public suits.

δίδ[οτ]αι <δὲ> δεκά[χους ... οὐκ ἔσ[τιν οὐ]δεί[ς: After πεντακισχιλίας Wilcken read δραχμὰς, but Kenyon in his Berlin ed. rejected this; after τρίχ[ο]υς τῷ Wilcken read ἐπ[—, Kaibel & Wilamowitz[3] restored [ὕστερον], and Kenyon read δ[ευτέρῳ]; Wilcken read μέχρι πεν[τή]κ[οντ]α μ[υ]ῶν, Kaibel & Wilamowitz[3] restored πεν[τακισ-χιλίων δραχμ]ῶν, Kenyon read πεν[τα]κ[ι]σχ[ιλί]ων. On all these points Mathieu & Haussoullier, Hommel (*op. cit.*, 22) and Oppermann follow Kenyon.

Kaibel & Wilamowitz[3] reconstructed this passage to distinguish four categories of lawsuit:

(*a*) for cases above 5,000 drachmae, 10 χόες for the first speech (*sc.* on each side) and 3 χόες for the second;

(*b*) for cases up to 5,000 drachmae, 7 χόες for the first speech and 2 χόες for the second;

(*c*) for δίκαι ἔμμηνοι (reading τα[ῖς] ἐν[μήνοις]), 5 χόες for the first speech and 2 χόες for the second;

(*d*) for διαδικασίαι, 6 χόες (and no second speech).

For the third category various scholars suggested cases up to 1,000 drachmae, the one dividing-line mentioned in 53. iii (ἐν[τὸς χ'], B. Keil, *Anonymus Argentinensis*, 238; ἐν[τὸς χιλίων], Φωτιάδης, Ἀθ. xvi 1904, 76; ἐν[τὸ]ς [ᾱ], Kenyon, Berlin ed. and O.C.T.). Hommel argued that in this chapter *A.P.* is giving the rules only for cases tried by juries of 401, that is, cases above 1,000 drachmae (cf. on §i), and so here restored ἐν[τὸ]ς [β̄] (*op. cit.*, 22 with n. 54, 79–83): this interpretation has won the approval of Oppermann and Gomme (*CR* xliv 1930, 64); Tovar gives β' in his text but *mil* in his translation; Fritz & Kapp and Moore retain Kenyon's 1,000. Though the assumption that equal numbers of cases in the four categories would come to trial is unlikely to have been fulfilled, Hommel's interpretation does in other respects seem to be the best that has been proposed.

The κλεψύδρα mentioned in the previous note implies a time allowance of 3 minutes per χοῦς or 36 minutes per amphora; earlier Keil had calculated from the hours of daylight in the month Posideon (vi) and from the eleven amphorae of A. II. *F.L.* 126, and had supported his calculation by his reading of surviving speeches, that we should allow 4 minutes per χοῦς or 48 minutes per amphora; it is possible but not certain that the number of minutes per χοῦς remained unchanged between the late fifth century and the late fourth. If a court tried one case in each of *A.P.*'s four categories, and there were only two parties to the διαδικασία, it would devote a maximum of 3½ hours or 4 hours 40 minutes, plus a few more minutes in ἀγῶνες τιμητοί (cf. 69. ii), to hearing speeches (cf. Hommel, *op. cit.*, 104–5). The clock was stopped during the official reading of documents (cf. below), so the actual presentation of the cases would take longer than this; but supporting speeches by συνήγοροι would have to be fitted into a litigant's own time allowance (Din. I. *Dem.* 114; cf. II. *Aristog.* 6, Hyp. II. *Phil.* 13).

On λόγοι πρότεροι and ὕστεροι see Lipsius, *A.R.*, 910–11, Harrison, *L.A.*, ii. 160–1: it is not certain that litigants were allowed a second speech in all private suits; on the other hand, whereas *A.P.* mentions an allowance of 6 χόες and no second speech in διαδικασίαι, in [D.] XLIII. *Mac.* 8 (speech c. 370–365: L. Gernet, Budé ed. of D.'s *Plaidoyers civils*, ii. 94) we read of a διαδικασία in which each litigant was allowed 1 amphora (= 12 χόες), and 3 χόες for a ὕστερος λόγος. Evidently the rules were changed between the 370's and the time of *A.P.* (cf. Keil's conclusion from the length of surviving speeches), and it may well be true that in the time of *A.P.* ὕστεροι λόγοι were never allowed in διαδικασίαι. ὕστεροι λόγοι seem not to have been allowed in public suits (D. XIX. *F.L.* 213 with Colin, *op. cit.*, 70–1, Harrison, *loc. cit.*).

67. iii] COMMENTARY ON THE *ATH. POL.*

67. iii. ὁ] δ' ἐ[φ' ὕδ]ωρ [εἰ]λη[χ]ὡς ἐπιλαμβάνει ... ἀναγι[γνώσκειν μέλλῃ: After ἐπιλαμβάνει we reach col. xxiv, the worst-preserved part of the papyrus. In this sentence the sense is clear, though the supplements are doubtful: the clock is stopped while documents are read out by the secretary. Kenyon follows Kaibel & Wilamowitz[3] in restoring ὅταν ψήφισμα ἦ] νόμον ἢ μαρ[τυρίαν ἢ σύμβολον and ἀναγι[γνώσκειν μέλλῃ·; Mathieu & Haussoullier, Hommel (*op. cit.*, 22) and Oppermann follow Blass[3] with ἐπειδὰν μέλλῃ τινὰ ἦ] νόμον ἢ μαρ[τυρίαν ἢ τοιοῦτόν τι and ἀναγι[γνώσκειν.: in favour of Blass, I note that it would be surprising to find ψήφισμα taking precedence over νόμον as the first example to be cited.

For the juror assigned to the water clock cf. 66. ii; for the employment of a secretary to read out documents cf. the secretary who did this at meetings of the boule and assembly (54. v). *A.P.* goes on to state that the clock is not stopped when timing is by the διαμεμετρημένη ἡμέρα, which gave litigants a much more generous allowance. Probably the διαμεμετρημένη ἡμέρα was used for all public suits (cf. next note): references to the stopping of the water while documents are read are plentiful in speeches in private suits (e.g. D. XLV. *Steph. i.* 8: the verb ἐπιλαμβάνειν is regularly used), but there are none in speeches in what are unquestionably public suits. Hommel, *op. cit.*, 95–6, is confident that the water was not stopped for documents in any public suits; Harrison, *L.A.*, ii. 161–2, accepts Hommel's application of the διαμεμετρημένη ἡμέρα to all public suits but nevertheless is more cautious on this point.

ὅταν δὲ] ἦ [πρὸς] διαμεμετρη[μένην τὴν ἡμέρα]ν ... τῷ ἀπο]λογ[ου-μ]ένῳ: Editors who follow Blass[3] and do not need μέλλῃ after ἀναγιγνώσκειν (cf. previous note) fill the space with ἐπειδὰν δὲ] ἦ; otherwise the text of Kenyon's Berlin ed. is generally accepted.

As earlier *A.P.* had to add information to explain what he had already said (cf. p. 698), so here he abruptly introduces the concept of the διαμεμετρημένη ἡμέρα and afterwards (it seems) explains it. Our earliest reference to a tripartite division of the day for a major trial occurs in Xenophon's account of the trial of the generals after Arginusae (cf. 34. i with commentary). Euryptolemus proposed that the generals should be tried either by the assembly, according to the decree of Cannonus, or by a δικαστήριον, and in either case διῃρημένων τῆς ἡμέρας τριῶν μερῶν, ἑνὸς μὲν ἐν ᾧ συλλέγεσθαι ὑμᾶς δεῖ καὶ διαψηφίζεσθαι ἐάν τε ἀδικεῖν δοκῶσιν ἐάν τε μή, ἑτέρου ἐν ᾧ κατηγορῆσαι, ἑτέρου δ' ἐν ᾧ ἀπολογήσασθαι (*H.* I. vii. 23: Marchant deletes ἐάν τε ἀδικεῖν ... μή, with its irregular use of ἐάν, Underhill joins those editors who delete the whole passage, but Hatzfeld deletes nothing and inserts ὅτῳ τρόπῳ πρέπει αὐτοὺς κρίνεσθαι before ἐάν τε ἀδικεῖν). A. II. *F.L.* 126, offering slaves for torture, says that there is still ample time for this: ἐνδέχεται δὲ τὸ λοιπὸν μέρος τῆς ἡμέρας ταῦτα πρᾶξαι· πρὸς ἕνδεκα γὰρ ἀμφορέας ἐν διαμεμετρημένῃ τῇ ἡμέρᾳ κρίνομαι; and A. III. *Ctes.* 197–8 says that εἰς τρία μέρη διαιρεῖται ἡ ἡμέρα ὅταν εἰσίῃ γραφὴ παρανόμων εἰς τὸ δικαστήριον: the first allowance of water is for the prosecutor, the second is for the defendant, and the third (when the defendant has been convicted) is for the assessment of the penalty. The expression διαμεμετρημένη ἡμέρα is found also in D. XIX. *F.L.* 120, [D.] LIII. *Nic.* 17. It has attracted various notes by lexicographers and scholiasts (Harp., Suid. [Δ 651], *Lex. Sabb.* [*JM(R)I* CCLXXXI. v May 1892, *Otd. kl. Fil.* 49 = K. Latte & H. Erbse, *Lexica Graeca Minora*, 49], *s.vv.*, schol. A. II. *F.L.* 126): they say that this division of the day was used for the greatest cases and, agreeing with Xenophon against Aeschines, that the three divisions were assigned one to the prosecutor, one to the defendant and one to the jurors (οἱ τοίνυν δημόσιοι καὶ μεγάλοι ἀγῶνες ... ἡ τρίτη τοῖς δικάζουσιν εἰς τὸ σκέψασθαι τὴν ψῆφον, first entry in *Lex. Sabb.*).

Aeschines can hardly be wrong about contemporary procedure. There is no reliable indication that Athenian jurors were allowed time to consider their verdict (cf. Colin, *op. cit.*, 73, Hommel, *op. cit.*, 96), and despite the calculations of Φωτιάδης (*Ἀθ.* xvi 1904, 36–41) it is hard to imagine that as much as a third of the day would be needed for the casting and counting of the votes of even the largest juries if efficiently organised; but it may be that the division of Xenophon and the scholia is an earlier version of the διαμεμετρημένη ἡμέρα. Probably by the time of *A.P.* the clock was used to time not the whole proceedings but the litigants' speeches, and we should infer from Aeschines that the third division of the day was assigned to speeches on the assessment in ἀγῶνες τιμητοί and was not needed in ἀγῶνες ἀτίμητοι. (It was supposed by Colin that the day was divided into four parts for ἀγῶνες τιμητοί [cf. p. 728]; by Hommel, *op. cit.*, 93–5, that the third part had to contain the vote on the verdict and, when necessary, the speeches and the vote on the assessment.)

Some have thought that only the more important public suits, with juries of 1,001 or more, were timed in this way; but according to §i a court regularly tried only one public suit in a day, so Hommel is probably right to suggest that this practice was followed for all public suits (*op. cit.*, 86–7, cf. Harrison, *L.A.*, ii. 161–2; contr. B. Keil, *Anonymus Argentinensis*, 248–50, Colin, *op. cit.*, 70, Gomme, *CR* xliv 1930, 65).

67. iv–68. i: Only Colin, *op. cit.*, 36–8, and Hommel, *op. cit.*, 23–4 cf. 92–5, have attempted a complete reconstruction of the remainder of this chapter and the beginning of the next: on pp. 724–5 I quote their texts; and in this note I cite by lines of col. xxxiv of the papyrus.

As reconstructed by Colin: col. xxxiv

67.iv διαμετ[ρεῖται δὲ πρὸς τὰς ἡμέ]ρας [το]ῦ Ποσιδεῶνος [μηνός, ὅτι εἶναι σύμμετ]ρο[ι δύνα]νται.
χρῶντ[αι δ' ἀμφορεῦσιν ια', οἳ δ]ια[νέμο]νται
τακτ[ὰ μέρη γ'· τούτων ἐν μὲν ἀ]ποτι[θέ]ασιν οἱ   10
δι[κ]ασ[ταὶ ἐπὶ τὰς ψήφους, τ]ὸ λ[οιπὸν δ'] ἴσον ἕ-
καστοι λ[αμβάνουσι, εἰκότως· οἱ πρό]τε[ροι] γὰρ ἔσπευδο[ν ἂν εἰς βραχὺ τῆς ἡμ]έ[ρας μέ]ρος ἐξωθεῖν τοὺς [ὑστέρους. ἵν' οὖν ἀ]εὶ [ἴσο]ν ὕδωρ
λαμβά[νωσι, δύο χωρὶς κάδοι] εἰ[σίν, ὁ] μὲν ἕτε-   15
ρος τοῖς δ[ιώκουσιν, ὁ δ' ἕτερος] το[ῖς] φεύγου[σ]ιν.
67.v ἐν δὲ τοῖς [τιμητοῖς ἀγῶσι, μέρο]ς ἴ[σον] ἐξεῖλε
τῷ διαψη[φισμῷ τῷ ἑτέρ]ῳ, δι[αιρ]εῖται δ' [ἡ ἡμ]έ[ρ]α
ἐπὶ τοῖς [δ'· τιμητοὶ δὲ τῶν ἀγώ]νω[ν, ὅ]σοις πρόσεστι δεσμ[ὸς ἢ θάνατος ἢ ἀτ]ιμία ἢ δήμευσις   20
χρημάτ[ων, καὶ οὐ κελεύει ὁ νόμος ὅ] τι χρὴ παθεῖν
68.i ἢ ἀποτεῖσαι. τὰ δὲ δημόσι]α τῶν [δικ]αστηρίων
ἐστὶ φ', [οἷς κρίνειν τὰς ἐλάσ]σο[υς διδό]ασιν· ὅταν
δὲ δέ[ῃ τὰς μείζους γραφ]ὰς ε[ἰς ἃ εἰ]σαγαγεῖν,
συν[έρχεται β' δικαστή]ρια εἰ[ς] τὴν ἡλιαίαν·   25
τα[ῖς δὲ μεγίσταις συνι]κν[εῖται] εἰς φ' καὶ ἃ
τρία [δικαστήρια.

Readings of Wilcken, of Kenyon (Berlin ed.) and of Dr J. D. Thomas, at beginning and end of ll. 10, 12, and at ends of other lines:

8   αρο...νται W   αρο...νται K   αντ̣αι̣, but Colin's supplement too long and αντ̣αι̣ not impossible, T
9   τ...τεντ̣αισ W   ια[...]τεντ̣αισ K   ενται (without σ), o impossible, T
10 τακλη——ἀ]ποτι̣[θέ]ασιν οἱ W   τακλι—— ἀπ]ο..ασιν οἱ K   τακ λ or τακτ possible —— ασιν possible but not ησιν, οι certain, T
11 οληι.. ἴσον ἕ- W   ολ..[..ε]ἰς ὃν ἕ- K
12 καστοι λ or μ —— τε[s] γὰρ ἐσ- W   καστοι λ or μ —— τε.[..] γὰρ ἐσ- K   καστοι μ preferable to λ T
13 ιστ̣...ρος ἐξω- W   πετ[..]ρος ἐξω- K   πετ̣ looks good T

COMMENTARY ON THE *ATH. POL.* [67. iv–68. i

As reconstructed by Hommel: col. xxxiv

67.iv διαμετ[ρεῖται δὲ πρὸς τὰς ἡμέ]ρας [το]ῦ Ποσι-
δεῶνος· [εἰσὶ γὰρ καὶ ταῖς ἄλλαις σύμμετ]ρο[ι α]ὐται.
χρῶντ[αι δ᾽ ἀμφορεῦσιν ια΄, οἳ δ]ια[νέμ]ονται
τακτὰ [μέρη· γ΄ μὲν ἀμφορέας ἀ]ποτί[θη]σιν ὁ 10
δι[κ]ασ[τὴς τῷ διαψηφισμῷ, τ]ὸ λ[οιπὸν δ᾽] ἴσον ἕ-
καστοι μ[έρος λαμβάνουσιν· πρό]τε[ρον] γὰρ ἔσπευδο[ν εἰς πάνυ βραχὺ τοῦ χρόνου μέ]ρος ἐξωθεῖν τοὺς [φεύγοντας, ὥστε τὸ ἐπι]λεῖ[πο]ν ὕδωρ
λαμβά[νειν· νῦν δὲ β΄ κάδοι] εἰ[σίν, ὁ] μὲν ἕτε- 15
ρος τοῖς δ[ιώκουσιν, ὁ δ᾽ ἕτερος] το[ῖς] φεύγου[σ]ιν.
67.v ἐν δὲ τοῖς [πρότερον χρόνοις ὕδ]ατό[ς τι] ἐξεῖλε
τῷ διαψη[φισμῷ τῷ δευτέρ]ῳ· δι[αιρ]εῖται δ᾽ [ἡ ἡμ]έ[ρ]α
ἐπὶ τοῖς [δημοσίοις τῶν ἀγώ]νω[ν, ὅ]σοις πρόσεστι δεσμ[ὸς ἢ θάνατος ἢ φυγὴ ἢ ἀτ]ιμία ἢ δήμευσις 20
χρημάτ[ων ἢ τιμῆσαι δ]ε[ῖ, ὅ] τι χρὴ παθεῖν
68.i ἢ ἀποτεῖ[σαι. τὰ δὲ δημόσι]α τῶν [δικ]αστηρίων
ἐστὶ φ[α΄, οἷς κρίνειν τοὺς ἐλάττου]ς δ[ιδό]ασιν· ὅταν
δὲ δέ[ῃ τὰς μείζους γραφ]ὰς ε[ἰς ἃ εἰ]σαγαγεῖν,
συν[έρχεται β΄ δικαστή]ρια εἰ[ς] τὴν ἡλιαίαν. 25
τα[ῖς δὲ μεγίσταις συνι]κν[εῖται] εἰς φ΄ καὶ ᾶ
τρία [δικαστήρια.

---

14 λει[πο]ν ὕδωρ W λει..ν ὕδωρ K λει better than αει T
15 ιν ὁ μὲν ἑτε– W εἰ[σίν, ὁ] μὲν ἑτε– K
17 σι.. ἐξ εἰσι W ατο[...] ἐξεῖλε K, lectio dubia μέρο]ς ἴ[σον impossible, ὕδ]ατο[ς doubtful, T
18 ....ειταιδ... W δι[αιρ]εῖται δ᾽ [ἡ ἡμ]έ[ρ]α K perhaps [ἡ ἡμ]έ<ρ>α T
19 κατ]ά[γ]νω[σι]ς οἷς πρόσ– W ἀγώ]νω[ν ὅ]σοις πρόσ– K
21 ε[. ὅ] τι χρὴ παθεῖν W μοις [ὅ] τι χρὴ παθεῖν K
23]ασιν ὅταν W σο..[..]ασιν ὅταν K neither σο nor σδ visible T
24 γραφ]ὰς [εἰ]σαγαγεῖν W γραφ]ὰς ε[ἰς ἃ εἰ]σαγαγεῖν K
26 κλε.. δ᾽ εἰς φ̄ καὶ χ̄ W κρα[.]. εἰς φ καὶ ᾶ K κγ acceptable, χ̄ good, T

67. iv–68. i] COMMENTARY ON THE *ATH. POL.*

It seems clear that to the end of ch. 67 (l. 22) *A.P.* is still concerned with the timing of proceedings in the courts, with ὕδωρ in l. 14 and δι[αιρ]εῖται δ' [ἡ ἡμ]έ[ρ]α in l. 18. The point of ll. 7–8 is clear: as their basis for the division of the day the Athenians take a day in Posideon, which is their sixth month and will normally have contained the shortest day; an allowance which was sufficient for business to be completed on the shortest day will have been more than sufficient for other times of the year (cf. schol. A. II. *F.L.* 126: φασὶν ὅτι τὰς ἡμέρας τοῦ Ποσιδεῶνος μηνὸς ἐκλεξάμενοι οἱ Ἀθηναῖοι ὡς συμμέτρους καὶ δυναμένας κατέχειν ἕνδεκα ἀμφορέας, πρὸς αὐτὰς καὶ ταῖς ἄλλαις ἡμέραις ἐσκευάζοντο τὴν κλεψύδραν). The length of the shortest day in Athens is given as 9 hrs 28 mins by Keil, *op. cit.*, 255, as 9 hrs 25·8 mins by Φωτιάδης, *op. cit.*, 10. Keil, finding a division of the day into eleven parts improbable, suggested that the court day was divided into twelve 'winter hours' of (fractionally under) 48 minutes, represented by an amphora of water, and each 'hour' was subdivided into 12 χόες of 4 minutes; one 'hour' was allowed for the allotments to set up the courts (cf. X., *loc. cit.*, and τοῦτο δὲ ἀπὸ μιᾶς ὥρας in schol. A. II. *F.L.* 126; I have not been able to stage a reenactment of the procedure, but suspect that this would be a rather ungenerous allowance for a day when many jurors were needed in several courts and most of the men registered offered themselves for service), and the rest of the day was available for the trying of the case, leaving four 'hours' each for prosecutor and defendant and three for voting and τίμησις (*op. cit.*, 255–6, cf. Colin, *op. cit.*, 66–73, Hommel, *op. cit.*, 87–95). To confirm his theory that a χοῦς lasted 4 minutes, Keil read aloud surviving court speeches and checked them against the allowances of 67. ii: with speeches later than *c.* 370 he found that he needed 4⅓ minutes for a χοῦς, but he thought that 4 minutes might be enough for a native Greek speaker; earlier speeches in the same categories are about one seventh longer (*op. cit.*, 246–54, 257–63). Φωτιάδης supposed Aeschines to mean that eleven amphorae were allowed not for the whole day but for each third of the day (*op. cit.*, 19–20, cf. Harrison, *L.A.*, ii. 162), but that both conflicts with the scholium and yields an unacceptably short time of 1 min. 25·6 secs for the χοῦς: Keil's interpretation of Aeschines must be right, and his calculations give a maximum time for the χοῦς which can hardly have been exceeded.

However, whereas speeches in private suits were longer before *c.* 370 than after, the fifth-century κλεψύδρα discussed on p. 720 is evidence for a χοῦς lasting only 3 minutes: if this standard remained unchanged in the fourth century, Aeschines' eleven amphorae would have lasted only 6 hrs 36 mins, and we could suppose that as with private suits (except that here the water was not stopped for documents) the measured time was an allowance not for the whole proceedings but simply for the speeches, for prosecution, defence and τίμησις, leaving the remainder of the day for the setting-up of the courts and the voting. A. Rome, *Acad. Roy. Belg., Bull. Cl. Lett.*[5] xxxviii 1952, 596–609, assumes a χοῦς of a little over 3 minutes and applies it to the major speeches of Demosthenes and Aeschines and to other speeches, concluding that Demosthenes must have spoken rather quickly, about 150 words per minute, whereas Aeschines and Isaeus will have uttered a more normal 130 words per minute (neither Keil nor Rome makes any allowance for the possibility that, especially in cases of political significance, the speech subsequently published might be longer than the speech delivered in court). We should not doubt that speeches were longer earlier than in the time of *A.P.*, nor (from [D.] XLIII. *Mac.* 8: cf. p. 721) that time allowances as measured in χόες were different earlier from those of the time of *A.P.*; Xenophon and Aeschines point to two different views of the third part of the διαμεμετρημένη ἡμέρα. It is possible that the 3-minute χοῦς of the fifth century was replaced by a 4-minute χοῦς in the fourth; but on Rome's calculations it seems possible that the 3-minute χοῦς was retained, and that makes it easier to accept Aeschines' view of the third part of the day, though at the price of accepting also that to fill the shortest day one must add (almost) five more amphorae to Aeschines' eleven for setting up the courts and voting. I am inclined to believe that in the time of Aeschines and *A.P.* the total allowance for speeches in an ἀγὼν δημόσιος τιμητός was eleven 36-minute amphorae, and to guess that the term διαμεμετρημένη ἡμέρα persisted from an ealier time when it was used, more appropriately, of the division indicated by Xenophon.

Colin and Hommel restore ll. 9–12 with a further explanation of the διαμεμετρημένη ἡμέρα: eleven amphorae of water are used; part is set aside for the voting, and the remainder is divided equally between prosecutor and defendant. The eleven amphorae in l. 9 may well be right (but schol. A. II. *F.L.* 126, quoted above, though it may well be derived from *A.P.* does not guarantee this, since the eleven amphorae are mentioned in the passage on which the scholiast is commenting). What follows is awkward, with δικασταί/δικαστής a subject of ἀποτιθέναι (Hommel, *op. cit.*, 93, supposes ὁ δικάστης to be the man in charge of the water clock, and the same man to be subject of ἐξεῖλε in l. 17), and ἕκαστοι (*sc.* ἀντίδικοι) introduced without explanation; and if I am right to rely on Aeschines for procedure in the time of *A.P.* we ought not to be told that part of the water is set aside for the voting.

In ll. 12–16 the imperfect ἔσπευδο[ν] indicates a reference to earlier practice, the only one in these chapters of *A.P.* (cf. p. 698); we have to accommodate ἐξωθεῖν τοὺς, ὕδωρ λαμβα[ν—, and in 15–16 a clear reference to prosecutors and defendants. The point must be that earlier (apparently, earlier than the law invoked in X. H. I. vii. 23) there was a single allowance for speeches on the two sides, so that the prosecutor could use more than his share of the time and reduce the time available for the defendant's reply; but now to prevent this the prosecutor and defendant are given their separate allowances of water. Hommel's πρότερον (as in *A.P.*'s other references to earlier practice, listed in the Introduction, p. 34 n. 178) is likelier than Colin's οἱ πρότεροι (as in 68. iv, of the prosecutors, who speak first). For the use of ἐξωθεῖν with reference to time cf. T. VI. 34. iii. κάδοι must remain doubtful: according to Phil. 328 F 187 the word κάδος was used παρὰ τοῖς παλαιοῖς for the measure known as an amphora; the only use of the word in a judicial context recorded by LSJ is Ar. *Av.* 1032, where commentators accept the scholiast's 'ballot box' (cf. schol. *Eq.* 1150, *Vesp.* 987, Poll. VIII. 123; καδίσκος is common in this sense; 68. iii–iv uses ἀμφορεύς).

Ll. 17–19 contain ἐξεῖλε (?) τῷ διαψη[φισμῷ and δι[αιρ]εῖται δ' [ἡ ἡμ]έ[ρ]α ἐπὶ τοῖς, to be followed in 19–22 by a passage dealing with penalties. Colin gives a text which takes no account of the aorist, and postulates a four-part division of the day for ἀγῶνες τιμητοί (cf. *op. cit.*, 70–1), for which there is no supporting evidence (as Hommel, *op. cit.*, 94, rightly objects). Hommel does take note of the aorist, and inserts a further reference to earlier practice: previously the third portion of water was set aside only in ἀγῶνες τιμητοί, whereas now (ll. 9–11) the third portion is prepared for all suits timed by the διαμεμετρημένη ἡμέρα (cf. *op. cit.*, 93–5)—but the imperfect ἐξῄρει would be more appropriate than the aorist, and as Hommel admits there was no need to time the voting at the end of the trial and it is hard to see why his 'earlier' practice should ever have been abandoned.

We are on firmer ground in ll. 19–22 (in l. 20 Hommel follows Kenyon's Berlin ed., where it is stated that the shorter supplements of Wilcken and of Blass[3], the latter accepted by Colin, are insufficient). This passage is concerned with penalties: πρόσεστι points to a penalty due to the state in addition to any satisfaction that may be due to the injured party (cf. προστιμᾶν in 63. iii, Lys. X. *Theomn.* i. 16 = D. XXIV. *Tim.* 105, D. XXIV. *Tim.* 39, 41); and, since cases incurring this penalty will have been a minority among cases where an assessment was required, Hommel's restoration of the text to refer to προστίμησις or simple τίμησις is probably right.

In ll. 22–7 *A.P.* moves to a new subject, the size of juries in public suits. We have been told in 53. ii that in private suits the jury is of 201 when the sum at issue is up to 1,000 drachmae and of 401 when it is above 1,000 drachmae; Hommel has argued that in 67. i–ii *A.P.* is concerned only with the more important private suits tried by juries of 401. We might have expected the size of juries to be dealt with earlier, in the chapters on the setting-up of the courts. Reconstructions of this passage are based on Harp., Phot., Suid. (*H* 219), ἡλιαία καὶ ἡλίασις, Poll. VIII. 123, *Lex. Patm. ad* D. XXIII. *Arist.* 28 (*BCH* i 1877, 137 = K. Latte & H. Erbse, *Lexica Graeca Minora*, 147), L.S. 262. 10 and D. XXIV. *Tim.* 9 with schol.: the smallest jury used in public suits was 501; for more important suits two or three panels were combined, to produce a jury of 1,001 or 1,501, and the name heliaea was retained for the court in which these larger juries sat.

The use in the fourth century of the odd one juror above the round hundred is confirmed by 53. iii, D. XXIV. *Tim.* 9, Tod 200, 207–8: the object is said to have been to avoid a tie (schol. D. XXIV. *Tim.* 9), and to prevent abstentions the courts were organised so that jurors had to vote to qualify for their stipend (68. ii *fin.*); yet in the time of *A.P.* as well as earlier we find it laid down that a tie counts as a verdict for the defendant (69. i *fin.* with commentary), and two inscriptions of the mid fourth century give the result of a trial in which only 499 votes were cast (cf. p. 733). We are not told how the odd juror was appointed: A. L. Boegehold supposes him to be the court official of 65. ii and 68. ii, which still leaves his method of appointment unknown (cf. pp. 708, 712); or possibly the presiding magistrate was regarded as a voting member of his court (this is not normally believed, but I know no text which rules it out). Juries were often referred to as a round number (e.g. φ′ καὶ ᾱ, in l. 26; φ′ καὶ χ̄ does not give an acceptable sense). In the fifth century we have no reference to the odd one,[61] and with jurors allotted to panels for the whole year (Ar. *Vesp.* 303–6, 1107–9) there was no guarantee that all would assemble on any occasion, but it should not be regarded as certain that fifth-century juries lacked the odd one (most of our references to a tie are from the fifth century, but this could indicate less strict precautions to ensure that all jurors voted rather than even-numbered juries; notice the fifty-one ephetae in homicide courts [57. iv with commentary]; round numbers in the fifth century are accepted by Bonner & Smith, *Administration of Justice*, i. 243–4, apparently rejected by Harrison, *L.A.*, ii. 47). Larger juries than *A.P.*'s 1,501 are mentioned earlier (6,000 in 415, And. I. *Myst.* 17; 2,000 in 404, Lys. XIII. *Agor.* 35), and also in one trial of the 330's or 320's (2,500, Din. I. *Dem.* 52, doubted by Lipsius, *A.R.*, 155–6). We are not told how it was decided what size of jury should be used for particular cases. For reference to a large jury as a plurality of δικαστήρια cf. D. XXIV. *Tim.* 9.

[61] The odd one juror was restored in *A.T.L.*, ii, D 11, 52, by J. H. Oliver, *TAPA* lxvi 1935, 179 with 195–6 (cf. *SEG* x 14); the line is left unrestored in *A.T.L.*, ii.

For the heliaea as instituted by Solon, a judicial session of the assembly to hear appeals against the verdicts of individual magistrates, see 9. i with commentary. Different Athenian uses of the word are analysed by Busolt & Swoboda, *G.S.*, ii. 1151 n. 3: the heliaea as a courtroom is mentioned by [D.] XLVII. *Ev. & Mnes.* 12, and Paus. I. 28. viii calls it τὸ δὲ μέγιστον καὶ ἐς ὃ πλεῖστον συνίασιν. For the building tentatively identified as the heliaea by the excavators of the Agora see H. A. Thompson & R. E. Wycherley, *The Athenian Agora*, xiv. 62–5, *Agora Guide*[3], 166–8, 308–9: this is in the south-west of the Agora, in the opposite corner to the most probable site of the court complex implied by *A.P.*'s account (cf. p. 700), which would offer some support to those who believe that without exception the Athenians used only one size jury on any one day (cf. pp. 714–15, where I argue against that view).†

68. ii. ψῆφοι δέ] εἰσιν ... ἀμφ[ο]τέρας λαμβάν[ωσι: Restored by Kenyon[1] from the quotation of this passage in Harp., Phot., Suid. (*T* 417), τετρυπημένη (which omits ἀμφοτέρας). Except on their timing *A.P.* has nothing to say about the presentation of the litigants' cases, and passes directly to the voting. A number of the ballots used in the courts have survived: they are discs of bronze (in a few cases, lead) with a solid or hollow axle running through them (the αὐλίσκος: for a different use of the word see 67. ii with commentary); many are inscribed ψῆφος δημοσία, a few bear a single letter (H. A. Thompson & R. E. Wycherley, *The Athenian Agora*, xiv. 56 with pl. 40b). The axles allowed a distinction between two kinds of ballot, such that it could be seen that each juror received one of each kind but how each juror voted could be concealed. It seems to be stated in §iv that the jurors took their ballots from a stand. Earlier each juror had a single ballot: see Boegehold, *Hesp.* xxxii 1963, 366–8, Harrison, *L.A.*, ii. 164–5.

For the four men λαχόντες ἐπὶ τὰς ψήφους cf. 66. ii.

τότε δ' ὁ ἐπὶ τοῦτο] εἰληχὼς ἀπολα[μβάνει τὰς βακτηρίας: τότε δ' ὁ ἐπὶ τοῦτο was restored by Kenyon in his Berlin ed. and O.C.T.; Mathieu & Haussoullier, Hommel (*op. cit.*, 25) and Oppermann prefer Thalheim's ὁ δὲ ταύτην τὴν ἀρχὴν (cf. 65. ii, of the man who issues the first σύμβολον to the jurors when they enter the court): whichever phrase we adopt, it is likely that the same man is meant here as in 65. ii (cf. *ad loc.*). There is a more serious disagreement as to what object the jurors surrendered at this point: Kenyon follows Φωτιάδης (*Ἀθ.* xv 1903, 31–2) in restoring τὰς βακτηρίας; Mathieu & Haussoullier, Hommel (*op. cit.*, 25, 70–1 n. 169, 97) and Oppermann prefer Thalheim's τὰ σύμβολα, supposing that the staff and βάλανος were surrendered when the first σύμβολον was received (cf. 65. iii with commentary); Colin, *op. cit.*, 39 with n. 1 (after accepting

Kenyon's interpretation of 65. iii), follows Thalheim here on the grounds that if we have the same official here as in 65. ii we should expect him to collect here the objects which he issued in 65. ii, but argues from 69. ii that the jurors must also have surrendered their staves at this point although *A.P.* does not say so. 69. ii states that the jurors receive their staves again if there is to be a τίμησις with a second vote, and, while Colin's more complicated solution cannot be proved wrong, it is simpler and better to regard that statement as decisive in favour of τὰς βακτηρίας here (cf. Gomme, *CR* xliv 1930, 65, K. K. Carroll, *Philol.* cxviii 1974, 274–6).

ἀνθ'] ᾦ[ν] εἷς ἕκαστος . . . ἐὰν μὴ ψηφίζηται: Mathieu & Haussoullier and Oppermann accept the text as reconstructed in Kenyon's Berlin ed. and O.C.T. At [μετὰ] τοῦ γ we reach col. xxxv of the papyrus, and from here to the end much less restoration is needed. Cf. Ar. *Vesp.* 752–3: ἵν' ὁ κῆρυξ φησί, "τίς ἀψήφιστος; ἀνιστάσθω." *A.P.* emphasises that a juror cannot receive this second σύμβολον unless he votes: presumably the jurors left their seats, gave up their staves and took their ballots (we are not told how the jurors were divided among four ballot-issuers), moved on to the two amphorae and voted, and then received the σύμβολα which they were to exchange for their stipend. What the juror received as his stipend was 3 obols (for the whole day's work; but in Lucian, *Bis Acc.* 12, 33, 3 obols are offered for each case tried): the papyrus twice uses γ, and commentators have supposed that the σύμβολον was marked Γ (e.g. Sandys; Hommel, *op. cit.*, 25); but the alphabetic system of numerals was not used before the Hellenistic period, so it is now thought that the σύμβολον was marked ||| (Boegehold, *Hesp.* xxix 1960, 394 with n. 5, cf. the translations of Fritz & Kapp, Moore). Boegehold mentions but immediately dismisses the possibility that this σύμβολον was that bearing the 'triobol' stamp on one face and one of the letters *A–K* on the other, which earlier commentators identified as the σύμβολον of 65. ii (cf. *ad loc.*): surviving specimens are of lead, whereas *A.P.* writes of bronze, but changes of material are possible (cf. p. 704, on the πινάκια), and it does not seem unlikely to me that μετὰ τοῦ γ should mean 'bearing the "triobol" stamp'.

68. iii. εἰσὶ δὲ ἀμφ[ο]ρεῖς [δύο . . . μὴ δύο [ὁ] αὐτὸς [ἐμβάλλ]ῃ: Cf. schol. Ar. *Eq.* 1150, citing 'Aristotle', *Vesp.* 987, Poll. VIII. 123. Elsewhere the ballot box is termed κάδος (schol. *Eq.*, Poll., *locc. citt.*: cf. p. 728) or καδίσκος (e.g. Phryn. Com. fr. 32 Kock, Lys. XIII. *Agor.* 37, [D.] XLIII. *Mac.* 10). Probably at an earlier stage in the history of the courts ordinary amphorae were used; but by the time of *A.P.* the ballot boxes were vessels made for that purpose.

Each juror receives two ballots, one for the prosecutor and one for the defendant: he drops the one that is to count in the bronze vessel, and the one that is not to count in the wooden. Two kinds of improper behaviour are envisaged and guarded against: the vessels can be dismantled, to show that no ballots have been inserted before the vote begins (in LSJ διαιρετός this passage should be listed with D.S. ii. 16. vi under sense i. 2, cf. περιαιρετός in T. ii. 13. v, not under a separate sense i. 1. b: the correct interpretation is given in the 1968 Supplement); and the bronze vessel has a lid with a hole (other uses of διαρρινᾶν cited in LSJ are from technical and medical writings of the Roman period) small enough to prevent more than one ballot from being dropped in together, so that no juror can abstain from voting by casting both his ballots into this vessel. The fifth-century amphorae had a wicker funnel (κημός) through which the ballots were dropped (Ar. *Eq.* 1150, *Vesp.* 99, with schol., Poll. viii. 123, discussed by Boegehold, *Hesp.* xxxii 1963, 367–8).

A.P. does not say how voting was organised in διαιδικασίαι to which there were more than two parties. By analogy with the system described here we may guess that there were as many ballot boxes, and each juror had as many ballots, as there were parties to the suit (claimants of equal standing apparently being treated as a single party), and one of each juror's ballots had a hollow axle for a favourable vote (Harrison, *L.A.*, ii. 165–6, citing [D.] xliii. *Mac.* 10, Isae. xi. *Her. Hagn.* 21).

68. iv. ἐπειδὰν δὲ διαψηφίζεσ[θ]αι ... ὅταν ἄρξωνται διαψη[φίζεσ]θαι: (Thalheim, followed by Sandys[2], restored ⟨ἂν⟩αγορεύει as in 69. i, cf. ἀνακηρύττει below, but this is not necessary.) An ἐπίσκηψις is a declaration of intent to prosecute a witness for perjury, in a δίκη ψευδομαρτυρίων (cf. Harrison, *L.A.*, ii. 192–7, and 59. vi with commentary): the maker of the declaration would not necessarily follow it up (e.g. Lys. xxiii. *Panc.* 14), and he might well not think it worth his while to do so if he won the substantive case; a last-minute ἐπίσκηψις might influence the jurors in his favour. The rule that ἐπισκήψεις must be made before the jurors vote is found also in Plat. *Legg.* xi. 937 b 3–7 (on the basis of which Kaibel & Wilamowitz[1] and subsequent editors have substituted ταῖς μαρτυρίαις for the papyrus' accusative); but in Hellenistic Alexandria the ἐπίσκηψις had to follow the announcement of the verdict (*P. Hal.* 1, 24–6). For the heralds cf. 64. iii with commentary.

ἔπειτα πάλιν ἀνακηρύττει· "ἡ τε[τρυπη]μένη ... το]ῦ ὕστερον λέγοντος": Cf. A. i. *Tim.* 79 (τὸ ἐκ τοῦ νόμου κήρυγμα· "τῶν ψήφων ἡ τετρυπημένη, ὅτῳ δοκεῖ πεπορνεῦσθαι Τίμαρχος, ἡ δὲ πλήρης, ὅτῳ μή"); *A.P.*'s version, of course, will be the formula actually used.

ὁ δὲ δικαστὴς ... εἰς [τὸν ξύλ]ινον: Hommel, *op. cit.*, 26 with n. 61, followed by Oppermann, restores λα[βόμ(εν)ος]: this is preferable to the λα[βὼν ἅμα] of Blass[4], adopted by Kenyon and other editors. ἐκ τοῦ λυχνείου τὰς ψήφους, πιέ[ζ]ων τὸν | [αὐλίσκον] τῆς ψήφου is the restoration of Π. Ν. Παπαγεώργιος, Ἀθ. iv 1892, 617 ([ἐκ]πιέ[ζει]), accepted by Kenyon (Berlin ed., O.C.T.) and Mathieu & Haussoullier; Wilcken read τὸ(ν) αὐ[λίσκον], and Blass[3] printed τὸ λυ[χνεῖον] (supposing λυχνεῖον to be synonymous with αὐλίσκος), but Kenyon in his Berlin ed. read the superscript letter at the end of the line as ν, and is supported by Dr J. D. Thomas; Hommel, *loc. cit.*, proposed ἐκ τοῦ αὐλίσκου τὰς ψήφους, πιέ[ζ]ων τὸ | [μέσον], but Oppermann rightly allows Kenyon's text to stand. The meaning should be that the juror takes his ballots from a stand resembling a lamp-stand, with two pans to hold the two kinds of ballots (Sandys[2]: as noted by Fritz & Kapp, 200 n. 200, this need not be incompatible with παραδιδόασιν in §ii), and when he moves on to vote he holds them with thumb and finger covering the ends of the axles, so that he can feel but no one can see which ballot he drops into which vessel.

69. i. πάντες δ' ἐπειδὰν . . . καὶ τὰ πλήρη [[δηλονότι [τοῖς ἀν]τι- [δί]κ[οις]]]: Kenyon in his Berlin ed. and O.C.T., followed by Colin (*op. cit.*, 40 with n. 1), Hommel (*op. cit.*, 27 with n. 62) and Tovar, reads καὶ τ]αῦτα ὅ[πως] αἱ κύρ⟨ιαι προ⟩κείμεναι εὐαρίθμη[τοι ὦσι]ν, καὶ τὰ [τρ]υπητὰ καὶ τὰ πλήρη, and (after Diels) deletes δηλονότι τοῖς ἀντιδίκοις as a gloss (he reads κεναρίθμη with a correction, perhaps εν, above). Wilcken read and Kaibel & Wilamowitz[3] restored ἵν'] αὐτα[ι φανεραὶ προ]κείμεναι [[καὶ]] εὐαρίθμη[τοι ὦσ]ι [[καὶ ⟨τὰ⟩ τε[τρ]υπημένα [καὶ] τὰ π[λ]ήρη δηλ(. . .)]] [τοῖς ἀν]τιδ[ί]κοις; Dr J. D. Thomas reads]υ . . υπητα but otherwise confirms Kenyon's readings. Sandys[2] and Mathieu & Haussoullier follow Kenyon except that (with Blass[3-4]) they retain δῆλα τοῖς ἀντιδίκοις at the end of the sentence; Oppermann follows Kaibel to εὐαρίθμη[τοι and Sandys[2] thereafter. Kenyon's may be accepted as the neatest solution, and there is no doubt about the general sense: a plurality of ὑπηρέται empty the bronze vessel (for ἐξερᾶν cf. Ar. *Vesp.* 993) and arrange the ballots on a board to be counted (λίθος in Ar. *Vesp.* 332; cf. the use of the diminutive ἀβάκιον in Alexis, fr. 15. 3 Kock, Polyb. v. 26. xiii); the board has holes into which the axles of the ballots are pegged. For the ὑπηρέται cf. 63. v with commentary.

οἱ δ[ὲ] ἐπὶ τὰς ψήφους [ε]ἰλη[χότες] . . . οὗ]τος νικᾷ: Presumably the same men are responsible for the counting of the ballots as were responsible for their issue (66. ii, 68. ii). IG ii[2] 1641, 30–3 = *I. de Délos* 104-26, C 7–10 and *I. de Délos* 104-26 *bis*, C 1–3, report the result of one trial: τῶν ψήφων αἱ τετρυπημέναι : Η : αἱ δὲ πλήρεις [:] ΗΗΗΡΔΔΔΔΓΙΙΙΙ.

ἂν δὲ ἴσαι, ὁ φ[εύ]γων: Since juries comprised one more than the round hundred (cf. p. 729), and the voting was organised so as to

69. i] COMMENTARY ON THE *ATH. POL.*

prevent any juror from abstaining (68. ii with commentary), ties ought not to have occurred. Yet the rule that a tie counts as a vote for the defendant is found in Aesch. *Eum.* 741, 752–3 (homicide trials before the Areopagus), Ant. v. *Caed. Her.* 51, Ar. *Ran.* 684–5, and still in A. III. *Ctes.* 252, cf. Arist. *Probl.* XXIX. 13. 951 A 20–952 B 16, 15. 952 B 36–953 A 2: perhaps the rule was needed earlier, and was retained but was only exceptionally needed (e.g. if a juror was taken ill during the day) under the system described by *A.P.*

69. ii. ἔ[π]ειτα πάλιν τιμῶσι, ἂν δέῃ τιμῆσαι: If the suit is an ἀγὼν τιμητός, and on the substantive issue the jury decides in favour of the prosecutor, there follow a further pair of speeches and a second vote on the penalty or damages: each litigant makes his own proposal and the jury has to decide between the two (cf. Plat. *Apol.* 35 E 1–38 B 9: Arist. *Pol.* II. 1268 A 1–6, B 11–22, criticises Hippodamus of Miletus for allowing each juror to make his own assessment). **τὸν αὐτὸν τρόπον ... πάλιν παραλαμβάνοντες:** The juror surrenders his 'triobol' σύμβολον, takes back his staff (cf. 68. ii), and returns to his place in the courtroom. Presumably the same procedure was followed when private suits were being tried and the court had another case to try (cf. Hommel, *op. cit.*, 107, supposing that the σύμβολον of 65. ii was reissued; contr. Colin, *op. cit.*, 76, supposing that the jurors collected four 'triobol' σύμβολα during the day). When the litigants have made their speeches the procedure of 68. ii–69. i is repeated, except that in connection with the assessment there is no need to invite ἐπισκήψεις.

ἡ δὲ τίμησίς ἐστιν πρὸς ἡμιχοῦν ὕδατος ἑκατέρῳ: This allows each litigant 1½ minutes by the standard of the Agora κλεψύδρα or 2 minutes by the calculations of Keil, or (implausibly) 42·8 seconds by the calculations of Φωτιάδης (cf. pp. 720, 726). According to A. III. *Ctes.* 197–8, when the διαμεμετρημένη ἡμέρα was used, in public suits, a third of the total time allowed for speeches was assigned to the τίμησις (cf. pp. 722–3), so probably the short allowance mentioned here is that granted in private suits (cf. Hommel, *op. cit.*, 106–7; Colin, *op. cit.*, 69–71, seems to think that it applied also to the lesser public suits for which he believes the διαμεμετρημένη ἡμέρα was not used).†

ἐπειδὰν δὲ αὐτοῖς ... ἐν τῷ μέρει οὗ ἔλαχον ἕκαστοι: For τὰ ἐκ τῶν νόμων cf. ἐξ ἑκάστων τῶν δίκων τῶν ἐκ τοῦ νόμου in 67. i. When the jurors have completed their duties for the day they are paid. Five of the jurors picked by lot when the court assembled are responsible for this: they receive instructions specifying how the payment is to be made and where in the courtroom jurors from the different tribes are to gather (66. iii), and they take the box containing the πινάκια of each tribe's jurors, call the jurors by name, and give them their stipend and πινάκιον in exchange for the 'triobol' σύμβολον (68. ii). The words ἐν τῷ μέρει οὗ ἔλαχον ἕκαστοι are obscure: they may refer to an allotment of two of the tribes to each of the five officials (Φωτιάδης, Ἀθ. xv 1903, 25–6, cf. Colin, *op. cit.*, 79–80); or the μέρη may be the 'parts' of the courtroom (e.g. Sandys[2]); less plausibly, Boegehold, *Hesp.* xxix 1960, 400, refers to the random order in which the officials drew the πινάκια from the boxes (which does not explain the aorist ἔλαχον). Two of the objects received by the juror at the beginning of the day remain unaccounted for: the βάλανος which first assigned him to his court (64. iv) and which he still had when he took his place in the court (65. iii, as restored by Φωτιάδης and Kenyon), and the σύμβολον which he received on entering the court and which he did not surrender when he voted (*pace* Thalheim's restoration of 68. ii). These must have been surrendered at some stage before the juror left the court, and all the official symbols must have been sorted to be reused when the courts next met (on the jurors' accumulation of symbols cf. Colin, *op. cit.*, 75–6; Thalheim's reconstruction of 65. iii and 68. ii, though I believe it to be wrong, has the advantage that it avoids this accumulation and does not leave any objects unaccounted for).

Here the scribe ends, in the middle of a line and in the middle of col. xxxvi of the papyrus (as the same scribe had ended in 46. i and the fourth scribe had ended at the end of ch. 63), and this time with an elaborate flourish. It is an abrupt ending to the text, but the last sentence is acceptable as the end of an account of the δικαστήρια. There is no need to doubt that this is the end of *A.P.* as known to the scribes who wrote the London papyrus; the modern reader would prefer a clearer indication of the work's conclusion, but it is not incredible that *A.P.* should have ended in this manner, and if not certain it is at any rate very probable that this is the end of *A.P.* as the author wrote it.

APPENDIX

I list here the points at which I doubt or reject the text of Kenyon' O.C.T. See commentary *ad locc.*

3. iii	ὥσπερ		30. iv	σῷα
5. iii	ἄρτια πάντ'		30. iv	κἄν τι
5. iii	φι[λαργυρ]ίαν		30. v	κληροῦν δὲ τὴν βουλὴν
7. iii	μὲ[ν ἄλλ]ας		30. v	χρηματίζεσθαι
7. iv	εἰκὼν Διφίλου		31. i	περὶ τοῦ ὅρκου
8. i	καὶ ⟨ἐκ⟩ τούτων		31. ii	καὶ ἄν τι
8. iv	δι' ὃ [τὸ ἐ]κτ[ίν]εσθαι		31. iii	ἵππαρχον ἕνα καὶ φυλάρχους δέκα
10. i	ποιῆσαι		31. iii	τοῖς ἀστοῖς
10. ii	ἔχ[ο]υσα		32. ii	Πεισάνδρου καὶ Ἀντιφῶντος καὶ Θηραμένους
12. i	ἀπαρκεῖ			
12. iii	οἱ δ'		33. ii	πολέμου τε
12. iii	[ῥέζ]ειν		34. i	Ἀργινούσσαις
12. iv	πρόσθεν δὲ		35. i	ἐκ τῶν χιλίων
12. iv	ὡς ἄν		35. ii	διοικεῖν
12. iv	κράτει νόμου		35. ii	πάγου καὶ . . . εἶχον, καὶ
12. iv	θεσμούς θ'		35. ii	μανιῶν ἢ γηρῶν ἢ
12. v	ἐν μεταιχμίῳ ὅρος		35. iii	ἔχαιρον
14. iv	δωδεκάτῳ		37. i	τυγχάνουσιν τὸ . . . [[ἢ]] τοῖς κατασκευάσασι
15. iv	παρεῖλε⟨το⟩			
16. ii	πρᾶος		38. i	ἔπεμπον
16. vii	παρ⟨ην⟩ώχλε[ι]		39. v	αὐτοχειρίᾳ ἔκτεινεν
16. vii	πολλὰ κλέ[α ἐ]θρ[ύλλο]υν		39. vi	εἶθ' . . . τοὺς ἐθέλοντας
16. x	πρᾶοι		40. iii	δημοκρατήσαντες
16. x	τυραννεῖν . . . [[ἐπὶ τυραννίδι]]		41. ii	ἐνάτῃ δέ, δημοκρατία
19. iii	ὑπὲρ Πάρνηθος		41. ii	καὶ ἡ τῶν δέκα
19. iii	μ(ετὰ) ταύτην		41. iii	ἀλλὰ πολλὰ σοφιζομένων
19. iii	αἰεί		42. v	δυεῖν
19. vi	ἑνὸς δεῖ πεντήκοντα		43. v	ἐπιχειροτονίαν
21. v	τοῖς τόποις		46. ii	καταγνόντος
22. ii	πέμπτῳ		47. ii	[ι'] ἔτη
22. iv	πρᾳότητι		48. iv	ἀ[γορ]αῖς
22. viii	τετάρτῳ		48. iv	γ' ἡ[μερῶν
22. viii	⟨μὴ⟩ κατοικεῖν		48. v	ταύτην εἰσάγουσιν
24. iii	καὶ τῶν συμμάχων		48. v	θεσμοθέτα[ις ἀ]ναγράφει
24. iii	συνεστήσαντο τὸν πόλεμον		48. v	ἐὰν παραλάβωσιν
24. iii	αἱ τοὺς φόρους ἄγουσαι		48. v	[ταύτην τὴν] εὔθυναν
25. i	ἑπτακαίδεκα		49. i	καλ[ὸν ἵππον ἔχ]ων
25. ii	περιεῖλε⟨το⟩		49. i	ἀλλ' ἀνάγουσι
25. iv	καὶ * * * ἀνῃρέθη		49. iii	παραδείγματα καὶ τὸν
26. i	†νεώτερον ὄντα†		50. ii	δυεῖν δραχμαῖς
27. ii	στρατείαις		50. ii	σπουδάσωσι
28. ii	Πεισίστρατος, τῶν εὐγενῶν καὶ γνωρίμων		54. ii	μόνοι ⟨οἱ⟩
			54. vii	ἐν τῷ αὐτῷ ἐγγίγνε[ται
28. iii	πρῶτος ὑποσχόμενος		54. vii	Ἡ]φαίσ[τια
29. v	ἔλαττον ἢ πεντακισχιλίοις		56. vi	κοινὰ [τὰ ὄντα νέμεσθαι]

737

APPENDIX

57. iv	Φρεάτου δικάζουσιν . . . ἐν πλοίῳ·		61. ii	ἐπιβολὴν ἐπιβάλλειν
			64. i	τότε] σείσαντος
57. iv	ταῦ[τ' ἐφέται]		64. iii	ὅ[ταν
57. iv	εἰδῇ τὸν		64. iii	ἐ[ξέλῃ]
58. i	[[καὶ]] τοῖς		65. iv	ἀριθμῷ [[τὰ πινάκια]]
58. ii	ἀποδοῦναι		66. ii	ἐφ' ἕκαστον ὦ]σιν
58. iii	αὐτὸς δ'		66. iii	π]ρόγ[ραμμ]α
58. iii	τοῦ ἀπο[σ]τασίου		67. i	ἀριθμῷ δ' [ἑ]ξ
59. ii	εἰσαγγέλλουσιν εἰς τὸν δῆμον		67. ii	ἔχουσ[αι μι]κρούς
59. v	τὰ ἴδια		67. ii	[[καὶ]] τὰς δίκας
60. ii	ἐλαίαν		67. ii	ἐν[τὸ]ς [ἇ]
60. iii	ἀργύρια καὶ χρυσία		67. iii	ψήφισμα ἢ] νόμον . . . ἀναγι-
61. i	χειροτονοῦσι δὲ καὶ			[γνώσκειν μέλλῃ· ὅταν
61. i	πολεμεῖ		68. ii	τότε δ' ὁ ἐπὶ τοῦτο]

BIBLIOGRAPHY

Part i lists all editions of, translations of and commentaries on *A.P.* that are known to me; part ii provides bibliographical details of books cited in this Commentary (including an author's collected essays, and *Festschriften*, but omitting such standard compilations as *C.A.H.* and *RE*, and also editions of and commentaries on texts other than *A.P.*). Articles in periodicals are cited in sufficient detail in the course of the Commentary, but special mention must be made of the following: *CR* v 1891 contains notes on and suggested emendations in *A.P.* by many scholars, in some cases reprinted from other British or continental periodicals (where the original is not easily accessible, I have cited *CR* rather than the original); *JAW* contains three surveys of work on *A.P.*, by V. von Schoeffer in xxi. i = lxxv 1893, 1–54 (1891–mid 1892), xxiii. i = lxxxiii 1895, 181–264 (1892–mid 1895: pp. 225–64 list suggested emendations), and by F. Reuss in xxxiii. iii = cxxvii 1905, 40–56 (1900–1904).

I. Editions, Translations and Commentaries

After items 1 and 2 the order of arrangement is by year of first edition, and within the year by alphabetical order of editors; where possible I give more precise indications of dates within 1891; an alphabetical index is appended. I normally omit (*a*) unaltered reprints (but when what has been called a new edition appears to be an unaltered reprint I say so; and when a book has been reprinted after it has been long out of print, usually by a different publisher or in a different series, I list it as 'reissued'), and (*b*) short extracts from *A.P.* in books devoted primarily to other works.

In describing editions I use the following standard terms: int[roduction], text, app[aratus criticus], trans[lation], comm[entary], notes [amounting to less than a full commentary]; I have not attempted to draw the line between elementary and advanced commentaries; except when otherwise stated, in editions divided into two volumes, vol. i contains introduction and text or translation and vol. ii contains commentary. For a note on some particularly important editions see Introduction, pp. 4–5. Editions which I have not seen are marked with an asterisk.

1. KENYON, F. G. English int.; text; *app.* (3rd ed. only); comm.; *testimonia*; schol. D. xxi. *Mid.* from same papyrus (3rd ed. only). London: British Museum, 30 January 1891 (preface

739

31 December 1890); 2nd ed. February 1891 (on the extent of the revision see *Academy* xxxix 1891, 210, 234); 3rd ed. 1892. *See also* items 11, 35, 42, 43.
2. SCOTT, E. J. L. Facsimile. London: British Museum, 1 March 1891 (preface 4 February); 2nd ed. August 1891 (preface 9 June).
3. *ΑΓΑΘΟΝΙΚΟΣ, A.* Modern Greek int.; text; *app.* Athens: Barth & Hirst (Μπάρτ καὶ Χίρστ), 1891 (first quarter, *JAW* xviii. Bibl. = lxx 1891, 31).
4. DYMES, T. J. English int.; trans. London: Seeley, July 1891 (preface 26 March).
5. FERRINI, C. Italian int.; text; *app.*; trans.; notes. Milan: Hoepli, 1891 (second quarter, *JAW vol. cit.*, 99); [2nd ed. (Bibl. Scr. Gr. & Rom. Hoepliana), 1893, simply a reprint].
6. HAGEN, H. German trans. Zurich: *Schweizerische Rundschau* ii 1891, iv. [39 or] 43–68, v. 185–210, vi. 323–58.*
7. HAUSSOULLIER, B. (with BOURGUET, E.; BRUNHES, J.; EISENMANN, L.) French int.; trans.; notes. (Bibl. Éc. Haut. Ét., sci. philol. et hist., lxxxix.) Paris: Bouillon, 1891 (preface November). *See also* item 45.
8. HERWERDEN, H. VAN, & LEEUWEN, J. VAN Latin int. (textual); line-by-line transcription; text; *app.*, schol. D. xxi. *Mid.* from same papyrus; full indexes. Leiden: Sijthoff, 1891 (preface August; third quarter, *JAW vol. cit.*, 153); reissued 1951. (*reissue.) [My references to Herwerden or to Leeuwen without further specification are to suggestions thus attributed in this edition.]
9. KAIBEL, G., & KIESSLING, A. G. German trans. Strasburg: Trübner, 1891 (preface 6 March; first quarter, *JAW vol. cit.*, 31); 2nd ed. 1891 (preface 26 April). *See also* items 10, 87.
10. KAIBEL, G., & WILAMOWITZ-MOELLENDORFF, U. VON Latin int. (textual); text; *app.*; *testimonia* (3rd ed. only). Berlin: Weidmann, July 1891; 2nd ed. 1891 (preface September); 3rd ed. (reporting readings of U. WILCKEN) 1898. [My references to Wilcken without further specification are to readings reported in this edition.] *See also* items 9, 87.
11. KENYON, F. G. English int.; trans.; notes. London: Bell, July 1891; 2nd ed. 1895. *See also* items 1, 35, 42, 43.
12. POLAND, F. German int.; trans.; notes. (Langenscheidtsche Bibliothek, Aristoteles, lxxviii/lxxix.) Berlin: Langenscheidt, 1891 (preface 25 May; but first quarter, *JAW vol. cit.*, 31).
13. POSTE, E. English trans.; notes; appendix; new readings in Milton, *Paradise Lost* (2nd ed. only). London: Macmillan, July 1891; 2nd ed. 1892.
14. REINACH, T. French int.; trans.; notes. Paris: Hachette, 1891 (preface June; fourth quarter, *JAW vol. cit.*, 213).

EDITIONS, TRANSLATIONS AND COMMENTARIES

15. SHUBIN, N. YA. Russian trans.; few notes. *JM(R)I* CCLXXV. v, vi, CCLXXVI. vii, viii, May, June, July, August 1891, *Otd. kl. Fil.* 58–70, 71–9, 1–11, 25–44; also published separately, St. Petersburg: Balasheva, 1891.
16. ZURETTI, C. O. Italian int.; trans.; notes. Turin: Loescher, 1891 (preface April).
17. BLASS, F. W. Latin int. (textual); text; *testimonia*; *app.* (Bibl. Teubneriana.) Leipzig: Teubner, 1892; 2nd ed. 1895; 3rd ed. 1898; 4th ed. 1903 (*addenda nova* added after publication of item 35). *See also* items 37, 51.†
18. BRUHN, E. Chs 5–22, 28–40. Text; German comm. With other texts in *Griechisches Lesebuch für Obersekunda*. 2 vols. Berlin: Weidmann, 1892.*
19. CWIKLINSKI, L. Polish trans. (or perhaps simply commentary or discussion: I. A. Robinson, in the dissertation cited in part ii of this Bibliography, has deleted the entry in his part i and inserted an entry in his part ii). Cracow: *Przegląd Polski* [xxvi 1891/2 or] xxvii 1892/3, 50 [or 51]–99.*
20. ERDMANN, M. German int.; trans.; notes; appendix. Leipzig: Neumann, 1892.
21. HUDE, K. K. T. Chs 1–41. Danish trans.; notes. (Studier fra Sprog- og Oldtidsforskning udgivene af det Philologisk-Historiske Samfund, viii.) Copenhagen: Klein, 1892. *See also* items 22, 23.
22. HUDE, K. K. T. Chs 1–41. Danish int.; text; comm. Copenhagen: Gyldendal, 1892. *See also* items 21, 23.
23. HUDE, K. K. T. 1st ed. chs 1–41, slightly revised from item 22; 2nd and 3rd edd. whole work. German int.; text; comm. Leipzig (2nd and 3rd edd. Leipzig and Berlin): Teubner, 1892; 2nd ed. 1916; [3rd ed., apparently simply a reissue, 1932]. *See also* items 21, 22.
24. WENTZEL, G. German int.; trans. (Universal-Bibliothek, 3010.) Leipzig: Reclam, 1892. *See also* items 35; 80.
25. KESEBERG, A. German trans.; notes. (*Jahresbericht über das Progymnasium zu Eupen*, 1892/3 = Progr.-No. 443, 1893.) Eupen: Mayer, 1893.
26. ΠΟΛΙΤΗΣ, N. Γ. Text. Athens, 1893.*
27. SANDYS, J. E. English int.; text; *app.*; *testimonia*; comm.; full indexes. London: Macmillan, 1893; 2nd ed. 1912; 2nd ed. reissued New York: A.M.S., 1971; 2nd ed. reissued New York: Arno, 1973.
28. PASZKIEWICZ, E. Polish trans. Sambor: *Sprawozdanie Dyrekcji Gimnazyum w Samborze za rok szkolny 1894 i 1895* (chs 1–41, 1894; 42–63, 1895).*

29. WIERZBICKI, J. Polish int., trans.; few notes. *Sprawozdanie Dyrekcyi C. K. Gimnazyum w Wadowicach za rok szkolny 1894*, pp. 3–69. Wadowic: Nakładem Funduszu Naukowego, 1894.
30. LOVIAGIN, A. Russian int.; text; *app.*; trans.; notes. St. Petersburg: Leibermann, 1895.
31. *ΠΑΠΑΓΕΩΡΓΙΟΥ, Δ. Γ.* Chs 1–41. Modern Greek int.; text; commentary. Athens, 1897.*
32. BARTH, W. (*ΜΠΑΡΤ, Γ.*) Chs 1–41. Modern Greek int.; text; comm. 2 vols. (i Συλλογὴ Ἑλλήνων Συγγραφέων, ii Σχόλια εἰς Ἕλληνας καὶ Ῥωμαίους Συγγραφεῖς.) Athens: Barth (*Μπάρτ*), 1898/9.
33. COSATTINI, A. Chs 1–41. Italian int.; text (based on item 17, 3rd ed.); comm.; appendixes. Florence: Le Monnier (Nuova Collezione di Autori Greci e Latini), 1900; 2nd ed. (text from item 45; Nuova Biblioteca dei Classici Greci e Latini) 1942. (*2nd ed.)
34. PRAŽÁK, J. Czech trans. (Bibliothéka klassiků řeckých a římských, vydavaná iii. trídou České akademie Číslo 2.) Prague: Wiesner, 1900.*
35. KENYON, F. G. Latin int. (textual); text; *app.*; *testimonia* (by Kenyon & G. WENTZEL); full indexes (by E. NEUSTADT). (Supplementum Aristotelicum, III. ii.) Berlin: Reimer, 1903. [Cited in this Commentary as Kenyon, Berlin ed.] See also items 1, 11, 42, 43; 24.†
36. KATSAROV", G. I. Bulgarian int.; trans.; notes; comm. (B"lgarska Biblioteka, v.) Sofia: Pridvorna Pechatnitsa Br. Proshekovi, 1904.
37. THALHEIM, T. F. A. Latin int. (textual); text; *testimonia*; *app.* (Bibl. Teubneriana.) Leipzig: Teubner, 1909; 2nd ed. 1914. See also items 17, 51.‡
38. *ΖΕΡΒΟΣ, Ι.* Modern Greek int.; trans.; notes. (Βιβλιοθήκη Φέξη Ἀρχαίων Ἑλλήνων Συγγραφέων.) Athens: Φέξης, 1911. See also item 58.
39. *ΓΟΥΔΗΣ, Δ.* Chs 1–41. Modern Greek int.; text; comm. Athens: Σακελλάριος, 1915.
40. *ΦΑΡΑΝΤΑΤΟΣ, Ν. Σ.* Chs 1–41. Modern Greek int.; text; comm. Athens: Σαλίβερος, 1916.
41. *ΠΑΝΤΕΛΑΚΗΣ, Ε. Γ.* Chs 1–41. Modern Greek int.; text; comm. Athens: Κορνάρος, 1917.
42. KENYON, F. G. Latin int. (textual); text; *app.* (O.C.T.) O.U.P., 1920. [Cited in this Commentary as Kenyon, O.C.T.] See also items 1, 11, 35, 43.
43. KENYON, F. G. English summary; trans.; notes (With E. S. Forster's [Arist.] *Oec.* in The Works of Aristotle translated into English under the editorship of W. D. Ross, x. ii.) O.U.P.,

EDITIONS, TRANSLATIONS AND COMMENTARIES

1920; whole of vol. x (with B. Jowett's Arist. *Pol.*) 1921. [Cited in this Commentary as Kenyon, Oxford Translation.] *See also* items 1, 11, 35, 42.†

44. HUSSEIN, T. Arabic trans.; notes. Cairo: Daar Al-Māaref Be. Misr, 1921; 2nd ed. 1967; reissued in The Complete Works of T. Hussein, viii. 281–439. Beirut: Daar Al-Ketaab Al-Lubnani, 1973. (*1st ed., 1973 ed.)

45. MATHIEU, G., & HAUSSOULLIER, B. French int.; trans.; notes; text; *app.* (Coll. Budé.) Paris: Les Belles Lettres, 1922; of later printings 2nd (1930), 4th (1952) and 5th (1958) claim to be revised, but see above, p. 701; text and trans. of 1st ed. both issued separately; text of 2nd ed. issued separately. *See also* item 7.

46. ΚΩΝΣΤΑΝΤΙΝΟΣ, Π. Κ. Chs 1–41. Modern Greek trans. Athens: Σαλίβερος, 1924.

47. FARRAN I MAYORAL, J. Catalan int.; text; *app.*; trans.; notes. (With Arist. *Poet.*) (Escriptors Grecs.) Barcelona: Fundació Bernat Metge, 1926; 2nd ed., revised by J. VERGÉS, 1946.

48. JACOBS, O. Chs 1–22, with omissions. German int.; text; notes. (With other relevant texts.) (Eclogae Graeco-latinae, xxvi.) Leipzig and Berlin: Teubner, 1926; 2nd ed. 1929; 3rd ed. 1933.

49. STOSCHEK, M. German int.; text; comm. 2 vols. (Aschendorffs Sammlung lateinischer und griechischer Klassiker.) Münster: Aschendorff, 1926/9; [2nd ed. of both vols, simply a reissue, 1952); 3rd ed. of vol. i, revised by O. LEGGEWIE, 1965. (*1st ed., 3rd ed.) *See also* item 78.

50. HARA, Z. Japanese int.; trans.; comm. Tokyo: Iwanami Shoten, 1928; 2nd ed. 1937. (*2nd ed.)

51. OPPERMANN, H. Latin int. (textual and bibliographical); text; *testimonia*; *app.*; full indexes. (Bibl. Teubneriana, 1094.) Leipzig: Teubner, 1928; repr. with *addenda* to bibliography (Stuttgart) 1961; repr. with further *addenda* 1968. *See also* items 17, 37.‡

52. ΠΑΠΑΝΔΡΕΑΣ, Γ. Modern Greek int.; trans. Athens: Σαλίβερος, 1929.

53. PIOTROWICZ, L. Polish int.; trans.; notes. (Tłomaczenia klasyków filozofji, Arystoteles, xvi.) Cracow: Gebethner & Wolff for Polish Academy of Sciences, 1931.*

54. ΣΤΑΜΑΤΑΚΟΣ, Ι. Text; Modern Greek trans.; paraphrase; comm. Athens: Δημητράκος, 1931.

55. CARSTENN, M. Chs 1–61. German int.; text based on item 51; comm. 2 vols. (Schöninghs griechische Klassiker, 18 a/b.) Paderborn: Schöningh, 1934; [2nd ed., apparently simply a reissue, 1947]. (*1st ed.)§

56. RACKHAM, H. English int.; text; *app.*; trans.; notes. (With Arist. *E.E.*, [Arist.] *V.V.*) (Loeb Classical Library, 285: Aristotle, xx.) London: Heinemann/Harvard U.P., 1935; revised repr. 1938; revised repr. 1952.
57. RADTSIG, S. I. Russian int.; trans.; comm. Moscow and Leningrad (2nd ed. simply Moscow): State Social-Economic Publishers, 1936; 2nd ed. 1937.
58. *ZEPBOΣ, I.* Modern Greek int.; text; trans.; notes. 2 vols. (Int. + 1–25; 26–69). (Βιβλιοθήκη Παπύρου, vii–viii.) Athens: Πάπυρος, 1937; 2nd ed. 1938. See also item 38.
59. MONDRUP, G. Danish int.; trans.; notes; appendixes. (Selskabet til historiske kildeskrifters oversaettelse, skrifter 12, raekke 1.) Copenhagen: Gyldendal, 1938.
60. *ΚΟΡΔΑΤΟΣ, Γ. Κ.*, & *ΚΟΤΖΙΟΥΛΑΣ, Γ.* Modern Greek int. (Κορδάτος); text, trans., notes (all Κοτζιούλας). (Βιβλιοθήκη Ἀρχαίων Ἑλλήνων Πεζογράφων καὶ Ποιητῶν.) Athens: Ζαχαρόπουλος, 1939.†
61. MURAKAWA, K. Japanese int.; trans.; comm. (With [Arist.] *Oec.*) (Complete works of Aristotle translated into Japanese, vol. xvi.) Tokyo: Kawade Shobo, 1939; 4th ed. (first to incorporate revisions) 1947. See also items 82, 85.
62. BAYDUR, S. Y. Turkish int.; trans.; few notes; date table. (Dünya edebiyatından tercümeler. Yunan klâsikleri, lxii.) Ankara: Maarif matbaası, 1943.
63. COON, C. S. Chs 42–69. English int.; trans. and notes from item 56; conclusion. With other texts in *A Reader for General Anthropology*, pp. 498–515. New York: Holt, 1948.
64. MAJNARIĆ, N. Serbo-Croat int.; trans.; notes. Zagreb: Izdavacki zavod Jugosl. akad. znan. i umjet., 1948.
65. STECCHINI, L. C. Chs 1–41. English trans. With other texts in University of Chicago, *History: Selected Readings*, i. 1–31. U. of Chicago P., 1948.* See also item 68.
66. TOVAR, A. Spanish int.; text; *app.*; trans.; notes. (Biblioteca española de escritores politicos.) Madrid: Instituto de Estudios Politicos, 1948; reissued (Classicos politicos, same publisher) 1970.
67. FRITZ, K. VON, & KAPP, E. English int.; trans.; notes; comm. (With a few other texts.) (Hafner Library of Classics, xiii.) New York: Hafner, 1950.
68. STECCHINI, L. C. English int.; trans.; notes. (With [X.] *A.P.*) Glencoe, Ill.: Free Press, 1950. See also item 65 (but this is a new translation).
69. THALER, O. Chs 1–41, with omissions. German int.; text; comm. 2 vols. (Am Born der Weltliteratur, c 7.) Bamberg:

EDITIONS, TRANSLATIONS AND COMMENTARIES

Bayerische Verlagsanstalt, 1953; 2nd ed. (Bamberg and Wiesbaden), 1969.

70. RITOÓK, Z., & SARKADY, J. Hungarian int. (Sarkady); text, *app.*, trans. (Ritoók, with verse translations by others); comm., appendix (Sarkady). (With [X.] *A.P.*) (Görög és latin írók, ii.) Budapest: Akadémiai Kiadó, 1954.
71. GIGON, O. German trans. (With Arist. *Pol.*) (Bibliothek der alten Welt, griechische Reihe: Aristoteles, iv.) Zurich: Artemis, 1955; [2nd ed. of Arist. *Pol.*, adding comm. on that but omitting *A.P.*, 1971].
72. VIANO, C. Italian int.; trans.; notes. (With Arist. *Pol.*) (Classici politici, ix.) Turin: U.T.E.T., 1955; [ed. of 1966 is simply reprint].
73. SHARMA, B. Hindi int.; trans.; notes. (With Arist. *Pol.*) (Series of books on assemblies, iv.) Lucknow: Government of Uttar Pradesh, 1956.*
74. GOHLKE, P. German int.; trans.; notes. (Aristoteles, Die Lehrschriften, VII. v.) Paderborn: Schöningh, 1958; included also with Arist. *Pol.* and [Arist.] *Oec.* in vol. xii of bound ed., 1959. (* bound ed.)
75. WARRINGTON, J. English int.; trans.; notes. (With Arist. *Pol.*) (Everyman's Library, 605.) London: Dent/New York: Dutton, 1959.
76. ASHERI, D., with MELTZER, A. Hebrew int.; trans.; notes (verse trans. by Meltzer, remainder by Asheri). (Philosophical Classics.) Jerusalem: Magnes Press, Hebrew University, 1967.
77. BARBARA, A. Arabic trans.; notes. Beirut: Dar El-Machreq for Comm. Intern. pour la Trad. des Chefs-d'oeuvre, 1967.*
78. HOHNEN, P. German int.; text; comm. 2 vols. (Aschendorffs Sammlung lateinischer und griechischer Klassiker.) Münster: Aschendorff, 4th ed. of vol. i and 3rd ed. of vol. ii, 1967, 4th ed. of vol. ii 1971; 5th ed. of vol. i 1975. (* 4th ed. of vol. i, 3rd and 4th edd. of vol. ii.) *For earlier edd.* see item 49.
79. LEVI, M. A. Italian comm. 2 vols. (1–22 + 23–69). (Testi e documenti per lo studio dell' antichità, xix.) Milan and Varese: Istituto Editoriale Cisalpino, 1968.
80. DAMS, P. German trans. (Universal-Bibliothek, 3010.) Stuttgart: Reclam, 1970.* *See also* item 24.
81. LAURENTI, R. Italian int.; trans.; notes; appendixes. (With Arist. *Pol.*) (Universale Laterza, 212.) Bari: Laterza, 1972.
82. MURAKAWA, K. Japanese int.; trans.; comm. (With T. Imamichi's Arist. *Poet.* and A. Miyauchi & A. Matsumoto's Arist. *Frag.* in Complete Works of Aristotle translated into

COMMENTARY ON THE *ATH. POL.*

Japanese, xvii.) Tokyo: Iwanami Shoten, 1972.* *See also* items 61, 85.
83. [ANON.] Modern Greek trans. (Βιβλιοθήκη Ἀρχαίων Ἑλλήνων Συγγραφέων.) Athens: Δαρεμᾶς, 1973.*
84. MOORE, J. M. English int.; trans.; comm. With [X.] *A.P.*, X. *Lac. P.* and other texts in *Aristotle and Xenophon on Democracy and Oligarchy*. London: Chatto and Windus/U. of California P., 1975.†
85. MURAKAWA, K. Japanese int.; trans.; comm. (Iwanami Bunkô, 33-604-7.) Tokyo: Iwanami Shoten, 1980. *See also* items 61, 82.‡

Not a text, translation or commentary, though alleged to be so in some early bibliographies (e.g. Sandys[1]):

—. BELAJEV, D. ['Nur eine Abhandlung': V. von Schoeffer, *JAW* XXXI. i = lxxv 1893, 18 with 21 no. 55.]*

The following works about *A.P.* deserve to be appended to this list:

86. KEIL, B. *Die solonische Verfassung in Aristoteles Verfassungs-geschichte Athens*, incorporating text, *app.*, comm. for chs 5–13. Berlin: Gärtner, 1892.
87. KAIBEL, G. *Stil und Text der Πολιτεία Ἀθηναίων des Aristoteles*, incorporating linguistic and textual commentary on whole work. Berlin: Weidmann, 1893; reissued Hildesheim and New York: Olms, 1973; reissue announced by Weidmann in 1978 catalogue. *See also* items 9, 10.
88. COLIN, G. 'Les Sept Derniers Chapitres de l'Ἀθηναίων Πολιτεία', incorporating trans. of 63–9 and reconstructed text of 67. iv–68. i. *REG* xxx 1917, 20–87.
89. HOMMEL, H. *Heliaia*, incorporating text and German trans. of 63–9. *Philol.* Supp. xix. ii 1927.§

Alphabetical index:

[Anon]	83	Dams	80	Hommel	89
Asheri	76	Dymes	4	Hude	21, 22, 23
Barbara	77	Eisenmann	7	Hussein	44
Barth	32	Erdmann	20	Jacobs	48
Baydur	62	Farran i Mayoral	47	Kaibel	9, 10, 87
Blass	17	Ferrini	5	Kapp	67
Bourguet	7	Fritz	67	Katsarov"	36
Bruhn	18	Gigon	71	Keil	86
Brunhes	7	Gohlke	74	Kenyon	1, 11, 35, 42, 43
Carstenn	55	Hagen	6	Keseberg	25
Colin	88	Hara	50	Kiessling	9
Coon	63	Haussoullier	7, 45	Laurenti	81
Cosattini	33	Herwerden	8	Leeuwen	8
Cwiklinski	19	Hohnen	78	Leggewie	49

746

EDITIONS, TRANSLATIONS AND COMMENTARIES

Levi	79	Reinach	14	Wilamowitz-	
Loviagin	30	Ritoók	70	Moellendorff	10
Majnarić	64	Sandys	27	Wilcken	10
Mathieu	45	Sarkady	70	Zuretti	16
Meltzer	76	Scott	2	Ἀγαθόνικος	3
Mondrup	59	Sharma	73	Γουδῆς	39
Moore	84	Shubin	15	Ζερβός	38, 58
Murakawa	61, 82, 85	Stecchini	65, 68	Κορδάτος	60
Oppermann	51	Stoschek	49	Κοτζιούλας	60
Neustadt	35	Thaler	69	Κωνσταντῖνος	46
Paskiewicz	28	Thalheim	37	Παντελάκης	42
Piotrowicz	53	Tovar	66	Πααπγεωργίου	31
Poland	12	Vergés	47	Πααπνδρέας	52
Poste	13	Viano	72	Πολίτης	26
Prazák	34	Warrington	75	Σταματάκος	54
Rackham	56	Wentzel	24, 35	Φαραντᾶτος	40
Radtsig	57	Wierzbicki	29		

II. Other Books

(See note on p. 739.)

ADCOCK, F. E., & MOSLEY, D. J. *Diplomacy in Ancient Greece.* Thames and Hudson, 1975.
ADKINS, A. W. H. *Merit and Responsibility*, O.U.P., 1960.
—— *Moral Values and Political Behaviour in Ancient Greece.* Chatto and Windus, 1972.
ADMIRALTY: NAVAL INTELLIGENCE DIVISION. *Greece.* 3 vols. 1944–5.
ANDREWES, A. *The Greek Tyrants.* Hutchinson, 1956.
—— *Probouleusis: Sparta's Contribution to the Technique of Government.* (Inaugural Lecture.) O.U.P., 1954.
Apophoreton. See Verein deutscher Philologen und Schulmänner.
ARDAILLON, E. *Les Mines du Laurion dans l'antiquité. Bibl. Éc. Fr. Ath. & Rome* lxxvii 1897.
ARMBRUSTER, O. *Über die Herrschaft der Dreissig zu Athen, 404/3 v. Chr.* Diss. Freiburg im Breisgau, 1913.
ASHERI, D. *Distribuzioni di terre nell' antica Grecia. Mem. Torino*[4] x 1966.
ATHENS: AGORA. *The Athenian Agora: A Guide to the Excavation and Museum.* Athens: A.S.C.S.A., [2]1962; [3]1976.
Athens Comes of Age. See Conference.
BAUMSTARK, A. *Syrisch-arabische Biographieen des Aristoteles; Syrische Commentare zur εἰσαγωγή des Porphyrios.* Leipzig: Teubner, 1900.
BAYNES, N. H. *Byzantine Studies and Other Essays.* Athlone Press, 1955.
BEAUCHET, L. *L'Histoire du droit privé de la république athénienne.* 4 vols. Paris: Chevalier-Marescq, 1897.

COMMENTARY ON THE *ATH. POL.*

BEAZLEY, J. D. *Attic Black-Figure Vase-Painters*. O.U.P., 1956.
—— *Attic Red-Figure Vase-Painters*. 3 vols. O.U.P., ²1963.
BECHTEL, F. *Die historischen Personennamen des Griechischen bis zur Kaiserzeit*. Halle: Niemeyer, 1917.
BELOCH, K. J. *Die attische Politik seit Perikles*. Leipzig: Teubner, 1884.
—— *Griechische Geschichte*. 4 vols in 8. Strasburg: Trübner/Berlin and Leipzig: De Gruyter, ²1912–27.
BERVE, H. *Die Tyrannis bei den Griechen*. 2 vols. Munich: Beck, 1967.
BEST, J. G. P. *Thracian Peltasts and their Influence on Greek Warfare*. Groningen: Wolters-Noordhoff, 1969.
BICKNELL, P. J. *Studies in Athenian Politics and Genealogy*. Hist. Einz. xix 1972.
BIONDI, B. *Studi in onore di B. Biondi*. 4 vols. Milan: Giuffrè, 1965.
BLANK, O. *Die Einsetzung der Dreissig zu Athen im Jahre 404 v. Chr.* (Diss. Freiburg im Breisgau.) Würzburg: Stürtz, 1911.
BOARDMAN, J. *Athenian Black Figure Vases*. Thames & Hudson, 1974.
BÖCKH, A. (rev. FRÄNKEL, M.) *Die Staatshaushaltung der Athener*. 2 vols. Berlin: Reimer, ³1886.
—— *Urkunden über das Seewesen des attischen Staates*. 2 vols. Berlin: Reimer, 1840.
BOEGEHOLD, A. L. 'Aristotle and the Dikasteria.' Diss. Harvard, 1958 (abstract published *HSCP* lxiii 1958, 526–8).
BOERNER, A. *De Rebus a Graecis inde ab Anno 410 usque ad Annum 403 Gestis Quaestiones Historicae*. (Dissertation.) Göttingen: Dieterich, 1894.
BONNER, R. J. *Evidence in Athenian Courts*. U. of Chicago P., 1905.
—— & SMITH, G. *The Administration of Justice from Homer to Aristotle*. 2 vols. U. of Chicago P., 1930/8.
BOWRA, C. M. *Essays presented to C. M. Bowra*. Oxford: Alden Press for Wadham College J.C.R. and M.C.R., 1970.
BRADEEN, D. W. *The Athenian Agora*, xvii. *Inscriptions: The Funerary Monuments*. Princeton: A.S.C.S.A., 1974.
BRENDEL, O. J. *Essays in Archaeology and the Humanities in Memoriam O. J. Brendel*. Mainz: Zabern, 1976.
BRILLANT, M. *Les Secrétaires athéniens*. (Bibl. Éc. Haut. Ét. cxci.) Paris: Champion, 1911.
BROMMER, F. (with others) *Denkmälerlisten zur griechischen Heldensage*. 4 vols. Marburg an der Lahn: Elwert, 1971–6.
—— *Vasenlisten zur griechischen Heldensage*. Marburg an der Lahn: Elwert, ³1973.
—— *Festschrift für F. Brommer*. Mainz: Zabern, 1977.
BUCHANAN, J. J. *Theorika: A Study of Monetary Distributions to the Athenian Citizenry during the Fifth and Fourth Centuries B.C.* Locust Valley, N.Y.: Augustin, 1962.

BUDGE, E. A. T. W. *By Nile and Tigris*. 2 vols. Murray, 1920.
BURN, A. R. *Persia and the Greeks: The Defence of the West, c. 546–478 B.C.* Arnold, 1962 (corr. 1970).
BURSY, B. *De Aristotelis Πολιτείας Ἀθηναίων Partis Alterius Fonte et Auctoritate*. (Dissertation.) Dorpat: Mattiesen, 1897.
BURY, J. B. *A History of Greece to the Death of Alexander the Great*. Macmillan, 1900; rev. MEIGGS, R., ^{4}1975.
BUSESKUL, W. *Afinskaja politija Aristotelja kak istotschik dlja isstorii gossudarsstwennowa sstroja Afinn*. Charkow: Silberberg, 1895.
BUSOLT, G. *Griechische Geschichte bis zur Schlacht bei Chaeroneia*. Vols i^2, ii^2, III. i, III. ii (to 404). Gotha: Perthes, 1893–1904.
—— (part rev. SWOBODA, H.) *Griechische Staatskunde*. 2 vols. (H.d.A. IV. i. 1.) Munich: Beck, 1920/6.
CAHN, H. A. *Kleine Schriften zur Münzkunde und Archaeologie*. Basle: Archäologischer Verlag, 1975.
CALHOUN, G. M. *Athenian Clubs in Politics and Litigation*. Bull. U. Texas cclxii (Humanistic Series xiv), 1913.
CAPPS, E. *Classical Studies presented to E. Capps*. Princeton U.P., 1936.
CARCOPINO, J. *L'Ostracisme athénien*. Paris: Alcan, ^{2}1935.
CASSOLA, F. *La Ionia nel mondo miceneo*. Naples: Edizioni Scientifiche Italiane, 1957.
CASSON, S. *Macedonia, Thrace and Illyria: Their Relations to Greece from the Earliest Times down to the Time of Philip Son of Amyntas*. O.U.P., 1926.
CAUER, F. *Hat Aristoteles die Schrift vom Staate der Athener geschrieben?* Stuttgart: Göschen, 1891.
CHRIMES, K. M. T. *Ancient Sparta: A Re-examination of the Evidence*. (Pub. U. Manchester ccciv; Historical Series lxxxiv.) Manchester U.P., 1949.
CLINTON, H. F. *Fasti Hellenici*. Vols i, ii^3, iii^2. O.U.P., 1834–51.
CLINTON, K. *The Sacred Officials of the Eleusinian Mysteries*. T. A. Philos. S. LXIV. iii 1974.
CLOCHÉ, P. *La Démocratie athénienne*. Paris: P.U.F., 1951.
—— *La Restauration démocratique à Athènes en 403 avant J.-C.* Paris: Leroux, 1915.
COHEN, E. E. *Ancient Athenian Maritime Courts*. Princeton U.P., 1973.
COLDSTREAM, J. N. *Geometric Greece*. Benn, 1977.
—— *Greek Geometric Pottery*. Methuen, 1968.
COLIN, G. *Xénophon historien d'après le livre II des Helleniques*. (Annales de l'Est, Mémoires, ii.) Paris: Les Belles Lettres, 1933.
CONFERENCE. *Athens Comes of Age: From Solon to Salamis*. Princeton: Archaeological Institute of America, 1978.
—— *IIe Conférence internationale d'histoire économique, 1962*. 2 vols. (Éc. Prat. Haut. Ét. VI. viii.) Paris and The Hague: Mouton, 1965.

—— *Actes du 2e congrès international d'épigraphie grecque et latine, 1952*. Paris: Maisonneuve, 1953.
—— *Atti del 3⁰ congresso internazionale di epigrafia greca e latina, 1957*. Rome: L'Erma di Bretschneider, 1959.
—— *Acta of the Fifth International Congress of Greek and Latin Epigraphy, 1967*. Blackwell, 1971.
—— *Actes du colloque 1972 sur l'esclavage*. (Ann. Litt. de l'U. de Besançon, clxiii; Centre de Recherches d'Histoire Ancienne, xi.) Paris: Les Belles Lettres, 1974.
—— Ἀρχαία Μακεδονία, [i.] *1968*. Thessalonica: "Ἴδρυμα Μελετῶν Χερσονήσου τοῦ Αἵμου (Institute for Balkan Studies), 1970.
—— TURNER, E. G. *The Terms Recto and Verso: The Anatomy of the Papyrus Roll*. (*Actes du XVe congrès international de papyrologie, 1977*, i; Papyrologica Bruxellensia xvi.) Brussels: Fond. Ég. Reine Elis., 1978.
CONNOR, W. R. *The New Politicians of Fifth-Century Athens*. Princeton U.P., 1971.
—— *Theopompus and Fifth-Century Athens*. Harvard U.P. for Center for Hellenic Studies, 1968.
CORNELIUS, F. *Die Tyrannis in Athen*. Munich: Reinhardt, 1929.
CROISET, M. *Aristophane et les partis à Athènes*. Paris: Fontemoing, 1906; trans. LOEB, J., *Aristophanes and the Political Parties at Athens*. Macmillan, 1909.
CRUSIUS, O. *Analecta Critica ad Paroemiographos Graecos*. Leipzig: Teubner, 1883.
CURTIUS, E. *Attische Studien*. 2 vols. Abh. Göttingen xi 1862, xii 1865.
DAUX, G. *Delphes au IIe et au Ier siècle*. Paris: Boccard, 1936.
—— *Mélanges helléniques offerts à G. Daux*. Paris: Boccard, 1974.
DAVIES, J. K. *Athenian Propertied Families, 600–300 B.C.* O.U.P., 1971.
—— *Democracy and Classical Greece*. Fontana/Harvester, 1978.
DAVISON, J. A. *From Archilochus to Pindar: Papers on the Literature of the Archaic Period*. Macmillan, 1968.
DAY, J. H., & CHAMBERS, M. H. *Aristotle's History of Athenian Democracy*. (U. Calif. Pub. Hist. lxxiii.) U. of California P., 1962.
DE LAIX, R. A. *Probouleusis at Athens: A Study of Political Decision-Making*. (U. Calif. Pub. Hist. lxxxiii.) U. of California P., 1973.
DELCOURT, M. *Oedipe, ou la légende du conquérant*. (Bibl. Fac. Phil. & Lett. U. Liége, civ.) Liége: Fac. Phil. & Lett., Paris: Droz, 1944.
DELEBECQUE, E. *Essai sur la vie de Xénophon*. Paris: Klincksieck, 1957.
DENNISTON, J. D. (rev. DOVER, K. J.) *The Greek Particles*. O.U.P., ²1954.
DE STE CROIX, G. E. M. *The Origins of the Peloponnesian War*. Duckworth, 1972.

OTHER BOOKS

Desrousseaux, A.-M. *Mélanges offerts à A.-M. Desrousseaux*. Paris: Hachette, 1937.
Deubner, L. (rev. Doer, B.) *Attische Feste*. Hildesheim: Olms, ²1966.
Dinsmoor, W. B. *The Archons of Athens in the Hellenistic Age*. Harvard U.P. for A.S.C.S.A., 1931.
Dodds, E. R. *The Ancient Concept of Progress and Other Essays on Greek Literature and Belief*. O.U.P., 1973.
Dorjahn, A. P. *Political Forgiveness in Old Athens*. (Northwestern U. Studies in the Humanities, xiii.) Evanston, Ill.: Northwestern U.P., 1946.
Dover, K. J. *Greek Popular Morality in the Time of Plato and Aristotle*. Blackwell, 1974.
Dow, S. *Prytaneis. A Study of the Inscriptions Honoring the Athenian Councillors. Hesp.* Supp. i 1937.
Duemmler, F. *Kleine Schriften*. 3 vols. Leipzig: Hirzel, 1901.
Düring, I. *Aristotle in the Ancient Biographical Tradition*. (Acta Universitatis Gothoburgensis, LXIII. ii; Studia Graeca et Latina Gothoburgensia v.) Stockholm: Almqvist och Wiksell, 1957.
Ehrenberg, V. L. *Aspects of the Ancient World*. Blackwell, 1946.
—— *Polis und Imperium*. Zurich and Stuttgart: Artemis, 1965.
—— *Ancient Society and Institutions: Studies presented to V. Ehrenberg*. Blackwell, 1966.
Eliot, C. W. J. *Coastal Demes of Attika. Phoen*. Supp. v 1962.
Eucken, R. *De Aristotelis Dicendi Ratione, i. Observationes de Particularum Usu*. (Dissertation.) Göttingen: Vandenhoeck und Ruprecht, 1866.
Febvre, L. *Éventail de l'histoire vivante: hommage à L. Febvre*. Paris: Colin, 1953.
Ferguson, W. S. *The Athenian Secretaries*. (Cornell Stud. Cl. Phil. vii.) New York: Macmillan, 1898.
—— *Hellenistic Athens*. Macmillan, 1911.
—— *The Treasurers of Athena*. Harvard U.P., 1932.
Fine, J. V. A. *Horoi: Studies in Mortgage, Real Security and Land Tenure in Ancient Athens. Hesp.* Supp. ix 1951.
Finley, M. I. *The Ancestral Constitution*. (Inaugural Lecture.) C.U.P., 1971.
—— *Studies in Land and Credit in Ancient Athens, 500–200 B.C.: The Horos-Inscriptions*. Rutgers U.P., 1952.
—— *The Use and Abuse of History*. Chatto and Windus, 1975.
—— *The World of Odysseus*. Chatto and Windus, ²1977.
Follet, S. *Athènes au IIe et au IIIe siècle: études chronologiques et prosopographiques*. Paris: Les Belles Lettres, 1976.
Fornara, C. W. *The Athenian Board of Generals from 501 to 404. Hist.* Einz. xvi 1971.

FORREST, W. G. *The Emergence of Greek Democracy: The Character of Greek Politics, 800–400 B.C.* Weidenfeld and Nicolson, 1966.
—— *A History of Sparta, 950–192 B.C.* Hutchinson, 1968.
FRÄNKEL, M. *Die attische Geschworengerichte: ein Beitrag zum attischen Staatsrecht.* Berlin: Reimer, 1877.
FRANCOTTE, H. *La Polis grecque.* Paderborn: Schöningh, 1907.
FREEMAN, K. *The Work and Life of Solon.* O.U.P. for U. of Wales, 1926.
FRENCH, A. *The Growth of the Athenian Economy.* Routledge, 1964.
FRITZ, K. VON *Schriften zur griechischen und römischen Verfassungsgeschichte und Verfassungstheorie.* Berlin and New York: De Gruyter, 1976.
FUKS, A. *The Ancestral Constitution.* Routledge, 1953.
FUSTEL DE COULANGES, N. D. *La Cité antique: étude sur le culte, le droit, les institutions de la Grèce et de Rome.* Paris: Durand, 1864; the edition which I cite is Hachette, ^{23}1916.
GARLAN, Y. *La Guerre dans l'antiquité.* Paris: Nathan, 1972; trans. LLOYD, J., *War in the Ancient World: A Social History.* Chatto and Windus, 1975.
GAUTHIER, P. *Symbola: les étrangers et la justice dans les cités grecques.* (Annales de l'Est, Mémoires, xlii.) U. de Nancy II, 1972.
GEAGAN, D. J. *The Athenian Constitution after Sulla. Hesp.* Supp. xii 1967.
GERNET, L. *Anthropologie de la Grèce antique.* Paris: Maspero, 1968.
—— *Droit et société dans la Grèce ancienne.* (U. de Paris, Pub. de l'Institut de Droit Romain, xiii.) Paris: Sirey, 1955.
GILBERT, G., trans. BROOKS, E. J., & NICKLIN, T. *The Constitutional Antiquities of Sparta and Athens.* Sonnenschein, 1895.
GLOTZ, G. *La Cité grecque.* Paris: La Renaissance du Livre, 1928; trans. MALLINSON, N., *The Greek City and its Institutions.* Routledge, 1929; rev. CLOCHÉ, P., Paris: Michel, 1953.
—— with COHEN, R., & ROUSSEL, P. *Histoire générale: histoire grecque.* 4 vols. Paris: P.U.F., 1926–38.
—— *Mélanges G. Glotz.* 2 vols. Paris: P.U.F., 1932.
GOMME, A. W. *Essays in Greek History and Literature.* Blackwell, 1937.
—— *More Essays in Greek History and Literature.* Blackwell, 1962.
—— *The Population of Athens in the Fifth and Fourth Centuries B.C.* (Glasgow U. Pub. xxviii.) Blackwell, 1933.
GOODWIN, W. W. *A Greek Grammar.* Macmillan, ^{2}1894.
—— *Syntax of the Moods and Tenses of the Greek Verb.* New York: St. Martin's Press, ^{3}1875 (rev. 1910).
GRAINDOR, P. *Album d'inscriptions attiques d'époque impériale.* 2 vols. (U. de Gand, Rec. Fac. Phil. & Lett. liii, liv.) Ghent: van Rysselberghe & Rombaut, Paris: Champion, 1924.

—— *Athenes de Tibère à Trajan.* (U. Égyptienne, Rec. Fac. Lett. viii.) Cairo: Misr, 1931.
GRAYSON, A. K. *Texts from Cuneiform Sources*, v. *Assyrian and Babylonian Chronicles.* Locust Valley, N.Y.: Augustin, 1975.
GRIFFITH, G. T. (ed.) *Alexander the Great: The Main Problems.* Heffer, 1966.
GROTE, G. *A History of Greece from the Earliest Period to the Close of the Generation Contemporary with Alexander the Great.* The edition which I cite is 'a new edition' in 12 vols. Murray, 1869 (with a reprint in 1884).
GUTHRIE, W. K. C. *A History of Greek Philosophy.* In progress, C.U.P., 1962–.
HAMMOND, N. G. L. *A History of Greece to 322 B.C.* O.U.P., ²1967.
—— *Studies in Greek History.* O.U.P., 1973.
—— [& GRIFFITH, G. T.] *A History of Macedonia.* In progress. O.U.P., 1972–.
HANSEN, M. H. *Apagoge, Endeixis and Ephegesis against Kakourgoi, Atimoi and Pheugontes.* (Odense U. Cl. Stud. viii.) Odense U.P., 1976.
—— *Eisangelia.* (Odense U. Cl. Stud. vi.) Odense U.P., 1975.
—— *The Sovereignty of the People's Court in Athens in the Fourth Century B.C. and the Public Action against Unconstitutional Proposals.* (Odense U. Cl. Stud. iv.) Odense U.P., 1974.
HARRELL, H. C. *Public Arbitration in Athenian Law.* U. Missouri Stud. XI. i 1936.
HARRISON, A. R. W. *The Law of Athens.* 2 vols. O.U.P., 1968/71.
HASPELS, C. H. E. *Attic Black-Figured Lekythoi.* 2 vols. (Éc. Fr. Ath., Travaux et Mémoires, iv.) Paris: Boccard, 1936.
HAVELOCK, E. A. *The Greek Concept of Justice, from its Shadow in Homer to its Substance in Plato.* Harvard U.P., 1978.
HEADLAM(-MORLEY), J. W. (rev. MACGREGOR, D. C.) *Election by Lot at Athens.* (Cambridge Historical Essays, iv.) C.U.P., ²1933.
HELBIG, W. *Les ἱππεῖς athéniens. Mém. Ac. Inscr. & Belles-Lettres* XXXVII. i 1904, 157–264; also published separately, Paris: Klincksieck, 1902.
HENRY, A. S. *The Prescripts of Athenian Decrees. Mnem.* Supp. xlix 1977.
HIGNETT, C. *A History of the Athenian Constitution to the End of the Fifth Century B.C.* O.U.P., 1952 (corr. 1958).
—— *Xerxes' Invasion of Greece.* O.U.P., 1963.
HILL, I. C. T. *The Ancient City of Athens.* Methuen, 1953.
HIRZEL, R. ἄγραφος νόμος. *Abh. Leipzig.* xx. i 1900–3.
HOMMEL, H. *Heliaia. Philol.* Supp. xix. ii 1927. (Cf. above, part i, item 89.)
HOPPER, R. J. *The Acropolis.* Weidenfeld and Nicolson, 1971.

—— *The Basis of the Athenian Democracy.* (Inaugural Lecture.) Sheffield U., 1957.
HUMPHREYS, S. C. *Anthropology and the Greeks.* Routledge, 1978.
HUXLEY, G. L. *Early Sparta.* Faber, 1962.
ISAGER, S., & HANSEN, M. H. *Aspects of Athenian Society in the Fourth Century B.C.* (Odense U. Cl. Stud. v.) Odense U.P., 1975.
JACOBY, F. *Abhandlungen zur griechischen Geschichtschreibung.* Leiden: Brill, 1956.
—— *Apollodors Chronik.* (Philologische Untersuchungen, xvi.) Berlin: Weidmann, 1902.
—— *Atthis: The Local Chronicles of Ancient Athens.* O.U.P., 1949.
JAEGER, W. W. *Aristoteles: Grundlegung einer Geschichte seiner Entwicklung.* Berlin: Weidmann, 1923; trans. ROBINSON, R., *Aristotle: Fundamentals of the History of his Development.* O.U.P., ²1948.
—— trans. FISKE, A. M. *Five Essays.* Montreal: Casalini, 1966.
—— *Scripta Minora.* 2 vols. Rome: Ed. di Storia e Letteratura, 1960.
JARDÉ, A. *Les Céréales dans l'antiquité grecque*, i. *La Production.* Paris: Boccard, 1925.
JEFFERY, L. H. *Archaic Greece: The City-States, c. 700–500 B.C.* Benn, 1976.
—— *The Local Scripts of Archaic Greece.* (Oxford Monographs on Classical Archaeology.) O.U.P., 1961.
JONES, A. H. M. *Athenian Democracy.* Blackwell, 1957.
JORDAN, B. *The Athenian Navy in the Classical Period.* U. Calif. Pub. Cl. Stud. xiii 1975.
JUDEICH, W. *Topographie von Athen.* (H.d.A. III. ii. 2.) Munich: Beck, ²1931.
KAGAN, D. *The Archidamian War.* Cornell U.P., 1974.
KAHRSTEDT, U. *Forschungen zur Geschichte des ausgehenden V. und des IV. Jahrhunderts.* Berlin: Weidmann, 1910.
—— *Griechisches Staatsrecht*, i. *Sparta und seine Symmachie.* Göttingen: Vandenhoeck und Ruprecht, 1922.
—— *Studien zum öffentlichen Recht Athens*, i. *Staatsgebiet und Staatsangehörige in Athen.* Stuttgart and Berlin: Kohlhammer, 1934.
—— *Studien zum öffentlichen Recht Athens*, ii. *Untersuchungen zur Magistratur in Athen.* Stuttgart: Kohlhammer, 1936.
KAIBEL, G. *Stil und Text der Πολιτεία Ἀθηναίων des Aristoteles.* Berlin: Weidmann, 1893. (Cf. above, part i, item 87.)
KEIL, B. *Anonymus Argentinensis.* Strasburg: Trübner, 1902.
—— *Die solonische Verfassung in Aristoteles Verfassungsgeschichte Athens.* Berlin: Gärtner, 1892. (Cf. above, part i, item 86.)
KELLY, T. *A History of Argos to 500 B.C.* U. of Minnesota P., 1976.
KENYON, F. G. *Greek Papyri in the British Museum: Catalogue, with Texts*, [i]. British Museum, 1893.
KIRCHNER, J. *Prosopographia Attica.* 2 vols. Berlin: Reimer, 1901/3.

OTHER BOOKS

KLAFFENBACH, G. *Die Astynomeninschrift von Pergamon. Abh.* Berlin 1953, vi.
KLEE, T. *Zur Geschichte der gymnischen Agone an griechischen Festen.* Leipzig and Berlin: Teubner, 1918.
KRAAY, C. M. *Archaic and Classical Greek Coins.* Methuen, 1976.
KRIEGEL, J. *Der Staatsreich der Vierhundert in Athen, 411 v. Chr.* (Dissertation.) Bonn: Georgi, 1909.
KROLL, J. H. *Athenian Bronze Allotment Plates.* (Loeb Cl. Monographs.) Harvard U.P., 1972.
KRON, U. *Die zehn attischen Phylenheroen: Geschichte, Mythos, Kult und Darstellungen. AM* Bhft. v 1976.
KÜHNER, R., rev. BLASS, F., & GERTH, B. *Ausführliche Grammatik der griechischen Sprache.* 2 vols. in 4. Hanover (and Leipzig): Hahn, 1890–1904.
LABARBE, J. *La Loi navale de Thémistocle.* (Bibl. Fac. Phil. & Lett. U. Liège, cxliii.) Paris: Les Belles Lettres, 1957.
LACEY, W. K. *The Family in Classical Greece.* Thames and Hudson, 1968.
LAIDLAW, W. A. *A History of Delos.* Blackwell, 1933.
LANE FOX, R. J. *Alexander the Great.* Allen Lane with Longmans, 1973.
LANG, M. L., & CROSBY, M. *The Athenian Agora,* x. *Weights, Measures and Tokens.* Princeton: A.S.C.S.A., 1964.
LANGLOTZ, E. *Charites: Studien zur Altertumswissenschaft [E. Langlotz gewidmet].* Bonn: Athenäum, 1957.
LARSEN, J. A. O. *Representative Government in Greek and Roman History.* (Sather Cl. Lectures, xxviii.) U. of California P., 1955.
LATTE, K. *Kleine Schriften zu Religion, Recht, Literatur und Sprache der Griechen und Römer.* Munich: Beck, 1968.
LEDL, A. *Studien zur älteren athenischen Verfassungsgeschichte.* Heidelberg: Winter, 1914.
LEWIS, D. M. *Sparta and Persia.* (Cincinnati Cl. Stud.[2] i.) Leiden: Brill, 1977.
LINDERS, T. *Studies in the Treasure Records of Artemis Brauronia found in Athens. Acta Instituti Atheniensis Regni Sueciae,* Series in 4°, xix 1972.
LINFORTH, I. M. *Solon the Athenian.* (U. Calif. Pub. Cl. Phil. vi.) U. of California P., 1919.
LIPSIUS, J. H. *Das attische Recht und Rechtsverfahren.* 3 vols in 4. Leipzig: Reisland, 1905–15.
—— *Griechische Studien H. Lipsius . . . dargebracht.* Leipzig: Teubner, 1894.
LOFBERG, J. O. *Sycophancy in Athens.* (Diss. Chicago). Menasha, Wis.: Collegiate P., 1917.
LOTZE, D. *Lysander und der peloponnesischer Krieg. Abh.* Leipzig LVII. i 1964.

LUCAS, J. R. *The Principles of Politics*. O.U.P., 1966 (corr. 1974).
LYNCH, J. P. *Aristotle's School: A Study of a Greek Educational Institution*. U. of California P., 1972.
MCCREDIE, J. R. *Fortified Military Camps in Attica. Hesp.* Supp. xi 1966.
MCDONALD, W. A. *The Political Meeting Places of the Greeks*. (Johns Hopkins St. Arch. xxxiv.) Johns Hopkins P., 1943.
MACDOWELL, D. M. *Athenian Homicide Law in the Age of the Orators*. Manchester U.P., 1963.
—— *The Law in Classical Athens*. Thames and Hudson, 1978.
MACKENDRICK, P. *The Athenian Aristocracy, 399 to 31 B.C.* (Martin Cl. Lectures, xxiii.) Harvard U.P. for Oberlin Coll., 1969.
MADDOLI, G. *Cronologia e storia: studi comparati sull' Athenaion Politeia di Aristotele*. Perugia: Pubbl. Ist. Stor. Fac. Lett. & Fil., 1975.
MARTIN, A. *Les Cavaliers athéniens*. (Bibl. Éc. Fr. Ath. & Rome, xlvii.) Paris: Thorin, 1887.
MASARACCHIA, A. *Solone*. Florence: La Nuova Italia, 1958.
MATHIEU, G. *Aristote, Constitution d'Athènes: essai sur la méthode suivie par Aristote dans la discussion des textes*. (Bibl. Éc. Haut. Ét. ccxvi.) Paris: Champion, 1915.
MEIER, M. H. E., & SCHÖMANN, G. F., rev. LIPSIUS, J. H. *Das attische Prozess*. 2 vols. Berlin: Calvary, 1883-7.
MEIGGS, R. *The Athenian Empire*. O.U.P., 1972.
MEISTERHANS, K., rev. SCHWYZER, E. *Grammatik der attischen Inschriften*. Berlin: Weidmann, 1900.
MERITT, B. D. *The Athenian Calendar in the Fifth Century*. Harvard U.P. for A.S.C.S.A., 1928.
—— *Athenian Financial Documents of the Fifth Century*. (Humanistic Series, xxvii.) U. of Michigan P., 1932.
—— *The Athenian Year*. (Sather Cl. Lectures, xxxii.) U. of California P., 1959.
—— & TRAILL, J. S. *The Athenian Agora*, xv. *The Inscriptions: The Athenian Councillors*. Princeton: A.S.C.S.A., 1974.
—— et al. *The Athenian Tribute Lists*. 4 vols. Harvard U.P. for A.S.C.S.A./Princeton: A.S.C.S.A., 1939–53.
—— Φόρος: *Tribute to B. D. Meritt*. Locust Valley, N.Y.: Augustin, 1974.
MEYER, E. *Forschungen zur alten Geschichte*. 2 vols. Halle: Niemeyer, 1892/8.
—— (rev. STIER, E.) *Geschichte des Altertums*. Final ed. 5 vols. in 9. Stuttgart: Cotta/Basle and Stuttgart: Schwabe, 1925–58.
MEYER, P. *Des Aristoteles Politik und die Ἀθ. π.* Bonn: Cohen, 1891.
MIKALSON, J. D. *The Sacred and Civil Calendar of the Athenian Year*. Princeton U.P., 1975.

OTHER BOOKS

MILLER, S. G. *The Prytaneion: Its Function and Architectural Form.* U. of California P., 1978.
MILNE, H. J. M. *Catalogue of Literary Papyri in the British Museum.* British Museum, 1927.
MOMMSEN, A. *Feste der Stadt Athen im Altertum, geordnet nach attischem Kalendar.* Leipzig: Teubner, 1898.
MORAUX, P. *Les Listes anciennes des ouvrages d'Aristote.* Louvain: Éd. Universitaires, 1951.
MORRISON, J. S., & WILLIAMS, R. T. *Greek Oared Ships, 900–322 B.C.* C.U.P., 1968.
MOSSÉ, C. *La Fin de la démocratie athénienne.* Paris: P.U.F., 1962.
—— *La Tyrannie dans la Grèce antique.* Paris: P.U.F., 1969.
MOTZKI, A. *Eubulos von Probalinthos und seine Finanzpolitik.* (Dissertation.) Königsberg in Preussen: Leupold, 1903.
MYLONAS, G. E. *Eleusis and the Eleusinian Mysteries.* Princeton U.P., 1962.
NICOLE, J. *L'Apologie d'Antiphon ou λόγος περὶ μεταστάσεως.* Geneva and Basle: Georg, 1907.
OLDFATHER, W. A. *Classical Studies in Honor of W. A. Oldfather.* U. of Illinois P., 1943.
OLIVER, J. H. *The Athenian Expounders of the Sacred and Ancestral Law.* Johns Hopkins P., 1950.
—— *Marcus Aurelius: Aspects of Civic and Cultural Policy in the East. Hesp.* Supp. xiii 1970.
OSTWALD, M. *Nomos and the Beginnings of the Athenian Democracy.* O.U.P., 1969.
PAGE, D. L. *Sappho and Alcaeus.* O.U.P., 1955.
PAOLI, U. E. *Studi sul processo attico.* Padua: C.E.D.A.M., 1933.
PARKE, H. W. *Festivals of the Athenians.* Thames and Hudson, 1977.
PEČÍRKA, J. *The Formula for the Grant of Enktesis in Attic Inscriptions.* Prague: *Acta Universitatis Carolinae, Philosophica et Historica Monographia,* xv 1966.
PÉLÉKIDIS, CH. *Histoire de l'éphébie attique des origines à 31 avant J.-C.* (Éc. Fr. Ath., Travaux et Memoires, xiii.) Paris: Boccard, 1962.
PERLMAN, S. (ed.) *Philip and Athens.* Heffer, 1973.
PHILIPPSON, A., ed. LEHMANN, H., & KIRSTEN, E. *Die griechischen Landschaften.* 4 vols in 8. Frankfurt am Main: Klostermann, 1950–9.
PICKARD-CAMBRIDGE, A. W. *The Dramatic Festivals of Athens.* O.U.P., 1953; rev. GOULD, J. P. A., & LEWIS, D. M., ^{2}1968.
—— *The Theatre of Dionysus in Athens.* O.U.P., 1946.
PITTAKYS, K. S. *L'Ancienne Athènes: ou la description des antiquités d'Athènes et de ses environs.* Athens: Antoniades, 1835.
PODLECKI, A. J. *The Political Background of Aeschylean Tragedy.* U. of Michigan P., 1966.

PORALLA, P. *Prosopographie der Lakedaimonier bis auf die Zeit Alexanders des Grossen.* (Dissertation.) Breslau: Max, 1913.

POUILLOUX, J. *La Forteresse de Rhamnonte.* (Bibl. Éc. Fr. Ath. & Rome, clxxix.) Paris: Boccard, 1954.

POWELL, J. U., & BARBER, E. A. (edd.) *New Chapters in the History of Greek Literature,* [i.] O.U.P., 1921.

PRÉAUX, C. *Le Monde grec; pensée, littérature, histoire, documents: hommages à C. Préaux.* Brussels: Éd. de l'U., 1975.

PRICE, M. J., & WAGGONER, N. M. *Ancient Greek Coinage: The Asyut Hoard.* Vecchi, 1975.

PRITCHETT, W. K. *The Choiseul Marble. U. Calif. Publ. Cl. Stud.* v 1970.

—— *The Greek State at War.* Vols i–ii. (Vol. i previously published as *Ancient Greek Military Practices,* i: *U. Calif. Pub. Cl. Stud.* vii 1971.) U. of California P., 1974.

—— *Marathon. U. Calif. Pub. Cl. Arch.* IV. ii 1960.

—— & MERITT, B. D. *The Chronology of Hellenistic Athens.* Harvard U.P. for A.S.C.S.A., 1940.

—— & NEUGEBAUER, O. *The Calendars of Athens.* Harvard U.P. for A.S.C.S.A., 1947.

QUASS, F. *Nomos und Psephisma: Untersuchung zum griechischen Staatsrecht.* (Zetemata, lv.) Munich: Beck, 1971.

RALPH, J. D. *Ephesis in Athenian Litigation.* (Dissertation.) U. of Chicago Libraries, 1941.

REINMUTH, O. W. *The Ephebic Inscriptions of the Fourth Century B.C. Mnem.* Supp. xiv 1971.

REUSCH, A. *De Diebus Contionum Ordinarium apud Athenienses. Dissertationes Philologicae Argentoratenses Selectae,* iii (Strasburg: Trübner, 1880), 1–138.

RHODES, P. J. *The Athenian Boule.* O.U.P., 1972.

RICHTER, G. M. A., with GUARDUCCI, M. *The Archaic Gravestones of Attica.* Phaidon, 1961.

ROBINSON, D. M. *Studies presented to D. M. Robinson.* 2 vols. St Louis, Miss.: Washington U., 1951/3.

ROBINSON, E. S. G. *Essays in Greek Coinage presented to S. Robinson.* O.U.P., 1968.

ROBINSON, I. A. 'Bibliography of Aristotle's *Constitution of Athens,* 1891–1951.' Unpublished dissertation: London U., School of Library, Archive and Information Studies, 1952.

RÖMISCH, E. *Studien zur älteren griechischen Elegie.* (Frankfurter Studien zur Religion und Kultur der Antike, vii.) Frankfurt am Main: Klostermann, 1933.

ROMILLY, J. DE *La Loi dans la pensée grecque des origines à Aristote.* (Coll. Budé.) Paris: Les Belles Lettres, 1971.

—— *The Rise and Fall of States according to Greek Authors.* (Jerome Lectures, xi.) U. of Michigan P., 1977.

OTHER BOOKS

Ross, W. D. *Aristotle.* Methuen, ⁵1949.
ROSSITER, S. (ed.) *Greece.* (The Blue Guides.) Benn, ³1977.
ROSTAGNI, A. *Miscellanea di studi Alessandrini in Memoria di A. Rostagni.* Turin: Bottega d'Erasmo, 1963.
RUSCHENBUSCH, E. *Untersuchungen zur Geschichte des athenischen Strafrechts.* (Graezistische Abhandlungen, iv.) Cologne and Graz: Böhlau, 1968.
—— Σόλωνος νόμοι: *Die Fragmente des solonischen Gesetzeswerkes mit einer Text- und Überlieferungsgeschichte. Hist.* Einz. ix 1966.
RZACH, A. *Charisteria A. Rzach . . . dargebracht.* Reichenberg: Stiepel, 1930.
SABINE, G. H. *Essays in Political Theory presented to G. H. Sabine.* Cornell U.P., 1948.
SAKELLARIOS, A. A. *Untersuchung des Textes der Ἀθηναίων Πολιτεία des Aristoteles.* Jena: Haerdle, 1898.
SALMON, E. T. *Polis and Imperium: Studies in Honour of E. T. Salmon.* Toronto: Hakkert, 1974.
SAMUEL, A. E. *Greek and Roman Chronology.* (H.d.A. I. vii.) Munich: Beck, 1972.
SANCTIS, G. DE *Ἀτθίς: Storia della reppublica Ateniese dalle origini alle riforme di Clistene.* Rome: Tipografia Poliglotta, 1898; . . . *alla età di Pericle.* Turin: Bocca, ²1912; rev. ACCAME, S., Florence: La Nuova Italia, ³1975. I cite the 1st ed. and the 2nd; the pagination of the 2nd is indicated in the margins of the 3rd.
—— *Scritti minori.* 6 vols in 7. Rome: Ed. di Storia e Letteratura, 1966–.
SARIKAKIS, TH. CH. *The Hoplite General in Athens.* Diss. Princeton, 1951.
SARTORI, F. *La crisi del 411 a.C. nell' Athenaion Politeia di Aristotele.* Padua: C.E.D.A.M., 1951.
—— *Le eterie nella vita politica ateniese del VI e V secolo a.C.* (U. di Padova, Pubbl. Ist. Stor. Ant. iii.) Rome: L'Erma di Bretschneider, 1957.
SCHACHERMEYR, F. *Forschungen und Betrachtungen zur griechischen und römischen Geschichte.* Vienna: Ö.A.W., 1974.
—— *Greece and the Eastern Mediterranean in Ancient History and Prehistory: Studies presented to F. Schachermeyr.* Berlin and New York: De Gruyter, 1977.
SCHAEFER, A. D. *Demosthenes und seine Zeit,* vol. III. ii. (Not revised in 2nd ed. of 1885–7.) Leipzig: Teubner, 1858.
SCHOEFFER, V. VON (SHEFFER, V.) *Afinskoe Grazhdanstvo i Narodnoe Sobranie,* i. (Moscow U., Otd. Ist.-Fil. Uch.) Moscow: Lissera i Romana, 1891.
—— *De Insulae Deli Rebus.* (Berl. Stud. Cl. Phil. u. Arch. IX. i.) Berlin: Calvary, 1889.

SCHÖMANN, G. F. *Die Verfassungsgeschichte Athens nach G. Grote's History of Greece kritisch geprüft.* Leipzig: Weidmann, 1854.
SCHREINER, J. C. S. *De Corpore Iuris Atheniensium.* Diss. Bonn, 1913.
SCHREINER, J. H. *Aristotle and Perikles: A Study in Historiography. SO* Supp. xxi 1968.
SCHWYZER, E. (*et al.*) *Griechische Grammatik.* 4 vols. (H.d.A. II. i.) Munich: Beck, 1934-71.
SEALEY, B. R. I. *Essays in Greek Politics.* New York: Manyland, 1967.
―― *A History of the Greek City States, ca. 700–338 B.C.* U. of California P., 1976.
SHEAR, T. L., JR. *Kallias of Sphettos and the Revolt of Athens in 286 B.C. Hesp.* Supp. xvii 1978.
SHUTE, R. *On the History of the Process by which the Aristotelian Writings arrived at their Present Form.* O.U.P., 1888.
SNODGRASS, A. M. *Archaeology and the Rise of the Greek State.* (Inaugural Lecture.) C.U.P., 1977.
STARR, C. G. *The Economic and Social Growth of Early Greece, 800–500 B.C.* New York: O.U.P., 1977.
STAVELEY, E. S. *Greek and Roman Voting and Elections.* Thames and Hudson, 1972.
STROUD, R. S. *The Axones and Kyrbeis of Drakon and Solon. U. Calif. Pub. Cl. Stud.* xix 1979.
―― *Drakon's Law on Homicide. U. Calif. Pub. Cl. Stud.* iii 1968.
STUPPERICH, R. *Staatsbegräbnis und Privatgrabmal im klassischen Athen.* Diss. Münster, 1977.
ŚWIDEREK, A. *La Propriété foncière privée dans l'Égypte de Vespasien et sa technique agricole d'après P. Lond. 131 Recto.* (Ac. Sci. Pol., Bibl. Ant. i.) Wrocław: Zakład Narodowy I. Ossolińskich, 1960.
THOMAS, D. H. 'Aristotle's Treatment of Historical Material in the *Politics*.' Unpublished dissertation: Oxford U., 1978.
THOMPSON, H. A. *The Tholos of Athens and its Predecessors. Hesp.* Supp. iv 1940.
―― & WYCHERLEY, R. E. *The Athenian Agora,* xiv. *The Agora of Athens: The History, Shape and Uses of an Ancient City Center.* Princeton: A.S.C.S.A., 1972.
THOMSEN, R. *Eisphora: A Study of Direct Taxation in Ancient Athens.* Copenhagen: Gyldendal, 1964.
―― *The Origin of Ostracism.* Copenhagen: Gyldendal, 1972.
TOYNBEE, A. J. *Some Problems of Greek History.* O.U.P., 1969.
TRAILL, J. S. *The Political Organization of Attica: A Study of the Demes, Trittyes and Phylai, and their Representation in the Athenian Council. Hesp.* Supp. xiv 1975.
TRAVLOS, J. *Pictorial Dictionary of Ancient Athens.* Thames and Hudson for D.A.I., 1971.

OTHER BOOKS

Turner, E. G. *Greek Manuscripts of the Ancient World.* O.U.P., 1971.
—— *Greek Papyri: An Introduction.* O.U.P., 1968.
Ure, P. N. *The Origin of Tyranny.* C.U.P., 1922.
Usener, H. *Vorträge und Aufsätze.* Leipzig and Berlin: Teubner, 1907.
Usteri, P. L. *Ächtung und Verbannung im griechischen Rechte.* (Diss. Zurich.) Berlin: Weidmann, 1903.
Verein deutscher Philologen und Schulmänner *Festschrift zur 36. Versammlung deutscher Philologen und Schulmänner..., 1882.* Karlsruhe: Braun, 1882.
—— *XLVII. Versammlung deutscher Philologen und Schulmänner Apophoreton überreicht von der Graeca Halensis.* Berlin: Weidmann, 1903.
Verrall, M. de G., & Harrison, J. E. *Mythology and Monuments of Ancient Athens.* Macmillan, 1890.
Wace, A. J. B., & Stubbings, F. E. (edd.) *A Companion to Homer.* Macmillan, 1962.
Wachsmuth, C. *Philologisch-historische Beiträge C. Wachsmuth... überreicht.* Leipzig: Teubner, 1897.
Wade-Gery, H. T. *Essays in Greek History.* Blackwell, 1958.
Webster, T. B. L. *Potter and Patron in Classical Athens.* Methuen, 1972.
Weidauer, L. *Probleme der frühen Elektronprägung.* Fribourg: Office du Livre, 1975.
Weil, R. *Aristote et l'histoire: essai sur la Politique.* Paris: Klincksieck, 1960.
Whitehead, D. *The Ideology of the Athenian Metic.* PCPS Supp. iv 1977.
Wilamowitz-Moellendorff, U. von *Aristoteles und Athen.* 2 vols. Berlin: Weidmann, 1893.
—— *Kleine Schriften.* 6 vols. in 7 Berlin: Weidmann/Akademie-Verlag, 1935–72.
—— & Robert, C. *Aus Kydathen.* (Philologische Untersuchugen, i.) Berlin: Weidmann, 1880.
Wilhelm, A. *Akademieschriften zur griechischen Inschriftenkunde.* 3 vols. (Opuscula, viii.) Leipzig: Zentralantiquariat der D.D.R., 1974.
Will, E. *Doriens et Ioniens.* (Pub. Fac. Lett. U. Strasbourg, cxxxii.) Paris: Les Belles Lettres, 1956.
Willetts, R. F. *Aristocratic Society in Ancient Crete.* Routledge, 1955.
—— *The Law Code of Gortyn. Kadmos* Supp. i 1967.
Wolff, H. J. *Die attische Paragraphe: Ein Beitrag zum Problem der Auflockerung archaischer Prozessformen.* (Graezistische Abhandlungen, ii.) Weimar: Böhlau, 1966.
—— *'Normenkontrolle' und Gesetzesbegriff in der attischen Demokratie. Sb.* Heidelberg 1970, ii.

WOODHOUSE, W. J. *Solon the Liberator: A Study of the Agrarian Problem in Attika in the Seventh Century.* O.U.P., 1938.
WYCHERLEY, R. E. *The Athenian Agora*, iii. *Literary and Epigraphical Testimonia.* Princeton: A.S.C.S.A., 1957.
—— *The Stones of Athens.* Princeton U.P., 1978.
ZUCKER, F. *Festschrift für F. Zucker.* Berlin: Akademie-Verlag, 1954.
ZÜRCHER, J. *Aristoteles Werk und Geist.* Paderborn: Schöningh, 1952.
ΑΡΒΑΝΙΤΟΠΟΥΛΟΣ, Α. Σ. Μέθοδος πρὸς ἔρευναν τοῦ Ἀττικοῦ ποινικοῦ δικαίου. Volos: Παρασκευοποῦλος, 1923.
Ἀρχαία Μακεδονία See Conference.
ΚΕΡΑΜΟΠΟΥΛΛΟΣ, Α. Δ. ʽΟ Ἀποτυμπανισμός· συμβολὴ ἀρχαιολογικὴ εἰς τὴν ἱστορίαν τοῦ ποινικοῦ δικαίου καὶ τὴν λαογραφίαν. (Βιβλ. Ἀθ. Ἀρχ. ʽΕτ. xxii.) Athens: ʽΕστία, 1923.

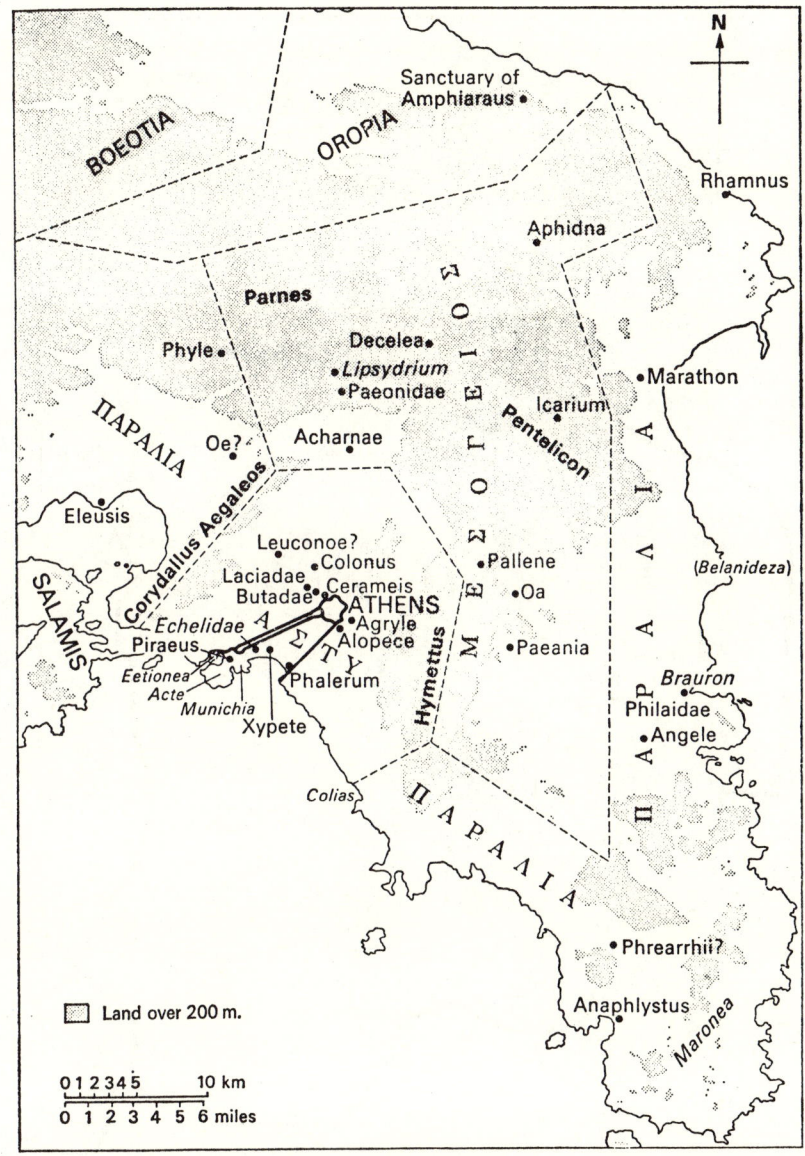

Fig. 3 Map of Attica

(Names of demes are in upright capital and lower case letters; names of Cleisthenes' three regions are in Greek capitals. Regional boundaries are purely schematic.)

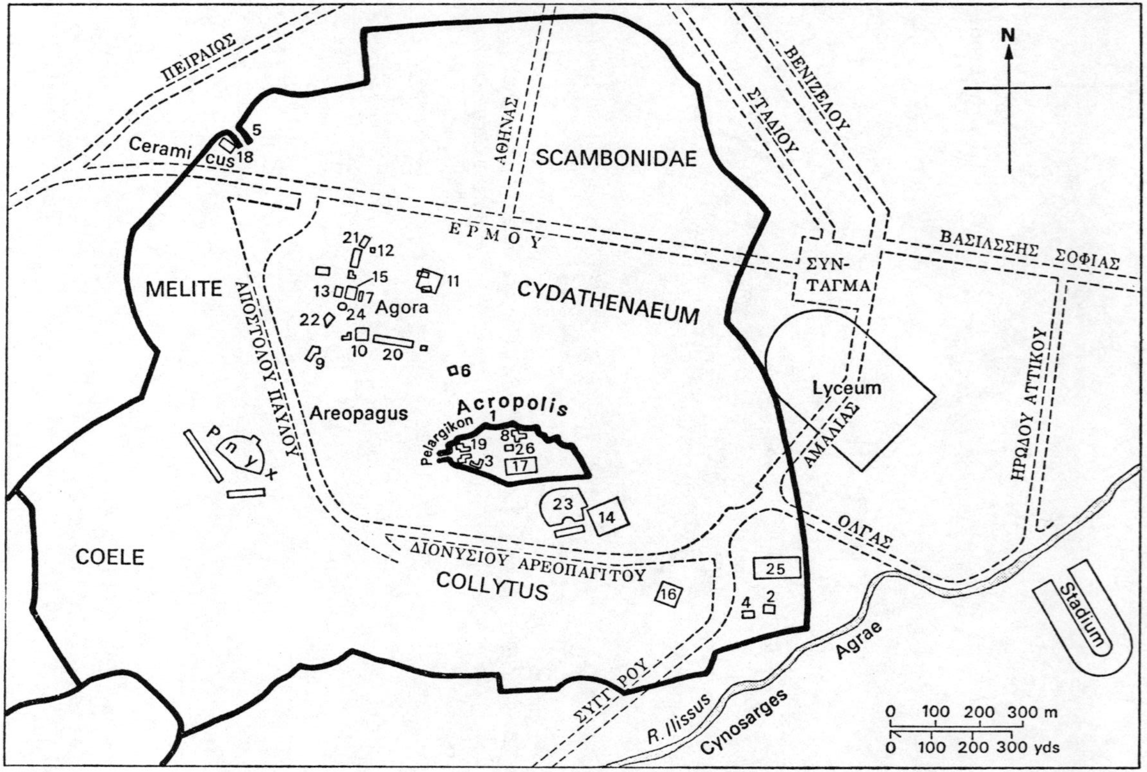

Fig. 4 Plan of Athens

Key to Fig. 4

1 Aglaurus, shrine of
2 Apollo $\Delta\epsilon\lambda\phi\acute{\iota}\nu\iota\sigma$, temple of
3 Brauronium
4 Delphinium, court at the
5 Dipylon Gate
6 Eleusinium
7 Eponymi, statues of
8 Erechtheum
9 Gaol
10 Heliaea
11 Lawcourts
12 Leocoreum
13 New Bouleuterium
14 Odeum
15 Old Bouleuterium = Metroum
16 Palladium, court at the
17 Parthenon
18 Pompeum
19 Propylaea
20 South Stoa
21 Stoa of the Basileus
22 Strategeum
23 Theatre of Dionysus
24 Tholos
25 Zeus $'O\lambda\acute{\upsilon}\mu\pi\iota\sigma$, temple of
26 $'O\pi\iota\sigma\theta\acute{o}\delta\sigma\mu\sigma\varsigma$ (?)

Names of demes are in capital letters;
principal modern streets are shown in pecked lines.

SELECT ADDENDA, 1992

These addenda include the addenda of 1981 printed in the original edition: an obelus (†), or where necessary a double obelus (‡) or a section mark (§), at the end of a paragraph in the main text refers to the material collected here; authors are given their initials at their first mention here, and books are given their full titles and publication details at their first mention here.

The original Addenda included a general reference to W. K. Pritchett, *The Greek State at War*, iii (U. of California P., 1979). The following works should also be consulted throughout:

the works added as items 85E, 85F 90 and 91 to Section I of the Bibliography, in the addenda to p. 746. (I review item 90 in *Polis* forthcoming.)

BLEICKEN, J. *Die athenische Demokratie.* Paderborn: Schöningh, 1985.
DEVELIN, R. *Athenian Officials, 684–321 B.C.* C.U.P., 1989.
HANSEN, M. H. *The Athenian Assembly in the Age of Demosthenes.* Oxford: Blackwell, 1987.
——— *The Athenian Democracy in the Age of Demosthenes.* Oxford: Blackwell, 1991.
SINCLAIR, R. K. *Democracy and Participation in Athens.* C.U.P., 1988.
STOCKTON, D. L. *The Classical Athenian Democracy.* O.U.P., 1990.

Notice also:

HANSEN, M. H. *Ecclesia* ⟨*I*⟩ = *The Athenian Ecclesia: A Collection of Articles, 1976–83.* (Opuscula Graecolatina, xxvi.) Copenhagen: Museum Tusculanum P., 1983.
———*Ecclesia II* = *The Athenian Ecclesia, II: A Collection of Articles, 1983–89.* (Opuscula Graecolatina, xxxi.) Copenhagen: Museum Tusculanum P., 1989.

14 On a 'tragic' view of the rise and fall of the *demos* in the fifth century see J. J. Keaney, *Studies ... S. Dow (G. R. & B. Mon.* x 1964), 161–3; on the use of Aristotelian dialectic in rationalising what the author found in his sources see D. L. Blank, *GR&BS* xxv 1984, 275–84.

18 *A.P.* is believed to be based essentially on the *Atthides* by E. Ruschenbusch, *Hermes* cix 1981, 316–26 (on *A.P.*'s sources for the Thirty see addendum to p. 420).

22 For further discussion of the 'Theramenes papyrus' see G. E. Peseley, *AHB* iii 1989, 29–35; H. R. Breitenbach, *Labor Omnibus Unus G. Walser* (*Hist.* Einz. lx 1989), 121–35.

ADDENDA

23 On Stesimbrotus see E. M. Carawan, *Hist.* xxxviii 1989, 144–61.
63 J. J. Keaney, *LCM* v 1980, 51–6, champions Aristotelian authorship against the arguments of Hignett.
66 On Eumolpus see R. M. Simms, *GR&BS* xxiv 1983, 197–208.
68, 243 The 360 γένη are taken seriously by F. Bourriot, *Recherches sur la nature du génos* (2 vols. Paris: Champion for U. de Lille III, 1976), 460–91, and by D. Roussel, *Tribu et cité* (Ann. Litt. U. Besançon cxciii. Paris: Les Belles Lettres, 1976), 79–87—supposing that these γένη are different from the γένη to be discussed below—and a belief in thirty military γένη was advanced by J. H. Oliver, *Hesp.* xlix 1980, 30–56, esp. 30–8; but I am still not inclined to see any historical reality in these γένη. S. C. Humphreys, *The Craft of the Ancient Historian . . . C. G. Starr* (U. P. of America, 1985), 214–5, wonders if the scheme has come to *A.P.* from Phanodemus, and compares the 5–12–720 in *P. Hib* i 28 (regulations for Ptolemais?).
69, 502 Discussion of γένη and phratries continues apace: Bourriot and Roussel suggest that we should think of γένη as priestly families rather than politically important families—but, even if they are technically correct, the priestly families of the early archaic period are likely to have been politically important too. The Demotionidae of *IG* ii² 1237 are regarded as a phratry by Bourriot and Roussel, and by C. W. Hedrick, Jr., *The Decrees of the Demotionidai* (Am. Cl. Stud. xxii. Atlanta: Scholars P., 1990).
70 The Alcmaeonids are considered not to be a γένος by Bourriot and Roussel, and by M. W. Dickie, *Phoen.* xxxiii 1979, 193–209.
76 γεννῆται are believed to be more or less equivalent to Eupatridae by Humphreys, *Sociologia del diritto* viii 1983, 38–44 at 42; but I disagree.
76 The archaeological evidence is said to suggest expansion from Athens in the dark age, to reoccupy land earlier abandoned, rather than centralisation on Athens: A. Andrewes, *C.A.H.*² III. iii. 380; W. G. Cavanagh in J. W. Rich & A. F. Wallace-Hadrill (edd.), *City and Country in the Ancient World* (Routledge, 1991), 107–8.
78, 99 M. Sakellariou, *REA* lxxviii–lxxix 1976–7, 11–21, envisages a federal state in the dark age, with an archon as supreme ruler and βασιλεῖς under him.
81 G. A. Lehmann, *Hist.* xxix 1980, 242–6, replies to Robertson.
82 P. J. Bicknell, *AC* liv 1985, 89–90, returns to Beloch's dating of Epimenides' purification to the end of the sixth century, but does not persuade me.
83 On the tradition of the Cylonian affair see R. Thomas, *Oral Tradition and Written Record in Classical Athens* (C.U.P., 1989),

ADDENDA

272–80. For further discussion of the πρυτάνιες τῶν ναυκράρων see S. D. Lambert, *Hist.* xxxv 1986, 105–12; Develin, *Klio* lxviii 1986, 68–70.

94   For complications in the history of settlement in Attica see J. McK. Camp, II, *Hesp.* xlviii 1979, 397–411; R. G. Osborne, *BSA* lxxxiv 1989, 297–302. For suggestions that some or all of the ἐκτήμοροι were working public land see P. B. Manville, *The Origins of Citizenship in Ancient Athens* (Princeton U. P., 1990), 93–123 (believing, as I do not, that πελάται differed from ἐκτήμοροι); T. E. Rihll, *JHS* cxi 1991, 101–27.

96   P. D. A. Garnsey in *Crux . . . G. E. M. de Ste Croix* (*Hist. Pol. Thought* vi. 1–2 1985 = Duckworth 1985), 62–75, argues that locally grown corn was not seriously insufficient until well into the sixth century, but I think this is too optimistic, and my pupil Mr J. M. M. Helm has found errors in his calculations.

99   See on 78.

103   Humphreys in *Tria Corda . . . A. Momigliano* (Bibl. di Athenaeum l. Como: New Press, 1983), 234, suggests that the thesmothetae were originally assessors to the three senior archons. For attempts to interpret the duty ascribed to them by *A.P.* see M. Gagarin, *TAPA* cxi 1981, 7–17; H. R. Immerwahr, *BASP* xxii 1985, 128 n. 20.

104, 211   Though I described it as secure, the identification of the cave of Aglaurus has turned out to be wrong: it is located even more securely at the east end of the Acropolis by an inscription published by G. S. Dontas, *Hesp.* lii 1983, 48–63. This has repercussions on the location of other buildings, and of the Old Agora; for an attempt to reconstruct an Old Agora east of the Acropolis see N. Robertson, *Hist.* xxxv 1986, 157–68.

104   See also W. Burkert, *Greek Religion* (Blackwell, 1985), 239–41.

105   In *Blue Guide: Athens*² (1981), atlas p. 10, the plan was corrected.

106   B. R. I. Sealey, *The Athenian Republic* (Penn State U. P., 1987), 68–9, after D. L. Anderson, suggests that both before Solon and after, until the institution of the παραγραφή procedure in the fourth century, the archon had the power to decide whether a case was admissible. Unfortunately we do not know how much power the archon had in the ἀνάκρισις in the fifth and fourth centuries.

107, 675   It is argued by W. G. Forrest & D. L. Stockton, *Hist.* xxxvi 1987, 235–40, and J. L. Marr, *LCM* xv 1990, 44–5, that the archons joined the Areopagus not at the end but at the beginning of their year of office; but 60. iii and the passages cited *ad loc.* point against it. R. W. Wallace, *The Areopagos Council, to 307 B.C.* (Johns Hopkins U. P., 1989), argues that the Areopagus was at first only a lawcourt, was made a council

ADDENDA

by Solon, and was not politically important except between 480 and 462: I am not persuaded.

112 καὶ ἐάμ as the beginning of Draco's law is accepted by Gagarin, *Drakon and Early Athenian Homicide Law* (Yale U. P., 1981).

119 On knowledge and belief about Solon in the fourth century see Hansen, *C&M* xl 1989, 71–99 = W. R. Connor et al., *Aspects of Athenian Democracy (C&M* Diss. xi. Copenhagen: Museum Tusculanum P., 1990), 71–99; Rhodes, in M. Piérart (ed.), *Aristote et Athènes* (Paris: Boccard for U. de Fribourg: Séminaire d'histoire ancienne, 1993), 53–64.

121 The ascription of Solon's reforms to his archonship in 594/3 is upheld by Wallace, *AJAH* viii 1983, 81–95.

126 See also G. E. M. de Ste Croix, *The Class Struggle in the Ancient Greek World* (Duckworth, 1981), 163.

127, 175 A. French, *Antichthon*, xviii 1984, 1–12, suggests that the liberation of the land and the return of men from abroad should be seen not as part of the economic reform but as the return of the exiled Alcmaeonids.

127 For reduction or cancellation of interest as a milder alternative to cancellation of debts cf. Aen. Tact. 14. i (perhaps of the 350's).

131 Discussion of κύρβεις and ἄξονες continues: Immerwahr, *BASP* xxii 1985, 123–35, believes that the κύρβεις were the original publication and the ἄξονες were invented for the transfer to the Stoa; Robertson, *Hist.* xxxv 1986, 147–76 at 147–53, suggests that Craterus was really citing the κύρβεις as a source for a law on festivals or public entertainment; Connor, *Anc. Soc.* xix 1988, 185–8, revives the theory that the κύρβεις contained ἱερά and the ἄξονες ὅσια. I still believe that the two words were alternative names for the same objects-with-their-contents.

135 For Thompson's views see *Hesp.* Supp. xix 1982, 136–7; Πρακτικά XII. Int. Congr. Class. Arch., *1983*, iv. (Athens: Ὑπουργεῖο Πολιτισμοῦ, 1988), 198–204. See also Robertson, art. cit.

138 In support of ζευγῖται as hoplites see D. Whitehead, CQ^2 xxxi 1981, 282–6.

145 For a dedication of a [ζευ]γίτες, who perhaps rose from being a θής, see D.A.A. 372 = *IG* i^3 831.

146, 182 Develin, *AC* xlviii 1979, 455–68, discusses the election of archons before and after Solon's reforms. M. Ostwald, *From Popular Sovereignty to the Sovereignty of Law* (U. of California P., 1986), 14, suggests that what lies behind the alleged appointments by the Areopagus is a δοκιμασία conducted by the Areopagus after election by the people. Against sortition in the time of Solon see Hansen, *C&M* xli 1990, 55–61.

151 Alternative etymologies and meanings for ναύκραρος have been

ADDENDA

suggested by B. Jordan, *Servants of the Gods* (Hypomnemata lv. Göttingen: Vandenhoeck & Ruprecht, 1979), ch. ii; J.-C. Billigmeier & A. S. Dusing, *TAPA* cxi 1981, 11–16; Rihll, *LCM* xii 1987, 10. V. Gabrielsen, *C&M* xxxvi 1985, 21–51, finds no firm foundation for any interpretation. I still think the traditional interpretation is as likely as any.

155 On εὔθυναι see I. Worthington, *AC* liv 1985, 235–9, guessing that the formal examination was instituted by Pisistratus; Ostwald, *From Popular Sovereignty*, 12–13, distinguishing between 'disciplinary control' and εὔθυναι of the classical kind.

157 In favour of authenticity, Manville, *TAPA* cx 1980, 213–21; against, E. David, *MH* xli 1984, 129–38 (suggesting that the law was fabricated in Theramenes' circle).

158 On the development of ἀτιμία see Manville, *art. cit.*; S. Vleminck, *LEC* xlix 1981, 251–65.

160 Hansen reaffirms his view of the heliaea in *GR&BS* xix 1978, 141–3 = *Ecclesia* ⟨*I*⟩, 153–5; *C&M* xxxiii 1981–2, 27–39 = *Ecclesia II*, 237–49.

168 Higher dates are championed again by D. Kagan, *AJA*^{2} lxxxvi 1982, 343–60, but he is answered by J. H. Kroll & N. M. Waggoner, *AJA*^{2} lxxxvii 1984, 325–40. The lowest dates yet (no Greek coins before 500) have been advanced by M. Vickers, *NC* cxlv 1985, 9–44, *REG* xcix 1986, 239–70, but he is answered by M. C. Root, *NC* cxlviii 1988, 1–12.

171 εἰς is deleted by R. Kassel, *ZPE* i 1983, 47.

173 ἀμφοτέροισι sc. ὤμοις Wilamowitz, *Griechisches Lesebuch*, ii (Berlin: Weidmann, ^{5}1932), 24, *ad* 47. 29; cf. A. S. F. Gow *ad* Theocr. x. 25; Kassel, *ZPE* l 1983, 47–8.

175 Cf. Anaximander, 12 B 1 Diels & Kranz.

175 See on 127.

181, 194 C. Reid Rubincam, *Phoen.* xxxiii 1979, 293–307, discusses the use of numerals in *A.P.*, offering a different schema for the years after Solon's archonship and suggesting that where the author qualifies a numeral he was unsure of the facts.

182 See on 146. D. Fehling, *Herodotus and his 'Sources'* (ARCA xxi. Leeds: Cairns, 1989), 235–6, suggests that ἔτη δύο καὶ δύο μῆνας is not authentically precise but an artificially constructed 'bonus number'.

183 T. J. Figueira, *Hesp.* liii 1984, 447–73, represents Damasias as a populist wanting to go beyond Solon, and the ten ἄρχοντες (which he accepts) as a product of aristocratic reaction.

185 See also M. H. Chambers, *Proc. VII Congr. FIEC, 1979* (Budapest: Akadémiai Kiadó, 1984), i. 69–72.

187 H. A. Shapiro in W. G. Moon (ed.), *Ancient Greek Art and Iconography* (U. Wisconsin P., 1983), 87–96, is unable to find

ADDENDA

much Neleid iconography in Athens in the second half of the sixth century.

190, 237 Against the doctrine that the view attacked was that of Hellanicus see D. Asheri, *Acme* xxxiv 1981, 15–31. For another discussion of the sources for the Alcmaeonids, Delphi and the ending of the tyranny see M. Zahrnt, *ZPE* lxxvi 1989, 297–307.

194 See on 181.

199 547/6 is championed by H. Kaletsch, *Hist.* vii 1958, 39–47; A. A. Mosshammer, *The Chronicle of Eusebius and Greek Chronographic Tradition* (Bucknell U. P., 1979), 255–79.

200 D. J. R. Williams, *AK* xxiii 1980, 137–45, revives the view of Beloch, $G.G.^2$, I. ii. 312–3, that the Spartan arbitrator Cleomenes (Pl. *Sol.* 10. vi) was king Cleomenes I and the final award belongs to the end of the sixth century.

206 Beloch's doublet theory is revived by J. H. Schreiner, *SO* lvi 1981, 13–17; the story of Phye is defended by Pritchett, *Greek State at War*, iii. 20–1, 41, and is interpreted as a significant act of ritual by Connor, *JHS* cvii 1987, 42–7.

207 συνῴκισε: ᾤκισε A. Gennadios, *CR* v 1891, 274; perhaps we should read συνῴκησε (cf. fr. 1 and 41. ii *init.*, on Ion), but the first scribe does not elsewhere write ι for η. With Cole cf. D. Viviers, *JHS* cvii 1987, 193–5.

211 See on 104.

211 See C. Sourvinou-Inwood, *Theseus as Son and Stepson* (*BICS* Supp. xl 1979); J. N. Davie, $G\&R^2$ xxix 1982, 25–34. Boardman is criticised by R. M. Cook, *JHS* cvii 1987, 167–9; he replies in *JHS* cix 1989, 158–9.

212 See W. B. Dinsmoor, Jr., *The Propylaia to the Athenian Akropolis*, i (Princeton: A.S.C.S.A., 1980), dating the earliest remains to the 480's.

213 Zs. Ritoók, *Aristoteles Werk und Wirkung P. Moraux* (Berlin: De Gruyter, 1985), i. 436–45, notes that *A.P.* has a more favourable view of Pisistratus than Arist. *Pol.*, and has had more influence on later writers.

215 ἵνα μήτε ... καὶ ὅπως: Kassel, *ZPE* l 1983, 48, takes me to task, citing Arist. *Rhet.* I. 1355 A 30–4 (οὐχ ὅπως ... ἀλλ' ἵνα ... καὶ ὅπως) and his *Der Text der aristotelischen Rhetorik* (Peripatoi, iii. Berlin & New York: De Gruyter, 1971), 121–3.

222 Notice also the ἀτιμία in *IG* ii² 43 = Tod 123, 54–63.

223 Gagarin, *TAPA* cxi 1981, 71–7, suggests that the original θέσμια belongs to the trial *in absentia* of the Cylonians, and the reaffirmation to Solon.

226 Viviers, *AC* lvi 1987, 12–16, after Gernet, suggests that the marriage with Timonassa was matrilocal.

228 See also R. G. Osborne, $PCPS^2$ xxxi 1985, 47–73.

ADDENDA

229 On οἱ περὶ see S. L. Radt, *ZPE* xxxviii 1980, 47–56; Kassel, *ZPE* l 1983, 48.

234 For scepticism on the exile of the Alcmaeonids, after Pallene and after Hipparchus' murder, see Thomas, *Oral Tradition*, 147–51; she further discusses the Alcmaeonids and the liberation of Athens at *op. cit.*, 238–64.

237 See on 190.

243 See on 68.

244 The view that one could not be a member of the college of archons more than once is doubted by Forrest & Stockton, *Hist.* xxxvi 1987, 235–40; but the traditional view is shown to be correct for the period 229–86 by S. V. Tracy, *CP* lxxxvi 1991, 201–4, and need not be doubted for the earlier period.

253, 518, 533, 611 Another area annexed by Athens (Paus. 1. 38. viii, cf. Str. 412. ix. ii. 31) but not included in Cleisthenes' organisation (*IG* i^2 943 = i^3 1162 = M&L 48, 96, cf. 400 = 511, 537 = 892) was Eleutherae, in the far north-west of Attica. It will have been annexed not later than the bringing of Dionysus' image to Athens, perhaps in the time of Pisistratus (cf. p. 627, but my addendum *ad loc.* notes a suggested alternative dating).

There has been much further discussion of the composition of trittyes and tribes. I note here P. Siewert, *Die Trittyen Attikas und die Heeresreform des Kleisthenes* (Vestigia xxxiii. Munich: Beck, 1982), arguing that *A.P.* is wrong and Cleisthenes' trittyes were equal trittyes, constructed to facilitate the mustering of the army; G. R. Stanton, *Chiron* xiv 1984, 1–41, defending *A.P.*'s regional trittyes; J. S. Traill, *Demos and Trittys* (Toronto: Athenians, 1986), revising his earlier studies and accepting that Cleisthenes' trittyes were equal trittyes; Bicknell, *GR&BS* xxx 1989, 83–100 at 87–8, arguing that the trittyes were unequal at first but made equal in the fourth century; Hansen, *C&M* xli 1990, 51–4, arguing that at first the trittyes were both regional and equal but in the fourth century some demes had to be reassigned to restore equality. I think it is a serious possibility that Cleisthenes' trittyes were equal trittyes.

E. Kearns, *Crux*, 189–207, emphasises the creation of new organisations and new cults rather than the undermining of the old (cf. Ostwald, *From Popular Sovereignty*, 139).

258 O. Murray in O. Murray & S. R. F. Price (edd.), *The Greek City from Homer to Alexander* (O.U.P., 1990), 14–15, claims that the classical phratries are totally different from those likely to have existed in the archaic period, and that we should infer from Arist. *Pol.* vi that Cleisthenes did create new phratries.

ADDENDA

266 Dover's position is not demolished by E. F. Bloedow, *Chiron* xi 1981, 65–72.

268 C. Pecorella Longo, *Hist.* xxix 1980, 257–81, makes the most sensible attempt yet to find a factual basis for the Vatican MS; and there is another treatment by Lehmann, *ZPE* xli 1981, 85–99. I am still inclined to think that the MS is simply wrong.

269 For further discussion of the Androtion fragment see K. R. Walters, RM^2 cxxvii 1984, 222–6; K. H. Kinzl, *Klio* lxxiii 1991, 28–45.

270 Ten years in exile did not prevent Pisistratus from returning to re-establish himself as tyrant.

271 For other prepared ostraca see D. J. Phillips, *ZPE* lxxxiii 1990, 123–48.

282 ⟨μή⟩ is championed by Figueira, *GR&BS* xxviii 1987, 281–305.

298 On the three islands see T. J. Quinn, *Athens and Samos, Lesbos and Chios, 478–404 B.C.* (Manchester U. P., 1981); and on the constitution of Chios see J. L. O'Neil, *Τάλαντα* x–xi 1978–9, 66–73.

301 D. Potter, *AJP* cviii 1987, 164–6, suggests τῶν φόρων τῶν συμμάχων καὶ τῶν τελῶν.

304 On the κατάστασις in the fourth century see G. R. Bugh, *The Horsemen of Athens* (Princeton U. P., 1988), 158, 169.

305 Hansen, *GR&BS* xxi 1980, 153–73, thinks seven hundred ἔνδημοι ἀρχαί about right.

309 On the connection between payment for orphans and the prytaneum see R. S. Stroud, *Hesp.* xl 1971, 280–301. 7, 10–12, with pp. 290–1.

312 See also C. W. Macleod, *JHS* cii 1982, 124–44 = *Collected Essays* (O.U.P., 1983), 20–40.

314 Sealey, *JHS* cxi 1991, 210, suggests that 'Lys.' fr. 178 is in fact from a speech of c. 340.

316 G. L. Cawkwell, *JHS* cviii 1988, 1–12, believes the guardianship to be a *cura morum*, and accepts Ephialtic νομοφύλακες.

317 On jurisdiction in the early fifth century see Sealey, *Classical Contributions ... M. F. McGregor* (Locust Valley: Augustin, 1981), 125–34; Ostwald, *From Popular Sovereignty*, 28–40; E. M. Carawan, *GR&BS* xxviii 1987, 167–208.

322 On the murder of Ephialtes see Stockton, CQ^2 xxxii 1982, 227–8; L. Piccirilli, *Ann. Pisa*^{3} xvii 1987, 9–17; Bicknell, *LCM* xiii 1988, 114–5; D. W. Roller, *Hist.* xxxviii 1989, 257–66.

326 See also D. Micalalla, *PP* xxxviii 1983, 113–23.

327 Andrewes' article is in *Classical Contributions*, 1–3. Hansen, *SO* lvi 1981, 9–32, makes a similar distinction but thinks the thetes are included in 53. vii.

ADDENDA

332 Walters, *CA* ii 1983, 314–36 at 333, suggests that Pericles' law never lapsed, and that what was banned in the fourth century was not a mixed marriage but the misrepresentation of a mixed marriage as a valid Athenian marriage. C. Vatin, *Recherches sur le mariage et la condition de la femme mariée à l'époque hellénistique* (B.E.F.A.R. ccxvi. Paris: Boccard, 1970), 125–6, notes that mixed marriages are found occasionally in the third century and often in the second.

333 See also Humphreys, *CJ* lxxiii 1977/8, 99 = *The Family, Women and Death* (Routledge, 1983), 24; Ruschenbusch, *Athenische Innenpolitik im 5. Jahrhundert v. Chr.* (Bamberg: Aku, 1979), 83–7; C. B. Patterson, *Pericles' Citizenship Law of 451–50 B.C.* (New York: Arno 1981); Walters, *art. cit.*; Patterson, *CA* ix 1990, 40–73. Patterson's suggestion that the requirement for citizenship had not been explicitly defined before Pericles' law may well be right.

338 M. M. Markle, III, *Crux*, 265–97, argues that members of juries and assemblies were πένητες = poor men who could not afford a life of leisure, but not πτωχοί = indigent; he discusses wages, prices and rations.

340 A date in the late 450's or after is proposed by C. W. Fornara & L. J. Samons, II, *Athens from Cleisthenes to Pericles* (U. of California P., 1991), 25–6.

342 Fornara & Samons, *op. cit.*, 160–1, suggest *c.* 437.

362 On the whole of this section see Andrewes in A. W. Gomme *et al.*, *A Historical Commentary on Thucydides*, v (O.U.P., 1981), esp. 184–256.

377 On Clitophon's amendment and the πάτριος πολιτεία see C. Mossé, *Eirene* xvi 1978, 81–9.

381 On the appointment of the Four Hundred E. M. Harris, *HSCP* xciii 1990, 243–80 at 259–61, prefers *A.P.* to Thucydides.

382 De Ste Croix replied to me in *The Class Struggle*, 291 with 605–6 nn. 30–1. R. Brock, *LCM* xiii 1988, 136–8, notes that nothing is said about justice and wonders if the Five Thousand became the heliaea as well as the assembly.

383 Brock, *JHS* cix 1989, 160–4, notices the oligarchs' fascination with numbers such as 5,000.

389 Harris, *art. cit.*, revives the theory of Ehrenberg and Ferguson.

391 B. M. Mitchell, *LCM* xvii 1992, 36–40, argues that the documents of chs. 30–1 were invented after the amalgamation of the two boards in 406—but I do not see why what was done then should not have been considered earlier.

402 It is not ἄν = ἐάν but ἤν = ἐάν which is 'gänzlich fremd ... der attischen Inschriften': there is a misprint in Meisterhans & Schwyzer.

ADDENDA

406 Meritt and Pritchett continued to reaffirm their opposing positions; but I abstain from piling up further references.

408 Two Antiphons: G. Pendrick, *Hermes* cxv 1987, 47–60. One Antiphon: J. S. Morrison, *PCPS*^{2} vii 1961, 49–58; H. C. Avery, *Hermes* cx 1982, 145–58; Gagarin, *GR&BS* xxxi 1990, 27–44.

414 Aristotelian examples may be found in H. Bonitz, *Index Aristotelicus* (I. Bekker [ed.], *Aristotelis Opera*, v. Berlin: Reimer, 1870), 155 A 1–4.

420 For further attempts to establish the relationships between the sources see Ruschenbusch, *Hermes* cix 1981, 316–26, *ZPE* xlv 1982, 91–4; P. Krentz, *The Thirty at Athens* (Cornell U. P., 1982), 131–52. Krentz prefers *A.P.*'s chronology to Xenophon's.

427 A constitutional requirement in the peace terms is accepted by P. J. Rahn, *Classical Contributions*, 110; Krentz, *op. cit.*, 42.

428 A. W. Lintott, *Violence, Civil Strife and Revolution in the Classical City, 750–330 B.C.* (Croom Helm, 1982), 161, thinks the ephors in §76 are the Spartan ephors; and at 264–5 he accepts the chronology of Lys. XIII for the conspiracy betrayed by Agoratus.

435 Whitehead, *JHS* c 1980, 208–13, agrees with my conclusion but suggests that the list may follow tribal order but not comprise three men from each tribe. It is argued that the number Thirty is deliberately copied from the Spartan *gerousia* (cf. the five 'ephors') by Krentz, *op. cit.*, 63–8; Whitehead, *Anc. Soc.* xii–xiv 1982–3, 105–30.

440 L. G. H. Hall, *CQ*^{2} xl 1990, 319–28, argues that the members of the Areopagus are unlikely to have supported the Thirty and the Thirty are unlikely to have strengthened the Areopagus, but the laws of Ephialtes and Archestratus which they annulled will have been laws specifying the duties which the Areopagus was still required to perform after 462/1.

448 In *A.P.* τρισχιλίους is a regularly accepted correction (from the commentary of Kenyon^1) of the papyrus' δισχιλίους: Krentz, *op. cit.*, 57 n. 1, champions δισχιλίους. Brock, *JHS* cix 1989, 160–4, notices the oligarchs' fascination with numbers such as 3,000.

458 Bugh, *Horsemen*, 123–4, argues that the cavalry were a privileged group not included in but additional to the Three Thousand.

460 The second Ten are accepted by M. B. Walbank, *Hesp.* li 1982, 93 with n. 47; Krentz, *op. cit.*, 97; T. C. Loening, *The Reconciliation Agreement of 403/402 B.C. in Athens* (*Hermes* Einz. liii 1987), 44–6. Loening's study should be consulted on the whole of chs. 39–40.

ADDENDA

461 P. E. Harding, *Hermes* cxvi 1988, 186–93, suggests that Pausanias was neither jealous of Lysander nor a covert democrat, but simply judged that the oligarchy at Athens was no longer viable.

476 Loening, *Hermes* cix 1981, 280–94, argues that Lysias received ἰσοτέλεια under this decree and affirmed his eligibility for it in his speech περὶ τῶν ἰδίων εὐεργεσιῶν.

477 On *IG* ii^2 10 = Tod 100 see (a) Krentz, *Phoen.* xxxiv 1980, 289–306, who dates it 403/2 (Euclides + demotic), does not restore the proposer, and believes that all beneficiaries were given ἰσοτέλεια; (b) M. J. Osborne, *Naturalization in Athens* (4 volumes in 3: Verh. Kon. Ac. Belg. xcviii 1981, ci 1982, cix 1983), who re-edits it as D 6, dates it 401/0, restores Thrasybulus as the proposer, and believes that the first category of beneficiaries were given citizenship and the second and third were given ἰσοτέλεια.

488 See Rhodes, *CJ* lxxiv 1979/80, 305–23; also P. Koerner, in E. C. Welskopf (ed.), *Hellenische Poleis* (Berlin: Akademie-Verlag, 1974), i. 132–46, who goes even further than I would in stressing the fourth century's departures from 'democracy'; Hansen, *Athenian Democracy*, esp. 296–304, who argues that the fourth-century democracy was a deliberately modified democracy.

491 For Hansen's further thoughts on the Pnyx see *GR&BS* xxiii 1982, 241–9 = *Ecclesia* ⟨*I*⟩, 25–34, *GR&BS* xxvi 1985, 241–50 = *Ecclesia II*, 129–41, *C&M* xxxvii 1986, 89–98 = *Ecclesia II*, 143–53: he now believes that Pnyx I and II had a capacity of 6,000 and that III was built in the time of Hadrian. Thompson, *Hesp.* Supp. xix 1982, 133–47 (esp. 138 n. 18 with 134–5), champions the smaller size for II, and links I with Ephialtes and II with the Thirty. Krentz, *AJA*^{2} lxxxviii 1984, 230–1, attributes II to the beginning of the Thirty's régime and III to Eubulus rather than Lycurgus.

493 That it is Heraclides of Clazomenae who is honoured in M&L 70 and that there therefore was a Peace of Epilycus is shown by an additional fragment identified by Walbank, *ZPE* xlviii 1982, 261–3, li 1983, 183–4. I therefore abandon my doubts (but H. B. Mattingly remains unpersuaded: *EMC* xxxii = ^{2}vii 1988, 322–4).

495 See also P. Gauthier, *Un Commentaire historique des Poroi de Xénophon* (Geneva: Droz / Paris: Minard, 1976), 190–3 with 193–5, arguing from X. *Vect.* iv. 51–2.

495 On the later history of the ἐφηβεία see especially Gauthier, *Chiron* xv 1985, 149–63.

497 On bastards and citizenship see also Sealey, *CA* iii 1984, 111–

ADDENDA

  33, *The Athenian Republic*, 19–23; and the works cited in the addendum to p. 333.

502 See on 69.

503 For an exploration of the connections between ἔφηβοι and tragedy see J. J. Winkler, *Representations*, summer 1985, 26–62.

503, 512, 591 On the basis of fourth-century population figures Ruschenbusch, *ZPE* xxxv 1979, 173–80, and a series of other articles in *ZPE*, most recently lxxv 1988, 194–6 (preferring the lower of the possible figures), argues that the thetes served as ἔφηβοι and διαιτηταί, and were eligible for membership of the boule, and that all who were eligible were automatically treated as candidates; contr. Rhodes, *ZPE* xxxviii 1980, 191–201 (preferring the higher figures). Hansen's major study of fourth-century population figures is *Demography and Democracy* (Herning: Systime, 1985), in which he prefers the higher figures but believes that the thetes served as ἔφηβοι and διαιτηταί; his most recent view on this question is that by the time of the reform of the ἐφηβεία 'service in principle applied to all citizens, but that it took a fair while for the principle to have full effect' (*Athenian Democracy*, 108–9, spelling out a conclusion towards which he was moving in *Three Studies in Athenian Demography* [Kon. Dansk. Vid. Selsk., Hist.-Fil. Med. lvi 1988], 3–6).

508 See on 491.

508 On the black cloaks as a symbol of the marginal status of the ἔφηβοι see P. Vidal-Naquet, *Le Chasseur noir* (Paris: Maspero, ²1983), 123–207 = *The Black Hunter* (Johns Hopkins U. P., 1986, 83–156.

514 Cf. Ruschenbusch, *ZPE* xxxvi 1979, 303–8.

517 The view that a quadrennium is intended is championed by Develin, *ZPE* lvii 1984, 133–8.

518 See on 253. J. K. Davies, *LCM* iv 1979, 151–6, suggested that *IG* i² 847 = i³ 1040 is a fragment of a fifth-century bouleutic list, showing the same quotas as in the fourth century; but H. Lohmann has argued that Atene can scarcely have been a deme, let alone one with a quota of 3 bouleutae, at the time of Cleisthenes, and that Piraeus can scarcely have deserved a quota of 9(?) before its development as Athens' harbour town (W. Eder [ed.], *Die athenische Demokratie im 4. Jahrhundert v. Chr.: Vollendung oder Verfall einer Verfassungsform?*, forthcoming).

521, 658 Hansen, *GR&BS* xx 1979, 243–6, argues that the courts sat on monthly but not on annual festival days, i.e. between 150 and 200 days in the year.

522 On ἐκκλησίαι σύγκλητοι and numbers of assemblies see Hansen, *GR&BS* xxiii 1982, 331–50 = *Ecclesia* ⟨*I*⟩, 83–102, *SO* lix

ADDENDA

1984, 13–19 = *Ecclesia II*, 167–75 (with F. W. Mitchel), *GR&BS* xxviii 1987, 35–50 = *Ecclesia II*, 177–94; and the replies of E. M. Harris, CQ^2 xxxvi 1986, 363–77, *AJP* cxii 1991, 325–41; S. V. Tracy, *ZPE* lxxv 1988, 186–8.

522 See Thompson in *Hesp.* Supp. xix 1982, 136–7, and (Old Bouleuterium after Ephialtes?) Πρακτικά *XII Int. Congr. Class. Arch.*, iv. 198–204.

524 Hansen replies in *JHS* c 1980, 89–95.

531 In favour of the lexicographers see Hansen, *Ecclesia* ⟨*I*⟩, 123–30.

531 C. Habicht points out to me that one man is known to have served twice as epistates of the proedri: Stratophon Στρατοκλέους Σουνιεύς, in 112/1 and 107/6 (*IG* ii² 1012, 7–9; 1011, 65, 74).

533 See on 253.

537 Meritt, *PAPS* cxxviii 1984, 123–33, revised M&L 56 and at 127–8 claimed to see proof that the generals served for the bouleutic year.

540 K. Latte, *RE* Supp. vii (1940), 1606–8 = *Kleine Schriften* (Munich: Beck, 1968), 400–3, argued for beheading: that view is rejected by P. A. Stadter, *A Commentary on Plutarch's Pericles* (U. of North Carolina P., 1989), 258–9.

541 Hansen, *Eisangelia*, 28, suggested εἰσαγ[γελλέτω μὲν].

545 That a decree or law which was attacked would not come into effect automatically if the γραφή failed, unless it had been carried before the γραφή was begun, was argued by J.-M. Hannick, *AC* l 1981, 393–7, but rejected by Hansen, *C&M* xxxviii 1987, 63–73 = *Ecclesia II*, 271–81.

547 On the fleet in 323/2 see N. G. Ashton, *BSA* lxxii 1977, 4–9.

553 For a review of recent work on the mines see J. Ellis Jones, $G\&R^2$ xxix 1982, 169–83. In the mines of Lusitania half of the ore was reserved for the *fiscus*, but Hadrian allowed the original lessee to buy out the *fiscus*' share for a lump sum of HS 4,000: Bruns, $F.I.R.^7$ 113 = Riccobono, $F.I.R.A.^2$, i. 104 = Smallwood, *Documents . . . Nerva, Trajan and Hadrian*, 439, 3–4 §1, 5–7 §2, 11–12 §5.

556 See Walbank, *Hesp.* li 1982, 74–98, following up D. M. Lewis's suggestion and assembling the fragments.

566 See also Bugh, *Horsemen*, 221–4. In *TAPA* cxii, 1982, 23–32, he suggests that the cavalry were under a cloud in the first half of the fourth century and the καταλογεῖς of 49. ii were introduced about the 340's to improve recruitment.

569 That the πέπλος was a large robe for Phidias' statue is suggested by Lewis, *Scr. Class. Isr.* v 1979/80, 28–9; contr. Kroll, *Hesp.* Supp. xx 1982, 65–76; W. Burkert, *Greek Religion* (Oxford:

ADDENDA

Blackwell, 1985), 92. Various novel suggestions about the festival and the πέπλος are made by Robertson, *HSCP* lxxxvii 1983, 241–88, *RM*² cxxviii 1985, 231–95.

573 The ἱερῶν ἐπισκευασταί are mentioned in Ἀρχ. Ἐφ. 1923, 36–42. 123, rescued from oblivion and dated 369/8 by D. Knoepfler, *Chiron* xvi 1986, 71–98.

575 On dung-collectors at Athens see E. J. Owens, *CQ*² xxxiii 1983, 44–50.

578 Gauthier, *RD* lix 1981, 5–28 at 22–3, suggests that a φορμός was the capacity of a mule-pannier. He doubts if there was any change in the boundaries between the duties of the σιτοφύλακες and of other officials.

581 Carawan, *GR&BS* xxv 1984, 111–21, suggests that by the time of *A.P.* execution without trial remained on the statute book but was no longer a serious possibility.

585 P. Millett in P. D. A. Garnsey *et al.* (edd.), *Trade in the Ancient Economy* (London: Chatto & Windus, 1983), 46, argues that this would be a loan to keep a business going, not to start one.

590 On the date of the change to written evidence see Ruschenbusch, *Symposion 1982* (*AGR* v 1989), 34–5 (*c.* 390); Rhodes, in Eder, *Die athenische Demokratie*, forthcoming (perhaps a period of overlap before the law cited by D. XLV. *Steph. i.* 44, *c.* 350, which required evidence in writing). Boegehold's ἐχῖνος lid is published in *Hesp.* Supp. xix 1982, 1–6 and revised by G. Soritz-Hadler, *Festschrift . . . A. Kränzlein* (Grazer Rechts- und Staatswissenschaftliche Studien, xliii. Graz: Leykam, 1986), 103–8: the words ἐξ ἀνακρίσεως are fully preserved, implying that the procedure mentioned by *A.P.* in connection with the arbitrators came to be used for other cases too.

591 See on 503. Ruschenbusch discusses matters concerned with the διαιτηταί in *Symposion 1982*, 31–40. Humphreys suggests that public arbitrators were instituted not at the beginning of the fourth century but by Cleisthenes to replace Pisistratus' δικασταὶ κατὰ δήμους (*Tria Corda*, 239–42), but this is perhaps what ought to have happened rather than what did happen.

594 S. I. Rotroff, *Hesp.* xlvii 1978, 196–209, argues from a dedication of 328/7 that the monument had only recently been completed then, in which case this passage would have to belong to the revision of *A.P.* (contr. Keaney as cited on p. 592): her inference is neat but not inevitable.

594 But (if it is true) Tisias of Oeneis was arbitrator when Apollodorus of Oeneis sued Phormio of ?Hippothontis (D. XLV. *Steph. i.* 8): perhaps the system guaranteed only that an arbitrator would not serve for a defendant of his own tribe.

597 According to Harp., Suid. (Λ 651) λογισταὶ καὶ λογιστήρια the

ADDENDA

logistae had to complete the examination of accounts within thirty days.

600 Secretaries are discussed by S. Alessandrì, *Ann. Pisa*³ xii 1982, 7–70, who rejects the view that γραμματεὺς τῆς βουλῆς and γραμματεὺς κατὰ πρυτανείαν are titles of the same secretary.

602 Rotation from 356/5 is confirmed by Ag. I. 7495 (354/3). Rotation from 366/5 is accepted by Alessandrì, *op. cit.*; Whitehead, *AHB* iii 1989, 102–6.

604 Hansen, *Athenian Democracy*, 168–9, 257, infers from what *A.P.* says here that citizens' proposals for new laws were discussed by the boule. Shortly before the publication of my original edition, the University of Durham spoiled my analogy by appointing a graduate to the post of Chief Clerk.

605 For a review of religious officials in Athens see R. S. J. Garland, *BSA* lxxix 1984, 75–123.

608 Pisistratus built a temple at Brauron according to Phot. (*B* 264) Βραυρωνιά, cited by S. Angiolollo, *PP* xxxviii 1983, 351–4. On the Brauronium in Athens see R. F. Rhodes & J. J. Dobbins, *Hesp.* xlviii 1979, 325–41 (no building before the fourth century?). On Aristophanes see Walbank, *CQ*² xxxi 1981, 276–81; on vase-paintings see L. Kahil, *Hesp.* l 1981, 255–63 (supporting a late-sixth-century Brauronium); on the festival of Brauronian Artemis see Robertson, *HSCP* lxxxvii 1983, 241–88, with the denunciation of Pritchett, *The Greek State at War*, iv (U. of California P., 1985), 94 n. 1.

608 The Gymnasium at Cynosarges has been found: *O. Ἀλεξάνδρη, ΑΔ* xxvii 1972, χρον. 65, 100–2, xxix 1974, χρον. 128–31.

611 See on 253. Walbank, *Hesp.* li 1982, 74–98, fr. d (= *IG* ii² 1579), 8 with p. 81, claims to find a non-citizen holding an official position in Salamis; Whitehead, *ZPE* xlvii 1982, 40–2, points out that the demarch in *IG* ii² 1672, 272–3, is the demarch of Sunium, not of Oropus.

611 On the Dionysia in Thoricus see Whitehead, *ZPE* lxii 1986, 213–20.

617 Cf. *IG* ii² 1237, 114–25, where the paternal grandfather is omitted. Osborne, *Naturalization*, iii–iv. 173–6, thinks a third generation is required by *A.P.* but not by [D.] LIX.

623 On the recruitment of choregi and choruses see D. M. MacDowell, *Symposion 1982*, 65–77.

624 Against a reduction to three comedians during the Peloponnesian War see W. Luppe, *Philol.* cxvi 1972, 53–75, G. Mastromarco, *Belfagor* xxx 1975, 469–73 (in *P. Oxy.* xxxv 2737 Plato is said to have been placed fourth). Traill, *Demos and Trittys*, 79–92, suggests that the ἐπιμεληταὶ τῆς φυλῆς were one from each trittys, and indeed were the τριττύαρχοι.

ADDENDA

625 On ἀντιδόσεις see Gabrielsen, C&M xxxviii 1987, 7–38. Lys. IV. *Vuln.* 1 cites an actual exchange of property. M. A. Christ, *TAPA* cxx 1990, 147–69, argues that there was more avoidance of liturgies than is commonly believed.

627 Connor, C&M xl 1989, 7–16 = *Aspects of Athenian Democracy*, 7–16, suggests that the acquisition of Eleutherae should be dated 506–501.

629 Carawan, GR&BS xxiv 1983, 209–26, stresses that interrogations when a case came to court are to be taken seriously; the issues were not all settled at the ἀνάκρισις.

637 R. G. Osborne, *Demos* (C.U.P., 1985), 175, notes that not only none of the Kerykes but only one attested Eumolpid belonged to the deme of Eleusis.

640 Some problems in homicide law are discussed by Gagarin, GR&BS xx 1979, 301–23; Hansen, GR&BS xxii 1981, 11–30.

643 On the distinction between intentional and unintentional homicide see W. T. Loomis, *JHS* xcii 1972, 86–95.

645 Sealey, *TAPA* cxiv 1984, 71–85, argues that the *Tetralogies* do not reflect late-fifth-century Athenian law.

646 Carawan, $RIDA^3$ xxxvii 1990, 47–67, suggests that these trials were originally for killers who had withdrawn into exile but who wished to plead innocence of intent and qualify for reconciliation.

648 That the ephetae continued to be drawn from the Areopagites is rejected by Sealey, *CP* lxxviii 1983, 275–96, *The Athenian Republic*, 70–7; accepted by Carawan, *CP* lxxxvi 1991, 1–16.

650 Enyalius appears as a separate deity in the Linear B tablets: M. Ventris & J. Chadwick, *Documents in Mycenaean Greek* (C.U.P., ^{2}1973), 311–12 with 476, no. 208, cf. 126 with 411.

650 Pritchett has wavered on 6 Boedromion: *The Greek State at War*, iii. 183–4 contr. 166.

651 See also Robertson, *EMC* xxxvii 1983, 78–92; Pritchett, *The Greek State at War*, iv. 94–259.

653 Fifth-century Athenian proxeny decrees are collected and re-edited by Walbank, *Athenian Proxenies of the Fifth Century B.C.* (Toronto and Sarasota: Stevens, 1978).

658 See on 521.

659 On ἀπόφασις see Carawan, GR&BS xxvi 1985, 111–40; Rhodes, in Eder, *Die athenische Demokratie*, forthcoming.

672 The athlothetae were also responsible for the crowns awarded at the Great Panathenaea to the kings of the Cimmerian Bosporus: *IG* ii^2 212 = Tod 167, 26–9.

673 Ar. fr. 48 Kock has τριημιωβόλιον.

674 Cf. the κάλπιδες of Callim. fr. 384. 35–6 Pfeiffer.

675 See on 107.

ADDENDA

675 ἀργύρια is defended by I. Avotins, CQ^2 xxxvii 1987, 231–3.
678 We can now be confident only that two of the generals of 323/2 were from the same tribe, even when a ναύαρχος is counted as a general: Develin, *Athenian Officials*, 408.
681 See Mossé in H. van Effenterre (ed.), *Points de vue sur la fiscalité antique* (Centre G. Glotz. Pub. Sorbonne, Études xiv 1979), 31–42 (the same συμμορίαι for εἰσφορά and for the trierarchy); Rhodes, *AJAH* vii 1982, 1–19 (different συμμορίαι); Gabrielsen, *C&M* xl 1989, 145–59 (different συμμορίαι).
687 On the tokens naming Pheidon, and also one naming a hipparch and one a general (?) sent to Samos, see Kroll & Mitchel, *Hesp.* xlix 1980, 87–96. On the hipparch and his cavalry in general see Bugh, *Horsemen*, 209–18.
695 Against Hansen see Gabrielsen, *Remuneration of State Officials in Fourth Century B.C. Athens* (Odense U. Cl. Stud. xi. Odense U. P., 1981).
696 Some men who are known to have served twice in the boule before A.D. 1 are listed by Rhodes, *ZPE* xxxviii 1980, 197–201, xli 1981, 101–2, and more could be added. For the archonship see on 244.
698, 701 Boegehold, *Studies . . . S. Dow*, 23–9 at 24, cites *P. Flor.* ii 112, and suggests that the word κληρωτήριον appeared already in Aristophanes' *Geras* of ?410 and that κληρωτήρια were introduced for dicastic allotments after the scandal of Anytus' acquittal (27. v).
701 R. Townsend, forthcoming, dates the court buildings in the north-east of the Agora to the hellenistic period.
701 See on 698.
719 Against the requirement to complete all trials in a day see Worthington, *JHS* cix 1989, 204–7; the best evidence for the requirement is Plat. *Apol.* 37 A–B.
719 The basis for Diels' proposal appears to be Anaximander, 12 A 11. iv Diels & Kranz (Hippolytus: emended, but with certainty). Wilcken's text is possible, but I now prefer Diels' αὐλ[ώδεις], with ἕκρους as noun.
730 ἡλιαία is used to denote a court in a fourth-century law, *Hesp.* xlix 1980, 258–88, ll. 28, 32–3; the excavators' heliaea is doubted by Hansen, *C&M* xxxiii 1981–2, 15–27 = *Ecclesia II*, 225–37.
734 MacDowell, CQ^2 xxxv 1985, 525–6, suggests ἥμισυ τοῦ ὕδατος.
741 Item 17: at end add reference to item 85E.
742 Item 35: reissued Berlin & New York: De Gruyter, 1960.*
742 Item 37: at end add reference to item 85E.
743 Item 43: revised in J. Barnes (ed.), *The Complete Works of Aristotle: The Revised Oxford Translation* (Bollingen Series, lxxi.

ADDENDA

Princeton U. P., 1984), ii. 2341–83; another revision in A. W. H. Adkins & P. White (edd.), *U. of Chicago Readings in Western Civilization*, i. *The Greek Polis* (U. of Chicago P., 1986), 229–78.
743 Item 51: at end add reference to item 85E.
743 Item 55: delete (*1st ed.).
744 Item 60: reissued (Βιβλιοθήκη Ἀρχαίων Συγγραφέων, xvii) n.d. (1977?).
746 Item 84: 2nd ed. 1983.
746 Add after item 85:
  85A. ΒΛΑΧΟΥ, Α. Σ. Modern Greek int.; trans.; few notes; appendixes. (With [X.] *A.P.*) Athens: Βιβλιοπώλειον τῆς Ἑστίας, 1980.
  85B. RHODES, P. J. English int.; comm. O.U.P., 1981; corr. repr. 1985; reissued with addenda, 1993. (= this book.) *See also* item 85D.
  85C. GARCÍA VALDÉS, M. Spanish int.; trans.; notes. (With [Ar.] *Oec.*) (Biblioteca Clásica Gredos, lxx.) Madrid: Gredos, 1984.
  85D. RHODES, P. J. English int.; trans.; notes. (Penguin Classics.) Harmondsworth: Penguin, 1984; corr. repr. 1986. *See also* item 85B.
  85E. CHAMBERS, M. H. Latin int. (textual and bibliographical); text; *testimonia*; *app.*; full indexes. (Bibl. Teubneriana.) Leipzig: Teubner, 1986. *See also* items 17, 37, 51; *also* 85F.
  85F. CHAMBERS, M. H. German trans.; comm. (Aristoteles' Werke in deutscher Übersetzung, x. i.) Berlin: Akademie-Verlag, 1990.* *See also* item 85E.
746 Add after item 89:
  90. KEANEY, J. J. *The Composition of Aristotle's Athenaion Politeia: Observation and Explanation.* New York: O.U.P., 1992.
  91. PIÉRART, M. (ed.) *Aristote et Athènes.* Paris: Boccard for U. de Fribourg: Séminaire d'histoire ancienne, 1993.

INDEX I

PASSAGES FROM ARISTOTLE

Italic numerals refer to the pages and notes of this book.

Categoriae
  12 B: *136*
Physica
  II. 194 B–195 A: *7*
    196 A: *171*
    198 A: *7*
  VI. 239 B: *443*
Meteorologica
  I. 351 A: *719*
  II. 363 A: *536*
De Anima
  I. 404 A: *575*
  II. 416 A: *320*
De Respiratione
  473 B–474 A: *719–20*
Historia Animalium
  I. 491 A: *58 n. 288*
  III. 511 B–515 A: *38*
  VI. 579 B: *224*
  VIII. 588 A: *232*
    589 A: *478*
  IX. 608 B: *232*
De Partibus Animalium
  I. 644 B–645 A: *58 n. 288*
De Motu Animalium
  703 A: *7 n. 24*
De Audibilibus
  804 B: *212*
Problemata
  II. 1. 866 B: *720*
  XV. 13. 913 A: *575*
  XVI. 8. 914 B–915 A: *720*
  XIX. 2. 917 B: *212*
  XXIX. 13. 951 A–952 B: *734*
    13. 951 A: *481*
    15. 952 B–953 A: *734*
Metaphysica
  Δ. 1013 A–B: *7*
    1015 A: *320*
  E. 1026 A–1027 A: *13*
Ethica Nicomachea
  I. 1102 B: *353*

  II. 1104 A: *9*
    1106 A–1109 B: *9*
  IV. 1125 B: *526*
    1126 A: *213*
  V. 1132 A: *502*
    1137 B: *329*
  VI. 1140 A: *578*
    1143 A: *213*
  VII. 1152 B: *604*
  VIII. 1160 A–B: *361*
    1160 B: *359*
  X. 1173 B: *445*
    1176 A: *604*
    1180 B–1181 B: *1, 58*
Magna Moralia
  I. 1188 B: *642*
  II. 1199 A: *157*
Ethica Eudemia
  III. 1232 B: *22*
  VII. 1241 B: *322*
[De Virtutibus et Vitiis]
  1251 B: *178, 213*
Politica
  I. 1252 B: *578*
    1252 B–1253 A: *7*
    1255 B: *330*
    1256 A: *441*
    1256 B: *7*
    1258 B: *143*
    1260 B: *360*
  II. 1260 B–1269 B: *38*
    1261 A–B: *116*
    1263 A: *330, 443*
    1264 A: *7 n. 30*
    1264 B: *116*
    1266 A: *481*
    1266 B: *171*
    1267 B: *72, 328, 357*
    1268 A: *72, 308–9, 453, 734*
    1268 B: *360, 370, 734*
    1269 A: *444*
    1269 B: *143, 330, 513*

PASSAGES FROM ARISTOTLE

Politica–contd.
1270 A: *490, 631*
1271 B: *97*
1272 A: *504*
1272 B: *97, 448, 484*
1273 A: *97, 117, 543*
1273 B: *328, 478*
1273 B–1274 A: *8, 10, 25, 60, 118–19, 146, 150, 159–60, 272–3*
1274 A: *61, 137, 140, 142–3, 155, 162–3, 172, 288, 296, 311, 316 n. 29, 323, 336–8, 361*
1274 B: *53, 60, 85, 110, 668*
III. 1275 A: *108, 116, 180, 666*
1275 B: *188, 242, 255, 333, 429, 483*
1276 A: *473*
1276 A–B: *479*
1276 B–1278 B: *361*
1278 A: *333, 496*
1278 B: *7, 97, 478*
1279 A–B: *7, 143, 361, 383*
1280 A–B: *666*
1280 A–1281 A: *7*
1281 A–B: *10, 490*
1281 B: *25, 60, 140, 146, 155, 162, 273, 316 n. 29*
1282 A: *138, 324*
1282 B: *10, 329*
1283 B: *360, 442*
1283 B–1284 A: *361*
1284 A: *61, 269, 298*
1284 B: *61, 269, 481*
1285 B: *10 n. 48, 99, 294, 304*
1286 A: *10, 490*
1286 B: *7 n. 30, 200*
1288 A: *481*
IV. 1288 B: *360*
1289 A: *97*
1289 B: *208*
1290 A: *322*
1290 B: *7 n. 24*
1291 B: *72*
1291 B–1292 A: *10–11, 301*
1292 A: *10, 116, 323, 329*
1292 A–B: *448*
1292 B–1293 A: *9, 11, 301*
1292 B: *214*
1293 A: *10, 329, 338, 448*
1293 A–B: *9*
1293 B: *97, 361*
1294 A–B: *117*
1295 A: *298*
1295 A–1297 A: *9, 186*
1296 A: *10, 118, 123, 171, 359*

1296 B: *262*
1296 B–1301 A: *32*
1296 B–1297 B: *496*
1297 A–B: *117*
1297 B: *286, 383, 473*
1298 A: *10, 116–17, 318, 329, 398, 523*
1298 B: *117, 146, 384*
1299 A: *116, 577*
1299 B–1300 A: *9–10, 489–90*
1300 A–B: *115–17, 146*
1300 B: *540, 587, 640, 643–4, 646*
V. 1301 B: *322*
1302 B: *61, 116, 269*
1303 A: *13 n. 69, 327*
1304 A: *10, 227, 283, 287–9, 322, 337*
1304 B: *29 n. 165, 60–1, 323, 368, 371, 447, 478*
1305 A: *179, 185, 294, 479, 623*
1305 A–B: *209*
1305 B: *10, 13 n. 68, 61, 116, 368, 409, 416, 430, 478*
1306 A: *13 n. 68, 208*
1306 B–1307 A: *479*
1307 B: *299*
1308 A: *116*
1308 B: *61, 107, 215, 269, 324*
1309 A: *213, 479, 623*
1309 A–B: *115–16, 293, 313*
1309 B: *35*
1310 B: *78, 185*
1311 A: *210, 230*
1311 A–B: *227*
1311 B: *58*
1312 B: *230*
1313 A–1314 A: *203*
1313 B: *214*
1314 A–1315 B: *10 n. 48, 203*
1314 B: *214*
1315 A: *210, 219, 359*
1315 B: *61, 192, 194, 196, 219–20, 223, 240*
1316 A–B: *8 n. 31*
VI. 1317 B–1318 A: *115–16*
1317 B: *9–10, 489–90, 692*
1318 B–1319 B: *11, 301*
1318 B: *214*
1319 A: *92, 214*
1319 B: *12, 61, 242, 250, 258, 261–2, 287, 333, 481, 496*
1320 B–1321 A: *12, 448*
1321 A: *116, 337, 454, 470*
1321 B–1323 A: *33*
1321 B: *390, 516, 535, 558–60,*

786

PASSAGES FROM ARISTOTLE

Politica–contd.
    573, 576, 596
    1321 B–1322 A: *580*
    1322 B: *392, 573, 597, 605*
  VII. 1324 B: *297*
    1327 A–B: *337*
    1328 A: *13* n. 69
    1328 B: *72*
    1330 B: *360*
    1331 A: *479*
    1331 B: *573, 576*
    1332 B: *116, 442*
    1333 A: *361*
  VIII. 1337 A: *360*
    1339 B–1342 B: *322–3*
    1341 A: *296*
[*Oeconomica*]
  II. 1347 A: *575*
    1347 B: *640*
    1348 B: *213*
Rhetorica
  I. 1354 A: *162, 718*
    1354 B: *162, 478*
    1355 B: *215*
    1357 B: *200*
    1359 B: *398, 523*
    1360 A: *322, 523*
    1366 A: *7, 649*
    1367 B: *229*
    1374 B: *572, 591*
    1375 A–1377 B: *590*
  II. 1384 B: *213, 694*
    1390 B: *326*
    1394 A: *215*
    1400 B: *110*
    1401 B: *230*
    1402 A: *604*
  III. 1404 B: *486*
    1419 A: *373, 381*
Poetica
    1448 B: *479, 486*

1449 A: *7* n. *30, 483*
1459 A: *13* n. 69
Fragments (ed. V. Rose. Leipz g: Teubner, 1886)
pp. 8–9 (D.L. v. 27): *1*
p. 16 (Hesychius' list): *1, 25, 131*
pp. 21–2 (Ptolemy's list): *1–2*
p. 258 (Ammonius, Elias): *1* n. 2, *2* n. 6
381–603: *2* n. 9
381 (*A.P.* fr. 1 Kenyon): *56, 65, 66–7*
382: *56*
384 (*A.P.* fr. 2): *56, 65, 67, 74–5*
385 (*A.P.* fr. 3): *56, 65, 67*
386: *56*
389: *56–7*
392: *56*
394: *56*
399: *56*
401: *56, 341*
406 (cf. 28. iii): *57*
415: *56*
439: *57, 601*
447 (cf. 54. ii): *57*
456: *56*
461: *57, 356–7*
A.P. fr. 4 Kenyon: *65, 76–7*
A.P. fr. 15 Kaibel & Wilamowitz[3]: *57*
500: *508*
504 (Phot. σκυτάλη): *1* n. 2
514a (p. 324): *2* n. 9
529: *58* n. *290*
558: 209
611: *2*
—§35: *694*
p. 431 (*Vit. Marc.* 23): *2* n. 6
p. 440 (*Vit. Vulg.* 23): *2* n. 6
p. 446 (*Vit. Lat.* 23): *2* n. 6

INDEX II

INSCRIPTIONS, PAPYRI AND OTHER MANUSCRIPTS

In the index of inscriptions I give references to *IG*, M&L and Tod (vol. ii) for all texts published in those collections, but otherwise give only the references that are used in this book. Modern numerals (1234567890) refer to serial numbers, old style numerals (*1234567890*) to pages and *italic* numerals to the pages and notes of this book. See also Ostraca, Tokens, Vases, in Index III.

INSCRIPTIONS

'Αρχαιολογικὴ 'Εφημερίς
  1918, 73–100, 95–7: *See* Reinmuth 15
  1953, *175–6*, 1: *552*
'Αρχαιολογικὸν Δελτίον
  vii–ix 1922–5, παρ. 52–4: *535*
  xxiv 1969, μελ. 1–5: *651*
  xxv 1970, μελ. 146, 5: *460*
Abh. Berlin
  1953, vi: *See* OGIS 483
American Journal of Philology
  lxvi 1945, 234–9: *See IG* ii² 2976
The Athenian Agora
  xv 12: *See* ii² 1740
    34: *See IG* ii² 223 c
    43: *See IG* ii² 1700
    53 = *Hesp.* x 11: *603*
    58 = *Hesp.* Supp. i 1: *601, 603*
    62 = *Hesp.* xxxvii, 1–24: *601, 603*
    89 = *Hesp.* xxxviii 1: *520*
  xvii 1–16: *328*
    23 = *IG* i² 954 + 957 + 964: *370, 685*
The Athenian Tribute Lists
  A 9: *See IG* i² 63
  A 10 = *IG* i² 64: *300*
  D 9 = *IG* i² 109: *371*
  D 11 = *IG* i² 22 = *SEG* x 14: *306, 371, 729 n. 61*
  D 22 = *IG* i² 60: *299*
  D 23 = *IG* i² 144 + 155: *654*
  List 1 = *IG* i² 191 + 197: *560*
Athenische Mitteilungen
  lxxii 1957, 156–64, 1 = Pouilloux,

Choix, 8: *695*
  lxvi 1961, 143–6, 2: *See* Reinmuth 6
  147, 3: *See* Reinmuth 7
Bulletin de Correspondance Hellénique
  lxxxiii 1959, 152–5: *See SIG*³ 276
California Studies in Classical Antiquity
  v 1972, 164–9, 2: *534*
Corpus Inscriptionum Graecarum
  2880: *399*
  3660: *139*
GRAYSON, *Assyrian and Babylonian Chronicles*
  104–11, 7 (Nabonidus Chronicle): *199*
Hesperia
  ii 1933, 1: *See IG* ii² 2811
    418–46: *See IG* ii² 1706
  iv 1935, 2: *68, 70, 151*
  v 1936, 9: *555–6*
    10: *553, 555–6, 559, 581, 624, 701 n. 60*
  vi 1937, 2: *577*
  vii 1938, 1: *131, 259, 589*
    2: *589*
    13: *See IG* ii² 143
    18: *621*
    20: *507*
    27: *See IG* ii² 1013
  viii 1939, 6: *529*
  ix 1940, 8: *See* Reinmuth 9
  x 1941, 1: *See SEG* xii 100
    2: *151*
    11: *See Agora* xv 53

INSCRIPTIONS, PAPYRI AND OTHER MANUSCRIPTS

Hesperia–contd.
    78: *475, 492, 534*
  xi 1942, 55: *385*
    329–37: *See SEG* x 2
  xiii 1944, 8: *577*
  xv 1946, 31 ⎫
  xvi 1947, 38 ⎭ *See IG* ii² 1579
  xix 1950, 1: *See SEG* xii 100
  xxii 1953, 223–99 + xxx 1961, 23–9:
    See SEG xiii 12–22 + xix 23–5
  xxiii 1954, 17: *See IG* ii² 1706
    183: *See SEG* xiv 65
  xxviii 1959, 239–47: *See SEG* xviii 13
  xxix 1960, 3: *See SEG* xix 119
    33: *See SEG* xix 133
  xxx 1961, 23–9: *See* xxii 1953,
    223–66
    23: *577*
  xxxii 1963, 1: *See SEG* xxi 80
    2*b*: *460*
  xxxvii 1968, 1–24: *See Agora* xv 62
    1: *577*
    50: *See SEG* xxv 180
  xxxviii 1969, 1: *See Agora* xv 89
  xl 1971, 4: *638*
    5: *621*
    6: *621*
    7: *355, 475, 487*
    Acr. 23 = *IG* ii² 30: *687*
    448–57: *See IG* ii² 1477
  xli 1972, Acr. 54: *See IG* ii² 1375
  xlii 1973, 1: *See IG* i² 772
  xliii 1974, 157–88: *329, 491, 520–1,
    540–1, 552–3, 557–8, 566, 574,
    576, 579, 587, 600, 657*
  xlviii 1979, 28: *625*
  xlix 1980, 258–88: *108, 634, 636–7*
  Supp. i 1937, 1: *See Agora* xv 58
  Supp. xiii 1970: *617 n. 49*
  Supp. xvii 1978: *568*
Hondius, *Novae Inscriptiones Atticae*
  x + xi = *IG* i³ 403: *607*
Inscriptiones Creticae
  iv 41: *94*
    72 (Gortyn Code): *94, 635*
Inscriptiones Graecae, i² (numbers in i³ in parentheses)
  1 (1) = M&L 14: *153, 253, 305*
  2 (233): *133 n. 8*
  3 (4 A): *391*
  4 (4 B): *213, 518*
  5 (5): *206, 605*
  6 (6): *See SEG* x 6
  10 (14) = M&L 40: *149, 251, 298,
    518, 531, 543, 696*

  16 (10) = M&L 31: *318, 531, 586,
    654–5, 667*
  19 (11) = M&L 67: *531*
  22 (21): *See A.T.L.*, D 11
  24 (35) = M&L 44: *552*
  27 (27): *See SEG* x 19
  28, *a* (23): *See SEG* x 23
  39 (40) = M&L 52: *384, 668*
  41 (41): *149, 661–2*
  44 (45): *304*
  45 (46) = M&L 49: *112, 330, 467,
    606*
  56 (156): *305*
  57 (61) = M&L 65: *373, 399, 498,
    526, 545, 578*
  60 (66): *See A.T.L.*, D 22
  63 (71) = *A.T.L.*, A 9, extr. M&L
    69: *300, 374–5, 399, 522, 583, 601*
  64 (77): *See A.T.L.*, A 10
  65 (68) = M&L 68: *307, 375, 583*
  66 (34) = M&L 46: *298, 307, 522,
    540, 562*
  71 (89): *See SEG* x 86
  73 (153): *545*
  74 (154) = *SEG* x 41: *545*
  76 (78) = M&L 73: *239, 371, 374,
    378, 385, 391, 543, 588*
  77 (131): *308*
  80 (7): *See SEG* xiv 3
  81 (79): *568*
  82 (80): *602*
  84 (82) = Sokolowski 13: *108, 494
    n. 35, 610, 638*
  87 (75): *602*
  88 (64): *374, 568*
  90 (76) = Tod 68: *468*
  91 (52 A) = M&L 58 A: *371, 375,
    391, 517, 522, 532, 550, 560*
  92 (52 B) = M&L 58 B: *371, 532,
    573*
  93 (174–5): *407*
  94 (84): *134, 391, 555–8*
  97 (60) = *SEG* xii 26: *308*
  98–9 (93) = M&L 78: *137*
  101 (96): *See SEG* xiv 9
  105 (117) = M&L 91: *379, 548*
  106 (106): *653*
  106a (107): *653*
  109 (99): *See A.T.L.*, D 9
  110 (102) = M&L 85: *70, 387, 409*
  114 (105): *34, 133, 384, 398, 441, 536*
  115 (104) = M&L 86: *69, 98, 109–
    12, 131, 134, 154, 387, 441, 600,
    641–9*
  116 (118) = M&L 87: *296, 299*

INSCRIPTIONS, PAPYRI AND OTHER MANUSCRIPTS

Inscriptiones Graecae, i²–contd.
122 (182): See SEG x 131
124 (124): *422*
127 (133): *561, 564*
139 (207): *532*
144 + 155 (91): See A.T.L., D 23
153 (24): *654*
154 (164): *653*
155: See 144
183–9 (251, 33, 58, 253, 254, 244, 245): *256*
185 (58) = SEG x 60: *636*
186 (253): *242*
188 (244): *115*
191 + 197 (259): See A.T.L., List 1
232–92 (292–362, 403–4): *531–2, 551*
232 (292): *517*
237–9 (297–9): *281*
237 (297): *391*
248 (309): *366*
251 + 252 (312) = SEG x 188: *366*
261–3 (322–4): *281*
272 (333): *366*
272 (part) + 273 (334): See SEG xxii 30–4
293 (363) + M&L 55: *391*
294 etc. (366): See SEG x 226
298 (373) = M&L 81: *366, 411*
301 (376): *344*
302 (370) = M&L 77: *460, 517, 561, 669–70*
304, a (375) = M&L 84: *355, 391, 413, 415, 565, 606, 669*
304, b + c (377) (b = Tod 92): *355, 696*
305 (378): *532*
313 (386): *532, 711*
314 (387): *532*
324 (369) = M&L 72: *460, 517, 532, 550, 560*
325–34 (421–30, 1047), extr. M&L 79: See SEG xiii 12–22 + xix 23–5
340 (437): *391*
354–5 (458–60) = M&L 54: *391, 551*
370 (472): *407*
372 (474): *557, 711*
373–4 (475–6): *691*
374 (476): *497, 568*
377 (402) = M&L 62 = I. de Délos 89: *556, 693*
393 (510): *149, 550*
400 (511): *685*
463 + 475 (507): *670*
770a (960): *370*

772 (974) = Hesp. xlii 1: *413*
837 (1023): See SEG x 345
842 (246): *672*
891 (1105): *212*
929 (1147) = M&L 33: *606*
943 (1163) = M&L 48: *259*
954 + 957 + 964: See Agora xvii 23
1024 (1256): *200*
Inscriptiones Graecae, i³ (items not listed above)
32: See SEG x 24
92: See IG ii² 27
98: See IG ii² 12
127: See IG ii² 1, 1–40
227: See IG ii² 8
403: See Hondius x + xi
498–500: See SEG x 353–5
508: See Raubitschek 327
509: See Raubitschek 328
1031: See M&L 6
1116–18: See SEG x 379
Inscriptiones Graecae, ii (v)
978b: See SEG i 126
Inscriptiones Graecae, ii²
1, 1–40 = M&L 94: *371, 545, 602*
1, 41–75 = Tod 97: *492, 534, 600, 602*
2: *492, 534*
8 = M&L 70 = IG i³ 227: *460, 493, 653*
10 = SEG iii 70 = Tod 100 = SEG xii 84: *436, 463, 475–7, 578*
12 = M&L 80 = IG i³ 98: *397*
27 = IG i³ 92: *371*
29 = Tod 116: *559*
30: See Hesp. xl, Acr. 23
43 = Tod 123: *131, 299, 440, 534*
46 = SEG xvii 17: *666–7*
53: *654*
103 = Tod 133: *70*
104 = Tod 134: *602*
105 + 523 = Tod 136: *602*
106 = Tod 135: *528, 602*
107 = Tod 131: *528–9, 602*
109: *602*
110 = Tod 143: *602*
111 = Tod 143: *602, 667*
112 = Tod 144: *221, 321, 685*
116 = Tod 147: *221*
120: *522, 571, 600–1, 604*
123 = Tod 156: *678*
124 = Tod 153: *52, 677–8*
125 = Tod 154: *374, 544*
127 = Tod 157: *602*
130: *653*

INSCRIPTIONS, PAPYRI AND OTHER MANUSCRIPTS

Inscriptiones Graecae, ii²-contd.
138–40: *600*
143 + 2813 = *Hesp.* vii 13 = *SEG* xv 89: *593*
144: See *SEG* xiv 18
179: *34, 667*
192: *528*
204: *374, 532, 534, 679, 706*
206: *653*
211 = Tod 166: *528, 653*
212 = Tod 167: *529*
215: *516*
218: *528*
222: *600, 694*
223 A: *548, 604*
223 B: *505, 548*
223 C = *Agora* xv 34: *505, 515, 571, 600, 603*
224: *600*
225: *600*
226 = Tod 173, *374, 655*
228: *602*
229: *602*
237 = Tod 178: *70, 654–5*
244: *549–50*
276: *528*
287: *653*
288: *653*
330: *522–3*
333: *214*
334: *606, 628, 670, 685*
336: *522–3, 528*
334 = Tod 189: *528*
338: *516*
345–7: *529*
351 + 624 = Tod 198: *671*
352: *523*
354: *505, 627*
380: *573–6, 611, 628*
404: *528*
448: *441*
456: *611*
457: *547, 671*
463: *552*
466: *397, 666*
478 = Reinmuth 17: *495, 506*
502: *528, 534*
505: *158, 359, 547*
523: See 105
553: *518*
585: *506*
624: See 351
649: *678 n. 56*
657: *568*
659: *573*

661 = *SIG*³ 384: *57, 636*
665: *506*
666: *158*
668: *621, 626*
672: *687*
682: *671, 678, 682*
683: *636*
772: *529*
784: *670*
807: *636*
847: *597, 608, 636*
892: *536–7*
875: See *SEG* xxi 436
896: *627*
945: *521*
954: *536–7*
955: *536–7*
956–9: *521*
956: *638, 676*
968: *568*
974: *627*
1006: *503–4, 505–6, 652*
1008: *611*
1011: *611, 638*
1013, and 2nd copy *Hesp.* vii 27: *576–7*
1034: *568–9*
1036 + 1060: *568–9, 670*
1046: *212*
1060: See 1036
1128 = Tod 162: *583*
1138–71: *256*
1151: *624*
1152: *624*
1156 = Reinmuth 2: *497, 504, 508, 593*
1159 = Reinmuth 19: *503–4*
1163: *705*
1172–1221: *256*
1174: *561*
1176: *611*
1177: *611*
1183: *561, 597*
1189 = Reinmuth 3: *504, 508*
1191: *612*
1194: *611*
1205 = *SIG*³ 916: *501*
1214: *252, 611*
1224: *687*
1225–8: *253*
1227: *611–12*
1230: *622*
1237: *69–70, 496–502, 562, 616*
1239: *259*

INSCRIPTIONS, PAPYRI AND OTHER MANUSCRIPTS

Inscriptiones Graecae, ii²-contd.
1241: *556–7*
1264: *550, 565*
1281: *678 n. 56*
1289: *589*
1302: *682*
1304: *608, 682*
1357: *151*
1370–1513: *551*
1370 + 1371: *391, 462*
1375 = *Hesp.* xli, ACR. 54: *480–1*
1388: *676*
1414: *550*
1415: *688*
1421–35: *675*
1421: *688*
1424a: *551*
1438: See *SEG* xix 129
1443: *513, 551*
1457 + 1458: *550*
1461: *676*
1462: *550*
1468: *550*
1477 = *Hesp.* xl, 448–57: *550*
1484: *550*
1485: *550*
1491: *682*
1492: *517*
1493–7: *551*
1493–5: *516*
1493: *550, 569*
1496: *605–6, 608, 611, 637–8*
1498: *366, 436*
1514–31: *607*
1554–9: See *SEG* xviii 36
1579 = *Hesp.* xv 31 = xvi 38 = *SEG* xvi 120: *556*
1590: *556*
1604*: See *SEG* x 353–5
1604–32: *545*
1611: *546, 687–8*
1612: *547*
1613: *546, 680*
1617: *680*
1622: *558*
1623: *52, 680–1, 688*
1624: *460*
1627: *52–3, 546–7, 558, 626*
1628: *52–3, 546, 688*
1629, extr. Tod. 200: *52–3, 546, 561, 680–1*
1631: *626, 663, 681*
1634 = *I. de Délos* 97: *694*
1635 = Tod 125 = *I. de Délos* 98: *606–7, 626, 694*

1640 = *I. de Délos* 104-12: *606–7*
1641 = *I. de Délos* 104-26: *701, 733*
1668: *547, 568*
1669: *553*
1670: *701*
1672: *441, 510, 556, 569, 575, 577, 605–11, 636–8, 687, 691, 695, 706*
1678 = *I. de Délos* 104-4: *553, 573*
1686: *355–6*
1696: *621*
1700 = *Agora* xv 43: *571, 601, 603*
1706 = *Hesp.* ii, 418–46 = xxiii 17 = *SEG* xiv 87: *614*
1710: *577*
1711: *577*
1713: *182*
1714: *614*
1717: *614, 692*
1721: *692*
1740 = *Agora* xv 12: *601, 604*
1749: *602, 605*
1924 + 2409 : *593*
1925: *593*
1926: *593–4*
1928: *213*
1942: *569*
1943: *569*
2037: *505*
2044: *505*
2090: *508*
2122: *504*
2292–2310: *304*
2308: *248*
2311: *638, 671, 675–6*
2313–17: *671*
2318: *312*
2336: *182*
2409: See 1924
2498: *556–7, 611–12*
2578: *622*
2579: *622*
2811 = *Hesp.* ii 1: *613, 620*
2813: See 143
2818: *624*
2834: *593*
2966: *688*
2971: *480*
2976 = *AJP* lxvi 1945, 234–9 = Reinmuth 8: *506*
3006: *638*
3013: *638*
3019: *638*
3023: *609, 638*
3063: *624*
3064 = *SEG* xviii 69: *624*

INSCRIPTIONS, PAPYRI AND OTHER MANUSCRIPTS

Inscriptiones Graecae, ii²–contd.
  3065–70: *624*
  3093: *611–12*
  3391: *576*
  3779: *638*
  4796: *211*
  4960: *405, 626*
  6320: *672*
Inscriptiones Graecae, iv sqq.
  iv 497: See SIG³ 594
  iv² (i) 68: *535*
    83 = SIG³ 796 B: *532*
  v (i) 1564 = Tod 99: *694*
  v (iii), p. xxxvi = Tod 202: *135*
  vii 414: See SEG i 126
    4252: *569*
    4253 = SIG³ 287: *523, 610*
    4254 = SIG³ 298: *214, 610*
  ix (i) 694: *383*
  ix² (i) 179: See SIG³ 629
  xi (ii) 161: *606–7*
    203: *606*
  xii (ii) 6 = Tod 201: *135*
    526 = Tod 191: *535*
    645: *535*
  xix (v) 444 = F.G.H. 239 (*Marmor Parium*): *74, 78, 123, 165, 181–2, 193, 225, 238, 276, 280, 281, 289, 422*
    647: *210*
  xii (viii) 51: *695*
  xiv 1297 = F.G.H. 252 (*Chronicon Romanum*): *193*
    1389: *637*
Inscriptiones Graecae ad Res Romanas Pertinentes
  iv 360: *508*
Inscriptions de Délos
  87: See Tod 99
  89: See IG i² 377
  92: *693*
  93 = Tod 85: *693*
  94: *693–4*
  97: See IG ii² 1634
  98: See IG ii² 1635
  100: *626, 694*
  103: *694*
  104: *694*
  104-4: See IG ii² 1678
  104-5: *573*
  104-6: *573*
  104-12: See IG ii² 1640
  104-23: *573*
  104-24: *573*
  104-26: See IG ii² 1641
  104-26 bis: *733*
Inscriptions of Cos
  27: *605*
  36 = SIG³ 1106: *605–6*
  382 = SIG³ 1107: *605*
Meiggs & Lewis
  2: *116*
  6: IG i³ 1031: *98–9, 120–1, 220, 234, 280*
  8: *153, 160 n. 13*
  14: See IG i² 1
  17: *136*
  20: *467*
  21: *275*; *and see* Ostraca, in Index III
  23: *114, 281, 290, 394, 497–8, 511, 595, 681*
  26: *289*
  30 A: *577*
  31: See IG i² 16
  33: See IG i² 929
  37: See IG i² 19
  40: See IG i² 10
  42 B = SIG³ 56: *160*
  44: See IG i² 24
  45: *298*
  46: See IG i² 66
  48: See IG i² 943
  49: See IG i² 45
  52: See IG i² 39
  54: See IG i² 354–5
  55: See IG i² 293
  58 A: See IG i² 91
  58 B: See IG i² 92
  62: See IG i² 377
  65: See IG i² 57
  68: See IG i² 65
  69: See IG i² 63
  70: See IG ii² 8
  72: See IG i² 324
  73: See IG i² 76
  77: See IG i² 302
  78: See IG i² 98–9
  79: See SEG xiii 12–22 + xix 23–5
  80: See IG ii² 12
  81: See IG i² 298
  84: See IG i² 304, a
  85: See IG i² 110
  86: See IG i² 115
  87: See IG i² 116
  91: See IG i² 105
  94: See IG ii² 1, 1–40
Orientis Graeci Inscriptiones Selectae
  5 = Welles 1 = *Staatsverträge* 428: *695*
  46: *214*

793

INSCRIPTIONS, PAPYRI AND OTHER MANUSCRIPTS

Orientis Graeci Inscriptiones–contd.
483 = *Abh.* Berlin 1953, vi: *573–5, 597*
POUILLOUX, *Choix d'inscriptions grecques*
8: See *AM* lxxii 1957, 1
POUILLOUX, *La Forteresse de Rhamnonte*
2: See Reinmuth 10
RAUBITSCHEK, *Dedications from the Athenian Akropolis*
326: See *IG* i² 463 + 475
327 = *IG* i³ 508: *670*
328 = *IG* i³ 509: *670*
REINMUTH, *Mnem.* Supp. xiv 1971
1 + *SEG* xxiii 78: *494 n. 35, 495, 621*
2: See *IG* ii² 1156
3: See *IG* ii² 1189
5: *52, 679*
6 = *AM* lxvi 1961, 2: *593*
7 = *AM* lxvi 1961, 3: *52, 679*
8: See *IG* ii² 2976
9 = *Hesp.* ix 8: *52, 505–6, 508, 579*
10 = Pouilloux, *La Forteresse*, 2: *506–8*
15 = 'Ἀρχ.'Ἐφ. 1918, 95–7: *52, 505, 507, 679*
17: See *IG* ii² 478
19: See *IG* ii² 1159
SOKOLOWSKI, *Lois sacrées des cités grecques*
13: See *IG* i² 84
166: See *I. of Cos* 27
177: See *I. of Cos* 36
Die Staatsverträge des Altertums
428: See *OGIS* 5
545: *135*
Supplementum Epigraphicum Graecum
i 126 = *IG* ii (v) 978b + vii 414: *610 n. 48*
iii 70: See *IG* ii² 10
ix 1: *115, 142*
x 2 = *Hesp.* xi, 329–37: *257*
6 = *IG* i² 6: *308, 605*
14: See *A.T.L.*, D 11
19 = *IG* i² 27: *298*
23 = *IG* i² 28, a: *298, 654*
24 = *IG* i³ 32: *338, 548*
41: See *IG* i² 74
60: See *IG* i² 185
86 = *IG* i² 71: *296, 371, 399*
123: *371*
131 = *IG* i² 122: *548*
142: *545*
188: See *IG* i² 251 + 252
226: *548*
345: *228*

353–5 = *IG* ii² 1604* = i³ 498–500: *565*
379 = *IG* i³ 1116–18: *212*
xi 667: *237*
xii 26: See *IG* i² 97
84: See *IG* ii² 10
87: *156, 221–3, 315, 440, 645*
100 = *Hesp.* x 1 = xix 1: *553, 556*
xiii 12–22 + xix 23–5 = *IG* i² 325–34 = *Hesp.* xxii, 223–99 + xxx, 23–9, extr. M&L 79: *491, 554–5, 797*
xiv 3 = *IG* i² 80: *314*
9 = *IG* i² 101: *299*
27: *212*
64: *685*
65 = *Hesp.* xxiii 183: *627*
87 = *Hesp.* xxiii 17: See *IG* ii² 1706
xv 89: See *IG* ii² 143 + 2813
xvi 120: See *IG* ii² 1579
xviii 17: See *IG* ii² 46
18 = *IG* ii² 144: *666*
19–20: *666*
415: *583*
xviii 13: *556, 628*
36 = *IG* ii² 1554–9: *578*
69: See *IG* ii² 3064
xix 23–5: See xiii 12–22
119 = *Hesp.* xxix 3: *516*
129 = *IG* ii² 1438: *600*
133 = *Hesp.* xxix 33: *555, 614*
xxi 80 = *Hesp.* xxxii 1: *355, 436*
435: *304, 564, 566*
436 = *IG* ii² 895: *686*
515: *624*
525: *303–4, 564, 566–7*
xxii 30–4 = *IG* i² 272 (part) + 273: *366*
xxiii 78: See Reinmuth 1
xxv 124: *537*
180 = *Hesp.* xxxvii 50: *701, 716*
*Sylloge Inscriptionum Graecarum*³
56: See M&L 42 B
276 = *BCH* lxxxiii 1959, 152–5: *695*
287: See *IG* vii 4253
298: See *IG* vii 4254
360: *135*
364: *396*
384: See *IG* ii² 661
410: *210*
495: *289*
531: *394*
578: *507*
591: *100*
594 = *IG* iv 497: *160*

INSCRIPTIONS, PAPYRI AND OTHER MANUSCRIPTS

*Sylloge Inscriptionum Graecarum*³–contd.
  629 = *IG* ix² (i) 179: *114*
  715: *160*
  796 B: *See IG* iv² (i) 83
  916: *See IG* ii² 1205
  976: *114*
  1060: *676*
  1061: *676*
  1106: *See I. of Cos* 36
  1107: *See I. of Cos* 382
Tod
  68: *See IG* i² 90
  85: *See I. de Délos* 93
  92: *See IG* i² 304, *b*
  97: *See IG* ii² 1, *41–75*
  99: *See IG* v (i) 1564
  100: *See IG* ii² 10
  116: *See IG* ii² 29
  123: *See IG* ii² 43
  124: *See IG* ii² 44
  125: *See IG* ii² 1635
  131: *See IG* ii² 107
  133: *See IG* ii² 103
  134: *See IG* ii² 104
  135: *See IG* ii² 106
  136: *See IG* ii² 105 + 523
  140: *165–6*
  142: *See IG* ii² 111
  143: *See IG* ii² 110
  144: *See IG* ii² 112
  147: *See IG* ii² 116
  153: *See IG* ii² 124
  154: *See IG* ii² 125
  156: *See IG* ii² 123
  157: *See IG* ii² 127
  162: *See IG* ii² 1128
  166: *See IG* ii² 211
  167: *See IG* ii² 212
  173: *See IG* ii² 226
  178: *See IG* ii² 237
  189: *See IG* ii² 337
  191: *See IG* xii (ii) 526
  198: *See IG* ii² 351 + 624
  200: *See IG* ii² 1629
  201: *See IG* xii (ii) 6
  202: *See IG* v (ii), p. xxxvi
  204: *494, 506, 685*
Welles, *Royal Correspondence in the Hellenistic Period*
  1: *See OGIS* 5

PAPYRI

Nicole, *L'Apologie d'Antiphon*
  = Antiphon, frs. 1–6 Blass & Thalheim = fr. iii Gernet = fr. B 1 Maidment: *22, 367*
P. Berol.
  163 = P. East Berlin 5009 (Berlin Papyrus of *A.P.*): *2–3, 65, 174–7, 180–2, 256–81*
P. Brux. E.
  6842 = 38b, Page, *Greek Literary Papyri: Poetry* = 73, Austin, *Com. Gr. Frag. Pap.*: *354*
P. Cair.
  43227 = 40, Page, *op. cit.* = 92, Austin, *op. cit.*: *345–6*
P. Eleph.
  ii [501]: *289*
P. Hal.
  1: *732*
P. Heid.
  182: *21–2, 323, 368*
P. Hib.
  i 14 = Lysias, fr. vi Gernet & Bizos: *303, 458, 475, 497, 544*

P. Lond.
  131 (London Papyrus of *A.P.*): *3–5, 56–7*; Commentary *passim*, esp. *84, 312, 486, 548, 699, 705, 715, 722–8, 735*
P. Mich.
  5982: *22, 359–60, 367–8, 421, 426*
P. Oxy.
  iv 664: *202*
  v 842 (*Hellenica Oxyrhynchia*): *393, 419, 425, 432, 450*
  xi 1364 = Ant. Soph. 87 B 44 Diels & Kranz: *329*
  xiii 1606 = Lysias, fr. i Gernet & Bizos: *446, 465, 472*
  xv 1800: *475, 477*
  xvii 2082 = *F.G.H.* 257a: 551
  xviii 2161 = Aeschylus, fr. 275 Lloyd-Jones = fr. 474 Mette: *90–1*
  xxxiv 2686: *659*
  unpublished fragment (cf. *A.P.* 7. iii): *4, 138–9*
P. Soc. It.
  vi 571: *693*

INSCRIPTIONS, PAPYRI AND OTHER MANUSCRIPTS

P. Strasb.
84: *546*

P. Teb.
i 14: *461*

WESSELY, *Studien zur Paläographie und Papyruskunde*
iv 1905, 111–13: *588–91, 595*

OTHER MANUSCRIPTS

MS Vat. Gr.
1144, 222^{r-v} = *AJP* xciii 1972, 87–91: *268*

2306, B = *TAPA* cvi 1976, 227–40 = *GR&BS* xviii 1977, 326–9 (Theophrastus): *116, 149, 551, 676–7*

INDEX III

GENERAL INDEX

There are complete indexes to the text of *A.P.* in Kenyon's Berlin ed. and Sandys[2], and substantial indexes in Oppermann. This index omits many words and names which appear only in a single passage in *A.P.* and are discussed *ad loc.*

ἀγαθός. With social connotations, 174, 177
ἀγορανόμοι. 575–6, cf. 32–3
ἄγροικοι. 72, 183–4, *See also* Classes
ἀγωνοθέται. 623, cf. 521
ἀδύνατοι. 570
ἀθλοθέται. 668–76, cf. 31–2, 308, 693
αἱρεῖν. Appoint, by any method, 53–4, 182, 329
ἀμείβεσθαι. 144–5
Ἄμμωνος. Sacred trireme, 687–8, cf. 39, 53, 55–7
ἀμφισβητεῖν. 38 n. 195, 39, 103, 123, 163, 360
ἀναγραφεῖς. In 411, 384–9, cf. 50, 406; in 410–399, 111–12, 387, 441–2
ἀνίεσθαι. 322–3, cf. 9–10, 288
ἀντιγραφεύς. 515, 601
ἀντίδοσις. 623–5, cf. 681
ἄξονες. *See* κύρβεις.
ἀπαγωγή. 379, 580–1, 640
ἀποδέκται. 557–60, cf. 32–3, 573, 587
ἀριστίνδην. 39, 83, 97–8
ἄρχων. More recent than βασιλεύς, 98–102, cf. 26–7, 37, 639; competition for office after Solon, 180–4, cf. 27, 179; irregular archonships, 181–2, 410–11, 436–7, 462–3, 481–2; list of archons, 98–9, 103, 120–1, 180, 220, 234, 280, *and see* Chronology; proclamation on property, 622; religious duties, 622–9, 672–5, cf. 35, 101–2, 639; judicial duties, 624–5, 629–36
— ἄρχοντες. Officials in general, 32–4, 510–12, 513–17, 689–97, cf. 549, 571, 613, 615; a. of Salamis, 610–11
—— The nine archons, 99–106, 612–68, cf. 31–2; ten with secretary, 147, 613–15, 668, 696, 700, 705–6, 708, 715; appointment before Solon, 60,
97–9, 146–7, 149–50; 'Draco', 113; from 594/3, 146–9, cf. 25, 27, 37, 53–4, 60; from 580/79, 182–3; from 508/7, 260, 273; from 487/6, 272–4, cf. 146–7; from 457/6, 329–30, cf. 147, 284; in 411, 396–7; in C4, 613–14, 689–91, cf. 31, 37, 147, 149; δοκιμασία, 511, 542–3, 612, 614–19; oath, 100–1, 135–6, 620–1, cf. 37; stipend, 382, 692–3; duties of whole college, 668, 696, 700, 705–6, 708, 715
ἄστυ. Cleisthenic region, 252–4
ἀστυνόμοι. 573–5, cf. 32–3, 596
ἀτέλεια. 509, 595, 625, 653, 682
ἀτιμία. 111, 158, 161–2, 222, 282–3, 581–2, 594, 702–3; recall of ἄτιμοι in 404, 430–1
αὐλίσκος. 719, 730
αὐλώδης. Possibly to be restored in 67. ii, 719
αὐξάνεσθαι. 287, 310, cf. 8
αὐτοκράτωρ. 373–4, 402, 409–10, 464. *See also* αὐτοτελής, κύριος.
αὐτοτελής. 106, 589
ἄφεσις. 399, 520–1

βασιλεύς. King of Athens, 65–9; annual magistrate, 77–8, 98–102; headquarters, 103–4, cf. 27, *and see* Stoa of the Basileus; religious duties, 636–9, cf. 101–2; sacred property, 556; wife's sacred marriage, 104–5, cf. 27; judicial duties, 639–50, cf. 668
Βουκολεῖον. 103–4, cf. 27
βούλευσις. Of homicide, 643–4; failure to delete discharged debtor, 663
βουλευτήριον. 522, 593–4; in 411, 405–6, 410; new β. built and old used to house records, 532, 557, 600

797

GENERAL INDEX

βουλή. 517-71; in laws and in *A.P.*, 14, 31-2, 34, 37, 512; 401 of 'Draco', 115-17; 400 of Solon, 153-4, cf. 141, 246, 400; 500 of Cleisthenes, 251; after Ephialtes, 317; in 411, 379-81, 389-99, 400, 405-7; in 404-403, 437-8, 452-3; appointment, 251-2, 517-18, 691; δοκιμασία, 542-3; oath, 145-6, 260, 263-4, 538; stipend, 304, 405, 691-2; duties: δοκιμασίαι, 500-2, 542-3, 564-8, 570-1, 614-19; supervision of ἀρχαί, 540-2, 549-71; navy, 545-8; buildings, 548-9; πέπλος, 568-9; judicial, 477-8, 489-90, 537-43, 549; secretaries and β., 599-605

βουλόμενος, ὁ. 159-60, 374, 444, 656

γένη 68-71, 75-6, cf. 84, 243, 257-8
γεωμόροι. 72. See also Classes
γεωργοί. 71-2, 74-5, cf. 67, 78, 183-4. See also Classes
γῆς ἀναδασμός. 15, 171, 174, 478-9, 622
γνώριμοι. 88-9, 96, 347, 349, 351, 355. See also προστάται
γραμματεῖς. 599-605, cf. 36-7, 52, 520; γ. θεσμοθέταις, 613-15, 668, 700, and see ἄρχοντες.
γραφαί. 159-60, 629-31, 639, 656, 660-3, 666-7, 717-19, 722-3, 728; γ. παρανόμων, 315-16, 357, 378, 544-5, 660; against Thrasybulus, 474-7; γ. νόμον μὴ ἐπιτήδειον θεῖναι, 315-16, 357, 544-5, 660
γυμνασίαρχοι. 638-9

δημαγωγός. 323-4, cf. 97, 335, 352, 358
δήμαρχοι. 256-7, cf. 215; δδ. of Oropus and Piraeus, 611
δημιουργοί. 71-2, 74-5, 183-4, cf. 67, 78. See also Classes
δημοκρατία. 261
δῆμος. Whole people, 88-9, 174-5; lower classes, 88-9, 172-3, 243-5, and see πλῆθος, προστάται; deme, before Cleisthenes, 81-2, 205, 254, 257; institutionalised by Cleisthenes, 251-8; in registration of citizens, 497-502, cf. 494; in appointments, 251-2, 518, 689-91
δημόσιοι. See Slavery
δημοτικός. 219
διαδικασία. 624-5, 629-40, 681, 720-1, 732

διαιτηταί. 589-96, cf. 36, 500, 572, 655-6
Διακρία. 184-8, cf. 28, 73-4, 179-80
διατάττειν. 136, 379-81
διαψηφισμός. See Citizenship
δικάζειν. Sometimes, preside in court, 586-7, 639-40, 648, cf. 318
δίκαι. 'Private' lawsuits, 159-60, 582-96, 632-3, 640-50, 652-7, 664-6, 667-8, 717-19, 728; δδ. ἔμμηνοι, 582-6, 665, 720-1; δδ. ἐμπορικαί, 57, 583-4, 664-5
δικασταὶ κατὰ δήμους. 215-16, 257, 284, 331, 563, 588. See also Forty
δικαστήρια. Development from ἡλιαία, 318-19, cf. 38, 106; discretion of, 159-63, 442-4, 489, cf. 26, 30; stipend, 338-44, 691, 716-17, 730-1, 734-5, cf. 284, 286, 302-3, 355-6, 514; bribery, 342-4; organisation, 657-8, 666, 668, 697-735, cf. 32-3, 36, 49, 52; panel of jurors, 302, 702-3; size of juries, 591, 714-15, 718, 728-9; special juries, 665; timing of trials, 715, 719-28, 734; voting in trials, 730-4; δοκιμασίαι, 500-2, 542-3, 614-19; εὔθυναι, 562-4, 577-9; πέπλος, 568-9; δ. at Piraeus, 646, 701. See also γραφαί, δίκαι and names of other procedures; ἔφεσις, ἡλιαία.
δίκη. In Solon, fr. 36 (12. iv), 175
διοικεῖν. Political administration, 39-40, 107-8, 203, 213, 287, 513; festivals, 101-2
διοίκησις. Finance, 309; ὁ ἐπὶ τῇ δ., 515-16, 552, cf. 35-6, 53
διωβελία. 355-7
δοκιμασία. 615, 663, 669; by Areopagus in early Athens, 316-18, cf. 150; of archons, 511, 542-3, 612, 614-19; of boule, 542-3; of ἀδύνατοι, 570, cf. 31; of cavalry, 564-8, cf. 31; of citizens, 497-502; δ. ῥητόρων, 357, 660 n. 53; δοκιμαστής of coins, 574, 576
δυοῖν. 509-10

ἐγκύκλιος. 330, 513
εἰκός. 26-7, 59
εἰσαγγελία. Different kinds, 57, 156, 524, 546; for major offences: 'Draco', 117; Solon, 156, 220; Ephialtes, 316-18, 320; in cc5-4, 221, 357, 378, 524-5, 564, 658, 664, 683;

798

GENERAL INDEX

εἰσαγγελία–contd.
νόμοις μὴ χρῆσθαι, 316–18, 378, 541–2, 564, 660, 662, 664; to διαιτηταί, 595–6; κακώσεως, 629–30
εἰσάγειν εἰς δικαστήριον. 563, 581, 583, 587, 597–8, 629, 640, 648, 657–8, 664, 683, 714–15
εἰσαγωγεῖς. 582–6; and δίκαι ἐμπορικαί, 57, 665
εἰσφορά. 137, 142, 153, 680–1
ἐκκλησία. Solon, 140–1, 154, 174–5; Cleisthenes legislates through, 241, 248–9, 376 n. 32; Ephialtes, 317–18; in 411, 363–5, 377–87, 396, 404–5, 411–12; in 404, 433–5; compelled or deceived (late c5), 29 n. 165, 369–70, 416, 423–4, 434; fickleness, 357; payment, 490–3, 691, cf. 9, 51, 355–6, 514; meetings, 521–31, 535–7, cf. 31–2, 507–8, 512; κυρία ἐ., 522–3, cf. 691; secretaries and ἐ., 601–5
ἐκκλησιάζειν. 39, 211–12
ἐκτήμοροι. 90–7, 111, 126–7
Ἑλληνοταμίαι. 139; in and after 411, 355, 391–3
ἔνδειξις. 379, 581–2, 661, 663, 675, 703
ἐπιβολαί. 161, 535, 564, 576, 587, 684; of boule, 540–2
ἐπιεικής. With social connotations, 324, 326–7, 343, 344–5; with moral, 326–8, 343
ἐπίθετα. More recent (festivals), 102, 639; usurpations (Areopagus), 108, 287, 314
ἐπίκληροι. See Inheritance
ἐπιλείπεσθαι. 39, 245, 341, 431
Ἐπιλύκειον. 105
ἐπιμεληταί. Διονυσίων, 627–8, cf. 52, 611; ἐμπορίου, 579; κρηνῶν, 516–17; μυστηρίων, 636–8, cf. 57–8; νεωρίων, 545–6; φυλῆς, 624, cf. 627; in 411, 392
ἐπιστάτης. προέδρων, 534–5, 660, cf. 31; πρυτάνεων, 531–3, cf. 31
ἐπιχειροτονεῖν. 452, 523, 659, 682–3, 686
ἐπώνυμοι. Of tribes, 105, 259, 562, 592–4; of year-classes, 121, 592–4
ἑταιρεῖαι. In 508, 243; in 404, 427–31
εὔθυναι. 'Draco', 114–15; before Ephialtes, 316–18, 335–6; after Ephialtes, 357, 547–8, 561–4, 587–8, 597–9, 661–2; for Thirty and ministers, 461–3, 469–71. See also λογισταί
εὐθυνεῖν. 155
εὐπατρίδαι. 71–2, 74–6, 185–7, cf. 67,

78–9, 98; weakened by Solon, 148, 150, 153, 179, 183–4. See also Classes
ἔφεσις. From archons, 106, 160–1, and see ἡλιαία; from boule, 540–3, 549; from διαιτηταί, 589–91, 595–6
ἐφέται. 646–9
ἔφηβοι. 502–10, cf. 31–3, 36–7, 51–2, 494–5, 592–3, 695

ζευγῖται. 138, 145; admitted to archonship, 329–31. See also Property classes

ἡλιαία. Solon's appeal court, 106, 160–2; under Pisistratus, 219; transformed into δικαστήρια, 318–19, cf. 38, 106; largest court of classical Athens, 701, 730

θαρρεῖν. 39, 267, 296, 337
θεσμοθέται. 102–3, 657–67, cf. 106, 563–4, 683; δίκαι ἐμπορικαί, 57, 584, 664–5; ἔνδειξις, 582, 661; εὔθυναι, 563–4, 661; θ. used of college of ten, 705–6, 715. See also γραμματεῖς
θεσμοθετεῖον. 106, 308, 520, 692–3
θεσμός. 86–7, 102–3, 109–12, 130, 177, 248, 440–1, 485
θεωρικόν, τὸ. 514–17, cf. 355–6, 492, 552, 558, 596–7
θῆτες. Labourers, 91, 138; Solonian class, 137–8; excluded from office, 140–1, 145–6, 510, 550–1; from ἔφηβοι and διαιτηταί, 36, 503, 591. See also Classes
θόλος. 105, 308, 520, 532–3

ἱερομνήμων. In Arist. Pol., 33; in Athens, 390
ἱεροποιοί. 605–10, cf. 36; in 411, 392
ἱκετεία. 527–8, cf. 321
ἵνα. 374–5, 403
ἵππαρχοι. 'Draco', 114, cf. 116; in 411, 390, 402–3; in c4, 566, 685–6; to Lemnos, 686–7
ἱππεῖς. Cavalry, 303–4, 564–8; in 404–403, 458; Solonian class, 138, 143–5, cf. 26, 148, 330, and see Classes

κατάλογος. Of hoplites, in c5, 327; of Five Thousand, 384–5; of Three Thousand, 449; of cavalry, 566–7
κατάστασις. 262–3, 495; false reading in 41. ii, 483–4, cf. 487

799

GENERAL INDEX

κῆρυξ. Of archons, 622, 692-3; in δικαστήρια, 709, 715
— Κήρυκες of Eleusinian cult, 465, 636-7, cf. 276, 280
κινεῖν. 329, 370
κλεψύδρα. 716, 719-28
κληρωτήρια. 704-9, cf. 36, 149, 512, 690-1, 700-1, 713-15
κοινός. τὰ κοινά, 39-40, 203, 297, cf. 213; καὶ ἰδίᾳ καὶ κοινῇ, 478; neutral, 130
κολάζειν. 39, 108, 155
κόσμος. Orderliness, 39, 108, 353-4, 504-5, 535, 627; religious equipment, 551
κυαμεύειν. 149. See also Sortition
κύρβεις and ἄξονες. 131-5, cf. 25, 61, 109, 111, 241 n. 20, 441
κύριος. 37, 402, 464, 540, 543, 589. See also αὐτοκράτωρ, αὐτοτέλης, ἐκκλησία
κωλακρέται. 139-40; abolished c. 411, 355, 391-2, 558

λαγχάνειν δίκην. 587
Λεωκόρειον. 231-2
λῆξις. In 411, 393-4, 403-4; claim to inheritance, 526
λῃτουργία. 382. See also γυμνασίαρχοι, τριήραρχοι, χορηγοί
λίθος. In front of Stoa of Basileus, 135-6, 620
λογισταί. Prytany-ly board, 560-1; annual board, 597-9. See also εὔθυναι
λοχαγοί, 685; cadet officers, 505

μὲν οὖν. 414-15
μερισμός. 559-60, 573
μεσόγειος. Cleisthenic region, 252-3
μέσος. μέση πολιτεία, 9-10, 186, 322-3, and see πάτριος πολιτεία; μεσότης of Solon, 119, 123-4
μεταβολή / μετάστασις. 7, 213, 286, 482-8
μεταδιδόναι / μετέχειν / παραδιδόναι πόλεως / πολιτείας / πραγμάτων. 158-9, 250, 335, 382-4, 411-12, 448, 453, 477, 496
μέτοικοι. 652-7, cf. 35, 334, 384, 497, 527, 664; homicide, 642-4, 654-5

ναυκραρίαι. 151-3, cf. 21, 73, 257; πρυτάνιες τῶν ναυκράρων, 80, 82, 152
Νίκαι. 551, 569
νομοθέται, νομοθεσία. 35, 102, 512-13,

601-4, cf. 441-2; secretaries and, 599-604
νόμος. And θεσμός, 112, 130, 177, 248, 440-1, 485; and ψήφισμα, 177, 248, 328-30, 489, 512-13, 516. See also Laws
νομοφύλακες. 315, 580

ξενοδίκαι. 655, 662

οἰκίαι. Households, 69-70, 245-6
ὅπως, ὅπως ἄν. 374-5, 377, 378-9, 395
ὅροι. 90, 94, 126, 175; ὅρος in Solon, fr. 37 (12. v), 179

παραγραφή. 473, 477-8
παραιβατεῖν. 21, 38, 206
παραλία. 184-8, cf. 28, 73-4, 179-80; Cleisthenic region, 252-3
πάρεδροι. Of εὔθυνοι, 561; of archons, 621-2
πάτριος. Law against tyranny, 222-3; π. πολιτεία, 115, 376-7, 416, 420, 427-34, 440-1. See also ἐπίθετα
πεδίον. 184-8, cf. 28, 73, 179-80
Πειραιεύς. Spelling, 439. See also Piraeus
πελάτης. 90-1, 95. See also ἑκτήμοροι
πέπλος. Of Athena, 568-9, 671-2
περί, οἱ. 228-9
περίπολοι. 494-5, 506, 508
πινάκια. 704-10, cf. 36, 512, 701, 713-14, 716-17, 734-5
πλῆθος. Assembly of citizens, 404-5; number of citizens, 333; lower classes, 88-9, 244-5, and see δῆμος, προστάται.
πληροῦν. 396-7, 702
ποιήματα. 24, 39, 49, 124
πολέμαρχος. More recent than βασιλεύς, 66, 78-9, 99-100, 652; powers in cc6-5, 264-6; religious duties, 101-2, 639, 650-2; judicial duties, 652-7, cf. 587
πόλις. Acropolis, 155-6; city, 209
πολιτεία. Constitution, 89-90, 163, 360, 493, 495-6; control of state, 244-5; citizenship, 90, 113; body of citizens, 39, 90, 116, 454, 457
πολιτικός. 203, 213, 228
πορισταί. 356
πράκτορες. 559
πρᾶος. 213, 220, 222, 272
προβολή. 36, 526-7, 659-60, 683

800

GENERAL INDEX

προβούλευσις. 525-31, 535-7, 543-5, cf. 31, 49
πρόβουλοι. 372-3
προγράφειν. 522, 534, 716-17
πρόεδροι. In 411, 380-1, 385; in C4, 533-5, 660
προστάται γνωρίμων, δήμου. 29, 43, 88-9, 97, 283-4, 292-4, 311, 323-4, 344-61, 447
προχειροτονία. 529-31, cf. 35, 49
πρυτανεῖον. 103-5; κύρβεις in, 133-5; σίτησις in, 308-9, 520, 693; homicide trials in, 648-9, cf. 49
πρυτάνεις. 'Draco', 114-15; instituted by Ephialtes (?), 317; in 411, 382; in CC5-4, 518-22, cf. 660; ππ. ναυκράρων, 80, 82, 152
πωλεῖν. Sell, 554; let contract, 552, 673
πωληταί. 552-7, cf. 35, 525, 690

ῥήτορες. 114, 511; Cleon, 352-4; δοκιμασία ῥητόρων, 357, 660 n. 53

σεισάχθεια. 125-30, cf. 20-1, 164-9
σημεῖον. 26-7, 37, 59, 147
σίτησις. See θεσμοθετεῖον, θόλος, πρυτανεῖον; also Stipends
σῖτος. Corn supply, 523, 577-9; fodder for cavalry, 565; maintenance for orphans, 635-6
σιτοφύλακες. 576-9, cf. 55-6
σκήπτεσθαι. 38, 633-4
σκῆψις. 625, 681
στρατεία, στρατιά. 282, 337, 451
στρατηγοί. 'Draco', 114, cf. 116; Cleisthenes, 264-5, 274; appointment in late C5-early C4, 265-6, 535-7; in 411, 379, 390, 401-2, 409-10, 510; appointment in late C4, 535-7, 676-9, cf. 52, 511; εὔθυναι, 661; σ. ἐπὶ τὴν χώραν, 508, 524, 679; σ. ἐπὶ τοὺς ὁπλίτας, 678-9; σσ. ἐπὶ τὸν Πειραιέα, 52, 506, 679; σ. ἐπὶ τὰς συμμορίας, 35, 52, 657, 679-82. See also Army
στρατιωτικά. 513-17, 552, 569, 674
συγγραφεῖς. 21, 372-81, 434-5, 437, 543-4
συκοφάνται. 444-5, 526-7
συμβαίνειν. 12-13, 323
σύμβολα. Judicial agreements with cities, 654-5, 666-7; tokens used in δικαστήρια, 713, 730-1, 735, and see Tokens
σύν. 240
σωτηρία. 373-4

ταμίαι. Of Athena and Other Gods, 27, 37, 147-8, 531-2, 549-51, 674; 'Draco', 113; in 411-410, 366, 391
— Of boule, 570-1. See also διοίκησις, θεωρικόν, στρατιωτικά
ταξίαρχοι. 684-5; in 411, 390, 402-3; cadet officers, 505
τάξις. duty, 107; hoplite manoeuvres, 508; property class, 142-3; state of affairs, 171; τ. τῆς πολιτείας, 39, 97, 484-5, 496
τελεῖν. 140, 618
τέλος. Final cause, 7-9; property class, 137, 142-3
τίθεσθαι ὅπλα. 157-8
τίμημα. Valuation for property classes, 136-7, 470-1; assessment for lawsuit, 563, 589
τίμησις. In lawsuits, 683, 703, 713, 723, 726-8, 734, and see τίμημα
τριήραρχοι. 679-82, cf. 35, 570; lawsuits, 586, 681
τριττύες. Ionian, 68-71, cf. 258; Cleisthenic, 252-4, cf. 256, 331, 435; ττ. πρυτάνεων, 533

ὑπεράκριοι. 184-8, cf. 28, 73-4, 179-80
ὑπηρέται. 439, 705, 710-11, 713. See also Slavery
ὑποφέρεσθαι. 310, 447, cf. 8, 287

φανερός. 130
φρατρίαι. 68-71, cf. 61, 76, 258, 496; spelling, 258-9. See also IG ii² 1237, in Index II
φυλαί. Ionian, 67-71, cf. 65, 78, 258, 400; Cleisthenic, 250-4, cf. 256, 259, 400, 435; classical democracy based on, 493-735 passim; 5 men from 10 tribes, 582, 596, 624, cf. 578; tribal rotation in offices, 601-2, 614, 694, cf. 259; judicial officers and defendant's tribe, 562, 582, 588, 590, 594; tenfold subdivision, 690-1, 706-9
φυλακὴ τῆς πολιτείας. 107, 117, 155, 315-17; τῆς χώρας, 524, 679
φύλαρχοι. In 411, 390, 402-3; in C4, 566, 686
φυλοβασιλεῖς. 150-1, 648-50
φύσει. 232

χειροτονεῖν and ψηφίζειν. 423, 492, 498-9, 619. See also Voting

801

GENERAL INDEX

χορηγοί. 622-6, cf. 35, 340-1; in demes, 611
χρειούς. In Solon, fr. 36 (12. iv), 175-6
χρηματίζειν. 399, 529

ψηφίζειν. See χειροτονεῖν
ψήφισμα. 177, 241, 248, 329, 489, 512-13, 516; secretaries and ψψ., 599-604

ᾠδεῖον. 670-1; trials at, 52, 701, 714

Acastus. Life archon, 30, 77-8, 100; in archons' oath, 100-1
Acropolis. Seized by Cylon, 80; by Pisistratus, 201, cf. 213; in 514, 231; in 510, 238-9; in 508, 246; in 404-403, 455; Areopagus' penalties recorded on, 155-6; κύρβεις on, 134-5; archons' oath on, 621; garrison, 304. See also πόλις
Acte. ἔφηβοι, 506; στρατηγός, 679, cf. 52
Aegina. War with Athens c7 (?), 95-6; cc6-5, 279-80; weights, measures, coinage, 164-8
Aegospotami. Battle, 416, 424, 426
Age. Classes, 495, 503, 572, 592-3, 596; age requirements, 116, 372-3, 385, 389-90, 396, 497-8, 504, 510, 591, 625-6, 635, 702-3; men over military age, 383
Aglaurus. Sanctuary of, 103, 211, 506
Agrae. 80
Agyrrhius. Introduces assembly pay, 492-3, cf. 355-6, 514
Alcibiades. σεισάχθεια leaked to ancestor, 128-9; in 411, 369-72; absent from A.P., 345, 354, 371
Alcmaeon (c6). First Alcmaeonid, 70; in Sacred War, 81, 83
Alcmaeonids. 186-7, 274-7, cf. 79; not a γένος, 70, 243; homes, 186, 254; and Cylon, 80-4; and Pisistratids, 204, 206-7, 233-7, 247-8, cf. 29, 47-8, 190-1, 289; Cleisthenes, 242, 254; victim of ostracism in 480's, 274-7; politics after 479, 289
Amasis. King of Egypt, 121, 169-70, 236
Amphiaraus. See Oropus
Andron. Father of Androtion, 19, 367
Androtion (F.G.H. 324). 15-30, cf. 108; on σεισάχθεια and coinage (F 34), 164-9, cf. 20-1, 28, 47, 54, 118, 125, 127; on fall of tyranny, 191, 236;

on ostracism (F 6) and 510-480, 240-1, 267-9, cf. 11, 20-1, 29, 289; on Pentecontaetia, 285; on συγγραφεῖς and revolutions of 411 (F 43), 366-8, cf. 21, 363; on 404-403 (FF 10-11), 21, 421
Anthemion. Equestrian statue, 143-5
Antiphon. Oligarch in 411, 19, 366, 407-8, 410, 413; defence, 22, 29, 367-8, 405, 408, and see Nicole, in Index II
Anytus. Son of Anthemion, 144; bribes a jury, 343-4; in 404-403, 431-3
Appointment of officials, 510-12, 689-91; ban on reappointment, 116, 390, 403, 515, 604, 696-7. See also Election, Sortition, and names of individual offices
Archinus. 15, 420, 431-3, 473-8
Areopagus. Membership, 106-7, 674; in early Athens, 75, 79, 106-8, 149-50, cf. 54, 60, 86; 'Draco', 117; Solon, 153-6, 220; Cleisthenes, 246, 260; battle of Salamis, 287-90, cf. 19, 21; after Persian Wars, 283-91, cf. 6, 8, 9-10, 15, 48-9, 54 n. 263, 485; reformed by Ephialtes, 309-22, cf. 8, 14, 19, 283, 336, 486; Thirty, 440; casual treatment in 2nd part of A.P., 85; homicide, 641-2, 646-9, cf. 667-8; sacred olives, 673-5; ἀπόφασις, 659
Arginusae. Battle, 415-16, 422-6, 722-3
Argos. Connection with Pisistratus, 199, 208, 225-7, 237. See also Pheidon
Aristides. Marathon, 280, 686 n. 58; ostracised, 277, 280-1; Delian League, 283-5, 294-7, 300; and Themistocles after Persian Wars, 27, 43, 283, 286, 292-4, 348-9, 486
Aristion. Proposer of Pisistratus' bodyguard, 200, 268
Aristocrates. 'Moderate' in 411, 413-14
Aristogiton. Tortured after Hipparchus' death, 26, 232-3. See also Harmodius
Aristomachus. ἐπιψηφίζων in 411, 362, 385-7, 404-5
Aristotle. Historical work of school, 58-63; composition of Pol., 58-9; authorship of A.P., 61-3; language, 37-40, 60; political judgments, 7, 60, 163, 323, 328-9, 358-61, 488-9; μέσον, 9-10, 123-4, 322-3; συμβαίνειν,

802

GENERAL INDEX

Aristotle—contd.
12–13, 323; analysis of constitutions, 32–3; on Draco, 85, 109–10; Solon, 118, 123–4, 146–8, 163; Pisistratids, 189, 192, 194–6, 214; Cleisthenes, 242, 250, 255–6, 258; ostracism, 269–70; Areopagus and Salamis, 287–8, cf. 10; Pericles and Ephialtes, 311–12, 336; demagogues, 323; adherence to laws, 10, 328–9, 488–9; Theramenes, 358–61; on 411, 368, 369–71, 409; on 404–403, 429–30

Army. Officers, 32–3, 517, 535–7, 676–88; selective enlistment, 327, 596. *See also* ἔφηβοι, ἱππεῖς, στρατηγοί and names of other offices

Asclepius. Procession for, 626–7

Atthides. 15–30, 88, 100, 179, 184, 239–41, 285, 416; on Areopagus, 108; on chronology of tyranny, 189, 191, 196–7; on fall of tyranny, 191, 236; on Salamis, 287–9. *See also* Androtion, Clidemus, Hellanicus, Phanodemus, Philochorus

Boeotia. *See* Thebes

Brauron. Home of Pisistratus, 187, 257–8; Brauronian Artemis, 607–8

Buildings. Boule's responsibility, 528–9, 568–9; ἱερῶν ἐπισκευασταί 572–3. *See also* names of individual buildings

Butadae. γένος and deme, 187, 257

Calendar. 36, 406–7, 518–19, 537, 606–10

Callias Διδυμίου. Ostracised in 440's, 271, 350
— Κρατίου Ostracised in 480's (?), 275–6
— Archon in 412/1, 405, 410, 422
— Archon in 406/5, 405, 422

Cecrops. First king of Athens, 66, 78

Cedon. 248

Cephisophon. Archon in 329/8, 37, 52, 55–6, 610

Charicles. Oligarch in 404–403, 430

Chios. δημοσίη βολή in c6, 153, 160 n. 13; in Delian League, 298–300

Chronology. Kings, 66; Cylon, 81–4; Draco, 109, cf. 121; Solon, 120–2, 127, 163–4, 223–4; after Solon, 180–2; tyranny, 191–9, cf. 27–8, 61; Cleisthenes, 240–1, 244, 248–9, 262–3, cf. 121; 510–480, 262–3, 266–7, 272, 274, 281, cf. 43; Pentecontaetia, 295–6, 309–10, 330, 337; of 411, 371, 405–7; of 404–403, 417–22, 436–7, 450–1, 462–3, cf. 30; in 2nd part of *A.P.*, 35, 37, 52, 55–6, 495, 516, 534, 546–8, 584, 601–3, 607, 610, 628, 698, 714; *A.P.* argues from, 26, 223–4; date of *A.P.*, 51–8

Cimon (c6). 198
— (c5). And Anthemion in 480, 144; Delian League, 294–5; Theseus' bones, 76–7, 211, 289, cf. 65; and Themistocles, 288–9, 292–3; prosecuted by Pericles, 312, 317, 325, 335–6; opponent of Ephialtes, 311–12, 317, 349, cf. 19; ostracised, 271, 311; *A.P.* mentions after Ephialtes' death, 284–6, 324–6, cf. 27; inferior leadership, 284–5, 324–8, cf. 23; generosity, 338–44, cf. 23; unaffected by citizenship law, 333; in ch. 28, 27, 286, 325, 349

Citizenship. In early Athens, 76, 331–2; after tyranny, 187–8, 255–6, cf. 12, 27; Cleisthenes, 249–51, 253, 255–6, cf. 12; Pericles' law, 331–4, cf. 12, 284; Phormisius' proposal, 432–3, 472; c4 law, 496–502, cf. 31–2, 331, 663; legitimate birth required, 36, 332, 496–7, 499–500; reduced rights of νεοπολῖται, 510–11, 617

City facilities. 571–9, 596–7, cf. 31, 33

Classes. In early Athens, 71–2, 74–6, 183–4, cf. 67, 78–9, *and see* εὐπατρίδαι. *See also* Age, Property

Cleisthenes. 240–72, cf. 11–12, 68–70, 485; archon in 525/4, 220, 234, 242, 243–4; opponent of Isagoras, 242–7, cf. 28, 249, 348; chronology, 240–1, 244, 248–9, 262–3, cf. 121; citizenship, 249–51, 253, 255–6, cf. 12; ostracism, 262, 266–70, cf. 11, 20; no new phratries, 61, 258; founder of democracy, 375–7, cf. 19
— Tyrant of Sicyon, 186, cf. 234, 332

Cleomenes. King of Sparta, 238, 246–7, 249, cf. 80

Cleon. 351–4, cf. 23, 25, 357

Cleophon. 354–7, 416, 424–6

Clidemus (*F.G.H.* 323). 15–30; on ναυκραρίαι (F 8), 21, 151–2, 257; on Phye (F 15), 21, 38, 205–6, 226; on fall of tyranny, 191, 236; on Salamis (F 21), 287–90, cf. 21

Clitophon. In 411, 362, 366, 375–7; in 404–403, 432–3

803

GENERAL INDEX

Coesyra. 204
Coinage. Beginnings of, 96, 152–3, 167–8; 'Draco', 113, 117; Solon, 164–9, cf. 20–1, 28, 47, 54, 127; use of triobol design, 704. *See also Hesp.* xliii 1974, in Index II
Collytus. Deme, 205
Colonus. Assembly in 411, 377–85, 405–6, cf. 23–4
Comedy. As source of *A.P.*, 16, 25, 285–6, 301–2, 354; performances, 623–4, 638, cf. 431, 492, 611
Confiscated property. 525–6, 554–5, 581–2; Pisistratus, 214
Constitutions. Studied by Aristotle's school, 1–2, 51, 58–63; 'Draco', *see* Draco; of 411, 385–405, cf. 49, 115
Creon. Archon in 683/2, 66, 79, 98–9
Critias. Alleged pamphlet by, 16, 18, 129; on Pericles and Cimon, 338–9; political career, 417, 429–30, 433–4, 448, 452–3, 456; absent from *A.P.*, 10, 345, 420–1, 430, cf. 371
Croesus. King of Lydia, allegedly visited by Solon, 169–70, cf. 121; rescues Miltiades, 187, 198; date of overthrow, 192, 198–9
Cylon. 79–84, cf. 28, 65, 79, 86, 88, 96, 245

Damasias. Archon in 582/1 and after, 180–4
Damon. Advises Pericles on jury pay, 284, 341–2; ostracised, 271, 342, 350
Damonides. *A.P.* omits name of son Damon, 341–2, cf. 56 n. 278
Debts. In early Athens, 90–7, 111; cancelled by Solon, 125–6, 184, 187–8, cf. 20; c4 law, 559, 599, 703
Delian League. 283–5, 291–309, cf. 8 n. 33, 10, 48–9, 288, 667. *See also* Navy
Delos. Purified by Pisistratus, 217; festivals held by Athens, 606–7, 626, 687–8, 693–5
Delphi. Supports Cylon, 80, 82; First Sacred War, 81, 83, 181; assists overthrow of tyranny, 190–1, 236–7, 247; names Cleisthenes' tribes, 259; ἱερομνήμων to, 390
Demetrius of Phalerum. Researcher for *A.P.* (?), 18, 86; abolishes liturgies, 623, 682
Democracy. A perversion, 7, 9; goal of Athenian development, 7–9; kinds of, 9, 10–12; Athens paradigm of, 299, 337; origin of, 14, 19, 74–7, 119, 159, 241, 261, 376–7, 484–6; restoration in 410, 414–15, cf. 486–7; restoration in 403, 416–22, 461–82, cf. 9, 49, 487; moderation of restored democracy, 471–80, cf. 10; character of c4 democracy, 487–93
Demophon. Son of Theseus, 79
Diasia. 80, 82
Diodorus Siculus. On tyranny, 189, 191, 216, 218, 228, 232–3; on Delian League, 295–6; on Ephialtes, 314; on 411–410, 368–70; on 404–403, 415–82
Dionysia. Great, 623–4, 627–8, cf. 52, 431, 492; rural, 611. *See also* Lenaea
Dionysus. Sacred marriage with βασίλιννα, 104–5, cf. 27
Diphilus. *See* Anthemion
Dithyrambic contests. 622–4, 638; on Salamis, 611
Documents. *A.P.*'s use of, 15, 23–5, 29–30, 49, 59; of 411, 365–7, 385–405; of 404–403, 420, 434, 452, 463–72. *See also* Cleisthenes, Draco, Laws, Solon
Draco. 109–18; Athens' first written laws, 96–7, 102, 485; extent of legislation, 98, 102, 109–11; homicide, 109–12, 641–9, *and see IG* i² 115, in Index II; other laws superseded by Solon, 110–11, 130–1; θεσμοί in 1st ed. of *A.P.*, 5 n. 21, 60, 86–7, 112, cf. 28, 84, 485; 'constitution' a late insertion, 5 n. 21, 53–6, 84–7, 484–5, cf. 27–8, 45–6, 60–1, 97, 137, 482
Dracontides. Decree instituting Thirty: 434–5, cf. 24

Eetionea. Fortified in 411, 453
Election. 31–2, 115–16, 513–17, 535–7, 601–4, 676–9. *See also* Voting, and names of individual offices
Eleusis. War in time of Ion, 66, 100; late incorporation in Athenian state, 76; in 404–401, 418, 452, 456, 463–81; ἔφηβοι, 508; Eleusinia, 608–9; Mysteries, 57–8, 465–6, 625–6, 636–7
Eleven. 579–82, cf. 32, 139, 309, 379, 664; under Thirty, 439, 469–71, cf. 580
Ephialtes. 309–19, cf. 14, 283, 486; and Themistocles, 283–5, 319–22, cf. 29,

804

GENERAL INDEX

Ephialtes–contd.
53–6, 61; and Pericles, 311–12, 336, cf. 61, 286; opposed by Cimon in ch. 28, 286, 325, 349, cf. 27; moves κύρβεις from Acropolis, 134–5; murdered, 321–2; reform undone by Thirty, 440; *A.P.*'s treatment favourable, 29–30, 283–5

Ephorus. Possible source of *A.P.*, 15–16; on tyranny, 20–1, 189, 191, 216, 218, 228, 232–3; on 411–410, 368; on 404–403, 20–1, 29, 419–21, 472. *See also* Diodorus Siculus

Epimenides. Purifies Athens after Cylon, 81–4, cf. 86, 88

Eretria. Pisistratus and, 208; in 411, 411

Euclides. Archon in 403/2, 331, 437, 462–3, 481–2

Eumelides. *See* Lysimachus

Festivals. 101–2, 605–10, 622–9, 636–9, 650–2. *See also* names of individual festivals

Five Thousand. In 411, 362–415, cf. 29, 486–7; list never published, 385–7, 413–14, cf. 50

Forty. 563, 587–90, 655–6, cf. 36. *See also* δικασταὶ κατὰ δήμους

Four Hundred. In 411, 362–415, cf. 23–4, 29, 60–1, 115, 181–2, 361, 453–4, 486–7. *See also* βουλή.

Gaol. 309, 580; boule and imprisonment, 540

Hagnon. 354, 373

Harmodius and Aristogiton. Murder Hipparchus, 228–32, cf. 27, 189–90; cult, 37, 190, 289, 308, 651–2

Harpactides. Archon in 511/0, 191–9, 240

Hegesias. Archon in 556/5, 191–9, 203

Hegesistratus. Son of Pisistratus, 199, 217, 226–7; *A.P.* wrongly identifies with Thessalus, 225, 229–30

Hellanicus. Possible source of *A.P.*, 21; list of kings, 66, 98; on end of tyranny, 189, 228, 233

Hephaestia. 610, 638

Heraclea. 608, 638–9

Heracles. Pisistratus and, 201, 205–6, 211

Heraclides. Epitome of πολιτεῖαι, 2, 65–79, 447. *See also* Aristotle, fr. 611, in Index I

— 'ὁ βασιλεύς', 492–3

Hermocreon. Archon in 501/0, 262–3, cf. 196

Herodotus. Source of *A.P.*, 15–30, 38; named as source, 205; knows few kings, 66; on Cylon, 79–84; on Solon, 118, 123, 136, 169–70; on rise of Pisistratus, 184–7, 189–213; on end of tyranny, 189–99, 223–40; on Cleisthenes, 241–7; on Themistocles' shipbuilding programme, 277–80; lacks opposition of γνώριμοι and δῆμος, 88; ring composition, 44

Hiatus. 40

Hipparchus Χάρμου. 240, 268–9, 271–2, 281–2, cf. 49

— Son of Pisistratus. Age, 198–9; character, 227–9; status after father's death, 189–90, 227–8, cf. 25; *A.P.* transfers love for Harmodius to Thessalus, 228–31, cf. 27–8, 30, 50, 54–5, 191; murdered, 231–3, cf. 189–90, 218

Hippias, son of Pisistratus. Age, 198–9; eldest son and principal heir, 189–90, 227–8, cf. 25; archon in 526/5, 197, 220; expelled, 233–40, cf. 28, 190–1

Hippomenes. Last ruler from Codridae, 65–6, 78–9, 98

Homicide, trials for. 109–12, 640–50, cf. 49, 655; in 403, 468

Hoplites. In oligarchic constitutions: 'Draco', 113; in 411, 382–4, 411–14. *See also* ἔφηβοι, ζευγῖται, στρατηγοί, Army

Hyperbolus. Ostracised 417–415, 269–71, 354

Hypsichides. Archon in 481/0, 281

Idomeneus. On Athenian politicians, 23

Imbros. Athenian cleruchy, 686–7, 695

Inheritance. Law of, 162–3, 442–4, 509, 526, 629–36, 657

Inscriptions. Used by *A.P.*, 24, 59, 143–5, 246, 593, 602–3

Insertions. In text of *A.P.*, 53–6, cf. 45–7, 50–1, 84–7, 182, 228, 284, 319–22, 484–5, 546–7, 577, 610, 688

Intermediate régime. In 411–410, 362–9, 410–15, cf. 10, 486–7

805

GENERAL INDEX

Ion. 65-73, cf. 78, 100, 483
Ionian migration. 66, 92, cf. 122
Iophon, son of Pisistratus. 226
Isagoras. Family, 241; opponent of Cleisthenes, 242-7, 249, cf. 28, 348; archon in 508/7, 243-6, cf. 181, 195-6, 249, 273-4
Isocrates. Teacher of Androtion, 17, 19; possible source of *A.P.*, 20, 108; on appointments in early Athens, 146-7; on tyranny, 203, 323; προστάται, 97, 345-6; δημαγωγοί, 323; language, 39-40

Land tenure. 71, 90-7, 126-7, 622. *See also* γῆς ἀναδασμός
Laws. Revision at end of c5, 109, 111-12, 134-5, 241, 376, 416, 441-2; Thirty and, 440-5, cf. 162; democracy and adherence to, 284, 328-9, cf. 10; source of *A.P.*, 33-5, 38-9, 49, 60, 443-4, 512, 516, 557, 571, 612, 633-4, 641-6, 674, 682, 684, 698-9. *See also* θεσμός, νόμος, φυλακή τῆς πολιτείας.
Lemnos. Athenian cleruchy, 686-7, 695
Lenaea. 623-4, 637-8, cf. 431, 492
Lipsydrium. Fortified against Hippias, 235
Lycurgus (c6). Leader of πεδίον, 187; perhaps missing from 28. ii, 347-8
— (c4). Financial office held by, 515-16, cf. 35-6, 53
Lygdamis. Tyrant of Naxos, 198, 208-10, 217
Lysander. Spartan commander, 416-20, 426-34, 436, 457, 460-1
Lysimachus. ὁ ἀπὸ τοῦ τυπάνου, 537-40, cf. 35, 37

Marathon, battle of. Date, 195-6, 266, 650; commemoration, 650; ostracism after, 271-2, 275; propaganda concerning, 289
Measures. As basis of Solonian classes, 141-2. *See also* Weights and measures
Medon. First life archon or last king, 77-8, 98, 100-1, cf. 30, 66
Megacles (c7). Opponent of Cylon, 80-3
— (c6). Leader of παραλία, 186-7, 204, 206-7, 234, cf. 10 n. 47, 70; perhaps missing from 28. ii, 347-8
— (c5). 204; ostracised, 274-5, 281, cf. 49
Megara. Acquired by Pandion, 73-4; supports Cylon, 79-80, cf. 96; war with Athens over Salamis, 81, 83, 199-200
Melobius. Supports institution of συγγραφεῖς in 411, 370, cf. 24, 362, 366-7, 375
Menestheus. Supplants Theseus, 77, 79
Metre. 41-2
Miltiades (c6). 187, 198, 217
— (c5). Archon in 524/3, 220; captures Lemnos, 686; battle of Marathon, 289; in *A.P.* in 28. ii only, 27, 348
Mines. 277-9, 552-4, 665
Mnasilochus. Oligarchs' archon in 411, 362, 410-11
Monotony, avoidance of. 42-4, 267, 275-6, 348-9, 351, 485-7, 550, 579, 605
Munichia. Fortified by Hippias, 233-4; in 404-403, 418, 455-6; ἔφηβοι, 506; στρατηγός, 679, cf. 52
Mysteries. 636-7, cf. 626-7; settlement of 403, 465-6. *See also* ἐπιμεληταί.
Mytilene. War with Athens over Sigeum, 96, 217, 226; in Delian League, 298-300

Navy. Themistocles' shipbuilding programme, 277-80, cf. 257; naval power, 283-5, 291-309, cf. 8 n. 33, 10, 48-9, 288, 336-7, 486, *and see* Delian League; boule and, 545-8, cf. 31; quadriremes and quinqueremes, 52-3, 55-6, 57, 546-7; sacred triremes, 687-8, cf. 39, 53, 55-7. *See also* ναυκραρίαι, τριήραρχοι.
Nicias. 351-2, 354, 358-9, cf. 10, 15, 26, 284

Oaths. Cylonian jurors, 83; to Solon's laws, 135; in 411, 373, 385, 400-1; in 403, 463; διαιτηταί, 620; δικασταί, 696, 718; ἔφηβοι, 494-5, 506; archons, 100-1, 135-6, 620-1, cf. 37; boule, 145-6, 260, 263-4, 538; cavalry, 567; litigants, 718; witnesses, 620
Olives. For Panathenaea, 672-5
Oropus. Athenian subject territory, 253, 610-11; cult of Amphiaraus, 505, 610-11
Orphans. Archon and, 629-36; maintenance of war orphans, 308-9, 508, cf. 355

806

GENERAL INDEX

Ostraca. Of c6, 200; of c5, 271, 275-7, 279, 280, 350, 355; Ceramicus hoard, 204, 275-6
Ostracism. Date and purpose, 267-71, cf. 11, 20-1, 61, 221, 262; in 480's, 267-71, cf. 49; territorial limits, 282-3; in c4, 526. *See also* names of victims

Paeania. Deme, 205, cf. 235
Pallene. Deme, 208-9. *See also* Chronology (of tyranny)
Pamphlets. Source of *A.P.*, 26, 286, 368. *See also* Critias, Theramenist; and P. Heid, P. Mich., in Index II
Panathenaea. Armed procession, 25-6, 232, cf. 210; administration, 606, 609, 638, 669-72, 675-6, 693; prizes, 569, 672-6; calendar, 609, 669; Panathenaic year, 517
Pandion. 73-4, cf. 65, 79
Parties, regional (c6). 184-8, cf. 28, 73, 179-80
Pausanias. King of Sparta. 419, 460-1
Payments. Stipends for assembly, 490-3, 691, cf. 9, 51, 355-6, 514; for officials and soldiers, 300-9, 691-5, cf. 337; for δικασταί, 338-44, 691, 716-17, 730-1, 734-5, cf. 284, 286, 302-3, 355-6, 514; in 411, 372, 381-2, 390, 405, 412-13; maintenance for ἀδύνατοι, 570; for war orphans, 308-9, 508, cf. 355; κατάστασις for cavalry, 304, 458, 565. *See also* διωβελία, θεωρικόν, σίτησις, σῖτος
Pericles. 334-45; prosecutes Cimon, 335-6, cf. 312, 317, 325; and Ephialtes, 311-12, 336, cf. 61, 286; against Cimon's generosity, 338-44, cf. 23, 284, 286; jury pay, 338-44, cf. 514; citizenship law, 331-4, cf. 12, 284, 496; Panathenaea, 670-1; opposed by Thucydides Μελησίου, 349-51; deterioration of politics after his death, 351-4, cf. 9, 15, 284, 344
Phanodemus. Possible source of *A.P.*, 17-18, 21
Phayllus. Member of Ten, 460
Pheidon, king of Argos. Measures, 165-6, cf. 153, 168
Philochorus (*F.G.H.* 328). On φρατρίαι (F 35), 69-70; on σεισάχθεια (F 114), 125-7; on Alcmaeonids and Delphi (F 115), 190-1, 236-7; on ostracism (F 30), 267, 270, 282, 526

Philocyprus. King of Soli (Cyprus), 121, 170
Philoneos. Archon in 528/7, 191-9, 223
Phormisius. Moderate democrat in 404-403, 432-3, 472
Phrynichus. Oligarch in 411, 407-10, cf. 372, 413; absent from text of *A.P.*, 408, cf. 61, 363
Phye. Poses as Athena for Pisistratus, 204-6, cf. 21, 226
Phyle. In 404-403, 450-2, cf. 417-22, 474-7; ἔφηβοι, 508
Piraeus. Ten governors in 404-403, 438-9, 469-71; occupied by democrats in 404-403, 455-61, cf. 474-7; administration under democracy, 573-4, 576, 578-9, 611; στρατηγοί, 697, cf. 52; lawcourts, 646, 701. *See also* Πειραιεύς, Acte, Munichia
Pisander. Oligarch in 411, 363-5, 371, 379-81, 407-8, 413
Pisistratus. Background, 187, cf. 79; προστάτης τοῦ δήμου, 184-6, 347-8, cf. 97, 199; tyranny, 189-240, cf. 14, 27-8, 88, 485, 627; and Solon, 170, 201-3, 224; sons, 189-90, 198-9, 224-30, cf. 24-5, 27-8, 30
— Son of Hippias, 24, cf. 239
Plato. On politicians, 323; on oligarchies of late c5, 371-2, 421, 429-30, 435, 438-9, 445, cf. 345 n. 31; on homicide, 640-50
Plutarch. On cc7-6, 79-202 *passim*, cf. 24 n. 153, 28, 224; on 480's, 270, 277-80; on later c5, 283-361 *passim*; wide reading, 22 n. 136; use of *A.P.*, 56 n. 278, 118, 131, 283, 287, 319, 322, 338, 341-2, 358
Pnyx. Meeting-place of assembly, 491, 507-8; in 411, 411
Population. 333-4, 383-4, 491, cf. 12, 696
Property classes. 'Draco', 117, cf. 113; Solon, 136-49; in cc5-4, 142, 145-6, 510, 550-1; archons, 148, 273, 284, 330-1, 618; ταμίαι, 148, 550-1, cf. 37
Public Works. 31, 568-9. *See also* Buildings, City facilities
Pylos. Melanthus, 79; Alcmaeonids, 186, cf. 79; Pisistratids, 187, cf. 79; lost to Sparta by Anytus, 344
Pythodorus. Decree instituting συγγραφεῖς in 411, 370, cf. 24, 362, 366, 375; archon in 404/3 (same

807

GENERAL INDEX

Pythodorus–contd.
man?), 370, 436–7, 462–3, 475–7, 481–2

Religious officials. 32. *See also* names of individual offices
Rhaecelus. Occupied by Pisistratus, 207
Rhamnus. ἔφηβοι, 508
Rhinon. Member of Ten in 403, 10, 15, 420, 460, 462
Ring composition. 44–9, cf. 30–2, 54 n. 267, 84, 86–7, 120, 149, 169, 180, 247–8, 513, 571–2, 596, 613

Salamis. Athens' early wars for, 81, 83, 199–200; subject territory, 253, 259–60, 610–12, 686, 693; battle and consequences, 283–5, 287–90, cf. 10, 19, 21, 48–9; in 404–403, 418, 456
Samos. Tyranny of Polycrates, 198, 210; in Delian League, 298–300; Athenian cleruchy in c4, 694–5, cf. 52
Satyrus. Henchman of Thirty, 430
Scolia. Used by *A.P.*, 15, 24–5, 59, 235, 240, 248
Scyros. Theseus' bones, 76–7, cf. 65, 211, 289; Athenian cleruchy, 686–7, 695
Sentence structure. 40–1, 124, 421–2, 461–2
Sigeum. Athens' early wars for, 96, 217, 226; Hippias' retreat, 247
Simonides. And tyrants, 228–9; and Themistocles. 289
Slavery. In early Athens, 90–7, 125–6, 175–6; for rejected claimants to citizenship, 499–502; lawsuits concerning slaves, 642–4, 665–6; public slaves, 439, 557, 597, 601, 604, 705, 710–13, 733
Solon. 118–79, cf. 45–7, 485; μεσότης, 119, 123–4; chronology, 120–2, 127, 163–4, 223–4; travels, 123–4, 169–70; linked with purification after Cylon, 81–4; προστάτης τοῦ δήμου, 97, 345–7; refuses to be tyrant, 122, 171; σεισάχθεια, 125–30, cf. 20–1, 47, 90, 622; story of leak, 128–30, cf. 15, 26; supersedes Draco's laws, 130–1, cf. 110–11; property classes, 136–49, cf. 113; archons moved to θεσμοθετεῖον, 106; beginning of democracy, 14, 19, 119, 376–7, 485; but did not intend all that followed, 8, 10, 119; not deliberately ambiguous, 162–3, cf. 26, 30, 440–5; survival of laws, 131–5, cf. 24–5, 27, 37, 61, 88, 102, 109, 119, 147, 152, 157–9, 160–1; poems used by *A.P.*, 118–20, 122–5, 171–9, cf. 15–16, 24, 28, 59
Sortition. For appointments, 31–2, 115–16, 148, 513, 601–3, 613, 689–91, *and see* names of individual offices; in δικαστήρια, 668, 700–17
Sources of *A.P.* 15–20, 33–5, and Commentary *passim*; *A.P.* condenses, 24, 49–50, 262, 286, 297–8, 300–1, 325–7, 348–9, 387–8, 392–3, 396, 403, 463–72, 496, 499–500, 519, 526–7, 529–31, 540–3, 591, 599–600, 605, 661; disagreements between, 25–8, 128, 129–30, 143–4, 191, 193, 285–6, 360–1, 380; language of, 38–40
Sparta. Overthrow of tyranny in Naxos, 210; in Athens, 190–1, 236–40; and Athens after Persian Wars, 291–5; paradigm of oligarchy, 299, 337; Messenian War of c5, 311, 325, 349; and Athens in 411, 369, 372, 384, 390, 410; peace offers 410–404, 416, 424–6; in 404–403, 454–5, 457, 466, 472, 478–9, *and see* Lysander, Pausanias; ἀγωγή, 504, 507; reckoning of ages, 498
Stesimbrotus. On Athenian politicians, 22–3, 29, 301, 328, 345–6, 350–1
Stipends. *See* Payments
Stoa of Basileus. 134–6, cf. 103, 106

Taxation. 142, 552, 555, 618, *and see* εἰσφορά; under tyranny, 214–15; of metics, 652–4
Ten. Successors of Thirty in 403, 415–82, esp. 456–9, 469, cf. 29, 30, 487; alleged second Ten, 459–61, cf. 15, 420–2, 469
Thargelia. 624, 628–9
Theatre. In Athens, 507–8; in Piraeus, 611
Thebes. And Pisistratus, 208; Boeotians opposed to Cleisthenes, 247; Boeotian murders Ephialtes, 322; Boeotian influence on 'future' constitution of 411, 389, 393
Themistocles. Background, 279; at Marathon, 686; in 480's, 274, 277–

GENERAL INDEX

Themistocles—contd.
80, cf. 25; provision of money before Salamis, 287–90, cf. 19, 21; opponent of Cimon after Persian Wars, 288–9; partner of Aristides, 283, 286, 292–4, 348–9, cf. 27, 43; and Ephialtes, 283–5, 319–22, cf. 29, 53–6, 61; condemned for medism, 317; Panathenaea, 670–1

Theophrastus. Member of Aristotle's school, 35 n. 184. *See also* MS Vat. Gr. 2306, in Index II

Theopompus. Archon in 411/0, 410–11 — (*F.G.H.* 115). On Athenian politicians, 23, 344–6, 350–1, 358; on Cimon (F 89), 338–40; on Cleon (F 92), 353–4; possible source of *A.P.*, 23, 130, 286, 301, 328, 338–9, 354

Theramenes. Teacher of Isocrates, 19; in 411, 363–5, 407, 409, 413–14; after Arginusae, 423–4; in 404, 417–22, 427–35, 447–55, cf. 30; προστάτης τῶν γνωρίμων, 354–5, 358–61, cf. 15, 26, 284; as moderate, 361, 413–14, 427–34, cf. 15 n. 75, 17; as democrat (D.S.), 427–8, 433–4; defence, 20, 29, 367, *and see* P. Mich., in Index II

Theramenist pamphlet. Alleged as source of *A.P.*, 15–18, 368, 421–2

Theseus. 74–7, 79, 484–5; bones brought from Scyros, 76–7, 211, 289, cf. 65; Thesea, 638, 651; coinage attributed to, 169; ostracism attributed to, 267–8

Theseum. Pisistratus' disarming located in, 210–11; murals, 289 n. 28; allotments in, 689–90

Thessalus. Son of Pisistratus, 228–31, cf. 24, 27, 49, 54–5, 191; *A.P.* wrongly identifies with Hegesistratus, 225, 229–30

Thessaly. Supports Pisistratids, 226, 238

Thirty. In 404–403, 415–82, cf. 23–4, 29–30, 162, 182, 487, 588

Thrasybulus. Democrat in 404–403, 417–22, 428, 450–2, 474–8

Three Thousand. In 404–403, 417, 448, 452–4

Thucydides Μελησίου. Opponent of Pericles, 349–51, cf. 15, 26, 284, 358–9; ostracised, 271, 350

— 'Ολόρου, historian. Source of *A.P.*, 15–30; on Cylon, 79–84; on tyranny, 191–9, 210, 215; on fall of tyranny, 224–34; on Themistocles, 277–80, 294, 319–20; on Pericles, 285, 313, 344; on 411, 362–415, cf. 15; use of sources, 24, 59; political views, 414; γνώριμοι and δῆμος, 88, 346

Tokens. 687, 689–90, 711–12, 730–1, 735

Tragedy. Performances, 622–3, 638, cf. 611; Aeschylus and politics, 312; Sophocles and public office, 373, 537

Tyranny. Laws against, 154–6, 220–3. *See also* Cylon, Hipparchus, Hippias, Pisistratus, Solon

Vases. 104, 144, 271, 272, 289 n. 28, 506, 508, 564, 675, cf. 205–6, 211, 670–2, 674

Vocabulary. 37–40

Voting. 154, 397, 498–9, 535, 568, 619; in δικαστήρια, 730–4. *See also* χειροτονεῖν and ψηφίζειν

Weights and measures. Solon, 164–9, cf. 20–1, 28, 47, 54; enforcement of standards, 575–6

Xanthippus. Ostracised, 276–7, 281; in 28. ii, 348, cf. 27, 277

Xenaenetus. Archon in 401/0, 475–7, 480–1

Xenophon. *Hellenica* possible source of *A.P.*, 15–16, 20, 29, 416–21, 447–9

[Xenophon], *A.P.* On responsibilities of boule (iii. 2), 398, 545; common source with *A.P.* on gaolers and orphans (iii. 4), 21 n. 130, 302, 308–9